Al-Muwaṭṭaʾ

Al-Muwaṭṭaʾ

by Mālik b. Anas (d. 179/795)

[The Recension of Yaḥyā b. Yaḥyā al-Laythī (d. 234/848)]

A translation of the Royal Moroccan Edition

Edited and translated by
Mohammad Fadel & Connell Monette

Published by the
Program in Islamic Law, Harvard Law School
Distributed by Harvard University Press
Cambridge, Massachusetts
2019

Library of Congress Control Number:
2019946147

Printed in the United States of America
ISBN 978-0-6742413-5-0

Arabic Edition Team

Editorial Committee

Dr. Mohamed Raoundi, Member of the High Council of Religious Scholars

Dr. Driss Ibn Daouia, President of the High Council of Religious Scholars, Larache Branch

Dr. Mohamed Azzeddine Mayar El Idrissi, President of the High Council of Religious Scholars, Marrakesh Branch

With the Assistance of:

Prof. Driss Elhamdaoui, Faculty of Islamic Law, Fez

Dr. Lahoucine Ait Said, Member of the High Council of Religious Scholars

Dr. Abdelhafid Doumar, Faculty of Humanities, Oujda

Dr. Abdellah Lansari, Representative of the Ministry of Endowments and Islamic Affairs, Marrakesh

Prof. Abdelmjid Mouhib, Dar al-Hadith al-Hasaniyya

Dr. Mohammed Guennoun Hassani, President of the High Council of Religious Scholars, Tangiers Branch

English Translation Team

Chief Editor

Dr. Connell Monette, Al Akhawayn University in Ifrane

Co-Editor and Mālikī Law Specialist

Dr. Mohammad Fadel, University of Toronto Faculty of Law

First Draft Translators

Dr. Ali Azeriah, Al Akhawayn University in Ifrane

Dr. Mohamed Ouakrime, Al Akhawayn University in Ifrane

Research Assistants

Shuaib Ally, University of Toronto

Lahoucine Amedjar, Al Akhawayn University in Ifrane

Dawud Nasir, Al Akhawayn University in Ifrane

Contents

English Translation of the Royal Moroccan Edition of Imam Mālik b. Anas' *Muwaṭṭa'*: An Introduction 1

Introduction to the Translation of the Royal Moroccan Edition of the *Muwaṭṭa'*, Recension of Yaḥyā b. Yaḥyā al-Laythī 7

Arabic Introduction to the Royal Moroccan Edition of the *Muwaṭṭa'* 39

Book 1: The Book of Obligatory Prayer (*Ṣalāt*) Times 73

Book 2: The Book of Ritual Purity (*Ṭahāra*) 83

Book 3: The First Book of Prayer (*Ṣalāt*) 109

Book 4: Forgetfulness in Prayer (*Sahw*) 129

Book 5: The Book of the Friday Congregational Prayer (*Ṣalāt al-Jumuʿa*) 131

Book 6: The Book of Prayer (*Ṣalāt*) during Ramadan 139

Book 7: The Book of the Night Prayer (*Ṣalāt al-Layl*) 141

Book 8: The Book of the Congregational Prayer (*Ṣalāt al-Jamāʿa*) 149

Book 9: The Book of Shortening the Prayer (*Ṣalāt*) 157

Book 10: The Book of the Two Feasts (*ʿĪd*) 177

Book 11: The Book of the Prayer of Danger (*Ṣalāt al-Khawf*) 181

Book 12: The Book of the Prayer for Rain (*Ṣalāt al-Istisqā'*) 187

Book 13 : The Book of the Prayer Direction (*Qibla*) 191

Book 14: The Book of the Quran 195

Book 15: The Book of Funerals (*Janā'iz*) 209

Book 16: The Book of the Alms-Tax (*Zakāt*) 221

Book 17: The Book of Fasting (*Ṣiyām*) 253

Book 18: The Book of the Night of Power (*Laylat al-Qadr*) 271

Book 19: The Book of Pious Seclusion (*Iʿtikāf*) 275

Book 20: The Book of Pilgrimage (*Ḥajj*) 281

Book 21: The Book of Campaigning for the Sake of God (*Jihād*) 357

Book 22: The Book of Sacrificial Animals (*Ḍaḥāyā*) 377

Book 23: The Book of the Newborn Sacrifice (*'Aqīqa*) 381
Book 24: The Book of Domesticated Animals Slaughtered for Ordinary Use (*Dhabā'iḥ*) 383
Book 25: The Book of Wild Animals (*Ṣayd*) 387
Book 26: The Book of Vows (*Nudhūr*) 393
Book 27: The Book of Mandatory Inheritance Shares (*Farā'iḍ*) 401
Book 28: The Book of Manumission (*'Atāqa*) and Patronage (*Walā'*) 421
Book 29: The Book of the Slave Who is a Party to a Manumission Contract (*Mukātab*) 435
Book 30: The Book of a Master's Designation of Slaves for Manumission Upon His Death (*Tadbīr*) 463
Book 31: The Book of Marriage (*Nikāḥ*) 473
Book 32: The Book of Divorce (*Ṭalāq*) 493
Book 33: The Book of Breastfeeding (*Raḍā'a*) 531
Book 34: The Book of Sales (*Buyū'*) 537
Book 35: The Book of Judicial Rulings (*Aqḍiya*) 599
Book 36: The Book of the Right of First Refusal (*Shuf'a*) 643
Book 37: The Book of Irrigation Partnerships (*Musāqāt*) 649
Book 38: Leasing Out (*Kirā'*) Farmland 657
Book 39: The Book of Investment Partnerships (*Qirāḍ*) 659
Book 40: The Book of Compensation (*'Aql*) Due for Battery 677
Book 41: The Book of Collective Oaths (*Qasāma*) 701
Book 42: The Book of Lapidation (*Rajm*) and Mandatory Criminal Punishments (*Ḥudūd*) 709
Book 43: The Book of Theft (*Sariqa*) 719
Book 44: The Book of Beverages 727
Book 45: The Book of Miscellaneous Matters 731

Glossary of Proper Names 787
Glossary of Terms 795
Bibliography 807
Index 811

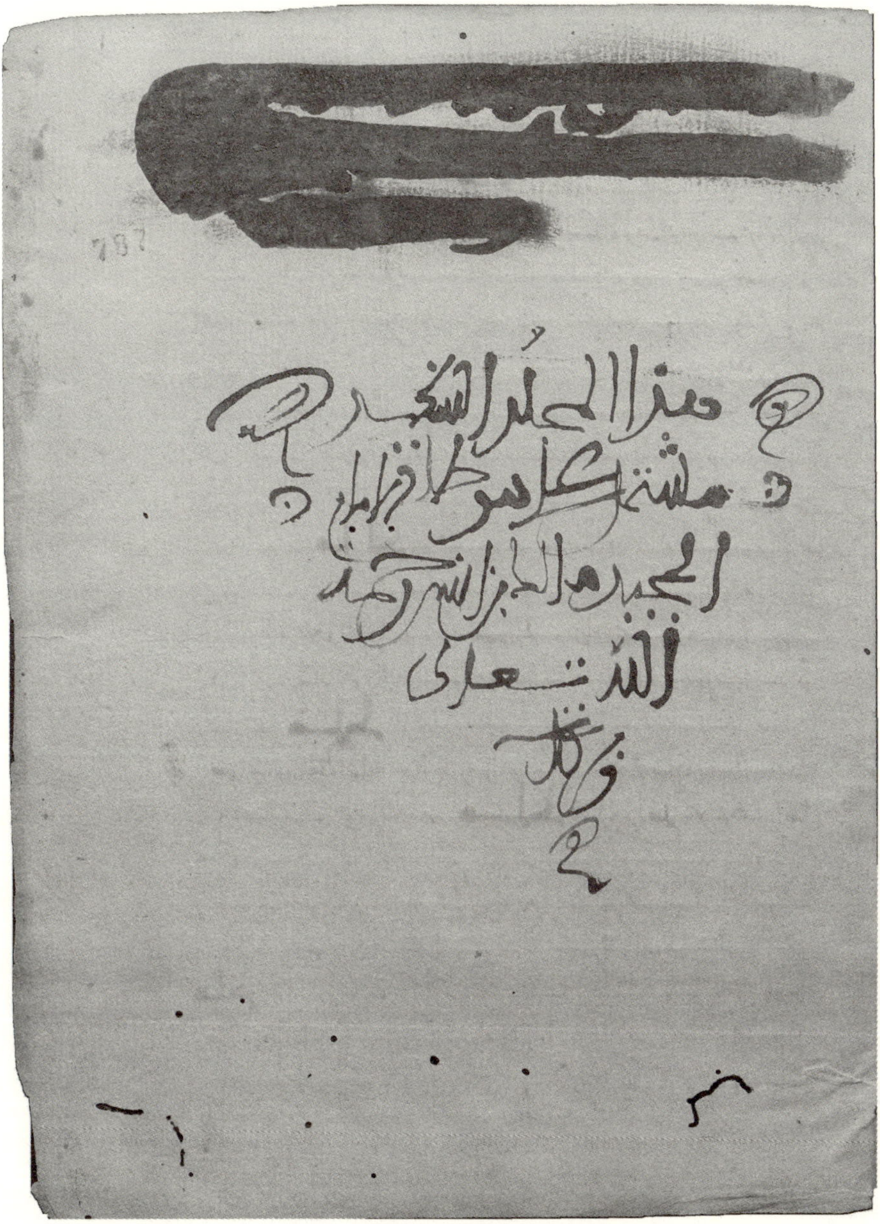

Kingdom of Morocco National Library, MS No. J787: Colophon of the *Muwaṭṭa*ʾ manuscript, copied by Ibn al-Ṭallāʿ, dated 595 AH.

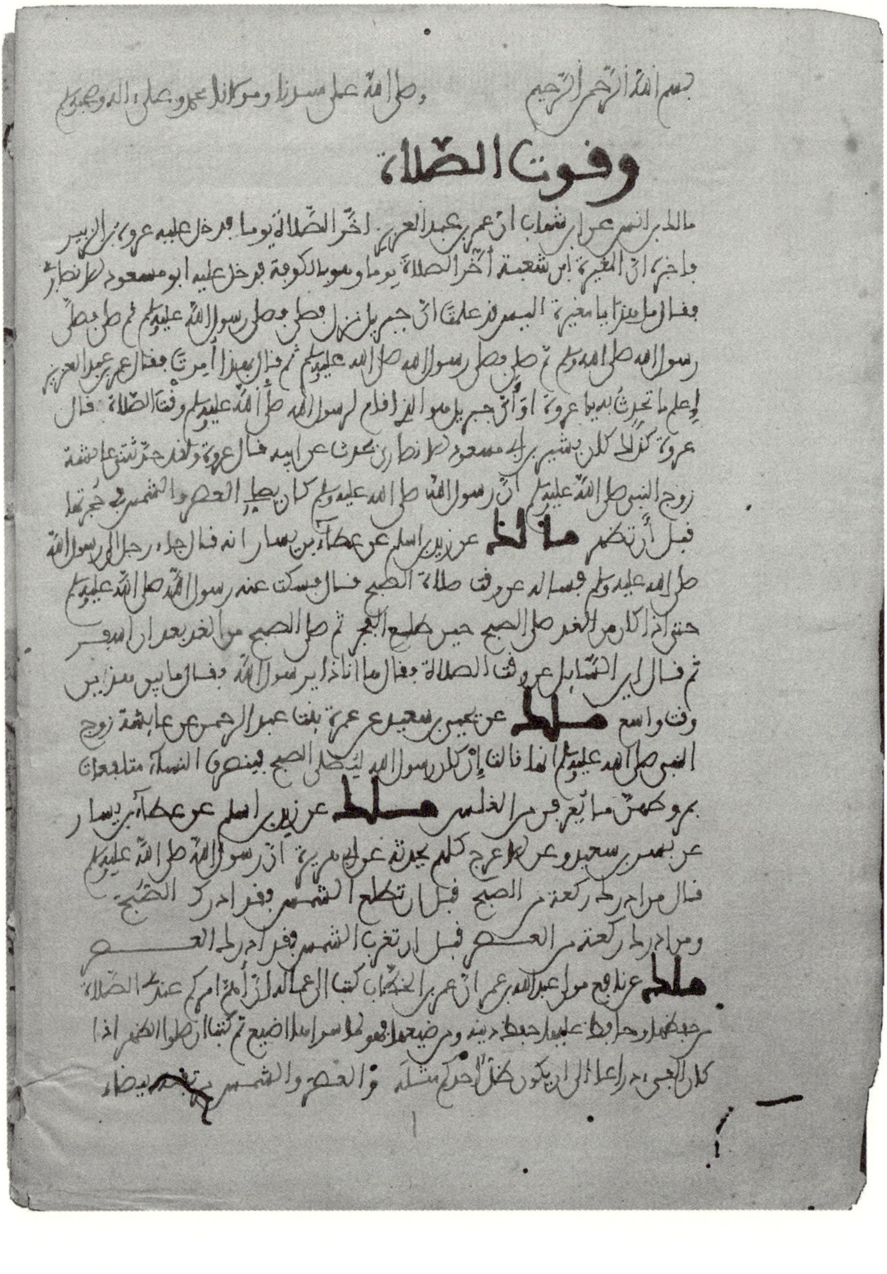

بسم الله الرحمن الرحيم وصلى الله على سيدنا ومولانا محمد وعلى آله وصحبه

وقوت الصلاة

Kingdom of Morocco National Library, MS No. J787, Folio 1: Excerpt of manuscript of the *Muwaṭṭaʾ*, copied by Ibn al-Ṭallāʿ, dated 595 AH.

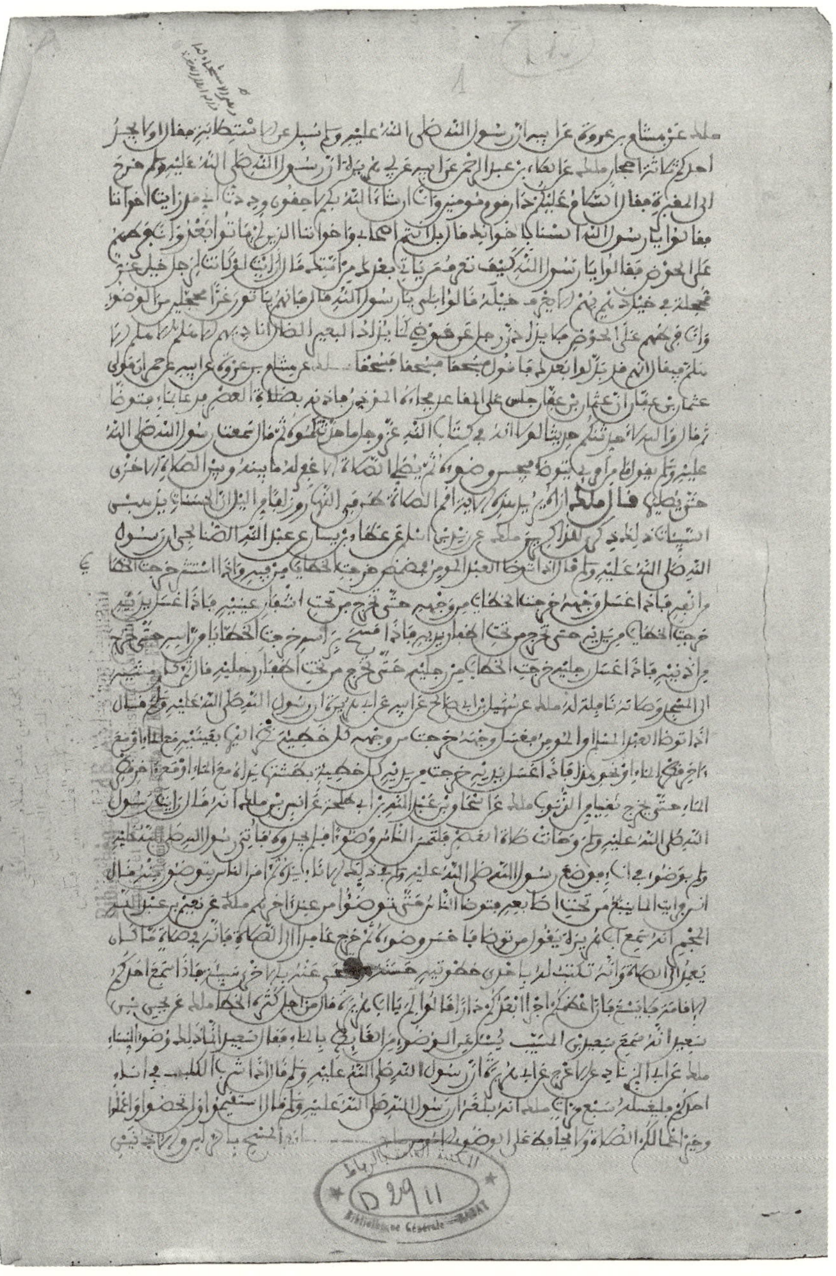

Kingdom of Morocco National Library, MS No. D2911, Folio 1: Excerpt of manuscript of the *Muwaṭṭa'*, copied by Ibn al-Labbād, dated 613 AH.

English Translation of the Royal Moroccan Edition of Imam Mālik b. Anas' *Muwaṭṭa'*: An Introduction

Background to the Translation

In summer 2011, President Idriss Ouaouicha of Al Akhawayn University in Ifrane (AUI) proposed to His Excellency Ahmed Toufiq, Minister of Islamic Affairs and Endowments of the Kingdom of Morocco, that the ministry sponsor the university to produce academic translations of some of the foundational texts in Mālikī law (*fiqh*). In the Mālikī school of Islamic jurisprudence, the two earliest and most important texts are the *Muwaṭṭa'* (eighth century CE) and *al-Mudawwana al-kubrā* (ninth century CE). Although nonspecialists had previously translated the *Muwaṭṭa'* into English, no academic press had published a peer-reviewed translation of this work. The absence of a scholarly translation of the *Muwaṭṭa'* made its use in North American universities problematic. Given the recent upsurge in interest in the academic study of Islamic law at leading universities in the United States (e.g., Harvard), Canada (e.g., Toronto, McGill), and Europe, the ministry agreed that the publication of academic translations of these works would be very timely. Further, Mālik's *Muwaṭṭa'* has always been considered a very special text, in that it not only provides the basis for a legal system but also tells a kind of story. Piece by piece, anecdote by anecdote, opinion by opinion, this collection of conversations, stories, and legal opinions coalesces into a powerful narrative space that can project the reader, like a time traveler, back into the world of the first, second, and third generations of the Muslim community of Medina. Medina was where the first public Muslim community was established, and from its humble beginnings there it grew into a universal religion. The *Muwaṭṭa'* tells the story of that ancient first community of Muslims, a community that straddled the time and space between Arabian paganism (known as the Days of Ignorance, or *jāhiliyya*), the Greco-Roman Hellenism of late antiquity, and the Zoroastrianism of the Sasanians, on the one hand, and the rise of a new Islamic order that would radically restructure the Mediterranean, Near Eastern, and Central

Asian worlds, on the other. The outlines of this new religious and cultural order, however, were only dimly coming into view when Mālik wrote the *Muwaṭṭaʾ*. The narrative space that he inhabited can be accessed only if the tone, nuance, and specific vocabulary of his text are properly translated into our modern vernacular.

But the *Muwaṭṭaʾ*'s importance lies not only in its status as a unique repository of communal memory (which it certainly is), but also in the special reverence with which Moroccan national culture, which historically is closely intertwined with the Mālikī school of law, cloaks the work. For these reasons, the ministry and the university agreed that the *Muwaṭṭaʾ* of Imam Mālik would serve as an excellent pilot for their joint translation project. The choice of the *Muwaṭṭaʾ* was especially timely in view of the then impending publication of the Royal Moroccan Edition of the *Muwaṭṭaʾ* (RME; the edition was eventually published in 1434/2013). The RME, which at the time was still being prepared by a team of Moroccan scholars in response to a request of His Majesty, the Commander of the Faithful, Muḥammad VI, King of Morocco, was to be the first critical edition of the Arabic text and was to be based on some of the most ancient North African and Andalusian manuscripts available. Minister Toufiq provided the university with an electronic copy of the RME's text, and President Ouaouicha promised that the university would revise the timetable and budget of the translation to align with the production of the RME. The university received the digital copy in 2013, and the printed version of the RME followed in 2016.

Previous Translations of the *Muwaṭṭaʾ*

As noted above, at the time the translation was begun there were two English-language, nonacademic translations of the *Muwaṭṭaʾ*, those of Muhammad Rahimuddin (1985) and Aisha Bewley (1989). Although both of these editions have proven useful to non-Arabic-speaking Muslims, a critical edition of the *Muwaṭṭaʾ* did not exist when Rahimuddin and Bewley undertook their respective translations. Moreover, neither translation was published under an academic imprint, and to our knowledge, neither translation was ever subjected to peer review.[1] Further, neither text included supplemental notes that could help the nonspecialist understand the legal issues presented in the text, a deficiency that further limited the usefulness of these translations for general readers.

1 Muhammad Rahimuddin, *Muwatta' Imam Malik* (Lahore: Sh. Muhammad Ashraf, 1985); Aisha Bewley, *Al-Muwatta of Imam Malik ibn Anas: The First Formulation of Islamic Law* (London: Kegan Paul, 1989). The Bewley translation was republished by Routledge in 2010. Merlin Swartz published an appreciative, if brief, review of the Bewley translation in *Middle East Studies Association Bulletin* 25, no. 1 (1991): 102–3.

Translation Team

To assure a translation of the highest quality, Al Akhawayn University employed a team of specialists: Dr. Ali Azeriah (AUI) and Dr. Mohamed Ouakrime (AUI) as first draft translators, Dr. Mohammad Fadel (University of Toronto Faculty of Law) as the Mālikī *fiqh* specialist and editor, and Dr. Connell Monette as chief editor and project coordinator. Graduate students Dawud Nasir (AUI), Lahoucine Amedjar (AUI), and Shuaib Ally (University of Toronto) also participated as research assistants. Special thanks are due to Dr. Walid Saleh (University of Toronto), who served as lead translator at the beginning of the project.

Method and Timeline of Translation

The translation of the RME began in January 2014. Each section was first translated by Drs. Azeriah and Ouakrime. The first draft relied heavily on consultation of primary and secondary Mālikī sources, including the very valuable annotations included in the notes of the RME by its editors, along with considerable assistance from the graduate assistants (Amedjar and Nasir). The first draft of the translation took approximately three years to complete (2014–2016). As each chapter of the *Muwaṭṭaʾ* was translated, it was sent to Drs. Fadel and Monette. In the second stage, Fadel independently reviewed the first-round translation, checking it against the Arabic original and revising it as needed to guarantee correct jurisprudential interpretation and conformity, when appropriate, with contemporary legal terminology. Fadel and Monette then jointly reviewed Fadel's revisions to the initial translation against the Arabic text of the RME to ensure that the tone of the original Arabic was conveyed as clearly as possible in idiomatic English, even if this required a departure from the literal sense or original grammatical structure of the text. They also confirmed that technical Arabic terms had been translated consistently throughout the text. The translation was finalized by reading it without reference to the Arabic original, with the sole aim of ensuring that the translation read smoothly in English.

The review and editing process began in 2015 and continued to mid-2018. As dictated by the context of the Arabic original, the translation has sometimes adopted a very formal, even archaic tone, while at other times, a colloquial style was deemed more appropriate. All in all, this multilayered process has yielded, we believe, a translation that is stylistically superior to previous translations and that provides a more faithful and accessible account of its substantive teachings, particularly the technical legal questions it addresses. Although the earlier English translations conveyed the general sense of the text, this translation benefits from the use of idiomatic English and of consistent English technical terms instead of Arabic transliterations. Because the *Muwaṭṭa'* is not only a collection of narratives but also a legal text, the use of modern legal terminology, wherever possible, is necessary and desirable to make it more accessible to modern legal scholars who are not specialists in Islamic law.

The result, we hope, is a translation that conveys both the sense and the sensibility of the Arabic text, using idiomatic English and substituting English terms for Arabic ones. Succinct clarificatory notes are provided to explain to the general reader what might otherwise appear obscure, if not unintelligible, issues while avoiding burdening the reader with excessive commentary. Because one of the aims of the Ministry of Islamic Affairs and Endowments is to make this important work accessible to pious English-speaking Muslims, the texts of supplications that appear in the original have been transliterated in full in the translation's notes.

We believe that this translation will be useful both to researchers who are interested in Islamic law but lack the necessary language skills to access primary texts, and to nonspecialists seeking deeper familiarity with Islamic law, whether as teachers of Islamic history, legal history, or religious studies or as students interested in learning more about Islamic law or early Islamic history. We are grateful to the Program in Islamic Law at Harvard Law School for agreeing to publish this important text, and for its decision to host an online companion to the translation on the SHARIAsource Portal. The online companion will include both the original Arabic text and the English translation, as well as supplementary materials that place the *Muwaṭṭa'* in its broader historical and social context. Importantly, the online companion will give readers and the scholarly community a forum for ongoing comments, criticisms, and suggestions for improving the translation—for example, by proposing revisions or corrections to the original translation or identifying areas of the text that could benefit from greater commentary.

The remainder of this introduction includes an abridged translation of the Arabic introduction to the RME and the translators' introduction to the English translation of the RME. We have omitted from the former portions that deal with the technical aspects of preparing the critical edition and that would interest only specialists in the study of manuscripts. We include, however, those portions of the Arabic introduction that elucidate the cultural background of contemporary Morocco that led to the project to produce a critical edition of the *Muwaṭṭa'*, the place of Imam Mālik in Morocco's religious identity, and the history of the *Muwaṭṭa'* in the Maghrib and Andalusia. The translators' introduction to the RME attempts to situate the *Muwaṭṭa'* in the broader sweep of the history of Islamic law and jurisprudence. It also provides a brief synopsis of the different views contemporary scholars have taken regarding the significance of the text for Islamic law and jurisprudence. The aim of the introduction is to assist nonspecialist readers in approaching the text. Accordingly, it provides a general overview of the text's structure, an introduction to Mālik's use of technical terms in his work, and our own views regarding the significance of the *Muwaṭṭaʾ* for understanding early Islamic legal history.

The abridged translation of the Arabic introduction, while necessary to gain a better understanding of the work's history, the place of the *Muwaṭṭaʾ* in Moroccan religious culture, and the labors that went into preparing the Royal Moroccan Edition, may be skipped by those readers interested in the *Muwaṭṭaʾ* primarily as an artifact of early Islamic legal history. Although the translation speaks for itself, we believe that reading the translators' introduction is helpful for understanding the text of the *Muwaṭṭaʾ*, especially for nonspecialist readers.

Transliteration and Editorial Conventions

The transliteration of Arabic terms generally follows the conventions of the *International Journal of Middle East Studies*. Nonspecialist readers should note the variant spellings of the words *ibn* ("son of") and *bint* ("daughter of"), which appear, respectively, as "Ibn" or "Bint" in the beginning of a name and as "b." or "bt." within a name, and *abū* ("father of"), which appears as "Abū" in the beginning of a name and as "Abī" within a name. Place-names and other anglicized Arabic words are not transliterated but rendered in their conventional English spellings. Accordingly, the translation uses "Iraq," not "ʿIrāq," and "Ramadan," not "Ramaḍān." The person who leads a Muslim congregation in prayers is called an "imam," since that term has entered the English language with the meaning of "prayer leader," but the word is transliterated (*imām*) when used to mean a public official or ruler. When the term is used honorifically in relation to Mālik b. Anas, it is capitalized ("Imam Mālik"). We have chosen to translate *Allāh*, which in Arabic is the proper name for the divinity, using the English word "God." The blessings that Muslims formulaically invoke upon the Prophet Muḥammad when his name is mentioned are noted parenthetically as "(pbuh)," meaning "peace be upon him." The chains of transmitters (*isnād*s) that introduce individual reports typically take the form "from X, from Y, that [text of report]." For the sake of improved readability, we have replaced the first "from X" with "X reported" even when the original text does not include a verb.

Technical terms are indicated by capitalization (e.g., the Morning Prayer). On the assumption that readers of the translation are not likely to read the text straight through, the transliteration of technical Arabic terms is provided immediately following the first use of the English term in each chapter; for example, "He performed the Morning Prayer (*ṣalāt al-ṣubḥ*)." In order to minimize the use of Arabic, the transliterated Arabic term is then not repeated until it appears again in a different chapter. This convention enables readers to locate Arabic technical terms easily without having to reference the translation's glossary, no matter where they begin reading.

Introduction to the Translation of the Royal Moroccan Edition of the *Muwaṭṭaʾ*, Recension of Yaḥyā b. Yaḥyā al-Laythī

Biography of Mālik b. Anas and His Place in the Sunnī Tradition

Mālik b. Anas, the author of the *Muwaṭṭaʾ*, lived through momentous changes in early Muslim society. Born in 93/711 in Medina during the reign of the Umayyad caliph al-Walīd b. ʿAbd al-Malik (r. 86–96/705–715), he witnessed the transformation of Islam from a primarily Arab religion into a cosmopolitan, multiethnic religion. By the time of his death in 179/795 during the reign of the fifth ʿAbbāsid caliph, Hārūn al-Rashīd (r. 170–93/786–809), the ʿAbbāsids had already been in power more than forty years after their successful overthrow of the Umayyads in 132/750. With the rise of the ʿAbbāsids and the founding of their new, cosmopolitan capital of Baghdad during the reign of their second caliph, Abū Jaʿfar al-Manṣūr (r. 136–58/754–775), the cultural center of gravity of the Muslim world began to shift decisively from Medina in the Hijaz to Iraq and the Muslim East. By Mālik's death, Medina was no longer an important center of learning, religious or otherwise, although it would remain central to Muslims' religious imagination and a site of pilgrimage. When Mālik was still a youth, however, Medina was the undisputed cultural center of the Muslim world, thus affording him the opportunity to learn from the most important religious figures of the Umayyad period. His residence in Medina also proved fortunate for his career as a teacher. Given Medina's status as a pilgrimage destination, Mālik taught scores of students from all over the nascent Islamic empire, but especially those hailing from the regions located to the west of the Hijaz—Egypt, North Africa, and Andalusia. Mālik was known as a meticulous and scrupulous scholar for the care he took in the transmission of the historical materials known as hadith. *Ḥadīth* literally means "story" or "tale," but in this case it refers generically to narrative materials purporting to tell the story of the Muslim community. The term would later come to be used almost exclusively to denote reports of incidents that occurred during the lifetime of the Prophet Muḥammad, but at this early stage in Muslim history, it was used more broadly to include any report about the community's past. Because of the care with which Mālik transmitted these materials and what appears to have been a conscious decision on his part to transmit to students only what he deemed the best-attested of the historical narratives that he had studied and collected,[1] he came to be considered an *imām*, an authority, in the science of hadith (*imām fī al-ḥadīth*). However, Mālik was not only an authority on the Muslim community's history as documented in hadith. He was also deemed an authority—an *imām*—on its law (*imām fī al-sunna*).

To appreciate Mālik's stature as a scholar within the Sunnī tradition, it is helpful to consider the number and identity of his students. According to Umar Abd-Allah Wymann-Landgraf, none of the putative founders of the other Sunnī schools of law had as many students from as many different regions of the Islamic world as did Mālik. Although a majority of his students hailed from Egypt, North Africa, and Andalusia, his students also came from the Levant and Iraq and even as far east as Khurāsān. Uniquely in a culture that prized seniority, his study circle attracted more students who were older than him than it did those who were his juniors.[2]

A principal reason for Mālik's fame as a legist was his book, *al-Muwaṭṭaʾ*. Mālik's *Muwaṭṭaʾ* constitutes the first authored treatise on Islamic law. Prior to Mālik's generation, Islamic law seems to have developed in the context of deliberations that took place in small gatherings of jurists. Although many of these earlier juristic deliberations were preserved, either as handwritten notes or via oral transmission, the generations of Muslim scholars before Mālik did not compose *books* of law. The *Muwaṭṭaʾ*, by contrast, represents an attempt to conceive of the law as an entirety, and even though it is not a comprehensive treatise, the structure and contents of the work clearly indicate that Mālik thought of the law as an independent object of knowledge that could be set out systematically in written form. Indeed, historical reports indicate that Mālik spent years editing and revising his text, which resulted in the transmission to posterity of numerous different recensions of the *Muwaṭṭaʾ*.[3] Many of these recensions are lost to history or have survived in only fragmentary form. The recension of the *Muwaṭṭaʾ* that is translated here is that of the Andalusian scholar Yaḥyā b. Yaḥyā al-Laythī (152–234/769–839). Yaḥyā would have studied the *Muwaṭṭaʾ* near the end of Mālik's life, and accordingly, his recension represents the last, or almost the last, "version" or

---

1 Umar F. Abd-Allah Wymann-Landgraf, *Mālik and Medina: Islamic Legal Reasoning in the Formative Period* (Boston: Brill, 2013), 46.

2 Wymann-Landgraf, *Mālik and Medina*, 48.

3 Wymann-Landgraf, *Mālik and Medina*, 60 (noting that Mālik authorized as many as seventy-three different recensions of the *Muwaṭṭaʾ* and that more than one thousand students transmitted the text).

"edition" Mālik prepared of the *Muwaṭṭa'*.[4] In any case, Yaḥyā's recension of the *Muwaṭṭa'* became the most widely used version of the text in the Islamic West, and the version most familiar to modern scholarship.[5]

The *Muwaṭṭa'*, however, is not the only source on Mālik's legal reasoning. Subsequent generations of Muslim jurists compiled Mālik's legal opinions into various books that came to serve as the sourcebooks (*ummahāt*) for what came to be known as the Mālikī school of law or, sometimes, the Medinese school (*madhhab ahl al-Madīna*). These sourcebooks that purported to document Mālik's legal reasoning were apparently drawn from the notes, recollections, and inferences of Mālik's students, and sometimes the students of Mālik's students. The most important of the sourcebooks in the later Mālikī tradition was the *Mudawwana*.[6] Compiled by Saḥnūn b. Saʿīd (d. 240/854), a North African jurist who hailed from Qayrawān in present-day

4 At least seven recensions of the *Muwaṭṭa'* have been published, although some are only fragmentary. Jonathan Brockopp, "Rereading the History of Early Mālikī Jurisprudence," *Journal of the American Oriental Society* 118, no. 2 (1998): 235.

5 Aside from Yaḥyā's recension, the recension of Muḥammad b. al-Ḥasan al-Shaybānī (d. 189/805) is also well known and was widely disseminated, at least among followers of what came to be known as the Iraqi school of jurisprudence (i.e., the Ḥanafīs). Shaybānī's recension, however, represents a substantially different text from the other recensions of the *Muwaṭṭa'*. Sarah Savant has documented, using computer analysis of the recensions of Yaḥyā, his near-contemporary Abū Muṣʿab al-Zuhrī (d. 242/856), and Shaybānī, that whereas the recensions of Yaḥyā and Abū Muṣʿab are virtually identical, with relatively minor differences in ordering, less than 25% of Shaybānī's recension overlaps with those of Yaḥyā and Abū Muṣʿab, and less than 10% of the latter two recensions is found in Shaybānī's. Savant concludes from these results that Shaybānī's recension is better understood as a commentary on the *Muwaṭṭa'* rather than as a recension of Mālik's text. This is not surprising insofar as Shaybānī remained loyal to the Iraqi tradition of Islamic law and was interested in transmitting only those portions of Mālik's work that were useful for Iraqi legal doctrine. Accordingly, he omits the entirety of Mālik's own legal reasoning in his recension, even though, as will be shown below, Mālik's reasoning represents a substantial portion of the book. Sarah Savant, "A Tale of 3 'Versions,'" KITAB website, September 10, 2017, http://kitab-project.org/2017/09/10/a-tale-of-3-versions/ (accessed September 29, 2018). See also Wymann-Landgraf, *Mālik and Medina*, 61–62 n. 119 (comparing Shaybānī's recension of the *Muwaṭṭa'* to that of Yaḥyā).

6 Saḥnūn b. Saʿīd, *al-Mudawwana*, 4 vols. (Beirut: Dār al-Fikr, 1986). Other sourcebooks include *al-Mustakhraja* of ʿUtbī (d. 255/868), *al-Wāḍiḥa* of ʿAbd al-Malik b. Ḥabīb (d. 238/852), and *al-Mawwāziyya* of Muḥammad b. Ibrāhīm b. Ziyād, known as Ibn al-Mawwāz (d. 269/882). See Mohammad Fadel, "The Social Logic of *Taqlīd* and the Rise of the *Mukhtaṣar*," *Islamic Law and Society* 3, no. 2 (1996): 218 n. 98. It should be noted, however, that many passages of the *Mudawwana* are verbatim quotations from the *Muwaṭṭa'*. See, for example, Wymann-Landgraf, *Mālik and Medina*, 6, 54 n. 87, 61 n. 118, and 368. The *Mustakhraja* is published as part of Ibn Rushd the Grandfather's (d. 520/1126) commentary on that text: Abū al-Walīd Muḥammad b. Rushd, *al-Bayān wa'l-taḥṣīl wa'l-sharḥ wa'l-tawjīh wa'l-taʿlīl fī masā'il al-Mustakhraja*, ed. Muḥammad Ḥijjī et al., 20 vols., 2nd ed. (Beirut: Dār al-Gharb al-Islāmī, 1988). Only small portions of *al-Wāḍiḥa* have been edited and published. See Beatrix Ossendorf-Conrad, *Das "K. al-Wadiha" des ʿAbd al-Malik b. Ḥabīb: Edition und Kommentar zu Ms. Qarawiyyin 809/40 (Abwab al-Tahara)* (Stuttgart: Franz Steiner, 1994), and ʿAbd al-Malik b. Ḥabīb, *al-Wāḍiḥa: Kutub al-ṣalāt wa-kutub al-ḥajj*, ed. Miklos Muranyi (Beirut: Dār al-Bashā'ir al-Islāmiyya, 2010). To our knowledge, no portion of the *Mawwāziyya* has yet been published.

Tunisia, the *Mudawwana* consists largely of a series of dialogues between Saḥnūn and one of Mālik's leading students, ʿAbd al-Raḥmān b. al-Qāsim (d. 191/806), in which Saḥnūn would ask Ibn al-Qāsim about Mālik's views on particular legal questions.[7] Ibn al-Qāsim would, in each case, then provide Saḥnūn with Mālik's opinion on the matter, if he believed he knew what it was. If he did not know Mālik's opinion on the question, he might, using conjecture, offer his *opinion* regarding what Mālik would have said about the question, had it been posed to Mālik directly. He would sometimes also share his own view on the issue under consideration. Saḥnūn occasionally also included the views of other students of Mālik, as well as the views of other Muslim scholars, in the course of elaborating a particular legal issue. However, it is clear that Saḥnūn anchored the *Mudawwana* in the voice of Mālik, and it later became the most important source of Mālikī positive law, eclipsing even the *Muwaṭṭaʾ* itself.[8]

While it is extremely unlikely that Mālik viewed himself as founding a legal school, the decisive impact he had on later generations of jurists who chose to follow his teachings ensured that he would hold an honored place in the hall of Sunnī sages. But his impact was not limited to those jurists who chose to follow him. One of his leading students, Muḥammad b. Idrīs al-Shāfiʿī (d. 204/820), identified closely with Mālik's teachings in his youth but went on to break with them and to take Islamic jurisprudence in a distinctly different direction, one perhaps more in keeping with the greater cosmopolitanism of the ʿAbbāsid Empire. In so doing, he established the Shāfiʿī school of law.[9] Mālik's influence was also felt in the Iraqi school of law, later known as the Ḥanafī school: Muḥammad b. al-Ḥasan al-Shaybānī, one of Abū Ḥanīfa's (d. 150/767) two most important disciples, spent substantial time studying with Mālik in Medina. He even transmitted a version of the *Muwaṭṭaʾ* to his own students, known as the *Muwaṭṭaʾ* of Muḥammad or the *Muwaṭṭaʾ* of Shaybānī.[10] Mālik also left an important legacy in the study of hadith: not only was he deemed an astute critic of reports and transmitters,

---

7 For example, in the first line of the opening chapter of the *Mudawwana*, titled "What has come down regarding ablutions (*wuḍūʾ*)," Saḥnūn wrote, "I said to ʿAbd al-Raḥmān b. al-Qāsim, 'With respect to ablutions, did Mālik specify a number of washings, one, two, or three?' He said, 'No, only that they be fulsome. Mālik did not specify a number of washings.'" Saḥnūn, *al-Mudawwana*, 1:2.

8 For an account of how the *Mudawwana* became the central text of Mālikī positive law, see Fadel, "Social Logic," 218–24.

9 Shāfiʿī not only authored his own extensive treatise on positive law, known as *al-Umm*, but also composed the first theoretical treatise on Islamic jurisprudence, known as *al-Risāla*. This latter work would lead in later generations to the development of theoretical jurisprudence, which came to be known as *uṣūl al-fiqh*, a branch of knowledge that was distinct from and independent of substantive law, which was simply known as *fiqh*.

10 Shaybānī also wrote a polemical refutation of the teachings of Mālik and the Medinese; see Muḥammad b. al-Ḥasan al-Shaybānī, *al-Ḥujja ʿalā ahl al-Madīna* (Beirut: ʿĀlam al-Kutub, 1983).

but many of the reports that he included in the *Muwaṭṭaʾ* about the Prophet Muḥammad were later incorporated into what became the most important Sunnī collections of hadith, such as those of Bukhārī and Muslim.

The Place of the *Muwaṭṭaʾ* in Modern Scholarship

English-language scholarship in Islamic studies has long recognized the centrality of the *Muwaṭṭaʾ* in the history of Islamic law and jurisprudence and in the rise of hadith. Much of this scholarship, however, has been concerned primarily with the provenance of the material Mālik cites in his book and with what it tells us about early conceptions of authority in the Muslim community. Historians of early Islamic law are divided with respect to two fundamental issues. The first is the historical authenticity of the narrative materials preserved in works such as the *Muwaṭṭaʾ*. The second is the nature of the Prophet Muḥammad's legislative authority in the early Muslim community, a debate centered around the meaning of the term Arabic term *sunna* (law), and the extent to which it bears an exclusively Prophetic association.

Skeptics, most prominently the great Orientalist Ignaz Goldziher,[11] the historian of Islamic law Joseph Schacht,[12] and their followers, believe that the historical reports found in the Arabic literary tradition, such as those in the *Muwaṭṭaʾ*, which attributed various legal and theological doctrines to earlier generations of the Muslim community or sometimes to the Prophet Muḥammad himself, were not to be taken at face value. Indeed, the general position of these skeptics is that all such historical reports should be deemed fabrications unless proven otherwise. Instead of viewing them as plausible historical accounts of the development of Islamic legal doctrines, the skeptics argue that literary sources such as the *Muwaṭṭaʾ* are useful only for determining the content of Islamic law at the time the works were composed, but that they tell us nothing about the legal practices or theological beliefs of prior generations of Muslims.

Traditional Muslim scholarship exhibited great concern for the integrity of transmitted historical materials, particularly if they had legal or theological significance. Accordingly, transmitters of traditions developed a custom of naming their sources. Ideally, every historical report would be prefaced by the names of the intermediate sources responsible for each stage of the report's transmission, beginning with the report's source and concluding with the person receiving the report. The chain of transmitters documenting the report's provenance was known as the *isnād*, literally "that which props [something] up." The content of the report, that which was

11 Ignaz Goldziher, *Muslim Studies* (London: Allen and Unwin, 1971).

12 Joseph Schacht, *The Origins of Muhammadan Jurisprudence* (Oxford: Clarendon Press, 1959).

"propped up" by the chain of transmitters, was called the *matn*. Scholars of the skeptical school, however, placed no credence in these chains of authorities, even suggesting that the more perfect the chain of authorities, the greater reason there was to suspect forgery. They noted that sometimes reports could be found in early works, such as the *Muwaṭṭa'*, with a chain of transmitters that was truncated, ended with a Companion (sing. *ṣaḥābī*, pl. *ṣaḥāba*) of the Prophet Muḥammad, or omitted intermediate sources, only to appear in later works, such as the hadith collection of Bukhārī, with a gapless chain of transmitters going back all the way to the Prophet Muḥammad. To account for this phenomenon, skeptical scholars suggested that later generations had invented chains of transmission to make it appear as though the doctrines originated with the Prophet or the early community.

The skeptics' belief that most historical reports found in early literary sources should be deemed spurious is closely connected to their belief that the early Muslim community did not see the Prophet Muḥammad as a legislator or, if they did believe him to be one, did not consider him the Muslim community's exclusive or supreme lawgiver. For them, the fact that a historical report places a theological or legal norm in the mouth of the Prophet is evidence that a faction of Muslims attempted to project their own normative views onto the Prophet Muḥammad to strengthen their position vis-à-vis other Muslims who might have held a different view; it is not evidence that the norm in fact originated in Prophetic teaching. When such a report is documented by a gapless chain of transmission, there is even greater reason to believe that the report was introduced later, rather than earlier, in Muslim history.

There is a curious form of circularity in casting doubt on the accuracy of a historical report on the grounds that it contains an appeal to a kind of authority whose grounds, it is asserted, were articulated only later. The danger of using normative standards regarding what does or does not count as a plausible legal argument in the early Muslim community to date particular texts comes out most clearly in the work of Norman Calder. Calder, who read in the *Muwaṭṭa'* a theory of the Prophet Muḥammad as the community's supreme legislator, used this reading to argue that, contrary to the common view of scholarship, the *Mudawwana* must have preceded the *Muwaṭṭa'*. It was Calder's view that because the Prophet's role as supreme legislator had become firmly established in legal theory only in the third Islamic century (ninth century CE), the *Muwaṭṭa'* must have been written substantially after Mālik's death, and thus its attribution to Mālik is, like the attributions of many traditions to the Prophet Muḥammad, fictitious.[13]

13 Norman Calder, *Studies in Early Muslim Jurisprudence* (Oxford: Clarendon Press, 1993). See Mohammad Fadel, "Authority in Ibn Abī Zayd al-Qayrawānī's *Kitāb al-nawādir wa-l-ziyādāt 'alā mā fī l-Mudawwana min ghayrihā min al-ummahāt*: 'The Chapter of Judgments' (*Kitāb*

Unsurprisingly, Muslim scholars have reacted to such claims impeaching the integrity of the Islamic legal tradition with derision and hostility. Numerous Muslim scholars have published books and articles in both English and Arabic defending the authenticity of the reports preserved by the early Muslim literary tradition and the antiquity of the Prophet Muḥammad's status as not only *a* legislator but as the *supreme* legislator of the Muslim community from the earliest days of the Muslim community. Perhaps the best example of this genre of writing is Muhammad al-Azami's *On Schacht's Origins of Muhammadan Jurisprudence*,[14] in which Azami attempted to refute Schacht's claim that Muslim jurists invented spurious chains of transmission in order to attribute, anachronistically, their preferred legal positions to the Prophet Muḥammad. Azami demonstrated that the phenomenon of the apparent backward proliferation of chains of authorities might be explained by the failure of skeptical scholars to consider the broad range of historical material available. While Mālik, for example, might have included a report with only a perfunctory chain of transmitters, another, contemporaneous authority might have transmitted the same report with the full chain of authorities. Azami also criticized Schacht and his followers for failing to distinguish between the use of traditions in works of law such as the *Muwaṭṭaʾ* and in the works of traditionists (scholars who specialized in the transmission of historical reports about the Prophet Muḥammad, known as *muḥaddithūn* or *ahl al-ḥadīth*). According to Azami, jurists were relatively indifferent to documenting the chains of authorities for every report they used in their legal reasoning. In short, Azami and other scholars with a positive view of the integrity of the Muslim tradition have demonstrated that there are numerous plausible explanations for the phenomenon of the backward proliferation of chains of authorities other than Schacht's suggestion of deliberate forgery.[15]

---

al-aqḍiya)," in *The Heritage of Arabo-Islamic Learning: Studies Presented to Wadad Kadi*, ed. Maurice A. Pomerantz and Aram A. Shahin (Boston: Brill, 2016), 208–9. However, the careful work of Miklos Muranyi, based on careful analysis and collation of thousands of pieces of early manuscript evidence found in North African libraries, has generally been taken as vindicating the traditional dating of the *Muwaṭṭaʾ* and the *Mudawwana*. See Joseph E. Lowry, review of *Die Rechtsbücher des Qairawāners Saḥnūn b. Saʿīd: Entstehungsgeschichte und Werküberlieferung* by Miklos Muranyi, *Journal of the American Oriental Society* 123, no. 2 (2003): 439 (stating that "Muranyi has surely disproved Calder's imaginative reconstruction" of the relative dating of the *Mudawwana* and the *Muwaṭṭaʾ*).

14 Muhammad M. al-Azami, *On Schacht's Origins of Muhammadan Jurisprudence* (Oxford: Oxford Centre for Islamic Studies and Islamic Texts Society, 1996).

15 See, for example, Nabia Abbott, *Studies in Arabic Literari Papyri*, 3 vols. (Chicago: University of Chicago Oriental Institute Publications, 1957), for evidence that the early Muslim community recorded traditions of the Prophet Muḥammad. See also Harald Motzki, *Analysing Muslim Traditions: Studies in Legal, Exegetical and* Maghāzī Ḥadīth (Boston: Brill, 2010), who attempts to develop a method for dating traditions that neither assumes that the chains of authorities are forgeries nor takes them as conclusive.

Whatever one's views regarding the dating of Muslim traditions generally and of the historical authenticity of the traditions that Mālik cites in the *Muwaṭṭa'* in particular, one can approach the *Muwaṭṭa'* without taking a stance on the provenance of either the work or the materials it contains. Contemporary readers are entitled to read it as an important artifact of Islamic legal history—indeed, of legal history generally[16]—that challenges us to understand it on its own terms, whether at the level of its implicit theory of law (jurisprudence, or what the later Islamic tradition would call *uṣūl al-fiqh*) or at the level of its specific legal doctrines (positive law, or what Islamic tradition refers to as *fiqh*). It is our hope as translators that our translation will render the text of the *Muwaṭṭa'* sufficiently accessible to nonspecialists to allow them to appreciate it with both questions in mind.

Calder has helpfully classified the modes of reasoning in early Islamic legal thought as falling broadly into two categories: *apostolic* and *discursive*.[17] Discursive arguments are characteristically dialogic in structure, often appearing in the guise of a question followed by an answer, or a statement followed by a response.[18] Arguments rooted in apostolic authority, by contrast, are exegetical in structure; that is, they are based on deciphering the meaning of an authoritative text, whether from the Quran, from the Prophet Muḥammad, or from some other authority figure. This division of arguments into those of authority versus those of discursive reason, moreover, is well known in the Islamic tradition, which itself broadly recognizes the distinction between arguments rooted in authority and those rooted in reason. The Islamic tradition uses various terms to refer to authority arguments, including *naql* (transmitted information), *sam'* (heard information), and *athar/khabar*/hadith (reported information), to name only a few. Likewise, there are a number of terms for rational (discursive) arguments, such as *ra'y* (considered opinion), *naẓar* (deliberation), and *qawl* (a view). Indeed, Islamic sources themselves describe early legal and theological disputes as being grounded in different conceptions of the relative authority of revelation and reason, sometimes labeling one group *aṣḥāb al-ḥadīth* (the partisans of transmitted authority) and its rivals *aṣḥāb al-ra'y* (the partisans of considered judgment).

Part of what makes the *Muwaṭṭa'* a challenging text is that it resists neat categorization as either a vindication of authoritative texts against rational argumentation or a vindication of rational argumentation over texts. In reading this work, therefore, the reader must attempt to understand how

16 To put the *Muwaṭṭa'* into a broader historical context, the Justinian Code, for example, was developed between 529 and 565 of the Common Era, only two centuries before Mālik.

17 Calder, *Studies*, 8 and 19.

18 Calder, *Studies*, 8 and 19 (noting that discursive arguments are often marked by an "I said, he said" [*qultu/qāla*] structure or introduced by the phrase, "What do you think [*a-ra'ayta*]?").

its author views the relationship between authority and reason. As the preceding discussion of scholarly debates regarding the provenance of the *Muwaṭṭaʾ* indicates, however, scholars have sometimes implicitly conflated jurisprudential questions with questions related to the authenticity of the materials on which such questions draw. One consequence is that some scholars essentially use jurisprudential arguments to derive conclusions regarding the authenticity of particular texts. Although we believe that this is a serious methodological error, it is nevertheless important for the reader to be aware of the different jurisprudential theories that modern scholars have attributed to the text. Awareness of the different accounts of the *Muwaṭṭaʾ*'s jurisprudence will help the reader approach the text with a better sense of its interpretive possibilities.

As seen in greater detail below, while there is a great deal of disagreement among modern scholars about Mālik's jurisprudence, there is convergence regarding certain features of the *Muwaṭṭaʾ* and its place in Islamic legal history. First, there is broad agreement that Mālik's jurisprudence represents, for lack of a better term, an "old" style of jurisprudence that was displaced with the rise of a "new" style of jurisprudence. This new style of jurisprudence is exemplified by the writings of Mālik's student Muḥammad b. Idrīs al-Shāfiʿī. In contrast to earlier generations of Muslim jurists, including Mālik himself, Shāfiʿī was deeply concerned with articulating a formal set of jurisprudential principles that could justify substantive legal doctrine. Although he began his study of the law as a student of Mālik, his peripatetic career, which led him to various regions of the ʿAbbāsid Empire, including Yemen, Iraq (especially the ʿAbbāsid capital, Baghdad), and finally Egypt, exposed him to the diversity of legal views within the Muslim world. In the course of these travels, moreover, Shāfiʿī regularly debated with local scholars, constantly challenging them to explain the grounds on which they justified their diverse doctrinal positions. His critical approach to substantive law ultimately led him to write treatises devoted exclusively to the jurisprudential questions of what are the material sources that constitute Islamic law and what are the proper means of inference (*istidlāl*) that may be used to interpret those material sources. The most famous of these theoretical reflections on jurisprudence is known simply as *The Epistle* (*al-Risāla*).[19]

Shāfiʿī articulated a formal system of jurisprudence based on three material sources of law—the Quran, Prophetic law (*sunna*), and the

19 There are two translations of this text into English, the first by Majid Khadduri, *Islamic Jurisprudence: Shāfiʿī's "Risāla"* (Baltimore: Johns Hopkins Press, 1961), and the second by Joseph E. Lowry, *The Epistle on Legal Theory: A Translation of al-Shāfiʿī's "Risālah"* (New York: New York University Press, 2013).

consensus of the Muslim community (*ijmāʿ*)—and one method of reasoning, analogy (*qiyās*). Shāfiʿī's theory of the sources of Islamic law is sometimes referred to as the "four sources" theory. Many scholars also assume that Shāfiʿī's four-source theory of the law later became the *universal* theory that defined Sunnism. For that reason, scholars sometimes refer to him as "the master architect" of Islamic law.[20]

Even a cursory skim of the *Muwaṭṭa'*, however, discloses that Mālik certainly recognized the authority of each of these three material sources insofar as he appealed, from time to time, to Quranic texts, to traditions attributed to the Prophet Muḥammad, and to a kind of consensus. It is also clear from the *Muwaṭṭa'* that Mālik sometimes engaged in analogical reasoning. Therefore, what is distinctive about Shāfiʿī's contribution?

Whereas there was no substantive difference with respect to the Quran between Mālik and other representatives of the "old" jurisprudence, on the one hand, and Shāfiʿī, on the other hand, Shāfiʿī applied much more demanding standards than did other jurists for what constituted evidence of Prophetic law, the *sunna*. Mālik, for example, accepted traditions attributed to the Companions of the Prophet Muḥammad, as well as traditions attributed to the next two generations of Muslims, known as the Followers (*tābiʿūn*) and the "followers of the Followers" (*tābiʿū al-tābiʿīn*), as evidence of Prophetic law. He also accepted as evidence traditions attributed to the Prophet Muḥammad that lacked a complete chain of transmitters attesting to the authenticity of the report. For example, Mālik frequently omitted the names of all the intermediary transmitters of the report between himself and the Prophet Muḥammad, and he would sometimes simply attribute the report to an unnamed source that he deemed to be trustworthy.[21]

Shāfiʿī, by contrast, admitted only traditions that satisfied the most rigorous criteria of authenticity—those that included the names of all the reporters who had participated in transmitting the report from the report's origination with the Prophet Muḥammad to himself. Shāfiʿī insisted that only reports with explicit and uninterrupted chains of transmission could serve as evidence of Prophetic law because although a Muslim is bound to obey Prophetic law, there must be objective proof that a particular norm is, in fact, part of Prophetic law before he is under an obligation to follow it. When a Muslim hears a Prophetic tradition,

20 See, for example, Wael Hallaq, "Was al-Shāfiʿī the Master Architect of Islamic Jurisprudence?," *International Journal of Middle East Studies* 25, no. 4 (1993): 593 (while denying that Shāfiʿī in fact was the "master architect" of Islamic jurisprudence, Hallaq argues that he was the first to articulate the "great synthesis" between rationalists and traditionists that is said to characterize Sunnī Islam).

21 See, for example, hadith no. 933 of the RME, where Yaḥyā gives the chain of transmitters as follows: "According to Mālik, a source he deemed reliable reported (*ʿan al-thiqa ʿindahu*)."

he will suffer confusion if he has no means to determine whether the teaching contained in the tradition is an authentic part of Prophetic law (and therefore to be obeyed) or a mistaken attribution to the Prophet Muḥammad or, worse still, a forgery (and therefore to be ignored). Only if the full chain of transmitters of the report is disclosed to the listener is he in a position to evaluate the soundness of the report's contents, because he is then able to determine whether the transmitters are reliable. If the listener can establish that each link in the chain of transmission is reliable, he can soundly conclude that the teaching in the report is part of Prophetic law and must be taken into account in determining his legal rights and obligations before God.

Accordingly, for Shāfiʿī, a report, even if attributed to the Prophet Muḥammad, is not admissible as evidence of Prophetic law unless two conditions are satisfied. First, the report must include a complete chain of transmission. And second, the transmitters of the report, at each stage of its transmission, must be known to be trustworthy. When these conditions are satisfied, the report is considered valid (*ṣaḥīḥ*) and its teachings become obligatory, even if only a few individuals (or, in the extreme case, only one) report the tradition, and even if the tradition goes against numerous other reports of the Prophet's Companions or their Followers. The only exception to this principle occurs when another source of law contradicts or otherwise qualifies the report's teachings. However, Shāfiʿī went to great lengths to demonstrate that many traditions attributed to the Prophet that were commonly thought to contradict other traditions or the Quran were not, in fact, contradictory and could, with proper knowledge of the Arabic language as well as the community's history, be harmonized.

This point marked another distinctive feature of Shāfiʿī's jurisprudence: when faced with texts that seemed to contradict one another, he attempted to harmonize them (*jamʿ*) rather than give effect to only one of them (*tarjīḥ*) and ignore the others. Shāfiʿī's approach to Prophetic law thus reduced the possibility of contradictions within the body of reports that constituted evidence of Prophetic law by simply excluding a vast amount of traditional material that did not meet his relatively stringent formal criteria of validity. However, Mālik and other jurists adhering to the "old" jurisprudence were more willing to accept reports while ignoring contrary reports without providing a clear basis for their choice, because they admitted a much broader set of reports as valid evidence of Prophetic law. Shāfiʿī's theory of what constituted Prophetic law and how it related to the other material sources of law gave pride of place to reports attributed to the Prophet Muḥammad that bore objective indicia of reliability in the form of complete chains of transmitters whom the Muslim community knew to be trustworthy.[22]

Shāfiʿī also articulated a doctrine of consensus (*ijmāʿ*) that essentially eviscerated it, neutering it as an effective source of law. Whereas the "old" jurisprudence often relied on assertions of consensus or agreement, these claims did not assert *universal* agreement or consensus. In most cases, claims of agreement or consensus indicated that a majority of jurists agreed on a particular principle of law, and not that *all* of them agreed. Furthermore, even these majoritarian agreements were not universal, but instead often reflected only local majorities of scholars. Accordingly, a claim of consensus or agreement often boiled down to the agreement of a majority of scholars in a particular location, such as the scholars of the Hijaz (Mecca and Medina), those of Iraq (Kufa and Basra), or the Levant. Shāfiʿī, however, understood consensus as requiring the agreement of *all* Muslims, not just the agreement of the learned. The effect of such an understanding of consensus was to reduce its purview to those elements of revealed law that were elementary, such as the obligations to pray, to fast, to pay the alms-tax, to perform the Pilgrimage, and so on, and to eliminate it as a source of law for the substantive regulation of either ritual or secular life. Another consequence of this narrow understanding of consensus was that it reinforced the status of valid Prophetic traditions as a preeminent, if not the dominant, source of Islamic law.

With respect to what constituted legitimate tools of legal reasoning, Shāfiʿī's theory was not original insofar as he recognized the validity of analogical reasoning. There is no doubt that the "old" jurisprudence made much use of analogy, a fact that is evident from the *Muwaṭṭa'*. What was unique about Shāfiʿī's theory of legal reasoning was that he argued that the *only* form of legitimate legal reasoning was analogy based on a rule set out in one of the three material sources of law—Quran, Prophetic law, or consensus. With this position, he pitted himself against the "old" jurisprudence, which was also willing to use other modes of practical reasoning to derive legal rules.

Mālik, for example, readily used the doctrine of "preclusion" or "blocking the means" (*sadd al-dharīʿa*) to prohibit conduct that, although lawful if viewed in isolation, could reasonably be expected to produce an unlawful result. Mālik would also sometimes take into account conceptions of the public

22 Wymann-Landgraf suggests that in many cases the disagreement between Mālik and Shāfiʿī regarding how Prophetic law should be understood turned on how much weight to give the Prophet Muḥammad's nonverbal conduct, with Mālik much more reluctant to take such conduct as evidence of Prophetic law. See, for example, Wymann-Landgraf, *Mālik and Medina*, 106 (noting that according to the Mālikīs, reports of the Prophet's actions are ambiguous and in need of further interpretation to determine their legal content).

good (*al-maṣlaḥa al-mursala*) in formulating legal rules without grounding his conclusions in a rule enshrined in one of the three material sources of law. Similarly, Iraqi jurists would sometimes adopt a rule that was contrary to analogical reasoning on the basis of what they called *istiḥsān*, which is often translated as "equity" or "juristic preference." Shāfiʿī, however, vociferously rejected these various modes of nontextual legal reasoning in his polemics with followers of the "old" jurisprudence, even authoring a treatise called "The Invalidation of *Istiḥsān*" (*Ibṭāl al-istiḥsān*).[23] Just as Shāfiʿī's approach to Prophetic law dramatically reduced the kinds of evidence admissible to prove the content of Prophetic law, his theory also significantly reduced the scope of legitimate legal reasoning by limiting it to analogical reasoning grounded in a rule found in one of the three material sources of law.

Finally, Shāfiʿī elevated the status of the individual legal interpreter over the community as a collective interpreter by recognizing an *individual* duty to engage in a search for the legal truth in situations in which the material sources did not provide an explicit answer to a legal question. This search for an answer to a legal question he called *ijtihād*, and he derived its necessity from the general obligation of Muslims to face the Kabah (a cube-shaped shrine located in Mecca) when they perform their daily prayers. If a Muslim is in the vicinity of the Kabah, his sense perception provides immediate and necessary knowledge of the proper direction of prayer. If, however, the Muslim is not in Mecca, he is obliged to infer the direction of the Kabah using natural signs, such as the location of stars, as well as other possible indicants to determine, to the best of his or her ability, the direction in which he ought to pray. By doing so, he has discharged his duty before God, whether or not his reasoning is correct.

According to Shāfiʿī, the same principle applies whenever a Muslim is faced with a practical question of law for which the revealed sources do not provide a clear answer. In such a case, the Muslim is obliged, to the extent of his ability, to seek evidence (*dalīl*) of what God's intended rule is by investigating the material sources of law in order to reach a reasoned judgment. Whether or not his conclusion is correct, he has satisfied his duty before God. By contrast, blindly following the opinion of another scholar or a group of scholars (a process known as *taqlīd*), at least in circumstances in which the Muslim has the capacity to understand the material sources of law directly, does not discharge his duty before God and therefore implicitly results in sin.[24]

---

23 Shāfiʿī's opposition to non-analogical modes of legal reasoning was so strident that he was commonly reported to have said, "Whoever reasons by *istiḥsān* has certainly invented law" (*man istaḥsana fa-qad sharaʿa*).

24 For details on Shāfiʿī's view of *ijtihād* and *taqlīd*, see Ahmed El Shamsy, "Rethinking *Taqlīd* in the Early Shāfiʿī School," *Journal of the American Oriental Society* 128, no. 1 (2008): 1–23.

Modern scholars' view of Shāfiʿī's contribution to Islamic jurisprudence inevitably colors their understanding of Mālik's approach to Islamic law as set out in the *Muwaṭṭa'*. It would not be much of an exaggeration to say that Schacht considered Shāfiʿī and his jurisprudence the *telos* toward which Islamic law was evolving and its natural equilibrium point. Indeed, one might even say that in Schacht's view, Islamic law did not become truly *Islamic* until Shāfiʿī, whose jurisprudential method sought to anchor every rule in a revealed source. For Schacht, the "old" jurisprudence was characterized by a different ethos, one that he referred to as the "living *sunna*." By this term he meant that the legal system of the early Muslim community was little more than an ad hoc, anonymous amalgamation of Arab customary laws and the laws of the conquered peoples of the Near East, with only a vague connection to Quranic ethical principles.

Prophetic law was not a constituent element of this living *sunna* in Schacht's conception. The fact that Mālik included in the *Muwaṭṭa'* traditions attributed to the Prophet Muḥammad did not contradict this conclusion, since Mālik clearly did not feel bound to give effect to all of the Prophetic traditions that he included. However, in Schacht's view, Mālik's inclusion of Prophetic traditions indicated that the idea of the living *sunna* as the basis of the Muslim community's law was already beginning to give way to a notion of an explicitly *Prophetic* law. But at least in Mālik's generation, scholars were still keen on defending the living *sunna* against the threat posed by Prophetic traditions, which were often transmitted by relatively small numbers of individuals. According to Schacht, Shāfiʿī's powerful defense of Prophetic law and his insistence on excluding secondary evidence and admitting only rigorously authenticated Prophetic traditions finally served the coup de grace to the living *sunna* and the "old" method of jurisprudence. Followers of the latter continued to adhere to the teachings of prior generations, but as a result of Shāfiʿī's impact, they could no longer justify their position on the grounds of either consensus or deference to prior authority. Accordingly, Schacht concluded, they had no choice but to fabricate Prophetic traditions to support their legal positions.

In Schacht's assessment, therefore, Shāfiʿī's legacy is mixed. Although Shāfiʿī succeeded in the articulation of a jurisprudence that transformed what had merely been the law of the Muslims into a self-consciously Islamic legal system, that very same jurisprudence also led to stasis in Islamic law and its ultimate demise. Because his jurisprudential theory reduced Islamic law to a process of law-finding that was limited to a body of fixed texts, once the body of Prophetic traditions had stabilized in the century after Shāfiʿī, Islamic law lost the adaptive qualities that had characterized the role of the living *sunna* in the "old" jurisprudence. As a result, Islamic law found it increasingly difficult, if not impossible, to adapt to changing circumstances, a feature that caused its deep crisis in the modern era.

Schacht's view of the "old" methods of jurisprudence does have some empirical basis in the *Muwaṭṭaʾ*. Mālik includes reports from numerous authority figures other than the Prophet Muḥammad. At times, he cites Prophetic traditions but explicitly points out that these traditions are not only not legally normative but actually contrary to the law. In such cases, Mālik often invokes the concept of "practice" (*ʿamal*). Indeed, post-Shāfiʿī jurisprudence would identify Mālik's conception of "the practice of the people of Medina" (*ʿamal ahl al-Madīna*) as a distinctive feature of what would become Mālikī substantive law. Schacht appears to treat Mālik's conception of the practice of the people of Medina as the paradigm of the living *sunna* that characterized the "old" jurisprudence and that was the direct object of Shāfiʿī's critique.

Other scholars, however, have denied that Mālik's conception of the practice of the people of Medina functioned as an alternative to Prophetic law in the manner Schacht suggested. Rather, according to them, Mālik understood "practice" to be a more reliable indicant of Prophetic law than were traditions narrated through single chains of transmission, even if the individual transmitters were known to be reliable.[25] Others agreed with Schacht in part, accepting his claim that the pre-Shāfiʿī law of the Muslim community was based on the living *sunna* in the sense that it was the product of the deliberations of the Muslim community at the time and hence dynamic. But they qualified Schacht's understanding of the living *sunna* by insisting that such deliberations and the development of the law were always conducted under the general rubric of Prophetic law, so it was an error to juxtapose the "old" conception of law with the idea of Prophetic law.[26]

However, these observations about the status of "practice" (*ʿamal*) in Mālik's jurisprudence in general and in the *Muwaṭṭaʾ* in particular are largely impressionistic and not based on a systematic reading of the text itself. The groundbreaking work of Umar Abd-Allah Wymann-Landgraf on the *Muwaṭṭaʾ*, by contrast, provides a systematic analysis of Mālik's approach to the law.[27] On the basis of a close analysis of Mālik's terminology in the

25 See, for example, Yasin Dutton, *The Origins of Islamic Law: The Qurʾan, the "Muwaṭṭaʾ" and Madinan ʿAmal*, 2nd ed. (New York: RoutledgeCurzon, 2002), 30 (arguing that although Mālik recognized the decisive role of Prophetic traditions in the derivation of Islamic law, he believed that they could be properly understood only by reference to the practice of the Muslim community).

26 See, for example, Fazlur Rahman, *Islamic Methodology in History* (Karachi: Karachi Central Institute of Islamic Research, 1965), 19. See also El Shamsy, "Rethinking *Taqlīd*," 3, where he equates Schacht's notion of the living *sunna* with Mālik's concept of practice but notes that Prophetic traditions "were clearly an important element" constituting the "living tradition."

27 Wymann-Landgraf, *Mālik and Medina*.

Muwaṭṭaʾ, Wymann-Landgraf argues convincingly that Mālik developed a sophisticated set of terms that he used to make systematic distinctions between rules of law based on historical authority and those based on discursive authority. Mālik denoted the former category of rules with the term *sunna* and the latter with the term *amr*. Moreover, Mālik's terminology also signaled to his readers the degree to which various legal rules were the subject of agreement in Medina. Accordingly, he would sometimes describe a rule as "the rule in our view" (*al-amr ʿindanā*) or "the agreed-upon rule among us" (*al-amr al-mujtamaʿ ʿalayhi ʿindanā*), the latter indicating a greater degree of acceptance among the Medinese than the former. Mālik also deployed many other terms, according to Wymann-Landgraf, to convey the range of views on particular legal issues, from terms indicating that the stated position was his own opinion to those marking the absence of known dissent on the rule in question.[28]

Wymann-Landgraf's analysis of Mālik's terminology calls into question Schacht's conception of the living *sunna* as an anonymous amalgam of ad hoc norms adopted in response to new problems in the community. On this account, Mālik's notion of the practice of the people of Medina entailed a complex set of interpretive and jurisprudential assumptions and practices. In some cases, these included the assumption of a continuing, unbroken line of "practice" that originated in the days of the Prophet Muḥammad. The legitimacy of such practice could not be doubted simply because a lone reporter transmitted a Prophetic tradition contrary to it, even if the transmitters of that report were otherwise reliable. Mālik's notion of practice also encompassed appeal to the systematic legal reasoning of scholars, sometimes individual and at other times collective, that was based on legal norms and not on revealed texts and so was broader than the legal analogy that Shāfiʿī endorsed as the only permissible tool of legal reasoning. It also included an idea of *relative* consensus and thus recognized points of agreement and disagreement within the community as well as the breadth of each. Finally, it recognized that certain legal norms—which Mālik called *sunna*—were themselves not justifiable in terms of systematic legal reasoning but rather defined the bounds within which systematic legal reasoning took place.[29]

Wymann-Landgraf thus argues that even before Shāfiʿī, Islamic law was deeply committed to formal legal reasoning (*ijtihād*), although it recognized a broader set of legitimate inferential tools than Shāfiʿī's limited

---

28 Mālik's other terms include, for example, "the agreed-upon rule among us, the one in respect of which there is no dissent" (*al-amr al-mujtamaʿ ʿalayhi ʿindanā alladhī lā ikhtilāfa fīhi*).

29 Because of the compelling nature of Wymann-Landgraf's argument, the translation strives to use consistent translations of Mālik's terminology and to provide transliterations of the key Arabic terms.

legal analogy. Accordingly, the notion of practice cannot be equated with a vague, ad hoc system of customary law, as Schacht's analysis would suggest. Moreover, even after Shāfiʿī, Muslim scholars trained in the Hijazi and Iraqi traditions (which later came to be known as the Mālikī and Ḥanafī schools,[30] respectively) continued to accept the legitimacy of the inferential techniques that Shāfiʿī had so vehemently rejected and to follow their own, broader, pre-Shāfiʿī conceptions of how Prophetic law may be established. Therefore, contrary to Schacht, Shāfiʿī's theory of the four sources never became the *common* Sunnī theory of law. The Mālikīs and the Ḥanafīs continued to reject Shāfiʿī's most distinctive jurisprudential claims regarding the role of Prophetic traditions as well as his narrow definition of consensus and his position that analogy was the only legitimate method of legal reasoning. Accordingly, they had no need to forge Prophetic traditions to defend their points of view. In addition, there is very little evidence to support Schacht's claim that post-Shāfiʿī jurists increasingly relied on Prophetic traditions to support their interpretations of controversial points of law, whether the reports were forged or authentic.[31]

For Ahmed El Shamsy, the crucial development inaugurated by Shāfiʿī's jurisprudence was not his emphasis on the centrality of the Prophet Muḥammad as a lawgiver but rather the gradual canonization of the Muslims' collective memory of the Prophet's mission. The process of canonization resulted in the transfer of religious authority from the community of Muslims to a body of texts that recorded the community's experience of revelation. The result was a sharp demarcation between the sacred time of the Muslim community's founding and its subsequent, "secular" history. Prior to canonization, the significance of the Muslim community's past necessarily had to be mediated through its living experience. But once canonization had clearly separated sacred time from secular time, there was no need for communal experience to access the Prophetic era; instead, the individual interpreter became the locus of understanding the present implications of the sacred founding moment. In the post-Shāfiʿī era, El Shamsy argues, Islamic law was characterized by communities of *interpretation* known as the schools of law (sing. *madhhab*, pl. *madhāhib*),

30 Followers of the Iraqi tradition of Islamic law were known as Ḥanafīs after the leading representative of that tradition, Abū Ḥanīfa.

31 At several points in his book, Wymann-Landgraf identifies a rule in the *Muwaṭṭaʾ* as a point of contention between Hijazi and Iraqi jurists but notes that neither side was able to produce a conclusive Prophetic tradition to vindicate its position, whether during Mālik's lifetime or over the succeeding generations. See, for example, Wymann-Landgraf, *Mālik and Medina*, 375 (noting that despite the antiquity of the disagreement between the Iraqis and the Medinese regarding how to distribute the estates of individuals who die in common circumstances, such as during battles, in shipwrecks, or under collapsed buildings, neither party was able to cite a hadith in support of its position).

rather than the communities of *tradition* that had prevailed in the first two centuries of Islam before Shāfiʿī.[32]

The ideological transformation sparked by canonization was paralleled by a sociological transformation that reinforced this cultural development. Whereas Mālik was born in an Islamic empire dominated by Arab Muslims and one in which Arab tribal origins were a distinct badge of privilege, by Shāfiʿī's death in the beginning of the third Islamic century, Muslim society had become ethnically cosmopolitan, and tribal membership was rapidly losing its social importance. The new order under the ʿAbbāsids, for example, increasingly relied on non-Arab Muslims to staff the empire's legal and administrative bureaucracy. In such a sociological milieu, it is not surprising that a conception of the law such as that advanced by Shāfiʿī, which cast the law as amenable to theoretical study along the lines of any other science, would displace a conception of the law rooted in shared experience. The kind of experience-based justification of law seemingly advocated by Mālik and other jurists of the "old" school seemed to marginalize, even if unintentionally, new Muslims, who by virtue of their more recent conversion could never be the discursive equals of "old" Muslims. Shāfiʿī's jurisprudence, by making a common body of texts that existed in the space of sacred time the exclusive source of religious and legal authority, had a leveling effect between old Muslims and new converts. Both groups existed in historical time and therefore were equidistant from the sacred time that held a monopoly over the new community's authority. Whereas Mālik was reported to have believed that "the people" should defer to the Medinese (*al-nās tabaʿ li-ahl al-Madīna*), for Shāfiʿī all Muslims stood in an equal relationship to the community's founding moment. The implicit social egalitarianism of Shāfiʿī's jurisprudence was in that respect more consonant with the spirit of the ʿAbbāsid age than was the communitarian model of law and authority found in the *Muwaṭṭaʾ*, which effectively denied that those who had not experienced life in the Prophet's community could reach a true understanding of Prophetic law.[33]

Overview of the *Muwaṭṭaʾ*

Although modern scholarship has provided many interesting and useful insights regarding the *Muwaṭṭaʾ* and its relationship to Mālik's jurisprudence, its engagements with the text have been overwhelmingly generic, and its conclusions have consequently been partial, incomplete, and in many cases reductive. To demonstrate their weaknesses, however, it is first necessary to

32 Ahmed El Shamsy, *The Canonization of Islamic Law: A Social and Intellectual History* (New York: Cambridge University Press, 2013), 4–6.

33 El Shamsy, *Canonization*, 91–92.

provide a fuller description of the text to show that there is no single theory that structures the relationship between authority and legal reason in Mālik's jurisprudence. Instead, context matters. As shown in greater detail below, some discussions in the *Muwaṭṭa'* are almost entirely dependent on what Calder would have called "apostolic" authority, that is, appeals to authoritative texts that call simply for exegesis, while other discussions are virtually devoid of historical texts and therefore consist almost entirely of discursive legal reasoning. One cannot fully grasp the jurisprudence of the *Muwaṭṭa'*, therefore, without also taking into account the distribution of different kinds of arguments across the work.

Accordingly, we will here provide an overview of the book's arrangement and contents, outline a taxonomy of the texts Mālik uses, and tally the distribution of these texts throughout the work, both in the aggregate and at the level of individual chapters. This overview, in turn, will allow the reader to better appreciate the relationship of authority and discursive reason in Mālik's jurisprudence.

Mālik arranged the *Muwaṭṭa'* in a series of parts that the modern reader would call chapters but that Mālik himself titled "books," each chapter representing one book (*kitāb*). The Royal Moroccan Edition (RME), which forms the basis of this translation, includes forty-five books, the first entitled the Book of Obligatory Prayer Times and the last called the Book of Miscellaneous Matters. Each book is typically divided into one or more sections, each with its own heading, with one or more texts included under each heading.[34] Although the manuscript does not number the texts, the editors of the RME have done so. According to their enumeration, the RME contains 2,815 distinct texts. The first twenty books of the *Muwaṭṭa'* pertain to ritual law, regulating the ordinary ritual practices of Islam commonly referred to as the "five pillars" of Islam as well as certain supererogatory rituals closely associated with those duties.[35] These texts make up almost 40% of the book's length if measured by word count,[36] and 45% of the

34 The only exception to this pattern is Book 38, which does not contain separate sections. Instead, it has a single section titled "Leasing Out Farmland." It is, however, clearly separate from Book 37, and it concludes with the statement, "The Book of Leasing Farmland has been completed, with praise to God."

35 The "five pillars" of Islam consist of the testimony of faith, daily prayer (*ṣalāt*), fasting (*ṣiyām*), almsgiving (*zakāt*), and pilgrimage (*ḥajj*). Mālik also includes texts that deal with various supererogatory forms of worship associated with these required rituals. One might question the inclusion of Book 16, the Book of the Alms-Tax (*zakāt*), among the chapters that deal with ritual law and instead classify it simply as part of the law of taxation in light of its objective character and the fact that it even touches on the tax obligations of non-Muslims. Of the chapters that treat ritual, the Book of the Alms-Tax is the second-longest, consisting of approximately 12,000 words and including 129 distinct texts.

36 Our translation contains approximately 270,000 words. The total word count of the first twenty books is approximately 100,000.

book's length if measured as a proportion of the total number of texts in the work.[37] If a broader understanding of ritual is used, however, it is also necessary to include Books 21–26. These books deal with religiously motivated conduct, even if it is not part of ordinary ritual life.[38] When these books are added to the first twenty books of the *Muwaṭṭaʾ*, the proportion of texts dealing with ritual law increases to approximately 43% of the book by word count[39] and approximately 51% by text count.[40]

Given the centrality of ritual to the *Muwaṭṭaʾ*, it is understandable that one might choose to describe this work as a book of religious law. However, the rest of the book, with the exception of its concluding chapter, deals with matters that lie squarely within what would conventionally be understood to be "secular" law: inheritance (3%); manumission of slaves (7%); marriage, divorce, and fosterage by suckling (*raḍāʿa*) (9%); sales (10%); judicial rulings (7%); preemption rights (1%); agricultural partnerships and the lease of agricultural land (1%); investment partnerships (3%); acts of battery (4%); collective oaths (1%);[41] scripturally determined criminal penalties (3%); and inebriating beverages (<1%).[42] The last chapter of the *Muwaṭṭaʾ*, the Book of Miscellaneous Matters (9%), consists of heterogeneous materials that include, among other things, anecdotes regarding the virtues of Medina and of the early Muslim community that made its home there, eschatological tales, and elaboration of various practices that were closely identified with Muslim identity, even if they did not rise to the status of legal obligations. The chapter concludes with a text affirming the world-historical role of the Prophet Muḥammad and, by implication, that of his community.

The shortest chapter of the *Muwaṭṭaʾ* is Book 4, Forgetfulness in Prayer (170 words). The longest is Chapter 20, the Book of Pilgrimage (29,000 words). The Book of Sales, however, is nearly as long, with almost 26,000 words. Indeed, secular topics, in the aggregate, cover approximately 50% of the book by word count, a fact that complicates characterization of the *Muwaṭṭaʾ* as a work of religious law.

37 The number of reports included through the end of Book 20 is 1,283 according to the enumeration of the RME.

38 These chapters deal with rules governing warfare with non-Muslims (*jihād*), religiously motivated sacrifices (*ḍaḥāyā* and *ʿaqīqa*), the sacrifice of domesticated animals for ordinary consumption (*dhabāʾiḥ*), hunting wild animals (*ṣayd*), and vows (*nudhūr*).

39 Books 21–26 contain approximately 15,000 words in total.

40 Books 21–26 include 165 texts.

41 A special procedure used to determine either guilt or liability in cases of unlawful killing when direct evidence of guilt or liability is unavailable.

42 The percentages referenced in this context are approximations based on word count, not number of texts.

To understand the kinds of authority Mālik draws on in the *Muwaṭṭa'*, some scholars have resorted to tallying the numbers of the different kinds of texts found in the *Muwaṭṭa'*,[43] but because the texts' lengths can vary dramatically, we believe a better measure of the relative importance of different kinds of texts is their length relative to the total size of the book. Furthermore, it is important to use an appropriate taxonomy of the *Muwaṭṭa'*'s texts. We have divided all the texts that appear in the *Muwaṭṭa'* into six categories:

- historical texts
- texts in which Mālik uses the term *amr*
- texts in which Mālik uses the term *sunna*
- texts that refer to the concept of practice (*'amal*), expressly or implicitly
- texts in which Mālik adopts one rule out of an unspecified set of potential rules solely because he prefers that solution, usually describing it as "the best" (*istiḥsān*) of the proposed solutions[44]
- rules that Mālik articulates in his own personal voice and that appear to represent his personal legal reasoning (*ijtihād*)

Some explanation of these categories is in order. A text is classified as historical if it purports to have been transmitted from an earlier generation, whether or not it is represented as originating with the Prophet Muḥammad. Usually, these texts are preceded by a chain of transmitters, although in many cases Mālik omits the chain and simply introduces a historical report by saying, "It reached me (*balaghanī*) . . ."

The second category of texts—*amr* texts—includes texts that describe a rule using the Arabic term *amr*, whatever its subsequent qualifications. According to Wymann-Landgraf, a rule described with this term originates in an exercise of discursive legal reasoning (*ijtihād*), and so Mālik also signals the degree to which the proposition enjoys general assent in his community by qualifying the *amr* with various descriptors. These texts thus convey rules that both are derived from discursive legal reasoning and enjoy

43 For example, Wael Hallaq, in rejecting Schacht's argument that Mālik did not recognize the authority of Prophetic traditions and instead favored local traditions representing the "living *sunna*," stated that "Mālik's *Muwaṭṭa'* . . . contains 898 Companion reports, but as many as 822 for the Prophet alone." Wael Hallaq, *The Origins and Evolution of Islamic Law* (New York: Cambridge University Press, 2005), 106. Without knowing either the proportion of the whole work represented by these numbers or the relative lengths of the different types of texts, however, it is difficult if not impossible to determine the relative weight of each kind of text in the overall structure of the *Muwaṭṭa'*.

44 Because Mālik uses the elative form of the word "good" (*aḥsan*) or "beloved" (*ahabb*) in these circumstances to justify his choice of rule, we have, for convenience, tallied such choices as instances of *istiḥsān* insofar as they are, quite literally, justified by virtue of Mālik's conclusion that the chosen rule is "better" or "more beautiful" or "more beloved" than the other possible solutions.

a certain degree of public recognition. When he describes a norm as *al-amr ʿindanā*, Mālik intends to communicate that the norm in question enjoys substantial support but is not without important detractors. We translate this expression as "the rule in our view." With *al-amr al-mujtamaʿ ʿalayhi ʿindanā*, Mālik means a norm that has *nearly* universal but not complete support in Medina. We translate that expression as "the agreed-upon rule among us." For a rule that apparently enjoys unanimous support, Mālik uses the expression *al-amr alladhī lā ikhtilāfa fīhi ʿindanā*, meaning that there are no known dissenters to the rule. We translate the expression as "the rule about which there is no dissent among us." There are various other qualifiers that Mālik uses to describe legal principles, but they are all included within the broad category of *amr* terms—rules derived through discursive legal reasoning that have gained a significant degree of public recognition.

The third category of texts—*sunna* texts—comprises texts that describe a rule using the Arabic term *sunna*. According to Wymann-Landgraf, in Mālik's usage a rule of this type originates in an authoritative past decision that cannot be justified through the exercise of discursive legal reason and thus may be reasonably compared to a statute. A *sunna* rule may or may not come from a decision of the Prophet Muḥammad,[45] but its crucial feature is that unlike an *amr* rule, it places boundaries on discursive reasoning and is inconsistent with the conclusions that discursive legal reasoning would reach.[46] Because the normativity of a *sunna* rule is based on history, we have translated it as a "long-established ordinance" to distinguish it in English from a rule derived through discursive legal reason. Like the term *amr*, however, it may be qualified by a subsequent phrase, as in *al-sunna ʿindanā*, which we translate as "the long-established ordinance among us," or *al-sunna allatī lā ikhtilāfa fīhā ʿindanā*, which we translate as "the long-established ordinance about which there is no dissent among us." Unlike *amr*, *sunna* is sometimes used in an absolute sense, in which case we translate it simply as "the long-established ordinance."[47] The statute-like quality of a *sunna* rule is also reflected in a qualification that is unique to it and not applied to *amr* rules, namely, the expression *maḍat al-sunna*. Mālik's use of the past tense of the verb *maḍā*, which means "to proceed" or "to issue," corroborates the intuition that a *sunna* rule is based on a decision

45 Wymann-Landgraf argues that a *sunna* rule may have originated in a decision of the Prophet Muḥammad, in the precedent of one of the early caliphs, or even in events prior to Islam. Wymann-Landgraf, *Mālik and Medina*, 4–5.

46 Wymann-Landgraf, *Mālik and Medina*, 5 ("the *sunna*-terms are systematically contrary to analogy with related Medinese precepts of law").

47 An example is hadith no. 248 of the RME. Significantly, after stating the rule, Mālik cites a Prophetic tradition in support of it.

made at a discrete moment in the past.[48] Because the grammatical subject is *sunna*—the rule itself—the phrase does not disclose who the decision maker was. We have therefore translated the expression *maḍat al-sunna* as "it has long been the established ordinance that..."

The fourth category of texts—practice (*ʿamal*) texts—raises interpretive issues not present in the prior three categories. Although the later Islamic tradition emphasizes Mālik's commitment to the "practice of the people of Medina" as a distinctive feature of his jurisprudence, he did not use the term *ʿamal* or any cognate term systematically to describe rules in the *Muwaṭṭaʾ* in the manner he did with the previous terms, *amr* and *sunna*.[49] It most commonly shows up in a negative sense, as in the expression "practice does not accord with this" (*laysa ʿalā hādhā al-ʿamal*).[50] Mālik sometimes uses this phrase or an equivalent one when he rejects what might at first glance appear a plausible candidate for a rule. In such a case, the absence of sociological evidence that the rule is followed corroborates the *legal* conclusion that, despite its initial plausibility, the potential rule is not, in fact, normative. Positive appeals to practice as proof that something is a rule are more difficult to detect, but we have identified several phrases that Mālik uses to endorse particular rules as effectively practice-based. Some of these phrases are as follows: "This is the rule that I found both the people and the learned of our town following" (*al-amr alladhī adraktu ʿalayhi al-nās wa-ahl al-ʿilm bi-baladinā*); "That is the rule that the people of knowledge in our city have always followed" (*wa-dhālika alladhī lam yazal ʿalayhi ahl al-ʿilm bi-baladinā*); "It has always been the case that" (*lam tazal*). Accordingly, any rule that Mālik justifies by reference to a sociological fact we have classified as falling into the fourth category of practice (*ʿamal*).

We chose to describe the fifth category of texts as *istiḥsān* even though Mālik does not use that term anywhere in the *Muwaṭṭaʾ*. The term *istiḥsān* is derived from the Arabic root *ḥ-s-n*, which denotes beauty or goodness. In later juristic discourse, it is associated with the jurist's preference for one rule over another, often in circumstances in which the application of strict analogy would lead to a result that the jurist finds contradictory to the spirit of the law. Accordingly, modern scholarship has sometimes translated

48 See M. M. Bravmann, *The Spiritual Background of Early Islam* (Leiden: Brill, 2009), 148 ("It should be especially stressed that the phrase *maḍat-i s-sunnatu bi* [or: *maḍat sunnatun bi*], far from reflecting the concept of 'the continuous practice of the community [the custom of the Muslims of the *past*],' as Schacht had assumed..., precisely emphasizes the character of the *sunnah* as 'a procedure created by an individual personality.'").

49 Wymann-Landgraf notes that despite the importance of practice to understanding the *Muwaṭṭaʾ*, "explicit references to it are rare"; *Mālik and Medina*, 71. Practice most commonly appears in the titles of sections within the book's chapters, where it is used a total of twenty-nine times, mostly in connection with matters of ritual law. Ibid., 400.

50 See, for example, Wymann-Landgraf, *Mālik and Medina*, 384.

it into English using terms such as "equity" or "juristic preference." The detractors of *istiḥsān* in the Islamic tradition frowned on its use or rejected it outright on the grounds that it substituted the subjective preference of the jurist for the objective evidence provided by revelation. Indeed, as already mentioned, Shāfiʿī authored a treatise titled "The Invalidation of *Istiḥsān*" (*Ibṭāl al-istiḥsān*).[51] Mālik, however, is widely understood to have endorsed *istiḥsān* wholeheartedly, to the point that later Mālikī jurists commonly quote him as having said, "*Istiḥsān* is nine-tenths of [legal] knowledge."[52] Although later Mālikī jurists associated *istiḥsān* closely with the idea of well-being (*maṣlaḥa*),[53] that is not the sense in which we are using it here. Rather, we classify a text as falling into the category of *istiḥsān* whenever Mālik expressly endorses the rule contained in the text on the basis of its inherent beauty or goodness. He takes this approach in situations in which he is apparently aware of numerous possible solutions to a legal problem and chooses one of them, calling it either the best (*aḥsan*) of the proposed solutions or the one he himself prefers (*aḥabb ilayya*).

The sixth and last category of texts consists of rules based on Mālik's personal use of legal reason. This categorization reflects the fact that a rule of this type is articulated in Mālik's own voice and is usually preceded by an explicit question directed to him: "Mālik was asked . . . Mālik replied . . ." More rarely, these texts appear in exegetical contexts in which he is explaining the meaning of a historical text.[54]

Based on the preceding taxonomy, the aggregate breakdown of the *Muwaṭṭa*''s texts[55] is as follows:

---

51 It should be noted that Shāfiʿī used *istiḥsān* in a much broader sense than did later Muslim jurisprudence to refer to a variety of non-analogical juristic arguments, including preclusion or "blocking the means" (*sadd al-dharīʿa*).

52 Later Mālikī jurists regularly attribute this statement to Mālik. See Aḥmad al-Raysūnī, *Naẓariyyat al-maqāṣid ʿinda al-Shāṭibī*, 4th ed. (Herndon, VA: International Institute of Islamic Thought, 1995), 70. The earliest Mālikī text that supports the attribution is the *Mustakhraja* of ʿUtbī, one of the foundational texts of the school. See Ibn Rushd, *al-Bayān wa'l-taḥṣīl*, 4:155 (quoting Aṣbagh, an early follower of Mālik, as saying, "*Istiḥsān* is more common in the law than analogy is, and I heard Ibn al-Qāsim say—and he would attribute it directly to Mālik—that Mālik would say, 'Nine-tenths of the law is *istiḥsān*'" [*al-istiḥsān fī al-ʿilm yakūn aghlab min al-qiyās wa-qad samiʿtu Ibn al-Qāsim yaqūl wa-yarwī ʿan Mālik annahu qāla tisʿat aʿshār al-ʿilm al-istiḥsān*]).

53 Raysūnī, *Naẓariyyat al-maqāṣid*, 70 (*istiḥsān* means taking into account well-being, *maṣlaḥa*, and fairness, *ʿadl*); Wymann-Landgraf, *Mālik and Medina*, 15.

54 See, for example, hadith no. 48 of the RME, where Mālik opines that one may perform ablutions in preparation for praying with water out of which a cat drank, *unless* one saw that the cat's mouth contained something that was impure, such as the blood from something that it had killed.

55 The percentages were calculated on the basis of word count, not number of reports. The total exceeds 100% because some reports incorporate more than one kind of argument and were thus included in more than one category.

Historical texts	*Amr* texts	*Sunna* texts	*ʿAmal* texts	*Istiḥsān* texts	Personal *ijtihād* texts
55%	11%	3%	5%	3%	26%

At first glance, this taxonomical breakdown of the *Muwaṭṭa*'s texts seems to vindicate scholars such as Dutton and Calder who have described the *Muwaṭṭa'* as primarily a work of hadith, in which Mālik himself appears incidentally and only as a commentator.[56] But if one considers the *distribution* of these texts across the chapters of the *Muwaṭṭa'*, a different picture emerges. Some chapters are predominantly historical, whereas others barely include any historical material whatsoever. For example, the two chapters with the greatest amount of historical material are the Book of Pilgrimage, which contains approximately 20,000 words of historical reports, and the Book of Miscellaneous Matters, with approximately 22,000 words of historical reports. These two books contain approximately 16% of the *Muwaṭṭa*'s historical materials. Yet even that number conceals important differences between these two chapters. Despite the heavy emphasis on the historical past in the Book of Pilgrimage, approximately 40% of the chapter's content consists of texts from the other five categories, with Mālik's personal opinions representing approximately 24% of the chapter. By contrast, approximately 96% of the Book of Miscellaneous Matters consists of historical reports. At the other extreme, only 6% of the Book of Investment Partnerships consist of historical reports, and 76% of its texts convey Mālik's personal legal reasoning. It would stretch credulity to describe Mālik's personal legal reasoning in this case as exegetical since he hardly included any historical material that would call for exegesis. A chapter with a distribution in the middle of these extremes might be the Book of the Alms-Tax, of which approximately 33% is historical material, 39% is Mālik's personal legal reasoning, 9% is *amr* rules, 7% is *istiḥsān* rules, 7% is *ʿamal* rules, and 4% is *sunna* rules.

To understand the *Muwaṭṭa*'s jurisprudence, therefore, it is not enough to describe, in the abstract, a generic approach based on a theoretical relationship between authority and legal reason without taking into account the legal context. The distribution of different kinds of texts indicates that Mālik clearly believed that certain kinds of arguments had greater salience in different areas of the law. It should not come as a surprise, then, that historical materials make up a substantial portion of sections of the *Muwaṭṭa'* dealing with matters that either fell squarely within ritual law

56 Dutton, *Origins*, 27 (describing the *Muwaṭṭa'* as a book of hadith); Calder, *Studies*, 8 and 23 (describing the *Muwaṭṭa'* as based on "apostolic authority," with texts of authority figures coming first, followed by Mālik's exegesis of those texts).

or functioned as identity markers in the early Muslim community; and it is likewise not surprising that the relative importance of historical reports declines sharply as one moves to areas of the law connected to more conventional legal topics, such as sales, inheritance, and property. If, as we have suggested, *amr* rules are most relevant in contexts characterized by a need for a common understanding, it makes sense that they would appear with relatively high frequency in the Book of Sales (24%) and the Book of Judicial Rulings (27%). Similarly, because *sunna* rules function as the equivalent of statutory norms that preempt the ordinary operation of systematic discursive legal reason, it is understandable that the chapter with the largest number of *sunna* rules in absolute terms is the Book of Judicial Rulings (11% of the chapter and containing 1,924 words in total).[57]

The aggregate breakdown of the texts of the *Muwaṭṭaʾ*, though, is revealing in one important way: much contemporary scholarship assumes that Mālik was merely a representative of the Hijazi school of law, and that the *Muwaṭṭaʾ* is simply a reflection of the median view of the law from the perspective of the Medinese. But these conclusions are clearly not tenable when one considers the *Muwaṭṭaʾ* in its entirety. There can be no denying that Mālik's voice in the *Muwaṭṭaʾ*—at least in the recension of Yaḥyā—is that of an independent legal authority, in some areas of the law if not in all of them. The notion that Mālik held a communitarian conception of the law[58] in contrast to the more individualistic orientation that Shāfiʿī would propose must accordingly be modified in light of the fact that some areas of the law in the *Muwaṭṭaʾ* appear to be derived almost entirely from Mālik's own reasoning, and in most of the *Muwaṭṭaʾ*'s chapters his voice is distinct from both the community's history and the community of scholars.

At the same time, Mālik's heavy reliance on *amr* terms and *sunna* terms reveals a jurisprudential theory that was substantially different from the one that Shāfiʿī proposed and that would revolutionize Islamic law in later centuries. Although Wymann-Landgraf is certainly correct that Schacht was mistaken in believing that Shāfiʿī's theory of the four sources became the universal theory of law among Sunnīs, the fact that post-Mālikī jurists formally retained a broader set of sources than that recognized by Shāfiʿī does not capture what we believe lay at the heart of Shāfiʿī's revolution against the kind of law Mālik advocated. For Shāfiʿī and the Muslim jurists who came after him, regardless of school, law was now a science, modeled along the lines of theology,[59] in which the legal scholar was assumed to

57 Other chapters display much higher *proportional* reliance on *sunna* rules. The chapter with the highest proportion of *sunna* texts (23%) is the Book of Pious Seclusion, a supererogatory practice associated with fasting.

58 El Shamsy, *Canonization*, 84.

59 El Shamsy, *Canonization*, 44.

be investigating the legal implications of the ontological reality of divine speech.[60] Although jurists could reasonably disagree about the content of divine speech and its legal implications, in principle only one interpretation was correct. Indeed, because the study of law was now conceived of as a science, it was possible for one jurist to be correct and the rest of the juristic community to be wrong.[61] By contrast, it appears that although Mālik believed that there were correct and incorrect interpretations of the law, he understood the law to be a project immanent to the Muslim community, and so its legal deliberations were political (broadly understood), not scientific. For that reason, Mālik included in his book numerous historical reports of the decisions of Umayyad-era political authorities.

In the *Muwaṭṭaʾ*, discursive legal reasoning was the tool-in-trade of the jurist, but it operated within limits established by historical authority, and even systematic legal reasoning was shaped by considerations of well-being and the public good rather than strict analogy. It is no coincidence, therefore, that there has been renewed interest in Mālikī jurisprudence given contemporary Muslims' interest in *maṣlaḥa* (the common good) and the closely related notion of *maqāṣid al-sharīʿa* (the purposes of the divine law) as a method of legal reform.[62] At the same time, the history of Mālik's jurisprudence as found in the *Muwaṭṭaʾ* and the fact that it rapidly became obsolete under the ʿAbbāsids suggest that the kind of jurisprudence Mālik followed in the *Muwaṭṭaʾ* was dependent on a particular set of institutions that might have been appropriate for a small city-state but were not scalable when Islam became the religion of a cosmopolitan empire and its followers were no longer limited to a conquering Arab elite.

This fact helps explain why later Mālikīs abandoned the elaborate terminology of the *Muwaṭṭaʾ*.[63] Although the *Muwaṭṭaʾ* remained an important text because of its connection with the school's putative founder, its importance for later Mālikīs was more sentimental than substantive. Saḥnūn's *Mudawwana*, a work that approached the law as a science, became the foundational text of Mālikī jurisprudence. Saḥnūn's goal in that work was to identify, whenever

60 El Shamsy, *Canonization*, 10.

61 El Shamsy is almost certainly correct when he describes Shāfiʿī's theory of the law as grounded in metaphysical realism; *Canonization*, 82. Two centuries later, after theoretical jurisprudence became firmly established as a discipline distinct from positive law, Muslim jurists and theologians would split into two camps on the question of metaphysical realism, with one group endorsing the notion that the goal of legal reasoning (*ijtihād*) was to obtain true metaphysical knowledge of the content of the divine law and the other denying that legal rules derived through interpretation had any connection to metaphysical reality. The former were known as the "fallibilists" (*mukhaṭṭiʿa*) and the latter as the "infallibilists" (*muṣawwiba*).

62 See, for example, Felicitas Opwis, "*Maṣlaḥa* in Contemporary Islamic Legal Theory," *Islamic Law and Society* 12, no. 2 (2005): 182–223 (giving an overview of the history of *maṣlaḥa* in medieval Islamic theoretical jurisprudence and its reception by contemporary Muslim legal scholars).

63 Wymann-Landgraf, *Mālik and Medina*, 274 and 289 n. 50.

possible, Mālik's opinion on a wide range of legal questions; when that was not possible, to reconstruct it based on the views of his various students; and when even that was not possible, to derive, through conjecture, what Mālik would have said about the question had it been posed to him. While Saḥnūn's deference to Mālik's views would no doubt have prompted objections from Shāfiʿī and his followers, Saḥnūn seemed to share Shāfiʿī's assumption that the goal of legal science is to obtain *true* knowledge of an ontological reality disclosed through the vehicle of divine speech. The only difference between the two would have concerned the question whether such truths could be obtained indirectly through deference to the views of a great scholar such as Mālik, or whether a jurist had to consider the evidence provided by divine speech independently for himself.[64]

In reading the *Muwaṭṭaʾ*, it is crucial to remember that although scholars may disagree as to why it took the form that it did, there is no dispute that Mālik did not intend it to be an exhaustive statement of the law. Many of its texts make sense only on the assumption that the reader is already familiar with basic principles of Islamic law. There is also a temptation to view the work as a mere primer on the foundational elements of Medinese law in the time of Mālik, functioning as an introduction to the weightier work, Saḥnūn's compilation of Mālik's legal teachings.[65] The fact that the *Mudawwana* certainly includes more cases than the *Muwaṭṭaʾ* does not, on its own, mean that the cases discussed in the *Muwaṭṭaʾ* are basic or rudimentary. To the contrary, many of the cases Mālik addresses are quite intricate and require a relatively advanced level of legal education to understand. For this reason, we have included a substantial amount of commentary in the notes in an attempt to make the stakes at issue clear to nonspecialist readers. Although it may very well be the case that Mālik intended the *Muwaṭṭaʾ* to serve as a restatement of the basic principles of Medinese law, that in no way implies that the *Muwaṭṭaʾ* is a book for beginners in legal science. In fact, familiarity with a broad range of legal principles is very helpful to comprehend the text, its arguments, and the positions it takes on a variety of questions.

We believe that this translation of the *Muwaṭṭaʾ* offers readers a window into what is now an archaic period of Islamic law, and that it will make this important work of legal history available to a much wider audience.

---

64 Ibn Farḥūn (d. 799/1396) quoted Saḥnūn as saying, "I heard Ibn al-Qāsim say, 'I have gladly and contentedly accepted Mālik b. Anas for the good of my soul, and I have placed him between me and Hell.' . . . And I have gladly and contentedly accepted Ibn al-Qāsim for the good of my soul, and I have placed him between me and Hell." Ibn Farḥūn, *Tabṣirat al-ḥukkām fī uṣūl al-aqḍiya wa-minhāj al-aḥkām*, 2 vols. (Cairo: Maktabat al-Kulliyyāt al-Azhariyya, 1986), 1:70.

65 Wymann-Landgraf, *Mālik and Medina*, 71–73 (suggesting that the *Muwaṭṭaʾ* lays out the foundations of Mālik's legal reasoning, along with that of the Medinese more generally, and thus "lays the groundwork for the *Mudawwana*").

Arabic Introduction to the Royal Moroccan Edition of the *Muwaṭṭaʾ*

The Members of the Editorial Committee of the *Muwaṭṭa'*[i]

[5] The Commander of the Faithful, may God preserve him, entrusted the Committee for the Renewal of Islamic Learning, which is itself an affiliate of the Secretariat General of the High Council of Religious Scholars, with the task of preparing a critical edition of the *Muwaṭṭa'* of Imam Mālik b. Anas, may God be pleased with him, drawing the Committee's attention to the defective nature of the various printed editions currently in public circulation. He directed the Committee to rely only on original manuscripts of the recension of Yaḥyā b. Yaḥyā al-Laythī al-Maṣmūdī.

The members who have been honored with the task of carrying out His Majesty's command are the following:

- Dr. Mohamed Raoundi, Member of the High Council of Religious Scholars
- Dr. Driss Ibn Daouia, President of the High Council of Religious Scholars, Larache Branch
- Dr. Mohamed Azzeddine Mayar El Idrissi, President of the High Council of Religious Scholars, Marrakesh Branch

The Committee sought the help of the following group of researchers:

- Prof. Driss Elhamdaoui, Faculty of Islamic Law, Fez
- Dr. Lahoucine Ait Said, Member of the High Council of Religious Scholars
- Dr. Abdelhafid Doumar, Faculty of Humanities, Oujda
- Dr. Abdellah Lansari, Representative of the Ministry of Endowments and Islamic Affairs, Marrakesh
- Prof. Abdelmjid Mouhib, Dar al-Hadith al-Hasaniyya
- Dr. Mohammed Guennoun Hassani, President of the High Council of Religious Scholars, Tangiers Branch

i We reproduce footnotes that are part of the original text using consecutive Arabic numerals. Footnotes provided by the translators of the Arabic introduction are indicated in consecutive lowercase Roman numerals. The numbers in brackets indicate the page numbers in the Royal Moroccan Edition.

Preface to the Critical Edition of the *Muwaṭṭa'*

In the Name of God, the Merciful, the Compassionate

Praise Be to God, Lord of the Worlds.

May God Grace Our Master, the Chosen and Trustworthy One, the Prophet Muḥammad, His Family, and His Companions, All of Them.

[7] To proceed: Knowledge and wisdom are the greatest legacy that God's prophets and messengers have left for humanity. Together, knowledge and wisdom constitute the noblest achievements that they have commended to humanity and urged their followers to pursue, acquire, and understand. Whoever acquires a share of this inheritance is fortunate beyond measure and the recipient of a most generous bequest.

It is well known that during the Prophetic era, throughout the era of the Rightly Guided Caliphs, and for a portion of the Umayyad era, people's attention was focused on the Book of God, Sublime is He. This involved writing it down and memorizing, reciting, discussing, and interpreting it. With regard to other sciences, however, peopled relied primarily on their memory, though a handful of them recorded some details pertaining to other sciences in their own notebooks.

Toward the end of the first century AH (718 CE), the then ruler of the Muslims, the caliph ʿUmar b. ʿAbd al-ʿAzīz, issued an official declaration permitting people to record sacred knowledge, to collect the various reports (*ḥadīth*) about the Messenger of God (pbuh), and to preserve them. He also ordered the scholars to spread this knowledge among the people and directed them to instruct them in the affairs of their religion and its rules. This is how the process of collecting, writing, and recording the sacred sciences began.

Around the time of the decline of the Umayyad dynasty and the rise of the ʿAbbāsids, the first books in Islamic civilization emerged, written in an improved form and layout with topics arranged in well-sequenced chapters, using precise documentation and editing. The people who undertook this scholarly leap forward were a group of pioneering second-generation Muslims (*tābiʿūn*),[ii] and their followers. Responsibility for scholarship at that time ended up in their hands, their names forever shining in the heavens among the stars of knowledge. The most prominent of these was the Imam of Medina, Mālik b. Anas (93–179/711–795).

This Imam became famous for two reasons: his prolific teaching and his authorship of books. Because of his rigorous scholarly methods and his careful attention to the accuracy and reliability of his teaching materials, he won over the hearts and minds of the students who traveled from far and wide to study with him. In turn, his own knowledge and reputation spread far and wide when his students returned to their homes. [8] His book, the *Muwaṭṭa'*, secured for him and for his knowledge fame throughout the many regions and cities in which Muslims reside and sealed his reputation as one of Islam's scholars throughout the ages.

The *Muwaṭṭa'* in the Islamic West

The first groups of religious scholars returned to their own people in the Maghrib, their packs laden with the first books of the scholars of the eastern Arab lands. One of these was the *Muwaṭṭa'* of Imam Mālik b. Anas. These scholars had great respect and admiration for this Imam, his moral character, and his noble qualities. They were impressed by the great knowledge and understanding that God had bestowed upon him, a knowledge that the people received with open arms. Their respect and admiration for Imam Mālik laid the ground for the future spread of Mālik's school of jurisprudence (*madhhab*) in the Maghrib and Andalusia. His reputation continued to grow, and his teachings continued to spread, and the number of those who followed his teachings continued to increase. Finally, the entirety of the Maghrib and Andalusia submitted to his *madhhab* and freely adopted his teachings as their law.

Since then, tremendous importance has been given to anything having a connection with Imam Mālik's book, the *Muwaṭṭa'*, and his *madhhab*. No one can claim to be a learned scholar of Islam in these regions unless he has first made a contribution in the service of this *madhhab*. All scholars recognize this to be a binding obligation on them and part of their established creed.

However, attention to Mālik and his school of jurisprudence reaches its apogee and achieves its highest degree of perfection when its source originates in the great protector of Islam and its community, the one on whose opinion and deliberations the people rely. This person is none other than the Commander of the Faithful, our master and protector, Muḥammad VI, the descendant of the trustworthy Prophet Muḥammad (pbuh). When he issued his noble command to the High Council of Religious Scholars to

ii The generation of Muslims who were born after the death of Muḥammad but who were contemporaries of the Companions (*ṣaḥāba*) of Muḥammad (pbuh).

prepare a critical edition of the *Muwaṭṭaʾ*, one free of the mistakes, flaws, and errors found in previous published versions, he offered this project in repayment of the debt the Moroccan nation owed to Imam Mālik and his school.

His Majesty, may God ennoble him, gave appropriate directives to the Committee that has been tasked with preparing a critical version of the *Muwaṭṭaʾ*: "We have commissioned the Permanent Committee for the Renewal of Islamic Learning to produce a scholarly and carefully prepared critical edition of the *Muwaṭṭaʾ* of Imam Mālik b. Anas, may God be pleased with him, an edition appropriate to the status it holds among Moroccans. We expect this Committee to rectify the flaws plaguing previously published editions by relying on the manuscripts of this text that are found uniquely in Morocco, resulting in a publication bearing a national imprint, worthy of Morocco as a shining beacon of Mālikī jurisprudence." (From a speech of the Commander of the Faithful to the High Council of Religious Scholars on the occasion of the expansion of the Scholarly Councils, delivered at the Royal Palace in Casablanca on May 30, 2004).

[9] The Royal Order to prepare a critical edition of the *Muwaṭṭaʾ*, issued by the Commander of the Faithful, His Majesty Muḥammad VI, the descendant of Alaouite sultans, in the fifteenth century AH (twenty-first century CE), parallels the action of the Commander of the Faithful Abū Jaʿfar al-Manṣūr, the founder of the ʿAbbāsid dynasty, when he advised Imam Mālik to compile the *Muwaṭṭaʾ* in the second century AH (eighth century CE).

The Editorial Committee spared no effort in carrying out, faithfully and with utmost sincerity, the royal directives set out in the speech of the Commander of the Faithful by seeking out and collecting rare and precious manuscripts of the *Muwaṭṭaʾ* with the goal of publishing the most accurate edition conforming to the recension of Yaḥyā b. Yaḥyā al-Laythī al-Maṣmūdī (d. 234/848), as transmitted over the generations by its most reliable transmitters. The Committee used reliable, original Moroccan manuscript copies of the text, ones used by the luminaries of Islamic jurisprudence in our land, which our scholarly libraries have carefully preserved, as is further explained below in this introduction to this edition. In this regard, the respected Editorial Committee deserves high praise for the excellent work it has done in its service to the Islamic sciences, which are of ancient vintage in our country, by editing the *Muwaṭṭaʾ*, clarifying its content, and rectifying errors in the manuscripts. This is the Editorial Committee's important contribution to the renewal of Islamic learning, culture, and wisdom, and to a sound civilizational and scientific revival. This work—praise be to God—meets the established requirements of a critical edition, and it adds to the work of previous scholars, especially insofar as this edition relied on particularly rare and precious manuscripts that had never before been available to scholars. This fact confers on this edition a distinctive nature that gives us fair cause to boast, in addition to giving it a distinctively Moroccan character.

Praise belongs to God.
Dr. Mohamed Yessef
Secretary General, High Council of Religious Scholars

Introduction to the Critical Edition of the *Muwaṭṭa'*[iii]

In the Name of God, the Merciful, the Compassionate

May God Grace Our Master Muḥammad, His Family, and His Companions and Grant Them Perfect Tranquility.

[11] Imam Mālik b. Anas, may God be pleased with him (93–179/711–795), was without peer. He was the foremost scholar of the Hijaz in the history of the dissemination of that knowledge that serves and preserves the purposes of the teachings of the Prophet Muḥammad (pbuh). Imam Mālik had outstanding qualities, the likes of which none had possessed before him, nor was any other scholar able to make a contribution to learning like his. His stature was assured insofar as the Prophet (pbuh) expressly foretold us of his career. Sufyān b. ʿUyayna (d. 198/813–4) reported from ʿAbd al-Malik b. Jurayj, who reported from Muḥammad b. Muslim b. Abī al-Zubayr al-Makkī, who reported from Abū Ṣāliḥ al-Sammān, who reported from Abū Hurayra, may God be pleased with him, that the Prophet (pbuh) said, "The people shall strike the flanks of their camels in their quest for knowledge, but they will not find a scholar more knowledgeable than the scholar of Medina."[iv]

[12] The great scholar of Prophetic traditions (*ḥāfiẓ*) Dhahabī (d. 748/1348), may God have mercy on his soul, said, "There was not in Medina a scholar after the generation of the followers (*tābiʿūn*) who was the like of Mālik in terms of his knowledge of Prophetic traditions and of Islamic law (*fiqh*), augustness, and memorization."

The reason for this unique praise of Mālik's knowledge and his jurisprudence that is set out in the *Muwaṭṭa'*, which is considered one of the books of knowledge containing the most accurate accounts of Prophetic traditions on earth, is that he was, in comparison to other scholars and

iii This English translation of the "Introduction to the Critical Edition of the *Muwaṭṭa'*" has been abridged for greater readability to the nonspecialist reader. For the complete original essay with its comprehensive annotation, please consult the original Arabic text. Footnotes containing references to Arabic reference works have been removed.

iv "Striking the flanks of their camels" is an expression for setting out on a lengthy journey. This report was included in *Sunan al-Tirmidhī*, the famous collection of Prophetic traditions that is considered one of the six most important such collections among Sunnīs.

critics of his time, [13] uniquely blessed with a combination of a critical intellect, profound understanding, a strong memory, and breadth and depth of learning. Scholars are in unanimous agreement that he, Mālik, is a proof that the Prophetic traditions he transmits are sound and that his orthodoxy is unimpeachable. They are also in agreement as to his integrity (*ʿadāla*), his observance of the Prophetic law (*sunan*), his unsurpassed knowledge of Islamic law, his skill in providing legal opinions (*fatwā*) to the people, his care in choosing what kinds of questions to answer, and the strength of his legal school's foundational principles. He inherited this knowledge from those Medinese scholars—whether they were sons of the Emigrants (*muhājirūn*) of Quraysh or sons of the Medinese (*anṣār*)—who preserved religious knowledge and spread it in Medina before him, and whose reports concerning Islamic teachings are probative in themselves by virtue of the agreement of discerning scholars.

[15] This Medinese scholarly inheritance constitutes the principal distinguishing characteristic of Mālik's approach to questions, such as his rigor in the criticism of reports. This inheritance gave him an advantage in choosing narrators of historical reports. He approached this question by determining narrators' reputation for reliability. He answered it by investigating their honesty, their care in transmitting reports, their devotion to the study of Prophetic traditions, their innocence from heresies that could influence the soundness of their reports, the consistency of their reports with what the most important authorities had narrated with respect to matters that do not permit controversy,[1] and the absence of contradiction between their reports and the inherited practice of the Medinese jurists.

Muslim scholars have approved of his unique methodology for selecting the sources and narrators of tradition in deriving legal doctrines and giving legal opinions. They have praised him for his scholarly method, for the range of his knowledge, for his keen insights into the chains of transmission (*isnād*), and his use of reliable texts. Such was his skill that Sufyān b. ʿUyayna said, "I have never seen anyone better than Mālik in acquiring knowledge.... May God have mercy on Mālik's soul. He was an expert in assessing both the narrators

1 Mālik checked reports of Prophetic traditions with a group of credible Medinese scholars who were steeped in narration and jurisprudence and who closely followed their predecessors. They are Nāfiʿ (the freedman of Ibn ʿUmar), Yaḥyā b. Saʿīd al-Anṣārī, Muḥammad b. Muslim b. Shihāb al-Zuhrī, Hishām b. ʿUrwa, Abū al-Zinād ʿAbd Allāh b. Dhakwān, Zayd b. Aslam, ʿAbd Allāh b. Abī Bakr b. Muḥammad b. ʿAmr b. Ḥazm, Rabīʿa b. ʿAbd al-Raḥmān, ʿAbd al-Raḥmān b. al-Qāsim b. Muḥammad b. Abī Bakr al-Ṣiddīq, Sālim Abū al-Naḍr, Isḥāq b. ʿAbd Allāh b. Abī Ṭalḥa, Sumayy b. Abī Bakr b. ʿAbd al-Raḥmān b. al-Ḥārith b. Hishām, Abū al-Zubayr al-Makkī Muḥammad b. Tadrus, Jaʿfar al-Ṣādiq, Dāwūd b. al-Ḥuṣayn, Ḥamīd b. Qays al-Makkī al-Aʿraj, Suhayl b. Abī Ṣāliḥ, Abū Suhayl Nāfiʿ b. Mālik (Mālik's uncle), and al-ʿAlāʾ b. ʿAbd al-Raḥmān b. Yaʿqūb.

and the scholars," referring to Mālik's critical assessment of narrators in a chain of transmission and of how people understood the meanings attached to the words contained in reports.

Abū al-Ḥātim b. Ḥabbān (d. 354/965) said about Mālik, "Mālik, may God have mercy on him, was the first Medinese jurist to assess carefully the narrators of Prophetic traditions. He would turn away from anyone whom he did not deem trustworthy in transmitting reports. He himself would narrate only reports he believed to be sound, and only from narrators whose narrations he considered reliable, requiring also that they possess legal knowledge, religiosity, virtue, and regular worship."

The proof of the truth of these critics' testimonials is present in the *Muwaṭṭa'*, where Mālik demonstrates the prodigious knowledge that he inherited from the Medinese scholars; it is also proven by the fact that his Medinese contemporaries received the book warmly. At the time of its appearance the *Muwaṭṭa'* was deemed the most reliable collection of Prophetic traditions and other historical reports about the early Muslim community. It was also considered the most beneficial such collection because, as anyone who spends any time reading it will realize, it was based on the Noble Quran, on widely transmitted Prophetic traditions that satisfied Medinese stipulations regarding their mode of transmission as well as their content, and on the inherited learning of the scholars among the Companions of the Prophet (pbuh) and the succeeding generation. Mālik relied on the learning of this last group in order to avoid false narrations and distorted comprehension of texts, even if contrary Prophetic traditions were supported by sound chains of transmission attributed to sources who were generally reliable in the sense used by those whose criticism of reports focused exclusively on the individuals transmitting the reports, rather than their contents.

[16] Imam Shāfiʿī (d. 204/820), who was Mālik's student, appreciated the importance of having a teacher so skilled in resolving matters of disagreement regarding Prophetic traditions. When Shāfiʿī still adhered to his old doctrine,[v] he would say on that very point, "If a report comes to you from the people of Medina, let no doubt enter your heart regarding its truth. As for a report that comes to you and appears to be very sound, yet is unknown in Medina—ignore it and pay no pay attention to it."

This [i.e., the teachings of the Medinese] is the "way of the believers," which Mālik would indicate by describing it as "the agreed-upon rule (*al-amr*) in

v Shāfiʿī was a peripatetic scholar who traveled throughout the eastern Arab lands. After studying with Mālik in Medina, Shāfiʿī went to Yemen and Iraq and finally settled in Egypt. Scholars have divided his writings into two phases, his "old doctrine" and his "new doctrine." His "new doctrine" represents his more mature thinking, in which his differences with Mālik and the Hijazi scholars are more apparent.

respect of which there is no dissent among us," "the rule among us in respect of which there is no dissent," "the rule in respect of which there is no dissent nor doubt among any of the scholars in our town," "the agreed-upon rule among us," "the long-established ordinance (*al-sunna*) in respect of which there is no dissent and which I found the people of my town following," "the long-established ordinance of the Muslims in respect of which there is no dissent," "the firmly established ordinance in respect of which there is no dissent," "the long-established ordinance among us in respect of which there is no doubt or dissent," "the long-established ordinance in respect of which there is no dissent among us and which the people have continually practiced," and "it has long been the ordinance, which I have found the scholars of our town following." What Mālik took from his scholarly predecessors was the necessity to preserve the Medinese example and to adhere to it closely. Even though the apparent sense derived from naming the school of jurisprudence after Mālik is that his doctrines were his independent thoughts, they are in fact the collective legacy of the Medinese scholars.

Imam Abū al-Ḥasan al-Ashʿarī (d. 324/936), may God have mercy on him, explained clearly why the school of jurisprudence that is named after Mālik is so named when he said,

> The school of the Medinese is named after Mālik b. Anas, may God be pleased with him, and anyone who follows the Medinese school is called a "Mālikī." Mālik, may God be pleased with him, only followed the methods of those scholars who preceded him; indeed, he was exceptionally deferential to them, but he both clarified the school's doctrines and extended them, and provided them with strong legal proofs and detailed explanations. He composed his book, the *Muwaṭṭaʾ*, and furthermore his students recorded volumes of notes from his lectures, as well as his opinions about legal matters. The Medinese school, therefore, was attributed to him because of all the cases he elucidated and the arguments he expounded.

[18] The opinion of Imam Mālik, may God be pleased with him, was founded on the practices of the Medinese, out of respect for the legacy of the Companions in Medina, their jurists' deep understanding of the law, and the practices of the pious Emigrants and Medinese, as well as on the methods of the leading scholars who resided there. It was their opinions that the people relied on whenever a difficult case arose. Mālik would say, "If it is knowledge that you seek, then make Medina your home, for the Quran was not revealed along the banks of the Euphrates in Mesopotamia."

[19] Mālik, may God have mercy on him, rejected the apparent sense of many reports of Prophetic traditions based on his method for accepting

reports, even when he sometimes learned them from teachers he deemed reliable. Sometimes he even transmitted such reports to his own students to let them know he was aware of them and would give them permission to present them to him for teaching, in accordance with his own standards for transmitting knowledge. He would sometimes reject these reports despite their apparent authenticity because they were odd or strange, and thus too weak to stand against contrary teachings of the Quran, a well-documented teaching of the Prophet (pbuh), well-established legal principles, or Medinese practice.

God decreed that the knowledge-hungry students of the Islamic West, when they visited Medina, the city of the Prophet (pbuh), during their performance of the pilgrimage to Mecca, would attend Imam Mālik's lectures. The depth of his knowledge and the wisdom of his judgment impressed them greatly. As a result, they took his knowledge back with them to their lands and disseminated his school of law there. His book, the *Muwaṭṭa'*, was what they most zealously sought to take back to their homes.

The *Muwaṭṭa'* of Imam Mālik b. Anas al-Aṣbaḥī, may God be pleased with him, is beyond dispute the earliest and most authentic written collection of Prophetic traditions. It is also the best-known work of Prophetic traditions as established by the greatest scholars of Prophetic traditions.

Mālik earned his reputation on the strength of his book and his status as a great Imam. He was also well known for his engagement with reports about the Prophet (pbuh), for his rigorous methodology in refuting or accepting traditions attributed to the Prophet (pbuh), and for his deep knowledge of the status of the narrators of Prophetic traditions. Because of his fame, students wished to study directly with the book's author, Mālik. Scholars from the Islamic West had the largest share in studying directly with Mālik. Evidence of this fact is found in the records of those scholars of the Islamic West, and Morocco in particular, who traveled to the city of the Prophet (pbuh) to meet Imam Mālik, to learn the *Muwaṭṭa'* from him in person, and to benefit directly from his knowledge.

The most prominent of these scholars was Yaḥyā b. Yaḥyā al-Laythī al-Maṣmūdī, may God be pleased with him, who took on this task and was lucky enough to meet Imam Mālik. Among the fruits of that meeting was that Yaḥyā was able to transmit the *Muwaṭṭa'* directly from Mālik. [20] This is the recension attributed to Yaḥyā, which he recounted with utmost care and attention and which, on account of these efforts, became widespread and famous. The people of the Maghrib participated in teaching it and preserving it, embracing it wholeheartedly. They considered it *their* recension that was not to be superseded by any other. For that reason, the sublime Royal Order to the Editorial Committee for the Renewal of Islamic Learning was a call to edit the *Muwaṭṭaʾ* on the basis of the recension of Yaḥyā b. Yaḥyā al-Laythī and in reliance on Moroccan manuscripts based on that recension.[vi]

This is an appropriate response to the needs of scholarship and a methodological necessity, especially if we take into consideration the fact that the *Muwaṭṭaʾ*, despite its importance, has not undergone, until now, a critical edition commensurate with the status and respect it enjoys in the hearts of Moroccans and its place in their history. Many flawed editions have been put into circulation, published by editors who were inadequately prepared for the task. The sublime Royal Order, therefore, came to correct this defective situation and to restore things to their proper order. This sublime Order established a clear work plan, drawing the Committee's attention to the defective editions currently in public circulation with a view to correcting the mistakes and distortions that were prevalent in those editions. His Majesty, may God honor him, ordered the Editorial Committee to rely on original manuscripts of the book, copies of which are found in our Moroccan libraries. He specifically referenced the commonly accepted recension of the *Muwaṭṭaʾ* in Morocco, that is, Yaḥyā b. Yaḥyā al-Laythī al-Maṣmūdī's recension, with the goal of producing a scholarly edition of this recension, which would be free of the errors plaguing prior published editions.

In response to the sublime Order, a scholarly committee under the auspices of the High Council of Religious Scholars was established. It appointed a select group of scholars from the High Council whose task it became to realize this noble project.

The first step the Committee took was to prepare scholarly reports regarding the condition of prior editions. The Committee spent a considerable amount of time reviewing previous editions, though it proved unfeasible to survey all of them because of the sheer volume of the editions of the *Muwaṭṭaʾ* that have appeared in recent centuries, from India to Morocco; therefore, only the editions readily available to the Committee were considered.

More than two centuries had elapsed since the first appearance of the Delhi lithograph edition of the *Muwaṭṭaʾ* in 1216/1801, followed by editions in India, Egypt, Tunisia, and Lebanon. The Moroccan lithographic press also contributed to this output, which [21] complicated the Committee's efforts.

It was not easy to obtain microfilms of these lithographs, which, in contemporary circumstances, would be deemed the equivalent of manuscripts. Accordingly, the Committee decided to direct its attention

vi Mālik continued to teach and revise the *Muwaṭṭaʾ* over many years. During this period, several of his students transmitted different versions of the *Muwaṭṭaʾ*. Scholars know these different versions by the names of Mālik's students who transmitted them to later generations. In this translation of the Arabic introduction, we refer to each of these different versions of the *Muwaṭṭaʾ* as a "recension" and to the subsequent transmission of a recension as a "transmission."

to edited editions and editions deemed equivalent to edited editions. The Committee then decided to ignore editions whose publishers, producers, or printers failed to indicate their manuscript sources, because in the absence of any information about the manuscript sources it becomes difficult if not impossible to adopt objective criteria for assessing the reliability of different versions or for selecting the most reliable transmission among the existing recensions and manuscript copies.

The printed editions that the Committee decided to use are the following:

1. The Egyptian edition of Muḥammad Fu'ād ʿAbd al-Bāqī

This two-volume edition appeared in Cairo in 1951. The scholarly community at that time was in need of an edition that was within easy reach and had some scholarly features. As a result, it was received warmly and enjoyed a good reputation. Its editor, may God have mercy on him, said that he had consulted six previous editions:

a. The edition by al-Bābī al-Ḥalabī and Sons published in Egypt in 1348/1929
b. The edition by the Egyptian publisher ʿAbd al-Ḥamīd Ḥanafī in 1353/1934
c. The Bāb al-Lūq edition in Cairo in 1280/1863
d. The edition by Fārūqī Printing House in India in 1291/1874
e. The Delhi edition, India, in 1307/1889
f. The Hūrīnī edition in 1280/1863

The late Muḥammad Fu'ād ʿAbd al-Bāqī did not use or cite any manuscripts, despite their prevalence in Egypt, the Levant, the Hijaz, and Turkey, to say nothing of those in Tunisia, Algeria, and Morocco. His edition is thus deficient in its documentation. His choices and preferences regarding narrations and words do not rest on scholarly grounds. Instead, they are the result of his own taste and whatever [22] meanings secondary sources, such as dictionaries, books of Prophetic traditions, or biographies of the narrators of Prophetic traditions, led him to. As a consequence, his edition suffers from some very serious errors, which became clear with the subsequent publication of other editions of the *Muwaṭṭa'*.

2. The edition of Bashshār ʿAwwād Maʿrūf

This two-volume edition was issued in 1996 in Beirut by Dār al-Gharb al-Islāmī. Because it was a later edition, and because of the expertise and knowledge of its editor, Dr. Bashshār ʿAwwād Maʿrūf, who was known for his considerable knowledge of manuscripts and editing methodology, many scholars hoped that it would surpass its predecessors. Because of the war in Iraq, however, Maʿrūf was limited to the manuscripts available domestically in Iraq. Moreover, he was able to consult only some commentaries, such as Ibn ʿAbd al-Barr's *al-Tamhīd* and Zurqānī's commentary, as well as the materials he found in some other editions, including the Egyptian Hurīnī edition, the Tunisian edition, and the edition of Fu'ād ʿAbd al-Bāqī. In producing his own edition, he relied on a derivative copy from the manuscript of the traditionist (*muḥaddith*) Ibn Masdī, who died in the year 366/976. The manuscript he used was dated to 749/1348.

3. The edition of Dr. Muṣṭafā al-Aʿẓamī

This edition appeared in the United Arab Emirates in Abu Dhabi in 1421/2000. The eight-volume edition was published by the Zayed Bin Sultan Al Nahyan Charitable and Humanitarian Foundation. The first volume was devoted to the introduction and preliminary materials, the second through fifth volumes to the text of the *Muwaṭṭa'*, and the sixth through eighth volumes to the indexes. The editor said that he relied on six manuscripts, two of which were Moroccan; unfortunately, he made only limited use of them, as the reader will see in our footnotes in the commentary on the two manuscripts. [23] It is clear that the editor made no real effort, whether in terms of correcting manuscripts against a master or in terms of comparing them to one another, and he made serious errors as a result.

Of course, reliance on the original, authenticated manuscripts of the *Muwaṭṭa'* is necessary to produce a superior edition. Moreover, scholars need to be aware of the circumstances surrounding the transmission of the *Muwaṭṭa'* from the time of its first appearance in the Islamic West via Yaḥyā b. Yaḥyā al-Laythī, as well as the circumstances surrounding its continued narration by subsequent generations of scholars who devoted themselves to its careful transmission to preserve its integrity.

One important consequence of Yaḥyā b. Yaḥyā al-Laythī's blessed trip to the eastern lands of the Arab world was that he was able to meet Imam Mālik and return with the *Muwaṭṭa'* to the Maghrib. It is true that many students from the Maghrib had preceded him in doing so, including ʿAbd al-Raḥmān b. Ziyād Shabṭūn,[vii] whose narration of the *Muwaṭṭa'* did not acquire the same reputation, continuity, and wide dissemination as Yaḥyā's. On his return from Medina, Yaḥyā took it upon himself to teach and promote the *Muwaṭṭa'*, as is evident from his impressive series of lectures, which attracted many students. After he passed away, his son, ʿUbayd Allāh (d. 289/901), continued the work of his father, spending all his time on the *Muwaṭṭa'*, which gave his recension

vii The editors of the RME probably mean Ziyād b. ʿAbd al-Raḥmān (d. 204/819).

wide fame, especially insofar as ʿUbayd Allāh narrated exclusively from his father, a task at which he excelled. It is obvious that someone who spends the entirety of his time with one recension is likely to perfect its transmission and to become an authority on it given the rarity of mistakes in vocalization and spelling, confused passages, and outright errors.

One of the factors that made ʿUbayd Allāh's narration particularly famous and widespread was the lengthy period of time he spent publicly teaching and the fact that he was blessed with long life. He outlived his peers, Ibn Waḍḍāḥ and Ibn Bāz, and so he became the necessary destination of Andalusian students seeking the briefest chain of authorities to Mālik's *Muwaṭṭaʾ*.[viii] Accordingly, he taught three generations of students—sons, fathers, and grandfathers—all of whom attended his lectures to hear Prophetic traditions from him. It is for good reason, then, that he is described as a teacher who connected grandsons to their grandfathers. Students too numerous to count studied the *Muwaṭṭaʾ* with ʿUbayd Allāh, but at their forefront were his family members, the most prominent of whom were his two nephews:

[24] **Abū ʿAbd Allāh Muḥammad b. ʿAbd Allāh b. Yaḥyā** (284–339/897–950), chief judge (*qāḍī al-jamāʿa*) of Cordoba. He learned Prophetic traditions from his uncle. History has preserved an autograph copy of a manuscript of his. Later generations of scholars would correct his brother Yaḥyā's narration of the *Muwaṭṭaʾ* against his.

His brother, **Abū ʿĪsā Yaḥyā** (d. 367/977), whose narration gained such fame and became so widespread that it eclipsed that of his brother, Abū ʿAbd Allāh. He lived sufficiently long to become the last living narrator of his generation, just like his father's uncle Abū Marwān ʿUbayd Allāh, giving his narration the distinction of having the smallest number of intervening authorities to Mālik. Accordingly, the people felt the need to hear his

---

viii The medieval Muslim scholarly tradition was deeply concerned with preserving the accuracy of an author's text against the encroachment of errors in its transmission over time. Such errors could result from misreading of the vocalization of certain words, spelling errors, or mistranscription of a passage, to name just a few. Accordingly, scholars preserved the chain of transmitters between each copy of a manuscript and the original copy of the work's author as a means to authenticate the accuracy of a manuscript's transmission. In this manuscript culture, the brevity of the chain of transmitters to the author was highly prized and was often a function of the vagaries of health. It was assumed that the smaller the number of links to the original author, the smaller the likely number of mistakes in the manuscript. The editors are here pointing out that because ʿUbayd Allāh was given a long life compared to others of his generation who studied the *Muwaṭṭaʾ* with his father and transmitted it, chains of transmission linking copies of the *Muwaṭṭaʾ* that went through ʿUbayd Allāh were shorter than those that went through his contemporaries. Accordingly, after the deaths of other teachers of the *Muwaṭṭaʾ* belonging to his generation, students preferred to study the text directly with ʿUbayd Allāh rather than with teachers of the next generation, even if the latter were more numerous and readily available, on account of the brevity of the chain of authorities produced by studying with ʿUbayd Allāh.

transmission of the *Muwaṭṭaʾ* in particular. He would transmit exclusively from the manuscript of his father's uncle, ʿUbayd Allāh, which he had fully mastered. His student Abū al-Walīd b. al-Faraḍī (351–403/962–1012), who used to attend his gatherings on the *Muwaṭṭaʾ*, would say, "I never saw a Cordoban gathering more auspicious than our gathering for the *Muwaṭṭaʾ*."

The young, the middle-aged, and the elderly heard the *Muwaṭṭaʾ* from him. They came from all walks of life, including the Commander of the Faithful al-Mustanṣir, al-Ḥakam b. ʿAbd al-Raḥmān (d. 366/976), or so Ibn al-Faraḍī reported.

The most famous narrators from Abū ʿĪsā Yaḥyā b. ʿAbd Allāh are the following:

Yūnus b. Mughīth Abū al-Walīd b. al-Ṣaffār (d. 419/1028), the chief judge of Cordoba and one of its most esteemed jurists (*faqīh*) and traditionists, steeped in the narration of Prophetic traditions. He was a man of considerable acumen and intelligence and participated widely in the affairs of his day. He was well known for his deep knowledge of the Arabic language and its arts and for his knowledge of jurisprudence. He learned such a large number of traditions from so large a number of teachers that he became renowned in his day as the traditionist in possession of the largest number of attested traditions, with the briefest chains of authorities to their sources. For that reason, people were delighted that he narrated the *Muwaṭṭaʾ* from Abū ʿĪsā, and they competed with one another in transmitting it from him because of the accuracy and precision of his transmission and its immediacy to Abū ʿĪsā, even though he also narrated directly from (*ḥaddatha ʿan*) other eminent traditionists in Andalusia. Other eminent traditionists beyond its borders, such as Abū Muḥammad b. Abī Zayd al-Qayrawānī (310–386/922–996) and Abū al-Ḥasan al-Dāraquṭnī (306–385/918–995), gave him authority (*ajāzahu*) to transmit their materials.[ix] Several eminent traditionists followed his transmission.

[25] **Ibn Fuṭays, Abū al-Muṭarrif ʿAbd al-Raḥmān b. Muḥammad al-Qurṭubī** (348–402/960–1012) was one of the master traditionists of his age. He narrated from his father Abū ʿAbd Allāh b. Mufarrij, Abū Jaʿfar b. ʿAbd

ix The medieval Arabic manuscript tradition distinguished between the various means by which a student might study a text. Here, it is reported that Yūnus b. Mughīth "transmitted directly from," indicating that he studied directly with the source of the transmitted text. This method of transmission is contrasted with his link to scholars outside of Andalusia who are described as having authorized him to transmit their materials. This latter mode of transmission was indirect insofar as the student did not study the text directly with the source, but the source nevertheless trusted the student sufficiently to permit him to transmit the materials to new students. In terms of reliability of transmission, direct transmission from a source was considered more reliable than indirect transmission by way of the source's permission. Ibn Abī Zayd al-Qayrawānī lived in Qayrawān, in what is today Tunisia, and was the leading Mālikī jurist of his day. Dāraquṭnī was a leading traditionist.

Allāh, Abū Zakariyā' b. 'Ā'idh, and Abū 'Īsā al-Laythī. Traditionists outside of Andalusia, including Abū Muḥammad b. Abī Zayd al-Qayrawānī and Abū al-Ḥasan al-Dāraquṭnī, also authorized him to narrate their materials.

Abū 'Amr 'Uthmān b. Aḥmad al-Qayjāṭī al-Qurṭubī (d. 431/1040). He was one of the most senior students of Abū 'Īsā, and his narration was one of the best-known routes to Abū 'Īsā. He was a man of integrity, abstemious, trustworthy, noble-mannered, and a careful narrator. The narrators who narrated from him were Abū 'Abd Allāh al-Khawlānī, the latter's son, and Muḥammad b. Shurayḥ. His narration arrived in Seville through Abū 'Abd Allāh al-Khawlānī, who was a skilled traditionist; his father gave him a good education from an early age, bringing him to study the *Muwaṭṭa'* with his own teachers. He sought the permission of the senior scholars of his age on his son's behalf to authorize his son to narrate their materials. As a result, his son obtained the advantage of having the shortest chain of authorities and the only route for the *Muwaṭṭa'* through Qayjāṭī. Qayjāṭī was among the last narrators to have reported the *Muwaṭṭa'* from Abū 'Īsā, who was himself among the last people to have reported it from 'Ubayd Allāh, who was the last person to have reported it from Yaḥyā. Abū al-Rabī' al-Kallā'ī later narrated the *Muwaṭṭa'* through this chain, and Abū al-'Abbās b. al-Ghammāz narrated it from him, according to al-Wādī Āshī, as mentioned in his bibliography (*barnāmij*).[x] [26] Abū 'Īsā's narration, therefore, became widespread and acquired great fame because of his three students, Abū al-Walīd b. Mughīth, Ibn Fuṭays, and Abū 'Amr al-Qayjāṭī.

[27] Alongside Abū 'Īsā, **Abū 'Umar al-Muntajālī al-Ṣadafī**, whose full name is Aḥmad b. Sa'īd b. Ḥazm al-Qurṭubī (d. 350/961), also narrated the 'Ubayd Allāh transmission of the *Muwaṭṭa'*. He was one of the most prominent traditionists of his era. He busied himself with the narration and study of Prophetic traditions and historical reports, and with the compilation of Prophetic traditions. His knowledge of these matters was encyclopedic. He studied with 'Ubayd Allāh and Ibn Lubāba. He then traveled to the eastern lands of the Arab world, where he met the then most prominent scholars of Prophetic traditions in Mecca, Egypt, and Qayrawān. Afterward he returned to Andalusia, having acquired great knowledge.

Abū 'Amr Aḥmad b. Muṭarrif al-Azdī, known as **Ibn al-Mashshāṭ al-Qurṭubī** (d. 352/963), also took part in the transmission of the 'Ubayd Allāh transmission of the *Muwaṭṭa'*. He heard Prophetic traditions from 'Ubayd Allāh and busied himself with their study. He led prayers in Cordoba

x A genre of writing particular to the Islamic West in which a scholar lists all the books he has studied, along with the chains of authorities that link him to those texts' authors. It accordingly purports to document both the contents of the scholar's education and the scholarly networks that transmitted the texts he studied over time.

after the nephew of ʿUbayd Allāh, Muḥammad b. ʿAbd Allāh b. Yaḥyā. He and Muntajālī were reliable sources for whoever wished to hear Laythī's recension of the *Muwaṭṭa'* via ʿUbayd Allāh's transmission. Accordingly, some of their students who subsequently narrated the *Muwaṭṭa'* combined their two transmissions, while others narrated it only through one of them.

Among the narrators who combine the two routes of transmission are the following:

Ibn Ḥūbīl al-Tujībī, Abū Bakr ʿAbd al-Raḥmān b. Aḥmad b. Muḥammad (329–409/940–1018), one of Cordoba's senior traditionists. He was a trustworthy transmitter of reports, precise in what he transmitted, and a scholar of Prophetic traditions. He narrated from Abū ʿĪsā, but he was most famous for combining Muntajālī's and Ibn al-Mashshāṭ's narrations of the *Muwaṭṭa'*.

[28] Abū al-Qāsim al-Ṭarābulsī took these two transmissions from him, as did Abū ʿAbd Allāh b. ʿAttāb. The scholar of Prophetic traditions Abū ʿAlī al-Jayānī narrated that transmission from the two of them. He heard it[xi] from Ibn ʿAttāb in 448/1056 and 453/1061, and read it[xii] to Ḥātim al-Ṭarābulsī in 447/1055. Their combined narrations gained fame through Ibn Ḥūbīl, who narrated this version from Abū ʿAlī al-Jayānī. The latter authorized the combined narration and taught it to Ibn ʿAttāb and Ṭarābulsī. It reached us in the person of Qāḍī ʿIyāḍ (476–544/1083–1149), through Abū ʿAbd Allāh Muḥammad b. ʿĪsā al-Tamīmī al-Sabtī, from Jayānī. Qāḍī ʿIyāḍ received authorization from Jayānī. He repeated this transmission in the opening pages of his work *al-Mashāriq*. Abū Bakr b. Khayr also mentioned it in his list of the chains of transmission for the *Muwaṭṭa'* in his *Fihrist*[xiii] from his teacher, Abū Bakr b. Ṭāhir al-Qaysī, who narrated it to him from an autograph manuscript of his, which he copied from Aṣīlī's manuscript, which the latter himself had copied from Abū ʿAlī al-Jayānī, who transmitted it from Ibn ʿAbd al-Barr at a study session that took place in Ibn ʿAbd al-Barr's house in Shāṭiba in 453/1061.

---

xi The phrase "he heard it from" indicates not only that the student studied the text directly with the source but that the source either read the text aloud to the students or that it was read aloud in his presence. This was considered an especially accurate way of transmitting a text because it gave the teacher of the text the opportunity to clarify any ambiguities that might be present in the written manuscript, such as spelling errors, ambiguous vocalizations, or unclear grammar. It also offered an opportunity for the students to incorporate valuable notes from the teacher that could be beneficial to understanding the text into their own manuscripts of it.

xii This phrase indicates that he read his manuscript copy of the *Muwaṭṭa'* to the named teacher. By reading his manuscript to a teacher, the student has an opportunity to correct his own manuscript against the teacher's knowledge, which strengthens the reliability of the student's manuscript in the eyes of later generations of students.

xiii The *fihrist*, like the *barnāmij*, is a genre of writing particular to the Islamic West. It is virtually synonymous with *barnāmij*.

Abū ʿUmar b. ʿAbd al-Barr (368–463/978–1070) was one of the scholars who transmitted the combined narration of the *Muwaṭṭaʾ* from his teacher, Abū ʿUmar b. al-Jasūr al-Umawī al-Qurṭubī, as indicated in the beginnings of the former's works *al-Tamhīd*, *al-Istidhkār*, and *al-Taqaṣṣī*.[xiv] Ibn ʿAbd al-Barr, on the other hand, also preserved the individual transmissions of Abū Muḥammad b. al-Mashshāṭ al-Aṣīlī (d. 392/1001) and Abū ʿAbd Allāh b. Abī Zamanīn (d. 399/1008), both of whom were eminent scholars of Prophetic traditions and jurisprudence, steeped in knowledge, with encyclopedic knowledge of Prophetic traditions.

Abū ʿAbd Allāh b. Abī Zamanīn's narration of the *Muwaṭṭaʾ* is found in Qāḍī ʿIyāḍ's *Ghunya* and is mentioned in the opening pages of his *Mashāriq* via his teacher Ibn Ḥamdīn al-Taghlibī, from Abū Zakariyāʾ al-Qulayʿī, from Ibn Abī Zamanīn.

He also preserved the individual transmission of Ibn al-Mashshāṭ through Abū ʿUmar b. al-Jasūr. It was through him that this transmission—that is, the route through Ibn ʿAbd al-Barr—gained fame. He narrated it in *al-Tamhīd* and in *al-Istidhkār*. Abū al-ʿAbbās al-Dānī narrated it using this transmission in *al-Īmāʾ*. Jayānī, Abū Baḥr b. al-ʿĀṣ, Ibn Abī Talīd, and other students of Ibn ʿAbd al-Barr also narrated the *Muwaṭṭaʾ* via this transmission.

To these two transmissions Qāḍī ʿIyāḍ adds a third, that of Muḥammad b. Qāsim b. Hilāl. Abū al-Qāsim Khalaf b. Yaḥyā b. Ghayth al-Ṭulayṭilī narrated it from him, as did Abū ʿAbd Allāh b. ʿAttāb. Qāḍī ʿIyāḍ mentions it again in *al-Ghunya* in the biography of his teacher, Abū ʿAbd Allāh al-Tamīmī, from Jayānī, from [Ibn] ʿAttāb. [29] It is laid out in *al-Ghunya* in the biography of his teacher, Abū ʿAbd Allāh al-Tamīmī, as mentioned by Abū Bakr b. Khayr, via the transmission of Abū ʿAlī al-Jayānī.

There are also other transmissions of the *Muwaṭṭaʾ* from Yaḥyā that did not receive the same care as the recensions of Ibn Waḍḍāḥ and Ibn Bāz. Among these is the transmission of Abū ʿUmar Aḥmad b. Nābit al-Taghlibī (274–360/887–970), which was overshadowed by Abū ʿĪsā's transmission. Abū Bakr b. Khayr, however, who preserved this transmission for us, indicated that his teacher Abū Muḥammad b. Khazraj confirmed that the transmission of Abū ʿUmar b. Nābit and that of Abū ʿĪsā are one and the same, because Ibn Nābit copied his version from the manuscript of Abū ʿUbayd Allāh, which was the one that Abū ʿĪsā used when he taught the *Muwaṭṭaʾ*. Abū Bakr b. Khayr transmitted this transmission from his teacher

xiv These are three famous books by Ibn ʿAbd al-Barr that circulated widely in the medieval Islamic world. The first focuses largely on the chains of authorities for the various reports found in the different recensions of the *Muwaṭṭaʾ*. The second focuses on the legal doctrines in the *Muwaṭṭaʾ* and compares them to the views of Muslim jurists from other regions of the Muslim world. The third focuses exclusively on the Prophetic traditions included in the *Muwaṭṭaʾ*. The first two are multivolume works, whereas the third is shorter.

Abū Muḥammad b. Khazraj, from Abū al-Qāsim Ismāʿīl b. Badr, known as Ibn al-Ghannām. The aforementioned Abū ʿUmar Aḥmad b. Nābit reported it to him from ʿUbayd Allāh.

Alongside the ʿUbaydī transmission there were the following transmissions:

1. **The Waḍḍāḥī transmission**, attributed to Muḥammad b. Waḍḍāḥ (d. 287/900)
2. **The Bāzī transmission**, attributed to Ibrāhīm b. Muḥammad b. Bāz (d. 274/887)

The first transmission took its name from Imam Muḥammad b. Waḍḍāḥ al-Qurṭubī, who was a famous Andalusian religious scholar. He accompanied Yaḥyā for a lengthy period of time and transmitted the *Muwaṭṭa'* from him. He traveled to the eastern Arab lands twice, but he did not give himself over to studying Prophetic traditions during those trips because of his asceticism, piety, and devotion to Sufism.

[30] His colleague Abū Isḥāq Ibrāhīm b. Muḥammad b. Bāz al-Qurṭubī also participated in the narration of Yaḥyā b. Yaḥyā's recension. He was an eminent traditionist and one of those who made significant contributions to the success of Yaḥyā b. Yaḥyā's recension of the *Muwaṭṭa'*. Numerous students recited the work in his presence. Like his colleague Ibn Waḍḍāḥ, he claimed that Yaḥyā had made some errors in his recension of the *Muwaṭṭa'*.

With time, Ibn Waḍḍāḥ's transmission acquired fame and circulated widely. People competed to transmit it and were eager to spread it. The Bāzī transmission, however, could not keep pace with the ʿUbaydī and Waḍḍāḥī transmissions. Only two narrators continued to mention it alongside the Waḍḍāḥī transmission:

Aḥmad b. Khālid b. al-Jabbāb Abū ʿUmar al-Qurṭubī (246–327/860–938). He studied with Ibn Bāz, Ibn Waḍḍāḥ, and other scholars of Prophetic traditions in Andalusia. He traveled to the eastern Arab lands, going as far as Sanaa in Yemen. He received ʿAbd al-Razzāq's *Muṣannaf*[xv] from Abū Yaʿqūb Isḥāq al-Dabrī and brought it back to Andalusia, where he headed circles for the study of Prophetic traditions and jurisprudence.

Muḥammad b. ʿAbd al-Malik b. Ayman Abū ʿAbd Allāh al-Qurṭubī (252–330/866–941). He studied Prophetic traditions with Ibn Waḍḍāḥ and Ibn Bāz and narrated from them. He traveled in the company of Qāsim b. Aṣbagh and met eminent traditionists and jurists, including ʿAbd Allāh

xv The *Muṣannaf* of ʿAbd al-Razzāq al-Ṣanʿānī (d. 211/826) is a collection of Prophetic traditions, reports from the first generations of Muslims, and early legal opinions. It was one of the earliest authored works on Prophetic traditions and Islamic law, appearing a generation after the *Muwaṭṭa'*.

b. Aḥmad b. Ḥanbal. He visited Baghdad and heard there *Kitāb al-Tārīkh* of Ibn Abī Khaythama, and he transmitted it from him. He authored a book of Prophetic traditions that reproduced the contents of *Sunan Abū Dāwūd*[xvi] but with chains of transmission that differed from those of Abū Dāwūd (*mustakhraj*).[xvii] The book was well received. He was a precise and trustworthy narrator from whom people narrated a great deal.

Among those who narrated from Ibn al-Jabbāb and Ibn Ayman is Abū Muḥammad ʿAbd Allāh b. ʿAlī b. Sharīʿa al-Lakhmī (d. 378/988), known as "the narrator" (*al-rāwiya*). He narrated the *Muwaṭṭaʾ* in the month of Dhū al-Ḥijja in the year 310/922.

As good fortune would have it, the National Library has an invaluable original copy of Ibn Waḍḍāḥ's narration. It is the original manuscript of Abū al-Ḥasan Shurayḥ, which he wrote with his own hand. It incorporates notes that include the words of Ibn Ayman and Ibn al-Jabbāb and those of their teacher, Ibn Waḍḍāḥ, [31] based on what Abū Muḥammad heard in 319/931, when he read it to Ibn Ayman, and what he heard in 320/932, when he read it back to Ibn al-Jabbāb. This is what Abū Bakr b. Khayr specifically mentioned in his chains of transmission of the *Muwaṭṭaʾ* in his *Fihrist*, as noted earlier.

Abū Bakr ʿAbbās b. Aṣbagh al-Hamadānī al-Ḥijārī (306–386/918–996), by contrast, narrated it only from Ibn Ayman, from Ibn Waḍḍāḥ and Ibrāhīm b. Bāz, and did not combine Ibn Ayman's transmission with Ibn al-Jabbāb's.

Abū Bakr was an accurate transmitter from whom the people benefited greatly. Abū al-ʿĀṣ Ḥakam b. Muḥammad b. Afrānk al-Judhāmī (d. 447/1055) narrated from him. Abū Bakr was from Cordoba and one of the city's traditionists. He studied Prophetic traditions in Andalusia and then traveled to the eastern Arab lands. On his way there he met Ibn Abī Zayd al-Qayrawānī and studied with him. Qayrawānī authorized him to teach his books. Abū Bakr performed the Pilgrimage (*ḥajj*), and on his return journey he studied in Egypt and copied the books of its scholars. He lived well into old age, so his transmissions, relative to those of his peers, have a shorter chain of authorities. As a result, many eminent traditionists, such as Abū Marwān al-Ṭabnī and Abū ʿAlī al-Jayānī, narrated through him.

---

xvi The *Sunan* of Abū Dāwūd al-Sijistānī (d. 275/888) is one of the six most important collections of Prophetic traditions in the Sunnī tradition. His collection focused on traditions that had legal relevance, hence the title *Sunan*, which means "laws."

xvii A *mustakhraj* is a genre of works in the science of Prophetic traditions in which the author seeks to replicate the Prophetic traditions found in another collection—in this case, the *Sunan* of Abū Dāwūd—but with chains of authorities that differ from those reported by the author of the original work. The purpose of such a work is to provide further authentication for the content of the traditions by adducing additional routes of the texts' transmission.

One of the well-known transmissions from Ibn Waḍḍāḥ is the transmission of **Qāsim b. Aṣbagh al-Bayānī** (244–340/858–951), transmissions of which are many and divided into several branches. Narrators transmitted it to one another and it spread widely, thanks to Ibn Aṣbagh's status, longevity, and reputation. Its transmission is from Ibn ʿAbd al-Barr, from his teacher Saʿīd b. Naṣr (d. 395/1004), from Qāsim.

Imam Qāsim b. Aṣbagh was a respected narrator of Prophetic traditions. He studied them in Andalusia from the region's eminent traditionists, such as Ibn Waḍḍāḥ, Baqī (201–276/817–889), and Abū ʿAbd Allāh al-Khushanī. He traveled to the eastern Arab lands in 274/887 in the company of Muḥammad b. Ayman and Ibn ʿAbd al-Aʿlā. He studied Prophetic traditions in Qayrawān, Egypt, and the Hijaz. He went as far as Iraq before bringing back to Andalusia much knowledge and a great many lengthy books directly from their eminent authors, such as Ibn Abī Khaythama's *Tārīkh* and the works of Ibn Qutayba, al-Mubarrad, and Thaʿlab. The people therefore preferred his transmission over those of his colleagues [32] Ibn [ʿAbd] al-Aʿlā and Muḥammad b. Ayman. The young and the old alike studied Prophetic traditions with him, and he served as a bridge between the generations, as stated by Ibn al-Faraḍī.

Among the scholars who studied the *Muwaṭṭaʾ* directly with Qāsim and narrated his recension of it are the following:

Abū Jaʿfar Aḥmad b. ʿAwn Allāh b. Ḥudayr al-Bazzāz (300–378/912–988). He studied with Qāsim b. Aṣbagh and Ibn Abī Dulaym. He traveled to Egypt, the Levant, and the Hijaz, where he heard Prophetic traditions from Ibn al-Aʿrābī in Mecca, from Khaythama in Levantine Tripoli, from Abū al-Maymūn al-Bajlī in Damascus, and from Ibn al-Sakan in Egypt. He was a traditionist and a trustworthy narrator. Abū ʿUmar al-Ṭalamankī (d. 429/1037), the Quran reciter, narrated this transmission from him.

Abū al-Walīd al-Waqshī narrated Ṭalamankī's recension. He was the most eminent scholar of his time in Prophetic traditions and the Arabic language. He busied himself with the correction and emendation of books. His linguistic annotations are found scattered across the margins of various copies of the *Muwaṭṭaʾ*, including the manuscript copies on which we have relied in preparing this critical edition. Abū al-Qāsim Ḥātim al-Ṭarābulsī also narrated the *Muwaṭṭaʾ* from Abū ʿUmar al-Ṭalamankī, as did Abū ʿAlī al-Jayānī.

Abū ʿUthmān Saʿīd b. Naṣr narrated the *Muwaṭṭaʾ* from both Qāsim and Wahb b. Masarra. Ibn ʿAbd al-Barr, as stated in *al-Tamhīd*, heard him recite it, word for word, from his copy, from Qāsim and Wahb, from Ibn Waḍḍāḥ.

Wahb b. Masarra al-Ḥajārī (d. 346/957). He was one of the most eminent traditionists, well acquainted with Prophetic traditions, their defects, and the biographies of their narrators. He was well known for his rigor and precision in the transmission of Prophetic traditions. The manuscripts of Ibn Waḍḍāḥ that he had studied were brought to him, and people read them to him in Cordoba.

[33] In his *Tamhīd*, *Istidhkār*, and *Taqaṣṣī*, Ibn ʿAbd al-Barr transmits the *Muwaṭṭaʾ* through various chains that go through Wahb b. Masarra, as well as a unique chain from Abū ʿUmar b. al-Jasūr, to whom Ibn ʿAbd al-Barr read the work, attributed to Ibn Abī Dulaym, from Abū al-Faḍl Aḥmad Qāsim al-Tāhartī, from both of them (that is, Ibn Abī Dulaym and Wahb b. Masarra, from Ibn Waḍḍāḥ), and added to Qāsim b. Aṣbagh's narration, transmitted by Ibn ʿAbd al-Barr via his teacher, Saʿīd b. Naṣr, from both of them (that is, Qāsim and Wahb, from Ibn Waḍḍāḥ).

Ibn Khayr narrated it via Abū ʿAlī al-Jayānī, from Abū Shākir al-Qabrī, from Abū Muḥammad al-Aṣīlī, from Abū al-Ḥazm Wahb, in Wādī al-Ḥijāra (Guadalajara) in 344/955.

Ibn ʿAbd al-Barr said, "There are some differences in the wording of ʿUbayd Allāh's narration and that of Ibn Waḍḍāḥ's narration, which I noted in my book."

Ibn ʿAbd al-Barr set forth his remarks in detail in *al-Tamhīd*, which helped greatly in preparing this critical edition. Works such as *al-Mashāriq* and *al-Īmāʾ* and other commentaries on the *Muwaṭṭaʾ* relied extensively on Ibn ʿAbd al-Barr's comments in *al-Tamhīd*. Ibn Khayr also transmitted them in his collections of Prophetic traditions from his two teachers Abū Muḥammad b. ʿAttāb, by way of authorization, and Abū al-Ḥasan Yūnus, by way of oral recitation, from Qāḍī Abū ʿUmar b. al-Ḥadhdhāʾ al-Tamīmī, who named his sources as follows: "ʿAbd al-Wārith b. Sufyān, from Qāsim b. Aṣbagh and Wahb b. Masarra, combining the two recensions, from Ibn Waḍḍāḥ."

Ibn Khayr also mentioned another chain of transmission to Wahb b. Masarra, from the recension of his teacher, Abū Muḥammad Ismāʿīl b. Khazraj, from his teacher, Abū ʿUthmān Saʿīd b. Aḥmad al-Qallās, from Wahb, from Ibn Waḍḍāḥ.

Among the transmissions from ʿUbayd Allāh to Ibn Waḍḍāḥ is the transmission of **Abū ʿAbd Allāh b. ʿAbd Allāh b. Abī Dulaym** (d. 338/949). Most of the reports that he transmitted came from Ibn Waḍḍāḥ. He was one of the most important narrators from Ibn Waḍḍāḥ. He was said to resemble him in terms of physical appearance and behavior. He was upright in character and a trustworthy narrator. Many people studied Prophetic traditions with him.

His transmission of the *Muwaṭṭaʾ* came from Ibn Waḍḍāḥ, coupled with that of Wahb b. Masarra, from Ibn ʿAbd al-Barr (as set out in the opening pages of *al-Tamhīd*), from his teacher Abū al-Faḍl al-Tāhartī, from both of them (Ibn Abī Dulaym and Wahb).

[34] This transmission became famous through Ibn ʿAbd al-Barr. Abū al-ʿAbbās al-Dānī mentioned it in his collection of the *Muwaṭṭa'*, from Abū ʿAlī al-Jayānī, from Ibn ʿAbd al-Barr. This is what is found in Abū Bakr b. Khayr.

In the fourth century AH (tenth century CE), the features of the *Muwaṭṭa'* were determined definitively. This was manifested in the disappearance of the Bāzī transmission and the continuation of the ʿUbaydī and Waḍḍaḥī transmissions. The change is confirmed by the notes, comments, and corrections made in the margins of our manuscript copies.

All this came about thanks to a new generation of students of the students of Ibn Waḍḍāḥ and ʿUbayd Allāh, the most prominent of whom was Imam Abū Muḥammad ʿAbd Allāh b. Ibrāhīm al-Aṣīlī al-Maghribī. He traveled to Cordoba in 342/953 and discovered brisk demand for the ʿUbaydī and Waḍḍaḥī narrations, so he listened to the ʿUbaydī narration from Muntajālī and Ibn al-Mashshāṭ.

During the fifth century AH (eleventh century CE), religious scholars made the *Muwaṭṭa'* an object of intense study. [35] The figure who made the greatest advancements in promoting the *Muwaṭṭa'* was the great Maghribi scholar of Prophetic traditions Ibn ʿAbd al-Barr al-Qurṭubī, whose transmission of the *Muwaṭṭa'* enjoyed great prominence. People adopted his transmission because of his respected status as a scholar and a reliable narrator of Prophetic traditions with an avid interest in the *Muwaṭṭa'*. The written works of Ibn ʿAbd al-Barr—namely, *al-Tamhīd*, *al-Istidhkār*, and *al-Taqaṣṣī*—became famous themselves among scholars, as did his recension of the *Muwaṭṭa'*. In his *Tamhīd*, Abū ʿUmar provides a good overview of the *Muwaṭṭa'* from Yaḥyā's recension, relying on the transmissions of ʿUbayd Allāh and Ibn Waḍḍāḥ. His commentary is confined exclusively to Yaḥyā's recension, treading the path of Moroccans who chose and preferred this recension because it was the version they had inherited from their teachers, which is why they preserved it so zealously. He prepared a commentary that was well documented, relying on the first ʿUbaydī transmission, which he had received via the route of Abū ʿUmar b. al-Jasūr, from Ibn al-Mashshāṭ and Muntajālī, from ʿUbayd Allāh.

The second transmission, Ibn Waḍḍāḥ's, was narrated by Saʿīd b. Naṣr from his teacher, from Qāsim b. Aṣbagh and Wahb b. Masarra, both of whom narrated it from Ibn Waḍḍāḥ, and via his teacher, Abū al-Faḍl al-Tāhartī, from Ibn Abī Dulaym and Wahb b. Masarra, both from Ibn Waḍḍāḥ.

[36] Ibn ʿAbd al-Barr noted differences between the two transmissions and mentioned them in his version. They are clearly detailed in his book *al-Tamhīd*, along with his comments. As a result, we were compelled to make regular use of his *Tamhīd* in preparing this critical edition. We had frequent recourse to it in cases of discrepancy between the transmissions

of ʿUbayd Allāh and Ibn Waḍḍāḥ, as though it were an edited version of the text.

Abū ʿAlī al-Jayānī, Ibn ʿAbd al-Barr's best student, continued to work on his teacher's project, adding other transmissions of the *Muwaṭṭaʾ*, one of which was that of Qāsim b. Aṣbagh and Wahb b. Masarra, both from Ibn Waḍḍāḥ, via his teacher, Abū ʿUmar b. al-Ḥadhdhāʾ (d. 467/1074), from ʿAbd al-Wārith b. Sufyān, from Qāsim b. Aṣbagh. Abū al-ʿAbbās al-Dānī mentioned this transmission in the opening of his *Īmāʾ*.

We found a transmission made up of the transmissions of three different narrators, Muntajālī, Ibn al-Mashshāṭ, and Abū ʿĪsā, all from ʿUbayd Allāh. We find this transmission in Abū Muḥammad b. ʿAṭiyya's *Fihrist*, from Abū ʿAlī al-Jayānī, from Abū ʿAbd Allāh b. ʿAttāb and Abū al-Qāsim al-Ṭarābulsī, both from Abū Bakr b. Ḥūbīl, from the three of them (Muntajālī, Ibn al-Mashshāṭ, and Abū ʿĪsā), from ʿUbayd Allāh.

We find Abū Bakr b. Ḥūbīl again recounting Ibn al-Mashshāṭ's transmission in particular, as mentioned by Qāḍī ʿIyāḍ at the beginning of *al-Mashāriq*.

Abū ʿAlī al-Jayānī also adds another individual to the list of narrators from ʿUbayd Allāh: Muḥammad b. Qāsim b. Hilāl. Qāḍī ʿIyāḍ reported the transmission of Abū ʿAlī al-Jayānī via Muḥammad b. Qāsim b. Hilāl, to which he added the transmissions of Ibn al-Mashshāṭ and Muntajālī, thus combining the three. We find this transmission in Qāḍī ʿIyāḍ's *al-Mashāriq* and in his *Ghunya* from Abū ʿAlī al-Jayānī, who authorized it, from Abū Isḥāq al-Lawātī, who learned it from him in Sabta, from Qāḍī Abū ʿĪsā b. Sahl, from Abū ʿAbd Allāh b. ʿAttāb, from Abū al-Qāsim Khalaf b. Yaḥyā b. Ghayth, from Ibn al-Mashshāṭ and Muntajālī, and Muḥammad b. Qāsim b. Hilāl. Mention has already been made of the multiple ʿUbaydī transmissions through the chain of authorities found in the *Fihrists* of Ibn ʿAṭiyya, ʿIyāḍ, and Ibn Khayr.

[37] Through Ibn ʿAṭiyya's *Fihrist*, we learn of two more transmissions of Abū ʿĪsā:

- The transmission of Abū al-Muṭarrif ʿAbd al-Raḥmān b. Muḥammad b. ʿĪsā b. Fuṭays al-Qurṭubī (d. 402/1011)
- The transmission of Abū ʿAbd Allāh Muḥammad b. ʿUmar b. al-Fakhkhār (d. 419/1028)

Abū Muḥammad b. ʿAṭiyya mentioned these two transmissions from the transmission of Abū ʿAlī al-Jayānī, from Ḥātim al-Ṭarābulsī, from both Ibn Fuṭays and Ibn al-Fakhkhār, from Abū ʿĪsā.

Abū al-Qāsim al-Ṭarābulsī adds a transmission from Abū ʿĪsā through the Quran reciter Abū ʿUmar al-Ṭalamankī. We drew a comparison between his transmission and that of Abū ʿAbd Allāh b. al-Fakhkhār, from Abū ʿĪsā.

Among the scholars who reported the transmission of the *Muwaṭṭa'* in a unique chain via Aḥmad b. al-Muṭarrif was Ibn al-Mashshāṭ, from 'Ubayd Allāh Abū 'Abd Allāh b. Abī Zamanīn (d. 399/1008). We find his transmission in the beginning of Qāḍī 'Iyāḍ's *Mashāriq*, from his teacher Abū 'Abd Allāh b. Ḥamdīn, from the latter's father, from Abū Zakariyā' Yaḥyā b. Muḥammad b. Ḥusayn al-Qulay'ī, from Ibn Abī Zamanīn.

Through Abū Muḥammad b. 'Aṭiyya and Qāḍī 'Iyāḍ, we come across a mention of two further transmissions from Abū 'Īsā:

- The transmission of Abū 'Uthmān Sa'īd b. Salama (d. 413/1022)
- The transmission of Abū Bakr Yaḥyā b. Wāfid (d. 404/1013)

Abū 'Abd Allāh b. 'Attāb transmitted both transmissions, but Ibn Wāfid raised doubts as to whether he had heard the entirety of the *Muwaṭṭa'* from Abū 'Īsā', the omitted parts being the Book of Pilgrimage (*ḥajj*) and portions of the Book of Obligatory Prayer (*ṣalāt*).

Nevertheless, the fifth-century individual who made the most lasting impact on the 'Ubaydī transmission was Abū 'Abd Allāh b. al-Ṭallā' (d. 497/1103). He lived a long life, in which he devoted himself to public teaching of the *Muwaṭṭa'*. He became famous for this, and people flocked to him to hear the work. His chain of narration was the shortest of the chains for the *Muwaṭṭa'*.

Through his chain of transmission, an ancient manuscript, written on a gazelle parchment, has come down to us; this manuscript is a copy of an original version. It was corrected and compared to the manuscript of the jurist and meticulous scholar of Prophetic traditions Abū 'Abd Allāh Muḥammad b. Salama al-Anṣārī. The date [38] of the manuscript's copying is Rabī' al-Thānī 613/July 1216. The date on which the comparison took place was probably not too far from the date of copying, because the word "comparison" suggests that it occurred during the life of Abū 'Abd Allāh b. Salama, who was in possession of the original manuscript that was used for the comparison. The manuscript's use of the expression *akramahu 'llāh* (May God honor him) is also consistent with the conclusion that Ibn Salama was alive at that time.

Abū 'Abd Allāh b. Salama's date of birth cannot be later than 580/1184, because he recited the *Muwaṭṭa'* to his father, Aḥmad b. Salama, who died in the year 597/1200. The comparison with his transmission must have taken place when he was at least thirty-five years old. This manuscript is precious because it was compared to and corrected against the manuscript of Abū 'Abd Allāh b. Salama, who was himself a meticulous narrator and well known for his rigor, and because of the precious marginal notes included in his manuscript. These notes included comparisons with other manuscripts, notes regarding divergences among various narrators of the *Muwaṭṭa'*, and other notes and explanations. All of these were then transferred to the copy from Ibn Salama's manuscript, with which it was compared.

Thus, this manuscript represents the ʿUbaydī transmission via Abū ʿĪsā, ʿUbayd Allāh's nephew, which helped us greatly.

Sixth-century AH (twelfth-century CE) scholars continued to transmit the *Muwaṭṭa'*, taking good care of it. The most prominent of them were the compilers of the famous *Fihrists*:

- Abū Muḥammad b. ʿAṭiyya al-Gharnāṭī
- Qāḍī ʿIyāḍ al-Sabtī
- Abū Bakr b. Khayr al-Fāsī

From a scrutiny of their collections of Prophetic traditions we derive a list of scholars who had strong interest in the *Muwaṭṭa'* and in its preservation and propagation. They include the following:

- Qāḍī Abū al-Qāsim b. Baqī, one of the grandchildren of the famous narrator Baqī b. Mukhallad
- Abū al-Ḥasan b. Mughīth, the grandson of Abū al-Walīd b. Mughīth
- Abū ʿAbd Allāh b. Abī al-Aṣbagh b. Abī al-Baḥr al-Zahrī [39]
- Abū ʿAbd Allāh b. Ḥamdīn al-Taghlibī
- Abū Isḥāq al-Lawātī
- Abū Marwān ʿAbd al-Malik b. al-Bājī
- Abū al-Ḥasan Shurayḥ
- Abū al-Ḥakam b. Najāḥ al-Lakhmī

Most of these scholars were students of Abū ʿAbd Allāh b. al-Ṭallāʿ, whose transmission achieved unprecedented fame due to the brevity of his chain of transmission. It was possible for anyone who narrated from him to trace the recension back to Mālik through only five intermediaries, which was the shortest chain of narration possible at the time.

Through these scholars, their counterparts, and their attention to the *Muwaṭṭa'*, Yaḥyā b. Yaḥyā's recension was handed down to us, with all of its differences in terms of people and texts and its various ambiguous readings of terms, along with scholars' sustained efforts to understand his meaning as evidenced by their marginalia and substantive notes, all of which we have taken into account in editing this work. We have tried very hard to ensure that our edition draws on the ʿUbaydī and Waḍḍāḥī transmissions, in addition to the commentaries and works of Moroccan scholars of the *Muwaṭṭa'* such as *al-Tamhīd* and *al-Mashāriq*. We were thus able, in our work, to rely on valuable and rare manuscripts, one of which is dated 421/1030 and was itself copied from the manuscript of Abū ʿUmar al-Muntajālī (d. 350/961). It was compared and corrected twice against the original text.

The first comparison and correction took place in 487/1094, against a manuscript of Muntajālī's text in which variances found in Ibn Waḍḍāḥ's transmission were noted.

The second took place in the middle of the sixth century AH, in 557/1161, when the manuscript was corrected against a handwritten manuscript of the chief judge Abū ʿAbd Allāh Muḥammad b. ʿAbd Allāh b. Abī ʿĪsā (d. 339/950), that is, more than ten years before Muntajālī's death. That manuscript, which was used as the basis for correcting our manuscript, is the equivalent of Muntajālī's because both of them recited the *Muwaṭṭaʾ* to ʿUbayd Allāh.

[40] This version has thus achieved the highest degree of accuracy and reliability, in addition to the abundance of marginalia and notes in it, which make it especially useful.

The man who was in charge of publicly teaching this manuscript was the traditionist Abū Bakr b. Rizq, one of the most famous traditionists of the sixth century AH. All transmissions of the *Muwaṭṭaʾ* from Yaḥyā in circulation at that time found their way to him. Abū Bakr recorded the various chains of transmission of the *Muwaṭṭaʾ* from his teachers on this copy. He narrated the *Muwaṭṭaʾ* via Abū Baḥr Sufyān b. al-ʿĀṣ, who was one of Ibn ʿAbd al-Barr's companions, which makes it necessary to make use of his version. It is as if this version, which was corrected against Muntajālī's manuscript and against that of Abū ʿAbd Allāh b. Abī ʿĪsā, had benefited from Ibn ʿAbd al-Barr's text as received from his teachers. In Ibn Rizq's collections of Prophetic traditions there are other transmissions that converge on ʿUbayd Allāh, such as the transmission of Abū al-Qāsim Aḥmad b. al-Qāsim b. Jābir b. ʿUbayda.

Ibn Rizq also has other collections of Prophetic traditions that cannot be mentioned here for lack of space—alas, would that it were otherwise! Among the texts adopted in the preparation of this new edition of the *Muwaṭṭaʾ* is the text of the accomplished philologist and narrator Abū al-Ḥasan Shurayḥ b. Muḥammad (d. 539/1144), one the teachers of Abū Bakr b. Khayr and a companion of Abū Muḥammad b. Ḥazm—what a great teacher and student they were! He wrote the text out with his own hand for his son, Muḥammad b. Shurayḥ (d. 567/1171), the reliable narrator of Prophetic traditions. ʿAbd Allāh b. Bulayṭ al-Qaysī (d. 530/1135), one of Shurayḥ's students, was able to compare his copy with that of Shurayḥ's son Muḥammad. ʿAbd Allāh b. Bulayṭ was one of Abū Bakr b. al-ʿArabī's (468–543/1075–1148) students. In Cordoba, ʿAbd Allāh b. Bulayṭ read Bukhārī's *Ṣaḥīḥ* with Abū al-Ḥasan b. Mughīth, the well-known transmitter of Ibn al-Sakan. He studied Prophetic traditions with Abū al-Qāsim b. Ḥabīsh and other famous traditionists of the era in 503/1109.

Accordingly, this manuscript boasts great value, reliability, and precision. Its value becomes evident in its scattered marginalia and textual notes. This text gives us the transmission of the *Muwaṭṭa'* via the transmission of Ibn Waḍḍāḥ along with that of Ibn Bāz through his students Ibn al-Jabbāb and Ibn Ayman.

At the end of the version is found an appendix that includes a record of the names of the most famous traditionists of the sixth century AH (twelfth century CE) until Shurayḥ. They include Ibn al-Aṣbagh al-Shaʿbānī, Abū Bakr b. al-Murābiṭ, Abū al-Qāsim al-Mawāʿīnī, Abū ʿAbd Allāh al-Balansanī, and Abū Muḥammad b. Mūjwāl al-Balansanī, and all of them studied this manuscript directly, either by reading it aloud to their teacher or by listening to it as it was read aloud in the presence of their teacher.

[41] There are three other copies that we used for purposes of comparison and correction. These were a great help to us in certain ambiguous cases; however, they do not match those other manuscripts in quality. We will, however, discuss and describe them when we discuss the manuscripts on which we relied to prepare this critical edition.

Having reviewed the various historical stages involved in the transmission of Yaḥyā b. Yaḥyā's recension of the *Muwaṭṭa'* in the course of its passing from one generation of scholars to the next, a process that focused efforts on this particular recension through its various chains of transmission and succeeded in preserving its text reliably, we can make the following observations in light of the manuscripts that we selected for use in the critical edition on the grounds of their quality, reliability, and precision.

Yaḥyā's recension would not have enjoyed such circulation and popularity were it not for his reputation, his popularity, and his intention to secure the place of the *Muwaṭṭa'* in Cordoba for as long as he lived. He was able to prepare a generation of transmitters led by his son ʿUbayd Allāh, along with a group of scholars who continued to transmit the *Muwaṭṭa'* after his death. His son ʿUbayd Allāh, in particular, was able to continue along the path of his father and prepare a generation of transmitters who followed his example and his recension; some of these transmitters were members of his family. In this way, each rising generation learned the recension from the preceding one. This process continued from one generation to the next until it became a widespread custom in all subsequent periods. In the ensuing centuries, there were leading scholars whose main concern was to transmit Yaḥyā's recension and to teach it publicly. The generation of ʿUbayd Allāh, Ibn Bāz, and Ibn Waḍḍāḥ was replaced, with respect to the ʿUbaydī transmission, by the generation of Muntajālī, Ibn al-Mashshāṭ, and Abū ʿĪsā, while Ibn Waḍḍāḥ's transmission was taken up by the generation of transmitters that included Ibn al-Jabbāb, Ibn Ayman, Ibn Abī Dulaym, Qāsim b. Aṣbagh, and Wahb b. Masarra. They were followed by another generation, which combined the two transmissions. This generation included Abū Muḥammad al-Bājī (d. 378/988), Abū Muḥammad al-Aṣīlī, Saʿīd b. Naṣr, Ibn Abī Zamanīn, and other scholars whose efforts culminated in the work of the generation of the fifth century AH, Abū ʿUmar al-Ṭalamankī, Abū al-Qāsim al-Ṭarābulsī, and the pioneering Ibn ʿAbd al-Barr, who became the undisputed leader in scholarship on the *Muwaṭṭa'*. Subsequent generations of scholars held him in awe and respect, both for his efforts in transmitting the *Muwaṭṭa'* to his students and for the encyclopedic works he authored about the *Muwaṭṭa'*. [42]

One important trait of Yaḥyā's recension of the *Muwaṭṭa'* is that its transmitters were long-lived, which enhanced its popularity. Because the *Muwaṭṭa'* was the work Imam Mālik, the Imam of Medina, it enjoyed a special place in the hearts of Moroccans. In a sense, a fifth-century Moroccan or Andalusian could get to know Mālik himself by studying the *Muwaṭṭa'* through Imam Abū ʿAbd Allāh b. al-Ṭallāʾ's transmission, since the latter was separated from Mālik by only four generations of transmitters: Abū al-Walīd Yūnus b. Mughīth, from Abū ʿĪsā al-Laythī, from ʿUbayd Allāh, from Yaḥyā b. Yaḥyā, from Mālik.

From the perspective of traditionists and the conventions of their science, the final version of an author's work is considered the best because it represents the last time he brings the text out to the public. There is no doubt that Yaḥyā b. Yaḥyā was the last person to have studied the *Muwaṭṭa'* with Mālik and received it from him. Yaḥyā studied with Mālik in the latter's final days, he attended Mālik's funeral, and he returned home bearing what he narrated from Mālik, that is, the *Muwaṭṭa'*, which makes his recension the most reliable. Despite the criticisms that may be leveled at Yaḥyā's recension, whether related to his omission of certain chapters such as the Book of Pious Seclusion (*iʿtikāf*) or alleged mistakes regarding some its expressions (which the editors identified by comparing his transmission with others), Yaḥyā's reputation and the value of his recension are beyond question. The people of Morocco adopted his recension of the *Muwaṭṭa'* as theirs and it formed the basis of their commentary tradition, a reality that the great Moroccan scholar Ibn ʿAbd al-Barr noted in the introduction to his *Tamhīd*. He said:

> I adopted Yaḥyā b. Yaḥyā's recension especially because of the place he occupies in the hearts of Moroccans because of his reliability, devotion, gracefulness, knowledge, and understanding, and because

of the consistent use of his recension, which our scholars learned from their teachers. I rely on his recension except in cases in which he omits an important Prophetic tradition dealing with a foundational matter of law; in such cases I mention it using another recension, God willing. Every people should adhere to the practice of its predecessors and follow their example in doing what is good, even when the behavior of others is likewise permissible and desirable.

[43] The Manuscripts Used in Preparing the Critical Edition of the *Muwaṭṭa*ʾ

His Majesty Muḥammad VI, the Commander of the Faithful, may God protect him, entrusted the Committee for the Renewal of Islamic Learning, which is an affiliate of the Secretariat General of the High Council of Religious Scholars, with the task of producing a critical edition of Imam Mālik's *Muwaṭṭa*ʾ, may God be pleased with him, in accordance with scientific standards, for an edition whose quality would surpass all other editions found in the Islamic libraries in the Muslim world, whether in the past or in the present, and which would be free of the many errors found in those other works. It is to be the first fruit of the Committee's ongoing efforts to publish scholarly and model works in a manner that is in conformity with the requirement of having attested chains of transmission satisfying the conditions of the traditionists and the methods of Moroccan scholars to preserve texts, whether orally or in writing.

His Majesty, may God preserve him, says, "Similarly, we are commissioning the standing Committee for the Renewal of Islamic Learning to produce a critical edition of Imam Mālik's *Muwaṭṭa*ʾ, may God be pleased with him, which will be scholarly and carefully prepared, commensurate with its subject and the status the subject enjoys among Moroccans. We expect this Committee to rectify the errors that have plagued previous editions by relying on the manuscripts of the *Muwaṭṭa*ʾ that are uniquely available in Morocco, and to publish a version that bears a national imprint, worthy of Morocco as a shining beacon of Mālikī jurisprudence."[2]

The Committee has taken the following steps to produce an accurate version of the *Muwaṭṭa*ʾ in accordance with the recension of Yaḥyā b. Yaḥyā al-Laythī (d. 234/848), as transmitted over successive generations by careful scholars through various paths of transmission, such as the narration of ʿUbayd Allāh b. Yaḥyā from his father, which is the first narration that springs to mind when the *Muwaṭṭa*ʾ is mentioned, despite the existence of numerous others. It is the transmission that Moroccans have relied on

2 From the speech of His Majesty, the Commander of the Faithful, during His Majesty's presiding over the first opening session of the proceedings of the High Council of Religious Scholars in the Royal Palace in Fez on July 8, 2005.

when they transmit, teach, and comment on the work, and explicate unusual words in it. They do not refer to any other recension of the text, even though these, too, have been transmitted through reliable chains of transmitters, as is clear in the bibliographies documenting their scholarly accomplishments (*fahārisuhum wa-athbātuhum wa-barāmijuhum*).

[44] In producing this new edition, we celebrate the great efforts of our religious scholars. We have compiled an inventory of their work within this edition and cited it when appropriate. We have marshaled, in preparing this edition, their great learning on matters related to the Arabic language and its unfamiliar words, to the work's jurisprudence, texts, and chains of authority, and to the biographies of its narrators. The work that produced this critical edition relied on original and reliable Moroccan manuscripts, which generations of our leading scholars have used in their education. All of this effort was in compliance with the Commander of the Faithful's sublime command and instructions. Our work has only confirmed what His Majesty originally said in his noble speech when he commissioned this task:

First, the previous published editions contain errors and faults, because they did not take care to confirm the reliability of their source texts or to follow scholarly methods of editing. We have spared no effort to avoid the errors, deviations, and distortions plaguing those editions.

Second, the principal manuscripts that formed the basis for comparisons between versions and determinations of reliability are the Moroccan manuscripts preserved in our archives and libraries. His Majesty referred to them in his sublime speech. They are six in number and were carefully selected out of the large number of manuscripts mentioned in the indexes of Moroccan libraries.[3] The most important of these six, in descending order

3 The most important of these are the indexes of the Ḥassani Library and the other Moroccan libraries such as the Tamkarūt Library, the Public Library in Rabat and all the precious libraries annexed to it such as the Muḥammad ʿAbd al-Ḥayy Library and the Jallāwī Library, the Royal Library in Rabat, Qarawiyyīn Library in Fez, the index of the manuscripts of the Grand Mosque in Meknes, the Public Library in Tarudant, and the guide to the manuscripts of the *ḥabūs* prepared by the Ministry of Religious Endowments and Islamic Affairs in Morocco. This index includes the Ḥabūs Library in the Mosque of Moulay ʿAlī Sharī in Ouezzane, the Ḥabūs Library affiliated to the Superintendence of Religious Endowments in Safi, the library of the Ḥabūs Islamic Institute in the Superintendence of Tetouan, the Library of Ḥabūs Manuscripts in the Superintendence of Zarhun, the library of the Ḥabūs Islamic Institute in the Superintendence of Salé, the Ḥabūs Library of al-Zāwiya al-Ḥamzāwiyya in Errachidia Province, the Ḥabūs Library of al-Masjid al-ʿAtīq in the Qaṣba of Essaouira, the Ḥabūs Library of the Grand Mosque in Tangier, the Ḥabūs Library of the Ancient School affiliated to the Superintendence of Qalaa Sraghna, the Ḥabūs Library in the Superintendence of Kasr Kbir, the Ḥabūs Library in Sidi Usidī Mausoleum in Tarudant, the Ḥabūs Library of the Regional Supreme Scientific Council of the Prefecture of Casablanca, the Ḥabūs Library of the Moulay Slimān Mosque in Abū al-Jaʿd in the Superintendence of Khoribga, and other famous libraries that boast a great number of titles that have stood the test of time, among which are the Sidi ʿAbd al-Salām Library, the Darqawiyya Library in Oujda, the Karzaziyya Library, the library of the Good Marabou Sidi ʿAbd al-Jabbār in Figuig, the library of the Grand Mosque

of importance, are the following:

[45] 1. A copy of the manuscript taken from al-Zāwiya al-Ḥamzāwiyya, which found its final destination in Tunis. It is one of the most precious manuscripts in terms of its accuracy and the care taken in its preparation. It was copied at the end of the fifth century AH (487/1094). Because this manuscript was compared and corrected against two other ancient manuscripts, which are described below, it is recognized as having the highest level of precision and reliability.

(a) The first manuscript was that of Abū ʿUmar al-Muntajālī (d. 350/961). He was among those who studied the *Muwaṭṭaʾ* with ʿUbayd Allāh b. Yaḥyā, from the latter's father, Yaḥyā b. Yaḥyā al-Laythī. Accordingly, there is only one transmitter between him and Yaḥyā, and that is ʿUbayd Allāh.

(b) The second manuscript was the autograph manuscript of the Chief Judge of Cordoba Abū ʿAbd Allāh Muḥammad b. ʿAbd Allāh b. Abī ʿĪsā. His manuscript was dictated in the presence of his father's uncle, Abū Marwān ʿUbayd Allāh b. Yaḥyā, from his father, Yaḥyā. Both its marginalia and its notes are of the utmost importance.

2. The manuscript copy of Abū ʿAbd Allāh b. al-Ṭallāʿ (d. 497/1103). This manuscript has a remarkably small number of links in its chain of transmitters, with grandchildren narrating from their grandfathers. It is a precious manuscript that was copied at the beginning of the seventh century AH (thirteenth century CE), replete with useful annotations, notes, and marginalia. It is distinguished by its careful spelling and proofreading and was written in beautiful, clear handwriting, with full vocalization that accords with both the narration and the rules of Arabic grammar. The owner of this manuscript, Abū ʿAbd Allāh b. al-Ṭallāʿ, narrates it from the Chief Judge Abū al-Walīd Yūnus b. ʿAbd Allāh al-Ṣaffār, from Abū ʿĪsā Yaḥyā b. ʿAbd Allāh, from his father, Yaḥyā. The manuscript was corrected against that of Abū al-ʿAbbās Aḥmad b. Salama al-Anṣārī, who holds the reputation of a trustworthy and credible narrator and was a companion of Ibn Qarqūl, Ibn Bashkawāl, and Ibn Khayr, all of whom were masters of transmission, accuracy, and reliability. This second manuscript is no less important than the first manuscript in terms of the abundance of quotations from other sources, annotations, and marginalia. We were able to incorporate

---

in al-ʿAwīda, the library of the Grand Mosque in Chefchaouen, the ʿIyāshiyya in Er-Rich, the Scientific Library in Beni Mellal, the Bzū Library, and the library of Moulay Idriss Zarhūn.

most of these annotations into the critical edition because we had in our possession the handwritten original of the manuscript, and although it was difficult to read some of them, in the end we were able to decode them. Another point of interest is that this manuscript was in the possession of two of the greatest traditionists of the Maghrib. The first was Abū ʿAbd Allāh b. Rashīd al-Sabtī (d. 721/1321), who put his name on it in 720/1320. The second was Abū ʿAbd Allāh al-Wādī Āshī (d. 749/1348), author of the famous *barnāmij*, who put his name on it in 728/1327.[xviii]

[46] 3. The copy of the traditionist, Quran reciter, scholar of the Arabic language, and grammarian Abū Muḥammad Shurayḥ b. Muḥammad b. Shurayḥ al-Ruʿaynī (d. 539/1144). He was one of the companions of Abū Muḥammad b. Ḥazm and one of the teachers of Abū Bakr b. Khayr al-Ishbīlī. He wrote the manuscript in his own hand in beautiful Maghribi script for his son, Muḥammad b. Shurayḥ (d. 567/1171). It was corrected at the hands of one of his students, the skilled and careful traditionist Abū Muḥammad b. Billīṭ, who gained fame, according to Ibn al-Abbār and Abū ʿAbd Allāh b. ʿAbd al-Malik al-Murrākushī, as a trustworthy and careful transmitter. Because of its accuracy and the care with which it was prepared, it is deemed an invaluable piece of work. Furthermore, it includes an impressive number of valuable marginalia and glosses, as well as notes on the textual differences among the various transmissions of the text and recensions of the *Muwaṭṭa'*. A great number of the most rigorous and famed scholars of Andalusia, whose excellence in the transmission of Prophetic traditions is expressly noted in various Andalusian sources, studied this manuscript in the six century AH (twelfth century CE), as explicitly evidenced by the record of study sessions noted on the manuscript.

[47] These three texts constitute the principal manuscripts that we used as a basis for our comparisons and corrections, and they suffice to produce a critical edition that meets the expectations of the Commander of the Faithful and fulfills the requirements set forth in his sublime speech.

We also made use of three other manuscripts as principal texts. These manuscripts also proved beneficial to us in cases in which we had doubts regarding some words. These texts are as follows:

4. A manuscript that was copied in 595/1198, collated and corrected, teeming with valuable marginalia and commentary.

---

xviii This is a reference to the custom of medieval scholars to add their names to a manuscript once they had formally studied it.

5. Another manuscript, written in the hand of ʿAbd Allāh b. Aḥmad b. Muḥammad b. al-Labbād in 613/1216. This manuscript would have been no less important than the previous ones had there not been substantial omissions in the first and middle parts of the book. Its marginalia, however, are very important.
6. Another manuscript contemporaneous to that of the previously mentioned Ibn al-Labbād. It has many important glosses that helped clarify the kinds of differences in the text's vocabulary, and the words' proper spelling and vocalization.

It is possible that there are other manuscripts that we were not able to examine in the private collections of scholars who are engaged in the study of Prophetic traditions or who acquired precious manuscripts representing the legacy of Islamic learning by way of inheritance, purchase, or some other means. Such persons preferred to keep their treasures to themselves and were content to benefit from what they have privately instead of sharing them with the community, deeming the sin of withholding them from those in need of them a trivial matter compared to the profit they hope to realize from their sale. There were no means available, however, to force them to share with the Committee whatever they had in their private collections, despite widespread dissemination of news of the project to produce a critical edition of the *Muwaṭṭaʾ* in accordance with the instructions of the Commander of the Faithful.

Our consolation in this respect is that, despite what was withheld from us, even if potentially important, we were able to use manuscripts with uninterrupted chains of transmission that had been studied by the giants of the sciences of Prophetic tradition in the dear lands of the Islamic West. Their chains of transmission, in our estimation, are unsurpassed in their brevity.[xix]

The Committee hopes that fair-minded scholars, those who understand the importance of producing scholarly, critical editions of the Islamic scholarly tradition, will appreciate the Committee's work, and that they will accept it in a spirit of scholarly charity that restrains unbalanced criticism that points out faults without recognizing merits. The Committee for the Renewal of Islamic Learning also hopes that the scholarly community will excuse it for the delay in completing this project. The delay resulted from the Committee's sense of the weightiness of the responsibility that had been entrusted to it. There were two principal reasons the Committee found this trust so burdensome. The first was the Commander of the Faithful's requirement that the Committee prepare a scholarly, critical edition of the *Muwaṭṭaʾ* that met the highest academic standards, was commensurate

xix See note viii above.

with the honor of the *Muwaṭṭa'* and its elevated status in the eyes of Moroccans, and corrected the mistakes of previous editions. The second was His Majesty's attachment to the *Muwaṭṭa'*, a book that all Moroccans agree is unsurpassed as a source of divine guidance by any but the Book of God, Sublime is He, and that is the distinctive foundational text of the Mālikī school itself.

None of that prevents the Committee from admitting that fulfilling this responsibility—in terms of satisfying the requirements of scholarly methodology, manifesting fidelity to the *Muwaṭṭa'*'s status, and paying careful attention to the text's transmission—was a challenging task. Given the nature of the task, and in light of the reality of the differences present in the various narrators' transmissions of the text, it is impossible to claim perfection. Carelessness, mistakes, and forgetfulness are present in all human beings. God, Sublime is He, has made mutual fairness and sincerity the cure to these defects. He decreed that the cure for error should take the form of beautiful reminders, whether by speech or by conduct. Authentic Islamic tradition reports that humans are, by their nature, forgetful, error-prone, and quick to succumb to temptation, but also that they instinctively seek to repent of their mistakes. It is therefore the virtue of the godly person to remember where his true welfare lies when he is duly reminded.

All praise belongs to God, Lord of the Worlds.

In the Name of God, the Merciful, the Compassionate

May God Grace Our Prophet Muḥammad and His Family and Grant Them Perfect Tranquility.

Book 1

The Book of Obligatory Prayer (*Ṣalāt*) Times

Chapter 1. The Times for the Performance of Obligatory Prayer (*Ṣalāt*)

The jurist Abū ʿAbd Allāh Muḥammad b. Faraj, may God be pleased with him, told us, in an oral reading of the *Muwaṭṭaʾ* in his presence by one of his students in his mosque in Cordoba at the beginning of the month of Rabīʿ al-Ākhir in the year 494 AH,[1] while I listened, that the judge Abū al-Walīd Yūnus b. ʿAbd Allāh b. Mughīth, the chief judge of Cordoba, known as Ibn al-Ṣaffār, may God have mercy on him, said that Abū ʿĪsā Yaḥyā b. ʿAbd Allāh b. Abī ʿĪsā told him from his father's paternal uncle ʿUbayd Allāh b. Yaḥyā, from his father, Yaḥyā, the following:[2]

1 The first day of that month would correspond to February 3, 1101 CE.

2 This set of names establishes the chain of transmission (*isnād*) by which the *Muwaṭṭaʾ* was transmitted from its author, Mālik b. Anas (d. 179/795), via his student Yaḥyā b. Yaḥyā (d. 234/849), who introduced the text to Andalusia and the Maghrib. This chain of transmission was highly valued because it was only three transmitters removed from the original source of this version of the *Muwaṭṭaʾ*, Yaḥyā b. Yaḥyā. Yaḥyā's recension of the *Muwaṭṭaʾ* is only one of several recensions of the Mālik's *Muwaṭṭaʾ*. It is, however, the best known, and the one that predominated in Andalusia and the Maghrib. Most other recensions of the *Muwaṭṭaʾ* have survived only in fragmentary form, with the exception of the recension of Muḥammad b. al-Ḥasan al-Shaybānī (d. 189/805). Shaybānī was one of the two principal students of Abū Ḥanīfa (d. 150/767) in Iraq and can be deemed one of the founders of the Ḥanafī school of law. Shaybānī studied for a time with Mālik b. Anas in Medina, where he read the *Muwaṭṭaʾ*. Because he did not follow Mālik's legal views, however, his recension of the text omits the bulk of Mālik's legal opinions and reasoning and retains only the portions of the text that Shaybānī found useful from the perspective of his own legal doctrine. After laying out this chain of authorities, the text hereafter names only the transmitters through whom Mālik received his material.

1. According to Mālik b. Anas, Ibn Shihāb[3] reported that one day, ʿUmar b. ʿAbd al-ʿAzīz[4] deferred the performance of an obligatory prayer. Upon his doing so, ʿUrwa b. al-Zubayr[5] came to him and told him that al-Mughīra b. Shuʿba[6] had once deferred the performance of an obligatory prayer when he was in Kufa. Seeing al-Mughīra's action, Abū Masʿūd al-Anṣārī had gone to him and said, "Mughīra, what are you doing? Don't you know that the Angel Gabriel descended and prayed in the presence of the Messenger of God (pbuh), and so the Messenger of God (pbuh) prayed; then Gabriel prayed, and so the Messenger of God (pbuh) prayed; then Gabriel prayed, and so the Messenger of God (pbuh) prayed; then Gabriel prayed, and so the Messenger of God (pbuh) prayed; and then Gabriel prayed, and so the Messenger of God (pbuh) prayed. The Messenger of God (pbuh) then said, 'Thus have I been commanded to perform the obligatory prayers.'"[7] ʿUmar b. ʿAbd al-ʿAzīz said to ʿUrwa, "Think carefully about what you are reporting! Was it really Gabriel who established for the Messenger of God (pbuh) the times for the performance of the obligatory prayers?" ʿUrwa said, "This is what Bashīr b. Masʿūd al-Anṣārī would relate from his father."

2. ʿUrwa said, "ʿĀʾisha, the wife of the Prophet (pbuh), told me that the Messenger of God (pbuh) would perform the Afternoon Prayer (*ṣalāt al-ʿaṣr*) while the sun was still shining in her chamber, before it faded from there."

3. According to Mālik, Zayd b. Aslam reported that ʿAṭāʾ b. Yasār said, "A man came to the Messenger of God (pbuh) and asked him about the time for the

---

3 Muḥammad b. Muslim b. ʿUbayd Allāh b. ʿAbd Allāh b. Shihāb, known as Ibn Shihāb al-Zuhrī (d. 124/742), was a prominent early Muslim historian and collector of hadith. He is one of Mālik's most important sources in the *Muwaṭṭaʾ*.

4 ʿUmar b. ʿAbd al-ʿAzīz b. Marwān (r. 99–101/717–720) was an Umayyad caliph who was highly esteemed in the Sunnī tradition for his learning and piety and is often referred to as the fifth of the Rightly Guided (*rāshidūn*) Caliphs. Mālik includes many decisions and opinions of ʿUmar b. ʿAbd al-ʿAzīz as precedents in the *Muwaṭṭaʾ*.

5 ʿUrwa b. al-Zubayr (d. 94/713) was the son of a prominent early convert to Islam, al-Zubayr b. al-ʿAwwām, and an important member of the early generation of Muslims known as the Followers (*tābiʿūn*) that followed the founding generation, known as the Companions (*ṣaḥāba*). ʿUrwa was known as one of the "seven jurists of Medina" and is an important source of legal rules for Mālik in the *Muwaṭṭaʾ*. The sources do not agree on the identity of these seven jurists, and as a result, more than seven have been named as such. Furthermore, some have suggested that the group of seven functioned as a council, in which case membership could have changed over time.

6 Al-Mughīra b. Shuʿba (d. 50/670) was a Companion of the Messenger of God (pbuh) who served as the governor of the garrison town of Kufa in southern Iraq during the term of the second of the Rightly Guided Caliphs, ʿUmar b. al-Khaṭṭāb (r. 13–23/634–644).

7 The Arabic is equivocal: the phrase "Thus have I been commanded to perform the obligatory prayers" could be read as a statement by the Angel Gabriel rather than the Messenger of God (pbuh), with the meaning "Thus have you been commanded to perform the obligatory prayers." The difference between the two readings hinges on vocalization, and manuscripts of the *Muwaṭṭaʾ* include both.

performance of the Morning Prayer (*ṣalāt al-ṣubḥ*). The Messenger (pbuh) did not answer him. The next morning, the Messenger performed the Morning Prayer when the blackness of the night had begun to lift. The next day, the Messenger (pbuh) performed the Morning Prayer when sunlight had just begun to appear. The Messenger (pbuh) then said, 'Where is the man who asked about the time of the Morning Prayer?' The man said, 'Here I am, Messenger of God!' The Messenger of God (pbuh) then said, 'Between these two is the time for the performance of the Morning Prayer.'"

4. According to Mālik, Yaḥyā b. Saʿīd reported from ʿAmra bt. ʿAbd al-Raḥmān[8] that ʿĀʾisha, the wife of the Prophet (pbuh), said, "When the Messenger of God would complete performance of the Morning Prayer, the women would depart from the mosque, wrapped in their shawls, and they would be unrecognizable on account of the darkness."

5. According to Mālik, Zayd b. Aslam reported from ʿAṭāʾ b. Yasār, from Busr b. Saʿīd, and from al-Aʿraj, all of whom told Zayd b. Aslam from Abū Hurayra, that the Messenger of God (pbuh) said, "Whoever performs one cycle (*rakʿa*) of the Morning Prayer before sunrise has performed the Morning Prayer within its designated time; and whoever performs one cycle of the Afternoon Prayer before sunset has performed the Afternoon Prayer in a timely fashion within its designated time."

6. According to Mālik, Nāfiʿ, the freedman (*mawlā*)[9] of ʿAbd Allāh b. ʿUmar,[10] reported that ʿUmar b. al-Khaṭṭāb wrote to his governors, "In my estimation, your most important duty is the obligatory prayer. Whoever guards it and performs it diligently guards his religion; whoever neglects his prayers is likely to be even more heedless of his other duties." He then added, "Perform the Noon Prayer (*ṣalāt al-ẓuhr*) beginning when a person's shadow is one arm's length until his shadow is equal to his own height; the Afternoon Prayer when the sun is high in the sky, white and clear, and when there is still enough time for a rider to travel six to ten kilometers[11]

8 ʿAmra bt. ʿAbd al-Raḥmān (29–106/649–724) was a prominent Follower to whom the sources attribute great knowledge. She was raised and educated by the Mother of the Believers, ʿĀʾisha bt. Abī Bakr al-Ṣiddīq. Mālik included many of her reports in the *Muwaṭṭaʾ*.

9 The Arabic term *mawlā* in this context means a manumitted slave. It can also refer to the slave's owner or manumitter.

10 ʿAbd Allāh b. ʿUmar (d. 73/693) was a Companion of the Messenger of God (pbuh) and the son of the second caliph, ʿUmar b. al-Khaṭṭāb. ʿAbd Allāh b. ʿUmar is a very important source for Mālik in the *Muwaṭṭaʾ*, with his words usually reported to Mālik by Nāfiʿ, ʿAbd Allāh's freedman. The chain Mālik → Nāfiʿ → ʿAbd Allāh b. ʿUmar is sometimes called "the golden chain" by virtue of the high regard Muslim scholars had for the reliability of reports transmitted through this chain.

11 This distance is roughly equivalent to two to three *farsakhs*. A *farsakh* is a unit of length equal to three *mīls*. A *mīl* is the equivalent of 3,500 arm's lengths, or a man's paces. A *farsakh* is

before the sun sets; the Sunset Prayer (*ṣalāt al-maghrib*) when the sun sets; and the Evening Prayer (*ṣalāt al-ʿishāʾ*) between the time that twilight disappears and the end of the first third of the night. Whoever goes to bed without performing the Evening Prayer—may his night be restless! Whoever sleeps without performing the Evening Prayer—may his night be restless! Whoever sleeps without performing the Evening Prayer—may his night be restless! Perform the Morning Prayer when the stars are clear and fill the sky."

7. According to Mālik, his paternal uncle Abū Suhayl b. Mālik reported from his father that ʿUmar b. al-Khaṭṭāb wrote to Abū Mūsā al-Ashʿarī, "Perform the Noon Prayer when the sun begins its descent from its zenith; the Afternoon Prayer when the sun is white and clear, before it becomes yellowish-orange; and the Sunset Prayer when the sun sets. Defer performance of the Evening Prayer into the night, provided that you do not fall asleep. Perform the Morning Prayer when the stars are clear and fill the sky, reciting therein two chapters of the long *Mufaṣṣal*[12] chapters of the Quran."

8. According to Mālik, Hishām b. ʿUrwa[13] reported from his father that ʿUmar b. al-Khaṭṭāb wrote to Abū Mūsā al-Ashʿarī, "Perform the Afternoon Prayer while the sun is white and clear, when there is still enough time for a rider to travel ten kilometers before the sun sets. Perform the Evening Prayer in the first third of the night, but if you defer it beyond that, then only until the middle of the night, and do not be among the heedless."

9. According to Mālik, Yazīd b. Ziyād reported from ʿAbd Allāh b. Rāfiʿ, the freedman of Umm Salama, the wife of the Prophet (pbuh), that he asked Abū Hurayra about the times for the performance of the obligatory prayers. Abū Hurayra said, "I'll tell you. Perform the Noon Prayer when your shadow equals your height; the Afternoon Prayer when your shadow is double your height; the Sunset Prayer when the sun sets; the Evening Prayer in the first

---

thus equal to 10,500 paces, and the distance mentioned in this report is between 21,000 and 31,500 paces. Ibn ʿAbd al-Barr, *al-Istidhkār al-jāmiʿ li-madhāhib fuqahāʾ al-amṣār wa-ʿulamāʾ al-aqṭār fīmā taḍammanahu al-Muwaṭṭaʾ min maʿānī al-raʾy waʾl-āthār* (Cairo: Muʾassasat al-Risāla, 1993), 1:237.

12 The "long" *Mufaṣṣal* chapters of the Quran form a subcategory of the *Mufaṣṣal* chapters. These begin with *al-Ḥujurāt* and conclude with *ʿAbasa* (chapters 49–80). See Zurqānī, *Sharḥ al-Zurqānī ʿalā Muwaṭṭaʾ al-Imām Mālik* (Cairo: Maktabat al-Thaqāfa al-Dīniyya, 2003), 1:86. Elsewhere, Zurqānī mentions various opinions over the starting point of the more inclusive category of the *Mufaṣṣal* chapters, which ends with the Quran's final chapter. He concludes that the category starts with *al-Ḥujurāt*, in accordance with the preponderant view of the Mālikīs and the Shāfiʿīs. Ibid., 1:306.

13 Hishām b. ʿUrwa b. al-Zubayr b. al-ʿAwwām (d. 146/763) was a prominent member of the second generation of Muslims, known as "the followers of the Followers" (*tābiʿū al-tābiʿīn*), and an important source for Mālik in the *Muwaṭṭaʾ*.

third of the night; and the Morning Prayer when it is still dark, meaning when dawn is just breaking."

10. According to Mālik, Isḥāq b. ʿAbd Allāh b. Abī Ṭalḥa reported that Anas b. Mālik said, "We would perform the Afternoon Prayer, and one could then walk to the dwellings of the tribe of ʿAmr b. ʿAwf and find them still in the midst of performing the Afternoon Prayer."

11. According to Mālik, Ibn Shihāb reported that Anas b. Mālik said, "We would perform the Afternoon Prayer, and one could then set off for Qubāʾ[14] and arrive there when the sun was still high in the sky."

12. According to Mālik, Rabīʿa b. Abī ʿAbd al-Raḥmān[15] reported that al-Qāsim b. Muḥammad[16] said, "In my experience, the Companions[17] always deferred performance of the Noon Prayer until later in the day, when it was cooler."

Chapter 2. The Time of the Friday Congregational Prayer (*Jumuʿa*)

13. According to Mālik, his uncle Abū Suhayl b. Mālik reported that his father said, "I used to notice that on Fridays, a cushion belonging to ʿAqīl b. Abī Ṭālib would be placed along the western wall of the Prophet's Mosque. Only when the shadow of the wall had completely covered the cushion would ʿUmar b. al-Khaṭṭāb enter the mosque for the Friday Congregational Prayer." Mālik's grandfather said, "After the prayer, we would return to our homes and nap, making up for the midmorning nap that we missed by going to the mosque."

14. According to Mālik, ʿAmr b. Yaḥyā al-Māzinī reported from Ibn Abī Salīṭ that ʿUthmān b. ʿAffān[18] performed the Friday Congregational Prayer in Medina and the Afternoon Prayer (*ṣalāt al-ʿaṣr*) in Malal.[19] Mālik said, "That

---

14 A place on the outskirts of Medina.

15 Nicknamed "Rabīʿa the legal reasoner" (*Rabīʿat al-raʾy*), he was an important Medinese jurist and teacher of Mālik, and an important source in the *Muwaṭṭaʾ*. Sources differ as to the date of his death but place it in either the fourth or the fifth decade of the second Islamic century, in 133/750, 136/753, or 142/759.

16 Al-Qāsim b. Muḥammad b. Abī Bakr al-Ṣiddīq (d. 107/752) was a member of the Followers and one of the "seven jurists of Medina." He served as an important source for Mālik in the *Muwaṭṭaʾ*.

17 The text literally uses the term "the people," but here it refers to the Companions, as al-Qāsim was one of the oldest members of the Followers. Hence, the practices he would have observed would have been those of the Companions who continued to live in Medina after the death of the Prophet Muḥammad (pbuh). Zurqānī, *Sharḥ al-Zurqānī*, 1:25.

18 ʿUthmān b. ʿAffān (r. 23–35/643–656) was the third of the Rightly Guided caliphs according to the Sunnīs.

19 A place on the way from Medina to Mecca. Some authorities place it at a distance of approximately 19 km (18 *mīls*) from Medina, whereas others say it is approximately 24 km (22 *mīls*)

was because he set out during the heat of the day and rode quickly—not because he performed the Friday prayer before noon."[20]

Chapter 3. Regarding a Person Who Performs Only One Cycle (*Rakʿa*) of a Prayer (*Ṣalāt*) with the Congregation

15. According to Mālik, Ibn Shihāb reported from Abū Salama b. ʿAbd al-Raḥmān,[21] from Abū Hurayra, that the Messenger of God (pbuh) said, "Whoever performs one cycle (*rakʿa*) of a prayer with the congregation has performed his prayer with the congregation."

16. According to Mālik, Nāfiʿ reported that ʿAbd Allāh b. ʿUmar b. al-Khaṭṭāb would say, "If you join the congregational prayer after the imam has already stood up from bowing, you have also missed the prostration (*sajda*) for that cycle of the prayer."

17. According to Mālik, it reached him that ʿAbd Allāh b. ʿUmar and Zayd b. Thābit would both say, "Whoever joins the congregational prayer before the imam stands up from bowing validly performs the prostration for that cycle of the prayer."

18. According to Mālik, it reached him that Abū Hurayra would say, "Whoever bows with the imam also validly performs the prostration for that cycle of prayer. Whoever joins the congregational prayer after the imam recites the *Fātiḥa*,[22] however, has missed out on a great deal of good."

Chapter 4. What Has Come Down regarding the Meaning of "*Dulūk* of the Sun" and "*Ghasaq* of the Night"[23]

19. According to Mālik, Nāfiʿ reported that ʿAbd Allāh b. ʿUmar would say, "The phrase '*dulūk* of the sun' means the beginning of its descent after midday."

20. According to Mālik, Dāwūd b. al-Ḥuṣayn said, "Someone told me that ʿAbd Allāh b. ʿAbbās[24] would say, 'The phrase "*dulūk* of the sun" is when

away, one *mīl* comprising 3,500 paces. Ibn ʿAbd al-Barr, *al-Istidhkār*, 1:254. Other authorities report the distance as 41 km. Yāqūt al-Ḥamawī, *Muʿjam al-buldān* (Beirut: Dār Ṣādir, 1995), 5:194.

20 Ibn ʿAbd al-Barr, *al-Istidhkār*, 1:254–55.

21 Abū Salama b. ʿAbd al-Raḥmān b. ʿAwf (d. 94/712) was a Follower and one of the "seven jurists of Medina." He is also an important source for Mālik in the *Muwaṭṭaʾ*.

22 The *Fātiḥa* is the first chapter of the Quran and must be recited in each cycle of prayer.

23 These two phrases appear in *al-Isrāʾ*, 17:78, where they serve to delineate times for the performance of prayers.

24 ʿAbd Allāh b. ʿAbbās (d. 68/687) was the paternal first cousin of the Prophet Muḥammad (pbuh). Although they were first cousins, the Prophet was many years Ibn ʿAbbās' senior and

shadows begin to point east; and, the phrase "*ghasaq* of the night" means the darkness of the night.'"

Chapter 5. Miscellaneous Matters Related to the Times of the Obligatory Prayers (*Ṣalāt*)

21. According to Mālik, Nāfiʿ reported from ʿAbd Allāh b. ʿUmar that the Messenger of God (pbuh) said, "The loss endured by someone who fails to perform the Afternoon Prayer (*ṣalāt al-ʿaṣr*) is the equivalent of losing his family and all his wealth."

22. According to Mālik, Yaḥyā b. Saʿīd reported that ʿUmar b. al-Khaṭṭāb departed after performing the Afternoon Prayer. He then ran into someone who had not attended it. ʿUmar asked the man, "What kept you from the Afternoon Prayer?" The man offered him an excuse, but ʿUmar replied, "You have only cheated yourself." Yaḥyā[25] said, "Mālik said, 'The terms "cheating" (*taṭfīf*) and "fidelity" (*wafāʾ*) may be applied to anything—not just to goods bought and sold in the market.'"

23. According to Mālik, Yaḥyā b. Saʿīd would say, "Many a worshipper will perform an obligatory prayer toward the end of its prescribed time, yet had he prayed it earlier, his reward for doing so would have been superior to, and greater than, his family and his wealth."

24. Yaḥyā said, "Mālik said, 'If someone is traveling and the prescribed time for a prayer comes, but he defers its performance either out of distraction or out of forgetfulness until he arrives home and remembers it, he should perform the prayer as a resident would, provided that the prescribed time for the performance of that prayer has not expired. If, however, he reaches home and the prescribed time has expired, he should perform the shortened prayer of a traveler, because his present obligation is to perform the equivalent of his previous obligation.' Mālik then said, 'This is the rule that I found both the people and the learned of our town[26] following' (*al-amr alladhī adraktu ʿalayhi al-nās wa-ahl al-ʿilm bi-baladinā*)."

---

raised the latter in his household in Medina from a young age. Ibn ʿAbbās later became well known as one of the scholars among the younger Companions. Muslim tradition assigns to him an especially prominent role as an expert in the exegesis of the Quran.

25 This Yaḥyā is Yaḥyā b. Yaḥyā al-Laythī, Mālik's student and the narrator of the *Muwaṭṭaʾ*, not Yaḥyā b. Saʿīd, Mālik's source for this hadith. In many instances in the *Muwaṭṭaʾ*, Yaḥyā b. Yaḥyā, after transmitting Mālik's report, includes an additional comment or question directed to Mālik, which is introduced simply by "Yaḥyā said." Sometimes the addition appears as a free-standing report, as in hadith no. 24.

26 That is, Medina.

25. Mālik said, "The term 'dusk' (*shafaq*) means the redness that appears at sunset. When that redness disappears, it is time for the Evening Prayer (*ṣalāt al-ʿishāʾ*), and the time for the Sunset Prayer (*ṣalāt al-maghrib*) has expired."

26. According to Mālik, Nāfiʿ reported that ʿAbd Allāh b. ʿUmar once fainted and lost consciousness. Once revived, he did not perform the prayers that he missed while unconscious. Mālik said, "This, in our view, and God knows best, is because the time for the performance of that prayer had already passed. If an unconscious person revives, however, and the time to pray has not yet expired, he should perform that prayer."

Chapter 6. Missing an Obligatory Prayer (*Ṣalāt*) Because of Oversleeping

27. According to Mālik, Ibn Shihāb reported from Saʿīd b. al-Musayyab[27] that when the Messenger of God (pbuh) returned from Khaybar,[28] he marched throughout the night and set up camp at the night's end. He said to Bilāl, "Keep a vigilant watch so you can wake us for the Morning Prayer (*ṣalāt al-ṣubḥ*)." The Messenger of God (pbuh) and his companions went to sleep, and Bilāl kept watch for as long as fate had decreed. Then he leaned against his mount, seeking some rest while facing the direction of the sunrise, but his eyelids became heavy, and he fell asleep. Neither the Messenger of God, nor Bilāl, nor anyone in the camp awoke until the sun was beating down on them. The Messenger of God was startled, and Bilāl said, "Messenger of God, the very same thing that overtook me overtook you." The Messenger of God (pbuh) said, "Let us decamp," and so they stirred their mounts and marched some distance. The Messenger of God (pbuh) then ordered Bilāl to halt so they could perform the prayer that they had missed. Bilāl gave the immediate call to prayer (*iqāma*),[29] and the Messenger of God (pbuh) led them in the Morning Prayer. After completing the prayer, he said, "Anyone who forgets to perform a prayer should perform it when he remembers it. God, Blessed and Sublime is He, says in His Book, 'Establish prayer in remembrance of Me.'"[30]

---

27 Saʿīd b. al-Musayyab (d. 94/712) was a prominent member of the Followers, one of the "seven jurists of Medina," and an important source for Mālik in the *Muwaṭṭaʾ*.

28 Khaybar, a fortified oasis town in the Hijaz, had been settled by Arabian Jews. The Muslims laid siege to the oasis town in year 7 of the Hijra (628 CE), following the conclusion of the Treaty of al-Ḥudaybiya. Khaybar is located approximately four days' march north of Medina. Zurqānī, *Sharḥ al-Zurqānī*, 1:141.

29 The immediate call to prayer—the *iqāma*—is performed directly prior to the performance of the prayer. It is a shortened version of the general call to prayer—the *adhān*—which is made at the beginning of the time for a designated prayer and is intended to announce to the community that the time for that prayer has started.

30 *Ṭāhā*, 20:14.

28. According to Mālik, Zayd b. Aslam said that the Messenger of God (pbuh) camped late one night on the road to Mecca. He charged Bilāl to awaken them when it was time for the Morning Prayer, but all of them, including Bilāl, slept through the dawn. They awoke only after the sun had already risen above them. The men awoke in a state of distress, so the Messenger of God ordered them to ride until they exited that valley, saying, "This is a valley in which a devil dwells." They rode, therefore, until they left it. The Messenger of God (pbuh) then ordered them to dismount and to perform ablutions for prayer. He commanded Bilāl to make the general call to prayer (*adhān*). The Messenger of God (pbuh) then led the people in prayer. When he turned to them and saw their distress, he said, "People, God takes our souls while we sleep, and had He desired, He would have returned them to us at a different moment in time. Accordingly, if one oversleeps and as a result misses a prayer, or forgets it, and then remembers it when he awakes, he should perform that prayer as he would normally have performed it during its prescribed time." The Messenger of God (pbuh) then turned to Abū Bakr al-Ṣiddīq[31] and said, "The Devil did indeed come to Bilāl while he was standing in prayer and convinced him to lie down. He continued to soothe him, just as a baby is soothed, until he went to sleep." The Messenger of God (pbuh) then called Bilāl, who reported to the Messenger of God (pbuh) a version of events similar to what the Messenger of God (pbuh) had told Abū Bakr. Abū Bakr then said, "I testify that you are indeed the Messenger of God.'"

Chapter 7. The Prohibition against Performing the Prayer (*Ṣalāt*) during the Hottest Part of the Day

29. According to Mālik, Zayd b. Aslam reported from ʿAṭāʾ b. Yasār that the Messenger of God (pbuh) said, "Severe heat comes from the breath of Hell. When it is extremely hot, defer performance of the prayer until it cools down." The Messenger of God (pbuh) also said, "Hell complained to its Lord, saying 'One part of me has consumed the other,' so He permitted it two breaths every year, one in the winter and one in the summer."[32]

30. According to Mālik, ʿAbd Allāh b. Yazīd, the freedman (*mawlā*) of al-Aswad b. Sufyān, reported from Abū Salama b. ʿAbd al-Raḥmān (and Mālik also narrated it from Muḥammad b. ʿAbd al-Raḥmān b. Thawbān),

31 Abū Bakr al-Ṣiddīq was one of the earliest converts to Islam, one of the Prophet's closest confidants and companions, and the father of ʿĀʾisha, a wife of the Prophet (pbuh). He was the first caliph (r. 11–13/632–634) of the Muslim community after the Prophet (pbuh) died.

32 This and other narrations draw a connection between extreme weather on earth and Hell. Both extreme heat and extreme cold are seen as deriving from the two breaths that Hell takes, one in the summer and one in the winter.

each from Abū Hurayra, that the Messenger of God (pbuh) said, "When it is extremely hot, defer performance of the prayer until it cools down, for the heat's severity comes from the breath of Hell." He also mentioned that "Hell complained to its Lord, so He permitted it two breaths every year, one in the winter and one in the summer."

31. According to Mālik, Abū al-Zinād reported from al-Aʿraj, from Abū Hurayra, that the Messenger of God (pbuh) said, "When it is extremely hot, defer performance of the prayer until it cools down, for the heat's severity comes from the breath of Hell."

Chapter 8. The Prohibition against Entering the Mosque with the Odor of Garlic on One's Breath and against Covering One's Mouth While Performing the Prayer (*Ṣalāt*)

32. According to Mālik, Ibn Shihāb reported from Saʿīd b. al-Musayyab that the Messenger of God (pbuh) said, "Anyone who eats garlic should keep away from our mosques, lest he annoy us with its odor."

33. According to Mālik, ʿAbd al-Raḥmān b. al-Mujabbar reported that he would notice that whenever Sālim b. ʿAbd Allāh[33] saw someone using his cloak to cover his mouth while performing his prayer, he would firmly yank it from the person's mouth until he removed it.

33 Sālim b. ʿAbd Allāh b. ʿUmar (d. 106/724) was a prominent member of the Followers and one of the "seven jurists of Medina." He is also an important source for Mālik in the *Muwaṭṭa'*.

Book 2
The Book of Ritual Purity (*Ṭahāra*)

Chapter 1. The Practice (*ʿAmal*) with Respect to the Performance of Ablutions (*Wuḍūʾ*)

34. According to Mālik, ʿAmr b. Yaḥyā al-Māzinī reported from his father that the latter said to ʿAbd Allāh b. Zayd b. ʿĀṣim, who was the grandfather of ʿAmr b. Yaḥyā al-Māzinī and a Companion of the Messenger of God (pbuh), "Can you show me how the Messenger of God would perform ablutions?" ʿAbd Allāh b. Zayd said, "Yes, I can." He called for a basin of water and poured some on his hands, washing each of them twice. He then rinsed his mouth and blew his nose three times each; then he washed his face three times; and then he washed each of his hands twice, up to the elbows. He then wiped his head with both of his hands, front to back and back to front, starting from his forehead, then running his hands over the back of his neck, and then returning them to where he had started. He then washed each of his feet.

35. According to Mālik, Abū al-Zinād reported from al-Aʿraj, from Abū Hurayra, that the Messenger of God (pbuh) said, "When someone performs ablutions, he should inhale water into his nose and then expel it. Whoever uses small stones to remove impurities from his body after defecating or urinating should use an odd number of them."

36. According to Mālik, Ibn Shihāb reported from Abū Idrīs al-Khawlānī, from Abū Hurayra, that the Messenger of God (pbuh) said, "Whoever performs ablutions should expel the water from his nose, and whoever uses small stones to remove impurities from his body after defecating or urinating should use an odd number of them."

37. Yaḥyā said, "I heard Mālik say, 'There is nothing objectionable in someone rinsing his mouth and nose with the same handful of water.'"

38. According to Mālik, it reached him that ʿAbd al-Raḥmān b. Abī Bakr visited ʿĀʾisha, the wife of the Prophet (pbuh), the day Saʿd b. Abī Waqqāṣ died. While there, he asked for a basin of water from which to perform ablutions. 'Ā'isha said to him, "'Abd al-Raḥmān, perform your ablutions diligently, for I heard the Messenger of God (pbuh) say, 'Unwashed heels are doomed to the fire of Hell!'"

39. According to Mālik, Yaḥyā b. Muḥammad b. Ṭaḥlā' reported from 'Uthmān b. 'Abd al-Raḥmān that his father told him that he heard that 'Umar b. al-Khaṭṭāb would use water rather than small stones to clean the area beneath his undergarment (*izār*).[34]

40. Yaḥyā said, "Mālik was asked about a man who, when performing ablutions, forgot and washed his face before rinsing his mouth, or washed his arms before washing his face. Mālik replied, 'Someone who washes his face before rinsing his mouth should go ahead and rinse his mouth, but he does not need to repeat washing his face. Someone who washes his arms before his face should go ahead and wash his face; however, he should then repeat washing his arms, so that he washes them after washing his face, provided he is in the same place, or nearby, when he remembers the proper order of ablutions.'"

41. Yaḥyā said, "Mālik was asked about a man who forgot to rinse his mouth or blow his nose, and then prayed. Mālik replied, 'He is under no obligation to repeat the performance of his prayer. He should, however, rinse his mouth and blow his nose prior to performing any subsequent prayers that he intends to pray.'"

Chapter 2. The Ablutions (*Wuḍū'*) of One Who Is Sleeping and Gets Up to Perform Prayer (*Ṣalāt*)

42. According to Mālik, Abū al-Zinād reported from al-A'raj, from Abū Hurayra, that the Messenger of God (pbuh) said, "When someone awakes from sleep, he should wash his hands before he places them in his ablution basin. No one knows where his hand passed the night."

43. According to Mālik, Zayd b. Aslam reported that 'Umar b. al-Khaṭṭāb said, "If someone sleeps lying down, he must perform ablutions prior to performing any prayer."

44. According to Mālik, Zayd b. Aslam reported that the verse, "Believers, when you arise to perform your prayers, wash your faces, your hands up to the elbows, and your feet up to the heels, and wipe your heads,"[35] is understood to refer to those who awake from their beds, that is, from sleep.

---

34 This is a reference to the difference of opinion over whether water was effective by itself for purifying the body of feces, or whether pebbles first had to be used to remove feces after defecation.

35 *Al-Mā'ida*, 4:6.

45. Yaḥyā said, "Mālik said, 'The rule in our view (*al-amr ʿindanā*)[36] is that one does not need to perform ablutions because of a nosebleed, or bleeding, or pus that seeps from the body. Ablutions are required only for impurities that exit from the penis or the anus, or on account of sleep.'"

46. According to Mālik, Nāfiʿ reported that Ibn ʿUmar would sleep while sitting and then wake up and perform his prayer without performing ablutions.

Chapter 3. The Substances That May Be Used for Ablutions (*Wuḍūʾ*)

47. According to Mālik, Ṣafwān b. Sulaym reported from Saʿīd b. Salama, a man from the people of Banū al-Azraq, from al-Mughīra b. Abī Burda of the tribe of Banū ʿAbd al-Dār, that al-Mughīra told Saʿīd that al-Mughīra heard Abū Hurayra say, "A man came to the Messenger of God (pbuh) and said, 'Messenger of God, we are a seafaring people and sail with only small amounts of fresh water. Were we to use that water for ablutions, we would go thirsty. May we perform our ablutions with seawater?' The Messenger of God (pbuh) said, 'Seawater purifies filth, and even its carrion may be eaten.'"

48. According to Mālik, Isḥāq b. ʿAbd Allāh b. Abī Ṭalḥa al-Anṣārī reported from Ḥumayda, the daughter of Abū ʿUbayda b. Farwa, that her maternal aunt Kabsha, the daughter of Kaʿb b. Mālik, who was married to Ibn Abī Qatāda, told Ḥumayda that one day Abū Qatāda came to her house, and she poured some water into an ablution basin for him to use. A cat then came and wanted to drink from the basin, so he tilted it until the cat could drink. Kabsha said, "He saw me staring at him and said, 'Niece, are you surprised that I would allow the cat to drink from my ablution basin?' I said, 'Yes.' He said, 'The Messenger of God (pbuh) said, "Cats are not impure. They come and go freely among you."'" Yaḥyā said, "Mālik said, 'There is no harm in letting a cat drink from one's ablution basin, unless one sees something impure on its mouth.'"

49. According to Mālik, Yaḥyā b. Saʿīd reported from Muḥammad b. Ibrāhīm b. al-Ḥārith al-Taymī, from Yaḥyā b. ʿAbd al-Raḥmān b. Ḥāṭib, that ʿUmar b. al-Khaṭṭāb went out with a riding party that included ʿAmr b. al-ʿĀṣī. They rode until they came to a cistern filled with water. ʿAmr b. al-ʿĀṣī said to its owner, "Do predators drink from your cistern?" ʿUmar b. al-Khaṭṭāb said, "You don't need to answer that, for we certainly each take turns drinking its water: we drink after them, and they drink after us."

36 Mālik uses the expression *al-amr ʿindanā* when the rule represents Mālik's view on an issue regarding which there was a predominant opinion among the Medinese legal experts as well as significant dissent. Umar F. Abd-Allah Wymann-Landgraf, *Mālik and Medina: Islamic Legal Reasoning in the Formative Period* (Leiden: Brill, 2013), 283.

50. According to Mālik, Nāfiʿ reported that ʿAbd Allāh b. ʿUmar would say, "In the time of the Messenger of God (pbuh), men and women would perform ablutions together."[37]

Chapter 4. Things That Do Not Necessitate Ablutions (*Wuḍū'*)

51. According to Mālik, Muḥammad b. ʿUmāra reported from Muḥammad b. Ibrāhīm, from a handmaiden of Ibrāhīm b. ʿAbd al-Raḥmān b. ʿAwf who bore him a child (*umm walad*),[38] that she inquired of Umm Salama, the wife of the Prophet (pbuh), about the following situation: "The trains of my garments are lengthy, and I walk in filthy places." Umm Salama said, "The Messenger of God said, 'The dust that comes in the filth's wake purifies the garment's train.'"

52. According to Mālik, on several occasions he saw Rabīʿa b. Abī ʿAbd al-Raḥmān coughing up small amounts of liquid in the mosque.[39] He would not, however, leave the mosque or perform ablutions as a consequence, until he had first concluded performance of his prayer.

53. Yaḥyā said, "Mālik was asked whether a man who coughed up a small amount of food must perform ablutions before performing his prayer. Mālik replied, 'He is not obliged to perform ablutions as a consequence, but he should gargle and wash his mouth.'"

54. According to Mālik, Nāfiʿ reported that ʿAbd Allāh b. ʿUmar prepared the corpse of one of the sons of Saʿīd b. Zayd for burial and carried him in the funeral procession. He subsequently entered the mosque and prayed, without first performing ablutions.

55. Yaḥyā said, "Mālik was asked whether vomiting necessitates ablution. Mālik replied, 'No; someone who vomits should gargle and wash his mouth, but ablution is not necessary.'"

Chapter 5. Not Performing Ablutions (*Wuḍū'*) on Account of Eating Roasted Food

56. According to Mālik, Zayd b. Aslam reported from ʿAṭā' b. Yasār, from ʿAbd Allāh b. ʿAbbās, that the Messenger of God (pbuh) ate a shoulder of lamb and then performed his prayer without performing ablutions.

---

37 Meaning from a single ablution basin, per a marginal note in one of the RME manuscripts.

38 An *umm walad* was a handmaiden who gave birth to her master's child. After giving birth to the child, the mother could not be sold, her child was free, and she would become free upon the earlier of her express manumission or her master's death.

39 The Arabic word *qalas* refers to a small amount of vomit that does not exceed a mouthful.

57. According to Mālik, Yaḥyā b. Saʿīd reported from Bushayr b. Yasār, the freedman (*mawlā*) of the tribe of Ḥāritha, that Suwayd b. al-Nuʿmān told Bushayr that he went out with the Messenger of God (pbuh) in the year of Khaybar.[40] When they reached al-Ṣahbāʾ, a place just outside Khaybar, the Messenger of God (pbuh) dismounted and performed the Afternoon Prayer (*ṣalāt al-ʿaṣr*). He then asked for the rations to be brought out, but there was nothing except some dried porridge (*sawīq*).[41] He ordered that it be prepared, so it was mixed with some water, and then the Messenger of God (pbuh) ate and we ate.[42] He then got up to perform the Sunset Prayer (*ṣalāt al-maghrib*), but he first rinsed his mouth, and we did the same. He then performed the Sunset Prayer without performing ablutions.

58. According to Mālik, both Muḥammad b. al-Munkadir and Ṣafwān b. Sulaym informed him from Muḥammad b. Ibrāhīm b. al-Ḥārith al-Taymī, from Rabīʿa b. ʿAbd Allāh b. al-Hudayr, that Rabīʿa shared an evening meal with ʿUmar b. al-Khaṭṭāb, after which ʿUmar prayed without first performing ablutions.

59. According to Mālik, Ḍamra b. Saʿīd al-Māzinī reported from Abān b. ʿUthmān[43] that ʿUthmān b. ʿAffān ate bread and meat, then rinsed his mouth, washed his hands, and wiped his face with them. He then prayed without first performing ablutions.

60. According to Mālik, it reached him that ʿAlī b. Abī Ṭālib and ʿAbd Allāh b. ʿAbbās did not perform ablutions after eating roasted food.

61. According to Mālik, Yaḥyā b. Saʿīd reported that he asked ʿAbd Allāh b. ʿĀmir b. Rabīʿa whether a man who had performed ablutions in preparation for performing a prayer but then ate roasted food before praying had to repeat his ablutions. ʿAbd Allāh said, "I saw my father do that very thing, and he would pray without first repeating his ablutions."

---

40 The year of Khaybar was 7/628.

41 *Sawīq* is a dish described as consisting of either ground wheat or ground barley that is cooked by itself or fried. It is then mixed into water or milk and eaten as a kind of porridge. Zurqānī, *Sharḥ al-Zurqānī*, 1:141.

42 The text's switch from the third person to the first person is not an uncommon feature of early Arabic texts that were originally transmitted orally.

43 Abān b. ʿUthmān served as the governor of Medina from 75/695 to 82/702 during the reign of the Umayyad caliph ʿAbd al-Malik b. Marwān (r. 65–86/685–705). ʿAbd al-Malik was credited with numerous administrative reforms, including Arabizing the language of administration and minting the first coins of the caliphate (before his reign, Muslims had simply adopted the coinage circulating in the conquered territories). He also built the Dome of the Rock in Jerusalem. For more on his contributions to the emerging Arabic-Islamic civilization, see Iḥsān ʿAbbās, "ʿAbd al-Malik b. Marwān wa-dawruhu fī thaqāfat ʿaṣrih," *Dirāsāt* 13, no. 1 (1986): 105–13.

62. According to Mālik, Abū Nu'aym Wahb b. Kaysān reported that he heard Jābir b. 'Abd Allāh al-Anṣārī say, "I saw Abū Bakr al-Ṣiddīq eat meat and then pray, without first repeating his ablutions."

63. According to Mālik, Muḥammad b. al-Munkadir reported that the Messenger of God (pbuh) was invited for a meal and offered bread and meat. So he ate, then performed ablutions and prayed. Later, the leftovers from that meal were brought to him, so he ate again. This time, however, he prayed without first performing ablutions.

64. According to Mālik, Mūsā b. 'Uqba reported from 'Abd al-Raḥmān b. Zayd al-Anṣārī that Anas b. Mālik returned from Iraq to Medina, and Abū Ṭalḥa and Ubayy b. Ka'b came to visit him. Anas offered them roasted food, and so they ate. Anas then got up and performed ablutions. Abū Ṭalḥa and Ubayy said to him, "What are you doing, Anas? Is this an Iraqi practice?" Anas said, "I wish I had never done it!" Abū Ṭalḥa and Ubayy both then prayed without first performing ablutions.

Chapter 6. Miscellaneous Matters Related to Ablutions (*Wuḍū'*)

65. According to Mālik, Hishām b. 'Urwa reported from his father that the Messenger of God (pbuh) was asked about cleaning oneself after defecating. He said, "Is it really difficult to find three small stones?"

66. According to Mālik, al-'Alā' b. 'Abd al-Raḥmān reported from his father, from Abū Hurayra, that the Messenger of God (pbuh) went to the cemetery and said, "Peace to you, dwelling place of a believing folk! We shall, God willing, join you here. How I wish that I could see our brethren!" Those who had gone with him to the cemetery said, "Messenger of God, are we not your brethren?" He said, "No; rather, you are my companions. My brethren are those who have not yet come. I shall lead them to the Pool in Paradise." They said, "Messenger of God, how will you recognize those of your community who come after your death?" He said, "Would a man whose horses' foreheads and legs are emblazoned with flashes of white not recognize them in the midst of a group of dark, black horses?" They said, "Certainly he would, Messenger of God!" He said, "My future followers will come on the Day of Judgment, shining and white from ablutions, and I shall lead them to the Pool in Paradise. Let no one be driven away from my Pool as though he were a lost camel. I will call out to such people, 'Come now! Come now!' It will be said, 'Indeed, they deviated after your death,' so I will say, 'So be gone! So be gone! So be gone!'"

67. According to Mālik, Hishām b. 'Urwa reported from his father, from Ḥumrān, a freedman (*mawlā*) of 'Uthmān b. 'Affān, that 'Uthmān b. 'Affān was sitting on one of the benches outside the Prophet's Mosque,[44] and the muezzin came and called him for the Afternoon Prayer (*ṣalāt al-ʿaṣr*). ʿUthmān called for water and performed his ablutions. He then said, "By God, I shall certainly tell you all something that I would not have narrated, were it not already in God's Book." He said, "I heard the Messenger of God (pbuh) say, 'No person performs ablutions diligently and then performs his prayer without God's forgiving the sins he commits between that prayer and the next prayer that he performs.'" Yaḥyā reported from Mālik, "I believe he was referring to this verse: 'Establish prayer at the ends of the day and for a portion of the night. Surely good deeds erase wicked deeds. That is a reminder for those keen to remember.'"[45]

68. According to Mālik, Zayd b. Aslam reported from ʿAṭāʾ b. Yasār, from ʿAbd Allāh al-Ṣunābiḥī, that the Messenger of God (pbuh) said, "When a faithful servant performs ablutions, and gargles and rinses his mouth, sins exit from his mouth. When he blows his nose, sins leave from his nostrils. When he washes his face, he cleanses his face of sin, even from under his eyelids. Sins leave his hands when he washes them, even from under his fingernails. Sins leave his head when he wipes it, even from his ears. Sins leave his feet when he washes them, even from under his toenails." The Messenger of God (pbuh) then said, "As a result, the faithful servant's walk to the mosque, and his performance of the prayer therein, accrue entirely to his credit."[46]

69. According to Mālik, Suhayl b. Abī Ṣāliḥ reported from his father, from Abū Hurayra, that the Messenger of God (pbuh) said, "When a submitting (or faithful) servant[47] performs ablutions and washes his face, all the sins he has looked upon with his eyes leave with the water (or 'with the last drop of water,' or a similar expression). When he washes his hands, every sin he has committed with his hands leaves with the water (or 'with the last drop of water').[48] As a result, he emerges absolved of sins."[49]

---

44 The text does not explicitly state that this was the Prophet's Mosque, but the presence of the benches and the muezzin indicates that it was a place of communal prayer and therefore almost certainly the mosque of the Prophet Muḥammad (pbuh). Accordingly, in this case and in others like it, we have translated "mosque" as "the Prophet's Mosque" to distinguish it from local or private places of worship that were also referred to as mosques.

45 *Hūd*, 11:114.

46 That is, ablution discharges the "debt" of sins that he has accrued, so the performance of the prayer and the walk to the mosque yield positive credits to his spiritual account.

47 The narrator of the text is uncertain whether the adjective modifying "servant" in the words attributed to the Prophet (pbuh) was *muslim*, meaning, literally, "submitting," or *muʾmin*, meaning "faithful."

48 The parentheses indicate the narrator's doubt regarding which expression the Prophet (pbuh) actually used.

49 Most commentators interpret this absolution as being limited to venial sins.

70. According to Mālik, Isḥāq b. ʿAbd Allāh b. Abī Ṭalḥa reported that Anas b. Mālik said, "I saw the Messenger of God (pbuh) when it was time for the Afternoon Prayer. The people were looking for water for ablutions, but they could not find any. Some water was brought to the Messenger of God (pbuh) in a basin for his ablutions. The Messenger of God (pbuh) put his hand inside that basin, and then he ordered the people to perform their ablutions from it." Anas then said, "I saw the water gush out from under his fingers until the last of them had performed his ablutions."

71. According to Mālik, Nuʿaym b. ʿAbd Allāh al-Mujmir reported that he heard Abū Hurayra say, "Whoever performs ablutions diligently and then sets out intending to perform the prayer is in a state of prayer so long as he intends to perform the prayer. For every stride he takes, a good deed is recorded and a sin is absolved. When one hears the immediate call to prayer (*iqāma*), one should not hurry, for the one whose home is furthest away receives the greatest reward." They said, "Why, Abū Hurayra?" He said, "Because of the many steps he must take to attend the prayer."

72. According to Mālik, Yaḥyā b. Saʿīd reported that he heard someone ask Saʿīd b. al-Musayyab about purification with water after defecation. Saʿīd said, "That manner of purification is only for women."

73. According to Mālik, Abū al-Zinād reported from al-Aʿraj, from Abū Hurayra, that the Messenger of God (pbuh) said, "If a dog drinks from one's basin, one should wash it seven times."

74. According to Mālik, it reached him that the Messenger of God (pbuh) said, "Be upright, even if perfection is unattainable, and perform good deeds constantly. The best of your deeds is the regular performance of prayer, and only a faithful servant persists in maintaining his ablutions."

Chapter 7. What Has Come Down regarding Wiping the Head and Ears

75. According to Mālik, Nāfiʿ reported that ʿAbd Allāh b. ʿUmar would take water with two of his fingers to his ears.

76. According to Mālik, it reached him that Jābir b. ʿAbd Allāh al-Anṣārī was asked whether a man could wipe his turban instead of his head. Jābir said, "No, not until he wipes his hair with water."

77. According to Mālik, Hishām b. ʿUrwa reported that his father, ʿUrwa b. al-Zubayr, would remove his turban and wipe his head with water.

78. According to Mālik, Nāfiʿ reported that he saw Ṣafiyya bt. Abī ʿUbayd, the wife of ʿAbd Allāh b. ʿUmar, remove her veil and wipe her head with water. Nāfiʿ was a child at the time.

79. Yaḥyā said, "Mālik was asked about wiping the turban and the veil instead of the head. He said, 'Neither a man nor a woman should wipe the turban or the veil. Each should wipe his or her head.'"

80. Yaḥyā said, "Mālik was asked about a man who performed ablutions but forgot to wipe his head and remembered only after the water from his ablutions had dried. Mālik said, 'I believe he should wipe his head, and if he has already prayed, he should repeat the performance of his prayer (*ṣalāt*).'"

Chapter 8. What Has Come Down regarding Wiping Leather Socks (*Khuff*)

81. According to Mālik, Ibn Shihāb reported from ʿAbbād b. Ziyād, one of the children of al-Mughīra b. Shuʿba,[50] that his father, al-Mughīra b. Shuʿba, said, "During the Tabūk campaign,[51] the Messenger of God (pbuh) once went to relieve himself, and I went with him, bringing water. After the Messenger of God (pbuh) finished, I poured water for him, so he washed his face. Then he tried to extend his hands through the openings of his cloak's sleeves but could not do so because of their tightness, so he brought them out from underneath the outer cloak and then washed his hands. He then wiped his head and his leather socks (*khuff*). The Messenger of God (pbuh) returned to camp to find ʿAbd al-Raḥmān b. ʿAwf leading them in prayer, having completed one cycle (*rakʿa*) of the prayer with them. The Messenger of God (pbuh) therefore joined them and prayed the remaining cycle of their prayer. The people were startled, so when the Messenger of God (pbuh) completed the performance of his prayer, he said, 'You all did well.'"

82. According to Mālik, Nāfiʿ and ʿAbd Allāh b. Dīnār both told him that ʿAbd Allāh b. ʿUmar visited Saʿd b. Abī Waqqāṣ in Kufa during the latter's tenure as its governor. ʿAbd Allāh b. ʿUmar saw him wiping his leather socks and faulted him for doing so. Saʿd said to him, "Ask your father, ʿUmar b. al-Khaṭṭāb, about this when you return to him in Medina." When ʿAbd Allāh b. ʿUmar returned, he forgot to ask his father about it. Later, when Saʿd came to Medina, he said, "Did you ask your father?" ʿAbd Allāh said, "No." ʿAbd Allāh b. ʿUmar then asked his father about it, and ʿUmar said, "If one puts on leather socks when one's feet are pure following ablutions, one thereafter needs only to wipe them." ʿAbd Allāh then said, "Even after defecation?" ʿUmar said, "Indeed, even after one has defecated."

50 The affiliation of ʿAbbād b. Ziyād to al-Mughīra is an error, committed by either Mālik or Yaḥyā.
51 A campaign to the Levant that took place in 9/630, the final campaign of the Prophet (pbuh).

83. According to Mālik, Nāfiʿ reported that ʿAbd Allāh b. ʿUmar urinated in the market. He then performed ablutions, washed his face and hands, and wiped his head. When he entered the mosque, he was asked to lead a funeral prayer. He wiped his leather socks and led the funeral prayer.

84. According to Mālik, Saʿīd b. ʿAbd al-Raḥmān b. Ruqaysh al-Ashʿarī said, "I once saw Anas b. Mālik on a day when he went to Qubā'. When he arrived, he urinated. A basin was brought to him, and he performed his ablutions. He washed his face and hands to the elbows, and wiped his head and his leather socks. He then went to the mosque and prayed."

85. Yaḥyā said, "Mālik was asked whether a man needs to repeat his ablutions if he performed the ablutions for prayer, then put on leather socks, then urinated, then took off his leather socks, and then put them on again. Mālik replied, 'He should remove his leather socks and then perform the ablutions. He should also wash his feet. Only someone who has put on leather socks when his feet are pure following ablutions may wipe them. Anyone who puts on leather socks without first having performed ablutions to ensure that his feet are pure is not permitted to wipe them.'"

86. Yaḥyā said, "Mālik was asked about a man who had performed ablutions while wearing leather socks but had forgotten to wipe them until the water from his ablutions had already dried, and then performed his prayer. Mālik replied, 'He should wipe his leather socks and repeat the performance of his prayer, but he need not repeat the ablutions.'"

87. Yaḥyā said, "Mālik was asked about a man who had washed his feet, then put on his leather socks, and then completed his ablutions. Mālik said, 'He should remove his leather socks and then perform his ablutions, washing his feet.'"

Chapter 9. The Practice (*ʿAmal*) with Respect to Wiping Leather Socks

88. According to Mālik, Hishām b. ʿUrwa reported that he saw his father wipe his leather socks. He said, "When he wiped his leather socks, he wiped only their upper portions, not their soles."

89. According to Mālik, he asked Ibn Shihāb about how one should wipe leather socks. Ibn Shihāb placed one hand under the leather sock and the other on top of it, and then moved them along its length. Yaḥyā said, "Mālik said, 'Of all the views that I have heard regarding this issue, Ibn Shihāb's view is the one I prefer most.'"

Chapter 10. What Has Come Down regarding Nosebleeds

90. According to Mālik, Nāfiʿ reported that if ʿAbd Allāh b. ʿUmar had a nosebleed while performing the prayer, he would pause his prayer, leave, and perform ablutions. He would then return and resume his prayer from where he had left off, without uttering a word.

91. According to Mālik, it reached him that if ʿAbd Allāh b. ʿAbbās' nose began to bleed while he was performing his prayer, he would pause his prayer, leave, wash the blood away, and then resume his prayer from where he had left off.

92. According to Mālik, Yazīd b. ʿAbd Allāh b. Qusayṭ al-Laythī reported that he saw Saʿīd b. al-Musayyab's nose bleed while he was performing the prayer. Saʿīd went to the chamber of Umm Salama, the wife of the Prophet (pbuh). A basin was brought to him, and he performed ablutions. He then returned and resumed his prayer from where he had left off.

Chapter 11. The Practice (*ʿAmal*) with Respect to Nosebleeds during the Performance of Prayer (*Ṣalāt*)

93. According to Mālik, ʿAbd al-Raḥmān b. Ḥarmala al-Aslamī said, "I saw Saʿīd b. al-Musayyab's nose bleed, to the point that the blood coming out his nose stained his fingers; nevertheless, he would perform the prayer without first performing ablutions."

94. According to Mālik, ʿAbd al-Raḥmān b. al-Mujabbar reported that he saw blood coming from Sālim b. ʿAbd Allāh's nose, to the point that the blood stained his fingers. He then would rub the blood off his fingers and perform his prayer without first performing ablutions.

Chapter 12. The Practice (*ʿAmal*) with Respect to Someone Overcome by Blood from a Wound or a Nosebleed

95. According to Mālik, Hishām b. ʿUrwa reported from his father that al-Miswar b. Makhrama informed ʿUrwa that he visited ʿUmar b. al-Khaṭṭāb the night he was stabbed and woke ʿUmar for the Morning Prayer (*ṣalāt al-ṣubḥ*). ʿUmar then said, "Yes! Those who forsake prayer (*ṣalāt*) have no part in Islam." ʿUmar perfomed his prayer, even though his wound was oozing blood.

96. According to Mālik, Yaḥyā b. Saʿīd reported that Saʿīd b. al-Musayyab asked his pupils, "What do you think of someone who is overcome by a severe nosebleed in the middle of the performance of his prayer, and the nosebleed does not stop?" Yaḥyā b. Saʿīd said that Saʿīd b. al-Musayyab then said, "I think that such a person should move his head to and fro rather than bow and prostrate, in order to prevent the blood from polluting his clothes or the prayer area." Yaḥyā said, "Mālik said, 'Of all the views that I have heard regarding this issue, that view is the one I prefer most.'"

Chapter 13. Ablutions (*Wuḍū'*) Due to Pre-Ejaculate (*Madhī*)[52]

97. According to Mālik, Abū al-Naḍr, the freedman (*mawlā*) of 'Umar b. 'Ubayd Allāh, reported from Sulaymān b. Yasār,[53] from al-Miqdād b. al-Aswad, that 'Alī b. Abī Ṭālib asked him to inquire of the Messenger of God (pbuh) on his behalf what a man should do if he engages in foreplay with his wife and pre-ejaculate emerges. 'Alī said, "Given that I am married to the Messenger of God's daughter, I am embarrassed to ask him." Al-Miqdād said, "I therefore asked the Messenger of God (pbuh) about that, and he said, 'When this happens to someone, he should rinse his penis with water and perform the ablutions that one would perform in order to pray.'"

98. According to Mālik, Zayd b. Aslam reported from his father that 'Umar b. al-Khaṭṭāb said, "Sometimes it rolls out of me, like small pearls. If this happens to someone, let him wash his penis and perform the ablutions that one does for prayers." He was referring to pre-ejaculate.

99. According to Mālik, Zayd b. Aslam reported that Jundab, the freedman of 'Abd Allāh b. 'Ayyāsh al-Makhzūmī, said, "I asked 'Abd Allāh b. 'Umar about pre-ejaculate, and he said, 'If this happens to you, wash your penis and perform the ablutions that you do for prayers.'"

Chapter 14. The Dispensation (*Rukhṣa*) to Forego Ablutions (*Wuḍū'*) as a Result of Pre-Ejaculate (*Madhī*)

100. According to Mālik, Yaḥyā b. Sa'īd reported from Sa'īd b. al-Musayyab that Yaḥyā b. Sa'īd heard a man ask Sa'īd b. al-Musayyab about pre-ejaculate. The man said, "Sometimes I notice some moisture while I am praying. Should I interrupt my prayer (*ṣalāt*)?" Sa'īd said to him, "Even if it were flowing down my thighs I would not stop until I completed performance of my prayer."

101. According to Mālik, al-Ṣalt b. Zuyayd said, "I asked Sulaymān b. Yasār what to do if I notice some moisture on my penis. He said, 'Rinse what is under your garment with water and ignore it.'"

---

52 *Madhī* refers to the pre-ejaculation liquid that emerges from the penis in connection with foreplay or other sexual arousal.

53 Sulaymān b. Yasār (d. 107/725) belonged to the generation of the Followers and was one of the "seven jurists of Medina." He served as an important source for Mālik in the *Muwaṭṭa'*.

Chapter 15. Performing Ablutions (*Wuḍū'*) on Account of Touching the Genitalia

102. According to Mālik, ʿAbd Allāh b. Abī Bakr reported from Ibn Muḥammad b. ʿAmr b. Ḥazm that he heard ʿUrwa b. al-Zubayr say, "I met with Marwān b. al-Ḥakam, and we discussed what necessitates the performance of ablutions. Marwān said, 'Touching one's penis necessitates ablutions.' ʿUrwa said, 'I did not know that.' Marwān b. al-Ḥakam then said, 'Busra bt. Ṣafwān informed me that she heard the Messenger of God (pbuh) say, "If someone touches his penis, he should perform ablutions."'"

103. According to Mālik, Ismāʿīl b. Muḥammad b. Saʿd b. Abī Waqqāṣ reported that Muṣʿab b. Saʿd b. Abī al-Waqqāṣ said, "I was holding pages of the Quran for Saʿd b. Abī al-Waqqāṣ, and I scratched myself. Saʿd said, 'Perhaps you touched your penis?'" Muṣʿab said, "I said, 'Yes, I did,' so Saʿd said, 'Go and perform ablutions.' I did and then came back."

104. According to Mālik, Nāfiʿ reported that ʿAbd Allāh b. ʿUmar would say, "If someone touches his penis, he must perform ablutions."

105. According to Mālik, Hishām b. ʿUrwa reported that his father would say, "Whoever touches his penis must perform ablutions."

106. According to Mālik, Ibn Shihāb reported that Sālim b. ʿAbd Allāh said, "I saw my father, ʿAbd Allāh b. ʿUmar, bathe and then perform ablutions, so I said to him, 'My dear father, doesn't bathing obviate the need for ablutions?' He said, 'Certainly, but sometimes I touch my penis while bathing, so I perform ablutions.'"

107. According to Mālik, Nāfiʿ reported that Sālim b. ʿAbd Allāh said, "I accompanied ʿAbd Allāh b. ʿUmar on a journey. I saw him perform ablutions after the sun had risen and then pray." Sālim said, "I then said to him, 'I have not previously seen you pray at this time!' ʿAbd Allāh b. ʿUmar said, 'After I performed ablutions for the Morning Prayer (*ṣalāt al-ṣubḥ*), I touched my penis but then forgot to repeat my ablutions, so I performed ablutions and repeated my prayer once I remembered.'"

Chapter 16. Ablutions (*Wuḍū'*) after a Man Kisses His Wife

108. According to Mālik, Ibn Shihāb reported from Sālim b. ʿAbd Allāh that his father, ʿAbd Allāh b. ʿUmar, would say, "A man's kissing his wife or touching her with his hand is a kind of intimate contact. Anyone who kisses his wife or touches her with his hand must perform ablutions."

109. According to Mālik, it reached him that ʿAbd Allāh b. Masʿūd would say, "Kissing one's wife necessitates ablution."

110. According to Mālik, Ibn Shihāb would say, "Kissing one's wife necessitates ablution."

Chapter 17. The Practice (*ʿAmal*) with Respect to the Removal of Ritual Preclusion (*Janāba*)[54]

111. According to Mālik, Hishām b. ʿUrwa reported from his father, from ʿĀʾisha, the Mother of the Believers, that when the Messenger of God (pbuh) would bathe on account of ritual preclusion, he would start by washing his hands. He would then perform ablutions as he would for the performance of prayer (*ṣalāt*). He would then dip his fingers into a basin of water and run his fingers through the roots of his hair. Then, scooping up water with both hands, he would pour it on his head three times. Finally, he would pour the basin's remaining water over his entire body.

112. According to Mālik, Ibn Shihāb reported from ʿUrwa b. al-Zubayr, from ʿĀʾisha, the Mother of the Believers, that when the Messenger of God (pbuh) would bathe on account of ritual preclusion, he would use a single basin of water containing approximately six liters of water.[55]

113. According to Mālik, Nāfiʿ reported that when ʿAbd Allāh b. ʿUmar bathed on account of ritual preclusion, he would begin by pouring water into his right hand and washing it. Then he washed his penis. Then he rinsed his mouth and blew his nose. Then he washed his face and sprinkled water in his eyes. Then he washed his right hand and then his left. Then he washed his head. Then he bathed and poured water over himself.

114. According to Mālik, it reached him that ʿĀʾisha, the Mother of the Believers, was asked about how a woman bathes on account of ritual

54 Islamic ritual law came to divide the impurities that result from bodily functions into two kinds, major (*ḥadath akbar*) and minor (*ḥadath aṣghar*). The latter involves any excretion from the genitalia or the anus, including the passing of gas. The former involves secretions related to the body's sexual functions, such as ejaculation for males and ejaculation, menstruation, and lochia (postpartum discharge) for females. The jurists refer to the state associated with these latter functions as *janāba*, translated here as "ritual preclusion." A person who is in a condition of ritual preclusion may not resume ordinary ritual life simply by performing ablutions (*wuḍūʾ*) but rather must complete a ritual bath (*ghusl*) and, in the case of a menstruating woman or a postpartum mother, must also wait for the blood or lochia, as applicable, to cease flowing before bathing. During this time, she is excused from the observance of ordinarily applicable ritual requirements. A person subject to ritual preclusion is known as *junub*. See Chapter 19 of the Book of Purity.

55 The editors of the RME explain that the unit specified in the report, *faraq*, is the equivalent of three measures (*ṣāʿ*). A measure is made up of four *mudds*, a *mudd* measuring approximately 500 grams. A *faraq*, therefore, contains approximately six kilograms of water, or six liters.

preclusion. She said, "She should pour three handfuls of water on her head and rub her head with her hands."

Chapter 18. The Obligation to Bathe When the Genitalia Touch

115. According to Mālik, Ibn Shihāb reported from Saʿīd b. al-Musayyab that ʿUmar b. al-Khaṭṭāb, ʿUthmān b. ʿAffān, and ʿĀʾisha, the wife of the Prophet (pbuh), would all say, "When one genital organ penetrates[56] another, bathing becomes obligatory."

116. According to Mālik, Abū al-Naḍr, the freedman (*mawlā*) of ʿUmar b. ʿUbayd Allāh, reported that Abū Salama b. ʿAbd al-Raḥmān b. ʿAwf said, "I asked ʿĀʾisha, the wife of the Prophet (pbuh), 'What necessitates a ritual bath (*ghusl*)?' She said, 'Do you know what you remind me of, Abū Salama? You are like a chick who hears the roosters crowing, so he crows with them.[57] When one genital organ penetrates another, bathing becomes obligatory.'"

117. According to Mālik, Yaḥyā b. Saʿīd reported from Saʿīd b. al-Musayyab that Abū Musā al-Ashʿarī went to ʿĀʾisha, the wife of the Prophet, and said to her, "A disagreement among the Companions of the Messenger of God (pbuh) over a certain question has brought me grief, but it is extremely embarrassing for me to bring it up with you." She asked, "What is it? Whatever you would ask your mother, you may ask me." He said, "Is bathing necessary if a man has intercourse with his wife but then loses his erection and does not ejaculate?" She said, "If one genital organ penetrates the other, bathing becomes obligatory." Abū Mūsā said, "I will never ask anyone else about this again."

118. According to Mālik, Yaḥyā b. Saʿīd reported from ʿAbd Allāh b. Kaʿb, the freedman of ʿUthmān b. ʿAffān, that Maḥmūd b. Labīd al-Anṣārī asked Zayd b. Thābit about a man who has intercourse with his wife but loses his erection and does not ejaculate. Zayd said to him, "He must bathe." Maḥmūd then said to him, "But Ubayy b. Kaʿb was of the opinion that bathing is not obligatory in that case." Zayd said to him, "Ubayy b. Kaʿb changed his mind about that before he died."

119. According to Mālik, Nāfiʿ reported that ʿAbd Allāh b. ʿUmar would say, "When one genital organ penetrates another, bathing becomes obligatory."

56 The literal word used for sexual organ in this report and the next one is *khitān*, a reference to circumcision, and it thus functions as a euphemism for penetrative sexual intercourse.

57 The point of ʿĀʾisha's analogy is that the narrator is too young to understand the question.

Chapter 19. The Ablutions (*Wuḍū'*) of One Ritually Precluded (*Junub*) When He Wishes to Sleep or Eat before He Bathes

120. According to Mālik, ʿAbd Allāh b. Dīnār reported that ʿAbd Allāh b. ʿUmar said, "ʿUmar b. al-Khaṭṭāb mentioned to the Messenger of God (pbuh) that sometimes he might have a wet dream at night. The Messenger of God (pbuh) said to him, 'Wash your penis, perform ablutions, and go back to sleep.'"

121. According to Mālik, Hishām b. ʿUrwa reported from his father that ʿĀ'isha, the wife of the Prophet (pbuh), would say, "If someone has intercourse with his wife and wishes to sleep before bathing, he should not sleep until he first performs ablutions as he would for the performance of prayer (*ṣalāt*)."

122. According to Mālik, Nāfiʿ reported that ʿAbd Allāh b. ʿUmar, when he wanted to sleep or eat when in a state of ritual preclusion, would wash his face and his hands to the elbows and then wipe his head. He would then eat or sleep.

Chapter 20. Repetition of Prayer (*Ṣalāt*) by One Ritually Precluded (*Junub*); His Bath If He Prayed and Did Not Remember; and His Washing of His Clothes

123. According to Mālik, Ismāʿīl b. Abī Ḥakīm reported that ʿAṭā' b. Yasār informed him that the Messenger of God (pbuh) one day began performance of an obligatory prayer but then signaled to the congregation with his hand to wait in their places, and left. He then returned, and traces of water were still on his body.

124. According to Mālik, Hishām b. ʿUrwa reported that Zuyayd b. al-Ṣalt said, "I went out one day with ʿUmar b. al-Khaṭṭāb to the Juruf,[58] only for him to realize that he had had a wet dream and prayed without first bathing. ʿUmar said, 'By God, it seems that I had a wet dream and didn't realize it, and I prayed without first bathing.' So he bathed, and washed the stains that he saw on his clothes, and sprinkled water on the rest. Then he made the general call to prayer (*adhān*) (or the immediate call to prayer, *iqāma*), and prayed after the morning sun had risen high."

125. According to Mālik, Ismāʿīl b. Abī Ḥakīm reported from Sulaymān b. Yasār that ʿUmar b. al-Khaṭṭāb set out early in the morning to his land in Juruf and noticed stains from a wet dream on his clothes. He said, "I have been afflicted with wet dreams ever since I became responsible for the

58 An agricultural village approximately 3–5 km outside of Medina.

people's affairs." He therefore bathed and washed the stains that he saw on his clothes. He then prayed after the sun had already risen.

126. According to Mālik, Yaḥyā b. Saʿīd reported from Sulaymān b. Yasār that ʿUmar b. al-Khaṭṭāb led the people in the Morning Prayer (*ṣalāt al-ṣubḥ*) and then set out while it was still early in the morning to his land in Juruf. He later discovered the stains of a wet dream on his clothes. He said, "Since we have been eating well, our vigor has been restored." So he bathed, and washed the stains from his clothes, and repeated the performance of his prayer.

127. According to Mālik, Hishām b. ʿUrwa reported from his father, from Yaḥyā b. ʿAbd al-Raḥmān b. Ḥāṭib, that he performed the Visitation (*ʿumra*)[59] with ʿUmar b. al-Khaṭṭāb and a band that included ʿAmr b. al-ʿĀṣī. ʿUmar set up camp at night on the road near a well, and he had a wet dream. It was nearly dawn, and none of them had any water. He rode off until he reached the well, and began to wash all visible stains from his clothes. He continued to do so until morning arrived. ʿAmr b. al-ʿĀṣī said to ʿUmar, "It is now morning, and we have other clothes you can wear, so put aside your clothes to be washed later." ʿUmar then said to him, "How strange that you should say this, Ibn al-ʿĀṣī! Maybe you have a change of clothes, but not everyone else does! By God, if I were to do that, it would become the rule. Instead, I will wash the visible stains, and sprinkle water on the rest."

128. Yaḥyā said, "Mālik said, regarding a man who finds stains from a wet dream on his clothes but does not know when it happened, nor does he remember his dream, 'He should bathe on the assumption that the wet dream occurred the last time he slept. If he subsequently performed any prayers, he should repeat the prayers performed since he last awoke, because a man may ejaculate without having had an erotic dream, or he may have an erotic dream without ejaculating. Accordingly, if he discovers stains from a wet dream on his clothes, he must bathe. That is because ʿUmar b. al-Khaṭṭāb repeated whatever prayer he had performed since he last slept, but not anything prior to that."

Chapter 21. A Woman's Obligation to Bathe If She Has an Erotic Dream Similar to a Man's

129. According to Mālik, Ibn Shihāb reported from ʿUrwa b. al-Zubayr that Umm Sulaym said to the Messenger of God, "If a woman has an erotic dream like a man, must she bathe (*ghusl*)?" The Messenger of God (pbuh) said, "Yes,

---

59 The Visitation (*ʿumra*) is a truncated pilgrimage to Mecca in which the pilgrim performs only some of the rites associated with the Pilgrimage (*ḥajj*).

she must." 'Ā'isha said to her, "Woe to you! As if women have such dreams!" The Messenger of God (pbuh) said to 'Ā'isha, "What a strange thing for you to say! Where else does a child's resemblance to its mother come from?"

130. According to Mālik, Hishām b. 'Urwa reported from his father, from Zaynab bt. Abī Salama, that Umm Salama, the wife of the Prophet (pbuh), said, "Umm Sulaym, the wife of Abū Ṭalḥa al-Anṣārī, went to the Messenger of God (pbuh) and said, 'Messenger of God, God is not embarrassed by the truth! Must a woman bathe when she has an erotic dream?' He said to her, 'Yes, if she notices any ejaculate.'"

Chapter 22. Miscellaneous Matters Related to Bathing (*Ghusl*) on Account of Ritual Preclusion (*Janāba*)

131. According to Mālik, Nāfi' reported that 'Abd Allāh b. 'Umar would say, "There is nothing objectionable in someone bathing with water left over from a woman's bath, provided she was not menstruating or otherwise ritually precluded (*junub*)."

132. According to Mālik, Nāfi' reported that 'Abd Allāh b. 'Umar would perform prayers while wearing the very clothes he had worn while in a state of ritual preclusion, even though he had sweated profusely while wearing them.

133. According to Mālik, Nāfi' reported that Ibn 'Umar's handmaidens would wash his feet and bring him his prayer mat even when they were menstruating.

134. Mālik was asked whether a man with multiple wives and handmaidens may have intercourse with one and then another without bathing in between. Mālik said, "There is nothing objectionable in his having intercourse with another one of his handmaidens while he is still in a state of ritual preclusion. He is prohibited from having intercourse with one of his wives on the day of another wife.[60] It is not objectionable, however, if he has intercourse with one handmaiden and then, while still in a state of ritual preclusion, has intercourse with another."

135. Yaḥyā said, "Mālik was asked about a man in a state of ritual preclusion for whom a bath was drawn. Without giving any thought to it, he put his finger into the water to see whether it was hot or cold. Mālik said, 'So long as there was no impure substance on his fingers, I do not believe that rendered the water impure.'"

60 That is, without that other wife's consent.

Chapter 23. Dry Ablutions (*Tayammum*)[61]

136. According to Mālik, ʿAbd al-Raḥmān b. al-Qāsim reported from his father that ʿĀʾisha, the Mother of the Believers, said, "We went with the Messenger of God (pbuh) on one of his journeys. When we arrived at Baydāʾ, or Dhāt al-Jaysh, I lost my necklace.[62] The Messenger of God (pbuh), along with everyone else, stopped to search for it. There was no water there, and they were short of water. People went to Abū Bakr al-Ṣiddīq and said, 'Have you seen what ʿĀʾisha has done? She has forced the Messenger of God (pbuh) and ourselves to halt our march in a waterless place, and we ourselves are running out of water.' Then Abū Bakr came to see me, and the Prophet was sleeping with his head on my lap. He berated me, saying, 'You have detained the Messenger of God (pbuh) and the people in a waterless place, and at a time when they are running out of water.' Abū Bakr reproached me sharply and without any restraint. He began to shove me at the waist with his hand, and I would have gotten up to leave, but for the fact that the Messenger of God (pbuh) was asleep with his head on my lap. The Messenger of God continued sleeping, waking up the next morning without any water for ablutions. God, Blessed and Sublime is He, then revealed the verse regarding dry ablutions. Usayd b. al-Khuḍayr said, 'This isn't the first of your many blessings, family of Abū Bakr!' We stirred the camel that I had been riding and found my necklace beneath it."

137. Yaḥyā said, "Mālik was asked about a man who performed dry ablutions for a prayer (*ṣalāt*) that was due. Then the time for the next prayer came. Must he perform dry ablutions again, or do the first ablutions suffice for him? Mālik said, 'He must perform dry ablutions for every prayer, for he is obliged to seek out water for every prayer. Only one who has sought out water and failed to find it is permitted to perform dry ablutions.'"

138. Yaḥyā said, "Mālik was asked whether a man who had performed dry ablutions may lead his companions in the performance of prayer, if they have performed their ablutions with water (*wuḍūʾ*). Mālik said, 'I prefer that someone else lead them, but were he to do so, I would not believe it to be objectionable.'"

139. Yaḥyā said, "Mālik said, regarding a man who could not find water and consequently performed dry ablutions in its place, stood up to pray, performed the opening magnification of God (*takbīr*),[63] and had begun to

---

61 *Tayammum* is an alternative means of performing ablution using sand or dirt in circumstances in which water is not reasonably available.

62 Baydāʾ and Dhāt al-Jaysh are vast desert expanses in the Hijaz.

63 Ritual prayer is begun when the worshipper raises his hands to his ears and states, "God is great" (*Allāhu akbar*).

pray when suddenly another man appeared with water—whether such a man should interrupt the performance of his prayer to perform ablutions: 'The first man should not interrupt his prayer but rather complete it in reliance on his dry ablutions. He should then perform ablutions for his subsequent prayers.'"

140. Mālik said, "When someone intends to pray but cannot find water and so acts in conformity with God's command by performing dry ablutions, he has faithfully obeyed God. Someone who performed ablutions with water is not any purer than the one who performed dry ablutions, nor is his prayer any better, because each of them was subject to a particular command, and each of them acted in accordance with what God ordered. The obligation to act in accordance with God's command to perform ablutions applies only to someone with water, and the command to perform dry ablutions applies only to someone who does not have water. Either ablution or dry ablution must be performed before anyone begins to pray."

141. Mālik said, regarding a man in a state of ritual preclusion (*junub*), "He may perform dry ablutions, read his daily portion of the Quran, and perform his supererogatory prayers, as long as he cannot find water. This is permissible only in situations in which it would have been permissible for him to perform an obligatory prayer with dry ablutions."

Chapter 24. The Practice (*ʿAmal*) with Respect to Performance of Dry Ablutions (*Tayammum*)

142. According to Mālik, Nāfiʿ reported that he and ʿAbd Allāh b. ʿUmar were returning from Juruf. When they reached al-Mirbad, ʿAbd Allāh dismounted and performed dry ablutions with some pure dust, wiping his face and his hands up to the elbows. Then he performed the prayer.

143. According to Mālik, Nāfiʿ reported that ʿAbd Allāh b. ʿUmar would perform dry ablutions by wiping up to the elbows.

144. Mālik was asked, "How is dry ablution performed, and how extensive is it?" He said, "A person performing dry ablutions strikes the ground once to stir up dust for the face, and strikes it again for the hands, wiping them up to the elbows."

Chapter 25. The Dry Ablutions (*Tayammum*) of Someone in a State of Ritual Preclusion (*Janāba*)

145. According to Mālik, ʿAbd al-Raḥmān b. Ḥarmala reported that a man asked Saʿīd b. al-Musayyab about a man in a state of ritual preclusion (*junub*) who performs dry ablutions and then prays, but later finds water. Saʿīd said, "Once he finds water, he must bathe to perform future prayers."

146. Yaḥyā said, "Mālik said, regarding a man who has a wet dream while traveling and has only enough water to perform ablutions but will not go thirsty before he reaches a source of water, 'He should wash his penis and anything else that has been stained using that water. He should then perform dry ablutions with pure dust, as God, Mighty and Exalted is He, has ordered, prior to praying.'"

147. Yaḥyā said, "Mālik was asked whether a man who can find only hard, salty soil and is in a state of ritual preclusion is permitted to perform dry ablutions. Further, is it forbidden to perform prayer on hard, salty soil? Mālik said, 'There is nothing objectionable in performing prayers (*ṣalāt*) on hard, salty soil or in using it for dry ablutions, because God, Blessed and Sublime is He, says in the Quran, "And seek out pure soil."[64] Whatever qualifies as "soil" may be used to perform dry ablutions, whether or not it is hard and salty or anything else.'"

Chapter 26. Permissible Sexual Intimacy between Husband and Wife during Menstruation

148. According to Mālik, Zayd b. Aslam reported that a man asked the Messenger of God (pbuh), "What intimacy is permissible with my menstruating wife?" The Messenger of God (pbuh) said, "Let her wrap her undergarment (*izār*) tightly, and do what you wish with her upper body."

149. According to Mālik, Rabīʿa b. Abī ʿAbd al-Raḥmān reported that ʿĀʾisha, the wife of the Prophet (pbuh), was lying next to him under one cover when she suddenly jumped up, startled. The Messenger of God (pbuh) said to her, "What's wrong? Are you bleeding?"—by which he meant "menstruating." She said, "Yes." He said, "Wrap your undergarment around yourself tightly, and then come back to bed."

150. According to Mālik, Nāfiʿ reported that ʿAbd Allāh b. ʿAbd Allāh b. ʿUmar sent a messenger to ʿĀʾisha, asking her whether a man may be intimate with his menstruating wife. She said, "She should wrap her undergarment tightly around her waist, and he may then be intimate with her, if he wishes."

151. According to Mālik, it reached him that Sālim b. ʿAbd Allāh and Sulaymān b. Yasār were both asked whether the husband of a menstruating woman may have intercourse with her after the end of her period but before she bathes. They both said, "No, not until she bathes."

64 *Al-Māʾida*, 5:6.

Chapter 27. The Cessation of a Menstruating Woman's Bleeding

152. According to Mālik, ʿAlqama b. Abī ʿAlqama reported that his mother, the freedwoman (*mawlāt*) of ʿĀʾisha, the Mother of the Believers, said, "Women would send to ʿĀʾisha bits of cotton they had used during their periods, with a slight yellow discoloration, asking whether they could now resume performing prayer (*ṣalāt*). She would say to them, 'Don't be hasty; wait until the discharge is completely clear,' meaning thereby that bleeding had stopped entirely."

153. According to Mālik, ʿAbd Allāh b. Abī Bakr reported from his paternal aunt, from the daughter of Zayd b. Thābit, that it had reached her that women would call for lamps in the middle of the night to determine whether they had stopped menstruating. She was critical of that, saying, "Women did not do this in the time of the Prophet (pbuh)."

154. Yaḥyā said, "Mālik was asked whether a woman whose period comes to an end but who cannot find water should instead perform dry ablutions. Mālik said, 'Yes, she should. She is in the same position as a ritually precluded man (*junub*): if he cannot find water, his obligation is to perform dry ablutions.'"

Chapter 28. Miscellaneous Matters regarding Menstruation

155. According to Mālik, it reached him that ʿĀʾisha, the wife of the Prophet (pbuh), said that a pregnant woman who is bleeding should refrain from the performance of prayers (*ṣalāt*).

156. According to Mālik, he asked Ibn Shihāb about a pregnant woman who is bleeding. The latter said, "She should refrain from the performance of prayers." Yaḥyā said, "Mālik said, 'That is the rule among us (*dhālika al-amr ʿindanā*).'"[65]

157. According to Mālik, Hishām b. ʿUrwa reported from his father that ʿĀʾisha, the wife of the Prophet (pbuh), said, "I would comb the hair of the Messenger of God (pbuh) even when I was menstruating."

158. According to Mālik, Hishām b. ʿUrwa reported from his father, from Fāṭima bt. al-Mundhir b. al-Zubayr, that Asmāʾ bt. Abī Bakr al-Ṣiddīq said, "A woman asked the Messenger of God (pbuh), 'What should a woman do if menstrual blood stains her clothes?' The Messenger of God (pbuh) said,

---

65 We distinguish Mālik's more common use of "the rule in our view is (*al-amr ʿindanā*) . . ." from his less frequent use of the phrase "that is the rule among us (*dhālika al-ʿamr ʿindanā*)," insofar as the latter is a complete statement of the law, whereas the former is the subject of a nominal sentence that introduces the rule. The latter usage is less common in the *Muwaṭṭaʾ*.

'She should rub the stain with moistened fingers and then splash it with water. She may then perform her prayer wearing those clothes.'"

Chapter 29. A Woman Who Suffers from Chronic Nonmenstrual Bleeding

159. According to Mālik, Hishām b. ʿUrwa reported from his father that ʿĀʾisha, the wife of the Prophet (pbuh), said, "Fāṭima bt. Abī Ḥubaysh said, 'Messenger of God, I do not stop bleeding. Should I stop praying?' The Messenger of God (pbuh) said to her, 'This is just blood from a vein, and not menstrual blood. When it's time for your period, refrain from praying, and when you believe your period has run its course, wash any blood from your body and resume performance of your prayers.'"

160. According to Mālik, Nāfiʿ reported from Sulaymān b. Yasār, from Umm Salama, the wife of the Prophet (pbuh), that during the time of the Messenger of God (pbuh) there was a woman who suffered from chronic bleeding. The woman asked Umm Salama to inquire about her condition with the Messenger of God. He said, "She should estimate the number of days and nights that she menstruated each month before she had this condition. She should refrain from prayer each month for that length of time. When the time ends, she should bathe, tighten her undergarments, and resume performance of her prayers."

161. According to Mālik, Hishām b. ʿUrwa reported from his father, from Zaynab bt. Abī Salama, that she knew Zaynab bt. Jaḥsh, who was married to ʿAbd al-Raḥmān b. ʿAwf.[66] She suffered from chronic bleeding, but she would bathe and pray.

162. According to Mālik, Sumayy, the freedman (*mawlā*) of Abū Bakr, reported that al-Qaʿqāʿ b. Ḥakīm and Zayd b. Aslam sent him to Saʿīd b. al-Musayyab to ask him how a woman suffering from chronic bleeding should bathe in order to pray. Saʿīd said, "She should bathe once daily and perform ablutions for every prayer (*ṣalāt*), and if the bleeding is substantial, she should change her undergarment."

163. According to Mālik, Hishām b. ʿUrwa reported that his father said, "A woman who suffers from chronic bleeding needs to bathe only once (per menstrual cycle), and after that she should perform ablution prior to every obligatory prayer."

---

66 The majority of the *Muwaṭṭa*ʾs transmitters believe that this is an error, and that it was Ḥabība bt. Jaḥsh, not Zaynab, who suffered from this condition.

164. Yaḥyā said, "Mālik said, 'The rule in our view (*al-amr ʿindanā*) is that the husband of a woman suffering from chronic bleeding may have intercourse with her during the time in which she is eligible to pray. The same applies in the case of a woman with postpartum bleeding, once the maximum length of time during which women ordinarily experience postpartum bleeding has elapsed. If she continues to bleed after that, her husband may have intercourse with her, and she is deemed to be the equivalent of a woman who suffers from chronic bleeding.'"

165. Yaḥyā said, "Mālik said, 'The rule in our view, regarding a woman suffering from chronic bleeding, is in accord with the report of Hishām b. ʿUrwa from his father. Of all the views that I have heard regarding this issue, it is the one I prefer most.'"

Chapter 30. What Has Come Down regarding the Urine of an Infant Boy

166. According to Mālik, Hishām b. ʿUrwa reported from his father that ʿĀ'isha, the wife of the Prophet (pbuh), said, "One day a baby boy was brought to the Messenger of God (pbuh), and the baby urinated on his clothes. The Messenger of God (pbuh) asked for water and poured it on the stain."

167. According to Mālik, Ibn Shihāb reported from ʿUbayd Allāh b. ʿAbd Allāh b. ʿUtba b. Masʿūd,[67] from Umm Qays bt. Miḥṣan, that she brought her infant son, who had not yet started to eat food, to the Messenger of God (pbuh). He sat the boy on his lap, and the baby urinated on his clothes. The Messenger of God (pbuh) called for water, and he sprinkled it on the stain but did not wash it.

Chapter 31. What Has Come Down regarding Urinating While Standing and Other Matters

168. According to Mālik, Yaḥyā b. Saʿīd said, "A bedouin entered the Prophet's Mosque in Medina, lifted up his clothes, and took out his penis to urinate. The people shouted at him, and a great commotion broke out. The Messenger of God (pbuh) said, 'Leave him alone!' So they did, and the man urinated. When the man finished, the Messenger of God (pbuh) asked for a bucket of water, which was poured on that spot."

---

67 ʿUbayd Allāh b. ʿAbd Allāh b. ʿUtba b. Masʿūd (d. 98/716) belonged to the generation of the Followers and was one of the "seven jurists of Medina." He served as an important source for Mālik in the *Muwaṭṭa'*.

169. According to Mālik, ʿAbd Allāh b. Dīnār said, "I saw ʿAbd Allāh b. ʿUmar urinate while he was standing."

170. Yaḥyā said, "Mālik was asked whether there were any precedents about washing the genitalia after urination or the anus after defecation. Mālik said, 'It reached me that some of those in the past would wash themselves[68] after defecating, and I prefer that the genitalia be rinsed after urination.'"

Chapter 32. What Has Come Down regarding Use of the Toothbrush (*Siwāk*)[69]

171. According to Mālik, Ibn Shihāb reported from Ibn al-Sabbāq that the Messenger of God (pbuh) said in one of his Friday sermons, "Assembly of Muslims! This is a day that God has made a feast, so bathe. Whoever has perfume should not be reluctant to use it, and use of the toothbrush is commended to you all."

172. According to Mālik, Abū al-Zinād reported from al-Aʿraj, from Abū Hurayra, that the Messenger of God (pbuh) said, "If I were not afraid of overburdening my community, I would have ordered them to use the toothbrush."

173. According to Mālik, Ibn Shihāb reported from Ḥumayd b. ʿAbd al-Raḥmān b. ʿAwf that Abū Hurayra said, "Had the Prophet (pbuh) not been fearful of overburdening his community, he would have ordered them to brush their teeth every time they performed ablutions (*wuḍūʾ*)."

---

68 Although the verb used is the same as that used for the performance of ablutions, it is being used in its ordinary sense of "to wash" in this context. Zurqānī, *Sharḥ al-Zurqānī*, 1:254.

69 *Siwāk* is a twig used as a toothbrush.

Book 3
The First Book of Prayer (*Ṣalāt*)

Chapter 1. What Has Come Down regarding the Call to Prayer (*Ṣalāt*)

174. According to Mālik, Yaḥyā b. Saʿīd said, "The Messenger of God (pbuh) wanted to take two pieces of wood that would be struck together to produce a sound, so the people could be gathered for the performance of prayer. ʿAbd Allāh b. Zayd al-Anṣārī, of the tribe of Banū al-Ḥārith b. al-Khazraj, dreamed that he saw two pieces of wood, so he said to himself, 'These two pieces of wood are similar to what the Messenger of God (pbuh) desires.' Someone in the dream said, 'Why don't you instead use your voice to make the call to prayer?' When he awoke, he went to the Messenger of God (pbuh) and mentioned the dream to him. The Messenger of God (pbuh) then ordained the use of the general call to prayer (*adhān*) instead of the two pieces of wood."

175. According to Mālik, Ibn Shihāb reported from ʿAṭāʾ b. Yazīd al-Laythī, from Abū Saʿīd al-Khudrī, that the Messenger of God (pbuh) said, "When you hear the general call to prayer, repeat the words of the muezzin."[70]

176. According to Mālik, Sumayy, the freedman (*mawlā*) of Abū Bakr b. ʿAbd al-Raḥmān, reported from Abū Ṣāliḥ al-Sammān, from Abū Hurayra, that the Messenger of God (pbuh) said, "If people only knew the blessings of the general call to prayer and of praying in the first row of the mosque, they would draw lots to prevent themselves from fighting over those blessings. If they knew of the blessings of attending the prayer early, they would race to it. If they knew of the blessings of the Evening Prayer (*ṣalāt al-ʿishāʾ*) and the Morning Prayer (*ṣalāt al-ṣubḥ*), they would have come crawling to the mosque to perform them."

177. According to Mālik, al-ʿAlāʾ b. ʿAbd al-Raḥmān b. Yaʿqūb reported that both his father and Isḥāq Abū ʿAbd Allāh told him that they heard Abū Hurayra say, "The Messenger of God (pbuh) said, 'If an obligatory prayer is

70 In Arabic *muʾadhdhin*, that is, the one making the call to prayer (*adhān*).

about to begin, do not come in a rush, but rather solemnly and calmly. Pray what you can with the congregation, and complete what you have missed when the prayer is finished. Anyone setting out to the mosque with the intention to pray is already in a state of prayer."

178. According to Mālik, ʿAbd al-Raḥmān b. ʿAbd Allāh b. ʿAbd al-Raḥmān b. Abī Ṣaʿṣaʿa al-Anṣārī al-Māzinī reported that his father told him that Abū Saʿīd al-Khudrī said to him, "I've noticed that you love sheep and the desert. When you are with your flock or out in the desert and you make the general call to prayer, raise your voice. Everyone and everything, human or jinn, who hears your call will testify in your favor on the Day of Judgment." Abū Saʿīd said, "I heard it from the Messenger of God (pbuh)."

179. According to Mālik, Abū al-Zinād reported from al-Aʿraj, from Abū Hurayra, that the Messenger of God said, "When the general call to prayer is made, the Devil flees, farting loudly so that he cannot hear the call to prayer. When the call to prayer is over, he returns until the immediate call to prayer (*iqāma*) is made, and then he again flees. When the latter is completed, he returns so as to penetrate a man's inner thoughts, saying, 'Remember this and that,' reminding him of things that he ordinarily would not remember, to the point that the man will even forget how much of the prayer he has performed."

180. According to Mālik, Abū Ḥāzim b. Dīnār reported that Sahl b. Saʿd al-Sāʿidī said, "There are two occasions on which the gates of Heaven are open, and rare is the supplicant whose petition is rejected: the general call to prayer, and lining up for battle for the sake of God."

181. Yaḥyā said, "Mālik was asked whether the general call to prayer on Fridays should be made before the time of the prayer itself. He said, 'It should not be made until the sun has reached its zenith and begun its decline.'"

182. Yaḥyā said, "Mālik was asked about the doubling of certain phrases in the general call to prayer and the immediate call to prayer, and the precise moment when people should stand up when the immediate call to prayer is made. Mālik said, 'No report has reached me about the general call to prayer or the immediate call to prayer. My view is based entirely on what I have seen the people do here in Medina. As for the immediate call to prayer, its phrases are not to be doubled.[71] That is the rule that the people of

71 According to the Mālikīs the phrases in the immediate call to prayer (*iqāma*) are said only once, with the exception of the magnification of God, which is said twice, both at the beginning and at the conclusion of the call. Accordingly, the Mālikī formula for the immediate call to prayer is as follows: "God is great, God is great; I testify that there is no god except God; I testify that Muḥammad is the Messenger of God; Hasten to perform prayer; Hasten to attain success;

knowledge in our town have always followed (*wa-dhālika alladhī lam yazal ʿalayhi ahl al-ʿilm bi-baladinā*). As for the moment when people should line up to perform the prayer after the immediate call to prayer has been made, I have not heard of any specific rule regarding when they should stand. I believe that this is a matter of each individual's capacity, for some can stand and join the line only slowly, whereas others can stand and join the line quickly. They cannot act as a single body in such a matter.'"

183. Yaḥyā said, "Mālik was asked whether some townspeople may perform an obligatory prayer together as a congregation, making only the immediate call to prayer but not the general call to prayer. Mālik said, 'That is sufficient. The general call to prayer is an obligation only for congregational mosques in which public worship is performed.'"

184. Yaḥyā said, "Mālik was asked about the practice of the muezzin's greeting the ruler and inviting him to enter the mosque to perform the prayer, and also about who was the first ruler to be greeted in this fashion. Mālik said, 'I have no evidence that greeting the ruler in this fashion took place in the early days of Islam.'"

185. Yaḥyā said, "Mālik was asked about a muezzin who made the general call to prayer for a specific group of people and then waited, but when no one came, he made the immediate call to prayer and prayed alone. Then, after he had finished, some people came. Should he repeat his prayer with them? Mālik said, 'He should not repeat his prayer, and whoever came after he had finished should pray on his own.'"

186. Yaḥyā said, "Mālik was asked about a muezzin who made the general call to prayer for a group of people and then began to pray supererogatory prayers. The others wanted to perform the obligatory prayer without waiting for the muezzin to complete his supererogatory prayers. Accordingly, they invited someone else to make the immediate call to prayer. Mālik said, 'That is fine; anyone can perform the immediate call to prayer, not just the muezzin.'"

187. Yaḥyā said, "Mālik said, 'It has always been the case (*lam tazal*) that the general call to the Morning Prayer is made before dawn. As for the other prayers, we have never heard their call being made before their time has commenced.'"

Performance of the prayer is due; God is great, God is great; There is no god except God" (*Allāhu akbar, allāhu akbar; ashhadu an lā ilāha illā 'llāh; ashhadu anna Muḥammadan rasūlu 'llāh; ḥayy ʿalā 'l-ṣalāt; ḥayy ʿalā 'l-falāḥ; qad qāmat al-ṣalāt; allāhu akbar, allāhu akbar; lā ilāha illā 'llāh*).

188. According to Mālik, it reached him that the muezzin went to ʿUmar b. al-Khaṭṭāb and announced to him the Morning Prayer. He found ʿUmar asleep, so he said, "Prayer is better than sleep." ʿUmar then admonished him, saying that this phrase should be used only when making the general call to the Morning Prayer.[72]

189. According to Mālik, his paternal uncle Abū Suhayl b. Mālik reported that his father said, "Nothing that the people do today is familiar to me, except the general call to prayer."

190. According to Mālik, Nāfiʿ reported that ʿAbd Allāh b. ʿUmar heard the immediate call to prayer while he was in al-Baqīʿ, so he walked quickly to the Prophet's Mosque.[73]

Chapter 2. Making the General Call to Prayer While Traveling or without Having Performed Ablutions (*Wuḍūʾ*)

191. According to Mālik, Nāfiʿ reported that ʿAbd Allāh b. ʿUmar made the general call to prayer (*ṣalāt*) on a cold, windy night. He added the phrase, "Pray in your saddles!" Then he said, "The Messenger of God (pbuh) would tell the muezzin on cold and rainy nights to say, as part of the general call to prayer, 'Pray in your saddles!'"

192. According to Mālik, Nāfiʿ reported that when traveling, ʿAbd Allāh b. ʿUmar would make only the immediate call to prayer (*iqāma*), not the general call to prayer, except for the Morning Prayer (*ṣalāt al-ṣubḥ*), for which he would make both. He also said, "The general call to prayer is the responsibility of those who lead the public in the performance of congregational prayer."

193. According to Mālik, Hishām b. ʿUrwa reported that his father told him, "When you are traveling, you may make the general call to prayer and the immediate call to prayer, if you so wish. Otherwise, you may dispense with the general call and just make the immediate call."

194. Yaḥyā said, "I heard Mālik say, 'There is nothing objectionable in making the general call to prayer while mounted.'"

---

72 Sulaymān b. Khalaf al-Bājī, *al-Muntaqā sharḥ al-Muwaṭṭaʾ*, 7 vols. (Cairo: Dār al-Kitāb al-Islāmī, n.d.), 1:138. Our translation follows the view of the majority of the *Muwaṭṭaʾ*'s commentators, even though it is contrary to the apparent sense of the report, which implies that ʿUmar b. al-Khaṭṭāb introduced the phrase "Prayer is better than sleep" into the call to the Morning Prayer.

73 Al-Baqīʿ is the cemetery of Medina, located next to the Prophet's Mosque.

195. According to Mālik, Yaḥyā b. Saʿīd reported that Saʿīd b. al-Musayyab would say, "When someone prays alone in a desolate stretch of desert, an angel prays on his right and another on his left; and when he makes the general call to prayer and the immediate call to prayer (or just the immediate call to prayer),[74] an angelic host, arrayed like mountains, prays behind him."

Chapter 3. The Length of Pre-Dawn after the General Call to the Morning Prayer (*Ṣalāt al-Ṣubḥ*)

196. According to Mālik, ʿAbd Allāh b. Dīnār reported from ʿAbd Allāh b. ʿUmar that the Messenger of God (pbuh) said, "Bilāl calls to the Morning Prayer when it is still dark and before dawn has broken, so eat and drink until Ibn Umm Maktūm makes the general call to prayer again."

197. According to Mālik, Ibn Shihāb reported from Sālim b. ʿAbd Allāh that the Messenger of God (pbuh) said, "Bilāl calls to the Morning Prayer when it is still dark and before dawn has broken, so eat and drink until Ibn Umm Maktūm makes the general call to prayer again." He said, "Ibn Umm Maktūm was blind, and he would make the call to prayer only after someone told him, 'It is morning, it is morning.'"

Chapter 4. Commencement of the Prayer (*Ṣalāt*)

198. According to Mālik, Ibn Shihāb reported from Sālim b. ʿAbd Allāh, from ʿAbd Allāh b. ʿUmar, that when the Messenger of God (pbuh) commenced performance of the prayer, he would raise both of his hands to the level of his shoulders, and when he stood up after bowing, he raised them again in a similar manner and said, "God hears those who praise Him. All praise belongs to You, our Lord!"[75] He did not do that, however, when he stood up following prostration.

199. According to Mālik, Ibn Shihāb reported that ʿAlī b. Ḥusayn b. ʿAlī b. Abī Ṭālib[76] said, "The Messenger of God (pbuh) would magnify God (say "God is great," *Allāhu akbar*) each time he changed position in the prayer. That was how he always performed the prayer until he met God."

200. According to Mālik, Yaḥyā b. Saʿīd reported from Sulaymān b. Yasār that the Messenger of God (pbuh) would raise his hands during prayer.

---

74 The narrator is unsure whether the report specifies both calls or just the immediate call.

75 *Samiʿa 'llāhu li-man ḥamidah, rabbanā wa-laka 'l-ḥamd.*

76 He is also known as Zayn al-ʿĀbidīn (d. 95/713) and was the great-grandson of the Prophet (pbuh). The Shīʿa consider him their fourth *imām*.

201. According to Mālik, Ibn Shihāb reported from Abū Salama b. ʿAbd al-Raḥmān b. ʿAwf that Abū Hurayra would lead them in the performance of prayer and would magnify God each time he changed position. When he finished, he would say, "By God, none of you perform your prayers in the manner of the Messenger of God (pbuh) as much as I do."

202. According to Mālik, Ibn Shihāb reported from Sālim b. ʿAbd Allāh that ʿAbd Allāh b. ʿUmar would magnify God each time he changed position during the performance of prayer.

203. According to Mālik, Nāfiʿ reported that when ʿAbd Allāh b. ʿUmar commenced the prayer, he would raise his hands to his shoulders, but when he stood up from bowing, he raised them to a point below them.

204. According to Mālik, Abū Nuʿaym Wahb b. Kaysān reported from Jābir b. ʿAbd Allāh that Jābir taught them to magnify God when performing the prayer. He said, "He commanded us to magnify God each time that we changed position in prayer."

205. According to Mālik, Ibn Shihāb would say, "If a man joins the congregation in time to complete one cycle (*rakʿa*) of the prayer and magnifies God once, that one declaration of God's greatness is sufficient to render his performance of the prayer valid." Yaḥyā said, "Mālik said, 'That is only the case if he intended by that declaration (*takbīra*) the magnification of God that commences the prayer.'"

206. Yaḥyā said, "Mālik was asked about a man who joined the congregational prayer but forgot to magnify God both at the prayer's commencement and at the first instance of bowing. Then, after completing one cycle of the prayer, he remembered that he had not made a declaration magnifying God on either occasion. He therefore magnified God in the second cycle of the prayer. Mālik said, 'I prefer that he deems his prayer to have begun with the second cycle of the prayer, not the first. If, however, he began the prayer with the imam, forgot to make a declaration magnifying God at the beginning of the prayer, but then said it at the first instance of bowing, that is sufficient to render his performance of the prayer valid, provided that he intended that declaration to be the one that is said at the prayer's commencement.'"

207. Yaḥyā said, "Mālik said, regarding someone who prays by himself and forgets to magnify God when he commences his prayer, 'He must begin his prayer anew.'"

208. Mālik said, regarding an imam who forgets to commence the prayer by magnifying God and does not remember until he finishes the prayer, "I believe that he and the congregation must repeat performance of the prayer. Even if the congregants magnified God, they must nevertheless repeat the prayer."

Chapter 5. Recitation of the Quran in the Sunset Prayer (*Ṣalāt al-Maghrib*) and the Evening Prayer (*Ṣalāt al-ʿIshāʾ*)

209. According to Mālik, Ibn Shihāb reported from Muḥammad b. Jubayr b. Muṭʿim that his father said, "I heard the Messenger of God (pbuh) reciting from 'The Mount' (*al-Ṭūr*)[77] during the Sunset Prayer (*ṣalāt al-maghrib*)."

210. According to Mālik, Ibn Shihāb reported from ʿUbayd Allāh b. ʿAbd Allāh b. ʿUtba b. Masʿūd, from ʿAbd Allāh b. ʿAbbās, that Umm al-Faḍl bt. al-Ḥārith heard Ibn ʿAbbās reciting 'The Emissaries' (*al-Mursalāt*),[78] so she said to him, "My dear son, your recitation of this chapter reminded me that this was the last thing I heard the Messenger of God (pbuh) recite during the Sunset Prayer."

211. According to Mālik, Abū ʿUbayd, the freedman (*mawlā*) of Sulaymān b. ʿAbd al-Malik, reported from ʿAbbād b. Nusayy, from Qays b. al-Ḥārith, that Abū ʿAbd Allāh al-Ṣunābiḥī said, "I came to Medina during the caliphate of Abū Bakr al-Ṣiddīq and I prayed the Sunset Prayer behind him. In each of the first two cycles, he recited the *Fātiḥa* and a short chapter chosen from the *Mufaṣṣal* chapters of the Quran.[79] He then stood for the third cycle of the prayer. I inched up so close to him that my clothes almost touched his, and I heard him recite the *Fātiḥa* and then this verse: 'Our Lord! Do not cause our hearts to go astray after You have guided us, and grant us mercy from Your presence! You are certainly the Granter of Favor!'"[80]

212. According to Mālik, Nāfiʿ reported that ʿAbd Allāh b. ʿUmar, when performing by himself the daily prayers that consist of four cycles,[81] would recite in each cycle the *Fātiḥa* and another chapter from the Quran. Sometimes he would recite two or three chapters in one cycle of an obligatory prayer. In the first two cycles of the Sunset Prayer, he would also recite the *Fātiḥa* and one chapter of the Quran.

---

77 Chapter 52 of the Quran.

78 Chapter 77 of the Quran.

79 On the *Mufaṣṣal* chapters, see note 12 above.

80 *Āl ʿImrān*, 3:8.

81 These prayers are the Noon Prayer (*ṣalāt al-ẓuhr*), the Afternoon Prayer (*ṣalāt al-ʿaṣr*), and the Evening Prayer (*ṣalāt al-ʿishāʾ*).

213. According to Mālik, Yaḥyā b. Saʿīd reported from ʿAdī b. Thābit al-Anṣārī that al-Barāʾ b. ʿĀzib said, "I prayed the Evening Prayer with the Messenger of God (pbuh), and he recited 'By the Fig and the Olive' (*al-Tīn wa'l-zaytūn*)."[82]

Chapter 6. The Practice (*ʿAmal*) with Respect to Recitation of the Quran

214. According to Mālik, Nāfiʿ reported from Ibrāhīm b. ʿAbd Allāh b. Ḥunayn, from his father, from ʿAlī b. Abī Ṭālib, that the Messenger of God (pbuh) prohibited the wearing of silk-lined clothes and gold rings, or reading the Quran when bowing during performance of the prayer.[83]

215. According to Mālik, Yaḥyā b. Saʿīd reported from Muḥammad b. Ibrāhīm b. al-Ḥārith al-Taymī, from Abū Ḥāzim al-Tammār, from al-Bayāḍī, that the Messenger of God (pbuh) came across people loudly reciting the Quran while performing their prayers. He said, "A praying man is in intimate conversation with his Lord, so he should think carefully about the means he uses to converse with Him. Therefore, do not raise your voices above one another when reciting the Quran."

216. According to Mālik, Ḥumayd al-Ṭawīl reported that Anas b. Mālik said, "I stood in prayer behind Abū Bakr al-Ṣiddīq, ʿUmar, and ʿUthmān, and none of them recited 'In the Name of God, the Merciful, the Compassionate' when they commenced the prayer (*ṣalāt*)."

217. According to Mālik, his paternal uncle Abū Suhayl b. Mālik reported that his father said, "When ʿUmar performed the prayer, we could hear him reciting the Quran while we were in the house of Abū Jahm in the neighborhood of al-Balāṭ."[84]

218. According to Mālik, Nāfiʿ reported that if ʿAbd Allāh b. ʿUmar missed any portion of the congregational prayer in which the imam recited audibly from the Quran, he would, once the imam had finished performance of the prayer, stand and recite aloud for himself that portion of the prayer that he was making up.

219. According to Mālik, Yazīd b. Rūmān said, "I would pray standing next to Nāfiʿ b. Jubayr b. Muṭʿim, and he would nudge me when he faltered in his recition of the Quran, so I would jog his memory while we were in the midst of praying."

---

82 Chapter 95 of the Quran.

83 The first two prohibitions apply only to men.

84 Balāṭ was a place in Medina between the Prophet's Mosque and the market. Muḥammad Zakariyyā al-Kāndihlawī, *Awjaz al-masālik ilā Muwaṭṭa' Mālik*, 17 vols. (Damascus: Dār al-Qalam, 2003), 2:144.

Chapter 7. Recitation of the Quran in the Morning Prayer (*Ṣalāt al-Ṣubḥ*)

220. According to Mālik, Hishām b. ʿUrwa reported from his father that Abū Bakr al-Ṣiddīq performed the Morning Prayer and recited from 'The Cow' (*al-Baqara*)[85] in each of its two cycles (*rakʿa*).

221. According to Mālik, Hishām b. ʿUrwa reported from his father, ʿUrwa, that he heard ʿAbd Allāh b. ʿĀmir b. Rabīʿa say, "We performed the Morning Prayer behind ʿUmar b. al-Khaṭṭāb and he slowly recited 'Joseph' (*Yūsuf*) and 'The Pilgrimage' (*al-Ḥajj*)."[86] I, ʿUrwa, said, "By God, in that case he must have begun to pray at dawn's first light!" ʿAbd Allāh said, "Indeed."

222. According to Mālik, Yaḥyā b. Saʿīd and Rabīʿa b. Abī ʿAbd al-Raḥmān reported from al-Qāsim b. Muḥammad that al-Furāfiṣa b. ʿUmayr al-Ḥanafī said, "I would have never learned *Yūsuf* but for the fact that ʿUthmān b. ʿAffān recited it so many times during the Morning Prayer."

223. According to Mālik, Nāfiʿ reported that ʿAbd Allāh b. ʿUmar, when traveling, would recite, in each cycle of the Morning Prayer, the *Fātiḥa* and a chapter from the first ten *Mufaṣṣal* chapters.

Chapter 8. What Has Come Down regarding the *Fātiḥa*

224. According to Mālik, al-ʿAlāʾ b. ʿAbd al-Raḥmān b. Yaʿqūb reported that Abū Saʿīd, the freedman (*mawlā*) of ʿĀmir b. Kurayz, told him that the Messenger of God (pbuh) called out to Ubayy b. Kaʿb while the latter was performing his prayer (*ṣalāt*). When he finished his prayer, the Messenger of God (pbuh) caught up with Ubayy and put his hand on Ubayy's hand just as Ubayy was trying to leave through the Mosque's door. The Messenger of God (pbuh) said, "I implore you not to leave the mosque until you learn a chapter the like of which was not revealed in the Torah or the Gospels or the *Furqān*."[87] Ubayy said, "I slowed down in the hope of accomplishing that, so I said, 'Messenger of God, what is this chapter you have promised me?' He said, 'What do you recite when you commence your prayer? I recited to him, 'All praise belongs to God, Lord of the Worlds' (*Al-ḥamdu lillāhi rabb al-ʿālamīn*),[88] until I had completed the *Fātiḥa*. The Messenger of God (pbuh) said, 'It is this very chapter. These are the seven oft-repeated verses (*al-sabʿ al-mathānī*), the Great Recitation (*al-qurʾān al-ʿaẓīm*),[89] that I was given.'"

85 Chapter 2 of the Quran.

86 Chapters 12 and 22 of the Quran, respectively.

87 *Furqān* is another name for the Quran, and it means the criterion that separates truth from falsehood.

88 The first verse of the *Fātiḥa*.

89 According to Bājī, the phrase *al-qurʾān al-ʿaẓīm* refers specifically to the Quran's first chapter, the *Fātiḥa*, on account of its numerous virtues. The phrase *al-sabʿ al-mathānī wa'l-qurʾān al-ʿazīm* is a reference to *al-Ḥijr*, 15:87. Bājī, *al-Muntaqā*, 1:155.

225. Yaḥyā told me, from Mālik, from Wahb b. Kaysān, that he heard Jābir b. ʿAbd Allāh say, "Anyone who performs one cycle (*rakʿa*) of prayer without reciting therein the *Fātiḥa* has not prayed, unless he is praying behind an imam."

Chapter 9. Recitation of the Quran behind the Imam When He Recites Silently

226. According to Mālik, al-ʿAlāʾ b. ʿAbd al-Raḥmān b. Yaʿqūb reported that he heard Abū al-Sāʾib, the freedman (*mawlā*) of Hishām b. Zuhra, say, "I heard Abū Hurayra say, 'I heard the Messenger of God (pbuh) say, "If anyone prays without reciting the *Fātiḥa*, his prayer is incomplete; it is incomplete; it is incomplete."' I said, 'Abū Hurayra, sometimes I am standing behind the imam, so how can I recite it?' Abū Hurayra poked me in the arm and said, 'Recite it silently, you Persian! I indeed heard the Messenger of God (pbuh) say, "God, Blessed and Sublime is He, said, 'I have divided prayer between Myself and my servant into two halves, half for Me and half for My servant, and My servant gets what he has requested.'" The Messenger of God (pbuh) said, "Recite, all of you! The worshipper says, 'All praise belongs to God, Lord of the Worlds,' and God says, 'My servant has glorified Me.' The worshipper says, 'The Merciful, the Compassionate,' and God says, 'My servant has praised Me.' The servant says, 'King of the Day of Judgment,' and God says, 'My servant has exalted Me.' The servant says, 'Only You do we worship and only from You do we seek help,' and God says, 'This verse is between Me and My servant, and My servant shall have what he requests.' The servant then says, 'Guide us to the righteous path, the path of those whom You have blessed, not of those upon whom is Your wrath or those who are astray,' and God says, 'These verses are for My servant, and My servant shall have what he requests.'"'"

227. According to Mālik, Hishām b. ʿUrwa reported from his father that he would recite the Quran silently behind the imam in those prayers in which the imam does not recite audibly.

228. According to Mālik, Yaḥyā b. Saʿīd reported from Rabīʿa b. Abī ʿAbd al-Raḥmān that al-Qāsim b. Muḥammad would recite the Quran silently behind the imam in those prayers in which the imam does not recite audibly.

229. According to Mālik, Yazīd b. Rūmān reported that Nāfiʿ b. Jubayr b. Muṭʿim would recite the Quran silently behind the imam in those prayers in which the imam does not recite audibly. Yaḥyā said, "Mālik said, 'Of all the views that I have heard regarding this issue, that is the one I prefer most.'"

Chapter 10. Abstention from Recitation When Standing behind the Imam in Those Prayers in Which the Imam Recites Audibly

230. According to Mālik, Nāfiʿ reported that ʿAbd Allāh b. ʿUmar, when asked whether the congregants behind the imam should recite the Quran, said, "The imam's recitation is sufficient for the congregants, but anyone who prays alone should recite for himself." Nāfiʿ said, "ʿAbd Allāh b. ʿUmar did not recite from the Quran when he prayed behind an imam."

231. Yaḥyā said, "I heard Mālik say, 'The rule in our view (*al-amr ʿindanā*) is that one recites from the Quran silently while standing behind the imam in those prayers in which the imam does not recite audibly, and one refrains from recitation altogether in those prayers in which the imam recites audibly."

232. According to Mālik, Ibn Shihāb reported from Ibn Ukayma al-Laythī, from Abū Hurayra, that the Messenger of God (pbuh) concluded performance of a prayer (*ṣalāt*) in which he had recited from the Quran audibly and then said, "Did any of you recite along with me during the previous prayer?" A man said, "Yes, I did, Messenger of God." The Messenger of God (pbuh) said, "Indeed, I was saying to myself, 'It is as if there were something tugging at my recitation.'" Thereafter, the people refrained from reciting from the Quran along with the Messenger of God (pbuh) in those prayers in which the Messenger of God (pbuh) recited audibly.

Chapter 11. What Has Come Down regarding the Saying of "Amen" after the Imam

233. According to Mālik, Ibn Shihāb reported from Saʿīd b. al-Musayyab and also from Abū Salama b. ʿAbd al-Raḥmān that they both told Ibn Shihāb from Abū Hurayra that the Messenger of God (pbuh) said, "When the imam says 'Amen,' say 'Amen.' If it happens that someone says 'Amen' at the moment the angels say 'Amen,' his previous sins are forgiven." Ibn Shihāb said, "The Messenger of God (pbuh) would say *āmīn* (amen)."

234. According to Mālik, Sumayy, the freedman (*mawlā*) of Abū Bakr b. ʿAbd al-Raḥmān, reported from Abū Ṣāliḥ al-Sammān, from Abū Hurayra, that the Messenger of God (pbuh) said, "When the imam recites the last verse of the *Fātiḥa*, say 'Amen,' for whoever happens to say it when the angels say it will have his previous sins forgiven."

235. According to Mālik, Abū al-Zinād reported from al-Aʿraj, from Abū Hurayra, that the Prophet (pbuh) said, "If someone says 'Amen,' and the angels in Heaven say 'Amen' at the same time, his previous sins are forgiven."

236. According to Mālik, Sumayy, the freedman of Abū Bakr, reported from Abū Ṣāliḥ al-Sammān, from Abū Hurayra, that the Messenger of God (pbuh) said, "When the imam says, 'God listens to those who praise Him,' say, 'God, our Lord, to You belongs all praise,' for whoever says it the moment the angels say it will have his previous sins forgiven."

Chapter 12. The Practice (*ʿAmal*) with Respect to Sitting during Performance of the Prayer (*Ṣalāt*)[90]

237. According to Mālik, Muslim b. Abī Maryam reported that ʿAlī b. ʿAbd al-Raḥmān al-Muʿāwī said, "ʿAbd Allāh b. ʿUmar saw me playing with pebbles while I was performing the prayer. When he finished the prayer, he commanded me not to do that, and said, 'Do instead as the Messenger of God (pbuh) did.' I said, 'And what did the Messenger of God (pbuh) do?' He said, 'When he sat in prayer, he would put his right palm on his right thigh, making a fist with his fingers, and pointing with his index finger; and he would place his left palm on his left thigh.' ʿAbd Allāh said, 'That is what he would do.'"

238. According to Mālik, ʿAbd Allāh b. Dīnār reported that ʿAbd Allāh b. ʿUmar once sat next to a man who had squatted and crossed his legs to one side during a four-cycle (*rakʿa*) prayer. ʿAbd Allāh b. Dīnār heard ʿAbd Allāh b. ʿUmar reproach the man for his poor posture after he finished the prayer. The man said, "But you do the same thing!" ʿAbd Allāh b. ʿUmar replied, "Yes, but I am old and frail."

239. According to Mālik, Ṣadaqa b. Yasār reported from al-Mughīra b. Ḥakīm that he saw ʿAbd Allāh b. ʿUmar lean on the front part of his feet when he sat up after prostrating in the prayer. When he finished, someone asked him about that, and ʿAbd Allāh b. ʿUmar explained, "This is not the correct way to pray; I do this only because I am old and frail."

240. According to Mālik, ʿAbd al-Raḥmān b. al-Qāsim reported that ʿAbd Allāh b. ʿAbd Allāh b. ʿUmar informed him that he would see ʿAbd Allāh b. ʿUmar cross his legs in the sitting position of the prayer. He said, "I therefore did as he did, but I was young at the time, and ʿAbd Allāh b. ʿUmar forbade me to do that. He said, 'The correct way to perform the prayer is to raise your right foot and fold your left foot.'" ʿAbd Allāh said, "I said to him, 'But you yourself do that.' He said, 'My feet are too weak to bear me.'"

---

90 In the Muslim prayer, the worshipper sits down between prostrations, at the end of the second cycle (*rakʿa*) of the prayer, and at the end of the prayer's concluding cycle. The worshipper recites a short prayer while seated between prostrations, the *tashahhud*, the attestation of faith, while seated at the conclusion of the second and concluding cycles of the prayer. The testimony of faith consists of the statement "I testify that there is no god except God, and that Muḥammad is His servant and messenger."

241. According to Mālik, Yaḥyā b. Saʿīd reported that al-Qāsim b. Muḥammad showed them how to sit when reciting the attestation of faith (*tashahhud*). He raised his right foot and folded his left, and sat on his left haunch, not on his left foot. Then he said, "ʿAbd Allāh b. ʿAbd Allāh b. ʿUmar showed this to me, and he told me that his father would do that."

Chapter 13. The Attestation of Faith (*Tashahhud*) in the Prayer (*Ṣalāt*)

242. According to Mālik, Ibn Shihāb reported from ʿUrwa b. al-Zubayr, from ʿAbd al-Raḥmān b. ʿAbd al-Qārī,[91] that he heard ʿUmar b. al-Khaṭṭāb say from the pulpit, teaching the people the attestation of faith:

> Greetings belong to God; pure actions belong to God; good words and prayers belong to God. Peace be upon you, Prophet, and His mercy. Peace be upon us and upon God's righteous servants. I attest that there is no god except God, and I attest that Muḥammad is His servant and messenger.[92]

243. According to Mālik, Nāfiʿ reported that when ʿAbd Allāh b. ʿUmar performed the attestation of faith, he would say:

> In the name of God. Greetings belong to God; prayers belong to God; pure actions belong to God. Peace be upon the Prophet, and God's mercy and blessings. Peace be upon us and upon God's righteous servants. I attest that there is no god except God. I attest that Muḥammad is the Messenger of God.[93]

He would say this at the end of the first two cycles of prayer. When he completed the attestation of faith, he would invoke God in whatever manner suited him. When he sat at the end of his prayer, he repeated the attestation of faith in a like manner, except that he would begin with the attestation of faith and then would invoke God in whatever manner suited him. When he had completed the attestation of faith and he wanted to conclude the prayer, he would say, "Peace be upon the Prophet, and God's mercy and His blessings. Peace be upon us and on God's righteous servants." He would then say "Peace be upon you" to whomever was on his right side, and he would reply to the imam. If someone said "Peace be upon you" from his left side, he would reply to him.

---

91 The name Ibn ʿAbd al-Qārī means "son of a slave from the Qārī tribe of Kināna."

92 *Al-taḥiyyātu lillāh, al-zākiyātu lillāh, al-ṭayyibātu wa'l-ṣalawātu lillāh. Al-salāmu ʿalayka ayyuhā 'l-nabiyyu wa-raḥmatu 'llāhi wa-barakātuh. Al-salāmu ʿalaynā wa-ʿalā ʿibādi 'llāhi 'l-ṣāliḥīn. Ashhadu an lā ilāha illā 'llāhu wa-ashhadu anna Muḥammadan ʿabduhu wa-rasūluh.*

93 *Bismi 'llāh. Al-taḥiyyātu lillāh, al-ṣalawātu lillāh, al-zākiyātu lillāh. Al-salāmu ʿalā 'l-nabiyyi wa-raḥmatu 'llāhi wa-barakātuh. Al-salāmu ʿalaynā wa-ʿalā ʿibādi 'llāhi 'l-ṣāliḥīn. Shahidtu an lā ilāha illā 'llāh. Shahidtu anna Muḥammadan rasūlu 'llāh.*

244. According to Mālik, ʿAbd al-Raḥmān b. al-Qāsim reported from his father, from ʿĀʾisha, the wife of the Prophet (pbuh), that she would say in the attestation of faith:

> Greetings, good words, prayers, and pure actions belong to God. I attest that there is no god except God, alone without partner, and that Muḥammad is God's servant and messenger. Peace be upon you, Prophet, and God's mercy and His blessings. Peace be upon us and upon God's righteous servants.[94]

She would then conclude performance of the prayer and say, "Peace be upon you."

245. According to Mālik, Yaḥyā b. Saʿīd reported that al-Qāsim b. Muḥammad informed him that ʿĀʾisha, the wife of God's Prophet (pbuh), would say in the attestation of faith:

> Greetings, good words, prayers, and pure actions belong to God. I attest that there is no god except God, and that Muḥammad is God's servant and messenger. Peace be upon you, Prophet, and God's mercy and His blessings. Peace be upon us and upon God's righteous servants."

She would then conclude the prayer and say, "Peace be upon you."

246. According to Mālik, he asked Ibn Shihāb and Nāfiʿ, the freedman (*mawlā*) of Ibn ʿUmar, whether a man who joins a congregational prayer after the imam has already performed one of the prayer's cycles (*rakʿa*) should say the attestation of faith with the imam in the second and fourth cycles of that prayer, even though these cycles are, for him, the first and third. They both said, "Yes, he should say the attestation of faith with him." Yaḥyā said, "Mālik said, 'That is the rule among us (*dhālika al-amr ʿindanā*).'"

Chapter 14. What Someone Should Do If He Changes Positions in Prayer Prior to the Imam

247. According to Mālik, Muḥammad b. ʿAmr b. ʿAlqama reported from Malīḥ b. ʿAbd Allāh al-Saʿdī that Abū Hurayra said, "As for the one who changes positions in prayer prior to the imam, a demon has grabbed him by the forelock."

94 *Al-taḥiyyāt, al-ṭayyibāt, al-ṣalawāt, al-zākiyātu lillāh. Ashhadu an lā ilāha illā 'llāhu waḥdahu lā sharīka lahu wa-anna Muḥammadan ʿabdu 'llāhi wa-rasūluh. Al-salāmu ʿalayka ayyuhā 'l-nabiyyu wa-raḥmatu 'llāhi wa-barakātuh. Al-salāmu ʿalaynā wa-ʿalā ʿibādi 'llāhi 'l-ṣāliḥīn.*

248. Yaḥyā said, "Mālik said, regarding someone who mistakenly stands up before the imam has completed his bowing or prostration, 'The long-established ordinance (*al-sunna*)[95] with respect to this issue is that he should return to the imam's position and not wait for the imam to catch up with him. Whoever waits for the imam to catch up has erred in the performance of his prayer, because the Messenger of God (pbuh) said, "The position of imam was established only so that he would be followed; therefore, do not contravene what he does." Also, Abū Hurayra said, "As for the one who changes positions in prayer prior to the imam, a demon has grabbed him by the forelock."'"

Chapter 15. What Someone Should Do If He Mistakenly Concludes His Prayer after Two Cycles (*Rakʿa*)[96]

249. According to Mālik, Ayyūb b. Abī Tamīma al-Sakhtiyānī reported from Muḥammad b. Sīrīn, from Abū Hurayra, that the Messenger of God (pbuh) once finished the prayer after two cycles, and Dhū al-Yadayn[97] asked him, "Has the length of the prayer (*ṣalāt*) been reduced or did you forget to complete it, Messenger of God?" The Messenger of God (pbuh) said, "Is Dhū al-Yadayn correct?" The people said, "Yes!" So the Messenger of God (pbuh) stood up and prayed another two cycles and said, "Peace be upon you," to conclude the prayer.[98] Then, however, he magnified God (said "God is great," *Allāhu akbar*) and prostrated in his usual fashion (or slightly longer), then sat up, then magnified God again and prostrated in his usual fashion (or slightly longer), then sat up.

250. According to Mālik, Dāwūd b. al-Ḥuṣayn reported that Abū Sufyān, the freedman (*mawlā*) of Ibn Abī Aḥmad, said, "I heard Abū Hurayra say, 'The Messenger of God (pbuh) performed the Afternoon Prayer (*ṣalāt al-ʿaṣr*), finishing after completing only two cycles. Then Dhū al-Yadayn stood up and said, "Has the length of the prayer been reduced, Messenger of God, or did you forget to complete it?" The Messenger of God (pbuh) said, "Neither happened."

95 Mālik refers to this rule using the term *sunna* rather than the alternative term *amr*. We have translated *sunna* as "long-established ordinance" and *amr* as "rule" following the argument of Wymann-Landgraf, who concluded that when Mālik describes a rule as *sunna*, the rule is usually contrary to analogy and derived from historical precedent, whereas he uses *amr* for rules that are derived through legal interpretation (*ijtihād*) and are therefore consistent with analogy.

96 Of the five obligatory daily prayers, only the Morning Prayer (*ṣalāt al-ṣubḥ*) consists of only two cycles (*rakʿa*).

97 Literally, "the man with two hands." His actual name was al-Khirbāq b. ʿAmr, from the Hijazi tribe of Banū Sulaym.

98 The prayer is concluded when the worshipper or, in a group prayer, the imam turns to his right while seated and says, "Peace be upon you" (*al-salām ʿalaykum*).

Dhū al-Yadayn then said, "One or the other certainly happened, Messenger of God!" The Messenger of God (pbuh) then turned to the congregation and asked them, "Is Dhū al-Yadayn correct?" They replied, "Yes!" The Messenger of God (pbuh) therefore stood up and completed what remained of the prayer, and then, after completing performance of the prayer by saying "Peace be upon you," prostrated twice from a sitting position.'"

251. According to Mālik, Ibn Shihāb reported that Abū Bakr b. Sulaymān b. Abī Ḥathma said, "It reached me that the Messenger of God (pbuh) once performed only two cycles of either the Noon (*ṣalāt al-ẓuhr*) or the Afternoon Prayer, concluding the prayer after only two cycles. Then Dhū al-Shamālayn,[99] a man from the tribe of Banū Zuhra b. Kilāb, said, 'Has the length of the prayer been reduced, Messenger of God, or did you forget to complete it?' The Messenger of God (pbuh) said, 'Neither has the length of the prayer been reduced, nor did I forget to complete it.' Dhū al-Shamālayn, however, said, 'One of those certainly happened, Messenger of God!' The Messenger of God (pbuh) turned to the congregation and said, 'Is Dhū al-Yadayn correct?' They said, 'Yes!' The Messenger of God (pbuh) therefore completed what remained of the prayer and then said 'Peace be upon you' to conclude performance of the prayer."

252. According to Mālik, Ibn Shihāb reported that Saʿīd b. al-Musayyab and Salama b. ʿAbd al-Raḥmān reported something similar to the previous report.

253. Yaḥyā said, "Mālik said, 'Every instance of forgetfulness that reduces the length of the prayer is remedied by the performance of a prostration before the conclusion of the prayer; and every instance of forgetfulness that lengthens the prayer is remedied by the performance of a prostration after its conclusion.'"

Chapter 16. Completing the Prayer When the Worshipper Has Doubts about His Performance of It

254. According to Mālik, Zayd b. Aslam reported from ʿAṭā' b. Yasār that the Messenger of God (pbuh) said, "If someone has doubts about his performance of the prayer and is unable to remember whether he has performed three or four cycles, he should perform one additional cycle (*rakʿa*) and prostrate twice from a sitting position before concluding the prayer. If the additional cycle is actually the fifth, the two additional prostrations are the equivalent of an additional cycle, rendering the number of cycles even. If the additional

99 A marginal note on the principal source manuscript of the RME identifies Dhū al-Shamālayn as ʿUmayr b. ʿAbd ʿAmr, an ally of the Banū Zuhra. He died in the Battle of Badr.

cycle is actually the fourth, the two additional prostrations offend and humiliate Satan."

255. According to Mālik, ʿUmar b. Muḥammad b. Zayd reported from Sālim b. ʿAbd Allāh that ʿAbd Allāh b. ʿUmar would say, "If someone has doubts about his performance of the prayer, he should determine what he believes he has omitted from it and perform it. He should then perform two prostrations from a sitting position on account of his forgetfulness."

256. According to Mālik, ʿAfīf b. ʿAmr al-Sahmī reported that ʿAṭāʾ b. Yasār said, "I asked ʿAbd Allāh b. ʿAmr b. al-ʿĀṣī and Kaʿb al-Aḥbār[100] about someone who is unable to remember whether he has performed three or four cycles of the prayer. They both said, 'He should perform an additional cycle and then perform two prostrations from a sitting position.'"

257. According to Mālik, Nāfiʿ reported that ʿAbd Allāh b. ʿUmar, when asked about forgetfulness in prayer, said, "He should determine what he thinks he has omitted from his prayer and perform it."

Chapter 17. Mistakenly Standing Up after Completing the Prayer or after Two Cycles (*Rakʿa*)

258. According to Mālik, Ibn Shihāb reported from al-Aʿraj that ʿAbd Allāh b. Buḥayna said, "The Messenger of God (pbuh) led us in the performance of two cycles of prayer, then got up and did not sit down before beginning the third cycle.[101] The people stood up with him, and when he finished his prayer (*ṣalāt*), we waited for him to conclude it by saying 'Peace be upon you.' Instead, however, he magnified God (said "God is great," *Allāhu akbar*) and performed two prostrations from a sitting position, then concluded by saying 'Peace be upon you.'"

259. According to Mālik, Yaḥyā b. Saʿīd reported from ʿAbd al-Raḥmān b. Hurmuz that ʿAbd Allāh b. Buḥayna said, "Once the Messenger of God (pbuh)

100 Kaʿb al-Aḥbār, according to Muslim accounts, was a Jewish scholar from Yemen who converted to Islam after the death of the Prophet Muḥammad (pbuh). Accordingly, he is reckoned among the Followers (*tābiʿūn*) rather than among the Companions (*ṣaḥāba*) of the Prophet Muḥammad (pbuh). According to Muslim tradition, he was responsible for introducing many elements of Jewish lore into Muslim understandings of the Quran, particularly Quranic stories of the prophets. His name was Kaʿb b. Mātiʿ al-Ḥimyarī, and after his conversion to Islam he left Yemen and migrated to the Levant.

101 According to the rules of ritual prayer, after performing the second prostration at the conclusion of the second prayer cycle (*rakʿa*) the worshipper sits and recites the attestation of faith (*tashahhud*). The worshipper should not stand to begin performance of the third *rakʿa* of the prayer until he has completed this recitation. According to this report, the Prophet (pbuh) erroneously omitted the sitting and stood up immediately upon conclusion of the second prostration at the end of the second *rakʿa*.

led us in the Noon Prayer (*ṣalāt al-ẓuhr*), and he stood up after the first two cycles, without sitting down. After he finished his prayer, he performed two prostrations, and only then did he conclude the prayer by saying 'Peace be upon you.'"

260. Yaḥyā said, "Mālik said, regarding someone who makes a mistake in his prayer out of absent-mindedness by performing an additional prayer cycle after already completing four, meaning that he stands up, recites the *Fātiḥa*, and bows but then, upon standing up after bowing, realizes that he has already completed the prayer: 'Such a person should resume a sitting position and not perform any additional prostrations. If he has already performed one of the two prostrations, I do not think he should perform the other. After he has finished his prayer by saying "Peace be upon you," he should then perform two additional prostrations from a sitting position.'"

Chapter 18. Looking at Distracting Things during Performance of the Prayer (*Ṣalāt*)

261. According to Mālik, ʿAlqama b. Abī ʿAlqama reported that ʿĀʾisha, the wife of the Prophet (pbuh), said, "Abū Jahm b. Ḥudhayfa gave the Messenger of God (pbuh) a fine, patterned Levantine cloak, and he went to the mosque to pray while wearing it. When he finished praying, he said to me, 'Return this cloak to Abū Jahm. I glanced at its patterns during performance of the prayer, and they nearly distracted me.'"

262. According to Mālik, Hishām b. ʿUrwa reported from his father that the Messenger of God (pbuh) wore a fine, patterned cloak, then gave it to Abū Jahm and took from Abū Jahm a plain, rough cloak in exchange. Abū Jahm said, "Messenger of God, why?" The Messenger of God (pbuh) said, "Because I looked at its patterns during prayer."

263. According to Mālik, ʿAbd Allāh b. Abī Bakr reported that Abū Ṭalḥa al-Anṣārī was praying in his orchard of date palms when a wild pigeon began flying to and fro, trying to find a way out. Pleased at the sight, he permitted his eyes to follow the bird as it fluttered around for a while. Then, when he set his mind back to his prayer, he found that he could not remember how much of it he had already completed. He said to himself, "This property of mine has surely become a trial for me," so he went to the Messenger of God (pbuh) and mentioned to him the trial that had befallen him on account of his orchard. He said, "Messenger of God! I freely give this orchard of mine to God as a gift, so dispose of it as you wish."

264. According to Mālik, ʿAbd Allāh b. Abī Bakr reported that a Medinese[102] man was praying in an orchard of his in the neighborhood of the Quff, a valley in Medina, during date season, and the branches of the palm trees were hanging down, laden with dates. He glanced at them, and the sight of the abundant fruit delighted him. When he set his mind back to his prayer, he found that he could not remember how much of his prayer he had already completed. He said to himself, "This property of mine has surely become a trial for me," whereupon he went to ʿUthmān b. ʿAffān, who was the caliph at that time, and mentioned to him what had happened. He said, "My orchard is a gift, so use it for any godly purpose." ʿUthmān b. ʿAffān sold it for 50,000, so that property became known as "The Fifty."

102 We use the adjective "Medinese" for the Arabic term *anṣār*, literally, "helpers," which refers to the Arabs who lived in Medina before the immigration of the Prophet (pbuh) and embraced Islam. They hailed from the tribes of Aws and Khazraj, but when they embraced Islam after inviting the Prophet Muḥammad (pbuh) to move there from Mecca, they became known as al-Anṣār to distinguish them from the Meccans and other non-Medinese Arabs who immigrated to Medina and who were known as the Emigrants (*muhājirūn*). Not all the Medinese embraced Islam immediately upon the Prophet's arrival to the town.

Book 4
Forgetfulness in Prayer (*Sahw*)

Chapter 1. The Practice (*ʿAmal*) with Respect to Forgetfulness in Prayer

265. According to Mālik, Ibn Shihāb reported from Abū Salama b. ʿAbd al-Raḥmān b. ʿAwf, from Abū Hurayra, that the Messenger of God (pbuh) said, "Whenever a person stands to pray, Satan comes to him and confuses him so that he is unable to recall how much he has prayed. Whoever finds himself in that situation should perform two prostrations from a sitting position."

266. According to Mālik, it reached him that the Messenger of God (pbuh) said, "I forget (or 'I am made to forget')[103] in order that I may establish a precedent."

267. According to Mālik, it reached him that a man asked al-Qāsim b. Muḥammad, "When I perform my prayers (*ṣalāt*), my imagination gets the better of me, and as a result I have no confidence regarding how much I have prayed." Al-Qāsim replied, "Continue praying, for these doubts will never cease. Even when you finish praying, you will say to yourself, 'I haven't completed my prayer.'"

103 The commentators on the *Muwaṭṭaʾ* disagree as to the meaning of the alternative phrases in this report. Some say that the narrator was not sure which of the two phrases the Prophet used, whereas others contend that the Prophet intentionally used both, because both situations occurred.

Book 5
The Book of the Friday Congregational Prayer (*Ṣalāt al-Jumuʿa*)

Chapter 1. The Practice (*ʿAmal*) with Respect to Bathing (*Ghusl*) for the Friday Congregational Prayer (*Ṣalāt al-Jumuʿa*)

268. According to Mālik, Sumayy, the freedman (*mawlā*) of Abū Bakr b. ʿAbd al-Raḥmān, reported from Abū Ṣāliḥ, from Abū Hurayra, that the Messenger of God said, "Whoever bathes on Friday as he would on account of ritual preclusion (*janāba*) and then sets out to the Friday Congregational Prayer in the first part of the day, it is as if he has offered a camel as a charitable sacrifice; if he sets out in the second part of the day, it is as if he has offered a cow as a charitable sacrifice; if he sets out in the third part of the day, it is as if he has offered an adult ram as a charitable sacrifice; if he sets out in the fourth part of the day, it is as if he has offered a hen as a charitable sacrifice; and if he sets out in the fifth part of the day, it is as if he has offered an egg as a charitable sacrifice. Then, when the imam comes to preach, the angels attend and listen to the lesson."

269. According to Mālik, Saʿīd b. Abī Saʿīd al-Maqburī reported that Abū Hurayra would say, "Bathing on Friday is obligatory for every male who has reached puberty, just as bathing to remove the state of ritual preclusion is obligatory."[104]

270. According to Mālik, Ibn Shihāb reported that Sālim b. ʿAbd Allāh said, "One of the Companions of the Messenger of God (pbuh) entered the Prophet's Mosque on Friday while ʿUmar b. al-Khaṭṭāb was delivering the sermon. ʿUmar said to the man, 'What time do you think it is?' The man said, 'Commander of the Faithful, I was in the market, and when I heard the general call to prayer (*adhān*), I came immediately, stopping only to perform ablutions.' ʿUmar said, 'Ablutions, when you know that the Messenger of God (pbuh) commended bathing on Friday?'"

---

104 The four schools of Sunnī jurisprudence agree that bathing is recommended but not obligatory for attending the Friday prayer.

271. According to Mālik, Ṣafwān b. Sulaym reported from ʿAṭā' b. Yasār, from Abū Saʿīd al-Khudrī, that the Messenger of God (pbuh) said, "Bathing on Friday is obligatory for every male who has reached puberty."

272. According to Mālik, Nāfiʿ reported from Ibn ʿUmar that the Messenger of God (pbuh) said, "Whoever attends the Friday Congregational Prayer should first bathe."

273. Yaḥyā said, "Mālik said, 'Whoever bathes early in the day on Friday, intending that bath to satisfy his obligation to bathe for the Friday Congregational Prayer, is not relieved of that obligation unless he bathes and departs directly for the mosque. That is because the Messenger of God said in Ibn ʿUmar's report, "Whoever attends the Friday Congregational Prayer should first bathe."'"

274. Mālik said, "If someone bathes on Friday, early or late, with the intention of bathing for the Friday Congregational Prayer, and something happens that invalidates his ablutions, he should repeat his ablutions, but he need not bathe again."

Chapter 2. What Has Come Down regarding Listening While the Imam Preaches on Friday

275. According to Mālik, Abū al-Zinād reported from al-Aʿraj, from Abū Hurayra, that the Messenger of God (pbuh) said, "If you say to your companion, 'Listen!' (while the imam is preaching on Friday),[105] you have spoken out of order."

276. According to Mālik, Ibn Shihāb reported that Thaʿlaba b. Abī Mālik al-Quraẓī told him that it was their practice during the time of ʿUmar b. al-Khaṭṭāb to pray supplementary prayers on Friday until ʿUmar came out. Once he came out and sat on the pulpit and the muezzin made the general call to prayer (*adhān*), they would stop praying. Thaʿlaba said, "We would sit and talk. When the general call to prayer was finished and ʿUmar b. al-Khaṭṭāb stood to give the sermon, we listened, and none of us would say a word." Ibn Shihāb said, "The entry of the imam brings to an end all other prayers, and his speech preempts all other conversations."

277. According to Mālik, Abū al-Naḍr, the freedman (*mawlā*) of ʿUmar b. ʿUbayd Allāh, reported from Mālik b. Abī ʿĀmir that ʿUthmān b. ʿAffān would regularly say in his sermon, rarely omitting it, "When the imam begins to preach on Friday, listen and pay attention. Certainly, the reward of someone

105 The parenthetical words are Mālik's, not the Prophet Muḥammad's (pbuh), according to a marginal note on the principal source manuscript of the RME.

who pays attention but cannot hear is similar to that of one who pays attention and hears. When the immediate call to prayer (*iqāma*) is made, straighten the rows and align your shoulders, because straightening the rows is part of perfecting the prayer." ʿUthmān b. ʿAffān would not begin the prayer by magnifying God (saying "God is great," *Allāhu akbar*) until the men to whom he had delegated the task of straightening the rows returned to him and reported that the rows were straight. Only then would he begin the prayer and magnify God.

278. According to Mālik, Nāfiʿ reported that ʿAbd Allāh b. ʿUmar saw two men talking while the imam preached on Friday, so he tossed some pebbles at them in order to quiet them.

279. According to Mālik, it reached him that a man sneezed while the imam was preaching on Friday. A man sitting next to him invoked God's mercy on the man who sneezed. The man later asked Saʿīd b. al-Musayyab whether that had been appropriate. Saʿīd prohibited the man from doing so, saying, "Don't do it again."

280. According to Mālik, he once asked Ibn Shihāb about talking on Friday during the interval after the imam descends from the pulpit but before he commences the prayer by magnifying God. Ibn Shihāb said, "There is nothing objectionable in that."

Chapter 3. What Has Come Down regarding Someone Who Joins the Friday Congregational Prayer (*Ṣalāt al-Jumuʿa*) in Time to Complete One Cycle (*Rakʿa*)

281. According to Mālik, Ibn Shihāb would say, "If someone joins the Friday Congregational Prayer in time to complete one cycle, he should pray an additional cycle." Yaḥyā said, "Mālik said that Ibn Shihāb said, 'That is the long-established ordinance (*al-sunna*).'"

282. Yaḥyā said, "Mālik said, 'That rule is what I found the learned people of our town following (*wa-ʿalā dhālika adraktu ahl al-ʿilm bi-baladinā*). That is because the Messenger of God (pbuh) said, "Whoever performs one cycle of prayer with the imam has perfomed the prayer with the imam."'"

283. Mālik said, regarding someone who is stuck in the midst of a great crowd during the Friday Congregational Prayer and is able to bow but cannot prostrate, either until the imam stands after performing his prostrations or until the imam has finished the prayer in its entirety, "He should prostrate when the people stand, if he is able to do so, provided that he has already bowed; however, if he is unable to prostrate at all until the imam has finished the prayer, then I prefer that he begin performance of his prayer anew and perform the Noon Prayer (*ṣalāt al-ẓuhr*), with four complete cycles."

Chapter 4. What Has Come Down regarding Someone Whose Nose Bleeds during the Friday Congregational Prayer (*Ṣalāt al-Jumuʿa*)

284. Yaḥyā said, "Mālik said, 'Whoever has a nosebleed on Friday while the imam is preaching and leaves, but does not return until the imam has finished the prayer, should instead pray the four cycles of the Noon Prayer.'"[106]

285. Yaḥyā said, "Mālik said, regarding someone who performs one cycle (*rakʿa*) of the Friday Congregational Prayer with the imam and then experiences a nosebleed, so he leaves and comes back, but only after the imam has completed the two cycles of the Friday Congregational Prayer in their entirety, 'He should complete the performance of the Friday Congregational Prayer from where he left off and perform the second cycle on his own, as long as he did not speak in the interval between the time he left the prayer and his return.'"

286. Mālik said, "Someone who suffers a nosebleed or any other condition that forces him to leave the Friday Congregational Prayer prior to its completion does not need the imam's permission to do so."

Chapter 5. What Has Come Down regarding the Meaning of the Word *Saʿy* in Connection with the Friday Congregational Prayer (*Ṣalāt al-Jumuʿa*)

287. According to Mālik, he asked Ibn Shihāb about the words of God, Blessed and Sublime is He, "When the call to prayer on Friday is proclaimed, *hasten earnestly* (*isʿaw*) to remember God."[107] Ibn Shihāb said, "ʿUmar b. al-Khaṭṭāb would recite it thus: 'When the call to prayer on Friday is proclaimed, *go* to remember God.'"[108]

288. Mālik said, "The meaning of *saʿy* in the Book of God is limited to 'deeds and actions.' God, Blessed and Sublime is He, says, 'And when he turns

106 In other words, the worshipper should pray the regular Noon Prayer (*ṣalāt al-ẓuhr*), which consists of four cycles (*rakʿa*), rather than make up the Friday Congregational Prayer, which consists of the sermon and only two cycles of prayer.

107 *Al-Jumuʿa*, 62:9.

108 The verse as found in the written rendition of the Quran uses the second-person masculine plural imperative of the verb *saʿā, isʿaw*, which means "to run" or "to hasten"; but according to Ibn Shihāb's report as narrated by Mālik, ʿUmar b. al-Khaṭṭāb recited this verse using the second-person masculine plural imperative of the verb *maḍā, imḍaw*, which means simply "to go," without the sense of haste. Early sources attribute to various Companions nonstandard readings of the Quran that are not consistent with its written text (*muṣḥaf*). These nonstandard readings are not part of the recited text of the Quran, but they may be used as evidence of the text's intended meaning.

away, he acts (*sa'ā*) in the land,'[109] and He says, 'But as for him who comes to you, acting (*yas'ā*) out of fear (of God),'[110] and He says, 'Then he turned his back, acting (*yas'ā*),'[111] and He says, 'Indeed, your deeds (*sa'yakum*) are diverse.'[112] The *sa'y* that God mentions in His Book, therefore, does not mean 'running on the feet' or 'severe exertion.' He intended specifically 'deeds and actions.'"

Chapter 6. What Has Come Down regarding the Ruler (*Imām*)[113] Who, While Traveling, Alights in a Village on Friday (*Jumu'a*)

289. Yaḥyā said, "Mālik said, 'If the ruler (*imām*) is traveling and alights in a town in which the Friday Congregational Prayer (*ṣalāt al-jumu'a*) is obligatory, and he leads the people there in the Friday prayer and preaches the sermon, the people of that village, and everyone else present, should perform the Friday Congregational Prayer with him."

290. Mālik said, "If the ruler, while traveling, gathers the people to perform the Friday Congregational Prayer in a village in which that prayer is not obligatory, it is not permissible for him to pray the Friday Congregational Prayer there, nor is it permissible for the villagers or for anyone else present there. The villagers and whoever else is present there who is not traveling should instead perform the Noon Prayer (*ṣalāt al-ẓuhr*) in its entirety."

291. Yaḥyā said, "Mālik said, 'The traveler is not eligible to pray the Friday Congregational Prayer. Instead, he performs two cycles of the Noon Prayer.'"

Chapter 7. What Has Come Down regarding the Special Moment on Friday

292. According to Mālik, Abū al-Zinād reported from al-A'raj, from Abū Hurayra, that the Messenger of God (pbuh) mentioned Friday and said, "There is a moment on Friday when God grants to any Muslim who is standing in prayer, beseeching Him for something at that very moment, whatever he asks." The Messenger of God (pbuh) used his hand to indicate how fleeting that moment is.

---

109 *Al-Baqara*, 2:205. The full text of the verse is *Wa-idhā tawallā sa'ā fī 'l-arḍi li-yufsida fīhā wa-yuhlika 'l-ḥartha wa'l-nasla wa'llāhu lā yuḥibbu 'l-fasād* ("When he turns away, he acts to corrupt the earth and to destroy crops and people; and God does not love destruction").

110 *'Abasa*, 80:8–9. The full text of the verses is *Wa-ammā man jā'aka yas'ā wa-huwa yakhshā.*

111 *Al-Nāzi'āt*, 79:22. The full text of the verse is *Thumma adbara yas'ā*. The next verse reads *Fa-ḥashara fa-nāda*, which means "So he called out and gathered his forces," referring to the Pharaoh.

112 *Al-Layl*, 92:4. The full text of the verse is *Inna sa'yakum la-shattā.*

113 In this context, *imām* does not mean a prayer leader but rather a public official, such as the caliph or the governor.

293. According to Mālik, Yazīd b. ʿAbd Allāh b. al-Hādī reported from Muḥammad b. Ibrāhīm b. al-Ḥārith al-Taymī, from Abū Salama b. ʿAbd al-Raḥmān, that Abū Hurayra said, "I went to Mount Sinai and there met Kaʿb al-Aḥbār. I sat with him, and he related to me teachings of the Torah, and I related to him teachings of the Messenger of God (pbuh). One of the things I told him was that the Messenger of God (pbuh) said, 'The most auspicious day upon which the sun rises is Friday. Adam was created on that day, and on it he fell from the Garden to the Earth; repentance was granted to him on that day, and on that day he died. The Hour of Divine Judgment is on that day. Every moving creature is attentive on Friday, from morning to sunset, in fear of the Hour, except for jinn and humans. There is a moment of time on Friday when God grants to any Muslim who is standing in prayer, beseeching Him for something at that very moment, whatever he asks.' Kaʿb said, 'That is one day every year.' I said, 'No, it is every Friday.' Kaʿb searched the Torah and said, 'The Messenger of God (pbuh) has spoken the truth.' I later met Baṣra b. Abī Baṣra al-Ghifārī, who said, 'Where are you coming from?' I said, 'From Mount Sinai.' Baṣra said, 'Had I seen you before you set out on your journey, you would never have left. I heard the Messenger of God (pbuh) say, "No one should set out on the back of a camel[114] to any mosque save for three: the Sacred Mosque (*al-masjid al-ḥarām*) of Mecca, this mosque of mine in Medina, or the Mosque of Jerusalem.[115]"' Later I met ʿAbd Allāh b. Salām.[116] I told him about my meeting with Kaʿb al-Aḥbār and what I had related to him regarding Friday. I also told him that Kaʿb had said, 'That is one day every year.' ʿAbd Allāh b. Salām said, 'Kaʿb was mistaken.' I said, 'Kaʿb later searched the Torah carefully and said, "Indeed, it is every Friday."' ʿAbd Allāh b. Salām said, 'Kaʿb has spoken the truth.' Then ʿAbd Allāh b. Salām said, 'I know which portion of the day it is.' I said, 'In that case, tell me, and don't keep it from me.' ʿAbd Allāh b. Salām said, 'It is the last moments of Friday.' I then asked, 'How can it be the last moments of Friday, when the Messenger of God (pbuh) said, "If a Muslim is standing in prayer, beseeching Him for something at that very moment?" That is not a time of prayer.' ʿAbd Allāh b. Salām said, 'Didn't the Messenger of God (pbuh) say, "Anyone who sits, awaiting the time of prayer, is in prayer until he prays"?' I said, 'Certainly.' He said, 'That is it, then.'"

114 The implication is that no conveyance should be used because one should go to the nearest possible mosque.

115 The Arabic text provides two different names for Jerusalem, *Īliyāʾ* and *Bayt al-Maqdis*. The Arabic version includes the gloss *yashukku*, meaning that the narrator is unsure which word was used for Jerusalem in the original report attributed to Abū Hurayra. It is unclear, however, which narrator this is.

116 ʿAbd Allāh b. Salām was a prominent Medinese Jew who converted to Islam during the Prophet Muḥammad's lifetime.

Chapter 8. Physical Appearance, Trampling over People in the Mosque, and Facing the Imam on Friday

294. According to Mālik, Yaḥyā b. Saʿīd reported that it reached him that the Messenger of God (pbuh) said, "There is nothing objectionable in having two garments that are worn only for the Friday Congregational Prayer (*ṣalāt al-jumuʿa*) in addition to the two garments one wears daily for work."

295. According to Mālik, Nāfiʿ reported that ʿAbd Allāh b. ʿUmar would set out for the Friday Congregational Prayer only after applying oil to his hair and perfume to his body, unless he was in the consecrated state (*muḥrim*) for the performance of either the Pilgrimage (*ḥajj*) or the Visitation (*ʿumra*).[117]

296. According to Mālik, ʿAbd Allāh b. Abī Bakr b. Ḥazm reported from someone who related it to him that Abū Hurayra would say, "It is better for someone to pray on the lava field outside of Medina than to sit in the mosque waiting for the imam to appear to deliver the sermon and then, when he does appear, to trample over people to reach the front rows."

297. Yaḥyā said, "Mālik said, 'The long-established ordinance among us (*al-sunna ʿindanā*) is that everyone faces the imam on Friday when he intends to give the sermon, whether they be seated in front of the imam, facing the direction of prayer (*qibla*),[118] or elsewhere."

Chapter 9. Recitation of the Quran in the Friday Congregational Prayer (*Ṣalāt al-Jumuʿa*), Sitting with One's Knees Drawn and Supported,[119] and Missing the Friday Congregational Prayer without an Excuse

298. According to Mālik, Ḍamra b. Saʿīd al-Māzinī reported that ʿUbayd Allāh b. ʿAbd Allāh b. ʿUtba b. Masʿūd said that al-Ḍaḥḥāk b. Qays asked al-Nuʿmān b. Bashīr, "What would the Messenger of God (pbuh) recite in the second

---

117 Mālik discusses the special rules regarding what a pilgrim may wear and use for personal hygiene and grooming, including perfume, in detail in the Book of Pilgrimage below.

118 In ordinary circumstances, the congregants are seated in front of the imam as he stands on the pulpit and gives the sermon during the Friday Congregational Prayer. The imam is positioned with his back to the direction of prayer, facing the congregants. Accordingly, the congregants are typically seated facing the imam and the direction of prayer (*qibla*). In some mosques, however, the pulpit may be so far from the *qibla* wall of the mosque that some congregants are seated behind the pulpit, not in front of it. In this case, according to Mālik, these congregants should turn and face the imam rather than continue facing the direction of prayer.

119 The title of this section mentions *iḥtibāʾ*, translated here as "sitting with one's knees drawn and supported," but the section contains no narrations about this practice despite the title. Zurqānī, *Sharḥ al-Zurqānī*, 1:408.

cycle of the Friday prayer after reciting 'The Congregation' (*al-Jumuʿa*)[120] in the first?" He said, "He would recite 'The Enveloping' (*al-Ghāshiya*)."[121]

299. According to Mālik, Ṣafwān b. Sulaym—and Mālik said, "I do not know whether this is from the Prophet (pbuh) or not"—said, "God places a seal upon the heart of anyone who misses the Friday Congregational Prayer three times without an excuse or illness."

300. According to Mālik, Jaʿfar b. Muḥammad reported from his father, "The Messenger of God (pbuh) would give two sermons during the Friday Congregational Prayer and would sit down between them."[122]

---

120 Chapter 62 of the Quran.

121 Chapter 88 of the Quran.

122 Jaʿfar b. Muḥammad, also known as Jaʿfar al-Ṣādiq (d. 148/765), was the great-great-great-grandson of the Prophet (pbuh) and the sixth *imām* of the Shīʿa. His father is Muḥammad b. ʿAlī Zayn al-ʿĀbidīn, known as Muḥammad al-Bāqir (d. 114/733), the fifth *imām* of the Shīʿa.

Book 6
The Book of Prayer (*Ṣalāt*) during Ramadan

Chapter 1. Encouraging People to Perform Prayers (*Ṣalāt*) during Ramadan

301. According to Mālik, Ibn Shihāb reported from ʿUrwa b. al-Zubayr, from ʿĀʾisha, the wife of the Prophet (pbuh), that the Messenger of God (pbuh) prayed in the mosque one night, and some people performed their prayers behind him. The next night he prayed in the mosque, and a good crowd of people showed up. They gathered again on the third and fourth nights, but the Messenger of God (pbuh) did not join them. In the morning, he said to them, "I saw what you did, and the only thing that stopped me from joining you was my fear that it would become obligatory for you." That was in Ramadan.

302. According to Mālik, Ibn Shihāb reported from Abū Salama b. ʿAbd al-Raḥmān b. ʿAwf, from Abū Hurayra, "The Messenger of God (pbuh) encouraged people to pray during the nights of Ramadan without ever definitively ordering it. He would say, 'Whoever spends the night in prayer during Ramadan, having faith in God and seeking reward exclusively from Him, shall have all his prior sins forgiven.'" Ibn Shihāb said, "When the Messenger of God (pbuh) died, that was still the case, and it continued in that fashion throughout the caliphate of Abū Bakr and for a period of time in the beginning of ʿUmar b. al-Khaṭṭāb's caliphate."

Chapter 2. What Has Come Down regarding Prayer at Night during Ramadan

303. According to Mālik, Ibn Shihāb reported from ʿUrwa b. al-Zubayr that ʿAbd al-Raḥmān b. ʿAbd al-Qārī said, "I went with ʿUmar b. al-Khaṭṭāb to the Prophet's Mosque in Ramadan, and people were scattered and spread out in groups, one man or another praying by himself and groups of people performing their prayers (*ṣalāt*) behind different individuals. ʿUmar said, 'By God, I certainly believe that were I to bring everyone together into one group behind one reciter, it would be better.' So he gathered them all into one group behind Ubayy b. Kaʿb." ʿAbd al-Raḥmān said, "I then went out with him to the mosque on another night, and the people were praying together behind one reciter. ʿUmar said, 'What a blessed innovation this is! But that part of the night that you miss while you sleep is more virtuous than that part of the night during which you pray,' meaning the last part of the night—for people would pray in the first part of the night."

304. According to Mālik, Muḥammad b. Yūsuf reported that al-Sāʾib b. Yazīd said, "ʿUmar b. al-Khaṭṭāb ordered Ubayy b. Kaʿb and Tamīm al-Dayrī[123] to lead the people in prayer and to perform eleven cycles (*rakʿa*)."[124] Al-Sāʾib b. Yazīd said, "The reciter of the Quran would recite from the moderately long chapters of the Quran (the *Miʾūn*)[125] to the point that we would have to lean on our staves because of exhaustion from standing for so long in prayer. We would not leave until the break of dawn."

305. According to Mālik, Yazīd b. Rūmān said, "During the time of ʿUmar b. al-Khaṭṭāb, people would pray twenty-three cycles during the night prayer in Ramadan."

306. According to Mālik, Dāwūd b. al-Ḥuṣayn reported that he heard al-Aʿraj say, "It was always the case in my experience that people cursed their enemies during Ramadan." He said, "The reciter of the Quran would recite 'The Cow' (*al-Baqara*)[126] in eight cycles, and if he finished it in twelve cycles, people would think he had made the prayer easy."

307. According to Mālik, ʿAbd Allāh b. Abī Bakr said, "I heard my father say, 'After finishing the nighttime prayer during Ramadan we would urge the servants to hurry with the preparation of food out of fear that dawn would break.'"

308. According to Mālik, Hishām b. ʿUrwa reported from his father that Abū ʿAmr Dhakwān, a slave of ʿĀʾisha, the wife of the Messenger of God (pbuh), whom she manumitted upon her death, would stand in prayer and recite the Quran for her during Ramadan."

---

123 Narrators of the *Muwaṭṭa*ʾ other than Yaḥyā b. Yaḥyā call him "Tamīm al-Dārī," not "Tamīm al-Dayrī."

124 Mālik's narration of this report is unique in specifying eleven cycles; other narrations have twenty-one.

125 Literally "the hundreds," these verses begin with chapter 19 of the Quran (*Maryam*) and contain approximately one hundred verses each. Zurqānī, *Sharḥ al-Zurqānī*, 1:420.

126 The second and longest chapter of the Quran, with 286 verses.

Book 7
The Book of the Night Prayer (*Ṣalāt al-Layl*)

Chapter 1. What Has Come Down regarding the Night Prayer (*Ṣalāt al-Layl*)

309. According to Mālik, Muḥammad b. al-Munkadir reported from Saʿīd b. Jubayr that a man agreeable to him told him that ʿĀʾisha, the wife of the Prophet (pbuh), told him that the Messenger of God (pbuh) said, "If anyone regularly performs prayer during the night but is sometimes overcome by sleep, God grants him the reward for the prayer he missed, and his sleep is a gift from God."

310. According to Mālik, Abū al-Naḍr, the freedman (*mawlā*) of ʿUmar b. ʿUbayd Allāh, reported from Abū Salama b. ʿAbd al-Raḥmān that ʿĀʾisha, the wife of the Prophet (pbuh), said, "I would be sleeping next to the Messenger of God (pbuh) with my legs outstretched, lying between him and the direction of prayer (*qibla*). Accordingly, when he prostrated, he would nudge me and I would fold my legs, and when he stood up, I would stretch them out again." She said, "In those days, houses did not have lamps."

311. According to Mālik, Hishām b. ʿUrwa reported from his father, from ʿĀʾisha, the wife of the Prophet (pbuh), that the Messenger of God (pbuh) said, "When someone becomes drowsy during the performance of prayer, he should lie down until he is rested. When someone prays while he is drowsy, he may not realize what he is saying. He may intend to seek forgiveness for himself but may end up cursing himself."

312. According to Mālik, Ismāʿīl b. Abī Ḥakīm reported that it reached him that the Messenger of God (pbuh) heard a woman praying at night, so he said, "Who is that?" Someone said, "It is al-Ḥawlāʾ bt. Tuwayt; she does not sleep at night." The Messenger of God (pbuh) disapproved, and it was clear from his face. He then said, "God, Blessed and Sublime is He, does not weary of rewarding good deeds before you grow weary of performing them. Therefore, only undertake for yourselves rites that you can reasonably sustain."

313. According to Mālik, Zayd b. Aslam reported from his father that during the night ʿUmar b. al-Khaṭṭāb would pray as much as he could,[127] but when the last hours of the night came, he would rouse his household for prayer, saying to them, "The prayer! The prayer!" Then he would recite the verse "Summon your family to pray, and be constant therein. We ask no sustenance from you; rather, we provide it for you, and the reward of the Hereafter is for righteousness."[128]

314. According to Mālik, it reached him that Saʿīd b. al-Musayyab would say, "Sleep before the Evening Prayer (*ṣalāt al-ʿishāʾ*) should be avoided, as should conversation afterward."

315. According to Mālik, it reached him that ʿAbd Allāh b. ʿUmar would say, "Voluntary prayers, whether performed during the day or during the night (*ṣalāt al-layl*), are performed in pairs of cycles (*rakʿa*), and each pair of cycles should be concluded by saying 'Peace be upon you.'" Yaḥyā said, "Mālik said, 'That is the rule among us (*dhālika al-amr ʿindanā*).'"

Chapter 2. The Prophet's (pbuh) Performance of the *Witr*[129] Prayer (*Ṣalāt al-Witr*)

316. According to Mālik, Ibn Shihāb reported from ʿUrwa b. al-Zubayr, from ʿĀʾisha, the wife of the Prophet (pbuh), that the Messenger of God (pbuh) would perform eleven cycles (*rakʿa*) of prayer in the night, five pairs of two cycles and then a single cycle at the end, thereby rendering the lot an odd number. When he had finished, he would lie down on his right side and sleep.

317. According to Mālik, Saʿīd b. Abī Saʿīd al-Maqburī reported from Abū Salama b. ʿAbd al-Raḥmān b. ʿAwf that he asked ʿĀʾisha, the wife of the Prophet (pbuh), "How did the Messenger of God (pbuh) pray during Ramadan?" She said, "Whether during Ramadan or at any other time, the Messenger of God (pbuh) would never exceed eleven cycles. He would pray four cycles—do not ask about their beauty or length!—and then he would pray another four—do not ask about their beauty or length!—and then he would pray three." ʿĀʾisha then said, "So I said, 'Messenger of God, do you sleep before you perform the last cycle?' He said, "ʿĀʾisha, my eyes sleep, but not my heart.'"

---

127 Literally, "as much as God willed for him."

128 *Ṭāhā*, 20:132.

129 *Witr* is the name for the last cycle of a nighttime prayer. Unlike the rest of the nighttime prayer, the *witr* prayer consists of just one prayer cycle. It is usually preceded by the performance of at least one prayer consisting of two cycles. These paired cycles are referred to collectively as *shafʿ*.

318. According to Mālik, Hishām b. ʿUrwa reported from his father that ʿĀʾisha, the Mother of the Believers, said, "The Messenger of God would pray thirteen cycles during the night, and then, when he heard the call to the Morning Prayer (*ṣalāt al-ṣubḥ*), he would pray two quick cycles."

319. According to Mālik, Makhrama b. Sulaymān reported from Kurayb, the freedman (*mawlā*) of Ibn ʿAbbās, that ʿAbd Allāh b. ʿAbbās informed Kurayb that he spent a night in the house of Maymūna, the wife of the Prophet (pbuh) and his maternal aunt. He said, "I was lying down along the breadth of the pillow, and the Messenger of God (pbuh) and his wife were lying down along its length. The Messenger of God (pbuh) slept until midnight or thereabouts, and when he woke up, he sat down and began to wipe away the sleep from his face with his hands. He then recited the last ten verses of 'The Family of ʿImrān' (*Āl ʿImrān*).[130] He then got up and proceeded to an old waterskin that was suspended from a hook and meticulously performed his ablutions from it. He then stood and prayed." Ibn ʿAbbās said, "I therefore stood up and did as he did, and went and stood by his side. The Messenger of God (pbuh) put his right hand on my head and affectionately rubbed my right ear. He then prayed two cycles, and another two, and another two, and another two, and another two, and another two. Then he performed a single cycle of prayer, at the conclusion of which he lay down until the muezzin came to him at the time of the Morning Prayer. He then prayed two quick cycles, went out, and performed the Morning Prayer."

320. According to Mālik, ʿAbd Allāh b. Abī Bakr reported from his father that ʿAbd Allāh b. Qays b. Makhrama informed him that Zayd b. Khālid al-Juhanī said, "Tonight, I shall carefully observe how the Messenger of God (pbuh) performs the Night Prayer." He said, "I rested my head on the threshold of his house (or his tent).[131] The Messenger of God (pbuh) awoke and prayed two very, very long cycles. Then he prayed two cycles that were shorter than the previous two. Then he prayed two cycles that were shorter than the previous two. Then he prayed two cycles that were shorter than the previous two. Then he prayed two cycles that were shorter than the previous two. Then he prayed two cycles that were shorter than the previous two. Then he performed one cycle of prayer, making thirteen cycles in all."

130 The third chapter of the Quran. The last ten verses of this chapter begin with "Indeed, in the creation of the heavens and the earth and in the alternation of night and day are signs for those with understanding."

131 Zurqānī quotes Bājī as saying that the uncertainty regarding whether Zayd rested on the threshold of his house or on that of the tent is on the part of the narrator, but that the more likely version is "his house." Zurqānī, *Sharḥ al-Zurqānī*, 1:440.

Chapter 3. The Command to Pray the *Witr* Prayer

321. According to Mālik, Nāfiʿ and ʿAbd Allāh b. Dīnār reported from ʿAbd Allāh b. ʿUmar that a man asked the Messenger of God (pbuh) about the Night Prayer (*ṣalāt al-layl*), so the Messenger of God (pbuh) said, "The Night Prayer is performed two cycles at a time, and if someone fears that the Morning Prayer (*ṣalāt al-ṣubḥ*) is approaching, he should conclude the prayer by performing one cycle (*rakʿa*) so as to make the number of cycles that he has performed odd."

322. According to Mālik, Yaḥyā b. Saʿīd reported from Muḥammad b. Yaḥyā b. Ḥabbān, from Ibn Muḥayrīz, that a man of the Banū Kināna called al-Mukhdajī heard a man in the Levant named Abū Muḥammad say, "Performance of the *witr* prayer is obligatory." Al-Mukhdajī said, "I therefore sought out ʿUbāda b. al-Ṣāmit. I approached him as he was heading to the mosque and informed him of what Abū Muḥammad had said. ʿUbāda said, 'Abū Muḥammad is mistaken. I heard the Messenger of God (pbuh) say, "The performance of five prayers is what God has imposed on His servants. Whoever performs them all, not missing any of them out of indifference to their obligatory character, has a covenant from God that He will cause him to enter Heaven. Whoever does not perform them lacks this covenant with God. Accordingly, if God wishes, He punishes him, and if He wishes, He admits him to Heaven."'"

323. According to Mālik, Abū Bakr b. ʿAmr reported that Saʿīd b. Yasār said, "I was traveling with ʿAbd Allāh b. ʿUmar along the road to Mecca. I grew anxious that dawn was approaching, so I dismounted and performed the *witr* prayer. I then caught up with ʿAbd Allāh b. ʿUmar, and he asked me, 'Where were you?' I said to him, 'I grew anxious that dawn was approaching, so I dismounted and performed the *witr* prayer.' ʿAbd Allāh said, 'Isn't the Messenger of God (pbuh) an example for you?' I said, 'By God, he certainly is.' He said, 'The Messenger of God (pbuh) would perform the *witr* prayer while mounted on his camel.'"

324. According to Mālik, Yaḥyā b. Saʿīd reported that Saʿīd b. al-Musayyab said, "Abū Bakr al-Ṣiddīq would perform the *witr* prayer before going to bed, and ʿUmar b. al-Khaṭṭāb would perform the *witr* prayer in the last hours of the night." Saʿīd b. al-Musayyab said, "As for me, I perform the *witr* prayer right before I go to bed."

325. According to Mālik, it reached him that a man asked ʿAbd Allāh b. ʿUmar whether the *witr* prayer was obligatory. ʿAbd Allāh b. ʿUmar said, "The Messenger of God (pbuh) performed the *witr* prayer, and the Muslims performed the *witr* prayer." The man kept on questioning him, and ʿAbd

Allāh b. ʿUmar continued to give him the same answer—"The Messenger of God (pbuh) performed the *witr* prayer, and the Muslims performed the *witr* prayer."

326. According to Mālik, it reached him that ʿĀʾisha, the wife of the Prophet (pbuh), would say, "Whoever is anxious that he might sleep until dawn, let him perform the *witr* prayer before he sleeps, and whoever believes he will awake during the last hours of the night, let him defer the performance of his *witr* prayer."

327. According to Mālik, Nāfiʿ said, "I was with ʿAbd Allāh b. ʿUmar in Mecca, and the sky was cloudy. ʿAbd Allāh grew anxious that dawn was approaching, so he performed one cycle of the *witr* prayer. Then the clouds dissipated, and he realized that it was still night, so he performed an additional cycle of prayer, thus making the total number of cycles that he had prayed that night even. He then performed additional cycles of prayer, two at a time, and when he became anxious that dawn was approaching, he performed one cycle of the *witr* prayer."

328. According to Mālik, Nāfiʿ reported that ʿAbd Allāh b. ʿUmar would conclude the last two cycles of the Night Prayer by saying, "Peace be upon you," and he would then perform one cycle of the *witr* prayer. Sometimes he would even ask for something he needed before completing the *witr* prayer.[132]

329. According to Mālik, Ibn Shihāb reported that Saʿd b. Abī Waqqāṣ would perform one cycle of the *witr* prayer immediately after completing the Evening Prayer (*ṣalāt al-ʿishāʾ*). Yaḥyā said, "Mālik said, 'The practice (*ʿamal*) among us is not in accord with this; rather, the minimum length of the *witr* prayer is three cycles.'"[133]

330. According to Mālik, ʿAbd Allāh b. Dīnār reported that ʿAbd Allāh b. ʿUmar would say that the Sunset Prayer (*ṣalāt al-maghrib*) was the *witr* prayer of the daytime prayers.[134]

331. Yaḥyā said, "Mālik said, 'Whoever performs the *witr* prayer at the beginning of the night, then sleeps, and then awakes and decides to perform additional cycles of prayer should perform two cycles at a time. Of all the views that I have heard, this is the one I prefer most.'"

---

132 In other words, the *witr* prayer, according to ʿAbd Allāh b. ʿUmar, consisted of one cycle of prayer, which was distinct from the pairs of cycles that were prayed previously through the night.

133 In other words, the odd cycle of the *witr* prayer should be preceded by at least one even pair (*shafʿ*) of cycles. Zurqānī, *Sharḥ al-Zurqānī*, 1:451.

134 The Sunset Prayer consists of an odd number of cycles, in contrast to the other four daily prayers, all of which have an even number of cycles.

Chapter 4. Performing the *Witr* Prayer after the Break of Dawn

332. According to Mālik, ʿAbd al-Karīm b. Abī al-Mukhāriq al-Baṣrī reported from Saʿīd b. Jubayr that ʿAbd Allāh b. ʿAbbās was asleep and then awoke, so he said to his servant, "Go see whether the people have prayed," his sight having left him by that time. The servant went out to have a look, and when he returned, he said, "The people have finished performance of the Morning Prayer (*ṣalāt al-ṣubḥ*)." ʿAbd Allāh got up, performed the *witr* prayer, and then performed the Morning Prayer.

333. According to Mālik, it reached him that ʿAbd Allāh b. ʿAbbās, ʿUbāda b. al-Ṣāmit, al-Qāsim b. Muḥammad, and ʿAbd Allāh b. ʿĀmir b. Rabīʿa had all performed the *witr* prayer after dawn broke.

334. According to Mālik, Hishām b. ʿUrwa reported from his father that ʿAbd Allāh b. Masʿūd said, "When I am performing the *witr* prayer, not even the immediate call (*iqāma*) to the Morning Prayer will interrupt me."

335. According to Mālik, Yaḥyā b. Saʿīd said, "ʿUbāda b. al-Ṣāmit acted as the imam for a group of people. One day, he went out to perform the Morning Prayer, and the muezzin began to make the immediate call to the Morning Prayer. ʿUbāda, however, told him to desist until he, ʿUbāda, had finished performing the *witr* prayer. Then ʿUbāda led them in the Morning Prayer."

336. According to Mālik, ʿAbd al-Raḥmān b. al-Qāsim said, "I heard ʿAbd Allāh b. ʿĀmir b. Rabīʿa say, 'I perform the *witr* prayer even when I hear the immediate call to the Morning Prayer' or 'after the break of dawn.'" ʿAbd al-Raḥmān was not certain which of the two expressions he had used.

337. According to Mālik, ʿAbd al-Raḥmān b. al-Qāsim reported that he heard his father, al-Qāsim b. Muḥammad, say, "I do indeed perform the *witr* prayer, even after dawn breaks." Yaḥyā said, "Mālik said, 'Only someone who oversleeps and fails to perform the *witr* prayer before the break of dawn should perform it after dawn breaks. No one should plan to perform it after dawn breaks.'"

Chapter 5. What Has Come Down regarding the Two Cycles (*Rakʿa*) of the Dawn Prayer (*Ṣalāt al-Fajr*)

338. According to Mālik, Nāfiʿ reported from ʿAbd Allāh b. ʿUmar that Ḥafṣa, the wife of the Prophet (pbuh), told him that once the muezzin had finished the general call (*adhān*) to the Morning Prayer (*ṣalāt al-ṣubḥ*), the Messenger of God (pbuh) would perform two quick cycles (*rakʿa*) of prayer before the immediate call (*iqāma*) to the Morning Prayer was made.

339. According to Mālik, Yaḥyā b. Saʿīd reported that ʿĀʾisha, the wife of the Prophet (pbuh), said, "The Messenger of God (pbuh) would perform the two cycles of the Dawn Prayer (*ṣalāt al-fajr*) so quickly that I would wonder whether or not he had even recited the *Fātiḥa*."

340. According to Mālik, Sharīk b. ʿAbd Allāh b. Abī Namir reported that Abū Salama b. ʿAbd al-Raḥmān said, "A group of people heard the immediate call to prayer, so they stood to pray.[135] Then the Messenger of God (pbuh) came and said, 'Are you performing two prayers at the same time? Are you performing two prayers at the same time?' That referred to the Morning Prayer and the two cycles that precede the Morning Prayer."

341. According to Mālik, it reached him that ʿAbd Allāh b. ʿUmar once missed the two cycles of the Dawn Prayer, so he made them up by performing them after sunrise.

342. According to Mālik, ʿAbd al-Raḥmān b. al-Qāsim reported from al-Qāsim b. Muḥammad something similar to that which Ibn ʿUmar had done.

135 According to Bājī, this group of people, instead of joining the congregation to pray the obligatory Morning Prayer (*ṣalāt al-ṣubḥ*), began to pray the two cycles of the supererogatory Dawn Prayer (*ṣalāt al-fajr*) that precedes it. Bājī, *al-Muntaqā*, 1:227.

Book 8

The Book of the Congregational Prayer (*Ṣalāt al-Jamāʿa*)

Chapter 1. The Superiority of Congregational Prayers (*Ṣalāt al-Jamāʿa*) over Individual Prayers

343. According to Mālik, Nāfiʿ reported from ʿAbd Allāh b. ʿUmar that the Messenger of God (pbuh) said, "A prayer (*ṣalāt*) performed with a congregation is twenty-seven times more virtuous than a prayer performed alone."

344. According to Mālik, Ibn Shihāb reported from Saʿīd b. al-Musayyab, from Abū Hurayra, that the Messenger of God (pbuh) said, "A prayer performed with a congregation is twenty-five times more virtuous than a prayer performed alone."

345. According to Mālik, Abū al-Zinād reported from al-Aʿraj, from Abū Hurayra, that the Messenger of God (pbuh) said, "By Him whose hand holds my soul! I am on the verge of ordering that wood be gathered, and it would be gathered; then I would make a command for prayer, and it would be held; then I would command a man to lead the prayer, and he would lead it; then I would search out those men who did not come to pray, and burn their houses down with them inside. By Him whose hand holds my soul! If any of them had believed that he would find at the mosque a meaty bone or two fine, small arrows,[136] he would have come to the mosque for the Evening Prayer (*ṣalāt al-ʿishāʾ*)."

---

136 The Arabic term in the text is *mirmātayn*, the dual form of *mirmāt*. Arab lexicographers identify two meanings for the term. The first refers to the meat from a cloven-hooved animal, and the second refers to a kind of arrow that was used by pre-Islamic Arabs either to learn archery or for sports such as target practice. The majority of the commentators seem to prefer the second interpretation of *mirmātayn*. Zurqānī, for example, concludes his commentary on this report by stating that it "entails condemnation of those who neglect to attend the [congregational] prayer by describing them as covetous of trivial things such as food or sport." Zurqānī, *Sharḥ al-Zurqānī*, 1:464. Bājī also prefers the second interpretation (Bājī, *al-Muntaqā*, 1:230), as do the editors of the RME.

346. According to Mālik, Abū al-Naḍr, the freedman (*mawlā*) of ʿUmar b. ʿUbayd Allāh, reported from Busr b. Saʿīd that Zayd b. Thābit said, "The most virtuous prayer is one performed in your home, except for the obligatory prayers."[137]

Chapter 2. What Has Come Down regarding the Evening Prayer (*Ṣalāt al-ʿIshā'*) and the Morning Prayer (*Ṣalāt al-Ṣubḥ*)

347. According to Mālik, ʿAbd al-Raḥmān b. Ḥarmala al-Aslamī reported from Saʿīd b. al-Musayyab that the Messenger of God (pbuh) said, "What separates us from the hypocrites is our attendance at the Evening Prayer (*ṣalāt al-ʿishā'*) and the Morning Prayer (*ṣalāt al-ṣubḥ*). They cannot bear them," or something to that effect.

348. According to Mālik, Sumayy, the freedman (*mawlā*) of Abū Bakr, reported from Abū Ṣāliḥ al-Sammān, from Abū Hurayra, that the Messenger of God (pbuh) said, "A man was once walking along a road when he discovered a thorny branch in the way, so he removed it from the road. God was so pleased by the man's act that He forgave his prior sins." The Messenger of God (pbuh) also said, "There are five kinds of martyrs: those who die of the plague, those who die of disease, those who die by drowning, those who die because of a collapsed building, and those killed for the sake of God."[138]

349. According to Mālik, Ibn Shihāb reported from Abū Bakr b. Sulaymān b. Abī Ḥathma that ʿUmar b. al-Khaṭṭāb noticed that Sulaymān b. Abī Ḥathma did not attend the Morning Prayer. Later that day, when ʿUmar b. al-Khaṭṭāb went to the market—Sulaymān's house was between the mosque and the marketplace—he walked past al-Shaffā', Sulaymān's mother. He said to her, "I didn't see Sulaymān at the Morning Prayer," and she replied, "He spent the night praying and overslept." ʿUmar said, "I would rather perform the Morning Prayer with the congregation than spend the whole night standing in prayer."

350. According to Mālik, Yaḥyā b. Saʿīd reported from Muḥammad b. Ibrāhīm that ʿAbd al-Raḥmān b. Abī ʿAmra al-Anṣārī said that ʿUthmān b. ʿAffān once attended the Evening Prayer in the Prophet's Mosque, and

---

137 I.e., the five obligatory daily prayers.

138 The narration on which the RME is based—that of ʿUbayd Allāh b. Yaḥyā, the son of Yaḥyā b. Yaḥyā—contains this report in a form that has no relevance to the chapter heading. Other narrators of the *Muwaṭṭa'* from Yaḥyā, however, include the following addition after the report about the five kinds of martyrs: "If people only knew the blessings of the general call to prayer (*adhān*) and of praying in the first row of the mosque, they would draw lots to prevent themselves from fighting over those blessings. If they knew of the blessings of attending the prayer early, they would race to it. And if they knew of the blessings of the Evening Prayer (*ṣalāt al-ʿishā'*) and the Morning Prayer (*ṣalāt al-ṣubḥ*), they would come crawling to the mosque to perform them."

noticing that only a few people were there, he lay down in the back and waited for more people to come. Ibn Abī ʿAmra came and sat down beside him. ʿUthmān asked him who he was, and he told him. ʿUthmān asked him how much of the Quran he had memorized, and he told him. Then ʿUthmān said to him, "If someone attends the evening congregational prayer, it is as if he had prayed half the night, and if he attends the morning congregational prayer, it is as if he had prayed the entire night."

Chapter 3. Repeating Performance of the Prayer (*Ṣalāt*) with the Imam

351. According to Mālik, Zayd b. Aslam reported from a man of the Banū al-Dīl called Busr b. Miḥjan, from his father, Miḥjan, that the latter had been in a gathering sitting with the Messenger of God (pbuh) when the general call to prayer (*adhān*) was made. The Messenger of God (pbuh) left and prayed and then returned, and Miḥjan was still sitting there. The Messenger of God (pbuh) asked him, "What kept you from praying with us? Aren't you a Muslim?" He said, "Yes I am, Messenger of God, but I already prayed with my family." The Messenger of God (pbuh) said to him, "When you're with the congregation, pray with them, even if you've already prayed."

352. According to Mālik, Nāfiʿ reported that a man asked ʿAbd Allāh b. ʿUmar, "I often perform the prayer in my house, and then I find the imam performing that very same prayer. Should I perform it again with him?" ʿAbd Allāh b. ʿUmar said to him, "Yes!" The man asked, "Which of the two prayers should I deem to be my obligatory prayer?" Ibn ʿUmar said to him, "Is that up to you? That decision belongs only to God. He decides which of the two was the obligatory prayer, as He wishes."

353. According to Mālik, Yaḥyā b. Saʿīd reported that a man asked Saʿīd b. al-Musayyab, "I perform the prayer in my house, and then I go to the mosque and find the imam praying that very same prayer. Should I perform it again with him?" Saʿīd b. al-Musayyab said, "Yes!" The man asked him, "Which of the two is my obligatory prayer?" Saʿīd said, "Is it you who decides which of the two is the obligatory prayer? That decision belongs only to God."

354. According to Mālik, ʿAfīf b. ʿAmr al-Sahmī reported from a man of the tribe of Banū Asad that he asked Abū Ayyūb al-Anṣārī, "I perform the prayer in my house, and then I go to the mosque and find the imam performing that very same prayer. Should I perform it again with him?" Abū Ayyūb said, "Yes, perform it with him, for whoever does so earns the reward of praying with a congregation, or its near equivalent."

355. According to Mālik, Nāfiʿ reported that ʿAbd Allāh b. ʿUmar would say, "Whoever performs the Sunset Prayer (*ṣalāt al-maghrib*) or the Morning

Prayer (*ṣalāt al-ṣubḥ*) and then finds the imam performing either of them should not pray either of them again."

356. Yaḥyā said, "Mālik said, 'There is nothing objectionable in someone repeating the performance of an obligatory prayer with the imam, even if he has already prayed it at home. The sole exception is the Sunset Prayer: if someone prays that twice, he makes its cycles even-numbered.'"

Chapter 4. The Practice (*ʿAmal*) with Respect to the Performance of the Congregational Prayer (*Ṣalāt al-Jamāʿa*)

357. According to Mālik, Abū al-Zinād reported from al-Aʿraj, from Abū Hurayra, that the Messenger of God (pbuh) said, "When someone leads a congregational prayer, he should be brief, because some congregants will be weak, some will be ill, and some will be aged. When someone performs a prayer (*ṣalāt*) alone, however, he may pray for as long as he wishes."

358. According to Mālik, Nāfiʿ said, "I stood behind ʿAbd Allāh b. ʿUmar for the performance of one of the prayers, and there was no one else except me. ʿAbd Allāh therefore gestured with his hand, motioning me to stand beside him on his right."

359. According to Mālik, Yaḥyā b. Saʿīd reported that once there was a man who led people in prayer in al-ʿAqīq.[139] ʿUmar b. ʿAbd al-ʿAzīz summoned him and prohibited him from continuing to do so. Mālik said, "The only reason he forbade him was that his paternity was unknown."

Chapter 5. The Imam's Performance of the Prayer (*Ṣalāt*) from a Sitting Position

360. According to Mālik, Ibn Shihāb reported from Anas b. Mālik, "The Messenger of God (pbuh) was riding a horse and was thrown off, suffering a deep bruise on his right side. Because of that, he performed one of the prayers from a sitting position, and we prayed behind him, also seated. When he completed the prayer, he said, 'The sole reason for having an imam lead the prayer is that the congregants have someone to follow. Therefore, when he prays standing, pray standing; when he bows, bow with him; when he gets up, get up with him; when he says, "God hears those who praise Him," say "Our Lord, unto you belongs all praise"; and when he prays from a sitting position, you should all pray from a sitting position.'"

361. According to Mālik, Hishām b. ʿUrwa reported from his father that ʿĀ'isha, the wife of the Messenger of God (pbuh), said, "The Messenger of

139 Al-ʿAqīq is a place near Medina. Bājī, *al-Muntaqā*, 6:28.

God (pbuh) once performed the prayer from a sitting position because he was in pain. A group of congregants, however, stood as they prayed behind him, but he signaled them to sit down. When he finished, he said, 'The sole reason for having an imam lead the prayer is that the congregants have someone to follow. When he bows, bow with him; when he gets up, get up with him; and when he prays from a sitting position, you should pray from a sitting position.'"

362. According to Mālik, Hishām b. ʿUrwa reported from his father that the Messenger of God (pbuh) once went to the mosque when he was ill. There he found Abū Bakr leading the congregation in the performance of an obligatory prayer. When he noticed the arrival of the Messenger of God (pbuh), Abū Bakr began to retreat, but the Messenger of God (pbuh) signaled him to stay put, and he sat down beside Abū Bakr. Abū Bakr followed the lead of the Messenger of God (pbuh) and the congregants followed Abū Bakr."

Chapter 6. The Superiority of Prayer (*Ṣalāt*) Performed Standing over Prayer Performed from a Sitting Position

363. According to Mālik, Ismāʿīl b. Muḥammad b. Saʿd b. Abī Waqqāṣ reported from a freedman (*mawlā*) of ʿAmr b. al-ʿĀṣī or of ʿAbd Allāh b. ʿAmr b. al-ʿĀṣī, from ʿAbd Allāh b. ʿAmr b. al-ʿĀṣī, that the Messenger of God (pbuh) said, "A prayer performed from a sitting position is equivalent to half of a prayer performed while standing."

364. According to Mālik, Ibn Shihāb reported that ʿAbd Allāh b. ʿAmr b. al-ʿĀṣī said, "When we arrived in Medina from Mecca, we came down with a severe bout of the fever endemic to Medina.[140] The Messenger of God (pbuh) then came to see the people and found them performing their supplementary prayers from a sitting position. The Messenger of God (pbuh) said, 'A prayer performed from a sitting position is equivalent to half of a prayer performed while standing.'"

Chapter 7. What Has Come Down regarding the Performance of Supplementary Prayers (*Ṣalāt*) from a Sitting Position

365. According to Mālik, Ibn Shihāb reported from Sāʾib b. Yazīd, from al-Muṭṭalib b. Abī Wadāʿa al-Sahmī, that Ḥafṣa, the wife of the Messenger of God (pbuh), said, "I had never seen the Messenger of God (pbuh) perform supplementary prayers from a sitting position until the year prior to his death, when he performed them seated. He would recite a chapter of the

140 Tradition holds that fever (likely malaria) was endemic to Medina and that many of the Emigrants (*muhājirūn*) contracted this disease soon after their arrival there.

Quran so slowly that it would take longer than lengthier chapters recited at his usual pace."

366. According to Mālik, Hishām b. ʿUrwa reported from his father that ʿĀʾisha, the wife of the Prophet (pbuh), told him that she had never seen the Messenger of God (pbuh) perform the Night Prayer (*ṣalāt al-layl*) from a sitting position until he grew old. He would then recite the Quran while seated; when he wanted to bow, he would stand up and recite approximately thirty or forty additional verses, and then he would bow.

367. According to Mālik, ʿAbd Allāh b. Yazīd and Abū al-Naḍr, the freedman (*mawlā*) of ʿUmar b. ʿUbayd Allāh, reported from Abū Salama b. ʿAbd al-Raḥmān, from ʿĀʾisha, the wife of the Prophet (pbuh), that the Messenger of God (pbuh) would perform the prayer from a sitting position. He would first recite while seated, and when he had about thirty or forty verses of the Quran left of his daily recitation, he would get up and recite them while standing. Then he would bow and prostrate, and would do the same in the second cycle.

368. According to Mālik, it reached him that ʿUrwa b. al-Zubayr and Saʿīd b. al-Musayyab would perform the supplementary prayers while in a sitting position.

Chapter 8. The Middle Prayer (*al-Ṣalāt al-Wusṭā*)

369. According to Mālik, Zayd b. Aslam reported from al-Qaʿqāʿ b. Ḥakīm that Abū Yūnus, the freedman (*mawlā*) of ʿĀʾisha, the Mother of the Believers, said, "ʿĀʾisha ordered me to write out a copy of the Quran for her and said, 'When you get to this verse, "Strictly observe the performance of your prayers, especially the middle prayer, and stand devoutly before God,"[141] tell me.' When I reached it, I told her, and she dictated to me, 'Strictly observe the performance of your prayers, especially the middle prayer and the Afternoon Prayer (*ṣalāt al-ʿasr*), and stand devoutly before God.' Then she said, 'I heard it from the Messenger of God (pbuh).'"

370. According to Mālik, Zayd b. Aslam reported that ʿAmr b. Rāfiʿ said, "I was writing a copy of the Quran for Ḥafṣa, the Mother of the Believers, and she said, 'When you get to this verse, "Strictly observe the performance of your prayers, especially the middle prayer, and stand devoutly before God,"[142] tell me.' So I told her when I reached it, and she dictated to me, 'Strictly observe the performance of your prayers, especially the middle prayer and the Afternoon Prayer, and stand devoutly before God.'"

141 *Al-Baqara*, 2:238.
142 *Al-Baqara*, 2:238.

371. According to Mālik, Dāwūd b. al-Ḥuṣayn reported that Ibn Yarbūʿ al-Makhzūmī said, "I heard Zayd b. Thābit say, 'The middle prayer is the Noon Prayer (*ṣalāt al-ẓuhr*).'"

372. According to Mālik, it reached him that ʿAlī b. Abī Ṭālib and ʿAbd Allāh b. ʿAbbās would say, "The middle prayer is the Morning Prayer (*ṣalāt al-ṣubḥ*)." Yaḥyā said, "Mālik said, 'Of all the views that I have heard regarding this issue, the view of ʿAlī b. Abī Ṭālib and ʿAbd Allāh b. ʿAbbās is the one I prefer most.'"

Chapter 9. The Dispensation to Perform Prayers (*Ṣalāt*) Wearing Only a Single Garment

373. According to Mālik, Hishām b. ʿUrwa reported from his father, from ʿUmar b. Abī Salama, that he had seen the Messenger of God (pbuh) perform prayers while wrapped in a single garment, putting both ends over his shoulders, in Umm Salama's house.

374. According to Mālik, Ibn Shihāb reported from Saʿīd b. al-Musayyab, from Abū Hurayra, that a man asked the Messenger of God about performing prayers while wearing only a single garment. The Messenger of God (pbuh) asked rhetorically, "Does everyone have two garments?"[143]

375. According to Mālik, Ibn Shihāb reported that Saʿīd b. al-Musayyab said, "Abū Hurayra was asked, 'Can a man pray while wearing only a single garment?' He said, 'Yes!' Then he was asked, 'Do you yourself do that?' He said, 'Yes, I do indeed pray while wearing only a single garment whenever my other garments are hanging out to dry.'"

376. According to Mālik, it reached him that Jābir b. ʿAbd Allāh would pray wearing only a single garment.

377. According to Mālik, Rabīʿa b. ʿAbd al-Raḥmān reported that Muḥammad b. ʿAmr b. Ḥazm would pray wearing a single long tunic.

378. According to Mālik, it reached him from Jābir b. ʿAbd Allāh that the Messenger of God (pbuh) said, "Whoever cannot find two garments should pray wearing one garment, wrapped around him. If the garment is short, let him wrap it around his waist."

379. Yaḥyā said, "Mālik said, 'In the case of a man who is praying wearing only a tunic, I prefer that he drape a garment, or the cloth from his turban, about his shoulders.'"

---

143 The Messenger (pbuh) is implying that some people possess only one garment, which necessarily is worn as an outer garment.

Chapter 10. The Dispensation Permitting a Woman to Perform Prayers (*Ṣalāt*) Wearing a Wrap and a Headcover

380. According to Mālik, it reached him that 'Ā'isha, the wife of the Prophet (pbuh), would pray in a wrap and a headcover.

381. According to Mālik, Muḥammad b. Zayd b. Qunfudh reported that his mother asked Umm Salama, the wife of the Prophet (pbuh), about the kinds of clothes a woman may wear when praying. Umm Salama said, "She should pray in a headcover and a long wrap, provided that it reaches down to her ankles and covers them."

382. According to Mālik, a source that he deemed to be reliable reported from Bukayr b. 'Abd Allāh b. al-Ashajj, from Busr b. Sa'īd, from 'Ubayd Allāh al-Khawlānī, that when 'Ubayd Allāh was in the care of Maymūna, the wife of the Messenger of God (pbuh), she would pray while wearing a long wrap and a headcover, without an undergarment around her waist.

383. According to Mālik, Hishām b. 'Urwa reported from his father that a woman sought his opinion regarding appropriate clothing for praying, saying, "Wearing a girdle around my waist is unbearable for me, so can I pray wearing only a wrap and a headcover?" He said, "Certainly, if the dress is long."

Book 9
The Book of Shortening the Prayer (*Ṣalāt*)

Chapter 1. Combining Two Prayers (*Ṣalāt*) When at Home and When Traveling

384. According to Mālik, Dāwūd b. al-Ḥuṣayn reported from al-Aʿraj that the Messenger of God (pbuh) combined performance of the Noon Prayer (*ṣalāt al-ẓuhr*) and the Afternoon Prayer (*ṣalāt al-ʿaṣr*) when traveling to Tabūk.

385. According to Mālik, Abū al-Zubayr al-Makkī reported from Abū al-Ṭufayl ʿĀmir b. Wāthila that Muʿādh b. Jabal told him that they set out with the Messenger of God (pbuh) to Tabūk, and that the Messenger of God combined performance of the Noon and Afternoon Prayers and of the Sunset (*ṣalāt al-maghrib*) and Evening (*ṣalāt al-ʿishāʾ*) Prayers during that campaign. He said, "One day, the Messenger of God (pbuh) deferred performing the prayer. He then went out and performed the Noon and Afternoon Prayers together. Then he went inside. Then he went out and performed the Sunset and Evening Prayers together. Then, he said, 'Tomorrow, God willing, you will arrive at the spring of Tabūk, but you will not get there before midmorning. Whoever gets there must not touch its water until I arrive.' When we arrived, we discovered that two men had gotten there ahead of us and that very little water was trickling from the spring. The Messenger of God (pbuh) therefore asked the two men, 'Did you put your hands in its water?' They said, 'Yes.' The Messenger of God (pbuh) cursed them, saying whatever God wished for him to say. Then everyone scooped up whatever water remained with their hands from the spring, little by little, until a small amount had been collected. The Messenger of God (pbuh) was able to wash his face and hands with that water and returned what was left of it to the spring. Then the spring began to flow profusely, and everyone was able to draw water from it. The Messenger of God (pbuh) then said, 'If you live long enough, Muʿādh, you will soon see this place filled with gardens.'"

386. According to Mālik, Nāfi' reported that 'Abd Allāh b. 'Umar said, "When he was marching quickly, the Messenger of God (pbuh) would combine the Sunset and Evening Prayers."

387. According to Mālik, Abū al-Zubayr al-Makkī reported from Sa'īd b. Jubayr that 'Abd Allāh b. 'Abbās said that the Messenger of God (pbuh) performed the Noon and Afternoon Prayers together and the Sunset and Evening Prayers together even when he was neither exposed to danger nor traveling." Yaḥyā said, "Mālik said, 'I believe it must have been raining.'"

388. According to Mālik, Nāfi' reported that whenever it rained and a local governor combined performance of the Sunset and Evening Prayers, 'Abd Allāh b. 'Umar would pray in the congregation behind him.

389. According to Mālik, Ibn Shihāb reported that he asked Sālim b. 'Ubayd Allāh whether performance of the Noon and Afternoon Prayers could be combined while traveling. He said, "Yes, there is nothing objectionable in that. Haven't you noticed how people perform their prayers at 'Arafāt?"[144]

390. According to Mālik, it reached him that 'Alī b. Ḥusayn would say, "When the Messenger of God (pbuh) wished to travel throughout the day, he would combine performance of the Noon and Afternoon Prayers, and when he wished to travel throughout the night, he would combine performance of the Sunset and Evening Prayers."

Chapter 2. Shortening the Prayer (*Ṣalāt*) While Traveling

391. According to Mālik, Ibn Shihāb reported that a man of the family of Khālid b. Asīd said to 'Abd Allāh b. 'Umar, "Abū 'Abd al-Raḥmān, in the Quran we find mentioned the Prayer of Danger (*ṣalāt al-khawf*) and the prayer when at home, but nothing about the prayer while traveling." 'Abd Allāh b. 'Umar said, "Nephew, God, Mighty and Majestic is He, sent us Muḥammad (pbuh), and we knew nothing of the divine law—so we do exactly as we saw him do."

392. According to Mālik, Ṣāliḥ b. Kaysān reported from 'Urwa b. al-Zubayr that 'Ā'isha, the wife of the Prophet (pbuh), said, "When originally ordained, each prayer consisted of only two cycles (*rak'a*) for both residents and travelers. Later, the prayer for travelers was maintained as it was in the beginning, but the prayer for residents was lengthened."[145]

393. According to Mālik, Yaḥyā b. Sa'īd reported that he said to Sālim b. 'Abd Allāh, "What was the latest you saw your father defer performance of

144 A mountain near Mecca where the central rites of the Pilgrimage are performed.
145 The Morning Prayer, however, still consists of two cycles.

the Sunset Prayer (*ṣalāt al-maghrib*) when traveling?" Sālim said, "The sun was setting when we were in Dhāt al-Jaysh, and he prayed the Sunset Prayer in al-ʿAqīq."[146]

Chapter 3. The Circumstances in Which Shortening the Prayer (*Ṣalāt*) Is Obligatory

394. According to Mālik, Nāfiʿ reported that ʿAbd Allāh b. ʿUmar, when he set out for the Pilgrimage (*ḥajj*) or the Visitation (*ʿumra*), would begin to shorten his prayers at Dhū al-Ḥulayfa.[147]

395. According to Mālik, Ibn Shihāb reported from Sālim b. ʿAbd Allāh, from his father, that he rode to Rīm and shortened his prayers on that trip. Yaḥyā said, "Mālik said, 'That distance is about four mail stages.'"[148]

396. According to Mālik, Nāfiʿ reported from Sālim b. ʿAbd Allāh that ʿAbd Allāh b. ʿUmar rode to Dhāt al-Nuṣub and shortened his prayers on that trip. Yaḥyā said, "Mālik said, 'The distance between Dhāt al-Nuṣub and Medina is four mail stages.'"

397. According to Mālik, Nāfiʿ reported from Ibn ʿUmar that he would shorten prayers when he traveled to Khaybar.

398. According to Mālik, Ibn Shihāb reported from Sālim b. ʿAbd Allāh that ʿAbd Allāh b. ʿUmar would shorten the prayers whenever he traveled for an entire day.

399. According to Mālik, Nāfiʿ reported that when he would travel with ʿAbd Allāh b. ʿUmar a distance of one mail stage or less, ʿAbd Allāh would not shorten his prayers.

400. According to Mālik, it reached him that ʿAbd Allāh b. ʿAbbās would shorten his prayers whenever he traveled a distance equivalent to that between Mecca and Ṭāʾif, that between Mecca and ʿUsfān, or that between Mecca and Jeddah. Yaḥyā said, "Mālik said, 'That is four mail stages.'" Yaḥyā said, "Mālik said, 'This is the opinion I prefer most regarding the minimum distance one must travel before shortening the prayers.'"

---

146 Dhāt al-Jaysh and al-ʿAqīq are places outside of Medina. The distance between the two is approximately 10.5 km (ten *mīls*).

147 An abandoned village on the way from Medina to Mecca. It lay at a distance of nine or ten days' march from Mecca. Zurqānī, *Sharḥ al-Zurqānī*, 2:356.

148 This is equivalent to approximately 52 km. A "mail stage," called a *barīd* in Arabic, is defined as twelve *mīls*, and a *mīl* is between 3,500 and 4,000 arm's lengths or man's paces. A distance of four mail stages, then, is roughly between 168,000 and 192,000 paces, or forty-eight *mīls*. See Edward Lane, *An Arabic-English Lexicon*, 8 vols. (London: Williams, 1863), 1:185.

401. Mālik said, "Someone who intends to travel should not shorten his prayers until he leaves the outskirts of the village, and he should not perform the prayers in full until he has reached the outskirts of his destination, or nearly so."

Chapter 4. The Prayer (*Ṣalāt*) of a Traveler Who Is Uncertain Whether He Will Stay or Go

402. According to Mālik, Ibn Shihāb reported from Sālim b. ʿAbd Allāh that ʿAbd Allāh b. ʿUmar would say, "I perform the prayers of a traveler so long as I have not conclusively decided to stay in a location, even if I remain in the same town for twelve nights, undecided whether to stay or to go."

403. According to Mālik, Nāfiʿ reported that Ibn ʿUmar spent ten nights in Mecca, shortening the performance of his prayers, except when he prayed behind the imam, in which case he prayed as the imam did.

Chapter 5. The Prayer (*Ṣalāt*) of a Traveler Who Decides to Stay

404. According to Mālik, ʿAṭāʾ al-Khurasānī reported that he heard Saʿīd b. al-Musayyab say, "Whoever decides to stay in a place for at least four nights when traveling should perform the prayer in full." Yaḥyā said, "Mālik said, 'Of all the views that I have heard, this is the one I prefer most.'"

405. Yaḥyā said, "Mālik was asked about the prayers of a captive. He answered, 'He prays in the manner of someone who resides there.'"

Chapter 6. The Prayer (*Ṣalāt*) of the Traveler Who Is a Ruler or Who Is Praying behind an Imam

406. According to Mālik, Ibn Shihāb reported from Sālim b. ʿAbd Allāh, from his father, that when ʿUmar b. al-Khaṭṭāb arrived in Mecca during his term as caliph, he would lead the Meccans in the performance of two cycles (*rakʿa*) of prayer, and then he would say, "People of Mecca! Complete your prayer in full, for we are a band of travelers."

407. According to Mālik, Zayd b. Aslam reported from his father, from ʿUmar b. al-Khaṭṭāb, a similar report.

408. According to Mālik, Nāfiʿ reported that ʿAbd Allāh b. ʿUmar would pray four cycles behind the imam at Minā,[149] but when he performed the prayer by himself there, he would perform only two cycles.

---

149 Minā is a plain located outside of Mecca where many of the rites of the Pilgrimage, including the symbolic stoning of the Devil, take place.

409. According to Mālik, Ibn Shihāb reported that Ṣafwān b. ʿAbd Allāh b. Ṣafwān said, "ʿAbd Allāh b. ʿUmar came to pay a visit to ʿAbd Allāh b. Ṣafwān when he was ill, and he led us in the performance of two cycles of prayer, at which point he finished and we stood up and completed it."

Chapter 7. Performing Supplementary Prayers (*Ṣalāt*) While Traveling during the Day and While Riding a Beast of Burden

410. According to Mālik, Nāfiʿ reported from ʿAbd Allāh b. ʿUmar that he would not perform any prayer beyond the obligatory prayers, whether before or after them, while traveling. In the dead of night, however, he might pray on the ground or in the saddle of his camel, whichever way it was facing.

411. According to Mālik, it reached him that al-Qāsim b. Muḥammad, ʿUrwa b. al-Zubayr, and Abū Bakr b. ʿAbd al-Rahmān would perform supplementary prayers while traveling.

412. Yaḥyā said, "Mālik was asked about the performance of supplementary prayers while traveling. He said, 'There is nothing objectionable in that, whether at night or during the day. It has reached me that some of the people of knowledge did so.'"

413. Mālik said, "It reached me that ʿAbd Allāh b. ʿUmar would see his son, ʿUbayd Allāh b. ʿAbd Allāh, performing supplementary prayers while traveling, and he did not criticize him for it."

414. According to Mālik, ʿAmr b. Yaḥyā al-Māzinī reported from Saʿīd b. Yasār that ʿAbd Allāh b. ʿUmar said, "I saw the Messenger of God (pbuh) praying while seated on a donkey on his way to Khaybar."

415. According to Mālik, ʿAbd Allāh b. Dīnār reported from ʿAbd Allāh b. ʿUmar that the Messenger of God (pbuh) would pray in his saddle while traveling, whichever direction his camel was facing. ʿAbd Allāh b. Dīnār said, "ʿAbd Allāh b. ʿUmar would also do that."

416. According to Mālik, Yaḥyā b. Saʿīd said, "I once saw Anas b. Mālik perform the prayer while seated on his donkey. He did not face the direction of Mecca. He bowed and prostrated by motioning, without putting his face on anything."

Chapter 8. The Midmorning Prayer (*Ṣalāt al-Ḍuḥā*)

417. According to Mālik, Mūsā b. Maysara reported from Abū Murra, the freedman (*mawlā*) of ʿAqīl b. Abī Ṭālib, that Umm Hānī, Abū Ṭālib's daughter, told him that in the year of the conquest of Mecca (*ʿām al-fatḥ*),[150] the Messenger of God (pbuh) performed eight cycles (*rakʿa*) of prayer while wrapped in a single garment.

418. According to Mālik, Abū al-Naḍr, the freedman of ʿUmar b. ʿUbayd Allāh, reported that Abū Murra, the freedman of ʿAqīl b. Abī Ṭālib, told him that he heard Umm Hānī, Abū Ṭālib's daughter, say, "I went to the Messenger of God (pbuh) in the year of the conquest of Mecca, and I found him bathing. His daughter Fāṭima was screening him with a piece of cloth." Umm Hānī said, "I greeted him, and he said, 'Who is that?' I said, 'I am Umm Hānī, Abū Ṭālib's daughter.' He said, 'Welcome, Umm Hānī.' When he finished bathing, he got up and performed eight cycles of prayer, wrapped in a single piece of cloth. When he finished, I said, 'Messenger of God, my brother, ʿAlī, has declared his intention to kill a man whom I have placed under my protection, so-and-so, the son of Hubayra.' The Messenger of God (pbuh) said, 'We have granted our protection to whomever you have granted protection, Umm Hānī.' Umm Hānī said, 'That was in the morning.'"

419. According to Mālik, Ibn Shihāb reported from ʿUrwa b. al-Zubayr that ʿĀʾisha, the wife of the Prophet (pbuh), said, "I never once saw the Messenger of God (pbuh) perform the Midmorning Prayer (*subḥat al-ḍuḥā*),[151] but I myself like to do it. At times, the Messenger of God (pbuh) would abstain from a practice he loved out of fear that the people might perform it and it would become obligatory."

420. According to Mālik, Zayd b. Aslam reported that ʿĀʾisha, the Mother of the Believers, would perform the Midmorning Prayer, which consisted of eight cycles, and she would say upon their completion, "Even if my parents were brought back to life for me, I would not give these up."

Chapter 9. Miscellaneous Matters Related to the Midmorning Prayer (*Ṣalāt al-Ḍuḥā*)

421. According to Mālik, Isḥāq b. ʿAbd Allāh b. Abī Ṭalḥa reported from Anas b. Mālik that his grandmother, Mulayka, invited the Messenger of God for food, and he ate some. Then the Messenger of God (pbuh) said, "Stand, for I shall lead you in prayer." Anas said, "I therefore stood up and brought out a mat that had turned black from prolonged use, and sprinkled it with

150 The year of the conquest refers to the year in which the Prophet (pbuh) returned triumphant to Mecca, year 9 of the Hijra (630 CE).

151 This text and others use the term *subḥa* in place of the more common word for prayer, *ṣalāt*, to distinguish this prayer from the obligatory ones. However, *subḥa* seems to have become archaic already by the time of Mālik, as indicated by the fact that he uses the more common term *ṣalāt* to refer to the Midmorning Prayer (*ṣalāt al-ḍuḥā*) in the title of this chapter.

some water. The Messenger of God (pbuh) stood on it, and the orphan and I made a line behind him, and the old woman stood behind us. He led us in the performance of two cycles (*rakʿa*) of prayer and then he left."

422. According to Mālik, Ibn Shihāb reported from ʿUbayd Allāh b. ʿAbd Allāh b. ʿUtba b. Masʿūd that his father said, "I went to see ʿUmar b. al-Khaṭṭāb when the day was at its hottest and found him performing supplementary prayers. I stood up behind him, and he motioned for me to stand beside him, on his right. When Yarfaʾ came, I stepped back, and we formed a row behind him."

Chapter 10. The Admonition against Walking in Front of a Person Performing Prayer

423. According to Mālik, Zayd b. Aslam reported from ʿAbd al-Raḥmān b. Abī Saʿīd al-Khudrī, from his father, that the Messenger of God (pbuh) said, "When someone is praying, he should not let anyone pass in front of him. He should repel such a person to the extent he can; and if the person refuses, he should fight him, for the person is most certainly a demon."

424. According to Mālik, Abū al-Naḍr, the freedman (*mawlā*) of ʿUmar b. ʿUbayd Allāh, reported from Busr b. Saʿīd that Zayd b. Khālid al-Juhanī sent him to Abū Juhaym, asking him what he had heard the Messenger of God (pbuh) say about a person who walks in front of someone performing the prayer. Abū Juhaym said, "The Messenger of God (pbuh) said, 'If the person passing in front of someone praying knew the enormity of his action, he would find it preferable to wait forty . . . rather than pass in front of him.'" Abū al-Naḍr said, "I do not know whether he said forty days, months, or years."

425. According to Mālik, Zayd b. Aslam reported from ʿAṭāʾ b. Yasār that Kaʿb al-Aḥbār said, "If the person passing in front of someone praying knew the enormity of his action, he would prefer to have the earth swallow him so as not to pass in front of him."

426. According to Mālik, it reached him that ʿAbd Allāh b. ʿUmar did not like to pass in front of women while they were praying.

427. According to Mālik, from Nāfiʿ, that ʿAbd Allāh b. ʿUmar would not pass in front of anyone who was praying, nor would he permit anyone to pass in front of him while he prayed.

Chapter 11. The Dispensation to Pass in Front of Someone Performing Prayer

428. According to Mālik, Ibn Shihāb reported from ʿUbayd Allāh b. ʿAbd Allāh b. ʿUtba b. Masʿūd that ʿAbd Allāh b. ʿAbbās said, "I arrived riding a female donkey—and I had just about come of age—while the Messenger of God (pbuh) was leading the people in prayer at Minā. There was a row of people praying, and I passed in front of some of them. I dismounted, sent the donkey off to graze, and joined the row of worshippers. No one, however, chided me for what I did."

429. According to Mālik, it reached him that Saʿd b. Abī Waqqāṣ would pass in front of some of the rows of worshippers while the prayer (*ṣalāt*) was in progress. Yaḥyā said, "Mālik said, 'I believe there is a broad dispensation to do that if the immediate call to prayer (*iqāma*) has been made, the imam has just begun the prayer by magnifying God (saying "God is great," *Allāhu akbar*), and it is impossible to enter the mosque and join the congregation without walking between the rows of worshippers.'"

430. According to Mālik, it reached him that ʿAlī b. Abī Ṭālib said, "Nothing that passes in front of a worshipper invalidates his prayer."

431. According to Mālik, Ibn Shihāb reported from Sālim b. ʿAbd Allāh that ʿAbd Allāh b. ʿUmar would say, "Nothing that passes in front of a worshipper invalidates his prayer."

Chapter 12. The Traveler's Barrier[152] during Prayer

432. According to Mālik, it reached him that ʿAbd Allāh b. ʿUmar would use his camel as a barrier when performing his prayer.

433. According to Mālik, Hishām b. ʿUrwa reported that his father would pray in the desert without a barrier.

Chapter 13. Brushing Away Small Stones during Performance of the Prayer (*Ṣalāt*)

434. According to Mālik, Abū Jaʿfar al-Qārī said, "I saw ʿAbd Allāh b. ʿUmar, when he prostrated during the prayer, gently brush away pebbles from the place where his forehead would touch the ground."

435. According to Mālik, Yaḥyā b. Saʿīd reported that it reached him that Abū Dharr would say, "Brushing away pebbles during performance of the

152 The Arabic term is *sutra*, and it refers to something that a worshipper uses as a kind of marker to signal to others to avoid walking in front of him while he is performing his prayer.

prayer may be done in only one sweep; but leaving them as they are is better than having red camels."[153]

Chapter 14. What Has Come Down regarding Straightening the Rows for the Performance of Prayer

436. According to Mālik, Nāfiʿ reported that ʿUmar b. al-Khaṭṭāb would take care to ensure that the rows of worshippers were straight and would magnify God (say "God is great," *Allāhu akbar*) and begin performance of the prayer only after he had been told that the rows had been straightened.

437. According to Mālik, his paternal uncle Abū Suhayl b. Mālik reported that his father said, "I was with Uthmān b. ʿAffān when it was time to pray. I was talking to him, asking him to give me an allowance from the treasury. I continued to talk to him even as he busied himself by stamping down some pebbles with his sandals. Finally, the men to whom he had delegated the task of straightening the rows returned and informed him that the rows had been straightened. He then said to me, 'Join a line of worshippers,' and then he magnified God and began the prayer."

Chapter 15. On Placing One Hand over the Other during Performance of the Prayer (*Ṣalāt*)

438. According to Mālik, ʿAbd al-Karīm b. Abī al-Mukhāriq al-Baṣrī said, "Some of the teachings of the prophets are 'If you feel no shame, then do as you please'; placing one hand on the other during the performance of prayer, the right hand on the left; breaking the fast promptly; and delaying the pre-dawn meal."

439. According to Mālik, Abū Ḥāzim b. Dīnār reported that Sahl b. Saʿd al-Sāʿidī said, "People were told to place the right hand on the left forearm during the performance of prayer." Abū Ḥāzim said, "I am certain that Sahl attributed this to the Messenger of God (pbuh)."

Chapter 16. The *Qunūt*[154] Supplication during the Morning Prayer (*Ṣalāt al-Ṣubḥ*)

440. According to Mālik, Nāfiʿ reported that ʿAbd Allāh b. ʿUmar did not utter the *qunūt* supplication during the performance of any prayer (*ṣalāt*).

---

153 "Red camels" (*ḥumr al-naʿam*) is an Arabic expression signifying good fortune.

154 *Qunūt* is the name of a supplication which, according to the Mālikīs, is made in the second cycle of the Morning Prayer (*ṣalāt al-ṣubḥ*) while the worshipper is standing upright after finishing recitation of the Quran but before bowing.

Chapter 17. The Prohibition against Performing the Prayer (*Ṣalāt*) When One Needs to Relieve Oneself

441. According to Mālik, Hishām b. ʿUrwa reported from his father that ʿAbd Allāh b. al-Arqam would lead his companions in prayer. One day, when they were about to perform a prayer, he went to relieve himself, and when he returned, he said, "I heard the Messenger of God (pbuh) say, 'Should anyone need to defecate, he should do so before praying.'"

442. According to Mālik, Zayd b. Aslam reported that ʿUmar b. al-Khaṭṭāb said, "Let no one pray while squeezing his thighs tightly together."

Chapter 18. Waiting for the Prayer (*Ṣalāt*) and Walking to the Mosque to Perform It

443. According to Mālik, Abū al-Zinād reported from al-Aʿraj, from Abū Hurayra, that the Messenger of God (pbuh) said, "The angels invoke God's blessings on anyone who lingers in the place where he performs his prayers, as long as he does not do anything to change his condition (*mā lam yuḥdith*). The angels say, 'God, forgive him! God, have mercy on him!'" Yaḥyā said, "Mālik said, 'I think his words "as long as he does not change his condition" refer to any act that invalidates ablutions.'"[155]

444. According to Mālik, Abū al-Zinād reported from al-Aʿraj, from Abū Hurayra, that the Messenger of God (pbuh) said, "A person is in a continuous state of prayer even if he is not performing a prayer as long as the thought of prayer preoccupies him, there being nothing stopping him from returning to his family other than his decision to wait to pray."

445. According to Mālik, Sumayy, the freedman (*mawlā*) of Abū Bakr, reported that Abū Bakr b. ʿAbd al-Raḥmān would say, "A person who sets out for the mosque in the morning or in the afternoon, with no other intention than to learn or to teach something good there, and then returns to his house is like a warrior fighting for the sake of God who has returned victorious with spoils."

446. According to Mālik, Nuʿaym b. ʿAbd Allāh al-Mujmir reported that he heard Abū Hurayra say, "If someone prays and then sits down in the place in which he prayed, the angels continue to bless him, saying, 'God, forgive him! God, have mercy on him!' If he gets up and leaves that place and sits down elsewhere in the mosque to await the next prayer, he remains in a state of prayer until he performs it."

155 Such acts include passing gas and relieving oneself.

447. According to Mālik, al-ʿAlāʾ b. ʿAbd al-Raḥmān b. Yaʿqūb reported from his father, from Abū Hurayra, that the Messenger of God (pbuh) said, "Shall I not tell you about the deeds through which God absolves your sins and raises your spiritual rank?[156] Performing your ablutions diligently when you are beset by adverse circumstances; walking great distances to the mosque; and waiting for one prayer after another. That indeed is vigilant defense of your outpost! That indeed is vigilant defense of your outpost! That indeed is vigilant defense of your outpost!"[157]

448. According to Mālik, it reached him that Saʿīd b. al-Musayyab said, "It is said that anyone who leaves the mosque after the call to prayer has been made without intending to return to join the congregation is a hypocrite."

449. According to Mālik, ʿĀmir b. ʿAbd Allāh b. al-Zubayr reported from ʿAmr b. Sulaym al-Zuraqī, from Abū Qatāda al-Anṣārī, that the Messenger of God (pbuh) said, "When someone enters the mosque, he should perform two cycles of prayer before he sits down."

450. According to Mālik, Abū al-Naḍr, the freedman of ʿUmar b. ʿUbayd Allāh, reported that Abū Salama b. ʿAbd al-Raḥmān said to him, "Didn't I see your master sit down without praying when he entered the mosque?" Abū al-Naḍr said, "He was referring to ʿUmar b. ʿUbayd Allāh, whom he was criticizing because ʿUmar entered the mosque and sat down before praying." Mālik said, "When someone enters the mosque, it is good for him to perform two cycles (*rakʿa*) of prayer before he sits down, but it is not obligatory."

Chapter 19. Placing the Hands on the Surface on Which One Places One's Face during Prostration

451. According to Mālik, Nāfiʿ reported that when ʿAbd Allāh b. ʿUmar prostrated, he would place the palms of his hands on the very surface on which he would put his face. Nāfiʿ said, "I saw him on a very cold day take his hands out from under his cloak and place them on the stony ground."

452. According to Mālik, Nāfiʿ reported that ʿAbd Allāh b. ʿUmar would say, "Whoever places his forehead on the ground in prostration should also place the palms of his hands there; and when he sits up, he should lift them from the ground, for the hands prostrate just like the face."

---

156 In Islamic eschatology, there are levels of punishment and reward. The closer one is to God in this life, the higher one's spiritual rank in the next life will be.

157 "Outpost" is the English translation of *ribāṭ*, which means a frontier outpost. Here the word is an allusion to the virtue of those serving in frontier outposts, guarding the frontiers of Islam against enemy attack.

Chapter 20. Turning and Clapping during the Performance of Prayer (*Ṣalāt*) When There Is a Need

453. According to Mālik, Abū Ḥāzim b. Dīnār reported from Sahl b. Saʿd al-Sāʿidī that the Messenger of God (pbuh) went to the clan of Banū ʿAmr b. ʿAwf to resolve a dispute that had broken out among them. The time to pray came, and the muezzin went to Abū Bakr and said, "Are you going to lead the people in the prayer, in which case I will make the immediate call to prayer (*iqāma*)?" Abū Bakr said, "Yes," and he began to pray. The Messenger of God (pbuh) then came and found the people praying. He continued walking until he stood in the first row. The people clapped when they noticed the Messenger of God (pbuh), but Abū Bakr was not one to turn around in his prayer. Only after the congregants' clapping became intense did Abū Bakr turn around and see the Messenger of God (pbuh). The Messenger of God (pbuh) motioned for him to stay put. Abū Bakr raised his hands and praised God in response to the command of the Messenger of God (pbuh). Then he stepped back until he stood in the first row. Then the Messenger of God (pbuh) stepped forward and led the prayer. When he finished, he said, "Abū Bakr, why didn't you stay where you were, as I instructed you?" Abū Bakr said, "It is not appropriate for Ibn Abī Quḥāfa[158] to pray in front of the Messenger of God (pbuh)." The Messenger of God (pbuh) then said to the congregants, "Why did you all clap so much? When something happens during the prayer, the men should say, 'Glory be to God' (*Subḥāna 'llāh*). When the men say, 'Glory be to God,' the imam will pay attention. Only women should clap."

454. According to Mālik, Nāfiʿ reported that Ibn ʿUmar did not turn around when performing his prayer.

455. According to Mālik, Abū Jaʿfar al-Qārī said, "I was praying, and ʿAbd Allāh b. ʿUmar was behind me, but I did not realize it. I then turned around, and he prodded me disapprovingly."

Chapter 21. What One Should Do When Joining the Prayer While the Imam Is Bowing

456. According to Mālik, Ibn Shihāb reported that Abū Umāma b. Sahl b. Ḥunayf said, "Zayd b. Thābit entered the mosque and found the people bowing, so he bowed and then advanced slowly until he reached the row of worshippers."

158 "Ibn Abī Quḥāfa" is a tongue-in-cheek reference by Abū Bakr to himself. "Abū Quḥāfa" was the name of his father, so "Ibn Abī Quḥāfa" is the "son of Abū Quḥāfa," i.e., Abū Bakr.

457. According to Mālik, it reached him that ʿAbd Allāh b. Masʿūd would move forward slowly while bowing.

Chapter 22. What Has Come Down regarding Invocation of God's Grace on the Prophet (pbuh)

458. According to Mālik, ʿAbd Allāh b. Abī Bakr b. Ḥazm reported from his father that ʿAmr b. Sulaym al-Zuraqī said, "Abū Ḥumayd al-Sāʿidī told me that they said, 'Messenger of God, how do we invoke God's grace upon you?' He said, 'Say, "God, grace Muḥammad and his wives and his offspring, just as You graced the family of Abraham; bless Muḥammad and his wives and his offspring, just as You blessed the family of Abraham. You are worthy of praise and glorious."'"[159]

459. According to Mālik, Nuʿaym b. ʿAbd Allāh al-Mujmir reported that Muḥammad b. ʿAbd Allāh b. Zayd al-Anṣārī told him that Abū Masʿūd al-Anṣārī said, "The Messenger of God (pbuh) came to us when we were at Saʿd b. ʿUbāda's gathering.[160] Bashīr b. Saʿd said to the Messenger of God (pbuh), 'God has commanded us to invoke His grace upon you, Messenger of God, but how should we do that?'" Abū Masʿūd said, "The Messenger of God (pbuh) remained so silent that we wished Bashīr had not asked him. The Messenger of God (pbuh) then said, 'Say, "God, grace Muḥammad and the family of Muḥammad, just as You graced Abraham, and bless Muḥammad and the family of Muḥammad, just as You blessed the family of Abraham, among all creatures; You are worthy of praise and glorious," and then say the "peace,"[161] as you have already learned it.'"[162]

460. According to Mālik, ʿAbd Allāh b. Dīnār said, "I saw ʿAbd Allāh b. ʿUmar standing at the grave of the Messenger of God (pbuh), invoking God's grace on the Messenger of God (pbuh) and on Abū Bakr and ʿUmar."

---

159 *Allāhumma ṣalli ʿalā Muḥammadin wa-azwājihi wa-dhurriyyatihi kamā ṣallayta ʿalā āli Ibrāhīm, wa-bārik ʿalā Muḥammadin wa-azwājihi wa-dhurriyyatihi kamā bārakta ʿalā āli Ibrāhīm, innaka ḥamīdun majīd.*

160 Saʿd b. ʿUbāda was the chief of the Khazraj, one of the two leading tribes of Medina before the Prophet Muḥammad's arrival. As the tribal chief, he would regularly meet with the leading men of the tribe.

161 That is, "And peace be upon you, Prophet, and God's mercy and His blessings." The editors of the RME note that the principal source manuscript included a note on the margin stating that the "peace" was a reference to this phrase, which is taken from the attestation of faith (*tashahhud*). See Book 3 (The First Book of Prayer), chapter 13.

162 The Arabic text of the prayer is *Allāhumma ṣalli ʿalā Muḥammadin wa-ʿalā āli Muḥammadin kamā ṣallayta ʿalā Ibrāhīm, wa-bārik ʿalā Muḥammadin wa-ʿalā āli Muḥammadin kamā bārakta ʿalā āli Ibrāhīm, fī ʾl-ʿālamīn, innaka ḥamīdun majīd.*

Chapter 23. The Practice (*ʿAmal*) with Respect to Miscellaneous Matters Related to Prayer (*Ṣalāt*)

461. According to Mālik, Nāfiʿ reported from Ibn ʿUmar that the Messenger of God (pbuh) would perform two cycles (*rakʿa*) of prayer before and after the Noon Prayer (*ṣalāt al-ẓuhr*), and after the Sunset Prayer (*ṣalāt al-maghrib*) he would perform two cycles at home. He would also perform two cycles of prayer after the Evening Prayer (*ṣalāt al-ʿishāʾ*). He would not, however, pray after the Friday Congregational Prayer (*ṣalāt al-jumuʿa*) until he had left the mosque and gone home, where he would perform two cycles of prayer.

462. According to Mālik, Abū al-Zinād reported from al-Aʿraj, from Abū Hurayra, that the Messenger of God (pbuh) said, "You see me standing in prayer in front of you. By God, neither your inner reverence nor your outward actions[163] during prayer are concealed from me, for I can see you from behind my back."

463. According to Mālik, Nāfiʿ reported from Ibn ʿUmar that the Messenger of God (pbuh) would go to Qubāʾ, sometimes riding and at other times walking.

464. According to Mālik, Yaḥyā b. Saʿīd reported from al-Nuʿmān b. Murra that the Messenger of God (pbuh) said, "What do you all believe about a drunkard, a thief, and a fornicator?" That was before specific rules about them had been revealed. They said, "God and His Messenger know best." He said, "These are vile deeds, and they warrant punishment. But the worst of thieves is the one who steals his prayer." They said, "How does one steal his prayer, Messenger of God?" He said, "He neither bows nor prostrates diligently."

465. According to Mālik, Hishām b. ʿUrwa reported from his father that the Messenger of God (pbuh) said, "Perform some of your prayers at home."

466. According to Mālik, Nāfiʿ reported that ʿAbd Allāh b. ʿUmar would say, "If a man is too ill to prostrate, he should motion with his head, not raise something to his forehead."

467. According to Mālik, Rabīʿa b. ʿAbd al-Raḥmān reported that if ʿAbd Allāh b. ʿUmar arrived at the mosque after the people had already performed the obligatory prayer, he would perform it immediately and not pray anything before it.

468. According to Mālik, Nāfiʿ reported that ʿAbd Allāh b. ʿUmar passed in front of a man who was praying and greeted him. The man said something in reply, so ʿAbd Allāh b. ʿUmar returned to him and said, "If someone is

163 In Arabic, *khushūʿikum wa-rukūʿikum*. We have understood the latter term as referring to the outward actions of the prayer in general, not just bowing.

greeted while he is praying, he should not reply using speech. Rather, he should wave with his hand."

469. According to Mālik, Nāfiʿ reported that Ibn ʿUmar would say, "If someone forgets to perform a prayer and remembers it only when he is praying with the imam, he should continue praying with the imam. Then, when the imam finishes that prayer, he should perform the prayer that he forgot and then repeat the other prayer that he previously performed with the imam."

470. According to Mālik, Yaḥyā b. Saʿīd reported from Muḥammad b. Yaḥyā b. Ḥabbān that his paternal uncle Wāsiʿ b. Ḥabbān said, "I was performing my prayer, and ʿAbd Allāh b. ʿUmar was resting his back against the wall in the direction of Mecca. When I finished praying, I got up, turned left, and went to him. ʿAbd Allāh b. ʿUmar then said, 'Why didn't you turn to the right?'" Wāsiʿ said, "I said, 'I saw you, so I came over.' ʿAbd Allāh said, 'You did well! Some might say, "Turn to your right," but when someone prays, he may leave in either direction, to his right or his left.'"

471. According to Mālik, Hishām b. ʿUrwa reported from his father, from an Emigrant man[164] whom he believed trustworthy, that he had asked ʿAbd Allāh b. ʿAmr b. al-ʿĀṣī, "Can I pray where camels rest next to their watering holes?" ʿAbd Allāh answered, "No; however, you can pray in a paddock for sheep and goats."

472. According to Mālik, Ibn Shihāb reported that Saʿīd b. al-Musayyab said, "In which prayer does one sit for every cycle?" Saʿīd answered, "The Evening Prayer, if one misses one cycle with the imam." Mālik said, "That is the long-established ordinance (*al-sunna*) for all prayers, namely, that one sits for the cycle that one has missed."

Chapter 24. Miscellaneous Matters Related to the Performance of Prayer (*Ṣalāt*)

473. According to Mālik, ʿĀmir b. ʿAbd Allāh b. al-Zubayr reported from ʿAmr b. Sulaym al-Zuraqī, from Abū Qatāda al-Anṣārī, that the Messenger of God (pbuh) would pray while carrying Umāma bt. Zaynab, the granddaughter of the Messenger of God (pbuh) and the daughter of Abū al-ʿĀṣ b. Rabīʿa b. ʿAbd Shams. When the Messenger of God (pbuh) prostrated, he would put her down, and when he stood up, he would lift her up again.

164 The Emigrants (*muhājirūn*) were those Muslims who emigrated from Mecca to Medina, in contrast to the Muslims native to Medina, who were called the "helpers" (*anṣār*).

474. According to Mālik, Abū al-Zinād reported from al-Aʿraj, from Abū Hurayra, that the Messenger of Allāh (pbuh) said, "Angels come to you in turns, one after the other; some by night, and others by day. They meet at the times of the Afternoon Prayer (*ṣalāt al-ʿaṣr*) and the Dawn Prayer (*ṣalāt al-fajr*). Those who have passed the night with you ascend, and God asks them—although He knows more than they do—'In what condition did you leave my servants?' They say, 'When we left them, they were praying, and when we came to them, they were praying.'"

475. According to Mālik, Hishām b. ʿUrwa reported from his father, from ʿĀ'isha, the wife of the Prophet (pbuh), that the Messenger of God (pbuh) said, "Tell[165] Abū Bakr to lead the congregation in prayer." ʿĀ'isha said, "Messenger of God, if Abū Bakr takes your place, his weeping will obscure his voice, so the congregation will not hear him. Ask ʿUmar instead to lead the congregation in prayer." The Messenger of God (pbuh) again said, "Tell Abū Bakr to lead the congregation in prayer." ʿĀ'isha said, "So I said to Ḥafṣa, 'Tell the Messenger of God (pbuh), "If Abū Bakr takes your place, his weeping will obscure his voice, and the congregation will not hear him. Ask ʿUmar instead to lead the congregation in prayer."' So she did." The Messenger of God (pbuh) said, "You are exactly like the women who betrayed Joseph." Then he said, "Tell Abū Bakr to lead the congregation in prayer!" Ḥafṣa said to ʿĀ'isha, "No good has ever come to me from listening to you."

476. According to Mālik, Ibn Shihāb reported from ʿAṭā' b. Yazīd al-Laythī that ʿUbayd Allāh b. ʿAdī b. al-Khiyār said, "When the Messenger of God (pbuh) was sitting with some people, a man approached him and spoke secretly to him. No one knew what the man had secretly told the Messenger of God (pbuh) until the Messenger of God (pbuh) spoke up. It turned out that he wanted permission to kill one of the hypocrites.[166] When the Messenger of God (pbuh) spoke up, he said to the man, 'Doesn't that man attest that there is no god but God, and that Muḥammad is the Messenger of God?' The man answered, 'Yes, indeed, but it is mere speech, and he has not said it sincerely.' The Messenger of God (pbuh) said, 'Does he not perform the prayers?' The man said, 'Yes, indeed, but only outwardly; he does not pray sincerely.' The Messenger of God (pbuh) said, 'Those are precisely the ones whom God has forbidden me to kill.'"

477. According to Mālik, Zayd b. Aslam reported from ʿAṭā' b. Yasār that the Messenger of God said, "God, do not make my grave an object that is

---

165 The imperative is in the plural (*murū*) and not directed at ʿĀ'isha personally.

166 The term "hypocrites" refers to a group of people in Medina who had outwardly embraced Islam but were not sincere followers of the Prophet Muḥammad and who secretly hoped for his defeat at the hands of his enemies.

worshipped!" Then he said, "God's wrath fell on those who made the graves of their Prophets into shrines."[167]

478. According to Mālik, Ibn Shihāb reported from Maḥmūd b. Labīd al-Anṣārī[168] that ʿItbān b. Mālik, who was blind, would lead his people in prayer, and that he said to the Messenger of God (pbuh), "Sometimes it is dark, or it rains or floods, and I am blind, so I can't make it to the mosque. Therefore, Messenger of God, please pray in a certain spot in my house so that I may use it as a regular place of prayer." The Messenger of God (pbuh) went to his home and said, "Where would you like me to pray?" The man pointed out to him a spot in his house, and the Messenger of God (pbuh) prayed there.

479. According to Mālik, Ibn Shihāb reported from ʿAbbād b. Tamīm, from his paternal uncle,[169] that he saw the Messenger of God (pbuh) lying down in the mosque, with one foot on top of the other.

480. According to Mālik, Ibn Shihāb reported from Saʿīd b. al-Musayyab that ʿUmar b. al-Khaṭṭāb and ʿUthmān b. ʿAffān would do likewise.

481. According to Mālik, Yaḥyā b. Saʿīd reported that ʿAbd Allāh b. Masʿūd said to someone, "You are living in a time when those who understand the Quran are many, but those who recite it are few; when the Quran's ordinances are preserved, but its wording is lost; when few beg, but many give; when prayers are long, but sermons are short; and when good deeds are preferred over desires. There will come a time, however, when those who understand the Quran will be few, but those who recite it many; when the wording of the Quran will be preserved, but its ordinances lost; when many will beg, but few give; when the sermons are long, but the prayers short; and when desires are preferred over good deeds."

482. According to Mālik, Yaḥyā b. Saʿīd said, "It has reached me that prayer will be considered before a servant's all other deeds. If God accepts his prayer, the rest of his deeds will be considered; however, if He does not accept it, none of the servant's other deeds will even be considered."

---

167 Zurqānī glosses this report with the comment that the word *masājid*, which ordinarily means "places of worship," is here intended either in its literal sense, i.e., as a place of prostration, or in the sense of direction of prayer. Consequently, the wrath of God would befall those who prostrate themselves on the graves of their prophets or worship the prophets' tombs. Zurqānī, *Sharḥ al-Zurqānī*, 1:595.

168 Other narrators of the *Muwaṭṭa'* identify this narrator as Maḥmūd b. Rabīʿ. Zurqānī, *Sharḥ al-Zurqānī*, 1:596.

169 He is ʿAbd Allāh b. Zayd b. ʿĀṣim al-Māzinī.

483. According to Mālik, Hishām b. ʿUrwa reported from his father that ʿĀʾisha, the wife of the Prophet (pbuh), said, "The good deeds that the Messenger of God (pbuh) loved the most were those that were performed constantly."

484. According to Mālik, ʿĀmir b. Saʿd b. Abī Waqqāṣ reported that his father said, "There were two brothers, and one of them died forty nights before the other. The virtues of the first were mentioned in the presence of the Messenger of God (pbuh), so he said, 'Was the other brother not a Muslim?' They said, 'He was, and not a bad one.' The Messenger of God (pbuh) said, 'Do you know what station he reached by virtue of his prayers? Prayer is like having a deep river at your door's edge, into which you plunge five times every day. How much filth do you think would remain? You certainly cannot imagine the station he reached simply by virtue of his prayers.'"

485. According to Mālik, it reached him that whenever a peddler selling goods would pass in front of ʿAṭāʾ b. Yasār in the mosque, the latter would call to him and ask, "What detained[170] you here, and what do you want?" If the peddler told him that he wanted to sell him something, ʿAṭāʾ would say to him, "Go to the market of this world, for this is exclusively the market of the Hereafter."

486. According to Mālik, it reached him that ʿUmar b. al-Khaṭṭāb built a courtyard near a corner of the mosque called al-Buṭayḥāʾ and said, "If someone wants to engage in idle talk, recite poetry, or raise his voice, he should go there."

Chapter 25. Miscellaneous Reports Encouraging the Performance of Prayer (*Ṣalāt*)

487. According to Mālik, his paternal uncle Abū Suhayl b. Mālik reported from his father that he heard Ṭalḥa b. ʿUbayd Allāh say, "A man from Najd[171] came to the Messenger of God (pbuh). His hair was disheveled and he spoke in a loud voice, but we could not make out what he was saying. It was not until he drew close to the Messenger of God (pbuh) that we discovered that he was asking about Islam. The Messenger of God (pbuh) said to him, 'There are five prayers during the day and the night.' The man said, 'Are there any other prayers I am obliged to perform?' The Messenger of God (pbuh) said, 'No, except if you choose to pray more.' The Messenger of God (pbuh) said, 'And fasting the month of Ramadan.' The man asked, 'Am

---

170 The text of the RME uses the Arabic expression *mā manaʿaka*. Other transmissions of the *Muwaṭṭaʾ* instead read *mā maʿaka* ("What is with you?").

171 A region of the central Arabian Peninsula to the east of the Hijaz.

I obliged to fast additional days?' The Messenger of God (pbuh) said, 'No, except if you choose to fast more.' Then the Messenger of God (pbuh) spoke of the alms-tax (*zakāt*). The man asked, 'Am I obliged to give away anything more?' The Messenger of God (pbuh) said, 'No, except if you choose to give more.' The man walked away, saying, 'By God, I shall do neither more nor less than this.' The Messenger of God (pbuh) said, 'He will be successful, if he is telling the truth.'"

488. According to Mālik, Abū al-Zinād reported from al-Aʿraj, from Abū Hurayra, that the Messenger of God (pbuh) said, "When people are asleep, Satan ties three knots at the back of their heads, and as he tightens each knot, he says, 'A long night lies ahead of you, so sleep well!' If someone wakes up and manages to remember God, the first knot is undone. If he performs ablutions, the second is undone. If he prays, the third is undone, and so he awakes with a spring in his step, and in good spirits; however, if he sleeps through the night, in the morning he awakes ill-tempered and lazy."

Book 10
The Book of the Two Feasts (*ʿĪd*)

Chapter 1. The Practice (*ʿAmal*) with Respect to Bathing (*Ghusl*) for the Two Feasts (*ʿĪd*), the General Call (*Adhān*) to the Feast Prayers (*Ṣalāt al-ʿĪd*), and the Immediate Call to Perform Them (*Iqāma*)

489. According to Mālik, he heard several of their knowledgeable men[172] say, "There has never been a general call to prayer or an immediate call to prayer prior to the performance of the prayers for the Feast of Breaking the Ramadan Fast (*ʿīd al-fiṭr*) or the Feast of the Sacrificial Animals (*ʿīd al-aḍḥā*) from the time of the Messenger of God (pbuh) down to this day." Mālik said, "That is the long-established ordinance among us about which there is no dissent (*al-sunna allatī lā ikhtilāfa fīhā ʿindanā*)."[173]

490. According to Mālik, Nāfiʿ reported that ʿAbd Allāh b. ʿUmar would bathe on the day of the Feast of Breaking the Ramadan Fast before he headed out early in the morning to the spot where the prayer would be performed.

Chapter 2. The Command to Perform the Prayer before the Sermons Are Delivered for the Feast Prayers (*Ṣalāt al-ʿĪd*)

491. According to Mālik, Ibn Shihāb reported that the Messenger of God (pbuh) would perform the prayer for the Feast of Breaking the Ramadan Fast (*ʿīd al-fiṭr*) and for the Feast of the Sacrificial Animals (*ʿīd al-aḍḥā*) before delivering the sermon.

492. According to Mālik, it reached him that Abū Bakr and ʿUmar b. al-Khaṭṭāb would do the same.

---

172 That is, learned men from the generation of the Followers, those who succeeded the Companions of the Messenger of God (pbuh) and met them, prayed with them, learned from them, and then taught those who came after them. Bājī, *al-Muntaqā*, 1:315.

173 Wymann-Landgraf, *Mālik and Medina*, 293. According to the classical Arabic dictionary *Lisān al-ʿArab*, the term *aḍḥā* is the plural of *aḍḥāh*, which means a sacrificial animal. We have therefore translated *ʿīd al-aḍḥā* as "the Feast of the Sacrificial Animals."

493. According to Mālik, Ibn Shihāb reported that Abū ʿUbayd, the freedman (*mawlā*) of Ibn Azhar, said, "I attended the Feast Prayers when ʿUmar b. al-Khaṭṭāb was caliph. He performed the prayer, and when he finished, he gave a sermon to the congregants, in which he said, 'The Messenger of God (pbuh) has indeed prohibited you from fasting on these two days: the day you conclude the fast of Ramadan and the day you eat from your sacrificial animals.'" Abū ʿUbayd said, "I was also present for the Feast Prayers when ʿUthmān b. ʿAffān was caliph. He came and performed the prayer, and when he finished, he gave a sermon, in which he said, 'It is the case that today two feasts of yours have fallen on the same day.[174] Anyone from ʿĀliya[175] is free to remain here to perform the Friday Congregational Prayer (*ṣalāt al-jumuʿa*) or to return home, as he wishes.'" Abū ʿUbayd said, "Then I was also present for the Feast Prayers when ʿAlī b. Abī Ṭālib performed them—when ʿUthmān was besieged. ʿAlī came and prayed, and when he finished, he gave the sermon."

Chapter 3. The Command to Eat before Heading Out on the Morning of the Feast of Breaking the Ramadan Fast (*ʿĪd al-Fiṭr*)

494. According to Mālik, Hishām b. ʿUrwa reported from his father that he would eat on the day of the Feast of Breaking the Ramadan Fast before going out in the morning to perform the prayer.

495. According to Mālik, Ibn Shihāb reported that Saʿīd b. al-Musayyab informed him that the people were instructed to eat on the day of the Feast of Breaking the Ramadan Fast before going out in the morning to perform the prayer. Yaḥyā said, "Mālik said, 'I do not think that people are required to do that on the day of the Feast of the Sacrificial Animals (*ʿīd al-aḍḥā*).'"

Chapter 4. What Has Come Down regarding Magnifying God (Saying "God Is Great," *Allāhu Akbar*) and Reciting the Quran during the Performance of the Feast Prayers (*Ṣalāt al-ʿĪd*)

496. According to Mālik, Ḍamra b. Saʿīd al-Māzinī reported from ʿUbayd Allāh b. ʿAbd Allāh b. ʿUtba b. Masʿūd that ʿUmar b. al-Khaṭṭāb asked Abū Wāqid al-Laythī about what the Messenger of God (pbuh) would recite in the prayers for the Feast of the Sacrificial Animals (*ʿīd al-aḍḥā*) and the Feast of Breaking the Ramadan Fast (*ʿīd al-fiṭr*). He said, "He would recite '*Qāf*, by the Glorious Quran' (*Qāf wa'l-Qurʾān al-majīd*) and 'The Hour is nigh, and the moon has been cleft in two' (*Iqtarabat al-sāʿatu wa'nshaqqa al-qamar*)."[176]

---

174 That is, the Feast Day had fallen on a Friday, which is a metaphorical feast day.

175 A place approximately 3 km from Medina.

176 The first verses of the Quran's fiftieth and eighty-fifth chapters, respectively.

497. According to Mālik, Nāfiʿ, the freedman of ʿAbd Allāh b. ʿUmar, said, "I attended the Feast Prayers for both the Feast of the Sacrificial Animals and the Feast of Breaking the Ramadan Fast when Abū Hurayra performed them. He would magnify God seven times in the first cycle (*rakʿa*) of the prayer before reciting the *Fātiḥa* and five times in the second cycle of the prayer before reciting the *Fātiḥa*." Yaḥyā said, "Mālik said, 'That is the rule among us (*dhālika al-amr ʿindanā*).'"

498. Yaḥyā said, "Mālik said, regarding someone who arrives at the place where the Feast Prayer is to be performed only to find that the people have already performed it, 'He is not obliged to perform the Feast Prayer, whether in that place or at home. If he does perform the Feast Prayer, whether there or at home, however, there is nothing objectionable in that. He should magnify God seven times in the first cycle of the prayer before reciting the *Fātiḥa* and five times in the second cycle before reciting the *Fātiḥa*.'"

Chapter 5. Refraining from Performing Supplementary Prayers (*Ṣalāt*) before and after the Feast Prayers (*Ṣalāt al-ʿĪd*)

499. According to Mālik, Nāfiʿ reported that ʿAbd Allāh b. ʿUmar did not perform any supplementary prayers on the day of the Feast of Breaking the Ramadan Fast (*ʿīd al-fiṭr*), either before or after the Feast Prayer.

500. According to Mālik, it reached him that Saʿīd b. al-Musayyab, after performing the Morning Prayer (*ṣalāt al-ṣubḥ*), would set out before the sun rose to the place where the Feast Prayer was to be performed.

Chapter 6. The Dispensation to Perform Supplementary Prayers (*Ṣalāt*) before and after the Feast Prayers (*Ṣalāt al-ʿĪd*)

501. According to Mālik, ʿAbd al-Raḥmān b. al-Qāsim reported that his father would perform four cycles of supplementary prayers before he set out early in the morning to the place where the Feast Prayer was to be performed.

502. According to Mālik, Hishām b. ʿUrwa reported from his father that he would perform supplementary prayers in the mosque on the day of the Feast of Breaking the Ramadan Fast (*ʿīd al-fiṭr*) before the performance of the Feast Prayer.

Chapter 7. The Early Morning Departure of the Ruler (*Imām*) on Feast Day (*ʿĪd*), and Waiting for the Sermon

503. Yaḥyā said, "Mālik said, 'It has long been the established ordinance about which there is no dissent among us (*maḍat al-sunna allatī lā ikhtilāfa* *fīhā 'indanā*) that the ruler sets out from his home to the place where the Feast Prayer is to be performed at a time that allows him to arrive there shortly after the sun rises, when it has become permissible to perform the Feast Prayer.'"

504. Yaḥyā said, "Mālik was asked whether a man who performs the prayer for the Feast of Breaking the Ramadan Fast (*'īd al-fiṭr*) with the imam may leave before he hears the sermon. Mālik said, 'He should not leave until the imam leaves.'"

Book 11

The Book of the Prayer of Danger (*Ṣalāt al-Khawf*)

Chapter 1. The Prayer of Danger (*Ṣalāt al-Khawf*)[177]

505. According to Mālik, Yazīd b. Rūmān reported from Ṣāliḥ b. Khawwāt, from someone[178] who had performed the Prayer of Danger (*ṣalāt al-khawf*) with the Messenger of God (pbuh) at the Battle of Dhāt al-Riqāʿ,[179] that one group of soldiers formed a row with him, while another faced the enemy. The Messenger of God (pbuh) performed one cycle (*rakʿa*) of the prayer with the group that was with him. Then he stood up and remained standing while they finished the second cycle of prayer themselves. Then they left and went to face the enemy. The other group then came, and so the Messenger of God (pbuh) prayed with them the one cycle of prayer that remained of his prayer. Then he remained seated while they finished by performing one cycle by themselves, and then he concluded the prayer by saying "Peace be upon you" (*taslīm*) with them.

506. According to Mālik, Yaḥyā b. Saʿīd reported from al-Qāsim b. Muḥammad, from Ṣāliḥ b. Khawwāt al-Anṣārī, that Sahl b. Abī Ḥathma al-Anṣārī told him that the Prayer of Danger is performed in the following manner: the imam stands with a group of soldiers while another group faces the enemy. The imam performs one cycle of prayer, prostrating with those who are with him. Then he stands up, and once he has arisen, he waits while they conclude the remaining cycle of prayer themselves. They finish their prayer, saying "Peace be upon you," and leave and go face the enemy,

177 As is clear from the texts included in this chapter, this form of prayer is particular to soldiers on a battlefield who are facing the enemy in combat.

178 Zurqanī identifies this anonymous source as either Sahl b. Abī Ḥathma or Ṣāliḥ b. Khawwāt's father, Khawwāt b. Jubayr, giving greater probability to the latter. Zurqānī, *Sharḥ al-Zurqānī*, 1:624.

179 According to the editors of the RME, the battle of Dhāt al-Riqāʿ took place in year 5 of the Hijra (626 CE). It was named after the multi-hued mountain where the battle took place, or on account of the multicolored banners that were flown by those fighting that day, or because many of the Muslims who fought in the battle suffered bloody feet from marching barefooted to the battlefield, which forced them to tie rags around their feet.

while the imam remains standing in place. Then the other soldiers who have not yet prayed come and form a row behind the imam and join the prayer by magnifying God (saying "God is great," *Allāhu akbar*).[180] The imam then bows and prostrates with them and concludes his prayer by saying "Peace be upon you." The soldiers then stand up and conclude the second cycle of prayer on their own, and then they finish their prayer by saying "Peace be upon you."

507. According to Mālik, Nāfiʿ reported that when ʿAbd Allāh b. ʿUmar was asked about the Prayer of Danger, he would say, "The imam and a group of soldiers step forward, and he performs one cycle of prayer with them, while another group, which has not yet prayed, stands between him and the enemy. When those who are with him have performed one cycle of the prayer, they change places with those who have not yet prayed—but because they have not yet finished their prayer, they do not say 'Peace be upon you.' Then the other group performs one cycle of the prayer with the imam. The imam then leaves, having finished his prayer by performing two cycles. Then each person in the two groups performs one cycle of prayer by himself. In this way, everyone in both groups will have performed two cycles of prayer. If it is too dangerous to follow this procedure, they should pray standing on their feet, or on their mounts, whether or not they are facing the direction of prayer." Yaḥyā said, "Mālik said that Nāfiʿ said, 'I believe that ʿAbd Allāh b. ʿUmar related this procedure from none other than the Messenger of God (pbuh).'"

508. According to Mālik, Yaḥyā b. Saʿīd reported that Saʿīd b. al-Musayyab said, "The Messenger of God (pbuh) performed neither the Noon Prayer (*ṣalāt al-ẓuhr*) nor the Afternoon Prayer (*ṣalāt al-ʿaṣr*) at the Battle of the Trench until the sun had set." Yaḥyā said, "Mālik said, 'Of all that I have heard regarding the Prayer of Danger, the report of al-Qāsim b. Muḥammad[181] from Ṣāliḥ b. Khawwāt is, in my opinion, the best.'"

Chapter 2. The Practice (*ʿAmal*) with Respect to the Performance of the Prayer on the Occasion of a Solar Eclipse (*Ṣalāt Kusūf al-Shams*)

509. According to Mālik, Hishām b. ʿUrwa reported from his father that ʿĀ'isha, the wife of the Prophet (pbuh), said, "A solar eclipse occurred in the time of the Prophet (pbuh), so he led the people in prayer. He stood and continued to stand for a long time, and then he bowed for a long time. He

---

180 This is the *takbīrat al-iḥrām*, which indicates that the worshipper has entered the state of formal prayer. He exits this state by concluding the prayer through the *taslīm*, which involves turning his head to the right and saying *Al-salām ʿalaykum* ("May peace be upon you").

181 That is, hadith no. 506 above.

then stood again for a long time, though not as long as before, and again bowed for a long time, but not as long as before. Then he stood up, and then prostrated. He did the same in the last cycle of the prayer (*rakʿa*). He then concluded the prayer, and the sun had reappeared. He gave a sermon, praised God, and then said, 'The sun and the moon are among God's signs. They are not blotted out from the sky on account of anyone's birth or death. When you see an eclipse, call out to God as supplicants, magnify Him, and give charity freely.' Then he said, 'Community of Muḥammad! By God, no one is angrier at the adultery of his servant or handmaiden than God Himself. Community of Muḥammad! By God, if you knew what I know, you would laugh little and weep much.'"

510. According to Mālik, Zayd b. Aslam reported from ʿAṭāʾ b. Yasār that ʿAbd Allāh b. ʿAbbās said, "A solar eclipse occurred, so the Messenger of God (pbuh) prayed, and the people prayed with him. He remained standing for a lengthy time, approximately the time it takes to recite 'The Cow' (*al-Baqara*)."[182] ʿAbd Allāh b. ʿAbbās said, "Then he bowed for a lengthy time. He then rose and stood for a long time, but not as long as before. Then he bowed again for a long time, but not as long as before. Then he prostrated. Then he stood up and remained standing for a long time, though not as long as before. Then he bowed for a long time, though not as long as before. He then rose and stood for a long time, though not as long as before. Then he bowed for a long time, though not as long as before. Then he prostrated. Then he finished, and the sun had reappeared. The Messenger of God (pbuh) then said, 'The sun and the moon are two of God's signs. They are not blotted out from the sky on account of anyone's birth or death. When you see an eclipse, remember God.' They said, 'Messenger of God! We noticed that you reached out for something while you were standing there, and then we saw you retreat.' He said, 'I saw Paradise, and I reached out for a bunch of its grapes, and had I taken them, you would have eaten from them for as long as the world endured. Then I saw Hell, and I had never seen anything like it before.[183] And I saw that most of its denizens are women.' They said, 'Why, Messenger of God?' He said, 'Because of their ingratitude.' Someone said, 'Are those women ungrateful to God?' He said, 'No, they are ungrateful to their husbands, and they are ungrateful for their husbands' kindness toward them. Even if a husband had always been kind to one of them, were she ever to see something bad from him, she would say, "I have never seen any good come from you."'"

182 The second and longest chapter of the Quran.

183 Another narration of the *Muwaṭṭaʾ* includes the phrase *afẓaʿ* ("more shocking"). Zurqānī, *Sharḥ al-Zurqānī*, 1:636.

511. According to Mālik, Yaḥyā b. Sa'īd reported from 'Amra bt. 'Abd al-Raḥmān, from 'Ā'isha, the wife of the Prophet (pbuh), that a Jewish woman came to her, begging. The Jewish woman said to 'Ā'isha, "May God protect you from the torment of the grave (*'adhāb al-qabr*)." 'Ā'isha asked the Messenger of God, "Is it true that people are tormented in their graves?" The Messenger of God (pbuh) said, "I seek God's protection from that."[184] Then, one morning, the Messenger of God (pbuh) set out on a mount, but there was a solar eclipse, so he returned by midmorning, passing by his wives' homes. He stood to pray, and the people stood behind him. He stood for a long time and then bowed for a long time. Then he stood up and remained standing for a long time, though not as long as before. Then he bowed for a long time, though not as long as before. Then he stood up, and then prostrated. Then he stood up and remained standing for a long time, though not as long as before. Then he bowed for a long time, though not as long as before. Then he stood up and remained standing for a long time, though not as long as before. Then he bowed for a long time, though not as long as before. Then he stood up again, and then prostrated. Then he finished the prayer and said whatever God wished him to say, and then he ordered them to seek God's protection from the torment of the grave.

Chapter 3. What Has Come Down regarding the Prayer of the Eclipse (*Ṣalāt al-Kusūf*)

512. According to Mālik, Hishām b. 'Urwa reported from Fāṭima bt. al-Mundhir that Asmā' bt. Abī Bakr said, "I went to see 'Ā'isha, the wife of the Prophet (pbuh), during a solar eclipse, and I found the people standing there in prayer, including her. So I said, 'What's going on? Why is everyone praying?' 'Ā'isha pointed toward the sky and said, 'Glory be to God!' So I said, 'Is the eclipse a sign?' She nodded her head in agreement." Asmā' said, "I therefore joined them and stood until I almost fainted, and so I began to pour water over my head. The Messenger of God (pbuh) then praised God and commended Him, and then said, 'There were things I had never seen before, but I have now seen them while standing in this very spot, even Heaven and Hell. It has been revealed to me that you will be tried in your graves, like (or close to) the way the Antichrist (*al-dajjāl*)[185] will try you.'" (I, Fāṭima, do not know which of the two phrases Asmā' used.) Asmā' said,

184 Bājī suggests that this report bears two possible meanings. The first is that the Prophet (pbuh) was seeking God's protection from the possibility that people could be tormented in their graves. The second assumes that the torment is real and that the Prophet (pbuh) was seeking God's protection from it. Bājī, *al-Muntaqā*, 1:329.

185 *Al-dajjāl* is a figure that features in Islamic eschatology and plays a role similar to that of the Antichrist in Christian eschatology as a false messiah who will seduce countless people to follow him before the appearance of the true messiah, who will defeat him.

"Each of you in his grave will be called and asked, 'What do you know about this man (the Messenger of God, pbuh)?' The believer (or 'the one with certain conviction'; I, Fāṭima, do not know which of the two phrases Asmāʾ used) will say, 'He is Muḥammad, the Messenger of God. He came to us with clear proofs and guidance, and we responded favorably to his message, believed in it, and followed him.' It will be said to him, 'Sleep peacefully, for now we know you are a true believer.' But the hypocrite (or 'the skeptic'; I, Fāṭima, do not know which of the two phrases Asmāʾ used) will say, 'I do not know. I heard people say something like that, so I said it too.'"

Book 12
The Book of the Prayer for Rain (*Ṣalāt al-Istisqā'*)

Chapter 1. The Practice (*'Amal*) with Respect to the Performance of the Prayer for Rain (*Ṣalāt al-Istisqā'*)

513. According to Mālik, ʿAbd Allāh b. Abī Bakr b. Ḥazm reported that he heard ʿAbbād b. Tamīm say, "I heard ʿAbd Allāh b. Zayd al-Māzinī say, 'The Messenger of God (pbuh) went to the place outside Medina where the Feast Prayers are performed in order to ask God for rain. When he faced Mecca, he turned his cloak inside out.'"[186]

514. Yaḥyā said, "Mālik was asked about the number of cycles (*rakʿa*) that should be performed during the Prayer for Rain. He said, 'Two cycles, but the imam performs them before giving the sermon. He prays two cycles, and then, facing the direction of Mecca, he turns his cloak inside out, delivers the sermon standing, and supplicates. He recites aloud from the Quran in both cycles of the prayer. When he reverses his cloak, he puts what was on his right side on his left, and what was on his left side on his right. The congregants, while sitting facing Mecca, should reverse their cloaks when the imam reverses his.'"

Chapter 2. What Has Come Down regarding the Prayer for Rain (*Ṣalāt al-Istisqā'*)

515. According to Mālik, Yaḥyā b. Saʿīd reported from ʿAmr b. Shuʿayb that when the Messenger of God (pbuh) prayed for rain, he would say, "God! Send rain to Your faithful servants and Your creatures! Spread Your mercy and renew the life of this dying land of Yours!"

---

186 Bājī indicates that this is an auspicious gesture to indicate the change from a state of drought to one of plenty. Bājī, *al-Muntaqā*, 1:332.

516. According to Mālik, Sharīk b. ʿAbd Allāh b. Abī Namir reported that Anas b. Mālik said, "A man came to the Messenger of God (pbuh) and said, 'Messenger of God, our herds are perishing, and travel has become impossible,[187] so supplicate God for rain.' The Messenger of God (pbuh) therefore supplicated God, and rain fell for an entire week." Anas continued, "A man then came to the Messenger of God (pbuh) and said, 'Messenger of God! Homes have been destroyed, roads have become impassable, and herds have perished from flooding.' The Messenger of God (pbuh) therefore said, 'God, send the rain only to the hills and mountains, to the river beds, and to the orchards!'" Anas said, "The clouds over Medina cleared up, like a robe being cast off."

517. Yaḥyā said, "Regarding someone who missed the Prayer for Rain (*ṣalāt al-istisqā'*) but attended the sermon and desired to pray it, either in the mosque or when he got home, Mālik said, 'The choice is his: he may choose to pray if he wishes, or choose not to.'"

Chapter 3. What Has Come Down regarding Seeking Rain by Means of the Stars

518. According to Mālik, Ṣāliḥ b. Kaysān reported from ʿUbayd Allāh b. ʿAbd Allāh b. ʿUtba b. Masʿūd that Zayd b. Khālid al-Juhanī said, "The Messenger of God (pbuh) performed the Morning Prayer (*ṣalāt al-ṣubḥ*) with us at al-Ḥudaybiya[188] after a rainy night. When he finished, he approached the people and said, 'Do you know what your Lord said?' They replied, 'God and His Messenger know best.' The Messenger of God (pbuh) said, 'God said, "Some of My servants awoke this morning believing in Me, while others awoke denying Me. Those who say, 'Rain fell on us through the Grace of God and His Mercy'—they believe in Me and reject the power of the stars. Those who say, 'Rain fell on us because of such-and-such stars'—they reject Me and believe in the power of the stars."'"[189]

519. According to Mālik, it reached him that the Messenger of God (pbuh) would say, "If a cloud forms over the Red Sea and then moves north toward the Levant, that cloud will bring heavy rain."[190]

---

187 Either because the camels are too weak to undergo journeys or because there is insufficient pasture to maintain them along the way.

188 A place outside of Mecca.

189 They reject God insofar as they ascribe natural events (in this case the falling of rain) to the stars, instead of recognizing that God is the true cause of the rainfall.

190 According to Zurqānī, Mālik included this report immediately after the preceding report to indicate that there is no harm in attributing causation to natural phenomena in a manner consistent with custom so long as the speaker does not intend thereby to affirm that the wind, not God, is the effective cause of the rain. Zurqānī, *Sharḥ al-Zurqānī*, 1:656.

520. According to Mālik, it reached him that when Abū Hurayra awoke to find that rain had fallen on the people, he would say, "Rain has fallen on us by the star of God's gracious intervention," and he would recite the verse "Whatever merciful blessings God decrees for the people—no one can withhold."[191]

191 *Al-Fāṭir*, 35:2.

Book 13

The Book of the Prayer Direction (*Qibla*)

Chapter 1. The Prohibition against Relieving Oneself While Facing the Prayer Direction (*Qibla*)

521. According to Mālik, Isḥāq b. ʿAbd Allāh b. Abī Ṭalḥa reported from Rāfiʿ b. Isḥāq, the freedman (*mawlā*) of the household (*āl*) of al-Shifāʾ who was known as "the freedman of Abū Ṭalḥa," that he heard Abū Ayyūb al-Anṣārī, one of the Companions of the Messenger of God (pbuh), say when he was in Egypt, "By God! I am at a loss regarding what to do with these water closets. The Messenger of God (pbuh) said, 'When someone defecates or urinates, he should not expose his genitals toward the prayer direction nor turn his back to it.'"

522. According to Mālik, Nāfiʿ reported from a Medinese man that he heard the Messenger of God (pbuh) prohibit someone from facing the prayer direction while defecating or urinating.

Chapter 2. The Dispensation to Face the Prayer Direction (*Qibla*) While Urinating or Defecting

523. According to Mālik, Yaḥyā b. Saʿīd reported from Muḥammad b. Yaḥyā b. Ḥabbān, from his paternal uncle Wāsiʿ b. Ḥabbān, that ʿAbd Allāh b. ʿUmar would say, "Some people say, 'When you sit to relieve yourself, avoid facing the prayer direction.'" ʿAbd Allāh said, "I went up on the roof of a house of ours and saw the Messenger of God (pbuh) squatting on two bricks to relieve himself, and he was facing Jerusalem." Then ʿAbd Allāh b. ʿUmar said, "Perhaps you are one of those people who pray on their haunches." Wāsiʿ said, "I said, 'I don't know, by God!'" Mālik said, "He means someone who prostrates but does not raise his body correctly from the ground; rather, he prostrates, clinging to the ground."[192]

---

192 Ibn ʿUmar was chastising Wāsiʿ for his confusion regarding the prohibition against relieving oneself in the prayer direction. According to him, the prohibition applied only in the countryside or the desert, not in a town with fixed structures. Ibn ʿUmar's comment about Wāsiʿ's

Chapter 3. The Prohibition against Spitting in the Prayer Direction (*Qibla*)

524. According to Mālik, Nāfiʿ reported from ʿAbd Allāh b. ʿUmar that the Messenger of God (pbuh) saw spittle on the wall facing the prayer direction (*qibla*), so he scraped it off. He then went to the people and said, "When someone is praying, he should not spit in front of himself, because God, Blessed and Sublime is He, is in front of him when he is performing the prayer."

525. According to Mālik, Hishām b. ʿUrwa reported from his father, from ʿĀ'isha, the wife of the Prophet of God (pbuh), that the Messenger of God (pbuh) saw spittle or mucus on the wall facing the prayer direction, so he scraped it off.

Chapter 4. What Has Come Down regarding the Prayer Direction (*Qibla*)

526. According to Mālik, ʿAbd Allāh b. Dīnār reported that ʿAbd Allāh b. ʿUmar said, "While the people were praying the Morning Prayer (*ṣalāt al-ṣubḥ*) at Qubā', a man came to them, saying, 'Last night the Messenger of God (pbuh) received revelation, a new verse of the Quran, commanding him to face the Kabah during the performance of prayer, so turn toward it!'[193] They had been facing north, the direction of the Levant, toward Jerusalem, so they turned and faced the Kabah."

527. According to Mālik, Yaḥyā b. Saʿīd reported that Saʿīd b. al-Musayyab said, "The Messenger of God (pbuh) prayed toward Jerusalem for sixteen months after his arrival in Medina. Then the prayer direction was changed two months before the Battle of Badr."[194]

528. According to Mālik, Nāfiʿ reported that ʿUmar b. al-Khaṭṭāb said, "Anywhere between the east and the west is an appropriate direction of prayer, as long as the worshipper is facing south toward God's House (the Kabah)."[195]

---

prayer is rhetorical, because only someone lacking knowledge would pray in the fashion he describes; therefore, he is implying that Wāsiʿ is ignorant.

193 Other narrations of this report use the past tense of the verb rather than the imperative, as found in the RME. Therefore, in those narrations, the passage reads "so they turned toward it" instead of "so turn toward it." The unvoweled Arabic spelling of the third-person plural is the same as that of the second-person plural imperative.

194 The Battle of Badr was the first major military encounter between the Muslims and the pagans of the Quraysh, and it resulted in a decisive victory for the Muslims even though they were substantially outnumbered by the pagans. It took place in year 2 of the Hijra (624 CE).

195 The statement was made in Medina, which lies to the north of Mecca.

Chapter 5. What Has Come Down regarding the Mosque of the Prophet (pbuh)

529. According to Mālik, Zayd b. Rabāḥ and ʿUbayd Allāh b. Abī ʿAbd Allāh reported from Abū ʿAbd Allāh al-Agharr, from Abū Hurayra, that the Messenger of God (pbuh) said, "A prayer in this mosque of mine is better than a thousand prayers performed in any other mosque, except the Sacred Mosque (*al-masjid al-ḥarām*) in Mecca."

530. According to Mālik, Khubayb b. ʿAbd al-Raḥmān reported from Ḥafṣ b. ʿĀṣim, from Abū Hurayra or from Abū Saʿīd al-Khudrī, that the Messenger of God (pbuh) said, "What lies between my home and my pulpit is one of the meadows of Paradise, and my pulpit sits on my fountain."[196]

531. According to Mālik, ʿAbd Allāh b. Abī Bakr reported from ʿAbbād b. Tamīm, from ʿAbd Allāh b. Zayd al-Māzinī, that the Messenger of God (pbuh) said, "What lies between my home and my pulpit is one of the meadows of Paradise."

Chapter 6. What Has Come Down regarding Women Going to the Mosque

532. According to Mālik, it reached him that ʿAbd Allāh b. ʿUmar said, "The Messenger of God (pbuh) said, 'Do not prohibit God's handmaidens from going to God's mosques.'"

533. According to Mālik, it reached him from Busr b. Saʿīd that the Messenger of God (pbuh) said, "A woman who attends the Evening Prayer (*ṣalāt al-ʿishāʾ*) should not apply perfume."

534. According to Mālik, Yaḥyā b. Saʿīd reported from ʿĀtika bt. Zayd b. ʿAmr b. Nufayl, the wife of ʿUmar b. al-Khaṭṭāb, that she would ask his permission to go to the mosque. But he would not respond, and exasperated, she would say, "By God! I am certainly going, unless you stop me." He never did, however.

535. According to Mālik, Yaḥyā b. Saʿīd reported from ʿAmra bt. ʿAbd al-Raḥmān that ʿĀʾisha, the wife of the Prophet (pbuh), said, "Had the Messenger of God (pbuh) lived to see what women do today, he would have forbidden them to go to mosques, just as the women of the Israelites were forbidden." Yaḥyā b. Saʿīd said, "I therefore said to ʿAmra, 'Was it the case that Israelite women were forbidden to go to mosques?' She said, 'Yes.'"

196 The Prophet (pbuh) was buried in his home, which is now known as his tomb.

Book 14
The Book of the Quran

Chapter 1. The Command to Perform Ablutions (*Wuḍūʾ*) before Touching the Quran

536. According to Mālik, ʿAbd Allāh b. Abī Bakr b. Ḥazm reported that the Messenger of God (pbuh) sent an edict to ʿAmr b. Ḥazm that included the commandment "Only the pure shall touch the Quran."

537. Yaḥyā said, "Mālik said, 'No one should carry a copy of the Quran in his satchel or cushion unless he is in a state of ritual purity.'" Mālik then said, "Had that been permissible, it would have been permissible to carry it within a leather cover even if there were some impure substance that could defile the copy on the hands of the person holding it. But in fact anyone who carries a copy of the Quran is prohibited from doing so when he is in a state of ritual impurity in order to respect and honor the Quran."

538. Mālik said, "The best view that I have heard regarding the verse 'None shall touch the Quran save those who are purified'[197] is that it is the equivalent of verses in the chapter 'The Prophet Frowned and Turned Away' (*ʿAbasa wa-tawallā*),[198] in which God, Blessed and Sublime is He, says, 'By no means! These verses are nothing other than a reminder—so whoever wishes, let him remember—preserved in noble scrolls, exalted in dignity, and purified, in the hands of angelic scribes, noble and righteous.'"[199]

Chapter 2. The Dispensation to Recite the Quran without Having Performed Ablutions (*Wuḍūʾ*)

539. According to Mālik, Ayyūb al-Sakhtiyānī reported from Muḥammad b. Sīrīn that ʿUmar b. al-Khaṭṭāb was with a group of people who were reciting

197 *Al-Wāqiʿa*, 56:79.

198 Chapter 80 of the Quran, *ʿAbasa* ("He frowned"), is so called after its first verse, which describes the Prophet Muḥammad frowning and turning away when a blind Muslim man interrupts his discussions with some of the leading men of Mecca.

199 *ʿAbasa*, 80:11–16.

the Quran, and he went to relieve himself. Then he returned and was heard reciting the Quran. A man said to him, "Commander of the Faithful, are you reciting the Quran without first performing ablutions?" ʿUmar said to him, "Who led you to believe that this is a problem? Was it Musaylima?"[200]

Chapter 3. What Has Come Down regarding Dividing the Quran into Sections

540. According to Mālik, Dāwūd b. al-Ḥuṣayn reported from al-Aʿraj, from ʿAbd al-Raḥmān b. ʿAbd al-Qārī, that ʿUmar b. al-Khaṭṭāb said, "Whoever misses the recitation of his nightly portion of the Quran but reads it between noon and the performance of the Noon Prayer (*ṣalāt al-ẓuhr*) has not missed it (or 'it is as if he recited it during the night')."[201]

541. According to Mālik, Yaḥyā b. Saʿīd said, "Muḥammad b. Yaḥyā b. Ḥabbān and I were sitting down, and Muḥammad called on a man to come over and said to him, 'Tell me what you have heard from your father.' The man said, 'My father told me that he went to Zayd b. Thābit and asked him, "What do you think about completing the recitation of the Quran in seven days?" Zayd said to him, "That is good, but I prefer to recite it in half a month or ten days, and if you wish, I will explain to you why." My father said, "In that case, please explain to me the reason!" Zayd said, "So that I might mull it over and examine it closely."'"

Chapter 4. What Has Come Down regarding the Quran

542. According to Mālik, Ibn Shihāb reported from ʿUrwa b. al-Zubayr that ʿAbd al-Raḥmān b. ʿAbd al-Qārī said, "I heard ʿUmar b. al-Khaṭṭāb say, 'I heard Hishām b. Ḥakīm b. Ḥizām recite "The Criterion" (*al-Furqān*)[202] differently from me, and I had learned how to recite it directly from the Messenger of God (pbuh) himself. I was about to interrupt Hishām, but instead I waited for him to finish. I then grabbed him by his cloak and took him to the Messenger of God (pbuh) and said, "Messenger of God, I heard

200 Musaylima b. Ḥabīb al-Ḥanafī claimed to be a prophet alongside Prophet Muḥammad (pbuh), so Muslims always refer to him as "the liar" (*Musaylima al-kadhdhāb*) because they consider him a false prophet. His tribe, the Banū Ḥanīfa, was defeated in battle after the Prophet Muḥammad's death during the apostasy wars that took place during the caliphate of Abū Bakr al-Ṣiddīq. Musaylima himself died in that battle.

201 The narrator is unsure as to the precise phrase used by ʿUmar b. al-Khaṭṭāb. According to Ibn ʿAbd al-Barr, Dāwūd b. al-Ḥuṣayn's version of this report is erroneous. The more reliable version is that narrated by Ibn Shihāb, which reads as follows: "Whoever overslept and missed his nightly portion of the Quran but recited it between the time of the Dawn Prayer and the Noon Prayer has the recitation recorded for him as if he had performed it during the night." Zurqānī, *Sharḥ al-Zurqānī*, 2:6.

202 Chapter 25 of the Quran.

this man recite 'The Criterion' differently from the way you taught me." The Messenger of God (pbuh) said, "Let him go," and then he said, "Recite!" Hishām recited in the same manner as I had heard him recite previously. The Messenger of God (pbuh) said, "That is how it was revealed." Then he said to me, "Recite!" and so I recited "The Criterion." The Messenger of God (pbuh) said, "That is how it was revealed. The Quran was revealed in seven modes, so recite it in whichever of those suits you."'"

543. According to Mālik, Nāfiʿ reported from ʿAbd Allāh b. ʿUmar that the Messenger of God (pbuh) said, "The man who has committed the Quran to memory is like the man who keeps a tight rein on his camels. If he keeps them reined in, he maintains control of them, but if he relaxes his grip, they wander off."[203]

544. According to Mālik, Hishām b. ʿUrwa reported from his father, from ʿĀʾisha, the wife of the Prophet (pbuh), that al-Ḥārith b. Hishām asked the Messenger of God (pbuh), "How does revelation come to you?" The Messenger of God (pbuh) said, "Sometimes, it comes to me with the sound of a bell, and that is the most severe on me. When it leaves me, I have retained what was said. At other times, the angel appears to me in the form of a man, and he speaks to me, and I retain what he says." ʿĀʾisha said, "I saw him experience an entire episode of revelation on a very cold day, and when it concluded, his forehead was drenched in sweat."

545. According to Mālik, Hishām b. ʿUrwa reported that his father said, "The chapter 'The Prophet Frowned and Turned Away' was revealed about ʿAbd Allāh b. Umm Maktūm. He came to the Messenger of God (pbuh) and said insistently, 'Muḥammad, let me get close to you.' At that very moment, one of the leading pagans was sitting with the Prophet (pbuh), so the Prophet (pbuh) decided to ignore ʿAbd Allāh and turned away from him, instead giving his full attention to the pagan. The Prophet (pbuh) said to the pagan, 'Father of so-and-so, do you have any objections to what I am saying?' The man replied, 'No, by the altars of the idols and the animals sacrificed there, I have no objections to what you're saying.' Then the verse 'The Prophet frowned and turned away because the blind man came to him' was revealed."[204]

546. According to Mālik, Zayd b. Aslam reported from his father that the Messenger of God (pbuh) was on a journey one night, and ʿUmar b. al-Khaṭṭāb was traveling with him. ʿUmar asked him about something, but

203 In other words, without regularly reciting what he has memorized, he is likely to forget what he has memorized or suffer confusion regarding the correct recitation.

204 *ʿAbasa*, 80:1–2.

the Prophet (pbuh) did not answer him; he asked him again, and again he did not answer him. He then asked him a third time, and a third time the Prophet (pbuh) did not answer him. ʿUmar said to himself, "ʿUmar! May your mother keen over you! You have annoyed the Messenger of God (pbuh)! Three times you asked him something, and not once did he respond." ʿUmar said, "I hurried my camel along so that I would be at the head of the people. I dreaded that a verse of the Quran would be revealed about me, and it was not long before I heard someone calling out for me. I said to myself, 'This is what I was dreading—that a verse of the Quran would be revealed about me.' I therefore went to the Messenger of God (pbuh) and greeted him. The Prophet (pbuh) said, 'A chapter of the Quran has been revealed to me this night, and it is surely more beloved to me than anything on which the sun has risen.' Then he recited, 'Verily, We have granted you a manifest victory.'"[205]

547. According to Mālik, Yaḥyā b. Saʿīd reported from Muḥammad b. Ibrāhīm b. al-Ḥārith al-Taymī, from Abū Salama b. ʿAbd al-Raḥmān, that Abū Saʿīd al-Khudrī said, "I heard the Messenger of God (pbuh) say, 'There shall emerge from among you a group of people who will cause you to consider your own prayers deficient when compared to theirs (or "your own fasting deficient when compared to theirs," or "your own deeds deficient when compared to theirs"). They will recite the Quran, but it does not go beyond their throats.[206] They exit from Islam just like an arrow passes through the body of the hunter's prey: the hunter looks at the arrowhead and sees no evidence that it penetrated the prey; the hunter looks at the shaft and sees no evidence that it penetrated the prey; the hunter looks at the fletching and sees no evidence that it penetrated the prey; and he looks at the notch at the arrow's end skeptically, to see whether it has any traces of blood from the prey.'"[207]

---

205 *Al-Fatḥ*, 48:1. According to Muslim tradition, this chapter of the Quran was revealed on the occasion of the Treaty of al-Ḥudaybiya. The treaty was initially controversial among the Prophet Muḥammad's Companions because it did not permit them to continue to Mecca to complete their Pilgrimage rites, which had been the ostensible reason that they had set out from Medina to Mecca. The treaty instead required them to return the following year. It also included what they believed were humiliating conditions, including requirements to return any Muslim refugees who escaped from Mecca to Medina back to the Meccans and to permit any Muslim in Medina who wished to renounce Islam and return to Mecca to do so. The Prophet Muḥammad also reportedly agreed to sign the treaty using his given name, Muḥammad b. ʿAbd Allāh, rather than his title, the Messenger of God. Nevertheless, the treaty proved to be instrumental to the ultimate defeat of the Meccans by the Muslims and the latter's triumphant return to Mecca a few years later.

206 That is, God will not accept their recitation of the Quran.

207 The sense of the report is that despite this group's excessive performance of ritual devotions—recitation of the Quran, performance of prayers, and fasting—they fail to internalize any of the essential meanings of Islam.

548. According to Mālik, it reached him that ʿAbd Allāh b. ʿUmar spent eight years learning 'The Cow' (*al-Baqara*).[208]

Chapter 5. What Has Come Down regarding Prostrations during Recitation of the Quran[209]

549. According to Mālik, ʿAbd Allāh b. Yazīd, the freedman (*mawlā*) of al-Aswad b. Sufyān, reported from Abū Salama b. ʿAbd al-Raḥmān that while leading them in prayer, Abū Hurayra recited the chapter 'When the sky is rent asunder,'[210] and he prostrated in it. When he finished leading the prayer, he told them that the Messenger of God (pbuh) had prostrated when he recited the same chapter.

550. According to Mālik, Nāfiʿ, the freedman of Ibn ʿUmar, reported that an Egyptian told him that ʿUmar b. al-Khaṭṭāb recited the chapter 'The Pilgrimage' (*al-Ḥajj*),[211] and he prostrated twice during his recitation of it. Then he said, "This chapter has been given the special virtue of having two prostrations."

551. According to Mālik, ʿAbd Allāh b. Dīnār said, "I saw ʿAbd Allāh b. ʿUmar perform two prostrations during his recitation of 'The Pilgrimage.'"

552. According to Mālik, Ibn Shihāb reported from al-Aʿraj that ʿUmar b. al-Khaṭṭāb recited the chapter that begins with 'By the star, when it falls.'[212] He prostrated during his recitation of it and then stood up and recited another chapter.

553. According to Mālik, Hishām b. ʿUrwa reported from his father that when ʿUmar b. al-Khaṭṭāb was on the pulpit delivering the Friday sermon, he recited verses of the Quran[213] that included a command to prostrate. He descended from the pulpit and prostrated, so we prostrated with him. He then recited the very same verses in another Friday sermon. When he saw the people readying themselves to prostrate, he said, "Take it easy! God has not obliged us to prostrate at this verse, but we may do so if we wish." ʿUmar b. al-Khaṭṭāb did not prostrate on that occasion, and he also prohibited them from prostrating at that time."

---

208 The second and longest chapter of the Quran.

209 This section refers to the numerous verses of the Quran that include affirmative commands to prostrate to God. Only some of these, however, are understood to impose an obligation to prostrate when one recites or hears the command. The precise instances of mandatory prostration are subject to dispute among Muslim jurists.

210 *Al-Inshiqāq*, 84:1.

211 Chapter 22 of the Quran.

212 *Al-Najm*, chapter 53 of the Quran.

213 The editors of the RME identify the verses that he read as part of *al-Naḥl*, the twenty-seventh chapter of the Quran.

554. Yaḥyā said, "Mālik said, 'It is not part of the practice (*ʿamal*) with respect to the recitation of Quranic verses that include a command to prostrate for the imam to descend from the pulpit and prostrate each time he recites a verse of the Quran that includes such a command.'"

555. Yaḥyā said, "Mālik said, 'The rule in our view (*al-amr ʿindanā*) is that there are only eleven mandatory prostrations in the Quran, and none of these are in the *Mufaṣṣal*.'"

556. Yaḥyā said, "Mālik said, 'No one should recite verses of the Quran that oblige prostration after performing the Morning Prayer (*ṣalāt al-ṣubḥ*) or Afternoon Prayer (*ṣalāt al-ʿaṣr*). This is because the Messenger of God (pbuh) forbade the performance of additional prayers after completion of the Morning Prayer until the sun had risen. Likewise, he forbade the performance of additional prayers after completion of the Afternoon Prayer until the sun had set. Prostration is a constituent part of prayer (*ṣalāt*); therefore, no one should recite any verses that require a prostration during these two periods of time.'"

557. Yaḥyā said, "Mālik was asked: If someone recites a verse from the Quran commanding a prostration, and a menstruating woman is listening, is it appropriate for her to prostrate? He said, 'Neither a man nor a woman should prostrate unless he or she is ritually pure.'"

558. Yaḥyā said, "Mālik was asked whether a man who hears a woman reciting a verse from the Quran commanding a prostration should prostrate with her. He said, 'He does not have to prostrate with her. Prostration is obligatory only for a group of people praying behind an imam. If the imam recites a verse from the Quran commanding a prostration, they prostrate with him. If someone hears another person who is not leading him in prayer recite a verse of the Quran commanding a prostration, he is not obliged to perform that prostration.'"

Chapter 6. What Has Come Down regarding the Recitation of "Say: He Is God, the Singular One" (*Qul Huwa 'Llāhu Aḥad*)[214] and "Blessed Is the One" (*Tabāraka*)[215]

559. According to Mālik, ʿAbd al-Raḥmān b. ʿAbd Allāh b. Abī Ṣaʿṣaʿa reported from his father, from Abū Saʿīd al-Khudrī, that he heard a man[216] reciting the

214 *Al-Ikhlāṣ*, 112:1.

215 *Al-Mulk*, 67:1. The entirety of the verse reads *Tabāraka 'lladhī bi-yadihi 'l-mulku wa-huwa ʿalā kulli shayʾin qadīr*. It means, "Blessed is the One in whose hand is absolute dominion [over the heavens and the earth] and who has power over all things."

216 The editors of the RME identify this man as Qatāda b. al-Nuʿmān. See also Zurqānī, *Sharḥ al-Zurqānī*, 2:27.

chapter of the Quran that begins with "Say: He is God, the singular one" (*Qul huwa 'llāhu aḥad*), repeating it again and again. When Abū Saʿīd al-Khudrī awoke the next day, he set out at dawn for the Messenger of God (pbuh) and mentioned it to him as though he, Abū Saʿīd, thought little of it. The Messenger of God (pbuh) said, "By Him whose hand holds my soul, that chapter is the equivalent of one-third of the Quran."

560. According to Mālik, ʿUbayd Allāh b. ʿAbd al-Raḥmān reported that ʿUbayd b. Ḥunayn, the freedman (*mawlā*) of the household (*āl*) of Zayd b. al-Khaṭṭāb, said, "I heard Abū Hurayra say, 'I was walking with the Messenger of God (pbuh) when he heard a man reciting the chapter of the Quran that begins with "Say: He is God, the singular one." The Messenger of God (pbuh) said, "He has become entitled to it." So I asked him, "What has he become entitled to, Messenger of God?" He said, "Paradise." I wanted to go to that man and give him the glad tidings, but I didn't want to miss breakfast with the Messenger of God (pbuh), so I preferred to stay and have breakfast with him.[217] Thereafter, I tried to find that man, but I discovered that he had already left.'"

561. According to Mālik, Ibn Shihāb reported that Ḥumayd b. ʿAbd al-Raḥmān b. ʿAwf told him that the chapter of the Quran that begins with "Say: He is God, the singular one" is one-third of the Quran, and the chapter of the Quran that begins with "Blessed is the One in whose hand is absolute dominion" (*Tabāraka 'lladhī bi-yadihi 'l-mulk*) will advocate on behalf of whoever has memorized it.

Chapter 7. What Has Come Down regarding Remembrance of God, Blessed and Sublime Is He

562. According to Mālik, Sumayy, the freedman (*mawlā*) of Abū Bakr, reported from Abū Ṣāliḥ al-Sammān, from Abū Hurayra, that the Messenger of God (pbuh) said, "Whoever says one hundred times each day, 'There is no god except God, alone without partner. To Him belongs the kingdom and all praise, and He has power over all things,'[218] receives a reward that is equivalent to that of someone who has manumitted ten slaves from bondage. He receives credit for one hundred good deeds, and one hundred of his sins are effaced. It shields him from Satan for that day until nightfall. None does a more virtuous act than he, except someone who outdoes him in reciting that supplication."

---

217 According to Zurqānī, Abū Hurayra was poor and dependent on the Prophet Muḥammad for his food, so he did not want to risk missing his morning meal by leaving the Prophet Muḥammad in order to seek out the man. Zurqānī, *Sharḥ al-Zurqānī*, 2:29.

218 *Lā ilāha illā 'llāhu waḥdahu lā sharīka lah, lahu 'l-mulku wa-lahu 'l-ḥamdu wa-huwa ʿalā kulli shay'in qadīr.*

563. According to Mālik, Sumayy, the freedman of Abū Bakr, reported from Abū Ṣāliḥ al-Sammān, from Abū Hurayra, that the Messenger of God (pbuh) said, "Whoever says 'Glory be to God and by His praise' (*Subḥāna 'llāhi wa-bi-ḥamdih*) one hundred times in a day is relieved of his sins, even if they are as profuse as the foam of the sea."

564. According to Mālik, Abū ʿUbayd, the freedman of Sulaymān b. ʿAbd al-Malik, reported from ʿAṭāʾ b. Yazīd al-Laythī that Abū Hurayra said, "Whoever glorifies God (by saying 'Glory be to God,' *Subḥāna 'llāh*) thirty-three times, magnifies God (by saying 'God is great,' *Allāhu akbar*) thirty-three times, praises God (by saying 'All praise belongs to God,' *Al-ḥamdu lillāh*) thirty-three times, and then makes his invocations a complete hundred by saying, 'There is no god except God, alone without partner. To Him belongs the kingdom and all praise, and He has power over all things,' after the completion of every prayer (*ṣalāt*), shall have his sins forgiven, even if they are as profuse as the foam of the sea."

565. According to Mālik, ʿUmāra b. Ṣayyād reported that he heard Saʿīd b. al-Musayyab say regarding the meaning of "the enduring good deeds" (*al-bāqiyāt al-ṣāliḥāt*)[219] that these are when God's servant says, "God is great," "Glory be to God," "All praise belongs to God," "There is no god except God" (*Lā ilāha illā 'llāh*), and "No might or power is there except through God" (*Lā ḥawla wa-lā quwwata illā billāh*).

566. According to Mālik, Ziyād b. Abī Ziyād said, "Abū al-Dardāʾ said, 'Shall I tell you which deed most benefits you, is most likely to elevate your spiritual rank, is purest in your Master's eyes, is better than giving gold and silver in charity, and is better than meeting your enemy on the battlefield, striking at their necks while they strike at yours?' They said, 'Certainly!' He said, "Remembrance of God.'" Ziyād b. Abī Ziyād said, "Abū ʿAbd al-Raḥmān Muʿādh b. Jabal said, 'No deed is more effective in saving someone from divine punishment than remembrance of God.'"

567. According to Mālik, Nuʿaym b. ʿAbd Allāh al-Mujmir reported from ʿAlī b. Yaḥyā al-Zuraqī, from his father, that Rifāʿa b. Rāfiʿ al-Zuraqī said, "One day, we were praying behind the Messenger of God (pbuh). When he stood up after bowing, he said, 'May God hear whoever praises Him' (*Samiʿa 'llāhu li-man ḥamidah*).[220] A man[221] who was praying behind him said, 'Our Lord! To You belongs all praise, abundantly, blessedly, and purely' (*Rabbanā wa-laka 'l-ḥamd ḥamdan kathīran ṭayyiban mubārakan fīh*). When the Messenger of

219 A Quranic expression; see, for example, *al-Kahf*, 18:46.

220 Alternately, the Arabic can be understood as "God hears whoever praises Him."

221 The editors of the RME identify this unnamed man as Rifāʿa b. Rāfiʿ, the narrator of this report.

God (pbuh) finished, he said, 'Who was it that spoke just now?' The man said, 'It was I, Messenger of God.' The Messenger of God (pbuh) said, 'I saw a good thirty-odd angels rushing about to see which of them would record it first.'"

Chapter 8. What Has Come Down regarding Supplications (*Duʿāʾ*)

568. According to Mālik, Abū al-Zinād reported from al-Aʿraj, from Abū Hurayra, that the Messenger of God (pbuh) said, "Every prophet has one special supplication through which he calls on God. I wish to save mine to intercede for my community in the Hereafter."

569. According to Mālik, Yaḥyā b. Saʿīd reported that it reached him that the Messenger of God (pbuh) would supplicate saying, "God, Cleaver of dawn from darkness, who makes the night a time of repose and who made the sun and the moon the means to reckon the passage of time! Discharge my debts, free me from need, and enable me to use my sight, hearing, and strength in Your cause."[222]

570. According to Mālik, Abū al-Zinād reported from al-Aʿraj, from Abū Hurayra, that the Messenger of God (pbuh) said, "No one who supplicates God should say, 'God, forgive me if You wish. God, have mercy on me if You wish.' Let him be resolute in his petition, because no one can compel God to do anything."

571. According to Mālik, Ibn Shihāb reported from Abū 'Ubayd, the freedman (*mawlā*) of Ibn Azhar, from Abū Hurayra, that the Messenger of God (pbuh) said, "A supplicant's petition to his Lord will be granted, unless he becomes impatient and says, 'I have petitioned my Lord, but my petition was denied.'"

572. According to Mālik, Ibn Shihāb reported from Abū 'Abd Allāh al-Agharr and from Abū Salama, both from Abū Hurayra, that the Messenger of God (pbuh) said, "When only one-third of the night remains, our Lord, Blessed and Sublime is He, descends to the lowest heaven of this world and says, 'Who is supplicating Me, so that I may fulfill his request? Who is petitioning Me, so that I may grant it to him? Who is seeking My forgiveness, so that I might forgive him?'"

573. According to Mālik, Yaḥyā b. Saʿīd reported from Muḥammad b. Ibrāhīm b. al-Ḥārith al-Taymī that ʿĀʾisha, the Mother of the Believers, said, "I was sleeping next to the Messenger of God (pbuh). At some point in the night I did not find him next to me, so I felt around for him until my hand touched his foot as he was prostrating. He was saying, 'I seek refuge in Your

222 *Allāhumma fāliqa 'l-iṣbāḥi wa-jāʿila 'l-layli sakanan wa'l-shamsa wa'l-qamara ḥusbānan, iqḍi ʿannī al-dayna wa'ghninī min al-faqr, wa-amtiʿnī bi-samʿī wa-baṣarī wa-quwwatī fī sabīlik.*

satisfaction from Your wrath, and in Your pardon from Your punishment, and in You from Yourself. My exaltation of You cannot do You justice; You can only be exalted as You have exalted Yourself.'"[223]

574. According to Mālik, Ziyād b. Abī Ziyād reported from Ṭalḥa b. ʿUbayd Allāh b. Kurayz that the Messenger of God (pbuh) said, "The best supplications are those made on the Day of ʿArafa.[224] The best thing that I and the prophets before me have declared is 'There is no god except God, alone without partner' (*Lā ilāha illā 'llāhu waḥdahu lā sharīka lah*)."

575. According to Mālik, Abū al-Zubayr al-Makkī reported from Ṭāwūs al-Yamānī, from ʿAbd Allāh b. ʿAbbās, that there was a supplication that the Messenger of God (pbuh) would teach them, just as he would teach them a chapter of the Quran. He would say, "I seek Your protection from the torments of Hell; I seek refuge in You from the torments of the grave; I seek refuge in You from the Antichrist (*al-dajjāl*); and I seek refuge in You from all the tribulations of life and death."[225]

576. According to Mālik, Abū al-Zubayr al-Makkī reported from Ṭāwūs al-Yamānī, from ʿAbd Allāh b. ʿAbbās, that when the Messenger of God (pbuh) stood to pray in the middle of the night, he would say, "God! All praise belongs to You. You are the Light of the heavens and the earth, all praise belongs to You. You are the Maintainer of the heavens and the earth, all praise belongs to You. You are the Lord of the heavens and the earth and all who are in them. You are the Truth; Your word is the Truth; and Your promise is the Truth. Meeting You after death is real. Heaven is real, Hell is real, and the Hour of Judgment is real. God! To You I have given myself up; in You I have placed my faith; and in You I have placed my trust. To You I have returned. Through You I have pleaded my case against my foes. To You I have looked for judgment. Forgive me what I have done, and what I may yet do; what I have kept hidden, and what I have made manifest. You are my God; there is no god but You."[226]

---

223 *Aʿūdhu bi-riḍāka min sakhaṭika wa-bi-muʿāfātika min ʿuqūbatika wa-bika minka; lā uḥṣī thanā'an ʿalayka; anta kamā athnayta ʿalā nafsika.*

224 The Day of ʿArafa is the climax of the annual Pilgrimage (*ḥajj*) to Mecca, when the pilgrims pass the day on the plains of ʿArafāt praying and supplicating God. It takes place on the ninth day of Dhū al-Ḥijja, the day before the Feast of the Sacrificial Animals (*ʿīd al-aḍḥā*) in which Muslims not participating in the Pilgrimage sacrifice an animal to commemorate Ibrāhīm's sacrifice of a ram in lieu of his son as mentioned in the Quran, *al-Ṣaffāt*, 32:102–7. In this translation, we refer to the geographical place using the plural form, ʿArafāt, but to the day on which the central ritual of the Pilgrimage is performed using the singular form, the Day of ʿArafa.

225 *Allāhumma innī aʿūdhu bika min ʿadhābi jahannam, wa-aʿūdhu bika min ʿadhābi 'l-qabr, wa-aʿūdhu bika min fitnati 'l-masīḥi 'l-dajjāl, wa-aʿūdhu bika min fitnati 'l-maḥyā wa'l-mamāt.*

226 *Allāhumma laka 'l-ḥamd, anta nūru 'l-samāwāti wa'l-arḍ, wa-laka 'l-ḥamd; anta qiyyāmu 'l-samāwāti wa'l-arḍ, wa-laka 'l-ḥamd; anta rabbu 'l-samāwāti wa'l-arḍi wa-man fīhinna; anta 'l-ḥaqq, wa-qawluka 'l-ḥaqq, wa-waʿduka 'l-ḥaqq, wa-liqā'uka ḥaqq; wa'l-jannatu ḥaqq,*

577. According to Mālik, ʿAbd Allāh b. ʿAbd Allāh b. Jābir b. ʿAtīk said, "ʿAbd Allāh b. ʿUmar came to us in Banū Muʿāwiya, one of the villages of the Medinese, and said, 'Do you know where the Messenger of God (pbuh) prayed in this mosque of yours?' I said to him, 'Yes!' and I pointed to a spot therein. He said to me, 'Do you know the three things for which he supplicated there?' I said, 'Yes!' He said, 'Do tell me about them.' I said, 'He petitioned God not to allow a non-Muslim enemy to prevail over the Believers, and not to destroy them through drought and starvation—and both of these were granted him. He also petitioned God not to permit the Believers to unleash their weapons against one another—but that was refused.' Ibn ʿUmar said, 'You have spoken the truth.' Then he said, 'Strife will continue until the Day of Judgment.'"

578. According to Mālik, Zayd b. Aslam would say, "Every supplicant who petitions God receives one of three outcomes: the petition is granted; it is stored up for him until the Hereafter; or it wipes out his sins."

Chapter 9. The Practice (*ʿAmal*) with Respect to Supplication (*Duʿā'*)

579. According to Mālik, ʿAbd Allāh b. Dīnār said, "ʿAbd Allāh b. ʿUmar saw me supplicating and pointing with two fingers, one from each hand. He told me not to do that."

580. According to Mālik, Yaḥyā b. Saʿīd reported that Saʿīd b. al-Musayyab would say, "After someone dies, his children's supplications elevate his spiritual rank." He pointed toward the sky and then he raised his hands.

581. According to Mālik, Hishām b. ʿUrwa reported that his father said, "The verse 'And neither declaim your prayer (*ṣalāt*) in a loud voice nor whisper it, but seek out a path between the two'[227] was revealed specifically about supplication."

582. Yaḥyā said, "Mālik was asked about supplicating during the performance of an obligatory prayer, and he said, 'That is not objectionable.'"

583. According to Mālik, it reached him that the Messenger of God (pbuh) would supplicate saying, "God, I ask You that I perform good deeds, and that I shun foul deeds, and that I love the deprived. If You desire to try the people, then take me to You, without subjecting me to a trial."[228]

---

wa'l-nāru ḥaqq, wa'l-sāʿatu ḥaqq; allāhumma laka aslamtu wa-bika āmantu wa-ʿalayka tawakkaltu wa-ilayka anabtu wa-bika khāṣamtu wa-ilayka ḥākamtu; fa'ghfir lī mā qaddamtu wa-akhkhartu, wa-asrartu wa-aʿlantu; anta ilāhī lā ilāha illā anta.

227 *Al-Isrā'*, 17:110.

228 *Allāhumma innī as'aluka fiʿla 'l-khayrāti wa-tarka 'l-munkarāti wa-ḥubba 'l-masākīn, wa-idhā aradta fī 'l-nāsi fitnatan fa'qbiḍnī ilayka ghayra maftūn.*

584. According to Mālik, it reached him that the Messenger of God (pbuh) said, "Anyone who calls people to guidance shall receive a reward similar to theirs, without diminishing their reward in the least. Anyone who calls people to sin shall bear a burden similar to theirs, without diminishing their burden in the least."

585. According to Mālik, it reached him that ʿAbd Allāh b. ʿUmar said, "God, make me an imam for those who are mindful of God."[229]

586. According to Mālik, it reached him that Abū al-Dardāʾ would awake in the middle of the night and say, "The eyes have slept, the stars have set, and You are the Living, the Self-Subsistent."[230]

Chapter 10. The Prohibition against the Performance of Prayer (*Ṣalāt*) after the Morning Prayer (*Ṣalāt al-Ṣubḥ*) and Afternoon Prayer (*Ṣalāt al-ʿAṣr*)

587. According to Mālik, Zayd b. Aslam reported from ʿAṭāʾ b. Yasār, from ʿAbd Allāh al-Ṣunābiḥī, that the Messenger of God (pbuh) said, "The sun rises, and with it the Devil's horns, but when it rises high, the horns leave it. When the sun reaches its zenith, the horns rejoin it. When the sun begins to decline, however, the horns again leave it. When the sun draws near the western horizon, the horns return, but when the sun disappears below the western horizon, the horns leave it again." The Messenger of God (pbuh) prohibited the performance of prayer at these times.

588. According to Mālik, Hishām b. ʿUrwa reported that his father said, "The Messenger of God (pbuh) would say, 'When the top of the sun appears over the horizon in the morning, defer prayer until it has risen completely. When the bottom of the sun disappears below the horizon, defer prayer until it has set completely.'"

589. According to Mālik, al-ʿAlāʾ b. ʿAbd al-Raḥmān said, "We visited Anas b. Mālik after the Noon Prayer (*ṣalāt al-ẓuhr*). Then he stood up to perform the Afternoon Prayer. When he finished, we mentioned (or 'Anas mentioned')[231] the obligation to perform the Afternoon Prayer promptly." Al-ʿAlāʾ b. ʿAbd al-Raḥmān said, "Anas said, 'I heard the Messenger of God (pbuh) say, "That is the prayer of the hypocrites! That is the prayer of the hypocrites! That is the prayer of the hypocrites! They sit indifferently until the sun becomes

229 *Allāhumma 'jʿalnī min aʾimmati 'l-muttaqīn.*
230 *Nāmat al-ʿuyūn wa-ghārat al-nujūm wa-anta 'l-ḥayyu 'l-qayyūm.*
231 The narrator of the report is uncertain who brought up the question of the prompt performance of the Afternoon Prayer.

yellow and is between the Devil's horns (or 'on the Devil's horn').[232] Then the hypocrite finally gets up and knocks out four cycles of prayer, pecking up and down like a bird, hardly remembering God at all."'"

590. According to Mālik, Nāfiʿ reported from ʿAbd Allāh b. ʿUmar that the Messenger of God (pbuh) said, "No one should plan to pray when the sun is rising or when it is setting."

591. According to Mālik, Muḥammad b. Yaḥyā b. Ḥabbān reported from al-Aʿraj, from Abū Hurayra, that the Messenger of God (pbuh) forbade the performance of supplementary prayers after the Afternoon Prayer until the sun had set and after the Morning Prayer until the sun had risen.[233]

592. According to Mālik, ʿAbd Allāh b. Dīnār reported from ʿAbd Allāh b. ʿUmar that ʿUmar b. al-Khāṭṭāb would say, "Do not plan to pray at either sunrise or sunset, for the Devil's horns rise with the rising of the sun, and they set with its setting." The narrator of the report said, "ʿUmar b. al-Khāṭṭāb would strike people who prayed at those times."[234]

593. According to Mālik, Ibn Shihāb reported that al-Sāʾib b. Yazīd saw ʿUmar b. al-Khāṭṭāb strike al-Munkadir b. Muḥammad b. al-Munkadir for praying after he had performed the Afternoon Prayer.

The Book of Prayer (*Ṣalāt*)[235] Has Come to an End, with Abundant Praise to God. May God Grace Muḥammad and His Family and Grant Them Perfect Tranquility.

---

232 The narrator of the report is uncertain whether Anas used the phrase "between the Devil's horns" or the phrase "on the Devil's horn."

233 Mālikī jurists interpret this and previous reports as indicating that performance of supplementary prayers at these times of the day is disfavored (*makrūh*) but not categorically forbidden (*ḥarām*).

234 The report is ambiguous as to the source of this comment, but Zurqānī quotes ʿAbd Allāh b. ʿAbbās as saying that he assisted ʿUmar b. al-Khaṭṭāb in punishing people who violated this prohibition. Zurqānī, *Sharḥ al-Zurqānī*, 2:67–68.

235 Here the RME reads "Book of Prayer (*ṣalāt*)," but this section of the *Muwaṭṭaʾ* actually includes several "books," beginning with the First Book of Prayer (*Kitāb al-ṣalāt al-awwal*) and concluding with the Book of the Quran.

Book 15

The Book of Funerals (*Janā'iz*)[236]

In the Name of God, the Merciful, the Compassionate

May God Grace Muḥammad and His Family.

Chapter 1. Washing the Deceased

594. According to Mālik, Jaʿfar b. Muḥammad reported from his father that the corpse of the Messenger of God (pbuh) was washed in a tunic.

595. According to Mālik, Ayyūb b. Abī Tamīma al-Sakhtiyānī reported from Muḥammad b. Sīrīn that Umm ʿAṭiyya al-Anṣāriyya said, "The Messenger of God (pbuh) came to us when his daughter[237] died and said, 'Wash her three times, or five times, or more than that, with water and lotus (*sidr*) tree leaves,[238] putting camphor (or "a little camphor")[239] in the final washing, and when you finish, let me know.'" She said, "When we finished, we told him, and he gave us his undergarment (*ḥiqw*) and said, 'Shroud her with this.'" By "undergarment" Umm ʿAṭiyya meant the garment that is wrapped around the waist.

596. According to Mālik, ʿAbd Allāh b. Abī Bakr reported that Asmāʾ bt. ʿUmays, the wife of Abū Bakr al-Ṣiddīq, washed Abū Bakr al-Ṣiddīq when he died. When she finished, she asked the Emigrants (*muhājirūn*) who were present, "I am fasting, and today is extremely cold. Must I bathe?" They said, "No."

---

236 *Janā'iz* is the plural of two different Arabic words, *janāza* and *jināza*. The commentators agree that these two words refer to the funeral bier and the corpse, respectively, but there is disagreement as to which word means which. This edition follows the view that *jināza* refers to the corpse and *janāza* to the bier.

237 The editors of the RME report that the deceased daughter was either Zaynab or Umm Kulthūm.

238 The *sidr* tree is known as the lotus tree, with the scientific name *Ziziphus lotus*. It also goes by the name *nabaq* in Arabic.

239 The narrator is uncertain whether the Prophet (pbuh) said "camphor" or "a little camphor."

597. According to Mālik, he heard the people of knowledge say, "If a woman dies and there are no women present to wash her, nor is her father, brother, son, or husband present, her face and hands should be rubbed with clean earth." Yaḥyā said, "Mālik said, 'If a man dies and only women are present, they should wipe his face and hands with clean earth.'"

598. Yaḥyā said, "Mālik said, 'We do not have a specified way to wash the dead, nor is its mode of performance determinate. Rather, the corpse is washed until it is clean.'"

Chapter 2. What Has Come Down regarding Shrouding the Dead

599. According to Mālik, Hishām b. ʿUrwa reported from his father, from ʿĀʾisha, the wife of the Prophet (pbuh), that the Messenger of God (pbuh) was shrouded in three rough white Saḥūlī[240] cotton cloths, none of which was a tunic or a turban.

600. According to Mālik, Yaḥyā b. Saʿīd reported that the Messenger of God (pbuh) was shrouded in three rough white Saḥūlī cotton cloths.

601. According to Mālik, Yaḥyā b. Saʿīd said, "It reached me that Abū Bakr al-Ṣiddīq asked ʿĀʾisha, the wife of the Prophet (pbuh), when he himself was ill, 'How many pieces of cloth were used to shroud the Messenger of God (pbuh)?' She answered, 'He was shrouded in three rough white Saḥūlī cotton cloths.' Abū Bakr said, 'Take this piece of cloth'—the one that he was wearing, which had been dyed red with either ochre or saffron—'wash it and then shroud me in it, along with two other pieces of cloth.' ʿĀʾisha said, 'Why is that?' Abū Bakr said, 'The living need new clothes more than the dead. This shroud of mine is needed only for the pus of a decaying cadaver.'"

602. According to Mālik, Ibn Shihāb reported from Ḥumayd b. ʿAbd al-Raḥmān b. ʿAwf that ʿAbd Allāh b. ʿAmr b. al-ʿĀṣī said, "The corpse of a deceased male is cloaked in a tunic, and his waist is wrapped. He is then shrouded with a third piece of cloth. If there is only one piece of cloth, he is shrouded in it."

Chapter 3. Walking ahead of the Corpse (*Jināza*)

603. According to Mālik, Ibn Shihāb reported that the Messenger of God (pbuh), Abū Bakr, and ʿUmar all walked at the head of the corpse in funeral processions in a steady and dignified manner, and so did the caliphs after them. ʿAbd Allāh b. ʿUmar did likewise.

240 According to the editors of the RME, these garments were called *saḥūlī* after the village in Yemen where they were made.

604. According to Mālik, Muḥammad b. al-Munkadir reported that Rabīʿa b. ʿAbd Allāh b. al-Hudayr told him that he (Rabīʿa) saw ʿUmar b. al-Khaṭṭāb walking at the head of the corpse in the funeral procession of Zaynab bt. Jaḥsh.

605. According to Mālik, Hishām b. ʿUrwa said, "I only ever saw my father at the front of a funeral procession." He said, "Then, when he arrived at al-Baqīʿ,[241] he would sit down to allow the procession to pass him."

606. According to Mālik, Ibn Shihāb said, "Walking behind the corpse in a funeral procession represents a mistaken understanding of the long-established ordinance (*al-sunna*)."[242]

Chapter 4. The Prohibition against Marching behind the Bier (*Janāza*) Holding Torches

607. According to Mālik, Hishām b. ʿUrwa reported from Asmāʾ bt. Abī Bakr that she said to her family, "When I die, burn incense over my clothes and perfume me, but do not sprinkle any perfume on my shroud, and do not march in the rear of my funeral procession holding torches."

608. According to Mālik, Saʿīd b. Abī Saʿīd al-Maqburī reported from Abū Hurayra that he asked that people refrain from marching behind his funeral procession while holding torches. Yaḥyā said, "I heard Mālik disapprove of that practice."

Chapter 5. What Has Come Down regarding Magnifying God (Saying "God Is Great," *Allāhu Akbar*) during Funerals (*Janāʾiz*)

609. According to Mālik, Ibn Shihāb reported from Saʿīd b. al-Musayyab, from Abū Hurayra, that the Messenger of God (pbuh) announced the death of al-Najāshī[243] to the people on the day he died, led them to the place of prayer, arranged them into rows, and magnified God four times.[244]

610. According to Mālik, Ibn Shihāb reported that Abū Umāma b. Suhayl b. Ḥunayf told him that a poor woman of no social standing[245] fell ill. Someone

---

241 Al-Baqīʿ is the cemetery of Medina.

242 However, other Muslim jurists, such as Abū Ḥanīfa and Thawrī, believe walking behind the deceased to be more virtuous. This view is also attributed to the fourth caliph and the Prophet Muḥammad's cousin and son-in-law, ʿAlī b. Abī Ṭālib.

243 The Christian ruler of Abyssinia, who gave asylum to some Muslims of Mecca whom the pagan Quraysh in Mecca had persecuted.

244 When Mālik refers to the fourfold magnifications of the funeral prayer, he means both the utterance of *Allāhu akbar* and the recitations of the Quran and supplications for the deceased that take place between the magnifications.

245 The Arabic word used here is *miskīna*, which comes from the root *s-k-n* and here denotes passivity due to the lack of a tribal affiliation that would afford standing in seventh-century Arabia.

informed the Messenger of God (pbuh) of her illness. It was customary for the Messenger of God (pbuh) to visit the poor and those of no social standing during their illnesses and to ask about them. He said, "Let me know when she dies." She died that night and was buried immediately without anyone telling the Messenger of God (pbuh) because they did not want to wake him up. When the Messenger of God (pbuh) awoke that morning, someone told him that she had passed. He said, "Didn't I tell you to let me know when she died?" They answered, "Messenger of God, we didn't want to wake you up in the middle of the night and drag you out of your house!" The Messenger of God (pbuh) then set out to her grave, arranged the people into rows, and magnified God four times.

611. According to Mālik, he asked Ibn Shihāb about a man who performs only some of the magnifications of God in the funeral prayer. Ibn Shihāb said, "He should complete the magnifications that he missed."

Chapter 6. What the Worshipper Should Say over the Corpse (*Jināza*)

612. According to Mālik, Saʿīd b. Abī Saʿīd al-Maqburī reported from his father that he asked Abū Hurayra how one should pray over the deceased. Abū Hurayra answered, "By the life of God, I will certainly tell you. I follow the body in the funeral procession from its outset. When the body is laid to rest in the grave, I magnify God, saying 'God is great' (*Allāhu akbar*). I then praise God and invoke God's grace on His Prophet. I then say, 'God! He is Your servant, the son of Your servant and Your handmaiden. He testified that there is no god save You, and that Muḥammad is Your servant and messenger, but You know him best. God! If he did well, amplify his good deeds; and if he sinned, overlook his sins. God! Do not deprive us of his reward, or try us after him.'"[246]

613. According to Mālik, Yaḥyā b. Saʿīd said, "I heard Saʿīd b. al-Musayyab say, 'I once prayed behind Abū Hurayra as he performed the funeral prayer over a deceased child who was too young to have ever committed a wrong, yet I heard him say, "God! Protect him from the torment of the grave."'"

614. According to Mālik, Nāfiʿ reported that ʿAbd Allāh b. ʿUmar would not recite the Quran when praying over the deceased.

246 *Allāhumma innahu ʿabduka wa-ibnu ʿabdika wa-ibnu amatika, kāna yashhadu an lā ilāha illā anta wa-anna Muḥammadan ʿabduka wa-rasūluka wa-anta aʿlamu bih. Allāhumma in kāna muḥsinan fa-zid fī iḥsānih, wa-in kāna musīʾan fa-tajāwaz ʿan sayyiʾātih. Allāhumma lā taḥrimnā ajrahu wa-lā taftinnā baʿdah.*

Chapter 7. Praying over the Deceased (*Jināza*) after the Morning Prayer (*Ṣalāt al-Ṣubḥ*) and Afternoon Prayer (*Ṣalāt al-ʿAṣr*)

615. According to Mālik, Muḥammad b. Abī Ḥarmala, the freedman (*mawlā*) of ʿAbd al-Raḥmān b. Abī Sufyān b. Ḥuwayṭib, reported that Zaynab bt. Abī Salama died while Ṭāriq was the governor of Medina.[247] Her funeral bier (*janāza*) was brought out after the Morning Prayer and was taken to al-Baqīʿ. Ibn Abī Ḥarmala said that Ṭāriq would perform the Morning Prayer at its outset, when it was still dark outside. Ibn Abī Ḥarmala then said, "I heard ʿAbd Allāh b. ʿUmar explain to her family, 'You can pray over her now, or you can wait until the sun has fully risen.'"

616. According to Mālik, Nāfiʿ reported that ʿAbd Allāh b. ʿUmar said, "The prayer over the corpse can be performed after the Afternoon Prayer or after the Morning Prayer, if they have been performed promptly at the beginning of their respective times."[248]

Chapter 8. Performing Prayers (*Ṣalāt*) over Corpses (*Janāʾiz*) in the Mosque

617. According to Mālik, Abū al-Naḍr, the freedman (*mawlā*) of ʿUmar b. ʿUbayd Allāh, reported from ʿĀʾisha, the wife of the Prophet (pbuh), that when Saʿd b. Abī Waqqāṣ died, she asked that his corpse be brought before her in the mosque so that she could supplicate God for him. Many criticized her for doing so, but ʿĀʾisha said, "How quickly they forget! The Messenger of God (pbuh) prayed over the corpse of Suhayl b. Bayḍāʾ in the mosque."

618. According to Mālik, Nāfiʿ reported that ʿAbd Allāh b. ʿUmar said, "They prayed over the corpse of ʿUmar b. al-Khaṭṭāb in the mosque."

Chapter 9. Miscellaneous Matters regarding Prayers over Corpses (*Janāʾiz*)

619. According to Mālik, it reached him that in Medina, ʿUthmān b. ʿAffān, ʿAbd Allāh b. ʿUmar, and Abū Hurayra would pray over the corpses of both men and women at the same time. They would place the male corpses next to the imam and the female corpses near the prayer niche (*qibla*).

---

247 According to the editors of the RME, Ṭāriq b. ʿAmr was the freedman (*mawlā*) of ʿUthmān b. ʿAffān and served as the governor of Medina during the caliphate of ʿAbd al-Malik b. Marwān.

248 For the Morning Prayer, this point in time is when it is still dark, before the rays of the sun fill up the sky, and for the Afternoon Prayer, it is when the sun is still high in the sky, before it descends and becomes orange.

620. According to Mālik, Nāfiʿ reported that when ʿAbd Allāh b. ʿUmar prayed over corpses, he would conclude his prayer audibly so that those standing nearby would hear him saying, "Peace be upon you."

621. According to Mālik, Nāfiʿ reported that ʿAbd Allāh b. ʿUmar would say, "No one should pray over a corpse (*jināza*) unless he is in a state of ritual purity."

622. Yaḥyā said, "I heard Mālik say, 'I know of no man of knowledge who disapproved of praying either over the corpse of an illegitimate child or over the corpse of the mother who gave birth to him or her.'"

Chapter 10. What Has Come Down regarding Burying the Dead

623. According to Mālik, it reached him that the Messenger of God (pbuh) died on Monday and was buried on Tuesday, and the people prayed over him individually, without anyone leading them in prayer. Some people said that he should be buried near the pulpit of his mosque in Medina, while others said he should be buried in al-Baqīʿ. Abū Bakr al-Ṣiddīq then came and said, "I heard the Messenger of God (pbuh) say, 'Every prophet has been buried in the very spot in which he died.'" They therefore dug a grave for him in that very spot. When it was time to wash his body, they intended to remove his tunic, but they heard a voice saying, "Do not remove it," so they did not remove his tunic, and he was washed with it still on his corpse.

624. According to Mālik, Hishām b. ʿUrwa reported that his father said, "There were two men in Medina who dug graves. One dug graves in accordance with the Medinese custom (*laḥd*), and the other dug graves in accordance with the Meccan custom (*shaqq*).[249] The people said, 'Whichever of the two shows up first will dig the grave of the Prophet (pbuh).' The Medinese man showed up first, so he dug the grave of the Messenger of God (pbuh) in accordance with the Medinese custom."

625. According to Mālik, it reached him that Umm Salama, the wife of the Prophet (pbuh), would say, "I refused to accept that the Messenger of God (pbuh) had actually died until I heard them digging the grave."

626. According to Mālik, Yaḥyā b. Saʿīd reported that ʿĀʾisha, the wife of the Prophet (pbuh), said, "I dreamed that three moons fell into my lap, so I recounted my dream to Abū Bakr al-Ṣiddīq." She said, "When the Messenger of God (pbuh) died and was buried in my house, Abū Bakr said to me, 'Here you are: this is one of your moons, and it is the best of the three.'"

---

249 The Meccan custom was to dig a deep vertical grave, whereas the Medinese custom was to dig a shallower grave with a niche in its wall.

627. According to Mālik, several sources whom he believed to be reliable reported that Saʿd b. Abī Waqqāṣ and Saʿīd b. Zayd b. ʿAmr b. Nufayl died in al-ʿAqīq and were brought to Medina to be buried there.

628. According to Mālik, Hishām b. ʿUrwa reported that his father said, "I do not want to be buried in al-Baqīʿ; I would prefer to be buried elsewhere. Only two sorts are buried there: oppressors—and I don't wish to be buried with them—and the righteous—and I don't wish their bones to be disinterred for my sake."

Chapter 11. Stopping for Funeral Processions (*Janāʾiz*) and Sitting at Graves

629. According to Mālik, Yaḥyā b. Saʿīd reported from Wāqid b. Saʿd b. Muʿādh, from Nāfiʿ b. Jubayr b. Muṭʿim, from Masʿūd b. al-Ḥakam, from ʿAlī b. Abī Ṭālib, that the Messenger of God (pbuh) would stand up for funeral processions and then sit down after they passed.

630. According to Mālik, it reached him that ʿAlī b. Abī Ṭālib would rest his head on graves and lie down on them. Yaḥyā said, "Mālik said, 'In our view, sitting on graves was forbidden only to prevent people from relieving themselves there.'"

631. According to Mālik, Abū Bakr b. ʿUthmān b. Sahl b. Ḥunayf reported that he heard Abū Umāma b. Sahl b. Ḥunayf say, "We would attend funeral processions, and the people in the back would not sit down until they had been given permission."

Chapter 12. The Prohibition against Keening over the Deceased

632. According to Mālik, ʿAbd Allāh b. ʿAbd Allāh b. Jābir b. ʿAtīk reported that his maternal grandfather, ʿAtīk b. al-Ḥārith b. ʿAtīk, told him that Jābir b. ʿAtīk told him that when ʿAbd Allāh b. Thābit was ill, the Messenger of God (pbuh) went to visit him but found him unconscious. He called out to him, but ʿAbd Allāh did not reply. The Messenger of God (pbuh) said, "To God we belong and to Him we return!" He then said, "We were too late to reach you, Abū Rabīʿ!" Then the womenfolk cried out and sobbed loudly, so Jābir told them to be quiet. The Messenger of God (pbuh) said, "Leave them be, but when the inevitable comes, let none of them keen." They said, "Messenger of God, what do you mean by 'the inevitable'?" He said, "When he dies." ʿAbd Allāh's daughter said, "By God, I really hoped that you would die a martyr, for you had already equipped yourself for battle." The Messenger of God said, "God has already rewarded him in accordance with his intention. And what is it, you think, that makes someone a martyr?" They said, "Dying on the battlefield for the sake of God." The Messenger of God said, "There are seven other kinds of martyrs: those who die of the plague; those who die of drowning; those who die of pleurisy; those who die of dysentery; those who die in a fire; those who die under a collapsed building; and women who die in childbirth."[250]

633. According to Mālik, ʿAbd Allāh b. Abī Bakr reported from his father, from ʿAmra bt. ʿAbd al-Raḥmān, that when someone mentioned to ʿĀʾisha, the Mother of the Believers, that ʿAbd Allāh b. ʿUmar had said, "The dead are tormented by the keening of the living," ʿAmra heard ʿĀʾisha say, "May God forgive Abū ʿAbd al-Raḥmān (i.e., ʿAbd Allāh b. ʿUmar). Certainly he did not intentionally lie, but he must have forgotten or misunderstood, for the Messenger of God (pbuh) passed by a deceased Jewish woman whose family was keening over her, and it was only then that he said, 'You are keening over her, yet she is being tormented in her grave.'"

Chapter 13. Fortitude in the Face of Tragedy

634. According to Mālik, Ibn Shihāb reported from Saʿīd b. al-Musayyab, from Abū Hurayra, that the Messenger of God (pbuh) said, "Hellfire will not touch any Muslim who endures the death of three children except momentarily, in fulfillment of God's oath."[251]

635. According to Mālik, Muḥammad b. Abī Bakr b. Ḥazm reported from his father, from Abū al-Naḍr al-Salamī, that the Messenger of God (pbuh) said, "Any Muslim who is bereaved of three children and bears it with fortitude shall be shielded from Hell." A woman who was with the Messenger of God (pbuh) said, "Or two, Messenger of God?" so he said, "Or two."

636. According to Mālik, it reached him from Abū al-Ḥubāb Saʿīd b. Yasār, from Abū Hurayra, that the Messenger of God (pbuh) said, "The believer endures the inevitable losses of children and relatives with fortitude and patience, until he meets God free of sin."

250 The terms plague, pleurisy, and dysentery are used as generic references to severe medical conditions.

251 This is a reference to the Quranic verse *Wa-in minkum illā wāriduhā* ("And each one of you shall certainly enter it [i.e., the fire of Hell]"). *Maryam*, 19:71. The sense of the report is that a person who has suffered the loss of three children is exposed to Hell only for a moment that suffices to make the Quranic statement literally true, but he or she avoids the substantive torment of Hell.

Chapter 14. Miscellaneous Reports about Fortitude in the Face of Tragedy

637. According to Mālik, ʿAbd al-Raḥmān b. al-Qāsim b. Muḥammad reported that the Messenger of God (pbuh) said, "Let my personal tragedies comfort Muslims in their own."[252]

638. According to Mālik, Rabīʿa b. Abī ʿAbd al-Raḥmān reported from Umm Salama, the wife of the Prophet (pbuh), that the Messenger of God (pbuh) said, "God grants the prayer of anyone who is struck by tragedy and then says—as God has commanded him—'To God we belong and to Him we return. God, reward me for patiently enduring my tragedy, and make tomorrow better than today!'" Umm Salama said, "When Abū Salama died, I said that, but I thought to myself, 'Who could be better for me than Abū Salama?'" But then God gave her His Messenger, who married her.

639. According to Mālik, Yaḥyā b. Saʿīd reported that al-Qāsim b. Muḥammad said, "One of my wives died, and Muḥammad b. Kaʿb al-Quraẓī came to offer his condolences. He told me about a learned Israelite who possessed great knowledge and was intensely devoted to worship. He had a wife whom he admired and adored. When she died, he was so grief-stricken over her that he withdrew into a room and locked himself in, withdrawing from the society of men. No one visited him. Then a woman heard about his condition, so she went to see him and said, 'I have an issue that requires me to obtain a legal opinion from him, and nothing less than speaking to him directly will satisfy me.' The people departed, but she remained at his door and said, 'I must see him.' Someone then went and said to him, 'There is a woman here who wishes to ask your opinion on some matter. She insists, saying, "All I want is to speak to him directly." The people have already dispersed, but she is refusing to leave your door.' He said, 'Let her in,' so she went in and said, 'I have come to seek your legal opinion on a matter.' He said, 'What about?' She said, 'I borrowed a piece of jewelry from a woman who is my neighbor, and I have worn it for long time and have even loaned it to others. Now she has demanded it back. Should I return it to her?' He said, 'Yes, by God!' The woman said, 'But I have had it for a long time.' He said, 'That is all the more reason for you to return it to her, insofar as she loaned it to you for a long time.' She said, 'Certainly, yes, may God have mercy on you! Do you then grieve over what God loaned you and then took back, even though He has a greater right to it than you?' Suddenly he perceived the reality of his situation, and God benefited him through her words."

252 For example, the Prophet (pbuh) had seven children, but only one of them, Fāṭima, outlived him.

Chapter 15. What Has Come Down regarding Disinterment

640. According to Mālik, Abū al-Rijāl Muḥammad b. ʿAbd al-Raḥmān reported that he heard his mother, ʿAmra bt. ʿAbd al-Raḥmān, say, "The Messenger of God cursed both men and women who desecrate graves," meaning those who disinter the dead.

641. According to Mālik, it reached him that ʿĀ'isha, the wife of the Prophet (pbuh), would say, "Breaking the bone of a Muslim who is dead is no different from doing so when he is alive," meaning that both acts are equally sinful.

Chapter 16. Miscellaneous Matters Related to Burial (*Janā'iz*)

642. According to Mālik, Hishām b. ʿUrwa reported from ʿAbbād b. ʿAbd Allāh b. al-Zubayr that ʿĀ'isha, the wife of the Prophet (pbuh), told him that she heard the Messenger of God (pbuh) say before he died, while his head was resting on her chest and she was listening to him closely, "God, forgive me and have mercy on me, and lodge me with the best company."

643. According to Mālik, it reached him that ʿĀ'isha, the wife of the Prophet (pbuh),[253] said, "The Messenger of God (pbuh) said, 'No Prophet dies before he is asked whether he wishes to depart.'" She said, "I heard him say, 'God! The best company!' so I knew that he was departing."

644. According to Mālik, Nāfiʿ reported that ʿAbd Allāh b. ʿUmar said, "The Messenger of God (pbuh) said, 'Every morning and evening, the dead are shown their destinations in the next life. If a person is one of the people of Paradise, his destination will be with them. If he is one of the people of Hell, his destination will be with them. He will be told, "But here you will stay until the Day of Resurrection."'"

645. According to Mālik, Abū al-Zinād reported from al-Aʿraj, from Abū Hurayra, that the Messenger of God (pbuh) said, "The earth consumes the entire human body except the tailbone. From it he was created, and from it he will be reconstituted."

646. According to Mālik, Ibn Shihāb reported that ʿAbd al-Raḥmān b. Kaʿb b. Mālik al-Anṣārī told him that his father, Kaʿb b. Mālik, would relate that the Messenger of God (pbuh) said, "The soul of the believer is a bird that wanders freely among the trees of Paradise until God restores it to his body on the day He resurrects him."

253 The Arabic text of the RME simply has *zawj ṣallā allāh ʿalayhi wa-sallam* without clarifying the omission of *al-nabī* or *rasūl allāh*. The printed edition of *Sharḥ al-Zurqānī* omits *zawj*.

647. According to Mālik, Abū al-Zinād reported from al-Aʿraj, from Abū Hurayra, that the Messenger of God (pbuh) said, "God, Blessed and Sublime is He, said, 'If My servant longs to meet Me, I long to meet him, and if he is loath to meet Me, I am loath to meet him.'"

648. According to Mālik, Abū al-Zinād reported from al-Aʿraj, from Abū Hurayra, that the Messenger of God (pbuh) said, "A man who never did a single pious deed instructed his family to burn him when he died and to scatter his ashes over land and sea. He feared that if God were to seize him, no one on earth would be made to suffer as he would. When the man finally died, his family did as he had instructed. God then ordered the land and the sea to gather all of the man's remains, wherever they might be. He then said to the man, 'Why did you do this?' The man said, 'Out of my dread for You, my Lord, and You know best.'" Abū Hurayra said, "So He forgave him."

649. According to Mālik, Abū al-Zinād reported from al-Aʿraj, from Abū Hurayra, that the Messenger of God (pbuh) said, "Every child is born in conformity with pristine nature (*fiṭra*). It is his parents who make him a Jew or a Christian. A child is like a camel that emerges from its mother perfectly formed. Do you notice anything about it that is mutilated?"[254] They asked him, "What happens to those who die as minors?" He said, "God knows best what they would have become had they reached adulthood."

650. According to Mālik, Abū al-Zinād reported from al-Aʿraj, from Abū Hurayra, that the Messenger of God (pbuh) said, "The Hour will not come until a man passing the grave of another says, 'If only I were in his place.'"

651. According to Mālik, Muḥammad b. ʿAmr b. Ḥalḥala al-Dīlī reported from Maʿbad b. Kaʿb b. Mālik that Abū Qatāda b. Ribʿī would relate that a funeral bier (*janāza*) once passed before the Messenger of God (pbuh), so he said, "Some are relieved, and others bring relief." They said, "Messenger of God, who is the one who is relieved, and who is the one who brings relief?" He said, "The faithful servant is the one who is relieved from the sufferings and adversities of this world, departing to God's mercy. The wicked servant's death brings relief to the people, land, trees, and beasts."

652. According to Mālik, Abū al-Naḍr, the freedman (*mawlā*) of ʿUmar b. ʿUbayd Allāh, said, "When ʿUthmān b. Maẓʿūn died and his funeral bier passed before the Messenger of God (pbuh), he said, 'You departed from this life without indulging in any of its pleasures.'"

254 The Prophet (pbuh) was referring to the Arab custom of cutting parts of camels, such as their noses or ears, as a way of marking them.

653. According to Mālik, ʿAlqama b. Abī ʿAlqama reported that his mother said, "I heard ʿĀ'isha, the wife of the Prophet (pbuh), say, 'The Messenger of God (pbuh) arose one night, put on his clothes, and went out. So I ordered Barīra, my handmaiden, to follow him. She followed him until he reached al-Baqīʿ, and he stood there in front of it for as long as God wished and then left. Barīra came back before him and told me what he had done, but I didn't mention it to him until he awoke the next morning, at which point I brought it up. He said, "I was dispatched to seek God's blessings and forgiveness for the sake of those interred there."'"

654. According to Mālik, Nāfiʿ reported that Abū Hurayra said, "Bury your dead quickly, for they are one of two sorts: the righteous, whom you deliver to a better world; or the wicked, whom you are well rid of."

The Book of Funerals (*Kitāb al-Janā'iz*) Has Come to an End, with Abundant Praise to God. May God Grace Our Prophet Muḥammad and His Family and Grant Them Perfect Tranquility.

Book 16

The Book of the Alms-Tax (*Zakāt*)[255]

In the Name of God, the Merciful, the Compassionate

Chapter 1. The Property That Is Subject to the Alms-Tax (*Zakāt*)

655. According to Mālik b. Anas, ʿAmr b. Yaḥyā al-Māzinī reported that his father said, "I heard Abū Saʿīd al-Khudrī say, 'The Messenger of God (pbuh) said, "No alms-tax (*ṣadaqa*)[256] is due on fewer than five camels; none is due on less than 600 grams (five *awāq*) of silver;[257] and none is due on less than 610 kilograms (five *awsuq*)[258] of cereal crops."'"

656. According to Mālik, Muḥammad b. ʿAbd Allāh b. ʿAbd al-Rahmān b. Abī Ṣaʿṣaʿa al-Anṣārī al-Māzinī reported from his father, from Abū Saʿīd al-Khudrī, that the Messenger of God (pbuh) said, "No alms-tax is due on less than 610 kilograms of dates; none is due on less than 600 grams of silver; and none is due on fewer than five camels."

---

255 The payment of the alms-tax (*zakāt*) is obligatory on those with means and constitutes one of the "five pillars" of Islam. The religious purpose of the alms-tax is to purify one's wealth, and for that reason it is levied only on Muslims. On the other hand, it also serves the social purpose of redistribution of wealth and income from the more fortunate to the poor, and from that perspective, it bears characteristics that make it resemble a tax, including the prospect that the state may enforce it coercively.

256 The Quran uses the words *ṣadaqa* and *zakāt* to refer to the payment of alms. Muslim jurists settled on the term *zakāt* to refer to the mandatory alms-tax and used the term *ṣadaqa* to refer to charity.

257 *Awāq* is the plural of *awqiya*, which is a measure of weight for silver. When the caliph ʿAbd al-Malik b. Marwān struck coins in Arabic for the first time, forty dirhams of pure silver represented the weight of one *awqiya*. Zurqānī, *Sharḥ al-Zurqānī*, 2:94. Each *awqiya* is approximately 125 grams according to the Ḥanafīs, but 119 grams according to the other Sunnī schools of law. ʿAlī Jumuʿa, *al-Makāyīl wa'l-mawāzīn al-sharʿiyya* (Cairo: al-Quds, 2001), 21. According to the majority of jurists, the weight of a silver dirham is approximately 2.975 grams, so the minimum amount of silver needed for liability for the alms-tax would have been between 595 and 625 grams. For ease of reference, we have pegged the amount at 600 grams.

258 *Awsuq* is the plural of *wasaq*, a measure of weight. Zurqānī, *Sharḥ al-Zurqānī*, 2:139. The majority of jurists, including the Mālikīs, define the *wasaq* as approximately 122 kilograms, but the Ḥanafīs define it as 195 kilograms. Jumuʿa, *al-Makāyīl*, 41. Mālikī jurists also define five *awsuq* as the amount of food that an individual needs to sustain himself for a year.

657. According to Mālik, it reached him that ʿUmar b. ʿAbd al-ʿAzīz wrote to his representative in Damascus about the alms-tax, saying, "The alms-tax is levied only on cereal crops, precious metals, and livestock." Mālik said, "The alms-tax is due on only three kinds of property: cereal crops, precious metals, and livestock."

Chapter 2. The Alms-Tax (*Zakāt*) on Gold and Silver

658. According to Mālik, Muḥammad b. ʿUqba, the freedman (*mawlā*) of al-Zubayr, reported that he asked al-Qāsim b. Muḥammad whether he must pay the alms-tax on a large sum of money that he received from a slave of his with whom he had entered into a manumission contract (*mukātab*), when the slave paid the contractual amount in advance in return for his immediate manumission. Al-Qāsim said, "Abū Bakr al-Ṣiddīq would not levy the alms-tax on money until a year had passed with the money in its owner's possession." He also said, "Whenever Abū Bakr gave the people their stipends, he would ask each one of them, 'Do you have in your possession any money on which the alms-tax is due?' and if someone said yes, Abū Bakr would withhold that amount from his stipend. If he said no, Abū Bakr would give the person his stipend in full."

659. According to Mālik, ʿUmar b. Ḥusayn reported from ʿĀ'isha bt. Qudāma that her father said, "Whenever I went to ʿUthmān b. ʿAffān to collect my stipend, he would ask me, 'Do you have any money in your possession on which the alms-tax is due?' If I said yes, he would deduct the amount owed on that money from my stipend, but if I said no, he would pay me my stipend in full."

660. According to Mālik, Nāfiʿ reported that ʿAbd Allāh b. ʿUmar would say, "Money is not subject to the alms-tax until a year passes with the money in its owner's possession."

661. According to Mālik, Ibn Shihāb said, "The first person to deduct the alms-tax directly from stipends was Muʿāwiya b. Abī Sufyān."[259]

---

259 Muʿāwiya b. Abī Sufyān was a member of the clan of the Banū Umayya, traditional rivals of the Banū Hāshim (the clan of the Prophet, pbuh). His father, Abū Sufyān, led the Meccan opposition to the Prophet Muḥammad (pbuh) and became a Muslim only when the Prophet (pbuh) returned to Mecca triumphant. Muʿāwiya, however, became a Muslim prior to the conquest of Mecca. He served as the governor of the Levant during the caliphates of ʿUmar b. al-Khaṭṭāb and ʿUthmān b. ʿAffān. When ʿUthmān was murdered, Muʿāwiya demanded that the killers be brought to justice and refused to recognize ʿAlī b. Abī Ṭālib as the rightful caliph, leading to the first civil war in Islamic history. After ʿAlī's murder, Muʿāwiya was recognized as the caliph in 41/660, and he moved the capital to Damascus. He reigned until the year 60/680. The reign of Muʿāwiya, who is conventionally considered the founder of the Umayyad dynasty, marks the end of the Rightly Guided Caliphate (*al-khilāfa al-rāshida*) and the beginning of dynastic rule. In this text, Muʿāwiya deducts *zakāt* from the stipends as taxes due on the stipends themselves, not to offset the alms-tax due on other money, as done in the previous reports.

662. Yaḥyā said, "Mālik said, 'The long-established ordinance about which there is no dissent among us (*al-sunna allatī lā ikhtilāfa fīhā ʿindanā*) is that the alms-tax is due on eighty-five grams (twenty dinars)[260] of pure gold, just as it is due on 600 grams of pure silver (200 dirhams).'"[261]

663. Yaḥyā said, "Mālik said, 'No alms-tax is due on twenty gold dinar coins if they are obviously underweight; however, if the number of underweight gold dinar coins is so great that their weight reaches the weight of twenty gold dinar coins of full weight, the alms-tax becomes due.'" Yaḥyā said, "Mālik said, 'No alms-tax is due on less than twenty pure gold dinars.'" Yaḥyā said, "Mālik said, 'No alms-tax is due on 200 silver dirham coins that are obviously underweight; however, if the number of underweight silver dirham coins is so great that their weight reaches the weight of 200 silver dirham coins of full weight, the alms-tax becomes due. If any underweight coins circulate in commerce and merchants accept them as though they were full-weight coins, the alms-tax is due on them, whether the coins are dirhams or dinars.'"

664. Mālik said, regarding a man who has 160 full-weight silver dirham coins at a time when the prevailing exchange rate in his town is eight dirhams for every gold dinar, "He is not obliged to pay the alms-tax on them.[262] The alms-tax is due only on twenty dinars of pure gold, or 200 silver dirhams."

665. Mālik said that a man who obtains five dinars, whether as a gain (*fāʾida*) from a prior investment or from any other source, then deploys the sum in trade, and then liquidates his investment less than a year later,[263] with the proceeds equaling or exceeding the minimum amount that is subject to the alms-tax (i.e., twenty gold dinars), is immediately obliged to pay the alms-tax on the amount realized. This is the case even if he liquidated the investment just one day before (or after) a year had passed from the date of the investment. He is not, however, again liable for the alms-tax on that money until a year passes from the day on which he last paid the alms-tax.[264]

---

260 A dinar is 4.25 grams of pure gold.

261 A dirham is approximately 2.975 grams of pure silver.

262 In other words, he is not obliged to pay the alms-tax on his silver coins even though they are, in worth, the equivalent of twenty gold dinars.

263 We have assumed here that the individual acquires a property for trade and then sells it at an opportune time. Such a trader the Mālikīs call a *muḥtakir*. The same principle, however, would also apply to a retail merchant, who acquires inventory and then sells it at whatever price is available in the market. Such a merchant the Mālikīs term a *mudīr*. In the latter case, if the value of the merchant's inventory reaches the minimum amount on which the alms-tax is due, he is required to pay the alms-tax, even though he hasn't liquidated his inventory.

264 Mālik, uniquely among all Sunnī jurists, adopts the position that once commercial profits reach the minimum required for liability to the alms-tax when added to the investor's cash basis in the investment, they are subject to the alms-tax immediately, not only after the passage of a year. The majority of jurists distinguish between profits and the cash basis of the

666. Yaḥyā said, "Mālik said, regarding a man who had ten dinars that he invested in trade and that grew to twenty dinars after one year, that he was obliged to pay the alms-tax immediately and could not defer payment for an additional year from the day on which the amount became subject to the alms-tax. This is because one year had already passed from the date when he first had ten dinars; however, no additional alms-tax is due on the money until one year passes from the day on which he last paid the alms-tax."

667. Yaḥyā said, "Mālik said, 'The agreed-upon rule among us (*al-amr al-mujtama' 'alayhi 'indanā*) concerning income gained from hiring out (*ijāra*) slaves, money that slaves pay their masters out of their own earnings (*kharāj*), rent (*kirā'*) on dwellings, and instalment payments received from a slave who is a party to a manumission contract (*mukātab*) is that no alms-tax is due on any of them, whether the amounts are small or large, until a year has passed from the day on which the owner took possession of the cash."[265]

668. Mālik said, regarding two or more partners who own gold and silver jointly, that if the share of any partner in the partnership is equal to or exceeds twenty gold dinars or 200 silver dirhams, the partner must pay the alms-tax on that share. No alms-tax, however, is due from a partner whose share is less than the minimum amount subject to the alms-tax. If the partners' combined shares exceed the minimum amount, but one partner's share is larger than those of the others, the alms-tax is taken from each partner in proportion to his share of the total, provided that each partner's share is at least equal to the minimum amount subject to the alms-tax. That is because the Messenger of God (pbuh) said, "No alms-tax is due on less than 600 grams of pure silver (five *awāq*)." Mālik said, "Of all the views that I have heard, this is the one I prefer most."

---

investment and therefore do not subject profits to the alms-tax until the investor has held the profits for a year. A minority of jurists levy the alms-tax on commercial profits immediately if the cash basis of the investment already satisfies the minimum amount required to impose the alms-tax and a year has passed since the original investment was made. Mālik is the only jurist to combine the cash basis of an investment with the profits realized on its disposition to impose an immediate obligation to pay the alms-tax, as long as the investor acquired the cash used for the original investment at least a year earlier. Zurqānī, *Sharḥ al-Zurqānī*, 2:145.

265 In this case, the alms-tax is not due immediately because the owner has not sold the asset and recovered his basis in the investment in cash. Such income is the equivalent, therefore, of newly received money, which the owner enjoys the right to deploy productively (*ḥaqq al-tanmiya*) before paying any tax on it. Accordingly, a year must pass with the money in the owner's possession before he becomes liable to pay the alms-tax on it, if the amount received was in excess of the required minimum. It the amount was less than the minimum required, however, he is entitled to hold it free of any obligation to pay the alms-tax until such time as the money in his possession reaches the minimum.

669. Yaḥyā said, "Mālik said, 'If a man has entrusted his gold and silver to various people, he must add up the total of these amounts and pay the alms-tax due on that sum.'"

670. Mālik said, "Whoever has acquired gold or silver is not obligated to pay any alms-tax on it until one year has passed from the day he acquired it."

Chapter 3. The Alms-Tax (*Zakāt*) Due on Mineral Wealth (*Maʿādin*) Extracted from the Earth

671. According to Mālik, Rabīʿa b. Abī ʿAbd al-Raḥmān reported from more than one source that the Messenger of God (pbuh) assigned the right to exploit the mines (*maʿādin*) of al-Qabaliyya, which were located in the direction of al-Furʿ,[266] to Bilāl b. al-Ḥārith al-Muzanī. No levy other than the alms-tax has ever been imposed on those mines up to this day.

672. Mālik said, "It is my view, and God knows best, that no alms-tax should be taken from mineral wealth until its output reaches the equivalent of eighty-five grams (twenty dinars) of gold or 600 grams (200 dirhams) of silver. Once that threshold has been reached, however, the alms-tax becomes due immediately. Thereafter, as long as the vein remains productive, all subsequent production is immediately subject to the alms-tax. If the vein is depleted, but later more can be extracted, the new supply is dealt with in the same way as the original case: payment of the alms-tax becomes due only when the renewed output reaches the minimum amount, as in the original case."[267]

673. Yaḥyā said, "Mālik said, 'Mines are treated like crops, insofar as the alms-tax is levied on mineral wealth in the same fashion as it is levied on crops. It is deducted from what comes out of the ground on the day it is extracted without waiting for a year to elapse, just as a tenth is taken from crops on the day of harvest without waiting for a year to pass.'"

Chapter 4. The Alms-Tax (*Zakāt*) Due on Buried Treasure (*Rikāz*)

674. According to Mālik, Ibn Shihāb reported from Saʿīd b. al-Musayyab and from Abū Salama b. ʿAbd al-Raḥmān, from Abū Hurayra, that the Messenger of God (pbuh) said, "The alms-tax due on buried treasure is one-fifth."

675. Yaḥyā said, "Mālik said, 'The rule about which there is no dissent among us and which I heard the people of knowledge affirm (*al-amr alladhī*

266 A place between Mecca and Medina.

267 In other words, no alms-tax is due until the output again reaches the equivalent of eighty-five grams (twenty dinars) of gold or 600 grams (200 dirhams) of silver.

lā ikhtilāfa fīhi 'indanā wa'lladhī sami'tu min ahl al-'ilm) is that "buried treasure" refers to valuables buried prior to Islam,[268] as long as its finder did not intentionally deploy any capital, expense, or hard labor or incur any other inconvenience in order to find it. If capital was required, however, and hard labor was incurred, and if the venture was only sometimes successful, then whatever is found is not considered buried treasure.'"

Chapter 5. Items on Which No Alms-Tax (*Zakāt*) Is Due: Jewelry, Gold Ore, and Amber

676. According to Mālik, 'Abd al-Raḥmān b. al-Qāsim reported from his father that 'Ā'isha, the wife of the Prophet (pbuh), was responsible for her fraternal nieces, who were orphans in her care. They had gold jewelry, but she did not pay the alms-tax on such jewelry.

677. According to Mālik, Nāfi' reported that 'Abd Allāh b. 'Umar would give his daughters and handmaidens gold jewelry but did not pay the alms-tax on that jewelry.

678. Yaḥyā said, "Mālik said, 'The alms-tax is due on gold ore and on any gold or silver jewelry that is not worn. It must be weighed annually, and one-fortieth is taken from it, provided that it weighs at least eighty-five grams (twenty dinars) in pure gold or 600 grams (200 dirhams) in silver. If it weighs less than that, no alms-tax is due. Jewelry is subject to the alms-tax only when it is kept for purposes other than ornamentation. Gold ore and broken jewelry that its owner intends to repair and wear later are equivalent to ordinary household items. For that reason, members of the household do not pay the alms-tax on them.'"

679. Yaḥyā said, "Mālik said, 'No alms-tax is due on pearls, musk, or amber.'"

Chapter 6. The Alms-Tax (*Zakāt*) Due on the Property of Orphans and on Commercial Investment of Orphans' Property

680. According to Mālik, it reached him that 'Umar b. al-Khaṭṭāb said, "Invest orphans' property in commerce; don't let the alms-tax deplete it."

681. According to Mālik, 'Abd al-Raḥmān b. al-Qāsim reported that his father said, "One of my brothers and I were in the care of 'Ā'isha. Because we were orphans and in her care, she would pay the alms-tax due on our property."

---

268 If the "buried treasure" could be dated to the Islamic era, it was considered lost property and had to be handed over to the state for safekeeping until the true owner could be found.

682. According to Mālik, it reached him that ʿĀʾisha, the wife of the Prophet (pbuh), would turn over the property of orphans in her care to merchants, who would invest that property in commerce for them.

683. According to Mālik, Yaḥyā b. Saʿīd reported that he purchased some property for his orphaned nephews who were in his care. It was later sold for a substantial profit.

684. Yaḥyā said, "Mālik said, 'There is nothing objectionable in investing orphans' property in commerce, if the person investing their property is trustworthy. Further, I do not believe that he is liable for any losses that might result.'"

Chapter 7. The Alms-Tax (*Zakāt*) Due on a Decedent's Estate (*Mīrāth*)

685. Mālik said, "If a man dies without having paid the alms-tax that is due on his property, it is to be collected out of the one-third of his property available for testamentary disposition,[269] but no more is to be taken. The payment of unpaid alms-tax is given priority over the payment of other bequests. I consider unpaid alms-tax to be the equivalent of a debt, which is why I believe it ought to be given priority over bequests." Mālik also said, "This is the case only when the deceased makes a testamentary disposition for payment of the unpaid alms-tax. If the deceased fails to leave such an instruction but his family pays it anyway, that is a good thing. However, the family is under no obligation to do so."

686. Yaḥyā said, "Mālik said, 'The long-established ordinance among us about which there is no dissent (*al-sunna ʿindanā allatī lā ikhtilāfa fīhā*) is that no alms-tax is due on inherited property that consists of debts, goods, realty, or male or female slaves until a year has passed from the date on which the items were sold and payment in cash was received or the debt was collected.'"

687. Yaḥyā said, "Mālik said, 'The long-established ordinance among us (*al-sunna ʿindanā*) is that no alms-tax is due on money[270] inherited by an heir until a year has passed from the date of the inheritance.'"

Chapter 8. The Alms-Tax (*Zakāt*) Due on Debt

688. According to Mālik, Ibn Shihāb reported from al-Sāʾib b. Yazīd that ʿUthmān b. ʿAffān would say, "This is the month in which the alms-tax is

269 A Muslim is permitted to make a testamentary disposition (i.e., a will) of up to one-third of the value of his estate. At least two-thirds of the decedent's estate must pass to the decedent's legal heirs.

270 That is, gold or silver.

due. Whoever owes a debt, therefore, should pay it. This way, every person receives what he is owed and may pay any alms-tax that is due out of the proceeds of such debts."

689. According to Mālik, Ayyūb b. Abī Tamīma al-Sakhtiyānī reported that ʿUmar b. ʿAbd al-ʿAzīz issued a decree with respect to money that a public official had misappropriated. He ordered that it be returned to its owner but that the alms-tax that had accumulated over the years should first be deducted. He later amended his prior decree with a subsequent decree, namely, that the alms-tax be taken from misappropriated money only once, because its rightful owner had effectively lost use of his property.[271]

690. According to Mālik, Yazīd b. Khuṣayfa reported that he asked Sulaymān b. Yasār whether a man who had money in hand but also owed a debt for the same amount was obliged to pay the alms-tax on that money. He said, "No."

691. Yaḥyā said, "Mālik said, 'The rule about which there is no dissent among us (*al-amr alladhī lā ikhtilāfa fīhi ʿindanā*) is that the creditor is not obliged to pay the alms-tax on a debt owed to him until he collects it. Even if it remains outstanding with the borrower for a number of years before he collects it, he need pay the alms-tax on it only once. If he collects an instalment of the debt on which no alms-tax is due (because it is less than the minimum amount liable to the alms-tax) but has other money on which the alms-tax is due, the instalment is added to the rest of his money, and he pays the alms-tax on the total sum.' Mālik said, 'If he has no liquid money other than that instalment of the debt that he collected, and it falls short of the minimum amount on which the alms-tax is due, he is not obliged to pay the alms-tax on it. He should, however, keep track of the instalments he has collected, for if he later collects additional instalments that, when added to that which he has already collected, exceed the minimum amount, he is obliged to pay the alms-tax on the total. Whether or not he has consumed prior instalments of the debt, he is obliged to pay the alms-tax on everything collected. Once the sum he has collected on the debt he is owed amounts to eighty-five grams (twenty dinars) of pure gold or 600 grams (200 dirhams) of silver, he pays the alms-tax on it. He thereafter pays the alms-tax on any subsequent amounts received, be they small or large, according to the amount received.' Mālik said, 'The proof that the alms-tax on a debt is to be paid only once, even if the debt was outstanding for several years before it was repaid, is that commercial goods may remain in a merchant's

271 This is because the alms-tax is due only on property that the owner could have profitably invested. In the case of misappropriated money, the true owner effectively lost control of his property and therefore lacked the opportunity to invest it profitably, thus relieving him of the obligation to pay alms-tax on it.

possession for many years before he sells them, but he pays the alms-tax on the prices he receives for them only once, in that year. This is so because neither the creditor nor the owner of commercial goods is obliged to use other property that he may own to pay the alms-tax due on the debt owed to him or on his commercial goods. The alms-tax that is due on an item of property is to be satisfied only from that particular item of property; the alms-tax due on one item of property need not be satisfied from another piece of property.'"

692. Yaḥyā said, "Mālik said, 'The rule in our view (*al-amr ʿindanā*) regarding a debtor who has enough commercial goods on hand to discharge any debt that he owes and who also has an amount of cash on which the alms-tax is due is that he must pay the alms-tax on that cash.'" Yaḥyā said, "Mālik said, 'If, however, the commercial goods and cash he has on hand are sufficient only to discharge his debt, he is not obliged to pay any alms-tax. He is obliged to pay the alms-tax only when his cash on hand exceeds his debt and the cash sum is at least the minimum amount on which the alms-tax must be paid.'"

Chapter 9. The Alms-Tax (*Zakāt*) Due on Commercial Goods

693. According to Mālik, Yaḥyā b. Saʿīd reported that Zurayq b. Ḥayyān (who was in charge of collecting the alms-tax in Egypt during the terms of al-Walīd, Sulaymān, and ʿUmar b. ʿAbd al-ʿAzīz)[272] said that ʿUmar b. ʿAbd al-ʿAzīz sent him an edict that said, "Inspect the goods in the possession of the Muslim merchants who pass your way. Assess the value of all of their cargo that is intended for immediate sale, deduct from that amount the value of eighty-five grams (twenty dinars) of gold, and take one-fortieth of the remainder in satisfaction of the alms-tax. However, if the value of the goods is less than eighty-five grams (twenty dinars) of gold, leave the cargo alone and do not take anything. As for non-Muslim merchants who are permanent residents in Muslim territory: assess the value of all of their cargo that is intended for immediate sale, deduct from that amount the value of 42.5 grams (ten dinars) of gold, and take one-fortieth of the remainder. But if the value of the goods is less than 42.5 grams (ten dinars) of gold, leave the cargo alone and do not take anything. Record the amount you take from them and give them a receipt, which suffices them until the same time next year."

694. Yaḥyā said, "Mālik said, 'The rule in our view (*al-amr ʿindanā*) regarding commercial goods that are intended for immediate sale is that if a man pays the alms-tax on his money, then buys commercial goods such as

272 Al-Walīd b. ʿAbd al-Malik b. Marwān (r. 86–96/705–715), Sulaymān b. ʿAbd al-Malik b. Marwān (r. 96–99/715–717], and ʿUmar b. ʿAbd al-ʿAzīz b. Marwān (r. 99–101/717–720) were successive Umayyad caliphs.

cloth, slaves, or similar things, and then sells them before a year has passed since he last paid the alms-tax, he does not pay alms-tax on the money that he receives from the sale of those goods until a year has passed from the day on which he paid the alms-tax on the original amount. If he does not sell the commercial goods for some years, however, he is not obliged to pay the alms-tax on them, and even if he retains the goods for a long time without selling them, he pays the alms-tax on them only once, when he sells them.'"

695. Yaḥyā said, "Mālik said, 'The rule in our view regarding a man who purchases wheat or dates with gold or silver for purposes of trade, retains them in his inventory until a year has passed, and then sells them is that he pays the alms-tax on the goods only at the time when he sells them. This is provided that the price he receives is at least the minimum amount on which the alms-tax is due. This case is different from that of crops that a man harvests from his land or of dates that he gathers from his palm trees.'"

696. Yaḥyā said, "Mālik said, 'As for money that a man invests in commercial trade but that does not yield sufficient profit for him to incur the alms-tax: the man should determine a month of the year when he appraises the monetary value of the commercial goods that he holds in inventory, adding to that sum any gold and silver coin or bullion he owns as of that date. If their aggregate sum is at least the minimum amount on which the alms-tax is due, he must then pay the alms-tax on that amount.'"

697. Mālik said, "The same principle applies to Muslims who trade and to those who do not. They have to pay the alms-tax only once every year, whether or not they engaged in commerce that year."

Chapter 10. What Has Come Down regarding Hoarding

698. According to Mālik, ʿAbd Allāh b. Dīnār said, "I heard ʿAbd Allāh b. ʿUmar, when asked what a 'hoard' (*kanz*)[273] was, say, 'It is money on which the alms-tax (*zakāt*) has not been paid.'"

699. According to Mālik, ʿAbd Allāh b. Dīnār reported from Abū Ṣāliḥ al-Sammān that Abū Hurayra would say, "On the Day of Resurrection, anyone who had money on which he failed to pay the alms-tax will see his wealth transformed into a smooth, poisonous, white-headed serpent with two venom-swollen glands bulging over its maw, which will seek him out until it grips him and says, 'I am your hoard.'"

273 A reference to *al-Tawba*, 9:34, which condemns those who hoard gold and silver and do not spend it to further godly ends.

Chapter 11. The Alms-Tax (*Ṣadaqa*)[274] on Livestock (*Māshiya*)

700. Mālik said that he had read ʿUmar b. al-Khaṭṭāb's edict (*kitāb*) regarding the alms-tax. He said, "I found written therein the following:

'In the Name of God, the Merciful, the Compassionate.

This is the edict clarifying the alms-tax with respect to livestock.

§1. On twenty-four camels or fewer, the alms-tax is due in sheep (*ghanam*): one yearling (*shāt*)[275] for every five camels. On anything above that, up to thirty-five camels, a she-camel in its second year is due or, if there is no she-camel in its second year, a male camel in its third year. On anything above that, up to forty-five camels, a she-camel in its third year is due. On anything above that, up to sixty camels, a she-camel in its fourth year is due. On anything above that, up to seventy-five camels, a she-camel in its fifth year is due. On anything above that, up to ninety camels, two she-camels, each in its third year, are due. On anything above that, up to 120 camels, two-she camels, each in its fourth year, are due. On any number of camels greater than 120, a she-camel in its third year is due for every forty camels and a she-camel in its fourth year is due for every fifty.

§2. On grazing sheep, if their number is between forty and 120, one yearling is due. On anything above that, up to 200 sheep, two yearlings are due. On anything above that, up to 300 sheep, three yearlings are due. On anything above that, for every one hundred sheep, one yearling is due. A ram is not to be given as payment of the alms-tax, nor is an old or injured animal, except as the alms-tax collector sees fit. Separate flocks should not be joined together to make one flock, nor should a mingled flock be divided into two or more flocks, in order to avoid paying the alms-tax. Whenever two or more persons commingle their flocks, any alms-tax that is collected must be apportioned between them proportionately.

§3. On silver, if it reaches 600 grams (five *awāq*), one-fortieth is levied.'"

---

274 It is Mālik's custom to refer to the alms payable on livestock as *ṣadaqa* rather than *zakāt*.

275 The Arabs in Mālik's time used *ghanam* to refer to both sheep and goats. For stylistic reasons, we have decided to translate the term as "sheep," with the understanding that it is also inclusive of goats. Arabs of that time also referred to individual sheep and goats of up to two years of age as *shāt*. We have chosen to translate this term as "yearling." English permits use of the word "yearling" for both newborn lambs and kids up to the completion of their second year.

Chapter 12. What Has Come Down regarding the Alms-Tax (*Zakāt*) on Cattle (*Baqar*)

701. According to Mālik, Ḥumayd b. Qays al-Makkī reported from Ṭāwūṣ al-Yamānī that Muʿādh b. Jabal al-Anṣārī took one calf in its second year from every thirty cows, and one cow in its third year from every forty cows.[276] Once a herd of less than thirty head was brought to him, so he refrained from taking anything from it, saying, "I have not heard anything about it from the Messenger of God (pbuh), so when I next meet him, I shall ask him." But the Messenger of God (pbuh) died before Muʿādh b. Jabal could return to Medina and ask him.[277]

702. Yaḥyā said, "Mālik said, 'The best view that I have heard regarding someone who owns flocks of sheep (*ghanam*) cared for by two or more shepherds in different places is that the several flocks are treated as one, and the owner pays the alms-tax on the combined amount. This case is analogous to that of a man who owns gold and silver, which he has entrusted to various people who are scattered about; he must add up all those deposits and pay the alms-tax that is due on the aggregate sum.'"

703. Yaḥyā said, "Mālik said, regarding a man who has both sheep (*ḍaʾn*) and goats (*maʿz*), 'They should be added up, and if together they reach the minimum amount on which the alms-tax is due, the alms-tax must be paid. It is certainly the case that they are both "sheep," and ʿUmar b. al-Khaṭṭāb's edict says, "On grazing sheep, if they reach forty, one yearling."'"

704. Mālik said, "If there are more sheep than goats, and the owner owes only one yearling, the alms-tax collector takes a lamb. If the goats are more numerous than the sheep, he takes a kid. If the goats and the sheep are equal in number, the alms-tax collector takes a yearling of either kind, as he wishes."

705. Yaḥyā said, "Mālik said, 'The same applies to Arabian and Bactrian camels.[278] They are added together to determine liability for the alms-tax. Indeed, they are both "camels." If there are more Arabian camels than Bactrians, and the owner owes only one camel, the alms-tax collector should take an Arabian. If, on the other hand, the Bactrians outnumber the Arabians, he should take a Bactrian. If they are equal in number, he may take whichever kind he wishes.'"

---

276 According to some authorities, the cow to be taken in the latter case should be in its fourth year. Zurqānī, *Sharḥ al-Zurqānī*, 2:170.

277 The Prophet Muḥammad (pbuh) had dispatched Muʿādh b. Jabal al-Anṣārī to Yemen to serve as his governor there during the last years of his mission.

278 Arabian camels have a single hump, whereas Bactrian camels, which are native to Central Asia, have two.

706. Yaḥyā said, "Mālik said, 'The same applies to cows and buffalo. They are added together to determine liability for the alms-tax. Indeed, they are both "cattle." If there are more cows than buffalo, and the owner owes only one cow, the alms-tax collector should take a cow. If there are more buffalo, he should take a buffalo. If they are equal in number, he may take whichever kind he wishes. If the alms-tax is due on both, it is taken from the two kinds.'"[279]

707. Yaḥyā said, "Mālik said, 'The alms-tax is not due from anyone who has acquired livestock, be it camels, cattle, or sheep, until a year has passed from the date of their acquisition, unless he previously owned an amount of livestock on which the alms-tax was due—either five camels, thirty cattle, or forty sheep. If he already owns five camels, thirty cattle, or forty sheep and then acquires additional camels, cattle, or sheep, whether by purchase, as a gift, or through inheritance, he must pay the alms-tax on the latter when he pays the alms-tax on the livestock that he already owned, even if a year has not passed from the date he acquired the additional livestock and even if the previous owner paid the alms-tax on the animals on the day before the new owner bought or inherited them. The new owner must pay the alms-tax on the newly acquired livestock when he pays the alms-tax due on the livestock that he already owned. This is the very same rule that applies to silver on which the owner paid the alms-tax and then used to buy goods from another man. When the second man sold the goods for the silver of the first man, the second man became liable to pay the alms-tax due on the silver he received in exchange for those goods—and so he must pay it. As a result, the first man paid the alms-tax on the silver the day before the purchase, and the second man then paid the alms-tax on that very same silver the next day when he took it in exchange for the goods he sold to the first man.'"

708. Yaḥyā said, "Mālik said, regarding a man who had too few sheep to incur liability for the alms-tax but then purchased or inherited a number of additional sheep sufficient by itself to render him liable for the alms-tax, that he is not obliged to pay alms-tax on any of his sheep until a year has passed from the day on which he acquired the additional sheep, whether they were purchased or inherited. That is because whenever an individual owns livestock—be they camels, cattle, or sheep—in a quantity less than that which renders him liable to pay the alms-tax, he does not own the requisite quantity of livestock to render him liable for subsequent acquisitions. That is to say, until he acquires the minimum amount of each kind of livestock on

279 As would be the case, for example, if there were thirty cows and thirty buffalo, in which case the alms-tax collector should take one calf from the cows and one calf from the buffalo.

which the alms-tax is due, he is not liable for subsequent acquisitions. Once he has acquired the minimum amount of livestock on which the alms-tax is due, however, whatever he subsequently acquires, whether much or little, is added to what he previously owned, and the alms-tax is payable at once on all of them."

709. Mālik said, "If a man has camels, cattle, and sheep, and the alms-tax is due with respect to each kind, and he then acquires an additional camel, cow, or yearling (*shāt*), he must include it with the rest of his livestock when he calculates and pays the alms-tax that is due on his livestock. Of all the views I have heard regarding this issue, that is the view I prefer most.'"

710. Mālik said, regarding a man who is obliged to pay the alms-tax on his livestock but does not have the specific animal required of him, "If what is due is a she-camel in her second year but he does not have one, a male camel in its third year is taken instead. If what is due is a she-camel in its third, fourth, or fifth year and the owner does not have one, he must purchase one to satisfy his obligation. The owner should not, in my opinion, give the alms-tax collector the monetary value of what is due."

711. Mālik said, regarding camels and cows used in transporting water, irrigation, and plowing, "I think that the alms-tax is due on all of these animals once their number reaches the minimum that renders the alms-tax obligatory."

Chapter 13. What Has Come Down regarding the Alms-Tax Payable by Those Who Commingle (*Khulaṭāʾ*)[280] Their Livestock

712. Yaḥyā said, "Mālik said, concerning two persons who have commingled (*khulaṭāʾ*) their livestock, 'If they share a shepherd, a stud, a pasture, and the water, the two are comminglers, as long as each of them can identify his own property. If one of them cannot distinguish his property from that of his companion, he is not a commingler; rather, he is a partner.[281] The alms-tax (*ṣadaqa*) is not obligatory on the comminglers until each one of them independently owns a quantity of livestock on which the alms-tax is

280 The Arabic term *khulaṭāʾ* (sing. *khalīṭ*) refers to two or more individuals who pasture their livestock together but do not own them in common.

281 Mālik is here distinguishing between two kinds of cooperative ventures in animal husbandry: in the first, called a *khulṭa*, the participants share only the inputs required for livestock raising, but each retains individual ownership of the animals in his flock by ensuring that his animals are marked in a way that distinguishes them from the animals of his colleague. In this case, the participants are called *khulaṭāʾ*, or "comminglers." But when the participants commingle their flocks in such a fashion that it is impossible to determine individual ownership of the specific animals that make up the commingled flock, they form a partnership (*sharika*) and are called partners (*shurakāʾ*, sing. *sharīk*).

due. An example that clarifies this principle is that of two comminglers, one of whom has forty or more yearlings (*shāt*) and the other has fewer than forty. In this case, the alms-tax is due only on the one who owns forty or more. No alms-tax is due on the commingler who owns fewer than that. If each one of them owns a quantity of livestock on which the alms-tax is due, the two flocks are assessed together to determine the amount of alms-tax that is due in the aggregate, and they are jointly liable for the alms-tax due on their commingled flock. If one of the two has a thousand yearlings, or some smaller number on which the alms-tax is due, and the other has forty or more yearlings, they are comminglers. Each one is liable to pay the alms-tax that is due on the entire flock in proportion to his share of the commingled property. The one with one thousand head is liable for his proportionate share of the alms-tax, and the one with forty head is liable for his proportionate share of the alms-tax.'"

713. Yaḥyā said, "Mālik said, 'Two persons who commingle their camels are the same as two who commingle their sheep (*ghanam*): they are jointly liable for the alms-tax due on the entirety of the commingled herd, provided that each of them owns the minimum number of camels on which the alms-tax is due. That is because the Messenger of God (pbuh) said, "No alms-tax is due on fewer than five camels," and ʿUmar b. al-Khaṭṭāb said, "If the number of grazing sheep reaches forty, one yearling is due." Of all the views I have heard regarding this issue, this view is the one I prefer most.'"

714. ʿUmar b. al-Khaṭṭāb said, "Animals that are grazed separately should not be joined together into one flock, nor should animals that are grazed together be separated into different flocks, in each case in order to avoid paying the alms-tax." Mālik said, "What he meant by that is that the owners of livestock should not do this. An example of what he meant by 'animals that are grazed separately should not be joined together into one flock' is the case of three men, each of whom owns forty yearlings. Accordingly, each is liable to pay the alms-tax on his flock. But when the alms-tax collector arrives, they commingle their flocks so that together they owe only one yearling. This is prohibited. An example of what he meant by 'nor should animals that are grazed together be separated into different flocks' is the case of two comminglers, each of whom owns 101 yearlings. Accordingly, they jointly owe three yearlings on their commingled flock. But when the alms-tax collector arrives, they separate their flocks so that each is liable to pay only one yearling. This is prohibited. That is why it is said, 'Animals that are grazed separately should not be joined together into one flock, nor should animals that are grazed together be separated into different flocks, in each case in order to avoid paying the alms-tax.' This is what I have heard about this issue."

Chapter 14. What Has Come Down regarding the Inclusion of Newborn Kids and Lambs (*Sakhl*) in Calculating the Alms-Tax

715. According to Mālik, Thawr b. Zayd al-Dīlī reported from a son of ʿAbd Allāh b. Sufyān al-Thaqafī, from his grandfather Sufyān b. ʿAbd Allāh, that ʿUmar b. al-Khaṭṭāb appointed him as an alms-tax collector.[282] He would include newborn kids and lambs (*sakhl*) in assessing alms-tax obligations. The people objected, saying, "Do you include newborn kids and lambs even though you do not accept them as payment?" When Sufyān returned to ʿUmar b. al-Khaṭṭāb, he mentioned this issue to him, and ʿUmar said, "Yes, we include even the newborn kid or lamb that the shepherd must carry on his back, but we do not accept it as payment. But neither do we take a fattened animal intended for slaughter (*akūla*), nor a mother nursing its child (*rubbā*), nor a pregnant ewe (*mākhiḍ*), nor a ram (*faḥl*). We take only six-month-old females or animals in their second year, because that is the median between the least valuable newborn sheep (*ghanam*) and the best, most valuable sheep." A *sakhla* is a newborn sheep; a *rubbā* is a female that has just given birth to a lamb and is nursing it; a *mākhiḍ* is a pregnant ewe; and an *akūla* is a sheep that is being fattened to be slaughtered for its meat.

716. Mālik said, regarding a scenario in which a man owns a number of sheep on which he is not liable to pay the alms-tax, but one day before the alms-tax collector's arrival his flock increases as a result of births to the point that it now reaches the minimum number on which the alms-tax is obligatory: "If the number of sheep, including their newborn offspring, reaches the level at which the alms-tax is due, the alms-tax is due on them that year. That is so because the newborn offspring are a result of the flock's natural growth. That distinguishes this case from that of flock increases resulting from purchase, gift, or inheritance. This case is similar to that of commercial goods whose value at the time of their acquisition is below the minimum amount on which the alms-tax is due but which, when sold by their owner, fetch a cash profit sufficient to render the alms-tax obligatory. In this case the owner pays the alms-tax on the profit and on the original capital amount in that year. Had the growth in his property been the result of an acquisition through purchase, gift, or inheritance, however, he would not have been obligated to pay the alms-tax on that growth until a year had passed from the day he acquired or inherited the additional property. Newborn sheep are part of the flock in the same way that the profit is part of the capital. They differ, however, in one aspect. When a man owns an

282 According to the editors of the RME, Sufyān was sent to the town of Ṭāʾif in the Hijaz, not far from Mecca.

amount of money on which the alms-tax is obligatory and then acquires additional money, he sets aside the newly aquired money and does not include it with his previously owned money when he calculates the alms-tax that is due on the latter. He does not add his newly acquired money to his previously owned money when calculating the alms-tax until a year has passed from the day on which he acquired the additional money. But if a man owns a flock of sheep or a herd of cattle or camels sizeable enough to render the alms-tax obligatory and then acquires an additional camel, cow, or yearling (*shāt*), he includes the new animal along with the others of its kind when paying the alms-tax on that kind of animal, provided again that he already owned a quantity of that particular kind of animal that made the alms-tax obligatory. This is the best of all the views that I have heard regarding this issue."

Chapter 15. The Practice (*ʿAmal*) with Respect to the Assessment of the Alms-Tax (*Ṣadaqa*) for Two or More Consecutive Years

717. Yaḥyā said, "Mālik said, 'The rule in our view (*al-amr ʿindanā*) concerning a man who is liable for the alms-tax on his herd of one hundred camels but who is not visited by the alms-tax collector until the alms-tax for the following year is due, by which time all but five camels of his herd have died, is that the alms-tax collector takes the alms-tax for the current and the previous year from the owner's five surviving camels, in this case amounting to two yearlings, one for each year. This is so because the alms-tax becomes due on the owner only on the day of assessment. Whether the animals have perished or multiplied, the alms-tax collector assesses the alms-tax on what the owner possesses on the day of assessment. Even if several years have passed without the owner paying the alms-tax due on his animals, the owner is not obliged to pay alms-tax on any livestock other than what the alms-tax collector finds in the owner's possession. If his animals had all perished, or if he owed several years of alms-tax on them but nothing was collected from him until his animals died out or their number withered to less than the minimum on which the alms-tax is due, he would not be obliged to pay any alms-tax, nor would he be liable for any alms-tax on the dead animals or on any other property that he previously owned.'"

Chapter 16. The Prohibition against Sharp Dealing When Collecting the Alms-Tax (*Ṣadaqa*) from the Public

718. According to Mālik, Yaḥyā b. Saʿid reported from Muḥammad b. Yaḥyā b. Ḥabbān, from al-Qāsim b. Muḥammad, that ʿĀʾisha, the wife of the Prophet (pbuh), said, "A flock of sheep (*ghanam*) consisting of animals collected as alms-tax was driven past ʿUmar b. al-Khaṭṭāb. He noticed that one of the animals had an udder swollen with milk. He asked, 'What is that animal doing here?' They said, 'It was collected as part of the alms-tax.' ʿUmar said, 'Its owner would not have given it voluntarily. Do not subject people to hardship. Do not take from Muslims the best of their animals, and avoid taking lactating females.'"[283]

719. According to Mālik, Yaḥyā b. Saʿīd reported that Muḥammad b. Yaḥyā b. Ḥabbān said, "Two men from the tribe of Ashja' told me that Muḥammad b. Maslama al-Anṣārī would come to them to collect the alms-tax. He would say to the livestock owners, 'Give me what you owe on your livestock.' He always accepted whatever yearling (*shāt*) the owner gave him, provided that it satisfied the owner's obligation."[284]

720. Yaḥyā said, "Mālik said, 'The long-established ordinance among us and that which I found the people of knowledge following (*al-sunna ʿindanā wa'lladhī adraktu ʿalayhi ahl al-ʿilm*) is that Muslims must not be subjected to sharp dealing when they pay their alms-tax (*zakāt*). Whatever they give of their property should be accepted from them.'"[285]

Chapter 17. Receiving Alms (*Ṣadaqa*) and Who Is Permitted to Receive Them

721. According to Mālik, Zayd b. Aslam reported from ʿAṭā' b. Yasār that the Messenger of God (pbuh) said, "Apart from the needy, only five categories of people may take property that has been collected as alms: a soldier campaigning for the sake of God; an administrator of the alms-tax; a debtor; someone who purchases with his own money property from a poor person who originally received that property as alms; and someone who receives as a gift property from his poor neighbor who originally received it as alms."

722. Mālik said, "The rule in our view (*al-amr ʿindanā*) regarding the distribution of alms is that it is determined exclusively by the good-faith judgment of the ruler (*wālī*). When distributing alms, the ruler ought to

283 According to the editors of the RME, the word *ṭaʿām* was understood by commentators to mean "milk." Zurqānī reports that Mālik was asked what ʿUmar's admonition meant, and he said it was a prohibition against the alms-tax collector's taking a lactating animal (*labūn*) as payment of the alms-tax. Zurqānī, *Sharḥ al-Zurqānī*, 2:182.

284 That is, he did not inquire too closely into the quality of the animal that was given in satisfaction of the obligation.

285 In other words, individual owners have the right to specify what of their property to give to the alms-tax collector in satisfaction of their obligation to pay the alms-tax. This does not mean, however, that the owners cannot be coerced to pay the alms-tax.

use his good-faith judgment to prioritize that category of eligible recipients that is in fact the most needy and numerous. It may well be the case that the class of beneficiaries that should receive the alms changes from one year to the next. In each case, preference is given to those who are needier and more numerous, whatever class that might be at the time at which the ruler exercises his good-faith judgment. This, in my experience, is in accord with the teachings of the people of knowledge of whom I approve. Administrators of the alms receive no fixed share of the alms. They receive only what the ruler (*imām*) specifies for them in good faith."

Chapter 18. What Has Come Down regarding Collecting the Alms-Tax (*Ṣadaqa*) and Strictly Enforcing Its Payment

723. According to Mālik, it reached him that Abū Bakr al-Ṣiddīq said, "Were they to refuse me even a length of rope used to hobble a camel, I would fight them over it."

724. According to Mālik, Zayd b. Aslam said, "Once ʿUmar b. al-Khaṭṭāb drank some milk and liked it very much. He asked the man who poured it for him where he had gotten it. The man told him that he and some others had gone to a well (whose name he mentioned), found some livestock that had been collected as alms-tax watering there, and milked some of the animals. He said, 'I put some of that milk in my waterskin, and this is it.' ʿUmar b. al-Khaṭṭāb then put his hand into his mouth and threw it up."

725. Yaḥyā said, "Mālik said, 'The rule in our view (*al-amr ʿindanā*) concerning anyone who withholds a determinate obligation owed to God and who cannot be persuaded by the Muslims to fulfill it voluntarily is that the Muslims are obliged to use force against him until he fulfills his duty.'"

726. According to Mālik, it reached him that an official in the government of ʿUmar b. ʿAbd al-ʿAzīz wrote to him about a man who had refused to pay the alms-tax (*zakāt*) that was due on his property. ʿUmar wrote back to him, instructing him, "Let the man be, and do not collect any alms-tax from him when you collect it from the other Muslims." Mālik said, "When the man heard about this, he became deeply ashamed, so he offered to pay the alms-tax that he had previously refused to pay. The official wrote back to ʿUmar and told him what had happened. ʿUmar wrote back to him and told him, 'Accept it from him.'"

Chapter 19. The Alms-Tax (*Zakāt*) Based on the Estimated Yield of Date Palms and Grapevines

727. According to Mālik, a source that he deemed reliable reported from Sulaymān b. Yasār and Busr b. Saʿīd that the Messenger of God (pbuh) said, "Regarding date palms and grapevines, if they are watered by rain, springwater, or an aquifer, one-tenth of their harvest is due as alms-tax; and if they are irrigated, one-twentieth is due."

728. According to Mālik, Ziyād b. Saʿd reported that Ibn Shihāb said, "The alms-tax (*ṣadaqa*) may not be discharged with poor-quality dates such as *juʿrūr*, *muṣrān al-faʾra*, or *ʿadhq Ibn Ḥubayq*.[286] Such dates should be included in the assessment, but they should not accepted as payment of the alms-tax." Mālik said, "This rule is the equivalent of the principle that applies to sheep (*ghanam*), whose newborns are included in the assessment but are not accepted as payment of the alms-tax. Sometimes a person might possess some property, including fresh dates, from which no alms-tax ought to be collected. An example is *burdī*[287] and similar varieties of high-quality dates. The alms-tax should be collected from neither the poorest-quality dates nor the highest-quality ones but only from median-quality dates."

729. Yaḥyā said, "Mālik said, 'The agreed-upon rule among us (*al-amr al-mujtamaʿ ʿalayhi ʿindanā*) concerning fresh fruit is that the yield of date palms and grapevines alone is estimated prior to harvest. Their yield is estimated at the time when the fruit first becomes viable and may lawfully be sold. This is because fresh dates and grapes may be eaten as they are, without first being dried. Accordingly, the owners are required to have the quantity of their crops estimated, and that estimate determines the amount of the alms-tax due from them. This is done to ease people's lives and to avoid constraining anyone in their affairs. Once made, the estimate of the quantity of these fruits is conclusive, and thereafter their owners are left alone and may do with them whatever they wish, including eating them. They then pay the alms-tax due on the fruit on the basis of the estimate, not of the amount actually harvested.'"

730. Yaḥyā said, "Mālik said, 'As for crops that are not eaten fresh—such as grains, which are eaten only after they have been harvested—they are never to be estimated. Rather, once such crops have been harvested, threshed, and sifted, leaving only the seeds, it is the duty of their owners to pay the applicable alms-tax on their crops, as long as the harvest produces at least the minimum on which the alms-tax is due. The owners of these crops

286 These are varieties of dates that are of extremely poor quality.
287 A high-quality variety of dates.

are trusted to pay what they owe without an alms-tax collector coming to collect it from them. This is the rule about which there is no dissent among us (*al-amr alladhī lā ikhtilāfa fīhi ʿindanā*).'"

731. Yaḥyā said, "Mālik said, 'The agreed-upon rule among us is that once the fruit of date palms becomes viable and may lawfully be sold, the owners of date palms are required to have the quantity of their dates estimated. Their liability for the alms-tax on their dates is determined conclusively on the basis of that estimate, and the alms-tax is collected from them in the form of dried dates at harvest. If a calamity happens to destroy the crop in its entirety after its output is estimated but before the crop is harvested, the owner is freed of the obligation to pay the alms-tax on that fruit. If part of the crop survives, however, and it weighs at least 610 kilograms (five *awsuq*) using the measure (*ṣāʿ*) of the Prophet (pbuh), the alms-tax is calculated only on that amount. The owner is not liable for the alms-tax in respect of the crops that the calamity destroyed. The same rule applies also to grapevines.'"

732. Yaḥyā said, "Mālik said, 'If a man has property that is scattered in various places or owns shares in scattered pieces of property, none of which is by itself large enough to incur liability for the alms-tax but which, when added together, constitute an amount on which the alms-tax would be due, he must aggregate them and pay the alms-tax that is due.'"

Chapter 20. The Alms-Tax (*Zakāt*) Due on Grains and Olives

733. According to Mālik, he asked Ibn Shihāb about the alms-tax due on olives, and Ibn Shihāb said, "One-tenth is due on them."

734. Yaḥyā said, "Mālik said, 'The one-tenth that is taken from olives is levied only after they have been pressed, provided that the weight of the olives is at least 610 kilograms (five *awsuq*). If the olives' weight is less than 610 kilograms, no alms-tax is due.'"

735. Yaḥyā said, "Mālik said, 'Olive trees are like date palms: if they are watered by rain, springwater, or an aquifer, one-tenth of the harvest is due, and if they are irrigated, one-twentieth is due. The output of olive trees, however, is not to be estimated.'"

736. Yaḥyā said, "Mālik said, 'The long-established ordinance among us (*al-sunna ʿindanā*) concerning edible grains that people can store is that one-tenth is taken from that which has been watered by rain, springwater, or an aquifer and that one-twentieth is taken from that which has been irrigated if in either case the harvest exceeds five *awsuq* (approximately

610 kilograms) using the original measure (*ṣāʿ*) of the Messenger of God (pbuh). The alms-tax is levied on anything in excess of 610 kilograms (five *awsuq*) in accordance with the rate that applies to it.'"

737. Mālik said, "The grains and pulses[288] that are subject to the alms-tax are wheat, barley, pearl barley (*sult*),[289] corn, millet, rice, lentils, peas, beans, sesame seeds, and similar grains that constitute staples. They are all subject to the alms-tax after they have been harvested and reduced to edible form. The people are taken at their word with respect to the quantity of their crops, and whatever they give as payment of the alms-tax is accepted."

738. Yaḥyā said, "Mālik was asked when the alms-tax on olives should be paid: before the expenses of storage are incurred or after? He said, 'Expenses are not taken into consideration. The owners of olives are asked about their crops just as the people who produce grains and legumes are. The alms-tax is taken from them on the basis of what they declare. Whoever declares 610 kilograms or more of olives pays one-tenth of its oil after his olives have been pressed. Whoever declares less than that does not have to pay alms-tax on his oil.'"

739. Yaḥyā said, "Mālik said, 'Whoever sells his cereal crops when they are ripe and ready in the husk is liable for the alms-tax that is due on them; their purchaser is not liable.'"

740. Yaḥyā said, "Mālik said, 'The sale of cereal crops is not valid until their grains are dry in the husk and they no longer need water.'"

741. Yaḥyā said, "Concerning the statement of God, Blessed and Sublime is He, 'Render what is due on it on the day of its harvest,'[290] Mālik said, 'It is a reference to the alms-tax, and God knows best. I heard people say that.'"

742. Yaḥyā said, "Mālik said, 'When someone sells his orchard or his land, including immature cereal crops or fruit, the purchaser is liable for the alms-tax, if any, on those cereals or fruit at harvest. If the cereal crops and the fruit are viable and ready for sale at the time of the transaction, the seller is liable for the applicable alms-tax unless the seller has stipulated that the purchaser be liable for paying the alms-tax.'"

---

288 Pulses include such legumes as peas, chickpeas, and lentils.
289 A type of barley with no husk.
290 *Al-Anʿām*, 6:241.

Chapter 21. Dates That Are Not Subject to the Alms-Tax (*Zakāt*)

743. Mālik said, "If a man has harvested 488 kilograms (four *awsuq*) of dried dates or the same amount of raisins,[291] wheat, or pulses, he is not required to add these crops together, and he is not liable for the alms-tax with respect to any of them—not the dates, the grapes, the wheat, or the pulses—until any one of them amounts to five *awsuq* (approximately 610 kilograms) using the measure (*ṣāʿ*) of the Prophet (pbuh), since the Messenger of God (pbuh) said, 'No alms-tax is due on less than 610 kilograms of dates.'"

744. Mālik said, "If any one of those categories amounts to 610 kilograms, the alms-tax is due, but if it does not reach that amount, no alms-tax is due. For example, a man who harvests 610 kilograms of dates, even if they are of different kinds and colors, adds them all together and must pay the alms-tax on them; however, if they do not add up to that amount, no alms-tax is due on them."

745. Yaḥyā said, "Mālik said, 'The same rule applies to the various kinds of cereal crops, such as brown wheat, white wheat, barley, and pearl barley, all of which are treated as one kind. If a man harvests an aggregate total of at least 610 kilograms of these grains, the alms-tax is due on the total. If, however, the combined total falls short of that amount, no alms-tax is due.'"

746. Mālik said, "The same rule applies to raisins of all kinds, whether black or red. If a man harvests (and dries) at least 610 kilograms of raisins, the alms-tax becomes due on them, but if the harvest falls short of that amount, no alms-tax is due."

747. Mālik said, "The same rule applies to pulses; they all fall into one category, like cereal crops, dates, and raisins, even if they differ in kind and color. Pulses include chickpeas, lentils, beans, and peas, as well as anything else the people understand to be pulses. If a man harvests at least 610 kilograms of pulses using the original measure of the Prophet (pbuh), even if the harvest is made up of different kinds of pulses, not just one kind, they are added together and the alms-tax is due on them." Yaḥyā said, "Mālik said, "Umar b. al-Khaṭṭāb distinguished between pulses and cereals when these were collected from the Nabateans.[292] He determined that pulses

291 This assumes that no conclusive estimate (*kharṣ*) of the harvest has been made. *Al-Mawsūʿa al-fiqhiyya*, 1st ed., 45 vols. (Kuwait: Kuwaiti Ministry of Endowments, 1983), 19:100. If, however, a conclusive estimate of the harvest has been made, Mālikīs assess liability for the alms-tax on grapes and dates on the basis of the estimated amount, not what the farmer actually harvested and dried, as set forth in report nos. 729 and 731 above.

292 According to the editors of the RME, in this context "the Nabateans" refers to the non-Arabic-speaking peoples of the Fertile Crescent.

constituted one category, of which he took one-tenth of the harvest, but of cereals and raisins he took one-twentieth.'"

748. Yaḥyā said, "Mālik said, 'If someone were to ask how it can be that pulses are added together for purposes of the alms-tax and the alms-tax is levied on the aggregate, even though one is permitted to trade two measures of one kind for one measure of another whereas cereals cannot be traded at a rate of two for one, one would say to him that gold and silver are likewise assessed together for purposes of the alms-tax, even though gold coins might be exchanged hand-to-hand for many times more in silver coins.'"[293]

749. Yaḥyā said, "Mālik said, regarding two men who jointly own date palms from which they harvest 976 kilograms (eight *awsuq*) of dates, 'They are not obliged to pay any alms-tax on the harvest. If one of them harvests 610 kilograms and the other 488 kilograms or less from the same piece of land, the alms-tax is due from the owner of the former amount, but no alms-tax is due from the one who harvested 488 kilograms or less.'"

750. Yaḥyā said, "Mālik said, 'This is the practice (*ʿamal*) that applies to all partners, whether the partnership involves cereal grains that have been harvested, dates cut from branches, or grapes off the vine. If each partner's share of the harvest is at least 610 kilograms, whether of dried dates, raisins, or cereals, he is liable for the alms-tax on them. But a partner whose share is less than 610 kilograms is not liable for the alms-tax. The alms-tax is paid only by someone whose harvest of cereals, dried dates, or raisins is at least 610 kilograms.'"

751. Yaḥyā said, "Mālik said, 'The long-established ordinance among us (*al-sunna ʿindanā*) regarding these categories—that is, dried dates, wheat, raisins, and cereals—is that whatever cash proceeds their owner receives from selling what he has stored up after paying the alms-tax due on his crops at the time of their harvest is not subject to the payment of an additional alms-tax until a year has passed from the day of the sale, so long as the crops were harvested from his own fields and were not acquired for purposes of commerce. This is the same rule that applies to foods, cereals, and commercial goods that someone acquires and keeps for a number of years, then sells for gold or silver. In that case, he is not liable to pay the alms-tax on the sale price until a year has passed from the day of the sale. If, however, these goods were intended for commerce, the owner must pay the

293 The question points out that in the law of sales, the various kinds of pulses are deemed to be of different genera, which permits them to be traded in unequal quantities. The implication is that there is a contradiction between their treatment as different genera in the law of sales and Mālik's insistence that they be treated as one category for the alms-tax.

alms-tax on them when he sells them, if he has held them for a year from the day on which he last paid the alms-tax on the cash used to purchase them.'"

Chapter 22. Fruits, Fodder, and Vegetables That Are Excluded from the Alms-Tax (*Zakāt*)

752. Mālik said, "The long-established ordinance about which there is no dissent among us and that which I have heard from the people of knowledge (*al-sunna allatī lā ikhtilāfa fīhā ʿindanā wa'lladhī samiʿtu min ahl al-ʿīlm*) is that no alms-tax (*ṣadaqa*) is due on any kind of fruit, whether pomegranates, peaches, figs, or anything else that is a fruit, whether or not it resembles them."

753. Mālik said, "No alms-tax is due on animal fodder or vegetables when they are harvested, nor is any alms-tax due on their sale price when sold, until one year has passed from the day of the sale and the receipt of payment."

Chapter 23. What Has Come Down regarding the Alms-Tax (*Ṣadaqa*) on Slaves, Horses, and Honey

754. According to Mālik, ʿAbd Allāh b. Dīnār reported from Sulaymān b. Yasār, from ʿIrāk b. Mālik, from Abū Hurayra, that the Messenger of God (pbuh) said, "A Muslim does not have to pay alms-tax on his slave or his horse."

755. According to Mālik, Ibn Shihāb reported from Sulaymān b. Yasār that the Levantines said to Abū ʿUbayda b. al-Jarrāḥ, "Levy the alms-tax on our horses and slaves," but he refused.[294] He then wrote to ʿUmar b. al-Khaṭṭāb, seeking his advice on this issue, and ʿUmar refused to authorize the proposed levy. The Levantines again requested the levy, and so Abū ʿUbayda again wrote to ʿUmar, who wrote back to him saying, "If the Levantines insist, collect the levy and then distribute its proceeds among them and grant their slaves a stipend out of the proceeds." Yaḥyā said, "Mālik said, "ʿUmar's statement, may God have mercy on his soul, to "distribute its proceeds among them" means "their poor.""'

756. According to Mālik, ʿAbd Allāh b. Abī Bakr b. Ḥazm said, "An edict (*kitāb*) came from ʿUmar b. ʿAbd al-ʿAzīz to my father[295] when he was at Minā, saying, 'Do not collect any alms-tax on honey or horses.'"

---

294 Abū ʿUbayda b. al-Jarrāḥ (d. 18/639) was the general who completed the conquest of the Levant during the caliphate of ʿUmar b. al-Khaṭṭāb and later served as his governor there until he died of the plague in Jordan.

295 Abū Bakr b. ʿAmr b. Ḥazm, the father of Mālik's source for this report, served as the judge of Medina. Zurqānī, *Sharḥ al-Zurqānī*, 2:202.

757. According to Mālik, ʿAbd Allāh b. Dīnār said, "I asked Saʿīd b. al-Musayyab about the alms-tax payable on Turkish horses, and he said, 'Since when is the alms-tax levied on horses?'"

Chapter 24. The Annual Poll-Tax (*Jizya*)[296] Levied on People of the Book (*Ahl al-Kitāb*)

758. According to Mālik, Ibn Shihāb said, "It reached me that the Messenger of God (pbuh) collected an annual poll-tax from the Zoroastrians of Bahrain, that ʿUmar b. al-Khaṭṭāb took such a tax from the Zoroastrians of Persia, and that ʿUthmān b. ʿAffān took it from the Berbers of the Maghrib."

759. According to Mālik, Jaʿfar b. Muḥammad b. ʿAlī reported from his father that ʿUmar b. al-Khaṭṭāb brought up the subject of the Zoroastrians and said, "I have no idea how to treat them." ʿAbd al-Raḥmān b. ʿAwf said, "I attest that I heard the Messenger of God (pbuh) say, 'Treat them as you treat the People of the Book (*ahl al-kitāb*).'"

760. According to Mālik, Nāfiʿ reported from Aslam, the freedman (*mawlā*) of ʿUmar b. al-Khaṭṭāb, that ʿUmar b. al-Khaṭṭāb specified the annual poll-tax payable by non-Muslims living in regions where gold was the dominant currency to be four gold dinars,[297] and that due from non-Muslims living where silver was the dominant currency to be forty silver dirhams.[298] In addition, they were required to provide provisions for Muslim travelers or for the Muslims dwelling in their midst and to quarter traveling Muslims, but for no more than three days.

761. According to Mālik, Zayd b. Aslam reported from his father that he said to ʿUmar b. al-Khaṭṭāb, "There is a blind she-camel in the herd of pack camels." Aslam said, "ʿUmar then said, 'Take it to a household that may benefit from it.' I said, 'But it is blind.' ʿUmar replied, 'They can herd it with the other camels.' I said, 'How can it eat from the ground when it is blind?' ʿUmar said, 'Was it one of the animals given by non-Muslims as part of their annual poll-tax or one of those given by Muslims as part of their alms-tax?' I said, 'Indeed, it was given by non-Muslims.' ʿUmar said, 'By God, you just want to eat it!' I said, 'It bears the brand of the annual poll-tax.'[299] ʿUmar

---

296 *Jizya* is the term for the annual poll-tax that was collected from adult male non-Muslims who were permanent residents of Islamic territories. *Ahl al-kitāb* refers to the adherents of pre-Islamic revealed religions who follow a written scripture, such as Christians and Jews.

297 Such as Egypt and the Levant.

298 Such as Iraq and the territories of the former Sassanian Empire.

299 Aslam was defending himself against the insinuation that he was seeking illegal (and self-serving) ends: had the camel been given by Muslims as part of the alms-tax, he would not have been entitled to any part of it, but since it had been given by non-Muslims as part of their poll-tax, he was eligible to benefit from it.

therefore ordered that it be slaughtered. He possessed nine platters, and whenever he came into possession of some fruit or other delicacy, he would place it on those platters and send them to the wives of the Prophet (pbuh). The platter he would send to his own daughter, Ḥafṣa,[300] would be the last of the nine. If one of the platters had less than the others, that one would be Ḥafṣa's lot. ʿUmar put some of the meat of the slaughtered camel on the platters and sent them to the wives of the Prophet (pbuh). He ordered that the rest of the meat of the slaughtered camel be prepared, and a banquet was held, to which he invited the Emigrants and the Medinese."

762. Yaḥyā said, "Mālik said, 'I do not think that livestock should be taken from non-Muslims who are permanent residents of Islamic territory beyond what is already included in their annual poll-tax.'"

763. According to Mālik, it reached him that ʿUmar b. ʿAbd al-ʿAzīz sent an edict to his governors that said, "Relieve anyone who has embraced Islam among the non-Muslim population of his obligation to pay the annual poll-tax."

764. Yaḥyā said, "Mālik said, 'It has long been the established ordinance (*maḍat al-sunna*) that no poll-tax is levied on the women or children of the People of the Book and that the poll-tax is levied only on non-Muslim males who have reached puberty.'"

765. Yaḥyā said, "Mālik said, 'Neither the People of the Book (*ahl al-dhimma*)[301] nor the Zoroastrians pay the alms-tax (*ṣadaqa*) on their palms, vines, crops, or livestock, because the alms-tax was imposed on Muslims to purify their wealth and to redistribute it among their poor, whereas the annual poll-tax was imposed on the People of the Book to humble them. As long as they stay in their native region where they came to terms with

---

300 ʿUmar's daughter Ḥafṣa was one of the wives of the Prophet Muḥammad (pbuh).

301 *Ahl al-dhimma* is the legal term for non-Muslims permanently residing in and under the protection of the Islamic state. It is a broader category than *ahl al-kitāb* insofar as it may apply, in Mālik's view, to any non-Muslim, even if he or she is not an adherent of a revealed religion. For that reason, a more accurate translation would be "protected people." In this text, however, Mālik seems to be referring to Christians and Jews in particular. "Protected people" are so called because they and the Muslims have undertaken mutual covenants, the non-Muslims promising to abide by the nonreligious provisions of Islamic law, to pay the annual poll-tax, and to refrain from supporting the enemies of the Islamic state, and the Muslims promising to accord the non-Muslims substantially the same rights (other than political rights) afforded to Muslims under Islamic law, including protection from all external enemies and internal aggression, whatever the source. Like any obligation, the Muslims' covenant of protection is intangible and exists solely by virtue of the capability of a person to undertake an obligation toward another. Muslim jurists call this capacity *dhimma*. A beneficiary of this undertaking is known as a *dhimmī*, i.e., a person who is entitled to call on the collective conscience of the Muslim community for protection.

the Muslims, they are exempt from all taxes on their property other than the annual poll-tax, as per their treaty with the Muslims. If, however, they do business in other Muslim lands, traveling back and forth between them, one-tenth of the value of their commercial property intended for current sale is taken as a tax. This is because the annual poll-tax was imposed on them only in accordance with the terms of the peace treaty to which they agreed with the Muslims and whose terms provided only that they be protected against their enemies while remaining in their own territories. Accordingly, whenever one of them leaves his home territory to do business elsewhere in Muslim lands, he is obliged to pay one-tenth of the value of his commercial goods intended for current sale when he sets out on a trading venture. This applies, for example, if he is an Egyptian going to the Levant, a Levantine going to Iraq, an Iraqi going to Medina or Yemen, or anything like that. Nor are any of the livestock, dates, or cereal crops of the People of the Book or the Zoroastrians subject to the alms-tax. That has long been the established ordinance (*maḍat bi-dhālik al-sunna*). Muslims are not to interfere with their religious practices, and their affairs continue as they otherwise were prior to Islam. If they travel back and forth between different Muslim territories several times in any one year, they are obliged to pay one-tenth of the value of their commercial goods each time they cross a border, because that privilege was not included in their original treaty with the Muslims, nor was it a right granted to them at that time in the original treaty. This is what I found the people of knowledge in our town following (*hādhā alladhī adraktu ʿalayhi ahl al-ʿilm bi-baladinā*).'"

Chapter 25. The Taxes (*ʿUshūr*) That Apply to the Crops of the Protected People

766. According to Mālik, Ibn Shihāb reported from Sālim b. ʿAbd Allāh, from his father, that ʿUmar b. al-Khaṭṭāb would collect from the Nabateans only one-twentieth of their cereals and olive oil in order to encourage increased delivery of these goods to Medina, but he would collect one-tenth of their pulses.

767. According to Mālik, Ibn Shihāb reported that al-Sāʾib b. Yazīd said, "I, along with ʿAbd Allāh b. ʿUtba b. Masʿūd, oversaw the market of Medina during the term of ʿUmar b. al-Khaṭṭāb, and we would collect one-tenth from the Nabateans."

768. According to Mālik, he asked Ibn Shihāb on what basis ʿUmar b. al-Khaṭṭāb would take one-tenth from the Nabateans. Ibn Shihāb said, "That is what was taken from them during the Days of Ignorance prior to Islam (*jāhiliyya*), so ʿUmar b. al-Khaṭṭāb maintained the same practice in Islam."

Chapter 26. Purchasing What Has Been Given as Alms (*Ṣadaqa*) and Taking It Back

769. According to Mālik, Zayd b. Aslam reported that his father said, "I heard ʿUmar b. al-Khaṭṭāb say, 'I once gave a noble horse to a man to ride to battle for the sake of God, but the man did not take care of it. I considered repurchasing it from him, thinking that he would sell it cheaply. I therefore asked the Messenger of God (pbuh) whether he thought that would be advisable, but he said, "Do not buy it, even if he offers to sell it for one dirham, because the person who takes back his gift is like a dog who eats his own vomit."'"

770. According to Mālik, Nāfiʿ reported from ʿAbd Allāh b. ʿUmar that ʿUmar b. al-Khaṭṭāb gave a man a horse to ride to battle for the sake of God but then wanted to buy it back from him, so he asked the Messenger of God (pbuh) whether he thought that would be advisable. The Prophet (pbuh) said, "Don't buy it, and don't take your gift back."

771. Yaḥyā said, "Mālik was once asked about a man who gave another man a gift and then discovered that it was now in the possession of a third person, who was offering it for sale. The original owner wanted to know whether he could buy it. Mālik said, 'That he refrain from so doing would be preferable in my opinion.'"

Chapter 27. Who Is Subject to an Obligation to Pay Alms (*Zakāt*) on the Occasion of the Feast of Breaking the Ramadan Fast (*ʿĪd al-Fiṭr*)

772. According to Mālik, Nāfiʿ reported that ʿAbd Allāh b. ʿUmar would pay the alms due on the occasion of the Feast of Breaking the Ramadan Fast for his young male slaves who lived in Wādī al-Qurā and in Khaybar.[302]

773. According to Mālik, the best view he had heard regarding what a man must pay as alms on the occasion of the Feast of Breaking the Ramadan Fast was that he should pay alms on behalf of all those whom he is legally obliged to support and for whom he must provide maintenance. He must pay, therefore, for his slaves who have entered into manumission contracts (*mukātab*) with him;[303] for his slaves whom he has declared to

302 Wādī al-Qurā is a place just outside of Medina. Khaybar is an oasis fortress town located approximately four days' march north of Medina. Both were sites of intense date cultivation. Zurqānī, *Sharḥ al-Zurqānī*, 2:214.

303 Such a contract is called *kitāba* or *mukātaba* and ordinarily involves the slave agreeing to purchase his freedom from his master. The contract will usually provide that the payment be made over time in instalments. A slave who has entered such a contract with his master is called a *mukātab* and enjoys full contractual capacity against third parties. For further details on the legal treatment of such slaves, see Book 29.

be manumitted upon his death (*mudabbar*);[304] and for all of his chattel slaves, be they present in his household or not, as long as they are Muslims, whether or not they are held for trade. He is not, however, obliged to pay alms for his slaves who are not Muslims.

774. Yaḥyā said, "Mālik said, concerning a runaway slave, 'Whether or not the master knows his slave's whereabouts, if the slave is likely to be still nearby and the master has reason to believe that he is still alive and will return, my view is that the master should pay alms for him. If the runaway has been missing for a lengthy period of time and his master has given up hope of his return, my view is that he is not obliged to pay alms for him.'"

775. Yaḥyā said, "Mālik said, 'Bedouin must pay the alms for the Feast of Breaking the Ramadan Fast just as settled people who live in villages must pay them. That is because the Messenger of God (pbuh) made it obligatory on every Muslim, free or slave, male or female.'"

Chapter 28. The Measure of the Alms (*Zakāt*) That Are Due on the Occasion of the Feast of Breaking the Ramadan Fast (*ʿĪd al-Fiṭr*)

776. According to Mālik, Nāfiʿ reported from ʿAbd Allāh b. ʿUmar that the Messenger of God (pbuh) imposed on Muslims, be they free or slave, male or female, alms due on the occasion of the Feast of Breaking the Ramadan Fast in an amount equal to one measure (*ṣāʿ*) of dates or barley.

777. According to Mālik, Zayd b. Aslam reported from ʿIyāḍ b. ʿAbd Allāh b. Saʿd b. Abī Sarḥ al-ʿĀmirī that he heard Abū Saʿīd al-Khudrī say, "We would pay the alms of the Feast of Breaking the Ramadan Fast with a measure of wheat, barley, dried dates, buttermilk, or raisins, using the measure of the Prophet (pbuh)."

778. According to Mālik, Nāfiʿ reported that ʿAbd Allāh b. ʿUmar would always pay the alms of the Feast of Breaking the Ramadan Fast in dried dates, except once, when he paid them in barley.

779. Mālik said, "The penance for a broken oath or the like, the alms due on the occasion of the Feast of Breaking the Ramadan Fast, and the alms-tax (*zakāt*) on grains for which one-tenth or one-twentieth is due—these are all paid using measures of 500 grams (a *mudd*), which is the measure used by the Prophet (pbuh), except in the case of *ẓihār*,[305] whose penance is

304 For further details on the legal treatment of such slaves, see Book 30.

305 *Ẓihār* was a pre-Islamic practice akin to divorce, in which a man would declare that his wife was to him like his mother's back, meaning that intimate relations with her were as inconceivable to him as having relations with his mother would be. The Quran imposed an obligation of penance on any man who used such a phrase toward his wife and then wished to return to her. *Al-Mujādila*, 58:2–3.

discharged using the measure of Hishām,[306] which is the larger of the two and approximately 650 grams."

Chapter 29. When the Alms (*Zakāt*) of the Feast of Breaking the Ramadan Fast (*ʿĪd al-Fiṭr*) Should Be Paid

780. According to Mālik, Nāfiʿ reported that ʿAbd Allāh b. ʿUmar would send the alms due for the Feast of Breaking the Ramadan Fast to the alms administrator two or three days before the feast.

781. According to Mālik, it was his view that the people of knowledge preferred to pay the alms due for the Feast of Breaking the Ramadan Fast after dawn had broken on the day of the feast but before they set out to the place of prayer.

782. Yaḥyā said, "Mālik said, 'There is great latitude, God willing, with respect to when the alms due for the Feast of Breaking the Ramadan Fast are to be paid; they can be paid before or after setting out for the prayer on the day of the feast."

Chapter 30. Those for Whom Payment of the Alms (*Zakāt*) of the Feast of Breaking the Ramadan Fast (*ʿĪd al-Fiṭr*) Is Not Obligatory

783. Yaḥyā said, "Mālik said, 'A man is not obliged to pay the alms due for the Feast of Breaking the Ramadan Fast for any slaves who belong to his slaves, for his own employees, or for his wife's slaves, except for any of those who serve him personally and whose services are indispensable to him.[307] He is not obliged to pay the alms for the Feast of Breaking the Ramadan Fast for any of his non-Muslim slaves, whether or not he holds them for trade.'"

The Book of the Alms-Tax (*Zakāt*) Has Come to an End, with Praise to God as Befits Him. May God Grace His Prophet Muḥammad and His Family and Grant Them Perfect Tranquility.

306 According to the editors of the RME, the Hishām referenced here is Hishām b. Ismāʿīl al-Makhzūmī, who served as the governor of Medina during the reign of ʿAbd al-Malik b. Marwān. The precise size of the *mudd* of Hishām, although recognized to be larger than that of the Prophet (pbuh), is a matter of some controversy among the Mālikīs, with some saying that it is the equivalent of one and two-thirds of the *mudd* of the Prophet (pbuh) and others claiming it equaled two *mudds* of the Prophet (pbuh). According to Bājī, as reported by the editors of the RME, Mālik adopted the measure of Hishām in this instance not because it had revelatory significance but because he believed it would definitively satisfy the penitent's obligation. A Prophetic *mudd* is approximately 500 grams, whereas a *ṣāʿ* is approximately 2,000 grams.

307 It is ambiguous whether this exception refers to all three mentioned categories or just the first.

Book 17

The Book of Fasting (*Ṣiyām*)

In the Name of God, the Merciful, the Compassionate

May God Grace Muḥammad and His Family
and Grant Them Perfect Tranquility.

Chapter 1. What Has Come Down regarding Sighting the Crescent Moon Indicating the Beginning and the End of the Ramadan Fast

784. According to Mālik, Nāfiʿ reported from ʿAbd Allāh b. ʿUmar that the Messenger of God (pbuh) was discussing Ramadan and said, "Don't fast until you see the crescent moon of Ramadan, and don't celebrate the Feast of Breaking the Ramadan Fast (*ʿīd al-fiṭr*) until you see the crescent moon of Shawwāl.[308] If the sky above you is cloudy, estimate when the moon should appear."

785. According to Mālik, ʿAbd Allāh b. Dīnār reported from ʿAbd Allāh b. ʿUmar that the Messenger of God (pbuh) said, "The month has twenty-nine days, so don't fast until you see the crescent moon of Ramadan, and don't celebrate the Feast of Breaking the Ramadan Fast until you see the crescent moon of Shawwāl. If the sky above you is cloudy, estimate when the moon should appear."

786. According to Mālik, Thawr b. Zayd al-Dīlī reported from ʿAbd Allāh b. ʿAbbās that the Messenger of God (pbuh) spoke once of Ramadan and said, "Don't fast until you see the crescent moon of Ramadan, and don't celebrate the Feast of Breaking the Ramadan Fast until you see the crescent moon of Shawwāl. If the sky above you is cloudy, then fast a complete month of thirty days."

308 The Islamic calendar is a lunar calendar consisting of twelve months of either twenty-nine or thirty days. Ramadan is the ninth month and Shawwāl the tenth of the Muslim calendar. Unlike the Jewish lunar calendar, the Muslim lunar calendar does not adjust itself periodically to realign with the solar calendar. Consequently, relative to the solar calendar, the Muslim calendar moves up every (solar) year by approximately eleven solar days.

787. According to Mālik, it reached him that the crescent moon was once seen in the afternoon during the term of ʿUthmān b. ʿAffān, but he did not break his fast until that evening, when the sun disappeared below the horizon.

788. Yaḥyā said, "I heard Mālik say that even if someone is by himself when he sees the crescent moon that indicates the beginning of Ramadan, he should still fast, because it is not permissible for him to eat on a day that he knows is part of Ramadan."

789. Mālik added, "If, however, someone is by himself when he sees the crescent moon at the beginning of Shawwāl, he must not break his fast, because people accuse those who are not fasting of being untrustworthy. Such untrustworthy persons, when discovered not to be fasting, often say, 'We've already seen the crescent moon.' Therefore, whoever sees the crescent moon of Shawwāl during the day should not break his fast but should continue fasting for the rest of that day. This is because the crescent moon belongs to the coming night."

790. Yaḥyā said, "I heard Mālik say, 'If people are fasting on the day of the Feast of Breaking the Ramadan Fast, erroneously thinking that it is part of Ramadan, and then a reliable source comes to them, telling them that the crescent moon of Ramadan was seen the day before they began observance of the Ramadan fast and that this day that they are fasting is the first day of Shawwāl,[309] they should immediately cease fasting when they receive this news. They do not, however, perform the Feast Prayer if the news reaches them after noon.'"

Chapter 2. Those Who Resolve to Fast before Dawn

791. According to Mālik, Nāfiʿ reported that ʿAbd Allāh b. ʿUmar would say, "Only someone who has resolved to fast before dawn breaks may fast."

792. According to Mālik, Ibn Shihāb reported that ʿĀʾisha and Ḥafṣa, two of the Prophet's (pbuh) wives, said something similar.[310]

Chapter 3. What Has Come Down regarding Breaking the Fast

793. According to Mālik, Abū Ḥāzim b. Dīnār reported from Sahl b. Saʿd al-Sāʿidī that the Messenger of God (pbuh) said, "People shall continue to prosper as long as they break their fast promptly."

---

309 In other words, it is not the thirtieth day of Ramadan, as they believed, but rather the first day of Shawwāl, that is, the day of the Feast of Breaking the Ramadan Fast.

310 These reports are the basis for the Mālikī rule that the fast is not valid unless the person fasting has made an intention to fast prior to the start of the day that he intends to fast. Because the day begins with the dawn, the person desiring to fast must resolve to do so before dawn breaks.

794. According to Mālik, ʿAbd al-Raḥmān b. Ḥarmala al-Aslamī reported from Saʿīd b. al-Musayyab that the Messenger of God (pbuh) said, "People shall continue to prosper as long as they break their fast promptly."

795. According to Mālik, Ibn Shihāb reported from Ḥumayd b. ʿAbd al-Raḥmān that before ʿUmar b. al-Khaṭṭāb and ʿUthmān b. ʿAffān broke the fast, they would perform the Sunset Prayer (*ṣalāt al-maghrib*) when they saw the darkness of the night approaching from the eastern horizon. Then they would break the fast after the prayer. That was during Ramadan.

Chapter 4. What Has Come Down regarding the Fasting of Someone Who Awakes in a State of Ritual Preclusion (*Junub*)

796. According to Mālik, ʿAbd Allāh b. ʿAbd al-Raḥmān b. Maʿmar al-Anṣārī reported from Abū Yūnus, the freedman (*mawlā*) of ʿĀʾisha, that he overheard a man standing at the door of the Messenger of God (pbuh) saying to him, "Messenger of God, I sometimes get up in the morning in a state of ritual preclusion, and I wish to fast." The Messenger of God (pbuh) said, "I, too, get up in the morning in a state of ritual preclusion, and I wish to fast, so I bathe and I fast." The man said to him, "But you are not like us: God has already forgiven whatever wrong you have done or might yet do." The Messenger of God (pbuh) became angry and said, "By God, I hope that no man is more fearful of God than me, nor more knowledgeable about what to avoid."

797. According to Mālik, ʿAbd Rabbih b. Saʿīd reported from Abū Bakr b. ʿAbd al-Raḥmān b. al-Ḥārith b. Hishām that ʿĀʾisha and Umm Salama, two of the wives of the Prophet (pbuh), said, "During Ramadan, the Messenger of God (pbuh) would awake in the morning in a state of ritual preclusion as a result of sexual intercourse—not from a wet dream—and then would fast."

798. According to Mālik, Sumayy, the freedman of Abū Bakr b. al-Ḥārith b. Hishām, reported that he heard Abū Bakr b. al-Ḥārith b. Hishām say, "My father and I were with Marwān b. al-Ḥakam[311] when he was the governor of Medina, and someone mentioned to him that Abū Hurayra was saying that whoever gets up in the morning in a state of ritual preclusion must not fast that day. Marwān said, 'I swear to you, ʿAbd al-Raḥmān,[312] you

311 He served as the governor of Medina twice during the caliphate of Muʿāwiya b. Abī Sufyān (r. 41–60/660–680).

312 According to the notes of the RME, the father of Abū Bakr, the source of this report, was ʿAbd al-Raḥmān, not al-Ḥārith, who was in fact Abū Bakr's grandfather. Abū Bakr's full name appears in other manuscript copies of the *Muwaṭṭaʾ* as Abū Bakr b. ʿAbd al-Raḥmān b. al-Ḥārith b. Hishām. The very next hadith, no. 799, which presents a truncated version of this report, mentions the source as "Abū Bakr b. ʿAbd al-Raḥmān."

shall immediately set off for ʿĀʾisha and Umm Salama, the Mothers of the Believers, and ask them both about that.' ʿAbd al-Raḥmān set off to see ʿĀʾisha, and I accompanied him. He greeted her and then said, 'Mother of the Believers, we were with Marwān b. al-Ḥakam, and someone mentioned that Abū Hurayra says that whoever awakes in the morning in a state of ritual preclusion cannot fast that day.' ʿĀʾisha said, 'No, it is not as Abū Hurayra says, ʿAbd al-Raḥmān. Would you shun the practice of the Messenger of God (pbuh)?' ʿAbd al-Raḥmān said, 'No, by God!' ʿĀʾisha said, 'I attest that the Messenger of God (pbuh) would get up in the morning during Ramadan in a state of ritual preclusion following sexual intercourse, not a wet dream, and then fast that day.' Then we left to go see Umm Salama, and ʿAbd al-Raḥmān asked her about the same issue, and she said substantially the same thing as ʿĀʾisha had. Then we left and returned to Marwān b. al-Ḥakam, and ʿAbd al-Raḥmān told him what they both had said. Marwān said, 'I swear to you, Abū Muḥammad, you shall ride my mount—it is at the gate—and go see Abū Hurayra, who is at his estate in al-ʿAqīq, and let him know what they said.' ʿAbd al-Raḥmān rode off and I accompanied him until we arrived at Abū Hurayra's estate. ʿAbd al-Raḥmān briefly made small talk with him and then raised this issue. Abū Hurayra said, 'I have no knowledge about this; I simply reported what someone told me.'"

799. According to Mālik, Sumayy, the freedman of Abū Bakr, reported from Abū Bakr b. ʿAbd al-Raḥmān, from ʿĀʾisha and Umm Salama, two of the wives of the Prophet (pbuh), that they said, "The Messenger of God (pbuh) would get up in the morning in a state of ritual preclusion following sexual intercourse, not a wet dream, and then would fast."

Chapter 5. What Has Come Down regarding the Dispensation for a Fasting Man to Kiss His Wife

800. According to Mālik, Zayd b. Aslam reported from ʿAṭāʾ b. Yasār that a man kissed his wife with desire while fasting in Ramadan, and he became extremely distressed.[313] He therefore dispatched his wife to inquire on his behalf about this. She went to see Umm Salama, the wife of the Prophet (pbuh), and raised this issue with her. Umm Salama told her that the Messenger of God (pbuh) would kiss her while he was fasting. So the woman returned and told her husband what Umm Salama had said, but he became even more distraught and exclaimed, "We are not like the Messenger of God (pbuh)! God permits whatever He wishes to the Messenger of God

313 Because sexual intercourse during the daylight hours is prohibited as part of fasting, the man feared that kissing his wife with sexual desire might have invalidated his fast.

(pbuh)." His wife returned to Umm Salama and found the Messenger of God (pbuh) there with her. The Messenger of God (pbuh) said, "What troubles this woman?" Umm Salama told him. He said, "Didn't you tell her that I do that myself?" She said, "I did indeed. She returned to her husband and told him so, but he only became more distressed and said, 'We are not like the Messenger of God (pbuh)! God permits whatever He wishes to the Messenger of God (pbuh).'" Then the Messenger of God (pbuh) grew angry and said, "By God, I am more fearful of God than any of you, and more knowledgeable of His limits."

801. According to Mālik, Hishām b. ʿUrwa reported from his father that ʿĀʾisha, the Mother of the Believers, would say, "The Messenger of God (pbuh) would certainly kiss *one* of his wives while fasting," and then she would giggle.

802. According to Mālik, Yaḥyā b. Saʿīd reported that ʿĀtika bt. Saʿīd b. Zayd b. ʿAmr b. Nufayl, the wife of ʿUmar b. al-Khaṭṭāb, would affectionately kiss ʿUmar's head while he was fasting, and he would not forbid her.

803. According to Mālik, Abū al-Naḍr, the freedman (*mawlā*) of ʿUmar b. ʿUbayd Allāh, reported that ʿĀʾisha bt. Ṭalḥa told him that she was with ʿĀʾisha, the wife of the Prophet (pbuh), when the former's husband, ʿAbd Allāh b. ʿAbd al-Raḥmān b. Abī Bakr al-Ṣiddīq (ʿĀʾisha's nephew), came in. He was fasting at the time, and ʿĀʾisha said to him, "What's stopping you from cuddling with your wife, kissing her, and being flirtatious with her?" He said, "May I kiss her, even though I am fasting?" She said, "Yes, why not?"

804. According to Mālik, Zayd b. Aslam reported that Abū Hurayra and Saʿd b. Abī Waqqāṣ permitted a fasting man to kiss his wife with desire.

Chapter 6. What Has Come Down Warning against Kissing When Fasting

805. According to Mālik, it reached him that ʿĀʾisha, the wife of the Prophet (pbuh), would say, whenever she brought up the fact that the Messenger of God (pbuh) would kiss his wives while fasting, "Which of you can exercise self-control like the Messenger of God (pbuh)?"

806. Mālik said, "Hishām b. ʿUrwa said that ʿUrwa b. al-Zubayr said, 'In my opinion, kissing rarely invites a fasting man to good.'"

807. According to Mālik, Zayd b. Aslam reported from ʿAṭāʾ b. Yasār that ʿAbd Allāh b. ʿAbbās was asked about a fasting man who wished to kiss his wife. ʿAbd Allāh permitted old men to do so, but discouraged young men.

808. According to Mālik, Nāfiʿ reported that ʿAbd Allāh b. ʿUmar would prohibit a fasting man from kissing and intimately touching his wife.

Chapter 7. What Has Come Down regarding Fasting While Traveling[314]

809. According to Mālik, Ibn Shihāb reported from ʿUbayd Allāh b. ʿAbd Allāh b. ʿUtba b. Masʿūd, from ʿAbd Allāh b. ʿAbbās, that the Messenger of God (pbuh) left for Mecca during Ramadan in the year of the conquest of Mecca (*ʿām al-fatḥ*) and fasted until he reached al-Kadīd.[315] He then broke his fast, as did everyone else. The people would put into practice whatever the Messenger of God (pbuh) had most recently done.

810. According to Mālik, Sumayy, the freedman (*mawlā*) of Abū Bakr b. ʿAbd al-Raḥmān, reported from Abū Bakr b. ʿAbd al-Raḥmān, from one of the Companions of the Messenger of God (pbuh), that while en route to Mecca in the year of the conquest, the Messenger of God (pbuh) commanded the people not to observe the fast. He said, "Strengthen yourselves for your enemy." However, the Messenger of God (pbuh) himself fasted. Abū Bakr b. ʿAbd al-Raḥmān said, "The one who narrated this report to me said, 'At al-ʿArj[316] I saw the Messenger of God (pbuh) pour water over his head, either because of thirst or because of the heat. Then someone said to the Messenger of God, "A group of people decided to fast, despite your instructions, when they realized that you were fasting."' When the Messenger of God was at al-Kadīd, therefore, he asked for a bowl of water and drank, so everyone broke their fast."

811. According to Mālik, Ḥumayd al-Ṭawīl reported that Anas b. Mālik said, "Once, we were traveling with the Messenger of God (pbuh) in Ramadan. Those who fasted did not rebuke those who did not; those who did not fast did not rebuke those who did."

812. According to Mālik, Hishām b. ʿUrwa reported from his father that Ḥamza b. ʿAmr al-Aslamī said to the Messenger of God (pbuh), "Messenger of God, I am a man who fasts. Shall I fast when I am traveling?" The Messenger of God said, "Fast or do not fast, as you wish."

---

314 The plain sense of the Quran—"So whoever of you is ill or traveling, let him fast an equivalent number of other days"—suggests that a Muslim should not fast during the month of Ramadan if he is ill or traveling. *Al-Baqara*, 2:185. As the reports in this chapter suggest, however, the early community understood this verse as granting a fasting person permission to refrain from fasting under these circumstances but not obliging him to do so.

315 A place between Medina and Mecca.

316 According to the editors of the RME, a place on the way to Mecca from Medina at a distance of approximately three *marāḥil* (approximately 312 km) from Medina. A *marḥala* is defined as a day's journey, or approximately twenty-four *mīl*s, that is, 104 km. Jumuʿa, *al-Makāyīl*, 56.

813. According to Mālik, Nāfiʿ reported that ʿAbd Allāh b. ʿUmar would not fast when traveling.

814. According to Mālik, Hishām b. ʿUrwa reported from his father that the latter would travel during Ramadan. Hishām said, "We would travel with him. ʿUrwa would fast and we would not, but he would not tell us to fast."

Chapter 8. What One Should Do If One Returns from or Intends to Set Out on a Journey during Ramadan

815. According to Mālik, it reached him that if ʿUmar b. al-Khaṭṭāb was traveling during Ramadan and knew that he would reach Medina by morning, he would fast that day.

816. Yaḥyā said, "Mālik said, 'Whoever is traveling and knows that he will reach his home early in the morning, but dawn breaks before he arrives, should fast that day. Whoever intends to travel in Ramadan, but dawn breaks and he has yet to depart, should fast that day.'"

817. Mālik said that if a man returns from a journey in Ramadan and is not fasting, and his wife is not fasting because she has just completed bathing after her period, he may have sexual intercourse with her.

Chapter 9. The Expiation for Breaking the Ramadan Fast

818. According to Mālik, Ibn Shihāb reported from Ḥumayd b. ʿAbd al-Raḥmān b. ʿAwf, from Abū Hurayra, that a man broke his fast in Ramadan and the Messenger of God (pbuh) ordered him to expiate his sin by manumitting a slave, fasting two successive months, or feeding sixty needy people. He said, "I don't have the means to manumit a slave." A large basket of dried dates was brought to the Messenger of God, so he said, "Take these and give them to the poor as charity." He said, "Messenger of God, there is no one poorer than myself." The Messenger of God (pbuh) laughed heartily and said, "Eat them!"

819. According to Mālik, ʿAṭāʾ b. ʿAbd Allāh al-Khurasānī reported that Saʿīd b. al-Musayyab said, "A bedouin came to the Messenger of God (pbuh), beating his chest and pulling out his hair, saying, 'I have perished!' The Messenger of God said to him, 'And why is that?' He said, 'I had intercourse with my wife while fasting in Ramadan.' The Messenger of God said to him, 'Can you manumit a slave?' The man said, 'No!' Then he said, 'Can you slaughter a camel and give away its meat?' He said, 'No!' The Messenger of God said, 'Have a seat.' A large basket of dried dates was brought to the Messenger of God, and he said, 'Take these and give them away as charity.'

So the man said, 'But there is no one poorer than myself.' The Messenger of God said to the man, 'Eat them, and fast one day in place of the day on which you had intercourse during Ramadan.'" Mālik said, "'Aṭā' said, 'I asked Sa'īd b. al-Musayyab, "How many dried dates were in that basket?" He said, "Between thirty and forty kilograms (fifteen to twenty *ṣā'*)."'"

820. Mālik said, "I heard the people of knowledge say that a man who is expiating his violation of the Ramadan fast and then violates that make-up fast by, for example, having intercourse with his wife that day or doing something else is not obliged to perform a second expiation. He only has to make up for that day." Mālik said, "Of all the views I have heard about this, this view is the one I prefer most."

Chapter 10. Cupping[317] a Man Who Is Fasting

821. According to Mālik, Nāfi' reported from 'Abd Allāh b. 'Umar that 'Abd Allāh b. 'Umar would be cupped while he was fasting. Nāfi' said, "He later gave it up and would be cupped only after he had broken his fast."[318]

822. According to Mālik, Ibn Shihāb reported that Sa'd b. Abī Waqqāṣ and 'Abd Allāh b. 'Umar would be cupped while they were fasting.

823. According to Mālik, Hishām b. 'Urwa reported from his father that he would be cupped while he was fasting, and he would not break his fast. Hishām said, "I only saw my father being cupped when he was fasting."

824. Mālik said, "Cupping is discouraged for those who are fasting out of fear that they will be weakened and become unable to complete their fast. In the absence of such a concern, it is not discouraged. If a man is cupped in Ramadan and then completes his fast, I do not think he is subject to any penalty, nor would I order him to make up the fast day on which he was cupped. Cupping is discouraged only when it poses a risk to completing the fast. Accordingly, whoever is cupped and feels well enough to keep the fast until evening is not subject to any penalty, nor must he make up that day."

Chapter 11. Fasting on the Day of 'Āshūrā'[319]

825. According to Mālik, Hishām b. 'Urwa reported from his father that 'Ā'isha, the wife of the Prophet (pbuh), said, "The day of 'Āshūrā' was a day

317 A common traditional medicinal practice, believed to improve blood circulation.

318 The editors of the RME report that one of the commentators of the *Muwaṭṭa'* interprets Ibn 'Umar's actions as reflecting his own perception of his ability to withstand cupping. Accordingly, when his health was good, he engaged in this practice while fasting, but when old age had weakened him, he would undergo cupping only after he had broken his fast so as to have the strength to endure the procedure.

319 'Āshūrā' is the tenth day of Muḥarram, the first month of the Islamic calendar.

on which the Quraysh would fast in the Days of Ignorance prior to Islam (*jāhiliyya*). The Messenger of God (pbuh) also observed it in those days. When the Messenger of God (pbuh) came to Medina, he continued to observe it and ordered the Muslims to observe it as well. When the Ramadan Fast was imposed, however, it became the obligatory fast, and the obligation to observe the Fast of ʿĀshūrāʾ lapsed. Therefore, whoever wishes may continue to fast on ʿĀshūrāʾ, and whoever wishes may refrain from it."

826. According to Mālik, Ibn Shihāb reported from Ḥumayd b. ʿAbd al-Raḥmān b. ʿAwf that he heard Muʿāwiya b. Abī Sufyān say from the pulpit of the Prophet's Mosque, on the day of ʿĀshūrāʾ in the year in which he performed the Pilgrimage (*ḥajj*), "People of Medina! Where are your learned men? I heard the Messenger of God (pbuh) say about this day, 'This is the day of ʿĀshūrāʾ; observance of a fast on this day has not been prescribed for you, but I observe it. Therefore, whoever wishes to observe it may do so, but whoever does not need not.'"

827. According to Mālik, it reached him that ʿUmar b. al-Khaṭṭāb dispatched a messenger to al-Ḥārith b. Hishām with the message, "Tomorrow is the day of ʿĀshūrāʾ. Fast, therefore, and command your family to fast as well."

Chapter 12. Fasting on the Two Feast Days (*ʿĪd al-Fiṭr* and *ʿĪd al-Aḍḥā*),[320] and Fasting Every Day

828. According to Mālik, Muḥammad b. Yaḥyā b. Ḥabbān reported from al-Aʿraj, from Abū Hurayra, that the Messenger of God (pbuh) prohibited fasting on the two feast days (*ʿīd al-fiṭr* and *ʿīd al-aḍḥā*).

829. According to Mālik, he heard the people of knowledge say, "There is nothing objectionable in fasting day after day, as long as one breaks the fast on the days on which the Messenger of God (pbuh) forbade fasting—the days of Minā,[321] the Feast of Breaking the Ramadan Fast, and the Feast of the Sacrificial Animals—in accordance with what has reached us." Mālik said, "Of all the views that I have heard about this, this view is the one I prefer most."[322]

---

320 These are the Feast of Breaking the Ramadan Fast and the Feast of the Sacrificial Animals, respectively. The latter takes place on the tenth day of Dhū al-Ḥijja and commemorates Abraham's sacrifice of a ram in lieu of his son.

321 These are the days during the Pilgrimage season when the pilgrims symbolically cast pebbles at the Devil at the conclusion of the Pilgrimage.

322 This opinion assumes that the person is fasting only during daytime hours and breaking his fast each evening.

Chapter 13. The Prohibition against Continuous Fasting (*Wiṣāl*)[323]

830. According to Mālik, Nāfiʿ reported from ʿAbd Allāh b. ʿUmar that the Messenger of God (pbuh) prohibited continuous fasting. They said, "But Messenger of God, don't you fast continuously?" He said, "My constitution is not like yours; God satisfies my hunger and thirst."

831. According to Mālik, Abū al-Zinād reported from al-Aʿraj, from Abū Hurayra, that the Messenger of God (pbuh) said, "Be wary of continuous fasting! Be wary of continuous fasting!" They said, "But don't you fast continuously, Messenger of God?" He said, "My constitution is not like yours. My Lord feeds me and quenches my thirst even as I sleep."

Chapter 14. The Fast of the Penitent Who Kills Another Unintentionally (*Qatl al-Khaṭaʾ*)[324] or Who Declares His Wife to Be Like the Back of His Mother (*Ẓihār*)

832. Yaḥyā said, "I heard Mālik say, 'If someone who killed another unintentionally or declared his wife to be like the back of his mother starts to fulfill the obligatory two consecutive months of fasting due as expiation, then contracts a debilitating illness that forces him to interrupt his fast, but then recovers from his illness and is strong enough to resume fasting, he must do so immediately, starting from the point at which he previously stopped.'"

833. Mālik said, "Similarly, a woman who is obliged to fast because she killed another unintentionally must not delay resumption of her fast once she completes her period. She resumes her fast from the last day she fasted."

834. Mālik said, "No one who is under an obligation to fast two consecutive months as commanded in the Book of God may interrupt his or her fast for reasons other than illness or menstruation. One may not travel and thereby break the fast." Mālik said, "Of all the views I have heard about that, this view is the best."

---

323 Fasting in Islam is limited to the hours between dawn and sunset. To fast continuously, therefore, is to continue one's fast into the night until the next day's fast.

324 A person who accidentally kills another is not subject to criminal penalty in Islamic law. If the accident took place in Muslim territory, compensation must be paid to the victim's family and a Muslim slave must be manumitted. If the accident took place outside of Muslim territory and the victim was a Muslim, the defendant must manumit a Muslim slave, but there is no obligation to pay compensation, unless the non-Muslim territory is at peace with the Muslims. If the defendant is unable to manumit a slave, he must expiate by fasting two consecutive months. *Al-Nisāʾ*, 4:92.

Chapter 15. What an Ill Man Does regarding His Fast

835. Yaḥyā said, "I heard Mālik say, 'The rule that I have heard from the people of knowledge (*al-amr alladhī samiʿtu min ahl al-ʿilm*) is that if an illness befalls a man and as a result fasting becomes very difficult for him and exhausts him, he may suspend his fast. The same principle applies to someone so ill that he finds it extremely difficult to stand for obligatory prayers—it being understood that only God knows the person's true condition and whether he has a genuine excuse. If it is in fact so, he performs the prayer from a seated position, because God's religion is ease. God has permitted a traveler to suspend his fast when he is traveling, even though the traveler is better able to fast than is a sick man who is not on a journey. God says in His Book, "So whoever of you is ill or traveling, let him fast an equivalent number of other days."[325] God has therefore permitted a traveler to suspend the fast when he is traveling, even though he is better able to fast than a sick man is. Of all the views that I have heard, this view is the one I prefer most, and it is the agreed-upon rule (*al-amr al-mujtamaʿ ʿalayh*).'"

Chapter 16. A Vow (*Nadhr*) to Fast, and Fasting for the Benefit of the Deceased

836. According to Mālik, it reached him from Saʿīd b. al-Musayyab that he was asked whether a man who had vowed to fast a month could observe additional voluntary fasts. Saʿīd said, "Let the man fulfill his vow first, and then he may observe other voluntary fasts."

837. Mālik said, "It reached me that Sulaymān b. Yasār held a similar view."

838. Yaḥyā said, "I heard Mālik say, 'If a man dies without having fulfilled a vow, whether the vow required him to manumit a slave, to fast, to give charity, or to slaughter a camel, but he made a testamentary disposition for this obligation to be discharged out of his estate, then the slave, the charity, or the camel is to be taken from the one-third of his estate subject to testamentary dispositions.[326] Fulfillment of the obligations arising out of such vows is given priority over his other testamentary dispositions, unless they are of a similar nature. That is because the obligations he owes in respect of unfulfilled vows and other obligatory matters[327] are not the equivalent of what he voluntarily promised to give away to others. Amounts

325 *Al-Baqara*, 2:185.

326 In Sunnī inheritance law, the testator is allowed to dispose of only one-third of his estate via testamentary disposition (i.e., a will). The rest of the estate is distributed in accordance with mandatory rules of distribution that specify the heirs and the share of the estate that each receives.

327 "Other obligatory matters" might include, for example, unpaid obligations to pay the alms-tax.

owed in respect of unfulfilled vows are satisfied exclusively out of the one-third of his estate set aside for testamentary dispositions, not from the entirety of the decedent's capital. Were it permissible for the decedent to settle such amounts from the capital of his estate, the decedent might well choose to defer payment of these obligations until he is on his deathbed and his property is about to pass to his heirs. Then, at that moment, he would acknowledge the obligations, even though a court could never have enforced them.[328] If such acknowledgments were binding, he might delay acknowledging them until he was on his deathbed and only then specify them, in which case they might be so large that they would consume the entirety of his estate. He is therefore not allowed to do that.'"[329]

839. According to Mālik, it reached him that ʿAbd Allāh b. ʿUmar would be asked, "Can someone fast or perform prayer on behalf of someone else?" He would reply, "No one can fast or perform prayer on behalf of someone else."

Chapter 17. What Has Come Down regarding Making Up Missed Days of Fasting for Ramadan or for Penance

840. According to Mālik, Zayd b. Aslam reported from his brother that once, on a cloudy day in Ramadan, ʿUmar b. al-Khaṭṭāb broke his fast thinking that the sun had set. A man came to him and said, "Commander of the Faithful, the sun is still visible!" ʿUmar said, "Calm down; this is not a big deal. We certainly acted in accordance with our best judgment." Yaḥyā said, "Mālik said, 'In our opinion, he meant, by "Calm down; this is not a big deal," that the day's fast could be made up—and God knows best—and that its burden is light and easy. What he was saying is that he would fast another day in its place.'"

841. According to Mālik, Nāfiʿ reported that ʿAbd Allāh b. ʿUmar would say, "Whoever does not observe the Ramadan fast because of an illness or travel should make up the days he missed by fasting them consecutively, as though they were in the month of Ramadan."

---

328 Although vows such as manumitting a slave, giving certain sums in charity, or sacrificing an animal for the poor involve tangible property interests, in these cases, in contrast to commitments to give a gift or manumit a specific slave, there is no specific beneficiary who could sue in court to compel fulfillment of the vow. Therefore, the obligation to perform the vow is binding only in a moral sense.

329 Mālik's ruling in this case is an exemplary instance of his use of the concept of *sadd al-dharīʿa* ("blocking the means" or "preclusion"). If a dying person has vowed to perform certain acts of charity but has failed to fulfill his vows during his lifetime, he can fulfill them in death only out of the one-third portion of his estate dedicated to bequests. Otherwise, Mālik reasoned, people could claim unfulfilled pious obligations, whether unfulfilled vows or unpaid alms-tax, on their deathbeds to deprive their legal heirs of their inheritance precisely at the time when they know that they will no longer be able to enjoy their property themselves.

842. According to Mālik, Ibn Shihāb reported that ʿAbd Allāh b. ʿAbbās and Abū Hurayra disagreed on the issue of making up days missed in Ramadan. One of them said, "They need not be fasted consecutively," and the other said, "They must be fasted consecutively." Ibn Shihāb said, "I do not know which one said, 'They need not be fasted consecutively.'"

843. According to Mālik, Nāfiʿ reported that ʿAbd Allāh b. ʿUmar would say, "If a man induces himself to vomit while fasting, he must make up that day, but if he vomits spontaneously, he is not obliged to make up that fasting day."

844. According to Mālik, Yaḥyā b. Saʿīd reported that he heard Saʿīd b. al-Musayyab being asked about making up missed days of fasting in Ramadan, and Saʿīd said, "In my opinion, it is best to make up missed days of Ramadan fasting consecutively, one after another."

845. Yaḥyā said, "I heard Mālik say, regarding someone who made up missed days of Ramadan fasting in a nonconsecutive fashion, 'He is not obliged to fast them again consecutively. What he fasted was sufficient for him. I would have preferred it, however, had he fasted them consecutively.'"

846. Yaḥyā said, "I heard Mālik say, 'Whoever eats or drinks inadvertently or absentmindedly in Ramadan, or during any other fast day that he is obliged to observe, must fast another day in that day's place.'"

847. According to Mālik, Ḥumayd b. Qays told him, "I was with Mujāhid[330] while he was circumambulating the Kabah, and a man came to him and asked him whether fasts that are imposed for penance must be fasted consecutively or whether they can be fasted nonconsecutively. I said to him, 'Yes, he can fast them nonconsecutively if he wishes.' Mujāhid said, 'He should fast them consecutively because in Ubayy b. Kaʿb's recitation of the Quran, they are referred to as three consecutive days.'"[331]

848. Mālik said, "I prefer that a person observing a fast that is specified in the Quran complete the fasting days consecutively."

849. Yaḥyā said, "Mālik was asked about how the woman described in the following case should perform her religious duties of prayer and fasting.

330 An early exegete of the Quran (d. 103/721) who was a student of the Companion ʿAbd Allāh b. ʿAbbās.

331 This report concerns the proper understanding of the verse "God does not take you to account for oaths that you make casually, but He does take you to account for those made in earnest. The penance of an oath made in earnest is feeding ten poor people from the very food that you feed your own family, or clothing them, or manumitting a slave. Whosoever is unable to do any of these should fast three days." *Al-Māʾida*, 5:89. What Mujāhid meant is that Ubayy b. Kaʿb understood the verse to command the penitent to fast the three required days consecutively.

Assume the woman begins her day fasting in Ramadan and then finds fresh blood suddenly flowing from her, even though it is not the usual time of her period. She then waits until evening to see if the bleeding continues, but she does not notice anything. Then, on the next day, she awakes, and fresh blood again flows from her, but in a smaller amount than the previous day. Then, a few days before her period, this bleeding comes to a complete stop. Mālik said, 'That was menstrual blood. When she sees it she should suspend her fast; later, she should make up the days she did not fast. When the blood's flow comes to a complete stop, she should bathe and resume her fast.'"

850. Yaḥyā said, "Mālik was asked whether someone who embraces Islam on the last day of Ramadan must make up the entirety of the Ramadan fast that he missed, or whether he must make up the fasting day of Ramadan on which he became Muslim. He said, 'He is under no obligation to make up any prior fasting days. Rather, he begins fasting from that day onward. I prefer that he make up the fasting day on which he embraced Islam insofar as he was a Muslim for part of that day.'"

Chapter 18. Making Up Voluntary Fasts

851. According to Mālik, Ibn Shihāb reported that 'Ā'isha and Ḥafṣa, two of the wives of the Prophet (pbuh), woke up and began to observe a voluntary fast, but then they received a gift of food, so they broke their fast and ate it. The Messenger of God (pbuh) came in and saw them. 'Ā'isha said, "Ḥafṣa, being blunt and bold like her father, spoke before me, saying, 'Messenger of God, 'Ā'isha and I began the morning observing a voluntary fast, but then we received a gift of food, so we broke our fast and ate it.' The Messenger of God (pbuh) said, 'Fast another day in this day's place.'"

852. Yaḥyā said, "I heard Mālik say, 'A man who eats and drinks inadvertently or absentmindedly during a voluntary fast does not have to make up that day; rather, he should continue his voluntary fast for the rest of that day and should not abandon it. If something occurs unexpectedly on the day of a voluntary fast that causes a man to interrupt his fasting, and if the only reason he interrupted his fast was for that valid excuse and he did not desire to break his fast, then he is not obliged to make it up. Neither do I believe that he is obliged to repeat the performance of a voluntary prayer (*ṣalāt*), if he interrupted it because of a physical need of the body that he could not restrain, and it was of the kind whose occurrence necessitates the performance of ablutions (*wuḍū'*) prior to praying.'"

853. Yaḥyā said, "Mālik said, 'It is not acceptable that a person should begin any voluntary pious act, whether prayer, fasting, the Pilgrimage (*ḥajj*), or a similar act, and then abandon it prior to having completed it in accordance with its mandatory rules.[332] Accordingly, if he begins performance of the prayer by magnifying God (saying "God is great," *Allāhu akbar*), he is not to stop until he has performed two complete cycles (*rakʿa*) of prayer; if he is fasting, he is not to break the fast until he has finished that day's fast; and if he begins performance of the Pilgrimage, he is not to return home until he has completed it. If he begins to circumambulate the Kabah, he is not to stop until he has completed seven circuits. Once he has begun such acts, he must complete them, unless something serious happens to him, such as a serious illness or any other event that generally excuses people from ritual obligations. This is because God, Blessed and Sublime is He, says in His Book, "Eat and drink until the white thread of dawn appears to you distinct from its black thread, and then complete your fast till the night appears."[333] Therefore, once he has begun the fast, he must complete it. God also said, "Complete the Pilgrimage and the Visitation (*ʿumra*) for the sake of God."[334] Consequently, even if a man has already performed the obligatory Pilgrimage but then undertakes a second Pilgrimage, he must not abandon the consecrated state (*iḥrām*) of a pilgrim[335] and return home in the unrestricted state (*ḥalāl*) of a nonpilgrim until he has completed that Pilgrimage. Anyone who begins a voluntary pious act (*nāfila*) must complete it, just as he must complete an obligatory pious act. This is the best view that I have heard.'"

Chapter 19. What a Person Offers in Lieu of Fasting If He Does Not Observe the Ramadan Fast on Account of Incapacity

854. According to Mālik, it reached him that Anas b. Mālik reached such an advanced age that he lost the ability to fast, so he would instead feed the poor.

855. Mālik said, "I do not believe feeding the poor is obligatory for someone too old to fast; but if he is able to do so, it is better for him. If a person offers food in lieu of fasting, he should give approximately 500 grams (one *mudd*) of food, using the measure of the Prophet, for every day he misses."

---

332 The phrase Mālik uses is *ʿalā sunnatih*.

333 *Al-Baqara*, 2:198.

334 *Al-Baqara*, 2:196. The Visitation also entails a journey to Mecca and the performance of certain rites there, but unlike the Pilgrimage, it may be performed at any time during the year, and its rites are circumscribed in comparison to those of the Pilgrimage.

335 When a person resolves to perform the Pilgrimage or the Visitation, he enters into a consecrated state, known as *iḥrām*, in which many acts that are ordinarily permissible are prohibited. Leaving this consecrated state is known as *iḥlāl* or *taḥallul*, which indicates that the restrictions that bound the pilgrim as long as he was performing the Pilgrimage or the Visitation have ended and he is now free to resume his normal life.

856. According to Mālik, it reached him that ʿAbd Allāh b. ʿUmar was asked what a pregnant woman should do if the fast becomes extremely difficult for her and she fears for her fetus. He said, "She should suspend her fast, and for every day she misses, she feeds a poor person approximately 500 grams of wheat, using the measure of the Prophet (pbuh)."

857. Mālik said, "The people of knowledge are of the view that she must make up the days that she misses, because God said, 'Whoever of you is ill or traveling, let him fast an equivalent number of other days.'[336] They see that condition as an illness, in combination with her fear for her child."

858. According to Mālik, ʿAbd al-Raḥmān b. al-Qāsim reported that his father would say, "If Ramadan arrives, and someone who was obliged to make up fasting days from the previous year's Ramadan has not done so yet, despite having been healthy enough to fast, that person must feed a poor person approximately 500 grams of wheat for every day of fasting that he missed, and he must still make up those missed days."

859. According to Mālik, it reached him that a similar view was held by Saʿīd b. Jubayr.

Chapter 20. Miscellaneous Matters Related to Making Up Missed Fasting Days

860. According to Mālik, Yaḥyā b. Saʿīd reported from Abū Salama b. ʿAbd al-Raḥmān that he heard ʿĀ'isha, the wife of the Prophet (pbuh), say, "Sometimes I would have fasting days from the previous Ramadan to make up but would not be able to fast them until Shaʿbān."[337]

Chapter 21. Fasting on a Day regarding Which There Is Doubt

861. According to Mālik, he heard the people of knowledge forbid people from fasting when they were uncertain whether it was the last day of Shaʿbān or the first day of Ramadan, if they fasted with the intention (*niyya*)[338] of fasting for Ramadan. Their opinion was that whoever fasted that day without having personally seen the crescent moon of Ramadan had to fast another day to make it up, even if it was subsequently determined that it had in fact been the first day of Ramadan. They did not, however, see any harm in observing a voluntary fast on that day.[339] Yaḥyā said, "Mālik

336 *Al-Baqara*, 2:190.
337 Shaʿbān is the month before Ramadan.
338 *Niyya* is the Arabic term for "intention." According to the Mālikīs, the proper intention is a prerequisite for the valid performance of every ritual act in Islamic law.
339 The principle here is that a condition for the validity of the Ramadan fast is certainty that it is in fact Ramadan. If a person is not certain that the day is part of Ramadan, he cannot fast it

said, 'This is the rule among us and the one I found the people of knowledge in our town following (*hādhā al-amr ʿindanā wa'lladhī adraktu ʿalayhi ahl al-ʿilm bi-baladinā*).'"

Chapter 22. Miscellaneous Matters Related to Fasting

862. According to Mālik, Abū al-Naḍr, the freedman (*mawlā*) of ʿUmar b. ʿUbayd Allāh, reported from Abū Salama b. ʿAbd al-Raḥmān that ʿĀʾisha, the wife of the Prophet (pbuh), said, "The Messenger of God (pbuh) would fast so many consecutive days (outside of Ramadan) that we wondered whether he ever stopped fasting. He would then go so long without fasting (outside of Ramadan) that we would wonder whether he ever fasted. I never saw the Messenger of God (pbuh) fast an entire month except in Ramadan, and I never saw him fast more days in any month outside of Ramadan than he did in Shaʿbān."

863. According to Mālik, Abū al-Zinād reported from al-Aʿraj, from Abū Hurayra, that the Messenger of God (pbuh) said, "Fasting is a shield, so a fasting man should neither utter obscenities nor lash out in anger. If someone challenges him to a fight or curses him, he should say, 'I am fasting, I am fasting.'"

864. According to Mālik, Abū al-Zinād reported from al-Aʿraj, from Abū Hurayra, that the Messenger of God (pbuh) said, "By Him whose hand holds my soul, a fasting man's unpleasant breath smells sweeter to God than musk does. God says, 'For My sake, he turns away from his carnal desires and puts aside his food and drink. Fasting is exclusively for Me, and I certainly shall reward it. Every good deed is rewarded tenfold up to seven hundred-fold—except for fasting, which is exclusively for Me, and I reward it without limit."

865. According to Mālik, his paternal uncle Abū Suhayl b. Mālik reported from his father that Abū Hurayra said, "When Ramadan arrives, the gates of Paradise are opened, the gates of Hell are closed, and the demons are locked up."

866. According to Mālik, he never heard the people of knowledge disapprove of using the toothbrush (*siwāk*) during Ramadan at any time of day, neither at the beginning nor at the end of the day. Mālik said, "I did not hear any of the people of knowledge disapprove of or forbid that."

867. Yaḥyā said, "I heard Mālik speak about whether it was desirable to fast six days in Shawwāl after the Feast of Breaking the Fast (*ʿīd al-fiṭr*). He said

---

on the assumption that it is. Even if it turns out that the day did, in fact, belong to Ramadan, he still needs to fast another day in its stead because the prerequisite for a valid Ramadan fast—knowledge that Ramadan has begun—was not satisfied.

that he knew of no person of knowledge and understanding who observed such a fast. Mālik also said, 'Neither has it reached me that any of the pious ancestors observed it. Furthermore, the people of knowledge disapprove of it and fear that it is an unauthorized innovation in religion, and that the ignorant and rough folk would assimilate such a fast to the Ramadan fast if they knew that the people of knowledge permitted it and if they saw them observing it.'"

868. Yaḥyā said, "I heard Mālik say, 'I never heard any of the people of knowledge and understanding or any of those who are exemplars of upright conduct prohibit fasting on Friday. Observing a fast on Fridays is good, and I knew of one person of knowledge who did so, and I believe that he singled out Friday for fasting.'"

The Book of Fasting (*Ṣiyām*) Is Complete. Praise Be to God as Befits Him, and God's Grace on Muḥammad, His Servant and Messenger.

Book 18
The Book of the Night of Power (*Laylat al-Qadr*)[340]

In the Name of God, the Merciful, the Compassionate

May God Grace Our Prophet Muḥammad and His Family
and Grant Them Perfect Tranquility.

Chapter 1. What Has Come Down regarding the Night of Power (*Laylat al-Qadr*)

869. According to Mālik, Yazīd b. ʿAbd Allāh b. Usāma b. al-Hādī reported from Muḥammad b. Ibrāhīm b. al-Ḥārith al-Taymī, from Abū Salama b. ʿAbd al-Raḥmān, that Abū Saʿīd al-Khudrī said, "The Messenger of God (pbuh) would spend the middle ten days of Ramadan in pious seclusion (*iʿtikāf*) in the mosque. One year, he went into pious seclusion until the night of the twenty-first day of Ramadan, which was ordinarily the night on which he would conclude his pious seclusion. He said, 'Those of you who have gone into pious seclusion with me should continue for the last ten days of Ramadan. I was granted a vision this night,[341] but then I was made to forget it. I saw myself prostrating that morning in a place of water and mud. Seek it during the last ten nights of Ramadan, and especially on every odd-numbered night of the last ten.'" Abū Saʿīd said, "It rained that night, and the mosque, whose roof was made of palm fronds, leaked. With my own eyes, I saw the Messenger of God (pbuh) leave the mosque the next morning with traces of water and mud on his forehead and nose."[342]

---

340 The Night of Power (*laylat al-qadr*) is mentioned explicitly in the Quran as the night on which God first revealed the Quran. It is a blessed night, and the Quran describes it as "better than a thousand months"; *al-Qadr*, 97:1–5. Numerous reports attributed to the Prophet Muḥammad (pbuh) identify the night as falling within the last ten nights of Ramadan, and of these ten nights, the odd-numbered nights are singled out for special veneration as candidates for the Night of Power.

341 That is, he was shown which night was the Night of Power.

342 He emerged on the morning of the twenty-first. In the Islamic calendar, the day begins with sunset. Accordingly, the morning of the day comes after its night.

870. According to Mālik, Hishām b. ʿUrwa reported from his father that the Messenger of God (pbuh) said, "Seek the Night of Power during the last ten nights of Ramadan."

871. According to Mālik, ʿAbd Allāh b. Dīnār reported from ʿAbd Allāh b. ʿUmar that the Messenger of God (pbuh) said, "Seek the Night of Power in the last seven nights of Ramadan."

872. According to Mālik, Abū al-Naḍr, the freedman (*mawlā*) of ʿUmar b. ʿUbayd Allāh, reported that ʿAbd Allāh b. Unays al-Juhanī said to the Messenger of God (pbuh), "Messenger of God, my house is quite a distance from the mosque. Tell me, is there a special night on which I should come?" The Messenger of God (pbuh) said to him, "Come on the twenty-third night of Ramadan."

873. According to Mālik, Ḥumayd al-Ṭawīl reported that Anas b. Mālik said, "The Messenger of God (pbuh) came out to us in Ramadan and said, 'I was granted a vision this Ramadan night,[343] but then two men quarreled violently, so it vanished. Seek it on the ninth, seventh, and fifth nights.'"[344]

874. According to Mālik, it reached him that some of the Companions of the Messenger of God (pbuh) dreamed that the Night of Power took place during the last seven nights of Ramadan. The Messenger of God (pbuh) said, "I see that your visions have all converged on the Night of Power being in the last seven nights of Ramadan, so whoever seeks it should do so in the last seven nights."

875. According to Mālik, he heard a person of knowledge whom he trusted say, "The Messenger of God (pbuh) was shown the lifespans of the people who had lived before him, or whatever God wished to show him concerning such things, and it was as though he feared that the lifespans of his community would be too short to accumulate the good deeds that others with their long lives had attained. So God gave him the Night of Power, which is better than a thousand months."[345]

876. According to Mālik, it reached him that Saʿīd b. al-Musayyab would say, "Whoever attends the Evening Prayer (*ṣalāt al-ʿishāʾ*) in the mosque on the Night of Power has a share of its reward."

---

343 That is, he was given a vision of the Night of Power.

344 He meant when there were nine, seven, and five days remaining of Ramadan, so on the twenty-first, twenty-third, and twenty-fifth nights, respectively.

345 According to the editors of the RME, a marginal note on the principal manuscript of the *Muwaṭṭaʾ* states that this hadith is one of four in the broader Islamic hadith tradition that were transmitted exclusively by Mālik.

The Book of the Night of Power (*Laylat al-Qadr*) Is Complete, with Abundant Praise to God. May God Grace Muḥammad and His Family.

Book 19

The Book of Pious Seclusion (*Iʿtikāf*)

In the Name of God, the Merciful, the Compassionate

May God Grace Muḥammad and His Family
and Grant Them Perfect Tranquility.

Chapter 1. Reports about Pious Seclusion (*Iʿtikāf*)

877. According to Mālik, Ibn Shihāb reported from ʿUrwa b. al-Zubayr, from ʿAmra bt. ʿAbd al-Raḥmān, that ʿĀʾisha, the wife of the Prophet (pbuh), said, "When the Messenger of God (pbuh) secluded himself in the mosque for pious purposes (*iʿtikāf*), he would sometimes place his head close to me[346] so that I could comb his hair. He would go into a roofed room only to relieve himself."

878. According to Mālik, Ibn Shihāb reported from ʿAmra bt. ʿAbd al-Raḥmān that whenever ʿĀʾisha went into pious seclusion, she would not even inquire about the sick except as she was walking, and would not stop to do so.

879. Yaḥyā said, "Mālik said, 'A person engaged in pious seclusion should not trouble himself with any worldly concerns, nor should he leave his place of pious seclusion in furtherance of them, whether for himself or others. He should leave it only to relieve himself. Were he to leave his place of pious seclusion for the sake of another person, then visitation of the sick, performance of the funeral prayer (*ṣalāt al-jināza*), and marching in a funeral procession would have the greatest claims over him.'"

880. Yaḥyā said, "Mālik said, 'A person engaged in pious seclusion is not actually in seclusion unless he refrains from everything that a person in pious seclusion avoids, such as visiting the sick, praying over the dead, and entering a roofed room, except to relieve himself.'"

346 The Prophet's house adjoined the mosque, making it possible for ʿĀʾisha to comb his hair while she stayed in her home and he was in the mosque.

881. According to Mālik, he asked Ibn Shihāb whether a man engaged in pious seclusion could enter a covered room to relieve himself. He said, "Yes, there is nothing objectionable in that."

882. Yaḥyā said, "Mālik said, 'The rule among us about which there is no dissent (*al-amr ʿindanā alladhī lā ikhtilāfa fīh*) is that it is not forbidden to engage in pious seclusion in a mosque that hosts the Friday Congregational Prayer (*ṣalāt al-jumuʿa*). The only reason, in my opinion, that one is discouraged from engaging pious seclusion in mosques that do not host the Friday prayer is the fear that someone secluded in such a mosque would have to leave that mosque to attend the prayer or otherwise miss it. If, however, a person is not under an obligation to attend the Friday Congregational Prayer elsewhere, I see no harm in his engaging in pious seclusion in a mosque that does not host the Friday prayer, because God, Blessed and Sublime is He, says, "While you are engaged in pious seclusion in the mosques."[347] God thus refers to all mosques without specifying any particular kind. For this reason, it is permissible for a person to go into pious seclusion in a mosque that does not host the Friday prayer as long as he is not under an obligation to leave it to attend the prayer in another mosque. Someone who is engaged in pious seclusion should spend the night only in the mosque in which he is secluded; however, he may sleep in his tent if it is in one of the mosque's courtyards. I have not heard that a person engaged in pious seclusion can pitch his tent in any place other than the mosque or one of its courtyards. One thing that indicates that a person engaged in pious seclusion must spend the night in the mosque is ʿĀ'isha's statement, "When the Messenger of God (pbuh) was engaged in pious seclusion, he would go into a roofed room only to relieve himself."'"

883. Yaḥyā said, "Mālik said, 'One should not engage in pious seclusion on the roof of the mosque or in the minaret—that is, in the chamber located there.'"

884. Yaḥyā said, "Mālik said, 'The person desiring to engage in pious seclusion should enter his desired place of seclusion before the sun sets on the night in which he wishes to begin his seclusion, so that he is ready to begin it at the beginning of the night on which he desires to engage in pious seclusion.'"

885. Yaḥyā said, "Mālik said, 'The person engaged in pious seclusion should devote himself entirely to pious devotion, thinking of nothing that would ordinarily preoccupy his thoughts, whether commerce or other matters. There is nothing objectionable, however, in his directing someone to look after his estate, the affairs of his family, the sale of some of his property, or

347 *Al-Baqara*, 2:186.

anything else that does not require his direct attention. There is nothing objectionable in his appointing someone else to do such things for him, so long as they are relatively mundane.'"

886. Yaḥyā said, "Mālik said, 'I have not heard any of the people of knowledge mention that it would be permissible for someone seeking to engage in pious seclusion to specify any conditions regarding how he will engage in it. Pious seclusion is nothing other than a complete act of worship, like prayer (*ṣalāt*), fasting, the Pilgrimage (*ḥajj*), and similar devotional acts, be they obligatory or voluntary. Anyone who performs any of these acts must perform them in accordance with the ordinances that have long been established (*bi-mā maḍā min al-sunna*) with regard to them. He may not introduce anything in respect of these devotional acts that differs from what the Muslims have always practiced (*mā maḍā ʿalayhi al-muslimūn*), whether it is a condition that he imposes before he begins his seclusion or something that he introduces after beginning it. The Messenger of God (pbuh) practiced pious seclusion, and the Muslims learned from him the ordinances (*sunna*) of pious seclusion.'"[348]

887. Yaḥyā said, "Mālik said, 'Pious seclusion and *jiwār*[349] are synonymous, and pious seclusion for a village-dweller is the same as it is for a bedouin.'"

Chapter 2. The Indispensable Elements of Pious Seclusion (*Iʿtikāf*)

888. According to Mālik, it reached him that al-Qāsim b. Muḥammad and Nāfiʿ, the freedman (*mawlā*) of ʿAbd Allāh b. ʿUmar, said, "Fasting must take place with pious seclusion. God, Blessed and Sublime is He, says in His Book, 'Eat and drink until the white thread of dawn appears to you distinct from its black thread, and then complete your fast till the night appears. And do not be intimate with your wives while you are engaged in pious seclusion in the mosques.'[350] God mentions pious seclusion only in connection with fasting." Yaḥyā said, "Mālik said, 'The rule among us is in accordance with that (*ʿalā dhālika al-amr ʿindanā*).' Fasting is a mandatory element of pious seclusion."

348 For Mālik and the Mālikīs, pious seclusion is a ritual like other rituals of Islam that is subject to certain rules, including that a person engaged in pious seclusion must fast and must remain in the mosque. Accordingly, if a person were, for example, to swear an oath that he will engage in a day of pious seclusion but then fail to fast, the oath would be ineffective, because its object is not a valid act of devotion insofar as pious seclusion requires the observance of a fast. Although the oath is not binding, if the person making the oath actually begins his act of pious seclusion, he is obliged to complete it in accordance with its rules. Bājī, *al-Muntaqā*, 2:81.

349 *Jiwār* literally means "presence in the vicinity of something," so Mālik is explaining that the word *jiwār* can be used interchangeably with the ordinary term for pious seclusion, *iʿtikāf*.

350 *Al-Baqara*, 2:186.

Chapter 3. The Departure of Someone Engaged in Pious Seclusion (*I'tikāf*) for the Feast of Breaking the Ramadan Fast (*'Īd al-Fiṭr*)

889. According to Yaḥyā b. Yaḥyā al-Laythī, Ziyād b. 'Abd al-Raḥmān[351] reported from Mālik b. Anas, from Sumayy, the freedman (*mawlā*) of Abū Bakr b. 'Abd al-Raḥmān, that Abū Bakr b. 'Abd al-Raḥmān was engaged in pious seclusion, and to relieve himself, he would pass through a roofed section of a closed room in Khālid b. al-Walīd's abode. He would not emerge from pious seclusion until he attended the prayer for the Feast of Breaking the Ramadan Fast with the Muslims."

890. According to Mālik, he had seen that when some of the people of knowledge went into pious seclusion during the last ten days of Ramadan, they would not return to their families until they had celebrated the Feast of Breaking the Ramadan Fast with the people. Yaḥyā said that Ziyād said, "Mālik said, 'This reached me from the people of virtue who have left us.'" Yaḥyā said that Ziyād said, "Mālik said, 'Of all the views I have heard regarding this issue, that is the one I prefer most.'"

Chapter 4. Making Up Incomplete Acts of Pious Seclusion (*I'tikāf*)

891. According to Mālik, Ibn Shihāb reported from 'Amra bt. 'Abd al-Raḥmān that the Messenger of God (pbuh) wanted to go into pious seclusion, and when he went to the place where he wished to perform it, he found some tents there. When he saw the tents, he asked about them and was told that they belonged to 'Ā'isha, Ḥafṣa, and Zaynab.[352] The Messenger of God (pbuh) said, "Do you think they intend piety by pitching them here?" Then he left and did not go into pious seclusion until Shawwāl, when he spent ten days in pious seclusion."

892. Yaḥyā said that Ziyād said, "Mālik was asked about a man who entered the mosque for pious seclusion during the last ten days of Ramadan and stayed there for one or two days. He then became ill, so he left the mosque. When he regains his health, is he under an obligation to make up the unfinished days of pious seclusion, and if so, during which month? Mālik said, 'He should, when he recovers, make up whatever days of pious

351 According to the editors of the RME, Ziyād b. 'Abd al-Raḥmān, known as Shabṭūn (d. 204/819), transmitted the *Muwaṭṭa'* to Yaḥyā b. Yaḥyā in Andalusia before Yaḥyā himself traveled east, where he was able to study directly with Imām Mālik. While in Medina, Yaḥyā heard the entirety of the *Muwaṭṭa'* from Mālik except for certain topics within the Book of Pious Seclusion. Because Yaḥyā was uncertain whether he had heard these passages directly from Mālik, he preserved them in his recension of the *Muwaṭṭa'* through Ziyād b. 'Abd al-Raḥmān's narration rather than his own.

352 Three of the Prophet Muḥammad's wives.

seclusion remain in Ramadan or in any other month. It reached me that the Messenger of God (pbuh) intended to engage in pious seclusion in Ramadan but then returned without doing it. When Ramadan ended, he went into pious seclusion for ten days in Shawwāl.'"

893. Yaḥyā said that Ziyād said, "Mālik said, 'Someone who is engaged in pious seclusion voluntarily and someone who is obliged to engage in pious seclusion[353] are similarly situated with respect to what is lawful for them and what is prohibited for them. I have not heard that the Messenger of God (pbuh) ever engaged in pious seclusion except voluntarily.'"

894. Yaḥyā said that Ziyād said, "Mālik said, 'A woman who goes into pious seclusion and then menstruates during the time of seclusion should return to her house. When her period finishes, she should immediately return to the mosque. She should not delay, and she should resume her seclusion from where she previously left off. Similar to that is the case of a woman who must fast two consecutive months and menstruates during that time. When her period comes to an end, she must promptly resume her fast from the point where she stopped.'"

895. According to Mālik, Ibn Shihāb reported that the Messenger of God (pbuh) would relieve himself in a roofed room when he was in pious seclusion.

896. Ziyād said that Mālik said, "The person engaged in pious seclusion should not leave to attend a funeral procession (*janāza*), even that of his own parents."

Chapter 5. Marriage during Pious Seclusion (*I'tikāf*)

897. Yaḥyā said that Ziyād said, "Mālik said, 'There is nothing objectionable in the conclusion by a person in pious seclusion of a marriage contract so long as there is no intimate contact.'"

898. Mālik said, "Also, a woman in pious seclusion may be betrothed so long as there is no intimate contact."

899. Mālik said, "Whatever is forbidden to a man engaged in pious seclusion with respect to his wife during the day is also prohibited to him during the night."

900. Mālik said, "It is unlawful for a man to touch his wife with desire while he is engaged in pious seclusion, nor may he receive any sexual gratification

353 Engaging in pious seclusion is in itself a voluntary act of piety. In certain circumstances, however, it may become obligatory, such as following a vow to engage in pious seclusion.

from her, whether through a kiss or anything else. I have not heard any of the people of knowledge prohibit either a man or a woman engaged in pious seclusion from marrying, so long as there is no intimate contact. Nor is it prohibited for a fasting person to marry. There is a difference between the marriage of someone engaged in pious seclusion and that of a pilgrim in the consecrated state (*iḥrām*). The pilgrim in the consecrated state is permitted to eat and drink, to visit the sick, and to attend funeral processions, but he may not wear perfume; the man or woman engaged in pious seclusion, by contrast, may use oil and perfume and groom his or her hair, but he or she is not permitted to attend funeral processions or funeral prayers or to visit the sick. Therefore, the law regarding the marriages of the two groups is different. This is on account of what have long been the established ordinances (*li-mā maḍā min al-sunna*) regarding the marriage of a pilgrim in the consecrated state, a person engaged in pious seclusion, and a fasting person.'"

The Book of Pious Seclusion (*Iʿtikāf*) Has Come to an End, with Praise to God for the Excellence of His Assistance.

Book 20
The Book of Pilgrimage (*Ḥajj*)

In the Name of God, the Merciful, the Compassionate

May God Grace Muḥammad and His Family
and Grant Them Perfect Tranquility.

Chapter 1. Bathing (*Ghusl*) in Preparation for Entering the Consecrated State (*Iḥrām*)[354]

901. According to Mālik, ʿAbd al-Raḥmān b. al-Qāsim reported from his father, from Asmāʾ bt. ʿUmays, that she gave birth to Muḥammad b. Abī Bakr at al-Baydāʾ.[355] When Abū Bakr mentioned that to the Messenger of God (pbuh), he said, "Tell her first to bathe and then to enter the consecrated state."

902. According to Mālik, Yaḥyā b. Saʿīd reported from Saʿīd b. al-Musayyab that Asmāʾ bt. ʿUmays gave birth to Muḥammad b. Abī Bakr at Dhū al-Ḥulayfa. Abū Bakr told her to bathe before entering the consecrated state.

903. According to Mālik, Nāfiʿ reported that ʿAbd Allāh b. ʿUmar would bathe in anticipation of entering the consecrated state before setting out on the Pilgrimage (*ḥajj*), again when he entered Mecca to circumambulate the Kabah, and in preparation for standing at ʿArafāt.

---

354 The actual title of this chapter is "Bathing in Order to Enter," with entry into the consecrated state being implied. When a person resolves to perform the Pilgrimage (*ḥajj*) or the Visitation (*ʿumra*), he enters into a consecrated state, known as *iḥrām,* in which many acts that are ordinarily permissible become prohibited. A person in the consecrated state is referred to as a *muḥrim*. Leaving this consecrated state is known as *iḥlāl* or *taḥallul*, which indicates that the restrictions that bound the pilgrim as long as he was performing the Pilgrimage or the Visitation have ended, and he is now free to resume his normal life.

355 A place between Mecca and Medina.

Chapter 2. The Bath (*Ghusl*) of the Person (*Muḥrim*) in the Consecrated State (*Iḥrām*)

904. According to Mālik, Zayd b. Aslam reported from Nāfiʿ, from Ibrāhīm b. ʿAbd Allāh b. Ḥunayn, from his father, that ʿAbd Allāh b. ʿAbbās and al-Miswar b. Makhrama once had a disagreement at al-Abwāʾ.[356] ʿAbd Allāh said, "A person in the consecrated state is permitted to wash his head," but al-Miswar b. Makhrama said, "No, he is not." ʿAbd Allāh b. Ḥunayn, the father of Ibrāhīm b. ʿAbd Allāh b. Ḥunayn, said, "ʿAbd Allāh b. ʿAbbās then sent me to Abū Ayyūb al-Anṣārī. I found him as he was bathing between the two posts of a well, covering himself with a piece of cloth. I greeted him, and he said, 'Who are you?' I said, 'I am ʿAbd Allāh b. Ḥunayn. ʿAbd Allāh b. ʿAbbās sent me to you to ask you how the Messenger of God (pbuh) would wash his head when he was in the consecrated state, if indeed he did so.' Abū Ayyūb put his hand on the garment and pulled it down until I could see his head and then said to the man who was pouring water for him, 'Pour!' So the man poured water over Abū Ayyūb's head. He then passed his hands from the front to the back of his head and back again to the front, and then he said, 'This is what I saw the Messenger of God (pbuh) do.'"

905. According to Mālik, Ḥumayd b. Qays reported from ʿAṭāʾ b. Abī Rabāḥ that ʿUmar b. al-Khaṭṭāb said to Yaʿlā b. Munya as he was pouring water on ʿUmar b. al-Khaṭṭāb when the latter was bathing, "Pour water on my head." Yaʿlā then said to him, "Are you trying to make me responsible?[357] If you tell me to pour, however, I will do so." ʿUmar b. al-Khaṭṭāb said to him, "Pour, the water will only make my head shaggier."[358]

906. According to Mālik, Nāfiʿ reported that whenever ʿAbd Allāh b. ʿUmar neared Mecca, he would spend the night at Dhū Ṭuwā, between the two mountain passes there. When morning came, he would perform the Morning Prayer (*ṣalāt al-ṣubḥ*) and then enter Mecca from the mountain pass on the highest side of the city. If he had set out to perform the Pilgrimage (*ḥajj*) or the Visitation (*ʿumra*), he would not enter Mecca until he had first bathed at Dhū Ṭuwā. He would also instruct everyone with him to bathe there before they entered Mecca.

---

356 A place in the direction of Mecca.

357 Yaʿlā was concerned that by pouring water on ʿUmar's head he might kill some insects in ʿUmar b. al-Khaṭṭāb's hair in violation of rules prohibiting a person in the consecrated state from killing any living thing.

358 In this report and the preceding one, the concern about washing the head arises out of the fear that washing the head too vigorously might cause the pilgrim to inadvertently kill an insect in the hair, thus violating the prohibition against killing any living thing while in the consecrated state.

907. According to Mālik, Nāfiʿ reported that ʿAbd Allāh b. ʿUmar would not wash his head when he was in the consecrated state unless he had a wet dream.

908. Yaḥyā said, "Mālik said, 'I heard the people of knowledge say that there is nothing objectionable in a person in the consecrated state washing his head with a palm leaf or the like, once he has cast his pebbles at Minā[359] and before he shaves his head. That is because once he throws the pebbles at Minā, it becomes permissible for him to kill lice, to shave his hair, to clean himself of filth, and to wear ordinary clothing.'"

Chapter 3. Clothing That May Not Be Worn While in the Consecrated State (*Iḥrām*)

909. According to Mālik, Nāfiʿ reported from ʿAbd Allāh b. ʿUmar that a man asked the Messenger of God (pbuh), "What clothing is a person in the consecrated state permitted to wear?" The Messenger of God (pbuh) said, "Do not wear tunics, turbans, trousers, hooded cloaks, leather socks—although if one cannot find sandals, one may wear leather socks after cutting them off below the ankles—or any clothes that have been dyed with saffron or *wars*."[360]

910. Yaḥyā said that Mālik was asked about a report in which the Prophet (pbuh) allegedly said, "If you cannot find an undergarment, wear trousers." Mālik said, "I have never heard this report, and it is inconceivable to me that someone in the consecrated state could wear trousers under any circumstances. Trousers are one of the items of clothing that the Messenger of God (pbuh) expressly prohibited those in the consecrated state from wearing. In contrast to the case of leather socks, he did not make an exception for trousers."

Chapter 4. Wearing Dyed Clothing While in the Consecrated State (*Iḥrām*)

911. According to Mālik, ʿAbd Allāh b. Dīnār reported from ʿAbd Allāh b. ʿUmar that the Messenger of God (pbuh) prohibited anyone in the consecrated state from wearing clothing that had been dyed with saffron or *wars*, and he said, "Whoever does not find sandals may wear leather socks after he cuts them off below the ankles."

---

359 A place outside of Mecca where the pilgrims cast pebbles symbolically at the Devil. This ritual takes place on the tenth, eleventh, and twelfth days of Dhū al-Ḥijja, the last month of the Muslim calendar. After throwing stones on the first day, the pilgrims are allowed to exit the consecrated state.

360 A yellowish or reddish dye produced from a plant found in Yemen.

912. According to Mālik, Nāfiʿ reported that he heard Aslam, the freedman (*mawlā*) of ʿUmar b. al-Khaṭṭāb, tell ʿAbd Allāh b. ʿUmar that ʿUmar b. al-Khaṭṭāb saw Ṭalḥa b. ʿUbayd Allāh wearing a dyed garment while he was in the consecrated state, whereupon ʿUmar said to him, "What is this dyed garment that I see you wearing, Ṭalḥa?" Ṭalḥa replied, "Commander of the Faithful, it's just clay." ʿUmar said, "You and your companions are leaders whom the people take as exemplars. Were an ignorant man to see what you are wearing, he might very well say that Ṭalḥa b. ʿUbayd Allāh wore dyed clothing when he was in the consecrated state. Accordingly, as long as you are in the consecrated state, do not wear any clothing that appears to have been dyed, even if, in fact, it has not been."

913. According to Mālik, Hishām b. ʿUrwa reported from his father, from Asmāʾ bt. Abī Bakr, that while in the consecrated state, she would wear clothes dyed with safflower, but not those dyed with saffron.

914. Yaḥyā said, "Mālik was asked whether someone entering the consecrated state could don clothing that had been perfumed, once the perfume's scent had dissipated. He said, 'Yes, as long as there is no visible trace of saffron or *wars* on it.'"

Chapter 5. Wearing a Pocket Belt (*Minṭaqa*) While in the Consecrated State (*Iḥrām*)

915. According to Mālik, Nāfiʿ reported that ʿAbd Allāh b. ʿUmar disapproved of a person in the consecrated state wearing a pocket belt.

916. According to Mālik, Yaḥyā b. Saʿīd reported that he heard Saʿīd b. al-Musayyab say, regarding a person in the consecrated state who is wearing a pocket belt under his clothes, "There is nothing objectionable in that, if he ties the ends together into a knot." Mālik said, "Of all the views I have heard regarding this issue, I prefer this one."

Chapter 6. Covering One's Face While in the Consecrated State (*Iḥrām*)

917. According to Mālik, Yaḥyā b. Saʿīd reported that al-Qāsim b. Muḥammad said, "Al-Furāfiṣa b. ʿUmayr al-Ḥanafī informed me that he saw ʿUthmān b. ʿAffān at al-ʿArj covering his face while he was in the consecrated state."

918. According to Mālik, Nāfiʿ reported that ʿAbd Allāh b. ʿUmar would say, "Everything above the chin is part of the head; therefore, someone in the consecrated state should not cover it."

919. According to Mālik, Nāfiʿ reported that ʿAbd Allāh b. ʿUmar shrouded his son Wāqid b. ʿAbd Allāh. He died at al-Juḥfa while he was in the consecrated state. ʿAbd Allāh covered his son's head and face and said, "Had we not been in the consecrated state, we would have perfumed his corpse."

920. Mālik said, "A man performs deeds only while he is alive. When he dies, his deeds come to an end."

921. According to Mālik, Nāfiʿ reported that ʿAbd Allāh b. ʿUmar would say, "A woman in the consecrated state should neither cover her face nor wear gloves."

922. According to Mālik, Hishām b. ʿUrwa reported that Fāṭima bt. al-Mundhir said, "We would cover our faces while we were in the consecrated state. Asmāʾ bt. Abī Bakr al-Ṣiddīq was with us at the time, and she did not object."

Chapter 7. What Has Come Down regarding Wearing Perfume during the Pilgrimage (*Ḥajj*)

923. According to Mālik, ʿAbd al-Raḥmān b. al-Qāsim reported from his father that ʿĀʾisha, the wife of the Prophet (pbuh), said, "I would apply perfume to the Messenger of God (pbuh) before he entered the consecrated state (*iḥrām*) and again when he exited it, before he circumambulated (*ṭawāf*)[361] God's House."

924. According to Mālik, Ḥumayd b. Qays reported from ʿAṭāʾ b. Abī Rabāḥ that a bedouin came to the Messenger of God (pbuh) when he was at Ḥunayn.[362] The bedouin was wearing a tunic that had traces of yellow on it. He said, "Messenger of God, I entered the consecrated state to perform the Visitation (*ʿumra*). What do you command me to do?" The Messenger of God (pbuh) said, "Remove your tunic, wash its yellowness off, and perform your Visitation in the same way as you would perform your Pilgrimage."

925. According to Mālik, Nāfiʿ reported from Aslam, the freedman (*mawlā*) of ʿUmar b. al-Khaṭṭāb, that ʿUmar b. al-Khaṭṭāb noticed the scent of perfume while he was at al-Shajara,[363] so he asked, "Who is wearing perfume?"

---

361 Circumambulation of the Kabah consists of making seven counterclockwise laps around the Kabah. It is performed during the Pilgrimage and the Visitation, and optionally by anyone who is in the Sacred Mosque. Some acts of circumambulation are obligatory parts of the Pilgrimage rites, including the circumambulation referred to in this report. Upon exiting the consecrated state following casting pebbles at Minā, the pilgrims march to Mecca to circumambulate God's House and then return to Minā. This circumambulation is known as *ṭawāf al-ifāḍa*, which we have translated as the "Circumambulation of the March," insofar as the pilgrims march to Mecca en masse to perform that obligatory circumambulation.

362 A valley located in the Hijaz that was the site of a major battle between the Muslims and the pagan tribes of Hawāzin and Thaqīf shortly after the Prophet (pbuh) conquered Mecca in year 8 of the Hijra (629 CE).

363 A place approximately 6–7 km outside of Medina.

Muʿāwiya b. Abī Sufyān said, "I am, Commander of the Faithful!" ʿUmar said, "It's *you*, by the life of God?" Muʿāwiya said, "Umm Ḥabība[364] applied perfume to me, Commander of the Faithful." ʿUmar said, "I insist that you go back and wash it off completely."

926. According to Mālik, al-Ṣalt b. Zuyayd reported from several members of his family that ʿUmar b. al-Khaṭṭāb noticed the scent of perfume while he was at al-Shajara. Kathīr b. al-Ṣalt was at his side. ʿUmar said, "Who is wearing perfume?" Kathīr said, "I am! I matted my hair and wanted to shave it." ʿUmar said, "Go to a *sharaba* and rub your head until you remove the perfume's scent," so Kathīr did so. Mālik said, "A *sharaba* is a pool dug at the base of a date palm in which water is collected."

927. According to Mālik, Yaḥyā b. Saʿīd, ʿAbd Allāh b. Abī Bakr, and Rabīʿa b. ʿAbd al-Raḥmān all reported that al-Walīd b. ʿAbd al-Malik asked Sālim b. ʿAbd Allāh and Khārija b. Zayd b. Thābit[365] if he could use perfume after he had cast pebbles at Minā and shaved his head but before he performed the Circumambulation of the March (*ṭawāf al-ifāḍa*). Sālim prohibited him from doing so, but Khārija b. Zayd b. Thābit allowed him to do it.

928. Mālik said, "There is nothing objectionable in a man applying oil to himself before he enters the consecrated state and before he sets out from Minā to God's House after casting his pebbles, as long as the oil does not have a scent."

929. Yaḥyā said, "Mālik was asked whether a person in the consecrated state could eat food that had saffron in it. He said, 'There is nothing objectionable in such a person eating it if it has been roasted, but if it has not been roasted he must not eat it.'"

Chapter 8. The Designated Stations (*Mawāqīt*) for Entering the Consecrated State (*Iḥrām*)

930. According to Mālik, Nāfiʿ reported from ʿAbd Allāh b. ʿUmar that the Messenger of God (pbuh) said, "The people of Medina should enter the consecrated state at Dhū al-Ḥulayfa,[366] the people of the Levant at al-Juḥfa,[367] and the people of Najd at Qarn."[368] ʿAbd Allāh b. ʿUmar said, "It reached me

364 Muʿāwiya's sister and a wife of the Prophet (pbuh).

365 Khārija b. Zayd b. Thābit (d. 99/717) was one of the "seven jurists of Medina" and a son of the prominent Companion and jurist Zayd b. Thābit.

366 An abandoned village on the way from Medina to Mecca. It lay at a distance of nine or ten days' march from Mecca. Of the various points at which pilgrims must enter the consecrated state, it is the furthest from Mecca. Zurqānī, *Sharḥ al-Zurqānī*, 2:356.

367 An abandoned village lying in a flood plain at a distance of five or six days' march from Mecca.

368 A mountain lying to the east of Mecca, two days' march away.

that the Messenger of God (pbuh) said, 'The people of Yemen should enter the consecrated state at Yalamlam.'"[369]

931. According to Mālik, ʿAbd Allāh b. Dīnār reported that ʿAbd Allāh b. ʿUmar said, "The Messenger of God (pbuh) commanded the people of Medina to enter the consecrated state at Dhū al-Ḥulayfa, the people of the Levant at al-Juḥfa, and the people of Najd at Qarn." ʿAbd Allāh b. ʿUmar said, "As for these three places, I heard them directly from the Messenger of God (pbuh). I was also told that the Messenger of God said, 'The people of Yemen should enter the consecrated state at Yalamlam.'"

932. According to Mālik, Nāfiʿ reported that ʿAbd Allāh b. ʿUmar once entered the consecrated state at al-Furuʿ.[370]

933. According to Mālik, a source he deemed reliable reported that ʿAbd Allāh b. ʿUmar once entered the consecrated state from Jerusalem.[371]

934. According to Mālik, it reached him that the Messenger of God (pbuh) entered the consecrated state at al-Jiʿirrāna[372] to perform the Visitation (*ʿumra*).

Chapter 9. The Practice (*ʿAmal*) with Respect to Entering the Consecrated State (*Iḥrām*)

935. According to Mālik, Nāfiʿ reported from ʿAbd Allāh b. ʿUmar that the Messenger of God (pbuh) would chant (*talbiya*), "I am at Your service, God, I am at Your service. I am at Your service; no partner have You. I am at Your service. Praise and blessings belong to You, as does the dominion. No partner have You."[373] Nāfiʿ said, "ʿAbd Allāh b. ʿUmar would add, 'I am at Your service, I am at Your service, I am at Your service and at Your call. Good is in Your hands; I am at Your service. The yearning is unto You, as is action.'"[374]

936. According to Mālik, Hishām b. ʿUrwa reported from his father that the Messenger of God (pbuh) would perform two cycles (*rakʿa*) of prayer in the mosque at Dhū al-Ḥulayfa, and then, when he mounted his camel and it stood up, he would begin chanting."

369 A place two days' march south of Mecca.

370 A place on the road from Medina to Mecca before Dhū al-Ḥulayfa, at a distance of four nights' journey from Mecca. Kāndihlawī, *Awjaz al-masālik*, 6:448.

371 Īliyāʾ, an Arabic name for Jerusalem.

372 A place between Mecca and Ṭāʾif, where the Prophet (pbuh) divided the spoils seized by the Muslims in the Battle of Ḥunayn in year 8 of the Hijra (629 CE).

373 *Labbayka allāhumma labbayk; labbayka lā sharīka laka labbayk; inna al-ḥamda wa'l-niʿmata laka wa'l-mulk; lā sharīka lak.*

374 *Labbayka labbayka labbayka wa-saʿdayk; wa'l-khayru bi-yadayka wa'l-raghbāʾ ilayka wa'l-ʿamal.*

937. According to Mālik, Mūsā b. ʿUqba reported from Sālim b. ʿAbd Allāh that he heard his father say, "You lie against the Messenger of God (pbuh) when you claim that he began his chanting at this very spot in your desert. The truth is that he only began to chant from the mosque," meaning the mosque at Dhū al-Ḥulayfa.

938. According to Mālik, Saʿīd b. Abī Saʿīd al-Maqburī reported from ʿUbayd b. Jurayj that he said to ʿAbd Allāh b. ʿUmar, "Abū ʿAbd al-Raḥmān, I have seen you do four things that I have not seen any of your companions do." He said, "What are they, Ibn Jurayj?" He said, "I noticed that you touch only the two Yemeni corners of God's House. I have seen you wear hairless leather sandals. I have seen you dye your clothes yellow. And when you were in Mecca and people began to chant when they saw the crescent moon of Dhū al-Ḥijja, I noticed that you did not begin to chant until the Day of Watering (*yawm al-tarwiya*)."[375] ʿAbd Allāh b. ʿUmar said, "As for the corners of God's House, I never saw the Messenger of God (pbuh) touch them beyond the two Yemeni corners. As for the sandals, I saw the Messenger of God (pbuh) wear hairless leather sandals and perform ablutions in them, so I like to wear them. As for the yellow dye, I noticed that the Messenger of God (pbuh) would use it to dye his clothes, so I decided to dye my clothes yellow like him. As for chanting upon entering the consecrated state, I never saw the Messenger of God (pbuh) do that until his mount rose and began to move forward."

939. According to Mālik, Nāfiʿ reported that ʿAbd Allāh b. ʿUmar would pray in the mosque at Dhū al-Ḥulayfa and then go outside and mount his camel. When his camel stood up with him firmly in the saddle, he would enter the consecrated state and begin to chant.

940. According to Mālik, it reached him that ʿAbd al-Malik b. Marwān began to chant at the mosque of Dhū al-Ḥulayfa when his mount stood up with him firmly in the saddle, relying on the advice that Abān b. ʿUthmān had given him.

Chapter 10. Raising the Voice When Beginning to Chant (*Talbiya*) upon Entering the Consecrated State (*Iḥrām*)

941. According to Mālik, ʿAbd Allāh b. Abī Bakr b. Ḥazm reported from ʿAbd al-Malik b. Abī Bakr b. al-Ḥārith b. Hishām, from Khallād b. al-Sāʾib al-Anṣārī, from his father, that the Messenger of God (pbuh) said, "Gabriel

---

375 The eighth day of Dhū al-Ḥijja. It is so named because on that day the pilgrims provision themselves with water from Mecca before heading out to Minā the next day to perform the rites of the Pilgrimage.

came to me and commanded me to tell my companions (or 'whoever is with me') to raise their voices when chanting (or 'upon entering the consecrated state')." He meant one of the two expressions.[376]

942. According to Mālik, he heard the people of knowledge say that a woman is not obliged to raise her voice when she chants, but she ought to chant loudly enough to be audible to herself.

943. Yaḥyā said, "Mālik said, 'A person in the consecrated state (*muḥrim*) should not raise his voice in chanting if he is in a mosque in which congregational prayers are held. In that case, his chanting should be audible only to himself and those near him. The exceptions are the Sacred Mosque (*al-masjid al-ḥarām*) in Mecca and the mosque at Minā. He should raise his voice in both of these places.'"

944. Mālik said, "I heard some of the people of knowledge recommend chanting at the conclusion of each prayer (*ṣalāt*) and at the top of every hill en route."

Chapter 11. Performing the Pilgrimage by Itself (*Ifrād*)[377]

945. According to Mālik, Abū al-Aswad Muḥammad b. ʿAbd al-Raḥmān reported from ʿUrwa b. al-Zubayr that ʿĀʾisha, the wife of the Messenger of God (pbuh), said, "We set out with the Messenger of God (pbuh) in the year of the Farewell Pilgrimage (*ḥajjat al-wadāʿ*).[378] Some of us entered the consecrated state (*iḥrām*) with the intention of performing only the Visitation (*ʿumra*), while others intended to perform both the Pilgrimage (*ḥajj*) and the Visitation. Others still intended to perform only the Pilgrimage. The Messenger of God (pbuh) entered the consecrated state with the intention to perform only the Pilgrimage. Those who had entered the consecrated state to perform the Visitation exited the consecrated state after completing the Visitation. Those who had entered the consecrated state to perform only the Pilgrimage or to perform both the Pilgrimage and the Visitation did not exit the consecrated state until the Day of the Slaughter of the Sacrosanct Animals (*yawm al-naḥr*)."[379]

---

376 In other words, the narrator is uncertain which of the two phrases the Prophet (pbuh) actually used. Regardless of the actual words spoken, the alternatives have the same meaning.

377 *Ifrād* refers to a pilgrim's performance of only the rites of the Pilgrimage (*ḥajj*), not those of the Visitation (*ʿumra*). In most cases, pilgrims perform both sets of rites on one trip.

378 This took place in year 10 of the Hijra (632 CE). It was so called because the Prophet (pbuh) died in that year.

379 *Yawm al-naḥr* falls on the tenth day of Dhū al-Hijja and overlaps with the Feast of the Sacrificial Animals. On this day, the pilgrims slaughter any sacrificial animals that they have brought with them on the Pilgrimage.

946. According to Mālik, ʿAbd al-Raḥmān b. al-Qāsim reported from his father, from ʿĀʾisha, the Mother of the Believers, that the Messenger of God (pbuh) performed the Pilgrimage by itself.

947. According to Mālik, Abū al-Aswad Muḥammad b. ʿAbd al-Raḥmān—Mālik said, "He was an orphan under the guardianship of ʿUrwa b. al-Zubayr"—reported from ʿUrwa b. al-Zubayr, from ʿĀʾisha, the Mother of the Believers, that the Messenger of God (pbuh) performed the Pilgrimage by itself.

948. According to Mālik, he heard the people of knowledge say, "A person who enters the consecrated state intending to perform the Pilgrimage by itself but then later wishes to perform the Visitation in addition to the Pilgrimage may not do so." Mālik said, "That is what I found the people of knowledge in our town following (*dhālika alladhī adraktu ʿalayhi ahl al-ʿilm bi-baladinā*)."

Chapter 12. Intending to Perform the Pilgrimage (*Ḥajj*) and the Visitation (*ʿUmra*) on the Same Trip (*Qirān*)[380]

949. According to Mālik, Jaʿfar b. Muḥammad reported from his father that al-Miqdād b. al-Aswad went to see ʿAlī b. Abī Ṭālib at al-Suqyā, where he was feeding some young camels a mash of crushed grains and leaves. Al-Miqdād said to ʿAlī, "This fellow, ʿUthmān b. ʿAffān, is prohibiting people from performing the Pilgrimage and the Visitation on the same trip." Al-Miqdād said, "ʿAlī stopped what he was doing, and traces of the crushed grains and leaves were still on his hands—and I will never forget the sight of the crushed grains and leaves on his forearms. He went to see ʿUthmān b. ʿAffān and said to him, 'Are you prohibiting people from performing the Pilgrimage and the Visitation on the same trip?' ʿUthmān said, 'That is my opinion.' ʿAlī left angrily, saying, 'I am at Your service, God, I am at Your service, for the Pilgrimage and the Visitation together on the same trip.'"

950. Mālik said, "The rule in our view (*al-amr ʿindanā*) is that someone who intends to perform the Pilgrimage and the Visitation together on the same trip should not cut a single strand of his hair, nor should he exit the consecrated state until he has slaughtered a sacrosanct animal (*hady*),[381] if he has one. He is to exit the consecrated state only at Minā on the Day of the Slaughter of the Sacrosanct Animals (*yawm al-naḥr*)."

---

380 *Qirān* refers to a person's intention to perform the Visitation and the Pilgrimage on the same occasion.

381 *Hady* refers to an animal that has been specifically designated for sacrifice at God's House.

951. According to Mālik, Muḥammad b. ʿAbd al-Raḥmān reported from Sulaymān b. Yasār that when the Messenger of God (pbuh) set out for the Pilgrimage in the year of the Farewell Pilgrimage (*ḥajjat al-wadāʿ*), some of his companions had the intention of performing the Pilgrimage by itself, some intended to perform both the Pilgrimage and the Visitation on the same trip, and some went with the sole intention of performing the Visitation. Those who intended to perform only the Pilgrimage or both the Pilgrimage and the Visitation did not exit the consecrated state until the Day of the Slaughter of the Sacrosanct Animals at Minā. Those who performed only the Visitation exited the consecrated state after completing the rites of the Visitation in Mecca.

952. According to Mālik, he heard some of the people of knowledge say, "A person who entered the consecrated state (*iḥrām*) with the intention to perform only the Visitation but who then later wants to perform the Pilgrimage as well may do so, as long as he has not circumambulated the House (*ṭawāf*), nor marched between the hillocks of Ṣafā and Marwa (*saʿy*).[382] In fact, ʿAbd Allāh b. ʿUmar did this. He said, 'If I am prevented from reaching God's House, we will do what we did when we were with the Messenger of God (pbuh).' He then turned to his companions and said, 'They are both subject to the same rule. I call you to witness that I am now resolved to perform the Pilgrimage, even though I originally set out to perform only the Visitation.'"

953. Mālik said, "The companions of the Messenger of God (pbuh) in the year of the Farewell Pilgrimage entered the consecrated state with the intention of performing only the Visitation, but then the Messenger of God (pbuh) said, 'Whoever has brought a sacrosanct animal (*hady*) with him should now resolve to perform the Pilgrimage in addition to the Visitation. He should not exit the consecrated state until he has completed the performance of both.'"

Chapter 13. The Cessation of Chanting (*Talbiya*)

954. According to Mālik, Muḥammad b. Abī Bakr al-Thaqafī reported that he asked Anas b. Mālik, while the two of them were en route early in the morning from Minā to ʿArafāt, "What was it that you did on this day with

382 *Saʿy* refers to the ritual of going back and forth seven times between the hillocks of Ṣafā and Marwa that is done during the Pilgrimage or the Visitation. It symbolizes Hajar's search for water for Ishmael, her son. Often the term *ṭawāf* is used to denote this rite instead of the term *saʿy*. Because the former term is also used to designate the practice of circumambulating the Kabah, later practice among the jurists was to limit *ṭawāf* to circumambulation and to use *saʿy* for marching between the hillocks of Ṣafā and Marwa. The reports Mālik cites in the *Muwaṭṭaʾ* reflect the older use of *ṭawāf* for both rites.

the Messenger of God (pbuh)?" He said, "Some of us chanted, and no one disapproved of it, while others magnified God (said 'God is great,' *Allāhu akbar*), and no one disapproved of it."

955. According to Mālik, Ja'far b. Muḥammad reported from his father that 'Alī b. Abī Ṭālib would chant during the Pilgrimage (*ḥajj*) until the sun set on the Day of 'Arafa, at which point he would stop. Yaḥyā said, "Mālik said, 'That is the rule that the people of knowledge among us have always followed (*dhālika al-amr alladhī lam yazal 'alayhi ahl al-'ilm 'indanā*).'"

956. According to Mālik, 'Abd al-Raḥmān b. al-Qāsim reported from his father, from 'Ā'isha, the wife of the Prophet (pbuh), that she would cease chanting when she arrived at 'Arafāt in the afternoon.

957. According to Mālik, Nāfi' reported that 'Abd Allāh b. 'Umar would cease chanting during the Pilgrimage once he reached the Sanctuary (*ḥaram*). After he had circumambulated God's House (*ṭawāf*) and marched between the hillocks of Ṣafā and Marwa (*sa'y*), he would resume chanting. He would continue chanting until the morning when he set out from Minā to 'Arafāt. He would cease chanting when he set out that morning. When he performed the Visitation (*'umra*), he would cease chanting once he entered the Sanctuary.

958. According to Mālik, Ibn Shihāb would say, "'Abd Allāh b. 'Umar would not chant while circumambulating God's House."

959. According to Mālik, 'Alqama b. Abī 'Alqama reported from his mother, from 'Ā'isha, the Mother of the Believers, that she would alight in 'Arafāt at Namira, but then she started going to another place called al-Arāk. 'Alqama's mother said, "'Ā'isha and her party would chant as long as they remained encamped, but once she mounted her animal and set out to 'Arafāt, she ceased chanting. 'Ā'isha would perform the Visitation in Mecca in the month of Dhū al-Ḥijja after the Pilgrimage was over. Then she stopped doing that. She would instead set out before the crescent moon of Muḥarram[383] for al-Juḥfa, where she would camp until she saw the crescent moon. When she saw the crescent moon, she would enter the consecrated state (*iḥrām*) with the intention of performing the Visitation."

960. According to Mālik, Yaḥyā b. Sa'īd reported that 'Umar b. 'Abd al-'Azīz set out on the morning of 'Arafa from Minā, when he unexpectedly heard the people magnifying God in a loud voice. He therefore dispatched the guard, who told them in a loud voice, "People! You should instead be chanting!"

---

383 Muḥarram is the first month of the Islamic lunar calendar, and it follows Dhū al-Ḥijja, the twelfth month of the Islamic calendar.

Chapter 14. The Time When Meccans and Non-Meccans in Mecca Enter the Consecrated State (*Iḥrām*)

961. According to Mālik, ʿAbd al-Raḥmān b. al-Qāsim reported from his father that ʿUmar b. al-Khaṭṭāb said, "Meccans! Why is it that while the pilgrims arrive here disheveled, you still have oil on your hair? You should enter the consecrated state when you first see the crescent moon of Dhū al-Ḥijja."

962. According to Mālik, Hishām b. ʿUrwa reported that ʿAbd Allāh b. al-Zubayr lived in Mecca for nine years. He would enter the consecrated state with the intention of performing the Pilgrimage (*ḥajj*) at the beginning of Dhū al-Ḥijja. ʿUrwa b. al-Zubayr was with him at that time and did the same.

963. Yaḥyā said, "Mālik said, 'If Meccans and any non-Meccans living in Mecca intend to perform the Pilgrimage, they should enter the consecrated state inside Mecca itself. They are not required to leave the Sanctuary (*ḥaram*) and enter the consecrated state outside its borders.'"

964. Mālik said, "If someone in Mecca enters the consecrated state with the intention of performing the Pilgrimage, he should defer circumambulation (*ṭawāf*) of God's House and marching between the hillocks of Ṣafā and Marwa (*saʿy*) until he returns from Minā. That is what ʿAbd Allāh b. ʿUmar would do."

965. Mālik was asked how a non-Meccan, whether from Medina or elsewhere, should perform the circumambulation if he enters the consecrated state with the intention of performing the Pilgrimage in Mecca at the beginning of Dhū al-Ḥijja. Mālik said, "He should defer the obligatory circumambulation, which is the one that is performed immediately before marching between the hillocks of Ṣafā and Marwa. He should, however, circumambulate as he wishes, performing two cycles (*rakʿa*) of prayer (*ṣalāt*) for every seven laps he completes. That is what the companions of the Messenger of God (pbuh) did when they entered the consecrated state with the intention of performing the Pilgrimage from Mecca. They delayed circumambulation around God's House and marching between the hillocks of Ṣafā and Marwa until they had returned from Minā. That is also what ʿAbd Allāh b. ʿUmar did. He entered the consecrated state with the intention of performing the Pilgrimage from Mecca at the beginning of Dhū al-Ḥijja, and he delayed circumambulation of God's House and marching between the hillocks of Ṣafā and Marwa until he returned from Minā."

966. Mālik was asked whether a Meccan who wishes to enter the consecrated state with the intention of performing the Visitation (*ʿumra*) may do so inside Mecca itself. He said, "No, he should rather leave the Sanctuary and enter the consecrated state beyond its borders."

Chapter 15. Garlanding Sacrosanct Animals (*Hady*) Does Not Necessitate Entering the Consecrated State (*Iḥrām*)

967. According to Mālik, ʿAbd Allāh b. Abī Bakr b. Ḥazm reported from ʿAmra bt. ʿAbd al-Raḥmān that she told ʿAbd Allāh b. Abī Bakr b. Ḥazm that Ziyād b. Abī Sufyān wrote to ʿĀʾisha, the wife of the Prophet (pbuh), saying, "ʿAbd Allāh b. ʿAbbās said, 'Whatever is prohibited for a pilgrim in the consecrated state is also prohibited for anyone who consecrates an animal and sends it to be slaughtered at God's House until the animal is actually slaughtered.' I have indeed consecrated an animal and sent it for slaughter to God's House, so give me your instructions about this, or instruct the person in charge of the sacrosanct animals.'" ʿĀʾisha said, "No, Ibn ʿAbbās is mistaken. I wove the garlands of the sacrosanct animals of the Messenger of God (pbuh) with my own hands, and then the Messenger of God (pbuh) garlanded the animals with his own hands. He then sent them with my father. Nothing that God had made licit for the Messenger of God (pbuh) prior to garlanding the animals subsequently became prohibited for him."[384]

968. According to Mālik, Yaḥyā b. Saʿīd said, "I asked ʿAmra bt. ʿAbd al-Raḥmān whether anything becomes prohibited for someone who sends a sacrosanct animal to God's House but stays in his hometown. She told me that she had heard ʿĀʾisha say, "Only those who enter the consecrated state and chant (*talbiya*) are subject to any prohibitions."

969. According to Mālik, Yaḥyā b. Saʿīd reported from Muḥammad b. Ibrāhīm b. al-Ḥārith al-Taymī, from Rabīʿa b. ʿAbd Allāh b. al-Hudayr, that he saw a man[385] covered in the fashion of a pilgrim in Iraq, so he asked the people there about him. They said, "He ordered that his animal be garlanded and sent to God's House, and for that reason he removed his clothes and donned the appearance of a pilgrim." Rabīʿa said, "I then met ʿAbd Allāh b. al-Zubayr

384 In other words, according to ʿĀʾisha, the Prophet (pbuh) did not consider the dispatch of animals for sacrifice at God's House during the Pilgrimage to require entering the consecrated state that is obligatory for pilgrims. Accordingly, after sending the animals the Prophet (pbuh) continued to engage in all the activities that would ordinarily be permissible for someone not in the consecrated state, including having intercourse with his wives, using perfume, and grooming, such as clipping the hair and nails. The practice of the Prophet (pbuh) in this case contradicted the opinion of Ibn ʿAbbās on which Ziyād b. Abī Sufyān had relied in his decision to impose on himself the restrictions of the consecrated state once he had sent a sacrosanct animal to be sacrificed at God's House, even though he was not performing the Pilgrimage himself.

385 According to the notes in the RME, other reports indicate that the man in question was ʿAbd Allāh b. ʿAbbās.

and mentioned it to him. He said, 'Islam does not sanction this act, by the Lord of the Kabah!'"

970. Yaḥyā said, "Mālik was asked about a man who set out for God's House with his own sacrosanct animal. The man marked it and garlanded it at Dhū al-Ḥulayfa but did not enter the consecrated state until he arrived al-Juḥfa. Mālik said, 'I dislike that, and the person who did that erred. One should neither garland nor mark one's sacrosanct animal until one enters the consecrated state. The exception to this rule is if the person does not desire to perform the Pilgrimage (*ḥajj*) but wishes only to send the animal to God's House while staying at home with his family.'"

971. Yaḥyā said, "Mālik was asked whether someone who is not in the consecrated state can set out with a sacrificial animal. He said, 'Yes, there is nothing objectionable in that.' Mālik was also asked about the dispute regarding whether someone who garlands a sacrosanct animal but does not intend to perform either the Pilgrimage or the Visitation (*ʿumra*) is subject to the prohibitions of the consecrated state. He said, 'The rule in our view, which we follow in respect of that question (*al-amr ʿindanā alladhī naʾkhudhu bihi fī dhālika*), is the opinion of ʿĀʾisha, the Mother of the Believers. She said, "The Messenger of God (pbuh) dispatched his sacrosanct animals to God's House and then stayed behind, and nothing that God had previously permitted for him subsequently became prohibited for him."'"

Chapter 16. What a Menstruating Woman Does during the Pilgrimage (*Ḥajj*)

972. According to Mālik, Nāfiʿ reported that ʿAbd Allāh b. ʿUmar would say, "A menstruating woman may enter the consecrated state (*iḥrām*) with the intention of performing either the Pilgrimage or the Visitation (*ʿumra*) if she so wishes, but she may not circumambulate God's House (*ṭawāf*) or march between the hillocks of Ṣafā and Marwa (*saʿy*). She should nevertheless attend all the rites of the Pilgrimage with the pilgrims, but she must neither circumambulate God's House nor march between the hillocks of Ṣafā and Marwa, nor can she approach the Sacred Mosque (*al-masjid al-ḥarām*) until she ceases menstruation and bathes."

Chapter 17. The Visitation (*ʿUmra*) during the Months of the Pilgrimage (*Ḥajj*)[386]

973. According to Mālik, it reached him that the Messenger of God (pbuh) performed the Visitation three times: in the year of al-Ḥudaybiya,[387] in the year of the Fulfilled Visitation,[388] and in the year of Jiʿirrāna.[389]

974. According to Mālik, Hishām b. ʿUrwa reported from his father that the Messenger of God (pbuh) performed the Visitation only three times: once in Shawwāl and twice in Dhū al-Qaʿda.

975. According to Mālik, ʿAbd al-Raḥmān b. Ḥarmala al-Aslamī reported that a man asked Saʿīd b. al-Musayyab, "May I perform the Visitation before performing the Pilgrimage?" Saʿīd said, "Yes, the Messenger of God (pbuh) performed the Visitation before the Pilgrimage."

976. According to Mālik, Ibn Shihāb reported from Saʿīd b. al-Musayyab that ʿUmar b. Abī Salama sought the permission of ʿUmar b. al-Khaṭṭāb to perform the Visitation in the month of Shawwāl. ʿUmar gave him permission, so he performed it. He then returned to his family without having performed the Pilgrimage.

Chapter 18. The Cessation of Chanting (*Talbiya*) during the Visitation (*ʿUmra*)

977. According to Mālik, Hishām b. ʿUrwa reported from his father that he would cease chanting during the Visitation when he entered the Sanctuary (*ḥaram*).

978. Yaḥyā said, "Mālik said, 'Whoever enters the consecrated state (*iḥrām*) at al-Tanʿīm[390] with the intention of performing the Visitation should cease chanting when he sees God's House.'"

979. Yaḥyā said, "Mālik was asked when a person from Medina or from another town other than Mecca who begins performance of the Visitation from one of the designated stations (*mawāqīt*) should cease chanting. He said, 'A person who enters the consecrated state at one of the designated

386 The months of the Pilgrimage are Shawwāl, Dhū al-Qaʿda, and Dhū al-Ḥijja, the tenth, eleventh, and twelfth months of the Islamic calendar, respectively.

387 This was year 6 of the Hijra (627 CE).

388 This Visitation took place in year 7 of the Hijra (628 CE) and reflected the agreement that the Prophet (pbuh) had reached with the Meccans the previous year at al-Ḥudaybiya.

389 Named after a place between Mecca and Ṭā'if where the Prophet (pbuh) divided the spoils seized by the Muslims in the Battle of Ḥunayn in year 8 of the Hijra (629 CE).

390 Of the designated stations at which pilgrims must enter the consecrated state, al-Tanʿīm is the closest to the Sacred Mosque. Zurqānī, *Sharḥ al-Zurqānī*, 2:406.

stations should cease chanting when he arrives at the Sanctuary.' He said, 'It has reached me that this was the practice of ʿAbd Allāh b. ʿUmar.'"

Chapter 19. What Has Come Down regarding the Decision to Perform the Pilgrimage (*Ḥajj*) in the Same Year after Performing the Visitation (*ʿUmra*) during the Pilgrimage Season (*Tamattuʿ*)[391]

980. According to Mālik, Ibn Shihāb reported that Muḥammad b. ʿAbd Allāh b. al-Ḥārith b. Nawfal b. ʿAbd al-Muṭṭalib told him that in the year in which Muʿāwiya b. Abī Sufyān performed the Pilgrimage, he heard Saʿd b. Abī Waqqāṣ and al-Ḍaḥḥāk b. Qays discussing the issue of someone deciding to perform the Pilgrimage after already performing the Visitation during the Pilgrimage season. Al-Ḍaḥḥāk b. Qays said, "Only someone ignorant of God's ordinances would do so." Saʿd said, "What you're saying is nonsense, my nephew!" Al-Ḍaḥḥāk said, "But ʿUmar b. al-Khaṭṭāb forbade it." Saʿd said, "The Messenger of God (pbuh), however, did it, and we did it with him."

981. Yaḥyā told me from Mālik, from Ṣadaqa b. Yasār, that ʿAbd Allāh b. ʿUmar said, "By God, I would rather perform the Visitation before the Pilgrimage and offer a sacrificial animal (*hady*) than perform the Visitation in Dhū al-Ḥijja after completing the Pilgrimage."[392]

982. According to Mālik, ʿAbd Allāh b. Dīnār reported that ʿAbd Allāh b. ʿUmar would say, "If someone performs the Visitation during the Pilgrimage season—that is, during Shawwāl, Dhū al-Qaʿda, or Dhū al-Ḥijja—before the Pilgrimage, then stays in Mecca until the Pilgrimage begins, and goes on to perform the Pilgrimage, he is performing *tamattuʿ*. Accordingly, he must offer any sacrificial animal that is conveniently available to him. If he cannot find one, he must fast three days during the Pilgrimage and seven days when he returns home." Mālik said, "That is the case only if he does not depart from Mecca until the Pilgrimage and then performs the Pilgrimage."

983. Mālik said that a Meccan who leaves Mecca to live elsewhere, then returns to perform the Visitation during the Pilgrimage season, and remains there until it is time to set off on the Pilgrimage is performing *tamattuʿ*. He must offer a sacrificial animal, or fast if he cannot find one. He is not to be treated as a Meccan.[393]

---

391 *Tamattuʿ* refers to the practice of entering the consecrated state (*iḥrām*) during the Pilgrimage season with the intention of performing the rites of the Visitation and subsequently reentering the consecrated state to perform the Pilgrimage.

392 A person who performs *tamattuʿ* must offer an animal as a sacrifice.

393 The rules of *tamattuʿ* apply only to non-Meccans.

984. Mālik was asked whether a non-Meccan who enters Mecca to perform the Visitation during the Pilgrimage season with the intention of settling there and then sets out to perform the Pilgrimage is deemed to be performing *tamattu'*. He said, "Yes, he is, and he is not deemed a Meccan, even if he intends to settle there. That is because when he entered Mecca, he was not yet a Meccan. In these circumstances, offering a sacrificial animal and fasting is obligatory for anyone who is not Meccan. Although this man intends to settle in Mecca, he might yet change his mind and leave. Therefore, he is not yet a Meccan."

985. According to Mālik, Yaḥyā b. Sa'īd reported that he heard Sa'īd b. al-Musayyab say, "Whoever performs the Visitation during Shawwāl, Dhū al-Qa'da, or Dhū al-Ḥijja and then stays in Mecca until the Pilgrimage begins is performing *tamattu'*, if he goes on to perfom the Pilgrimage. He therefore must offer any sacrificial animal that is conveniently available to him. If he cannot find one, he must fast three days during the Pilgrimage and seven days when he returns home."

Chapter 20. Circumstances in Which the Rules of *Tamattu'* Do Not Apply

986. Yaḥyā said, "Mālik said, 'Someone who performs the Visitation (*'umra*) in the months of Shawwāl, Dhū al-Qa'da, or Dhū al-Ḥijja, then leaves Mecca and returns to his people, but then performs the Pilgrimage (*ḥajj*) in that very year is not obliged to offer a sacrificial animal (*hady*). Only someone who performs the Visitation during the Pilgrimage season, then stays in Mecca until the time of the Pilgrimage, and then performs the Pilgrimage must offer a sacrificial animal.'"

987. Mālik said, "Anyone who hails from outside of Mecca but moves to Mecca and makes it his permanent home and subsequently performs the Visitation during the Pilgrimage season and then begins his Pilgrimage from Mecca is not performing *tamattu'*. Therefore, he is not obliged to offer a sacrificial animal or to fast. He is treated in the same way as the people of Mecca are because he resides there."

988. Mālik was asked about a Meccan who leaves Mecca to participate in the defense of a frontier town, or who sets off on a journey and then returns to Mecca with the intention of staying there. He enters Mecca to perform the Visitation during the Pilgrimage season and then sets out to perform the Pilgrimage from there. He begins his Visitation at the designated station (*mīqāt*) of the Prophet (pbuh) or at another place before it. He may or may not have family in Mecca. Is a person in such circumstances deemed to be perfoming *tamattu*ʿ? Mālik said, "He is not obliged to offer a sacrificial animal or to fast in the manner of someone performing *tamattu*ʿ. That is because God, Blessed and Sublime is He, says in His Book, 'That obligation is due from those whose families are not settled in the precinct of the Sacred Mosque.'"[394]

Chapter 21. Miscellaneous Matters regarding the Visitation (*ʿUmra*)

989. According to Mālik, Sumayy, the freedman (*mawlā*) of Abū Bakr b. ʿAbd al-Raḥmān, reported from Abū Ṣāliḥ al-Sammān, from Abū Hurayra, that the Messenger of God (pbuh) said, "Performance of the Visitation atones for sins committed since the last Visitation, and the only reward for a righteously performed Pilgrimage (*ḥajj*) is Paradise."

990. According to Mālik, Sumayy, the freedman of Abū Bakr, reported that he heard Abū Bakr b. ʿAbd al-Raḥmān say, "A woman went to the Messenger of God (pbuh) and said, 'I had completed my preparations for the Pilgrimage when something happened that prevented me from setting out.' The Messenger of God (pbuh) said to her, 'Perform the Visitation during Ramaḍān, because performing the Visitation during that month is like performing the Pilgrimage.'"

991. According to Mālik, Nāfiʿ reported from ʿAbd Allāh b. ʿUmar that ʿUmar b. al-Khaṭṭāb said, "Perform the Pilgrimage and the Visitation at separate times. Performing the Visitation outside the Pilgrimage season makes both your Pilgrimage and your Visitation more complete."

992. According to Mālik, it reached him that when ʿUthmān b. ʿAffān set out to perform the Visitation, he would sometimes not dismount from his animal until he had returned.

993. Yaḥyā said, "Mālik said, 'The Visitation is a long-established ordinance (*sunna*), and we know of no Muslim who has ever deemed it dispensable.'"

994. Mālik said, "I do not think that anyone should perform the Visitation more than once a year."

995. Mālik said, regarding a man who has sexual intercourse with his wife while performing the Visitation, "He must offer a sacrificial animal (*hady*) and perform a second Visitation, which he should begin after he finishes the one he invalidated by having intercourse. He should enter the consecrated state (*iḥrām*) in the same place where he entered it for the prior Visitation that he invalidated, unless he entered the consecrated state at a designated station (*mīqāt*) more distant than the designated station at which he

394 *Al-Baqara*, 2:196.

would ordinarily enter the consecrated state. He is not obliged to enter the consecrated state in a place further away than his designated station."

996. Mālik said, "If someone enters Mecca with the intention of performing the Visitation and proceeds to circumambulate (*ṭawāf*) God's House and march between the hillocks of Ṣafā and Marwa (*saʿy*) while either being in a state of ritual preclusion (*junub*) or having neglected to first perform ablutions (*wuḍūʾ*) and then, having completed the rites of the Visitation, has sexual intercourse with his wife and only then remembers that he failed to bathe or perform ablutions prior to performing the Visitation's rites, he should bathe or perform ablutions and then circumambulate God's House and march between the hillocks of Ṣafā and Marwa one more time, perform another Visitation, and offer a sacrificial animal. The woman whose husband had sexual intercourse with her while she was in the consecrated state (*muḥrima*) must do the same."

997. Mālik said, "Whoever wishes to leave the Sanctuary (*ḥaram*) in Mecca to perform a Visitation may enter the consecrated state at al-Tanʿīm—that suffices him, God willing, and he need not go any further. Virtue, however, lies in entering the consecrated state at the station that the Messenger of God (pbuh) designated, and it lies further away than al-Tanʿīm."

Chapter 22. Contracting Marriage While in the Consecrated State (*Iḥrām*)

998. According to Mālik, Rabīʿa b. Abī ʿAbd al-Raḥmān reported from Sulaymān b. Yasār that the Messenger of God (pbuh) sent his freedman (*mawlā*) Abū Rāfiʿ and another Medinese man to conclude his marriage contract with Maymūna bt. al-Ḥārith. The Messenger of God (pbuh) was in Medina at that time before he departed and entered the consecrated state (*iḥrām*).

999. According to Mālik, Nāfiʿ reported from Nubayh b. Wahb of the tribe of Banū ʿAbd al-Dār that ʿUmar b. ʿUbayd Allāh sent a message to Abān b. ʿUthmān, who was in charge of the Pilgrimage caravan at that time, while both of them were in the consecrated state, saying, "I want to contract the marriage of Ṭalḥa b. ʿUmar to Shayba b. Jubayr's daughter, and I want you to attend." Abān rebuked him for that, saying, "I heard ʿUthmān b. ʿAffān say, 'The Messenger of God (pbuh) said, "A man in the consecrated state should not himself marry, contract marriage for another, or become engaged."'"

1000. According to Mālik, Dāwūd b. al-Ḥuṣayn reported that Abū Ghaṭafān b. Ṭarīf al-Murrī told him that his father, Ṭarīf, married a woman while he was in the consecrated state, and ʿUmar b. al-Khaṭṭāb rescinded the marriage.

1001. According to Mālik, Nāfiʿ reported that ʿAbd Allāh b. ʿUmar would say, "A person who is in the consecrated state should not get married himself, become engaged to marry, or arrange the marriage of another."

1002. According to Mālik, it reached him that Saʿīd b. al-Musayyab, Sālim b. ʿAbd Allāh, and Sulaymān b. Yasār were asked whether a person in the consecrated state could marry. They said, "Such a person should neither get married himself nor arrange the marriage of another."

1003. Mālik said that a man in the consecrated state could, if he so wishes, revoke the divorce of his wife, provided that she is still in her waiting period (*ʿidda*) from her marriage to him.[395]

Chapter 23. Cupping While in the Consecrated State (*Iḥrām*)

1004. According to Mālik, Yaḥyā b. Saʿīd reported from Sulaymān b. Yasār that the Messenger of God (pbuh) once had the top of his head cupped while he was in the consecrated state (*iḥrām*) at Laḥyay Jamal, a place on the way to Mecca.

1005. According to Mālik, Nāfiʿ reported that ʿAbd Allāh b. ʿUmar would say, "A person in the consecrated state should not be cupped unless it is necessary to do so, and he has no other alternative."

1006. Yaḥyā said, "Mālik said, 'A person in the consecrated state should not be cupped, unless it is necessary to do so.'"

Chapter 24. The Wild Animals (*Ṣayd*) That a Person in the Consecrated State (*Muḥrim*) Is Permitted to Eat[396]

1007. According to Mālik, Abū al-Naḍr, the freedman (*mawlā*) of ʿUmar b. ʿUbayd Allāh al-Tamīmī, reported from Nāfiʿ, the freedman of Abū Qatāda al-Anṣārī, from Abū Qatāda, that he, along with others, set out with the Messenger of God (pbuh) toward Mecca. Abū Qatāda and a group of his companions fell behind the rest of the party. His companions were in the consecrated state, but he was not. Then, all of a sudden, he encountered a wild ass, so he quickly mounted his horse. He asked his companions to give him his whip, but they ignored him. He then asked them to pass him his spear, and they again ignored him. So he grabbed it himself and charged at the ass, killing it. Some of the companions of the Messenger of God (pbuh)

---

395 *ʿIdda* is the period of time a woman must wait before remarrying after her divorce from her husband or following his death. In an ordinary case of divorce, the husband may revoke his divorce and renew the marriage with his wife during this period. The waiting period is usually three menstrual cycles.

396 The Quran prohibits persons in the consecrated state from killing wild animals. *Al-Māʾida*, 5:95.

ate from it, while others refused. When they finally caught up with the Messenger of God (pbuh), they asked him about eating that meat, and he said, "That is simply food that God has given you."

1008. According to Mālik, Hishām b. 'Urwa reported from his father that al-Zubayr b. al-'Awwām would include strips (*ṣafīf*) of dried antelope meat in his provisions while he was in the consecrated state. Mālik said, "*Ṣafīf* are dried strips of meat."

1009. According to Mālik, Zayd b. Aslam reported that 'Aṭā' b. Yasār told him, from Abū Qatāda, the same report about the wild ass that Abū al-Naḍr reported, except that in Zayd b. Aslam's report the Messenger of God (pbuh) said, "Is any of its meat left?"

1010. According to Mālik, Yaḥyā b. Sa'īd said, "Muḥammad b. Ibrāhīm b. al-Ḥārith al-Taymī told me, from 'Īsā b. Ṭalḥa b. 'Ubayd Allāh, from 'Umayr b. Salama al-Ḍamrī, from al-Bahzī, that the Messenger of God (pbuh) set out for Mecca while in the consecrated state. When they reached al-Rawḥā',[397] a wounded wild ass unexpectedly appeared, and the Messenger of God (pbuh) was informed. He said, 'Leave it be. The hunter who wounded it is certain to show up soon.' Then al-Bahzī, who was the one who shot it, came to the Messenger of God (pbuh) and said, 'Messenger of God, do what you wish with this ass.' The Messenger of God (pbuh) then commanded Abū Bakr to divide its flesh among the company. Then they marched on until they arrived at a well between al-Ruwaytha[398] and al-'Arj, where they happened on an antelope lying in the shade with an arrow stuck in its side. He said that the Messenger of God (pbuh) ordered a man to guard it to make sure that no one interfered with it until all of them had passed."

1011. According to Mālik, Yaḥyā b. Sa'īd reported that he heard Sa'īd b. al-Musayyab relate from Abū Hurayra that when he reached al-Rabadha while he was on his way back to Medina from Baḥrayn, he encountered a caravan of Iraqis who were in the consecrated state. They asked him whether they could eat the meat of some wild animals that some of the people of al-Rabadha had. He told them that they could. Abū Hurayra said, "Later, I had second thoughts about what I told them, so when I arrived in Medina, I mentioned what had happened to 'Umar b. al-Khaṭṭāb, and he said, 'What was your advice to them?' 'I said to them, "Eat it."' 'Umar b. al-Khaṭṭāb said, 'Had you told them anything else, you would have been in real trouble,'" meaning that 'Umar would have rebuked him.

397 A place outside of Medina.
398 A place between Mecca and Medina. Zurqānī, *Sharḥ al-Zurqānī*, 2:416.

1012. According to Mālik, Ibn Shihāb reported from Sālim b. ʿAbd Allāh that he heard Abū Hurayra tell ʿAbd Allāh b. ʿUmar that a group of people in the consecrated state crossed paths with him in al-Rabadha, and they asked him for his opinion about the permissibility of partaking of the wild animal meat that was being eaten by a group of people who were not in the consecrated state.[399] He told them that in his opinion it was permissible for them to do so. He said, "Then I went to ʿUmar b. al-Khaṭṭāb in Medina and asked him about that, and he said, 'What advice did you give them?'" Abū Hurayra said, "I said, 'I advised them that it was permissible to eat.' ʿUmar said, 'Had you advised them otherwise, I would have punished you severely.'"

1013. According to Mālik, Zayd b. Aslam reported from ʿAṭāʾ b. Yasār that Kaʿb al-Aḥbār once came from the Levant to Medina in the company of a group of mounted men. All of them were in the consecrated state. After they had completed part of their journey, they chanced on the meat of some wild animals. Kaʿb advised them that in his opinion it was permissible for them to eat it. ʿAṭāʾ said, "When they arrived and saw ʿUmar b. al-Khaṭṭāb, they told him what had happened, and he said, 'Who advised you to do so?' They said, 'Kaʿb.' He said, 'Indeed, I had appointed him as your commander until your return.' Then, when they were on their way to Mecca, a swarm of locusts crossed their path, so Kaʿb advised them to capture and eat them. When they returned to ʿUmar b. al-Khaṭṭāb, they told him what had happened, and he said, "Kaʿb, what led you to advise them that they could do so?" Kaʿb said, "Locusts are a kind of seafood." ʿUmar said, "How do you know that?" Kaʿb said, "Commander of the Faithful, by Him whose hand holds my soul, they are nothing but the sneeze of a whale, which happens twice a year."[400]

1014. Mālik was asked whether a person in the consecrated state is permitted to purchase wild animal meat that he may find on the way to Mecca. He said, "I disapprove and forbid the sale of the meat of wild animals that were hunted solely for the purpose of selling their meat to pilgrims. There is nothing objectionable, however, in a pilgrim purchasing the meat

399 In other words, the group of people who had not entered the consecrated state had hunted and killed the animals.

400 Later Mālikī commentators on the *Muwaṭṭaʾ* such as Ibn ʿAbd al-Barr and Bājī find this hadith problematic, noting that all jurists, to their knowledge, deem locusts land animals, and that even Kaʿb, as evidenced by a subsequent report in the *Muwaṭṭaʾ*, understood that it was prohibited to kill locusts while in the consecrated state. See hadith no. 1250 below. Ibn ʿAbd al-Barr and Bājī explain ʿUmar's reticence to condemn Kaʿb's action in this case—he neither affirmed Kaʿb's claim about locusts nor denied it—as deference to the possibility that it was based on knowledge that Kaʿb—who was originally Jewish—might have obtained from pre-Islamic scriptural sources. Ibn ʿAbd al-Barr, *al-Istidhkār*, 4:131; Bājī, *al-Muntaqā*, 2:245.

of a wild animal from someone he encounters on the way, provided that the meat was not hunted for the purpose of selling it to pilgrims."

1015. Mālik said that someone who had in his possession a captive wild animal, whether obtained by hunting or by purchase, did not need to free it when he entered the consecrated state, and that there would be nothing objectionable in his leaving it in the care of his family while he performed the Pilgrimage (*ḥajj*).

1016. Mālik said that a person in the consecrated state is permitted to catch fish in seas, rivers, ponds, and similar bodies of water.

Chapter 25. The Wild Animals (*Ṣayd*) That a Person in the Consecrated State (*Muḥrim*) Is Not Permitted to Eat

1017. According to Mālik, Ibn Shihāb reported from ʿUbayd Allāh b. ʿAbd Allāh b. ʿUtba b. Masʿūd, from ʿAbd Allāh b. ʿAbbās, from al-Ṣaʿb b. Jaththāma al-Laythī, that he gave a wild ass to the Messenger of God (pbuh) while he was at al-Abwāʾ (or at Waddān),[401] but the Messenger of God (pbuh) returned it to him. He said, "When the Messenger of God saw the disappointment in my face, he said, 'We refused it only because we are in the consecrated state.'"

1018. According to Mālik, ʿAbd Allāh b. Abī Bakr reported that ʿAbd Allāh b. ʿĀmir b. Rabīʿa said, "I saw ʿUthmān b. ʿAffān at al-ʿArj. It was a hot summer day and he was in the consecrated state. He had covered his face with a red woolen cloth. Later, someone brought him meat from a wild animal, so he told his companions, "Eat!" They said, "Aren't you going to eat?" He said, "I am not in the same position as you. It was hunted and killed only for my sake."

1019. According to Mālik, Hishām b. ʿUrwa reported from his father that ʿĀʾisha, the Mother of the Believers, said to him, "Nephew, the restrictions of the consecrated state last only ten days. If there is any doubt in your mind, shun it." Mālik said, "She meant eating the meat of a wild animal."

1020. Mālik said, regarding a man in the consecrated state for whose sake a wild animal had been captured and cooked and who ate its meat knowing that it had been hunted for his sake, that the man was obliged to offer an equivalent animal as a sacrifice in compensation for that wild animal.[402]

1021. Mālik was asked whether it would be preferable for someone in the consecrated state who is facing the possibility of starvation to hunt and kill a wild animal or to eat carrion. He said, "He should rather eat carrion,

401 Al-Abwāʾ is a mountain and Waddān is a valley, and both lie in the vicinity of al-Juḥfa, one of the designated stations (*mīqāt*) at which pilgrims must enter the consecrated state.

402 *Al-Māʾida*, 5:95.

because God, Blessed and Sublime is He, has not given a dispensation to anyone in the consecrated state to capture and eat a wild animal under any circumstances, but He did give a dispensation to eat carrion in circumstances of possible starvation."

1022. Mālik said, "If someone in the consecrated state kills or slaughters a wild animal, no one may eat it, whether the person is in the consecrated state or not, because it was not lawfully slaughtered. Whether the killing was accidental or intentional, the animal is not permissible to eat." Mālik said, "I heard this rule from numerous persons."

1023. Mālik said that if someone kills and eats a wild animal, he is subject to only a single act of expiation, as is the case with someone who kills a wild animal but does not eat it.

Chapter 26. The Rule regarding Wild Animals (*Ṣayd*) within the Precincts of the Sanctuary (*Ḥaram*)[403]

1024. Mālik said, "It is not permissible to eat any wild animal captured within the precincts of the Sanctuary, nor is it permissible to eat a wild animal if it was captured and killed beyond its precincts, if a hound had been set after it within the Sanctuary's precincts. Anyone who does so must offer compensation for that animal. As for someone who sets his hound on a wild animal outside the Sanctuary's precints, and it pursues and captures the animal within the Sanctuary's precincts, he may not eat the animal, but he is not obliged to offer an animal in compensation, unless he set his hound on it in the vicinity of the Sanctuary's precincts. If he did, then he must offer compensation."

Chapter 27. Determination of the Compensation Due for Unlawfully Killed Wild Animals (*Ṣayd*)

1025. Yaḥyā said, "Mālik said, 'God, Blessed and Sublime is He, says, "O you who believe! Do not kill wild animals while you are in the consecrated state. Whoever does so intentionally must offer in compensation a domesticated animal similar to the one he killed, as determined by two of your just men, as an offering brought to the Kabah; or he shall offer, as expiation, food to the indigent, or the equivalent of that in fasts, so that he may taste of the gravity of his deed."[404] Someone who captures a wild animal when he is not

403 There is no dispute that the rules laid out here apply to the Meccan Sanctuary. However, jurists disagree whether these rules also apply to the Sanctuary of Medina. The Mālikīs hold that they do, whereas the Ḥanafīs argue that they do not. Bājī, *al-Muntaqā*, 2:252.

404 *Al-Mā'ida*, 5:95.

in the consecrated state and then later kills it when he is in that state is in the same position as someone who purchases and kills a wild animal while in the consecrated state. Because God has forbidden killing it, whoever does so must offer compensation for it. The rule in our view (*al-amr ʿindanā*) is that whoever kills a wild animal while in the consecrated state must offer compensation determined by arbitrators.'"

1026. Mālik said, "The best view that I have heard regarding a person who kills a wild animal while in the consecrated state and is under an obligation to offer compensation for that animal as determined by two arbitrators is that the value of the wild animal that he has killed is determined in terms of its equivalent in a staple food.[405] He must feed each poor person a 500-gram measure (*mudd*) of such food. Alternatively, he may fast a number of days equal to the number of poor people he would have had to feed.[406] If their number is ten, he fasts ten days, and if it is twenty, he fasts twenty days. He must fast whatever number it is, even if it exceeds sixty."

1027. Yaḥyā said, "Mālik said, 'I have heard that a person who is not in the consecrated state and kills a wild animal within the Sanctuary's precincts must offer the same compensation that would be imposed on a person who killed a wild animal while he was in the consecrated state.'"

Chapter 28. The Animals That a Person in the Consecrated State (*Muḥrim*) May Kill

1028. According to Mālik, Nāfiʿ reported from ʿAbd Allāh b. ʿUmar that the Messenger of God (pbuh) said, "There are five animals that a person in the consecrated state may kill without sinning: ravens, kites, scorpions, rats, and vicious dogs."[407]

1029. According to Mālik, ʿAbd Allāh b. Dīnār reported from ʿAbd Allāh b. ʿUmar that the Messenger of God (pbuh) said, "A person in the consecrated state is permitted to kill five kinds of animals without sinning: scorpions, rats, vicious dogs, ravens, and kites."

---

405 In other words, the value of the slain wild animal is calculated in measures of a staple food, such as wheat or barley.

406 This means that the food equivalent of the slain wild animal, as determined by the arbitrators, is then divided by 500 to establish how many poor people must be fed. For example, if the pilgrim kills a wild animal and the arbitrators determine that its equivalent in barley is 5,000 grams, the pilgrim is obliged to feed ten poor persons (5,000/500 = 10), or fast ten days.

407 It was understood that the Prophet (pbuh) had singled out the raven and the kite because of their propensity to abscond with the pilgrims' food. The category of the vicious dog was considered by the jurists to include any kind of predatory animal that could threaten a human being, such as a lion, a panther, or the like.

1030. According to Mālik, Hishām b. ʿUrwa reported from his father that the Messenger of God (pbuh) said, "There are five kinds of vicious animals, and these may be killed within the precincts of the Sanctuary (*ḥaram*): rats, scorpions, ravens, kites, and vicious dogs."

1031. According to Mālik, Ibn Shihāb reported that ʿUmar b. al-Khaṭṭāb decreed that snakes within the Sanctuary's precincts were to be killed.

1032. Yaḥyā said, "Mālik said, regarding the intended meaning of the 'vicious dog' that may be killed within the Sanctuary's precincts, 'Whatever bites people, attacks them, and terrorizes them, whether a lion, a cougar, a lynx, or a wolf, is included within "vicious dog." However, a person in the consecrated state may not kill predators that do not ordinarily attack people, such as hyenas, foxes, cats, and similar predators. If he kills one of these, he must offer compensation for it.'"

1033. Mālik said, "The only kinds of harmful birds that those in the consecrated state may kill are those that the Prophet (pbuh) specifically mentioned: ravens and kites. If someone in the consecrated state kills any other kind of bird, he must offer compensation for it."

Chapter 29. What a Person in the Consecrated State (*Muḥrim*) Is Permitted to Do

1034. According to Mālik, Yaḥyā b. Saʿīd reported from Muḥammad b. Ibrāhīm b. al-Ḥārith al-Taymī, from Rabīʿa b. ʿAbd Allāh b. al-Hudayr, that he saw ʿUmar b. al-Khaṭṭāb, while he was in the consecrated state, removing ticks from a camel of his and casting them into the mud at al-Suqyā.[408] Yaḥyā said, "Mālik said, 'I do not approve of that.'"

1035. According to Mālik, ʿAlqama b. Abī ʿAlqama reported that his mother said, "I heard ʿĀʾisha, the wife of the Prophet (pbuh), being asked whether a person in the consecrated state could relieve his itching by scratching his body.[409] She said, 'Yes he can, even abrasively. Even if my hands were bound and I could only scratch myself using my feet, I would certainly do so.'"

1036. According to Mālik, Ayyūb b. Mūsā reported that ʿAbd Allāh b. ʿUmar, while he was in the consecrated state, once looked in the mirror at something that was irritating his eye.

1037. According to Mālik, Nāfiʿ reported that ʿAbd Allāh b. ʿUmar discouraged people in the consecrated state from removing mites and ticks from their

408 A village between Mecca and Medina.

409 The question is motivated by the concern that vigorous scratching of the body might kill the insect that is the cause of the itching.

camels. Mālik said, "Of all the views that I have heard regarding this issue, that view is the one I prefer most."

1038. According to Mālik, Muḥammad b. ʿAbd Allāh b. Abī Maryam reported that he asked Saʿīd b. al-Musayyab about a fingernail of his that broke while he was in the consecrated state. Saʿīd said to him, "Cut it off."[410]

1039. Yaḥyā said, "Mālik was asked whether a man in the consecrated state who complains of an earache may pour drops of unperfumed moringa (*bān*) oil into his ear. He said, 'I see nothing objectionable in that, and even if he were to swallow it, I would still not object.'"

1040. Mālik said, "There is nothing objectionable about someone in the consecrated state lancing an abscess or a boil, or cutting a vein, if he needs to do so."

Chapter 30. Performance of the Pilgrimage (*Ḥajj*) on Behalf of Someone Else

1041. According to Mālik, Ibn Shihāb reported from Sulaymān b. Yasār that ʿAbd Allāh b. ʿAbbās said, "Al-Faḍl b. ʿAbbās was riding behind the Messenger of God (pbuh) on the same animal when a woman of the tribe of Khathʿam appeared, seeking his opinion on a religious matter. Al-Faḍl began to look at her, and she returned his glance, so the Messenger of God (pbuh) turned al-Faḍl's face away from her to the other side. She said, 'Messenger of God! By the time that God made the Pilgrimage a firm obligation, my father had become a very old man and was unable to sit securely on his camel. Should I perform the Pilgrimage on his behalf?' He said, 'Yes!' That took place during the Farewell Pilgrimage (*ḥajjat al-wadāʿ*)."[411]

Chapter 31. What Has Come Down regarding Someone Whose Pilgrimage (*Ḥajj*) or Visitation (*ʿUmra*) Is Interdicted by an Enemy

1042. Mālik said, "Whoever is prevented from completing his journey to God's House by an enemy is freed of the restrictions of the consecrated state (*iḥrām*). He is to slaughter his sacrificial animal (*hady*) and shave his head at the place where he was interdicted. He is under no obligation to make up that Pilgrimage or Visitation."

410 The question is motivated by the fact that one of the restrictions associated with the consecrated state (*iḥrām*) is the prohibition of many forms of personal grooming, such as clipping the nails.

411 According to the editors of the RME, it was Ibn Shihāb, not Ibn ʿAbbās, who said, "That took place during the Farewell Pilgrimage."

1043. According to Mālik, it reached him that the Messenger of God (pbuh) and his companions exited the consecrated state at al-Ḥudaybiya. They then slaughtered their sacrificial animals, shaved their heads, and were freed of all the restrictions of the consecrated state without ever circumambulating God's House (*ṭawāf*) and without their sacrificial animals reaching the Kabah. No reports indicate that the Messenger of God (pbuh) commanded any of his companions or anyone else who was with him at that time to make up any of these unperformed acts or to complete their performance.

1044. According to Mālik, Nāfiʿ reported that when ʿAbd Allāh b. ʿUmar set out from[412] Mecca to perform the Visitation during the Time of the Strife (*fitna*),[413] he said, "If I am prevented from reaching God's House, we will do what we did when we were with the Messenger of God (pbuh)." He entered the consecrated state with the intention of performing the Visitation because the Messenger of God (pbuh) had intended to perform the Visitation in the year of al-Ḥudaybiya.[414] But later, ʿAbd Allāh b. ʿUmar reflected on his decision and said to himself, "Aren't the Pilgrimage and the Visitation both subject to the same rules?" So he turned to his companions and said, "They are subject to the same rules. I call you to witness that I have obliged myself to perform the Pilgrimage along with the Visitation." He then set off, and when he reached God's House, he circumambulated once, concluding that this satisfied his obligations.[415] He then offered his sacrificial animal.

1045. Mālik said, "This is the rule in our view (*al-amr ʿindanā*) concerning someone whom an enemy interdicts from God's House, just as the Prophet (pbuh) and his companions were interdicted. However, if anything other than an enemy prevents a person from reaching God's House, he is not released from the consecrated state. In all other cases, he remains subject to the restrictions of the consecrated state until he arrives at God's House."

---

412 The text of the RME uses the preposition *min*, "from," here, but the notes to the text suggest that this is an error, and the correct preposition is *ilā*, "to," which would mean that he set out for, not from, Mecca.

413 A reference to the civil war that took place between the rival caliphates of ʿAbd al-Malik b. Marwān, who was based in Damascus, and ʿAbd Allāh b. al-Zubayr (d. 73/692), who was based in Mecca. Ibn ʿUmar's trip to Mecca that is referenced in this incident took place in year 72 of the Hijra (691 CE), the year that ʿAbd al-Malik's governor, al-Ḥajjāj b. Yūsuf al-Thaqafī (d. 95/714), laid siege to ʿAbd Allāh b. Zubayr's forces in the Hijaz. See Ibn ʿAbd al-Barr, *al-Istidhkār*, 4:169–70; Zurqānī, *Sharḥ al-Zurqānī*, 2:439–40.

414 In the year of al-Ḥudaybiya (6/628), the Messenger of God (pbuh) and his Companions set out for Mecca, but the Meccans prevented them from reaching their destination. The Muslims concluded a truce with the Meccans that allowed them to return the next year to perform the Pilgrimage rites.

415 In other words, ʿAbd Allāh b. ʿUmar concluded that he needed to circumambulate only once, even though he was performing both the Visitation and the Pilgrimage. Bājī, *al-Muntaqā*, 2:276.

Chapter 32. What Has Come Down regarding Someone Who Has Been Prevented from Reaching God's House by Something Other Than an Enemy

1046. According to Mālik, Ibn Shihāb reported from Sālim b. ʿAbd Allāh that ʿAbd Allāh b. ʿUmar said, "Whomever illness prevents from reaching God's House may not exit the consecrated state (*iḥrām*) until he circumambulates (*ṭawāf*) God's House and marches between the hillocks of Ṣafā and Marwa (*saʿy*). If the circumstances of his illness are such that he can heal only if he dons a garment or applies a medicinal perfume, he should do so and offer compensation."

1047. According to Mālik, Yaḥyā b. Saʿīd reported that it reached him that ʿĀʾisha, the wife of the Prophet (pbuh), would say, "Only arrival at God's House releases a person in the consecrated state from its restrictions."

1048. According to Mālik, Ayyūb b. Abī Tamīma al-Sakhtiyānī reported that a man of extremely advanced age from Basra[416] said, "I set out for Mecca, and on the way there I broke my thigh. I sent a message to Mecca. At that time, ʿAbd Allāh b. ʿAbbās, ʿAbd Allāh b. ʿUmar, and other learned people were there, but none of them permitted me to exit the consecrated state. Consequently, I stayed put at that well for seven months until I healed. I exited the consecrated state only by performing the Visitation (*ʿumra*)."

1049. According to Mālik, Ibn Shihāb reported from Sālim b. ʿAbd Allāh that ʿAbd Allāh b. ʿUmar said, "Whomever illness prevents from arriving at God's House cannot exit the consecrated state until he circumambulates God's House and marches between the hillocks of Ṣafā and Marwa."

1050. According to Mālik, Yaḥyā b. Saʿīd reported from Sulaymān b. Yasār that Maʿbad b. Ḥuzāba al-Makhzūmī was thrown off his mount on the way to Mecca while he was in the consecrated state. He inquired after learned people nearby, and he was able to find ʿAbd Allāh b. ʿUmar, ʿAbd Allāh b. al-Zubayr, and Marwān b. al-Ḥakam. He told them what had happened to him. Each of them directed him to take whatever medication he needed and to offer compensation for doing so. Then, once he healed, he should perform the Visitation and exit the consecrated state. He would then be obliged to perform the Pilgrimage (*ḥajj*) the following year and to offer whatever sacrificial animal (*hady*) was conveniently available to him. Mālik said, "The rule among us is in accordance with that (*ʿalā dhālika al-amr ʿindanā*) with respect to anyone who is impeded by something other than an enemy."

416 The Arabs founded the garrison town of Basra after their conquest of Iraq.

1051. Yaḥyā said, "Mālik said, "Umar b. al-Khaṭṭāb commanded Abū Ayyūb al-Anṣārī and Habbār b. al-Aswad, who missed the Pilgrimage because they arrived on the Day of the Slaughter of the Sacrosanct Animals (*yawm al-naḥr*),[417] to exit the consecrated state by performing the Visitation. He told them that they were permitted to return home free of the consecrated state's restrictions, but that they were under an obligation to perform the Pilgrimage in an upcoming year and to offer a sacrificial animal or, if unable to find one, to fast three days during the Pilgrimage and seven upon returning to their families.'"

1052. Mālik said, "Anyone who has been prevented from performing the Pilgrimage after entering the consecrated state, whether on account of illness or something else, or by a mistake in calculating the days of the month, or because the crescent moon was hidden from him, falls into the category of the impeded (*muḥṣar*) and must do what the impeded do."

1053. Mālik was asked about a Meccan who enters the consecrated state with the intention of performing the Pilgrimage but then breaks a bone, is afflicted with diarrhea, or goes into labor. He said, "Any Meccan to whom this happens is considered impeded and has the same obligations as non-Meccans when they are prevented from performing the Pilgrimage."

1054. Mālik said, regarding someone who comes to perform the Visitation during the Pilgrimage season and then, after completing the Visitation's rites, enters the consecrated state in Mecca to perform the Pilgrimage but then suffers a broken bone or another disabling affliction that prevents him from attending ʿArafāt with the people, "I think that he should stay where he is until he regains his health. Then he should depart the Sanctuary, reenter Mecca from beyond its precincts, circumambulate God's House, and march between the hillocks of Ṣafā and Marwa. Then he may exit the consecrated state. He is then obliged to perform the Pilgrimage in an upcoming year and to offer a sacrificial animal."

1055. Yaḥyā said, "Mālik said, regarding someone who enters the consecrated state in Mecca with the intention of performing the Pilgrimage, then circumambulates God's House and marches between the hillocks of Ṣafā and Marwa, and then falls ill and so is unable to attend ʿArafāt with the people, 'If he misses the Pilgrimage, he should, if he can, leave the Sanctuary and then reenter it with the intention of performing the Visitation. He then circumambulates God's House and marches between the hillocks of Ṣafā and

417 In order to perform the Pilgrimage successfully, the pilgrim must be present at ʿArafāt for at least a portion of the ninth day of Dhū al-Ḥijja. In this case, the two men arrived only on the tenth day and were therefore unable to perform the Pilgrimage.

Marwa again, because he did not intend the initial performance of these rites to be for the Visitation. For this reason, he must repeat them. He is still obliged to perform the Pilgrimage in an upcoming year and to offer a sacrificial animal. If he is not a Meccan, and a disabling illness befalls him that prevents him from performing the Pilgrimage but he has already circumambulated God's House and marched between the hillocks of Ṣafā and Marwa, he should exit the consecrated state by performing the Visitation. Therefore, he should circumambulate God's House and march between the hillocks of Ṣafā and Marwa a second time, because his initial performance of these rites was intended for the Pilgrimage. He remains obliged to perform the Pilgrimage in an upcoming year and to offer a sacrificial animal.'"

Chapter 33. What Has Come Down regarding the Construction of the Kabah

1056. According to Mālik, Ibn Shihāb reported from Sālim b. ʿAbd Allāh that ʿAbd Allāh b. Muḥammad b. Abī Bakr al-Ṣiddīq told ʿAbd Allāh b. ʿUmar from ʿĀʾisha that the Prophet (pbuh) said, "Did you know that your people, when they built the Kabah, were not faithful to the dimensions of Abraham's original structure?"[418] She said, "I said in response, 'Messenger of God, shouldn't you restore it to the way Abraham built it?' The Messenger of God (pbuh) said, 'I would, if only your people had not emerged from their idolatry just yesterday!'" ʿAbd Allāh b. ʿUmar said, "If indeed ʿĀʾisha heard this from the Messenger of God (pbuh), I believe that the Messenger of God (pbuh) refrained from touching the two corners adjacent to the Ḥijr[419] only because the physical structure of God's House was not in conformity with what Abraham had built."

1057. According to Mālik, Hishām b. ʿUrwa reported from his father that ʿĀʾisha, the Mother of the Believers, said, "It makes no difference to me whether I perform my prayer inside the Ḥijr or within God's House."

1058. According to Mālik, he heard Ibn Shihāb say, "I heard one of our learned men say that the Ḥijr was demarcated with a wall only out of a desire to force people to circumambulate beyond it and thus to guarantee that their circumambulation (*ṭawāf*) would encompass the entirety of the original perimeter of God's House."

418 He meant that it was smaller than the original structure, which was rectangular rather than cubic.

419 The Ḥijr is the section of the Sanctuary immediately north of the Kabah that is marked with a semicircular wall. The wall is reported to indicate the original foundations of the Kabah as built by Abraham. In light of ʿĀʾisha's report, ʿAbd Allāh b. ʿUmar interpreted the Prophet's decision to refrain from touching the two corners of the Kabah adjacent to the Ḥijr as reflecting the fact that the existing corners were not the corners of the original structure.

Chapter 34. Pacing Briskly with Short Steps (*Raml*) during Circumambulation (*Ṭawāf*)

1059. According to Mālik, Jaʿfar b. Muḥammad reported from his father that Jābir b. ʿAbd Allāh said, "I saw the Messenger of God (pbuh) pace briskly with short steps (*raml*) as he completed three laps around God's House, starting from the Black Stone."[420] Mālik said, "That is the practice that the people of knowledge in our town have always followed (*dhālika al-amr alladhī lam yazal ʿalayhi ahl al-ʿilm bi-baladinā*)."

1060. According to Mālik, Nāfiʿ reported that ʿAbd Allāh b. ʿUmar would circumambulate God's House three times, walking briskly with short steps and beginning from the Black Stone. He would then circumambulate it four times while walking.

1061. According to Mālik, Hishām b. ʿUrwa reported that when his father ʿUrwa circumambulated God's House, he would move at a brisk pace for the first three laps, reciting the following couplet in a low voice:

> God, there is no god but You,
> And You revive the dead after You made them die.[421]

1062. According to Mālik, Hishām b. ʿUrwa reported from his father that he saw ʿAbd Allāh b. al-Zubayr enter the consecrated state (*iḥrām*) at al-Tanʿīm with the intention of performing the Visitation (*ʿumra*). Hishām said, "Then my father saw him march three laps at a quick pace around God's House."

1063. According to Mālik, Nāfiʿ reported that if ʿAbd Allāh b. ʿUmar entered the consecrated state in Mecca, he would neither circumambulate God's House nor march between the hillocks of Ṣafā and Marwa (*saʿy*) until he returned from Minā. Moreover, when he entered the consecrated state in Mecca, he would not circumambulate God's House with a quick pace.

Chapter 35. Saluting (*Istilām*) the Corners of the Kabah during Circumambulation (*Ṭawāf*)

1064. According to Mālik, it reached him that when the Messenger of God (pbuh) completed circumambulation of God's House, he would perform

---

420 According to the editors of the RME, when the Prophet (pbuh) and his companions came to Mecca to perform the Visitation in year 7 of the Hijra (628 CE) in accordance with the Treaty of al-Ḥudaybiya, which had been concluded the previous year, the pagans of Mecca spread rumors that the Prophet and his companions had become weak and sickly as a result of the fevers that were endemic to Medina. The Prophet, therefore, ordered his companions to circumambulate God's House three times at a brisk pace, using short steps, to show the pagans that they were strong and in good health.

421 *Allāhumma lā ilāha illā anta, wa-anta tuḥyī baʿda an amattā.*

two cycles (*rakʿa*) of prayer (*ṣalāt*), and when he wanted to leave the Kabah to march between the hillocks of Ṣafā and Marwa (*saʿy*), he would salute the corner of the Kabah that contained the Black Stone before leaving.

1065. According to Mālik, Hishām b. ʿUrwa reported that his father said, "The Messenger of God (pbuh) said to ʿAbd al-Raḥmān b. ʿAwf, 'What is your practice, Abū Muḥammad, with respect to saluting the corner of the Kabah that contains the Black Stone?' ʿAbd al-Raḥmān said, 'Sometimes I salute it, and sometimes I don't.' The Messenger of God (pbuh) said, 'That's exactly right.'"

1066. According to Mālik, Hishām b. ʿUrwa reported that his father, ʿUrwa, would salute all four corners of the Kabah when he circumambulated God's House, and that he would not fail to salute the Yemeni corner unless physically prevented from doing so.

Chapter 36. Kissing the Black Stone When Saluting (*Istilām*) the Corner Containing It

1067. According to Mālik, Hishām b. ʿUrwa reported from his father that ʿUmar b. al-Khaṭṭāb said to the Black Stone, while he was circumambulating God's House, "You are just a stone, and had I not seen the Messenger of God (pbuh) kiss you, I would not do so." Then he kissed it.

1068. Mālik said, "I have heard some people of knowledge express the preference that a person who circumambulates God's House touch his hand to his mouth after removing it from the Yemeni corner."

Chapter 37. The Two Cycles (*Rakʿa*) of Prayer (*Ṣalāt*) after Circumambulation (*Ṭawāf*)

1069. According to Mālik, Hishām b. ʿUrwa reported from his father that he would not perform two sets of seven laps around God's House consecutively without praying between them. He would perform two cycles of prayer after every set of seven laps. Sometimes he would pray at Abraham's Standing Place,[422] sometimes elsewhere.

1070. Yaḥyā said, "Mālik was asked whether it was permissible for someone to complete two or more sets of seven laps consecutively around God's House and then pray whatever number of cycles he owed in respect of those sets of seven laps, if that would be easier for him. He said, 'That is improper. The long-established ordinance (*al-sunna*) is that after each set of seven laps, one must perform two cycles of prayer.'"

---

422 *Maqām Ibrāhīm*, where Abraham is believed to have stood as he built the Kabah.

1071. Mālik said, regarding someone who begins to circumambulate God's House and then loses track of how many laps he has completed and ends up completing eight or nine, "He should stop once he knows that he has exceeded the correct number and then perform two cycles of prayer, ignoring any additional laps. Nor should he add to the nine laps that he has performed to reach fourteen and then perform prayers for the two sets of seven together, because the long-established ordinance with respect to circumambulation is that every set of seven laps is followed by the performance of two cycles of prayer."

1072. Mālik said, "If a person performs the two cycles of prayer due upon completion of circumambulation but entertains doubts as to whether he in fact completed seven laps, he should go back and circumambulate further until he is certain that he has completed them. He should then repeat the performance of the two cycles of prayer, because the prayer performed upon the completion of circumambulation is valid only after completion of seven laps."

1073. Mālik said, "As for someone whose ritual purity becomes nullified while he is circumambulating God's House or while he is marching between the hillocks of Ṣafā and Marwa (*saʿy*), or between the two rites, and if he has completed some or all of the seven laps of circumambulation but has not yet performed the two cycles of prayer due upon completion of circumambulation, he should perform ablutions (*wuḍūʾ*) and then perform the circumambulation and the two cycles of prayer afresh."

1074. Mālik said, "As for marching between the hillocks of Ṣafā and Marwa, the nullification of a person's ritual purity does not stop him from completing that rite, but no one should begin marching unless he is in a state of ritual purity after ablutions."

Chapter 38. Performing Prayer (*Ṣalāt*) after Circumambulation (*Ṭawāf*) Following the Morning Prayer (*Ṣalāt al-Ṣubḥ*) and Afternoon Prayer (*Ṣalāt al-ʿAṣr*)

1075. According to Mālik, Ibn Shihāb reported from Ḥumayd b. ʿAbd al-Raḥmān b. ʿAwf that ʿAbd al-Raḥmān b. ʿAbd al-Qārī told him that he circumambulated God's House with ʿUmar b. al-Khaṭṭāb after the Morning Prayer had been performed. When ʿUmar finished his circumambulation, he looked up and saw that the sun had not yet risen, so he mounted his camel and rode until he reached Dhū Ṭuwā,[423] where he dismounted and performed two cycles (*rakʿa*) of prayer.

423 A valley in Mecca.

1076. According to Mālik, Abū al-Zubayr al-Makkī said, "I saw ʿAbd Allāh b. ʿAbbās circumambulate God's House after the Afternoon Prayer had concluded. He then went into his room, and I do not know what he did."

1077. According to Mālik, Abū al-Zubayr al-Makkī said, "I noticed that upon the conclusion of the Morning and Afternoon Prayers, God's House would empty, and no one would circumambulate it."

1078. Mālik said, "If a person has completed some laps of his circumambulation and then the Morning or Afternoon Prayer is called, he should pray with the imam and then complete the rest of his seven laps, beginning where he left off; however, he should not perform the prayer for circumambulation until the sun rises or sets." Mālik said, "There is nothing objectionable in delaying performance of the two cycles of prayer until one performs the Sunset Prayer (*ṣalāt al-maghrib*)."

1079. Mālik said, "There is nothing objectionable in completing a single performance of circumambulation, consisting of seven laps, after the Morning and Afternoon Prayers, but no one should perform more than one set of seven. If a person performs the circumambulation after the Morning Prayer, he defers performance of the two cycles of prayer until the sun rises, as ʿUmar b. al-Khaṭṭāb did. If he does so after the Afternoon Prayer, he defers them until the sun sets. If the sun has set, he can perform them immediately, if he so wishes, or he can defer them until he performs the Evening Prayer. There is nothing objectionable in that."

Chapter 39. Bidding Farewell to God's House[424]

1080. According to Mālik, Nāfiʿ reported from ʿAbd Allāh b. ʿUmar that ʿUmar b. al-Khaṭṭāb said, "Let no pilgrim depart for home until he has circumambulated God's House, for the final rite of the Pilgrimage (*ḥajj*) is circumambulation (*ṭawāf*)."

1081. Mālik said, regarding ʿUmar b. al-Khaṭṭāb's statement "The final rite of the Pilgrimage is circumambulation," "We believe, and God knows best, that it is because of the statement of God, Blessed and Sublime is He, 'Whoever honors the rites of God—that comes truly from the hearts' piety,'[425] and His statement 'Then their destination is the Ancient House.'[426] Accordingly, all rites should begin and conclude at the Ancient House (*al-bayt al-ʿatīq*)."[427]

---

424 This is a reference to the concluding ritual act of the Pilgrimage, which is to circumambulate God's House. This final act of circumambulation is known as the Farewell Circumambulation (*ṭawāf al-wadāʿ*).

425 *Al-Ḥajj*, 22:32.

426 *Al-Ḥajj*, 22:33.

427 The "Ancient House" is another name for the Kabah.

1082. According to Mālik, Yaḥyā b. Saʿīd reported that a man once left Mecca without bidding farewell to God's House, reaching as far as Marr Ẓahrān.[428] When ʿUmar b. al-Khaṭṭāb learned of this, he ordered the man to return in order to do it.

1083. According to Mālik, Hishām b. ʿUrwa reported that his father said, "Whoever performs the Circumambulation of the March (*ṭawāf al-ifāḍa*) has completed the Pilgrimage in the eyes of God. If, however, there is nothing detaining him, it is fitting that circumambulation of God's House be the very last thing he does in Mecca. If, however, something detains him or prevents him from circumambulating, God deems his Pilgrimage to be complete without it."

1084. Mālik said, "If a man doesn't realize that the last thing he should do before leaving Mecca is to circumambulate God's House, and he departs without doing so, he is not under any specific obligation to do anything, provided that he performed the Circumambulation of the March. If he is nearby, however, he ought to return, circumambulate, and then depart."

Chapter 40. Miscellaneous Matters Related to Circumambulation (*Ṭawāf*)

1085. According to Mālik, Abū al-Aswad Muḥammad b. ʿAbd al-Raḥmān b. Nawfal reported from ʿUrwa b. al-Zubayr, from Zaynab bt. Abī Salama, that Umm Salama, the wife of the Prophet (pbuh), said, "I once complained to the Messenger of God (pbuh), saying, 'I am ill.' He told me, 'Circumambulate God's House while riding behind the people.'" She said, "I therefore circumambulated while the Messenger of God (pbuh) prayed next to God's House. He was reciting 'By the mount, and by a Book transcribed.'"[429]

1086. According to Mālik, Abū al-Zubayr al-Makkī reported that Abū Māʿiz al-Aslamī ʿAbd Allāh b. Sufyān told him that while he was sitting with ʿAbd Allāh b. ʿUmar, a woman appeared, asking ʿAbd Allāh's opinion on a matter of religious law. She said, "I set out intending to circumambulate God's House, but just as I arrived at the door of the Sacred Mosque (*al-masjid al-ḥarām*), I began to bleed, so I left until the bleeding stopped. Then I set out again, but when I arrived at the door of the Sacred Mosque, the bleeding resumed, so I again left until the bleeding stopped. Then I set out again, but when I arrived at the door of the Sacred Mosque a third time, the bleeding started up again." ʿAbd Allāh b. ʿUmar said, "That is merely the work of the Devil. Bathe and wrap a cloth tightly around your waist and between your legs, and then circumambulate."

---

428 A valley at a distance of eighteen *mīl*s (about 19 km) from Mecca.

429 *Al-Ṭūr*, 52:1–2.

1087. According to Mālik, it reached him that when Saʿd b. Abī Waqqāṣ was tardy in arriving in Mecca and feared that he would not make the Pilgrimage (*ḥajj*), he would set out to ʿArafāt immediately, without first circumambulating God's House and marching between the hillocks of Ṣafā and Marwa (*saʿy*). He would perform these rites later, when he returned from Minā. Mālik said, "There is wide latitude for that, God willing."

1088. Yaḥyā said, "Mālik was asked, 'Can a man who is performing an obligatory circumambulation of God's House stop and talk with another man?' He said, 'I don't think it's a good idea for him to do that.'"

1089. Mālik said, "No one should circumambulate God's House or march between the hillocks of Ṣafā and Marwa unless he is in a state of ritual purity."

Chapter 41. Starting with Ṣafā When Performing the March between the Hillocks of Ṣafā and Marwa (*Saʿy*)

1090. According to Mālik, Jaʿfar b. Muḥammad b. ʿAlī reported from his father that Jābir b. ʿAbd Allāh said, "I heard the Messenger of God (pbuh) say as he was leaving the Sacred Mosque (*al-masjid al-ḥarām*) for Ṣafā, 'We begin with that with which God began.'[430] And so he began his march at Ṣafā."

1091. According to Mālik, Jaʿfar b. Muḥammad b. ʿAlī reported from his father, from Jābir b. ʿAbd Allāh, that when the Messenger of God (pbuh) stopped atop the hillock of Ṣafā, he would magnify God (say "God is great," *Allāhu akbar*) three times and then say, "There is no god except God, alone without partner; to Him belongs the kingdom and all praise, and He has power over all things." Jābir said, "He would say this three times and then supplicate. He would then do the same at the top of the hillock of Marwa."

1092. According to Mālik, Nāfiʿ reported that he heard ʿAbd Allāh b. ʿUmar supplicate on top of the hillock of Ṣafā, saying, "God! You indeed did say, 'Call on Me, and I will respond to you,'[431] and You do not break Your promise. I therefore beseech You: just as You have guided me to Islam, do not take it away from me, and take my soul as a Muslim."

Chapter 42. Miscellaneous Matters Related to the March between the Hillocks of Ṣafā and Marwa (*Saʿy*)

1093. According to Mālik, Hishām b. ʿUrwa reported that his father said, "I said to ʿĀʾisha, the Mother of the Believers—and I was but a youth at the

---

430 A reference to *al-Baqara*, 2:158, "Indeed, the hillocks of Ṣafā and Marwa are among the sacred rites of God."

431 *Al-Ghāfir*, 40:60.

time—'Have you considered the statement of God, Blessed and Sublime is He, "Indeed! The hillocks of Ṣafā and Marwa are among the sacred rites of God. No sin is there for the one seeking God's House as a pilgrim or a visitor to march between them"?[432] Doesn't that mean, therefore, that if someone were not to march between them, he would incur no sin?' ʿĀʾisha said, 'No, that's completely wrong. Were it as you say, it would have been "There is no sin for him in not marching between them." This verse was revealed on account of the Medinese. Before Islam they would make a pilgrimage for the sake of Manāt.[433] The shrine of Manāt was located near Qudayd,[434] and they would refuse to march between Ṣafā and Marwa. When Islam came, they asked the Messenger of God (pbuh) about marching between Ṣafā and Marwa, and so God, Blessed and Sublime is He, revealed the verse, "Indeed! The hillocks of Ṣafā and Marwa are among the sacred rites of God. No sin is there for the one seeking God's House as a pilgrim or a visitor to march between them."'"

1094. According to Mālik, Hishām b. ʿUrwa reported that Sawda bt. ʿAbd Allāh b. ʿUmar was with ʿUrwa b. al-Zubayr, and she set out on foot to march between the hillocks of Ṣafā and Marwa as part of either the Pilgrimage (*ḥajj*) or the Visitation (*ʿumra*). Because she was a heavyset woman, she started to march after performing the Evening Prayer (*ṣalāt al-ʿishāʾ*), when the people had departed, and managed to complete marching only at the time of the first call to the Morning Prayer (*ṣalāt al-ṣubḥ*); that is, she completed her march between the call to the Evening Prayer and the first call to the Morning Prayer. Hishām said, "If ʿUrwa saw anyone going between the two hillocks while mounted on a beast, he would admonish them in the strongest language. Feeling ashamed, they would make excuses by feigning illness. He would say to us in private about such people, 'They have failed to perform God's rites properly and so lost their opportunity for a full reward.'"

1095. Yaḥyā said, "Mālik said, 'If someone forgets to march between the hillocks of Ṣafā and Marwa during the performance of the Visitation and does not remember until he is far away from Mecca, he must return and march. Even if, in the meantime, he has had intercourse with a woman, he must still return and march to complete the unfinished rites of that Visitation. He is then obliged to perform another Visitation and to offer a sacrificial animal (*hady*).'"

432 *Al-Baqara*, 2:158.
433 Manāt was one of the principal goddesses worshipped by the pre-Islamic Arabians.
434 A village between Mecca and Medina.

1096. Yaḥyā said, "Mālik was asked about a man who meets another man when marching between the hillocks of Ṣafā and Marwa and stops to talk to him. Mālik said, 'I discourage him from doing so.'"

1097. Mālik said, "If someone forgets part of his circumambulation (*ṭawāf*) or becomes uncertain about it, but does not remember the matter until he is marching between the hillocks of Ṣafā and Marwa, he should cease marching and go and circumambulate God's House until he is certain that he has completed seven laps. Then he prays the two cycles (*rakʿa*) of the prayer (*ṣalāt*) for circumambulation. He then begins his march between the hillocks of Ṣafā and Marwa anew."

1098. According to Mālik, Jaʿfar b. Muḥammad b. ʿAlī reported from his father, from Jābir b. ʿAbd Allāh, that when the Messenger of God (pbuh) descended from the top of Ṣafā and Marwa, he walked until his feet reached the bottom of the valley, at which point his gait quickened until he emerged from it.

1099. Mālik said, regarding a man who, out of ignorance, marches between the hillocks of Ṣafā and Marwa before circumambulating God's House, "He must go back and circumambulate God's House and then march between the hillocks of Ṣafā and Marwa. If he does not realize this until he has left Mecca and is far away, he must return to Mecca, circumambulate God's House, and march between the hillocks of Ṣafā and Marwa. If, in the meantime, he has had intercourse with a woman, he must nonetheless return, circumambulate God's House, and march between the hillocks of Ṣafā and Marwa to complete the unfinished rites of that Visitation. He must, however, perform another Visitation at a later date and offer a sacrificial animal."

Chapter 43. Fasting on the Day of ʿArafa

1100. According to Mālik, Abū al-Naḍr, the freedman (*mawlā*) of ʿUmar b. ʿUbayd Allāh, reported from ʿUmayr, the freedman of ʿAbd Allāh b. ʿAbbās, from Umm al-Faḍl bt. al-Ḥārith, that some people were arguing in front of her on the Day of ʿArafa about whether the Messenger of God (pbuh) was fasting. Some of them said he was, and others said he was not. She said, "To find out, I sent him a bowl of milk when he had halted his mount at ʿArafāt, and he drank."

1101. According to Mālik, Yaḥyā b. Saʿīd reported from al-Qāsim b. Muḥammad that ʿĀʾisha, the Mother of the Believers, would fast on the Day of ʿArafa. Al-Qāsim said, "When the imam[435] would begin to leave at dusk on

435 That is, the leader of the Pilgrimage caravan.

the Day of ʿArafa, I noticed that she would stay put until the people left. She would then ask for something to drink and break her fast with."

Chapter 44. What Has Come Down regarding Fasting during the Days of Minā

1102. According to Mālik, Abū al-Naḍr, the freedman (*mawlā*) of ʿUmar b. ʿUbayd Allāh, reported from Sulaymān b. Yasār that the Messenger of God (pbuh) prohibited fasting on the Days of Minā.

1103. According to Mālik, Ibn Shihāb reported that the Messenger of God (pbuh) sent ʿAbd Allāh b. Ḥudhāfa out during the Days of Minā to circulate among the people and to tell them, "Certainly, these are days for eating and drinking, and for the remembrance of God."

1104. According to Mālik, Muḥammad b. Yaḥyā b. Ḥabbān reported from al-Aʿraj, from Abū Hurayra, that the Messenger of God (pbuh) prohibited fasting on two days: the Day of the Feast of Breaking the Ramaḍān Fast (*ʿīd al-fiṭr*) and the Day of the Feast of the Sacrificial Animals (*ʿīd al-aḍḥā*).

1105. According to Mālik, Yazīd b. ʿAbd Allāh b. al-Hādī reported from Abū Murra, the freedman of Umm Hānī, the wife of ʿAqīl b. Abī Ṭālib, that ʿAbd Allāh b. ʿAmr b. al-ʿĀṣī told him that he went to see his father, ʿAmr b. al-ʿĀṣī, and found him eating. He said, "My father asked me to eat, so I said to him, 'I am fasting.' He said to me, 'These are the days that the Messenger of God (pbuh) prohibited us from fasting, and during which he ordered us to eat and drink.'" Mālik said, "These are the Festival Days (*ayyām al-tashrīq*)[436] that follow the Feast of the Sacrificial Animals."

Chapter 45. What Qualifies as a Consecrated Animal (*Hady*)

1106. According to Mālik, Nāfiʿ reported from ʿAbd Allāh b. Abī Bakr b. Muḥammad b. ʿAmr b. Ḥazm that the Messenger of God (pbuh) offered in sacrifice a camel that had once belonged to Abū Jahl b. Hishām,[437] either during the Pilgrimage (*ḥajj*) or during the Visitation (*ʿumra*).

1107. According to Mālik, Abū al-Zinād reported from al-Aʿraj, from Abū Hurayra, that the Messenger of God (pbuh) saw a man driving forward a camel, so he told him, "Ride it!" The man said, "But Messenger of God, it is

---

436 The days of *tashrīq* are the eleventh, twelfth, and thirteenth days of Dhū al-Ḥijja.

437 Abū Jahl b. Hishām was one of the fiercest opponents of the Prophet Muḥammad (pbuh) in Mecca and one of the chief persecutors of early Muslims. His actual name was ʿAmr b. Hishām b. al-Mughīra, and he was known as Abū al-Ḥakam. The name "Abū al-Ḥakam" connoted wisdom and sagacity, so the early Muslims renamed him "Abū Jahl," meaning ignorant and impetuous, on account of his ferocious opposition to Islam. He died in the Battle of Badr.

consecrated for sacrifice." The Messenger of God then said to him, "Ride it, confound you!" at least two or three times.

1108. According to Mālik, ʿAbd Allāh b. Dīnār reported that he noticed that ʿAbd Allāh b. ʿUmar would offer for sacrifice a pair of camels during the Pilgrimage and only one camel during the Visitation. ʿAbd Allāh b. Dīnār said, "During a Visitation that he was performing, he encamped in the environs of Khālid b. Asīd's home. I saw him slaughter a camel of his as it stood there. I saw him pierce its throat with his spear tip until it emerged from under its shoulder."

1109. According to Mālik, Yaḥyā b. Saʿīd reported that ʿUmar b. ʿAbd al-ʿAzīz once offered a camel for sacrifice during a Pilgrimage or a Visitation.

1110. According to Mālik, Abū Jaʿfar al-Qārī reported that ʿAbd Allāh b. ʿAyyāsh b. Abī Rabīʿa al-Makhzūmī once offered two camels for sacrifice, one of which was a strong, speedy camel.

1111. According to Mālik, Nāfiʿ reported that ʿAbd Allāh b. ʿUmar would say, "If a she-camel that has been consecrated for sacrifice gives birth, her calf should be brought along so they may be sacrificed together, and if there is no animal to bear it, it should be borne on its mother's back until it is slaughtered with her."

1112. According to Mālik, Hishām b. ʿUrwa reported that his father said, "If you are compelled to use your consecrated animal, ride it, but without unduly burdening it. If you are in need of its milk, drink only after its calf has drunk, and when you slaughter it, slaughter its calf with it."

Chapter 46. The Practice (*ʿAmal*) with Respect to the Treatment of Consecrated Animals (*Hady*) En Route to God's House

1113. According to Mālik, Nāfiʿ reported from ʿAbd Allāh b. ʿUmar that when he consecrated an animal for sacrifice in Medina, he would garland it and mark it at Dhū al-Ḥulayfa. He would first garland it and then mark it. He would perform both acts in the same place, with the animal facing the direction of Mecca. He would garland it with two sandals and mark it on its left side. It would then be driven with him until it, along with everyone else, halted at ʿArafāt. Then Ibn ʿUmar would drive it along when everyone left ʿArafāt for Minā. When he arrived at Minā on the morning of the Day of the Slaughter of the Sacrosanct Animals (*yawm al-naḥr*), he would slaughter it before shaving or cutting his hair. He would slaughter the sacrosanct animals himself, standing them up in a line and turning them toward Mecca. He would then eat some of that meat and give some away.

1114. According to Mālik, Nāfiʿ reported that when ʿAbd Allāh b. ʿUmar stabbed the hump of his sacrosanct animal to mark it, he would say, "In the name of God; God is great."

1115. According to Mālik, Nāfiʿ reported that ʿAbd Allāh b. ʿUmar would say, "A sacrosanct animal is any animal that has been garlanded, marked, and brought to ʿArafāt."

1116. According to Mālik, Nāfiʿ reported that ʿAbd Allāh b. ʿUmar would drape his consecrated animals in fine white Egyptian linens, single-toned wool garments, and multihued garments. He would then send these garments to the Kabah and have the Kabah draped with them.

1117. According to Mālik, he asked ʿAbd Allāh b. Dīnār, "What did ʿAbd Allāh b. ʿUmar do with the drapings of his animals, once the Kabah began to be draped with this covering?" He said, "He would give them away in charity."

1118. According to Mālik, Nāfiʿ reported that ʿAbd Allāh b. ʿUmar would say regarding sacrificial animals and sacrosanct animals, "They should be at least two years old."[438]

1119. According to Mālik, Nāfiʿ reported that ʿAbd Allāh b. ʿUmar would neither tear the drapes of his sacrosanct animals nor drape them until he left Minā in the early morning for ʿArafāt.

1120. According to Mālik, Hishām b. ʿUrwa reported that his father would say to his sons, "My sons, none of you should ever offer as a sacrifice to God an animal that you would be ashamed to offer to a noble man. God is surely the noblest of the noble, and the worthiest to have the choicest selection designated for Him."

Chapter 47. The Practice (*ʿAmal*) regarding What to Do with Consecrated Animals (*Hady*) That Are Injured or That Wander Off and Are Lost

1121. According to Mālik, Hishām b. ʿUrwa reported from his father that the steward of the consecrated animals of the Messenger of God (pbuh) said, "Messenger of God, what should I do with a consecrated animal that gets injured?" The Messenger of God (pbuh) said to him, "You should slaughter any such camel. Then cast its garlands into its blood and abandon its meat, leaving it for the people to eat."

---

438 "Sacrificial animals" are the animals that nonpilgrims offer in sacrifice on the Day of the Feast of the Sacrificial Animals (*ʿīd al-aḍḥā*), whereas "sacrosanct animals" refers to the animals that pilgrims slaughter on the Day of the Slaughter of the Sacrosanct Animals (*yawm al-naḥr*).

1122. According to Mālik, Ibn Shihāb reported that Saʿīd b. al-Musayyab said, "If someone voluntarily sends a camel to God's House for sacrifice, but it gets injured en route so he slaughters it and then abandons its meat, leaving it for the people to eat, he is not under any further obligation. If, however, he eats some of it or urges someone else to eat of it, he is obliged to provide a substitute for it."

1123. According to Mālik, Thawr b. Zayd al-Dīlī reported from ʿAbd Allāh b. ʿAbbās something similar to that.

1124. According to Mālik, Ibn Shihāb said, "If someone consecrates a camel for sacrifice, whether as compensation for an animal he hunted, in fulfillment of a vow (*nadhr*), or on account of deciding to perform the Pilgrimage (*ḥajj*) after having set out to perform only the Visitation (*ʿumra*), and some misfortune befalls it en route, he must provide a substitute camel."

1125. According to Mālik, Nāfiʿ reported that ʿAbd Allāh b. ʿUmar said, "If someone has consecrated a camel for sacrifice in fulfillment of a vow, and it wanders off and is lost or dies, he must provide a substitute animal. If, however, he offered it voluntarily, he may provide a substitute if he wishes, but he is not obliged to do so."

1126. According to Mālik, he heard the people of knowledge say, "If the person who offers a sacrosanct animal does so as compensation for an animal that he hunted and killed while in the consecrated state, on account of discontinuing his Pilgrimage due to illness, or as compensation for any defect in the performance of his Pilgrimage, he may not eat from it."

Chapter 48. The Consecrated Animal (*Hady*) Due from Someone Who Has Intercourse with His Wife While in the Consecrated State (*Muḥrim*)

1127. According to Mālik, it reached him that ʿUmar b. al Khaṭṭāb, ʿAlī b. Abī Ṭālib, and Abū Hurayra were asked about a man who has intercourse with his wife while in the consecrated state during the Pilgrimage (*ḥajj*). They said, "Both of them shall continue on their way until they complete their Pilgrimage. Each must then perform the Pilgrimage again in an upcoming year and offer a sacrosanct animal as compensation for their illicit intercourse." Mālik said, "ʿAlī b. Abī Ṭālib said, 'When they enter the consecrated state in an upcoming year to perform the Pilgrimage, they are to be separated until they complete it.'"

1128. According to Mālik, Yaḥyā b. Saʿīd reported that he heard Saʿīd b. al-Musayyab say, "People! What do you say about a man who has intercourse with his wife while he is in the consecrated state?" Yaḥyā said, "None of them had a response, so Saʿīd said, 'It once happened that a man had intercourse with his wife while in the consecrated state, so he sent a message to Medina, inquiring about the consequences. Someone there responded to the question, saying, "They should be separated until the coming year.' Saʿīd b. al-Musayyab, however, disagreed, saying about that case, 'No; rather, they should continue on their way and complete the Pilgrimage that they invalidated by having intercourse. When they are done, they may return home. If they live to the next year, they must perform another Pilgrimage and offer a sacrosanct animal as expiation. They should enter the consecrated state at the same place where they entered it for the previous Pilgrimage, which they invalidated. They should, however, remain apart until they complete their Pilgrimage.'" Mālik said, "Both the man and the woman must offer a sacrosanct animal."

1129. Mālik said that a man who had intercourse with his wife during the Pilgrimage, whether before or after standing at ʿArafāt but before casting pebbles at Minā, is obliged to offer a sacrosanct animal and to perform another Pilgrimage in an upcoming year. Mālik said, "But if intercourse with his wife took place after he cast his pebbles at Minā, he need only perform the Visitation (*ʿumra*) and offer a sacrosanct animal; he is not obliged to perform another Pilgrimage in an upcoming year."

1130. Mālik said, "Penetration itself, even if there is no ejaculation, invalidates the Pilgrimage and the Visitation and therefore necessitates the offering of a sacrosanct animal."

1131. Mālik said, "Ejaculation renders such an offering compulsory, even if it results from intimate contact short of intercourse. As for a man who ejaculates as a result of some erotic thoughts, I do not think he is obliged to do anything."

1132. Mālik said, "If a man were to kiss his wife, and no ejaculation takes place, he is obliged to offer a sacrosanct animal, but his Pilgrimage is still valid."

1133. Mālik said, "A woman who willingly has intercourse with her husband while she is in the consecrated state, even if she does so several times, whether during the Pilgrimage or during the Visitation, needs to offer only one sacrosanct animal and to perform the Pilgrimage in an upcoming year. If he had intercourse with her during the Visitation, she must make up the Visitation that she invalidated by having intercourse and offer a sacrosanct animal."

Chapter 49. The Sacrosanct Animal (*Hady*) Offered by a Person Who Set Out for but Missed the Pilgrimage (*Ḥajj*)[439]

1134. According to Mālik, Yaḥyā b. Sa'īd said, "Sulaymān b. Yasār told me that Abū Ayyūb al-Anṣārī set out with the intention of performing the Pilgrimage. When he reached al-Nāziya[440] while en route to Mecca, he lost his camels. He finally caught up with 'Umar b. al-Khaṭṭāb in Mecca on the Day of the Slaughter of the Sacrosanct Animals (*yawm al-naḥr*)[441] and told him what had happened. 'Umar said, "Do what someone performing the Visitation (*'umra*) would do, after which you will be released from the restrictions of the consecrated state (*iḥrām*). And if you live to see the Pilgrimage in an upcoming year, set out for the Pilgrimage and offer whatever sacrosanct animal is conveniently available to you."[442]

1135. According to Mālik, Nāfi' reported from Sulaymān b. Yasār that Habbār b. al-Aswad arrived on the Day of the Slaughter of the Sacrosanct Animals just as 'Umar b. al-Khaṭṭāb was slaughtering his animals. He said, "Commander of the Faithful, we mistook the date, and so we wrongly believed that today was the Day of 'Arafa."[443] 'Umar said, "You and those who came with you—go to Mecca and circumambulate the Kabah (*ṭawāf*), and slaughter a sacrosanct animal, if you have one, then shave or cut your hair and return home. Then, next year, set out once again to perform the Pilgrimage and offer a sacrosanct animal, but if you cannot obtain one, fast three days during the Pilgrimage and seven upon returning home."

1136. Mālik said, "Whoever combines performance of the Pilgrimage with performance of the Visitation and then misses the Pilgrimage must perform the Pilgrimage in an upcoming year, again combining the Pilgrimage with the Visitation and offering two sacrosanct animals, one for the combined Pilgrimage and Visitation of the current year and one for the Pilgrimage he missed on the previous occasion."

---

439 A pilgrim misses the Pilgrimage if he fails to arrive at 'Arafāt by the ninth day of Dhū al-Ḥijja, whether because of getting lost, because of miscalculating the date, or for any other reason that delayed his arrival.

440 A well between Mecca and Medina.

441 This is the tenth day of Dhū al-Ḥijja, when the pilgrims sacrifice their animals and are released from the prohibitions of the consecrated state.

442 In this case, at least a yearling (*shāt*). Zurqānī, *Sharḥ al-Zurqānī*, 2:497.

443 The ninth day of Dhū al-Ḥijja.

Chapter 50. Offering a Sacrosanct Animal (*Hady*) as Expiation for Intercourse with One's Wife before Performance of the Circumambulation of the March (*Ṭawāf al-Ifāḍa*)[444]

1137. According to Mālik, Abū al-Zubayr al-Makkī reported from ʿAṭāʾ b. Abī Rabāḥ, from ʿAbd Allāh b. Abbās, that he was asked about a man who had intercourse with his wife while he was at Minā before he performed the Circumambulation of the March. Ibn ʿUmar told the man to offer a sacrosanct animal, either a cow or a camel, as sacrifice.

1138. According to Mālik, Thawr b. Zayd al-Dīlī reported that ʿIkrima, the freedman (*mawlā*) of Ibn ʿAbbās, said, "I believe it is only Ibn ʿAbbās who said, 'Whoever has intercourse with his wife before performing the Circumambulation of the March must undertake a Visitation (*ʿumra*) and offer a sacrosanct animal in sacrifice as expiation.'"

1139. According to Mālik, he heard Rabīʿa b. Abī ʿAbd al-Raḥmān express a view similar to the one that ʿIkrima reported from Ibn ʿAbbās regarding this case. Mālik said, "Of all the views that I have heard about this issue, that view is the one I prefer most."

1140. Mālik was asked about a man who forgot to perform the Circumambulation of the March until he left Mecca to return home. He said, "It is my opinion that if he has not yet had intercourse with women, he must return and perform the Circumambulation of the March, but even if he has, he should still return and perform the Circumambulation of the March, then perform a Visitation and offer a sacrosanct animal in sacrifice. He should not, however, purchase his sacrificial animal from Mecca and slaughter it there. Rather, if he did not bring one with him from whence he set out to perform the Visitation, he should purchase the sacrificial animal in Mecca, take it beyond the precincts of the Sanctuary (*ḥaram*), and then bring it back to Mecca. Only then may he slaughter it."

---

444 The Circumambulation of the March (*ṭawāf al-ifāḍa*) is a fundamental pillar (*rukn*) of the Pilgrimage and must be performed in order to complete the Pilgrimage. It is performed any time after the Day of ʿArafa (the ninth of Dhū al-Ḥijja). It is so called because the pilgrims march en masse from their campsites at Minā to Mecca, where they perform the rite of circumambulation, usually after slaughtering their animals and casting pebbles at Minā. After completing the circumambulation, they return to Minā, where they spend the night.

Chapter 51. The Meaning of "a Sacrosanct Animal (*Hady*) Conveniently Available for Sacrifice"[445]

1141. According to Mālik, Jaʿfar b. Muḥammad reported from his father that ʿAlī b. Abī Ṭālib would say, "The phrase 'a sacrosanct animal conveniently available for sacrifice' means a yearling (*shāt*)."

1142. According to Mālik, it reached him that ʿAbd Allāh b. ʿAbbās would say, "The phrase 'a sacrosanct animal conveniently available for sacrifice' means a yearling."

1143. Yaḥyā said, "Mālik said, 'Of all the views that I have heard regarding this issue, that view is the one I prefer most, because God, Blessed and Sublime is He, says in His Book, "O you who believe! Do not kill wild animals while you are in the consecrated state. Whoever does so intentionally must offer in compensation a domesticated animal similar to the one he killed, as determined by two of your just men, as an offering brought to the Kabah."[446] Among the domesticated animals that have been judged to be equivalent to wild animals are yearlings, and God has referred to them as "sacrosanct animals offered for sacrifice" (*hady*).[447] This is something about which there is no dissent among us (*lā ikhtilāfa fīhi ʿindanā*). Indeed, how could anyone entertain a doubt about it? It is undoubtedly the case that if a pilgrim kills a wild animal whose equivalent domesticated animal is smaller than a cow or a camel, he is obliged to offer a yearling. It is also undoubtably the case that if a pilgrim kills a wild animal whose equivalent domesticated animal is smaller than a yearling, he is obliged to expiate through fasting or feeding the poor.'"

1144. According to Mālik, Nāfiʿ reported that ʿAbd Allāh b. ʿUmar would say, "The phrase 'a sacrosanct animal conveniently available for sacrifice' means a camel or a cow."

1145. According to Mālik, ʿAbd Allāh b. Abī Bakr reported that a freedwoman (*mawlāt*) of ʿAmra bt. ʿAbd al-Raḥmān named Ruqayya informed him that she went to Mecca with ʿAmra bt. ʿAbd al-Raḥmān. She said, "ʿAmra and I entered Mecca on the Day of Watering (*yawm al-tarwiya*).[448] She then

445 This chapter title is taken from the Quranic phrase *mā 'staysara min al-hady*, which refers to the obligation of a pilgrim who is unable to complete his Pilgrimage to offer an animal as a sacrifice. *Al-Baqara*, 2:196.

446 *Al-Māʾida*, 5:95.

447 Mālik's point is that since judges have deemed the sacrifice of a yearling appropriate compensation for a wild animal killed by a pilgrim, and since the Quran refers to the animal that judges declare equivalent to the slain animal as *hady*, the word *hady* must include yearlings among its potential referents.

448 *Yawm al-tarwiya*, the eighth day of Dhū al-Ḥijja, was so named because on that day the pilgrims would provision themselves with water from Mecca before heading out the next day to ʿArafāt and the plains of Minā, where no water was available.

circumambulated God's House (*ṭawāf*) and marched between the hillocks of Safā and Marwa (*saʿy*). She went to the rear of the Sacred Mosque and asked me, 'Do you have a pair of scissors?' I said, 'No.' She said, 'Find one for me,' so I looked until I found one and brought it to her. She then grabbed her braids and cut some of her hair. Then, on the Day of the Slaughter of the Sacrosanct Animals (*yawm al-naḥr*), she slaughtered a yearling."[449]

Chapter 52. Miscellaneous Reports regarding Sacrosanct Animals (*Hady*)

1146. According to Mālik, Ṣadaqa b. Yasār al-Makkī reported that a Yemeni man with braided hair came to ʿAbd Allāh b. ʿUmar and said, "Abū ʿAbd al-Raḥmān, I have come with the intention of performing only the Visitation (*ʿumra*)." ʿAbd Allāh said to him, "Had I been with you, or had you asked me, I would have told you to combine the Visitation with the Pilgrimage (*ḥajj*)." The man said, "Well, what's done is done." ʿAbd Allāh b. ʿUmar said, "Trim some of the hair that is flying around your head and offer an animal as a sacrifice."[450] Then an Iraqi woman said, "Abū ʿAbd al-Raḥmān, what animal should he offer?" ʿAbd Allāh b. ʿUmar said, "His sacrosanct animal." She said to him, "And what is his sacrosanct animal?" ʿAbd Allāh b. ʿUmar said, "Even if I had nothing to slaughter other than a yearling (*shāt*), I would prefer to do that rather than fast."

1147. According to Mālik, Nāfiʿ reported that ʿAbd Allāh b. ʿUmar would say, "A woman in the consecrated state (*iḥrām*) may not comb her hair until she exits that state by trimming her braids; and if she has consecrated an animal for sacrifice, she should not trim her hair until she has first slaughtered her animal."

1148. According to Mālik, he heard a man of knowledge say, "A man and his wife should not consecrate the same animal for sacrifice; rather, each must offer his or her own animal."

1149. Yaḥyā said, "Mālik was asked about a person who had been entrusted with sacrosanct animals to be slaughtered during the Pilgrimage season but who intended to perform only the Visitation. Should he slaughter the animals immediately upon exiting the consecrated state once he completes

449 The significance of the report about ʿAmra is that her actions indicate that she had failed to complete the intended Pilgrimage and was thus performing only a Visitation, which meant that she was under an obligation to offer as a sacrifice "an easily available animal." The fact that she offered a yearling supports Mālik's view that the phrase "an animal conveniently available for sacrifice" means a yearling.

450 The most likely explanation for why ʿAbd Allāh told the man to offer a sacrificial animal is that he resolved to perform the Pilgrimage after completing the Visitation. This is known as *tamattuʿ*, and a pilgrim who performs it is required to offer an animal in sacrifice.

the rites of the Visitation, or should he postpone slaughtering them until the Pilgrimage season, after he has completed his Visitation and exited the consecrated state? Mālik said, 'No, he should defer slaughtering them until the Pilgrimage, but he should exit the consecrated state immediately upon completing his Visitation.'"

1150. Mālik said, "Anyone who has been ordered to offer an animal as compensation for having killed a wild animal or who must do so for violating any other prohibition of the consecrated state may only offer the sacrifice in Mecca, because God, Blessed and Sublime is He, says, 'an offering brought to the Kabah.'[451] As for fasting or charity in lieu of offering an animal, that is to be performed outside of Mecca, wherever the person wishes to do it."

1151. According to Mālik, Yaḥyā b. Sa'īd reported from Ya'qūb b. Khālid al-Makhzūmī that Abū Asmā', the freedman (*mawlā*) of 'Abd Allāh b. Ja'far, told him that he was with 'Abd Allāh b. Ja'far, and they left together from Medina. They met Ḥusayn b. 'Alī, may God be pleased with him, at al-Suqyā,[452] and Ḥusayn was ill at the time. 'Abd Allāh b. Ja'far stayed with Ḥusayn until 'Abd Allāh feared that he would miss the Pilgrimage. He therefore departed from Ḥusayn's side but sent to Medina for 'Alī b. Abī Ṭālib and Asmā' bt. 'Umays, and they came to Ḥusayn. Ḥusayn pointed to his head, so 'Alī ordered that it be shaved. 'Alī b. Abī Ṭālib then slaughtered a camel on Ḥusayn's behalf there at al-Suqyā. Yaḥyā b. Sa'īd said, "Ḥusayn had set out with 'Uthmān b. 'Affān on his trip to Mecca."

Chapter 53. Stopping at 'Arafāt and Muzdalifa

1152. According to Mālik, it reached him that the Messenger of God (pbuh) said, "One may encamp anywhere at 'Arafāt, except for the middle of 'Urana, and one may encamp anywhere at Muzdalifa, except for the middle of Muḥassir."[453]

1153. According to Mālik, Hishām b. 'Urwa reported that 'Abd Allāh b. al-Zubayr would say, "Everyone should know that they may encamp anywhere at 'Arafāt, except for the middle of 'Urana, and that they may encamp anywhere at Muzdalifa, except for the middle of Muḥassir."

451 *Al-Mā'ida*, 5:95.

452 Al-Suqyā is a place on the road from Medina to Mecca. Zurqānī, *Sharḥ al-Zurqānī*, 2:378.

453 'Urana and Muḥassir are places in the vicinity of 'Arafāt and Muzdalifa, respectively. Stopping at 'Arafāt on the ninth day of Dhū al-Ḥijja is the central requirement of the Pilgrimage. At sunset on the tenth day, the pilgrims depart from 'Arafāt for the plain of Muzdalifa, where they spend the night and gather the pebbles that they will then cast symbolically at the pillars in Minā on the eleventh, twelfth, and thirteenth days of Dhū al-Ḥijja.

1154. Mālik said, "God, Blessed and Sublime is He, says, 'Let there be no sexual intercourse (*rafath*), wickedness (*fusūq*), or wrangling (*jidāl*) during the Pilgrimage (*ḥajj*).'[454] *Rafath* means sexual intercourse with women, and God knows best. God, Blessed and Sublime is He, says, 'Sexual intercourse (*rafath*) with your wives is licit for you on the nights of the fast.'[455] *Fusūq* refers to sacrifices made to the altars of idols, and God knows best. God, Blessed and Sublime is He, says, 'Or wickedness (*fisq*), consecrated to other than God.'[456] And '*jidāl* during the Pilgrimage' refers to the Quraysh's practice of camping at the Mashʿar al-Ḥarām at Quzaḥ in Muzdalifa, while the Arabs and others would camp at ʿArafāt. They would argue with one another, each group saying, 'We are more upright,' so God said, 'For every people We have established a rite which they follow: let them not then dispute with you about that; but do call to Your Lord, for you are assuredly following a clearly marked, straight path.'[457] That is what we have come to believe is the meaning of 'wrangling during the Pilgrimage,' and God knows best. I heard that explanation from the people of knowledge."

Chapter 54. Stopping at ʿArafāt without Ritual Purity or While Mounted

1155. Yaḥyā said, "Mālik was asked whether a man may stop at ʿArafāt or Muzdalifa, cast pebbles at Minā, or march between the hillocks of Ṣafā and Marwa (*saʿy*) while in a state of ritual impurity. He said, 'A man in a state of ritual impurity may perform all the rites that a menstruating woman may perform during the Pilgrimage (*ḥajj*) without incurring any liability.[458] Virtue, however, lies in performing all of these rites while in a state of ritual purity, and a person should never intend to perform them while in a state of ritual impurity.'"

1156. Yaḥyā said, "Mālik was asked whether a rider who wishes to stop at ʿArafāt must dismount, or whether he may remain on his animal. He said, 'No, indeed he should remain mounted, unless some illness befalls him or his mount, in which case there is none more indulgent in accepting excuses than God.'"

---

454 *Al-Baqara*, 2:197.

455 *Al-Baqara*, 1:187. Mālik's point is that the Quran uses the term *rafath* to mean sexual intercourse.

456 *Al-Anʿām*, 6:145.

457 *Al-Ḥajj*, 22:67.

458 In other words, if he performs these rites while in a state of ritual impurity, his performance of them is valid and he need not perform them again, nor offer a sacrifice as penance.

Chapter 55. Stopping at ʿArafāt by Someone Who Misses the Pilgrimage (*Ḥajj*)

1157. According to Mālik, Nāfiʿ reported that ʿAbd Allāh b. ʿUmar would say, "Whoever fails to reach ʿArafāt prior to the breaking of dawn on the night of Muzdalifa has missed the Pilgrimage, and whoever manages to reach it before the breaking of dawn on the night of Muzdalifa has fulfilled the Pilgrimage."

1158. According to Mālik, Hishām b. ʿUrwa reported that his father said, "Whoever has yet to arrive at ʿArafāt when dawn breaks on the night of Muzdalifa has failed to perform the Pilgrimage, and whoever reaches ʿArafāt on the night of Muzdalifa before dawn breaks has performed the Pilgrimage."

1159. Yaḥyā said, "Mālik said that a slave who is manumitted at ʿArafāt is not relieved of the obligation to perform the Pilgrimage that is mandatory for every Muslim. If he had not entered the consecrated state (*iḥrām*) while he was a slave, however, he may enter the consecrated state immediately upon his manumission, and if he manages to reach ʿArafāt that same night before dawn breaks, he will have satisfied his obligation to perform the obligatory Pilgrimage. If he fails to enter the consecrated state before dawn breaks on the night of Muzdalifa, however, he is the equivalent of someone who misses the Pilgrimage on account of failing to reach ʿArafāt before the dawn breaks on the night of Muzdalifa. Accordingly, he remains obliged to perform the Pilgrimage that is obligatory for all Muslims."[459]

Chapter 56. Sending Women and Children Ahead from Muzdalifa to Minā

1160. According to Mālik, Nāfiʿ reported from Sālim and ʿUbayd Allāh, the sons of ʿAbd Allāh b. ʿUmar, that their father would send his wife and young children ahead from Muzdalifa to Minā so that they could perform the Morning Prayer (*ṣalāt al-ṣubḥ*) there and cast their pebbles before the great mass of the people arrived from Muzdalifa.[460]

459 Every Muslim is obligated to perform the Pilgrimage once in his or her lifetime, provided he or she has the means to do so. This obligation, however, can only be satisfied by a free person. In this case, although the slave who is manumitted on the Day of ʿArafa has performed all the rites of the Pilgrimage before his manumission, he was not a free man when he entered the consecrated state (*iḥrām*). Therefore, in Mālik's view, his performance of the Pilgrimage does not meet the conditions of the Pilgrimage without the further steps of reentering the consecrated state and reaching ʿArafāt in time.

460 The pilgrims spend the ninth day of Dhū al-Ḥijja at ʿArafāt and the night of the tenth day on the plains of Muzdalifa. In the ordinary case, they pray the Morning Prayer (*ṣalāt al-ṣubḥ*) at Muzdalifa and only then set out to Minā. According to this report, ʿAbd Allāh b. ʿUmar would

1161. According to Mālik, Yaḥyā b. Saʿīd reported from ʿAṭāʾ b. Abī Rabāḥ that a freedwoman (*mawlāt*) of Asmāʾ bt. Abī Bakr informed him, "We reached Minā with Asmāʾ bt. Abī Bakr when it was still dark. Worried, I said to her, 'We've arrived, and it's still dark.' Asmāʾ then said, 'We did this very thing with those who were more virtuous than you.'"[461]

1162. According to Mālik, it reached him that Ṭalḥa b. ʿUbayd Allāh would send the women of his household and his young children ahead from Muzdalifa to Minā.

1163. According to Mālik, he heard one of the people of knowledge disapprove of casting pebbles at Minā before dawn breaks on the Day of the Slaughter of the Sacrosanct Animals (*yawm al-naḥr*), but it was nevertheless licit for whoever had done so to slaughter their sacrificial animals.

1164. According to Mālik, Hishām b. ʿUrwa reported that Fāṭima bt. al-Mundhir informed him that she saw Asmāʾ bt. Abī Bakr at Muzdalifa ordering the person who led her and her companions in the Morning Prayer to perform it precisely at the break of dawn, whereupon she would mount her animal and proceed to Minā without stopping.

Chapter 57. Marching with the Body of the Pilgrims

1165. According to Mālik, Hishām b. ʿUrwa reported that his father said, "I was sitting with Usāma b. Zayd when someone asked him to describe the pace of the Messenger of God (pbuh) when he marched with the body of the pilgrims during the Farewell Pilgrimage (*ḥajjat al-wadāʿ*). Usāma said, 'He would march at a brisk pace (*al-ʿanaq*), but when he found a gap, he would speed up (*naṣṣa*).'" Mālik said, "Hishām said, '*Al-naṣṣ* is faster than *al-ʿanaq*.'"

1166. According to Mālik, Nāfiʿ reported that ʿAbd Allāh b. ʿUmar would spur his mount in the valley of Muḥassir a stone's throw at a time.

Chapter 58. What Has Come Down regarding the Slaughter of Consecrated Animals (*Hady*) during the Pilgrimage (*Ḥajj*)

1167. According to Mālik, it reached him that the Messenger of God (pbuh) addressed the people at Minā, saying, "This is where the consecrated animals are slaughtered. They may be slaughtered anywhere in Minā." Mālik

send his wives and minor children from Muzdalifa to Minā in the middle of the night so that they could avoid the crowds.

461 Asmāʾ's freedwoman expressed surprise that they arrived at Minā in the darkness, because pilgrims travel to Minā after spending the night at Muzdalifa, which implies that they generally arrive at Minā only with the first light of the morning.

said, "He also said during performance of the Visitation (*ʿumra*), 'This is the place of slaughter,' meaning the hillock of Marwa. He also said, 'Sacrificial animals may be slaughtered anywhere in the wide valleys or narrow passes of Mecca.'"

1168. According to Mālik, Yaḥyā b. Saʿīd said, "ʿAmra bt. ʿAbd al-Raḥmān informed me that she heard ʿĀʾisha, the Mother of the Believers, say, 'We set out with the Messenger of God (pbuh) from Medina with five nights remaining in the month of Dhū al-Qaʿda.[462] We believed that we had set out only to perform the Pilgrimage,[463] but as we approached Mecca, the Messenger of God (pbuh) ordered those of us who had not brought sacrosanct animals with them to exit the consecrated state (*iḥrām*) after circumambulating God's House and marching between the hillocks of Ṣafā and Marwa (*saʿy*).' ʿĀʾisha said, 'On the Day of the Slaughter of the Sacrosanct Animals (*yawm al-naḥr*), some beef was brought to us, so I said, "What is this?" They told me that the Messenger of God (pbuh) had slaughtered it on behalf of his wives.'" Yaḥyā b. Saʿīd said, "I mentioned this report to al-Qāsim b. Muḥammad, and he said, 'By God, ʿAmra reported this story to you precisely as it occurred.'"

1169. According to Mālik, Nāfiʿ reported from ʿAbd Allāh b. ʿUmar, from Ḥafṣa, the Mother of the Believers, that she said to the Messenger of God (pbuh), "Why is it that the people have exited the consecrated state but you have not, even though you have completed the rites of your Visitation?" He said, "I have matted my hair and garlanded my animals, so I shall not exit the consecrated state until I slaughter them."

Chapter 59. The Practice (*ʿAmal*) with Respect to the Slaughter of the Sacrosanct Animals (*Hady*)

1170. According to Mālik, Jaʿfar b. Muḥammad reported from his father, from ʿAlī b. Abī Ṭālib, that the Messenger of God (pbuh) slaughtered some of his consecrated animals himself and had others slaughter the rest.

1171. According to Mālik, Nāfiʿ reported that ʿAbd Allāh b. ʿUmar said, "Whoever vows to slaughter a consecrated camel for the sake of God should garland it with two sandals around its neck and mark its side with a shallow

462 The eleventh month of the Islamic calendar and the month immediately preceding Dhū al-Ḥijja, the month in which the Pilgrimage takes place. Its name reflects the fact that in the pre-Islamic period it was a truce month in which the Arabs would not engage in fighting.

463 That is, when they departed from Medina they were not aware that it was possible to perform the Visitation during the months designated for performance of the Pilgrimage. The rest of the report explains that the Prophet (pbuh) ordered some of those who were with him to perform only the rites of the Visitation, not those of the Pilgrimage.

cut from his blade. Then he should slaughter it at God's House, or at Minā on the Day of the Slaughter of the Sacrosanct Animals (*yawm al-naḥr*); there is no other appropriate place. Whoever vows to sacrifice an unconsecrated camel or cow, however, may slaughter it wherever he wishes."[464]

1172. According to Mālik, Hishām b. ʿUrwa reported that his father would slaughter his animals while they were standing.

1173. Mālik said, "It is not permissible for a person to shave his head before he has slaughtered his sacrosanct animals. Further, no one should slaughter his animals before dawn breaks on the Day of the Slaughter of the Sacrosanct Animals; rather, everything should take place on that day—slaughter, donning clothes, grooming the body, and shaving—and none of it should occur before that day."

Chapter 60. Shaving the Head

1174. According to Mālik, Nāfiʿ reported from ʿAbd Allāh b. ʿUmar that the Messenger of God said, "May God have mercy on those who shave their heads." They asked him, "What about those who merely trim their hair, Messenger of God?" He said, "May God have mercy on those who shave their heads." They said, "But what about those who merely trim their hair, Messenger of God?" He said, "And on those who merely trim their hair."

1175. According to Mālik, ʿAbd al-Raḥmān b. al-Qāsim reported from his father that he would enter Mecca at night to perform the Visitation (*ʿumra*), whereupon he would circumambulate God's House (*ṭawāf*) and march between the hillocks of Ṣafā and Marwa (*saʿy*) but would delay shaving his head until the morning. ʿAbd al-Raḥmān said, "He would not, however, return to God's House to circumabulate it again until he had first shaved his head." He said, "He would enter the Sacred Mosque (*al-masjid al-ḥarām*) and perform the *witr* prayer there, but he would not approach God's House."

1176. Mālik said, "'Grooming' (*tafath*) consists of shaving the head, donning clothes, and similar things."

1177. Mālik was asked whether there was a dispensation permitting a man who forgets to shave his head at Minā during the Pilgrimage (*ḥajj*) to shave it in Mecca instead. He said, "There is broad latitude in this matter, but I prefer that he shave his head at Minā."

---

464 The two oaths are distinguished by the use in the first oath of the term *badana*, which in the Arabs' usage was limited to animals that had been consecrated to be taken to Mecca by pilgrims and thus were called *hady*. The term *jazūr* was used to signify an unconsecrated animal of the same type.

1178. Mālik said, "The rule about which there is no dissent (*al-amr alladhī lā ikhtilāfa fīh*) is that no one should shave his head or trim his hair until he has slaughtered a consecrated animal (*hady*), if he has one; and that he is not released from the restrictions of the consecrated state (*iḥrām*) until he exits that state at Minā on the Day of the Slaughter of the Sacrosanct Animals (*yawm al-naḥr*). That is because God, Blessed and Sublime is He, says in His Book, 'And do not shave your heads until the sacrosanct animals reach their destination.'"[465]

Chapter 61. Trimming the Hair

1179. According to Mālik, Nāfiʿ reported that when ʿAbd Allāh b. ʿUmar finished the Ramaḍān fast and desired to perform the Pilgrimage (*ḥajj*), he would not cut his hair nor trim his beard until he completed the Pilgrimage. Mālik said, "That is not obligatory."

1180. According to Mālik, Nāfiʿ reported that when ʿAbd Allāh b. ʿUmar shaved his head at the conclusion of the Pilgrimage or the Visitation (*ʿumra*), he would trim his beard and moustache.

1181. According to Mālik, Rabīʿa b. Abī ʿAbd al-Raḥmān reported that a man came to al-Qāsim b. Muḥammad and said, "I performed the Circumambulation of the March (*ṭawāf al-ifāḍa*) with my wife and then led her off the main path to a trail in the mountains. I approached her, intending to have intercourse with her, but she said, 'I have not yet cut my hair.' I therefore tore some of her hair with my teeth and then had intercourse with her." Rabīʿa said, "Al-Qāsim b. Muḥammad laughed and said, 'Tell her to cut her hair with scissors.'"

1182. Mālik said, "In a case like this, I prefer that an animal be slaughtered. That is because ʿAbd Allāh b. ʿAbbās said, 'Whoever overlooks any of his rites should slaughter an animal.'"

1183. According to Mālik, Nāfiʿ reported from ʿAbd Allāh b. ʿUmar that he once met a man from his own people called al-Mujabbar who performed the Circumambulation of the March but did not first shave his head or trim his hair, not realizing that he was obliged to do so. ʿAbd Allāh, therefore, ordered him to return to Minā, shave his head or trim his hair, and then return to God's House and perform the Circumambulation of the March.

1184. According to Mālik, it reached him that when Sālim b. ʿAbd Allāh wanted to enter into the consecrated state (*iḥrām*), he would ask for scissors and trim his moustache and beard before setting off and entering the consecrated state.

---

465 *Al-Baqara*, 2:196.

Chapter 62. Matting the Hair

1185. According to Mālik, Nāfiʿ reported from ʿAbd Allāh b. ʿUmar that ʿUmar b. al-Khaṭṭāb said, "Whoever braids his hair should shave his head and not make it look as though it has been matted with gum."

1186. According to Mālik, Yaḥyā b. Saʿīd reported from Saʿīd b. al-Musayyab that ʿUmar b. al-Khaṭṭāb said, "Whoever braids, ties, or mats his hair with gum must shave his head."

Chapter 63. Performance of the Prayer (*Ṣalāt*) Inside God's House, Shortening Performance of the Prayer, and Hastening the Sermon at ʿArafāt

1187. According to Mālik, Nāfiʿ reported from ʿAbd Allāh b. ʿUmar that the Messenger of God (pbuh) entered the Kabah with Usāma b. Zayd, Bilāl b. Rabāḥ, and ʿUthman b. Ṭalḥa al-Ḥajabī. He closed the door behind him and stayed there for a while. ʿAbd Allāh said, "I then asked Bilāl when he came out what the Messenger of God (pbuh) had done while inside the Kabah. He said, 'He stood with one column to his left, two to his right, and three behind him, and then he prayed. At that time, God's House contained six columns.'"

1188. According to Mālik, Ibn Shihāb reported that Sālim b. ʿAbd Allāh said, "Abd al-Malik b. Marwān wrote to al-Ḥajjāj b. Yūsuf,[466] commanding him to defer to ʿAbd Allāh b. ʿUmar on any matters concerning the Pilgrimage (*ḥajj*)." Sālim said, "On the Day of ʿArafa, ʿAbd Allāh b. ʿUmar went to al-Ḥajjāj b. Yūsuf when the sun reached its zenith, and I was with him. ʿAbd Allāh cried out to al-Ḥajjāj from outside his tent, saying, 'Where is this fellow?' Al-Ḥajjāj came out, wrapped in a blanket dyed with safflower, and said, 'What troubles you, Abū ʿAbd al-Raḥmān?' He said, 'Hurry up and leave, if you desire to abide by the long-established ordinance (*al-sunna*).' Al-Ḥajjāj said, 'Right now?' He said, 'Yes.' Al-Ḥajjāj then said, 'Give me a moment so that I may wash up, and then I will set off.' ʿAbd Allāh dismounted and waited until al-Ḥajjāj emerged. Al-Ḥajjāj walked between me and my father, and I said to him, 'If you intend to abide by the long-established ordinance today, abbreviate the sermon and perform the prayer (*ṣalāt*) promptly.' Al-Ḥajjāj then turned to look at ʿAbd Allāh b. ʿUmar in order to hear his opinion. When ʿAbd Allāh noticed that, he said, 'Sālim is correct.'"

466 Al-Ḥajjāj b. Yūsuf al-Thaqafī (d. 95/715) was the governor of Iraq during the caliphate of ʿAbd al-Malik b. Marwān.

Chapter 64. Performance of the Prayer (*Ṣalāt*) at Minā on the Day of Watering (*Yawm al-Tarwiya*) and Performance of the Friday Prayer (*Ṣalāt al-Jumu'a*) at Minā and 'Arafāt

1189. According to Mālik, Nāfi' reported that 'Abd Allāh b. 'Umar would perform the Noon (*ṣalāt al-ẓuhr*), Afternoon (*ṣalāt al-'aṣr*), Sunset (*ṣalāt al-maghrib*), Evening (*ṣalāt al-'ishā'*), and Morning (*ṣalāt al-ṣubḥ*) Prayers at Minā. He would then set off for 'Arafāt when the sun rose.

1190. Mālik said, "The rule about which there is no dissent among us (*al-amr alladhī lā ikhtilāfa fīhi 'indanā*) is that the imam does not recite the Quran loudly during performance of the Noon Prayer at 'Arafāt, that he gives a sermon to the people on the Day of 'Arafa, and that the specific prayer that is performed at 'Arafāt is the Noon Prayer. The Noon Prayer is always performed on the Day of 'Arafa, even if it falls on a Friday. It is limited to two cycles (*rak'a*) of prayer because of traveling."

1191. Mālik said that the leader of the pilgrim caravan should not perform the Friday Prayer if Friday happens to fall on the Day of 'Arafa, on the Day of the Slaughter of the Sacrosanct Animals (*yawm al-naḥr*), or on any of the three Festival Days (*ayyām al-tashrīq*).

Chapter 65. Performance of the Prayer (*Ṣalāt*) at Muzdalifa

1192. According to Mālik, Ibn Shihāb reported from Sālim b. 'Abd Allāh, from 'Abd Allāh b. 'Umar, that the Messenger of God (pbuh) performed the Sunset Prayer (*ṣalāt al-maghrib*) and the Evening Prayer (*ṣalāt al-'ishā'*) together at Muzdalifa.

1193. According to Mālik, Mūsā b. 'Uqba reported from Kurayb, the freedman (*mawlā*) of Ibn 'Abbās, that he heard Usāma b. Zayd say, "The Prophet (pbuh) departed from 'Arafāt with the pilgrims, and when he reached the valley before Muzdalifa, he dismounted, urinated, and then performed ablutions (*wuḍū'*), using a minimal amount of water. I said to him, 'It is time for prayer, Messenger of God!' He said, 'Prayer lies ahead of you.' He then mounted his camel and rode. When he arrived at Muzdalifa, he dismounted and performed ablutions, using a copious amount of water. Then the immediate call to prayer (*iqāma*) was made, and he performed the Sunset Prayer. After that, every person settled his camel down where he would camp. Then the immediate call to prayer was made for the Evening Prayer. The Prophet (pbuh) performed it without having offered any supplementary prayer between it and the Sunset Prayer."

1194. According to Mālik, Yaḥyā b. Saʿīd reported from ʿAdī b. Thābit al-Anṣārī that ʿAbd Allāh b. Yazīd al-Khaṭmī informed him that Abū Ayyūb al-Anṣārī reported to him that during the Farewell Pilgrimage (*ḥajjat al-wadāʿ*) he performed the Sunset and Evening Prayers together at Muzdalifa with the Messenger of God (pbuh).

1195. According to Mālik, Nāfiʿ reported that ʿAbd Allāh b. ʿUmar would perform the Sunset and Evening Prayers together at Muzdalifa.

Chapter 66. Performance of the Prayer (*Ṣalāt*) at Minā

1196. Yaḥyā said, "Mālik said, regarding the people of Mecca, 'When they perform the Pilgrimage (*ḥajj*), they are to shorten their prayers at Minā, praying two cycles (*rakʿa*) instead of four, until they return to Mecca.'"

1197. According to Mālik, Hishām b. ʿUrwa reported from his father that the Messenger of God (pbuh) shortened the prayer to two cycles while at Minā. Abū Bakr and ʿUmar b. al-Khaṭṭāb did the same, as did ʿUthmān b. ʿAffān during the first half of his term as caliph, but thereafter he performed it in full.

1198. According to Mālik, Ibn Shihāb reported from Saʿīd b. al-Musayyab that when ʿUmar b. al-Khaṭṭāb came to Mecca, he led the people in prayer but performed only two cycles of prayer. When he finished, he said, "People of Mecca, complete the remaining two cycles of your prayer, for we are travelers!" Then ʿUmar b. al-Khaṭṭāb performed two cycles of prayer at Minā, but we have heard nothing suggesting that he said anything to them about performing an additional two cycles.

1199. According to Mālik, Zayd b. Aslam reported from his father that ʿUmar b. al-Khaṭṭāb led the people in the performance of two cycles of prayer at Minā.[467] When he finished, he said, "People of Mecca, complete the remaining two cycles of your prayer, for we are travelers!" ʿUmar then performed two cycles of prayer at Minā, but we have heard nothing suggesting that he said anything to them about performing an additional two cycles.

1200. Mālik was asked whether Meccans should perform two or four cycles of prayer at ʿArafāt. He was also asked whether the leader of the pilgrims' caravan, if he is a Meccan, should perform two or four cycles of prayer for the Noon Prayer (*ṣalāt al-ẓuhr*) and Afternoon Prayer (*ṣalāt al-ʿaṣr*) at ʿArafāt. He was also asked how Meccans should perform their prayer during their stay at Minā. Mālik said, "Meccans, during their stay at Minā

467 This is an error in the manuscript. It should read "Mecca," as do other transmissions of the *Muwaṭṭa'*.

and ʿArafāt, should pray only two cycles for each prayer until they return to Mecca. The leader of the pilgrims' caravan, if he is a Meccan, should also pray only two cycles of prayer at ʿArafāt and during the days spent at Minā. If there happens to be someone who resides in Minā, he should perform the full four cycles of prayer. If someone resides in ʿArafāt, he also should perform the full four cycles."[468]

Chapter 67. The Prayer (*Ṣalāt*) of a Resident of Mecca or Minā

1201. Yaḥyā said, "Mālik said, 'Whoever arrives in Mecca at the beginning of the month of Dhū al-Ḥijja and then begins performance of the Pilgrimage (*ḥajj*) should perform the full four cycles (*rakʿa*) of his prayers until he leaves Mecca for Minā, whereupon he should perform only two cycles. That is because he resolved to stay in Mecca for more than four nights.'"[469]

Chapter 68. Magnifying God (Saying "God Is Great," *Allāhu Akbar*) during the Three Festival Days (*Ayyām al-Tashrīq*)[470]

1202. According to Mālik, Yaḥyā b. Saʿīd reported that it reached him that ʿUmar b. al-Khaṭṭāb had set out on the morning of the Day of the Slaughter of the Sacrosanct Animals (*yawm al-naḥr*) just after the sun had risen. He magnified God, so the people did likewise. Then he went out a second time that same day, later in the morning, and again magnified God, so the people did likewise. He went out a third time in the afternoon and magnified God, so the people did likewise. Their chants of "God is great" were continuous and in unison, so their sound reached all the way from Minā to God's House in Mecca, and the Meccans knew that ʿUmar had set out to cast pebbles at ʿAqaba.

1203. Mālik said, "The rule in our view (*al-amr ʿindanā*) is that God is to be magnified during the three Festival Days after the conclusion of each of the daily prayers. This practice begins with the Noon Prayer (*ṣalāt al-ẓuhr*) on the Day of the Slaughter of the Sacrosanct Animals, and it concludes with the performance of the Morning Prayer (*ṣalāt al-ṣubḥ*) on the last of the three Festival Days. The people, together with the imam, magnify God at the conclusion of each of these daily prayers."

1204. Mālik said, "Magnifying God during the three Festival Days is obligatory for both men and women, whether in a group or individually, and

468 It would be unusual for anyone to be a resident of either Minā or ʿArafāt insofar as neither was a place of permanent residence; both were populated only during the Pilgrimage season.

469 In other words, someone who arrives in Mecca on the first of Dhū al-Ḥijja will necessarily spend more than four nights in Mecca before setting out for Minā.

470 These are the eleventh, twelfth, and thirteenth days of Dhū al-Ḥijja.

whether they are present at Minā or far away in distant lands. The people of Mecca follow the lead of the pilgrims' imam and the people at Minā in this respect, because they follow them when they return to Mecca and exit the consecrated state, so they have the same relationship with them as they had before the pilgrims entered the consecrated state. As for those who are not performing the Pilgrimage (*ḥajj*), they follow the pilgrims only with respect to magnifying God during the three Festival Days. The 'numbered days'[471] are the three Festival Days."

Chapter 69. The Prayer (*Ṣalāt*) of the Pilgrim Pausing at Muʿarras[472] and at Muḥaṣṣab[473]

1205. According to Mālik, Nāfiʿ reported from ʿAbd Allāh b. ʿUmar that the Messenger of God (pbuh) made his camel kneel down on the plain at Dhū al-Ḥulayfa, and he prayed there. Nāfiʿ said, "ʿAbd Allāh b. ʿUmar did the same."

1206. Mālik said, "No one should pass through Muʿarras on his way back to Mecca from Minā without praying there. If he passes through it outside the scheduled prayer times, he should stay there until it is time for the performance of a prayer and then pray there in a manner that seems appropriate to him. It reached me that the Messenger of God (pbuh) stopped there to rest on his journey and that ʿAbd Allāh b. ʿUmar also stopped there."

1207. According to Mālik, Nāfiʿ reported that ʿAbd Allāh b. ʿUmar would perform the Noon Prayer (*ṣalāt al-ẓuhr*), the Afternoon Prayer (*ṣalāt al-ʿaṣr*), the Sunset Prayer (*ṣalāt al-maghrib*), and the Evening Prayer (*ṣalāt al-ʿishāʾ*) at Muḥaṣṣab and then would enter Mecca at night and circumambulate God's House.

Chapter 70. The Prohibition against Spending the Night in Mecca during the Nights of Minā

1208. According to Mālik, Nāfiʿ said, "They said that ʿUmar b. al-Khaṭṭāb would dispatch men to usher people who were encamped beyond the limits of ʿAqaba back into Minā."[474]

---

471 This is Mālik's explanation of the Quranic phrase *ayyām maʿdūdāt* in the verse that reads, "And remember God for a number of days" (*Wa'dhkurū 'llāha fī ayyāmin maʿdūdāt*). *Al-Baqara*, 2:203.

472 A place on the plain of Dhū al-Ḥulayfa on the way to Mecca from Minā where the Prophet (pbuh) stopped to pray.

473 A plain between Mecca and Minā.

474 In the absence of a valid excuse, pilgrims are required to spend the nights of the eleventh, twelfth, and thirteenth days of Dhū al-Ḥijja at Minā, and ʿAqaba constitutes the outer boundary of Minā in the direction of Mecca. Accordingly, any pilgrim who spends the night beyond Minā's borders has violated one of the rules of the Pilgrimage.

1209. According to Mālik, Nāfiʿ said, "They said that ʿUmar b. al-Khaṭṭāb said, 'Let no pilgrim spend any of the nights of Minā beyond the borders of ʿAqaba.'"

1210. According to Mālik, Hishām b. ʿUrwa reported that his father said, regarding the question of spending the night in Mecca during the nights of Minā, "No pilgrim should spend the night anywhere except Minā."

Chapter 71. Casting Pebbles at ʿAqaba[475]

1211. According to Mālik, it reached him that ʿUmar b. al-Khaṭṭāb would stop at the first two of the three pillars where the pilgrims cast pebbles for such a long time that anyone standing there would grow weary.

1212. According to Mālik, Nāfiʿ reported that ʿAbd Allāh b. ʿUmar would stop at the first two of the three pillars where the pilgrims cast pebbles for a long time, magnifying God (saying "God is great," *Allāhu akbar*), glorifying Him (saying "Glory be to God," *Subḥāna 'llāh*), praising Him (saying "All praise belongs to God," *Al-ḥamdu lillāh*), and supplicating Him, but he would not stop at the last station at ʿAqaba.

1213. According to Mālik, Nāfiʿ reported that ʿAbd Allāh b. ʿUmar would exclaim "God is great" every time he cast a pebble.

1214. According to Mālik, he heard one of the people of knowledge say, "The pebbles that are cast at the pillars should be the size of slingshot pebbles." Mālik said, "My preference, however, is for pebbles slightly larger than that."

1215. According to Mālik, Nāfiʿ reported that ʿAbd Allāh b. ʿUmar would say, "Whoever is still at Minā when the sun sets on either of the first two of the three Festival Days (*ayyām al-tashrīq*) must not leave Minā before casting pebbles at the pillars the following day."

1216. According to Mālik, ʿAbd al-Raḥmān b. al-Qāsim reported from his father that after the people cast their pebbles at the pillars on the third day, they would leave on foot, heading every which way. The first to depart mounted was Muʿāwiya b. Abī Sufyān.

1217. According to Mālik, he asked ʿAbd al-Raḥmān b. al-Qāsim where his father would stand when he cast pebbles at the last pillar. He said, "Wherever it was easy for him to do so."

---

475 The three stone pillars at ʿAqaba represent the places at which the Devil attempted to dissuade Abraham from meeting certain tests that God had set for him (*al-Baqara*, 2:124). The pilgrims cast pebbles at these stones in a symbolic act of rejecting the Devil.

1218. Mālik was asked whether pebbles could be cast on behalf of a child or someone who was sick. He said, "Yes, and the sick person should take care to know when the pebbles are thrown on his behalf so that he can magnify God where he is in his camp and slaughter an animal. If he recovers during the three Festival Days, he should go and cast pebbles himself and then offer a sacrosanct animal (*hady*) as a sacrifice."

1219. Mālik said, "I do not think that someone who has not performed ablutions (*wuḍūʾ*) prior to casting his pebbles or marching between the hillocks of Ṣafā and Marwa (*saʿy*) needs to repeat the performance of either ritual, but he should not intentionally omit his ablutions."

1220. According to Mālik, Nāfiʿ reported that ʿAbd Allāh b. ʿUmar would say, "Pebbles are cast at the pillars during the three Festival Days only after the sun has reached its zenith."

Chapter 72. The Dispensation concerning Casting Pebbles

1221. According to Mālik, ʿAbd Allāh b. Abī Bakr b. Ḥazm reported from his father that Abū al-Baddāḥ ʿĀṣim b. ʿAdī informed him from his father, ʿAdī, that the Messenger of God (pbuh) allowed camel herders to spend the night outside of Minā and to cast their pebbles on the Day of the Slaughter of the Sacrosanct Animals (*yawm al-naḥr*), and then to cast pebbles on the next two days and on the day the pilgrims depart Minā.

1222. According to Mālik, Yaḥyā b. Saʿīd reported that he heard ʿAṭāʾ b. Abī Rabāḥ mention that camel herders had been allowed to cast their pebbles at night, but he said this had been during the early days of Islam.

1223. Mālik said, "In our view—and God knows best—the explanation for the report in which the Messenger of God (pbuh) gave a dispensation to camel herders to permit them to delay casting their stones is that they cast their pebbles on the Day of the Slaughter of the Sacrosanct Animals and then again two days later, that being the first day when pilgrims may depart Minā. First they cast pebbles for the previous day, and then they cast pebbles for that day. This is because a person makes up an action only after it has become compulsory for him. Further, if it is obligatory for him to do something but the time for its performance has ended, he must make it up later. Accordingly, if the camel herders decide to leave Minā in these circumstances, they may do so insofar as they have fulfilled their obligations. If they decide to spend the night, however, they must cast their pebbles with everyone else on the last day of departure, and only then may they leave."

1224. According to Mālik, Abū Bakr b. Nāfiʿ reported from his father that a niece of Ṣafiyya bt. Abī ʿUbayd bled at Muzdalifa after giving birth, so she and Ṣafiyya were late, arriving at Minā after sunset on the Day of the Slaughter of the Sacrosanct Animals. When they arrived, ʿAbd Allāh b. ʿUmar told both of them to go and cast their pebbles. He did not believe they were subject to any additional obligation.

1225. Mālik was asked about someone who forgot to cast pebbles at one of the pillars on one of the days of Minā, not remembering until night fell. He said, "He should go cast his pebbles at any time, whether day or night, as soon as he remembers that he has not done so, just as someone who forgets to perform a prayer and then remembers performs it immediately, whether day or night. If, however, he remembers after departing from Minā when he is in Mecca, or after he has left Mecca, he must offer a sacrosanct animal (*hady*) as a sacrifice."

Chapter 73. The Pilgrims' March (*Ifāḍa*) to God's House from Minā

1226. According to Mālik, Nāfiʿ and ʿAbd Allāh b. Dīnār reported from ʿAbd Allāh b. ʿUmar that ʿUmar b. al-Khaṭṭāb delivered a sermon to the people at ʿArafāt in which he instructed them about the rules of the Pilgrimage (*ḥajj*). Among the things that he told them was, "When you arrive at Minā, whoever casts his pebbles is freed of the restrictions that had applied to him as a pilgrim, except with respect to sexual intercourse with women and the prohibition against the use of perfume. Let no one, therefore, have sexual intercourse or touch perfume until he has first circumambulated God's House (*ṭawāf*)."

1227. According to Mālik, Nāfiʿ and ʿAbd Allāh b. Dīnār reported from ʿAbd Allāh b. ʿUmar that ʿUmar b. al-Khaṭṭāb said, "Whoever has finished casting his pebbles, shaved his head or trimmed his hair, and slaughtered a sacrosanct animal (*hady*), if he had one, is released from the restrictions that bound him, except with respect to sexual intercourse with women and perfume. He is not released from these restrictions until he has first circumambulated God's House."

Chapter 74. How a Menstruating Woman Enters Mecca

1228. According to Mālik, ʿAbd al-Raḥmān b. al-Qāsim reported from his father that ʿĀʾisha, the Mother of the Believers, said, "We set out with the Messenger of God (pbuh) in the year of the Farewell Pilgrimage (*ḥajjat al-wadāʿ*). We entered the consecrated state (*iḥrām*) to perform the Visitation (*ʿumra*). Then the Messenger of God (pbuh) said, 'Whoever brought with him sacrosanct animals (*hady*) should intend to perform both the Pilgrimage (*ḥajj*) and the Visitation. He should therefore continue to observe the restrictions of the consecrated state until he completes both sets of rituals.' When I arrived in Mecca, I was menstruating and so was unable to circumambulate God's House (*ṭawāf*) or to march between the hillocks of Ṣafā and Marwa (*saʿy*). I complained about that to the Messenger of God (pbuh), so he said, 'Undo your braids and comb your hair, and then enter the consecrated state for the Pilgrimage and leave aside the Visitation for now.' So I did, and when we completed the Pilgrimage, the Messenger of God (pbuh) sent me with my brother, ʿAbd al-Raḥmān b. Abī Bakr al-Ṣiddīq, to al-Tanʿīm, where I again entered the consecrated state and then performed the Visitation. The Messenger of God (pbuh) said, 'This substitutes for the Visitation that you were unable to perform when you first arrived.' As for those who had entered the consecrated state to perform only the Visitation, they circumambulated God's House and marched between the hillocks of Ṣafā and Marwa, and then they were released from the consecrated state. If they subsequently set out on the Pilgrimage, they circumambulated God's House a second time when they returned from Minā. As for those who had entered the consecrated state to perform only the Pilgrimage or to perform the Pilgrimage and the Visitation together, they circumambulated God's House only once, after returning from Minā."

1229. According to Mālik, Ibn Shihāb reported from ʿUrwa b. al-Zubayr, from ʿĀʾisha, a report similar to the preceding one.

1230. According to Mālik, ʿAbd al-Raḥmān b. al-Qāsim reported from his father that ʿĀʾisha, the Mother of the Believers, said, "I was menstruating when I entered Mecca, so I was unable to circumambulate God's House or to march between the hillocks of Ṣafā and Marwa. I complained to the Messenger of God (pbuh), so he said, 'Do everything the pilgrims do except for circumambulating God's House and marching between Ṣafā and Marwa until your period ends and you bathe.'"

1231. Yaḥyā said, "Mālik said, regarding a woman who enters the consecrated state for the Visitation and enters Mecca hoping to perform the Pilgrimage, but who is menstruating and thus unable to circumambulate God's House, 'If she fears that she will miss the Pilgrimage (if she waits for her period to end), she should enter into the consecrated state for the Pilgrimage and offer a sacrosanct animal (*hady*) as a sacrifice, in which case she is just like someone who has combined performance of the Pilgrimage and the Visitation (*qirān*). In this case, circumambulating God's House once fulfills her obligations. If the menstruating woman has, by the time her period begins, already circumambulated God's House and offered the two cycles (*rak'a*) of prayer that are due thereafter, she then marches between the hillocks of Ṣafā and Marwa, stands at 'Arafāt and Muzdalifa, and casts the pebbles at 'Aqaba even as she continues to menstruate. She must refrain, however, from performing the Circumambulation of the March (*ṭawāf al-ifāḍa*) until she has bathed at the conclusion of her period."

Chapter 75. A Menstruating Woman's Performance of the Circumambulation of the March (*Ṭawāf al-Ifāḍa*)

1232. According to Mālik, 'Abd al-Raḥmān b. al-Qāsim reported from his father, from 'Ā'isha, the Mother of the Believers, that Ṣafiyya bt. Ḥuyayy began to menstruate. 'Ā'isha said, "I mentioned this to the Messsenger of God (pbuh), who asked, 'Will we need to wait for her?' He was told, however, that she had already performed the Circumambulation of the March (*ṭawāf al-ifāḍa*), so he said, 'In that case, we need not wait.'"

1233. According to Mālik, 'Abd Allāh b. Abī Bakr b. Ḥazm reported from his father, from 'Amra bt. 'Abd al-Raḥmān, from 'Ā'isha, the Mother of the Believers, that she said to the Messenger of God (pbuh), "Messenger of God! Safiyya bt. Ḥuyayy's period has started." The Messenger of God (pbuh) said, "Will we need to wait for her? Hasn't she already performed the Circumambulation of the March with you women?" The women said, "Indeed she has." He said, "Then you may depart for home."

1234. According to Mālik, Abū al-Rijāl Muḥammad b. 'Abd al-Raḥmān reported from 'Amra bt. 'Abd al-Raḥmān that when 'Ā'isha, the Mother of the Believers, went on the Pilgrimage with women who, she feared, might menstruate, she would dispatch them quickly from Minā to perform the Circumambulation of the March on the Day of the Slaughter of the Sacrosanct Animals (*yawm al-naḥr*). Therefore, if they subsequently began to menstruate, she would not need to wait for them to complete their periods before she could head home. They could all return home together, even if these women were menstruating, provided that they had already performed the Circumambulation of the March.

1235. According to Mālik, Hishām b. 'Urwa reported from his father, from 'Ā'isha, the Mother of the Believers, that the Messenger of God (pbuh) asked about Ṣafiyya bt. Ḥuyayy and was told that her period had started. The Messenger of God (pbuh) said, "Perhaps we need to wait for her?" They said, "Messenger of God, she has already performed the Circumambulation of the March." The Messenger of God (pbuh) therefore said, "In that case, we need not wait."

1236. Mālik said that Hishām said that 'Urwa said that 'Ā'isha said, "We mention these precedents to the people, but they nevertheless continue to send their women ahead of them, even though it does not benefit the women themselves. If what they say were correct,[476] there would be more than six thousand menstruating women who had already performed the Circumambulation of March at Minā, waiting for their periods to end."

1237. According to Mālik, ʿAbd Allāh b. Abī Bakr reported from his father that Abū Salama b. ʿAbd al-Raḥmān informed him that Umm Sulaym bt. Milḥān had asked the Messenger of God (pbuh) what to do when her period started (or she gave birth)[477] after she had performed the Circumambulation of the March on the Day of the Slaughter of the Sacrosanct Animals. The Messenger of God (pbuh) gave her permission to leave, so she left.

1238. Mālik said, "A woman who menstruates at Minā must remain there until she performs the Circumambulation of the March, and there are no exceptions to this. If, however, she begins to menstruate after performing the Circumambulation of the March, she may return to her home. We have reports of a dispensation that the Messenger of God (pbuh) granted in this respect to menstruating women."

1239. Mālik said, "If a woman menstruates while at Minā before she has performed the Circumambulation of the March, her bleeding detains her there for no more than the maximum length of time that menstrual blood ordinarily flows."[478]

Chapter 76. The Compensation Due for Killing Birds and Wild Animals

1240. According to Mālik, Abū al-Zubayr al-Makkī reported that ʿUmar b. al-Khaṭṭāb decreed that a ram is to be offered in sacrifice as compensation for the killing of a hyena, a female goat for the killing of a gazelle, a she-goat that is less than a year old but has been weaned from her mother for the killing of a rabbit, and a four-month-old kid for a jerboa.[479]

1241. According to Mālik, ʿAbd al-Malik b. Qurayr reported from Muḥammad b. Sīrīn that a man came to ʿUmar b. al-Khaṭṭāb and said, "A

476 ʿĀʾisha is here rebutting the claim that the Farewell Circumambulation (*ṭawāf al-wadāʿ*) is obligatory. Since the Prophet (pbuh) permitted Ṣafiyya to return home after having completed the Circumambulation of the March (*ṭawaf al-ifāḍa*), by implication the Farewell Circumambulation is not obligatory. Moreover, ʿĀʾisha explains that if it were the case that the Farewell Circumabulation were indeed obligatory, there would be large numbers of women at Minā waiting for their periods to end so that they could perform the Farewell Circumambulation.

477 The narrator is uncertain which of the two took place.

478 Mālik's rule here is that if a woman begins to menstruate at Minā, she may not perform the obligatory Circumambulation of the March until either her bleeding ceases or the maximum length of an ordinary menstrual period is reached.

479 These rules apply to individuals who kill wild animals while in the consecrated state (*muḥrim*) or within the precincts of the Meccan Sanctuary (*ḥaram*).

friend of mine and I raced our horses along a narrow mountain trail, and we killed a gazelle. We were both in the consecrated state (*iḥrām*). What do you think we need to do?" ʿUmar turned to a man who was sitting next to him and said, "Come, let the two of us reach a judgment together." They ruled against the man and decreed that he must sacrifice a female goat as compensation. The man turned away, saying, "*This* is the Commander of the Faithful? He needs the help of another man to rule about a gazelle?" ʿUmar overheard what the man said, so he called him back and asked him, "Are you familiar with the chapter of the Quran called 'The Table' (*al-Māʾida*)?" He said, "No." ʿUmar said, "Do you know this man who judged alongside me?" The man said, "No." ʿUmar then said, "If you had told me that you were familiar with *al-Māʾida*, I would have slapped you hard. God, Blessed and Sublime is He, says in His Book, 'determined by two of your just men, as an offering brought to the Kabah.'[480] This man alongside me is ʿAbd al-Raḥmān b. ʿAwf."

1242. According to Mālik, Hishām b. ʿUrwa reported that his father would say, "A cow must be sacrificed for killing a female wild antelope, and a yearling (*shāt*) for a female gazelle."

1243. According to Mālik, Yaḥyā b. Saʿīd reported that Saʿīd b. al-Musayyab would say, "A yearling is due for killing a Meccan dove."

1244. Mālik said, regarding a Meccan who enters the consecrated state to perform either the Pilgrimage (*ḥajj*) or the Visitation (*ʿumra*) and who, while he is gone, locks the Meccan dove chicks that he is raising in his room, causing them to die, "He must, in my opinion, offer one yearling as a sacrifice for each dove chick that died as a result of his actions."

1245. Mālik said, "I have always heard (*lam azal asmaʿ*) that a person in the consecrated state (*muḥrim*) who kills an ostrich must offer a camel as a sacrifice in compensation."

1246. Mālik said, "In my opinion, one-tenth of the price of a camel must be given for destroying an ostrich egg, just as the compensation for the fetus of a free woman is a minor slave, either a boy or a girl. The fair market value of a minor slave is fifty dinars, and that is one-tenth of the compensation due for the mother's life."

1247. Mālik said, "Any bird belonging to the eagle, falcon, or vulture family counts as a wild animal (*ṣayd*), the killing of which requires a sacrifice, just as a sacrifice is required for any other wild animal that a person in the consecrated state kills."

480 *Al-Māʾida*, 5:195.

1248. Mālik said, "And for anything for whose killing a sacrifice is required, the sacrifice due for killing the young is the same as that due for killing the old. This resembles the case of the compensation due for the accidental killing of a free person; whether he be young or old, the same compensation is due."

Chapter 77. What Is Due from Someone Who Kills Locusts While in the Consecrated State (*Muḥrim*)

1249. According to Mālik, Zayd b. Aslam reported that a man came to ʿUmar b. al-Khaṭṭāb and said, "Commander of the Faithful, I killed some locusts with my whip while I was in the consecrated state." ʿUmar said to him, "Give some food to the needy as penance."

1250. According to Mālik, Yaḥyā b. Saʿīd reported that a man came to ʿUmar b. al-Khaṭṭāb and asked him about a locust he killed while he was in the consecrated state. ʿUmar therefore said to Kaʿb,[481] "Come, let us judge." Kaʿb said, "One dirham." Umar said to Kaʿb, "Spoken like a rich man! Indeed, a single date is better than a locust!"

Chapter 78. What Is Due for Shaving One's Head before Slaughtering One's Consecrated Animal (*Hady*)

1251. According to Mālik, ʿAbd al-Karīm b. Mālik al-Jazarī reported from ʿAbd al-Raḥmān b. Abī Laylā, from Kaʿb b. ʿUjra, that he was with the Messenger of God (pbuh) in the consecrated state (*muḥrim*) when he suffered an infestation of lice in his hair. The Messenger of God (pbuh) ordered him to shave his head and said to him, "Fast three days, or feed six poor people two handfuls of food each, or offer a yearling (*shāt*) as a sacrifice. Whichever of these you do suffices for your action."

1252. According to Mālik, Ḥumayd b. Qays reported from Mujāhid b. al-Ḥajjāj, from Ibn Abī Laylā, from Kaʿb b. ʿUjra, that the Messenger of God (pbuh) said, "It appears that you have an infestation of lice in your hair." Kaʿb said, "I said, 'Yes, Messenger of God.'" The Messenger of God (pbuh) said, "Shave your head and fast three days, or feed six poor people, or offer a yearling as a sacrifice."

1253. According to Mālik, ʿAṭāʾ b. ʿAbd Allāh al-Khurasānī said, "An old man at the Buram Market in Kufa[482] told me that Kaʿb b. ʿUjra said, 'The Messenger of God (pbuh) came to me as I was stoking the fire underneath

---

481 Kaʿb b. Mātiʿ, known as Kaʿb al-Aḥbār. Zurqānī, *Sharḥ al-Zurqānī*, 2:577.

482 The Muslims established the town of Kufa after their conquest of Iraq during the caliphate of ʿUmar b. al-Khaṭṭāb.

my companions' cooking pot. My head and beard were filled with lice. He caught hold of my forehead and said, "Shave your hair and fast three days, or feed six poor people!" The Messenger of God (pbuh) knew that I had no animal to offer as a sacrifice.'"

1254. Yaḥyā said, "Mālik said, regarding the penance due for shaving one's hair because of a lice infestation, that the rule (*al-amr*) is that no penance is due until the pilgrim does something requiring penance. Penance becomes obligatory only after he performs an act that obliges it. He may fulfill that duty once it arises wherever he wishes, whether by sacrificing an animal, fasting, or giving food to the poor, whether in Mecca or anywhere else."

1255. Mālik said, "A person in the consecrated state is not permitted to pluck out any of his hair, nor to shave or trim it, until he exits the consecrated state, unless his hair becomes infested with lice. In this case, he must shave his hair and offer penance as ordered by God, Blessed and Sublime is He. Nor is it appropriate that he cut his nails, kill lice, or remove them from his head, skin, or clothes and cast them aside. If someone in the consecrated state does any of these things, he must offer a handful of food as penance."

1256. Mālik said, "Any person in the consecrated state who plucks hair from his nose or armpit, or rubs his body with a mixture that removes his body hair, or shaves the hair around a head wound when needed, or shaves his neck in order to use cupping glasses—whoever does any of these things, whether out of forgetfulness or ignorance, must offer penance. A person who is to be cupped while in the consecrated state should not shave the areas where the cupping glasses are to be placed on his body."

1257. Mālik said, "Whoever shaves his head out of ignorance before casting pebbles at ʿAqaba must offer penance."

Chapter 79. What Is Due from Someone Who Omits, in Whole or in Part, a Ritual of the Pilgrimage (*Ḥajj*) or the Visitation (*ʿUmra*)

1258. According to Mālik, Ayyūb b. Abī Tamīma reported from Saʿīd b. Jubayr that ʿAbd Allāh b. ʿAbbās said, "Whoever forgets (or fails) to perform a ritual of the Pilgrimage or the Visitation should slaughter an animal." Ayyūb said, "I do not know whether he said 'fails' or 'forgets.'"

1259. Mālik said, "If what is involved here is a sacrosanct animal (*hady*), it can only be sacrificed in Mecca. If it involves penance for failure to perform any of the rituals, the sacrifice may take place wherever the person wishes."

Chapter 80. Miscellaneous Matters Related to What Is Due for Breaching the Rules of the Pilgrimage (*Ḥajj*) or the Visitation (*ʿUmra*)

1260. Mālik said, regarding someone who intentionally wears clothes inappropriate for the consecrated state (*iḥrām*), trims his hair, or uses perfume despite the absence of a compelling necessity, merely because offering what is due for breaching these rules is easier for him than complying with the rules, "No one should ever do this. These dispensations are valid only in circumstances of necessity. Anyone who does these things intentionally, however, must nevertheless render what is due for violating the rules."

1261. Yaḥyā said, "Mālik was asked whether a person who breaks a rule of the Pilgrimage or of the Visitation is obliged to offer a specific act of penance, be it fasting, feeding the poor, or slaughtering an animal, or whether he is free to choose among these three options. He was also asked what kind of animal would be satisfactory, the quantity of food that must be given, and how many days must be fasted. He was also asked whether the penance can be deferred, or whether it must be performed immediately. Mālik said, 'Everything in God's Book relating to acts of penance is stated in terms of alternatives. Accordingly, anyone under such an obligation is free to choose among them; whichever option he prefers, he does. As for slaughtering an animal, a yearling (*shāt*) is sufficient. As for fasting, it is three days. And as for feeding the poor, it consists of feeding six poor individuals two 500-gram measures (*mudd*) of food each, using the original measure of the Prophet (pbuh).'"

1262. Mālik said, "I heard one of the people of knowledge say, 'If a man in the consecrated state (*muḥrim*) shoots an arrow and hits and kills a wild animal (*ṣayd*) unintentionally, he must perform penance. Similarly, if someone who is not in the consecrated state shoots an arrow in the Sanctuary (*ḥaram*) and hits and kills a wild animal unintentionally, he must also perform penance, because intentional acts (*ʿamd*) and unintentional acts (*khaṭaʾ*) are treated in the same way in this respect.'"[483]

1263. Mālik said, regarding a group of people who together kill a wild animal while they are in the consecrated state or while they are within the

483 Both cases involve the killing of a wild animal that is protected from harm, but the reason for its protection is different in each case. In the first case, the person is categorically prohibited from harming wild animals by virtue of being in the consecrated state. In the second case, the person is not in the consecrated state, but the wild animal is sacrosanct because of its physical presence within the boundaries of the Sanctuary, which grants the animal protection from harm. Accordingly, even someone who is not in the consecrated state must perform penance if he accidentally kills such an animal.

precincts of the Sanctuary, "I think that each one of them is required to offer penance. If there is a judgment that they must offer a sacrosanct animal (*hady*), each of them should offer a sacrosanct animal. If there is a judgment that they should fast, each of them should fast. Their case is similar to that of a group of people who, without intending to do so, kill someone. In that case the required penance is that each one of them manumits a slave, or each one of them fasts for two consecutive months."

1264. Mālik said, "Whoever shoots or kills a wild animal after casting pebbles at ʿAqaba or shaving his head but before performing the Circumambulation of the March (*ṭawaf al-ifāḍa*) is obliged to offer penance, because God, Blessed and Sublime is He, says, 'When you exit the consecrated state, you may hunt.'[484] A person who has not yet performed the Circumambulation of the March is still prohibited from having intercourse with women and using perfume, so he has not yet exited the consecrated state."

1265. Mālik said, "A person in the consecrated state who cuts down trees within the precincts of the Sanctuary is not required to perform penance. No report of a judgment against someone for doing so has come to our attention, but his deed is most wicked nonetheless."

1266. Mālik said, regarding someone who, out of ignorance or forgetfulness, fails to fast three days during the Pilgrimage or falls ill while fasting and thus fasts them only once reaches his native land, that he should offer a sacrosanct animal as penance, if he finds one, and if he does not, he should fast three days when he reaches his people and seven days after that.

Chapter 81. Miscellaneous Matters Related to the Pilgrimage (*Ḥajj*)

1267. According to Mālik, Ibn Shihāb reported from ʿĪsā b. Ṭalḥa that ʿAbd Allāh b. ʿAmr b. al-ʿĀṣī said, "The Messenger of God (pbuh) stopped to let the people at Minā to ask him questions. A man came to him and said, 'Messenger of God, I shaved my head but then realized that I had not yet slaughtered my sacrosanct animals (*hady*).' The Messenger of God (pbuh) said, 'Slaughter them, and do not worry.' Then another man came to him and said, 'Messenger of God, I slaughtered my animals and then realized that I had not yet cast my pebbles at ʿAqaba.' The Messenger of God (pbuh) said, 'Go cast your pebbles, and do not worry.' Every time the Messenger of God (pbuh) was asked a question that day about a mistake in the timing of the performance of a ritual of the Pilgrimage, whether before or after its appointed time, he always told the questioner, 'Do it, and do not worry.'"

484 *Al-Māʾida*, 5:2.

1268. According to Mālik, Nāfiʿ reported from ʿAbd Allāh b. ʿUmar that every time the Messenger of God (pbuh) returned from a military expedition, the Pilgrimage, or the Visitation (*ʿumra*), he would magnify God (say "God is great," *Allāhu akbar*) three times at the top of every hill. He would then say, "There is no god except God, alone without partner. To Him belongs the kingdom and all praise, and He has power over all things. We return to Him, repent to Him, serve Him, and prostrate to Him; and to Him we give praise. God faithfully fulfilled His Promise, granted victory to His servant, and through His power alone defeated the Confederates."[485]

1269. According to Mālik, Ibrāhīm b. ʿUqba reported from Kurayb, the freedman (*mawlā*) of Ibn ʿAbbās, that the Messenger of God (pbuh) once passed a woman who was sitting in plain sight in the litter of her camel. Someone said to her, "This is the Messenger of God." She then held up the forearms of a child who was with her and asked, "May this child perform the Pilgrimage, Messenger of God?" He answered, "Yes, and you will be rewarded for it."

1270. According to Mālik, Ibrāhīm b. ʿAbd Allāh b. Abī ʿAbla reported from Ṭalḥa b. ʿUbayd Allāh b. Karīz that the Messenger of God (pbuh) said, "There is no day on which Satan is more degraded, more of an exile, more contemptible, and more enraged than the Day of ʿArafa. This is because of what he sees that day: the continuous descent of God's mercy and God's forgiveness of even the gravest of sins. The Battle of Badr, however, was even worse for him." Someone asked, "What did he see that day?" He said, "Verily, he saw the Archangel Gabriel himself, arranging the ranks of the angelic host."

1271. According to Mālik, Ziyād b. Abī Ziyād, the freedman of ʿAbd Allāh b. ʿAyyāsh b. Abī Rabīʿa al-Makhzūmī, reported from Ṭalḥa b. ʿUbayd Allāh b. Karīz that the Messenger of God (pbuh) said, "The best supplication is the supplication made on the Day of ʿArafa, and the best words that I and the prophets before me have said are, 'There is no god except God, alone without partner.'"

1272. According to Mālik, Ibn Shihāb reported from Anas b. Mālik that the Messenger of God (pbuh) entered Mecca in the year of the conquest

485 "The Confederates" refers to the pagan alliance that the Quraysh assembled in year 5 of the Hijra (627 CE). The Muslims were able to defeat them by digging defensive trenches around Medina. For this reason, this campaign became known as the Battle of the Trench. The pagans, although greatly outnumbering the Muslims, were not prepared to undertake a lengthy siege, and as a result they eventually withdrew in defeat after their attempt at a siege failed to break the Muslims' defenses.

(*ʿām al-fatḥ*) with a helmet on his head.[486] When he took it off, a man came to him and said, "Ibn Khaṭal is clinging to the curtains of the Kabah." The Messenger of God (pbuh) said, "Put him to death."[487] Mālik said, "Ibn Shihāb said, 'On that day, the Messenger of God (pbuh) was not in the consecrated state (*muḥrim*), and God knows best.'"[488]

1273. According to Mālik, Nāfiʿ reported that ʿAbd Allāh b. ʿUmar was traveling from Mecca, and when he arrived at Qudayd,[489] he received a message from Medina. He returned to Mecca, entering it without entering the consecrated state.

1274. According to Mālik, Ibn Shihāb provided a report similar to the previous one.

1275. According to Mālik, Muḥammad b. ʿAmr b. Ḥalḥala al-Dīlī reported from Muḥammad b. ʿImrān al-Anṣārī that his father said, "ʿAbd Allāh b. ʿUmar came upon me as I was resting under a tall tree on the road to Mecca, and he said, 'Why did you stop under this tall tree?' I replied, 'I wanted to rest under its shade.' He said, 'Nothing else?' I said, 'No, that was the only reason I stopped.' Then ʿAbd Allāh b. ʿUmar said, 'The Messenger of God (pbuh) said, "If you happen to be between the Akhshabayn[490] near Minā," pointing to the east with his hand, "there is a valley there called al-Surar, wherein is a tall tree, under which the umbilical cords of seventy prophets were cut."'"

1276. According to Mālik, ʿAbd Allāh b. Abī Bakr b. Ḥazm reported from Ibn Abī Mulayka that ʿUmar b. al-Khaṭṭāb passed by a woman suffering from leprosy who was circumambulating God's House. He said to her, "Handmaiden of God, do not cause the people harm! Why don't you stay at home?" Hearing this, she went home. Later, a man happened upon her and said, "The one who confined you to your home is dead, so you can come out

486 The "year of the conquest" (*ʿām al-fatḥ*) refers to the year in which the Prophet (pbuh) successfully returned to Mecca from Medina and received the surrender of the Quraysh. This event took place in the eighth year of the Hijra (630 CE).

487 Ibn ʿAbd al-Barr reports in the *Istidhkār* the explanation provided by the early historian Ibn Isḥāq for the Prophet's (pbuh) order to kill Ibn Khaṭal. The latter had embraced Islam, and the Prophet (pbuh) had appointed him a tax collector and dispatched him to collect taxes with a Medinese man and the latter's Muslim freedman. Ibn Khaṭal quarreled with the freedman, killing him, and then apostatized and fled to Mecca, where he lampooned the Prophet (pbuh) in satirical verse. Ibn ʿAbd al-Barr, *al-Istidhkār*, 4:404.

488 According to Muslim scholars, the fact that the Prophet (pbuh) was not in the consecrated state on that day was a special dispensation granted by God. In another report, the Prophet (pbuh) is quoted as saying, "God permitted Mecca to me for an hour in the day," that is, the day he returned to Mecca in triumph.

489 A place on the road from Mecca to Medina.

490 Two mountains located near the plain of Minā.

now." She replied, "I am not one who would obey him while he is alive, only to disobey him when he is dead."

1277. According to Mālik, it reached him that ʿAbd Allāh b. ʿAbbās would say, "The Multazam lies between the corner of the Black Stone (*rukn*)[491] and Abraham's Standing Place (*maqām*)."[492]

1278. According to Mālik, Yaḥyā b. Saʿīd heard Muḥammad b. Yaḥyā b. Ḥabbān relate that a man passed Abū Dharr[493] at al-Rabadha, and Abū Dharr asked him, "Where do you wish to go?" The man said, "I intend to perform the Pilgrimage." Abū Dharr said, "Is there anything else drawing you on your journey?" He said, "No." Abū Dharr said, "Well, then, continue on your way, seeking only God's pleasure." The man said, "I left and kept going until I reached Mecca and stayed there for a long time. Then I saw the people crowding around a man, so I pushed them aside to see him, and it was the same old man I had met at al-Rabadha, namely, Abū Dharr. When he saw me, he recognized me and said, 'This is what I meant when I first spoke to you.'"

1279. According to Mālik, he asked Ibn Shihāb about making the Pilgrimage conditional.[494] Ibn Shihāb said, "Would anyone do that?" And he disapproved of it.

1280. Yaḥyā said, "Mālik was asked whether it was permitted to gather fodder for one's mount in the precincts of the Sanctuary. He said, 'No.'"

Chapter 82. The Pilgrimage (*Ḥajj*) for a Woman Unaccompanied by a Close Male Relative

1281. Yaḥyā said, "Mālik said, concerning a woman who has never performed the Pilgrimage, that if she does not have a close male relative to accompany her, or if she has one but he cannot accompany her, she is not to abandon what God has imposed on her regarding the Pilgrimage. Instead, she should go with a group of women."

---

491 That is, the corner of the Kabah where the Black Stone is located.

492 The place where Abraham (pbuh) is said to have stood as he built the Kabah.

493 A Companion of the Prophet of God (pbuh) known for his piety and asceticism.

494 This would entail a person's placing a condition on his intention to perform the Pilgrimage such that if the condition came to pass, he could terminate his Pilgrimage before completing it without consequences.

Chapter 83. The Fast of a Pilgrim Who Adds (*Mutamatti'*) the Pilgrimage (*Ḥajj*) after Completing the Visitation (*'Umra*)[495]

1282. According to Mālik, Ibn Shihāb reported from 'Urwa b. al-Zubayr that 'Ā'isha, the Mother of the Believers, would say, "Anyone who combines performance of the Visitation with performance of the Pilgrimage must fast if he cannot obtain a sacrosanct animal (*hady*) for sacrifice between first entering the consecrated state (*iḥrām*) to perform the Pilgrimage and the Day of 'Arafa. If he has not fasted prior to the Day of 'Arafa, he should fast the days of Minā."

1283. According to Mālik, Ibn Shihāb reported from Sālim b. 'Abd Allāh, from 'Abd Allāh b. 'Umar, that his opinion on this matter was the same as 'Ā'isha's.

The Book of Pilgrimage (*Ḥajj*) Has Been Completed, with Much Praise to God, and May God Grace Muḥammad and His Family and Grant Them Perfect Tranquility.

495 In other words, the pilgrim performs *tamattu'*.

Book 21
The Book of Campaigning for the Sake of God (*Jihād*)

In the Name of God, the Merciful, the Compassionate

Your Assistance We Seek, O God!

Chapter 1. Exhorting the People to Campaign for the Sake of God (*Jihād*)

1284. According to Mālik, Abū al-Zinād reported from al-Aʿraj, from Abū Hurayra, that the Messenger of God (pbuh) said, "Someone who is campaigning for the sake of God (*mujāhid*) is like someone who is constant in fasting and prayer and never wearies of them, until he returns home."

1285. According to Mālik, Abū al-Zinād reported from al-Aʿraj, from Abū Hurayra, that the Messenger of God (pbuh) said, "For whoever sets out to campaign for the sake of God, provided that his only motive for leaving his home is the campaign and a firm conviction in the truth of His words, God has undertaken to grant either Heaven or a safe return to his home with whatever reward or booty he has obtained."

1286. According to Mālik, Zayd b. Aslam reported from Abū Ṣāliḥ al-Sammān, from Abū Hurayra, that the Messenger of God (pbuh) said, "For some men, horses are a source of divine reward. For other men, they are a source of protection in this life. For a third group of men, they shall be a burdensome sin in the next life. Those men who shall receive a divine reward for their horses—they are those who acquire them for the sake of God, letting them graze at length on meadows and grasslands. Whatever the horses eat while tethered there count as good deeds for their owners. Should the horses escape their tethers and cross a hillock or two, their tracks and droppings also count as good deeds for their owners. If they cross a river and drink, although their owners did not intend for them to drink at that place, those actions also count as good deeds, and so their owners are rewarded for them. As for those who acquire horses as a means of personal wealth and independence but do not forget God's claims to the horses—these horses protect their owners in this life. As for those who acquire horses out of pride, to show off, and out of hostility to the Muslims—the horses are a burdensome sin to their owners." The Messenger of God (pbuh) was asked about donkeys, so he said, "No specific revelation about them was given to me, except this comprehensive and unique verse: 'Then shall anyone who has done an atom's weight of good see it! And anyone who has done an atom's weight of evil shall see it.'"[496]

1287. According to Mālik, ʿAbd Allāh b. ʿAbd al-Raḥmān b. Maʿmar al-Anṣārī reported that ʿAṭāʾ b. Yasār said, "The Messenger of God (pbuh) said, 'Shall I tell you who has the best standing? Someone who takes hold of the reins of his horse to campaign in the way of God. Shall I tell you who has the best standing after him? Someone who keeps to himself with a small herd, regularly performs his prayers (*ṣalāt*), pays the alms-tax (*zakāt*), and worships God without associating anything with Him.'"

1288. According to Mālik, Yaḥyā b. Saʿīd said, "ʿUbāda b. al-Walīd b. ʿUbāda b. al-Ṣāmit informed me, from his father, that his grandfather said, 'We pledged our loyalty to the Messenger of God (pbuh), agreeing that we would hear and obey, in ease and in hardship, and in what was agreeable as well as in what was disagreeable to us, that we would not resist the commands of those in authority, and that we would speak (or act)[497] for the truth in all circumstances, without fearing rebuke, for the sake of God.'"

1289. According to Mālik, Zayd b. Aslam said, "Abū ʿUbayda b. al-Jarrāḥ wrote a letter to ʿUmar b. al-Khaṭṭāb, telling him about the Byzantine hosts that were massing, and his fear of them. ʿUmar wrote back to him, saying, 'Now then, whatever hardship befalls a faithful servant of God, God shall grant him relief thereafter, and it is inconceivable that one circumstance of hardship can overcome two circumstances of ease.[498] God says in His Book, "O you who believe! Persevere, be constant and firm in the face of your foes, and be mindful of God, that perhaps you may prosper."'"[499]

Chapter 2. The Prohibition against Taking the Quran into Enemy Territory

1290. According to Mālik, Nāfiʿ reported that ʿAbd Allāh b. ʿUmar said, "The Messenger of God (pbuh) prohibited taking the Quran into enemy territory." Mālik said, "This is only out of fear that the enemy might seize it."

496 *Al-Zalzala*, 99:7–8.

497 The narrator is uncertain whether the original word in the report was "speak" or "act."

498 An apparent allusion to *al-Sharḥ*, 94:5–6, which states, "For with hardship, there is ease; with hardship, there is ease."

499 *Āl ʿImrān*, 3:200.

Chapter 3. The Prohibition against Killing Women and Children during Military Expeditions

1291. According to Mālik, Ibn Shihāb reported that a son of Kaʿb b. Mālik (Mālik said, "I believe that Ibn Shihāb said it was ʿAbd al-Raḥmān b. Kaʿb") said, "The Messenger of God (pbuh) instructed those who were sent out to kill Ibn Abī al-Ḥuqayq[500] not to kill women and children. One of them said, 'Ibn Abī al-Ḥuqayq's wife exposed us through her screaming, so I raised my sword against her, but then I recalled the Messenger's prohibition, so I refrained from striking her. Otherwise, we would have finished her off.'"

1292. According to Mālik, Nāfiʿ reported that during one of his military expeditions, the Messenger of God (pbuh) saw the corpse of a slain woman. The sight angered him, and he prohibited the killing of women and children.

1293. According to Mālik, Yaḥyā b. Saʿīd reported that Abū Bakr al-Ṣiddīq dispatched some armies to the Levant. He then set out on foot with Yazīd b. Abī Sufyān, who was the commanding officer of one of the four armies, to accompany them. People claimed that Yazīd said to Abū Bakr, "Either ride together with me, or I will dismount." Abū Bakr al-Ṣiddīq replied, "Neither will you dismount, nor will I ride with you. I deem these steps of mine to be my contribution to the campaign for God's sake." He added, "You will encounter people who claim to have devoted themselves completely to God's service.[501] Leave them be, in accordance with their claims. You will encounter a people who have shaved the hair from the middle of their heads—so lop off their heads with your swords. I charge you to refrain from ten things: do not kill a woman or a child, or an aged, decrepit man; do not cut down fruit-bearing trees; do not destroy any built-up place; do not slaughter a yearling (*shāt*) or a camel, except for food; do not burn or drown date palms;[502] do not misappropriate booty from the battlefield; and do not be cowardly."

1294. According to Mālik, it reached him that ʿUmar b. ʿAbd al-ʿAzīz wrote to one of his provincial governors, telling him, "It has reached us that when the Messenger of God (pbuh) dispatched a raiding party, he would tell them, 'Set out in the name of God, knowing that you are campaigning for the sake of God. You are fighting those who deny Him. Do not misappropriate booty

---

500 Ibn Abī al-Ḥuqayq was a Jewish poet and warrior who played a significant role in marshaling support for the pagan alliance that laid siege to Medina in AH 5 (627 CE). After the Muslims defeated this alliance, Ibn Abī al-Ḥuqayq fled to the oasis town of Khaybar. The Prophet (pbuh) later sent a group of Medinese in his pursuit, and they successfully laid an ambush for him and killed him.

501 Abū Bakr is referring to monks who cloister themselves in cells in the desert.

502 Other narrations of the *Muwaṭṭa'* have "bees" in the place of "date palms," the only difference between the two in Arabic being a dot over one of the three letters: نحل (bees) versus نخل (date palms).

from the battlefield, do not be treacherous, do not mutilate the bodies of your fallen enemies, and do not kill a child.' Convey this message to your armies and raiding parties, if God wills, and may peace be upon you."

Chapter 4. What Has Come Down regarding Fidelity to a Grant of Safe Passage (*Amān*)

1295. According to Mālik, a man of Kufa reported that ʿUmar b. al-Khaṭṭāb wrote to the commander of an army that he had dispatched to Persia, "I have come to understand that some of your men pursue the enemy, tracking him down to his refuge, high up in the mountains. Then one of the Muslims will cry out to him in Persian, '*Mattaras*!' meaning 'Fear not!' in that language. But when the Persian surrenders, the Muslim kills him. By Him whose hand holds my soul, when I find the soldiers who do this, I will behead them." Yaḥyā said, "I heard Mālik say, 'This report is not one that is commonly accepted, and in any case, practice (*ʿamal*) is not in accordance with it.'"

1296. Yaḥyā said, "Mālik was asked whether a gesture of the hand indicating a grant of safe passage (*amān*) had the same effect as a verbal grant of safe passage. He said, 'Yes, and I think it proper that the soldiers understand that they may not kill anyone to whom they have promised safety, even if by a mere gesture. A peaceful gesture, to my mind, is the equivalent of express speech. Moreover, it reached me that ʿAbd Allāh b. ʿAbbās said, "Any people who breaks its covenants shall find itself under its enemy's domination."'"

Chapter 5. The Practice (*ʿAmal*) with Respect to Someone Who Contributes Matériel in Support of a Campaign for the Sake of God

1297. According to Mālik, Nāfiʿ reported from ʿAbd Allāh b. ʿUmar that whenever he contributed matériel in support of a campaign for the sake of God, he would say to the recipient, "Once you reach Wādī al-Qurā, you may do with it what you wish."[503]

1298. According to Mālik, Yaḥyā b. Saʿīd reported that Saʿīd b. al-Musayyab would say, "If a man is given matériel to use during a military expedition and he manages to reach the battlefield with it, it becomes his personal property."

1299. Yaḥyā said, "Mālik was asked about a man who had made a binding undertaking to participate in a military expedition. He readied himself by acquiring all the gear he needed. Then, when he resolved to set out, both of his parents (or one of them) told him not to go. Mālik said, 'I do not think he

503 An oasis not far from Medina on the way to the Levant where the army would muster for the march north.

should disobey them; rather, he should defer his plan to a subsequent year. As for his gear, I think he should store it until he sets out in the subsequent year. If he is concerned that his gear might become useless with the passage of time, he should sell it and keep the proceeds so that he can buy appropriate gear at the time of the upcoming campaign. If he is sufficiently wealthy, however, he will be able to obtain the appropriate gear whenever he sets out. Accordingly, he may do whatever he wishes with his current gear.'"

Chapter 6. Miscellaneous Reports on Excess Shares of Booty (*Nafl*) Distributed after the Conclusion of a Campaign

1300. According to Mālik, Nāfiʿ reported from ʿAbd Allāh b. ʿUmar that the Messenger of God (pbuh) dispatched a raiding party that included ʿAbd Allāh b. ʿUmar in the direction of Najd.[504] They successfully made off with a large number of camels, and their shares came to twelve (or eleven) camels each.[505] Each soldier in the raid was then given an extra camel in addition to his allotted share of the booty taken in the raid.[506]

1301. According to Mālik, Yaḥyā b. Saʿīd reported that he heard Saʿīd b. al-Musayyab say, "When the time came to divide booty seized on the battlefield, the soldiers deemed a camel the equivalent of ten yearlings (*shāt*)."

1302. Yaḥyā said, "I heard Mālik say, regarding a wage laborer who accompanies a campaign, 'If he attends the battle and is with the soldiers during the fight, and if he is a free man, he receives a share of any booty captured. If not, then he has no claim.'" Yaḥyā also said, "I heard Mālik say, 'Only someone who is present at the time of fighting, in my opinion, is entitled to a share of the booty.'"

Chapter 7. What Is Exempt from the One-Fifth Rule Governing Booty

1303. Yaḥyā said, "I heard Mālik speak of people from enemy territory who are found on the coastlines of Muslim territory. They deny they are soldiers and claim instead to be merchants who have been cast ashore by the sea. However, the Muslims are unable to determine whether their claim is true.

504 The large, barren plateau located to the east of the Hijaz in the center of the Arabian Peninsula.

505 The narrator is uncertain whether the share of each participant in the raid was twelve or eleven camels.

506 The rule governing the distribution of booty seized on the battlefield is that four-fifths is to be divided among the soldiers who participate in the campaign, and one-fifth goes to the state. *Al-Anfāl*, 8:41. The additional camel given to each soldier that is mentioned in this report refers to the excess shares of booty that were allotted to the soldiers out of the one-fifth share belonging to the state.

They do know, however, that these people's boats have been shipwrecked or that they have been overcome by thirst, and that they disembarked onto Muslim territory without prior permission. Mālik said, 'In my opinion, what to do with them is a decision that belongs to the ruler (*imām*); he decides how to treat them in accordance with his considered judgment. I do not think that they and their property should be deemed booty.'"[507]

Chapter 8. What Muslims on Campaign May Lawfully Consume of the Enemy's Property before Payment of the One-Fifth Due to the State

1304. Yaḥyā said, "I heard Mālik say, 'There is no harm, in my opinion, in the Muslims' eating whatever food they find in enemy territory while on a campaign there, before the booty is distributed.'"

1305. Mālik said, "I believe that camels, cattle, and sheep (*ghanam*) are the equivalent of 'food' in this case. Muslims can eat these whenever they enter enemy territory on a campaign, just as they eat the food they find there. If the rule were that food and animals could only be eaten after the army had divided the booty among themselves at the end of the campaign, it would cause great harm to armies. I have no objection to Muslims who are on the campaign eating any of these things, as long as what they consume does not exceed what is customary or what necessity requires. No Muslim, however, should store any of these items with the intention of bringing them back to his family."

1306. Yaḥyā said, "Mālik was asked about a soldier who, while in enemy territory, seizes some food, eats from it, and takes provisions from it. He then finds at the end of the campaign that some is left over. May he keep the leftovers for himself and eat them later with his family, or sell them before he returns to his native land and benefit from the proceeds of the sale? Mālik said, 'If he sold them while he was campaigning, I believe he should deliver the sale price he received to the army, because it is part of the Muslims' booty. If he arrives home with them, however, I have no objection if he eats them or otherwise makes use of them, if their amount is trivial.'"

Chapter 9. Restitution of Property Originally Belonging to Muslims That the Enemy Seized before the Booty Is Divided

1307. According to Mālik, it reached him that a slave of ʿAbd Allāh b. ʿUmar had run away, and one of his horses had escaped, and the enemy captured

507 In other words, the Muslims who captured them are not entitled to four-fifths of the prisoners' property; rather, the prisoners and their possessions come under the full control of the state, and the ruler is to determine their fate.

each of them. The Muslims later seized both in battle and returned them to ʿAbd Allāh b. ʿUmar before the booty was divided.

1308. Yaḥyā said, "I heard Mālik say that if the Muslims discover, before the distribution of the booty, that some of the booty they have taken from the enemy consists of property that originally belonged to Muslims,[508] such property is to be returned to its original owners. However, no claims of restitution are admissible with respect to such property after it has been divided among the soldiers."

1309. Yaḥyā said, "Mālik was asked about the owner of a young male slave whom the enemy had captured and made off with. The Muslims then recaptured him from the enemy. Mālik said, 'His owner has the best claim to him. He need not pay a purchase price for the slave, his fair value, or the cost of his upkeep, provided that the booty has not yet been divided. If the booty has been divided, however, and the slave has already been given to another, the original master may redeem his former slave if he wishes from the new master, but only after he pays the new master a mutually agreeable price.'"

1310. Regarding a scenario in which a slave woman who has given birth to the child of her Muslim master (*umm walad*) is subsequently captured by the enemy, but then the Muslims recapture her from the enemy and include her in the booty that is divided among the soldiers, but after the booty has been divided her original master recognizes her, Mālik said, "She should not, in my opinion, be enslaved, and the ruler must ransom her. If the ruler fails to do so, her former master must ransom her; he may not abandon her to her new master. I do not think that the person who received her as booty is permitted to enslave her or deem her licit for intercourse. Her status renders her the equivalent of a free woman. Her original master is obliged to ransom her in this case, just as he is obliged to ransom her had she injured another person.[509] This case is the equivalent of that one. He is not free to permit the mother of his child to be enslaved, nor is he permitted to allow her to become the subject of unlawful intercourse."

1311. Yaḥyā said, "Mālik was asked about the case of a man who sets out for enemy territory either to ransom prisoners captured by the enemy or to engage in commerce in enemy territory. While there, the man purchases

508 This includes property belonging to non-Muslims who are under the protection of the Islamic state (*dhimmīs*).

509 According to Mālik, when a slave injures another person, the slave's master must either compensate the injured party with money or property or forfeit the slave to the injured party. However, if the slave is the mother of his child, he is not allowed to forfeit her to the injured party.

from the enemy a slave or a free person that the enemy has captured,[510] or he receives one or the other as a gift. Mālik said, 'As for the free captive, the price that the man pays for him constitutes a debt that the captive owes to the man who ransomed him from the enemy, but the free captive may not be enslaved. If the enemy freely gave the captive to the man, the captive owes him nothing, unless the man gave the captors a gift in return. In that case, that reciprocal gift constitutes a debt that the captive is obliged to pay, and it is treated as the equivalent to what the man would have paid to free him, as in the previous case. As for the slave, his former master is free to take him back from the man who purchased him from the enemy by paying the sale price to him. If the former master wishes to abandon the slave to the man who purchased him from the enemy, however, he may do so. If, on the other hand, the enemy freely gave the slave to the man, then his former master has a superior claim to the slave and may reclaim him without paying anything to the man who retrieved him from the enemy, unless the man gave something to the slave's captors as a gift in return. In this case, the original master pays the man holding the slave whatever he paid to the slave's captors as a reciprocal gift, if he wants the slave returned to him.'"[511]

Chapter 10. What Has Come Down regarding the Plunder of Deceased Enemy Soldiers as an Extra Share of Booty

1312. According to Mālik, Yaḥyā b. Saʿīd reported from ʿAmr b. Kathīr b. Aflaḥ, from Abū Muḥammad, the freedman (*mawlā*) of Abū Qatāda, that Abū Qatāda b. Ribʿī said, "We set out with the Messenger of God (pbuh) in the year of the Battle of Ḥunayn.[512] When the two armies met, the Muslim forces were initially in disarray. I saw a pagan getting the better of one of the Muslims. I turned around and came at him from behind, striking the pagan with my sword on his shoulder blade. He turned and lunged at me, grabbing me so tightly that I could smell death oozing from him. When death finally overtook him, I pulled free of his grasp. Then I saw ʿUmar b. al-Khaṭṭāb and said, 'What's wrong with us today?' He said, 'The matter is in God's hands.'

510 Mālik is distinguishing here between the case of a person who was free under Islamic law at the time the enemy captured him and who therefore can never be enslaved under Islamic law and a person who was a slave in Islamic territory at the time the enemy captured him and who retains his status as a slave until he is manumitted.

511 Mālik here appears to be referring to the custom of reciprocal gift giving as a substitute for paying an explicit ransom for captives. Mālik treats the reciprocal gift as though it were, in fact, an explicit ransom payment.

512 A major battle fought between the Muslims and the tribes of Hawāzin and Thaqīf shortly after the Prophet (pbuh) conquered Mecca. The battle took place in the Hijaz, and despite the great numbers of the Muslims they were almost defeated, but the battle eventually turned to their favor and ended in a decisive Muslim victory.

At last we found our resolve after the initial setback. The Messenger of God (pbuh) said, 'Whoever slew an enemy soldier and can prove it is entitled to strip him of his effects.' When I heard this, I stood up and said, 'Who will vouch for me?' and then sat down. The Messenger of God (pbuh) said, 'Whoever slew an enemy soldier and can prove it is entitled to strip him of his effects.' I stood up again and said, 'Who will vouch for me?' and then sat down. Then the Messenger of God (pbuh) said it a third time, so I stood up a third time. The Messenger of God (pbuh) said, 'What is your claim, Abū Qatāda?' So I told him what had happened. Someone present said, 'He's telling the truth, Messenger of God. I already have the dead man's effects, so give him something of equivalent value that will satisfy him!' Then Abū Bakr said, 'No, by God! The Messenger (pbuh) did not intend that one of God's lions should fight for God and His Messenger, and then you take the spoils of his struggle.' So the Messenger of God (pbuh) said, 'He has spoken the truth. Give Abū Qatāda the dead man's effects.' He gave them to me, and I sold the plate armor, and with that money I bought date palms in Banū Salima, and this was the first property I acquired as a Muslim."[513]

1313. According to Mālik, Ibn Shihāb reported that al-Qāsim b. Muḥammad said, "I heard a man ask ʿAbd Allāh b. ʿAbbās about the meaning of the word *anfāl*. Ibn ʿAbbās said, 'Horses and the personal effects of a slain warrior are included in the term *anfāl*.'[514] Then the man asked his question again, so Ibn ʿAbbās repeated his previous answer. Then the man said, 'The *anfāl* that God mentioned in His Book, what is it?' The man kept asking Ibn ʿAbbās until the latter grew weary of his questions and said, 'Do you know who this man reminds me of? He is like Ṣabīgh whom ʿUmar b. al-Khaṭṭāb punished.'"[515]

1314. Yaḥyā said, "Mālik was asked whether someone who slays an enemy in battle is allowed to keep the personal effects of the slain warrior without

513 The ordinary rule that applies to the division of battlefield spoils (*ghanīma*) is that the spoils are gathered into one pool, out of which one-fifth is given to the state and the remaining four-fifths are divided equally among the soldiers who participated in the campaign. Mālik understood the individual right of a Muslim soldier to take the effects of an enemy warrior whom he personally killed as constituting an excess share of booty (*nafl*), which comes out of the one-fifth share of the state. This entitlement is thus contingent on the ruler's permission and not a freestanding right of the soldiers, as Mālik makes clear in hadith no. 1314. This view contrasts with that of the Shāfiʿīs, who hold that soldiers always have a superior claim to the personal possessions of enemy soldiers whom they kill on the battlefield.

514 Insofar as Ibn ʿAbbās believed that the personal effects of a slain enemy warrior are considered *anfāl*, that is, excess shares of booty, his definition supports Mālik's view, stated expressly in the following hadith (no. 1314), that the right to take possession of the personal effects of a slain enemy warrior is contingent on the ruler's prior permission.

515 Ṣabīgh was reported to have repeatedly asked ʿUmar b. al-Khaṭṭāb about the meanings of obscure passages of the Quran that were not relevant to the proper understanding or practice of Islam. When ʿUmar became convinced that Ṣabīgh was not sincere in his questions, he had him punished and exiled for a period of time.

the prior permission of the ruler (*imām*). He said, 'No one is allowed to do so without the prior permission of the ruler, and the ruler may give such permission only after the exercise of good-faith judgment (*ijtihād*). The only report that has reached me in which the Messenger of God (pbuh) said, "Whoever slew an enemy soldier is entitled to strip him of his effects," was from the Battle of Ḥunayn.'"

Chapter 11. What Has Come Down regarding the Grant of Excess Shares of Booty (*Nafal*) Out of the State's One-Fifth Share

1315. According to Mālik, Abū al-Zinād reported that Saʿīd b. al-Musayyab said, "People were given extra shares of booty out of the one-fifth share." Mālik said, "That is the best view I have heard on this issue."

1316. Yaḥyā said, "Mālik was asked whether excess shares of booty could be awarded out of spoils taken in the first battle of a campaign. He said, 'That is determined by the good-faith judgment (*ijtihād*) of the ruler (*imām*).[516] We Medinese do not have a definitive rule on this question beyond following the good-faith judgment of the responsible public official (*sulṭān*). No evidence has reached me to indicate that the Messenger of God (pbuh) always granted excess shares of booty to soldiers in his campaigns, although I am aware that he did give excess shares of booty in some of his campaigns, such as at the Battle of Ḥunayn. This is permitted, however, only in accordance with the good-faith judgment of the ruler, whether after the first battle of the campaign or after any subsequent battle.'"

Chapter 12. The Cavalry's Share of the Booty

1317. Mālik said, "It reached me that ʿUmar b. ʿAbd al-ʿAzīz would say, 'The cavalryman receives two shares of booty for every one given to the infantryman.'" Mālik added, "That is what I have always heard to be the rule (*wa lam azal asmaʿ dhālika*)."

1318. Yaḥyā said, "Mālik was asked whether a man who brought several horses to the campaign was entitled to a share for each horse. He said, 'I have not heard anything about that case. I do not believe, however, that he is entitled to receive a share for any horse other than the one he rode in battle.'"

1319. Mālik said, "I believe that draft horses and half-Arabian horses are also deemed to count as horses. God, Blessed and Sublime is He, says in His Book, 'And (He has created) horses, mules, and donkeys for you to ride.'[517]

516 The reference to the ruler would also include the ruler's authorized delegate, such as the relevant battlefield commander or a governor.

517 *Al-Naḥl*, 16:8.

God also said, 'Against them, marshal your strength as best you can and make ready the steeds of war, striking awe into God's enemies and yours.'[518] It is my view that draft horses and half-Arabians are indeed horses and are therefore entitled to shares of booty from a campaign, if the commanding officer incorporates them in the campaign. Saʿīd b. al-Musayyab once said, when he was asked whether the alms-tax (*ṣadaqa*) was levied on draft horses, 'Is the alms-tax levied on horses?'"

Chapter 13. What Has Come Down regarding the Misappropriation of Booty (*Ghulūl*)

1320. According to Mālik, ʿAbd Rabbih b. Saʿīd reported from ʿAmr b. Shuʿayb that when the Messenger of God (pbuh) departed from Ḥunayn toward al-Jiʿirrāna,[519] the soldiers were so adamant in demanding their shares of the spoils after the Battle of Ḥunayn that his she-camel was backed into a tree, with the Prophet (pbuh) still mounted on its back. His cloak became entangled in the tree's branches, and it was torn off his back. The Messenger of God (pbuh) said, "Give me back my cloak! Do you really doubt whether I will divide among you the spoils that God has bestowed on you this day? By Him whose hand holds my soul, if God had bestowed on you livestock equal to the number of acacia trees on the plain of Tihāma,[520] I would have divided them among all of you, and then you certainly would not think me either a miser, a coward, or a liar." When the Messenger of God (pbuh) dismounted, he stood among the soldiers and said, "Hand over even a thread and needle that you might have taken from the enemy, for misappropriation of booty (*ghulūl*) results in disgrace, fire, and shame on the Day of Resurrection." The Messenger of God (pbuh) then picked up a ball of camel hair (or something else) from the ground and said, "By Him whose hand holds my soul, only one-fifth of the spoils that God has bestowed on you goes to me, and even that," and he pointed to the camel hair, "I shall divide among you."

1321. According to Mālik, Yaḥyā b. Saʿīd reported from Muḥammad b. Yaḥyā b. Ḥabbān that Zayd b. Khālid al-Juhanī said, "A man died at the Battle of Ḥunayn,[521] and they told the Messenger of God (pbuh) so that he might perform the man's funeral prayer." Zayd stated that the Messenger of God

518 *Al-Anfāl*, 8:60.

519 A small village northeast of Mecca.

520 The acacia is a thorny bush found in abundance in Tihāma, the thin coastal plain of the Arabian peninsula that runs parallel to the Red Sea.

521 This narration of the *Muwaṭṭa'* identifies the man as having died at the Battle of Ḥunayn, which is an error. The correct version of the story says that he died at Khaybar, an oasis in the Hijaz controlled by a Jewish tribe, which is more consistent with the facts reported in this story. Bājī, *al-Muntaqā*, 3:200.

(pbuh) said, "*You* pray over your companion!" The color drained from their faces at those words. Zayd stated, "The Messenger of God (pbuh) said, 'Your companion misappropriated booty while campaigning for the sake of God.' We then opened the dead man's pack and found there some beads that had belonged to some Jews, not even amounting to two silver coins."

1322. According to Mālik, Yaḥyā b. Saʿīd reported from ʿAbd Allāh b. al-Mughīra b. Abī Burda al-Kinānī that it reached him that the Messenger of God (pbuh) went to each of the tribes to supplicate God on their behalf, except for one tribe. ʿAbd Allāh b. al-Mughīra said, "That tribe's men discovered that one of them had hidden in his saddle bag a necklace that he had misappropriated from the spoils. The Messenger of God (pbuh) went to see them, and he magnified God (said 'God is great,' *Allāhu akbar*) over the people in the same way as is done over the deceased."[522]

1323. According to Mālik, Thawr b. Zayd al-Dīlī reported from Abū al-Ghayth Sālim, the freedman (*mawlā*) of Ibn Muṭīʿ, that Abū Hurayra said, "We set out with the Messenger of God (pbuh) in the year of the Battle of Ḥunayn. The only booty we seized consisted of cloth and equipment, no gold or silver. Rifāʿa b. Zayd gifted the Messenger of God (pbuh) a young black slave named Midʿam. The Messenger of God (pbuh) resolved to march toward Wādī al-Qurā. When we arrived at Wādī al-Qurā, Midʿam was unsaddling the mount of the Messenger of God (pbuh) when a stray arrow struck and killed him. The people said, 'He has the good fortune of Paradise.' The Messenger of God (pbuh) said, 'No, by Him whose hand holds my soul, the cloak that he misappropriated at the Battle of Ḥunayn, before the spoils were divided, is ablaze on his body.' When the people heard this, a man brought a sandal-lace or two to the Messenger of God (pbuh), who said, 'A sandal-lace or two of fire.'"

1324. According to Mālik, Yaḥyā b. Saʿīd reported that it reached him that ʿAbd Allāh b. ʿAbbās said, "Whenever it becomes normal among a people to misappropriate booty, their hearts are gripped with fear and they lose their courage. So, too, whenever fornication becomes widespread among a people, death follows close in its wake. Whenever a people fail to give full measure in trade, their livelihoods are destroyed. Whenever a people judge falsely, murder spreads among them. Whenever a people do not

522 According to Ibn ʿAbd al-Barr, the narrator of this hadith, ʿAbd Allāh b. al-Mughīra b. Abī Burda al-Kinānī, is an obscure figure, and as a result this report is not of sufficient strength to establish a rule. As for the Prophet's (pbuh) magnification of God over the people, Ibn ʿAbd al-Barr is at a loss to explain the meaning of the act, but he concludes that since the report is weak, there is no need to expend great effort to comprehend its precise meaning beyond affirming that misappropriation of the spoils of war is a great sin. See RME, 1:481 n. 8.

faithfully fulfill their covenants with their enemies, their enemies come to dominate them."

Chapter 14. Martyrs for the Sake of God

1325. According to Mālik, Abū al-Zinād reported from al-Aʿraj, from Abū Hurayra, that the Messenger of God (pbuh) said, "By Him whose hand holds my soul, would that I could fight for the sake of God, be killed, and then be revived, so that I could be killed, revived, and killed again." After reporting this, Abū Hurayra would repeat three times, "I swear by God this is true."

1326. According to Mālik, Abū al-Zinād reported from al-Aʿraj, from Abū Hurayra, that the Messenger of God (pbuh) said, "God looks with pleasure at two men, one of whom kills the other but each of whom nonetheless enters Paradise. The first fights for the sake of God and is killed; and then, by God's grace, the killer repents, fights for the sake of God, and dies as a martyr."

1327. According to Mālik, Abū al-Zinād reported from al-Aʿraj, from Abū Hurayra, that the Messenger of God (pbuh) said, "By Him whose hand holds my soul, anyone wounded while campaigning for the sake of God—and God knows best who such people are—will appear on the Day of Resurrection with blood gushing from his wound: its color is that of blood, but its scent is that of musk."

1328. According to Mālik, Zayd b. Aslam reported that ʿUmar b. al-Khaṭṭāb would say, "God, let me not die at the hand of a man who has performed even a single prostration that he could use as evidence against me on the Day of Resurrection!"

1329. According to Mālik, Yaḥyā b. Saʿīd reported from Saʿīd b. Abī Saʿīd al-Maqburī, from ʿAbd Allāh b. Abī Qatāda, that his father said, "A man came to the Messenger of God (pbuh) and said, 'Messenger of God, if I am slain while campaigning for God's sake, showing patience and hoping for a reward from God, advancing toward and not fleeing from the enemy, will God pardon my sins?' The Messenger of God (pbuh) said, 'Yes.' As the man turned away, the Messenger of God (pbuh) called him back (or ordered that the man be called back) and said to him, 'Could you repeat your question?' The man repeated his question, and the Prophet (pbuh) said to him, 'Yes; everything except for your debts. That is what Gabriel told me.'"

1330. According to Mālik, Abū al-Naḍr, the freedman (*mawlā*) of ʿUmar b. ʿUbayd Allāh, reported that it reached him that the Messenger of God (pbuh) said about the martyrs of the Battle of Uḥud, "I certainly do testify on their behalf." Then Abū Bakr al-Ṣiddīq said, "Aren't we, Messenger of God, their brethren? We embraced Islam just as they did, and we struggled for God's sake just as they did." The Messenger of God (pbuh) said, "Certainly you did, but I have no idea what you will do after I die." Abū Bakr wept inconsolably and then said, "What—shall we still be alive even after you are dead?"

1331. According to Mālik, Yaḥyā b. Saʿīd said, "The Messenger of God (pbuh) was sitting nearby as a grave was being dug in Medina. A man looked into the grave and said, 'An awful bed indeed for the believer.' The Messenger of God (pbuh) said, 'Baneful is that which you say.' The man said, 'But that is not what I meant, Messenger of God! I only meant that dying as a martyr is more virtuous.' Then the Messenger of God (pbuh) said, 'There is nothing equivalent to martyrdom, but there is no place on earth I would rather have contain my grave than this patch of ground here.' He repeated this three times."

Chapter 15. What Constitutes Martyrdom

1332. According to Mālik, Zayd b. Aslam reported that ʿUmar b. al-Khaṭṭāb would say, "God, I ask that You grant me martyrdom and that I die in Your Messenger's city!"[523]

1333. According to Mālik, Yaḥyā b. Saʿīd reported that ʿUmār b. al-Khaṭṭāb said, "The believer's nobility lies in his mindfulness of God; his piety consists of the stock of his good deeds; and his manliness lies in his moral character. Courage and cowardice are instincts that God places in whomsoever He wills. Thus, the coward flees even from his own father and mother, whereas the courageous even risk their lives for trivial things. Death in battle is but one kind of death, and the martyr is someone who has given his life for the sake of God in expectation of His reward."

Chapter 16. The Practice (*ʿAmal*) with Respect to Preparing Martyrs for Burial

1334. According to Mālik, Nāfiʿ reported from ʿAbd Allāh b. ʿUmar that ʿUmar b. al-Khaṭṭāb was washed, shrouded, and prayed over even though he was a martyr; may God have mercy on him.

1335. According to Mālik, it reached him that the people of knowledge would say, "Martyrs are not to be washed, nor is a funeral prayer to be performed over them. Rather, they are to be buried in the clothes in which they were slain." Yaḥyā said, "Mālik said, 'That rule is for someone who dies on the battlefield and whose corpse is recovered only after his death. As for

523 ʿUmar is referring here to Medina.

someone who is carried away from the battlefield wounded but alive and who survives for some period of time before succumbing to his wounds, he is to be washed and the funeral prayer is to be performed over him, just as was done in the case of ʿUmar b. al-Khaṭṭāb.'"

Chapter 17. What Is Reprehensible to Give in Support of a Campaign for the Sake of God

1336. According to Mālik, Yaḥyā b. Saʿīd reported that ʿUmar b. al-Khaṭṭāb would requisition 40,000 camels each year, assigning one man per camel to the Levant and two men per camel to Iraq. An Iraqi came to him and said, "Provide Suḥaym and me with a mount." ʿUmar b. al-Khaṭṭāb said to him, "I admonish you to tell the truth! By God, tell me, is Suḥaym just a waterskin?"[524] The man said, "Yes."

Chapter 18. Exhorting the People to Campaign for the Sake of God (*Jihād*)

1337. According to Mālik, Isḥāq b. ʿAbd Allāh b. Abī Ṭalḥa reported that Anas b. Mālik said, "When the Messenger of God (pbuh) went to Qubāʾ, he would visit Umm Ḥarām bt. Milḥān, and she would feed him. At that time, she was married to ʿUbāda b. al-Ṣāmit. One day, the Messenger of God (pbuh) paid her a visit, and she fed him. She sat down to delouse his hair, and he fell asleep. Then he awoke, smiling. She said, 'Why are you smiling, Messenger of God?' He said, 'Some of my community appeared to me in my dream, campaigning for God's sake, sailing the open seas, kings on thrones'" (or "like kings on thrones"; Isḥāq was unsure). Anas said, "She said, 'Messenger of God, supplicate God that He make me one of them.' He supplicated God as she requested, put his head down, and went back to sleep. Then he woke up, smiling. She said, 'Why are you smiling, Messenger of God?' He said, 'Some of my community appeared to me in my dream, campaigning for God's sake, kings on thrones (or "like kings on thrones"),' as he said the first time. She said, 'Messenger of God, supplicate God that He make me one of them.' He said, 'You will be among the very first.'" Isḥāq said, "She participated in a naval campaign organized by Muʿāwiya b. Abī Sufyān, and as she came ashore, she was thrown from her horse and died."

1338. According to Mālik, Yaḥyā b. Saʿīd reported from Abū Sāliḥ al-Sammān, from Abū Hurayra, that the Messenger of God (pbuh) said, "Were I indifferent to the hardship facing my community, I would have always accompanied

524 "Suḥaym," in addition to being a proper name, is also used generically to refer to a waterskin. The man was trying to deceive ʿUmar b. al-Khaṭṭāb into giving him a camel solely for his own use.

every raiding party that set out for God's sake. But I cannot find a sufficient number of animals for them to ride, nor do they have a sufficient number of their own animals on which they could ride. Therefore, they would be distressed if I set out to campaign and they stayed behind. Alas, would that I could fight for God's sake, be killed, and then be revived, then be killed again, then be revived, and then be killed again!"

1339. According to Mālik, Yaḥyā b. Saʿīd said, "At the Battle of Uḥud, the Messenger of God (pbuh) said, 'Who will get me news of Saʿd b. al-Rabīʿ al-Anṣārī?' A man replied, 'I will, Messenger of God.' The man set off, wandering among the dead, and then Saʿd b. al-Rabīʿ said to him, 'What is your business?' The man said, 'The Messenger of God (pbuh) sent me to look for you so I could find out what happened to you.' Saʿd said, 'Return to him and give him my salutations. Then tell him that I have been stabbed twelve times and am mortally wounded. And tell the men that if the Messenger of God is killed today, they have no excuse before God if even one of them survives.'"

1340. According to Mālik, Yaḥyā b. Saʿīd reported that the Messenger of God (pbuh) was exhorting the people to struggle against the enemy, and he mentioned Paradise while a Medinese man was nearby, eating dates. Hearing this, the man said, "I would indeed be covetous of this world were I to remain seated here until I finish these." Then, he tossed them aside, grabbed his sword, and fought until he was killed.

1341. According to Mālik, Yaḥyā b. Saʿīd reported that Muʿādh b. Jabal said, "Campaigns are of two kinds. The first kind is a campaign in which valuable property is spent on equipment, the soldiers are in agreement, the commanding officers are obeyed, and disorder is avoided. This is a campaign that is good from beginning to end. The second kind is a campaign in which nothing of value is spent in preparation, the soldiers are quarrelsome, insubordination in the ranks is rife, and disorder prevails. This is the kind of campaign in which a man who fights returns bereft of reward."

Chapter 19. What Has Come Down regarding Horses and Horse Racing, and Spending in Support of a Campaign for the Sake of God

1342. According to Mālik, Nāfiʿ reported from ʿAbd Allāh b. ʿUmar that the Messenger of God (pbuh) said, "Blessings shall lie in the forelocks of horses until the Day of Resurrection."

1343. According to Mālik, Nāfiʿ reported from ʿAbd Allāh b. ʿUmar that the Messenger of God (pbuh) would hold a horse race for those horses that were lean and muscled from their years of racing. The race would begin at al-Ḥafyāʾ and end at Thaniyyat al-Wadāʿ.[525] He would hold another race for horses that were in the early stages of their training. That race would begin from Thaniyyat al-Wadāʿ and end at the Mosque of Banū Zurayq.[526] ʿAbd Allāh b. ʿUmar sometimes raced with them.

1344. According to Mālik, Yaḥyā b. Saʿīd reported that he heard Saʿīd b. al-Musayyab say, "There is no harm in providing a purse for the winner of a horse race if a third person provides it, on the condition that the winner takes the purse but the loser owes nothing."[527]

1345. According to Mālik, Yaḥyā b. Saʿīd reported that the Messenger of God (pbuh) was seen using his cloak to wipe the face of his horse. He was asked why he did that, and he replied, "God reproached me tonight on account of my horses."[528]

1346. According to Mālik, Ḥumayd al-Ṭawīl reported from Anas b. Mālik that the Messenger of God (pbuh) set out for Khaybar[529] and arrived there at night. It was his practice that if he reached his enemy in the darkness of night, he would not launch an attack until daybreak. In the morning, the Jews went out to their fields with their spades and large baskets, and when they saw him, they said, "It is Muḥammad! By God, it is Muḥammad and his army!" The Messenger of God (pbuh) said, "God is great! May Khaybar fall! Indeed, when we come to a people's territory, it is a baneful morning for those who have been warned."

1347. According to Mālik, Ibn Shihāb reported from Ḥumayd b. ʿAbd al-Raḥmān b. ʿAwf, from Abū Hurayra, that the Messenger of God (pbuh) said, "Whoever spends anything of his property for God's sake shall be addressed in Paradise with the words, 'O servant of God, this indeed is excellent!' Whoever performed prayer shall be called from the Gate of Prayer; whoever fought for God's sake shall be called from the Gate of Jihād; whoever gave charity shall be called from the Gate of Charity; and whoever fasted shall be called from the Gate of al-Rayyān."[530] Abū Bakr al-Ṣiddīq said,

525 Thaniyyat al-Wadāʿ is the place where those leaving Medina would be bid farewell, and al-Ḥafyāʾ is a location outside of Medina between five and seven *mīl*s from Thaniyyat al-Wadāʿ. Zurqānī, *Sharḥ al-Zurqānī*, 3:71.

526 The Banū Zurayq was a Medinese clan, and the mosque in their settlement was approximately one *mīl* from Thaniyyat al-Wadāʿ. Zurqānī, *Sharḥ al-Zurqānī*, 3:71.

527 Gambling is strictly prohibited in Islam.

528 In other words, God had told the Prophet (pbuh) to be more gentle with his horses.

529 Khaybar, an oasis town located approximately four days' march north of Medina, was a site of intense date cultivation by a Hijazi Jewish community. The Prophet (pbuh) campaigned against them after making peace with the Meccans at al-Ḥudaybiya. Khaybar surrendered after a brief siege.

530 *Rayyān* is the opposite of *ʿaṭshān*, which means "thirsty," or what a fasting person must endure patiently. Accordingly, the "Gate of *al-Rayyān*" may be understood literally as the "Gate of the Quenched" because those admitted to Paradise will never suffer thirst again.

"Messenger of God, anyone who is called from one of these gates surely does not need to be called from the others, but is it possible that someone might be called from all of them?" The Messenger of God (pbuh) said, "Yes, and I hope that you are one of them."

Chapter 20. The Proprietary Rights of Protected People (*Ahl al-Dhimma*) Who Later Embrace Islam to Their Land

1348. Yaḥyā said, "Mālik was asked about a ruler (*imām*) who agreed to accept payment of the poll-tax (*jizya*) from a people in exchange for peace. They then faithfully paid the levy. The questioner said, 'Do you think that those of them who embrace Islam become proprietors of their land, or should the land and such individuals' other property belong to the Muslims?' Mālik said, 'It depends. If one of those who have entered into a peace treaty with the Muslims[531] embraces Islam, he has a greater entitlement to his land and property than do the other Muslims. But if one of those who were conquered[532] and whose lands were taken by force later embraces Islam, his land and property belong to the other Muslims. This is because those who were conquered were dispossessed of their lands by force of arms, and so their property devolved upon the Muslims. By contrast, those who concluded a peace treaty with the Muslims and were not conquered by force of arms remained in possession of their persons and their property at the time they made peace with the Muslims. Their peace treaty confirmed their property rights. Consequently, they have no duties beyond those set out in their peace treaty.'"

Chapter 21. The Burial of Multiple Bodies in a Single Grave out of Necessity and Abū Bakr's Discharge of the Promises of the Prophet (pbuh) after His Death

1349. According to Mālik, ʿAbd al-Raḥmān b. ʿAbd Allāh b. ʿAbd al-Raḥmān b. Abī Ṣaʿṣaʿa reported that it reached him that a flood partially uncovered the grave of ʿAmr b. al-Jamūḥ and ʿAbd Allāh b. ʿAmr, two Medinese (*anṣār*) from the tribe of Banū Salima, exposing their bodies.[533] They had been buried together in one grave next to the flood plain. Both had been martyred at the Battle of Uḥud. Their grave was excavated and their bodies exhumed so that they could be reinterred somewhere other than the flood plain. When their

531 In Arabic, such people are literally called "people of the treaty" (*ahl al-ṣulḥ*), meaning that their rights have been secured by their entering into a treaty with the Muslim conquerors.

532 In Arabic, such people are called "people of conquest" (*ahl al-ʿanwa*), meaning that the Muslim conquerors subdued them by force.

533 According to Zurqānī, the Banū Salima was a branch of the Khazraj, one of the two major Arab tribes in Medina prior to Islam. Zurqānī, *Sharḥ al-Zurqānī*, 3:79.

bodies were exhumed, it was discovered that they had not yet decomposed, and it was as though they had just died yesterday. One of them, who had been wounded, had placed his hand over his wound and had been buried in that posture. His hand was lifted from the wound and then released, and it returned to its original position. Forty-six years had elapsed between the Battle of Uḥud and the day when their bodies were exhumed.

1350. Yaḥyā said, "Mālik said, 'There is no harm in burying two or three men together in the same grave out of necessity, with the oldest being placed nearest to Mecca.'"

1351. According to Mālik, Rabīʿa b. Abī ʿAbd al-Raḥmān said, "Abū Bakr received some property from Baḥrayn, so he said, 'Anyone who received an undertaking or a promise from the Messenger of God (pbuh) should come see me.' Jābir b. ʿAbd Allāh went to him, and Abū Bakr gave him three complete handfuls."[534]

The Book of Campaigning for the Sake of God (*Jihād*) Is Complete, through God's Most Excellent Assistance, with Praise to Him.

534 A handful means both hands. Zurqānī, *Sharḥ al-Zurqānī*, 3:81.

Book 22

The Book of Sacrificial Animals (*Ḍaḥāyā*)[535]

In the Name of God, the Merciful, the Compassionate

Chapter 1. Animals That May Not Be Sacrificed

1352. According to Mālik, ʿAmr b. al-Ḥārith reported from ʿUbayd b. Fayrūz, from al-Barāʾ b. ʿĀzib, that the Messenger of God (pbuh) was asked which animals should not be offered in sacrifice. He waved his hand and said, "Four types." (Al-Barāʾ was waving his hand, saying, "My hand is shorter than that of the Messenger of God, pbuh.") "Animals that are manifestly lame, blind in one eye, ill, or emaciated and lacking any fat."

1353. According to Mālik, Nāfiʿ reported that ʿAbd Allāh b. ʿUmar would not consecrate camels for the Pilgrimage (*ḥajj*) or offer sheep or goats in sacrifice on the Feast of the Sacrificial Animals (*ʿīd al-aḍḥā*) unless the animals in both cases were at least two years old and free of physical defects. Yaḥyā said, "Mālik said, 'Of all the views I have heard, this view is the one I prefer most.'"

Chapter 2. The Prohibition against Slaughtering the Sacrificial Animal (*Ḍaḥiyya*) before the Imam Departs from the Communal Prayer Ground

1354. According to Mālik, Yaḥyā b. Saʿīd reported from Bushayr b. Yasār that Abū Burda b. Niyār slaughtered his sacrificial animal before the Messenger of God (pbuh) slaughtered his animal on the day of the Feast of the Sacrificial Animals (*ʿīd al-aḍḥā*). Abū Burda later asserted that the Messenger of God (pbuh) ordered him to slaughter a second animal, to which Abū Burda said, "I can find only a one-year-old kid,[536] Messenger of God!" The Messenger of God (pbuh) said, "If all you can find is a kid, then by all means slaughter it."

---

535 *Ḍaḥāyā* is the plural of *ḍaḥiyya*. It refers to animals sacrificed on *ʿīd al-aḍḥā*, the Feast of the Sacrificial Animals, by those Muslims who are not performing the Pilgrimage (*ḥajj*). The Feast of the Sacrificial Animals coincides with the day on which the pilgrims at Minā slaughter their sacrosanct animals (*hady*). Mālik refers to that day in the context of Pilgrimage as *yawm al-naḥr*, the Day of the Slaughter of the Sacrosanct Animals.

536 That is, a baby goat.

1355. According to Mālik, Yaḥyā b. Saʿīd reported from ʿAbbād b. Tamīm that ʿUwaymir b. Ashqar slaughtered his sacrificial animal before he set out to attend the prayer for the Feast of the Sacrificial Animals. When he mentioned that to the Messenger of God (pbuh), the Prophet ordered him to slaughter a second animal.

Chapter 3. What Is Desirable in Sacrificial Animals (*Ḍaḥāyā*)

1356. According to Mālik, Nāfiʿ reported that ʿAbd Allāh b. ʿUmar once offered an animal in sacrifice in Medina. Nāfiʿ said, "He ordered me to purchase for him a mighty horned ram, one that I would slaughter on his behalf on the Feast of the Sacrificial Animals (*ʿīd al-aḍḥā*) at the communal prayer ground. I did as he asked, and then the meat was taken to ʿAbd Allāh b. ʿUmar, who shaved his head for the occasion. He was ill and did not attend the Feast Prayer with the people that day. ʿAbd Allāh b. ʿUmar would say, 'Shaving the head is not obligatory for someone who offers an animal in sacrifice on the Feast of the Sacrificial Animals,' but that is what he himself did."

Chapter 4. Preserving the Meat of Sacrificial Animals (*Aḍāḥī*)[537]

1357. According to Mālik, Abū al-Zubayr al-Makkī reported from Jābir b. ʿAbd Allāh that the Messenger of God (pbuh) prohibited the consumption of the meat of sacrificial animals (*ḍaḥāyā*) after three days had passed from their slaughter. Later, he then said, "Eat, take provisions from, and store the meat of the sacrificial animals."

1358. According to Mālik, ʿAbd Allāh b. Abī Bakr reported that ʿAbd Allāh b. Wāqid said, "The Messenger of God (pbuh) forbade us to eat the meat of sacrificial animals after three days had passed from their slaughter." ʿAbd Allāh b. Abī Bakr said, "I mentioned this to ʿAmra bt. ʿAbd al-Raḥmān, who said, "Abd Allāh b. Wāqid is correct. I heard ʿĀʾisha, the wife of the Prophet (pbuh), say, "A group of needy bedouin came to Medina at the time of the Feast of the Sacrificial Animals (*ʿīd al-aḍḥā*) during the lifetime of the Messenger of God (pbuh). The Messenger of God (pbuh) declared, 'Store enough meat to last you for only three days, and give the rest away in charity.' Some time later, some people went to the Messenger of God (pbuh) and mentioned to him that it had been their ordinary practice to benefit from their sacrificial animals fully, by melting and collecting their fat and making waterskins, among other things. The Messenger of God (pbuh) said, 'And what of it?' or something to that effect.[538] They said, 'But you prohibited us from consuming the meat of the sacrificial animals after

537 *Aḍāḥī* is the plural of *uḍḥiyya*, like *ḍaḥāyā* is the plural of *ḍaḥiyya*; both refer to animals sacrificed on the Feast of the Sacrifical Animals (*ʿīd al-aḍḥā*).

538 The narrator is unsure of the Prophet's (pbuh) precise words.

three days had passed from their slaughter.' The Messenger of God (pbuh) said, 'That was only on account of that group of needy people (*dāffa*) who came to you on that occasion. So eat from the sacrifical animals, give some away in charity, and preserve what is left of their meat for yourselves.'""[539] By *dāffa*, he meant the group of needy people who came to Medina.

1359. According to Mālik, Rabīʿa b. Abī ʿAbd al-Raḥmān reported from Abū Saʿīd al-Khudrī that when he returned from a journey, his family offered him some meat. He said to them, "Did you take care to make sure that this meat is not that of sacrificial animals?" They said, "Well, it is." Abū Saʿīd said, "But didn't the Messenger of God prohibit us from eating it?" They said, "The Messenger of God (pbuh) made a new rule regarding this matter after you departed." Abū Saʿīd left and inquired about the prohibition, and he was told that the Messenger of God (pbuh) indeed had said, "I had prohibited you from consuming the meat of sacrificial animals after three days had passed from their slaughter, but now you may eat from it, give charity from it, and preserve what remains of it. Further, I had prohibited you from storing dried fruit in basins of water, but now you may do so, remembering that everything that inebriates is prohibited. Likewise, I had previously prohibited you from visiting graves, but now you may visit them, provided you do not say '*hujran*,'" that is, do not say something foul.

Chapter 5. Shared Ownership of Sacrificial Animals (*Ḍaḥāyā*) and the Number of People Who Can Share in a Sacrificial Cow, Yearling (*Shāt*), or Camel

1360. According to Mālik, Abū al-Zubayr al-Makkī reported that Jābir b. ʿAbd Allāh said, "In the year of al-Ḥudaybiya,[540] we, together with the Messenger of God (pbuh), slaughtered one camel for seven of us and one cow for seven of us."

1361. According to Mālik, ʿUmāra b. Ṣayyād reported that ʿAṭāʾ b. Yasār informed him that Abū Ayyūb al-Anṣārī informed him, "It used to be customary that we would offer only one yearling (*shāt*) as a sacrifice (*uḍḥiyya*). A man would slaughter it for himself and his entire household.

539 In other words, the Prophet (pbuh) prohibited his community from consuming more than three days' worth of the sacrificial animals' meat and ordered them to give away the rest in order to ensure that the needs of this specific group of destitute visitors had been met. He did not intend to prohibit Muslims from storing the meat of sacrificial animals in the future.

540 Al-Ḥudaybiya is a valley between ten and fifteen *mīls* (approximately 9 to 14 km) from Mecca on the road to Jeddah. Zurqānī, *Sharḥ al-Zurqānī*, 3:117. The "year of al-Ḥudaybiya" was the sixth year of the Hijra (628 CE) and is so named because in that year the Prophet (pbuh) made a peace treaty with the Meccans in al-Ḥudaybiya. The treaty permitted the Muslims to return the following year to perform the Pilgrimage (*ḥajj*).

Thereafter pride set in, so it became a game in which the people, out of pride, strove to outdo one another in their sacrifices."

1362. Yaḥyā said, "Mālik said, 'The best view that I have heard regarding single camels, cows, or sheep is that a man can slaughter any of these on behalf of himself and his household, provided that he owns the animal outright. He slaughters it on his household's behalf, and he shares it with them. As for a group of people coming together to buy a camel, a cow, or a sheep and sharing it either for slaughter at the Pilgrimage (*ḥajj*) or for the Feast of the Sacrificial Animals (*ʿīd al-aḍḥā*), with each one of them contributing his *pro rata* share of its price and taking his *pro rata* share of its meat—that is a detestable practice.[541] We have heard the report that there should be no shared ownership of an animal that is designated for slaughter at the Pilgrimage. Rather, an animal should be slaughtered exclusively on behalf of a single household.'"

1363. According to Mālik, Ibn Shihāb said, "The Messenger of God (pbuh) never slaughtered anything on behalf of himself and his household other than a single camel or a single cow." Yaḥyā said, "Mālik said, 'I do not know which of the two Ibn Shihāb said.'"

Chapter 6. Offering a Sacrificial Animal (*Ḍaḥiyya*) on Behalf of a Fetus in Its Mother's Womb[542]

1364. According to Mālik, Nāfiʿ reported that ʿAbd Allāh b. ʿUmar said, "Animals may be offered in sacrifice for two days after the first day of the Feast of the Sacrificial Animals (*ʿīd al-aḍḥā*)."

1365. According to Mālik, it reached him that ʿAlī b. Abī Ṭālib said something similar to that.

1366. According to Mālik, Nāfiʿ reported that ʿAbd Allāh b. ʿUmar would not offer a sacrificial animal on behalf of an unborn fetus in the womb of its mother.

1367. Yaḥyā said, "Mālik said, 'Offering an animal (*ḍaḥiyya*) in sacrifice is an act of great merit, but it is not obligatory. Yet it is not acceptable, in my opinion, for someone who can afford the price of a sacrificial animal to refrain from offering a sacrifice.'"

The Book of Sacrificial Animals (*Ḍaḥāyā*) Is Complete, and Praise Belongs to God, the Lord of the Worlds.

---

541 The Mālikīs take the position that the slaughter of a jointly owned animal in the manner described by Mālik renders the sacrifice invalid.

542 Other narrations of the *Muwaṭṭaʾ* include in the chapter title the phrase "and Mention of the Number of Days in the Feast of the Sacrificial Animals.".

Book 23
The Book of the Newborn Sacrifice (*ʿAqīqa*)

In the Name of God, the Merciful, the Compassionate

May God Grace Muḥammad and His Family
and Grant Them Perfect Tranquility.

Chapter 1. What Has Come Down regarding the Newborn Sacrifice (*ʿAqīqa*)

1368. According to Mālik, Zayd b. Aslam reported from a man of the Banū Ḍamra that his father said that the Messenger of God (pbuh) was asked about the newborn sacrifice, and he said, "I dislike disloyalty in children (*ʿuqūq*)," as though he disliked the name of the practice.[543] The Messenger of God said, "If a man to whom a child is born wishes to slaughter an animal in celebration of the newborn's birth, he should do so."

1369. According to Mālik, Jaʿfar b. Muḥammad reported that his father said, "Fāṭima, the daughter of the Messenger of God (pbuh), weighed the hair of each of her children, Ḥasan, Ḥusayn, Zaynab, and Umm Kulthūm, when they were born. Then she gave in charity the silver equivalent of the weight of the child's hair."

1370. According to Mālik, Rabīʿa b. ʿAbd al-Raḥmān reported that Muḥammad b. ʿAlī b. Ḥusayn said, "Fāṭima, the daughter of the Messenger of God (pbuh), weighed the hair of her sons, Ḥasan and Ḥusayn, and she gave in charity the silver equivalent of the weight of each child's hair."

Chapter 2. The Practice (*ʿAmal*) with Respect to the Newborn Sacrifice (*ʿAqīqa*)

1371. According to Mālik, Nāfiʿ reported that ʿAbd Allāh b. ʿUmar never refused the request of any member of his household who asked him to

543 The Arabic word for the practice of slaughtering an animal on the birth of a child is *ʿaqīqa*, which is derived from the same root as the word for a child's disloyalty to his parents, *ʿuqūq*.

perform a newborn sacrifice. He would slaughter a yearling (*shāt*) for any child born, whether male or female.

1372. According to Mālik, Rabīʿa b. ʿAbd al-Raḥmān reported that Muḥammad b. Ibrāhīm b. al-Ḥārith al-Taymī said, "I heard my father say that performing the newborn sacrifice is desirable, even if only with a sparrow."

1373. According to Mālik, it reached him that an animal was slaughtered on the occasion of the births of Ḥasan and Ḥusayn, the sons of ʿAlī b. Abī Ṭālib.

1374. According to Mālik, Hishām b. ʿUrwa reported that his father, ʿUrwa b. al-Zubayr, would slaughter a yearling on the birth of each of his children, whether male or female.

1375. Mālik said, "The rule in our view (*al-amr ʿindanā*) regarding the newborn sacrifice is that whoever performs it should slaughter a yearling for each child, whether the child is male or female. The newborn sacrifice is not obligatory, but it is commendable and one of the norms that the people among us have always practiced (*min al-amr alladhī lam yazal ʿalayhi al-nās ʿindanā*). The position of someone who performs the newborn sacrifice is equivalent to that of someone who slaughters an animal (*nusuk*) for the Pilgrimage (*ḥajj*) or offers a sacrificial animal (*ḍaḥāyā*) on the Feast of the Sacrificial Animals (*ʿīd al-aḍḥā*). Accordingly, it is not permissible to slaughter an animal that is blind in one eye, emaciated, wounded, or sick; neither are its meat or skin to be sold. Its bones are to be broken,[544] its meat eaten by the family, and some of it given away as charity. The child shall not be smeared with any of its blood."[545]

The Book of the Newborn Sacrifice (*ʿAqīqa*) Is Complete, and Praise Belongs to God.

544 Breaking the bones of the sacrificial animal is permissible but not obligatory according to Zurqānī. The practice is undertaken to defy a pre-Islamic Arab taboo against breaking the bones of sacrificial animals. Zurqānī, *Sharḥ al-Zurqānī*, 3:151.

545 The prohibition against smearing the newborn with blood reflects a rejection of pre-Islamic pagan practices. Jurists instead recommend applying perfume to the child. Bājī, *al-Muntaqā*, 3:104.

Book 24

The Book of Domesticated Animals Slaughtered for Ordinary Use (*Dhabā'iḥ*)[546]

In the Name of God, the Merciful, the Compassionate

May God Bless Muḥammad and His Family.

Chapter 1. Invoking the Name of God When Slaughtering a Domesticated Animal (*Dhabīḥa*)

1376. According to Mālik, Hishām b. ʿUrwa reported that his father said, "The Messenger of God (pbuh) was asked, 'Messenger of God, bedouin come from the desert, laden with slaughtered meat to sell, but we do not know whether they invoked the name of God when they slaughtered it. Are we permitted to buy their meat?' The Messenger of God (pbuh) said, 'Invoke the name of God over the meat, and eat it.'" Mālik said, "That was in the early days of Islam."

1377. According to Mālik, Yaḥyā b. Saʿīd reported that ʿAbd Allāh b. ʿAyyāsh b. Abī Rabīʿa al-Makhzūmī ordered one of his young male slaves to slaughter an animal, and when he was about to do so, ʿAbd Allāh said, "Invoke the name of God." The boy said, "I have." ʿAbd Allāh said, "Invoke the name of God, curse you!" The boy said, "I did!" ʿAbd Allāh b. ʿAyyāsh then said to the boy, "By God, I shall not eat any of its meat!"

546 Whereas the preceding chapters concerned the slaughter of sacrosanct or sacrificial animals, this chapter deals with the slaughter of animals unconnected to any religious ritual.

Chapter 2. What Necessity Permits in Connection with the Slaughter (*Dhakāt*) of Domesticated Animals[547]

1378. According to Mālik, Zayd b. Aslam reported from ʿAṭāʾ b. Yasār that a Medinese man from the Banū Ḥāritha was tending a milch camel of his at Uḥud,[548] when it suddenly showed signs of imminent death. Having nothing else with him, he slaughtered it using a sharp stake. The Messenger of God (pbuh) was later asked about what the man had done, so he said, "There is nothing objectionable in that. You are free to eat it."

1379. According to Mālik, Nāfiʿ reported from a Medinese man, from Muʿādh b. Saʿd (or Saʿd b. Muʿādh), that a handmaiden of Kaʿb b. Muʿādh was tending a flock of her sheep in Salaʿ[549] when one of her sheep suffered a mortal injury. Just before it died, she managed to get to it and slaughtered it using a stone. The Messenger of God (pbuh) was later asked about what she had done, so he said, "There is nothing objectionable in that. You are free to eat it."

1380. According to Mālik, Thawr b. Zayd al-Dīlī reported from ʿAbd Allāh b. ʿAbbās that he was asked about animals that Arab Christians slaughter. He said, "There is nothing objectionable in eating them," but he recited this verse of the Quran: "And whoever of you takes them as his protector surely is one of them."[550]

1381. According to Mālik, it reached him that ʿAbd Allāh b. ʿAbbās would say, "Any animal whose carotid arteries have been cut may be eaten."

1382. According to Mālik, Yaḥyā b. Saʿīd reported that Saʿīd b. al-Musayyab would say, "In case of necessity, any animal that has been slaughtered with a cutting edge, even if dull, may be eaten."

---

547 In the ordinary course of things, according to the Mālikīs, a Muslim is not permitted to eat the meat of an animal unless it has been properly slaughtered. The most common method of slaughter is to use a sharp blade to cut both carotid arteries. The animal must be dispatched with one deep cut of the blade across the neck that severs both carotids. The blood must flow spontaneously and profusely from the arteries by virtue of the continued action of the animal's heart. This proves that the animal died from blood loss and not from some other cause. Otherwise, the animal is considered carrion (*mayta*) and its flesh is prohibited from consumption.

548 A mountain near Medina.

549 A small mountain in Medina.

550 *Al-Māʾida*, 5:51. The point of citing this verse is to imply that although it is permissible for a Muslim to eat meat slaughtered by Christians, it is preferable for him to eat meat slaughtered by Muslims.

Chapter 3. Techniques of Slaughter That Render Meat Impermissible for Consumption

1383. According to Mālik, Yaḥyā b. Saʿīd reported from Abū Murra, the freedman (*mawlā*) of ʿAqīl b. Abī Ṭālib, that he asked Abū Hurayra about a yearling (*shāt*) that had been slaughtered, but then part of it twitched. Abū Hurayra told him it was permissible for him to eat from it. He then asked Zayd b. Thābit, who said, "A dead animal may at times twitch," but Zayd nevertheless prohibited him from eating it out of fear that the animal had not been properly slaughtered.[551]

1384. Mālik was asked about a sheep that was badly injured as the result of a fall from a height. Its owner reached it and promptly slaughtered it, and its blood gushed out, but it did not move when it was slaughtered. Mālik said, "If he slaughtered it while it was still breathing and its eyes were still blinking, then he may eat from it. Otherwise he may not."

Chapter 4. Slaughtering the Fetus in the Slaughtered Animal's Womb

1385. According to Mālik, Nāfiʿ reported that ʿAbd Allāh b. ʿUmar would say, "When a she-camel is slaughtered, the fetus in her womb is also considered legally slaughtered, provided that it is fully formed and its hair has started to grow. But when it exits its mother's womb, it should be slaughtered so as to drain its body of blood."

1386. According to Mālik, Yazīd b. ʿAbd Allāh b. Qusayṭ al-Laythī reported that Saʿīd b. al-Musayyab would say, "The fetus of an animal that has been properly slaughtered is itself deemed to have been properly slaughtered, provided that its body is formed and its hair has begun to grow."

551 In other words, Zayd believed that the animal might have been still alive and therefore had not been slaughtered properly. In that case it would be carrion and could not be consumed.

Book 25

The Book of Wild Animals (*Ṣayd*)

Chapter 1. Refraining from Eating What Has Been Killed with a Dull Stick or a Stone

1387. According to Mālik, Nāfiʿ said, "While I was at Jurf,[552] I threw a stone at two birds and hit both of them. One of them died immediately, so ʿAbd Allāh b. ʿUmar cast it aside. He tried to slaughter the second one with an axe, but it died before he managed to slaughter it, so he cast it aside too."

1388. According to Mālik, it reached him that al-Qāsim b. Muḥammad disapproved of eating any animal killed by a dull stick or clay pellets.

1389. According to Mālik, it reached him that Saʿīd b. al-Musayyab disapproved of killing domesticated animals with weapons that are used to kill wild animals (*ṣayd*), such as arrows.

1390. Mālik said, "There is nothing objectionable, in my opinion, in eating a wild animal that has been killed with a dull stick, provided that the stick struck a major artery or a vital organ and penetrated it, leading to the animal's death."[553] Yaḥyā said, "I heard Mālik say, 'God, Blessed and Sublime is He, says, "O you who believe! God shall certainly test you through wild animals within reach of your hands and your lances."[554] Any beast that a man subdues by means of his hand, his spear, or any weapon of his, provided that the weapon pierces it and reaches its vital organs, falls into the category of "wild animal," in accordance with what God has said.'"

1391. According to Mālik, he heard the people of knowledge say, "When a hunter hits his target but some other factors contribute to the animal's death, such as the animal's plunging into a body of water or a hound's bringing it down, that wild animal is not to be eaten unless it is certain that

---

552 A place in Medina.

553 Mālikī jurists understand this ruling to apply only to cases in which the animal is killed with a sharpened edge of the stick, not with a dull side of it. Bājī, *al-Muntaqā*, 3:121.

554 *Al-Māʾida*, 5:94.

it was the hunter's arrow that killed it or pierced its vital organs. There should be no doubt that the hunter is the one who killed the animal and that it lost its life after it was hit."

1392. Yaḥyā said, "I heard Mālik say, 'There is nothing objectionable in a man eating a wild animal even if he did not witness its death, provided he sees his hound's bite marks on the animal or his arrow stuck in its body, and further provided that he does so before night passes. If night has passed, however, the animal should not be eaten.'"

Chapter 2. What Has Come Down regarding Wild Animals (*Ṣayd*) Captured by Hounds (*Muʿallamāt*)[555]

1393. According to Mālik, Nāfiʿ reported that ʿAbd Allāh b. ʿUmar said regarding hounds, "You may eat whatever they capture, whether they have killed it or not."

1394. According to Mālik, he heard Nāfiʿ say, "ʿAbd Allāh b. ʿUmar said, 'Eat the wild animal that your hounds have captured, whether or not they have eaten from it.'"

1395. According to Mālik, it reached him from Saʿd b. Abī Waqqāṣ that he was asked about eating a wild animal killed by a hound. Saʿd said, "You may eat it, even if the hound has left only a single bite."

1396. According to Mālik, he heard the people of knowledge say, regarding the case of wild animals killed by falcons, eagles, hawks, and other birds of prey, "If the bird has been trained to hunt and has the same skill as a hound, there is nothing objectionable in eating what it kills, provided that the name of God was invoked when the hunter released the bird."

1397. Yaḥyā said, "Mālik said, 'The best view that I have heard regarding a wild animal that a hunter retrieves from a falcon's claws or a hound's jaws but then fails to slaughter promptly, with the result that the animal later dies of its wounds, is that it is not lawful to eat.'"

1398. Mālik said, "The same rules applies to a wild animal that the hunter could have slaughtered while it was alive in the falcon's claws or the hound's jaws but neglected to do so, with the result that the falcon or the hound kills the animal. It is impermissible to eat such an animal."

1399. Mālik said, "The same rule also applies when a hunter shoots and hits a wild animal but it remains alive, and he negligently fails to slaughter it and then it dies. It is impermissible to eat such an animal."

555 The Quran expressly permits the eating of wild animals captured by hounds. *Al-Māʾida*, 5:4.

1400. Mālik said, "The agreed-upon rule among us (*al-amr al-mujtamaʿ ʿalayhi ʿindanā*) is that if a Muslim hunts using a Zoroastrian's hound, releasing it in pursuit of a wild animal, and the hound takes the animal down, killing or capturing it, he is permitted to eat that animal. There is nothing objectionable in eating it, even if the Muslim does not slaughter the animal. This case is no different from that of a Muslim who slaughters an animal using a Zoroastrian's knife, or shoots and kills a wild animal with a Zoroastrian's bow or arrow. In each of these cases, he kills the wild animal using items that are the Zoroastrian's personal property. In each case, the meat of the wild animal he hunted and killed and that of the animal he slaughtered is permissible, and there is nothing objectionable in eating it. But if a Zoroastrian hunts with a Muslim's hound, releasing it in pursuit of a wild animal, and the hound takes it down, the animal is not to be eaten unless a Muslim first slaughters it. That case is no different from that of a wild animal that a Zoroastrian shoots and kills using a Muslim's bow and arrow, and it is the same as the case of a Zoroastrian who uses a Muslim's knife to slaughter an animal. Neither animal would be permissible for a Muslim to eat."[556]

Chapter 3. What Has Come Down regarding the Capture of Sea Creatures

1401. According to Mālik, Nāfiʿ reported that ʿAbd al-Raḥmān b. Abī Hurayra asked ʿAbd Allāh b. ʿUmar about eating sea creatures that had been washed ashore. ʿAbd Allāh prohibited him from eating them. Nāfiʿ said, "Then ʿAbd Allāh left and asked to see a written copy of the Quran. When he consulted it, he found the verse that reads, 'Lawful to you are the sea's creatures and vegetation.'[557] Afterward, ʿAbd Allāh b. ʿUmar sent me to ʿAbd al-Raḥmān b. Abī Hurayra with the message that there is nothing objectionable in eating such creatures."

1402. According to Mālik, Zayd b. Aslam reported that Saʿd al-Jārī, the freedman (*mawlā*) of ʿUmar b. al-Khaṭṭāb, said, "I asked ʿAbd Allāh b. ʿUmar about the permissibility of eating a fish that had been killed by another fish, or a fish that had died from the cold." He said, "There is nothing objectionable in doing so." Saʿd said, "I then asked ʿAbd Allāh b. ʿAmr b. al-ʿĀṣī the same question, and he gave a similar answer."

556 The principle underpinning this discussion is that Muslims are not permitted to eat the meat of animals slaughtered by Zoroastrians, although they are permitted to eat meat slaughtered by Christians and Jews.

557 *Al-Māʾida*, 5:96.

1403. According to Mālik, Abū al-Zinād reported from Abū Salama b. ʿAbd al-Raḥmān that neither Abū Hurayra nor Zayd b. Thābit believed it objectionable to eat fish that had washed ashore.

1404. According to Mālik, Abū al-Zinād reported from Abū Salama b. ʿAbd al-Raḥmān that some people from al-Jār[558] came and asked Marwān b. al-Ḥakam about eating fish that had washed ashore. He said, "There is nothing objectionable in that." He said, "Go ask Zayd b. Thābit and Abū Hurayra, then come back and tell me what the two of them said." They went and asked the two of them the same question they had asked Marwān. They both said, "There is nothing objectionable in that." They then returned to Marwān and told him what the two had said. Marwān said, "I told you so."

1405. Mālik said, "There is nothing objectionable in eating fish that a Zoroastrian catches, because the Messenger of God (pbuh) said, 'The water of the sea is purifying—even dead sea creatures are lawful to eat.'

1406. Mālik said,"Because sea creatures may even be eaten when they are dead, it makes no difference who catches them."

Chapter 4. The Prohibition against Eating Any Predatory Animal with Canines

1407. According to Mālik, Ibn Shihāb reported from Abū Idrīs al-Khawlānī, from Abū Thaʿlaba al-Khushanī, that the Messenger of God (pbuh) said, "It is impermissible (*ḥarām*) to eat any predatory animal with canines."[559]

1408. According to Mālik, Ismāʿīl b. Abī Hakīm reported from ʿAbīda b. Sufyān al-Ḥaḍramī, from Abū Hurayra, that the Messenger of God (pbuh) said, "It is impermissible to eat any predatory animal that has canines." Yaḥyā said, "Mālik said, 'That is the rule among us (*dhālika al-amr ʿindanā*).'"

Chapter 5. The Riding Animals That One Should Avoid Eating

1409. Mālik said, "The best of the views that have been reported regarding eating horses, mules, and donkeys is that they should not be eaten. God, Blessed and Sublime is He, says, 'He created horses, mules, and donkeys for

---

558 A village near Medina.

559 Yaḥyā is the only narrator of the *Muwaṭṭa'* to transmit this report with the word *ḥarām*, indicating outright prohibition. Other narrators of the *Muwaṭṭa'* use instead the verb *nahā*, "to prohibit": "The Messenger of God (pbuh) prohibited the eating of any predatory animal with canines." The difference is important insofar as the verb *nahā* can also be understood to express disapproval, not necessarily prohibition. The position of the Mālikī school on this question, in fact, is that consumption of such animals is disapproved (*makrūh*), not prohibited.

you to ride and as ornamentation.'[560] Likewise, God, Blessed and Sublime is He, says regarding livestock, 'That you may use some to ride and some for food';[561] and God, Blessed and Sublime is He, says, 'That they may mention God's name in gratitude for the provision He has allotted to them of domesticated livestock';[562] and also, 'So eat of it, and feed the poor who show dignified restraint in their homes (*qāniʿ*), and those who gather around you (*muʿtarr*), hoping for provision.'"[563] Yaḥyā said, "Mālik said, 'I heard that *bāʾis*[564] means the poor and that *muʿtarr* means visitors.'" Yaḥyā said, "Mālik said, 'So God mentioned horses, mules, and donkeys in connection with riding and adornment, and He mentioned livestock in connection with riding and eating.'" Yaḥyā said, "Mālik said, '*Qāniʿ* also means the poor.'"

Chapter 6. What Has Come Down regarding the Use of the Hides of Dead Animals (*Mayta*)

1410. According to Mālik, Ibn Shihāb reported from ʿUbayd Allāh b. ʿAbd Allāh b. ʿUtba b. Masʿūd that ʿAbd Allāh b. ʿAbbās said, "The Messenger of God (pbuh) once gave a yearling (*shāt*) as a gift to a freedman (*mawlā*) of Maymūna, the wife of the Prophet (pbuh). Later, while going for a walk, he passed by the yearling's corpse, and he said to the people there, 'Why haven't you taken advantage of its hide?' They replied, 'Messenger of God, it died of natural causes.' The Messenger of God (pbuh) said, 'Only eating from it is prohibited.'"

1411. According to Mālik, Zayd b. Aslam reported from Ibn Waʿla al-Miṣrī, from ʿAbd Allāh b. ʿAbbās, that the Messenger of God (pbuh) said, "When a hide has been tanned, it becomes pure."

1412. According to Mālik, Yazīd b. ʿAbd Allāh b. Qusayṭ reported from Muḥammad b. ʿAbd al-Raḥmān b. Thawbān, from his mother, from ʿĀʾisha, the wife of the Prophet (pbuh), that the Messenger of God (pbuh) decreed that the hides of unslaughtered animals should be tanned and put to good use.

Chapter 7. What Has Come Down regarding Someone Whom Necessity Compels to Eat Carrion (*Mayta*)

1413. Mālik said, "The best of the views that have been reported regarding a starving man who finds carrion is that he may eat from it until his hunger is satisfied. Then he should take whatever he can carry of it as provisions

560 *Al-Naḥl*, 16:8.
561 *Al-Ghāfir*, 40:79.
562 *Al-Ḥajj*, 22:34.
563 *Al-Ḥajj*, 22:36.
564 *Al-Ḥajj*, 22:28.

for the remainder of his journey. If he later finds an alternative, he should throw the carrion away."

1414. Yaḥyā said, "Mālik was asked whether a starving man is permitted to eat carrion if dates, crops, or sheep (*ghanam*) belonging to someone else are present in that location. Mālik said, 'If he believes that the owners of the dates, crops, or sheep would accept his claim of dire hunger and not deem him a thief and therefore seek to have his hand amputated, I believe he may eat of any of those items, but only in an amount sufficient to satisfy his hunger. He is not permitted, however, to carry anything away with him as provisions for the rest of his journey. I prefer that he do that rather than eat carrion. If he fears, however, that they will not believe his claim of dire hunger and that they will accuse him of having stolen their property, then in my opinion it is better for him to eat the carrion. In this situation, he enjoys a broad dispensation. Nevertheless, I fear that some people who are not actually starving will transgress and falsely claim necessity in order to permit themselves to take other people's property, crops, and dates.'" Yaḥyā said, "Mālik said, 'This is the best view that I have heard.'"

The Book of Slaughter (*Dhakāt*) of Domesticated Animals[565] Is Complete, with Abundant Praise to God in the Manner That Befits Him, and His Grace on Muḥammad, His Servant and Messenger.

565 Although there is a clear mismatch between the concluding title of this chapter and its opening title, which was "The Book of Wild Animals (*Ṣayd*)," the prior chapter, "The Book of Domesticated Animals Slaughtered for Ordinary Use," lacked a concluding invocation.

Book 26

The Book of Vows (*Nudhūr*)

In the Name of God, the Merciful, the Compassionate

May God Grace Muḥammad and His Family and Grant Them Perfect Tranquility.

Chapter 1. When Vows (*Nudhūr*) to Take a Journey on Foot Are Binding

1415. According to Mālik, Ibn Shihāb reported from ʿUbayd Allāh b. ʿAbd Allāh b. ʿUtba b. Masʿūd, from ʿAbd Allāh b. ʿAbbās, that Saʿd b. ʿUbāda asked the opinion of the Messenger of God (pbuh) regarding the following case: "My mother died, having made a vow (*nadhr*) that she did not fulfill." The Messenger of God (pbuh) said, "Fulfill it on her behalf."

1416. According to Mālik, ʿAbd Allāh b. Abī Bakr reported that his paternal aunt told him from his grandmother that she had vowed to walk to the Qubāʾ mosque, but she died without doing so. ʿAbd Allāh b. ʿAbbās told her daughter that in his opinion, she should fulfill her mother's vow by walking to that mosque.

1417. Yaḥyā said, "I heard Mālik say, 'No one should fulfill the unfulfilled vow to walk made by another person.'"[566]

1418. According to Mālik, ʿAbd Allāh b. Abī Ḥabība said, "When I was still a young man, I said to someone, 'If a man says, "I am under an obligation to walk to God's House," but he does not say, "I have vowed to walk to God's House," he is under no obligation to do so.' That man replied, 'How about I give you this cucumber'—he had one in his hand—'if you say, "I am under an obligation to walk to God's House?"' I said, 'Sure,' and said, 'I am under an obligation to walk to God's House.' I was still young at that time. I did not

566 According to Zurqānī, Mālik rejected the preceding two reports and recognized an oath to walk to a mosque as binding only if the mosque in question was the Sacred Mosque in Mecca. Zurqānī, *Sharḥ al-Zurqānī*, 3:57.

set out to God's House. Then later, when I had matured, that man told me, 'You are obliged to walk to God's House, as we previously agreed.' I went to Saʿīd b. al-Musayyab and asked him about that, and he said, 'You are under an obligation to walk to God's House,' so I did." Yaḥyā said, "Mālik said, 'This is the rule among us (*hādhā al-amr ʿindanā*).[567]'"

Chapter 2. What Has Come Down regarding Someone Who Vows (*Nadhr*) to Walk to God's House

1419. According to Mālik, ʿUrwa b. Udhayna al-Laythī said, "I set out with one of my grandmothers, who had vowed to walk to God's House. Along the way, she grew weary and could not go on. She then dispatched one of her freedmen (*mawlā*) to go ask ʿAbd Allāh b. ʿUmar what she should do, and I went with him. He conveyed her question to ʿAbd Allāh b. ʿUmar, who said to him, 'Tell her to mount her camel and to complete her journey. Later, if she is able to do so, let her fulfill her vow by resuming her walk from the point at which she stopped due to her exhaustion.'" Yaḥyā said, "I heard Mālik say, 'In our opinion, she must offer a sacrosanct animal (*hady*) in addition to fulfilling her vow when she becomes able to do so.'"

1420. According to Mālik, it reached him that Saʿīd b. al-Musayyab and Abū Salama b. ʿAbd al-Raḥmān held the same opinion as ʿAbd Allāh b. ʿUmar.

1421. According to Mālik, Yaḥyā b. Saʿīd said, "I made a vow to walk to God's House, but then I came down with a sharp pain in my kidney and could not continue to walk. I therefore decided to mount my camel, and I rode until I reached Mecca, where I consulted ʿAṭāʾ b. Abī Rabāḥ and others.[568] They said, 'You are obliged to offer a sacrosanct animal.' Later, when I went to Medina, I asked the people there about my case. They ordered me to fulfill my vow by resuming my journey on foot from the point at which I stopped, and so I did."

1422. Yaḥyā said, "I heard Mālik say, 'The rule in our view (*al-amr ʿindanā*) regarding someone who says, "I am under an obligation to walk to God's House," is that if he becomes incapable of completing the journey on foot, he should ride in order to complete it. Later, he should return to the spot at which he became incapacitated and resume walking in order to fulfill his vow. If he is still unable to complete his journey, let him walk as much as he can and then ride for the remaining distance. He must also offer a

567 In other words, it is not necessary for a person to use the word "vow" in order to impose a pious obligation on himself: any phrase whose apparent sense implies such an obligation, so long as the act is itself an act of piety, is sufficient to create the obligation.

568 These are Meccan scholars from the generation that succeeded the Companions of the Prophet of God (pbuh). These are known as Followers (*tābiʿūn*).

sacrosanct animal, either a camel or a cow, or a yearling (*shāt*) if that is all he can find.'"[569]

1423. Mālik was asked about someone who says to another, "I will convey you to God's House." Mālik said, "If he intended by this expression to carry that other person on his shoulders and thereby to wear himself out on that other person's account, he is under no obligation to fulfill such an undertaking.[570] Instead, he should journey on foot as a person normally would and offer a sacrosanct animal. If he had no specific intention with respect to that phrase, he should set out for the Pilgrimage (*ḥajj*), riding on the back of an animal, and take that other man with him. This is because he said, 'I will convey you to God's House.' However, if the other man declines to set out on the Pilgrimage with him, he is absolved of any further duty toward him, and he has fulfilled any obligation that he might have owed that other man."

1424. Yaḥyā said, "Mālik was asked about someone who made so many oaths on pain of walking to God's House—such as not to talk to his brother or his father, and so on—that it was impossible for him to fulfill all of his obligations upon breaking the oaths. Even if he attempted to fulfill what he was obliged to do for breaking his oaths each year, he could not possibly live long enough to fulfill all of what he imposed on himself through his numerous oaths. Mālik was asked whether fulfilling one of his oaths would suffice him, or whether he was bound by all of them. Mālik said, 'I know of nothing that would relieve him of his obligations other than fulfilling what he bound himself to do. Let him walk for as long as he is able, and let him draw himself near to God by performing as many good deeds as he can.'"

Chapter 3. The Practice (*ʿAmal*) with Respect to Walking to the Kabah

1425. Mālik said, "The best of the views that have been reported from the people of knowledge regarding a man or a woman who swears an oath on pain of walking to God's House and then breaks that oath is that if the oath-breaker attempts to satisfy the obligations of the broken oath by walking to perform the Visitation (*ʿumra*), he or she continues to walk until he or she finishes marching between the hillocks of Ṣafā and Marwa (*saʿy*). At that point, the obligations of the oath have been completely fulfilled. However, if the oath-breaker took on the obligation to perform the Pilgrimage (*ḥajj*) on foot, he or she must walk until Mecca, and once there, the oath-breaker continues on foot until all the rites of Pilgrimage

569 In other words, a yearling is acceptable only if he cannot easily obtain a camel or a cow.

570 That is because a vow is binding only if it entails an act of piety, and undertaking an act with the intention of imposing hardship (*mashaqqa*) on oneself is not an act of piety.

have been completed, including the Circumambulation of the March (*ṭawāf al-ifāḍa*)." Yaḥyā said, "Mālik said, 'The obligation to walk, when made in a vow or an oath, may only be fulfilled through performance of the Pilgrimage or the Visitation.'"

Chapter 4. A Vow (*Nadhr*) That Is of No Effect Because It Involves Disobedience to God

1426. According to Mālik, Ḥumayd b. Qays and Thawr b. Zayd al-Dīlī both informed him—one of their versions being lengthier than the other—that the Messenger of God (pbuh) saw a man standing in the sun, so he said, "What is the matter with him?" They said, "He vowed not to speak, stand in the shade, or sit down, and to fast." The Messenger of God (pbuh) said, "Tell him that he should speak, enjoy the shade, and sit, but that he should complete his fast." Mālik said, "I have not heard anything to indicate that the Messenger of God (pbuh) ordered that man to perform any penance (*kaffāra*) for breaking his vow; rather, the Messenger of God (pbuh) ordered him to fulfill only that part of his vow that was an act of devotion to God and to abandon the part that was impious."

1427. According to Mālik, Yaḥyā b. Saʿīd reported that he heard al-Qāsim b. Muḥammad say, "A woman came to ʿAbd Allāh b. ʿAbbās and said to him, 'I made a vow to slaughter my son.' Ibn ʿAbbās told her, 'Do not slaughter your son, but rather do penance for your oath.' Then an old man who was present with Ibn ʿAbbās said, 'How can there be penance for something like this?' Ibn ʿAbbās said, 'God said, "Those of you who declare their wives to be like the backs of their mothers,"[571] and then He imposed penance for saying that, as you know.'"

1428. Yaḥyā said, "I heard Mālik say, 'What the Messenger of God (pbuh) meant when he said, "Whoever makes a vow in disobedience to God should not disobey Him," was that if a man vows to walk to some distant place, such as the Levant, Egypt, or al-Rabadha,[572] or to undertake any other act that does not entail an act of devotion to God in the event that he talks to so-and-so or does some other specified act, he is under no obligation to fulfill the consequences of his oath, whether or not he talks to that person or otherwise breaks his oath. None of the consequences specified in these oaths entail devotion to God. Only vows that impose an act of devotion to God must be fulfilled.'"

571 *Al-Mujādila*, 58:2.

572 Al-Rabadha is a settlement in the Arabian Peninsula located some 200 km to the northeast of Medina on the pilgrimage route from Iraq to Mecca.

Chapter 5. Casual Speech[573] in Oaths (*Yamīn*)[574]

1429. According to Mālik, Hishām b. ʿUrwa reported from his father that ʿĀʾisha, the Mother of the Believers, would say, "Casual speech in an oath is when a person says, 'By God, no! By God, no!'"

1430. Yaḥyā said, "Mālik said, 'The best view I have heard regarding this question is that casual speech in connection with an oath is when a person swears to the truth of something, believing with certainty that it is indeed so, but then it turns out not to be as he believed it to be. That is what is meant by casual speech in connection with an oath.'"

1431. Yaḥyā said, "Mālik said, 'A binding oath takes place, for example, when a man swears that he will not sell his garment for ten dinars but then sells it for that price anyway, or swears that he shall beat his young slave but then does not, and similar things. This is the kind of oath that imposes penance (*kaffāra*) on its maker if he fails to perform it, but no penance is due for an oath made in casual speech.'"

1432. Yaḥyā said, "Mālik said, 'As for someone who swears over something while knowing that he is sinning, or swears to the truth of something while knowing that he is lying, in order to please someone or to apologize to someone or to gain property thereby—his sin is too great to be remedied by penance.'"

Chapter 6. Oaths (*Yamīn*) Whose Violation Does Not Warrant Penance (*Kaffāra*)

1433. According to Mālik, Nāfiʿ reported that ʿAbd Allāh b. ʿUmar would say, "Whoever says 'By God!' and then 'God willing' but then does not do what he swore to do does not violate his oath."

1434. Yaḥyā said, "Mālik said, 'The best view I have heard regarding the inclusion of an exception in an oath is that it should be interpreted in favor of the man who made the oath, so long as he did not interrupt his speech and his speech was a continuous whole, one part following the other, before he went silent. Once he goes silent, however, and stops speaking, it is too late for him to make an exception to his oath.'"

573 Mālik's discussion of "casual speech" in connection with oaths is an allusion to *al-Baqara*, 2:225, which reads, "God does not take you to account for oaths you make casually, but He takes you to account for what your hearts have earned."

574 An oath (*yamīn*) differs from a vow (*nadhr*) in that the object of a vow must be an act of piety, whereas an oath has binding consequences on its maker even if it entails an impious act, such that if he fails to fulfill the oath, he is obliged to perform an act of penance (*kaffāra*). It is impermissible to fulfill an oath that requires its maker to commit a sin, such as "I swear that if you do such-and-such, I will kill you." In this case, the oath is deemed automatically broken upon the occurrence of the specified event, and its maker must offer penance.

1435. Mālik said, regarding a man who swears an oath to the effect that if he violates his oath, he is a denier of God or a polytheist, and who then indeed violates his oath, "He is not required to offer penance, nor is he an unbeliever or a polytheist, unless his heart inwardly denies God or accepts other deities alongside Him. He should seek God's forgiveness and not do that again, for what he did was certainly wicked."

Chapter 7. Oaths (*Yamīn*) Whose Violation Requires Penance (*Kaffāra*)

1436. According to Mālik, Suhayl b. Abī Ṣāliḥ reported from his father, from Abū Hurayra, that the Messenger of God (pbuh) said, "Whoever swears an oath and then comes to believe that another course of action would be better should break his oath, do what is better, and offer penance for violating his oath."

1437. Yaḥyā said, "I heard Mālik say, 'Whoever says, "I am under the obligation of a vow (*nadhr*)," without specifying what he must do if he violates it, must offer the penance due for breaking an oath if he fails to fulfill his vow. As for merely confirming an oath, that is when someone swears in respect of one particular thing and repeats the oath several times, such as when he says, "By God, I will not give him less than such-or-such," repeating that phrase several times—like three times or more. Only one act of penance is due for violating that oath, and it is the penance due for the violation of an oath.'"

1438. Mālik said, "If a man swears an oath, saying, 'By God, I shall not eat this food, wear this garment, or enter this room,' and it is a single oath, he owes only one act of penance if he violates the oath. That is precisely the same result as when a man says to his wife, 'You are divorced if I clothe you in this garment or permit you to go to the mosque,' and that is a single, continuous statement. If he violates either condition of the oath, he is obliged to divorce his wife, but he incurs no further consequences if he later violates the oath again. The violation of the oath in this case, regardless of any further violations, is limited to the original violation."[575]

575 What Mālik means is that a single oath that entails numerous commitments is terminated on the first instance of its violation. Accordingly, the person who swears a single oath to refrain from doing X, Y, or Z but then violates the oath by doing, for example, X is obliged to offer penance for that violation but is then free to do X, Y, or Z in the future. This contrasts with the case of a person who swears three separate oaths—to refrain from doing X, to refrain from doing Y, and to refrain from doing Z, respectively. Because these are independent oaths, violation of and penance for one does not eliminate any obligations arising out of the other two.

1439. Mālik said, "The rule in our view (*al-amr ʿindanā*) is that a woman's vow binds her even without her husband's prior permission. She must fulfill it immediately if its effect is limited to her own person and does not cause harm to her husband. If it does harm him, the time of performance is deferred until such time as she can fulfill it without causing him harm. The obligation continues to bind her until she fulfills it."

Chapter 8. The Practice (*ʿAmal*) with Respect to Penance (*Kaffāra*) for Violating an Oath (*Yamīn*)

1440. According to Mālik, Nāfiʿ reported that ʿAbd Allāh b. ʿUmar would say, "Whoever swears an oath, confirming it either through repetition or by invoking God's holy names, and then violates it must free a slave or clothe ten poor persons. Whoever swears an oath but does not confirm it and then violates it must feed ten poor persons, giving each of them 500 grams (one *mudd*) of wheat; but if he is not able to do so, he must fast three days."

1441. According to Mālik, Nāfiʿ reported from ʿAbd Allāh b. ʿUmar that he would offer penance for oaths that he had violated by feeding ten poor people, giving each one of them 500 grams of wheat. If he had confirmed the oath, he would free several slaves.

1442. According to Mālik, Yaḥyā b. Saʿīd reported that Sulaymān b. Yasār said, "I found that when the people performed penance for violating their oaths by feeding the poor, they would give 500 grams of wheat in accordance with the Prophet's measure. They believed that this satisfied their obligation."

1443. Yaḥyā said, "Mālik said, 'The best view I have heard regarding someone who chooses to offer penance for violating his oath by clothing the poor is that he gives one garment to each man and a tunic and a head covering to each woman. This is the minimum clothing that a person needs to perform his or her prayers.'"

Chapter 9. Miscellaneous Reports regarding Oaths (*Yamīn*)

1444. According to Mālik, Nāfiʿ reported from Ibn ʿUmar that the Messenger of God (pbuh) once found ʿUmar b. al-Khaṭṭāb mounted on his camel in the midst of a group of riders. ʿUmar was swearing oaths in the name of his father. The Messenger of God (pbuh) said, "God prohibits you from swearing oaths in the names of your fathers. If someone wishes to swear an oath, he should do so in God's name, or be silent."

1445. According to Mālik, it reached him that the Messenger of God (pbuh) would say, "No, by the One who turns hearts, from one side to the other!"

1446. According to Mālik, 'Uthmān b. Ḥafṣ b. 'Umar b. Khalda reported from Ibn Shihāb that it reached him that Abū Lubāba b. 'Abd al-Mundhir said, at the time that God brought him to Islam, "Messenger of God, should I abandon the land of my people, the place where I have committed sin, and dwell next to you, and part from my property, giving it freely to God and His Messenger (pbuh)?" The Messenger of God (pbuh) said, "One-third of your property is plenty."[576]

1447. According to Mālik, Ayyūb b. Mūsā reported from Manṣūr al-Ḥajabī, from his mother, from 'Ā'isha, the Mother of the Believers, that she was asked about a man who said, "All my property is dedicated to preserving the door of the Kabah." 'Ā'isha said, "He may perform penance for this statement in the same way that he would for an oath that he violated."

1448. Yaḥyā said, "Mālik said, regarding someone who says, 'I have placed my property in God's service,' and then breaks his oath, 'He is to place one-third of his property in God's service, and that is on account of what has come down about what the Messenger of God (pbuh) said in the case of Abū Lubāba.'"[577]

The Book of Vows (*Nudhūr*) Has Been Completed, with Abundant Praise to God.

576 Although this report is not directly related to oaths or vows, Mālikī jurists limit the applicability of vows or oaths that involve donating one's property to a pious purpose to one-third of the person's property, presumably in reliance on this report and others like it.

577 See hadith no. 1446 above.

Book 27
The Book of Mandatory Inheritance Shares (*Farā'iḍ*)

In the Name of God, the Merciful, the Compassionate

May God Grace Muḥammad and His Family and Grant Them Perfect Tranquility.

Chapter 1. The Inheritance Rights (*Mīrāth*) of Children

1449. According to Mālik, "The agreed-upon rule among us and the one that I found the people of knowledge in our town following (*al-amr al-mujtama' ʿalayhi ʿindanā wa'lladhī adraktu ʿalayhi ahl al-ʿilm bi-baladinā*) concerning determinate inheritance shares (*farā'iḍ*)[578] is that in the matter of the inheritance of children from their father or their mother, when the father or the mother dies leaving male and female children, the male receives twice the share of the female. If there are only female children and they number two or more, they receive two-thirds of the estate between them. If there is only one child and the child is female, she receives one-half of the estate.[579] If another person besides the children has a determinate share in the estate, and one of the children is male, the division of the estate begins with the determinate share of the heir who is not a child, and what remains is shared among the children in accordance with their proportional rights to the estate, that is, with the male receiving twice the female's share. If there are no living children, grandchildren from sons are treated exactly the same as the children of the decedent would

578 Heirs in Islamic law are of two types. The first type of heir has a determinate share in the estate, called a *farīḍa* or a *farḍ*. The second type, known as *ʿaṣaba*, consists broadly of the male paternal near-relations of the deceased. In distributing an estate, one first allocates any determinate shares owed to heirs. Whatever is left over is the surplus, *faḍl*, which is then divided among the closest living paternal near-relations of the decedent, following the principle that the male receives twice the share of the equivalent female.

579 In this case, as in the immediately preceding case of the two daughters, the daughters receive a determinate share of the estate, namely, two-thirds in the case of two daughters and one-half in the case of a single daughter.

have been had they lived—the grandsons like the decedent's sons and the granddaughters like the decedent's daughters. They inherit as their fathers would have inherited, and they preempt (*ḥajb*) others from sharing in the estate just as the children would have preempted other heirs.[580] If there are both children of the decedent and children of the decedent's sons living at the time of the decedent's death, and there is a living male among the children of the decedent, the grandchildren do not share in the estate.[581] If there are no living male children but there are two or more daughters, any granddaughters from the decedent's deceased son do not inherit with the decedent's daughters,[582] unless there is a male relative along with these granddaughters who has the same relationship to the decedent as they do, or a more distant (*aṭraf*) one. The existence of that male relation results in the inclusion of all the granddaughters from the decedent's sons in the class of paternal near-relations, provided that they are at least as closely related to the decedent as he is.[583] Together, they share whatever surplus (*faḍl*) remains from the estate after determinate shares have been distributed,[584] with the male receiving twice the female's share. If there is no surplus, however, the paternal near-relations receive nothing. If the only living child is a female, she receives one-half of the estate as a determinate share, and the daughters of a deceased son of the decedent, whether one or more, share one-sixth of the estate, as long as the deceased son's relationship to the decedent is the same as that of the decedent's daughters.[585] If there is

580 The principle of preemption in Islamic inheritance law applies in determining the rights of the paternal near-relations (*ʿaṣaba*) after the determinate shares have been distributed. Under this principle, the existence of a nearer relation precludes a more distant relation from sharing in the estate; an uncle, for example, preempts the claims of a nephew. The principle also distinguishes claimants whose relations to the decedent are equally close but of unequal strength; for example, a full-brother preempts a half-brother when they stand to inherit from the decedent in the capacity of paternal near-relations rather than as recipients of a determinate share.

581 This is because the decedent left a living son. That living son of the decedent preempts the claims of the children of the decedent's dead children.

582 In this case, the daughters of the decedent preempt the claims of the granddaughters.

583 In other words, if the decedent's deceased son had no living sons at the time of the decedent's death, the deceased son's daughters have no claim to the decedent's estate. If, however, the deceased son of the decedent had a living son, the deceased son's daughters would be included among the paternal near-relations who do have a claim to the estate under the principle established in the next sentence.

584 If the decedent leaves only two daughters and two granddaughters from a deceased son, as well as an appropriate male descendant, the two daughters receive two-thirds of the estate as a determinate share. The paternal near-relations, consisting of the granddaughters and the male heir, divide the remaining one-third among themselves, adhering to the ratio of the male's receiving twice the female's share.

585 Had the decedent left two or more daughters, they would have shared two-thirds of the estate. In this case, once the only living daughter receives her determinate share of one-half of the estate, one-sixth is left of the potential two-thirds share allocated to the daughters. The daughters of the decedent's dead son are given this leftover share, which is divided among them equally.

a male who has the same relationship to the decedent as do the daughters of the decedent's dead son, the granddaughters are entitled neither to a determinate share nor to one-sixth. If a surplus remains after those with determinate shares have received their shares, whatever is left goes to the male and to whatever daughters of the decedent's sons have the same or a closer relationship as he has to the decedent, the male receiving twice the female's share. More distant relations receive nothing. If there is no surplus after the determinate shares have been distributed, however, none of the paternal near-relations receives anything. This is in accordance with what God, Blessed and Sublime is He, says in His Book: 'God implores you, regarding your children: to the male, a share equal to that of two females. And if there are only daughters, two or more, they receive two-thirds of the estate, and if there is only one daughter, she receives one-half.'[586] And *aṭraf* means 'more distant.'"

Chapter 2. The Inheritance Rights (*Mīrāth*) of the Husband from His Wife and of the Wife from Her Husband

1450. Mālik said, "If the wife dies leaving no children or grandchildren from deceased sons, the husband receives one-half of her estate. If, however, she leaves children or male or female grandchildren from a deceased son, her husband receives one-fourth of her estate after her testamentary bequests (*waṣiyya*) are fulfilled and her personal debts are paid. If the husband dies leaving no children or grandchildren from deceased sons, the wife receives one-quarter of his estate. If, however, he leaves children or male or female grandchildren from a deceased son, his wife receives one-eighth of his estate after his testamentary bequests are fulfilled and his personal debts are paid. This is in accordance with what God, Blessed and Sublime is He, says in His Book: 'Half of your wives' estates belongs to you[587] if they leave no children. But if they leave a child, your share is one-fourth of their estates after the fulfillment of any testamentary bequests they have made and the payment of their personal debts. And their share in your estate is one-fourth if you leave no children. But if you leave a child, your wives receive one-eighth after the fulfillment of any testamentary bequests you have made and the payment of your debts.'"[588]

586 *Al-Nisā'*, 4:11.
587 Throughout this verse, the pronoun "you" is in the male plural form.
588 *Al-Nisā'*, 4:12.

Chapter 3. The Inheritance Rights (*Mīrāth*) of Mothers and Fathers from Their Children

1451. Yaḥyā said, "Mālik said, 'The agreed-upon rule about which there is no dissent and which I found the people of knowledge in our town following (*al-amr al-mujtamaʿ ʿalayhi alladhī lā ikhtilāfa fīhi wa'lladhī adraktu ʿalayhi ahl al-ʿilm bi-baladinā*) concerning the father's inheritance from his son or daughter is that if the decedent leaves children or grandchildren from a son, the father receives one-sixth of the estate as a determinate share (*farīḍa*). If the decedent does not leave any children or male grandchildren from a son, the division of the estate begins with the determinate shares of any heirs other than the father. They are given their determinate shares first, and whatever surplus (*faḍl*) remains afterward belongs to the father, even if it is more than one-sixth of the estate. If less than one-sixth would remain, however, the father receives one-sixth of the estate as a determinate share.'"

1452. Mālik continued,[589] "If the mother's son or daughter dies and leaves male or female children, or grandchildren from a son, or two or more male or female siblings, whether half-siblings or full, her inheritance from her child is one-sixth."

1453. Mālik continued, "If the decedent does not leave any children, grandchildren from a son, or two or more siblings, the mother receives one-third of the estate, except in two cases involving the determinate shares of others. The first case is when a man dies and leaves his wife and both his parents, in which case his wife receives one-fourth of the estate and his mother takes one-third of what remains, that is, one-fourth of the entire estate. The second case is when a woman dies, leaving her husband and both her parents, in which case the husband receives one-half and her mother receives one-third of what remains, that is, one-sixth of the entire estate.[590] This is in accordance with what God, Blessed and Sublime is He, says in His Book: 'Parents each receive one-sixth of the estate if the decedent left children. If he did not leave children and both his parents inherit from him, the mother receives one-third of the estate. If the decedent left siblings (*ikhwa*), the mother receives one-sixth of the estate.'[591] The applicable ordinance has long established (*maḍat al-sunna*) that *ikhwa* means two or more siblings."

---

589 Mālik's speech continues in this report and the following one, even though he is not explicitly named in the original text.

590 The decedent's father, by implication, receives two-thirds of what remains, that is, one-third of the entire estate.

591 *Al-Nisāʾ*, 4:11.

Chapter 4. The Inheritance Rights (*Mīrāth*) of Half-Siblings on the Mother's Side

1454. Yaḥyā said, "Mālik said, 'The rule in our view (*al-amr ʿindanā*) is that half-siblings on the mother's side do not inherit anything from their deceased sibling if the decedent leaves children or male or female grandchildren from a son. Nor do they inherit anything if the father or paternal grandfather of the deceased sibling is still alive. In all other cases, however, they do inherit, whether male or female, receiving one-sixth of the estate as a determinate share (*farīḍa*). If there are two of them, each receives one-sixth of the estate, but if there are more than two half-siblings on the mother's side, they share one-third of the estate, dividing it entirely among themselves, with the male receiving twice the female's share.[592] This is in accordance with what God, Blessed and Sublime is He, says in His Book: "If a man or a woman dies, leaving neither ascendants nor descendants but leaving a brother or a sister, the sibling receives one-sixth of the estate, but if there are more than one, they share one-third of the estate."[593] In this case, males and females are treated the same.'"

Chapter 5. The Inheritance Rights (*Mīrāth*) of Full Siblings

1455. Yaḥyā said, "Mālik said, 'The rule in our view (*al-amr ʿindanā*) is that siblings do not inherit anything from a decedent who leaves sons, grandsons from a son, or his father. They do, however, inherit, along with the decedent's daughters and granddaughters from the decedent's sons, any unallocated surplus (*faḍl*) from the estate in their capacity as the decedent's male paternal near-relations (*ʿaṣaba*), on the condition that the decedent has not left a paternal grandfather. In this case, the estate is divided by first fulfilling the claims of other heirs with determinate shares (*farīḍa*) in the estate. If any part of the estate is unallocated after that, the siblings, whether male or female, divide it among themselves in accordance with God's Book, the male receiving twice the female's share. If, however, there is no surplus, the siblings receive nothing. If the decedent did not leave a father, a paternal grandfather, a child, or a male or female grandchild from a son, his sister receives one-half of his estate as a determinate share, but if the decedent in this case leaves two or more sisters, they share two-thirds of the estate. If, however, the decedent also leaves a brother, none of the sisters is entitled

592 The RME's version of the text here differs materially from other versions of Yaḥyā's transmission of the *Muwaṭṭaʾ*, which instead have "dividing it equally (*bil-sawiyya*) among themselves, the male receiving the share of the female." The RME's version appears to be erroneous, as indicated by the previous sentence in the report, which affirms that each half-sibling, regardless of gender, receives one-sixth.

593 *Al-Nisāʾ*, 4:12.

to a determinate share, whether they are one or many. In this latter case, division of the estate begins with the other heirs who have determinate shares in the estate. After the determinate shares have been distributed, whatever surplus remains goes to the siblings, the male receiving twice the female's share, except in one case in which the siblings are not entitled to anything in their capacity as siblings but rather are compelled to share what is given to half-siblings on the mother's side. That case is that of a woman who dies leaving her husband, her mother, half-sisters from the mother's side, and siblings. Her husband receives one-half of the estate, her mother receives one-sixth, and her half-siblings on her mother's side receive one-third. No surplus is left to be allocated after that. For this reason, the full siblings share in this case the one-third previously allocated to their half-siblings, with the male receiving twice the female's share. The reason for this is that they are all siblings of the decedent on the mother's side, and they inherit only because of their common relationship with the mother. This is in accordance with what God, Blessed and Sublime is He, says in His Book: "If a man or a woman dies, leaving neither ascendants nor descendants but leaving a brother or a sister, the sibling receives one-sixth of the estate, but if there are more, they share one-third of the estate."[594] Because they are all siblings of the decedent on the mother's side, they share in this case for that reason.'"

Chapter 6. The Inheritance Rights (*Mīrāth*) of Half-Siblings on the Father's Side

1456. Yaḥyā said, "Mālik said, 'If the decedent dies without leaving siblings, the rule in our view (*al-amr ʿindanā*) regarding the inheritance rights of half-siblings on the father's side is the same as that which applies to siblings. Half-brothers on the father's side are treated just as full brothers are, and half-sisters on the father's side are treated just as full sisters are. They are not, however, entitled to share in the determinate share (*farīḍa*) awarded to half-siblings on the mother's side like siblings are, because in contrast to the latter, half-siblings on the father's side do not share a common mother with half-siblings on the mother's side.'"

1457. Mālik said, "If the decedent dies leaving siblings as well as half-siblings on the father's side, and there is at least one male among the siblings, half-siblings on the father's side do not inherit anything. Assuming, however, that all of the siblings are females and none are males, if there is only one full sister, she receives one-half of the estate as a determinate share and the half-sisters on the father's side receive one-sixth of the estate

594 *Al-Nisā'*, 4:12.

as a determinate share, the two shares thus collectively accounting for two-thirds of the estate. If, however, there is a male among the half-siblings on the father's side, the half-sisters do not receive one-sixth of the estate as a determinate share. Rather, the estate is first divided among the heirs with determinate shares, who receive their shares first. If any surplus (*faḍl*) remains, it is awarded to the half-siblings on the father's side, the male receiving twice the female's share. If no surplus remains, they receive nothing. If the full siblings are two or more females, they receive two-thirds of the estate as a determinate share, and the half-sisters on the father's side receive nothing. If, however, at least one of the half-siblings on the father's side is male, there is an exception. In this case, the estate is first divided among those who have determinate shares. After they have been given their shares, if any surplus remains, it is awarded to the half-siblings on the father's side, the male receiving twice the female's share. If no surplus remains, they receive nothing. Half-siblings on the mother's side, when there are also full siblings and half-siblings on the father's side, receive one-sixth of the estate if there is only one and one-third of the estate if there are two or more, the male receiving twice the female's share.[595] Males and females are treated the same in this case."

Chapter 7. The Inheritance Rights (*Mīrāth*) of Grandfathers

1458. According to Mālik, Yaḥyā b. Saʿīd reported that it reached him that Muʿāwiya b. Abī Sufyān wrote to Zayd b. Thābit, asking him about the grandfather's share in the decedent's estate. Zayd b. Thābit wrote back to him, saying, "You wrote to me asking about the inheritance rights of grandfathers, and God knows best, for this is a matter on which only the caliphs have given a judgment; the Prophet (pbuh) has not. I was with the two caliphs who preceded you, and I saw them award the grandfather one-half of the estate when the decedent died leaving only one brother, and one-third of the estate when the decedent died leaving two brothers. They never awarded the grandfather less than one-third of the estate, even if the decedent left more than two siblings."[596]

1459. According to Mālik, Ibn Shihāb reported from Qabīṣa b. Dhu'ayb that ʿUmar b. al-Khaṭṭāb is the one who established the grandfather's determinate share (*farīḍa*) of the estate that the people award him today.

---

595 Here, too, the RME's version of the text differs materially from other transmissions of Yaḥyā's *Muwaṭṭa'*, which instead have "the male receiving the share of the female." The RME's version seems to be erroneous, as indicated by the last sentence of the report, which implies that half-brothers and half-sisters are to be treated in the same way in this case.

596 This rule assumes that the father of the decedent predeceased him.

1460. According to Mālik, it reached him that Sulaymān b. Yasār said, "'Umar b. al-Khaṭṭāb, 'Uthmān b. 'Affān, and Zayd b. Thābit each awarded the grandfather the determinate share of one-third of the estate when the only other heirs of the decedent were siblings."

1461. Yaḥyā said, "Mālik said, 'The agreed-upon rule among us and the one I found the people of knowledge in our town following (*al-amr al-mujtamaʿ ʿalayhi ʿindanā wa'lladhī adraktu ʿalayhi ahl al-ʿilm bi-baladinā*) is that the paternal grandfather does not inherit anything if the father is alive. However, if the decedent dies leaving male children or paternal grandsons, the grandfather receives a determinate share of one-sixth. In all other cases, when the decedent dies without leaving a sibling on his father's side, the estate is first divided among those who have determinate shares. If one-sixth or more is left of the estate, it belongs to the grandfather as surplus (*faḍl*), but if the surplus is not at least one-sixth of the estate, the grandfather is given a determinate share of one-sixth.'"

1462. Mālik said, "When there are heirs in addition to the grandfather and the siblings who also have determinate shares in the decedent's estate, the division of the estate begins with those other heirs who have determinate shares. After they receive their shares, the surplus is awarded to the grandfather and the siblings. It is then determined which distribution would be most favorable for the grandfather, and he is awarded the most favorable of three possible distributions: the one-third of the surplus that he and the siblings receive; what he would receive if he were given the same share as each of the siblings; or one-sixth of the entire estate. He receives whichever of these three options is most favorable to him. Then any remaining surplus goes to the siblings, the male receiving twice the female's share. There is one specific case that is an exception to this rule. That is the case of a woman who dies leaving her husband, her mother, a sister, and her paternal grandfather. In this case, the husband's determinate share is one-half, the mother's is one-third, the grandfather's is one-sixth, and the sister's is one-half, but the total of these shares exceeds the full value of the estate. Accordingly, the determinate shares of the husband and the mother must be reduced, and the grandfather's one-sixth share and the sister's one-half share must be combined and treated as though they were a joint claim of siblings. Their joint claim is then divided into thirds, the male receiving twice the female's share. Consequently, the grandfather receives two-thirds and the sister one-third of their joint claim."[597]

597 This case came to be known in the legal tradition as *al-akdariyya*. The difficulty in the case stems from the fact that the determinate shares in this instance exceed the estate, since the husband should receive one-half of the decedent's estate (3/6), the mother should receive

1463. Yaḥyā said, "Mālik said, 'The inheritance rights of half-siblings on the father's side, when the decedent dies leaving his paternal grandfather but no siblings, are the same as the inheritance rights of siblings in the previous case; half-brothers on the father's side are like full brothers, and half-sisters on the father's side are like full sisters. If, however, the decedent dies leaving both full siblings and half-siblings on the father's side, the full siblings subsume the grandfather into their class through the relationship with the deceased father (the grandfather's son), with the result that, by virtue of their numbers, they deprive the grandfather of the bulk of the inheritance. Their status as siblings on the mother's side does not subsume the grandfather, because if the decedent died leaving only them and the grandfather, they would not inherit anything and the entire estate would be awarded to the grandfather. Therefore, whatever the siblings receive comes after the grandfather's share, but only with respect to siblings, not half-siblings on the father's side. When there are siblings in this case, half-siblings on the father's side receive nothing, unless the only sibling is a sister. If there is only one sister, she subsumes the grandfather through her status as a sibling on the father's side, however many half-siblings there may be.[598] Whatever is allotted to them and to her, she takes her share before they take theirs until she has received her determinate share of the estate, which is one-half of the entire estate. If whatever is allocated to her and her half-brothers on the father's side exceeds one-half of the entire estate, the surplus is allocated to her half-siblings on the father's side, the males receiving twice the females' share. If there is no surplus, however, they receive nothing.'"

---

one-third (2/6), the grandfather should receive one-sixth (1/6), and the sister should receive one-half (3/6). The jurists solve the dilemma by increasing the denominator to nine (a procedure they termed *'awl*), thereby reducing the claim of each heir. The result in this case is that the husband receives three-ninths, the mother two-ninths, the grandfather one-ninth, and the sister three-ninths. This distribution creates another problem, however, insofar as the sister receives three times as much as the grandfather, even though the general rule is that in the absence of surviving children, the grandfather's share is at least equal to that of the decedent's brother, which in turn should be twice the share of the decedent's sister. The jurists' solution to this problem is to combine the grandfather's one-ninth share with the sister's three-ninths share and then split the combined share at the ratio of two to one, the grandfather receiving two-thirds and the sister one-third of the four-ninths share. The result is that the grandfather receives 8/27 of the estate (2/3 * 4/9) and the sister receives 4/27. The husband's share is 9/27 and the mother's is 6/27. In this case, then, the determinate shares of the husband, the mother, and the sister are reduced in order to guarantee that the grandfather is treated at least as favorably as a brother would have been. This analysis is elided in the actual text of the *Muwaṭṭa'*, but it is necessary to make sense of the report's concluding sentence.

598 In this case, the decedent dies leaving a daughter. She is entitled to one-half of the estate as a determinate share (*farīḍa*). Because she is a descendant of the decedent and the decedent died leaving half-siblings on the father's side, they now get to inherit whatever surplus (*faḍl*) remains as paternal near-relations (*'aṣaba*).

Chapter 8. The Inheritance Rights (*Mīrāth*) of Grandmothers

1464. According to Mālik, Ibn Shihāb reported from ʿUthmān b. Isḥāq b. Kharasha that Qabīṣa b. Dhuʾayb said, "A grandmother came to Abū Bakr al-Ṣiddīq, asking him about her inheritance rights. Abū Bakr said to her, 'God's Book is silent about your rights, nor do I know of anything in the ordinances of the Messenger of God (*sunnat rasūl allāh*) (pbuh) that would provide you with anything. Give me some time, and let me ask the people about your case.' He then asked the people about her case, and al-Mughīra b. Shuʿba said, 'I was present when the Messenger of God (pbuh) awarded a grandmother one-sixth of the estate.' Abū Bakr asked, 'Were there any other witnesses to this?' Muḥammad b. Maslama al-Anṣārī stood up and corroborated what al-Mughīra b. Shuʿba had said. Abū Bakr al-Ṣiddīq therefore issued a ruling in the woman's case on the basis of their report. Later, the same decedent's other grandmother came to ʿUmar b. al-Khaṭṭāb, inquiring about her inheritance rights. He said to her, 'God's Book is silent about your rights, and all previous decisions in this matter have been resolved in favor of other heirs. I shall not add any new determinate shares (*farāʾiḍ*) to the law. There is, however, that one-sixth share. If the decedent dies leaving both grandmothers, they may share it, but if only one survives, it is awarded to her in its entirety.'"

1465. According to Mālik, Yaḥyā b. Saʿīd reported that al-Qāsim b. Muḥammad said, "Two surviving grandmothers came to Abū Bakr al-Ṣiddīq, so he wanted to award one-sixth of the estate to the grandmother on the mother's side. A Medinese man said to him, 'Aren't you excluding the only one from whom the decedent would have inherited, if both of the grandmothers had died and he were alive?'[599] Abū Bakr therefore changed his mind and ruled that the one-sixth should be shared between the two of them."

1466. According to Mālik, ʿAbd Rabbih b. Saʿīd reported that Abū Bakr b. ʿAbd al-Raḥmān b. al-Ḥārith b. Hishām would allot a determinate share only to the two grandmothers together.

1467. Yaḥyā said, "Mālik said, 'The agreed-upon rule among us about which there is no dissent and which I found the people of knowledge in our town following (*al-amr al-mujtamaʿ ʿalayhi ʿindanā alladhī lā ikhtilāfa*

599 The decedent was the grandchild of the two grandmothers, but as the preceding cases have made clear, only the children of sons are entitled to inherit from their grandparents. Abū Bakr's initial decision therefore would have excluded the paternal grandmother from inheriting from her grandchild, even though in the opposite case of her death and his survival, the grandchild could have inherited from her. By contrast, the grandchild would not inherit from his maternal grandmother if his mother—the grandmother's daughter—predeceased her.

fīhi wa'lladhī adraktu ʿalayhi ahl al-ʿilm bi-baladinā) is that the maternal grandmother does not inherit anything when the mother of the decedent is still alive, but in all other cases, she is given a determinate share of one-sixth of the estate. In addition, the paternal grandmother does not inherit anything when either the mother or the father of the decedent is still alive, but in all other cases, she is given a determinate share of one-sixth of the estate.'"

1468. Yaḥyā said, "Regarding a scenario in which both maternal and paternal grandmothers or great-grandmothers are alive and the decedent dies leaving neither a father nor a mother, Mālik said, 'I heard that if the survivors are the maternal grandmother and the paternal great-grandmother,[600] the former receives the one-sixth share of the estate at the expense of the latter, but if the survivors are the paternal grandmother and the maternal great-grandmother or if both of them are of the same generation, they divide the one-sixth share equally between them.'"

1469. Yaḥyā said, "Mālik said, 'None of the female ascendants have a share in the inheritance except for the two grandmothers.[601] It reached me that the Messenger of God (pbuh) awarded a grandmother a share of the estate, and then Abū Bakr inquired about it and a reliable source informed him that the Messenger of God (pbuh) had awarded the grandmother a share of the estate, so he enforced that rule for the benefit of the grandmother. Then the other grandmother appeared before ʿUmar b. al-Khaṭṭāb, seeking her share of the estate, so he said, 'I shall not add any new determinate shares to the law. If the decedent dies leaving both grandmothers, they may share the relevant share, but if only one survives, it is awarded to her in its entirety.'" Yaḥyā said, 'Mālik said, 'We have never heard of anyone granting a share in the estate to a female ascendant other than the two closest grandmothers, from the advent of Islam to the present day.'"

Chapter 9. The Inheritance Rights (*Mīrāth*) of Heirs Who Are Neither Ascendants Nor Descendants (*Kalāla*)

1470. According to Mālik, Zayd b. Aslam reported that ʿUmar b. al-Khaṭṭāb asked the Messenger of God (pbuh) about the inheritance rights of heirs who are neither ascendants nor descendants. The Messenger of God (pbuh)

600 Literally, if the maternal grandmother is the "closer" of the two survivors to the decedent in generational terms.

601 So, for example, if the decedent is survived by both grandmothers and a great-grandmother, only the grandmothers inherit. However, note that the term "grandmother" includes "great-grandmother." Therefore, if the decedent dies leaving two great-grandmothers, they would share equally the one-sixth allocated to the grandmother.

said, "The verse that was revealed in the summer at the end of 'The Women' (*al-Nisā'*) provides sufficient guidance."[602]

1471. Yaḥyā said, "Mālik said, 'The rule in our view about which there is no dissent and which I found the people of knowledge in our town following (*al-amr ʿindanā alladhī lā ikhtilāfa fīhi wa'lladhī adraktu ʿalayhi ahl al-ʿilm bi-baladinā*) is that the rules regarding the inheritance rights of those who are neither ascendants nor descendants apply in two different situations. The first is that of the verse that was revealed at the beginning of *al-Nisā'*,[603] in which God, Blessed and Sublime is He, says, "If a man or a woman dies, leaving neither ascendants nor descendants but leaving a brother or a sister, the sibling receives one-sixth of the estate, but if there are more, they share one-third of the estate."' Yaḥyā said, "Mālik said, 'This is the case in which maternal half-siblings would not have inherited had the decedent died leaving either a child or a parent.'"

1472. Yaḥyā said, "Mālik said, 'The second situation is that of the verse at the end of *al-Nisā'*,[604] in which God, Blessed and Sublime is He, says, "They ask you about a ruling; say, 'God answers your inquiry about those who die leaving no descendants. If a man dies leaving no child but leaving a sister, she receives one-half of the estate, and he inherits from her in the same fashion if she dies without leaving a child. If there are two sisters, they take two-thirds of the estate, but if they are brothers and sisters, they share two-thirds of the estate, the male receiving twice the female's share.' Thus does God make clear to you His law, lest you go astray. And God knows well all things."' Mālik said, 'This is the case in which siblings and half-siblings on the father's side take the surplus (*faḍl*) of the estate as paternal near-relations (*ʿaṣaba*) when the decedent dies without leaving a descendant. Therefore, the siblings and half-siblings on the father's side share with the grandfather in this situation, that is, when a decedent dies without leaving a descendant or an ascendant.'"[605]

1473. Yaḥyā said, "Mālik said, 'The grandfather inherits alongside the siblings in this case because his claim to the estate is stronger than theirs. That is because he inherits one-sixth of the estate even when the decedent leaves male children, whereas the siblings do not inherit anything in that case. How can he not be like one of them when he inherits one-sixth of the

---

602 *Al-Nisā'*, 4:176.

603 *Al-Nisā'*, 4:12.

604 *Al-Nisā'*, 4:176.

605 According to Mālik, the term *kalāla* applies to two circumstances. The first is when the decedent leaves neither ascendants nor descendants. The second is when the decedent leaves neither descendants nor parents but does leave a paternal grandfather.

decedent's estate even when the decedent leaves children? How can he not share in one-third of the estate with the siblings when the half-siblings on the mother's side share the one-third of the estate with them? The grandfather is the one who preempts the half-siblings on the mother's side from inheriting, and his presence as an heir excludes them from a claim to the estate. He therefore has a stronger entitlement to what would have been due to them because their claims lapse on his account. Had the grandfather not taken the one-third in question, it surely would have been allocated to the half-siblings on the mother's side. He has only taken that which would never have been given to the half-siblings on the father's side. The half-siblings on the mother's side have a greater claim to that one-third than do the half-siblings on the father's side, and the grandfather himself has a better claim to it than do the half-siblings on the mother's side.'"

Chapter 10. What Has Come Down regarding the Inheritance Rights (*Mīrāth*) of the Paternal Aunt (*'Amma*)

1474. According to Mālik, Muḥammad b. Abī Bakr b. Muḥammad b. 'Amr b. Ḥazm reported from 'Abd al-Raḥmān b. Ḥanẓala al-Zuraqī that someone informed him that an elderly freedman (*mawlā*) of the Quraysh known as Ibn Mirsā said, "I was sitting with 'Umar b. al-Khaṭṭāb, and when he finished performance of the Noon Prayer (*ṣalāt al-ẓuhr*), he said, 'Yarfā, bring me that document!' meaning the document that he had drafted regarding the inheritance rights of the paternal aunt. Meanwhile, 'Umar was asking others for their views about her inheritance rights, seeking the best advice of the people. When Yarfā finally brought the document, 'Umar called for a small vessel or a bowl of water in which he plunged the document to erase it. He then said, 'Had God approved of you, He would have confirmed you.'"

1475. According to Mālik, Muḥammad b. Abī Bakr b. Ḥazm reported that he would often hear his father say, "'Umar b. al-Khaṭṭāb would say, 'How strange is the case of the paternal aunt! Her estate is inherited, but she does not inherit!'"

Chapter 11. The Inheritance Rights (*Mīrāth*) of Male Paternal Near-Relations (*'Aṣaba*)

1476. Yaḥyā said, "Mālik said, 'The agreed-upon rule among us about which there is no dissent and which I found the people of knowledge in our town following (*al-amr al-mujtamaʿ ʿalayhi ʿindanā alladhī lā ikhtilāfa fīhi wa'lladhī adraktu ʿalayhi ahl al-ʿilm bi-baladinā*) with respect to the inheritance rights of male paternal near-relations is that the decedent's brother has a stronger claim to the estate than does the half-brother on the father's side. The half-brother on the father's side has a stronger claim to the estate than do the brother's children. The brother's children have a stronger claim to the estate than do the children of the half-brother on the father's side. The children of the half-brother on the father's side have a stronger claim to the estate than do the children of the brother's sons. The children of the half-brother on the father's side have a stronger claim to the estate than does the paternal uncle who is a brother of the father. The paternal uncle who is a brother of the father has a stronger claim to the estate than does the paternal uncle who is a half-brother on the father's side. The paternal uncle who is a half-brother on the father's side has a stronger claim to the estate than do the children of the paternal uncle who is a brother. The son of the paternal uncle who is a half-brother on the father's side has a stronger claim to the estate than does the father's paternal uncle who is a brother.'"

1477. Yaḥyā said, "Mālik said, 'Everything that I have been asked concerning the inheritance rights of paternal near-relations is resolved according to this principle: Determine the relationship of the decedent to those presenting conflicting claims to his estate among his paternal near-relations. If one of the paternal near-relations shares a common father with the decedent whereas the other paternal near-relations share only a more distant paternal ancestor with the decedent, award the estate to that paternal near-relation who shares with the decedent the closest common ancestor, rather than to a paternal near-relation with a more distant common paternal ancestor. If they all share the same paternal ancestor, one who connects them all, then closest common descent with the decedent is the relevant consideration. Accordingly, if the decedent leaves only one half-brother on the father's side, give the entirety of the estate to him rather than to a more distant relation, even if the further-removed relation shares common male and female ascendants with the decedent. If all the paternal near-relations are separated from the common paternal ancestor by the same number of generations, such that they all share a common paternal ancestor with the decedent and are all either half-siblings on the father's side or full siblings, they share the entirety of the estate. If the father of any of them is a full brother of the decedent's father whereas the others are the children of the decedent's father's half-brothers on the father's side, the entirety of the estate goes to the children of the decedent's full brother, excluding the children of the half-brother on the father's side. This is in accordance with what God, Blessed and Sublime is He, says: "But some kin have greater rights than others in God's Book. And God knows well all things."'"[606]

---

606 *Al-Anfāl*, 8:75. Mālik's theory of priority among the claims of the decedent's paternal near-relations takes into account two variables. The first is the nature of the relationship to

1478. Yaḥyā said, "Mālik said, 'The paternal grandfather has a stronger claim to the estate than do the children of the decedent's full brother and a stronger claim than does the decedent's paternal uncle, who is a full brother of the decedent's father. The son of the decedent's full brother, however, has a stronger claim than the grandfather does to be the patron of the decedent's freedmen.'"[607]

Chapter 12. Persons with No Inheritance Rights (*Mīrāth*)

1479. Yaḥyā said, "Mālik said, 'The agreed-upon rule among us about which there is no dissent and which I found the people of knowledge in our town following (*al-amr al-mujtamaʿ ʿalayhi ʿindanā alladhī lā ikhtilāfa fīhi wa'lladhī adraktu ʿalayhi ahl al-ʿilm bi-baladinā*) is that the son of a half-brother on the mother's side, the maternal grandfather, the paternal uncle who is a half-brother of the decedent's father on the mother's side, the maternal uncle (*khāl*), the great-grandmother (that is, the mother of the mother's father), the daughter of the full brother, the paternal aunt (*ʿamma*), and the maternal aunt (*khāla*) do not inherit anything by virtue of their kinship to the decedent. No woman who is more distantly related to the decedent than those mentioned above inherits anything by virtue of her kinship to the decedent. No woman inherits anything unless she was specifically designated as an heir. God, Blessed and Sublime is He, mentioned in His Book the inheritance rights of the mother from her children, the inheritance rights of daughters from their fathers, the inheritance rights of the wife from her husband, the inheritance rights of half-sisters on the father's side, and the inheritance rights of half-sisters on the mother's side. Further, the grandmother has a right to inherit by virtue of what has come down from the Prophet (pbuh). Likewise, a woman inherits the estates of any of her deceased former slaves that she herself manumitted, because God, Blessed and Sublime is He, says in His Book, "For they are your brothers in faith and your freedmen."'"[608]

---

the decedent—son, brother, male first cousin, nephew, etc.—and the second is the generation. As a rule, a brother of the decedent has a stronger claim to the estate in his capacity as a paternal near-relation than does a paternal half-brother, but a paternal half-brother has a stronger claim than does the decedent's paternal uncle, even if the decedent and the paternal uncle share both a male and a female ascendant, such as the decedent's paternal grandparents, who are the parents of both the decedent's father and his paternal uncle.

607 Bājī explains the different treatment of the right to be the patron of the decedent's freedmen as compared to inheritance with reference to the fact that patronage (*walāʾ*) is not properly speaking part of the estate but instead passes on exclusively according to the principles of agnatic succession and not the logic of the fixed shares of inheritance. Accordingly, the fixed share (*farīḍa*) that the grandfather enjoys in inheritance does not give him a superior claim to act as the patron of the decedent's freedmen; this role instead falls to the decedent's nephew from his full brother insofar as the nephew and the decedent share the common agnatic ancestor of the decedent's father (who is the nephew's grandfather), making him closer to the decedent in this respect than the grandfather is. Bājī, *al-Muntaqā*, 6:245.

608 *Al-Aḥzāb*, 33:4.

Chapter 13. The Estates (*Mīrāth*) of Non-Muslims

1480. According to Mālik, Ibn Shihāb reported from ʿAlī b. Ḥusayn b. ʿAlī, from ʿAmr b. ʿUthmān b. ʿAffān, from Usāma b. Zayd, that the Messenger of God (pbuh) said, "A Muslim does not inherit from a nonbeliever."

1481. According to Mālik, Ibn Shihāb reported that ʿAlī b. Ḥusayn b. ʿAlī b. Abī Ṭālib informed him that ʿAqīl and Ṭālib had inherited from Abū Ṭālib, but ʿAlī had not. ʿAlī b. Ḥusayn b. ʿAlī b. Abī Ṭālib said, "That is why we abandoned our share of al-Shiʿb."[609]

1482. According to Mālik, Yaḥyā b. Saʿīd reported from Sulaymān b. Yasār that Muḥammad b. al-Ashʿath informed him that a paternal aunt of his, who was Jewish or Christian, died. Muḥammad b. al-Ashʿath mentioned this to ʿUmar b. al-Khaṭṭāb and asked him who should inherit her estate. ʿUmar b. al-Khaṭṭāb said, "Her coreligionists inherit her estate." Muḥammad b. al-Ashʿath then went to ʿUthmān b. ʿAffān and asked him for his opinion. ʿUthmān said, "Do you think I have forgotten what ʿUmar b. al-Khaṭṭāb said to you? Her coreligionists inherit her estate."

1483. According to Mālik, Yaḥyā b. Saʿīd reported from Ismāʿīl b. Abī Ḥakīm that a Christian slave whom ʿUmar b. ʿAbd al-ʿAzīz had manumitted died. Ismaʿīl said, "ʿUmar b. ʿAbd al-ʿAzīz then ordered me to transfer his property to the public treasury."

1484. According to Mālik, a source that he deemed reliable reported that he heard Saʿīd b. al-Musayyab say, "ʿUmar b. al-Khaṭṭāb would not allow any non-Arab to share in the distribution of an estate, unless he was was born among the Arabs."[610]

1485. Mālik said, "If a pregnant woman comes from enemy territory and gives birth in Arab territory, it is her child, and he inherits from her if she dies and she inherits from him if he dies, receiving her share of his estate as specified in God's Book."

1486. Mālik said, "The agreed-upon rule among us, and the long-established ordinance about which there is no dissent and that which I found the people of knowledge in our town following (*al-amr al-mujtamaʿ ʿalayhi ʿindanā wa'l-sunna allatī lā ikhtilāfa fīhā wa'lladhī adraktu ʿalayhi ahl al-ʿilm*

609 The ancestral home of the Banū Hāshim, the clan of the Prophet (pbuh) in Mecca.

610 This is a reference to claims to kinship-based inheritance rights made by individuals born in territories beyond the frontiers of the Islamic state that were subsequently incorporated into the Islamic state. ʿUmar b. al-Khaṭṭāb did not recognize such claims because of the evidentiary problems they posed. If, however, the non-Arab claimants had been born within the frontiers of the Islamic state, they could present reliable Muslim witnesses to confirm their claims of kinship to the decedent.

bi-baladinā), is that a Muslim does not inherit the estate of a non-Muslim, whether on account of paternal kinship, patronage, or a maternal relationship, nor does he preempt the claim of any other heir to his share of the estate. This applies to every person who does not inherit: even though he may be the closest heir, he does not preempt anyone else from his or her share of the estate."[611]

Chapter 14. Those Who Died during Battle in Unknown Circumstances or Died in Other Unknown Circumstances

1487. According to Mālik, Rabīʿa b. Abī ʿAbd al-Raḥmān and several of their scholars reported that those killed in the Battles of the Camel, Ṣiffīn, and al-Ḥarra did not inherit from one another. Later, the Battle of Qudayd took place,[612] and none of the fallen was permitted to inherit anything from the estate of a fallen relation, unless it was known with certainty which of the two died first. Yaḥyā said, "I heard Mālik say, 'That is the rule about which there is no dissent, nor do any of the people of knowledge in our town have any doubt regarding it (*dhālika al-amr alladhī lā ikhtilāfa fīhi wa-lā shakka ʿinda aḥad min ahl al-ʿilm bi-baladinā*).'"

1488. Mālik said, "This is the rule that is followed in the case of two persons who are heirs of one another and die, whether by drowning, being killed, or any other cause of death, if it is not known which of the two was the first to die. When it is unknown which of them died first, neither inherits anything from the other. Rather, their estates are divided among those who remain of their respective heirs. Each decedent's heirs inherit from their respective relatives."

1489. Yaḥyā said, "I heard Mālik say, 'No one inherits from another person if there is any doubt about his claim. No one inherits from another person except on the basis of certain knowledge and the testimony of witnesses. This is because a man and his freedman whom his father had manumitted

611 Accordingly, were a non-Muslim man to die leaving a Muslim son and a non-Muslim daughter, the son would not reduce his non-Muslim sister's share from one-half of the estate to one-third, as would be the case if they were all Muslims.

612 Battles that took place between Muslims in the early civil wars over the caliphate. The Battle of the Camel involved the forces of ʿĀʾisha, the Mother of the Believers, Ṭalḥa, and al-Zubayr against the forces of ʿAlī b. Abī Ṭālib; the Battle of Ṣiffīn involved the forces of ʿAlī b. Abī Ṭālib against those of Muʿāwiya b. Abī Sufyān; the Battle of al-Ḥarra involved the forces of ʿAbd al-Malik b. Marwān, commanded by al-Ḥajjāj b. Yūsuf al-Thaqafī, against those of the Medinese; and the Battle of Qudayd involved a group of Khawārij who took over Medina temporarily during the reign of the last Umayyad caliph, Marwān b. Muḥammad (r. 126–132/744–750). "Khawārij" literally means "secessionists," and it refers to Muslims who seceded from the general body of the Muslim community with the aim of establishing their own government. In this early period, they would have consisted of Muslims of non-Qurayshī descent.

might die at the same time, and the Arab man's sons will say, "Our father certainly inherited the estate of the freedman (*mawlā*)." But they are not entitled to inherit the estate of the freedman in the absence of knowledge and testimony that he died before their father. Instead, the people closest to the freedman inherit his estate.'"

1490. Yaḥyā said, "Mālik said, 'This is also the rule that applies to the case of two full brothers who die, one leaving children and the other childless. They also leave a half-brother on the father's side, and it is unknown which of the two died first. Accordingly, the estate of the childless man goes to his half-brother, and the children of his full brother get nothing.'"[613]

1491. Yaḥyā said, "Mālik said, 'Another instance of that rule is when the paternal aunt (*ʿamma*), her nephew, her niece, and the latter's paternal uncle (*ʿamm*) all die, and the order of their deaths is unknown. If it is unknown who died first, the paternal uncle does not inherit anything from his niece, and the nephew does not inherit anything from his paternal aunt.'"

Chapter 15. The Estate of a Repudiated Child (*Walad al-Mulāʿana*)[614] and the Estate of an Illegitimate Child (*Walad al-Zinā*)

1492. According to Mālik, it reached him that ʿUrwa b. al-Zubayr would say, regarding the estate of a repudiated child and the estate of an illegitimate child, "When he dies, his mother inherits his estate in accordance with her rightful share as set out in God's Book; likewise, his half-siblings on his mother's side take their rightful share. If she is a freedwoman (*mawlāt*), her patrons inherit whatever remains of the estate. If she is an Arab woman,[615] she takes her rightful share of the estate, and his half-siblings on his mother's side take their rightful share of the estate, and whatever remains becomes property of the Muslim community." Mālik said, "A position similar

---

613 In this case, if it were known that the childless brother predeceased the brother with children, his estate would be divided equally between the half-brother and the full brother. Upon the full brother's death, his children would then inherit this property in turn, thus receiving property that had originally belonged to the estate of the childless brother. Under Mālik's rule, however, the court is to divide the estate of the childless brother as though the brother with children had no claim at all, with the result that the half-brother takes the entirety of the childless brother's estate instead of sharing it with his nephews and nieces.

614 Mālik is referring here to the formal procedure by which a husband may accuse his wife of adultery. This procedure involves the husband swearing four times in public that he is truthful in his accusation, followed by a fifth oath invoking God's damnation on himself should he be is lying. The wife can rebut the charge by swearing four public oaths denying the charge, followed by a fifth oath invoking God's anger on herself should she be lying. Once the husband completes the five oaths, any child that the woman subsequently delivers is affiliated only to her. *Al-Nūr*, 24:6–9. If the father, however, later retracts his accusation against the wife and acknowledges the child, he receives eighty lashes as punishment for slander. *Al-Nūr*, 24:4.

615 What is meant by "Arab" here is that she was born free.

to this reached me from Sulaymān b. Yasār. This is also the opinion that I found the people of knowledge of our town express regarding this question (*ʿalā dhālika adraktu raʾy ahl al-ʿilm bi-baladinā*)."

Book 28

The Book of Manumission (*ʿAtāqa*) and Patronage (*Walāʾ*)

Chapter 1. Manumission of a Partial Interest (*Shirk*) in a Slave

1493. According to Mālik, Nāfiʿ reported from ʿAbd Allāh b. ʿUmar that the Messenger of God (pbuh) said, "Whoever manumits his partial interest in a slave and owns a sufficient amount of other property to allow him to pay the slave's full price is obliged to give the slave's co-owners their share of the slave's price after his fair market value has been fairly appraised. Otherwise, only the former's share in the slave is manumitted."[616]

1494. Mālik said, "The agreed-upon rule among us (*al-amr al-mujtamaʿ ʿalayhi ʿindanā*) regarding a slave whose master, using a testamentary disposition effective upon his death, manumits a slave of his in part—be it one-third, one-fourth, or one-half—or a portion of his share in a co-owned slave is that the only portion of the slave that is effectively manumitted is the portion that the master expressly manumitted in his will out of the interest he owns in the slave.[617] This is because the manumission of that portion of the slave became due and effective only after the decedent's death. The master was free, as long as he was alive, to retract or fulfill the promise of manumission that he included in his will. When the slave's manumission took effect after the master's death by virtue of his bequest, the testator no longer had any rights to the property in his estate except in respect of that over which he had testamentary rights. The remaining portion of his

616 In other words, if four people co-own a slave, each having a one-quarter interest in the slave, and one of the part-owners manumits his share of the slave, the manumitting co-owner is obliged to buy out the remaining three-quarters of the slave from his co-owners after the slave's fair market value has been appraised. Once he pays the co-owners three-quarters of the slave's price, the slave becomes fully free. This requirement, however, applies only if the manumitting co-owner can afford the compensation due to his fellow co-owners. Otherwise, the co-owners retain their interest in the slave, and the slave is one-quarter free and three-quarters slave.

617 In other words, if the deceased master owns one-half of a slave and manumits one-half of his interest in the slave in his will, one-quarter of the slave is effectively manumitted.

slave was not effectively manumitted because others, namely, his heirs, now owned his property. How, then, could the remaining portion of the slave be manumitted in contravention of the ownership rights of another group of people who neither initiated the manumission nor ratified it? Nor would they take the status of patrons of the freedman (*mawlā*), nor would the law grant them the right of patronage. It was only the decedent who actually performed the manumission, and the law accordingly granted him the right of patronage. Therefore, the costs of the manumission should not be paid out of someone else's property. If, however, the decedent provided in his will that the remaining, unmanumitted portion of the slave be manumitted out of his property, such a provision would bind both his fellow co-owners of the slave and his heirs. His fellow co-owners cannot refuse to carry out such an instruction so long as the cost is paid out of the one-third of the decedent's interest in the estate that is available for testamentary disposition.[618] Moreover, the provision also binds the heirs because it does not cause any injury to their rights in the estate."

1495. Mālik said, "If someone manumits one-third of his slave while he is ill, intending the manumission to take effect immediately, the slave is automatically manumitted in his entirety, provided that the value of the slave is not more than one-third of the master's property at that time. This is because the ill man is not in the position of someone who manumits one-third of his slave after his death: such a person, had he lived, could have retracted his decision, in which case his partial manumission would never have taken effect. By contrast, the slave whose master pronounces an immediately effective one-third manumission during his deathbed illness is entitled to have the manumission completed by operation of law if the master recovers from his illness and lives. If the master dies as a result of the illness, the slave is also entitled to have the manumission completed, provided that the slave's value is not more than one-third of the master's property at the time of his death. This is because the decedent's directions regarding his property, so long as they do not exceed one-third of the property, are effective, just as a healthy person's directions regarding his property are effective with respect to all of his property."

Chapter 2. Conditional Manumission

1496. Yaḥyā said, "Mālik said, 'A man who manumits his slave with immediate effect, such that the slave's testimony becomes effective in court, his inviolability is perfected, and his estate can be passed to his heirs,

618 A decedent in Islamic law may dispose of only one-third of his property by testamentary disposition.

cannot impose conditions in connection with that manumission as he could with his slave, nor can he impose anything on the former slave that would resemble bondage. This is because the Messenger of God (pbuh) said, 'If someone manumits his interest in a slave, the slave's co-owners are to be given their share of his price after the slave's value is fairly appraised, and the slave is fully manumitted, regardless of the owner's intention.'"

1497. Mālik said, "If he is the sole owner of the slave, his obligation to complete the slave's manumission without undermining the manumission with any kind of bondage is even more binding."

Chapter 3. Manumitting Slaves When One Owns No Other Property

1498. According to Mālik, Yaḥyā b. Saʿīd reported from several people, from al-Ḥasan b. Abī al-Ḥasan, from Muḥammad b. Sīrīn, that a man in the time of the Messenger of God (pbuh) freed six slaves that belonged to him at the time of his death. The Messenger of God (pbuh) drew lots among them, manumitting one-third of them. Mālik said, "It reached me that the man's only property was those slaves."

1499. According to Mālik, Rabīʿa b. Abī ʿAbd al-Raḥmān reported that in the time of Abān b. ʿUthmān's term as governor of Medina, a man manumitted all of his slaves. Abān b. ʿUthmān ordered that the slaves be divided into three groups, and he then drew lots, stating that the group on which the decedent's lot fell would be freed. The one-third of the slaves represented by the lot that Abān drew were manumitted.

Chapter 4. Disposition of a Slave's Property When He Is Manumitted

1500. According to Mālik, he heard Ibn Shihāb say, "The applicable ordinance has long established (*maḍat al-sunna*) that a slave's property follows him when he is manumitted." Mālik said, "Something that corroborates the rule that a slave's property follows him upon his manumission is that the property of a slave who is a party to a manumission contract (*mukātab*)[619] follows the slave. This is because a manumission contract is also a contract of patronage (*walāʾ*) upon the contract's completion.[620] The property of a slave or of a slave under a manumission contract is not treated in the same manner as a slave's children are. Rather, children are deemed physical extensions of the slaves themselves. They are not deemed part of their

619 Such a contract is known as *kitāba*.

620 Mālik is arguing that since the master of a slave who is a party to a manumission contract enjoys the right of patronage of that slave upon the latter's performance of the contract, and since there is no disagreement that such a slave retains all his property, it must be the case that any slave who is manumitted retains all his personal property after he is manumitted.

property.[621] This is because the long-established ordinance about which there is no dissent (*al-sunna allatī lā ikhtilāfa fīhā*) is that a slave's property follows him after he is manumitted, but his children do not, and that the property of a slave who is a party to a manumission contract follows him, but his children do not."

1501. Mālik said, "Another thing that further corroborates this rule is that if a slave or a slave who is a party to a manumission contract becomes insolvent, his property, including any handmaiden of his who has borne him a child (*umm walad*), is taken to satisfy the claims of his creditors, but his creditors may not take his children, because they are not part of his property."

1502. Mālik said, "Another thing that also further corroborates this rule is that when a slave is sold and the purchaser stipulates inclusion of the slave's property in the contract of sale, the slave's children are not included in the slave's property under the contract."

1503. Mālik said, "Another thing that also further corroborates this rule is that if a slave injures someone in a manner requiring compensation, he and his property may be taken in compensation, but his children may not."

Chapter 5. Manumission of Handmaidens Who Have Given Birth to Their Masters' Children (*Umm Walad*) and Miscellaneous Matters Relating to Judicial Rulings regarding Manumission

1504. According to Mālik, Nāfiʿ reported from ʿAbd Allāh b. ʿUmar that ʿUmar b. al-Khaṭṭāb said, "Any master whose handmaiden has given birth to his child (*umm walad*) may neither sell her nor give her as a gift or bequeath her as part of his estate. He may continue to use her as a slave, but when he dies, she becomes free."

1505. According to Mālik, it reached him that a handmaiden went to ʿUmar b. al-Khaṭṭāb, her master having beaten her or struck her with a red hot iron. ʿUmar decreed that she be manumitted.

1506. Mālik said, "The rule in our view (*al-amr ʿindanā*) is that a man's manumission of a slave is not effective if his total debts exceed his property.

621 Mālik views the ownership interest of a master in his slave as consisting of two parts: the first concerns the body of the slave (*raqaba*), and the second concerns the usufruct. The income a slave generates for his master or for himself is part of the slave's usufruct, and under Mālik's rule, when the slave becomes free he becomes the full owner of whatever property he has acquired for himself, insofar as that property originated in usufruct. Children, however, are not part of usufruct under Mālik's principle, and therefore they are deemed an extension of the slave's body or even part of the slave's body.

Likewise, a minor's manumission of a slave is not effective before he attains puberty or reaches the age of puberty. Finally, the manumission of someone under an order of interdiction that prevents him from freely disposing of his own property (*al-mūlā ʿalayh*) is not effective, even if he has undergone puberty, until the authority to dispose of his own property is restored to him."

Chapter 6. Acts of Manumission That Are Effective in Discharging Obligations to Manumit Slaves

1507. According to Mālik, Hilāl b. Usāma reported from ʿAṭāʾ b. Yasār that ʿUmar b. al-Ḥakam[622] said, "I went to the Messenger of God (pbuh) and said, 'Messenger of God, a handmaiden of mine was herding some of my sheep (*ghanam*). When I went to check on her, she had lost a yearling (*shāt*), so I asked her what had happened. She said that a wolf killed and ate it. I became angry with her and, being human, I lost my temper and slapped her in the face. I am now under an obligation to manumit a slave,[623] so should it be her?' The Messenger of God (pbuh) said to the girl, 'Where is God?' She replied, 'In the sky.' The Messenger of God (pbuh) said, 'Who am I?' She said, 'You are the Messenger of God.'[624] The Messenger of God (pbuh) said, 'Manumit her.'"

1508. According to Mālik, Ibn Shihāb reported from ʿUbayd Allāh b. ʿAbd Allāh b. ʿUtba b. Masʿūd that a Medinese man came to the Messenger of God (pbuh) with a black handmaiden of his and said to him, "Messenger of God, I am under an obligation to manumit a believing slave. If you deem her a believer, I shall manumit her." The Messenger of God (pbuh) asked her, "Do you testify that there is no god but God?" She said, "Yes." He said, "Do you testify that Muḥammad is the Messenger of God?" She said, "Yes." He said, "Do you firmly believe in resurrection after death?" She said, "Yes." The Messenger of God (pbuh) said, "Manumit her."

1509. According to Mālik, it reached him that al-Maqburī said, "Abū Hurayra was asked whether a man who is under an obligation to manumit a slave can discharge his obligation by manumitting a slave born of adultery." Abū Hurayra said, "Yes, that would discharge his obligation."

---

622 The correct name of this transmitter is Muʿāwiya b. al-Ḥakam, as explained by the editors of the RME.

623 Bājī suggests that the narrator either caused the girl serious injury when he hit her or was already under an obligation to free a slave for some other reason. Bājī, *al-Muntaqā*, 6:274.

624 The Prophet (pbuh) asked her these questions to determine whether she was a Muslim. When a Muslim is obliged to manumit a slave as an act of penance, the slave must be Muslim. See hadith no. 1514 and no. 1516.

1510. According to Mālik, it reached him that Faḍāla b. ʿUbayd al-Anṣārī, who was a Companion of the Messenger of God (pbuh), was asked whether a man who is under an obligation to free a slave can discharge his obligation by manumitting a slave born of adultery. He said, "Yes, that satisfies his obligation."

Chapter 7. Acts of Manumission That Are Ineffective in Discharging Obligations to Manumit Slaves

1511. According to Mālik, it reached him that ʿAbd Allāh b. ʿUmar was asked whether a person under an obligation to manumit a slave could fulfill his obligation by purchasing a slave whose seller makes the sale conditional on the slave's manumission. He said no.

1512. Mālik said, "That is the best view I have heard regarding slaves who are acquired to fulfill an obligatory duty of manumission: the one who is obliged to manumit a slave may not purchase a slave subject to the seller's condition that he manumit the slave. Were he to do so, he would not have manumitted someone entirely subject to bondage, insofar as the slave's price is reduced in accordance with the seller's stipulation that the slave be manumitted."

1513. Mālik said, "There is nothing objectionable, however, in someone purchasing a slave on the condition that the buyer manumit him if it is a voluntary act of manumission."

1514. Mālik said that the best view that he had heard regarding someone who is under an obligation to manumit a slave is that he cannot fulfill his obligation by manumitting a slave belonging to the following categories: a Christian or Jewish slave; a slave who is a party to a manumission contract (*mukātab*); a slave whose master has designated him for manumission upon the master's death (*mudabbar*); a handmaiden who has borne her master a child (*umm walad*); a slave to be manumitted upon the expiration of a determined term; or a blind slave.

1515. Mālik said, "There is nothing objectionable in someone voluntarily manumitting a Christian, Jewish, or Zoroastrian slave, because God, Blessed and Sublime is He, says in the Book regarding prisoners, 'Therefore release them freely (*mannan*) or ransom them.'[625] Manumission means releasing freely (*mann*)."[626]

---

625 *Muḥammad*, 47:4.

626 For Mālik, manumission of any slave, regardless of religion, is meritorious, but if the manumitter is under a duty to manumit a slave, whether as an act of penance (*kaffāra*) or as the result of a vow (*nadhr*), the duty can be satisfied only by manumitting a Muslim slave. See,

1516. Mālik said, "As for those slaves whose manumission God has expressly commanded in the Book, only the manumission of believing slaves discharges that obligation."

1517. Mālik said, "The same rule applies to feeding poor persons in satisfaction of the duty to perform penance: only the feeding of Muslims satisfies the duty. No one following a religion other than Islam should be fed in satisfaction of that obligation."[627]

Chapter 8. Manumission by a Living Person on Behalf of a Dead One

1518. According to Mālik, ʿAbd al-Raḥmān b. Abī ʿAmra al-Anṣārī reported that his mother wanted to make a bequest for the purpose of manumitting a slave, but she postponed it until the next morning. Then she died in her sleep. ʿAbd al-Raḥmān said, "I then asked al-Qāsim b. Muḥammad whether God would reward her if I manumitted a slave on her behalf." Al-Qāsim replied that Saʿd b. ʿUbāda said to the Messenger of God (pbuh), "My mother died. Would God reward her were I to manumit a slave on her behalf?" The Messenger of God (pbuh) said, "Yes."

1519. According to Mālik, Yaḥyā b. Saʿīd said, "ʿAbd al-Raḥmān b. Abī Bakr died in his sleep, so his sister ʿĀʾisha, the wife of the Prophet (pbuh), manumitted a large number of slaves on his behalf." Mālik said, "Of all the views that I have heard regarding this question, this view is the one I prefer most."

Chapter 9. The Virtue in Manumitting Slaves, and the Manumission of an Adulteress and an Illegitimate Child

1520. According to Mālik, Hishām b. ʿUrwa reported from his father, from ʿĀʾisha, the wife of the Prophet (pbuh), that the Messenger of God (pbuh) was asked which slaves earn the greatest merit for those who manumit them. The Messenger of God (pbuh) said, "Those who are the dearest in price and the most valuable to their owners."

1521. According to Mālik, Nāfiʿ reported from ʿAbd Allāh b. ʿUmar that he manumitted an illegitimate child and his mother.

---

for example, *al-Nisāʾ*, 4:92, which provides that the penance for the unintentional killing of a person is "freeing a Muslim slave" (*taḥrīr raqaba muʾmina*).

627 Mālik is here speaking of how to discharge an obligation of penance (*kaffāra*), not whether it is permissible to give charity to non-Muslims.

Chapter 10. Patronage (*Walā'*) Belongs to the Manumitter

1522. According to Mālik, Hishām b. ʿUrwa reported from his father that ʿĀ'isha, the wife of the Prophet (pbuh), said, "Barīra came and said, 'I have entered into a manumission contract with my people for nine measures of silver (*awāq*),[628] one measure payable each year, so please assist me.' I replied, 'If your people have no objection, I will give them the entirety of the price at once, provided that the right of patronage (*walā'*) belongs to me.' Barīra then went to her people and presented my offer to them, but they rejected it. She returned to me and found the Messenger of God (pbuh) sitting there. She said to me, 'I made them the offer, but they refused me, insisting that the right of patronage remains with them.' The Messenger of God (pbuh) heard that, so he asked her about what was going on. I informed him about the matter, and he said, 'Take her and demand that the right of patronage belong to you as condition of the agreement. The right of patronage belongs exclusively to the one who manumits the slave.' I did as I was told, and the Messenger of God (pbuh) stood among the people, and praised God and honored Him. Then he said, 'Why is it that some people impose conditions that are not stipulated in God's Book? Any condition that is not in God's Book is void, even if there be one hundred such conditions in an agreement. God's judgment is more worthy of respect, and God's condition is firmer. The right of patronage belongs exclusively to the one who manumits the slave.'"

1523. According to Mālik, Nāfiʿ reported from ʿAbd Allāh b. ʿUmar that ʿĀ'isha, the Mother of the Believers, wanted to acquire a handmaiden in order to manumit her, so her owners said, "We are prepared to sell her to you, provided that the right of patronage remains with us." She mentioned this to the Messenger of God (pbuh), who said, "Let that not deter you, for the right of patronage belongs exclusively to the one who manumits the slave."

1524. According to Mālik, Yaḥyā b. Saʿīd reported from ʿAmra bt. ʿAbd al-Raḥmān that Barīra came to seek the assistance of ʿĀ'isha, the Mother of the Believers, in discharging her obligations under a manumission contract. ʿĀ'isha said, "If your people have no objection, I am ready to pay what you owe in its entirety and manumit you immediately." Barīra communicated that offer to her owners, who said, "No, not unless the right of patronage stays with us."

1525. Yaḥyā said, "Mālik said that Yaḥyā b. Saʿīd said, "Amra claimed that ʿĀ'isha mentioned this to the Messenger of God (pbuh), who said, "Purchase

628 Sing. *awqiya*. Nine *awāq* of silver are equivalent to a little more than 1,000 grams.

her and manumit her, for the right of patronage belongs exclusively to the one who manumits the slave.""'

1526. According to Mālik, ʿAbd Allāh b. Dīnār reported from ʿAbd Allāh b. ʿUmar that the Messenger of God (pbuh) prohibited the sale and gifting of the right of patronage.

1527. Mālik said, regarding a slave who purchases his freedom from his master on the condition that he has the right to choose whomever he wishes as his patron, "Such an arrangement is not permissible. The right of patronage belongs exclusively to the one who manumits the slave. Even if a master permitted his freedman (*mawlā*) to choose whomever he wished as his patron, it would not be permissible, because the Messenger of God (pbuh) said, 'The right of patronage belongs exclusively to the one who manumits the slave,' and the Messenger of God (pbuh) prohibited the sale and gifting of the right of patronage. If it were permissible for the master to grant the slave that condition and to permit him to choose as his patron whomever he wished, it would amount to a gift of the right of patronage."

Chapter 11. The Right of Patronage (*Walāʾ*) in Respect of the Freedman's Descendants

1528. According to Mālik, Rabīʿa b. Abī ʿAbd al-Raḥmān reported that al-Zubayr b. al-ʿAwwām bought a slave and then manumitted him. The slave had children from a free woman (who had formerly been a slave), and when al-Zubayr freed him, the former declared, "The children are my freedmen." The latter, however, said, "It is rather their mother's former owners who are our patrons." They took their dispute to ʿUthmān b. ʿAffān, and he ruled that they were the freedmen of al-Zubayr.

1529. According to Mālik, it reached him that Saʿīd b. al-Musayyab was asked, regarding a slave who had children from a free woman (who had formerly been a slave), "Who has the right of patronage (*walāʾ*) with respect to the children?" Saʿīd said, "If their father dies while still a slave, not having been manumitted, the right of patronage belongs to their mother's patrons."

1530. Mālik said, "A similar case is that of the children of freed slaves, when their fathers have accused their wives, the mothers of the children, of adultery (*mulāʿana*). Such children are affiliated to their mother's patrons. When such a child dies without an heir, the patrons inherit his estate. If he commits battery, they are required to contribute to the payment of any compensation that is due to the victim. If his father acknowledges the child, however, the child is affiliated to the father, and the right to the child's patronage goes to his father's patrons. The child's estate reverts to them in the event that he dies without heirs. They are also required to contribute to the payment of any compensation that is due to the victim of any battery committed by the child. His father, in this case, is subject to the mandatory punishment for falsely accusing the mother of adultery."

1531. Mālik said, "This is also the rule that applies to an Arab woman whose husband has publicly accused her of adultery but then comes to acknowledge her child. The child in this case is in the same position as the child in the previous case, except that whatever remains of his estate after his mother and siblings have taken their respective shares belongs to the Muslim community as long as he is unaffiliated to his father. The repudiated child of the freedwoman (*mawlāt*) is inherited only by his mother and her patrons until such time as his father acknowledges him. That is because until he is acknowledged as his father's child, he has neither a father nor paternal near-relations (*ʿaṣaba*). If his father acknowledges him, however, thereby establishing his paternal descent, whatever remains of his estate belongs to his paternal near-relations."

1532. Mālik said, "The agreed-upon rule among us (*al-amr al-mujtamaʿ ʿalayhi ʿindanā*) regarding the grandchildren of a freed slave when their father is still a slave but their mother is a freedwoman is that the right of patronage to the grandchildren is transferred from the mother's patron to the grandfather. The grandfather inherits the grandchildren's estates as long as their father remains a slave. If their father is manumitted, however, the right of patronage is transferred from the grandfather to the father's patrons. But if the father dies while still a slave, the grandchildren's estates and the right to their patronage go to the grandfather. And if the slave has two free sons and one of them dies while his father is still a slave, the right of patronage and the right of inheritance go to the grandfather, the father's father."

1533. Mālik said, regarding the case of a handmaiden who is manumitted while pregnant but whose husband remains a slave and is manumitted later, either before or after she delivers her baby, "The right of patronage to the fetus goes to whoever manumitted the mother. This is because the child had been destined for bondage before the mother was manumitted. This child is not in the position of a child whose mother becomes pregnant with him after her manumission. That is because the right of patronage to a child whose mother becomes pregnant with him after her manumission goes to his father's patrons once the father is manumitted."

1534. Mālik said, regarding a slave who seeks his master's permission to manumit one of his own slaves and whose master permits him to do so,

"The right of patronage to the manumitted slave, in this case, belongs to the first slave's master, not the master who manumitted him (i.e., the first slave), even if the first slave is subsequently manumitted."

Chapter 12. Inheritance of the Right of Patronage (*Walāʾ*)

1535. According to Mālik, ʿAbd Allāh b. Abī Bakr reported from ʿAbd al-Malik b. Abī Bakr b. ʿAbd al-Raḥmān b. al-Ḥārith b. Hishām that his father told him that al-ʿĀṣī b. Hishām died leaving three sons, two from a first wife and one from a second. One of the sons from the first wife subsequently died, leaving property and freedmen. His full brother inherited al-ʿĀṣī's property and the right of patronage to his freedmen. Then this full brother died. He left his own son and his half-brother on his father's side. His son said, "Whatever my father acquired from his brother, whether property or the right of patronage to the freedmen, is now mine." His uncle said, "That is not the case. Only the property is yours, not the right of patronage to the freedmen. Is it not the case that had the first of my deceased brothers died today, I would have inherited him?" They took their dispute to ʿUthmān b. ʿAffān, who ruled that the decedent's half-brother on his father's side should inherit the right of patronage to the freedmen.

1536. According to Mālik, ʿAbd Allāh b. Abī Bakr b. Ḥazm reported that his father told him that he was sitting with Abān b. ʿUthmān when a group from the tribe of Juhayna and another group from the tribe of Banū al-Ḥārith b. al-Khazraj came, asking him to resolve a dispute that had broken out between them. There was a woman from Juhayna who was married to a man from Banū al-Ḥārith b. al-Khazraj named Ibrāhīm b. Kulayb. The woman died, leaving property and freedmen, and her son and husband inherited her. Then her son died, and his heirs said, "The right of patronage to the freedmen should go to us, just as her son had that right." The people from Juhayna said, "That is not the case, for they are the freedmen of our female relation, and when her son died, we should get the right of patronage with respect to them, and we inherit them upon their death." Abān b. ʿUthmān ruled that the right of patronage to the freedmen belonged to the group from Juhayna.

1537. According to Mālik, it reached him that Saʿīd b. al-Musayyab said, regarding a man who died leaving three sons and freedmen that he himself had manumitted and who was then followed in death by two of his sons, who left children of their own, "The third son, who is still alive, inherits exclusively the right of patronage to the freedmen. When he dies, his children and his nephews inherit the right of patronage to the freedmen on an equal basis."

Chapter 13. The Estates of Abandoned Slaves (*Sā'iba*) and the Right of Patronage (*Walā'*) of Someone Who Manumits a Jewish or a Christian Slave

1538. According to Mālik, he asked Ibn Shihāb about abandoned slaves, and Ibn Shihāb said, "The abandoned slave may enter into a relationship of patronage with anyone who agrees to be his patron. If he dies without entering into a relationship of patronage, his estate belongs to the Muslim community, and they are required to contribute to the payment of any compensation (*ʿaql*) due for any batteries[629] he may commit."

1539. Mālik said, "The best opinion that has been reported about an abandoned slave is that he is not entitled to enter into a relationship of patronage with someone on the sole basis of an agreement with that person. Rather, the right of patronage with respect to an abandoned slave defaults to the Muslim community, his estate goes to the Muslim community, and the Muslim community is required to contribute to the payment of any compensation due for batteries that he commits."

1540. Mālik said, regarding a Jew or a Christian whose slave converts to Islam and who consequently manumits the slave before a judicial sale is ordered,[630] "The right of patronage (*walā'*) of freedmen such as these belongs to the Muslim community. Even if the Jewish or Christian master subsequently converts to Islam, he shall never enjoy the right of patronage to that slave." Mālik said, "On the other hand, if a Jew or a Christian manumits a slave who is a follower of his own religion and the manumitted slave then converts to Islam, and then the master himself converts to Islam, the right of patronage is restored to the master. This is because it had validly come into existence in his favor on the day he manumitted the slave."

1541. Mālik said, "If a Christian or a Jew has Muslim children, the Muslim children inherit the right of patronage to the freedmen of their Jewish or Christian father in the event that the freedmen convert to Islam before their former master does. If the manumitted slave is a Muslim when he is manumitted, however, the Muslim children of the Christian or the Jew do

629 In common law, a battery in most jurisdictions is an intentional injury to the body of another person. When the injury is unintentional, it is called negligence. In Islamic law, the term for battery is *jināya*, and it includes both intentional and unintentional injuries to the body of another. However, the duty of close relations or, in this case, of the Muslim community to contribute to the compensation due to the victim arises only if the battery was unintentional. Accordingly, in this translation, we use the term battery for both intentional and unintentional violations of bodily integrity.

630 Under Islamic law, non-Muslims were not permitted to own Muslim slaves. If they came to own a Muslim slave, whether by conversion, gift, inheritance, or other means, the Muslim slave would be sold by judicial order and the price received given to the non-Muslim master.

not receive the right of patronage to the Muslim slave, because in this case the Jewish or Christian master has no claim to the right of patronage. The right of patronage to a manumitted Muslim slave belongs exclusively to the Muslim community."

The Book of Manumission Has Been Completed, with Praise to God in the Manner That Befits Him, and May God Grace Muḥammad, His Prophet, and His Family.

In the Name of God, the Merciful, the Compassionate

May God Grace Muḥammad and His Family and Grant Them Peace.

Book 29

The Book of the Slave Who Is a Party to a Manumission Contract (*Mukātab*)[631]

Chapter 1. Judicial Rulings (*Qaḍāʾ*) with Respect to the Slave Who Is a Party to a Manumission Contract (*Mukātab*)

1542. According to Mālik, Nāfiʿ reported that ʿAbd Allāh b. ʿUmar would say, "The slave who is a party to a manumission contract remains a slave as long as any portion of his contract remains unperformed."

1543. According to Mālik, it reached him that ʿUrwa b. al-Zubayr and Sulaymān b. Yasār would say, "The slave who is a party to a manumission contract remains a slave as long as any portion of his contract remains unperformed." Yaḥyā said, "Mālik said, 'And that is my opinion as well.'"

1544. Mālik said, "If a slave who is a party to a manumission contract dies before performing the contract but leaves property in an amount greater than what he owed, and if he has children who were born during the term of his contract or if he included them within the scope of his contract, they inherit whatever remains of his property after the outstanding amount has been paid."

1545. According to Mālik, Ḥumayd b. Qays al-Makkī reported that a slave who was a party to a manumission contract belonging to the son of

631 A slave who is a party to a manumission contract is still a slave, but he is in important respects almost free, as the reports in this book indicate. Such a slave enjoys the right, among other things, to enter contracts on his own behalf, and he is obliged to discharge his obligations to third parties, whether arising out of his contracts or caused by his perpetration of battery. However, if the slave repudiates or is deemed to have repudiated the manumission contract, he reverts to his previous status as a chattel slave (*ʿabd mamlūk*) under the complete control of his master.

al-Mutawakkil died in Mecca. At the time of his death, he still owed amounts under his manumission contract as well as other debts to third parties. He also left a daughter. The governor of Mecca was uncertain about how to adjudicate these claims, so he wrote to ʿAbd al-Malik b. Marwān, seeking his view. ʿAbd al-Malik wrote back, saying, "Begin with the debts owed to the third parties and then pay the unpaid amounts due under the contract. Whatever remains, divide it between his daughter and his former master."[632]

1546. Yaḥyā said, "Mālik said, 'The rule in our view (*al-amr ʿindanā*) is that the slave's master is not obliged to enter into a manumission contract with his slave upon the slave's request. I have not heard of anyone in authority who ever compelled anyone to enter into a manumission contract with his slave. I did hear, however, that some of the people of knowledge, when asked about the verse "Contract with them for their manumission, if you perceive any good in them,"[633] would recite these two verses in response: "When you exit the consecrated state, hunt,"[634] and "And when the Friday congregational prayer is concluded, disperse throughout the land and seek out God's bounty."[635] This is simply a matter in which God has granted people permission without imposing an obligation.'"[636]

1547. Mālik said, "I heard some of the people of knowledge say, regarding the statement of God, Blessed and Sublime is He, in His Book, 'Give them out of God's property, over which God has given you stewardship,'[637] that it refers to the case of a man who enters into a manumission contract with his slave and then freely remits a specified portion of the contract's final instalment." Mālik said, "This is what I heard from the people of knowledge, and I found the practice of the people among us (*ʿamal al-nās ʿindanā*) to be in accordance with that."

1548. Mālik said, "It reached me that ʿAbd Allāh b. ʿUmar entered into a manumission contract with one of his slaves for 35,000 dirhams. He then later reduced the final instalment of the contract by 5,000 dirhams."

---

632 If any property remains after satisfying the claims of the third-party creditors and the obligations of the deceased slave under the manumission contract, the manumitted slave's daughter inherits one-half in accordance with her stipulated Quranic share. The former master has the right of patronage (*walāʾ*) in respect of the manumitted slave and therefore takes the remainer of the decedent's estate.

633 *Al-Nūr*, 24:33.

634 *Al-Māʾida*, 5:2.

635 *Al-Jumuʿa*, 62:10.

636 The point being made by the citation of these verses is that despite their use of the imperative mood, no one believes that the first verse imposes an obligation to hunt or that the second verse imposes an obligation to engage in commerce. By analogy, the mere fact that the imperative mood is used in the verse about manumission contracts does not, by itself, establish an obligation to enter into a manumission contract with any slave who requests it.

637 *Al-Nūr*, 24:33.

1549. Mālik said, "The rule in our view is that when a master enters into a manumission contract with his slave, the contract includes the slave's property but not his children, unless the slave expressly stipulates their inclusion in the contract."

1550. Yaḥyā said, "I heard Mālik say, regarding a slave who has entered into a manumission contract with his master and who himself owns a handmaiden who, unbeknownst to both the master and himself, was pregnant from the slave at the time they entered into the contract, 'The slave's unborn child is not included in the manumission contract because the slave did not expressly include it in the contract when he was still the master's property. As for the handmaiden, she belongs to the slave because she was part of his property at the time he entered into the manumission contract.'"

1551. Mālik said, regarding a slave who enters into a manumission contract with his owner, a free woman, and the woman then dies, leaving the slave to her husband and her son, "If the slave dies before completing payment of all the instalments due under his contract, the husband and the son divide the slave's estate in accordance with God's Book. If he pays all the instalments due under the contract and then dies, his estate goes to the former owner's son, and the husband receives nothing."[638]

1552. Yaḥyā said, "Mālik said, regarding a slave who is a party to a manumission contract and who then enters into a manumission contract with his own slave, 'Such a matter is to be investigated. If he was motivated to do this only to show favoritism to his own slave, and that comes to be known, for example, through evidence that he lessens the slave's burden, that contract is not binding. If, on the other hand, he was motivated by a desire to obtain additional property and extra funds to help him pay the instalments due under his contract, it is binding.'"

1553. Mālik said, regarding a man having intercourse with a handmaiden of his who is a party to a manumission contract with him, "If she becomes pregnant, she has a choice: if she wishes, she may choose to take the status of a mother of the master's child (*umm walad*) and cancel her manumission contract; or she may continue performance of her contract. But if she does not become pregnant, she remains subject to the terms of her manumission contract."

638 In the first case, in which the slave dies with outstanding instalments left under the manumission contract, he is still legally a slave, and therefore the husband and the son inherit the estate of the slave in accordance with each man's respective share in the decedent's estate. In the second case, in which the slave dies after completing payment of all the instalments due under the contract, he dies as a free person, so his estate goes to his patron. In this case, that would be the woman's son, insofar as he is the descendant of the person who manumitted the slave.

1554. Yaḥyā said, "Mālik said, 'The agreed-upon rule among us (*al-amr al-mujtamaʿ ʿalayhi ʿindanā*) regarding a slave whom two men own in common is that neither of them may individually enter into a manumission contract in respect of his own share in the slave, whether or not his co-owner consents; rather, both of them must jointly agree to enter into the contract. This is because this is a contract that promises the slave manumission. In the case of a partial contract, even if the slave were to perform the contract, he would be only half-free, and the co-owner with whom the slave contracted would not be obliged to complete the slave's manumission. That result contradicts what the Messenger of God (pbuh) said: "If someone manumits his interest in a slave, the slave's co-owners are to be given their share of his price after the slave's value is fairly appraised, and the slave is fully manumitted."'"

1555. Yaḥyā said, "And Mālik then said, 'If no one other than the parties to the contract knows of its existence until the slave has performed the contract, in whole or in part, the master who contracted with the slave must return whatever the slave paid him and share it with his partner in accordance with their respective interests in the slave; the manumission contract is invalidated, and the slave is restored to his original condition.'"

1556. Mālik said, regarding a scenario in which a slave is a party to a manumission contract and is owned in common by two men, one of whom has granted him an extension in the payment of an instalment due to him under the contract while the other has refused to grant a similar extension and so the former has collected only part of what he is owed, and the slave then dies, leaving insufficient property to discharge the remaining instalments under the manumission contract: "The co-owners share whatever property the slave left, pro rata, in accordance with each one's proportional share of the slave's unpaid obligation. If, on the other hand, the slave left property in excess of what is due, each one of them takes in accordance with his share. If the owner, the party entering into the manumission contract with the slave, leaves a surplus beyond what is due under the contract, each one of them takes what he is owed under the contract, in accordance with his share, and whatever remains is divided equally between them.[639] If the

639 The text of the RME differs materially from other recensions of Yaḥyā's *Muwaṭṭa'* in the two-sentence passage beginning with "If, on the other hand," and concluding with "divided equally between them." The RME includes the following sentence not found in other versions: *Fa-in taraka al-mukātib faḍlan ʿan kitābatihi akhadha kull wāḥid minhumā mā baqiya min al-kitāba*. This addition is likely a scribal error. If it were omitted, the text would be translated as follows: "If, on the other hand, the slave left property in excess of what is due under the manumission contract, each one of them takes what he is owed under the contract, in accordance with his share, and whatever remains is divided equally between them." This

slave repudiates the contract and if the co-owner who refused to grant the slave an extension collected more of what was due to him than his co-owner did, the slave continues to be co-owned, in equal shares. The co-owner who collected more than his fellow co-owner is under no obligation to share the additional payment he collected from the slave, because he agreed to manumit the slave only in accordance with the terms of the manumission contract to which his co-owner expressly consented. If one of the co-owners remits part of what he is owed but the other co-owner collects what is due to him, and then the slave is unable to perform the rest of the contract, the slave continues to be their common property. The co-owner who collected more is under no obligation to share whatever excess payment he received with his fellow co-owner, because he did nothing more than collect what he was owed. This is similar to the case of a single contract of debt owed to two creditors. One of them grants the debtor an extension, while the other insists on prompt payment, collecting part of what he is owed. Then the debtor becomes insolvent. In that case, the creditor who received partial payment is not obliged to share that partial payment with the creditor who granted an extension."

Chapter 2. Guaranty of a Manumission Contract

1557. Yaḥyā said, "Mālik said, 'The agreed-upon rule among us (*al-amr al-mujtamaʿ ʿalayhi ʿindanā*) is that when a group of slaves jointly contract for their manumission, they act as mutual guarantors of one another's obligations. Accordingly, should any of them die, they are not entitled to any reduction in their obligations. If one of them were to throw up his hands and say, "I can't do it," his fellows are entitled to engage him in some kind of employment that he can reasonably endure, thereby assisting one another in discharging their obligations, so that he is manumitted if they are manumitted, and he remains a slave if they remain slaves.'"

1558. Mālik said, "The agreed-upon rule among us is that when a master enters into a manumission contract with his slave (*mukātab*), the master is not allowed to benefit from another person's guaranty of the slave's performance of the contract should the slave die or abandon the contract. Such a guaranty is not part of the long-established ordinances of the Muslims (*sunnat al-muslimīn*). This is because if a third party guarantees the slave's obligation to his master under the manumission contract and the master enforces that obligation against the guarantor, the master would be unjustly enriched by the guarantor's property. The master neither sold

---

version makes more sense, but we have nonetheless preserved the apparent error for the sake of of fidelity to the text of the RME.

him the slave, in which case what the master took from the guarantor would have been the price of something that is now the guarantor's property, nor was the slave manumitted, in which case the payment of the guaranty would have been the price of establishing the slave's inviolability. Thus, if a slave who is a party to a manumission contract repudiates (or is deemed to have repudiated) the contract, he reverts to his former status as a chattel slave (*'abd mamlūk*) of his master. This is because a manumission contract is not an enforceable debt in respect of which the master may benefit from a guaranty. Rather, it is a way for the slave to be manumitted if he performs it. If a slave who is a party to a manumission contract dies with outstanding debts, his master is not allowed to claim payment of what he is owed under the manumission contract out of the slave's estate, in contrast to the slave's third-party creditors, who are entitled to repayment out of the dead slave's property. The slave's third-party creditors have a greater claim than the master to the slave's estate. If a slave who is a party to a manumission contract repudiates the contract, he reverts to his former status as a chattel slave of his master, even if he is indebted to third-party creditors. In this case, the slave remains liable with respect to the debts he owes to the third-party creditors, but they are payable only out of any property the slave presently has or might have in the future. The third-party creditors have no right to share ownership of the slave's person with his master."

1559. Yaḥyā said, "Mālik said, 'When a group of slaves jointly enter into a single manumission contract, and they share no ties of kinship through which they would inherit from one another, they are mutual guarantors of one another's obligations. None is manumitted until all are manumitted through payment of all of the obligations under the contract. If one of them dies, leaving property in excess of the entire amount they collectively owe, that property is used to satisfy the entirety of their joint obligation, with any surplus going to the deceased slave's master. None of the surplus goes to the other slaves who entered the manumission contract along with the deceased slave. The master of the dead slave may also recoup from the other slaves the amounts that were paid from the deceased slave's property, in accordance with their shares. The deceased slave was only their guarantor. Consequently, they must reimburse his estate for the property that was used to pay for their manumission.[640] If the deceased slave had free children who had been born before the manumission contract was concluded but who were not included in the manumission contract, they do not inherit from him because the slave was manumitted only after he died.'"

640 In this case, the master's only claims against his former slaves are those of a creditor; the slaves, although indebted to their former master, are now free.

Chapter 3. Accelerated Prepayment (*Qaṭāʿa*) of a Manumission Contract[641]

1560. According to Mālik, it reached him that Umm Salama, the wife of the Prophet (pbuh), would agree to accept prepayment in gold and silver[642] in discharge of manumission contracts from any slaves of hers with whom she had made such contracts.

1561. Mālik said, "The agreed-upon rule among us (*al-amr al-mujtamaʿ ʿalayhi ʿindanā*) concerning a slave who is a party to a manumission contract (*mukātab*) and who is owned by two partners in common is that neither of them may accept from the slave prepayment of his share of the manumission contract without the other's consent. This is because the partners own both the slave and his property. Accordingly, neither of them is permitted to take any of their commonly owned property without his partner's consent. Were it the case that only one of them accepted prepayment from the slave, and that transaction were deemed valid, and then the slave died, whether or not the slave left property, the partner who accepted prepayment would not have a claim to any of the dead slave's property; nor could that partner refund what the dead slave had given him as advance payment of the manumission contract and then retroactively resume his status as the slave's co-owner. When a co-owner accepts prepayment of the manumission contract with his partner's consent, however, and the slave then repudiates the contract, that partner has the right to refund the prepayment that the slave made and retroactively reclaim his proportional ownership of the slave. If, in this case, the slave dies leaving property, the partner whose claim under the manumission contract was unsatisfied can satisfy his claim in full out of the deceased slave's property. Then, whatever remains of the slave's property is divided between the partner who accepted prepayment and the other partner who did not, in accordance with their respective shares in the slave. If one of them accepted prepayment of the contract while the other partner insisted on the original payment terms, and the slave then repudiated the contract, the partner who accepted prepayment is given a choice: 'If you wish, you may share with your partner half of the prepayment that you took from the slave, in which case you will co-own the slave equally. If you

641 Such prepayment is a transaction between a slave who has already entered a manumission contract and his master. The transaction involves the slave offering to pay the master immediately a reduced amount in exchange for immediate manumission.

642 Mālik mentions Umm Salama's precedent of accepting a reduced prepayment in gold and silver to make clear that in his opinion this transaction was exempt from the general rules prohibiting the accelerated payment of commercial debts denominated in gold and silver in exchange for a reduction in the debtor's contractual obligation. See Ibn ʿAbd al-Barr, *al-Istidhkār*, 7:397–98.

refuse to share the prepayment with your partner, the slave becomes the sole property of your partner, who maintained his rights under the contract in their entirety.'"

1562. Mālik said, regarding a scenario in which a slave whom two partners own in common is a party to a manumission contract with them, and his offer of prepayment of the contract is accepted by one of the partners with the other partner's consent; the partner who insisted on the original payment terms then receives instalments from the slave under the contract in an amount equivalent to or in excess of what the other partner accepted as prepayment of the entire contract; and the slave then repudiates the contract: "The slave remains their common property, because the partner collected only what was owed to him from the slave. If, on the other hand, he collected less than what the partner who accepted prepayment from the slave received, and then the slave repudiates the contract, the partner who accepted prepayment is free to do one of two things. If he agrees to share with his partner half of what he received from the slave in excess of what his partner received, the slave again becomes their commonly owned property. If he refuses, however, the slave becomes the sole property of the partner who insisted on the original payment terms. If the slave dies leaving property and the partner who accepted prepayment agrees to give his partner half of the amount that he received from the slave in excess of what his partner received, they divide the slave's estate equally. If the one who maintained his rights under the manumission contract received an equal or greater amount compared to the partner who accepted prepayment, the slave's estate belongs to both of them, because he took only his due."

1563. Mālik said, regarding a scenario in which a slave owned in common is a party to a manumission contract, and one of the co-owners agrees to accept prepayment of the contract for half of what is due to him with his partner's consent, but then the co-owner who maintained his rights under the manumission contract collects less from the slave than what the partner who accepted prepayment received, and then the slave repudiates the contract: "If the partner who accepted prepayment agrees to share with his partner half of the amount that he received in excess of his partner, the slave once again becomes their commonly owned property. If he refuses to do so, however, the partner who maintained his rights under the contract takes over his partner's share in the slave. An example of this would be a slave owned by two men in common in equal shares. They then jointly enter into a contract of manumission with the slave. Then, with the permission of his partner, one of the co-owners agrees to accept prepayment from the slave for one-half of his claim under the contract, that being one-fourth of the entire slave. The slave then repudiates the contract. In this case, the partner who accepted prepayment has two choices. He is told, 'If you wish, share with your partner half of the excess amount that you received from the slave relative to what your partner received, in which case the slave becomes your common property in equal proportions.' If he refuses to share that excess amount with his partner, the other partner takes the one-fourth interest of the partner who accepted prepayment exclusively for himself. He also maintains his own one-half interest in the slave. That amounts to three-fourths of the slave. The partner who accepted prepayment of one-half of what he was owed under the contract is given one-fourth of the slave, because he refused to share what he received in respect of the one-fourth of the slave for which he had accepted prepayment."

1564. Mālik said, regarding a scenario in which the master of a slave who is a party to a manumission contract accepts prepayment from him for a reduced amount, resulting in his complete manumission, but then imposes on the manumitted slave the unpaid amount under the contract as a debt, and the slave then dies, owing debts to third parties: "The master's claim, arising out of the unpaid amount under the original manumission contract, is not included along with the claims of the third-party creditors against the deceased debtor's property. The claims of the third-party creditors must be satisfied first."

1565. Mālik said, "The slave who is a party to a manumission contract may not offer to prepay what he owes his master if he owes debts to third parties, if the result would be that he would be insolvent upon his manumission. This is because the third-party creditors have a greater claim to the slave's property than his master does. He is thus not permitted to do that."

1566. Mālik said, "The rule in our view (*al-amr ʿindanā*) is that there is nothing objectionable in the scenario of a master who has entered into a manumission contract with his slave for a specific amount of gold later agreeing to remit some of that amount on condition that the slave pays the reduced amount immediately. The only reason some people disapprove of it is that they deem this exchange the equivalent of the case of a debt owed by one man to another, in respect of which the creditor agrees to reduce the amount owed in exchange for the debtor's immediate payment of the reduced amount. However, this is not the equivalent of a debt. Rather, the slave's immediate prepayment of a reduced amount to his master is in exchange for immediate manumission, as a result of which the slave receives the right to inherit and to testify in court, as well as the full protections of criminal law, including against slander. He also receives the inviolability that manumission entails. He has not sold dirhams for dirhams, nor gold for gold; instead, his case is more like that of a master who says to his slave-boy, 'Give me such-and-such a number of dinars, and I will set you free.' Later, the master unilaterally remits some of that amount, saying, 'If you give me some lesser amount, I will set you free.' The master's initial statement does not establish a determinate contractual debt. If it were a determinate contractual debt, the master would be entitled to share the slave's property with the slave's third-party creditors in respect of whatever the slave still owed him under the manumission contract if the slave were to die or become insolvent without having met his obligations under the manumission contract."[643]

Chapter 4. Batteries (*Jirāḥ*) Committed by a Slave Who Is a Party to a Manumission Contract (*Mukātab*)

1567. Yaḥyā said, "Mālik said, 'The best view I have heard regarding a slave who is a party to a manumission contract and who causes someone else an injury grave enough to require compensation is that if he has property sufficient to pay the required compensation as well as what he owes under his manumission contract, he must first pay the compensation due. In this case, he continues to enjoy his rights under the manumission contract. If he is unable, however, to pay the required compensation, he is deemed to have repudiated his manumission contract. This is because his obligation to pay compensation for the battery (*jurḥ*) takes priority over his right to complete performance of the manumission contract. Further, if he is unable to pay the compensation due for his battery, his master is given a choice. If he wishes, he may pay the compensation due for the injury and retain his slave, who in this case reverts to being a chattel slave (*'abd mamlūk*). Alternatively, if the master wishes, he may surrender the slave to the injured party. The master is not required to do anything beyond surrendering his slave.'"

1568. Yaḥyā said, "Mālik said, 'If a group of slaves jointly enter into a manumission contract, and then one of them commits a battery that requires compensation, he and his fellow slaves who are parties to the same manumission contract will be told, "You are all jointly liable for payment of the compensation due for that battery." If they satisfy that obligation, they

643 Mālik's analysis of the manumission contract analogizes it to a unilateral contract or a reward contract (*ju'l*), which, in Mālik's doctrine, binds the offeror once the offeree begins performance. The offeree remains free to repudiate the contract at any time, but only upon completion of the contract does the offeree become entitled to the reward promised by the offeror. In the case of a manumission contract, the slave is being offered freedom as a reward for obtaining an agreed-upon sum of money or other property. Once the slave accepts this offer, the master is not free to repudiate the offer, whereas the slave is. Because it is a unilateral reward contract, moreover, it does not constitute a debt, and therefore the master is free to reduce what the slave must deliver in order to receive his reward.

retain their rights under their manumission contract, but if they do not, they are deemed to have repudiated their manumission contract, and their master is given a choice. If he wishes, he may pay the compensation due for the battery, in which case the slaves all revert to their former status as his chattel slaves. Alternatively, he may surrender the perpetrator to the victim. In this case, the others revert to their former status as his chattel slaves because of their failure to pay the compensation due for the battery perpetrated by their fellow.'"

1569. Mālik said, "The rule about which there is no dissent among us (*al-amr alladhī lā ikhtilāfa fīhi ʿindanā*) is that if a slave who is a party to a manumission contract is injured and is entitled to compensation for that injury, or if one of his children included with him under the manumission contract is injured, the measure of compensation to which they are entitled is the diminution in their fair market value. Whatever compensation is paid in respect of them is given to their master, who owns the right to payment under the manumission contract. Any amount the master collects in compensation for such injuries must be deducted from the amount the slave owes under the manumission contract. An example of this rule is a situation in which the manumission contract is for 3,000 dirhams and the compensation received by the master is 1,000 dirhams; once the slave pays his master 2,000 dirhams, the slave is manumitted. If the unpaid portion of the contract is 1,000 dirhams and the compensation received for the injury is 1,000 dirhams, the slave is manumitted immediately. If, on the other hand, the amount due to the master in respect of the injury to his slave exceeds the outstanding amount under the manumission contract, the master keeps only an amount equal to that which he is owed, and the slave is manumitted. Whatever amount remains after the contract has been fully paid belongs to the slave. In no case should any of the compensation due for an injury be paid directly to the slave, lest he consume it or dissipate it. Should it happen that he later repudiates the manumission contract (or is deemed to have repudiated it), he might revert to his master mutilated, perhaps one-eyed, with only one hand, or otherwise crippled. His master entered into a manumission contract with the slave relying on the slave's possessions and his prospective earnings, not in anticipation of receiving compensation for injuries to the slave or his children and being subjected to the risk that the slave may consume the compensation or otherwise dissipate it. For this reason, any compensation received for injuries to the slave, his children born during the term of the manumission contract, or his children included as part of the manumission contract is paid directly to his master. The slave is given credit for these amounts at the conclusion of the contract."

Chapter 5. The Sale of a Slave Who Is a Party to a Manumission Contract (*Mukātab*)

1570. Mālik said, "The best view that has been reported regarding a man who purchases a manumission contract,[644] if that manumission contract is to be paid in gold dinars or silver dirhams, is that he must pay for the contract using goods that are due immediately and are delivered without any delay. This is because if the purchaser were to defer payment of the contract's purchase price, the transaction would amount to settling one debt through another debt,[645] and payment of one debt by means of another debt is unlawful."

1571. Mālik said, "If the master who has entered into a manumission contract with his slave has specified payment in terms of particular goods, be they camels, cattle, sheep (*ghanam*), or slaves, a purchaser may purchase that contract from the master for gold, silver, or goods—provided that the goods are different from the goods specified in the manumission contract—on the condition that the purchaser agrees to pay immediately and makes delivery without any delay."

1572. Mālik said, "The best view I have heard regarding a slave who is a party to a manumission contract and whose contract is sold is that he has a greater right to purchase his own manumission contract than any third party does, provided that he can deliver to his master in cash the price at which the master has agreed to sell the contract. This is because his act of self-purchase amounts to manumission, and manumission is given priority over any other bequests that a testator may make in his will.[646] However, if one of the co-owners of a slave sells his share in the slave, be it one-half, one-third, one-quarter, or any other share, after all the co-owners have entered into a manumission contract with that slave, the slave does not enjoy a right of first refusal (*shufʿa*) to purchase that share. That is because the purchase of a fractional interest in himself is the equivalent of a prepayment (*qaṭāʿa*) of the manumission contract with only one of the

---

644 In other words, the purchaser is paying for the right to receive the payments due from the slave under the manumission contract.

645 In this case, if the manumission contract provides for the future payment of gold or silver instalments, the purchaser of the manumission contract is acquiring a right to be paid in gold and silver in the future. If the purchaser acquires this right by promising the master future payment of instalments in gold and silver, the agreement amounts to the seller settling his future obligations to the purchaser by means of the purchaser's future obligations to the seller.

646 If a person dies and provides for the disposition of some of his assets in a will, and the property he intends to dispose of exceeds one-third of his assets, any slaves whom he has designated for manumission are to be manumitted before any of the other testamentary dispositions are distributed, even if that means that some testamentary dispositions will not be fulfilled as a result.

slave's co-owners. A slave owned in common is not permitted to prepay the share of any of his masters in his manumission contract unless the others agree. Moreover, he does not attain complete freedom through acquisition of what is being offered for sale. He is still barred from complete ownership of his own property. Finally, if he purchases only a partial interest in himself, there is the risk that he later repudiates (or is deemed to have repudiated) the manumission contract because his ability to pay what he owes under the manumission contract has been reduced through his purchase of that partial interest. Therefore, the slave's purchase of a partial interest in himself is not the equivalent of the slave's buying himself completely, unless the co-owners who retain an interest in the manumission contract give him permission. If they do, he has a greater right to acquire the partial interest that is being sold."

1573. Mālik said, "The sale of one or more instalments (*najm*) due from a slave who is a party to a manumission contract is not permissible. This is because of material uncertainty in the consideration (*gharar*).[647] If the slave repudiates (or is deemed to have repudiated) the contract, his debt is canceled. If the slave dies owing debts to third parties or goes bankrupt, the purchaser of an instalment due under the manumission contract is not entitled to make a claim to the slave's assets along with his third-party creditors. The purchaser of an instalment due under a manumission contract has only the rights of the slave's master. The slave's master is not entitled to make a claim to the slave's assets alongside third-party creditors on the basis of the unpaid amounts of the manumission contract. Rather, their claims are paid first. The same rule applies to the slave's earnings that the slave owes to the master: the master may not recoup them out of the slave's assets until the third-party creditors' claims have first been satisfied."

1574. Mālik said, "There is nothing objectionable in a slave who is a party to a manumission contract purchasing his obligations under that contract from his master, with payment in either specie (*'ayn*)[648] or goods, which may be the same as or different from the genus of the payment specified in the contract, whether he pays promptly or defers payment."[649]

647 In Islamic contract law, there can be no uncertainty with respect to the material terms of the contract, whether arising out of indefiniteness in the description of the consideration or relating to uncertainty regarding the ability of the party to perform the obligation.

648 *'Ayn* is used generically in Islamic law to refer to either gold or silver.

649 Mālik's point here is that the manumission contract is not a commercial contract between the slave and his master. Accordingly, ordinarily applicable rules regarding the means by which debt obligations may be satisfied do not apply. For this reason, a slave is permitted to prepay what he owes under a manumission contract using the same genus of payment as that owed under the original contract, whereas a third party could not do so.

1575. Mālik said, regarding a slave who is a party to a manumission contract and dies leaving a handmaiden who has borne him children (*umm walad*) and minor children, whether from her or from another woman, who are incapable of earning money and thus at risk of being deemed to have repudiated the manumission contract, "The father's handmaiden, whether or not she is the childrens' mother, should be sold, but only if she would fetch a price sufficient to discharge the entirety of what they owe under the manumission contract to secure their manumission. The father would not have objected to selling her if he feared that he would be deemed to have repudiated the manumission contract. Consequently, if there is a concern that the children will repudiate (or be deemed to have repudiated) the manumission contract, their father's handmaiden should be sold and the proceeds from her sale applied to the discharge of the childrens' obligations under the manumission contract. If, on the other hand, the price she would fetch is insufficient to discharge their obligations under the manumission contract, and neither she nor they are capable of earning money, all of them revert to their prior status as chattel slaves of their master."[650]

1576. Mālik said, "The rule in our view (*al-amr ʿindanā*) regarding a scenario in which a person purchases the obligations of a slave who is a party to a manumission contract but the slave dies before discharging those obligations is that the purchaser of the contract inherits the slave's estate. Alternatively, if the slave repudiates (or is deemed to have repudiated) the contract, the purchaser becomes the slave's master. If the slave is able to discharge his obligations under the manumission contract to the purchaser, he is manumitted; however, the right of patronage (*walāʾ*) with respect to the manumitted slave nevertheless belongs to the master with whom the slave first entered the manumission contract. The purchaser of his obligations under the manumission contract receives none of the rights of patronage."

Chapter 6. What Has Come Down regarding the Work of a Slave Who Has Entered a Manumission Contract (*Mukātab*)

1577. According to Mālik, it reached him that ʿUrwa b. al-Zubayr and Sulaymān b. Yasār were both asked about a male slave who entered into a manumission contract with his master for himself and his children and then died: were the slave's children entitled to work for manumission under the

650 In order for this hypothetical case to make sense, one must assume that the deceased slave included his children within the terms of his manumission contract. His handmaiden, insofar as she was his personal property, would not have needed to be specified in the contract, because under Mālik's rule, a slave who is a party to a manumission contract retains whatever personal property he has upon discharge of his obligations under the contract.

terms of their father's manumission contract, or were they simply chattel slaves? They said, "Indeed, they are entitled to work pursuant to the terms of their father's manumission contract, but they are not entitled to any reduction of the amount owed as a result of their father's death." Mālik said, "If the children are minors and incapable of working, there is no obligation to wait until they are older to resolve their status: they are the slaves of their father's master, unless the dead slave left sufficient property to pay the instalments they owe to the master until they are able to work. If he did leave enough to cover the instalments, their amount is paid on the children's behalf out of the dead slave's property, and the children are left alone until they are old enough to work. Then, if they discharge what they still owe, they are manumitted, but if they repudiate (or are deemed to have repudiated) the contract, they revert to their former status as chattel slaves."

1578. Mālik said, regarding a slave who is a party to a manumission contract and dies leaving property insufficient to discharge what he owes under the contract, children who were included within the manumission contract, and a handmaiden who bore him children (*umm walad*) who desires to work in order to obtain money to discharge their obligations under the manumission contract, "The deceased slave's property should be given to her if she is sufficiently trustworthy to preserve it and healthy enough to work. If, however, she is not healthy enough to work nor sufficiently trustworthy to preserve the property, she should not receive anything. In that case, she and the slave's children revert to their prior status as chattel slaves of the deceased slave's master."

1579. Mālik said, "If a group of slaves who are unrelated to one another jointly enter into a manumission contract, and some of them repudiate (or are deemed to have repudiated) the contract while the others work, earning money successfully until all of them are manumitted, those who successfully worked for money are entitled to a contribution from those who repudiated (or were deemed to have repudiated) the contract in accordance with their proportionate share of what they paid on their fellows' behalf, because they are all guarantors for one another."

Chapter 7. The Accelerated Manumission of a Slave (*Mukātab*) Who Discharges What He Owes under the Manumission Contract before Its Maturity Date

1580. According to Mālik, he heard Rabīʿa b. Abī ʿAbd al-Raḥmān and others mention that a slave who had entered into a manumission contract with his master, al-Furāfiṣa b. ʿUmayr al-Ḥanafī, offered to prepay the entire balance due under his manumission contract, but al-Furāfiṣa refused. The slave then went to Marwān b. al-Ḥakam, who was the governor of Medina at the time, and complained to him. Marwān summoned al-Furāfiṣa and renewed the offer to him, but al-Furāfiṣa again refused to accept it. Marwān, therefore, ordered that the money be taken from the slave and placed in the public treasury for safekeeping. He then said to the slave, "Go; you have been manumitted." When al-Furāfiṣa heard of Marwān's decision, he went and took possession of the money.

1581. Mālik said, "The rule in our view (*al-amr ʿindanā*) is that a slave who is a party to a manumission contract may pay his master all of his instalments before their maturity dates. His master may not refuse him, because payment in full of what he owes relieves the slave of every condition and obligation of service or travel that the master could impose on him. Moreover, a person's manumission is not complete if any trace of bondage over him remains, nor in this case would his inviolability under the law be complete, his testimony admissible before a judge, his estate passable to his heirs, or his other affairs valid. His master is not permitted, therefore, to require any service of him after his manumission."

1582. Mālik said, regarding a slave who is a party to a manumission contract and becomes afflicted with a severe illness, consequently wishing to pay all the instalments due to his master at once so that his free heirs may inherit him—none of them, however, being his own children, because they were not included in the manumission contract—"That is permissible for him, because by doing so he completes his inviolability under the law and renders his testimony admissible before a judge, his acknowledgment of debts owed to third parties binding, and his bequests enforceable. His master may not refuse him that by claiming, 'He is trying to deprive me of his property.'"[651]

Chapter 8. The Estate of a Slave Manumitted through a Manumission Contract (*Mukātab*)

1583. According to Mālik, it reached him that Saʿīd b. al-Musayyab was asked about a slave whom two men owned in common and who entered into a manumission contract with both of them. One of the two decided to manumit his share of the slave, and then the slave died, leaving substantial property.

651 If the slave died as a result of his illness and he had not been allowed to discharge what he owed under the manumission contract before his death, the slave's property would pass to the master. Mālik rejects the master's argument that the slave's decision to pay the outstanding amount should be invalidated because it took place on the slave's deathbed, even though gratuitous deathbed transfers are ordinarily not valid. Mālik's argument is that the transfer in this case is not gratuitous, because it results in the slave's freedom.

Saʿīd said, "The amount still outstanding under the manumission contract is paid to the one who maintained the manumission contract, and whatever remains of the decedent's estate is divided between them equally."[652]

1584. Mālik said, "When a slave who is a party to a manumission contract is manumitted and then dies, the nearest living male kin of his manumitter on the day of his death, be they children or male paternal near-relations (*ʿaṣaba*), inherit him. This is the rule for every person who has been manumitted: his estate goes to his manumitter's nearest male kin as of the day of his death, be they children or paternal near-relations, and his estate passes according to the right of patronage (*walāʾ*)."[653]

1585. Mālik said, "Brothers who are parties to a manumission contract are in the same position as the children of a slave who is a party to a manumission contract, provided that they jointly entered a single manumission contract and further that none of them has any children of his own whom he included in his own manumission contract from its outset or who were born to him during the term of the manumission contract. In this case—that is, where there are no children—the brothers inherit one another, should one of them die. However, if one of them has children either born during the term of the manumission contract or included in the manumission contract from its outset, and he dies leaving property, that property is used to satisfy the unpaid amount under the manumission contract. If it is sufficient to discharge the amount, the deceased brother's children are manumitted. Moreover, any remaining surplus property (*faḍl*) belonging to the deceased brother goes to his children, not to his brothers."

Chapter 9. Conditions Imposed by the Master on His Slave (*Mukātab*) at the Time of the Manumission Contract

1586. Yaḥyā said, "Mālik said, regarding a scenario in which a man enters into a manumission contract with his slave for an amount of gold or silver and imposes on him an additional condition, such as undertaking a journey, performing a service, or slaughtering an animal, expressly specifying these additional things, and the slave successfully pays all the instalments under the contract before they are due: 'Once he pays all of his instalments, even if any of these conditions remain unfulfilled, he immediately becomes free,

652 In this case, the former masters inherit the slave's estate as a right of patronage (*walāʾ*), not as owners of the property.

653 This rule applies only to the extent that the manumitted slave dies without any familial heirs or the familial heirs do not exhaust the manumitted slave's estate. In either case, the right of patronage allows the manumitter or the nearest male relation of the manumitter to inherit the slave's estate or the undistributed surplus (*faḍl*) of the slave's estate.

and his inviolability under the law is perfected. The condition that his master had imposed on him, be it travel, service, or some other, similar thing that requires the slave's personal performance, is to be examined. He is excused from any requirement that requires his personal performance, and the master has no claim against him with respect to such things. As for matters that do not require the slave's personal performance, such as the slaughter of an animal, the preparation of clothing, or anything else that the slave is to deliver to the master, such matters are deemed the equivalent of a payment of gold and silver coins. An appraisal is made of the fair market value of these services in money, and the slave must then pay it in addition to the instalments that are due under the contract. He is not manumitted until he pays these amounts in addition to his instalments.'"[654]

1587. Mālik said, "The agreed-upon rule among us about which there is no dissent (*al-amr al-mujtamaʿ ʿalayhi ʿindanā alladhī lā ikhtilāfa fīh*) is that a slave who is a party to a manumission contract and whose master dies before the slave is able to perform the manumission contract is subject to the same rule as a slave whose master has agreed to manumit him after the slave provides him ten years of service but whose master dies before the ten years have elapsed: the remaining time of his service belongs to the master's heirs, and the right of patronage (*walāʾ*) belongs to the one who entered into the manumission contract with the slave, his male children, or his male paternal near-relations (*ʿaṣaba*)."[655]

1588. Mālik said, regarding a man who says to his slave at the time of entering into a manumission contract with him, "You may neither travel, nor marry, nor leave my domicile without my permission, and if you do any of these things without my permission, I am entitled to cancel the manumission contract": "The master is not entitled to cancel the manumission contract unilaterally, even if the slave does one or more of these things. Rather, the master should file a complaint with the authorities. A slave who is a party to a manumission contract is not entitled to travel, marry, or leave his master's domicile without the master's prior permission, whether or not the master stipulated any of these things in the manumission contract.

---

654 Mālik distinguishes here between two kinds of conditions that a master could impose on his slave in a manumission contract. The first is a condition that can be fulfilled only by the slave himself. In Mālik's opinion, such a condition is void and provides the master no claim against the slave. The second is a condition that the slave can fulfill by paying someone to do it. In this case, Mālik's rule is that the slave is obliged to pay to the master the fair value of the service involved as part of the amount due under the manumission contract.

655 In other words, the deceased master's heirs inherit the slave, subject to the terms of the manumission contract. The master's death does not terminate the manumission contract with the slave, nor does it deprive the master's male heirs of the right of patronage (*walāʾ*) if the slave performs the contract and is manumitted.

This is because a master might very well enter into a manumission contract for one hundred dinars, for example, knowing that the slave already has in his possession one thousand dinars, or even more than that, but then the slave goes out and marries a woman, giving her a dower that consumes the entirety of his property and bankrupting himself, with the result that he is forced to repudiate the manumission contract, and the master is left with a penniless slave. Or the slave sets out on a journey, and his instalments mature while he is away and he is thus unable to pay them. He is not free to do that, nor would his manumission contract give him the liberty to do it. Such matters and others like them remain subject to his master's control. If he wishes, the master may permit the slave to do any of these things, and if he wishes, he may forbid him."

Chapter 10. The Rights of Patronage (*Walāʾ*) When a Slave Who Is a Party to a Manumission Contract (*Mukātab*) Manumits His Own Slave

1589. Mālik said, "If a slave who is a party to a manumission contract manumits a slave of his own, the manumission is of no effect unless the first slave's master ratifies it. If the master approves the first slave's decision to manumit the second slave, and if, sometime later, the first slave is manumitted, the right of patronage (*walāʾ*) with respect to the second slave goes to the first slave. If the first slave dies before he is manumitted, however, the right of patronage to the second slave goes to the master of the first slave. If the second slave dies after having been manumitted but before the first slave's manumission, the master of the first slave (and not the first slave himself) inherits the second slave's property."[656]

1590. Mālik said, "The same applies if a slave who is a party to a manumission contract enters into a manumission contract with his own slave, and the second slave is manumitted before the first. The right of patronage with respect to the second slave, in this case, goes to the first slave's master, as long as the first slave has yet to be manumitted. Once the first slave is manumitted, however, the right of patronage with respect to the second slave, who was manumitted earlier, reverts to the first slave. If the first slave dies before performing his manumission contract or repudiates (or is deemed to have repudiated) it, and leaves free children, they do not inherit the right of patronage with respect to their father's slave, because the right of patronage was never vested in their father. The

656 The principle that governs this case is that the first slave's manumission of the second slave is valid only if the master of the first slave approves it. Even if the master approves it, however, the first slave does not receive the benefits of patronage until he himself is manumitted. Therefore, should the first slave die before he is manumitted, or should the second slave die before the first slave is manumitted, the master steps into his shoes in each case.

right of patronage would only have been vested in him after he himself had been manumitted."

1591. Mālik said, regarding a scenario in which a slave is owned in common by two men who have together entered into a manumission contract with him, one waiving what the slave owes him under the contract but the other insisting on payment in full, and the slave then dies, leaving property: "The one who insisted on payment in full is paid what is owed him, and then they divide the remaining property between them equally, as would have been the case had the decedent died as a slave. This is because what the first co-owner did was not tantamount to an act of manumission but rather constituted a waiver of his right to a sum of money. A similar case corroborates this conclusion. Take the case of a man who dies leaving a slave who is a party to a manumission contract as well as male and female heirs. Then one of the heirs manumits his share of the slave. That would not entitle the heir to claim any portion of the right of patronage with respect to the slave. Had this been a case of manumission, however, the right of patronage would have been established for whichever of the heirs manumitted him, male or female. Another similar case that corroborates this is one in which one of the heirs manumitted his share of the slave and then the slave repudiated (or was deemed to have repudiated) the contract: the remaining, unmanumitted portion of the slave would not be subject to mandatory appraisal in order to calculate what the manumitting heir owes to the other heirs. Had this been a case of manumission, however, an appraisal of the unmanumitted value of the slave would have been required, that sum would have been due out of the manumitting heir's own property, and the slave would be immediately manumitted, in accordance with the statement of the Messenger of God (pbuh), who said, 'If someone manumits his interest in a slave, the slave's value is fairly appraised, and the appraised value is deducted from the manumitter's property and given to his co-owners in proportion to their shares in the slave. If he lacks sufficient property, only that portion of the slave that has been manumitted is in fact manumitted.'"

1592. Mālik said, "Another point that corroborates this is that it is a long-established ordinance of the Muslims about which there is no dissent (*sunnat al-muslimīn allatī lā ikhtilāfa fīhā*) that whoever manumits his interest in a slave who is a party to a manumission contract is not then compelled to complete the slave's manumission out of his own property. Were he so compelled, he would hold the exclusive right of patronage in respect of this slave."

1593. Mālik said, "Another point that corroborates this is that it is a long-established ordinance of the Muslims that the right of patronage goes to whoever made the manumission contract with the slave. The female heirs of the master who made the manumission contract do not inherit any right to patronage of the slave, even if they manumitted their interests in the slave after they inherited him. It is rather the case that the right of patronage goes only to the manumitting master's male children or to his male paternal near-relations (*ʿaṣaba*)."

Chapter 11. Invalid Manumission of a Slave Who Is a Party to a Manumission Contract (*Mukātab*)

1594. Yaḥyā said, "Mālik said, 'If a group of slaves have jointly entered into a single manumission contract, their master is not permitted to manumit any one of them without first consulting the other parties to the manumission contract and obtaining their consent. If they are minors, however, there is no point in consulting them, and such a manumission would not bind them in any case.'"

1595. Mālik said, "This is because it may very well be that the specific manumitted slave could labor for the benefit of all of them and would be able to discharge successfully their obligations under the contract, thereby securing the manumission of them all. Realizing this, the master intentionally manumits the one slave among them who is clearly able to discharge all of their obligations, the one in whom lies the deliverance of them all from bondage. As a consequence, the remaining slaves are forced to repudiate (or will be deemed to have repudiated) their obligations under the manumission contract. The master does this only out of a desire to realize profit and gain for himself. Accordingly, his manumission of that slave has no binding effect on the remaining slaves.[657] The Messenger of God (pbuh) said, 'No one should harm another or repay one injury with another,' and that is the worst form of injury."

1596. Mālik said, regarding slaves who jointly enter a single manumission contract, "Their master may manumit those of them who are old and decrepit, or who are minors incapable of contributing anything toward the discharge of the contract, or who are too weak to work and incapable of assisting in the performance of the contract in any way. The manumission of such slaves is valid and binding."

657 Mālikīs disagree, however, regarding whether the remaining slaves may consent to the manumission of one of their group, with some authorities concluding that their consent to such a manumission renders it valid and binding and others arguing that their consent is insufficient to render the manumission valid since it increases the risk that the remaining slaves will be re-enslaved. All Mālikīs agree, however, that if any of the slaves are minors, the master's manumission of one of the adult slaves is always invalid. Bājī, *al-Muntaqā*, 7:34.

Chapter 12. Miscellaneous Reports on What Has Come Down regarding the Manumission of a Slave Who Is a Party to a Manumission Contract (*Mukātab*) and the Manumission of His Handmaiden Who Has Borne Him a Child (*Umm Walad*)

1597. Yaḥyā said, "Mālik said, regarding a scenario in which a man enters into a manumission contract with his slave and the slave then dies without having paid the manumission contract in full, leaving his handmaiden who has borne him children (*umm walad*) and enough other property to discharge what he owed at his death: 'His handmaiden reverts to being a chattel slave, because he died before he was manumitted. Moreover, he did not leave children who would have become manumitted upon payment of the balance due under the manumission contract. Had that been the case it would have resulted in the manumission of their father's handmaiden as an effect of their manumission.'"

1598. Mālik said, regarding a slave who is a party to a manumission contract and who manumits a slave of his own or gives away some of his own property in charity, in each case without the prior knowledge of his master, who discovers the actions only after the slave has been manumitted: "These actions bind the former slave, and he cannot repudiate them. Had the slave's master known about them before the slave was manumitted and rescinded them and refused to ratify them, they would not bind him after his manumission: if at that time the former slave still has in his possession the slave whom he previously attempted to manumit and the property that he previously attempted to give away as charity, he is not obliged either to manumit the slave or to give away the property unless he now does so willingly, of his own free will."

Chapter 13. Testamentary Dispositions (*Waṣiyya*) in Respect of a Slave Who Is a Party to a Manumission Contract (*Mukātab*)

1599. According to Mālik, the best view that he had heard concerning a slave who is a party to a manumission contract and whose master manumits him while the master is on his deathbed was the following: "The slave's fair market value should be appraised to establish the best price he could fetch if he were to be sold. If the slave's fair market value is less than what remains outstanding under the manumission contract, that amount is deducted from the one-third of the decedent's estate available for testamentary dispositions, and no consideration is given to the nominal sum of unpaid dirhams owing under the manumission contract.[658] This is because if someone were to kill

658 What Mālik is saying here is that for the purpose of determining whether the testamentary disposition exceeds the one-third permitted to every decedent, the relevant figure is the fair

the slave, the killer would be liable to pay only the slave's fair market value on the day he killed him, and if someone were to injure the slave, the perpetrator would be liable to pay only the compensation due in respect of the slave's injury on the day of the injury. In both cases, no consideration is given to the nominal sum of dinars and dirhams specified in the manumission contract, because as long as anything remains unpaid under the manumission contract, the slave remains a slave. However, if the unpaid amount under his manumission contract is less than the slave's fair market value, only the amount still due under the manumission contract is deducted from the decedent's estate. That is because in this case the decedent did no more than waive the amount still due to him from the slave. Accordingly, it is the equivalent of a testamentary disposition (*waṣiyya*) made by the decedent in favor of the slave in that amount. This point can be illustrated by the following example. If the fair market value of the slave who was a party to the manumission contract was one thousand dirhams, and if only one hundred dirhams remained outstanding under that contract, and then his master made a testamentary disposition in the slave's favor in the amount of the one hundred dirhams that the slave still owed, it would be deducted from the one-third of the master's property that he may use for testamentary dispositions. The result would be that the slave becomes free."[659]

1600. Mālik said, regarding a man who, while on his deathbed, enters into a manumission contract with his slave, "The slave's fair market value prior to his entering the manumission contract should be determined. If the slave's fair market value is less than one-third of the dying man's estate, the manumission contract is valid. This point can be illustrated by the following example. If the slave's fair market value were 1,000 dinars, and his master entered into a manumission contract while on his deathbed with the slave for 200 dinars, and one-third of the master's estate at that time amounted to 1,000 dinars, that contract would be valid, and the amount would be merely a testamentary disposition that the master made in the slave's favor out of one-third of his estate.[660] If, however, the master has made numerous testamentary

market value of the slave, not the amount owed under the contract, at least when the fair market value of the slave is less than what the slave owes under the contract. Accordingly, were a master, on his deathbed, to manumit a slave who was a party to a manumission contract, and the slave owed 1,000 dirhams, for example, and the entire value of the deceased master's estate was 2,000 dirhams, the master's heirs could claim that the deathbed manumission was invalid because it represented one half of the master's estate. Mālik rejects this analysis and argues that the relevant amount is the fair market value of the slave, not the contractual obligation. Consequently, if the fair market value of the slave in this case is less than 667 dirhams, the deathbed manumission would be effective.

659 This hypothetical assumes that the value of the dead master's estate is at least 300 dirhams.

660 The amount referred to here is the 800-dinar difference between the slave's fair market value and the money due under the manumission contract.

dispositions to several people, and the fair market value of the slave exhausts the one-third of the decedent's estate available for testamentary dispositions, the disposition in favor of the slave is given priority over the other dispositions. This is because a manumission contract is a form of manumission, and manumission takes priority over testamentary dispositions involving ordinary property. The value of those other dispositions, however, is made part of the manumission contract, and their beneficiaries may claim them from the slave. The heirs of the decedent are given a choice: they can satisfy the decedent's testamentary dispositions to the beneficiaries in full and retain their rights under the slave's manumission contract, or they can turn over the slave, along with whatever he now owes under the manumission contract, to the beneficiaries of the decedent's testamentary dispositions. This is because the slave now represents the entirety of the one-third of the decedent's estate out of which testamentary dispositions could have been made. The heirs of any decedent whose testamentary dispositions exceed one-third of his estate may object and say, 'That which our decedent has bequeathed exceeds one-third of his property, and he has taken what is not his.' His heirs, in such cases, are given a choice. They are told, 'Your decedent has made testamentary dispositions, as you know, in an amount exceeding one-third of his estate. If you wish, you may ratify those testamentary dispositions in accordance with the decedent's wishes; or you may turn over the entirety of the one-third of the decedent's estate to the beneficiaries.' If the heirs hand over the slave, owing what he owes under the manumission contract, to the beneficiaries, and if he discharges his obligations under the manumission contract, they must accept that sum in lieu of their testamentary dispositions, in accordance with their respective shares.[661] However, if the slave repudiates (or is deemed to have repudiated) the contract, he reverts to being a chattel slave of the beneficiaries of the testamentary dispositions. He does not revert to the heirs, because they waived their claim to him when they exercised their option. In addition, the beneficiaries bear the risk of his loss from the moment he is handed over to them. If he dies, they have no recourse against the heirs. Conversely, if he dies without discharging his obligations under the manumission contract and leaves property worth more than he owed, his property goes to the beneficiaries and not to the heirs. If the slave discharges his obligations under the manumission contract, he is manumitted, with the right to patronage (*walā'*) over him going to the male paternal near-relations (*'aṣaba*) of the former owner who made the manumission contract with him."

661 In other words, if the decedent made equal bequests in favor of three beneficiaries, they each take one-third of the sums collected in respect of the manumission contract in lieu of the specific bequests the decedent made in their favor.

1601. Mālik said, regarding a scenario in which a slave who is a party to a manumission contract owes his master 10,000 dirhams under that contract, and the master, at the time of his death, unilaterally reduces that amount by 1,000 dirhams: "The slave should be appraised and his fair market value determined. If the slave's fair market value is equal to 1,000 dirhams, for example, the amount owing under the manumission contract is reduced by one-tenth, which in relation to the slave's fair market value equals one hundred dirhams, that is, one-tenth of the slave's fair market value. Accordingly, one-tenth of the amount owed under the manumission contract is immediately waived. The deduction is treated as though it were a cash payment to the slave out of the one-third of the master's estate that is available for testamentary dispositions. This is the same result as it would be had the entire amount under the manumission contract been waived. Had the master indeed done that, only the slave's fair market value of 1,000 dirhams would have been deducted from the one-third of the master's estate available for testamentary dispositions. Further, if the amount waived had been one-half of the amount due, one-half of the slave's fair market value would have been deducted from the one-third of the master's estate available for testamentary dispositions.[662] Regardless of the precise amount the master waives in respect of the slave's obligation, its impact on the property available for testamentary dispositions is always calculated in this fashion."

1602. Yaḥyā said, "Mālik said, 'If a man on his deathbed unilaterally reduces his slave's obligation under his manumission contract by 1,000 dirhams from an original amount of 10,000 dirhams, but he does not specify whether the reduction should be applied to the first instalment of the contract or the last, each instalment should be reduced by one-tenth.'"[663]

1603. Mālik said, "If a man on his deathbed reduces his slave's obligation under the manumission contract by 1,000 dirhams and specifies which instalment (or instalments) is to be reduced, whether the contract's first

662 Mālik's rule, as set out in hadith no. 1599, provides that in cases in which the amount outstanding under the manumission contract exceeds the slave's fair market value, only the fair market value of the slave is relevant to determining whether the master has exceeded the one-third of his estate out of which he is entitled to make testamentary dispositions. Accordingly, if the fair market value of the slave is 1,000 dirhams, the amount outstanding under the manumission contract is 10,000 dirhams, and the master, in his testamentary disposition, waives 1,000 dirhams, Mālik concludes that one-tenth of the slave's fair market value must be deducted from the one-third available to the deceased master for testamentary dispositions. This result follows from Mālik's rule in hadith no. 1599 that if the master were to manumit outright a slave who is a party to a manumission contract, the only relevant consideration in determining whether the master's manumission is valid is the slave's fair market value at the time of the deathbed manumission: if it is less than one-third of the deceased master's estate, it is valid, regardless of the size of the unpaid amount on the contract.

663 Mālik assumes here that the contract consists of ten equal instalments. Otherwise, the reduction would be applied proportionally to all the instalments due under the contract.

or its last instalment, and the original obligation under the manumission contract is 3,000 dirhams, for example, the slave must be appraised to determine his fair market value in cash. Then, the slave's cash value is divided between the contract's instalments. The initial instalment of 1,000 dirhams is allocated its proportional share of the slave's cash value in accordance with the brevity of its term and its difference relative to the cash value of that instalment. Then the second instalment of 1,000 dirhams is also allocated its proportional share of the slave's cash value in accordance with its difference relative to the cash value of the second instalment. Then the third instalment of 1,000 dirhams is also allocated its proportional share of the slave's cash value in accordance with its difference relative to the cash value of the third instalment, and so on and so forth, until all the instalments are taken into consideration, with each later instalment being allocated its share of the cash value in accordance with its place in the schedule of payments, whether immediate or deferred. This is because the value of a deferred amount is less than the value of an amount paid before it, even if the stated amount of each instalment is the same. Then the proportionate value of the one-third reduction in the slave's obligation, taking into account the difference between the value of the instalment and its stated amount, is deducted from the one-third of the master's estate available for testamentary dispositions. Whether the difference is small or great, the value of the waiver is calculated in this manner."[664]

1604. Mālik said, regarding a scenario in which a man makes a testamentary disposition to another man of one-fourth of his slave with whom he has entered into a manumission contract and also manumits one-fourth of

664 The following example illustrates how this rule is applied. Suppose a master has entered into a manumission contract with his slave for 9,000 dirhams, payable in three annual instalments of 3,000 dirhams, in each case paid at the end of the calendar year. On his deathbed, however, the master reduces the amount owed under the manumission contract by the 3,000 dirhams of the third and final instalment. Mālik's general rule in such cases is that the value of the waiver (determined by its proportion to the slave's fair market value) is deducted from the one-third of the decedent's estate available for testamentary dispositions. Application of this principle is complicated here, however, by the time value of money, that is, the fact that prior payments are more valuable than later payments are. Mālik solves this problem by determining the fair market value of the slave at the time of the master's death and then determining the relationship of the stated amounts of the instalments under the manumission contract to their fair market value, taking into account the time value of money. In this case, suppose that the fair market value of the slave at the time of the master's death is 9,000 dirhams, but the slave will be permitted to obtain his freedom if he is able to pay three annual instalments of 3,000 dirhams at the end of each calendar year. Because of the time value of money, the value of the 3,000-dirham waiver is in fact less than one-third of the slave's fair market value, and it is that value which must be calculated in order to deduct the proper amount from the deceased master's estate. Accordingly, although the nominal amounts of the instalments are the same, the first instalment is more valuable than the second, and the second more valuable than the third. On the assumption the master made no other testamentary dispositions, the master's deathbed waiver will be valid if the present value of the waiver of the future instalment is less than the value of one-third of the deceased master's estate.

his interest in that same slave, and the master then dies, followed by his slave, who leaves a substantial amount of property that more than satisfies his obligations under the manumission contract: "The heirs of the master and the beneficiary of the testamentary disposition are given what they are owed under the manumission contract.[665] They then divide whatever surplus remains between them. The beneficiary of the testamentary disposition receives one-third of any surplus that remains, and the master's heirs receive the remaining two-thirds. This is because a slave who is a party to a manumission contract remains a slave so long as any obligation under the manumission contract is outstanding. Therefore, the slave's estate in this case passes only by virtue of ownership (not patronage)."

1605. Yaḥyā said, "Mālik said, regarding a slave who is a party to a manumission contract and whose master manumits him on his deathbed, 'If manumission of the slave would exhaust the one-third of the decedent's estate available for testamentary dispositions, the slave is manumitted in proportion to what the one-third of the decedent's estate can bear, and the amount due under his manumission contract is reduced by that same proportion. If, for example, the slave owed 5,000 dirhams, his fair market value in cash at the time of his master's death was 2,000 dirhams, and one-third of the decedent's estate was 1,000 dirhams, then one-half of the slave would be manumitted. In addition, the amount due under his manumission contract would be reduced by one-half (to 2,500 dirhams).'"

1606. Mālik said, regarding a man who manumits one of his slaves in his will and directs his heirs to enter into a manumission contract with another one of his slaves, "Manumission takes priority over entrance into a manumission contract, if the value of the testamentary disposition exceeds one-third of the decedent's estate."

The Book of the Slave Who Is a Party to a Manumission Contract (*Mukātab*) Is Complete, with Abundant Thanks to God.

665 The division of the amounts owed under the manumission contract is unaffected by the partial manumission. Therefore, the master's heirs receive three-fourths of the unpaid amount under the contract, and the beneficiary of the testamentary disposition receives one-fourth. Any surplus property in the slave's estate is distributed in accordance with their respective ownership interests in the slave. The master, after manumitting one-quarter of his interest in the slave, has a three-fourths interest in the slave. When the master dies, his testamentary disposition of one-fourth of the slave to the beneficiary becomes effective, leaving him with only a one-half interest and giving the beneficiary a one-quarter interest. The master's heirs inherit the decedent's one-half interest, while the beneficiary retains his one quarter interest. The master's heirs thus receive twice the share of the beneficiary of any property the slave may leave after the unpaid amounts under the manumission contract have been satisfied. See Bājī, *al-Muntaqā*, 7:38.

Book 30

The Book of a Master's Designation of Slaves for Manumission upon His Death (*Tadbīr*)

In the Name of God, the Merciful, the Compassionate

May God Grace Muḥammad and His Family
and Grant Them Perfect Tranquility.

Chapter 1. The Judicial Rule (*Qaḍāʾ*) regarding the Status of the Children of a Handmaiden Who Is Designated for Manumission upon Her Master's Death (*Mudabbara*)

1607. Mālik said, "The rule in our view (*al-amr ʿindanā*) regarding a handmaiden designated for manumission upon her master's death who gives birth to children after the designation but predeceases the master who designated her for manumission is that her children step into her shoes. The designation of freedom granted to her applies to them to precisely the same extent. Their mother's death does not undermine their position in any way. Accordingly, when the one who designated her for manumission dies, they are manumitted, as long as their value does not exceed one-third of the master's property."[666]

1608. Mālik said, "Children always take the status of their mother. If she is free and gives birth after her manumission, her children are free. And if she is designated for manumission upon her master's death, or if she is a party to a manumission contract (*mukātaba*), or if she is to be manumitted after the passage of a number of specified years or the completion of a designated service, or if part of her is free, or if she is pledged as collateral, or if she has borne children to her master (*umm walad*), her children in each case have the same status as their mother, and they are manumitted when she is."

1609. Mālik also said, regarding a woman designated for manumission upon her master's death who is pregnant at the time of the designation,

666 The father of the children in this case is not the handmaiden's master.

"Her children take her status. This rule is equivalent to that governing the case of a man who manumits a handmaiden of his who, unbeknownst to him, is pregnant. The long-established ordinance (*al-sunna*) with respect to such a woman is that her children's status is derivative of hers, so they are manumitted when she is."

1610. Mālik also said, "The same rules applies were a man to purchase a handmaiden who, unbeknownst to him, is pregnant. Both the pregnant woman and that which is in her womb belong to the purchaser, whether or not he expressly stipulates that."

1611. Mālik also said, "It is not permissible in the previous case for the seller to reserve what is in the handmaiden's womb for himself, because that introduces into the contract material uncertainty (*gharar*), which reduces her price, and the seller cannot know whether he will or will not receive a benefit from it. Such a reservation is the equivalent of selling a fetus still in its mother's womb. Such a sale is not permissible, because it entails material uncertainty."

1612. Mālik said, regarding a slave who is designated for manumission upon his master's death or is a party to a manumission contract, and who purchases a handmaiden and has sexual intercourse with her, resulting in her pregnancy and the birth of children, "In both cases, the children of the handmaiden take the same status as their father: they are manumitted when he is manumitted, and they are slaves as long as he remains a slave. Upon his manumission, his handmaiden who bore him children is delivered to him and becomes his exclusive property."

Chapter 2. Miscellaneous Matters That Have Come Down Related to Designating Slaves for Manumission upon Their Master's Death (*Tadbīr*)

1613. Yaḥyā said, "Mālik said, regarding a scenario in which a slave designated for manumission upon his master's death (*mudabbar*) tells his master, 'Manumit me now, and I will give you fifty dinars, paid in instalments,' and the master says, 'Yes; you are free, and you are indebted to me in the amount of fifty dinars, of which you will pay me ten every year for five years,' and the slave accepts that, but then two or three days later the master dies: 'His manumission is valid, and he is obliged to pay the fifty dinars. His testimony in court is now admissible. He is now inviolable as a free man, has the right to pass his estate to heirs, and is fully liable for his crimes. His master's death does not, however, in any way reduce his debt.'"

1614. Mālik said, regarding a scenario in which a man designates a slave of his for manumission upon his death and then dies, leaving property at hand and elsewhere, but the property at hand is insufficient to permit the slave's manumission:[667] "The slave, along with his personal property and whatever he earns, should be sequestered until the value of the master's property located elsewhere has been determined. Once that value is added to the property at hand, if the slave's value is less than one-third of all the property that the master left behind, the slave's manumission becomes effective. The slave also retains his personal property and whatever he has earned in the interim. If the property that the master left behind is less than two times the slave's value, however, only that portion of the slave that equals one-third of the value of the deceased master's estate is manumitted, but he nonetheless retains his personal property."[668]

Chapter 3. Testamentary Dispositions (*Waṣiyya*) Related to Designating Slaves for Manumission upon Their Master's Death (*Tadbīr*)

1615. Yaḥyā said, "Mālik said, 'The rule in our view (*al-amr ʿindanā*) is that whoever makes a testamentary disposition (*waṣiyya*), whether in good health or in illness, and manumits a slave as part of that testamentary disposition may change it as long as he is alive or even rescind it in its entirety, however he wishes. If, however, he designates a slave for manumission upon his death (*tadbīr*), he is bound by the designation and may not rescind it.'"

1616. Mālik said, "The children born to a handmaiden whose master manumits her in his will rather than in his lifetime via designation are not manumitted upon her manumission. This is because her master may change his will if he so wishes or rescind it whenever he likes. Therefore, she has not received the benefit of manumission during his lifetime. Her position is the equivalent of that of a handmaiden whose master says, 'If so-and-so remains with me until I die, she shall be free.' When that condition is fulfilled, she becomes free, but before that time he can, if he so wishes, sell her along with her children, because he did not include her children as beneficiaries of what he granted her."

---

667 In other words, the slave's value exceeds the value of one-third of the deceased master's property at hand.

668 So, for example, if the fair market value of the dead master's estate was 3,000 dirhams and the fair market value of the slave was 1,500 dirhams, only two-thirds of the slave—1,000 dirhams' worth—would be manumitted.

1617. Mālik said, "A manumission granted in a testamentary disposition is different from the designation of a slave for manumission upon the master's death. The long-established ordinance (*mā maḍā min al-sunna*) distinguishes between the two. Were it the case that a manumission effected in a testamentary disposition is the equivalent of designating a slave for manumission upon the master's death, no testator would be able to change a testamentary disposition, including anything in it pertaining to manumission. The testator's property would become immobilized, and he would not be able to benefit from it."

1618. Yaḥyā said, "Mālik said, regarding a man who, while in good health, designates a group of his slaves for manumission after his death but has no property other than those slaves, 'If he designated some of them for manumission before the others, priority is given to the first of the slaves so designated, followed by the next, and so on, until one-third of the value of the master's property is reached. If he designated them all for manumission at the same time by saying on his deathbed in one single, continuous statement, "So-and-so is free and so-and-so is free, if something happens to me during my illness," or if he designated all of them for manumission in a single declaration, they each share equally in the value of the master's one-third of the estate, none of them having priority over the others. This is simply a testamentary disposition. Accordingly, they are entitled only to one-third of the decedent's estate, to be divided among them in equal shares, so one-third of each of them is manumitted, whatever their number may be. If any of these scenarios takes place during the master's deathbed illness, none of the slaves is given priority over the others.'"[669]

1619. Mālik said, regarding a master who designates his slave-boy for manumission upon his death and then dies, leaving no property other than that slave, but with the slave possessing his own property, "One-third of the slave is manumitted, and the slave's property remains in his possession."

1620. Mālik said, regarding a slave whose master designates him for manumission after his death and who then enters into a manumission contract with his master, after which the master dies, leaving no property other than the slave, "One-third of the slave is manumitted, and one-third of his obligations under the manumission contract is canceled, but he is still obligated to pay the remaining two-thirds outstanding under the manumission contract."

---

669 What Mālik means here is that even if the master made consecutive declarations designating his favorite slaves for manumission, because he did so while on his deathbed the designations are treated as testamentary dispositions. Consequently, no priority is granted on the basis of the order of the master's declarations, contrary to the rule that applies if the master makes the declarations while in good health.

1621. Mālik said, regarding a man who manumits one-half of a slave of his during his deathbed illness, giving immediate effect to the manumission, either in half or even in full, and who has previously designated another slave of his for manumission upon his death, "Priority is given to the slave whom the master designated for manumission upon his death over the slave manumitted during the master's deathbed illness in the event that the value of the deathbed manumission, when combined with the value of the previously designated slave, exceeds one-third of the decedent's estate. This is because a man cannot rescind a prior designation for manumission that he made for his slave, nor may he perform any act after making such a designation that would undermine its effectiveness. When the designated slave is manumitted after the master's death, anything that remains of the master's one-third share available for testamentary dispositions should then be applied toward a full manumission of the slave whom the master attempted to manumit one-half of while on his deathbed. If that cannot be accomplished within what is left of the decedent's one-third of the estate, the slave is manumitted up to whatever is left of the one-third after the value of the slave previously designated for manumission has been deducted."

Chapter 4. A Man Having Intercourse with His Handmaiden after Designating Her for Manumission upon His Death (*Tadbīr*)

1622. According to Mālik, Nāfiʿ reported that ʿAbd Allāh b. ʿUmar designated two of his handmaidens for manumission after his death, and he had intercourse with both of them after the designation.

1623. According to Mālik, Yaḥyā b. Saʿīd reported that Saʿīd b. al-Musayyab would say, "A man may have intercourse with his handmaiden despite having designated her for manumission upon his death, but he may neither sell nor gift her, and her children take the same status that she has."

Chapter 5. The Sale of a Slave Designated for Manumission upon His Master's Death (*Mudabbar*)

1624. Yaḥyā said, "Mālik said, 'The agreed-upon rule among us (*al-amr al-mujtamaʿ ʿalayhi ʿindanā*) concerning a slave designated for manumission upon his master's death is that his master may not sell him nor otherwise undermine his status, which the master himself has granted him, in any way. If the master becomes insolvent, his creditors are not permitted to sell the slave as long as his master is alive. Should the master die leaving no debts, the slave is charged against the one-third of the master's estate available for testamentary dispositions, because the master reserved the slave's service for himself as long as he lived. The master may not benefit from the slave's service all his life and then manumit him only at the moment of his death, thus depriving his heirs by reducing the value of his estate. If the master dies leaving no property other than the slave, one-third of the slave is manumitted and the remaining two-thirds go to the master's heirs. If the master dies leaving debts that exceed the value of his slave, the slave is sold in satisfaction of the debt. This is because the slave may be manumitted only out of the one-third available for testamentary dispositions. Should the debt reach only one-half of the slave's value, only one-half of the slave is sold to satisfy the debt, and then one-third of the portion of the slave that remains after the debt is manumitted.'"[670]

1625. Mālik said, "The sale of a slave designated for manumission is invalid. No one is permitted to purchase him, unless the slave purchases himself from his master, in which case the sale is valid. Alternatively, it is permissible for someone to give the master some property on the condition that he manumit the slave immediately. That is also valid. However, the right to the slave's patronage (*walā'*) in this latter case goes to the master who designated the slave for manumission."

1626. Mālik said, "It is not permissible for the master of a slave designated for manumission to sell the slave's labor to a third party. This is because such a transaction involves material uncertainty in the consideration (*gharar*), insofar as it is impossible to know how long the master will live. That results in material uncertainty that is not appropriate in a contract."[671]

1627. Mālik said, regarding a slave who is owned in common by two men, one of whom designates his share of the slave for manumission upon his death, "They must jointly appraise the slave's fair market value. If the designating co-owner purchases his co-owner's share in the slave, the slave is deemed to be designated for manumission in his entirety. If, however, the designating co-owner does not purchase his co-owner's share in the slave, the designation of the slave's freedom is repealed, unless the non-designating co-owner desires to give his share of the slave to the designating co-owner in exchange for the fair market value of his share in the slave. If the non-designating co-owner gives the designating co-owner his share of the slave in exchange for the share's fair market value, that binds

670 In other words, one-sixth of the slave is manumitted.

671 What Mālik has in mind here is a contract that would entail the master's transferring to a third party all of the master's rights to the slave's future labor. Because the slave becomes free immediately upon the master's death, the purchaser of the slave's labor cannot know with reasonable certainty what he is acquiring: the purchaser could enjoy the rights to the slave's labor for the next twenty years, or his rights could lapse the next day, if the master suddenly and unexpectedly dies.

the designating co-owner. Consequently, in this case the slave becomes designated for manumission in his entirety."

1628. Mālik said, regarding a scenario in which a Christian designates a Christian slave of his for manumission, and then the slave becomes a Muslim: "The master is to be separated from the slave, but the slave's earnings are to be given to his Christian master. The slave should not be sold until his situation becomes clear. Should the Christian die, leaving a debt, the debt may be discharged out of the proceeds received from selling the slave. However, if the master dies leaving property sufficient to pay the debt, the slave is manumitted."

Chapter 6. Batteries (*Jirāḥ*) Committed by a Slave Designated for Manumission upon His Master's Death (*Mudabbar*)

1629. According to Mālik, it reached him that ʿUmar b. ʿAbd al-ʿAzīz ruled that if a slave designated for manumission upon his master's death causes injury to a third party, the slave's master may deliver his share of the slave to the injured party. If the master does so, the injured party may put the slave to use and collect the compensation due to him for his injury out of the proceeds from the slave's labor. In this case, if the slave discharges his obligation to the injured party before his master dies, he returns to his master.

1630. Mālik said, "The rule in our view (*al-amr ʿindanā*) regarding a slave designated for manumission who causes injury to a third party and whose master subsequently dies, leaving no property other than that slave, is that one-third of the slave is manumitted and then the compensation due in respect of the battery is divided into three equal parts. One-third is borne by that part of the decedent's estate from which the slave was manumitted, and the other two-thirds are borne by the two-thirds of the decedent's estate that goes to the heirs. Accordingly, the heirs may, if they wish, give the victim their share of the slave, or they may give him two-thirds of the compensation due and retain their share of the slave. This is because the liability for compensation arose only as a result of the slave's battery, not from any contractual debt of the master. Therefore, the injurious conduct of the slave is not of the kind that would invalidate the master's previous acts of manumission and designation of that slave for manumission.[672] If,

672 In this case, the master has died leaving no property other than a slave designated for manumission upon the master's death, and the slave has injured a third party, giving rise to an obligation of compensation. Mālik's rule in such a case is that one-third of the slave becomes manumitted upon the master's death in accordance with the master's prior designation of the slave. Because the master left no other property, however, only one-third of the slave can be manumitted, with the remaining two-thirds passing to the master's heirs. The obligation arising out of the slave's battery, meanwhile, attaches to the person of the slave himself.

on the other hand, the master owes a contractual debt to third parties in addition to the liability arising out of the slave's battery, the portion of the slave necessary to satisfy both sets of obligations is sold. Priority is given to payment of the obligation arising out of the slave's battery, which is satisfied first out of the proceeds received from the slave's sale. Only once that obligation is satisfied is the master's contractual debt repaid. Then, once both prior obligations have been discharged, the disposition of whatever share of the slave remains is then resolved in the following fashion: one-third of the remaining share of the slave is manumitted, and the remaining two-thirds goes to the master's heirs. This is because the compensation due as a result of the slave's battery takes greater priority than does payment of his master's contractual debt. This is because if a man dies, leaving a slave designated for manumission who has a fair market value of 150 dinars, and if that slave happens to have dealt a free man a blow to the head causing an open wound in his skull, thereby resulting in an obligation to compensate the victim in the amount of fifty dinars, and if the slave's master owes a contractual debt of fifty dinars, priority is given to the payment of the fifty dinars that constitute the compensation for the injury. This amount is collected from the price received from the sale of the slave, in whole or in part. Only after that is paid in full is the master's debt satisfied. Finally, what is left of the slave is then disposed of, one-third being manumitted and two-thirds going to the master's heirs. The obligation to pay compensation for the battery takes a higher priority against the slave's person than does his master's contractual debt, and the contractual debt has a greater priority than does the master's designation of the slave for manumission, which in these circumstances becomes the equivalent of a testamentary disposition. A testamentary disposition can be satisfied only out of the one-third of the decedent's estate available for testamentary dispositions.[673] Accordingly, no part of the master's designation of the slave

---

Accordingly, the slave, one-third of whom is now manumitted, is himself liable for one-third of the obligation. The heirs are liable for the remaining two-thirds, in accordance with their ownership interest in the slave. They are free to give the injured party their two-thirds interest in the slave, or they may pay the injured party two-thirds of the compensation due and retain their interest in the slave.

673 To give another, more detailed example, a master dies leaving no property other than a slave designated for freedom. Before the master's death, the slave committed a battery against a third party, giving rise to an obligation to pay twenty-five dinars of compensation to the injured party. The master also leaves an unpaid contractual debt of twenty-five dinars. In this case, Mālik's rule is that fifty dinars' worth of the slave must be sold to satisfy these two obligations. If the fair market value of the slave is one hundred dinars, one-half of the slave would be sold and the fifty dinars received would be used to discharge the two obligations. Of the remaining one-half of the slave, one-third would be manumitted pursuant to the master's designation of the slave for manumission, so one-sixth of the slave becomes free. The heirs would then take two-thirds of the remaining one-half of the slave, that is, one-third of the

for manumission can take effect as long as the master has outstanding debts. In such circumstances, the master's designation of the slave becomes a testamentary disposition, and God, Blessed and Sublime is He, says, 'After the payment of testamentary dispositions made by the decedent, or repayment of debts.'"[674]

1631. Mālik said, "If one-third of the decedent's estate is sufficient to absorb the entirety of the designated slave's fair market value, he is manumitted immediately upon his master's death. The compensation owed for his battery becomes the former slave's personal obligation, for which he remains liable after his manumission, even if what is due is the compensation owed for the unlawful killing of a free man.[675] This rule applies only if the master died without owing any contractual debt."[676]

1632. Mālik said, regarding a scenario in which a slave who has been designated for manumission injures a third party, and his master, instead of compensating the injured party, hands him over to the victim but then dies, leaving an unpaid debt and no property other than the slave, and the heirs say, "We will abandon the slave to the victim," while the creditor says, "But I am prepared to offer more for him than the amount of the compensation due to the victim": "If the creditor in fact pays more than the amount of the compensation due to the victim, his claim to the slave is superior to the victim's, but the debt owed by the master's estate is reduced only by the difference between the amount that the creditor pays for the slave and the amount of the compensation due to the victim. But if the creditor does not pay more than what is owed to the victim, he has no claim to the slave."[677]

---

slave. The other half of the slave is owned by whatever third party purchased the one-half sold to raise the cash necessary to discharge the amounts owed at the time of the master's death. If, however, the fair market value of the slave does not exceed fifty dinars, then the entirety of the slave would be sold to satisfy the obligations outstanding at the time of the master's death. If the amount realized through the sale is less than fifty dinars, the victim of the slave's battery is paid first, and the master's contract creditors are entitled to receive only whatever remains of the proceeds from the sale of the slave.

674 *Al-Nisā'*, 4:12.

675 The issue here is that the master could, in lieu of paying the full compensation due to the injured party, have simply delivered the slave to the injured party and relieved himself of all liability. Now that the slave is free, however, he is obliged to pay the indemnity in full and may not, for example, turn himself over to the victim to be his slave.

676 The manumitted slave has no personal liability for his master's contractual debts, provided that the estate is large enough to satisfy them.

677 For example, a slave, S, who has been designated for manumission by his master, M, upon the master's death, commits a battery against X, resulting in a duty to compensate X in the amount of one hundred dinars. M surrenders S to X in lieu of paying him the amount. M then dies, owing 150 dinars to a creditor, C, and possessing no property beyond S. In this situation, if C offers 125 dinars for S, he can take S from X, but the debt owed to him by M (now M's estate) is only reduced from 150 to 125 dinars. X can now collect the 100 dinars he is owed from the estate. The estate still owes C 125 dinars, but since it lacks sufficient assets, C is not

1633. Mālik said, regarding a scenario in which a slave designated for manumission injures a third party but possesses his own property, and the master refuses to pay the compensation due to the victim in order to redeem the slave from the victim's possession: "The victim can collect the compensation due to him out of the slave's property. If the slave's property is sufficient to discharge the compensation due, the victim can collect the entire amount out of the slave's property. In this case, the slave is then returned to his master. However, if the slave's property is insufficient to compensate the victim in full, the victim can deduct it from the compensation due to him and then employ the slave until he collects the balance of the compensation owed for his injury."

Chapter 7. Batteries (*Jirāḥ*) Committed by a Handmaiden Who Has Borne Her Master a Child (*Umm Walad*)

1634. Yaḥyā said, "Mālik said, regarding a handmaiden who has borne her master a child (*umm walad*) and who injures a third party, 'The master is solely liable for the compensation due to the victim, and he must satisfy it out of his own property, unless the compensation due exceeds her fair market value. In the latter case, her master is not obliged to pay more than her fair market value. This is because when the master of a slave, whether male or female, surrenders the slave in satisfaction of his obligation to indemnify the slave's victim, he is never obliged to do more, even if the compensation due is substantially in excess of the slave's fair market value. Because the long-established ordinance (*mā maḍā min al-sunna*) precludes the master from delivering to the victim his handmaiden who has borne him a child, when he pays to the victim her fair market value, it is as though he has delivered her to the victim. He is under no obligation to do more. That is the best view I have heard regarding this question. The master is not obliged to bear liability for batteries (*jināya*) committed by his handmaiden beyond her fair market value.'"

The Book of Designating Slaves for Manumission upon the Master's Death (*Tadbīr*) Is Complete, with Praise Due to God.

able to collect the debt. By purchasing S from X, however, C will presumably have the ability to recover some of the amount owed to him. See Bājī, *al-Muntaqā*, 7:50.

Book 31
The Book of Marriage (*Nikāḥ*)

In the Name of God, the Merciful, the Compassionate

May God Grace Muḥammad and His Family
and Grant Them Perfect Tranquility.

Chapter 1. What Has Come Down regarding Proposals of Marriage (*Khiṭba*)

1635. According to Mālik, Muḥammad b. Ḥabbān reported from al-Aʿraj, from Abū Hurayra, that the Messenger of God (pbuh) said, "No suitor should propose to a woman if another has already made her a proposal (*khiṭba*)."

1636. According to Mālik, Nāfiʿ reported from ʿAbd Allāh b. ʿUmar that the Messenger of God (pbuh) said, "No suitor should propose to a woman if another has already made her a proposal." Mālik said, "In our opinion, and God knows best, the explanation for this statement of the Messenger of God (pbuh) is that it applies to the case of a suitor who proposes to a woman, and the woman responds positively; they agree on a determinate dower (*ṣadāq*), having come to a mutual agreement to marry; and she makes stipulations for her own benefit in the terms of the marriage contract. That is the category of woman to whom other suitors may not propose. The statement of the Prophet (pbuh) was not intended to apply to a suitor who proposes to a woman, but she does not find his proposal agreeable, nor does she respond positively to him. In such a case, other suitors are not prohibited from proposing to that woman. Were it otherwise, much mischief would result."

1637. According to Mālik, ʿAbd al-Raḥmān b. al-Qāsim reported that his father would say, regarding the statement of God, Blessed and Sublime is He, "You commit no wrong whether you allude indirectly to marriage or keep it hidden in your hearts,"[678] that it applies to a situation in which a suitor

678 *Al-Baqara*, 2:235.

says to a widow while she is still in her waiting period (*ʿidda*),[679] mourning her deceased husband, and therefore prohibited from remarrying, "You are certainly precious to me," or "I really like you," or "God is certain to provide you good fortune and provisions," or similar statements.

Chapter 2. Consulting the Virgin (*Bikr*) and the Matron (*Ayyim*) regarding Their Marriages

1638. According to Mālik, ʿAbd Allāh b. al-Faḍl reported from Nāfiʿ b. Jubayr b. Muṭʿim, from ʿAbd Allāh b. ʿAbbās, that the Messenger of God (pbuh) said, "The matron has a stronger claim than her guardian does with regard to her own marriage, and the virgin, too, must be consulted with regard to her marriage—but her silence constitutes consent on her part."[680]

1639. According to Mālik, it reached him that Saʿīd b. al-Musayyab said, "ʿUmar b. al-Khaṭṭāb said, 'A woman's marriage is contracted only after the approval of either her guardian (*walī*), a man of good judgment from her kin, or a responsible public official (*sulṭān*).'"

1640. According to Mālik, it reached him that al-Qāsim b. Muḥammad and Sālim b. ʿAbd Allāh contracted the marriages of their virgin daughters without first consulting them. Mālik said, "The rule among us is in accordance with that (*ʿalā dhālika al-amr ʿindanā*) concerning the marriage of virgins."

1641. Mālik said, "A virgin's disposition of her own property is not effective until she enters her marital home and her competence in the management of that property is proven."

1642. According to Mālik, it reached him that al-Qāsim b. Muḥammad, Sālim b. ʿAbd Allāh, and Sulaymān b. Yasār would say that a virgin girl was bound by the marriage contract that her father contracted for her, even if he did so without her consent.

679 A period of time following a woman's divorce from her husband or her husband's death during which she may not remarry. Following a divorce, this period is usually around three months; for a widow, it is ordinarily 130 days. *Al-Baqara*, 2:234.

680 This rule reflects the understanding that a previously married woman is not embarrassed to express her desire for marriage, whereas a girl who has not previously been married is too bashful to say openly that she desires marriage. Therefore, her silence is taken to be tantamount to her acceptance of the proposal, whereas in the case of a previously married woman, her consent is evidenced only by an explicit statement.

Chapter 3. What Has Come Down regarding the Dower (*Ṣadāq*) and Gifts to the Guardian (*Ḥibāʾ*)

1643. According to Mālik, Abū Ḥāzim b. Dīnār reported from Sahl b. Saʿd al-Sāʿidī that a woman went to the Messenger of God (pbuh) and said, "Messenger of God, I have freely given myself to you in marriage!" She stood there for a long time, waiting for a reply. When the Messenger of God (pbuh) did not respond, a man stood up and said, "Messenger of God, let me marry her, if you do not wish to do so." The Messenger of God (pbuh) said, "Do you have anything to offer her as a dower?" The man said, "Only this undergarment of mine." The Messenger of God (pbuh) said, "But if you were to give that to her, you would not have an undergarment for yourself. Find something else." The man said, "But I cannot find anything else." The Messenger of God (pbuh) said to him, "Find something, even an iron ring." The man then went looking for something but failed, finding nothing he could offer as a dower. Finally, the Messenger of God (pbuh) said to him, "Have you memorized any verses of the Quran?" The man said, "Yes, I know such-and-such a chapter all the way through to such-and-such a chapter," naming them. The Messenger of God (pbuh) said, "I give her to you in marriage,[681] and her dower is your knowledge of the Quran."

1644. According to Mālik, Yaḥyā b. Saʿīd reported that Saʿīd b. al-Musayyab said, "ʿUmar b. al-Khaṭṭāb said, 'Whoever marries a woman afflicted with insanity or leprosy and consummates the marriage with her must give her the entirety of her dower but may recover that amount from her guardian (*walī*).'"

1645. Mālik said, "In those circumstances, her husband may recover the dower from her guardian only when the guardian who arranged her marriage to him was her father, her brother, or anyone else in a position to have reasonably known about her condition. If, however, the guardian who arranged her marriage to him was her paternal first cousin, a freedman (*mawlā*), or anyone else in her extended family—someone who would not have been in a reasonable position to know about her condition, he is not liable to compensate the husband. In that case, the woman must return to the husband whatever was given to her as a dower, retaining only the amount that would have made intercourse licit."[682]

---

681 The Prophet's (pbuh) act of giving the woman in marriage should not be seen as a sacrament but rather as a case of the Prophet's (pbuh) acting as the woman's guardian or representative for the purpose of entering into the marriage contract.

682 In other words, she is entitled to keep the legal minimum dower, which is one-quarter of a dinar. Zurqānī, *Sharḥ al-Zurqānī*, 3:197.

1646. According to Mālik, Nāfiʿ reported that the daughter of ʿUbayd Allāh b. ʿUmar (whose mother was the daughter of Zayd b. al-Khaṭṭāb) was married to one of the sons of ʿAbd Allāh b. ʿUmar. However, the groom died before bringing her to the marital home and without specifying a determinate dower for her.[683] Her mother then attempted to collect her dower, but ʿAbd Allāh b. ʿUmar said that she was not entitled to one, and that had she been so entitled, he would not have deprived her of it, and that he was not acting unjustly toward her. The mother disagreed, refusing to accede to Ibn ʿUmar's argument. They then appointed Zayd b. Thābit to arbitrate between them. He ruled that she was not entitled to a dower but that she was entitled to inherit from her deceased husband.[684]

1647. According to Mālik, it reached him that ʿUmar b. ʿAbd al-ʿAzīz had, during his term as caliph, sent a decree to one of his governors, saying, "If the person contracting a marriage for a woman, whether he is her father or anyone else, stipulates in connection with the marriage contract that the groom is to give him any kind of gift (*ḥibāʾ*), the gift belongs to the bride, if she claims it for herself."

1648. Mālik said, regarding a woman whose father arranges her marriage and stipulates that the groom give him a gift, that whatever gift is stipulated as a condition of the marriage belongs to the daughter, not the father, if she claims it. If, however, her husband fails to bring her to the marital home, whether as a result of death or of divorce, he (or in case of his death, his heirs) may reclaim one-half of the gifts that were given as a condition of the marriage.

683 Marriage in the early Islamic community (and up to the present day in many Muslim societies) took place in two stages. The first was entrance into the marriage contract, and the second was the beginning of the bride's cohabitation with her husband. The two events, in most cases, did not occur at (or around) the same time. Rather, a period of time, which could be substantial, would normally pass between the time of the marriage contract and the bride's performance of the marriage contract in the form of leaving her natal home and entering her marital home. Given these arrangements, if the husband died before the marriage contract was fulfilled, disputes sometimes arose with regard to dower and inheritance, as reflected in this case.

684 This form of marriage is called "the marriage of delegation" (*nikāḥ al-tafwīḍ*) In it, the dower is undetermined at the time of the contract, and the husband holds the power to determine the amount of the dower at a later date. If the dower later specified by the husband amounts at least to her fair dower (*ṣadāq al-mithl*), she is bound to the contract. If the husband proposes a dower that exceeds the legal minimum but is less than the fair dower, she is entitled to refuse the marriage; and if he proposes a dower that is below the minimum, the marriage is invalid. This type of marriage applies also to other scenarios not relevant to this incident. Bājī, *al-Muntaqā*, 3:281. Had the dower been specified at the time of the contract, and the husband died prior to the marriage's consummation, she would have been entitled to half of the specified dower. Because the dower had not been specified in this case, she was not entitled to anything.

1649. Mālik said, regarding a father who contracts a marriage for his son, who is a minor without property of his own, "The father is liable for the dower, if the son has no property as of the date the marriage is contracted. If the son does have property as of that date, the dower is payable out of the son's property, unless the father states expressly in the contract that he himself is liable for the dower. Such a marriage binds the son, as long as he is a minor and subject to his father's guardianship."

1650. Mālik said, regarding a scenario in which a man divorces his virgin wife before bringing her to the marital home, and then her father waives the one-half of the dower that was her due, "The husband is permitted to accept whatever reduction in the dower owed the father grants him. This is because God, Blessed and Sublime is He, says in His Book, 'Unless they waive it.'[685] 'They' in this phrase refers to wives who have taken up residence in the marital home with their husbands but were divorced prior to the marriage's consummation. The phrase 'or the one in whose hand is the marriage contract waives it'[686] refers to the virgin daughter's father or the handmaiden's master. That is what I have heard about this case, and that is the rule that applies among us (*alladhī ʿalayhi al-amr ʿindanā*)."

1651. Mālik said that a Jewish or Christian woman who is married to a Jew or a Christian and who converts to Islam before she is brought to the marital home is not entitled to any dower.

1652. Mālik said, "I am of the view that no woman may be married with a dower of less than one-quarter of a dinar, this being the minimum amount that, if stolen, mandates amputation of the hand."

Chapter 4. Marital Privacy (*Irkhā' al-Sutūr*)

1653. According to Mālik, Yaḥyā b. Saʿīd reported from Saʿīd b. al-Musayyab that ʿUmar b. al-Khaṭṭāb ruled that when a woman marries a man and marital privacy takes place, the dower (*ṣadāq*) becomes mandatory.

1654. According to Mālik, Ibn Shihāb reported that Zayd b. Thābit would say, "When a man brings his bride to the marital home and marital privacy takes place, the dower becomes mandatory."

1655. According to Mālik, it reached him that Saʿīd b. al-Musayyab would say, "If the husband visits his wife in her home, his claim is credited over hers; however, if she visits him in his home, her claim is credited over his." Mālik said, "I believe this refers to a dispute about the occurrence of sexual

685 *Al-Baqara*, 2:237.
686 *Al-Baqara*, 2:237.

intercourse. If he visits her in her home and she says, 'He had intercourse with me,' and he says, 'I did not have intercourse with her,' his claim is credited over hers. If she visits him in his home, however, and he says, 'I did not have intercourse with her,' and she says, 'He had intercourse with me,' her word is credited over his."[687]

Chapter 5. Residing with a Virgin Bride (*Bikr*) and with a Bride Who Is a Matron (*Ayyim*) at the Outset of the Marriage

1656. According to Mālik, ʿAbd Allāh b. Abī Bakr b. Muḥammad b. ʿAmr b. Ḥazm reported from ʿAbd al-Malik b. Abī Bakr b. ʿAbd al-Raḥmān b. al-Ḥārith b. Hishām al-Makhzūmī, from his father, that when the Messenger of God (pbuh) married Umm Salama and she awoke in his chambers, he said to her, "I, as your husband, have full respect for you. Accordingly, if you wish, I will spend the next seven nights with you, and then I will spend the next seven nights with my other wives. Alternately, if you prefer, I will spend the next three nights with you, and then visit each of my other wives in turns." She replied, "Let it be three nights."

1657. According to Mālik, Ḥumayd al-Ṭawīl reported that Anas b. Mālik would say, "A virgin bride is entitled to seven consecutive nights with her husband at the outset of her marriage, and a matron is entitled to three consecutive nights."[688] Mālik said, "That is the rule among us (*dhālika al-amr ʿindanā*)."

1658. Mālik said, "If a man has a wife other than the one he just married, he shall split his time equally between them after the wedding nights. However, he should not count the nights he spent with the newest bride against her."

Chapter 6. Nonbinding Stipulations in a Marriage Contract (*Nikāḥ*)

1659. According to Mālik, it reached him that Saʿīd b. al-Musayyab was asked about a woman who stipulated in her marriage contract that her husband could not relocate her from her home town. Saʿīd b. al-Musayyab said, "He may relocate her despite the stipulation, if he so wishes."

1660. Mālik said, "The rule in our view (*al-amr ʿindanā*) is that if the husband stipulates something for the benefit of his wife, even if it is in the

687 This refers to a case that would arise after the bride and groom have entered into their marriage contract but the bride has yet to join the husband in the marital home, and there is a dispute as to whether sexual intercourse has taken place. If it has taken place, the bride is entitled to the full dower. If it has not taken place and she is divorced before joining her husband in the marital home, she is entitled to only one-half of the dower.

688 This rule applies at the outset of a marriage when the husband has more than one wife.

marriage contract—for example, that he will not marry another woman or take a concubine while married to her—this condition is of no effect, unless it is accompanied by an oath of divorce or manumission of a slave. Such an oath creates obligations for him and therefore binds him."

Chapter 7. The Marriage (*Nikāḥ*) of a Man Who Marries a Woman Solely for the Purpose of Allowing Her to Remarry Her Previous Husband (*Muḥallil*), and Similar Cases

1661. According to Mālik, al-Miswar b. Rifāʿa al-Quraẓī reported from al-Zubayr b. ʿAbd al-Rahmān b. al-Zabīr that Rifāʿa b. Simwāl divorced his wife Tamīma bt. Wahb three times at the time of the Messenger of God (pbuh). She then married ʿAbd al-Raḥmān b. al-Zabīr. Because he found her unattractive, he was not able to consummate the marriage, so he divorced her. Then Rifāʿa, her first husband who had already divorced her three times, expressed a desire to remarry her, so he asked the Messenger of God (pbuh) whether he could. The latter, however, prohibited Rifāʿa from remarrying her, saying, "You may not remarry her unless she consummates a marriage with another man and then is divorced or widowed."[689]

1662. According to Mālik, Yaḥyā b. Saʿīd reported from al-Qāsim b. Muḥammad, from ʿĀʾisha, the wife of the Prophet (pbuh), that she was asked whether a man who divorced his wife three times could remarry her after she married another man who divorced her before consummating the marriage. She said, "No, not unless another husband consummates a marriage with her and then she is divorced or widowed."

1663. According to Mālik, it reached him that al-Qāsim b. Muḥammad was asked whether a man who had divorced his wife three times could remarry her if, after her divorce, she married another man but was widowed before they could consummate the marriage. Al-Qāsim b. Muḥammad said, "It is not permissible for her first husband to remarry her in this case."

1664. Mālik said, regarding a man who marries a woman solely for the purpose of making it permissible for her to remarry her previous husband, "He is not permitted to maintain the marriage unless he enters into a new, valid contract with that woman. However, if they consummated the marriage under the invalid marriage contract, she is nevertheless entitled to her dower."

---

689 The Quran permits a man to divorce his wife and remarry her twice, but upon the third divorce, he may not remarry her again until she first marries and is either divorced or widowed from another husband. *Al-Baqara*, 2:230.

Chapter 8. Women Who May Not Be Married Simultaneously to the Same Man

1665. According to Mālik, Abū al-Zinād reported from al-Aʿraj, from Abū Hurayra, that the Messenger of God (pbuh) said, "No one may be simultaneously married to a woman and her paternal aunt (*ʿamma*), or to a woman and her maternal aunt (*khāla*)."

1666. According to Mālik, Yaḥyā b. Saʿīd reported that Saʿīd b. al-Musayyab would say, "It is prohibited for a woman to be married to a man who is at the same time married to her paternal or maternal aunt, or for a man to have intercourse with a handmaiden who is carrying another man's child."

Chapter 9. Regarding the Impermissibility of Marriage (*Nikāḥ*) between a Man and His Mother-in-Law

1667. According to Mālik, Yaḥyā b. Saʿīd said, "Zayd b. Thābit was asked whether a man who married a woman and then divorced her before consummating the marriage might then marry her mother. Zayd b. Thābit said, 'No; the prohibition against marriage to mothers-in-law is absolute, without qualification. An exception to the prohibition is made only in the case of stepdaughters (*rabāʾib*).'"[690]

1668. According to Mālik, multiple sources reported that when ʿAbd Allāh b. Masʿūd was in Kufa, he was asked for his opinion about the legality of a man's marriage to his mother-in-law after his marriage to her daughter had come to an end without the marriage ever having been consummated. ʿAbd Allāh opined that in this case the marriage to the mother-in-law was valid. But he later went to Medina and asked whether his ruling had been correct. He was told that he had erred, and that the exception applied only to stepdaughters. Ibn Masʿūd then returned to Kufa, and before even reaching his home, he went directly to the man whom he had previously told that it was permissible for him to marry his former mother-in-law and ordered him to separate from her.

1669. Mālik said that if a man marries his mother-in-law and has intercourse with her, "His wife[691] becomes absolutely forbidden to him; he must immediately separate from the both of them; and he may never

---

690 In other words, the marriage contract with the daughter renders her mother, the mother-in-law, a perpetually prohibited marriage partner for the husband, whether or not the marriage with the daughter is consummated. By contrast, the bride's daughter (the husband's step-daughter) remains a licit marriage partner for the husband if he divorces the bride without having consummated the marriage. *Al-Nisāʾ*, 4:23.

691 That is, his wife who is the daughter of the mother-in-law whom he has now also married.

remarry either one. This is the rule only if he actually had intercourse with the mother-in-law. If he did not, and merely contracted a marriage with her, the daughter of the mother-in-law remains his lawful wife, but he must separate from the mother-in-law."

1670. Mālik said, "If a man marries his mother-in-law and has intercourse with her, the mother-in-law is forever forbidden to him. So, too, is she forever forbidden to his son and his father. Any sisters-in-law[692] also become forbidden to him, as does the mother-in-law's daughter to whom he is currently married."

1671. Mālik said, "Fornication does not introduce any such bars to marriage, because God, Blessed and Sublime is He, said, 'your wives' mothers.'[693] He made only the fact of marriage a criterion for barring marriage, without mentioning fornication. Therefore, every marriage that is licit in form, pursuant to which the man has intercourse with the wife, is treated as a licit marriage for purposes of creating bars to marriage. This is what I have heard, and the practice of the people among us is in accordance with that (*alladhī ʿalayhi amr al-nās ʿindanā*)."

Chapter 10. A Man's Marriage (*Nikāḥ*) to the Mother of a Woman with Whom He Has Had Illicit Sexual Relations

1672. Mālik said, regarding a man who had illicit intercourse with a woman and was then duly punished in accordance with the law, "He may nevertheless marry her daughter, and so may his son, if he wishes. That is because his intercourse with her was illicit. What God, Blessed and Sublime is He, made a bar to marriage was sexual relations within a relationship that, at a minimum, appears to be a valid marriage (*shubhāt al-nikāḥ*). God, Blessed and Sublime is He, says, 'And do not marry women whom your fathers have married.'[694] Accordingly, should a man marry a woman during her waiting period (*ʿidda*), pursuant to a contract that appears to be licit, and then has intercourse with her, his son may never marry her. That is because his father married her and had intercourse with her under the claim that his actions were lawful. Consequently, he cannot be punished for that act, and any children born as a result would be his. Moreover, just as the man's son is now prohibited from ever marrying that woman, so, too, is the father forever prohibited from marrying the woman's daughter, because he had intercourse with her mother within the bounds of what appeared to be a valid marriage contract."

---

692 That is, daughters of the mother-in-law.
693 *Al-Nisāʾ*, 4:23.
694 *Al-Nisāʾ*, 4:22.

Chapter 11. Miscellaneous Reports regarding What Is Impermissible in Regard to Marriage (*Nikāḥ*)

1673. According to Mālik, Nāfiʿ reported from ʿAbd Allāh b. ʿUmar that the Messenger of God (pbuh) prohibited marriage contracts that entail one man agreeing to give his daughter in marriage to another man who, in turn, gives his own daughter in marriage to the first man, with the result that no dower (*ṣadāq*) is exchanged.[695]

1674. According to Mālik, ʿAbd al-Raḥmān b. al-Qāsim reported from his father, from ʿAbd al-Raḥmān and Mujammiʿ, both sons of Yazīd b. Jāriya al-Anṣārī, from Khansāʾ bt. Khidhām al-Anṣāriyya, that her father contracted a marriage for her at a time when she was a matron (*thayyib*). She, however, did not want that marriage, so she went and complained to the Messenger of God (pbuh), who then invalidated the father's contract of marriage (*nikāḥ*).

1675. According to Mālik, Abū al-Zubayr al-Makkī reported that ʿUmar b. al-Khaṭṭāb was presented with the case of a marriage whose only witnesses were one man and one woman. He said, "This is a secret marriage, and I do not permit it to stand. Had I been the first to rule on such a case, I would have ordered the parties to be stoned to death for adultery."

1676. According to Mālik, Ibn Shihāb reported from Saʿīd b. al-Musayyab, from Sulaymān b. Yasār, that Ṭulayḥa al-Asadiyya was married to Rushayd al-Thaqafī, and he divorced her. She then remarried during her waiting period. ʿUmar b. al-Khaṭṭāb punished her and her new husband, giving each of them several blows with a stick. He then separated them from one another, saying, "Any woman who marries during her waiting period, as long as her new husband has not taken her to the marital home, shall be divorced from the new husband, and then she must complete the remaining portion of her waiting period from her first husband, after which the second man is treated the same as any prospective suitor. However, if the second man took her to the marital home before the expiration of her waiting period, they are separated from one another; she completes her waiting period from the first husband; she completes her waiting period from the second husband; and she and her second husband are forever prohibited from marrying each other." Mālik said, "Saʿīd b. al-Musayyab said, 'She is entitled to her dower, since the second man believed he contracted a lawful marriage with her.'"

1677. Mālik said, "The rule in our view (*al-amr ʿindanā*) concerning a free woman whose husband dies and who completes the widow's waiting period of four months and ten days is that she is not permitted to remarry if she

---

695 This type of marriage is referred to as *shighār*.

entertains any doubts about her period and fears she might be pregnant. She must not remarry until she is certain that she is not pregnant."

Chapter 12. Marriage (*Nikāḥ*) to a Handmaiden When Already Married to a Free Woman

1678. According to Mālik, it reached him that ʿAbd Allāh b. ʿAbbās and ʿAbd Allāh b. ʿUmar were both asked about a man who was married to a free woman and then wanted to marry a handmaiden alongside her. They both disapproved of the simultaneous marriage to a free woman and a handmaiden.

1679. According to Mālik, Yaḥyā b. Saʿīd reported that Saʿīd b. al-Musayyab would say, "A man is not to marry a handmaiden alongside his free wife, unless the free woman agrees to it. If she does, she is allotted two out of every three nights."[696]

1680. Mālik said, "A free man is not to marry a handmaiden when he has sufficient means to marry a free woman, nor is he to marry a handmaiden when he cannot afford to marry a free woman, unless he fears that he will commit fornication. That is because God, Blessed and Sublime is He, says in His Book, 'If any of you lack the means to wed free believing women, they may wed believing girls from among those whom your right hands possess.' God, Glorious and Exalted is He, also said, 'That concession is granted only to those of you who fear hardship (*ʿanat*).'[697] 'Hardship' here means fornication."

Chapter 13. What Has Come Down regarding a Man Who Comes to Own a Woman as a Handmaiden after Having Been Married to Her and Divorcing Her

1681. According to Mālik, Ibn Shihāb reported from Abū ʿAbd al-Raḥmān that Zayd b. Thābit would say, regarding a man who divorces his wife, who is a handmaiden at the time, three times and then subsequently purchases her, that he may not have intercourse with her until she first marries another man and is either divorced or widowed from him.

---

696 The basic rule in a polygamous marriage is that the husband is obligated to divide his nights equally among his wives, which means that in the ordinary case, if he has two wives, he spends every other night with each wife. In this case, the proposed rule treats the wife who is a slave as entitled to half the rights of the free woman and thus as entitled to spend only every third night with the husband.

697 *Al-Nisāʾ*, 4:25. Marriage of a free man to slave women was frowned upon since the children of such a union would be enslaved, the background principle being that the child takes the status of the mother. Accordingly, it was permitted only in exigent circumstances, such as when a man lacked the means to marry a free woman and feared committing the sin of fornication.

1682. According to Mālik, it reached him that both Sa'īd b. al-Musayyab and Sulaymān b. Yasār were asked whether a slave whose master arranged his marriage to one of the master's handmaidens and who then divorced her three times and then subsequently received her from his master as a gift could lawfully have intercourse with the handmaiden by virtue of his ownership of her. They both said, "No, not until she marries another man and is either divorced or widowed from him."

1683. According to Mālik, he asked Ibn Shihāb about a man who married a handmaiden who was a chattel slave. He then purchased her, having already divorced her once. Ibn Shihāb said, "She is lawful for him by virtue of his ownership of her, but only because he did not divorce her three times. If he divorces her two more times, then she will no longer be licit for him by virtue of his ownership of her until she marries another man and is divorced or widowed."

1684. Mālik said that if a man marries a handmaiden, and she bears him a child, and then he purchases her, she does not take the status of a handmaiden who bore her master a child (*umm walad*) by virtue of that child, because at the time of the child's birth, she belonged to someone else. She takes the status of a handmaiden who bore her master a child only when she bears him a child while in his ownership after his purchase of her. Mālik said, "If he purchased her while she was pregnant with his child, however, and she delivers the child in his home, then, in our opinion, she takes the status of a handmaiden who bore her master a child as a result of that pregnancy, and God knows best."

Chapter 14. What Has Come Down regarding the Prohibition against a Master Having Intercourse with Two Sisters, or a Mother and Her Daughter, by Virtue of His Ownership of Them

1685. According to Mālik, Ibn Shihāb reported from 'Ubayd Allāh b. 'Abd Allāh b. 'Utba b. Mas'ūd, from his father, that 'Umar b. al-Khaṭṭāb was asked whether a master who owned both a woman and her daughter could have sexual intercourse with both, one after the other. 'Umar said, "I do not like the idea of intercourse with the two of them," and he ordered him not to do that.

1686. According to Mālik, Ibn Shihāb reported from Qabīṣa b. Dhu'ayb that a man asked 'Uthmān b. 'Affān whether a master who owned two sisters could have intercourse with both of them. 'Uthmān said, "One verse of the Quran seems to permit it, and another seems to prohibit it.[698] As for me, I

698 What 'Uthmān b. 'Affān means is that verses in the Quran that permit intercourse with handmaidens do not mention any restriction with respect to sisters. On the other hand, the Quran prohibits a man from marrying two sisters simultaneously.

would not do that." Qabīṣa said, "The man then left ʿUthmān b. ʿAffān and met another Companion of the Messenger of God (pbuh), so he asked him the same question. The Companion said, "If I had anything to say about it, and I came across somebody doing that, I would punish him in an exemplary fashion." Ibn Shihāb said, "I think the Companion in question was ʿAlī b. Abī Ṭālib."

1687. According to Mālik, it reached him from al-Zubayr b. al-ʿAwwām that he was of the same opinion. Mālik said, "If a man owns a handmaiden and has intercourse with her, and then desires to have intercourse with her sister, he may not do so until he renders intercourse with the first sister prohibited to him through marriage (*nikāḥ*), manumission, entering into a manumission contract with her, or the like, or contracts a marriage for her, to his slave or to someone else's slave."

Chapter 15. The Prohibition against Intercourse with a Handmaiden Who Belonged to One's Father

1688. According to Mālik, it reached him that ʿUmar b. al-Khaṭṭāb gifted a handmaiden to his son and said to him, "Do not touch her, for I have seen her nude."[699]

1689. According to Mālik, ʿAbd al-Raḥmān b. al-Mujabbar said, "Sālim b. ʿAbd Allāh gifted a handmaiden to his son but said to him, 'Do not have intercourse with her—for I myself was intent on doing so but failed in my attempt.'"

1690. According to Mālik, Yaḥyā b. Saʿīd reported that Abū Nahshal b. al-Aswad said to al-Qāsim b. Muḥammad, "I saw a handmaiden of mine naked in the moonlight, and I sat with her as a man would sit with his wife, but she told me that she was menstruating. I left, and after that I never drew near her again. If I gift her to my son, may he have intercourse with her?" Al-Qāsim forbade the son from having intercourse with the handmaiden.

1691. According to Mālik, Ibrāhīm b. Abī ʿAbla reported from ʿAbd al-Malik b. Marwān that he gifted a handmaiden to one of his companions. He asked about her sometime later, and the man said, "I have been thinking about giving her as a gift to my son, so that he may enjoy her." ʿAbd al-Malik said, "Marwān was certainly a more pious man than you! He once gifted his son a handmaiden and told him, 'Do not draw near her, for I once saw her bare leg.'"

---

699 "Touch" here stands for intercourse.

Chapter 16. The Prohibition against Marrying (*Nikāḥ*) Handmaidens of the People of the Book (*Ahl al-Kitāb*)

1692. Mālik said, "It is not licit to marry a Jewish or Christian handmaiden, because God, Blessed and Sublime is He, says, 'Chaste believing women and chaste women of the people who were given the Book before you are lawful to marry,'[700] and these are free Jewish and Christian women. And God, Blessed and Sublime is He, says, 'If any of you lack the means to wed free believing women, they may wed believing girls from among those whom your right hands possess,'[701] and these are the believing handmaidens. It is our opinion that God has made licit marriage to handmaidens only if they are believers; He did not make licit marriage to handmaidens of the People of the Book, be they Jewish or Christian. Intercourse with a Jewish or Christian handmaiden, however, is licit for her master by virtue of the right of ownership."

1693. Mālik said, "Intercourse with a Zoroastrian handmaiden is not licit by virtue of the right of ownership."

Chapter 17. What Has Come Down regarding Chastity (*Iḥṣān*)[702]

1694. According to Mālik, Ibn Shihāb reported that Saʿīd b. al-Musayyab said, "The Quranic phrase 'the chaste among the women' refers to women who have husbands, and it is a reference to the fact that God prohibited adultery and fornication."

1695. According to Mālik, Ibn Shihāb reported that it reached him from al-Qāsim b. Muḥammad that they would both say, "If a free man marries a slave woman and consummates the marriage, she makes him, from a legal perspective, 'chaste.'"

1696. Mālik said, "Everyone that I encountered held the view that a free man's marriage to a handmaiden, if consummated, renders him 'chaste.'"

1697. Mālik said, "A male slave renders a free woman 'chaste' if he marries her and has intercourse with her pursuant to a marriage (*nikāḥ*). A male slave, however, is not rendered 'chaste' as a result of his marriage to a free woman unless he is manumitted while married to her and then has intercourse with her. If he divorces her before he is manumitted, however, he does not become 'chaste' until he marries after his manumission and then consummates that marriage."

---

700 *Al-Mā'ida*, 5:5.

701 *Al-Nisā'*, 4:25.

702 The concern about the meaning of the word "chastity" stems from its function in determining the punishment of those who engage in illicit sexual activity, a chaste person being subject to a more severe punishment than one lacking such status.

1698. Mālik said, "If a handmaiden is married to a free man, and he divorces her before she is manumitted, his marriage to her does not render her 'chaste.' She does not become 'chaste' until she marries after her manumission, and then her husband has intercourse with her. That endows her with the status of chastity."

1699. Mālik said, "If a handmaiden is married to a free man, and she is manumitted before he divorces her, he renders her 'chaste,' but only if he has intercourse with her after her manumission."

1700. Mālik said, "The consummated marriage of a free Muslim male to a free Christian or Jewish woman or to a Muslim handmaiden renders him 'chaste.'"

Chapter 18. Temporary Marriage (*Nikāḥ al-Mutʿa*)[703]

1701. According to Mālik, Ibn Shihāb reported from ʿAbd Allāh and al-Ḥasan, the sons of Muḥammad b. ʿAlī b. Abī Ṭālib, from their father, from ʿAlī b. Abī Ṭālib, that on the Day of Khaybar, the Messenger of God (pbuh) prohibited temporary marriages (*nikāḥ al-mutʿa*) and eating the flesh of domesticated donkeys.

1702. According to Mālik, Ibn Shihāb reported from ʿUrwa b. al-Zubayr that Khawla bt. Ḥakīm went to ʿUmar b. al-Khaṭṭāb and told him that Rabīʿa b. Umayya had entered into a temporary marriage with a woman of mixed descent,[704] and she became pregnant. Her words shook ʿUmar b. al-Khaṭṭāb, and he came out dragging his cloak, saying, "This is the temporary marriage that the Prophet (pbuh) forbade. Had I made its prohibition sufficiently well known earlier,[705] I would certainly have had them stoned."

Chapter 19. The Marriage (*Nikāḥ*) of Slaves

1703. According to Mālik, he heard Rabīʿa b. Abī ʿAbd al-Raḥmān say, "A slave may marry four women." Mālik said, "This is the best view I have heard about that matter."

1704. Mālik said, "The case of a slave's marriage is different from that of a man who marries a woman solely for the purpose of allowing her to remarry her previous husband (*muḥallil*). This is because if his master consents to

---

703 A temporary marriage is one that includes the stipulation of a specific date on which the marriage automatically dissolves. According to Sunnīs, this type of marriage is invalid. The Shīʿa, however, consider it valid.

704 In other words, the woman involved in this marriage was the product of a union between an Arab male and a non-Arab female. Such children were known as *muwalladūn* to distinguish them from children born of Arab mothers.

705 See Bājī, *al-Muntaqā*, 3:335.

his marriage (*nikāḥ*), it is valid and the law recognizes it; however, if his master does not consent to his marriage, the slave and his wife must be separated. By contrast, in the case of a man who marries a divorced woman solely for the purpose of allowing her to remarry her previous husband, the couple is separated in all cases, if indeed the sole purpose of the marriage was to allow her to remarry her previous husband."[706]

1705. Mālik said that if a husband or a wife comes to own his or her spouse, the ownership interest of each in his or her spouse, as applicable, results in the automatic dissolution of the marriage. Such a dissolution, however, is not deemed a divorce. Accordingly, if they subsequently remarry, the separation is not counted as one of their three divorces.[707]

1706. Mālik said, "Should a wife who owns her husband manumit him while she is in her waiting period from him, they may not return to one another without a new marriage contract."

Chapter 20. The Marriage (*Nikāḥ*) of a Non-Muslim Wife Who Converts to Islam before Her Husband Does

1707. According to Mālik, Ibn Shihāb reported that it reached him that during the time of the Messenger of God (pbuh) there were women who converted to Islam while still living in their native lands and who did not immigrate to Medina, their husbands still being nonbelievers at the time. One of these women was the daughter of al-Walīd b. Mughīra. She was married to Ṣafwān b. Umayya. She became a Muslim on the day the Muslims returned to Mecca in triumph. Her husband, Ṣafwān b. Umayya, fled that very day as a result of Islam's victory. The Messenger of God (pbuh) then dispatched Ṣafwān's paternal first cousin, Wahb b. ʿUmayr, in pursuit of him. The Messenger of God (pbuh) gave Wahb his cloak to give to Ṣafwān as a token of a grant of safe passage (*amān*). The Messenger of God (pbuh)

706 Mālik's point here is that a slave's marriage, even if it depends on the master's consent for its effectiveness, is valid on its face, whereas a marriage intended to remove the bar from the woman's remarriage to her previous husband is void *ab initio*.

707 This might happen, for example, if the two were both slaves when they first married. The husband is then manumitted, and the enslaved spouse is given to him as a gift, or vice versa. In such a case, because a person may not be married to his or her *own* slave (although it is permissible for a free person to marry the slave of another), the marriage is dissolved. The master is then given the opportunity to manumit the slave and, if he so chooses, to remarry his former spouse. As free people, they may contract their own marriages, whereas as long as they were slaves, their masters contracted their marriages on their behalf. Mālik thus does not assume that they would wish to continue a marriage contracted under conditions of slavery once they are free. At the same time, however, the dissolution of the marriage is not held against them in the event that they in fact wish to be married as free persons. Accordingly, Mālik does not count the dissolution as one of the three divorces that are incident to a freely contracted marriage.

called on Ṣafwān to embrace Islam and to join him in Medina. If that were agreeable to him, the Messenger of God (pbuh) would accept him among the ranks of the Muslims; otherwise, the Messenger of God (pbuh) would grant him a two-month respite. When Ṣafwān came to the Messenger of God (pbuh) bearing his cloak, he called out to the Messenger of God (pbuh), crying over the heads of the people, "Muḥammad! This ambassador of yours, Wahb b. ʿUmayr, came to me with your cloak, and he said that you called on me to join you, and if that were agreeable to me, I could accept it, and if not, you would grant me a two-month respite." The Messenger of God (pbuh) said, "Come down and join us, Abū Wahb!" He said, "By God, I shall not join you until you clarify some things for me." The Messenger of God (pbuh) said, "Certainly! The respite I have granted you is now for four months." The Messenger of God (pbuh) then set out toward the Hawāzin[708] at Ḥunayn.[709] He dispatched a messenger to Ṣafwān, with instructions to borrow from him arms and equipment. Ṣafwān asked, "Am I free to refuse?" The messenger replied, "Of course you are free to refuse!" Ṣafwān therefore agreed to lend out the arms and equipment that were in his possession, and then he set out with the Messenger of God (pbuh) to the battle, even though he was still a nonbeliever. Ṣafwān fought at Ḥunayn and the siege of Ṭāʾif[710] while still a nonbeliever. Although his wife was a Muslim, the Messenger of God (pbuh) never separated the two. Ṣafwān later embraced Islam, and his marriage to his wife remained intact throughout.

1708. According to Mālik, Ibn Shihāb said, "No more than one month elapsed between Ṣafwān's wife's embrace of Islam and his own. We are not aware of any case involving a woman who immigrated to Medina for the sake of God and His Messenger (pbuh) while her husband remained a nonbeliever dwelling in the land of unbelief that did not conclude in a divorce. The only exception to this rule was if the nonbelieving husband embraced Islam, immigrated to Medina after his wife, and arrived before her waiting period (*ʿidda*) had expired."

1709. According to Mālik, Ibn Shihāb reported that Umm Ḥakīm bt. al-Ḥārith b. Hishām was married to ʿIkrima b. Abī Jahl. She embraced Islam on the day the Muslims returned to Mecca in triumph. Her husband ʿIkrima fled that very day as a result of Islam's victory, taking refuge in Yemen. Umm Ḥakīm set out after him, finally catching up with him there, and she urged him to embrace Islam, so he did. He went to the Messenger of God (pbuh)

---

708 A tribal federation in the Hijaz that continued to resist the Prophet (pbuh) even after Mecca fell.

709 A valley in the vicinity of Mecca where the Prophet (pbuh) and the Muslims met a large army of the Hawāzin and its allies and, despite initial reversals, ended up securing a decisive victory against them.

710 A leading city of the Hijaz controlled by the tribe of Thaqīf.

in that same year. When the Messenger of God (pbuh) saw ʿIkrima, he welcomed him warmly, going out to greet him without even first bothering to put on his cloak. ʿIkrima shortly thereafter pledged his loyalty to him. The marriage of ʿIkrima and Umm Ḥakīm continued without interruption.

1710. Mālik said, "When a man embraces Islam before his wife does, his wife is asked whether she would like to convert as well. If she refuses, divorce takes place between the two, because God, Blessed and Sublime is He, says in His Book, 'But hold not to the marriage bonds of unbelieving women.'"[711]

Chapter 21. What Has Come Down regarding the Wedding Feast (*Walīma*)

1711. According to Mālik, Ḥumayd al-Ṭawīl reported from Anas b. Mālik that ʿAbd al-Raḥmān b. ʿAwf came to the Messenger of God (pbuh) with traces of saffron on him. The Messenger of God (pbuh) asked him about that, so he told him that he had just married. The Messenger of God (pbuh) asked him, "How much of a dower did you give her?" ʿAbd al-Raḥmān answered, "The weight of five dirhams in gold."[712] The Messenger of God then said, "Host a wedding feast, even if it consists of only a single yearling (*shāt*)!"

1712. According to Mālik, Yaḥyā b. Saʿīd said, "It reached me that the Messenger of God (pbuh) hosted wedding feasts that were so modest that neither bread nor meat was served."

1713. According to Mālik, Nāfiʿ reported from ʿAbd Allāh b. ʿUmar that the Messenger of God (pbuh) said, "Anyone invited to a wedding feast ought to attend."

1714. According to Mālik, Ibn Shihāb reported from al-Aʿraj that Abū Hurayra would say, "The vilest food is that of a wedding feast to which the rich are invited but from which the poor are excluded. Anyone who refuses to attend a wedding feast has disobeyed God and His Messenger."

1715. According to Mālik, Isḥāq b. ʿAbd Allāh b. Abī Ṭalḥa reported that he heard Anas b. Mālik say, "A tailor once invited the Messenger of God (pbuh) to partake in some food that he had prepared. I went with the Messenger of God (pbuh) to share in that food. The tailor offered him some soup with pumpkin in it, along with barley bread. I watched the Messenger of God

---

711 *Al-Mumtaḥana*, 50:10.

712 The Arabic text states that he gave her a date pit's (*nawāt*) weight worth of gold. Commentators suggest that this is the equivalent in weight of five dirhams. See Muḥammad b. ʿAbd al-Ḥaqq al-Yafuranī, *al-Iqtiḍāb fī gharīb al-Muwaṭṭa' wa-iʿrābihi ʿalā al-abwāb* (Riyadh: Maktabat al-ʿUbaykān, 2001), 2:114.

(pbuh) pluck out and eat the chunks of pumpkin from the bowl. Ever since that day, I have loved pumpkin."

Chapter 22. Miscellaneous Reports about Marriage (*Nikāḥ*)

1716. According to Mālik, Zayd b. Aslam reported that the Messenger of God (pbuh) said, "When someone marries a free woman or acquires a handmaiden, he should take her by the forelock and make an invocation, seeking God's blessings. And when he purchases a camel, let him grab the top of its hump and seek refuge with God from Satan."

1717. According to Mālik, Abū al-Zubayr al-Makkī reported that a suitor came to a man and mentioned that he desired to marry that man's sister. The man then told the suitor that she had committed fornication. Word of that conversation reached ʿUmar b. al-Khaṭṭāb. He struck the man, or was on the verge of doing so, saying to him, "What business is that of yours, such that you would reveal it to the suitor?"

1718. According to Mālik, Rabīʿa b. Abī ʿAbd al-Raḥmān reported that al-Qāsim b. Muḥammad and ʿUrwa b. al-Zubayr would say, regarding a man who had four wives and divorced one of them three times, that he could, if he wished, marry again without first waiting for the divorced wife to complete her waiting period (*ʿidda*).[713]

1719. According to Mālik, Rabīʿa b. Abī ʿAbd al-Raḥmān reported that al-Qāsim b. Muḥammad and ʿUrwa b. al-Zubayr gave that opinion to al-Walīd b. ʿAbd al-Malik b. Marwān[714] the year he came to Medina. Al-Qāsim b. Muḥammad told Rabīʿa, however, that al-Walīd had divorced his wife on three separate occasions, not all at once.

1720. According to Mālik, Yaḥyā b. Saʿīd reported that Saʿīd b. al-Musayyab said, "One cannot claim jest with respect to three things: marriage (*nikāḥ*), divorce (*ṭalāq*), and manumission (*ʿitq*)."

1721. According to Mālik, Ibn Shihāb reported from Rāfiʿ b. Khadīj that he married the daughter of Muḥammad b. Maslama al-Anṣārī. She remained with him until she grew old. He then married a younger woman, and he preferred her over his first wife. His first wife therefore asked him to divorce her. He divorced her once, but then, when her waiting period had nearly concluded, he revoked the divorce and resumed marital relations with her. However, his favoritism for the younger wife remained, so she again asked

713 This is because he divorced her three times and thus may not take her back as a wife. Because he cannot revoke the divorce during her waiting period, he is free to marry a fourth woman.

714 An Umayyad caliph who reigned from 86 to 96 of the Hijra (705–715 CE).

him for a divorce. He divorced her a second time, but again he revoked the divorce and resumed marital relations with her. But still his favoritism for the younger wife remained, so his first wife again asked for a divorce. This time, however, he said, "As you wish, but only one divorce remains. If you wish, you may stay and resign yourself to the fact that I prefer her to you; or if you wish, I will divorce you a third and final time and separate from you permanently." She said, "No; I would rather stay, despite your preference for her." Accordingly, he remained married to her in that state of affairs. Rāfiʿ did not believe that he had committed a sin by keeping his first wife, despite his preference for the second.

The Book of Marriage (*Nikāḥ*) Has Been Completed, with Praise to God, the Lord of the Worlds.

Book 32
The Book of Divorce (*Ṭalāq*)

In the Name of God, the Merciful, the Compassionate

May God Grace Muḥammad and His Family
and Grant Them Perfect Tranquility.

Chapter 1. What Has Come Down regarding the Absolute Declaration of Divorce (*Batta*)[715]

1722. According to Mālik, it reached him that a man said to ʿAbd Allāh b. ʿAbbās, "I divorced my wife one hundred times. Am I bound to do anything else as a consequence?" Ibn ʿAbbās said to him, "Your wife was divorced from you absolutely by virtue of the first three divorces you uttered; the rest were mere blasphemy."

1723. According to Mālik, it reached him that a man went to ʿAbd Allāh b. Masʿūd and said, "I divorced my wife eight times." Ibn Masʿūd said, "And what were you told was the consequence?" The man said, "I was told that she has now parted from me." Ibn Masʿūd said, "Whoever said that to you spoke truthfully. God has clarified the proper manner of divorce for whoever wishes to enact one. As for someone who follows an ambiguous path, we bind him to what he says. Do not make things ambiguous for yourselves and then expect us to relieve you of your burden. The outcome of such statements shall be in accordance with precisely what you say."[716]

1724. According to Mālik, Yaḥyā b. Saʿīd reported from Abū Bakr b. Ḥazm that ʿUmar b. ʿAbd al-ʿAzīz said, "How do people construe the absolute

---

715 *Batta* literally means "absolute." In the context of divorce, it refers to an absolute declaration of divorce after which the man may not remarry the woman until she has married and consummated a marriage with another man and then been divorced or widowed from him.

716 ʿAbd Allāh b. Masʿūd is contrasting the clear procedure outlined in the Quran for a lawful divorce whose rules are clear with unlawful expressions of divorce, such as those mentioned in reports 1723 and 1724, whose consequences are unclear. According to ʿAbd Allāh b. Masʿūd, in such circumstances the man should be bound by what he has said as a deterrent against deviating from the clear rules provided by God to govern such situations.

declaration of divorce?" I (Abū Bakr) said to him, "Abān b. ʿUthmān deemed it to count only as one divorce." ʿUmar b. ʿAbd al-ʿAzīz then said, "Were divorce to be final only after one thousand declarations of divorce, an absolute declaration of divorce would have exhausted them all immediately. Whoever uses an absolute declaration of divorce has struck the target lying at the furthest limit."

1725. According to Mālik, Ibn Shihāb reported that Marwān b. al-Ḥakam would rule that when a man divorces his wife using an absolute declaration of divorce, it constitutes a triple divorce. Mālik said, "Of all the views that I have heard with respect to that issue, this view is the one I prefer most."

Chapter 2. What Has Come Down regarding *Khaliyya, Bariyya,*[717] and Similar Expressions

1726. According to Mālik, it reached him that ʿUmar b. al-Khaṭṭāb received an inquiry from Iraq about a man who said to his wife, "Your rope is on your back."[718] ʿUmar b. al-Khaṭṭāb wrote back to his governor, directing him to order the man to meet ʿUmar in Mecca during the upcoming Pilgrimage (*ḥajj*) season. While ʿUmar was circumambulating God's House, the man met him and greeted him. ʿUmar then asked him, "Who are you?" The man said, "I am the one who was ordered to appear before you." ʿUmar said to him, "Tell me, by the Lord of this structure, what did you mean when you said, 'Your rope is on your back'?" The man said to ʿUmar, "Had you asked me to swear in any place other than this one, I would not have spoken truthfully. What I intended by that expression was to leave my wife." ʿUmar b. al-Khaṭṭāb said, "In that case, you shall receive what you intended."

1727. According to Mālik, it reached him that ʿAlī b. Abī Ṭalib would say about a man who said to his wife, "You are forbidden to me," that this meant three divorces had taken place. Mālik said, "This is the best view that I have heard about that matter."

1728. According to Mālik, Nāfiʿ reported that ʿAbd Allāh b. ʿUmar would say about the expressions *khaliyya* and *bariyya* that each of them is tantamount to three divorces.

1729. According to Mālik, Yaḥyā b. Saʿīd reported from al-Qāsim b. Muḥammad that a man was married to a certain tribe's handmaiden. One

717 Both are euphemisms for divorce.

718 The Arabic expression is *ḥabluki ʿalā ghāribik*. In saying this, the man is comparing his wife to a beast of burden, which is ordinarily kept under the direction of its owner by the owner holding its rope. By saying that her rope is on her back, the speaker is saying that she is free to go wherever she wishes and is no longer under his control as her husband.

day, he said to her people, "Do with her as you wish." Everyone understood this to be tantamount to a divorce.

1730. According to Mālik, he heard Ibn Shihāb say, regarding a man who says to his wife, "You owe me nothing, and I owe you nothing," that this is tantamount to three divorces and is the equivalent of an absolute declaration of divorce (*batta*).

1731. Mālik said, regarding a man who says to his wife, "You are *khaliyya*, or *bariyya*, or *bā'ina*," "Each of these expressions is tantamount to three divorces of the wife if he has brought her to the marital home. As for the bride who has yet to enter the marital home, it is left to the man's conscience to specify whether he intended one or three divorces. If he says he intended one divorce, he must swear an oath corroborating that, after which he is merely one of the woman's prospective suitors. This is because if the husband has brought the woman to the marital home, nothing except three divorces can release her from the bond of marriage. A single divorce, however, is sufficient to release a bride from the bond of marriage if her husband never brought her to the marital home. This is the best view that I have heard about that matter."

Chapter 3. What Kind of Delegation of Authority to Divorce (*Tamlīk*)[719] Is Effective in Dissolving the Marriage Bond

1732. According to Mālik, it reached him that a man went to ʿAbd Allāh b. ʿUmar and said, "Abū ʿAbd al-Raḥmān! I delegated to my wife the power to divorce herself, and then she did. What do you think is the result?" Ibn ʿUmar said, "I believe that the matter is as she decided." The man said, "Don't say that, Abū ʿAbd al-Raḥmān!" Ibn ʿUmar said, "Me? You are the one who is responsible!"

1733. According to Mālik, Nāfiʿ reported that ʿAbd Allāh b. ʿUmar would say, "When a man delegates to his wife authority to divorce herself, the judge must give effect to her decision. The only exception to this is if the husband denies having given her absolute authority of divorce and says, 'I intended to grant her the power to effect only one divorce.' If he swears an oath corroborating that claim, he is entitled to reclaim her as his wife, as long as she is in her waiting period (*ʿidda*)."

719 This refers to a formula in which the husband delegates to his wife the power to divorce herself from him.

Chapter 4. Delegations of Authority to Divorce (*Tamlīk*) That Result in Only One Divorce

1734. According to Mālik, Saʿīd b. Sulaymān b. Zayd b. Thābit reported that Khārija b. Zayd b. Thābit informed him that he was sitting with Zayd b. Thābit when Muḥammad b. Abī ʿAtīq came to him with tears in his eyes. Zayd said to him, "What's wrong with you?" He said, "I delegated to my wife authority to divorce herself (*tamlīk*), so she did and left me." Zayd said to him, "And what made you do that?" He said, "Fate!" Zayd then said to him, "You may reclaim her as your wife, if you wish, for that was only one divorce. Your right to reclaim her is stronger than her right to leave you."

1735. According to Mālik, ʿAbd al-Raḥmān b. al-Qāsim reported from his father that a man from the tribe of Thaqīf delegated to his wife authority to divorce herself. She then said, "You are utterly divorced!" He was silent, and she repeated, "You are utterly divorced!" He then said, "Shut your mouth!" She then repeated, "You are utterly divorced!" He again said, "Shut your mouth!" They took their dispute to Marwān b. al-Ḥakam, who asked the man to swear that he had delegated to her the power to effect only one divorce. When the husband did so, Marwān ordered her to return to her husband. Mālik said, "ʿAbd al-Raḥmān said, 'This judgment satisfied al-Qāsim, and he considered it to be the best view that he had heard about that matter.' This is the best view I have heard about that issue, and it is the view I prefer most."

Chapter 5. Delegations of Authority to Divorce (*Tamlīk*) That Do Not Dissolve the Marriage Bond

1736. According to Mālik, ʿAbd al-Raḥmān b. al-Qāsim reported from his father, from ʿĀʾisha, the Mother of the Believers, that she approached the family of Qarība bt. Abī Umayya to arrange her marriage to ʿAbd al-Raḥmān b. Abī Bakr. They agreed to give her to him in marriage. Her family subsequently found reason to object to ʿAbd al-Raḥmān, saying, "We accepted this marriage only for the sake of ʿĀʾisha." ʿĀʾisha then sent for ʿAbd al-Raḥmān and informed him about his in-laws' objections to him. He therefore decided to give Qarība the choice of whether to stay with him or to leave, and she chose to stay with her husband. That delegation was not deemed a divorce (*ṭalāq*).[720]

720 What this report makes clear is that the mere decision by a husband to delegate to his wife the power to effect a divorce does not constitute a divorce. Only when the wife actually exercises the power delegated to her does a divorce take place. In this case, because Qarība declined to exercise the power of divorce ʿAbd al-Raḥmān granted her, no divorce was deemed to have taken place.

1737. According to Mālik, ʿAbd al-Raḥmān b. al-Qāsim reported from his father that ʿĀʾisha, the wife of the Prophet (pbuh), arranged the marriage of Ḥafṣa bt. ʿAbd al-Raḥmān to al-Mundhir b. al-Zubayr while ʿAbd al-Raḥmān was away in the Levant. When ʿAbd al-Raḥmān returned, he said, "Is something like this done to someone like me? Is the authority of someone like me transgressed so lightly?" ʿĀʾisha therefore spoke to al-Mundhir b. al-Zubayr, and he said, "I will place the matter in ʿAbd al-Raḥmān's hands to do as he wishes." ʿAbd al-Raḥmān said, "I am not one who would repeal something that you, ʿĀʾisha, have decided." Ḥafṣa, therefore, stayed with al-Mundhir, and that delegation was not deemed a divorce.

1738. According to Mālik, it reached him that ʿAbd Allāh b. ʿUmar and Abū Hurayra were both asked about a man who delegated to his wife authority to divorce herself, and she declined to do so. They both said, "Delegation of that authority is not in itself a divorce."

1739. According to Mālik, Yaḥyā b. Saʿīd reported that Saʿīd b. al-Musayyab said, "When a man delegates to his wife authority to divorce herself, and she chooses to stay with him and not to leave him, that delegation is not tantamount to a divorce."

1740. Mālik said, regarding a woman to whom her husband has delegated authority to divorce herself, "When her husband delegates to her authority to divorce herself and then they go their separate ways, without her having exercised that power in the least, nothing remains of the authority. It lasts only for so long as they are present together in the place where it was given to her."[721]

Chapter 6. Oaths of Abstinence from Sexual Relations with One's Wife (*Īlāʾ*)

1741. According to Mālik, Jaʿfar b. Muḥammad reported from his father that ʿAlī b. Abī Ṭālib would say, "When a man swears an oath of abstinence from sexual relations with his wife, no immediate divorce (*ṭalāq*) takes place. When four months have elapsed from the time he made his oath, however, he is brought before a judge and is ordered either to divorce his wife or to revoke his oath." Mālik said, "That is the rule among us (*dhālika al-amr ʿindanā*)."

1742. According to Mālik, Nāfiʿ reported that ʿAbd Allāh b. ʿUmar would say, "Should a man swear an oath to abstain from sexual relations with his wife,

721 In other words, when the husband delegates to the wife authority to divorce herself, she must exercise that authority in the meeting in which he grants her that authority. Once the meeting comes to an end and they separate, her authority to divorce herself lapses.

and should four months elapse from that date, he is brought before a judge, at which time he must either divorce her or revoke his oath. Divorce does not take effect immediately after four months have elapsed from the time of his oath. He must first be brought before a judge."

1743. According to Mālik, Ibn Shihāb reported that Sa'īd b. al-Musayyab and Abū Bakr b. 'Abd al-Raḥmān would both say about a man who swears an oath to abstain from sexual relations with his wife, "If four months have elapsed from the time of the oath, one divorce takes place. He can, however, retract it and reclaim her as his wife as long as she is still in her waiting period (*'idda*)."

1744. According to Mālik, it reached him that in cases involving a man who swore an oath to abstain from sexual relations with his wife, Marwān b. al-Ḥakam would rule that if four months had elapsed from the time of the oath, one divorce took place. The husband, however, could retract it and reclaim her as his wife as long as she was still in her waiting period. Mālik said, "Ibn Shihāb's opinion was in accordance with that."

1745. Mālik said, "If a man swears an oath to abstain from sexual relations with his wife, four months pass, he is brought before a judge and divorces her but then revokes the divorce and reclaims her as his wife, but he still refuses to have sexual relations with her prior to the expiration of her waiting period, he loses his right to reclaim her as his wife, unless he has an excuse for not resuming sexual relations with his wife, such as illness, imprisonment, or a similar reason. If he does have an excuse, she continues to be subject to his right to reclaim her as his wife. If her waiting period has come to an end, however, and he remarries her but again fails to have sexual relations with her until another four months have passed, is again brought before a judge, and refuses to revoke his oath, in this case divorce takes place immediately upon the conclusion of the four months by virtue of the first oath of abstention from sexual relations. This is because he has no right to reclaim her as his wife the second time because he married her and then divorced her without ever consummating the marriage. Accordingly, she has no obligation to observe a waiting period for his benefit, and he has no right to reclaim her as his wife."

1746. Mālik said, regarding a scenario in which a man swears an oath to abstain from sexual relations with his wife, is brought before a judge after four months have passed, divorces her, and then reclaims her as his wife but does not resume sexual relations with her for another four months, and she is still in her waiting period from the first divorce:[722] "He is not brought before

722 Mālik is here speaking of a woman with an irregular period that lasts more than a month. In the ordinary case, the waiting period of a woman who is divorced as a consequence of a

a judge a second time, and no additional divorce is deemed to have occurred. If he manages to have sexual relations with her before her waiting period expires, he is entitled to remain married to her; however, if her waiting period comes to an end before he has sexual relations with her, he has no right to reclaim her. This is the best view that I have heard about that issue."

1747. Mālik said, regarding a man who swears an oath to abstain from sexual relations with his wife and then divorces her, with the four-month waiting period after the oath elapsing before the expiration of his wife's waiting period from the divorce, "If he was brought before a judge and did not revoke his oath, two divorces are deemed to result. But if the waiting period for the divorce ended before the four months of his oath elapsed, his oath is not deemed to constitute a divorce. That is because the four-month term whose expiration would have required that he be brought before a judge ended at a time when she was no longer married to him."

1748. Mālik said, "An oath in which a man swears to abstain from sexual relations with his wife for a day or a month, even if he then actually abstains for more than four months, is not the kind of oath that leads to divorce. The rule that a man must be brought before a judge in the case of an oath to abstain from sexual relations with his wife applies only when the term of that oath is more than four months. I do not believe that a man who swears an oath to abstain from sexual relations with his wife for four months or less has made the kind of oath that can lead to a divorce. This is because when the time comes for him to be brought before a judge, his oath has come to an end. He is thus not subject to the judge's jurisdiction."

1749. Mālik said, "A man who swears an oath to abstain from sexual relations with his wife until she has weaned her newborn child has not sworn the kind of oath that could result in a divorce."[723]

---

husband's oath to abstain from sexual intercourse is shorter than the four-month waiting period granted to the husband to retract the oath. In this case, however, because the woman's period is longer than a month, there is a a conflict between the husband's right to reclaim her as his wife and his obligation to divorce for failure to have intercourse with her for a period of four months. Mālik resolves this conflict by giving greater priority to the husband's right to reclaim his wife until her waiting period expires by not treating the husband's second failure to have intercourse with his wife as resulting in a second divorce.

723 The reason such an oath is excluded from the general rule governing oaths to refrain from sexual relations with a wife is the assumption that the husband swears the oath to prevent the possibility that the newborn's mother could become pregnant while still nursing the infant, which would end her ability to breastfeed the newborn, thereby injuring the child. Therefore, such an oath is understood to be motivated by the desire to preserve the health of the newborn, not by a desire to harm the wife by depriving her of sexual relations.

1750. Mālik said, "It reached me that ʿAlī b. Abī Ṭālib was asked about that kind of oath,[724] and he did not consider it to be the kind of oath that could result in a divorce."

Chapter 7. Oaths of Abstinence from Sexual Relations (*Īlāʾ*) Made by Slaves

1751. According to Mālik, he asked Ibn Shihāb about slaves who swear oaths to abstain from sexual relations with their wives. Ibn Shihāb said, "A rule similar to that for free men applies to them. The slave is legally responsible for his oath, but its term is only two months, after which he is brought before a judge, at which point he must either divorce his wife or revoke his oath."

Chapter 8. A Free Man Who Compares His Wife to the Back of His Mother (*Ẓihār*)[725]

1752. According to Mālik, Saʿīd b. ʿAmr b. Sulaym al-Zuraqī reported that he asked al-Qāsim b. Muḥammad about a man who swore an oath that if he should marry such-and-such a woman, she would be divorced.[726] Saʿīd said, "Al-Qāsim b. Muḥammad said, 'There was once a man who said that such-and-such a woman, should he ever marry her, would be like his mother's back to him. ʿUmar b. al-Khaṭṭāb ordered him not to go near her, if he did marry her, without first completing the penance required of a man who compares his wife to his mother's back.'"

1753. According to Mālik, it reached him that a man asked both al-Qāsim b. Muḥammad and Sulaymān b. Yasār about a man who had compared a woman to his mother's back before marrying her. They said, "If he does marry her, he may not go near her until he completes the penance that is obligatory for a man who compares his wife to his mother's back."

1754. According to Mālik, Hishām b. ʿUrwa reported that his father said, regarding a man who, in one statement, compared all four of his wives to his mother, that he was obliged to perform only one act of penance.

---

724 Mālik is here referring to the previous case, no. 1749.

725 A reference to the pre-Islamic practice of a man saying to his wife, "You are to me as my mother's back," a euphemism for saying that sexual relations with her are forbidden to him, just as sexual relations with his mother would be. The Quran condemned this practice, requiring men who utter it to manumit a slave or, if they are unable to do so, either to fast for two consecutive months or to feed sixty indigent persons before they can resume marital relations with their wives. *Al-Mujādila*, 58:2–4.

726 This is known as a conditional divorce, or a "suspended" divorce, in the sense that divorce takes place only upon the fulfillment of an external condition that is specified in the oath. In this case, the condition that would make the divorce effective is the very marriage itself. Such an oath has the effect of precluding the woman from being a potential wife.

1755. According to Mālik, Rabīʿa b. Abī ʿAbd al-Raḥmān reported something similar. Mālik said, "The rule among us is in accordance with that (*ʿalā dhālika al-amr ʿindanā*). God, Blessed and Sublime is He, says regarding the penance of a man who compares his wife to the back of his mother, 'A slave must be manumitted before they may touch one another. . . . But whoever is unable to manumit a slave must fast two consecutive months before they may touch one another. If he is unable to fast two consecutive months, he must instead feed sixty indigent persons.'"[727]

1756. Mālik said, regarding a man who compares his wife to the back of his mother on several different occasions, "He is obliged to perform only one act of penance. Had he compared his wife to the back of his mother once, then performed penance for it, and then done it again, however, he would need to perform a second act of penance."

1757. Mālik said, "Whoever compares his wife to the back of his mother and then has sexual relations with her before performing penance is obliged to perform only one act of penance. He must, however, refrain from further sexual relations with her until he completes his penance, and he must ask for God's forgiveness. This is the best view that I have heard."

1758. Mālik said, "The same rule applies if the husband compares his wife to the back of any of person whom he is not permitted to marry, whether on account of descent or of suckling."[728]

1759. Mālik said, "Were a woman to compare her husband to a man whom she is forbidden to marry, she would not be obliged to perform penance."

1760. Mālik said, regarding the words of God, Blessed and Sublime is He, "Those who compare their wives to the backs of their mothers but then wish to revoke their words,"[729] "I heard that this applies to a man who compares his wife to his mother's back but nevertheless resolves to remain married to her and to continue to have sexual relations with her. If he has so resolved, penance becomes obligatory for him. If he divorces her, however, and does not resolve, after comparing her to his mother, to remain married to her and to continue having sexual relations with her, he is under no obligation to perform penance. But if he subsequently remarries her, he may not touch her until he has performed the penance due of a man who compares his wife to his mother."

---

727 *Al-Mujādila*, 58:2–4.

728 The latter category refers to a foster sister who nursed from the same breast as the man or the foster mother who nursed him. In Islamic law, children who nurse from the same woman are deemed foster siblings and may not marry one another. The nursing woman is deemed the nursing child's foster mother and therefore ineligible for marriage with him.

729 *Al-Mujādila*, 58:3.

1761. Mālik said, regarding a man who compares his handmaiden to his mother, "If he subsequently wishes to have sexual relations with her, he is under an obligation to perform the penance due of a man who compares his wife to his mother."

1762. Mālik said, "A man who has compared his wife to his mother's back is not deemed to have sworn an oath to refrain from sexual relations with his wife (*īlā'*), unless he did so maliciously and has no intention of revoking his statement."

1763. According to Mālik, Hishām b. 'Urwa reported that he had heard someone ask 'Urwa b. al-Zubayr about a man who said to his wife, "Any woman I marry alongside you, as long as you live, shall be like my mother's back to me." 'Urwa b. al-Zubayr said, "Manumitting a slave absolves him of that oath."

Chapter 9. Slaves Who Compare Their Wives to the Backs of Their Mothers (*Ẓihār*)

1764. According to Mālik, he asked Ibn Shihāb about a slave who compares his wife to his mother's back. Ibn Shihāb said, "His case is similar to that of a free man." Mālik said, "He means that the rule applies to him just as it applies to a free man."

1765. Mālik said, "A slave is bound to perform penance when he compares his wife to his mother's back, and the slave's fast of penance is two months."

1766. Mālik said, regarding a slave who compares his wife to his mother's back, "He is not deemed to have sworn an oath to refrain from sexual relations with his wife (*īlā'*). This is because he would not complete the obligatory fast of penance before he would be required to divorce his wife had he sworn an oath to refrain from sexual relations with her."[730]

730 Mālik explains that when a slave swears an oath to refrain from sexual relations with his wife, he has two months in which to either revoke the oath and resume sexual relations with her or divorce her; but if he compares her to his mother's back, he is prohibited from having sexual relations with her until he completes the obligatory fast of penance. Therefore, it would be impossible for him to comply with the rule governing oaths to refrain from sexual relations with a wife *and* the rule of penance for comparing his wife to his mother's back. By contrast, a free man is given four months, not two, to revoke his oath to refrain from sexual relations with his wife or to divorce her. Consequently, a free man can complete his obligatory penance by fasting two consecutive months and then still have two months to decide whether to revoke his oath or divorce his wife.

Chapter 10. What Has Come Down regarding an Option to Divorce (*Khiyār*)

1767. According to Mālik, Rabīʿa b. Abī ʿAbd al-Raḥmān reported from al-Qāsim b. Muḥammad that ʿĀʾisha, the Mother of the Believers, said, "Three laws were made on account of Barīra.[731] The first was that when she was manumitted, she was given a choice whether to remain married to her husband.[732] The second was that the Messenger of God (pbuh) said with respect to her manumission, 'The right of patronage (*walāʾ*) belongs to the one who manumits the slave.' The third was when the Messenger of God (pbuh) came home one day and found a pot of meat boiling. Bread and condiments were brought to him out of the house's provisions, but no meat. The Messenger of God (pbuh) said, 'Didn't I see a pot full of boiling meat?' They said, 'Yes, indeed, Messenger of God, but that meat was already intended to be given to Barīra as charity, and you don't accept charity.' The Messenger of God (pbuh) said, 'It is charity for her, but a gift to us.'"

1768. According to Mālik, Nāfiʿ reported that ʿAbd Allāh b. ʿUmar would say, regarding a handmaiden who is manumitted while still married to a slave, that she is given the choice to leave him. That option endures until she allows him to have sexual relations with her.

1769. Mālik said, "If her husband has sexual relations with her, but she says that she did not know that she had the right to leave him, her statement is viewed with suspicion, and her claim of ignorance is not credited. Therefore, her option to leave him lapses after she allows him to have sexual relations with her."[733]

1770. According to Mālik, Ibn Shihāb reported from ʿUrwa b. al-Zubayr that a freedwoman (*mawlāt*) of the tribe of Banū ʿAdī named Zabrāʾ informed him that when she was still a handmaiden, she had been given in marriage to another slave. Later, she was manumitted. She said, "Ḥafṣa, the wife of the Prophet (pbuh), sent for me. She called me over and said, 'Listen, I will be giving you some important news, but I do not want you to act on it hastily. You now have the authority to divorce yourself. You will continue to enjoy this authority until you allow your husband to have sexual relations with you. Once he does, however, your authority to divorce yourself will lapse.' I said, 'In that case, it is divorce, then divorce, and then divorce.'" She therefore divorced herself from him three times.

---

731 A freedwoman of ʿĀʾisha.

732 Prior to her manumission, she had been married to a slave named Mughīth.

733 If, on the other hand, she claims ignorance of the fact that she had been manumitted, she retains the option to leave her slave husband, even if she had allowed him to have sexual relations with her after her manumission. Bājī, *al-Muntaqā*, 4:57.

1771. According to Mālik, it reached him that Saʿīd b. al-Musayyab said, "If a man marries a woman, and he suffers from madness or a contagious condition, she may stay with him or leave him, as she wishes."

1772. Yaḥyā said, "Mālik said, 'If a handmaiden is married to a slave and then is manumitted before the husband takes her to the marital home or before they consummate the marriage, and she chooses to leave him, she receives none of her dower. The divorce is deemed to constitute only one divorce. That is the rule among us (*dhālika al-amr ʿindanā*).'"

1773. According to Mālik, he heard Ibn Shihāb say, "If a man gives his wife the choice to stay with him or to leave him, and she chooses to stay with him, it is not deemed to be a divorce." Mālik said, "That is the best view that I have heard."

1774. Mālik said, regarding a woman whose husband gives her the choice of staying with him or leaving him, "If she chooses to leave him, she is deemed to have been divorced three times. If her husband were to say, 'I only gave you authority to exercise one divorce,' he would be told that such a limitation is not permissible. That is the best view that I have heard."

1775. Mālik said, "If he gives her the right to choose whether to stay with him or to leave him, and she says, 'I accept one divorce,' and he says, 'I did not intend that; rather, I only gave you the option to leave me absolutely and irrevocably,' but she insists on accepting only one divorce and continues dwelling with him, that does not count as a divorce."

Chapter 11. What Has Come Down regarding Divorce Effected by the Wife's Payment of Property to the Husband (*Khulʿ*)

1776. According to Mālik, Yaḥyā b. Saʿīd reported that ʿAmra bt. ʿAbd al-Raḥmān informed him from Ḥabība bt. Sahl al-Anṣārī that she was married to Thābit b. Qays b. Shammās. One morning, the Messenger of God (pbuh) set out to perform the Morning Prayer (*ṣalāt al-ṣubḥ*) only to find Ḥabība bt. Sahl standing at his door in the darkness. The Messenger of God (pbuh) said, "Who is there?" She said, "Messenger of God, I am Ḥabība bt. Sahl." He said, "What's wrong?" She said, "Neither am I fit to be a wife for Thābit b. Qays, nor is he fit to be a husband for me." When her husband, Thābit b. Qays, later showed up, the Messenger of God (pbuh) said, "Here stands Ḥabība bt. Sahl, and she has already said her piece." Ḥabība then said, "Messenger of God, everything that he has given me is still with me." The Messenger of God (pbuh) said to Thābit b. Qays, "Take it all back from her," and so he did. She then returned to live with her family.

1777. According to Mālik, Nāfiʿ reported from a freedwoman (*mawlāt*) of Ṣafiyya bt. Abī ʿUbayd that she gave everything she owned to her husband in exchange for a divorce. ʿAbd Allāh b. ʿUmar did not find that to be objectionable.

1778. Yaḥyā said, "Mālik said, regarding a woman who gives her husband property in exchange for a divorce, 'If it later comes to be known that her husband caused her injury, made her life miserable, and treated her unfairly, the divorce is upheld and he must return her property to her. This is what I would hear, and it is what is in accordance with the rule of our people (*alladhī ʿalayhi amr al-nās ʿindanā*).'"

1779. Mālik said, "There is nothing objectionable in a woman giving to her husband more than he gave her in order to remove herself from the marriage."

Chapter 12. The Divorce (*Ṭalāq*) of a Woman Who Has Given Property to Her Husband in Exchange for a Divorce (*Mukhtaliʿa*)

1780. According to Mālik, Nāfiʿ reported that Rubayyiʿ bt. Muʿawwidh b. ʿAfrāʾ and her paternal aunt (*ʿamma*) went to ʿAbd Allāh b. ʿUmar, and she informed him that she had removed herself from her marriage by giving her husband some property during the term of ʿUthmān b. ʿAffān. News of this had reached ʿUthmān b. ʿAffān, and he had not objected. ʿAbd Allāh b. ʿUmar said, "Her waiting period (*ʿidda*) is that of a woman whose husband has divorced her."

1781. According to Mālik, it reached him that Saʿīd b. al-Musayyab, Sulaymān b. Yasār, and Ibn Shihāb all said that the waiting period of a woman who gives her husband property in exchange for a divorce is the same as that of a woman whose husband has divorced her: three menstrual cycles.

1782. Mālik said, regarding a woman who gives her husband property in exchange for a divorce, that she may not return to him until a new marriage has been contracted. If he contracts a second marriage with her prior to the expiration of her waiting period but divorces her before having sexual relations with her, she is not obliged to observe a second waiting period in respect of the second marriage. She must, however, complete the first waiting period, resuming it from the date on which it was interrupted. Mālik said, "This is the best view I have heard about that matter."

1783. Mālik said, "If a woman gives her husband some property in exchange for a divorce, and he divorces her several times in one continuous phrase, those multiple divorces bind him. If, however, he is silent after the first expression of divorce, whatever subsequent expressions of divorce he makes are of no effect."

Chapter 13. What Has Come Down regarding Mutual Imprecation (*Liʿān*)[734]

1784. According to Mālik, Ibn Shihāb reported that Sahl b. Saʿd al-Sāʿidī informed him that ʿUwaymir al-ʿAjlānī had gone to ʿĀṣim b. ʿAdī al-Anṣārī and said to him, "ʿĀṣim, what do you think a man should do if he finds a male stranger alone with his wife? Should he kill him, only for you to have him put to death as punishment? What should he do? ʿĀṣim, do ask the Messenger of God (pbuh) on my behalf about this situation." ʿĀṣim then asked the Messenger of God (pbuh) the question that ʿUwaymir had raised. However, the Messenger of God (pbuh) abhorred ʿĀṣim's question, finding fault in it. Eventually, ʿĀṣim could no longer bear the criticisms of the Messenger of God (pbuh), so he ceased asking for an answer. When ʿĀṣim returned home, ʿUwaymir again went to see him and said, "ʿĀṣim, what did the Messenger of God (pbuh) tell you?" ʿĀṣim said to ʿUwaymir, "You have not brought any good to me. The Messenger of God (pbuh) abhorred the question that you asked me to ask him." ʿUwaymir said, "By God, I shall not desist until I ask him myself about it!" Therefore, he set off to see the Messenger of God (pbuh) and found him sitting among the people, whereupon he said, "Messenger of God, what do you think a man who finds a male stranger alone with his wife should do? Should he kill him, only for you to have him put to death as punishment? What should he do as an alternative?" The Messenger of God (pbuh) said, "A rule concerning you and your companion has already been revealed. Go fetch her." Sahl said, "They imprecated one another in front of the Messenger of God (pbuh). The people and I were present as this happened, and when they finished their mutual imprecations, ʿUwaymir said, 'Messenger of God, were I to remain married to her, I would surely appear to be a liar.' Therefore, he divorced her three times without any prompting from the Messenger of God (pbuh)." Mālik said, "Ibn Shihāb said, 'That subsequently became the basis for the ordinance governing mutual imprecation (*sunnat al-mutalāʿinīn*).'"[735]

1785. According to Mālik, Nāfiʿ reported from ʿAbd Allāh b. ʿUmar that during the time of the Messenger of God (pbuh), a man imprecated his wife

734 *Liʿān* or *mulāʿana* is the procedure to be followed when a husband accuses his wife of adultery but lacks the four eyewitnesses the Quran requires to prove the act (*al-Nūr*, 24:4). Its name derives from the requirement that the spouses call down God's curse on themselves if they are lying. The Quran's rules on mutual imprecation involve the husband swearing four times that he witnessed his wife commit an act of adultery, followed by a fifth oath that he should be damned if he is lying. The wife defends herself by swearing four times that her husband is a liar and a fifth oath that she should suffer God's anger if he is truthful. *Al-Nūr*, 24:6–9.

735 What he means is that whenever a husband and a wife engage in mutual imprecation, a triple divorce automatically takes place.

and denied paternity of the child she was bearing. The Messenger of God (pbuh) separated them and affiliated the child only to the woman.

1786. Mālik said, "God, Blessed and Sublime is He, says, 'And the husband who accuses his wife of adultery but has no witnesses other than himself may prove his claim by testifying four times in God's name that he is truthful in his accusation and then the fifth time that he solemnly invokes God's curse on himself if he is a liar. But she may avert punishment if she testifies four times in God's name that he is a liar and then the fifth time that she solemnly calls down God's wrath on herself if he is truthful.'"[736]

1787. Mālik said, "The ordinance among us (*al-sunna ʿindanā*) decrees that a couple who engage in mutual imprecation may never marry one another again. If the husband retracts his accusation, he is punished for slander and the child is affiliated to him, but he is still forever prohibited from remarrying his wife. The ordinance among us about which there is neither doubt nor dissent is in accordance with this (*ʿalā hādhā al-sunna ʿindanā allatī lā shakka fīhā wa-lā ikhtilāf*)."

1788. Mālik said, "If a man leaves his wife pursuant to an absolute divorce, one for which he has no right of revocation, and she is found to be pregnant, and he then denies paternity of the child she is carrying while she claims that he is the father, and her claim is plausible, as long as a length of time has not passed that would raise doubts about her claim, and so it cannot be known whether the child is his, he must imprecate her if he wishes his denial of paternity to be effective. That is the rule among us (*dhālika al-amr ʿindanā*), and it is what I have heard."

1789. Mālik said, "If a man divorces his wife three times, knowing she is pregnant, but then accuses her of having committed adultery, claiming that he saw her commit adultery with his own eyes before he divorced her, he is punished for slander and is not permitted to imprecate her.[737] If he denies having had knowledge of her pregnancy after divorcing her three times, however, he is permitted to imprecate her. This is what I have heard."

1790. Mālik said, "A slave is in the same position as a free man regarding accusations of adultery and imprecation; the rules that apply to a free man apply to him, except that the punishment for slander is not applied to anyone who accuses a handmaiden of adultery."

---

736 *Al-Nūr*, 24:6–9.

737 This is because only a husband has the right to initiate imprecation. By divorcing her without initiating charges against her even though, by his own admission, he knew that she had committed adultery, he essentially waived his right to imprecate her. On the other hand, if he was ignorant of her pregnancy at the time he divorced her, he may imprecate her in order to deny paternity of her child.

1791. Mālik said, "Muslim handmaidens and free Christian and Jewish women may imprecate their free Muslim husbands if the husband has married one of these women and consummated the marriage with her. This is because God, Blessed and Sublime is He, says in His Book, 'And those who accuse their wives,'[738] and they are wives. The rule among us is in accordance with this (*'alā hādhā al-amr 'indanā*)."

1792. Mālik said, "If a slave marries a free Muslim woman, a Muslim handmaiden, or a free Christian or Jewish woman, he may imprecate her."

1793. Mālik said, "If a man imprecates his wife but then retracts his accusation and contradicts himself after having sworn one or two of the oaths, but not all of them, he is punished for slander but is not separated from his wife as long as he did not swear the fifth oath of imprecation."

1794. Mālik said, "If a man divorces his wife, and after three months pass the woman says, 'I am pregnant,' but the husband wishes to deny paternity, he must imprecate her."

1795. Mālik said, regarding a handmaiden who is a chattel slave (*ama mamlūka*) and whose husband imprecates her and then buys her, "He may not have sexual relations with her, even though he owns her. That is because it has long been the established ordinance (*al-sunna maḍat*) that two persons who have engaged in mutual imprecation may never be intimate with one another again."

1796. Mālik said, "If a man imprecates his wife before he brings her to the marital home, she is entitled to only half of her dower (*ṣadāq*)."

Chapter 14. The Estate (*Mīrāth*) of a Child Born to a Couple Who Separated by Mutual Imprecation (*Mulā'ana*)

1797. According to Mālik, it reached him that 'Urwa b. al-Zubayr would say, regarding a child born to a couple who separated by mutual imprecation or an illegitimate child (*walad al-zinā*), that when such a child dies, the child's mother takes out of the child's estate the share due to her as specified in God's Book, and the child's maternal half-brothers take the shares specified for them. If she is a freedwoman (*mawlāt*), the rest of the estate goes to her patrons. If she is an Arab woman, she takes what is hers from the estate by right, and his maternal half-brothers take their rights, and whatever remains of the estate goes to the public treasury of the Muslims. Mālik said, "A similar opinion has reached me from Sulaymān b. Yasār. This is the opinion that I found the people of knowledge in our town following (*'alā dhālika adraktu ra'y ahl al-'ilm bi-baladinā*)."

---

738 *Al-Nūr*, 24:6.

Chapter 15. The Divorce of a Virgin (*Bikr*) Bride

1798. According to Mālik, Ibn Shihāb reported from Muḥammad b. ʿAbd al-Raḥmān b. Thawbān that Muḥammad b. Iyās b. al-Bukayr said, "A man divorced his wife three times before bringing her to the marital home. After doing so, he changed his mind and wished to marry her, so he went looking for a legal opinion that would permit him to do so. I went with him to ask on his behalf. He asked ʿAbd Allāh b. ʿAbbās and Abū Hurayra about his situation, and they both said, 'We do not think that you may marry her until she first marries another husband.' He said, 'But my divorce of her should only count as one.'[739] Ibn Abbās said, 'You threw away the good fortune that was yours.'"

1799. According to Mālik, Yaḥyā b. Saʿīd reported from Bukayr b. ʿAbd Allāh b. al-Ashajj, from al-Nuʿmān Abū ʿAyyāsh al-Anṣārī, that ʿAṭāʾ b. Yasār said, "A man came to ʿAbd Allāh b. ʿAmr b. al-ʿĀṣī and asked about a man who divorced his wife three times before consummating the marriage with her. I interjected, 'All that's needed to divorce a virgin (*bikr*) is one divorce.' ʿAbd Allāh b. ʿAmr b. al-ʿĀṣī then said to me, 'You're good for nothing but telling tales! One divorce separates her from her husband, but three divorces make her prohibited to him until she marries another husband.'"

1800. According to Mālik, Yaḥyā b. Saʿīd reported that Bukayr b. ʿAbd Allāh b. al-Ashajj informed him from Muʿāwiya b. Abī ʿAyyāsh al-Anṣārī that he was sitting with ʿAbd Allāh b. al-Zubayr and ʿĀṣim b. ʿUmar. Muʿāwiya said, "Muḥammad b. Iyās b. al-Bukayr appeared before them and said, 'A bedouin man divorced his wife three times before bringing her to the marital home. What do you two think about that?' ʿAbd Allāh b. al-Zubayr said, 'We have no opinion on this question. Why don't you go find ʿAbd Allāh b. ʿAbbās and Abū Hurayra and ask them. Come back and let us know what they said. I just left them now with ʿĀʾisha.' Muḥammad therefore left in search of them. When he found them, he posed his question to them. Ibn ʿAbbās said to Abū Hurayra, 'Give him an answer, Abū Hurayra! He certainly posed a tough one.' Abū Hurayra said, 'One divorce separates her from her husband, but three render her forbidden to him until she marries another husband.' Ibn ʿAbbās said the same thing." Mālik said, "The rule among us is in accordance with that (*ʿalā dhālika al-amr ʿindanā*)."

739 Bājī reports two possible meanings the man could have intended when he said he divorced her only once. The first is that although he divorced her three times, he intended only one divorce. The second is that although he divorced her three times, the utterances should be deemed to constitute only one divorce because the wife never entered the marital home. This latter interpretation is held by other jurists. Bājī, *al-Muntaqā*, 4:83.

1801. Mālik said, "When a man marries a matron (*thayyib*) but does not bring her to the marital home, the same rules that apply to a virgin bride apply to her: one divorce separates her from her husband, and three render her prohibited to him until she marries another husband."

Chapter 16. The Divorce (*Ṭalāq*) of a Man on His Deathbed (*Marīḍ*)

1802. According to Mālik, Ibn Shihāb reported from Ṭalḥa b. ʿAbd Allāh b. ʿAwf (Ibn Shihāb said, "And he knew more about this case than they did,") and from Abū Salama b. ʿAbd al-Raḥmān b. ʿAwf that ʿAbd al-Raḥmān b. ʿAwf divorced his wife with an absolute declaration of divorce (*batta*) while he was on his deathbed, but ʿUthmān b. ʿAffān nevertheless permitted her to inherit from him, even though her waiting period (*ʿidda*) had expired before he died.[740]

1803. According to Mālik, ʿAbd Allāh b. al-Faḍl reported from al-Aʿraj that ʿUthmān b. ʿAffān permitted Ibn Mukmil's former wives to inherit from him. He had divorced them while he was on his deathbed.

1804. According to Mālik, he heard Rabīʿa b. Abī ʿAbd al-Raḥmān say, "It reached me that ʿAbd al-Raḥmān b. ʿAwf's wife asked him to divorce her. He said to her, 'When your next period comes to an end, come ask me for a divorce.' She did not, however, menstruate again until he became seriously ill. After her period finally came and ended, she went and asked him for a divorce. He then divorced her either three times or once, but in either case no other divorces remained that he could have exercised against her, so whatever kind of divorce it was, it was her third and therefore final divorce from him. ʿAbd al-Raḥmān b. ʿAwf was seriously ill at the time and died later from that illness, and ʿUthmān b. ʿAffān permitted his former wife to inherit from him, even though her waiting period expired before he died."

1805. According to Mālik, Yaḥyā b. Saʿīd reported that Muḥammad b. Yaḥyā b. Ḥabbān said, "My grandfather Ḥabbān had two wives, one a Hāshimite and the other Medinese. He divorced the Medinese wife while she was breastfeeding. A year later he died, and she had not yet menstruated. She said, 'I am entitled to inherit from him,' but the Hāshimite wife disagreed. The two took their dispute to ʿUthmān b. ʿAffān, who decided that the Medinese wife was entitled to inherit. The Hāshimite wife rebuked ʿUthmān, so he said, 'Don't blame me—this is the doing of your first cousin. He advised us to rule in this manner.' He meant ʿAlī b. Abī Ṭālib."

---

740 According to Mālikīs, if a man divorces his wife while he is terminally ill, his ex-wife is nevertheless entitled to her determinate share of his estate, even if her waiting period has expired and she has remarried, to counter the possibility that the decedent divorced her in order to deprive her of her share in his estate.

1806. According to Mālik, he heard Ibn Shihāb say, "If a man divorces his wife three times while he is on his deathbed, she nonetheless inherits from him."

1807. Mālik said, "If he divorces her while he is on his deathbed, but before bringing her to the marital home, she receives half of her dower (*ṣadāq*) and is entitled to her share of the estate, but she need not observe a waiting period. If, however, he has brought her to the marital home and then divorces her, she is entitled to the entirety of her dower and her share of the estate. The virgin bride (*bikr*) and the matron (*thayyib*) are treated the same in our view."

Chapter 17. What Has Come Down regarding Parting Gifts (*Mutʿa*) upon Divorce (*Ṭalāq*)

1808. According to Mālik, it reached him that ʿAbd al-Raḥmān b. ʿAwf divorced one of his wives, so he gave her a handmaiden as a parting gift.

1809. According to Mālik, Nāfiʿ reported that ʿAbd Allāh b. ʿUmar would say, "Every divorced woman is entitled to a parting gift, except one who is divorced after her dower has been specified but before her marriage has been consummated. In such circumstances, her receipt of one-half of the specified dower ought to suffice her."

1810. According to Mālik, Ibn Shihāb said, "Every divorced woman is entitled to a parting gift." Mālik said, "Something similar to that reached me from al-Qāsim b. Muḥammad."

1811. Mālik said, "There is no fixed amount for the parting gift in our opinion, neither a minimum nor a maximum."

Chapter 18. What Has Come Down regarding a Slave's Divorce (*Ṭalāq*)

1812. According to Mālik, Abū al-Zinād reported from Sulaymān b. Yasār that Nufayʿ, who was either a party to a manumission contract (*mukātab*) with Umm Salama, the wife of the Prophet (pbuh), or one of her chattel slaves, was married to a free woman. He divorced her twice and then wanted to reclaim her as his wife. However, the wives of the Prophet (pbuh) ordered him to ask ʿUthmān b. ʿAffān whether he could do so. He ran into him at the stairs of the mosque, and ʿUthmān was holding Zayd b. Thābit's hand. Nufayʿ asked them both whether he could reclaim her as his wife. Before he could finish speaking, they both interrupted him and said, "She is prohibited to you; she is prohibited to you."

1813. According to Mālik, Ibn Shihab reported from Saʿīd b. al-Musayyab that Nufayʿ, who was a party to a manumission contract with Umm Salama, the wife of the Prophet (pbuh), divorced his free wife twice, so he asked ʿUthmān b. ʿAffān's opinion as to whether he could reclaim her as his wife. ʿUthmān said, "No; she is prohibited to you."

1814. According to Mālik, ʿAbd Rabbih b. Saʿīd reported from Muḥammad b. Ibrāhīm b. al-Ḥārith al-Taymī that Nufayʿ, who was a party to a manumission contract with Umm Salama, the wife of the Prophet (pbuh), sought out Zayd b. Thābit's opinion. He said, "I divorced a free woman twice. May I reclaim her as my wife?" Zayd b. Thābit said, "No; she is prohibited to you."

1815. According to Mālik, Nāfiʿ reported that ʿAbd Allāh b. ʿUmar would say, "If a slave divorces a woman twice, whether she is free or a slave, she becomes prohibited to him until she marries another husband. The waiting period (*ʿidda*) for a free wife is three menstrual periods, and for a slave woman two."

1816. According to Mālik, Nāfiʿ reported that ʿAbd Allāh b. ʿUmar would say, "If a person gives his slave permission to marry, the right of divorce belongs to the slave, and no one else may exercise his power to divorce. There is no harm, however, in a master divesting his slave of the slave's handmaiden, or divesting the master's handmaiden of her own handmaiden."

Chapter 19. What Has Come Down regarding the Maintenance of a Handmaiden Who Is Divorced While She Is Pregnant

1817. Yaḥyā said, "Mālik said, 'Neither a free man nor a slave who divorces a handmaiden who is a chattel slave (*mamlūka*), nor a slave who divorces a free woman irrevocably, is obligated to provide maintenance for her even if she is pregnant, so long as he has no right to reclaim her as his wife.'"

1818. Mālik said, "A free man is not obliged to pay for a wet nurse to suckle his son if his son is a slave belonging to another tribe; nor is a slave obliged to maintain a child out of his own property unless his master is also the owner of that child. If the slave's child is not the master's property, the slave may not use his own property to maintain the child except with his master's prior permission."

Chapter 20. What Has Come Down regarding the Waiting Period (*ʿIdda*) of a Woman Whose Husband Has Gone Missing

1819. According to Mālik, Yaḥyā b. Saʿīd reported from Saʿīd b. al-Musayyab that ʿUmar b. al-Khaṭṭāb said, "Any woman whose husband has gone missing, and his whereabouts are unknown, shall wait four years, whereupon she observes a waiting period of four months and ten days, at the conclusion of which she may lawfully remarry."

1820. Mālik said, "If she marries after completing her waiting period, her former husband, if he turns up, has no claim to her, whether or not her new husband has taken her to the marital home. That is the rule among us (*dhālika al-amr ʿindanā*). If her first husband reaches her before she remarries, however, he has a greater claim to her."

1821. Mālik said, "In my experience, the people rejected the position that some people attributed to ʿUmar b. al-Khaṭṭāb, namely, 'If her first husband returns after she has remarried, he may either recover the dower he gave her or reclaim his wife.'"

1822. Mālik said, "It reached me that ʿUmar b. al-Khaṭṭāb said, regarding a scenario in which a man divorced his wife while he was away from her on a journey and then decided to revoke the divorce and reclaim her as his wife, but she was aware only of the divorce and not of its revocation and therefore remarried, that her first husband, the one who divorced her, has no claim to her, whether or not her second husband has taken her to the marital home." Mālik said, "Of all the views that I have heard on this matter and on the matter of the missing husband, this is the one I prefer most."

Chapter 21. What Has Come Down regarding the Meaning of *Aqrāʾ*,[741] the Waiting Period (*ʿIdda*) after Divorce (*Ṭalāq*), and Divorcing a Menstruating Woman

1823. According to Mālik, Nāfiʿ reported that during the time of the Prophet (pbuh), ʿAbd Allāh b. ʿUmar divorced his wife while she was menstruating. ʿUmar b. al-Khaṭṭāb asked the Messenger of God (pbuh) about that. The Messenger of God (pbuh) said, "Tell him to revoke his divorce and reclaim her as his wife. He should then keep her until her period comes to an end and she bathes, and until she has another period, it comes to an end, and she bathes. Then he may remain married to her or divorce her, as he wishes; however, if he wishes to divorce her, he may not have sexual relations with

741 *Aqrāʾ* (also *qurūʾ*) is the plural of *qurʾ*, used in the Quran to designate the length of a divorced woman's waiting period (*ʿidda*). *Al-Baqara*, 2:228: "Divorced women shall wait three *qurūʾ*" (before the divorce is final and they may remarry). *Qurʾ* belongs to a class of words in the Arabic language known as *aḍdād*, "opposites," because they bear two meanings that are opposites of one another, in this case menstruation (*ḥayḍ*) and the cessation of menstruation (*ṭuhr*). This fact has practical consequences in the law of divorce, where the Mālikīs believe that *qurʾ* refers to the onset of the monthly period whereas the Ḥanafīs hold that it refers the end of the period. Accordingly, under Mālikī jurisprudence, a divorced woman may remarry once her third period after her divorce begins, whereas under Ḥanafī jurisprudence, she must wait until the conclusion of her third period after her divorce.

her prior to divorcing her.[742] That is the waiting period (*ʿidda*) that God has ordered to be observed with respect to divorced women."

1824. According to Mālik, Ibn Shihāb reported from ʿUrwa b. al-Zubayr, from ʿĀʾisha, the wife of the Prophet (pbuh), that Ḥafṣa bt. ʿAbd al-Raḥmān b. Abī Bakr al-Ṣiddīq left the marital home when the blood of her third period after her divorce began to flow. Ibn Shihāb said, "This incident was later brought to ʿAmra bt. ʿAbd al-Raḥmān's attention, and she said, "ʿUrwa spoke the truth. Some people took her to task regarding what she did, saying, "God, Blessed and Sublime is He, says in His Book, 'three periods' (*qurūʾ*).""[743] ʿĀʾisha said, 'You have all spoken the truth. Do you all know what "periods" (*aqrāʾ*) are? They are nothing other than the cessation of bleeding after menstruation.'"

1825. According to Mālik, Ibn Shihāb said, "I heard Abū Bakr b. ʿAbd al-Raḥmān say, 'I have never encountered any of our jurists contesting this,' meaning that this was ʿĀʾisha's opinion."[744]

1826. According to Mālik, Nāfiʿ and Zayd b. Aslam reported from Sulaymān b. Yasār that al-Aḥwaṣ died in the Levant when the blood of his wife's third period began to flow. He had just divorced her, so Muʿāwiya b. Abī Sufyān wrote to Zayd b. Thābit to ask him whether her waiting period had come to an end. Zayd wrote back to him, "Once her blood began to flow for the third time after her divorce, she became free of any obligations toward him and he became free of any obligations toward her. She does not inherit from him, nor he from her."

1827. According to Mālik, it reached him that al-Qāsim b. Muḥammad, Sālim b. ʿAbd Allāh, Abū Bakr b. ʿAbd al-Raḥmān, Sulaymān b. Yasār, and Ibn Shihāb would all say, "Once the divorced woman's blood flows for the third time after her divorce, she is separated from her husband, they no longer inherit from one another, and he no longer has the right to reclaim her as his wife."

1828. According to Mālik, Nāfiʿ reported that ʿAbd Allāh b. ʿUmar would say, "If a man divorces his wife, she becomes free of any obligations toward him and he of any toward her once her blood flows for the third time after her divorce." Mālik said, "That is the rule among us (*dhālika al-amr ʿindanā*)."

---

742 By having sexual relations with her the husband would be exercising his right to reclaim her as his wife, in which case he would need to repeat the entire process in order to divorce her.

743 *Al-Baqara*, 2:228.

744 The meaning of this text is ambiguous. Read in isolation, it could suggest that all the early jurists of Medina agreed with ʿĀʾisha's interpretation of the meaning of "period." However, a later hadith in this chapter, no. 1827, suggests that they accepted the view of Ḥafṣa as set out in hadith no. 1824, namely, that "period" refers to the onset of bleeding, not its conclusion.

1829. According to Mālik, al-Fuḍayl b. ʿUbayd Allāh, the freedman (*mawlā*) of al-Mahrī, reported that al-Qāsim b. Muḥammad and Sālim b. ʿAbd Allāh would say, "When a woman is divorced, once her blood flows for the third time after her divorce, she has separated from her husband, and she may remarry."

1830. According to Mālik, it reached him that Saʿīd b. al-Musayyab, Ibn Shihāb, and Sulaymān b. Yasār would all say, "The waiting period for a woman who gave her husband property in exchange for a divorce (*mukhtaliʿa*) is three periods."

1831. According to Mālik, he heard Ibn Shihāb say, "A divorced woman's waiting period is measured by her periods, even if a long time elapses between each one."

1832. According to Mālik, Yaḥyā b. Saʿīd reported from a Medinese man that his wife asked him to divorce her, so he said, "When your period begins, let me know." When it began, she let him know, and he said, "Let me know when it ends." When the bleeding ceased and she bathed, she told him, so he divorced her. Mālik said, "This is the best view I have heard about that issue."

Chapter 22. What Has Come Down regarding the Divorced Woman's Observance of the Waiting Period (*ʿIdda*) in Her House, If She Was Divorced There

1833. According to Mālik, Yaḥyā b. Saʿīd reported that he heard both al-Qāsim b. Muḥammad and Sulaymān b. Yasār mention that Yaḥyā b. Saʿīd b. al-ʿĀṣī had divorced ʿAbd al-Raḥmān b. al-Ḥakam's daughter using an absolute declaration of divorce (*batta*) and then sent her away from the marital home. ʿĀʾisha, the Mother of the Believers, sent a message to Marwān b. al-Ḥakam, who was then the governor of Medina, saying, "Fear God, and return the woman to her home." According to Sulaymān's report, Marwān said to her, "ʿAbd al-Raḥmān has the upper hand over me in this case." According to al-Qāsim's report, however, Marwān said to her, "Haven't you heard of the case of Fāṭima bt. Qays?" ʿĀʾisha said, "Fāṭima's case is not relevant!" Marwān said, "If ill manners and insults are what you believe explains Fāṭima's case, then there is more than enough ill will between those two to satisfy you."[745]

745 According to al-Qāsim, Marwān justified his nonintervention in the dispute with reference to a precedent involving Fāṭima bt. Qays, but ʿĀʾisha dismissed that case as exceptional and not to be relied on. Marwān replied to ʿĀʾisha by arguing that Fāṭima's case was in fact on point, insofar as she did not observe the waiting period in the marital home on account of the very poor relations she had with her husband's family. He pointed out that things were in fact

1834. According to Mālik, Nāfiʿ reported that the daughter of Saʿīd b. Zayd b. ʿAmr b. Nufayl was married to ʿAbd Allāh b. ʿAmr b. ʿUthmān. He irrevocably divorced her, and she left the marital home before her waiting period expired. ʿAbd Allāh b. ʿUmar criticized her action.

1835. According to Mālik, Nāfiʿ reported that ʿAbd Allāh b. ʿUmar divorced a wife of his. She lived in the house of Ḥafṣa, the wife of the Prophet (pbuh), which lay on ʿAbd Allāh's usual path to the mosque. He therefore began to take another route to the mosque, one that went behind the houses, so as to avoid asking for her permission to pass. He continued to do so until he reclaimed her as his wife.

1836. According to Mālik, Yaḥyā b. Saʿīd reported that Saʿīd b. al-Musayyab was asked who is liable for the rent of a woman who lives in a rented house at the time her husband divorces her. Saʿīd said, "Her husband." Someone interjected, "What if her husband lacks sufficient resources?" He said, "Then she must pay the rent." The questioner said, "What if she lacks sufficient resources?" He said, "Then the governor must pay the rent."

Chapter 23. What Has Come Down regarding the Maintenance (*Nafaqa*) Due to a Divorced Woman

1837. According to Mālik, ʿAbd Allāh b. Yazīd, the freedman (*mawlā*) of al-Aswad b. Sufyān, reported from Abū Salama b. ʿAbd al-Raḥmān b. ʿAwf, from Fāṭima bt. Qays, that Abū ʿAmr b. Ḥafṣ divorced her using an absolute declaration of divorce (*batta*) while he was away in the Levant. He dispatched his agent to her with some barley, but she spurned it. He[746] said, "By God, we owe you nothing." She went to the Prophet (pbuh) and told him what had happened. He said, "Your husband is not obliged to provide you with maintenance (*nafaqa*)." He then ordered her to observe her waiting period (*ʿidda*) in Umm Sharīk's house. Later, upon reflection, he said, "This is a woman whom my companions visit frequently. Finish your waiting period at ʿAbd Allāh b. Umm Maktūm's house, for he is blind. There you will have privacy, and you can undress without embarrassment. When your waiting period is complete and you may remarry, let me know." She said, "When I had completed my waiting period, I mentioned to the Prophet (pbuh) that both Muʿāwiya b. Abī Sufyān and Abū Jahm b. Hishām sought my hand. The Messenger of God (pbuh) said, 'Abū Jahm's staff is always on his shoulder,[747]

---

worse between ʿAbd al-Raḥmān's daughter and her husband than they had been between Fāṭima and her husband's family. Ibn ʿAbd al-Barr, *al-Istidhkār*, 6:158.

746 The antecedent of the pronoun is ambiguous, but the context dictates that it must be the agent of Fāṭima's husband.

747 That is, he travels frequently.

and Muʿāwiya is a penniless pauper. Why not marry Usāma b. Zayd instead?'" She said, "But I dislike him." But the Prophet (pbuh) again said, "Marry Usāma b. Zayd." She said, "So I married him, and God provided much good in that marriage, and I was very fortunate to have been with him."

1838. According to Mālik, he heard Ibn Shihāb say, "A woman who has been divorced three times should not leave her house until she completes her waiting period and is free to remarry. She is not, however, entitled to maintenance from her husband during her waiting period unless she is pregnant, in which case she continues to receive maintenance until she gives birth." Mālik said, "That is the rule among us (*dhālika al-amr ʿindanā*)."

Chapter 24. What Has Come Down regarding the Waiting Period (*ʿIdda*) for a Handmaiden Whose Husband Divorces Her

1839. Yaḥyā said, "Mālik said, 'The rule in our view (*al-amr ʿindanā*) regarding a slave's divorce of a wife who is herself a slave at the time of the divorce (*ṭalāq*) and who is manumitted before her waiting period expires is that her waiting period remains that of a handmaiden and does not become that of a free woman. The fact that she has been manumitted does not change the length of her waiting period. Whether or not her husband is entitled to reclaim her as his wife, her waiting period does not change.'"

1840. Mālik said, "The same principle applies to a mandatory criminal punishment (*ḥadd*)[748] imposed on a slave who is manumitted after being convicted of a crime but before the punishment is carried out: his punishment is that of a slave, not that of a free person."

1841. Mālik said, "A free man may divorce his wife who is a handmaiden up to three times, but her waiting period is only two periods. A slave married to a free woman may divorce her no more than twice, and her waiting period is three periods."

1842. Mālik said, "If a man is married to a handmaiden and then purchases and manumits her, she must observe the waiting period of a handmaiden as long as he has not had intercourse with her after purchasing her. If he has intercourse with her between purchasing her and manumitting her, however, she need only wait for the beginning of her period."[749]

---

748 *Ḥudūd*, sing. *ḥadd*, are a set of criminal acts that, according to classical Islamic law, carry mandatory punishments when properly proven. They include the crimes of theft (*sariqa*), brigandage (*ḥirāba*), fornication and adultery (*zinā*), slander (*qadhf*), wine-drinking (*shurb al-khamr*), rebellion (*baghy*), and apostasy (*ridda*).

749 This latter procedure is known as *istibrāʾ*, and it is not the same as the scripturally mandated waiting period that applies to a divorced wife. In this case, the husband's marriage to the slave woman is automatically dissolved when he purchases her, because a man cannot own

Chapter 25. Miscellaneous Matters regarding the Waiting Period (*ʿIdda*) after Divorce (*Ṭalāq*)

1843. According to Mālik, Yaḥyā b. Saʿīd and Yazīd b. ʿAbd Allāh b. Qusayṭ al-Laythī reported that Saʿīd b. al-Musayyab said, "ʿUmar b. al-Khaṭṭāb said, 'Any woman who is divorced and completes one or two menstrual cycles before her menstruation ceases must wait nine months. If it becomes clear that she is pregnant, delivery of the child brings her waiting period to an end. If she is not pregnant, her waiting period is an additional three months after the end of the initial nine months, at the conclusion of which she may remarry.'"

1844. According to Mālik, Yaḥyā b. Saʿīd reported that Saʿīd b. al-Musayyab would say, "The right to initiate divorce is particular to men, and the obligation to observe the waiting period (*ʿidda*) is particular to women."

1845. According to Mālik, Ibn Shihāb reported that Saʿīd b. al-Musayyab said, "The waiting period of a woman whose bleeding is irregular and continuous is one year."

1846. Yaḥyā said, "Mālik said, 'The rule in our view (*al-amr ʿindanā*) regarding a divorced woman who stops menstruating when her husband divorces her is that she waits nine months. If she does not menstruate during that period of time, she observes a waiting period of three months. If she menstruates a second time before the end of the three-month period, she reverts to a waiting period determined by menstruation, not the passage of months. If another nine months elapse before she menstruates a third time, she observes a waiting period of three months. If she menstruates a third time, she has completed the waiting period as determined by menstruation, but if the nine months elapsed without menstruation, she must observe another three-month waiting period, and only then may she remarry. At any time before the expiration of the waiting period, however, her husband may reclaim her as his wife, unless he has already divorced her irrevocably.'"

1847. Mālik said, "The long-established ordinance among us (*al-sunna ʿindanā*) is that when a man divorces his wife but retains the right to reclaim her, then exercises his right to reclaim her before she completes her waiting period, and then divorces her again, she does not resume her waiting period from where she left off, even if he did not have intercourse with her. Rather, she must start anew, beginning a new waiting period from

his wife. By having intercourse with her before he manumits her, he is exercising his prerogative as master to have intercourse with her. When he later manumits her, therefore, her only obligation is that of a handmaiden whose master has had intercourse with her, namely, to wait for the beginning of her period to ensure that she is not pregnant.

the day he divorced her the second time. By reclaiming her even though he had no desire for her, he wronged himself and erred."

1848. Yaḥyā said, "Mālik said, 'The rule in our view (*al-amr ʿindanā*) regarding a non-Muslim woman who embraces Islam when her husband is a nonbeliever and whose husband then converts to Islam is that he remains her husband as long as she is still in her waiting period. Once her waiting period has concluded, however, he has no claim to her. If he remarries her after the conclusion of her waiting period, that initial separation is not to be counted as a divorce; rather, it is treated as something that Islam nullified without a divorce.'"[750]

Chapter 26. What Has Come Down regarding the Two Arbitrators[751]

1849. According to Mālik, it reached him that ʿAlī b. Abī Ṭālib said that the two arbitrators whom God, Blessed and Sublime is He, mentioned in the verse, "If you fear a rift between the two of them, appoint two arbitrators, one from his people and the other from hers. If the couple desire reconciliation, God will bring them together, for God is knowledgeable and well-acquainted with all things,"[752] may divorce the couple or keep them together.

1850. Mālik said, "That is the best view I have heard expressed by the people of knowledge; namely, the decision of the two arbitrators as to whether the man and the woman should be divorced or remain together is binding."

Chapter 27. A Man's Oath (*Yamīn*) of Divorce (*Ṭalāq*) before Marriage

1851. According to Mālik, it reached him that ʿUmar b. al-Khaṭṭāb, ʿAbd Allāh b. ʿUmar, ʿAbd Allāh b. Masʿūd, Sālim b. ʿAbd Allāh, al-Qāsim b. Muḥammad, Ibn Shihāb, and Sulaymān b. Yasār all said, "If a man swears to divorce a woman before he marries her but then marries her anyway in violation of his oath, the oath of divorce binds him."

1852. According to Mālik, it reached him that ʿAbd Allāh b. Masʿūd would say that if someone says, "Every woman I ever marry I hereby divorce upon my marriage to her," without designating a specific tribe or woman, his

750 In other words, the dissolution of a marriage because of the non-Muslim wife's conversion to Islam followed by the failure of her husband to convert to Islam within her waiting period (*ʿidda*) is deemed the legal equivalent of an annulment (*faskh*), not of a divorce (*ṭalāq*). The difference is relevant in the event that the now ex-husband later converts to Islam and remarries his former wife. If he does so, he will be permitted to divorce her three times, not merely twice.

751 The Quran provides for the appointment of two arbitrators if the husband and wife are fighting and marital breakdown is feared. *Al-Nisāʾ*, 4:35.

752 *Al-Nisāʾ*, 4:35.

statement is of no legal consequence. Mālik said, "That is the best view I have heard regarding that issue."

1853. Mālik said, regarding a man who says to his wife, "You are divorced," or declares, "Every woman I ever marry I hereby divorce upon my marriage to her," or "All my property shall go to charity," if he fails to do something that he specifies in his oath—and then does not fulfill the oath, "His wives are indeed divorced, just as he said. As for his statement 'Every woman I ever marry I hereby divorce upon my marriage to her,' if he did not name a specific woman, tribe, or region or a similar qualification, the statement is of no legal consequence, and he may marry any woman he wishes. As for his property, however, he need only give away one-third of it, not all of it."

Chapter 28. The Length of Time Given to a Man to Consummate His Marriage with His Wife

1854. According to Mālik, Ibn Shihāb reported that Saʿīd b. al-Musayyab would say, "Whoever marries a woman and is unable to consummate the marriage immediately is given one year to do so. If he does so within that period of time, he may remain with his wife, but if he fails to do so, they will be separated."

1855. According to Mālik, he asked Ibn Shihāb, "From what date is the deadline to consummate the marriage counted? Is it from the day he brings her to the marital home, or the day she sues him before the judge or the governor?" He said, "No, it is certainly counted from the day she sues him before the responsible public official (*sulṭān*)."

1856. Mālik said, "As for someone who has consummated the marriage with his wife and then loses interest in her, I have not heard anything about a deadline being set for him, nor are they to be separated for that reason."

Chapter 29. Miscellaneous Matters Related to Divorce (*Ṭalāq*)

1857. According to Mālik, Ibn Shihāb said, "It reached me that the Messenger of God (pbuh) said to a man from the tribe of Thaqīf who had ten wives when he embraced Islam, 'Retain four of them, and leave the rest.'"

1858. According to Mālik, Ibn Shihāb said, "I heard each of Saʿīd b. al-Musayyab, Ḥumayd b. ʿAbd al-Raḥmān b. ʿAwf, ʿUbayd Allāh b. ʿAbd Allāh b. ʿUtba b. Masʿūd, and Sulaymān b. Yasār say that he heard Abū Hurayra say that he heard ʿUmar b. al-Khaṭṭāb say, 'As for a woman whose husband divorces her once or twice and then leaves her be until her waiting period comes to an end and it becomes licit for her to remarry, and who then marries another man, who predeceases her or divorces her, and who then remarries her first husband—such a woman stays with this husband in accordance with the number of divorces that remain from her prior marriage to him.'" Mālik said, "That is in accordance with the long-established ordinance among us about which there is no dissent (*wa-ʿalā dhālika al-sunna ʿindanā allatī lā ikhtilāfa fīhā*)."

1859. According to Mālik, Thābit al-Aḥnaf reported that he contracted a marriage with a former handmaiden of ʿAbd al-Raḥmān b. Zayd b. al-Khaṭṭāb who had borne ʿAbd al-Raḥmān a child (*umm walad*). Thābit said, "ʿAbd Allāh b. ʿAbd al-Raḥmān b. Zayd b. al-Khaṭṭāb called for me, so I went to see him. I went in and was surprised to see a whip and two iron cuffs placed before me and two of his slaves sitting next to him. He said, 'Divorce her or, by the One by whom oaths are sworn, I shall do to you such-and-such.' Terrified, I said, 'Divorce it is, one thousand times!' I then left his house and caught up with ʿAbd Allāh b. ʿUmar on the road to Mecca. I told him what had happened, and he became extremely angry. He said, 'That is not a divorce, and she is not forbidden to you, so return to your wife.' I was not at ease until I went to ʿAbd Allāh b. al-Zubayr, who at the time was the governor of Mecca, and told him what had happened and what ʿAbd Allāh b. ʿUmar had told me. ʿAbd Allāh b. al-Zubayr said to me, 'Indeed, she is not forbidden to you, so return to your wife.' He then wrote to Jābir b. al-Aswad al-Zuhrī, who was then the governor of Medina, ordering him to punish ʿAbd Allāh b. ʿAbd al-Raḥmān and to tell him not to come between me and my wife. I then went to Medina, and Ṣafiyya, ʿAbd Allāh b. ʿUmar's wife, prepared my bride for the marriage and brought her to my home, with the knowledge of ʿAbd Allāh b. ʿUmar. I then invited ʿAbd Allāh b. ʿUmar to the wedding feast on my wedding day, and he came."

1860. According to Mālik, ʿAbd Allāh b. Dīnār said, "I heard ʿAbd Allāh b. ʿUmar recite, 'Prophet, when you divorce women, divorce them at the beginning—*qubul*—of their waiting periods.'"[753] Mālik said, "He meant that a man should divorce his wife only once, after her period has ended."[754]

1861. According to Mālik, Hishām b. ʿUrwa reported that his father said, "It was previously the case that a man could divorce his wife and reclaim her before her waiting period (*ʿidda*) expired even if he had divorced her a thousand times. Then a man decided to be spiteful toward his wife, so

753 *Al-Ṭalāq*, 65:1.

754 According to this report, ʿAbd Allāh b. ʿUmar inserted the word *qubul* ("beginning") immediately before *ʿiddatihinna* ("their waiting periods") in the Quranic verse he was reciting as a clarification of the verse's meaning; the word is not actually part of the verse. Mālik's comment related to that specific word.

he divorced her, and when she had nearly concluded her waiting period, he exercised his right to reclaim her, and then divorced her again, saying, 'No, by God! Neither shall I return you to my house, nor shall I ever let you become eligible for remarriage.' So God, Blessed and Sublime is He, revealed 'Divorce is only twice, and after that, he either retains her equitably or releases her with generosity.'[755] Thereafter, the new rule regarding divorce applied both to men who had previously divorced their wives and to those who had not."

1862. According to Mālik, Thawr b. Zayd al-Dīlī reported that a man would divorce his wife and then reclaim her, even though he had no desire for her, nor a desire to live with her, only to lengthen her waiting period and to vex her. God, Blessed and Sublime is He, therefore revealed "Do not retain them to vex them so that you may transgress their rights; whoever does so has wronged his own soul."[756] God admonished such men with that verse.

1863. According to Mālik, it reached him that Saʿīd b. al-Musayyab and Sulaymān b. Yasār were asked about the effectiveness of a drunken man's divorce. They each said, "A drunken man's divorce binds him, and if he kills someone while drunk, he is subject to retaliation." Mālik said, "That is the rule among us (*dhālika al-amr ʿindanā*)."

1864. According to Mālik, it reached him that Saʿīd b. al-Musayyab would say, "If a man is unable to maintain his wife, they are to be separated." Mālik said, "That is what I found the people of knowledge in our town following (*ʿalā dhālika adraktu ahl al-ʿīlm bi-baladinā*)."

Chapter 30. The Waiting Period (*ʿIdda*) of a Widow

1865. According to Mālik, ʿAbd Rabbih b. Saʿīd b. Qays reported that Abū Salama b. ʿAbd al-Raḥmān said, "ʿAbd Allāh b. ʿAbbās and Abū Hurayra were asked about the waiting period of a pregnant woman whose husband dies, leaving her a widow. Ibn ʿAbbās said, 'The lengthier of the two periods.' Abū Hurayra, however, said, 'Once she gives birth, she may remarry.'" Abū Salama b. ʿAbd al-Raḥmān then went to Umm Salama, the wife of the Prophet (pbuh), and asked her that very same question, and she said, "Subayʿa al-Aslamiyya gave birth two weeks after her husband's death, and two men approached her with proposals of marriage. One was a young man and the other was middle-aged. She was clearly inclined toward the young man, so the middle-aged man said, 'You may not yet marry.' Her family was away at the time, and he entertained a hope that when they returned, they would

755 *Al-Baqara*, 2:229.
756 *Al-Baqara*, 2:231.

prefer him and prevail on her to accept him rather than the younger suitor. But she went to the Messenger of God (pbuh) and told him of her situation. He said, 'You are free to marry now, so marry whomever you wish.'"

1866. According to Mālik, Nāfiʿ reported from ʿAbd Allāh b. ʿUmar that he was asked about a woman whose husband dies while she is pregnant. ʿAbd Allāh b. ʿUmar said, "Once she gives birth, she may remarry." A Medinese man who was present with him informed him that ʿUmar b. al-Khaṭṭāb had said, "Once she has delivered, even if her husband's corpse is still warm on his deathbed, unburied, she is eligible to remarry."

1867. According to Mālik, Hishām b. ʿUrwa reported from his father that al-Miswar b. Makhrama informed him that Subayʿa al-Aslamiyya gave birth a few nights after her husband died. The Messenger of God (pbuh) said to her, "You are free to marry, so marry whomever you wish."

1868. According to Mālik, Yaḥyā b. Saʿīd reported from Sulaymān b. Yasār that ʿAbd Allāh b. ʿAbbās and Abū Salama b. ʿAbd al-Raḥmān b. ʿAwf disagreed about a married woman who gives birth a few nights after her husband's death. Abū Salama said, "Once she gives birth, she may remarry." Ibn ʿAbbās said, "She may remarry only at the expiration of the longer of the two terms: the end of her pregnancy or the waiting period of a widow." Then Abū Hurayra came and said, "I agree with my nephew" (that is, Abū Salama), so they sent Kurayb, the freedman (*mawlā*) of ʿAbd Allāh b. ʿAbbās, to Umm Salama, the wife of the Prophet (pbuh), to ask her about this issue. He came back to them and told them that she had said that Subayʿa al-Aslamiyya had given birth a few nights after the death of her husband. Subayʿa mentioned her situation to the Messenger of God (pbuh), who said to her, "You may remarry, so marry whomever you wish." Mālik said, "This is the rule that the people of knowledge in our town have always followed (*al-amr alladhī lam yazal ʿalayhi ahl al-ʿilm bi-baladinā*)."

Chapter 31. The Widow's Seclusion in the Marital Home Until She Can Remarry

1869. According to Mālik, Saʿīd b. Isḥāq b. Kaʿb b. ʿUjra reported from his paternal aunt, Zaynab bt. Kaʿb b. ʿUjra, that al-Furayʿa bt. Mālik b. Sinān, the sister of Abū Saʿīd al-Khudrī, informed her that al-Furayʿa had gone to the Messenger of God (pbuh) to ask him for permission to return to her people, the Banū Khudra, a Medinese tribe. Her husband had set out in search of some of his slaves who had run away, and when he caught up with them near al-Qadūm,[757] they killed him. Al-Furayʿa said, "I asked the Messenger

757 A place six *mīl*s from Medina. Zurqānī, *Sharḥ al-Zurqānī*, 3:338.

of God (pbuh) for permission to return to my people, the Banū Khudra. My husband did not leave me in a house that he owned, nor did he leave me maintenance (*nafaqa*). The Messenger of God (pbuh) said, 'Yes.' Therefore I set out to leave, but when I had reached the courtyard of his house, the Messenger of God (pbuh) called out to me, or had me summoned, and asked, 'What did you say?' I repeated the story that I had previously told him concerning my husband. He now said, 'Stay in the marital home until the prescribed term comes to an end.' Accordingly, I observed the entirety of my waiting period (*ʿidda*) of four months and ten days there. When ʿUthmān b. ʿAffān became caliph, he once sent for me and asked me about where a widow should observe her waiting period. I told him what had happened in my case, and he followed it and ruled in accordance with it."

1870. According to Mālik, Ḥumayd b. Qays al-Makkī reported from ʿAmr b. Shuʿayb, from Saʿīd b. al-Musayyab, that ʿUmar b. al-Khaṭṭāb would send widows who had come from the desert back to their homes, prohibiting them from performing the Pilgrimage (*ḥajj*) until their waiting periods had come to an end.

1871. According to Mālik, Yaḥyā b. Saʿīd reported that it reached him that al-Sāʾib b. Khabbāb died, and his wife went to ʿAbd Allāh b. ʿUmar and told him about her husband's death. She also mentioned to him that they owned some farmland at Qanāt[758] and asked him whether it would be appropriate for her to stay the night there. However, he prohibited her from doing so. As a result, she would leave Medina before dawn and arrive at their farm in the morning, remaining there through the day. She would then return to Medina when night fell and spend the night in the marital home.

1872. According to Mālik, Hishām b. ʿUrwa reported that his father would say, regarding a bedouin woman whose husband died, that she was free to travel and camp wherever her people travel and pitch their tents. Mālik said, "That is the rule among us (*dhālika al-amr ʿindanā*)."

1873. According to Mālik, Nāfiʿ reported that ʿAbd Allāh b. ʿUmar would say, "Neither a widow nor a woman who has been divorced three times should spend the night anywhere other than the marital home until her waiting period expires."

758 A district on the outskirts of Medina.

Chapter 32. The Waiting Period (*ʿIdda*) of a Handmaiden Who Has Borne Her Master a Child (*Umm Walad*) When Her Master Dies

1874. According to Mālik, Yaḥyā b. Saʿīd said, "I heard al-Qāsim b. Muḥammad say, 'Yazīd b. ʿAbd al-Malik separated some men from their wives. Their wives had previously been handmaidens who had borne children for their now deceased masters (*umm walad*). Their current husbands married them after the former handmaidens had waited one or two menstrual periods after their masters' deaths. Yazīd, however, separated them from their husbands until they completed the waiting period (*ʿidda*) of a widow, four months and ten days.' Al-Qāsim b. Muḥammad then said, 'Glory be to God! God says in His Book, "And those of you who die and leave wives behind,"[759] but these handmaidens are not wives.'"

1875. According to Mālik, Nāfiʿ reported that ʿAbd Allāh b. ʿUmar said, "The waiting period for a handmaiden who has borne her master a child is one menstrual period after her master dies."

1876. According to Mālik, Yaḥyā b. Saʿīd reported that al-Qāsim b. Muḥammad would say, "The waiting period for a handmaiden who has borne her master a child is one menstrual period after her master dies." Mālik said, "That is the rule among us (*dhālika al-amr ʿindanā*)." Mālik said, "If she is a woman who does not menstruate, her waiting period is three months."

Chapter 33. The Waiting Period (*ʿIdda*) of a Handmaiden When Her Husband or Master Dies

1877. According to Mālik, it reached him that Saʿīd b. al-Musayyab and Sulaymān b. Yasār would both say, "The waiting period of a handmaiden whose husband dies is two months and five nights." Mālik said, "A similar opinion has been attributed to Ibn Shihāb."

1878. Mālik said, regarding a scenario in which a slave divorces his wife, who is herself a handmaiden, but does not do so irrevocably, so he retains the right to reclaim her as his wife, and then he dies while she is still observing her waiting period from the divorce (*ṭalāq*): "She observes the waiting period that applies to a handmaiden whose husband has died, two months and five nights. If, however, she is manumitted before her waiting period expires, but she chooses not to leave him, and then he dies during her waiting period from the divorce, she must complete the waiting period that applies to a free woman who has been widowed, namely, four months

759 *Al-Baqara*, 2:234.

and ten days. This is because the widow's waiting period came into effect after her manumission. Accordingly, her waiting period is now that of a free woman. That is the rule among us (*dhālika al-amr ʿindanā*)."

Chapter 34. What Has Come Down regarding Withdrawal before Ejaculation (*ʿAzl*)

1879. According to Mālik, Rabīʿa b. Abī ʿAbd al-Raḥmān reported from Muḥammad b. Yaḥyā b. Ḥabbān that Ibn Muḥayrīz said, "I entered the Prophet's Mosque and saw Abū Saʿīd al-Khudrī. I sat next to him and asked him about withdrawal before ejaculation (*ʿazl*). Abū Saʿīd al-Khudrī said, 'We were with the Messenger of God (pbuh) on a military campaign against the Banū al-Muṣṭaliq,[760] and we managed to seize some Arab female captives. We longed for women at the time, and our long deprivation from them had become unbearable for us. At the same time, however, we also wished to ransom them. So we resolved that were we to have intercourse with them, we would practice withdrawal in order to avoid impregnating the captives. But we wondered: Can we engage in withdrawal before asking the permission of the Messenger of God (pbuh), given that he is with us? Therefore, we asked him for his opinion, and he said, "It will make no difference whether you do so or not. Every soul from now until the Day of Judgment that is meant to be, shall certainly be."'"

1880. According to Mālik, Abū al-Naḍr, the freedman (*mawlā*) of ʿUmar b. ʿUbayd Allāh, reported from ʿĀmir b. Saʿd b. Abī Waqqāṣ, from his father, that he would practice withdrawal.

1881. According to Mālik, Abū al-Naḍr, the freedman of ʿUmar b. ʿUbayd Allāh, reported from Ibn Aflaḥ, the freedman of Abū Ayyūb, from a handmaiden of Abū Ayyūb who bore him a child (*umm walad*), that he would practice withdrawal.

1882. According to Mālik, Nāfiʿ reported from ʿAbd Allāh b. ʿUmar that he did not practice withdrawal and that he disapproved of it.

1883. According to Mālik, Ḍamra b. Saʿīd al-Māzinī reported from al-Ḥajjāj b. ʿAmr b. Ghaziyya that he was sitting with Zayd b. Thābit when Ibn Qahd, a man from Yemen, came to him and said, "Abū Saʿīd, I have handmaidens, and I am more enamored with them than with any of my wives. I would not, however, be at all happy if any of them became pregnant, so may I practice withdrawal?" Zayd b. Thābit turned to al-Ḥajjāj and said, "What is your opinion, Ḥajjāj?" Al-Ḥajjāj said, "I then said, 'May God forgive you,

760 This raid took place in year 6 of the Hijra (627 CE).

Zayd, for we sit with you only to learn, not to answer people's questions.' Zayd then said, 'Give him your legal opinion.' I therefore said to Ibn Qahd, 'They are your fields, so if you wish, water them, and if you wish, leave them dry.'" Al-Ḥajjāj said, "I used to hear that from Zayd." Zayd said, "He has spoken truthfully."

1884. According to Mālik, Ḥumayd b. Qays al-Makkī reported that a man known as Dhafīf said, "Ibn ʿAbbās was asked about withdrawal, so he summoned a handmaiden of his and said, 'Tell them.' The question appeared to embarrass her, however, so he said, 'That settles it. I myself practice it,' meaning that he practiced withdrawal."

1885. Mālik said, "A man may practice withdrawal with a free wife only with her permission, but practicing it without the permission of his handmaiden is unobjectionable."

1886. Mālik said, "Whoever is married to a handmaiden, however, may not practice withdrawal without her people's permission."

Chapter 35. What Has Come Down regarding Mourning a Dead Husband (*Iḥdād*)

1887. According to Mālik, ʿAbd Allāh b. Abī Bakr b. Muḥammad b. ʿAmr b. Ḥazm reported from Ḥumayd b. Nāfiʿ that Zaynab bt. Abī Salama informed him of the following three reports. Zaynab said, "I called on Umm Ḥabība, the wife of the Prophet (pbuh), to pay my condolences when her father, Abū Sufyān b. Ḥarb, died. Umm Ḥabība called for a yellow-colored perfume, or some other kind of perfume. After it was brought to her, she rubbed it on a handmaiden and then wiped the sides of her face with what was left. She then said, 'By God, I have no need for perfume, but I heard the Messenger of God (pbuh) say, "No woman who believes in God and the Last Day may mourn a dead person for more than three nights, except for her husband, whom she may mourn for four months and ten days."'" Zaynab said, "Then I called on Zaynab bt. Jaḥsh, the wife of the Prophet (pbuh), to offer my condolences when her brother died. She called for some perfume and put some on. She then said, 'By God, I have no need for perfume, but I heard the Messenger of God (pbuh) say, "No woman who believes in God and the Last Day may mourn a dead person for more than three nights, except for her husband, whom she may mourn for four months and ten days."'"

1888. Zaynab[761] said, "I also heard my mother, Umm Salama, the wife of the Prophet (pbuh), say, 'A woman came to the Prophet (pbuh) and said,

761 This is the third of the three reports that Zaynab said she knew of.

"Messenger of God, my daughter has been widowed, and her eyes are aching. Can she apply kohl to them?" The Messenger of God (pbuh) said, "No!" two or three times. He was saying no to everything she asked. He then said, "Mourning is only for four months and ten days. During the Days of Ignorance prior to Islam (*jāhiliyya*), a widow would only cast off a piece of dung on the one-year anniversary of her husband's death.""" Ḥumayd b. Nāfiʿ said, "I then asked Zaynab, 'What is the significance of the widow's throwing away a piece of dung on the one-year anniversary of her husband's death?' Zaynab said, 'In the Days of Ignorance before Islam, when a husband died, his widow would enter a miserable hut (*ḥifsh*), don her worst clothes, and apply neither perfume nor anything else until one year had elapsed. Then she would be brought an animal—a donkey, a sheep, or a bird—and she would rub it (*taftaḍḍu*). Rarely would these animals survive. She would then leave the hut and be given a piece of dung that she would cast away. She could then resume the use of perfume or any other form of bodily grooming as she wished.'" Mālik said, "A *ḥifsh* is a small, dirty tent, and *taftaḍḍu* means using something to rub her skin, like a charm (*nushra*)."

1889. According to Mālik, Nāfiʿ reported from Ṣafiyya bt. Abī ʿUbayd, from ʿĀ'isha and Ḥafṣa, two of the wives of the Prophet (pbuh), that the Messenger of God (pbuh) said, "It is not permissible for a woman who believes in God and the Last Day to mourn the deceased for more than three nights, except for her husband."[762]

1890. According to Mālik, it reached him that Umm Salama, the wife of the Prophet (pbuh), told a woman who was in mourning for her husband and whose eyes were swollen and in pain, "Apply medicinal kohl to them at night, and wipe it off during the day."

1891. According to Mālik, it reached him that Sālim b. ʿAbd Allāh and Sulaymān b. Yasār would both say, regarding a widow in mourning for her husband, "If she fears that the inflammation of her eyes will damage her vision or that she has been afflicted with an infection, she should use kohl and treat herself with medicine or kohl, even if it contains perfume." Mālik said, "If there is a necessity, God's law is ease."[763]

1892. According to Mālik, Nāfiʿ reported that Ṣafiyya bt. Abī ʿUbayd suffered from an infection in her eyes while she was in mourning for her

762 The Prophet's (pbuh) intention was to prohibit the mourning rites of the Days of Ignorance before Islam, not to prohibit grieving the loss of a loved one, as is clear from the content of the reports in this chapter.

763 In other words, if the mourning woman is ill, she may use materials that would otherwise be prohibited to her under the rules of mourning because her illness justifies a dispensation (*rukhṣa*) to depart from the ordinarily applicable rules.

husband, ʿAbd Allāh b. ʿUmar, but she did not apply kohl until her eyes burned from pain.

1893. Mālik said, "A widow may anoint herself with olive oil, sesame oil, and the like on the condition that it contains no perfume."

1894. Mālik said, "A widow mourning her dead husband is not to wear jewelry, rings, anklets, or the like. She is not to wear any colourful, striped garment, unless it is coarse. She is not to wear any cloth that is dyed, unless it is dyed in black. Finally, she is not to comb her hair, except with lotus-tree leaves or the like, and then only if doing so does not dye or otherwise beautify her hair."

1895. According to Mālik, it reached him that the Messenger of God (pbuh) called on Umm Salama while she was in mourning for her deceased husband, Abū Salama, and she had applied an ointment to her eyes. He said, "What is this, Umm Salama?" She said, "It is only an ointment, Messenger of God." He said, "Apply it only at night, and remove it during the day."

1896. Mālik said, "A young girl who is widowed but has not yet had a menstrual period mourns her deceased husband in the same manner as an adult woman does. She must also refrain from doing everything that an adult woman in mourning avoids."

1897. Mālik said, "A handmaiden who is widowed mourns her deceased husband for two months and five nights, like the length of her waiting period (*ʿidda*)."

1898. Mālik said, "A handmaiden who has borne her master a child (*umm walad*) need not mourn him when he dies, nor must a handmaiden mourn her deceased master. Mourning is only an obligation for wives."

1899. According to Mālik, it reached him that Umm Salama, the wife of the Prophet (pbuh), would say, "A mourning woman may comb her hair with lotus tree leaves and oil, so long as it is not scented."

The Book of Divorce (*Ṭalāq*) Has Been Completed, with Praise to God, the Lord of the Worlds.

Book 33

The Book of Breastfeeding (*Raḍāʿa*)

In the Name of God, the Merciful, the Compassionate

May God Grace Muḥammad and His Family
and Grant Them Perfect Tranquility.

Chapter 1. Breastfeeding (*Raḍāʿa*) of the Young

1900. Yaḥyā related to me from Mālik, from ʿAbd Allāh b. Abī Bakr, from ʿAmra bt. ʿAbd al-Raḥmān, that ʿĀʾisha, the Mother of the Believers, informed her that the Messenger of God (pbuh) was once with her when she heard a man's voice requesting permission to enter Ḥafṣa's room. ʿĀʾisha said, "Messenger of God, a man requests permission to enter your house." The Messenger of God (pbuh) said, "It must be so-and-so," referring to a paternal uncle of Ḥafṣa by breastfeeding (*raḍāʿa*). ʿĀʾisha then said, "Messenger of God, had so-and-so been alive," referring to her own paternal uncle by breastfeeding, "would he have been allowed to come and go freely to visit me?" The Messenger of God (pbuh) said, "Yes; breastfeeding makes taboo what birth makes taboo."[764]

1901. According to Mālik, Hishām b. ʿUrwa reported from his father that ʿĀʾisha, the Mother of the Believers, said, "My paternal uncle by breastfeeding came and requested permission to see me. I did not permit him to do so before I could ask the Messenger of God (pbuh). The Messenger of God (pbuh) came, so I asked him. He said, 'He is your paternal uncle, so allow him to enter.' I then said, 'Messenger of God, it was a woman who breastfed me, not a man!' He said, 'Nevertheless, he is in the position of your paternal uncle. Let him in, so he can see you.' This event took place after seclusion[765]

764 That is, just as people are prohibited from marrying certain close relations sharing common descent, breastfeeding creates bars to marriage between the breastfed child and the breastfeeding woman and, by extension, her close relatives.

765 The Quran imposed a special norm of seclusion on the wives of the Prophet (pbuh) in *al-Aḥzāb*, 33:33, and an absolute prohibition on their remarriage after his death in *al-Aḥzāb*, 33:53.

had been imposed on us." ʿĀʾisha later explained, "Whatever is taboo by birth is also taboo by breastfeeding."

1902. According to Mālik, Ibn Shihāb reported from ʿUrwa b. al-Zubayr that ʿĀʾisha, the Mother of the Believers, informed him that Aflaḥ, the brother of Abū al-Quʿays, who was her paternal uncle by breastfeeding, once came and requested permission to see her after the obligation of seclusion had been revealed. She said, "I did not grant him permission to see me, and when the Messenger of God (pbuh) came, I told him what had happened. He ordered me, however, to allow Aflaḥ to see me."

1903. According to Mālik, Thawr b. Zayd al-Dīlī reported that ʿAbd Allāh b. ʿAbbās would say, "Any breastmilk that is swallowed within the first two years of a newborn's life, even if it is only one swallow, makes taboo whatever birth makes taboo."

1904. According to Mālik, Ibn Shihāb reported from ʿAmr b. al-Sharīd that ʿAbd Allāh b. ʿAbbās was asked about a man who was married to two women, one of whom breastfed a slave-boy, while the other breastfed a handmaiden; could the boy marry the girl? He said, "No; they share the same father through breastfeeding."

1905. According to Mālik, Nāfiʿ reported that ʿAbd Allāh b. ʿUmar would say, "The prohibitions of breastfeeding affect only someone who was breastfed in infancy; a non-infant who breastfeeds is not subject to those taboos."

1906. According to Mālik, Nāfiʿ reported that Sālim b. ʿAbd Allāh informed him that when he, Sālim, had been an infant and still breastfed, ʿĀʾisha, the Mother of the Believers, had sent him to her sister, Umm Kulthūm bt. Abī Bakr, saying to her, "Breastfeed him ten times so that he may come and go freely in my house." Sālim said, "Umm Kulthūm breastfed me three times, but then she became ill and could not complete the ten feedings. As a result, I could not come and go freely in ʿĀʾisha's presence, because Umm Kulthūm had not finished the requisite number of feedings."

1907. According to Mālik, Nāfiʿ reported that Ṣafiyya bt. Abī ʿUbayd informed him that Ḥafṣa, the Mother of the Believers, sent ʿĀṣim b. ʿAbd Allāh b. Saʿd to her sister, Fāṭima bt. ʿUmar b. al-Khaṭṭāb, when he was an infant, telling her to breastfeed him ten times so that he could come and go freely in her presence when he became an adult. Fāṭima did as Ṣafiyya instructed, and as a result, he went freely to her when he became an adult.

1908. According to Mālik, ʿAbd al-Raḥmān b. al-Qāsim reported that his father informed him that ʿĀʾisha permitted men to come and go freely in her presence only if her sisters or paternal nieces had breastfed them. She did not give such permission to men whom her sisters-in-law had breastfed.

1909. According to Mālik, Ibrāhīm b. ʿUqba reported that he asked Saʿīd b. al-Musayyab about breastfeeding, and Saʿīd said, "Any breastfeeding that takes place during the first two years of an infant's life, even if it involves only one drop of breastmilk, is sufficient to produce the same taboo that birth produces. Whatever breastmilk is ingested thereafter, however, is just food that the child eats." Ibrāhīm b. ʿUqba said, "I then asked ʿUrwa b. al-Zubayr for his opinion. His opinion was similar to that of Saʿīd b. al-Musayyab."

1910. According to Mālik, Yaḥyā b. Saʿīd said, "I heard Saʿīd b. al-Musayyab say, 'Only the breastfeeding of an infant still in his cradle has the effect of producing the same taboo that birth produces. Breastfeeding thereafter does not nourish the child or cause him to grow.'"

1911. According to Mālik, Ibn Shihāb would say, "Breastfeeding, whether in a large amount or a small one, produces the same taboo that birth produces, on both the male and the female side."[766]

1912. Yaḥyā said, "I heard Mālik say, 'Breastfeeding, whether in a small amount or a large one, during the first two years of an infant's life produces the same taboo that birth produces. Any breastfeeding that occurs thereafter, whether much or little, does not produce the same taboo that birth produces; it is merely food.'"

Chapter 2. What Has Come Down regarding Breastfeeding (*Raḍāʿa*) an Adult

1913. According to Mālik, Ibn Shihāb reported that he was asked about breastfeeding an adult. Ibn Shihāb said, "ʿUrwa b. al-Zubayr informed me that Abū Ḥudhayfa b. ʿUtba b. Rabīʿa, who was a Companion of the Messenger of God (pbuh) and who fought at the Battle of Badr, had adopted Sālim, the one who is now known as Sālim the freedman (*mawlā*) of Abū Ḥudhayfa, just as the Messenger of God (pbuh) had adopted Zayd b. Ḥāritha. Abū Ḥudhayfa, deeming Sālim his son, had arranged to have him marry his niece, Fāṭima bt. al-Walīd b. ʿUtba b. Rabīʿa. She was one of the first Muslim women of Mecca to emigrate to Medina, and one of the most suitable unmarried women of the Quraysh. When God, Blessed and Sublime is He, revealed in His Book the verses concerning Zayd b. Ḥāritha, including the verse 'Call them by their real fathers' names; that is more just in God's sight. But if you do not know their real fathers' names, they are your brothers in faith and your freedmen,'[767] all adopted males, such as Sālim and Zayd, took the names of their real fathers. If no one knew who such a man's father was, he was

766 In other words, just as the nursing woman becomes the foster mother of the infant, the nursing woman's husband becomes the infant's foster father, and his brothers become the infant's foster paternal uncles.

767 *Al-Aḥzāb*, 33:5.

known as the freedman of the person who had manumitted him. Sahla bt. Suhayl, Abū Ḥudhayfa's wife, of the clan of Banū ʿĀmir b. Luʾayy, then went to the Messenger of God (pbuh) and said, 'Messenger of God, we always thought of Sālim as a son. He would come and go in my presence while I was dressed only in the clothing I wear in private. We have only one room in our house. What do you think we should do?' According to what has reached us, the Messenger of God (pbuh) told her, 'Breastfeed him five times, and you will be in the same position as his birth mother as a result.' She did so, and consequently considered him her foster son. ʿĀʾisha, the Mother of the Believers, relied on that as a precedent for any man whom she wanted to allow to come and go freely in her presence. Accordingly, she would tell her sister, Umm Kulthūm bt. Abī Bakr al-Ṣiddīq, and her daughters to breastfeed anyone whom she desired to admit freely to her presence. The other wives of the Prophet (pbuh), however, would not permit anyone who had been breastfed as an adult to come and go freely in their presence. They said, 'No, by God, we believe that the advice the Messenger of God (pbuh) gave Sahla bt. Suhayl was merely a special dispensation for her to breastfeed Sālim, one that does not apply to anyone else. No one, by God, shall come and go freely in our presence by such means.' These were the views that the wives of the Prophet (pbuh) had regarding the effects of breastfeeding an adult male."

1914. According to Mālik, ʿAbd Allāh b. Dīnār said, "A man came to ʿAbd Allāh b. ʿUmar while I was with him in the chamber of justice (*dār al-qaḍāʾ*) to ask him about the legal consequences of breastfeeding an adult. ʿAbd Allāh b. ʿUmar said, 'A man once came to ʿUmar b. al-Khaṭṭāb and said, "I have a handmaiden with whom I would have sexual relations. My wife sought her out and forced the handmaiden to drink her breastmilk. The next time I saw my wife, she said, 'Keep your distance from her, for by God, I have breastfed her.'" ʿUmar said, "You may punish your wife, if you wish, and resume having sexual relations with the handmaiden. The only breastfeeding that produces a taboo is breastfeeding that takes place during infancy."'"

1915. According to Mālik, Yaḥyā b. Saʿīd reported that a man told Abū Mūsā al-Ashʿarī, "I accidentally sucked some of my wife's breastmilk and swallowed it." Abū Mūsā said, "I can only conclude that it is now forbidden for you to keep her as a wife." ʿAbd Allāh b. Masʿūd said, "Take care in the opinions you give this man," so Abū Mūsā said, "What is your opinion, then?" ʿAbd Allāh b. Masʿūd said, "The only breastfeeding that produces a taboo is that which takes place during an infant's first two years of life." Abū Mūsā said, "People, you should not ask me about anything as long as this learned man is among you."

Chapter 3. Miscellaneous Matters regarding Breastfeeding (*Raḍāʿa*)

1916. According to Mālik, ʿAbd Allāh b. Dīnār reported from Sulaymān b. Yasār and from ʿUrwa b. al-Zubayr, from ʿĀʾisha, the Mother of the Believers, that the Messenger of God (pbuh) said, "What is taboo by virtue of birth is taboo by virtue of breastfeeding."

1917. According to Mālik, Muḥammad b. ʿAbd al-Raḥmān b. Nawfal said that ʿUrwa b. al-Zubayr informed him, from ʿĀʾisha, the Mother of the Believers, that Judāma bt. Wahb al-Asadiyya informed ʿĀʾisha that she heard the Messenger of God (pbuh) say, "I was of a mind to prohibit *ghīla*, but I remembered that the Romans and Persians have no such restrictions, and their children are fine." Yaḥyā said, "Mālik said, '*Ghīla* is when a man has sexual relations with his wife while she is breastfeeding.'"[768]

1918. According to Mālik, ʿAbd Allāh b. Abī Bakr b. Muḥammad b. ʿAmr b. Ḥazm reported from ʿAmra bt. ʿAbd al-Raḥmān that ʿĀʾisha, the wife of the Prophet (pbuh), said, "Originally, the Quran provided that ten definitive instances of breastfeeding were required to produce the taboo that birth produces. That was later abrogated and reduced to five definitive instances of breastfeeding. At the time the Prophet (pbuh) died, this was still being recited as part of the Quran." Yaḥyā said, "Mālik said, 'The practice (*ʿamal*) is not in accord with this.'"

The Book of Breastfeeding (*Raḍāʿa*) Is Complete.
Praise Belongs to God, the Lord of the Worlds.

768 The basis for the belief that this would harm the nursing child is that the nursing mother might become pregnant and consequently cease lactating, and the newborn would then not receive adequate nourishment from the mother.

Book 34
The Book of Sales (*Buyūʿ*)

In the Name of God, the Merciful, the Compassionate

May God Grace Muḥammad and His Family
and Grant Them Tranquility.

Chapter 1. What Has Come Down regarding Nonrefundable Deposits (*Bayʿ al-ʿUrbān*[769])[770]

1919. According to Mālik, a source that he deemed reliable reported from ʿAmr b. Shuʿayb, from his father, from his grandfather, that the Messenger of God (pbuh) prohibited sales involving nonrefundable deposits. Mālik said, "In our view, and God knows best, such a sale takes place when a man buys a slave or a handmaiden, or hires a pack animal, and then tells the seller or the lessor, as the case may be, 'I'll give you a dinar, or dirham, or something more or less than that, on the condition that if I complete the purchase or decide to rent the animal, what I previously gave you is included in the final purchase price or final rent. However, if I do not complete the purchase of the merchandise or end up leasing the animal, whatever I gave you previously is yours to keep, with no obligation on your part to return it."

1920. Mālik said, "The rule in our view (*al-amr ʿindanā*) is that there is no objection to trading an Arabic-speaking slave who has commercial experience for several Abyssinian slaves or several slaves of any other race who are not his equal in fluency, commercial expertise, judgment, and skill. There is no objection if someone trades on credit one slave for two or more slaves whose attributes differ from those of first slave, provided that the date of delivery is specified and the slaves clearly differ in their qualities. If they resemble one another, however, to the extent that they are

769 Also known as *ʿarbūn* and *arbūn*.

770 This is the correct chapter heading. The published edition of the RME, however, contains the erroneous chapter title "Breastfeeding (*Raḍāʿa*) of the Young."

near-substitutes for one another, it is prohibited to trade one slave for two on credit, even if the slaves are of different races."

1921. Mālik said, "There is nothing objectionable in selling what you are to receive from that prior transaction before you take full possession of it, as long as you paid its price in cash and the purchaser is not the same person who originally sold you that merchandise."

1922. Mālik said, "If someone sells a pregnant female, whether a handmaiden or livestock, he may not retain ownership of the mother's fetus, because that would result in a sale with material uncertainty in the consideration (*gharar*). In these circumstances, one cannot know whether the fetus is male or female, handsome or ugly, deformed or fully formed, or alive or dead, but all of these are factors that affect its price."

1923. Mālik said, regarding a scenario in which a man who buys a male slave or a handmaiden for one hundred dinars on credit, and then the seller regrets the sale and asks the purchaser to cancel the transaction for ten dinars, payable in cash or on credit, and agrees in exchange to waive the one hundred dinars that the purchaser owes the seller: "There is nothing objectionable in that. Such a transaction is not permissible, however, if the purchaser is the one who regrets the sale and asks the seller to rescind it, offering to pay the seller ten dinars either in cash or on credit, due after the date specified in the original sale. The reason this latter transaction is prohibited is that it is as if the seller is selling to the purchaser the one hundred dinars that the purchaser already owes him, but in advance of its maturity date, for a handmaiden and ten dinars in cash, or on credit after the originally specified date. This transaction therefore implicitly involves the sale of gold for gold on credit terms, which is prohibited."[771]

1924. Mālik said, regarding someone who sells to another man a handmaiden for one hundred dinars on credit and then repurchases her at a higher price, also on credit but after the expiry of the original credit

771 The difference between the cases is the following. In the first case, the seller is effectively repurchasing the slave that he sold to the purchaser with a mark-up, in this case of ten dinars. Such a resale raises no legal problems. In the second case, however, because the purchaser owes the seller one hundred dinars and is now offering the seller ten dinars and the return of the slave in exchange for cancellation of the debt, it is as though the purchaser is purchasing the debt he owes for the price of the slave and ten dinars. This entails the deferred exchange of gold (the one hundred dinars) for gold (the ten dinars), which is not permitted. Another possible analysis of the second transaction, and the one adopted by Bājī, is that it involves a sale combined with a loan, pursuant to which the purchaser agrees to prepay ten dinars of the original debt and sells the slave back to the seller in exchange for cancellation of the original hundred-dinar obligation. Mālikīs do not consider a sale combined with a loan valid. Bājī, *al-Muntaqā*, 4:164.

term: "This is an impermissible transaction. An illustration of this rule is the case of a man who sells a handmaiden on credit and then repurchases her on credit after the expiry of the original credit term. For example, he sells her for thirty dinars, due in one month, and then repurchases her for sixty dinars, due in one year or in half a year. The result is that the very goods that he originally sold, in this case the handmaiden, are restored to him. Meanwhile, the second party (the original purchaser) gives the first party (the original seller) thirty dinars, payable in thirty days, against an obligation by the first party to pay sixty dinars to the second party in one year or half a year. This is, in effect, a credit sale of thirty dinars for sixty dinars, which is not permissible."

Chapter 2. The Property of a Chattel Slave (*Mamlūk*)

1925. According to Mālik, Nāfiʿ reported from ʿAbd Allāh b. ʿUmar that ʿUmar b. al-Khaṭṭāb said, "If a man sells a chattel slave, and the slave himself owns some property, the property remains the seller's, unless the purchaser stipulates its inclusion in the contract of sale."

1926. Mālik said, "The agreed-upon rule among us (*al-amr al-mujtamaʿ ʿalayhi ʿindanā*) is that if the purchaser stipulates the inclusion of the chattel slave's property in the contract of sale, the slave's property goes to the purchaser, whether it be cash, debt, or goods, known or unknown, even if it turns out that the value of the slave's property exceeds his sale price, whether he was purchased for cash, debt, or goods. This is because the master is not liable to pay the alms-tax in respect of the slave's property. If the slave owns a handmaiden, his ownership of her permits him to have sexual relations with her. If the slave is manumitted or becomes a party to a manumission contract, his personal property remains with him. If he goes bankrupt, his creditors are entitled to seize his property, and his master is not answerable for any portion of his debts."

Chapter 3. The Seller's Liability (*ʿUhda*) for Defects

1927. According to Mālik, ʿAbd Allāh b. Abī Bakr b. Muḥammad b. ʿAmr b. Ḥazm reported that Abān b. ʿUthmān and Hishām b. Ismāʿīl made regular reference in their Friday sermons to the seller's liability for defects in male and female slaves appearing within three days of their purchase, and for defects appearing within one year thereof.[772]

772 Both Abān and Hishām served as governors of Medina. Bājī understands this report as indicating that both of them were keen on communicating these rules clearly to the public by mentioning them regularly in their Friday sermons. Bājī, *al-Muntaqā*, 4:172–73.

1928. Mālik said, "The seller is responsible for any defects that appear in a slave, male or female, for a period of three days after the purchase of the slave. The seller is also responsible for a period of one year from the date of the slave's sale for the specific defects of insanity (*junūn*), elephantiasis (*judhām*), and leprosy (*baraṣ*).[773] Once a year has passed, the seller is free of liability for anything that subsequently happens to the slave."

1929. Mālik said, "Anyone who sells a male or female slave, whether the seller be an heir or a non-heir,[774] on the condition that he not be held liable for any defects whatsoever is in fact absolved of liability for any defects that subsequently appear in the slave, unless the seller knew of the defect and concealed it. If he knew of the defect and concealed it, the contractual waiver of liability is not effective, and the sale is rescinded. In our opinion, the seller's liability for defects exists only in the case of the sale of slaves."[775]

Chapter 4. Defects (*ʿAyb*) in Slaves

1930. According to Mālik, Yaḥyā b. Saʿīd reported from Sālim b. ʿAbd Allāh that ʿAbd Allāh b. ʿUmar sold a slave-boy of his for 800 dirhams, with a disclaimer of liability for any defects. After the sale, the boy showed signs of illness, and the purchaser said to ʿAbd Allāh, "The boy has a disease that you did not disclose to me." They took their dispute to ʿUthmān b. ʿAffān, and the man said, "He sold me a slave-boy with a disease that he failed to disclose to me." ʿAbd Allāh, however, said, "I sold the boy with a disclaimer of liability." ʿUthmān ruled that ʿAbd Allāh had to swear an oath that at the time of the sale he had no knowledge that the slave suffered from any disease. ʿAbd Allāh refused to swear the oath. As a result, the sale was rescinded, and the slave was returned to him. The slave subsequently recovered, and ʿAbd Allāh then sold him for 1,500 dirhams.

---

773 Elephantiasis leads to the loss of limbs, whereas leprosy does not. Mohammed Ghaly, *Islam and Disability: Perspectives in Theology and Jurisprudence* (London: Routledge, 2010), 17.

774 An heir who is selling an inherited slave bears no personal liability for any post-sale defects that arise in the slave, whether within three days or one year. Any such liability is instead borne collectively by all the heirs. Bājī, *al-Muntaqā*, 4:179.

775 Mālik divides sales into three categories with respect to the seller's liability for defects. The first consists of sales of items that are subject to the three-day and one-year warranties; these apply exclusively to slaves. The second involves the sale of anything that the seller could have damaged through mishandling or fraud. Mālik provides no determinate time period for the warranty in sales of this category; rather, the purchaser is entitled to bring an action to rescind such a sale upon discovery of the defect. The third kind of sale is a *caveat emptor* sale in which the seller disclaims all warranties unless it can be shown that he knew of the existence of a defect and concealed it. The view Mālik expresses in this report refers exclusively to the first category of sales.

1931. Mālik said, "The agreed-upon rule among us (*al-amr al-mujtamaʿ ʿalayhi ʿindanā*) is that if someone purchases a handmaiden and then she becomes pregnant, or he purchases a slave whom he then manumits, or any other condition arises in the slave subsequent to the purchase that makes his return impossible, but reliable evidence is introduced proving that a defect existed when the slave was still in the seller's possession, or that fact comes to be known either because the seller admits it or through other means, the purchaser is entitled to have the fair market value of the male or female slave on the purchase date determined by appraisal, taking the defect into account. The purchaser is then given a partial refund of his purchase price in proportion to the difference between the fair market value of the slave in the absence of the defect and his fair market value as is."[776]

1932. Mālik said, "The agreed-upon rule among us is that if a man buys a slave and then finds a defect in him that would ordinarily permit him to rescind the sale, return the slave to the seller, and receive a full refund of the purchase price, but after the purchaser took possession of the slave a second, substantial defect—such as the loss of a limb or an eye or something similar—arose, the purchaser of the slave is entitled to choose the more favorable of the following two options. If he wishes, he may receive a refund of the slave's purchase price in an amount proportional to the reduction in the slave's value arising out of the initial defect, calculated as of the day he purchased the slave. Alternatively, if he wishes, he may reimburse the seller for the diminution in the slave's value arising out of the second defect, return the slave to to the seller, and receive a full refund of the purchase price.[777] If, however, the slave dies while in the purchaser's possession, the slave's fair market value on the date of purchase, taking the defect into account, is determined. Then the purchase price is taken into account.[778] If, for example, the fair market value of the slave, assuming him to have been free of the defect, was one hundred dinars as of the purchase date, and his

776 Because the condition of the slave has materially changed after the purchase, whether because of pregnancy, manumission, or some other reason, the purchaser cannot simply return the slave to the seller and receive a refund of the purchase price. Consequently, his remedy is limited to a proportional refund. If, for example, the defect results in a 20 percent reduction in the slave's fair market value, the purchaser is entitled to a refund of 20 percent of the purchase price.

777 In other words, if the purchaser chooses to return the defective slave, the seller can deduct from the refunded purchase price the diminution in the slave's value caused by the subsequent defect in the slave. Therefore, if the slave's original purchse price had been one hundred dinars, but the second defect, which arose while the slave was in the purchaser's possession, caused a diminution of ten dinars in the slave's value, the seller need refund to the purchaser only ninety dinars, if the purchaser exercises his option to rescind the sale.

778 Mālik presumably takes the contract price as definitive of the slave's fair market value as of the date of purchase in the absence of the undisclosed defect.

fair market value with the defect as of the purchase date was eighty dinars, the purchaser is entitled to a refund of the difference between the two. The slave's value is calculated as of the date the slave was purchased."

1933. Mālik said, "The agreed-upon rule among us is that if someone discovers a defect in his handmaiden after having sexual intercourse with her and then returns her to the seller, he must reimburse the seller for the reduction in her fair market value if she was a virgin (*bikr*). If, however, she was a matron (*thayyib*), he bears no liability to the seller arising out of his intercourse with her, insofar as he bore the risk of loss for anything that happened to her while she was in his possession."[779]

1934. Mālik said, "The agreed-upon rule among us is that a person who sells a male or female slave or an animal, whether the seller is an heir or anyone else, and disclaims liability for any defects in the sold item is not liable for any defect that subsequently appears in the sold item, unless he knew of the defect and concealed it. If he knew of the defect and concealed it, his disclaimer of liability is ineffective, the sale is rescinded, and the sold item is returned to him."

1935. Mālik said, regarding a scenario in which one handmaiden is exchanged for two others, and then a defect that permits the return of one of the two is discovered, "First, the fair market value of the one handmaiden who was exchanged for the two is determined, and then the sale price (in this case, her appraised value) is taken into account. Then the fair market value of the two handmaidens is determined, on the assumption that the defective handmaiden was free of the defect. In other words, they are both appraised on the assumption that they are healthy and free of defects. Then the purchase price of each of the two handmaidens is determined by allocating the appraised value of the one handmaiden who was exchanged for the two between the two other handmaidens in proportion to their respective values, each of the two taking her share of that joint value, the more valuable of the two in proportion to her higher value, and the less valuable one in proportion to her value.[780] Then the fair market value of the handmaiden with the defect is taken into account, and the purchaser, upon returning her to the seller, receives a partial refund of the purchase price

779 In other words, because the purchaser's possession of the handmaiden was lawful, and because anything that happened to her until she was returned to the seller was at the purchaser's risk, he was entitled to have intercourse with her.

780 In other words, if the fair market value of the one handmaiden was appraised at one hundred dinars, and the fair market value of the two handmaidens, on the assumption that they were free of defects, was appraised at fifty and twenty-five dinars, respectively, the first of the two is worth twice as much as the second. Accordingly, the deemed price of the first of the two handmaidens would be sixty-seven dinars and that of the second thirty-three dinars.

in proportion to that handmaiden's share of the total value, whether that share is great or small. The fair market value of the two handmaidens is determined as of the date the purchaser took possession of them."

1936. Mālik said, regarding a man who buys a slave and hires him out to others, charging either a high or a low price for the slave's labor, and then finds a defect in the slave that would rescind the sale, "The purchaser returns the slave to the seller on account of that defect, but the purchaser retains whatever he collected from hiring out the slave to others or whatever the slave produced while in his possession. That is the rule that the community in our town has followed (*al-amr alladhī kānat ʿalayhi al-jamāʿa bi-baladinā*).[781] This is because were someone to purchase a slave who then builds him a house, the house's fair market value would be several times greater than that of the slave himself. If the purchaser were then to discover a defect in the slave that results in the rescission of the sale, and he elected to return the slave to the seller, the purchaser would not be obliged to pay the seller for the work that the slave did for him while the slave was in his possession. For the same reason, the purchaser in this case is entitled to retain any amount he collected from hiring out the slave to others, because the purchaser bore the risk of the slave's loss while the slave was in his possession. That is the rule among us (*dhālika al-amr ʿindanā*)."

1937. Mālik said, "The rule in our view regarding a man who buys a group of slaves in a single transaction and then discovers that one of them was stolen or has a defect is that the condition of the stolen or defective slave is taken into account. If that slave is the best of the lot or the most valuable of them, or if the lot of them was purchased in order to obtain that particular slave, and he is the one that everyone recognizes as the best of the lot were it not for that defect, the entire deal may be rescinded. If, on the other hand, the slave that is discovered to be stolen or defective represents only a trifling portion of the group's collective value and is not considered the best of the lot, and the deal was not concluded in order to acquire that particular slave, nor is he the one that everyone recognizes as the best of the lot, then that particular slave, whether stolen or defective, may be returned to the seller, and the purchaser is given a refund in an amount equal to the ratio of that slave's fair market value to the overall purchase price paid for the slaves."[782]

781 This is the first and only time Mālik uses this expression in the *Muwaṭṭaʾ*.

782 In other words, in the second hypothetical case, if the purchase price of the entire group of slaves was 1,000 dinars, and the defective slave was appraised at one hundred dinars, the purchaser would be entitled to a refund of 10 percent of the purchase price.

Chapter 5. Regarding the Sale of a Handmaiden and Stipulations Related to Her Sale

1938. According to Mālik, Ibn Shihāb reported that ʿUbayd Allāh b. ʿAbd Allāh b. ʿUtba b. Masʿūd told him that ʿAbd Allāh b. Masʿūd purchased a handmaiden from his wife, Zaynab al-Thaqafiyya. She stipulated in the contract that if he planned to sell her to a third party, she would have the right to purchase her from him for the price offered by the third party. ʿAbd Allāh asked ʿUmar b. al-Khaṭṭāb about the effect of such a condition. ʿUmar said, "You may not have sexual relations with her as long as another person benefits from a condition attached to her."[783]

1939. According to Mālik, Nāfiʿ reported that ʿAbd Allāh b. ʿUmar would say, "A man may not have intercourse with a handmaiden unless he has an unfettered right to sell her, gift her to another, keep her, or do whatever he wishes with her."

1940. Mālik said, regarding someone who purchases a handmaiden on the condition that he will neither sell nor gift her to a third party or under another, similar condition, "The purchaser in this case is not permitted to have intercourse with her. That is because he is permitted neither to sell nor to gift her. If he is unable to exercise either of those rights with respect to her, his ownership of her is incomplete. This is because the contract has excluded him from the exercise of certain ownership rights, which are now under the control of others. If a contract of sale includes such a condition, it is invalid, and the sale is void."[784]

Chapter 6. The Prohibition against a Master Having Intercourse with a Married Handmaiden

1941. According to Mālik, Ibn Shihāb reported that ʿAbd Allāh b. ʿĀmir gifted to ʿUthmān b. ʿAffān a married handmaiden whom he had purchased in Basra. ʿUthmān said, "I will not touch her unless her husband divorces her." Ibn ʿĀmir reached a settlement with her husband, who then divorced her.

---

783 In ʿUmar's opinion, the right of first refusal that ʿAbd Allāh granted his wife when he purchased the handmaiden from her had the effect of giving the wife a claim to the handmaiden. As a result, the handmaiden was not completely under his ownership, and therefore sexual relations with her were not permissible.

784 According to Mālik's analysis of this case, the contract of sale is void because it fails, by its terms, to give the purchaser essential rights related to the ownership of the item purchased. Therefore, the purchaser does not, as a legal matter, fully own the handmaiden, and he consequently has no right to have sexual relations with her. Rather, he holds the handmaiden with the obligation to return her to the seller and receive a refund of the purchase price.

1942. According to Mālik, Ibn Shihāb reported from Abū Salama b. ʿAbd al-Raḥmān b. ʿAwf that ʿAbd al-Raḥmān b. ʿAwf purchased a handmaiden and then discovered that she was married, so he returned her to the seller.

Chapter 7. What Has Come Down regarding Ownership of Dates That Mature after the Orchard Has Been Sold

1943. According to Mālik, Nāfiʿ reported from Ibn ʿUmar that the Messenger of God (pbuh) said, "If someone sells date palms after they have been pollinated, their fruit belongs to the seller, unless the purchaser stipulates their inclusion in the sale."

Chapter 8. The Prohibition against Selling Dates before They Mature

1944. According to Mālik, Nāfiʿ reported from Ibn ʿUmar that the Messenger of God (pbuh) prohibited the sale of dates before they had matured, prohibiting the seller from offering to sell them and the purchaser from offering to purchase them.

1945. According to Mālik, Ḥumayd al-Ṭawīl reported from Anas b. Mālik that the Messenger of God (pbuh) prohibited the sale of dates before they "brighten" (*tuzhī*). He was asked, "What does 'brighten' mean?" He said, "When they turn red."

1946. The Messenger of God (pbuh) said, "Suppose God prevents the dates from maturing. In that case, on what basis could the seller justify taking his brother's property?"

1947. According to Mālik, Abū al-Rijāl Muḥammad b. ʿAbd al-Raḥmān b. Ḥāritha reported from his mother, ʿAmra bt. ʿAbd al-Raḥmān, that the Messenger of God (pbuh) prohibited the sale of dates until they were safe from blight.

1948. Mālik said, "Selling dates before they mature is a kind of material uncertainty in the consideration (*gharar*) that renders the contract void."

1949. According to Mālik, Abū al-Zinād reported from Khārija b. Zayd b. Thābit, from Zayd b. Thābit, that he would not sell his dates until the Pleiades were visible.[785]

1950. Mālik said, "The rule in our view (*al-amr ʿindanā*) regarding the sale of melons, cucumbers, watermelons, and carrots is that once they have begun to mature, their sale is permissible and binding. After they are sold,

785 The Pleiades are the constellation of stars known as the "seven sisters" in English and as *thurayyā* in Arabic, and they were visible at the end of May.

whatever subsequent growth occurs in these crops belongs to the purchaser until their season concludes and they die. There is no predetermined limit to the length of their seasons; it is generally known to people by experience. Sometimes, however, they are stricken by blight that reduces the output of the crops before the customary time. Therefore, if a blight strikes a third or more of the crop as a result of a calamity (*jāʾiḥa*), the purchase price should be reduced by that amount."

Chapter 9. Trading Fresh Dates for Dried Dates (*Bayʿ al-ʿAriyya*)

1951. According to Mālik, Nāfiʿ reported from ʿAbd Allāh b. ʿUmar, from Zayd b. Thābit, that the Messenger of God (pbuh) granted the owner of date palms a dispensation (*rukhṣa*) permitting him to trade his unharvested fresh dates, to be delivered to the purchaser at harvest time, for the purchaser's dried dates, delivered immediately, on the basis of the estimated quantity of his future crop.[786]

1952. According to Mālik, Dāwūd b. al-Ḥuṣayn reported from Abū Sufyān, the freedman (*mawlā*) of Ibn Abī Aḥmad, from Abū Hurayra, that the Messenger of God (pbuh) granted a dispensation to trade fresh dates, using an estimate of their quantity, for dried dates in an amount less than five *awsuq* (or "five *awsuq*").[787] Dāwūd was not certain, so he said, "Five, or less than five, *awsuq*."

1953. Mālik said, "Unharvested dates are exchanged for their equivalent in dried dates on the basis of an estimate of their quantity. Their quantity is carefully estimated while they are still hanging on the date palm's branches without any attempt to weigh them. This was permitted because it was deemed to be the equivalent of a contract for the repurchase of goods (*tawliya*), the rescission of a contract for the benefit of the purchaser (*iqāla*), and a kind of partnership (*shirk*). Had it been deemed the equivalent of other kinds of sales, no one would have agreed to treat another person as his partner in a trade involving food until that other person had first taken possession of the food; nor would a seller ever have relieved a purchaser of his obligations under a contract involving the sale of food until the

786 Ordinarily, such a transaction would be invalid for two reasons. The first is that it violates the rules of *ribā* that prohibit the deferred trade of food (*ribā al-nasīʾa* or *ribā al-nasāʾ*). The second is that it involves material uncertainty in the consideration (*gharar*), insofar as the quantity of the fresh dates being traded is not known with certainty at the time of the trade but is instead only estimated. Moreover, the generally applicable rule is that it is not permissible to exchange dates for dates, except in like quantities. Accordingly, it is generally prohibited to trade fresh dates for dried ones, because it is impossible to confirm whether their quantities are equal since fresh dates shrink when dried.

787 Approximately 122 kilograms.

purchaser had first taken possession of such food; nor would a seller ever have agreed to repurchase the goods of a contract from a purchaser until the purchaser had first taken possession of such goods."[788]

Chapter 10. A Calamity (*Jā'iḥa*) That Affects an Unharvested Crop of Dates (*Thimār*) or Grains (*Zar'*) after Their Sale

1954. According to Mālik, Abū al-Rijāl Muḥammad b. ʿAbd al-Raḥmān reported that he heard his mother, ʿAmra bt. ʿAbd al-Raḥmān, say, "In the time of the Messenger of God (pbuh), a man once purchased the dates of an orchard prior to their harvest. He cared for them, staying in the orchard with them until it became obvious to him that the crop had withered while still on the branch. Accordingly, he asked the orchard's owner to give him a discount on the purchase price or to cancel the sale entirely, but the owner swore that he would not. The purchaser's mother went to the Messenger of God (pbuh) and told him what had happened. The Messenger of God (pbuh) then said, 'Indeed, the seller swore a wicked oath.' The orchard's owner came to learn of that conversation, so he went to the Messenger of God (pbuh) and said, 'Messenger of God, I will give it[789] to him.'"

1955. According to Mālik, it reached him that ʿUmar b. ʿAbd al-ʿAzīz ruled that a seller must grant the purchaser a reduction in the contract price in the case of a calamity that befalls the sold crop between the time of sale and the time of harvest. Mālik said, "The rule among us is in accordance with that (*ʿalā dhālika al-amr ʿindanā*)."

1956. Mālik said, "The definition of a calamity that requires the seller to give the purchaser a discount on the contract price is destruction of one-third or more of the sold crop. Any damage to the crop that is less than one-third does not count as a calamity."

Chapter 11. What a Seller May Exclude in a Contract Involving the Sale of Fresh Dates (*Thamar*)

1957. According to Mālik, Rabīʿa b. Abī ʿAbd al-Raḥmān reported that al-Qāsim b. Muḥammad would sell his orchard's crop of fresh dates but exclude some of them from the sale.

1958. According to Mālik, ʿAbd Allāh b. Abī Bakr reported that his grandfather Muḥammad b. ʿAmr b. Ḥazm sold the crop of fresh dates from one of

788 Mālik is analogizing the dispensation permitting the trade of unharvested fresh dates for dried dates to other exceptional contracts by virtue of the common factor that the motive in each case is to do a favor to the counterparty rather than to secure commercial gain.

789 That is, either a reduction in the purchase price or a cancellation of the contract.

his orchards, the one known by the name al-Afrāq, for 4,000 dirhams, but he excluded from the sale the equivalent of 800 dirhams' worth of dried dates (*tamr*).[790]

1959. According to Mālik, Abū al-Rijāl Muḥammad b. ʿAbd al-Raḥmān b. Ḥāritha reported that his mother, ʿAmra bt. ʿAbd al-Raḥmān, would sell her crops of fresh dates but exclude some from the contract.

1960. Mālik said, "The agreed-upon rule among us (*al-amr al-mujtamaʿ ʿalayhi ʿindanā*) is that if a man sells his crop of fresh dates from his orchard, he can exclude up to one-third of the crop, but no more, and there is no objection to excluding less than one-third of his crop from the sale."

1961. Mālik said, "There is nothing objectionable in a man selling his crop of fresh dates from his orchard but excluding from the contract the dates of one or more palm trees, which he chooses and specifies to the purchaser. That is because the orchard's owner is excluding from the contract only that which was originally part of his own orchard, and the exclusion is thus nothing more than the orchard's owner holding something back from his own orchard and retaining it for himself. In fact, he never sold that thing; rather, he sold only the unexcluded portion of his orchard's crop."

Chapter 12. What Is Prohibited with Respect to the Sale of Dried Dates (*Tamr*)

1962. According to Mālik, Zayd b. Aslam reported that ʿAṭāʾ b. Yasār said, "The Messenger of God (pbuh) said, 'When trading dried dates for dried dates, exchange like for like.' Someone said to the Messenger of God (pbuh), 'Your representative in Khaybar takes one measure (*ṣāʿ*)[791] of dates for two.' The Messenger of God (pbuh) said, 'Summon him to appear before me.' The representative was summoned and brought before the Messenger of God (pbuh), who asked him, 'Do you take one measure of dates for two?" He said, 'Messenger of God, they will not trade me high-quality dates (*janīb*) for low-quality dates (*jamʿ*) in equivalent amounts.' The Messenger of God (pbuh) said, 'Sell the low-quality dates for coins, and then use the coins to purchase the high-quality dates.'"

1963. According to Mālik, ʿAbd al-Ḥamīd b. Suhayl b. ʿAbd al-Raḥmān b. ʿAwf reported from Saʿīd b. al-Musayyab, from Abū Saʿīd al-Khudrī and Abū Hurayra, that the Messenger of God (pbuh) appointed a man to serve as his representative in Khaybar. The representative once brought the Prophet

790 The Arabic term for dried dates is *tamr*, whereas fresh dates are called *thamar* (pl. *thimār*).
791 A measure used by the Medinese at the time of the Prophet (pbuh). Modern scholars have estimated it to be the equivalent of two kilograms. Jumuʿa, *al-Makāyīl*, 37.

(pbuh) some high-quality dried dates. The Messenger of God (pbuh) said to him, "Are all the dried dates of Khaybar of such high quality?" The governor said, "By God, Messenger of God, no; but we purchase one measure of this kind for two measures of lower-quality dates, and two measures of this kind for three measures of that." The Messenger of God (pbuh) said, "Don't do that. You should instead sell the low-quality dates for coins, and then use the coins to purchase the high-quality dates."

1964. According to Mālik, ʿAbd Allāh b. Yazīd reported that Zayd, also known as Abū ʿAyyāsh, told him that he asked Saʿd b. Abī Waqqāṣ about trading hulled barley (*bayḍāʾ*) for pearl barley (*sult*). Saʿd asked him, "Which of the two is larger (*afḍal*)?"[792] Zayd said, "The hulled barley." Saʿd prohibited him from engaging in that trade. Saʿd said, "I heard the Messenger of God (pbuh) say, when he was queried about trading fresh dates for dried ones, 'Don't fresh dates shrink when they are dried?' They answered yes, so he forbade that trade."

Chapter 13. Trading Indeterminate Amounts (*Muzābana*) and Sharecropping (*Muḥāqala*)

1965. According to Mālik, Nāfiʿ reported from ʿAbd Allāh b. ʿUmar that the Messenger of God (pbuh) prohibited the exchange of indeterminate amounts (*muzābana*), meaning the trade of fresh dates (*thamar*) for a determinate amount of dried dates (*tamr*) by measure, and the trade of grapes on the vine for a determinate amount of raisins.[793]

1966. According to Mālik, Dāwud b. al-Ḥuṣayn reported from Abū Sufyān, the freedman (*mawlā*) of Ibn Abī Aḥmad, from Abū Saʿīd al-Khudrī, that the Messenger of God (pbuh) prohibited indeterminate trades and sharecropping (*muḥāqala*). "Indeterminate trades" means exchanging dried dates for fresh dates that are still hanging on the branches of palm trees, and "sharecropping" means leasing land in exchange for threshed wheat (*ḥinṭa*).

1967. According to Mālik, Ibn Shihāb reported from Saʿīd b. al-Musayyab that the Messenger of God (pbuh) prohibited indeterminate trades and sharecropping, "indeterminate trades" referring to trading fresh dates for

792 Bājī concludes that *afḍal* in this context refers not to the quality of the items being considered but rather to their quantity, as evidenced by the hadith that Saʿd uses to justify his response to Zayd. Bājī, *al-Muntaqā*, 4:242.

793 The reason these two trades are indeterminate is that fresh dates and grapes shrink when they are dried, and it is thus impossible to know whether they are the equivalent in quantity of the dried dates and raisins that are given in exchange for the fresh dates and grapes, respectively.

dried dates and "sharecropping" referring to the purchase of unharvested wheat (*zarʿ*) for threshed wheat and to the lease of land for threshed wheat. Ibn Shihāb said, "I asked Saʿīd b. al-Musayyab about leasing land in exchange for gold or silver. He said, 'There is nothing objectionable in that.'"

1968. Mālik said, "The Messenger of God (pbuh) prohibited indeterminate trades. This prohibition is understood as covering the sale of anything that is indeterminate, that is, whose volume, weight, or number is unknown, for something whose measure, weight, or number is known. An example of such a trade is when one man says to another who owns food, such as threshed wheat or dried dates, that is heaped up in mounds for sale, or piles of goods, such as camel fodder, date pits, clover, safflower, cotton, flax, or silk, whose quantities, whether measured by volume, weight, or number, are unknown, 'Measure out these goods of yours, or get someone to do so on your behalf,' or 'Weigh what can be weighed,' or 'Count what can be counted.' He then says, 'Even if the total amount in the pile falls short of such-and-such volume, weight, or number, I shall nevertheless accept the deal as final, provided that anything in excess of that specified amount shall be mine. I bear the risk of what falls short of the specified amount, and I keep what exceeds it.' That is not a sale, but rather a kind of bet (*mukhāṭara*) involving material uncertainty (*gharar*) and gambling (*qimār*). This is because he is not agreeing to purchase any specific thing from the seller in exchange for a specific price that he will pay him; rather, he guarantees to him the price of a determinate volume, weight, or number on the condition that he can keep any amount in the pile in excess of that. If, however, the goods happen to amount to less than specified, the seller takes the purchaser's property without giving him adequate consideration in exchange. Nor can the seller be deemed to receive that excess property as a gift, cheerfully given to him by the purchaser. Accordingly, this transaction resembles gambling, and anything similar to it is subject to the same objection."

1969. Mālik said, "The same principle applies to the case of someone telling another who has cloth for sale, 'I will take this cloth of yours and make from it and give you back such-and-such a number of hooded cloaks, each measuring such-and-such. If the cloth is insufficient to produce that number of hooded cloaks, I will make up the difference in order to give you the entirety of what I promised you. If, however, the cloth yields a number of hooded cloaks that exceeds the stipulated number, I get to keep the extras.' Alternatively, he says to the seller, 'I will take this cloth of yours and make from it and give you back so many tunics, each one measuring such-and-such. If the cloth is insufficient to produce that number of tunics, I will make up the difference. If, however, the cloth yields tunics in excess of that number, I get to keep the extras.' Alternatively, he says to a man who has cattle hides or camel hides for sale, 'I will take these leather hides of yours and make from them sandals similar to this one' (which he shows to the seller), 'and if it turns out that I deliver to you fewer than one hundred pairs of sandals from your leather, I will make up the difference, but if the leather is sufficient to produce more than one hundred pairs, I get to keep the excess pairs.' A similar case is when a man says to another who has moringa seeds for sale, 'I will press your seeds, and if the oil I extract falls short of such-and-such an amount, I will give you the difference, but whatever is in excess of that I get to keep.' All of these cases, and any that are like them or resemble them, amount to indeterminate trades, which are neither lawful nor binding. The same principle applies when a man says to another who has camel fodder, date pits, cotton, flax, herbs, or safflower, 'I will purchase this camel fodder from you for such-and-such a number of measures (*ṣāʿ*) of similar camel fodder, these date pits for such-and-such a number of measures of similar date pits,' or a similar offer with regard to the man's safflower, cotton, flax, or herbs. All of these trades would be examples of what we have called 'indeterminate trades.'"

Chapter 14. Miscellaneous Matters Related to the Sale of Fresh Dates (*Thamar*)

1970. Yaḥyā said, "Mālik said, 'There is nothing objectionable in purchasing fresh dates growing on specific palm trees or in a specific orchard or purchasing milk that is in the udder of specific sheep (*ghanam*) if the purchaser takes possession immediately after paying the purchase price. This case is the equivalent of the purchase of some oil, one or two dinars' worth, out of a closed container. The purchaser gives the seller his gold and asks him to pour him the amount that he has purchased. There is nothing objectionable in that. If the container cracks, however, and the oil spills before the seller can measure out the oil, the purchaser is entitled to nothing other than a refund of his gold, and the transaction is canceled. There is nothing objectionable in having a standing order for the cash purchase of items that are offered for sale in the market on a daily basis, such as milk after it has been expressed from the animal's udder, or freshly harvested dates, the purchaser receiving his order daily. However, if the purchaser has given the seller his money but the supply runs out before the purchaser receives his full order, the seller must refund the purchaser an amount of money proportional to the unfilled part of the order. Alternatively, if the purchaser can come to a mutual agreement with the seller, he may take other goods instead, provided that the purchaser stays with the seller until he takes possession of what is owed to him. An agreement in which they agree on what the seller will give the purchaser in lieu of the original obligation but the purchaser departs before taking possession of that second obligation would be prohibited. This is because the second transaction would now involve settling a current debt with a future debt, and the settlement of a current debt with a future debt has been prohibited. Therefore, if the second transaction is not settled promptly, it is forbidden. No deferral or postponement is allowed in the second transaction.[794] This is because a credit term is permissible only if the item sold on credit is subject to a reasonably precise description and the delivery date is specified. The seller in a credit sale is obliged only to deliver the goods that are generically described in the contract to the purchaser. He is not under an obligation to deliver specific goods that have been previously identified, as is the case in a cash transaction. Therefore, in the case of a credit sale, the parties do not specify which orchard or animal is the source of the dates or milk that the seller must deliver to the purchaser.'"

1971. Mālik was asked about a man who purchases another man's date orchard. That orchard has various kinds of date palms, including *ʿajwa*, *kabīs*, *ʿidhq*, and others.[795] The purchaser wishes to exclude from the sale the fruit of one or several of the palm trees of his choice. Mālik said in response, "That is not valid, because if the purchaser does so, he omits from the purchase the fruit of a palm tree whose yield is, for example, fifteen measures (*ṣāʿ*) in exchange for the fruit of another tree of a different variety whose yield is, say, ten measures. If, on the other hand, he includes in the purchase the fruit of the tree whose yield is fifteen measures in exchange for omitting the fruit of the tree that yields ten measures, it is as though he has exchanged one kind of dates for another kind of dates in unequal amounts. This is similar to the case of someone who offers to give another man who has heaps of three different varieties of dried dates offered for sale—fifteen measures of one variety, ten measures of the second, and twelve measures of the third—one dinar in exchange for permitting him to choose whichever of the three heaps he wishes. This kind of a transaction is therefore not valid."[796]

794 In this case, the parties had originally entered into a cash transaction, and when the seller ran out of goods, he and the purchaser agreed to substitute alternative goods for the original goods. If it turns out that the seller does not have those alternative goods on hand, the two parties cannot agree to have the seller deliver the goods the next day. Either they must choose substitute goods that the seller has on hand, or the seller must immediately refund the purchaser's money.

795 These are different varieties of high-quality dates.

796 Unlike in the previous case, in which the seller was reserving a portion of his orchard's fruit for himself, in this case the purchaser is seeking to exclude the fruit of certain trees in the orchard from the sale. Mālik concludes that this is not permissible because it implicitly results in an exchange of dates in unequal measures and because there is material

1972. Yaḥyā said, "Mālik was asked about the rights of a purchaser who purchases from an orchard's owner some fresh dates for one dinar in advance of their harvest, should the crop be damaged before delivery." Mālik said, "The purchaser makes an accounting with the orchard's owner of the fresh dates that were delivered to him and receives a refund from the seller in proportion to the undelivered amount. If the purchaser, for example, took possession of two-thirds of a dinar's worth of fresh dates, he receives a refund of one-third of a dinar. If he took possession of three-quarters of a dinar's worth of fresh dates, he receives a refund of a quarter dinar. Alternatively, the purchaser and the seller may come to a mutual agreement whereby the purchaser can choose to receive his refund out of the seller's inventory of dried dates or any other goods the seller has for sale if the purchaser is willing to accept such alternative goods in lieu of his refund. If he does choose to accept dried dates or other goods in lieu of his refund, this second transaction must be settled immediately and not deferred. This is the equivalent of the case of someone who rents out a specific camel of his to someone for use on a journey; or hires out to another a specific slave-boy of his who is a tailor, carpenter, or another kind of worker to perform one or another task; or rents out his house. In each of these cases, he receives payment in advance for hiring out the slave-boy, renting out the house, or renting out the camel. Then something happens to the camel, the slave-boy, or the house, such as death or something else that makes performance of the contract impossible. In such a case, the owner of the camel, the slave-boy, or the house must refund the unused portion of the rent of the camel, the wage of the slave-boy, or the rent of the house to the purchaser of these services once the owner has determined how much of the contract the lessee has consumed. If the lessee has received half of the benefits for which he has paid, he receives a refund of one-half. Whether he was able to receive little or much of the contract's benefit, the lessee receives a refund from the owner in an amount equal to the unperformed portion of the contract. In all of these cases, however, if payment is made in advance for the use of a specific thing, the contract is valid only if the one paying in advance takes immediate possession of the item (the slave, the camel, or the home) being rented or hired out from its owner or, in the case of a purchase, if the purchaser immediately begins to take possession of the fresh dates from the orchard's owner. The exchange should be immediate in such cases, and neither deferral of performance nor inclusion of a future date of performance is acceptable. An example of an invalid transaction

indeterminacy in the consideration (*gharar*), as suggested by his analogy to the case of a person offering money to a fruit seller in exchange for the right to purchase whichever heap of fruit he wishes.

is when one man says to another, 'I will now pay for this camel of yours, known as "such-and-such," and then ride it to the Pilgrimage (*ḥajj*),' but does so at a time when the Pilgrimage season is still several months away, or when a man says something similar to that with respect to a slave or a home. Indeed, were he to enter into such a transaction, it would be as if he were paying the other man money in advance on the condition that if that camel is present and healthy at the time specified, he is entitled to hire it out at the previously determined price; however, if something, such as death, were to happen to it between the time of the advance and the time of performance, he receives a refund. What had been a prepayment to the lessor effectively becomes a loan. What makes a difference in these two cases is immediate possession by the person making the payment. Whoever takes possession of what he has hired or rented has resolved the material uncertainty in the consideration (*gharar*) present in the previous transaction and is not involving himself in a prohibited loan (*salaf*); instead, he is receiving a determinate consideration. Indeed, an example of this principle is someone purchasing a male or female slave, taking immediate possession of him or her, and paying for the slave in cash. If, in this case, a defect appears in the slave during the one-year term in which the seller remains liable for defects, the purchaser receives a refund of the purchase price from the seller and returns the slave to the seller. There is nothing objectionable in that. This has long been the established ordinance (*bi-hādhā maḍat al-sunna*) with respect to the seller's liability for defects in slaves that arise subsequent to their sale. By contrast, whoever hires out a particular slave or rents out a particular camel with performance in each case being deferred to the future has entered into an invalid transaction. The lessee neither takes possession of what he has rented or hired nor provides advance payment against a generic debt that is enforceable as such against his counterparty."[797]

797 The problem with this transaction, as Mālik sees it, is that the obligation is specific to a determinate thing, that is, a specific slave, camel, or house, which may or may not be still in existence at the time of the contract's performance and may or may not be still fit to perform the function intended by the person making the advance payment. Accordingly, the loan does not, technically speaking, result in a debt (*dayn*), since a debt, in Islamic law, must be generic in nature. Rather, the contract generates a specific obligation (*ʿayn*), which can be satisfied only through delivery of that particular camel, slave, or home. The non-generic nature of the obligation entails the risk that the item may perish prior to the time of performance, and this, in turn, renders it vulnerable to material indeterminacy in the consideration, making the contract invalid. Alternatively, the proposed transaction can be viewed as a loan in exchange for an option granted to the lender. But this is also invalid, because loans, in Islamic law, must be wholly for the benefit of the borrower, with no benefit accruing to the lender. In this case, however, the lender receives the benefit of renting out the camel or the home or hiring the slave in the future, at a price determined today.

Chapter 15. The Sale of Fruit (*Fākiha*)

1973. Yaḥyā said, "Mālik said, 'The agreed-upon rule among us (*al-amr al-mujtamaʿ ʿalayhi ʿindanā*) is that anyone who purchases fruit (*fākiha*), whether fresh or dried, may not resell it until he has taken possession of it. Nor may fresh or dried fruit be traded one for another, except hand to hand.[798] Fruit capable of being dried, stored, and consumed later may not be exchanged for fruit of the same kind, except hand to hand and like for like. If they are two different kinds of fruit, however, there is nothing objectionable in exchanging two measures of one kind for one measure of another, provided that the exchange is hand to hand. But if such an exchange is settled in the future, it is invalid. Fruit and vegetables that cannot be dried and stored but must be consumed while fresh, such as melons and their like, cucumbers, watermelons, carrots, lemons, bananas, pomegranates, and the like, and fruit that, when dried, are no longer "fruit" are not like the fruit that can be stored and remain "fruit." I believe it to be a trivial thing to exchange one measure of one kind of such fruit for two measures of another, provided that the exchange is hand to hand. As long as settlement is not deferred to the future in any way, such exchanges are unobjectionable.'"

Chapter 16. Exchanging Gold for Silver, Whether Bullion (*ʿAyn*) or Unprocessed (*Tibr*)

1974. According to Mālik, Yaḥyā b. Saʿīd said, "The Messenger of God (pbuh) ordered the two Saʿds[799] to sell a gold or silver vessel that had been captured in battle. They sold it at a ratio of three measures of the vessel for four measures of its like in bullion or, possibly, four measures of the vessel for three measures of its like in bullion. The Messenger of God (pbuh) said to them, 'You have taken an excess, so you must rescind the sale.'"

1975. According to Mālik, Mūsā b. Abī Tamīm reported from Abū al-Ḥubāb Saʿīd b. Yasār, from Abū Hurayra, that the Messenger of God (pbuh) said, "A dinar of gold for a dinar of gold, and a dirham of silver for a dirham of silver, with no excess between the two."

1976. According to Mālik, Nāfiʿ reported from Abū Saʿīd al-Khudrī that the Messenger of God (pbuh) said, "No one should exchange gold for gold except in like quantities, even if the difference between them is small; no one should exchange silver for silver except in like quantities, even if the difference between them is small; and no one should exchange either gold or silver at hand for gold or silver that is absent, that is, to be delivered later."

798 In other words, both parties perform their obligations under the contract immediately, with no deferral of performance permitted to either party.

799 Saʿd b. ʿUbāda and Saʿd b. Abī Waqqāṣ.

1977. According to Mālik, Ḥumayd b. Qays al-Makkī reported that Mujāhid said, "I was with ʿAbd Allāh b. ʿUmar when a goldsmith came and said, 'Abū ʿAbd al-Raḥmān! I fashion gold into jewelry and the like, and then sell what I make at a price that is greater than its weight in gold, the excess being compensation for my hands' labor.' ʿAbd Allāh ordered him to refrain from doing so. The goldsmith continued to press ʿAbd Allāh on this point, yet ʿAbd Allāh refused to change his opinion. Finally, he arrived at the gate of the mosque, or at an animal that he wished to mount and ride. ʿAbd Allāh said to the man, 'A gold dinar for a gold dinar and a silver dirham for a silver dirham, with no difference between the two. This is the covenant of our Prophet (pbuh) with us, and our covenant with you.'"

1978. According to Mālik, it reached him from his grandfather, Mālik b. Abī ʿĀmir, that ʿUthmān b. ʿAffān said, "The Messenger of God (pbuh) said to me, 'No one should exchange one gold dinar for two, nor one silver dirham for two.'"

1979. According to Mālik, Zayd b. Aslam reported from ʿAṭā' b. Yasār that Muʿāwiya b. Abī Sufyān once sold a gold or silver drinking vessel for more than its equivalent weight in gold or silver. Abū al-Dardā' said to him, "I heard the Messenger of God (pbuh) prohibit such exchanges, except in like quantities." Muʿāwiya said to him, "I don't see anything objectionable in that." Abū al-Dardā' said, "Who here will defend Muʿāwiya against me? Here I am, informing him that the Messenger of God (pbuh) prohibited such an exchange, and there he is, telling me what his opinion is! I shall not dwell with you here in this land peacefully and quietly!" After saying this, Abū al-Dardā' set off to Medina to see ʿUmar b. al-Khaṭṭāb and informed him about his dispute with Muʿāwiya. ʿUmar b. al-Khaṭṭāb issued an edict to Muʿāwiya that said, "No one should exchange gold for gold or silver for silver except for its like and in equal quantities."

1980. According to Mālik, Nāfiʿ reported from ʿAbd Allāh b. ʿUmar that ʿUmar b. al-Khaṭṭāb said, "No one should exchange gold for gold except for a like quantity, even if the difference between them is small. No one should exchange silver for silver except for a like quantity, even if the difference between them is small. No one should exchange silver for gold if one of the two is not at hand and the other is present. Even if he asks you only to return home to fetch what he owes you, do not permit him to defer payment. I fear that if you do so, the exchange will be unlawful (*ramā'*)." *Ramā'* is a kind of unlawful gain (*ribā*).

1981. According to Mālik, ʿAbd Allāh b. Dīnār reported from ʿAbd Allāh b. ʿUmar that ʿUmar b. al-Khaṭṭāb said, "No one should exchange gold for gold except in like quantities, even if the difference between them is small. No one should exchange silver for silver except in like quantities, even if the difference between them is small. No one should exchange either gold or silver that is at hand for gold or silver that is not. Even if he asks you only to return home to fetch what he owes you, do not permit him to defer payment. I fear that if you do so, the exchange will be unlawful (*ramā'*)." *Ramā'* is a kind of unlawful gain (*ribā*).

1982. According to Mālik, it reached him that al-Qāsim b. Muḥammad said, "'Umar b. al-Khaṭṭāb said, 'One gold dinar for one gold dinar, one silver dirham for one silver dirham, one measure of food for one measure of food, and no deferred obligation in exchange for something delivered immediately.'"

1983. According to Mālik, Abū al-Zinād reported that he heard Sa'īd b. al-Musayyab say, "The rules of unlawful gain (*ribā*) apply only to exchanges involving gold or silver, or to items that are weighed or measured by volume and that are eaten or drunk."

1984. According to Mālik, Yaḥyā b. Sa'īd reported that he heard Sa'īd b. al-Musayyab say, "Clipping gold and silver coins is a form of 'corruption in the land.'"[800]

1985. Mālik said, "There is nothing objectionable in purchasing gold with silver or purchasing silver with gold by estimate, without first weighing it, if it is unprocessed or wrought into jewelry. No one, however, should estimate the number of silver coins or gold dinars being purchased without first inspecting and counting them. If someone purchases coins by estimate, he is only seeking to profit from the uncertainty present in the exchange that results from a failure to count the coins and from purchasing them through estimation. That is not the kind of exchange that Muslims recognize as valid. As for unprocessed gold and jewelry that are sold by weight, there is nothing objectionable in selling these by estimate, provided they are sold in the same way that wheat and dried dates and similar foodstuffs are sold by estimate, even though the volume or weight of such things may be measured out. There is nothing objectionable in using estimation to conclude exchanges of that sort."

1986. Mālik said, "Whoever purchases a copy of the Quran, a sword, or a ring using gold dinars or silver dirhams, and the purchased item contains some gold or silver, he must determine the value of the item purchased. If the purchased item contains gold and was purchased with gold dinars, and

800 A reference to the Quranic phrase *al-fasād fī al-arḍ*, which appears numerous times in the Quran and signifies antisocial behavior.

if one-third or less of the item's value is attributable to the gold it contains, the transaction is permissible and there is nothing objectionable in it, provided that it is concluded hand to hand, with no deferral of payment. If the purchased item contains silver and was purchased with silver dirhams, and if one-third or less of the item's value is attributable to the silver it contains, the transaction is permissible and there is nothing objectionable in it, provided that it is concluded hand to hand. That has always been lawful in the opinion of the people among us (*wa-lam yazal dhālika min amr al-nās ʿindanā*)."

Chapter 17. What Has Come Down regarding the Exchange (*Ṣarf*) of Currency

1987. According to Mālik, Ibn Shihāb reported from Mālik b. Aws b. al-Ḥadathān al-Naṣrī that he wanted to exchange one hundred gold dinars for silver coins. Mālik b. Aws said, "Ṭalḥa b. ʿUbayd Allāh called me over and we bargained until we agreed on a price. He took my gold coins and inspected them by flipping them back and forth in his hand. He then said, 'Wait until my treasurer comes from al-Ghāba.' ʿUmar b. al-Khaṭṭāb had overheard our conversation, so he said, 'By God, don't part ways with him until you receive what he owes you. The Messenger of God (pbuh) said, "The exchange of gold for silver results in an unlawful gain (*ribā*) unless it is concluded hand to hand. The exchange of wheat for wheat results in an unlawful gain unless it is concluded hand to hand. The exchange of dried dates for dried dates results in an unlawful gain unless it is concluded hand to hand. The exchange of barley for barley results in an unlawful gain unless it is concluded hand to hand."'"

1988. Mālik said, "If a man exchanges a gold dinar for several silver dirhams and then discovers that one of the silver dirhams he received was counterfeit, so he wants to return it, the transaction must be rescinded. He should return the silver dirhams and retrieve his gold dinar. What is prohibited in these exchanges can be understood from the words of God's Messenger (pbuh), who said, 'The exchange of gold for silver results in an unlawful gain unless it is concluded hand to hand,' and the words of ʿUmar b. al Khaṭṭāb, who said, 'Even if he asks you only to return home to fetch what he owes you, do not permit him to defer payment.' When he later attempts to return the counterfeit silver dirham that he received from the original exchange and to take a legitimate one in its place, his claim becomes the equivalent of a debt or a deferred payment, and for this reason, the transaction becomes prohibited. Therefore, the original exchange must be rescinded in its entirety. ʿUmar b. al-Khaṭṭāb intended by his words that there be no present exchanges of gold and silver or present exchanges involving food if payment is to be made later in gold, silver, or food. No delay or deferral is permitted in any exchange involving any of these items, be they of one kind or of different kinds."

Chapter 18. Exchanging Gold for Gold and Silver for Silver by Weight (*Murāṭala*)

1989. According to Mālik, Yazīd b. ʿAbd Allāh b. Quṣayṭ reported that he saw Saʿīd b. al-Musayyab exchange gold for gold by weight. He would place his gold in one hand of the scale, while his counterparty would place his own gold in the other. When the tongue of the scales was balanced, each took and gave.

1990. Mālik said, "The rule in our view (*al-amr ʿindanā*) about exchanging gold for gold and silver for silver by weight is that there is nothing objectionable in taking eleven gold dinars for ten, provided that the exchange is concluded immediately and the two sets of exchanged coins are equal in weight, even if the number of coins is different. The same rule applies to the exchange of silver dirhams."

1991. Mālik said, "If someone exchanges gold for gold or silver for silver by weight and there is, for example, a difference of 3.35 grams (one *mithqāl*)[801] between the two, and the party with the smaller amount of gold offers to give the other party the value of the difference in silver, for example, or perhaps in some other good, the second party should reject the offer. The offer is repugnant and a pretext (*dharīʿa*) for the procurement of an unlawful gain (*ribā*). The reason is that were it permitted for him to purchase the excess 3.35 grams by paying its value in silver as if he had purchased it independently, it would be permitted for him to engage in that transaction intentionally in order to render the original exchange with his counterparty licit. However, if the other party had sold him only the excess 3.35 grams of gold independently, without anything else, he would not have received one-tenth of the price that he would receive for it if he sells it along with the rest of the gold in order to make the transaction licit. Accordingly, it is a pretext intended to render an illicit transaction—something that is prohibited—licit."[802]

---

801 Muḥammad Ṣubḥī b. Ḥasan Ḥallāq, *al-Īḍāḥāt al-ʿaṣriyya lil-maqāyīs wa'l-makāyīl wa'l-awzān wa'l-nuqūd al-sharʿiyya* (Sanaa: Maktabat al-Jīl al-Jadīd, 2007), 204.

802 Similarly, it is illicit to exchange, for example, one-half of a high-quality gold dinar for one dinar of low-quality gold. The parties wishing to make such a trade might circumvent the prohibition by having the person with the low-quality dinar include some additional good in the trade in exchange for two high-quality dinars. In this case, it appears that the parties have agreed to exchange one poor-quality dinar for one high-quality dinar, and some other good

1992. Mālik said, regarding a man who wishes to exchange gold for gold by weight and so offers to give his counterparty genuine gold coins of ancient vintage along with an amount of low-quality, unminted gold (*tibr*) in exchange for clipped gold coins of Kufan origin, such Kufan coins being held in disregard by the people and the two quantities of gold being equal in weight, "That exchange is impermissible. The reason it is prohibited is that the owner of the high-quality gold uses the superior quality of his gold coins as a way to sell the poor-quality, unminted gold that he throws into the sale. Were it not for the superior quality of the first man's gold over that of his counterparty, the counterparty would never agree to exchange the poor-quality, unminted gold by weight for his Kufan gold. This case is the equivalent of the case of a man who wanted to purchase three measures (*ṣāʿ*), approximately six kilograms, of high-quality dried dates (*ʿajwa*) for two measures and one quarter-measure (*mudd*), approximately four and a half kilograms, of *kabīs* dates.[803] He was told, however, that such an exchange was not permissible.[804] So he instead proposed to exchange two measures of *kabīs* dates and one measure of low-quality *ḥashaf* dates for the three measures of *ʿajwa* dates in order to make the exchange licit.[805] But that is also not permissible, because the owner of the high-quality *ʿajwa* dates would never agree to give him one measure of *ʿajwa* for one measure of poor-quality *ḥashaf* without the inclusion of the high-quality *kabīs* dates in the exchange. Another example is if someone says to another person, 'Sell me three measures of white wheat for two and a half measures of Levantine wheat.' In response, the other person says, 'This exchange is permissible only in like quantities,' so he proposes instead to exchange two measures of Levantine wheat and one of barley, intending thereby to make the transaction between them licit. That is not permissible, however, because he would never have been willing to exchange one measure of white wheat for one measure of barley, had that trade been offered independently. He

---

for the other high-quality dinar. The economic reality of the transaction, however, is that they have exchanged the low-quality dinar for one-half of one of the high-quality dinars—the prohibited transaction—and the other good for one and a half high-quality dinars. For this reason, the Mālikīs do not allow a contract for the exchange of gold and silver to include the sale of any additional item. Abū Ḥanīfa, however, did permit such sales to take place alongside contracts for the exchange of currency. Therefore, he permitted the sale of one hundred gold dinars in a bag for two hundred gold dinars, reasoning that half of the sale price applied to the hundred dinars in the bag and the other half was the price of the bag itself. Bājī, *al-Muntaqā*, 4:277.

803 Two full measures (*ṣāʿ*) and one small measure (*mudd*), the latter being approximately 500 grams.

804 This transaction would not be permissible because dates may be exchanged only in like quantities.

805 It now appears to be a licit exchange because the dates are being exchanged in equal quantities.

agreed to make that offer to him only on account of the superior quality of the Levantine wheat over the white wheat. That exchange is therefore not permissible, and it is similar to the case of the unminted gold that we described previously."

1993. Mālik said, "In exchanges involving gold, silver, and food, the legitimate exchange of which depends on the exchange of like quantities, it is not permissible to include with a high-quality, marketable commodity an item that is of poor quality and lacks a ready market and that is included only to make the exchange licit and to make lawful through that exchange something that was proscribed. It is impermissible because inclusion of an undesirable item alongside the sale of a desirable item leads to the violation of an established rule. The party proposing the inclusion of the poor-quality item does so only in the hope that he will be able to realize the superior value of the high-quality good he is offering for sale. Accordingly, he offers his counterparty something that, had he offered it on its own, his counterparty would never have accepted nor given any heed to. It is in fact the case that the counterparty agrees to accept the low-quality good only because he also takes the item that is superior to his own. Therefore, no transaction involving gold, silver, or food should include any additional commodity that meets this description, namely, of being a low-quality product that lacks a ready market. If someone who owns low-quality food genuinely wishes to sell it for something else, he should offer it for sale independently, without including it in the sale of anything else. There is nothing objectionable in its sale in that fashion."

Chapter 19. Credit Sales Involving Food (*ʿĪna*) and Similar Exchanges

1994. According to Mālik, Nāfiʿ reported from ʿAbd Allāh b. ʿUmar that the Messenger of God (pbuh) said, "No one should resell food that he has purchased before he has taken full possession of it."

1995. According to Mālik, ʿAbd Allāh b. Dīnār reported from ʿAbd Allāh b. ʿUmar that the Messenger of God (pbuh) said, "Anyone who purchases food should not resell it until he has taken possession of it."

1996. According to Mālik, Nāfiʿ reported that ʿAbd Allāh b. ʿUmar said, "During the time of the Messenger of God (pbuh), we would purchase food, and then the Prophet would send someone to tell us that before we could sell it, we needed to transport it away from the place where we purchased it and sell it somewhere else."

1997. According to Mālik, Nāfiʿ reported that Ḥakīm b. Ḥizām purchased some food intended for the public, following an order from ʿUmar b.

al-Khaṭṭāb. Ḥakīm sold the food before he had taken full possession of it. Word of this reached ʿUmar, who rescinded the sale and said, "Do not resell food that you have purchased before you have taken full possession of it."

1998. According to Mālik, it reached him that during the time that Marwān b. al-Ḥakam was the governor of Medina, certificates (*ṣukūk*) were issued entitling the holders to receive specified quantities of food from the stocks stored in the market of al-Jār.[806] The people set about trading these certificates among themselves, even though they had not yet taken possession of the food represented by the certificates. Zayd b. Thābit and one of the Companions of the Messenger of God (pbuh) went to see Marwān b. al-Ḥakam to complain about this. They said, "Have you permitted the people to obtain unlawful gains (*ribā*), Marwān?" He said, "I seek God's protection! What do you have in mind?" They said, "These certificates that you have issued to the people: they have made a market out of them, buying and selling them among themselves. They resell them before taking full possession of the underlying food." Marwān then dispatched the guard, ordering them to find the certificates, to seize any that were in the possession of persons other than their original recipients, and to return them to their designated recipients.

1999. According to Mālik, it reached him that a man wished to purchase food from another man on credit. The would-be seller took the would-be purchaser to the market and began to show him heaps of food, saying, "Which of these would you like me to sell you?" The would-be buyer said, "Are you selling me something not already in your possession?" The two of them then went to ʿAbd Allāh b. ʿUmar and described to him their situation. ʿAbd Allāh said to the would-be purchaser, "Do not purchase from him something that is not currently in his possession," and to the would-be seller, "Do not offer to sell something that is not currently in your possession."

2000. According to Mālik, Yaḥyā b. Saʿīd reported that he heard Jamīl b. ʿAbd al-Raḥmān al-Muʾadhdhin say to Saʿīd b. al-Musayyab, "I purchase whatever I can of the certificates that are issued to the people in respect of their stipends. These certificates entitle their holders to receive specified quantities of food from the stocks stored in the market of al-Jār. I then seek to sell a determinate amount and kind of food for cash against my obligation to deliver that kind of food to the purchaser on a determinate date in the future." Saʿīd said to him, "Do you intend to settle your obligations to your counterparties out of the food that you expect to receive through your prior purchase of the certificates?" He said, "Yes." Saʿīd then ordered him to refrain from this practice.

806 According to the editors of the RME, this was a port located on the coast of the Hijaz where food would be collected prior to its distribution.

2001. Mālik said, "The agreed-upon rule about which there is no dissent (*al-amr al-mujtamaʿ ʿalayhi alladhī lā ikhtilāfa fīh*) is that whoever purchases food, whether wheat, barley, pearl barley, sorghum, pearl millet, or any of the various kinds of pulses, or anything similar to pulses on which the alms-tax is due, or any kind of condiment, including oil, clarified butter (ghee), honey, vinegar, cheese, milk, sesame oil, or similar condiments, may not resell it until he has taken full possession of it."

Chapter 20. Credit Sales Involving Food That Are Prohibited

2002. According to Mālik, Abū al-Zinād reported that he heard both Saʿīd b. al-Musayyab and Sulaymān b. Yasār prohibit the sale of wheat today for gold payable later and the subsequent purchase by the seller using the gold owed to him of dried dates (*tamr*) until the seller has first taken possession of the gold due to him pursuant to the first transaction.[807]

2003. According to Mālik, Kathīr b. Farqad reported that he asked Abū Bakr b. Muḥammad b. ʿAmr b. Ḥazm about someone who sells food today for gold payable later and then, using the gold owed to him, buys dried dates before taking possession of the gold. Abū Bakr disapproved of that practice and prohibited it.

2004. According to Mālik, Ibn Shihāb reported something similar to that. Mālik said, "Saʿīd b. al-Musayyab, Sulaymān b. Yasār, Abū Bakr b. Muḥammad b. ʿAmr b. Ḥazm, and Ibn Shihāb only prohibited the sale of wheat today for gold payable at a later date followed by the purchase of dried dates by the seller of the wheat before taking possession of the gold owed to him if the seller purchases the dates from the purchaser of the wheat. There is nothing objectionable, however, in his using the gold he is owed from the sale of the wheat, even before he takes possession of the gold, to purchase dried dates from someone other than the purchaser of the wheat. In that case, he assigns to the man from whom he buys the dried dates his claim against the purchaser of the wheat as payment for the dried dates. I asked several men of knowledge about this, and none of them found it objectionable."

Chapter 21. Advance Payment for Food

2005. According to Mālik, Nāfiʿ reported that ʿAbd Allāh b. ʿUmar said, "There is nothing objectionable in someone advancing to another the purchase price of food that will be delivered in the future, as long as the food has been described with sufficient precision, the price and the date of

807 Without possession of the gold, this transaction would amount to the sale of food for food on credit, and it is prohibited for that reason.

delivery are determinate, and the price was not advanced for the purchase of a specific harvest of grains on their stalks or dates on their trees before each has matured and is ready for sale."

2006. Mālik said, "The rule in our view (*al-amr ʿindanā*) regarding a contract involving advance payment for food at a determinate price and for a determinate date is that if, at the time of delivery, the purchaser discovers that the seller does not have a sufficient supply of food to fulfill his obligation and consequently agrees to relieve the seller of his obligation by canceling the sale, he may take back from the seller only the money that he advanced him, or the very thing that he advanced him in consideration for the food if he paid in kind and not in money. He is not to purchase anything else from the seller in exchange for the item that he advanced until he has received his refund from him. The reason is that if he accepts something other than that which he gave the seller, or if he substitutes for it something other than the food that he contracted to purchase from the seller, the transaction would amount to selling food before taking full possession of it. However, the Messenger of God (pbuh) forbade the sale of food before one has taken full possession of it. It is impermissible for a purchaser who regrets a transaction to tell the seller, 'Relieve me of this contract, and I will give you some time to refund what I paid you.' The people of knowledge prohibit this, because when the seller's obligation to deliver the food became due, the purchaser effectively agreed to defer the seller's obligation in exchange for the seller's agreement to cancel the contract. That is a sale of food on credit before one has taken full possession of it.[808] This is illustrated by the following example. When the delivery of the food is due, the purchaser decides he no longer wants it. Instead, he decides to take one dinar, payable in the future. However, this is not a cancellation of the sale. Something qualifies as a cancellation only if neither the purchaser nor the seller obtains an additional benefit. If, however, the second transaction entails an increased benefit, such as the inclusion of a term to defer payment (*nasīʾa*), or any other term that gives one of them an advantage over the other, or anything from which one of them benefits but the other does not, the new agreement is not a cancellation. If they agree to such terms, the cancellation instead becomes a second contract of sale. An exception was recognized in the case of cancellation, partnership, and resale to the seller (*tawliya*) as long as no

---

808 This is because the purchaser was owed a determinate amount of food, such as one hundred bushels of wheat. Instead of taking possession of it, however, he entered into a new contract whose terms were the mirror image of the original contract: he would effectively resell the hundred bushels of wheat to the original seller in exchange for future payment of the original price he paid. But as Mālik points out, the purchaser has not taken possession of the bushels of wheat, so he is not permitted to resell it.

increase or decrease in, or deferral of performance of, the original terms of the agreement is introduced. If any such increase, decrease, or deferral is introduced, the deal becomes a second sale, in which case it is lawful only to the extent that its terms conform to those of a lawful contract, and it is prohibited to the extent that its terms are considered unlawful. If someone pays in advance for some Levantine wheat, there is nothing objectionable in his accepting as payment Egyptian wheat, provided that the date of delivery has expired. The same rule applies to anyone who pays in advance for any of the various kinds of food. There is nothing objectionable in his accepting a kind of food that is superior or inferior to the one specified in the contract once the date of delivery has expired. This is illustrated by the following example. If a man pays in advance for Egyptian wheat, there is nothing objectionable in his accepting either barley or Levantine wheat instead. If he pays in advance for high-quality dates (*ʿajwa*), there is nothing objectionable in his accepting lower-quality dates. If he pays in advance for red raisins, there is nothing objectionable in his accepting black ones. In each of these cases, the conditions are that the exchange takes place after the date of delivery has expired and that the amount taken is the equivalent of the amount for which the purchaser paid in advance."

Chapter 22. Exchanging Food for Food in Like Quantities

2007. According to Mālik, it reached him that Sulaymān b. Yasār said, "Saʿd b. Abī Waqqāṣ ran out of fodder for his donkey, so he said to his slave-boy, 'Get some of our wheat and trade it for barley, but don't accept in exchange anything other than the same amount.'"

2008. According to Mālik, Nāfiʿ reported that Sulaymān b. Yasār informed him that ʿAbd al-Raḥmān b. al-Aswad b. ʿAbd Yaghūth ran out of fodder for his animal, so he said to his slave-boy, "Get some of our wheat and trade it for barley, but don't accept in exchange anything other than the same amount."

2009. According to Mālik, a similar report reached him from al-Qāsim b. Muḥammad, from Ibn Muʿayqīb al-Dawsī. Mālik said, "That is the rule among us (*dhālika al-amr ʿindanā*)."

2010. Mālik said, "The agreed-upon rule among us (*al-amr al-mujtamaʿ ʿalayhi ʿindanā*) is that wheat is not exchanged for wheat, nor dried dates for dried dates, nor dried dates for raisins, nor wheat for raisins, nor one kind of food for any other kind of food, unless the exchange is settled immediately. If performance is deferred in any such transaction, the transaction is invalid and prohibited. The same rule applies to all condiments: they may not be exchanged, one for another, unless the exchange is settled immediately."

2011. Mālik said, "Neither food nor condiments, if they are of the same kind, may be exchanged at a ratio of two to one. One measure of wheat may not be exchanged for two measures of wheat, nor one measure of dates for two measures of dates, nor one measure of raisins for two measures of raisins, nor any other similar grains or condiments, if they are of the same type, even if the exchange is hand to hand. This is the same rule that applies to the exchange of silver for silver and gold for gold. No inequality in the amounts of the exchanged items is permitted in such exchanges. They are permitted only if equivalent amounts are exchanged and the exchange is settled hand to hand. If, on the other hand, there is a clear difference between the exchanged items, whether they are eaten or drunk, and whether they are measured by weight or by volume, there is nothing objectionable in exchanging them at a ratio of two to one, provided that the exchange is hand to hand. Accordingly, there is nothing objectionable in exchanging one measure of dates for two measures of wheat, one measure of dates for two measures of raisins, or one measure of wheat for two measures of ghee. If the exchanged items of food are different, there is nothing objectionable in exchanging two measures for one, or more than two measures for one, provided that the exchange is hand to hand. If settlement is deferred, however, the transaction is not permitted.[809] It is not permissible to exchange one mound of wheat for another, but there is nothing objectionable in exchanging one mound of wheat for one mound of dates, provided that the exchange is settled hand to hand.[810] That is because there is nothing objectionable in exchanging wheat for dates on the basis of their estimated quantities. Whenever the food or condiments being exchanged differ in kind, and the difference is obvious, there is nothing objectionable in exchanging one kind for the other kind without precise knowledge of their quantities, provided that the exchange is settled hand to hand. If, however, settlement is deferred, it is prohibited. Exchanging these items on the basis of their estimated rather than precise quantities is no different from purchasing them with gold and silver on the basis of their estimated quantities: someone may purchase wheat with silver on the basis of the estimated quantity of the wheat, and dates with gold on the basis of the estimated quantity of the dates. That is licit, and there is nothing objectionable in it. But if, on the other hand, someone prepares a mound of

809 In other words, if the contract permits one or both parties to perform their obligations under the contract at some time in the future.

810 The exchange of a mound of wheat for a mound of wheat is not permissible even if it is settled hand to hand, because the parties cannot be certain that equal quantities of wheat are being exchanged. By contrast, the parties' ignorance of the precise quantities being exchanged in the second transaction, that of wheat for dates, is irrelevant, because it is permissible to exchange wheat for dates in unequal amounts.

food for sale and knows its measure but sells it on the basis of an estimate of its quantity without disclosing the actual quantity to the purchaser, the sale is invalid. If the purchaser wishes to return the food to the seller, he may do so on account of the fact that the seller withheld from him knowledge of the actual quantity of the food that was sold, and because the seller misled him. This is the rule that applies to all sales of food or similar items whose precise quantity—whether by weight, volume, or number—is known to the seller, but which he sells to the purchaser on the basis of a mere estimate, without disclosing to the purchaser that he has precise knowledge of its quantity. In such circumstances, the purchaser may, if he so wishes, rescind the sale and return the purchased items to the seller. It has always been the case that the people of knowledge prohibited such a practice (*wa-lam yazal ahl al-ʿilm yanhawna ʿan dhālika*). There is no good in the exchange of one loaf of bread for two, nor in that of a large one for a small one, if one weighs more than the other. If care is taken that only like amounts are exchanged, however, there is nothing objectionable in that, even if they have not been weighed. The exchange of one measure of butter and one measure of milk for two measures of butter is invalid. Such a trade is subject to the same rule that we previously explained concerning the sale of different kinds of dates, such as the exchange of two measures of high-quality *kabīs* dates and one measure of low-quality *ḥashaf* dates for three measures of high-quality *ʿajwa* dates. In that case, one of the parties said to the other, 'Two measures of *kabīs* for three measures of *ʿajwa* is not permitted,' so he included the one measure of *ḥashaf* in the exchange solely to render the transaction licit. The owner of the milk offered to include his milk along with his butter in the proposed exchange only so that he could take advantage of the superior quality of his butter over the other man's butter and thus accomplish his actual goal of exchanging one measure of butter for two. There is nothing objectionable in exchanging flour for wheat in like quantities. That is because the owner of the flour separated the flour and exchanged it for an equal quantity of wheat. Had he offered, however, to exchange half a measure of flour and half a measure of wheat for a measure of wheat, the proposed exchange would be subject to the same rule that we previously explained. Such a trade is invalid because when the owner offered to include the flour in the trade, he was only seeking to take advantage of the superior quality of his wheat, and that makes the trade invalid."[811]

811 In other words, the real substance of the transaction is the trade of half a measure of wheat for one full measure of wheat, with the one-half measure of flour being included solely for the purpose of satisfying the requirement that like quantities be traded.

Chapter 23. Miscellaneous Matters regarding the Sale of Food

2012. According to Mālik, Muḥammad b. ʿAbd Allāh b. Abī Maryam reported that he asked Saʿīd b. al-Musayyab the following question: "I am someone who purchases certificates (*ṣukūk*) representing the right to receive food stored in the market of al-Jār. I might contract the purchase of a certificate for one dinar and half a dirham. Should I satisfy my obligation to pay the half-dirham using half a dirham's worth of food?" Saʿīd said, "No; you should pay the one dinar and another dirham in its entirety, and take half a dirham's worth of food from the seller as change."[812]

2013. According to Mālik, it reached him that Muḥammad b. Sīrīn would say, "Do not sell grain that has yet to be harvested until its husk has whitened."

2014. Mālik said, "If someone buys food for a determinate price to be delivered on a determinate date, but then on the date when delivery is due the seller of the food says, 'I have no food to deliver, so sell me the food that I owe you and I will pay you for it in the future,' and the purchaser, the person with the claim to the food, says in response, 'That is invalid; the Messenger of God (pbuh) prohibited the sale of food before one has taken full possession of it,' so the obligor, the party who is under the obligation to deliver the food, says to the purchaser, his obligee, 'In that case, sell me some other food on credit so that I can settle my debt to you'[813]—such a contract would also be invalid because the obligee, the purchaser under the original contract, would be giving the obligor, the seller under the original contract, food under the terms of the second contract just to permit the seller to return that very food to the purchaser under the first contract. In this case, the gold that the obligor would give the obligee under the second contract serves as payment for the food that the obligor under the first contract was originally required to deliver to the obligee, and the food that the obligor gives the obligee serves merely as a device to render the transaction between the two licit. Should they enter into such a transaction, it would amount to selling food before taking full possession of it."

---

812 Even though the contract specified half a dirham, there was no such thing as a half-dirham coin. The purchaser was thus asking whether he could satisfy his obligation under the contract by paying half a dirham's worth of food. Saʿīd rejected the idea presumably because it would have entailed a deferred trade of food (that is, the purchaser giving half a dirham's worth of food today against the future delivery of some amount of food). Saʿīd instead suggested that the purchaser pay a full dirham, leading the seller to owe him a debt of half a dirham. There is nothing objectionable in the seller satisfying that debt with food in the value of half a dirham.

813 In other words, the seller, finding himself unable to deliver the promised goods to the purchaser and realizing that he cannot settle his obligation by having the obligee sell the obligation to him on credit, asks the obligee to enter into a new contract pursuant to which the obligee would sell him on credit new food, which the original seller could then use to satisfy his original delivery obligation to the obligee.

2015. Mālik said, regarding a scenario in which a man is owed food acquired via purchase from a second man, who is himself owed an equivalent amount of food by a third man, and the obligor (the second man) says to his obligee (the first man), "I will assign to you my claim against an obligor of mine who owes me food in an amount equivalent to that of the food I owe you": "If the obligation of the second man arose out of a contract of sale, and he wishes to satisfy his obligee by assigning to him his claim to food that also arises out of a contract of purchase with a third party, the assignment would be invalid because it amounts to the sale of food before full possession of it has been taken. If, however, the third man's obligation to deliver food to the second man arises out of a loan that is due, and not a sale, there is nothing objectionable in the second man assigning the debt he is owed to his obligee, because that debt does not represent the proceeds of a sale."[814]

2016. Mālik said, "It is impermissible to sell food before taking full possession of it, given that the Messenger of God (pbuh) prohibited that. Despite that prohibition, the people of knowledge agree that there is nothing objectionable in the purchaser forming a partnership (*shirk*) with the seller, selling the food back to the seller at cost (*tawliya*), or rescinding a sale of food or other goods, in each case before the purchaser has taken full possession of the food. That is because the people of knowledge deem such actions acts of goodwill (*maʿrūf*) and not sales. These transactions are similar to the case of a man who lends another man silver dirhams that are underweight but is paid back in silver dirhams of full weight, resulting in an excess. The transaction is nevertheless permissible and binding. By contrast, had he purchased a number of underweight silver dirhams from another man using a like number of full-weight silver dirhams, the transaction would not have been permissible. Further, had the lender stipulated, when lending the borrower the underweight silver dirhams, that he be repaid in full-weight silver dirhams, that, too, would have been impermissible. A similar rule to this one is the prohibition by the Messenger of God (pbuh) of sales involving indeterminate amounts of goods (*muzābana*), even though he granted permission to exchange unharvested fresh dates for dried dates on the basis of an estimate of their quantity at harvest. He distinguished between these two transactions because the former is a commercial transaction (*ʿalā al-wajh al-mukāyasa wa'l-tijāra*), in which each party is seeking a gain, whereas the latter is an exchange based on goodwill with no commercial intent."

---

814 The reasoning here is that the Prophet Muhammad's (pbuh) prohibition applies specifically to the sale of food that one has not yet taken possession of, not to food that one is owed as a result of a loan.

2017. Mālik said, "No one should purchase food for one-fourth, one-third, or any fractional share of a silver dirham payable on a future date on the condition that the obligation to pay the fractional share of the silver dirham be settled in an amount of food of equal value. There is nothing objectionable, however, in purchasing food for a fractional share of a silver dirham payable on a date in the future and then, when it is time to pay, giving the seller one silver dirham and taking as change some other good in an amount equal to the difference between the one silver dirham and the fraction of the silver dirham. That is because the purchaser paid the fractional share of the dirham he owed in silver and took in exchange for the rest of the dirham some other good, and there is nothing objectionable in that."[815]

2018. Mālik said, "There is nothing objectionable in a man leaving one silver dirham with a merchant and then taking from him a determinate good with a price of one-fourth, one-third, or some other determinate fraction of that silver dirham each day. If, however, that good does not have a stable price, so the man says, 'I will take from you each day an amount of that good in accordance with its current price,' that would not be permissible because there is material uncertainty in the consideration (*gharar*). One day the price declines, and the next day it rises. In this case, the parties would not have come to a definitive agreement before they parted ways."

2019. Mālik said, "If a man sells a mound of food on the basis of its estimated quantity and does not reserve any portion of it for himself, but then wishes to repurchase some of what he sold to the purchaser, he may repurchase only what he could have reserved for himself in the first sale, and that would be no more than one-third of the food originally sold. Should he repurchase more than one-third of the original amount sold, the purchase would transform the original transaction into one involving an indeterminate quantity, rendering the contract prohibited. Accordingly, he may repurchase from the purchaser only that which he might have reserved for himself in the original sale. He would have been allowed to reserve for himself no more than one-third of it. This is the rule about which there is no dissent among us (*hādhā al-amr alladhī lā ikhtilāfa fīhi ʿindanā*)."

815 Mālik objects to the first transaction because it amounts to a deferred trade of food for food: the purchaser takes food immediately and then settles the debt later in food, albeit in an amount specified with reference to a cash price. This amounts to selling the food before taking full possession of it.

Chapter 24. Withholding Goods from the Market and Awaiting the Best Price

2020. According to Mālik, it reached him that ʿUmar b. al-Khaṭṭāb said, "No one should withhold goods from our market. No one with excess amounts of gold on their hands shall use that wealth to acquire the provisions of God that have alighted in our domain and then withhold them from us. As for those who toil in the cold of winter and the heat of summer, bringing goods to our market, they are ʿUmar's guests and free to sell their goods or withhold them, as God wishes."[816]

2021. According to Mālik, Yūnus b. Yūsuf reported from Saʿīd b. al-Musayyab that ʿUmar b. al-Khaṭṭāb once crossed paths with Ḥāṭib b. Abī Baltaʿa, who was selling raisins of his in the market. ʿUmar said to him, "Either raise your price or leave our market."

2022. According to Mālik, it reached him that ʿUthmān b. ʿAffān prohibited withholding goods from the market.

Chapter 25. What Is Permitted with Respect to the Exchange of Livestock (*Ḥayawān*), One for Another, and Advance Payment Therefor

2023. According to Mālik, Ṣāliḥ b. Kaysān reported from Ḥasan b. Muḥammad b. ʿAlī b. Abī Ṭālib that ʿAlī b. Abī Ṭālib once sold a camel of his named ʿUṣayfirā for twenty camels to be delivered on a future date.

2024. According to Mālik, Nāfiʿ reported that ʿAbd Allāh b. ʿUmar purchased a riding camel for four camels, which he was obliged to deliver to the seller at al-Rabadha.

2025. According to Mālik, he asked Ibn Shihāb about selling livestock two for one, with delivery in the future. Ibn Shihāb said, "There is nothing objectionable in that."

2026. Mālik said, "The agreed-upon rule among us (*al-amr al-mujtamaʿ ʿalayhi ʿindanā*) is that there is nothing objectionable in someone exchanging a camel for a camel like it, along with hand-to-hand payment of some silver dirhams. Moreover, there is nothing objectionable in exchanging a camel for a like camel hand to hand, along with some additional silver dirhams payable later. It is not permissible, however, to agree to exchange a camel for a like camel along with some additional silver dirhams, with the silver

816 In other words, a person who imports food into the city is free to sell his goods on whatever terms he wishes, including withholding them from the market in the hope that their price will increase, whereas someone who acquires goods in the domestic retail market is not permitted to withhold them from the market in the hope of higher prices.

being paid immediately but the exchange of the camels being deferred to a future date.[817] Neither is it permissible to agree to defer the exchange of both the camels and the silver coins."

2027. Mālik said, "There is nothing objectionable in exchanging one excellent riding camel for two or more pack-camels that are of inferior quality. Even if they descend from the same stallion, there is nothing objectionable in purchasing two camels for one, with delivery to take place in the future, if they differ from one another in an obvious fashion. On the other hand, if they resemble one another, whether or not they are of the same type, two may not be exchanged for one, if delivery is to take place in the future. An example of what would be prohibited in this respect is exchanging one camel for two when there is no difference between them in terms of descent or capacity to undertake long journeys. If the case is as I have described to you, do not exchange two camels for one, with delivery taking place in the future. There is nothing objectionable, however, in someone selling whatever livestock he has purchased on credit before he has taken full possession of them, provided that it is to someone other than the one who sold them to him, and provided further that he sells them for cash."

2028. Mālik said, "An agreement to pay in advance for livestock that is to be delivered on a specified date in the future, whose characteristics have been reasonably specified, and whose price has been paid in cash is permitted. Both the seller and the purchaser are bound by their agreed-upon description of the animal to be delivered. That has been one of the continuous practices of the people that they deem binding among themselves and the validity of which the people of knowledge in our town have always upheld (*wa-lam yazal dhālika min ʿamal al-nās al-jāʾiz baynahum wa'lladhī lam yazal ʿalayhi ahl al-ʿilm bi-baladinā*)."

Chapter 26. Impermissible Exchanges Involving Livestock (*Ḥayawān*)

2029. According to Mālik, ʿAbd Allāh b. ʿUmar reported that the Messenger of God (pbuh) prohibited the sale of the offspring of a camel's offspring (*ḥabal ḥabala*). Such sales had been customary among the people in the Days of Ignorance prior to Islam (*jāhiliyya*). A man would purchase a camel for its meat (*jazūr*) but pay only when a fetus, at the time present in a she-camel's womb, successfully gave birth to its own calf.[818]

817 This transaction is prohibited because it takes on the appearance of a loan of money in which the lender is earning a profit in the form of the camel to be received in the future.

818 The commentators differ in their understanding of why this transaction is prohibited. One interpretation is that this pre-Islamic transaction is invalid because of the indeterminacy of

2030. According to Mālik, Ibn Shihāb reported that Saʿīd b. al-Musayyab said, "The rules of unlawful gain (*ribā*) do not apply to exchanges involving animals. However, three specific exchanges involving animals were prohibited: the sale of *maḍāmīn*, the sale of *malāqīḥ*, and the sale of future offspring of a fetus still in its mother's womb (*ḥabal ḥabala*)."[819] Mālik said, "*Maḍāmīn* refers to what is in the wombs of female camels, and *malāqīḥ* refers to the offspring of male camels."[820]

2031. Mālik said, "No one should purchase a specific animal unless it is present at the time of the sale, even if the prospective purchaser has already inspected it and found it acceptable, if he is to pay for it in cash, whether he inspected it recently or at some time in the past. The reason that a sale without such an inspection is prohibited is that the seller benefits immediately from the price he receives from the purchaser, but he cannot know whether the commodity has remained in the condition in which it was when the purchaser last inspected it. Therefore, such a sale is prohibited. It is not objectionable, however, if the seller's obligation is not the delivery of a specific animal but rather that of a generic animal, described with reasonable precision."

Chapter 27. Exchanging Livestock (*Ḥayawān*) for Meat

2032. According to Mālik, Zayd b. Aslam reported from Saʿīd b. al-Musayyab that the Messenger of God (pbuh) prohibited the exchange of livestock for meat.

2033. According to Mālik, Dāwūd b. al-Ḥuṣayn reported that he heard Saʿīd b. al-Musayyab say, "One way in which the people before Islam gambled was by exchanging the meat of an animal for one or two yearlings (*shāt*)."

---

the term, since it is defined with reference to an indefinite future event, namely, the fetus's giving birth to its own child. The second interpretation is that the transaction is invalid because the object of the sale is the as-yet unborn future camel—a nonexistent item. From an economic perspective, the seller presumably receives an above-market price for the camel that he is giving the purchaser, insofar as it has reached the end of its useful life and its only remaining use is to be slaughtered for meat. However, he will receive payment only if and when the specified condition takes place in the future. The purchaser, meanwhile, benefits immediately from the meat of the camel but will not be obliged to pay for it before the passage of several years, if ever. If the condition does not arise, he effectively obtains the camel for free. Accordingly, the transaction is simply a bet on the future fertility not just of the mother but of her daughter as well.

819 The third case refers to the transaction described in the previous hadith, no. 2029.

820 What is purported to be sold in the sale of *malāqīḥ* is the offspring that results from a male's mating with a female. Such a sale is invalid because it is impossible to know whether any offspring will be produced from the mating.

2034. According to Mālik, Abū al-Zinād reported that Saʿīd b. al-Musayyab would say, "Exchanging an animal for meat is prohibited." Abū al-Zinād said, "I said to Saʿīd b. al-Musayyab, 'What do you think of a man who purchases a camel that is long in the tooth for ten yearlings?' Saʿīd said, 'If he purchases the camel in order to slaughter it for its meat, it is not a valid sale.'" Abū al-Zinād said, "Everyone I encountered among the people forbade the exchange of animals for meat. That prohibition was also set out in the letters of appointment that the governors Abān b. ʿUthmān and Hishām b. Ismāʿīl issued to their subordinate officers. They all prohibited such an exchange."

Chapter 28. Exchanging Meat for Meat

2035. Yaḥyā said, "Mālik said, 'The agreed-upon rule among us (*al-amr al-mujtamaʿ ʿalayhi ʿindanā*) concerning the meat of cattle, camels, and sheep (*ghanam*) and the meat of wild animals similar to them is that the meat of one should not be exchanged for the meat of another except in like quantities and only if the exchange takes place hand to hand. It is not objectionable, however, if the meat is not weighed, if care is taken that like quantities are exchanged, and if the exchange takes place hand to hand.'"

2036. Mālik said, "There is nothing objectionable in exchanging fish for beef, camel meat, mutton, or the meat of wild animals similar to them, two for one or more than two for one, provided that the exchange takes place hand to hand. If the agreement permits delay in the performance of the transaction, however, it is not a good sale."

2037. Mālik said, "In my opinion, all meat from fowl constitutes a genus different from both the meat of four-legged domesticated animals and the meat of fish, and so I see nothing objectionable in exchanging one of these for the other in dissimilar quantities hand to hand; however, no delay is permitted in the exchange of such items."

Chapter 29. What Has Come Down regarding Payment for a Dog

2038. According to Mālik, Ibn Shihāb reported from Abū Bakr b. ʿAbd al-Raḥmān b. al-Ḥārith b. Hishām and Abū Masʿūd al-Anṣārī that the Messenger of God (pbuh) prohibited payment for a dog, the earnings of a prostitute, and the money of a soothsayer. "The earnings of a prostitute" refer to what a woman receives in exchange for illicit intercourse, and "the money of a soothsayer" refers to the bribe he receives in exchange for revealing his visions.

2039. Mālik said, "I dislike that a seller should benefit from payment for a dog, whether it is a hunting dog or not. This is on account of what has been transmitted from the Messenger of God (pbuh) forbidding payment for a dog."[821]

Chapter 30. Loans and the Exchange of Goods One for Another

2040. According to Mālik, it reached him that the Messenger of God (pbuh) prohibited the bundling of a sale and a loan in one transaction. Mālik said, "An example of this is if one man says to another, 'I will purchase your goods from you for such-and-such amount, if you lend me such-and-such.' If they enter into an agreement on these terms, the contract is not permissible. If, however, the party who made the loan a condition for entering into the transaction waives it, the sale becomes binding."

2041. Mālik said, "There is nothing objectionable in exchanging one unit of plain linen, Shaṭawī linen,[822] or fine Qaṣabī linen[823] for several units of Itribī, Qassī, or Zīqa[824] linen, nor is there anything objectionable in exchanging one unit of fine Harawī or Marwī[825] cotton cloth for several Yemeni cloaks, shawls, and similar garments made of rough cotton fabric, one for two or three, if the exchange takes place hand to hand. Should the goods be of the same kind, however, and performance of the transaction is deferred, it is not a good sale. If performance is deferred, it is a good sale only if the exchanged items are clearly different kinds of goods. When the goods are similar to one another, even if they have different names, exchanging one for two on a deferred basis is not permitted. An example of a prohibited exchange is if someone takes two units of fine Harawī cotton cloth for one unit of fine Marwī or Qūhī cotton cloth to be delivered in the future, or two units of Furqubī linen for one unit of Shaṭawī linen. If these various types of cloth have the same generic attributes, two units of them may not be exchanged for one to be delivered in the future. There is nothing

---

821 Mālik's view in the *Muwaṭṭa'* is that a dog, even a hunting dog, is not a legitimate object of sale. Other Mālikī sources, however, report that he distinguished between the sale of dogs whose ownership is permissible, such as hunting dogs and dogs used to guard livestock and crops, and the sale of dogs whose ownership is impermissible. According to these sources, it is permissible to sell and keep the payment received for the former type of dog. Bājī, *al-Muntaqā*, 5:28. Later Mālikīs also disagreed regarding whether Mālik's expression of dislike in the *Muwaṭṭa'* should be understood to mean that the sale of dogs is prohibited or that it is merely disfavored (*makrūh*).

822 Linen cloth from a village in Egypt called Shaṭā.

823 Qaṣabī linen is a particularly soft kind of linen cloth. Bājī, *al-Muntaqā*, 5:30; Zurqānī, *Sharḥ al-Zurqānī*, 3:459.

824 Itrībī, Qassī, and Zīqa are types of rough linen cloth, in contrast to the Shaṭawī and Qaṣabī linens, which are soft. Bājī, *al-Muntaqā*, 5:30.

825 Cotton cloth from the Persian towns of Herat and Merv, respectively.

objectionable in selling any of these items before taking full possession of them to someone other than the original seller, provided that the purchase price was paid in cash."

Chapter 31. Advance Payment for Goods

2042. According to Mālik, Yaḥyā b. Saʿīd reported that al-Qāsim b. Muḥammad said, "I heard a man ask ʿAbd Allāh b. ʿAbbās about a man who paid in advance for some fine pieces of linen (*sabā'ib*) and who wished to sell them before taking full possession of them. Ibn ʿAbbās said, 'That is silver for silver,' and forbade the sale."

2043. Mālik said, "In our opinion, and God knows best, Ibn ʿAbbās prohibited that previous transaction only because the seller in the second transaction wanted to sell the linen back to the very person who sold it to him in the first transaction, at a price greater than what he had originally paid. Had he sold the linen to a third person, however, the second transaction would have been unobjectionable."

2044. Mālik said, "The agreed-upon rule among us (*al-amr al-mujtamaʿ ʿalayhi ʿindanā*) regarding advance payment for slaves, livestock, or other goods is that the purchaser can pay in advance for such goods provided that they are described with sufficient precision and a determinate date is specified for their delivery. When the seller's obligation to deliver becomes due, the purchaser is not permitted to sell any of the goods back to the seller at a price higher than the amount that he initially advanced for them before first taking full possession of them. That is because if he were to do so, it would amount to an unlawful gain (*ribā*). In the latter scenario, by giving the seller dinars or dirhams, the purchaser transfers his title to them to the seller, which permits the seller to benefit from them. When the term expires and the seller is obliged to deliver the goods, the purchaser does not take possession of them but instead sells them back to their original owner at a price higher than what he paid in advance for them. The result is that the seller returns the advance payment to the purchaser along with the payment of an additional sum of money."[826]

2045. Mālik said, "When someone makes an advance payment of gold or silver for the future delivery of a quantity of generically described livestock (*ḥayawān*) or goods on a determinate date, and the seller's obligation becomes due, there is nothing objectionable in the purchaser selling the goods back to the original seller, whether before or after the date of delivery, in exchange for substitute goods in whatever amount they may

826 In other words, the transaction ends up being a loan at interest.

be, provided that the purchaser takes immediate possession of such goods. If the seller's obligation, however, was to deliver food, the purchaser is not permitted to sell that food back to the original seller until he first takes full possession of it. But the purchaser may, before taking delivery, resell the goods that he is entitled to receive from the original seller for gold or silver or any other goods to anyone other than the original seller, provided he is paid promptly. Were he to defer payment of the price for those goods, the second transaction becomes invalid because it violates the prohibition against exchanging one debt for another (*al-kāliʾ bil-kāliʾ*).[827] *Al-kāliʾ bil-kāliʾ* refers to an agreement in which a creditor sells a debt owed to him for a new debt owed to him by another."

2046. Mālik said, "When someone pays in advance for the future delivery of goods on a determinate date, and those goods are neither solid nor liquid foods, the purchaser may resell those goods for money or other goods before taking full possession of them to whomsoever he wishes, other than the original seller who sold them to him. He may not sell the goods back to the original seller, except in exchange for promptly delivered substitute goods. In the latter case, even if the seller's obligation to deliver has not yet become due, there is nothing objectionable in the purchaser selling the goods that are the subject of the seller's obligation back to their original owner for substitute goods, provided that they are clearly different in kind from those specified in the original contract and that the purchaser takes prompt possession of the substitute goods."

2047. Mālik was asked about the following case: Someone pays gold dinars or silver dirhams in advance for the future delivery of four generically described measures of cloth, but when the seller's obligation becomes due and the purchaser seeks to collect what is owed to him, he discovers that the seller does not have in his inventory what he promised to deliver. Instead, he finds that the seller has only cloth of an inferior quality to the kind specified in the contract. The seller proposes the following arrangement to him: "In lieu of what I owe you, I will give you eight measures of this cloth, the cloth that I have." Mālik said, "There is nothing objectionable in that, provided that the purchaser takes immediate possession of the eight measures of cloth that the seller is offering him before they part ways. If the seller's obligation to deliver the eight measures of cloth is deferred, however, the second sale is invalid. If they agreed to this arrangement before the original

827 In this case, the purchaser is owed delivery of certain goods by the seller. He is permitted to sell that obligation to a third party, but the third party must pay immediately for the right to take delivery from the original seller. If the original purchaser were to sell his right to receive delivery to a third party on credit terms, he would be exchanging one debt owed to him for a second debt owed to him, which is prohibited.

obligation became due, it would also be invalid, unless the measures of substitute cloth that the seller is offering the purchaser were not of the same kind as those specified in the original contract."[828]

Chapter 32. The Sale of Copper, Iron, and Similar Items That Are Sold by Weight

2048. Yaḥyā said, "Mālik said, 'The rule in our view (*al-amr ʿindanā*) regarding everything that is sold by weight other than gold and silver, such as copper, brass, lead, iron, animal fodder, figs, cotton, and similar things sold by weight, is that there is nothing objectionable in exchanging two measures for one of the same kind hand to hand. There is nothing objectionable in exchanging 280 grams (one *riṭl*)[829] of iron for twice that amount of iron, or a similarly unequal exchange of brass. A deferred exchange of these items in unequal quantities, however, is not a good sale. If the exchanged items are clearly of two different kinds, there is nothing objectionable in exchanging them in unequal quantities on a deferred basis. However, if the two kinds resemble one another but have different names, such as lead (*raṣāṣ*) and black lead (*ānuk*), and brass (*shabah*) and yellow brass (*ṣufr*), I believe that their deferred exchange in unequal quantities is prohibited. There is nothing objectionable in selling these kinds of purchased items in advance of delivery, even before the purchaser takes full possession of them, provided that the purchaser sells them to someone other than their original seller and that the purchase price for the second transaction is paid immediately, if they were originally purchased on the basis of volume or weight. If, on the other hand, the original goods were purchased by estimate, the purchaser may resell them to a third party either for cash or on credit. That is because in this case the purchaser, not the original seller, is responsible for their delivery, because he purchased them on the basis of an estimate. By contrast, if the purchaser purchased the items by weight or volume, he is not liable for their delivery in the second transaction until he has actually measured out the items and taken them fully into his possession. Of all the views that I have heard regarding these matters, this is the one I prefer most. The people among us have always acted in accordance with this rule (*wa-huwa alladhī lam yazal ʿalayhi amr al-nās ʿindanā*).'"

---

828 This is because pieces cloth of the same kind, even if their quality differs, may be exchanged in unequal quantities only if the transaction takes place immediately.

829 The *riṭl* was a measure of weight that was used throughout the Islamic world but varied significantly from one region to another. The *riṭl* in the Hijaz, where Mālik lived, was reported to have been the equivalent in weight of 120 silver dirhams, which was approximately 280 grams. Ḥallāq, *al-Īḍāḥāt al-ʿaṣriyya*, 175.

2049. Mālik said, "The rule in our view regarding the sale of items that are sold by volume or weight and that are neither solid nor liquid food, such as safflower, date pits, camel fodder, henna, and similar things, is that there is nothing objectionable in the hand-to-hand exchange of unequal amounts of any of these kinds of items, as long as the exchange is not deferred. Further, if the exchanged items are clearly different, there is nothing objectionable in the exchange of unequal amounts of these items on a deferred basis. In addition, there is nothing objectionable in selling purchased items of these kinds before taking full possession of them, if the purchaser sells them for cash to someone other than the original seller who first sold him the goods."

2050. Mālik said, "Exchanging any item[830] that people find beneficial, even gravel or gypsum, in unequal amounts on a deferred basis results in an unlawful gain (*ribā*). So, too, does exchanging equal amounts of any beneficial item on a deferred basis and adding something else to the exchange."

Chapter 33. The Prohibition against Two Sales in One

2051. According to Mālik, it reached him that the Messenger of God (pbuh) prohibited two sales in one.

2052. According to Mālik, it reached him that one man said to another, "Purchase this camel for me. Pay for it in cash, and I will purchase it from you on credit." ʿAbd Allāh b. ʿUmar was asked about that sale, and he disapproved of it and forbade it.[831]

2053. According to Mālik, it reached him that al-Qāsim b. Muḥammad was asked about a man who purchased some goods with the option of paying either ten dinars in cash or fifteen on credit. He expressed his disapproval of that sale and forbade it.[832]

2054. Mālik said, regarding someone who purchases goods from another for either ten dinars in cash or fifteen on credit, with the purchaser becoming entitled to the goods by virtue of payment of either one of the two prices,

830 He means goods that are neither solid nor liquid food.

831 In this transaction, the proposed agreement encompasses two contracts: the first contract entails the first purchaser acquiring a camel from a third party by paying for it in cash, and the second contract entails the sale of that very camel by the first purchaser to the second purchaser, i.e., the person proposing the arrangement, on credit, presumably in an amount in excess of the cash price initially paid by the first purchaser for the camel. Mālikī commentators point out that this transaction involves not only two contracts in a single agreement but also, implicitly, a loan at interest, and so it would be invalid on both grounds. Bājī, *al-Muntaqā*, 5:39.

832 The defect in this transaction is that the price was not specified at the time the parties entered into the contract, so it violates the rule that the price must be determinate in order for a valid contract to come into existence.

“This is not allowed, because if he delays payment of the ten dinars in cash, the price becomes fifteen dinars on credit, and if he pays the ten dinars in cash, it is as though he is purchasing fifteen dinars for ten.”[833]

2055. Mālik said, regarding a man who purchases goods from another man for either one dinar in cash or one young, generically described yearling (*shāt*) on credit, with the purchaser being bound by one of the two prices, “This is not permitted and should not be done, because the Messenger of God (pbuh) prohibited two sales in one, and this is a case of two sales in one.”

2056. Mālik said, regarding a man who says to another, “I’m prepared to purchase from you either fifteen measures (*ṣāʿ*) of these *ʿajwa* dates of yours or ten measures of these Ṣayḥānī dates of yours, or fifteen measures of this low-quality wheat of yours or ten measures of this Levantine wheat of yours, in each case for one dinar, with my retaining the right to specify which of the two trades I desire upon payment”: “This is forbidden and illicit. That is because he offered to take ten measures of the Ṣayḥānī dates but then spurned them, instead taking fifteen measures of the *ʿajwa* dates, or he offered to take fifteen measures of low-quality wheat but then spurned them, taking instead ten measures of Levantine wheat. That is forbidden and illicit. In addition, it resembles the subject of the prohibition in the command forbidding two sales in one, as well as the prohibition against the exchange of unequal quantities of the same kind of food.”

Chapter 34. Sales Involving Material Uncertainty in the Consideration (*Gharar*)

2057. According to Mālik, Abū Ḥāzim b. Dīnār reported from Saʿīd b. al-Musayyab that the Messenger of God (pbuh) prohibited sales involving material uncertainty in the consideration.

2058. Mālik said, “An instance of a sale involving indeterminate consideration and the mutual assumption of price risk (*mukhāṭara*) is when someone makes an offer to another person who has lost an animal or whose slave has run away, the purchase price of each having been fifty dinars, saying, ‘I’ll purchase it from you for twenty dinars.’ In this case, if the purchaser succeeds in finding the lost animal or the runaway slave, the seller loses thirty dinars, but if he does not, the seller gets twenty dinars

833 In other words, the contract is invalid because the price has not been determined as of the date of the parties’ agreement. It could be that the seller has the option of determining which price prevails, or the purchaser has this option, or both of them do. If the latter is the case, it is obvious that the parties have not reached any agreement at all with respect to price, so no contract could be deemed to exist.

from the purchaser without having given him anything in exchange. This sale suffers from another defect as well, insofar as it is impossible to know whether the value of the lost article, if it indeed is found, has increased or decreased in the meantime, or whether any defects have arisen in it. This type of agreement represents an extreme form of mutual assumption of price risk."

2059. Mālik said, "The rule in our view (*al-amr ʿindanā*) is that the purchase and sale of fetuses, whether human or not, is another instance of a sale involving the mutual assumption of price risk and indeterminate consideration, because it is not known whether the fetus will be born alive, and if it is, whether it will be handsome or ugly, well-formed or defective, or male or female. All of these factors, however, are relevant to making the newborn more or less desirable, with its fair market value being one amount if it has a particular set of features and a different amount with a different set of features."

2060. Mālik said, "It is not permissible to sell a female and to reserve what is in her womb. An example of this is when a seller says, 'The price for my yearling (*shāt*), which produces a lot of milk, is three dinars, but I will sell it to you for two dinars and reserve what is in its womb for myself.' This offer is prohibited because it entails indeterminate consideration and mutual assumption of price risk."

2061. Mālik said, "It is not licit to exchange olives for olive oil, sesame seeds for sesame oil, or butter for ghee, because it is an exchange that involves indeterminate amounts (*muzābana*). The purchaser who purchases seeds and similar things in exchange for a specified amount of a substance that is extracted from the thing purchased, such as olives for olive oil, does not know whether what will be extracted from what he purchased will be less or more than what he gave,[834] resulting in a transaction that involves indeterminate consideration and mutual assumption of price risk. Another instance of this principle is an exchange involving moringa seeds (*ḥabbat al-bān*) for moringa seed oil (*salīkha*). It involves indeterminate consideration, because that which is extracted from the moringa seeds is nothing other than moringa seed oil. There is nothing objectionable, however, in exchanging moringa seeds for scented moringa seed oil, because the latter has been

834 In other words, if someone acquires one measure of olives in exchange for one measure of olive oil, even though the amounts exchanged are known with precision, the transaction nevertheless involves indeterminate consideration, because it is impossible for the person acquiring the olives to know whether the amount of the oil that is to be extracted from those olives will be equal to, greater than, or smaller than the amount of the oil he gave his counterparty. Therefore, there is material indeterminacy in the consideration and a substantial risk of inequality in the exchange. Each of these constitutes a sufficient reason to invalidate the sale.

scented, mixed, and transformed through processing from its initial state as raw moringa seed oil into another item."

2062. Mālik said, regarding a man who sold goods to another party, guaranteeing to the purchaser that he would not incur any loss on the resale of the goods, "This is an invalid transaction, and it involves mutual assumption of price risk. This can be explained by the following analysis: It is as though the seller hired the purchaser, with the latter's wage deriving from the profit, if any, obtained from the resale of the goods. However, if the purchaser sells the goods at cost or less, he receives nothing beyond the cost of the goods, and his labor is uncompensated. This is not a valid transaction, and the purchaser in this case is entitled to receive a wage in accordance with the amount of labor he has expended in selling the goods, with whatever loss or profit is realized from the sale of the goods accruing exclusively to the goods' original owner. This rule applies only if the condition of the goods has changed substantially while in the purchaser's possession or if the goods were sold to a third party.[835] If neither has occurred, the transaction between them is simply rescinded."

2063. Mālik said, "As for the case of someone who purchases goods from another in a final and conclusive sale but then regrets the transaction and says to the seller, 'Give me a reduction in the price,' but the seller refuses, saying instead, 'Sell it, and I will reimburse you for any losses,' there is nothing objectionable in that. That is because it does not involve the mutual assumption of price risk. It is nothing more than a discount that the seller freely gives to the purchaser, and it is not a condition of their original contract. The rule among us is in accordance with that (*dhālika alladhī ʿalayhi al-amr ʿindanā*)."

Chapter 35. Sales by Touch (*Mulāmasa*) and Tossing (*Munābadha*)

2064. According to Mālik, Muḥammad b. Yaḥyā b. Habbān and Abū al-Zinād reported from al-Aʿraj, from Abū Hurayra, that the Messenger of God (pbuh) prohibited sales by touch (*mulāmasa*) and by tossing (*munābadha*). Mālik said, "*Mulāmasa* is when a man purchases a piece of cloth merely by touching it, without first unfolding it or examining what is in it, or when he purchases it in the darkness of the night, without knowing what is in it. *Munābadha* is when a man tosses a piece of cloth of his to another man and the latter throws his own piece of cloth to the first man, with neither of them examining the cloth he has taken. Instead, each of them says, 'This one

835 In other words, the rule that Mālik sets out here applies only if the purchaser successfully resells the goods or if the goods are materially transformed while in his possession.

is for that one.' This is what is meant by the prohibition of sales by touch and tossing."

2065. Mālik said, regarding a rough cloak that is unwrapped within its packaging or Egyptian cloth that is folded and packed, "It is not permissible to sell them without first unfolding them or allowing the contents of the containers to be examined. Otherwise, their sale would be a case of indeterminate consideration (*gharar*), and a kind of 'sale by touch.'"

2066. Mālik said, "The sale of bolts of cloth in reliance on a merchant's inventory list is different from the sale of a rough cloak that is unwrapped within its packaging, or cloth that is folded and packed, or things of that nature. The rule that is in force (*al-amr al-maʿmūl bih*) distinguishes between the two sales, and an awareness of that difference is present in people's hearts and has long been the case in the practices of those engaged in it (*mā maḍā min ʿamal al-māḍīn fīh*). This has been a continuous part of people's mutual contracts and mutual commerce in respect of which they have found nothing objectionable (*lam yazal min buyūʿ al-nās waʾl-tijāra baynahum allatī lā yarawna bihā baʾsan*). That is because the practice of selling bolts of cloth in reliance on a merchant's inventory list without first unfolding the bolts is not intended to result in a profit from material uncertainty in the consideration (*gharar*). Therefore, it does not resemble a 'sale by touch.'"

Chapter 36. Selling Goods at an Agreed-Upon Rate of Profit (*Murābaḥa*)

2067. Mālik said, "The rule in our view (*al-amr ʿindanā*) regarding someone who purchases cloth in one town and then transports it for sale to another town, where he sells it at an agreed-upon rate of profit, is that none of his brokers' fees, the costs of folding, straightening, or other upkeep of his merchandise, or the rent of warehouse space are included in the price on the basis of which the seller calculates his profit. The seller is entitled to include in the item's price the expense incurred in transporting the cloth, but he may not receive a profit on this expense unless he first discloses that information in its entirety to the potential purchaser. There is nothing objectionable in the seller receiving a profit on that expense from purchasers if the purchasers have knowledge of it. As for expenses arising out of bleaching, tailoring, and dyeing the cloth, as well as similar matters, they are deemed part of the cloth itself, and accordingly profit is calculated on such expenses, just as it is calculated on the cloth itself. If the seller sells the cloth without first disclosing the cost of the items that are to be excluded from the calculation of the profit, and then the cloth's condition changes[836] while it is in the possession of the purchaser, the cost of the transportation is reimbursable to the seller, but he is not entitled to any profit in respect thereof. If the cloth's condition has not changed while in the possession of the purchaser, however, the sale between them is rescinded, unless they come to a lawful, amicable settlement."

2068. Mālik said, concerning a man who purchases goods using either gold or silver on a day on which the exchange rate is ten silver dirhams for one gold dinar, and who then sells the goods either in a different city or in the city where he purchased them, in both cases at an agreed-upon rate of profit according to the exchange rate prevailing at the place and date of the second sale: "If he originally purchased the goods using silver dirhams but then sold them for gold dinars, or if he originally purchased them for gold dinars and then sold them for silver dirhams, and if the goods remained in their original condition, the seller is given an option to affirm the sale or to cancel it. If the goods are no longer in their original condition, however, the purchaser is entitled to keep the goods if he pays the seller the price that the seller initially paid for them. In this case the seller is entitled to whatever profit results from the previously agreed-upon rate of profit that the purchaser had agreed to give him on the basis of the seller's original purchase price."

2069. Mālik said, "If a man sells to a purchaser goods that he, the seller, himself purchased in an arm's length transaction for one hundred dinars, receiving an agreed-upon profit of one dinar on every ten spent, and then it is discovered that the seller paid only ninety dinars for the goods, and in the meantime, the condition of the goods changed while they were in the purchaser's possession, the seller is given an option. If he wishes, he may claim the fair market value of his goods on the day his purchaser took possession of them, unless their fair market value on that day was higher than the price at which he sold them to his purchaser. In no case can he collect more than the purchase price of 110 dinars. Alternatively, if the seller wishes, he can claim the capital sum of his goods, ninety dinars, plus the profit to which he was entitled on their sale to his purchaser, nine dinars. If that sum is less than their fair market value on the day his purchaser took possession of them, however, the seller is free to choose between the fair market value of his goods and his capital sum plus the agreed-upon profit, that is, ninety-nine dinars."

836 The cloth's condition may "change" if, for example, the purchaser uses it to tailor a garment, it is destroyed by fire or some other cause, or its market price changes significantly.

2070. Mālik said, "If a man sells goods on the basis of an agreed-upon rate of profit, mistakenly saying to his purchaser, on the basis of a faulty inventory list (*barnāmij*), 'These goods cost me one hundred dinars,' and then it is discovered that their cost was actually 120 dinars, the purchaser is given an option. If he wishes, he may give the seller the fair market value of the goods on the day he took possession of them, or if he wishes, he may give the seller the price that the seller originally paid for the goods, plus the profit that the purchaser had agreed to give the seller, whatever that may be, unless the goods' fair market value would be less than the price at which the seller originally purchased the goods. The purchaser is not entitled to force the seller to accept a price that is less than what the seller originally paid, because the purchaser agreed to purchase the goods from the seller on the basis of his costs plus an agreed-upon rate of profit. Indeed, the owner of the goods brought his claim out of a desire to seek additional profit. The seller's error does not provide the purchaser grounds for demanding a reduction in the price he initially paid for the goods on the basis of their faulty description in the merchant's inventory list."

Chapter 37. Sales in Reliance on a Merchant's Inventory List (*Barnāmij*)

2071. Yaḥyā said, "Mālik said, 'Regarding a scenario in which a group of people jointly purchase goods such as cloth or slaves, and then someone comes to learn about their deal and says to one of them, "I am well informed about the description and condition of the cloth that you just purchased from so-and-so, and I would like to purchase your share of that cloth, giving you a profit of such-and-such for it," and the offeree says, "I accept your offer," so the first man gives the second the agreed-upon price, including the agreed-upon profit, and then takes his place in the group as a partner to the original transaction, but when they examine the cloth that they agreed to purchase, they find it disagreeable and conclude that the price they paid was excessive in light of the cloth's poor quality: The rule in our view (*al-amr ʿindanā*) is that the new partner is bound by his agreement with the former partner and has no right to rescind it as long as the new partner purchased the goods in reliance on a merchant's inventory list or a reasonably precise description of the goods sold from the former partner."

2072. Mālik said, regarding a scenario in which a merchant arrives bearing various kinds of cloth wrapped in numerous bundles, and when prospective purchasers approach him to bargain over his goods, he reads out to them his inventory list (but does not open up his bundles for their visual inspection), saying, "In each bundle is such-and-such a number of Basran wraps, and such-and-such a number of fine Sābirī[837] wraps of such-and-such size," and he specifies for them the various kinds of cloth he has for sale by their type, and says, "Buy them from me on the basis of these representations," and so they purchase the bundles relying on his representations about their content, but when they open the bundles, they conclude that they paid too much for them and regret their decisions: "They are bound by their agreement with him, if the goods conform to the description in his inventory list that formed the basis of his offer to them. That is the rule that the people among us have continually followed and that they regard as binding among themselves (*hādhā al-amr alladhī lam yazal al-nās ʿalayhi ʿindanā yujīzūnahu baynahum*), as long as the goods conform to the merchant's inventory list and do not differ from it."

Chapter 38. Sales with a Right of Rescission (*Khiyār*)

2073. According to Mālik, Nāfiʿ reported from ʿAbd Allāh b. ʿUmar that the Messenger of God (pbuh) said, "Both parties to a sale are free to rescind their agreement as long as they have not gone their separate ways, except in a sale with an option to rescind." Mālik said, "In our view, a contractual option to rescind is not subject to a determinate limit, nor is there any rule in force (*amr maʿmūl bih*) with respect to it."

2074. According to Mālik, it reached him that ʿAbd Allāh b. Masʿūd would relate that the Messenger of God (pbuh) said, "Whenever a dispute arises between the purchaser and the seller in a contract of sale, the purchaser bears the burden of proving the truth of his claim, unless they agree to rescind their contract."

2075. Mālik said, regarding a scenario in which a man sells goods to another, telling the purchaser when it is time to conclude the sale, "I'll sell them to you only on the condition that I first get the opinion of so-and-so, and if he thinks the terms are appropriate, the sale will be final, but if he does not, the deal between us is off," and they contract on that basis, but the purchaser later regrets agreeing to this condition before the seller has had a chance to get the other person's view of the terms of the deal: "That sale binds both of them in accordance with their agreement, and the purchaser does not have the option to rescind it. He is bound by the contract if the person to whom he granted the option, that is, the seller, chooses to enforce it."

2076. Mālik said, "The rule in our view (*al-amr ʿindanā*) regarding a man who purchases goods from another and then disagrees with the seller about the price, with the seller saying, 'I sold it to you for ten dinars,' and

837 A reference to a Persian town where such wraps were manufactured.

the purchaser saying, 'I purchased it from you for five dinars,' is that the seller is told, 'You may choose to give the goods to the buyer for the price he claims, or you may choose to swear by God that you sold your goods only for the amount that you claim.' If the seller swears accordingly, the purchaser is told, 'Either take the goods for the price the seller claims, or swear by God that you purchased them for only the amount that you claim.' If the purchaser, too, swears as requested, he is relieved of the contract, and that is because each of them is in the position of being a claimant against the other party."[838]

Chapter 39. What Has Come Down regarding Unlawful Gains (*Ribā*) with Respect to Debts

2077. According to Mālik, Abū al-Zinād reported from Busr b. Saʿīd that ʿUbayd Abū Sāliḥ, the freedman (*mawlā*) of al-Saffāḥ,[839] said, "I sold some cloth of mine to the people of Nakhla on credit. I then intended to leave for Kufa, so they proposed to me that I reduce the amount due in exchange for immediate payment.[840] I asked Zayd b. Thābit about that, and he said, 'No; I command you to neither accept such an offer nor make such an offer to your creditor.'"

2078. According to Mālik, ʿUthmān b. Hafṣ b. Khalada reported from Ibn Shihāb, from Sālim b. ʿAbd Allāh, from ʿAbd Allāh b. ʿUmar, that he was asked about a creditor who offers to reduce the stated amount of a debt, maturing on a future date, if the debtor agrees to pay the remaining balance immediately. ʿAbd Allāh disapproved of such an agreement and prohibited it.

2079. According to Mālik, Zayd b. Aslam said, "In the Days of Ignorance prior to Islam (*jāhiliyya*), 'unlawful gain' (*ribā*) was understood to consist of the following transaction: someone was owed an obligation from another, due on a future date, and when payment of the obligation became due, the creditor would say to the debtor, 'Will you pay me what you owe, or will

---

838 The ordinary rule of evidence is that the claimant is obliged to prove the truth of his claim, and if the claimant has no such evidence, the defendant need only swear an oath denying the claim in order to have it dismissed. In this case, as Mālik sees the dispute, both the seller and the purchaser are claimants against each other; neither has affirmative evidence proving his claim, but each is willing to swear an oath denying the truth of his opponent's claim. Accordingly, the claims of both are dismissed.

839 Al-Saffāḥ was the title of the first ʿAbbāsid caliph, ʿAbd Allāh b. Muḥammad b. ʿAlī b. ʿAbd Allāh b. ʿAbbās b. ʿAbd al-Muṭṭalib (r. 132–136/750–754).

840 The debtors in this case are presumed to be offering prepayment using property of the same genus as in the original debt—for example, offering seventy-five dinars to settle a debt with a face value of one hundred dinars. If, however, the debtors were offering to settle the debt with some other kind of property, such as cloth in lieu of the dinars set out in the contract, that would be acceptable.

you increase the principal sum owed and defer payment to the future?' If the debtor paid, the creditor would accept payment, but if he did not, the creditor would increase the principal sum of the debt owed to him and extend the maturity date further into the future."

2080. Mālik said, "When a debtor owes a creditor an obligation that is due on a determinate date in the future, the practice that is forbidden and about which there is no dissent among us (*al-amr al-makrūh alladhī lā ikhtilāfa fīhi ʿindanā*) is the creditor's agreement to reduce the amount of the obligation in exchange for the debtor's prompt payment of the reduced amount. We consider that practice to be the equivalent of a scenario in which a creditor agrees to defer collection of his debt from his debtor after it has matured, and the debtor agrees to increase his obligation to the creditor. That is, without doubt, the very essence of unlawful gain."

2081. Mālik said, regarding a scenario in which a debtor owes his creditor one hundred dinars, payable on a determinate date in the future, and when payment is due, the debtor says to his creditor, "Sell me some goods whose cash price is one hundred dinars for 150 dinars on credit": "This is not a permissible sale. The people of knowledge have always prohibited it (*lam yazal ahl al-ʿilm yanhawna ʿanh*). Such a transaction is prohibited because the creditor is merely giving his debtor the price of the very thing that he first sold to the debtor, deferring the debtor's obligation to pay the first one hundred dinars to the new maturity date that the debtor just suggested to him, and then increasing the debt that his debtor owes him by fifty dinars in exchange for agreeing to postpone the maturity date of his debtor's obligation. That is prohibited and invalid. Moreover, it resembles the report of Zayd b. Aslam regarding the practices of the people in the Days of Ignorance before Islam. When their debts matured, the creditors would say to their debtors, 'Either pay up or increase the debt,' and if they paid up, the creditors accepted their payment, but if not, the debtors increased the amount of the debt they owed to the creditors, and the creditors granted their debtors an extension of the maturity date."

Chapter 40. Miscellaneous Matters Related to Debts and the Transfer of Debts

2082. According to Mālik, Abū al-Zinād reported from al-Aʿraj, from Abū Hurayra, that the Messenger of God (pbuh) said, "A solvent debtor who puts off payment of his debts when they are due commits a wrong. If a debtor tells his creditor to pursue his claim against a solvent third-party debtor who owes a debt to the first debtor, the creditor should pursue his claim against the third-party debtor, not against his original debtor."

2083. According to Mālik, Mūsā b. Maysara reported that he heard a man say to Saʿīd b. al-Musayyab, "I am someone who sells on credit." Saʿīd replied, "Sell only what you already have on your camel," meaning, in your possession.

2084. Yaḥyā said, "Mālik said, regarding a scenario in which a man purchases goods from another on the condition that the seller deliver them to him on a determinate date in the future, aiming either to take advantage of an anticipated increase in market demand for that good or to fulfill a need at the time that he stipulates, and then the seller fails to make a timely delivery of the goods, delivering them after the stipulated delivery date, so the purchaser wishes to reject them and return them to the seller: 'The purchaser cannot do that, and he is bound by the contract. Had the seller delivered the goods prior to the specified delivery date, however, the purchaser would not have been obliged to take them.'"

2085. Mālik said, regarding a scenario in which someone purchases food and measures it out, and then someone comes to purchase it from him, so the first purchaser informs the prospective purchaser that he has already weighed it out and taken full possession of it, and the prospective purchaser is willing to accept the seller's representation regarding the food's quantity and to purchase it on that basis: "There is nothing objectionable in such a sale, if the price is paid in cash; however, if the food is sold on this basis for delivery on a determinate date in the future, the sale is prohibited unless the second purchaser measures out the goods received by the first purchaser for himself. The sale on credit is forbidden only because it is a means to the realization of an unlawful gain (*ribā*), and there is a risk that the transaction will be performed in this way without the food ever being measured, whether by weight or by volume. Therefore, if the sale is for delivery on a determinate date in the future, it is prohibited, and there is no dissent about that among us (*lā ikhtilāfa fīhi ʿindanā*)."

2086. Mālik said, "No one should purchase a debt, whether owed by a present debtor or an absentee one, without that debtor's acknowledgment of the debt, nor should anyone purchase a debt owed by a deceased debtor, even if the purchaser knows what property the deceased has left in his estate. That is because purchasing such a debt involves material indeterminacy in the consideration (*gharar*), because it is impossible to know whether the debt will be fulfilled or not. The prohibition involved in this case can be illustrated through the case of a person who purchases the debt owed by an absentee or deceased debtor. It is unknown what other debt the debtor might owe. If the deceased in fact owes other debts, the price that the purchaser paid to acquire the deceased's debt is lost without the purchaser receiving anything of value in return. This transaction also suffers from another defect insofar as he is purchasing something without anyone being liable to him for its delivery. Accordingly, if the deceased's debt is not fulfilled, the price that the purchaser paid for it is lost without his receipt of anything of value in return. The transaction thus involves an indeterminate consideration, which makes it invalid. A further distinction has been made between the rule that prohibits a person from selling something not in his possession but permits him to accept payment in advance for something that he does yet not own, and the rule governing an intermediary (*ṣāḥib al-ʿīna*) who extends credit to finance a sale. The intermediary comes to the market bearing his gold, which he wishes to use to purchase things solely for the purpose of reselling them on credit. He says to the merchants in the market, 'Here are ten dinars. What goods would you like me to purchase for you to then sell back to you on credit?' It is as though the man were selling his ten dinars in cash for fifteen dinars payable on a determinate date in the future. For this reason the transaction is prohibited and is deemed nothing other than a ruse to obtain an unlawful gain."

Chapter 41. What Has Come Down regarding Partnership (*Shirka*) and Resale at Cost (*Tawliya*)

2087. Mālik said, regarding someone who offers various kinds of cloth for sale but excludes some on the basis of their particular marks, "There is nothing objectionable in his making his offer conditional on his right to choose among the garments bearing a particular mark those that he will reserve for himself. If, however, his offer does not stipulate that he will choose among them when he makes his reservation, then it is my belief that he becomes a partner in the specific pieces of cloth that are purchased from him, because two garments may share the same mark, but their prices may nevertheless differ."

2088. Mālik said, "The rule in our view (*al-amr ʿindanā*) is that there is nothing objectionable in forming a partnership (*shirk*), reselling at cost (*tawliya*), or rescinding a sale (*iqāla*) for the benefit of the purchaser, whether the sale involves food or anything else and whether or not possession has been taken, provided that the original payment is in cash and that there is no profit, loss, or delay. If profit, loss, or delay is involved on the part of either of the parties to the transaction, it is treated as a new sale. In the latter case, the sale's legality or illegality is determined by the rules that define lawful and unlawful sales generally. In this case, the transaction is neither a partnership, nor a resale at cost, nor a cancellation."

2089. Mālik said, "In a scenario in which a person purchases goods, whether cloth or slaves, and finalizes the deal, and then a man asks him to become his partner in the transaction, and the purchaser acquiesces, and then both of them pay the purchase price to the goods' owner, and then a claim is made against the goods which results in the removal of the goods from their possession, the new partner is entitled to recover the price he paid from the man who involved him as a partner, and the one who made him a partner pursues the seller of the goods for reimbursement of their price. This does not apply if the original purchaser stipulated to his prospective partner at the time of their agreement or at the time of the contract with the seller, but before any claims were made against the goods, that the seller would bear all liability for any defects in the goods. But if a claim is then made against the goods, and the sale cannot be rescinded, such a condition stipulated by the original purchaser is invalid, and he bears sole liability for whatever defects are present in the goods."[841]

2090. Mālik said, regarding a man who says to another, "Purchase these goods and let us own them as partners, and if you pay my share on my behalf I will sell them for you," "That is not a good sale insofar as the second man said, 'Pay my share, and I will sell them for you.' That amounts to a loan extended by the second man to the first on the condition that the first man sell the goods on behalf of the second. Were the goods to be destroyed or perish before their sale, the man who paid the price could recover from his partner the portion of the price that he paid on his behalf. This transaction, therefore, is a case of a loan that brings benefits to the creditor, and it is thus invalid."

2091. Mālik said, "If a man purchases goods and becomes fully entitled to them, and then another man says to him, 'If you make me your partner in these goods, I will sell them all for you,' that would be lawful and there is nothing objectionable in it. The reason for that is that this is a new sale, in which the goods' owner sells his partner half of his goods on the condition that his partner sell the half of the goods that he, the first owner, still owns."

Chapter 42. What Has Come Down regarding the Debtor's Insolvency (*Iflās*)

2092. According to Mālik, Ibn Shihāb reported from Abū Bakr b. ʿAbd al-Raḥmān b. al-Ḥārith b. Hishām that the Messenger of God (pbuh) said,

---

841 The second partner in this case is permitted to hold the first partner liable for the defect, because the first partner effectively sold the second partner an interest in the goods. By acting as a seller of goods, the first partner is liable to the purchaser of those goods for any relevant defects. In the second scenario, however, the second partner is purchasing the goods directly from the original seller, not from the first partner. Accordingly, when the defect arises, he sues the original seller and not the first partner.

"Whenever a man sells goods to another, and the purchaser becomes insolvent without the seller having received anything of the purchase price owed to him, but he discovers his goods still in the buyer's possession, unchanged from the condition in which he had sold them to him, he has a greater entitlement to take them than the purchaser's other creditors do. If the purchaser has died without paying his debt to the seller, however, the seller of the goods must, even if he finds his goods intact, nevertheless share them with the decedent's other creditors."

2093. According to Mālik, Yaḥyā b. Saʿīd reported from Abū Bakr b. Muḥammad b. ʿAmr b. Ḥazm, from ʿUmar b. ʿAbd al-ʿAzīz, from Abū Bakr b. ʿAbd al-Raḥmān b. al-Ḥārith b. Hishām, from Abū Hurayra, that the Messenger of God (pbuh) said, "If a debtor becomes insolvent, and then a creditor of his finds his goods still in the debtor's possession in their original condition, the creditor has a greater entitlement to take them than any of the debtor's other creditors do."

2094. Mālik said, regarding a scenario in which a man sells another some goods but the purchaser becomes insolvent without discharging his debt, "If the seller finds any of his property still in the debtor's possession in its original condition, he is entitled to repossess whatever he finds. Even if the purchaser has sold some of the goods and distributed them to others, the claim of the first owner of the goods—that is, the seller—to the remaining goods still in the purchaser's possession is superior to the claims of the purchaser's other creditors. The fact that the purchaser has distributed to others some of what he purchased does not preclude the seller from taking possession of whatever intact property he still finds in the purchaser's possession. However, if the seller collected any portion of the payment owing to him in respect of the goods, he may, if he so wishes, return the payment to the purchaser and instead repossess whatever intact property of his he finds in the purchaser's possession and, to settle his claims arising out of property that is no longer in the purchaser's possession, share pro rata with the purchaser's other creditors whatever value still remains in the purchaser's property."[842]

2095. Mālik said, "If someone sells goods such as wool thread or other raw material or a plot of land to another on credit, and then the purchaser makes some improvements to those goods, such as building a house or

842 In a situation in which the creditor has received partial payment of the debt owed by his insolvent purchaser, the creditor is given a choice between retaining the payment received and forgoing the right to repossess his intact goods or returning the payment received to the insolvent purchaser and seizing whatever intact goods of his are still in the insolvent purchaser's possession.

weaving the wool into cloth, but then becomes insolvent, the creditor in this case has no right to claim, for example, 'The plot of land and whatever improvements have been built on it are mine.' Rather, the plot of land, along with any improvements the purchaser has made on it, are appraised together, and then the value of the plot is determined independently and the value of the improvements is determined independently. The seller of the plot of land and any other creditors are then treated as co-owners of the entire parcel, each in proportion to his share. The seller of the plot makes a claim on the parcel in proportion to his claim against the purchaser, and the other creditors make claims in proportion to their claims against the purchaser. An example illustrating this rule is a plot of land whose aggregate value is 1,500 dirhams, the value of the plot alone being 500 dirhams and the value of the improvements being 1,000 dirhams. In this case, the seller of the plot is entitled to one-third of the value of the entire parcel, and the other creditors are entitled to the remaining two-thirds. The same principle applies to wool thread and any other similar thing if the debtor has made improvements to the property but is burdened by a debt that he is unable to pay. This is the practice in such matters (*hādhā al-ʿamal fīh*). As for intact goods to which the purchaser has not made any improvements but that sell well and have undergone an increase in their price with the result that the seller desires to repossess them for himself and the other creditors want to retain them for their own benefit, the other creditors have a choice between paying the seller the goods' purchase price in full, without any reduction, or abandoning the goods to him. If, on the other hand, the price of the goods has decreased, the original seller has the option of repossessing his goods, forgoing any recourse to the rest of the debtor's property, or he may elect to become one of the general creditors and take his pro rata share of the debtor's property, abandoning the claim to his specific goods."

2096. Mālik said, regarding the insolvency of someone who has purchased on credit a handmaiden or a female beast of burden that gave birth while in his possession before he became insolvent, "The handmaiden or the beast of burden, as applicable, and her offspring revert to the seller, unless the other creditors want her, in which case they must pay the seller what he is owed in full, and then they may keep her and her child."

Chapter 43. What Is Permissible with Respect to Loans (*Salaf*)

2097. According to Mālik, Zayd b. Aslam reported from ʿAṭāʾ b. Yasār that Abū Rāfiʿ, the freedman (*mawlā*) of the Messenger of God (pbuh), said, "The Messenger of God (pbuh) once borrowed a young male camel. He later received camels that were submitted as part of the alms-tax (*ṣadaqa*).

The Messenger of God (pbuh) then directed me to return a camel to the lender, but I said to him, 'I could find only fine seven-year-old camels in the herd.' The Messenger of God (pbuh) said, 'Give him one of them. The best of people are those who repay their debts in the best way.'"

2098. According to Mālik, Ḥumayd b. Qays al-Makkī reported that Mujāhid said, "'Abd Allāh b. 'Umar borrowed a number of dirhams from someone, and when he later repaid his debt, he did so with higher-quality coins. The man said, 'Abū 'Abd al-Raḥmān! These coins are superior to the ones I lent you!'[843] 'Abd Allāh said, 'I know, but I am happy to do this.'"

2099. Mālik said, "It is not objectionable if a person who has borrowed gold, silver, food, or animals repays his lender with something better than that which he borrowed from him, provided that he was not required to do so by a prior stipulation, promise, or custom as part of the loan. But if the terms of repayment were imposed through a stipulation, a promise, or a custom as part of the loan, it is forbidden, and there is no good in it. That is because the Messenger of God (pbuh) gave a good seven-year-old camel in repayment to the man who lent him a young camel, and because 'Abd Allāh b. 'Umar borrowed some dirhams and repaid the loan with higher-quality coins. When the borrower does so voluntarily and freely, not pursuant to a prior stipulation, promise, or custom as part of the loan, the excess payment is licit and unobjectionable."

Chapter 44. What Is Impermissible with Respect to Loans (*Salaf*)

2100. According to Mālik, it reached him that 'Umar b. al-Khaṭṭāb disapproved of someone lending food to another person on the condition that he repay it in a different town, saying, "What about the transport?" He meant the cost of transporting the food to the other town.

2101. According to Mālik, it reached him that a man went to 'Abd Allāh b. 'Umar and said, "Abū 'Abd al-Raḥmān! I made a loan to someone on the condition that he repay me with something better than what I lent him." 'Abd Allāh said, "That is an unlawful gain (*ribā*)." The man said, "What do you advise me to do then, Abū 'Abd al-Raḥmān?" 'Abd Allāh said, "There are three kinds of loans: a loan that you make for the sake of God, so look to God to reward you for that loan; a loan that you make for the sake of your friend, so look to your friend to reward you for that loan; and finally, a loan that you make in which you advance something wholesome and receive in return something foul, that foul thing being an unlawful gain." The man said, "What do you direct me to do in this case, then, Abū 'Abd al-Raḥmān?" He said, "I

843 That is, they had a higher silver content.

think that you should tear up your agreement. If he gives you back what you loaned him in kind, accept it; if he gives you less than what you loaned him and you are satisfied with it, God will reward you; and if he gives you more than what you loaned him, freely and voluntarily, that is an act of gratitude on his part. And God will certainly reward you for giving him any extra time to repay you."

2102. According to Mālik, Nāfiʿ reported that he heard ʿAbd Allāh b. ʿUmar say, "No one who makes a loan should stipulate anything other than its repayment."

2103. According to Mālik, it reached him that ʿAbd Allāh b. Masʿūd would say, "A person who makes a loan may not stipulate that it be repaid with something better than what he gave. If the lender stipulates even a handful of fodder in addition to what he loaned, that is an unlawful gain."

2104. Mālik said, "The agreed-upon rule among us (*al-amr al-mujtamaʿ ʿalayhi ʿindanā*) is that there is nothing objectionable in a person borrowing an animal with specific designated characteristics. In such a case, he is obliged to repay the loan by giving back an animal with similar features. Handmaidens are excluded from this rule since lending them out may become a means of making permitted something that is not permissible, and that is not acceptable. An example of what is prohibited in this respect is a man who borrows a handmaiden and then has intercourse with her as he wishes. Later, he returns that very same handmaiden to her owner. That is not licit, nor valid, and the people of knowledge have always prohibited it, refusing to make an exception for anyone in this matter (*lam yazal ahl al-ʿilm yanhawna ʿanhu wa-lā yurakhkhiṣūna fīhi li-aḥad*)."

Chapter 45. What Is Prohibited in Bargaining and Trading

2105. According to Mālik, Nāfiʿ reported from ʿAbd Allāh b. ʿUmar that the Messenger of God (pbuh) said, "Do not make an offer after someone else has made a firm offer."

2106. According to Mālik, Abū al-Zinād reported from al-Aʿraj, from Abū Hurayra, that the Messenger of God (pbuh) said, "Do not leave the city to meet caravans outside the city's borders in order to trade with them before they arrive at the market; do not make an offer after someone else has made a firm offer; do not advance fictitious bids (*najsh*); let no townsman sell on behalf of a bedouin; and do not bind the udders of camels and sheep (*ghanam*). Whoever purchases such an animal is permitted to choose the most favorable of the following two options, after milking it: he may keep the animal if he is satisfied with it, or he may return it along with two kilograms (one *ṣāʿ*) of dates if he dislikes it." Mālik said, "What the Messenger of God (pbuh) meant when he said 'Do not make an offer after someone else has made a firm offer,' as far as we have come to understand it, and God knows best, is that he prohibited a man from outbidding another for something offered for sale only when it is clear that the seller has come to an agreement with a prospective purchaser, and all that is left to do is weigh the gold, establish liability for defects, and similar matters, such that it is apparent that the seller has substantially come to an agreement with the prospective purchaser. Making a new offer in these circumstances is what the Prophet (pbuh) prohibited, and God knows best."

2107. Mālik said, "There is nothing objectionable in holding a public auction for the sale of goods in which numerous people are permitted to bid against one another. Were it the case that people must refrain from bidding after the first bid is made, goods would be sold at unreasonably low prices, which would harm the well-being of sellers with respect to their goods. The rule among us has always been in accordance with this (*lam yazal al-amr ʿindanā ʿalā hādhā*)."

2108. According to Mālik, Nāfiʿ reported from ʿAbd Allāh b. ʿUmar that the Messenger of God (pbuh) prohibited fictitious bids. Mālik said, "*Najsh* is when someone offers another more for his goods than they are really worth, without an actual intent to purchase them, with a view to having other bidders take their cue from his fictitious bid and raise their offers in response."

Chapter 46. Miscellaneous Matters Related to Sales

2109. According to Mālik, ʿAbd Allāh b. Dīnār reported from ʿAbd Allāh b. ʿUmar that a man mentioned to the Messenger of God (pbuh) that he regularly made poor deals in the market. The Messenger of God (pbuh) said, "When you bargain, say 'No trickery!'" Mālik said, "Whenever this man bargained after that, he would say, 'No trickery!'"

2110. According to Mālik, Yaḥyā b. Saʿīd reported that he heard Saʿīd b. al-Musayyab say, "If you go to a place whose people give full measure, stay there as long as you can, and if you go to a place whose people do not, stay there no longer than is necessary."

2111. According to Mālik, Yaḥyā b. Saʿīd reported that he heard Muḥammad b. al-Munkadir say, "God loves a man who is liberal when he sells, liberal when he buys, liberal when he pays his debts, and liberal when he collects what others owe him."

2112. Yaḥyā said, "Mālik said, regarding a man who purchases camels or sheep (*ghanam*), cloth, slaves, or other goods using estimation, 'Sales based on estimates are not permitted for goods that are sold by number and that are amenable to a precise enumeration.'"

2113. Yaḥyā said, "Mālik said, 'There is nothing objectionable in someone giving another person some of his own goods to sell after having appraised their fair market value, and saying to him, "If you manage to sell the goods for the price that I have determined for you, I'll give you one dinar," or some other amount that he specifies for him and about which they come to a mutual agreement, "but if you don't sell them, you get nothing," insofar as the owner of the goods specified a sale price for his goods and a wage that the other person would receive if he successfully sold them and specified that if he failed, he would get nothing. This is similar to the case in which someone says to another, "If you are able to recover my runaway slave or my stray camel, I'll give you such-and-such." This is a reward, not a wage, and had it been deemed a wage, this would not have been a valid employment contract.'"

2114. Mālik said, "As for a man being given goods and told, 'Sell them at whatever price you can, and I'll give you such-and-such,' that is, for every dinar some portion that the owner of the goods specifies, this is not a valid contract because each time he sells the goods at a lower price, he reduces what is due to him in accordance with what was specified in the agreement. This involves material indeterminacy in the consideration (*gharar*) insofar as he does not know how much he will receive for his labor."

2115. According to Mālik, he asked Ibn Shihāb about a man who leases a beast of burden and then hires it out for more than he himself is paying for it. Ibn Shihāb said, "There is nothing objectionable in that."

The Book of Sales Has Been Completed, with Praise to God for His Beautiful Assistance.

Book 35
The Book of Judicial Rulings (*Aqḍiya*)

In the Name of God, the Merciful, the Compassionate

May God Grace Muḥammad and His Family and Grant Them Perfect Tranquility.

Chapter 1. The Merits of Good Faith in Litigation

2116. According to Mālik, Hishām b. ʿUrwa reported from his father, from Zaynab bt. Abī Salama, from Umm Salama, the wife of the Prophet (pbuh), that the Messenger of God (pbuh) said, "I am only a human being. You bring your disputes to me. Sometimes one of you is more eloquent than the other in pleading his case, and as a result I rule in his favor on the basis of what he has told me. Accordingly, if I rule in favor of a party, giving him something that rightfully belongs to the other, he should refuse it in its entirety, for in that case I am only awarding him a piece of Hell."

2117. According to Mālik, Yaḥyā b. Saʿīd reported from Saʿīd b. al-Musayyab that a Muslim and a Jew brought a dispute to ʿUmar b. al-Khaṭṭāb. ʿUmar determined that the Jew was in the right and so ruled in his favor. The Jew said to him, "By God, you have judged rightly." ʿUmar poked him with his whip and said, "What makes you so sure?" The Jew said, "We believe that every judge, as long as he determines to rule justly, has an angel on his right and an angel on his left, the twain guiding him and succoring him, so that he may rule rightly. If he turns his back on justice, however, they ascend to heaven and abandon him."

Chapter 2. On Giving Truthful Testimony

2118. According to Mālik, ʿAbd Allāh b. Abī Bakr b. Ḥazm reported from his father, from ʿAbd Allāh b. ʿAmr b. ʿUthmān, from Abū ʿAmra al-Anṣārī, from Zayd b. Khālid al-Juhanī, that the Messenger of God (pbuh) said, "Do you know who makes the best witness? The one who gives his testimony before it is demanded of him and relates it before he is questioned about it."

2119. According to Mālik, Rabīʿa b. Abī ʿAbd al-Raḥmān reported that an Iraqi man went to ʿUmar b. al-Khaṭṭāb and said, "I have come to complain to you about a pitiable state of affairs, one that has no beginning or end." ʿUmar said to him, "What is it?" The man said, "Perjury has spread to every corner of our land." ʿUmar then said to him, "Is that indeed so?" The man said, "Yes, indeed." ʿUmar said, "By God, no man may be detained under the law of Islam except on the basis of the testimony of honest witnesses."

2120. According to Mālik, it reached him that ʿUmar b. al-Khaṭṭāb said, "Neither the testimony of a party to the case nor that of someone having an interest in the outcome of a case is admissible."

Chapter 3. The Judicial Ruling (*Qaḍā'*) regarding the Admissibility of Testimony (*Shahāda*) of a Witness Who Has Been Duly Punished for Slander

2121. According to Mālik, it reached him from Sulaymān b. Yasār and others that they had been asked whether the testimony of a man who has been duly punished for slander is admissible. They said, "Yes, if he has subsequently manifested sincere remorse."

2122. According to Mālik, he heard someone ask Ibn Shihāb this question, and his view was the same as that of Sulaymān b. Yasār.

2123. Yaḥyā said, "Mālik said, 'That is the rule among us (*dhālika al-amr ʿindanā*). This is because God, Blessed and Sublime is He, says, "Those who slander chaste women but produce not four witnesses in support of their allegations—scourge them with eighty lashes and never again accept their testimony, for these are the wicked transgressors; save those who repent thereafter and make right. God, indeed, is Oft-Forgiving, Compassionate."'"[844]

2124. Yaḥyā said, "Mālik said, 'The rule about which there is no dissent among us (*al-amr alladhī lā ikhtilāfa fīhi ʿindanā*) is that the testimony of someone who has been duly punished for slander but has subsequently manifested sincere remorse and thereafter acted uprightly is admissible. Of all the views that I have heard regarding that question, this is the one I prefer most."

844 *Al-Nūr*, 24:4–5.

Chapter 4. The Judicial Ruling (*Qaḍā'*) regarding Reliance on the Testimony of a Single Witness (*Shāhid*) and the Claimant's Oath (*Yamīn*)

2125. According to Mālik, Jaʿfar b. Muḥammad reported from his father that the Messenger of God (pbuh) decided cases on the basis of the testimony of a single witness and the claimant's oath.

2126. According to Mālik, Abū al-Zinād reported that ʿUmar b. ʿAbd al-ʿAzīz sent a prescript to ʿAbd al-Ḥamīd b. ʿAbd al-Raḥmān b. Zayd b. al-Khaṭṭāb, who was at the time the governor of Kufa, stating, "Pass judgment on the basis of the testimony of a single witness and the claimant's oath."

2127. According to Mālik, it reached him that Abū Salama b. ʿAbd al-Raḥmān and Sulaymān b. Yasār were both asked, "Is it valid for a judge to decide a case relying on the testimony of a single witness and the claimant's oath?" Each of them said, "Yes."

2128. Yaḥyā said, "Mālik said, 'It has long been the established ordinance (*maḍat al-sunna*) that judgment is given in accordance with the testimony of a single witness and the claimant's oath. If the claimant swears an oath corroborating his witness's testimony, he is entitled to what he claims is his due. If he declines, however, and refuses to swear such an oath, the defendant is given the opportunity to swear. If he does, the claim against him is dismissed. If the defendant refuses to swear, however, the claimant is granted his claim against the defendant.'"

2129. Mālik said, "That rule applies solely to cases involving disputes about property (*amwāl*). It is not applicable in any case involving the mandatory rules (*ḥudūd*), criminal or otherwise, nor in cases involving marriage (*nikāḥ*), divorce (*ṭalāq*), manumission (*ʿatāqa*), theft (*sariqa*), or slander (*fariyya*). Anyone who says, 'But a claim of manumission involves property,' is mistaken. It is not at all as he claims. Were this statement true, a slave could produce a single witness to testify that his master has manumitted him, and then the slave could swear an oath corroborating that testimony and be adjudicated a free person. Alternatively, a slave could produce a witness in support of his claim to some property, in which case he could swear an oath corroborating the testimony of his witness and be awarded his claim, just as a free person would have been offered the oath in similar circumstances. Neither, however, is the case."

2130. Yaḥyā said, "Mālik said, 'The long-established ordinance among us (*al-sunna ʿindanā*) is that if a slave produces a single witness who testifies to the fact of his manumission, his master is asked to swear an oath denying that he manumitted him. If he does so, the slave's claim fails and is dismissed. The long-established ordinance among us concerning divorce is the same. If a woman brings forward a single witness claiming that her husband divorced her, her husband is asked to swear an oath denying that he did. If he takes the oath, her claim of divorce is dismissed. Accordingly, the long-established ordinance regarding the testimony of a single witness in claims of divorce and manumission is the same, namely, that the husband and the master are each obliged to swear an oath denying the claim. Manumission, moreover, is an instance of a mandatory rule of law,[845] and the testimony of women is thus not admissible as proof in such cases. That is because when a slave is manumitted, his inviolability under the law becomes perfected, and he is entitled to the full protection of the law just as he becomes fully culpable for violating it:[846] if he commits fornication after having attained chastity, he must be stoned to death; if he is killed, his killer is subject to being put to death for taking his life; and upon his death, his property is recognized as an inheritable estate (*mīrāth*), which he can pass to his legal heirs (rather than his property reverting to his master). Someone might dispute this, saying, "Say a master manumits his slave, and someone appears claiming to be a creditor of the master; if the creditor produces a single male witness and two female witnesses who testify in support of his claim, their testimony is sufficient to establish the creditor's right against the master and, if the master's only property is that slave, to repeal the slave's manumission," the point of this objection being to establish that women's testimony is admissible in cases involving manumission. That example, however, cannot be understood in such a fashion; rather, it is the equivalent of a case in which a man manumits his slave, and then a creditor of the slave's master appears and asserts his claim against the master, relying on the testimony of a single witness and his own oath corroborating the witness's testimony, thereby entitling the claimant to judgment in his favor, which results, if the master has no property other than the slave, in a repeal of the slave's manumission. Alternatively, it is the equivalent of the case of a man who has a history of dealings and transactions with the slave's master and who asserts that the slave's master owes him some money. In this case the master is told, "Swear an oath, saying, 'I do

845 In this text Mālik uses the term *ḥadd* to refer to a mandatory, non-waivable rule of law. By contrast, in later legal thought *ḥadd* (pl. *ḥudūd*) is usually associated with the mandatory scriptural penalties for the crimes of theft, alcohol consumption, fornication and adultery, slander, apostasy, brigandage, and rebellion. Later jurists classified any non-waivable rule more broadly as a "claim of God" (*ḥaqq allāh*), in contrast to a claim that was potentially subject to waiver and was known as a "claim of man" (*ḥaqq al-ʿabd*).

846 Under Islamic law, slaves had diminished culpability for violations of criminal law. On the other hand, at least according to the Mālikīs, a slave did not enjoy all the protections of criminal law, such as protection against slander.

not owe him what he claims.'" If the master declines, however, and refuses to take the oath, the claimant becomes entitled to swear an oath in support of his claim, and if he does so, his claim against the slave's master is upheld. That judgment, too, might repeal the slave's manumission, if the master's debt is affirmed in this fashion and he has no property other than the slave. It is also the equivalent of the case of a man who marries a handmaiden, whereupon the handmaiden's master goes to the man and says, "You and so-and-so purchased my handmaiden from me for such-and-such an amount of dinars," but the handmaiden's husband denies that. The handmaiden's master, however, produces a single male witness and two female witnesses who testify in support of the master's claim, thereby establishing that the handmaiden was, in fact, sold to her husband and the other man, vindicating the master's claim and thereby rendering the husband's marriage to the handmaiden forbidden. That results in a mandatory divorce between the husband and the handmaiden, even though the testimony of females is generally not admissible to prove a divorce. Another example of this rule is the case of a man who slanders a free man and so is subject to the legally specified penalty for slander. Then, a man and two women come and testify that the person slandered was a chattel slave (*ʿabd mamlūk*), a fact that excuses the slanderer from criminal liability for the crime of slander after liability had already been established. This is the case even though the testimony of women is not admissible to prove criminal cases of slander. Another case that is similar to these, in which the rule applied in court differs from what has long been the established ordinance, is that of two women who testify to the birth of an infant, resulting in the infant's right to inherit and the right of the infant's heirs to inherit the infant's estate, if the infant should die. This is the rule even though no man testified alongside the two women, nor was there an oath by a claimant to corroborate their testimony. Such cases may even involve substantial amounts of property, including gold, silver, real property, orchards, slaves, and other valuables. Yet had two women testified directly as to the ownership of even a single dirham, or an amount lesser or greater than that, their testimony, by itself, would not have been sufficient to resolve the case in the absence of the testimony of an additional male witness, or the claimant's oath corroborating their testimony.'"[847]

847 In this lengthy text, Mālik is distinguishing between incidental and direct effects of testimony. The testimony of a female, to the extent that it is admissible to establish a financial liability, may have the incidental effect of invalidating the manumission of a slave in situations in which the master of the slave would be unable to pay the debt that was proven in part by the woman's testimony except by selling the slave. In this case, the effect of the woman's testimony on the slave's status, according to Mālik, is indirect and thus does not constitute evidence that she is entitled to testify directly as to whether a slave is free or enslaved. The same distinction between direct and indirect effects of testimony is emphasized in the other cases that Mālik cites in support of his position.

2131. Mālik said, "Some people say, 'It is not permitted to decide a case on the basis of the testimony of a single witness and the oath of the claimant, relying on the statement of God, Blessed and Sublime is He, and what He says is the truth, "And if there be not two male witnesses, then a single male witness and two female witnesses, such as are agreeable witnesses to you."'[848] These people say that if the claimant is not able to produce a single male witness and two female witnesses, he is not entitled to anything, and he is not given the opportunity to swear an oath corroborating the testimony of his single witness in order to prove his claim."[849]

2132. Mālik said, "One argument against anyone who holds that position—namely, that it is impermissible for a judge to rule on the basis of the testimony of a single witness and the claimant's oath—would be to say to him, 'You certainly agree that were someone to claim that another man owed him some property, and the defendant swore, "I do not owe him what he claims," the case against him would be dismissed. You also agree that if the defendant refused to swear that oath, and the claimant swore, "My claim is indeed true," his claim against the defendant would be upheld. No one disputes this rule, nor is there any dissension regarding it in any Muslim town.' But on what grounds did our opponent accept that rule? Where in God's Book did he find it? Insofar as he accepts the validity of the latter rule, he ought to accept the rule regarding the testimony of a single witness along with the claimant's oath, even though there is no mention of it in God's Book. What has long been established as an ordinance in the law certainly suffices to resolve that question. It may be the case, however, that someone may sincerely wish to comprehend the grounds of the correct opinion and to understand the argument. The preceding discussion provides a sufficient clarification of these issues, if God, Sublime is He, wills."

Chapter 5. The Judicial Ruling (*Qaḍā'*) regarding a Decedent Who Dies with Debts Owed to Him and with Debts That He Owes, and There Is Only a Single Witness (*Shāhid*) to Prove Each Claim

2133. Yaḥyā said, "I heard Mālik say, concerning a decedent to whom a debt is owed and against whom third parties have asserted a debt, with only a single witness available to prove each claim and with the heirs

848 *Al-Baqara*, 2:282.

849 The "people" whom Mālik is refuting here are the Ḥanafīs (the jurists of Iraq). They believed that a claimant needs to have the testimony of two male witnesses in support of his claim in order to win his case, and if he lacks two male witnesses, the only admissible substitute is the testimony of one male witness and two female witnesses. Accordingly, the Ḥanafīs rejected the Medinese practice of allowing the claimant to swear an oath corroborating the testimony of a single male witness or of two female witnesses.

refusing to swear an oath alongside the testimony of their single witness to vindicate their claims, 'If the decedent's creditors swear an oath corroborating the testimony of their single witness, they are given what they claim. If anything remains of the decedent's property, the heirs get nothing of it.[850] That is because they were given an opportunity to swear oaths supporting their claims, but they refused. The exception to this rule is if they say, "We did not know that the decedent's property would be sufficient to discharge his obligations," it being known that they refused to swear only for that reason. In that case, I believe that they should be permitted to swear the oath and take whatever remains of the decedent's estate after his debt had been repaid.'"[851]

Chapter 6. The Judicial Ruling (*Qaḍāʾ*) regarding the Validity of Claims (*Daʿwā*)

2134. According to Mālik, Jamīl b. ʿAbd al-Raḥmān al-Muʾadhdhin reported that he would be present with ʿUmar b. ʿAbd al-ʿAzīz whenever he adjudicated the people's disputes. When a claimant appeared before him, asserting a claim against another, he would first determine whether there was any history of dealings or transactions between the two. If there was, he would force the defendant to take an oath denying the claimant's claim; but if there wasn't, he would not require the defendant to swear an oath denying the claim.

2135. Mālik said, "The rule among us is in accordance with that (*ʿalā dhālika al-amr ʿindanā*). Accordingly, when a person makes a claim (*daʿwā*) against another, the claim must first be examined to determine whether there have been any dealings or transactions between the two parties. If yes, the defendant is required to take an oath denying the claimant's claim. If he swears an oath denying the claim, the case against him is dismissed. Should he refuse to swear, however, and instead demands that the claimant swear an oath in support of his claim, and the claimant does so, then the claimant prevails."

850 That is, of the debt owed to the decedent, not of what is left of the estate after the decedent's debts to third parties have been fully discharged.

851 This is because the decedent's debts must first be discharged before the heirs can take their share of the estate. Therefore, if they believe that the estate is too small to discharge the decedent's debts, they might refuse to swear oaths corroborating the debts owed to the decedent in the reasonable belief that they would not personally benefit from taking such oaths. When they discover that the estate had sufficient assets to cover the decedent's debts, they are now in a position to benefit from taking the oaths, and for that reason, Mālik is prepared to give them a second chance to swear.

Chapter 7. The Judicial Ruling (*Qaḍā'*) regarding the Testimony of Minors (*Shahādat al-Ṣibyān*)

2136. According to Mālik, Hishām b. ʿUrwa reported that ʿAbd Allāh b. al-Zubayr used to rule in accordance with the testimony of minors in cases involving batteries (*jirāḥ*) that the minors caused one another.

2137. Yaḥyā said, "I heard Mālik say, 'The rule in our view (*al-amr ʿindanā*) is that the testimony of minors is admissible in cases involving batteries that they cause one another, but it is not admissible against third parties. Their testimony is admissible only in cases involving batteries that they cause one another, not for any other claim. Moreover, even in such cases, their testimony is admissible only if it is taken before they go their separate ways, are coached, or are otherwise instructed as to what to say. If they go their separate ways before testifying, their testimony is inadmissible, unless upright witnesses were called to record the minors' testimony before they went their separate ways.'"

Chapter 8. What Has Come Down regarding Perjured Oaths Taken on the Pulpit (*Minbar*) of the Prophet (pbuh)

2138. According to Mālik, Hāshim b. Hāshim b. ʿUtba b. Abī Waqqāṣ reported from ʿAbd Allāh b. Nisṭās, from Jābir b. ʿAbd Allāh al-Anṣārī, that the Messenger of God (pbuh) said, "Whoever swears falsely on my pulpit has reserved for himself a place in Hell."

2139. According to Mālik, al-ʿAlā' b. ʿAbd al-Raḥmān reported from Maʿbad b. Kaʿb al-Salamī, from his brother, ʿAbd Allāh b. Kaʿb b. Mālik al-Anṣārī, from Abū Umāma, that the Messenger of God (pbuh) said, "If anyone deprives a Muslim of a rightful claim of his by means of a false oath, God shall deprive him of Paradise and punish him with Hell." They said, "Even if it is a trivial matter, Messenger of God?" He said, "Even if it concerns only a branch of the salvadora tree! Even if it concerns only a branch of the salvadora tree! Even if it concerns only a branch of the salvadora tree!" He said it three times.

Chapter 9. Miscellaneous Reports about Swearing Oaths (*Yamīn*) on the Pulpit (*Minbar*)

2140. According to Mālik, Dāwūd b. al-Ḥuṣayn reported that he heard Abū Ghaṭafān b. Ṭarīf al-Murrī say, "A dispute broke out between Zayd b. Thābit and Ibn Muṭīʿ regarding a house they owned in common. They brought their case to Marwān b. al-Ḥakam, who was the governor of Medina at the time. Marwān ruled that Zayd should swear an oath on the Prophet's pulpit. Zayd said, 'No, I should rather swear for Ibn Muṭīʿ in this very spot where I am now standing.' Marwān, however, said, 'No, by God; when the rights of others are at stake, the oath must be taken on the pulpit.' Zayd proceeded to swear that his claim was certainly truthful, and he continued to refuse to swear on the pulpit. Marwān was astonished at his behavior."

2141. Yaḥyā said, "Mālik said, 'No one should be compelled to swear an oath on the pulpit with respect to any claim whose value is less than a quarter of one dinar, and that is three dirhams.'"

Chapter 10. Impermissible Forfeiture Clauses in Connection with Pledges (*Rahn*)

2142. According to Mālik, Ibn Shihāb reported from Saʿīd b. al-Musayyab that the Messenger of God (pbuh) said, "Pledges may not be forfeited." Yaḥyā said, "Mālik said, 'What that means, in our opinion, and God knows best, is that a debtor may give a pledge to his creditor as security for his debt, with the pledge being worth more than the debt. The debtor then says to the creditor, "If I repay my debt to you in a timely fashion," and the debtor specifies the date of repayment, "you will return to me my pledge, but if I do not, you may take the pledge, in its entirety, for yourself." That is invalid and illicit. In fact, this is precisely what was forbidden. Even if the pledge's owner manages to pay off his debt only after its maturity date, he is still entitled to redeem his pledge. It is my opinion that such a condition is invalid.'"

Chapter 11. The Judicial Ruling (*Qaḍāʾ*) regarding Pledges (*Rahn*) of Unharvested Fruit (*Thamar*) and Livestock (*Ḥayawān*)

2143. Yaḥyā said, "I heard Mālik say, regarding someone who pledges an orchard of his to secure a debt due on a determinate date in the future, and the orchard's fruit ripens and is ready for harvest before the debt matures, 'The orchard's fruit is not subject to the pledge that applies to the orchard's trees, unless the secured creditor (*murtahin*) has expressly stipulated its inclusion in the pledge. If a secured creditor accepts a handmaiden as a pledge, however, and she is pregnant or becomes pregnant after she is given to him as a pledge, her child remains with her and becomes subject to the pledge.'"

2144. Mālik said, "The reason that the fruit of an orchard is treated differently from the child of a handmaiden is that the Messenger of God (pbuh) said, 'If an orchard of date palms is sold after the date palms have been pollinated, the seller is entitled to their fruit, unless the buyer stipulates otherwise.'"

2145. Mālik said, "The rule about which there is no dissent among us (*al-amr alladhī lā ikhtilāfa fīhi ʿindanā*) is that whoever purchases a pregnant handmaiden or livestock that is pregnant is entitled to the fetus, whether or not the purchaser so stipulates. Date palms, however, are not treated like livestock, nor are the dates they produce treated like a fetus in the womb of its mother." Yaḥyā said, "Mālik said, 'Something else that clarifies the difference in the applicable rules is the fact that people may pledge the fruit of their date palms without ever pledging the trees themselves. No one, however, would pledge a fetus in its mother's womb without also pledging the mother, whether pledging slaves or livestock.'"

Chapter 12. The Judicial Ruling (*Qaḍā'*) regarding Pledges (*Rahn*) of Livestock (*Ḥayawān*)

2146. Yaḥyā said, "I heard Mālik say, 'The rule about which there is no dissent among us (*al-amr alladhī lā ikhtilāfa fīhi ʿindanā*) regarding the question of who bears the risk of loss with respect to pledges while they are in the possession of the secured creditor (*murtahin*) is that if the pledge involves property such as land, homes, livestock, or any other property whose loss is manifest to all, the pledgor (*rāhin*) bears the loss of its value, without reducing the secured creditor's claim against the debtor in the least.[852] If, on the other hand, the true cause of the pledge's loss can be known only from the secured creditor's own statement, the secured creditor bears the loss of its fair market value.[853] He is told, "Describe the pledge." After he does so, he swears an oath affirming the truth of his statement, and an oath affirming the amount owed to him by the debtor.[854] Expert appraisers then estimate the pledge's fair market value in accordance with his statement. If the fair market value of the pledge is greater than the amount of the debt that the secured creditor claims, the pledgor receives the excess value from the secured creditor.[855] If, however, the fair market value of the pledge is less than the amount the secured creditor claims, the pledgor is given the

852 For example, if a debtor borrows 1,000 dinars from a creditor and gives the creditor his home as a pledge to secure his obligation of repayment, and the house then collapses as a result of an earthquake or another act of God, the debtor's debt is not reduced by an amount equal to the fair market value of the pledge; the debtor continues to owe the creditor the 1,000 dinars.

853 For example, if a debtor borrows 1,000 dinars from a creditor and gives the creditor jewelry as a pledge to secure his obligation of repayment, and the secured creditor then claims the jewelry was stolen, destroyed, or otherwise lost, the debtor's debt is reduced by an amount equal to the fair market value of the pledge.

854 Mālik is assuming that the parties in this case dispute both the value of the lost pledge and the amount of the debt that the debtor owes the creditor.

855 For example, if the secured creditor claims he is owed a debt of 1,000 dinars, and the fair market value of the collateral, according to the secured creditor's own testimony, is 1,200 dinars, the secured creditor owes the debtor 200 dinars.

opportunity to swear an oath affirming the secured creditor's statement, and if he does, the difference between the secured creditor's claim against the debtor and the pledge's fair market value is canceled.[856] However, if the pledgor refuses to swear the oath, the secured creditor is entitled to the difference between the amount of his claim against the debtor and the pledge's fair market value.[857] If the secured creditor says, "I have no idea what the actual value of the pledge is," then the pledgor is asked to provide a description of the pledge and to corroborate that statement with an oath. If he does so, his claim is taken as true, provided that it is not unreasonable.'" Yaḥyā said, "Mālik said, 'That is the rule that applies if the secured creditor himself took possession of the pledge and did not put it in escrow in the hands of a third party.'"

Chapter 13. The Judicial Ruling (*Qaḍā'*) on Pledges (*Rahn*) Held in Common by Two Secured Creditors

2147. Yaḥyā said, "I heard Mālik say, regarding a scenario in which a pledge is held in common by two secured creditors (*murtahin*), and then when the debt matures, one of the two seeks to sell his interest in the pledge whereas the other agrees to defer collection of his share of the debtor's obligation for one more year, 'If it is possible to divide the pledged property without diminishing the fair market value of that portion of the pledge held by the secured creditor who has agreed to defer collection of his interest in the debt, one-half of the pledged property held in common is sold for the benefit of the secured creditor seeking immediate repayment, and his claim against the debtor is satisfied out of those proceeds. However, if there is a fear that partition of the pledged property will diminish its value, the pledge is sold in its entirety, and the claim of the secured creditor who demanded the sale of the pledged property is satisfied out of the proceeds. If the secured creditor who has agreed to defer collection of his claim is agreeable, he may give his one-half share of the proceeds from the sale of the pledge to the pledgor (*rāhin*) and become an unsecured creditor. If he is unwilling to do so, however, he is given an opportunity to swear an oath, saying, "I agreed to defer collection of my claim against the debtor only on the condition

856 For example, if the secured creditor claims he is owed 1,000 dinars, and the fair market value of the collateral, according to the secured creditor's own testimony, is 800 dinars, the secured creditor's claim against the debtor is limited to the collateral's fair market value, and the additional 200 dinars that he claims is canceled. It should be noted that in this case the amount of the debt is also in dispute, not just the fair market value of the collateral.

857 For example, if the secured creditor claims he is owed 1,000 dinars, and the fair market value of the collateral, according to the secured creditor's own testimony, is 800 dinars, and the debtor is unwilling to swear an oath affirming the secured creditor's description of the collateral, the secured creditor is entitled to pursue the debtor for 200 dinars.

that my security interest in the pledge would remain as it is." If the secured creditor swears this oath, he is permitted to collect what is owed to him immediately out of the proceeds from the sale of the pledge.'"[858]

2148. Yaḥyā said, "I heard Mālik say, concerning a slave whose master pledges him as security for a debt and who has his own property, 'The slave's own property is not included in the master's pledge of the slave, unless the secured creditor expressly stipulates otherwise.'"

Chapter 14. The Judicial Ruling (*Qaḍāʾ*) on Miscellaneous Matters Related to Pledges (*Rahn*)

2149. Yaḥyā said, "I heard Mālik say, regarding a scenario in which a secured creditor (*murtahin*) takes possession of some goods as a pledge, and these goods perish while in his possession, and the debtor acknowledges the debt and agrees with the secured creditor as to its amount but they contest the fair market value of the pledge, with the pledgor (*rāhin*) saying, 'Its value was twenty dinars,' and the secured creditor saying, 'No, its value was ten dinars,' and the agreed amount of the debt being twenty dinars: 'The one who was in possession of the pledge is told, "Describe it." After doing so, he is asked to swear an oath affirming the truth of his statement, whereupon expert appraisers estimate the pledge's fair market value on the basis of that statement. If the estimated fair market value of the pledge exceeds the amount of the debt that the pledge secured, the secured creditor is told, "Refund the difference to the pledgor." However, if the estimated fair market value of the destroyed pledge is less than the amount of the debt which the pledge secured, the secured creditor is entitled to collect the deficiency from the pledgor. If the estimated fair market value of the pledge is equal to the secured creditor's claim, the pledge represents repayment of his claim.'"

2150. Yaḥyā said, "I heard Mālik say, 'The rule in our view (*al-amr ʿindanā*) regarding a debtor and a secured creditor who disagree about the amount of the debt secured by the pledge that the debtor gave the secured creditor, with the pledgor saying to the secured creditor, "I gave you this pledge as security for an obligation of ten dinars," and the secured creditor saying, "No, I took it from you as security for an obligation of twenty dinars," and the pledge consists of property that is manifest and in the secured creditor's possession, is that the secured creditor is first given the opportunity to swear an oath corroborating his claim as to the amount of the debt, provided that his claim does not exceed the pledge's fair market value. If his claim

858 In other words, although he agreed to allow the debtor an additional year to repay the debt, the secured creditor is now allowed to collect his debt immediately because he has been deprived of the benefit of his pledge.

regarding the amount of the debt neither exceeds the pledge's fair market value nor is less than it, the secured creditor is entitled to take the pledge in repayment of his claim against the debtor. He is given the first opportunity to establish the value of the debt by means of his oath because he had possession of the pledge. However, the pledgor may, in such circumstances, instead choose to pay the secured creditor the amount that he claims and affirms by oath, and to redeem his pledge. But if the fair market value of the pledge is less than the twenty dinars that the secured creditor claims is owed to him, the secured creditor is given the opportunity to swear an oath affirming his entitlement to the twenty dinars that he claims he is owed. If he does so, the pledgor is told, "Either you give him the amount he demands and has affirmed with his oath and then redeem your pledge, or you swear an oath affirming the truth of your claim regarding the amount of the debt secured by your pledge. If you do the latter, you will not be liable for the excess of the secured creditor's claim over the pledge's fair market value." If the pledgor takes the oath, his liability is limited to the pledge's fair market value, but if he does not, he is bound to pay the entire amount the secured creditor claimed and affirmed through his oath. If the pledge perishes, and the parties contest both the amount of the underlying debt owed and the value of the pledge securing it, with the secured creditor saying, "I held the pledge as security for a debt of twenty dinars and the fair market value of the pledge was ten dinars," and the debtor saying, "No, it secured a debt of only ten dinars and its fair market value was twenty dinars," then the secured creditor is told, "Describe the pledge." Once he does so, he is required to swear an oath affirming his description of the pledge, whereupon expert appraisers provide an estimate of its fair market value in light of that statement. If the estimated fair market value of the pledge is greater than the amount the secured creditor claims he is owed, he is given the opportunity to swear an oath affirming his claim. If he does so, the pledgor is given the difference between the estimated fair market value of the pledge and the creditor's claim regarding the amount of the debt. If, however, the pledge's estimated fair market value is less than the amount the secured creditor claims is owed to him, the secured creditor is given an opportunity to swear an oath affirming the amount of the debt he claims was secured by the pledge. If he does so, the debtor may offset the amount he owes the secured creditor up to the estimated fair market value of the pledge. The debtor is then given the opportunity to swear an oath denying that he owes the secured creditor any amount in excess of the pledge's fair market value. This is because in this situation the party in possession of the pledge is in the position of someone making a claim against the pledgor, so he bears the burden of proving his claim. Accordingly, if the debtor takes this oath, he is not liable for the excess amount claimed by the secured creditor. If, on the other hand, the debtor refuses to swear the oath, he is bound to pay the excess of the amount claimed by the secured creditor over the pledge's fair market value.'"

Chapter 15. The Judicial Ruling (*Qaḍāʾ*) regarding the Rental (*Kirāʾ*) of Beasts of Burden (*Dawābb*) and Breaches of the Rental Contract (*Taʿaddī*)

2151. Yaḥyā said, "I heard Mālik say, 'The rule in our view (*al-amr ʿindanā*) concerning a man who rents a beast of burden (*dābba*) to take him to a specified destination but then breaches the contract by taking it to a destination beyond that specified in the rental contract is that the animal's owner is given an option. If he wishes, he may demand the additional rent (*kirāʾ*) that would have been due for the lessee's (*mustakrī*) actual destination, plus the contractually specified rent and the return of his beast of burden. Alternatively, if the owner so wishes, he may demand the fair market value of his animal at the spot at which the lessee breached the contract, in addition to the contractually specified rent that had accrued up to the time of the breach.[859] If the contract was for a one-way rental and the lessee reached his specified destination before breaching the contract, the animal's owner is entitled to the full amount specified in the contract. If, on the other hand, the lessee rented the animal for a round trip and breached the contract only after reaching the contractually specified final destination, the owner is entitled only to half of the contract's rent. That is because one half of the rent was for the outward journey and the other half was for the return. Instead of returning with the animal after reaching his destination, however, the breaching party took it to another destination, thereby breaching the contract. In this case, only half of the rent had accrued at the time of the breach. Had the beast of burden died, for example, when it reached the contractual destination, thereby preventing the lessee from completing the round trip, the lessee would not have been liable to the animal's owner for its value, and the owner could claim only half the rent specified in the contract. Breaching parties are generally treated in accordance with this

859 By breaching the contract, the lessee has effectively usurped ownership of the animal. Accordingly, Mālik gives the animal's owner the right, if he so wishes, to force the lessee to pay him the fair market value of the animal as of the moment of the usurpation. In addition, the owner is entitled to collect the rent that had accrued under the contract up to the moment of the breach. For example, if the lessee covered 75% of the distance to the contractually specified destination before breaching the contract by directing the animal to another destination, the animal's owner has the option to take 75% of the rent owed to him (assuming the contract was for a one-way rental), plus the fair market value of the animal as of the time of the breach. If he selects this option, however, the lessee becomes the owner of the animal.

rule. The same rule applies, therefore, when an entrepreneur takes money from an investor to invest in an investment partnership (*qirāḍ*), and the investor says to him, "Do not use the investment capital to purchase such-and-such animals and goods," expressly specifying the excluded items and forbidding the entrepreneur to invest in them because the investor has no desire to invest in a venture trading in such goods. However, despite the investor's instructions, the entrepreneur invests in the very articles he was prohibited from acquiring, desiring thereby to assume liability for the venture's capital and to make off with the entirety of the venture's profit at the expense of the investor. If an entrepreneur breaches his undertakings to his investor in such a manner, the investor is given a choice. If the investor wishes, he can affirm his share in the venture's capital despite the entrepreneur's failure to respect his conditions and take his share of the venture's profits in accordance with their agreement. Alternatively, he can hold the entrepreneur, who took possession of the investor's capital but did not respect the terms of the investment, liable for the amount of his capital contribution.[860] The same rule applies to an agent who accepts commercial goods from an owner who orders him to trade his goods for other, specified goods. The agent, however, breaches the contract, using the owner's capital to acquire goods other than those that the owner specified. In this case, the owner of the goods is given a choice. If he wishes, he can take the goods the agent purchased using his capital. Alternatively, he is also entitled, if he wishes, to hold the agent liable for the value of his capital.'"

Chapter 16. The Judicial Ruling (*Qaḍā'*) regarding Women Coerced into Sexual Intercourse (*Mustakraha*)

2152. According to Mālik, Ibn Shihāb reported that ʿAbd al-Malik b. Marwān ruled in a case involving a woman who had been coerced into sexual intercourse that she is entitled to receive her dower (*ṣadāq*) from the perpetrator.

2153. Yaḥyā said, "I heard Mālik say, 'The rule in our view (*al-amr ʿindanā*) concerning a man who rapes a woman, whether a virgin (*bikr*) or a matron (*thayyib*), is that if she is a free woman, the perpetrator is liable for her fair

860 The rule that Mālik articulates is intended to deter the entrepreneur from intentionally breaching the terms of the investment contract in order to create the impression that the entrepreneur is holding the capital as a loan from the investor. In that case, whatever profit the entrepreneur earns from investing the capital would belong to him in its entirety. To deter such behavior, Mālik allows investors to choose whatever remedy leaves them better off: either to share in the venture's realized profit, despite the fact that the entrepreneur violated the terms of their agreement, or to treat the investment as a loan, in which case the entrepreneur is required to return the investor's capital in full, even if the venture fails to earn any profit.

dower, and if she is a handmaiden, he is liable for the diminution in her fair market value. The rapist (*mughtaṣib*) is also subject to criminal punishment, whereas the victim (*mughtaṣaba*) is under no criminal liability whatsoever for the act. If the rapist is a slave, monetary liability falls on his master, unless he wishes to surrender the slave to the victim.'"

Chapter 17. The Judicial Ruling (*Qaḍā'*) regarding the Destruction of Livestock (*Ḥayawān*) and Food Belonging to Another

2154. Yaḥyā said, "I heard Mālik say, 'The rule in our view (*al-amr ʿindanā*) concerning someone who destroys livestock without the permission of its owner is that he is liable to the owner for its fair market value as of the day on which he destroyed it. He is not obliged to replace it with similar livestock, nor is he entitled to give the owner similar livestock in compensation for what he destroyed. Rather, he is obligated to pay its fair market value as of the date he destroyed it. Fair market value is a better measure of the loss incurred from the perspective of both the owner and the perpetrator, whether the destroyed property is livestock or goods.'"

2155. Yaḥyā said, "I heard Mālik say, 'Anyone who takes food without its owner's permission is obliged to return a similar amount of the same food of the same quality. Food, in this case, is like gold and silver: someone who takes another person's gold without the owner's permission must replace it with gold, and someone who takes another person's silver without the owner's permission must replace it with silver. Livestock is not subject to the same rule as gold: the long-established ordinance (*al-sunna*) and the practice in force (*al-ʿamal al-maʿmūl bih*) have made a distinction between them.'"

2156. Yaḥyā said, "I heard Mālik say, 'If some property is deposited for safekeeping with another party, and the latter sells it, intending to benefit himself, and successfully realizes a profit from the sale, he is entitled to retain the profit entirely for himself because he assumed the risk of loss for the property that had been left with him for safekeeping until such time as he returned it to its owner.'"

Chapter 18. The Judicial Ruling (*Qaḍā'*) regarding Someone Who Apostatizes from Islam

2157. According to Mālik, Zayd b. Aslam reported that the Messenger of God (pbuh) said, "Strike the neck of anyone who changes his religion."

2158. Yaḥyā said, "I heard Mālik say, 'We think—and God knows best—that the meaning of the words of the Messenger of God (pbuh), "Strike the neck of anyone who changes his religion," is that it refers to people who abandon Islam for another religion, such as Manicheans[861] and their like. Such individuals, when they are discovered, are to be killed at once, without being given an opportunity to repent of their apostasy and to reaffirm their adherence to Islam. That is because it is impossible to know whether their repentance is genuine, for previously they had concealed their disbelief while outwardly professing Islam. I do not believe that such people should be given an opportunity to repent, nor can their statements be taken at face value. As for someone who openly abandons Islam for another religion, he is given an opportunity to repent. If he repents and returns to Islam, he is to be left alone, but if he does not, he is to be put to death. That rule also applies in the case of a group of people who abandon Islam: I believe that they ought to be called back to Islam and asked to repent, and if they repent and return to Islam, their outward professions are to be taken at face value. If they do not repent, however, they are to be put to death. We think—and God knows best— the Messenger of God (pbuh) did not have in mind those who leave Judaism for Christianity or Christianity for Judaism, nor those who change their faith to any of the other faiths known to humanity, except for Islam. The people intended by these words are only those who openly abandon Islam for another religion, and God knows best.'"

2159. According to Mālik, ʿAbd al-Raḥmān b. Muḥammad b. ʿAbd Allāh b. ʿAbd al-Qārī reported that his father said, "A man came to ʿUmar b. al-Khaṭṭāb at the behest of Abū Mūsā al-Ashʿarī, who was ʿUmar's governor in Iraq at the time. ʿUmar asked him about the people's affairs, and the man gave him a report. ʿUmar then asked him, 'Do you have any strange news?' He said, 'Yes, a man became an unbeliever after he had embraced Islam.' ʿUmar said, 'What did you do with him?' He said, 'We arrested him and then executed him.' ʿUmar said, 'Why didn't you detain him for three days, feeding him every day a loaf of bread, and call on him to repent, in the hope that he would repent and return to God's way?' ʿUmar then exclaimed, 'O God! I was not present; I did not give any orders; and I certainly was not pleased by the news when it reached me!'"

Chapter 19. The Judicial Ruling (*Qaḍāʾ*) regarding Someone Who Discovers a Stranger Alone with His Wife

2160. According to Mālik, Suhayl b. Abī Ṣāliḥ al-Sammān reported from Abū Hurayra that Saʿd b. ʿUbāda said to the Messenger of God (pbuh), "What do

861 The Arabic term here is *zanādiqa* (sing., *zindīq*). This term would later be used generically to mean "heretics," but in this text, Mālik has in mind Manicheans in particular, whom he accuses of feigning outward adherence to Islam while maintaining adherence to their pre-Islamic faith.

you propose I do if I find a stranger alone with my wife? Shall I leave him be until I can find four witnesses and bring them to the scene?" The Messenger of God (pbuh) said, "Yes."

2161. According to Mālik, Yaḥyā b. Saʿīd reported from Saʿīd b. al-Musayyab that a man in the Levant found a stranger alone with his wife, so he killed him, or her, or both of them.[862] Muʿāwiya b. Abī Sufyān did not know how to resolve the case, so he wrote to Abū Mūsā al-Ashʿarī, asking him to seek the view of ʿAlī b. Abī Ṭālib. Abū Mūsā therefore asked ʿAlī's opinion about the case. ʿAlī said to him, "This is not a case that has occurred in my jurisdiction. I insist that you give me the details." Abū Mūsā said, "Muʿāwiya b. Abī Sufyān wrote to me, asking me to get your view." ʿAlī then said, "I am Abū Ḥasan: if the man failed to produce four witnesses, he must be handed over with a rope around his neck to the families of his victims."[863]

Chapter 20. The Judicial Ruling (*Qaḍāʾ*) regarding an Abandoned Child (*Manbūdh*)

2162. According to Mālik, Ibn Shihāb reported from Sunayn Abū Jamīla, a man from the tribe of Banū Sulaym, that during the rule of ʿUmar b. al-Khaṭṭāb he found an abandoned child. He said, "I took him to ʿUmar b. al-Khaṭṭāb, and he said, 'What prompted you to assume custody of this soul?' I said, 'I found it in danger, so I took it.' ʿUmar's advisor said, 'Commander of the Faithful, he is a good man!' ʿUmar said, 'Is that so?' His advisor said, 'Yes, indeed.' ʿUmar therefore said to me, 'Go, and you may keep the child! The child, however, is free.[864] You have the right to oversee his affairs (*walāʾ*),[865] and we shall provide for his needs out of the treasury.'"

2163. Yaḥyā said, "I heard Mālik say, 'The rule in our view (*al-amr ʿindanā*) concerning an abandoned child is that he is a free person, and the right to his patronage belongs to the Muslim community. They are his legal heirs, and they are monetarily responsible for any batteries he may commit.'"

---

862 According to the notes to the RME, a marginal note in the manuscript indicated that the husband killed both his wife and the stranger.

863 In other words, the family or families of the victim or victims have the right to put the husband to death in retaliation (*qiṣāṣ*) for his killing of the stranger, his wife, or the both of them, as the case may be.

864 ʿUmar is explaining to Sunayn that even though the child is of unknown lineage, he is to be treated as a free person, not a slave.

865 Mālik here uses the word *walāʾ*, which ordinarily refers to the right of patronage to a freed slave, to mean the right to act as the abandoned child's guardian. Bājī, *al-Muntaqā*, 6:4.

Chapter 21. The Judicial Ruling (*Qaḍāʾ*) regarding Affiliating a Child to His Father

2164. According to Mālik, Ibn Shihāb reported from ʿUrwa b. al-Zubayr that ʿĀʾisha, the wife of the Prophet (pbuh), said, "ʿUtba b. Abī Waqqāṣ, in his last will and testament, declared to his brother, Saʿd b. Abī Waqqāṣ, the following: 'I am the true father of the son of Zamʿa's handmaiden, so find the boy, your nephew, and raise him.' In the year the Muslims returned in victory to Mecca, Saʿd found the child and took him, saying, 'He is my brother's son. He entrusted his care to me.' ʿAbd b. Zamʿa objected to Saʿd's actions and said, 'No; he is my brother, the son of my father's handmaiden, and born on my father's bed.' They took their dispute to the Messenger of God (pbuh). Saʿd said, 'Messenger of God, he is my nephew, my brother's son, and my brother entrusted his care to me at his death.' ʿAbd b. Zamʿa said, 'No, certainly he is my brother, the son of my father's handmaiden, and born on his bed.' The Messenger of God (pbuh) said, 'He is your brother, ʿAbd b. Zamʿa.' The Messenger of God (pbuh) then said, 'The child belongs to the marriage bed, and the fornicator gets nothing.' He then said to Sawda bt. Zamʿa, 'Conceal yourself from him when he is in your presence.' This was on account of the resemblance that the Prophet (pbuh) observed between the child and ʿUtba b. Abī Waqqāṣ. The child did not see her again for the rest of his life."

2165. According to Mālik, Yazīd b. ʿAbd Allāh b. al-Hādī reported from Muḥammad b. Ibrāhīm b. al-Ḥārith al-Taymī, from Sulaymān b. Yasār, from ʿAbd Allāh b. Abī Umayya, that a woman was widowed and observed her waiting period (*ʿidda*) of four months and ten days. She then remarried when it became lawful for her to do so. She had been with her new husband for only four and a half months when she delivered a fully formed child. Her husband went to ʿUmar b. al-Khaṭṭāb and told him what had happened. ʿUmar summoned some venerable old women who had been alive during the Days of Ignorance prior to Islam (*jāhiliyya*) and asked them their opinion of what had happened. One of the women said, "I'll tell you what happened to this woman. Her husband died around the same time she became pregnant, and as a result she began to bleed, and the child in her womb weakened and ceased to grow. Then, when she remarried, her new husband had intercourse with her, and his semen reached the fetus. As a result, the fetus began to move about in her womb again, and grew." ʿUmar credited her statement and consequently dissolved the couple's marriage. He said, "Indeed, I have heard nothing but good about each of you." The child, however, was affiliated to the deceased husband.

2166. According to Mālik, Yaḥyā b. Saʿīd reported from Sulaymān b. Yasār that after the advent of Islam, ʿUmar b. al-Khaṭṭāb would affiliate children born during the Days of Ignorance prior to Islam to whoever claimed them. One day, two men appeared before ʿUmar, each of them claiming to be the father of a woman's child. ʿUmar summoned a physiognomist (*qāʾif*) to examine the child's features and to determine which of them was the likely father. The physiognomist looked at both of them and said, "They are both his father." ʿUmar b. al-Khaṭṭāb, angered by his statement, struck him with his whip and then summoned the woman and said to her, "Tell me your story." She said, "This one (pointing to one of the men) used to come to me while I tended my people's camels. He continued to visit me until both of us believed that I was pregnant. Then he stopped visiting me, and I bled. Then this one (meaning the other man) began to visit me. As a result I do not know which of the two is the father." The physiognomist then said, "God is great (*Allāhu akbar*)!" ʿUmar said to the child, "Choose whichever of the two you wish to be your father."

2167. According to Mālik, it reached him that either ʿUmar b. al-Khaṭṭāb or ʿUthmān b. ʿAffān once ruled on a case involving a woman who concealed her true status when she married her husband, falsely representing that she was a free woman. She then gave birth to numerous children by him. ʿUmar (or ʿUthmān) ruled that the husband must redeem his children from slavery by giving their master a like number of slaves. Yaḥyā said, "I heard Mālik say, 'Their fair market value is the most equitable remedy in this case, God willing.'"

Chapter 22. The Judicial Ruling (*Qaḍāʾ*) regarding the Inheritance of Affiliated Children (*Mustalḥaq*)

2168. Yaḥyā said, "I heard Mālik say, 'The agreed-upon rule among us (*al-amr al-mujtamaʿ ʿalayhi ʿindanā*) concerning a man who dies leaving sons, one of whom says, "My father told me that so-and-so is his son," is that the testimony of a single male is insufficient to establish paternity.[866] An acknowledgment of paternity by one of the decedent's sons who reports his father's statement binds no one other than that son and is effective only with respect to that son's share of his father's estate. The one in whose favor the testimony was made, therefore, is given his share from only that portion of property that is in the possession of the son who acknowledged him as his father's son. The following example illustrates this rule. If a man dies leaving two sons and 600 dinars, each of them is entitled to take 300

866 The rule, according to Mālik, is that paternity may only be established through the testimony of two male witnesses. *A fortiori*, the testimony of a single female would be insufficient to establish paternity. That is why in this hypothetical case Mālik assumes that all of the decedent's children are male.

dinars. If, however, one of the two sons testifies that his deceased father acknowledged that so-and-so is also his son, the son who testified owes the son who is thus affiliated to the deceased father one hundred dinars. That represents one-half of the inheritance that the newly affiliated child would deserve if his affiliation to the deceased father had been indisputably proven. If the other son also subsequently acknowledges the affiliated child as his father's son, the affiliated child takes the remaining one hundred dinars from the other brother, thereby receiving his inheritance right in full and indisputably establishing his affiliation to the deceased father. His legal position is the same as that of a woman who acknowledges that her son or husband died owing a debt, while the rest of the heirs deny it. In that case she is obliged to pay the creditor in whose favor she acknowledged the existence of an unpaid debt what would be her proportionate share of that debt had it been conclusively proven and therefore binding on all the heirs. If she was the widow of the decedent and inherited one-eighth of the estate, she would pay the decedent's creditor one-eighth of his debt; if she was the decedent's daughter and inherited one-half of the estate, she would pay the decedent's creditor one-half of his debt. It is in accordance with this principle that the amount that any female heir who acknowledges a debt owed by her decedent must pay to the decedent's creditor is determined. By contrast, were a male heir to testify in the same way as such a female heir, stating that the decedent died owing a debt to so-and-so, the creditor would be given an opportunity to swear an oath corroborating the testimony of the male heir. If the creditor does so, he is awarded the entirety of his claim against the estate. This case is not similar to the previous one involving a female heir, because the testimony of a single male is effective in establishing the debt's existence, and it permits the creditor to recover the entire amount he claims if he swears an oath corroborating the testimony of his single male witness. However, if the creditor in this case declines to swear such an oath, he receives repayment only from the inheritance of the heir who acknowledged the creditor's claim in proportion to that heir's share of the decedent's debt. That is because that heir acknowledged the creditor's debt, while the other heirs denied it. The heir's acknowledgment is binding on him."

Chapter 23. The Judicial Ruling (*Qaḍā'*) regarding Handmaidens Who Bear Their Masters' Children (*Umm Walad*)

2169. According to Mālik, Ibn Shihāb reported from Sālim b. ʿAbd Allāh, from his father, that ʿUmar b. al-Khaṭṭāb said, "Men are having sexual relations with their handmaidens and then abandoning them and denying paternity of their children. Any master who admits to having had sexual relations with his handmaiden will be deemed the father of her child. Whether he claims to have practiced withdrawal (*ʿazl*) or not will not matter."[867]

2170. According to Mālik, Nāfiʿ reported that Ṣafiyya bt. Abī ʿUbayd informed him that ʿUmar b. al-Khaṭṭāb said, "Men are having sexual relations with their handmaidens, and then leaving them to come and go as they wish. Any master who admits to having had sexual relations with his handmaiden will be deemed the father of her child. Send them out of your homes or keep them inside; it will not matter."[868]

2171. Yaḥyā said, "I heard Mālik say, 'The rule in our view (*al-amr ʿindanā*) regarding a handmaiden who bears a child for her master is that if she commits a battery (*jināya*), her master is liable only up to her fair market value. Even if the injury she caused exceeds her fair market value, he is not liable for more than that.'"

Chapter 24. The Judicial Ruling (*Qaḍāʾ*) regarding the Reclamation of Unused Land (*Mawāt*)

2172. According to Mālik, Hishām b. ʿUrwa reported from his father that the Messenger of God (pbuh) said, "Anyone who puts to productive use unused land shall become its owner, but no right will grow out of an unjust root (*ʿirq ẓālim*)." Yaḥyā said, "Mālik said, '"An unjust root" refers to anything that was dug, taken, or planted without right.'"[869]

2173. According to Mālik, Ibn Shihāb reported from Sālim b. ʿAbd Allāh, from his father, that ʿUmar b. al-Khaṭṭāb said, "Anyone who puts to productive use unused land shall become its owner." Yaḥyā said, "Mālik said, 'The rule among us is in accordance with that (*ʿalā dhālika al-amr ʿindanā*).'"

Chapter 25. The Judicial Ruling (*Qaḍāʾ*) regarding Access to Water

2174. According to Mālik, ʿAbd Allāh b. Abī Bakr b. Muḥammad b. ʿAmr b. Ḥazm reported that it reached him that the Messenger of God (pbuh) said,

---

867 In other words, the master will not be able to deny paternity by claiming that he had engaged in birth control. The only defense Mālikī jurists permit to a master who admits to having had sexual relations with his handmaiden but who denies paternity of her child is the claim that he ceased having sexual relations with her, that she subsequently menstruated (*istibrāʾ*), and that he did not resume sexual relations with her afterward. Bājī, *al-Muntaqā*, 6:20.

868 In this report, ʿUmar affirms the absolute liability of masters for the children of their handmaidens if they admit to having had sexual relations with them. Accordingly, a master will not be permitted to disclaim paternity on the grounds that another man had sexual relations with his handmaiden while she was outside the home.

869 In other words, digging a well on someone else's land, seizing and cultivating land belonging to someone else, or planting fruit trees or vines on someone else's land will not result in legitimate rights, in contrast to such acts taken on land that is free of any prior claims.

regarding the flood channels of Mahzūr and Mudhaynīb,[870] "The upstream user may retain floodwater until it reaches the ankles. Thereafter, he must release the remainder and let it flow to the downstream user."

2175. According to Mālik, Abū al-Zinād reported from al-Aʿraj, from Abū Hurayra, that the Messenger of God (pbuh) said, "Excess water from a well in the countryside may not be withheld to deter others from pasturing their herds in the well's vicinity."[871]

2176. According to Mālik, Abū al-Rijāl Muḥammad b. ʿAbd al-Raḥmān reported that his mother, ʿAmra bt. ʿAbd al-Raḥmān, told him that the Messenger of God (pbuh) said, "No one should be excluded from even the puddles surrounding a well."[872]

Chapter 26. The Judicial Ruling (*Qaḍāʾ*) regarding Easements (*Mirfaq*)

2177. According to Mālik, ʿAmr b. Yaḥyā al-Māzinī reported from his father that the Messenger of God (pbuh) said, "No one is to cause harm, nor repay one injury with another."

2178. According to Mālik, Ibn Shihāb reported from al-Aʿraj, from Abū Hurayra, that the Messenger of God (pbuh) said, "One should not forbid his neighbor from placing a wooden peg in his wall."[873] Abū Hurayra then said, "Why is it that you people nonetheless shun this act of neighborliness? By God, I shall most certainly continue to admonish you about this until you observe it."

2179. According to Mālik, ʿAmr b. Yaḥyā al-Māzinī reported from his father that al-Ḍaḥḥāk b. Khalīfa dug an irrigation canal that began in al-ʿUrayḍ.[874] He

870 Two flood valleys in Medina.

871 Mālikīs interpreted this report as referring to a well that is dug in the countryside on property that is not privately owned. In such a case, the person who dug the well has the right of first use to the well's water for his own animals, but he must not seek to retain exclusive access to the pasture available in the vicinity of his well by forbidding the herds of others to use the well's excess water. Bājī, *al-Muntaqā*, 6:34–35.

872 Mālikīs interepreted this statement as applying to two situations. The first involves a well that is owned in common, with the co-owners taking turns to use the well water for their respective irrigation needs: a co-owner is not entitled to prevent any other co-owner's use of the well water in quantities that cause no harm to the other co-owner(s), regardless of the details of their co-use arrangement. The second involves a well that is wholly owned by a single individual. In this case, his neighbor has no right to any of the well's water except if his own well has collapsed. In this case, he may obtain a judicial order granting him access to his neighbor's well while he repairs his own well. Bājī, *al-Muntaqā*, 6:38–39.

873 Both Mālikīs and Ḥanafīs interpreted this hadith as a commending the wall's owner for permitting his neighbor to use it out of good will, but not as imposing a legally enforceable duty upon him to do so. Bājī, *al-Muntaqā*, 6:43.

874 A flood channel close to Medina.

wanted to extend it through property belonging to Muḥammad b. Maslama (whose property lay between his own and al-ʿUrayḍ), but Muḥammad refused to give him permission. Al-Ḍaḥḥāk said to him, "Why do you forbid me to do so, even though it would be advantageous for you? You could draw water from it whenever you wish, and it causes you no harm." Muḥammad continued to refuse, however, so al-Ḍaḥḥāk raised the issue with ʿUmar b. al-Khaṭṭāb. ʿUmar summoned Muḥammad and ordered him not to interfere with al-Ḍaḥḥāk's plan, but Muḥammad still refused to cooperate. Exasperated, ʿUmar said to him, "Why do you wish to prevent your brother from doing something that will benefit you both? You can draw water from it when you wish, and it causes you no harm." Muḥammad, however, continued to refuse to give his permission. ʿUmar, his patience now having run out, said, "By God, he can certainly pass the canal through Muḥammad's property, in spite of him!" ʿUmar therefore gave al-Ḍaḥḥāk permission to extend the canal over Muḥammad's property, so al-Ḍaḥḥāk did.

2180. According to Mālik, ʿAmr b. Yaḥyā al-Māzinī reported that his father said, "ʿAbd al-Raḥmān b. ʿAwf owned a stream that passed through my grandfather's orchard. ʿAbd al-Raḥmān wished to divert it to a corner of the orchard that was closer to his property, but the owner of the garden refused to give him permission. ʿAbd al-Raḥmān raised the issue with ʿUmar b. al-Khaṭṭāb, who ruled in favor of ʿAbd al-Raḥmān and gave him permission to divert the stream."

Chapter 27. The Judicial Ruling (*Qaḍāʾ*) regarding the Partition (*Qasm*) of Properties

2181. According to Mālik, Thawr b. Zayd al-Dīlī said, "It reached me that the Messenger of God (pbuh) said, 'The ownership rights in respect of any home or land that was partitioned during the Days of Ignorance prior to Islam (*jāhiliyya*) remain as they are in accordance with that partition; however, ownership rights in respect of any home or land that was not partitioned prior to the advent of Islam shall be partitioned in accordance with the law of Islam.'"

2182. Yaḥyā said, "I heard Mālik say, regarding a decedent who left property in ʿĀliya and Sāfila,[875] 'Rain-fed land is not to be partitioned along with irrigated land, unless the decedent's heirs agree to do so. Rain-fed land is, however, partitioned along with spring-fed land, if they are of similar quality. If the decedent's properties that are to be partitioned are in the same district and reasonably close to one another, each piece of land is to

875 Two districts in Medina.

be appraised separately and then partitioned among the decedent's heirs. Dwellings and homes are to be dealt with in the same way.'"

Chapter 28. The Judicial Ruling (*Qaḍā'*) on Crop Damage Caused by Tended (*Ḍawārī*) and Untended (*Maḥrūsa*) Livestock

2183. According to Mālik, Ibn Shihāb reported from Ḥarām b. Sa'd b. Muḥayyiṣa that a she-camel belonging to al-Barā' b. 'Āzib once entered a man's orchard, causing great damage to it. The Messenger of God (pbuh) ruled that it is the responsibility of the orchard's owner to protect it during the day from untended livestock, but whatever damage such livestock cause at night is the responsibility of the livestock's owners.

2184. According to Mālik, Hishām b. 'Urwa reported from his father, from Yaḥyā b. 'Abd al-Raḥmān b. Ḥāṭib, that some slaves belonging to Ḥāṭib once stole a she-camel belonging to a man from the Muzayna tribe, and they slaughtered and ate it. The case was brought to 'Umar b. al-Khaṭṭāb. He initially found them guilty of theft and ordered Kathīr b. al-Ṣalt to amputate their hands as punishment. Then, however, 'Umar thought better of it and changed his mind, saying to Ḥāṭib, "I think you must have been starving them. By God, I have resolved to impose a hefty fine on you!" He then asked the man from Muzayna, the stolen camel's owner, "How much was your she-camel worth?" The man said to him, "By God, I had turned down offers of 400 dirhams for her." 'Umar said to Ḥāṭib, "Give him 800 dirhams in compensation for his she-camel." Yaḥyā said, "I heard Mālik say, 'Payment of double the destroyed animal's fair market value is not in accordance with the practice among us (*laysa 'alā dhālika al-'amal 'indanā*);[876] rather, it has long been the rule of the people among us (*maḍā amr al-nās 'indanā*) that the person who destroys a camel or another animal belonging to another person is liable to its owner for its fair market value as of the day he wrongfully seized it.'"

Chapter 29. The Judicial Ruling (*Qaḍā'*) regarding Someone Who Injures Livestock Belonging to Another

2185. Yaḥyā said, "I heard Mālik say, 'The rule in our view (*al-amr 'indanā*) regarding someone who injures livestock belonging to another is that the one who inflicted the injury is liable to the injured animal's owner for any diminution in its value.'"

---

876 "The practice among us" is the translation of the Arabic *al-'amal 'indanā* proposed by Wymann-Landgraf, *Mālik and Medina*, 417.

2186. Yaḥyā said, "I heard Mālik say, regarding a camel that charges a man who, fearing for his own life, kills or injures the animal, that if the man can produce witnesses to testify that the animal was heading toward him or charging him, he is absolved of compensating its owner for the animal's fair market value. If he has no evidence to prove his claim other than his own word, however, he is liable for the camel's fair market value."

Chapter 30. The Judicial Ruling (*Qaḍāʾ*) regarding What Is Given to Artisans

2187. Yaḥyā said, "I heard Mālik say, regarding a scenario in which a person gives a dyer some cloth to dye, and he does, and the owner later says, 'I did not order you to use that dye,' but the dyer says, 'Yes, you did': 'The dyer's statement regarding what happened is to be credited. The same rule applies to disputes between tailors and goldsmiths and their customers, provided that, in each case, the artisan swears an oath in support of his claim, and his claim is in accordance with the ordinary practices of his craft. If that is not the case, his version of events is not credited, and the customer is given the opportunity to swear an oath in support of his claim. If the customer refuses to do so, however, and instead asks the dyer or other artisan, as the case may be, to take the oath, the artisan is then asked to swear an oath in support of his claim.'"[877]

2188. Yaḥyā said, "I heard Mālik say, regarding a dyer who receives a garment but mistakenly returns it to someone other than its true owner, and that person then wears it, 'The one to whom the garment was mistakenly given is not liable for any subsequent damage to the garment; rather, the dyer is liable to the garment's true owner for any such damage, but only if the man who wore the garment did not know that it was given to him mistakenly. If, however, he wore it knowing that it was not his, he is liable for the damages.'"

Chapter 31. The Judicial Ruling (*Qaḍāʾ*) regarding the Guaranty of Debts (*Ḥamāla*) and Settling Obligations by Assignment (*Ḥiwāla*)

2189. Yaḥyā said, "I heard Mālik say, 'The rule in our view (*al-amr ʿindanā*) regarding a debtor who assigns to his creditor the right to collect what a third-party debtor owes him is that if the third-party debtor goes bankrupt or dies, leaving insufficient property to discharge the creditor's claim, the creditor has no claim against the first debtor, nor does he have a right of

877 In this case, since the customer refuses to swear an oath in support of his claim, the artisan prevails if he agrees to swear an oath in support of his claim. But if the artisan also refuses to swear such an oath, the customer prevails.

recourse against him. This is the rule about which there is no dissent among us (*al-amr alladhī lā ikhtilāfa fīhi ʿindanā*). By contrast, if another man agrees to guarantee a debtor's debt for the benefit of the creditor in reliance on a debt that a second debtor owes the guarantor, but that guarantor dies or goes bankrupt, the creditor is still entitled to collect his debt from the first debtor.'"[878]

Chapter 32. The Judicial Ruling (*Qaḍāʾ*) regarding Someone Who Purchases a Defective Garment

2190. Yaḥyā said, "I heard Mālik say, 'If someone purchases a garment that has a defect, such as a burn mark or anything else, and the seller knew of it, and testimony is introduced against him proving that he knew of the defect or he admits having had knowledge of the defect at the time of the sale, and then the purchaser further damages it by, for example, ripping it, further reducing the garment's value, and only then discovers the original defect, he is nevertheless entitled to return it to the seller and is not liable for any diminution in the garment's value resulting from his actions.'"

2191. Mālik said, "If someone purchases defective cloth, whether damaged by burn marks or marred by other blemishes, and the seller claims that he was ignorant of those defects at the time of the sale, and the purchaser has already cut the cloth into smaller pieces or dyed it, the purchaser is given a choice: if he wishes, he may receive a rebate based on the diminution in the value of the cloth as a result of the burn marks or other blemishes, and retain the cloth; or if he wishes, he may return the cloth to the seller and receive a refund of its purchase price, offset by an amount equal to the diminution in the cloth's value resulting from his cutting or dyeing of the cloth. He may exercise either option. If the purchaser has dyed the cloth and thereby made it more valuable, the purchaser has another choice. He may elect to receive a reduction in the price of the cloth in an amount equal to the diminution in the cloth's fair market value resulting from the defect, and retain the cloth. Alternatively, he may choose to become a co-owner of the cloth along with the seller. In this latter case, the defective cloth's value must be determined. If it is ten dirhams, for example, and the increase in value produced by the dyeing is five dirhams, they become co-owners of the garment, each in accordance with his share of the cloth. On this basis, the increase in the cloth's value is applied toward its purchase price."[879]

878 An assignment contract (*ḥiwāla*) entails the complete discharge of the original debtor, whereas in a guaranty contract (*ḥamāla*) the original debtor remains liable to pay the underlying obligation in all cases.

879 In other words, if the purchaser chooses the second option, the increase in the cloth's value after the sale as a result of the dyeing is deemed part of the purchase price paid by the

Chapter 33. Noneffective Gifts

2192. According to Mālik, Ibn Shihāb reported that both Ḥumayd b. ʿAbd al-Raḥmān b. ʿAwf and Muḥammad b. al-Nuʿmān b. Bashīr told him from al-Nuʿmān b. Bashīr that his father, Bashīr, took him to the Messenger of God (pbuh) and said, "I have gifted this son of mine one of my own slave-boys." The Messenger of God (pbuh) said, "Have you given each of your children a similar gift?" He said, "No." The Messenger of God (pbuh) said, "In that case, you should rescind it."

2193. According to Mālik, Ibn Shihāb reported from ʿUrwa b. al-Zubayr that ʿĀ'isha, the wife of the Prophet (pbuh), said that Abū Bakr al-Ṣiddīq had gifted her the harvest of approximately 2,440 kilograms of dates (twenty *awsuq*)[880] from date palms located on his property in al-Ghāba. When he was on his deathbed, he said, "My dear daughter, there is no one, by God, whom I would rather prefer to see wealthy after my death than you, nor is there anyone whose poverty after my death would be more unbearable for me than yours. I did indeed gift you the harvest of 2,440 kilograms of dates from my date orchard. If only you had harvested them and taken possession of them, they would be yours! Now, however, they are the property of my heirs, you, and your two brothers and your two sisters. Accordingly, divide them in accordance with God's Book." ʿĀ'isha said, "Dearest father! By God, even if the gift had been more than that, I would have relinquished my claim to the dates and shared them with my siblings, but Asmā' is my only sister! Who is the second?" Abū Bakr said, "Bint Khārija[881] is pregnant, and I dreamed that she will give birth to a girl."

2194. According to Mālik, Ibn Shihāb reported from ʿUrwa b. al-Zubayr, from ʿAbd al-Raḥmān b. ʿAbd al-Qārī, that ʿUmar b. al-Khaṭṭāb said, "Why do some of you give your sons gifts but then retain possession of them, so that if the son dies, you say, 'This is my property and in my possession; I never gave it to anyone,' but when you are on your deathbeds, you say, 'It is my son's; I gifted it to him previously'? Any gift whose possession is deferred until the donor is on his deathbed and that would otherwise belong to his heirs upon his death is void."

---

purchaser. Accordingly, in Mālik's example, the purchaser is entitled to one-third ownership of the cloth. The purchaser is also entitled to a refund of his original purchase price.

880 In other words, Abū Bakr gifted her the output of the date orchard up to the amount of 2,440 kilograms (twenty *awsuq*), but not the orchard itself. Any dates the orchard produced above that amount would belong to the owner of the orchard, presumably Abū Bakr himself.

881 According to the editors of the RME, Bint Khārija was a Medinese wife of Abū Bakr who was pregnant when Abū Bakr died. Her name is reported in the sources as either Ḥabība or Malīka. Abū Bakr reportedly married her after her Medinese husband died at the Battle of Uḥud, which took place in year 3 of the Hijra (625 CE). She reportedly gave birth to a daughter after Abū Bakr's death, and ʿĀ'isha named the girl Umm Kulthūm.

Chapter 34. Effective Gifts

2195. Yaḥyā said, "I heard Mālik say, 'The rule in our view (*al-amr ʿindanā*) regarding someone who gives another a gift without expectation of receiving a like gift in return and so summons witnesses to attest to the gift is that such a gift is effective in transferring ownership of the gifted thing to the recipient, unless the donor dies before the recipient takes possession of it. If the donor attempts to retain possession of the gift even after bringing witnesses to attest to the gift, he is allowed to do so. If the recipient, the gift's owner, claims it, he is entitled to take possession of it.'"

2196. Mālik said, "If someone gives another a gift but later denies having done so, the recipient may establish his right to the gift by producing a witness who testifies that the donor did indeed give the recipient that item of property as a gift, whether the gift consists of goods, gold, silver, or livestock. In this case, the plaintiff-recipient must swear an oath corroborating his single witness's testimony in order to prove his claim against the defendant-donor. If he refuses to take the oath, however, the donor must then swear an oath denying the recipient's claim. If the donor refuses to take that oath, he is required to deliver to the recipient whatever the latter claims the defendant gave to him as a gift. This is the rule that applies if the recipient has one witness willing to testify to the fact of the gift. If he has no such witness, however, he is not entitled to anything."

2197. Mālik said, "If someone gives another a gift without expectation of receiving a like gift in return, and the recipient dies before taking possession of the gift, the recipient's heirs step into his shoes. However, if the donor dies before the recipient has taken possession of his gift, the recipient is not entitled to anything. That is because he was given a gift but failed to take possession of it. If the donor desires to retain possession of the gift after bringing witnesses to attest to the gift at the time he made it, he is not allowed to do so. If the recipient, that is, the gift's owner, brings a claim to take possession of the gift, he is entitled to take it from the donor."

Chapter 35. The Judicial Ruling (*Qaḍāʾ*) regarding Gifts

2198. According to Mālik, Dāwūd b. al-Ḥuṣayn reported from Abū Ghaṭafān b. Ṭarīf al-Murrī that ʿUmar b. al-Khaṭṭāb said, "Whoever gives a gift to assist his near-kin or with the aim of charity may not retract it. However, if someone gives a gift with the expectation of receiving a like gift in return, he may retract it if he is not given a satisfactory gift in return."

2199. Yaḥyā said, "I heard Mālik say, 'The agreed-upon rule among us (*al-amr al-mujtamaʿ ʿalayhi ʿindanā*) regarding a gift made in expectation of receiving a like gift in return is that if the value of the first gift changes while in the recipient's possession, whether increasing or decreasing, the recipient's obligation with respect to the reciprocal gift he is obliged to give to the donor is determined by the first gift's fair market value as of the day the recipient took possession of it.'"

Chapter 36. Retraction (*Iʿtiṣār*)[882] of Gifts of Support (*Ṣadaqa*)

2200. Yaḥyā said, "I heard Mālik say, 'The rule in our view about which there is no dissent (*al-amr ʿindanā alladhī lā ikhtilāfa fīh*) is that if someone makes a gift to his son, intending thereby to provide for his support (*ṣadaqa*), and the son takes possession of it, or if the son is a ward under his father's supervision and the father summons witnesses to attest to the gift, he may not later reclaim any part of it, because there is no retraction of a gift given for support once it has been made.'"

2201. Yaḥyā said, "I heard Mālik say, 'The agreed-upon rule among us (*al-amr al-mujtamaʿ ʿalayhi ʿindanā*) regarding anyone who makes a gift to his son or otherwise gives him something that is not intended for his support is that he may retract the gift as long as the recipient son has not subsequently contracted a debt to third parties who trusted him to repay them thanks to the gift from his father. In that case his father is not entitled to retract any portion of the gift in view of the debts that his son has contracted with third parties.'"

2202. Yaḥyā said, "Mālik said, 'Or, it may happen that a father gives gifts to his son or his daughter, and a woman marries the son because of his wealth and the gifts his father has given him, and then the father wishes to retract the gifts, or a man marries the daughter whose father has given her gifts, giving her a large dower (*ṣadāq*) on account of her wealth and property and the gifts her father gave her, and then the father says, "I am taking all of it back." He is not permitted to reclaim anything that he has given his son or his daughter if the circumstances are similar to what I have described above.'"

Chapter 37. The Judicial Ruling (*Qaḍāʾ*) regarding Gifts of a Life Estate (*ʿUmrā*)[883]

2203. According to Mālik, Ibn Shihāb reported from Abū Salama b. ʿAbd al-Raḥmān, from Jābir b. ʿAbd Allāh al-Anṣārī, that the Messenger of God

882 Islamic law recognizes a limited right of a father to retract gifts made to his children. This right is known as *iʿtiṣār*.

883 A gift becomes a life estate if the donor qualifies the term of the gift with reference to either the donor's lifetime or the recipient's lifetime. Such a gift consists of a property's usufruct (*manāfiʿ*), not of the property itself; the latter remains the property of the donor or, if he dies before the term of the gift expires, his heirs.

(pbuh) said, "Whoever is given a gift of a life estate (*ʿumrā*) for himself and his descendants[884] has effectively received an absolute gift; it never reverts back to the donor because he has made a gift that is subject to the rules of inheritance."[885]

2204. According to Mālik, Yaḥyā b. Saʿīd reported from ʿAbd al-Raḥmān b. al-Qāsim that he heard Makḥūl al-Dimashqī asking al-Qāsim b. Muḥammad about gifts of a life estate and about the people's opinions on such gifts. Al-Qāsim said, "I have always seen the people observe the conditions attached to the properties they have received from others and demand observance of the conditions they impose on the properties they give to others." Yaḥyā said, "I heard Mālik say, 'The rule among us is in accordance with that (*ʿalā dhālika al-amr ʿindanā*). A property that is subject to a life estate reverts to the donor, as long as he did not say, "It is for you and your descendants."'"

2205. According to Mālik, Nāfiʿ reported that ʿAbd Allāh b. ʿUmar inherited the house of Ḥafṣa bt. ʿUmar. Ḥafṣa had given the daughter of Zayd b. al-Khaṭṭāb the right to live there as long as she lived. When Zayd's daughter finally died, ʿAbd Allāh b. ʿUmar took possession of the property, believing that he owned it outright.

Chapter 38. The Judicial Ruling (*Qaḍāʾ*) regarding Lost Property Found by a Third Party (*Luqaṭa*)

2206. According to Mālik, Rabīʿa b. Abī ʿAbd al-Raḥmān reported from Yazīd, the freedman (*mawlā*) of al-Munbaʿith, that Zayd b. Khālid al-Juhanī said, "A man came to the Messenger of God (pbuh) and asked him what he should do with some lost property that he found. The Prophet (pbuh) said, 'Note its particular details carefully and publicize it for a year. If its owner shows up and claims it, give it to him, but if not, you may do with it what you wish.' The man then said, 'What about a stray sheep (*ghanam*), Messenger of God?' The Prophet (pbuh) said, 'It is either yours, your brother's, or the wolf's.' The man then said, 'And what about a stray

884 Descendants (*ʿaqib*), for this purpose, include both males and females of a given generation, but only the descendants of the male children in the next generation. The descendants of female children, whether male or female, are not included under the term *ʿaqib*.

885 The editors of the RME report that Ashhab (d. 204/819), a prominent student of Mālik, claimed that Mālik rejected this report, stating that it is not in accordance with the practice (*ʿamal*) of the people of Medina and that he wished it had been erased from the *Muwaṭṭaʾ*. According to Ibn al-Qāsim, Mālik's most prominent student, Mālik stated that a gift of a life estate to a person and his sons reverts to its donor if the donor is alive and to the donor's heirs once he dies. All gifts of usufruct, therefore, eventually revert to the ownership of the donor or the donor's heirs, unless the gift was expressly designated an endowment (*ḥabs*) at the time of the gift.

camel?' The Prophet said, 'What business is that of yours? A camel can find water for itself and trek throughout the land by itself, drinking water when it finds it and eating bushes that it finds along the way, until such time as its owner finds it.'"

2207. According to Mālik, Ayyūb b. Mūsā reported from Muʿāwiya b. ʿAbd Allāh b. Badr al-Juhanī that his father informed him that he had alighted once at the campsite of a group of people while he was on his way to the Levant. While there, he found a purse containing eighty dinars, which he took for safekeeping. He mentioned his discovery to ʿUmar b. al-Khaṭṭāb, and ʿUmar said to him, "For one year, publicize the find at the entrance to the mosque, and mention it to everyone who comes from the Levant. When one year has elapsed, you may do with it as you wish."

2208. According to Mālik, Nāfiʿ reported that a man once found some lost property, so he went to ʿAbd Allāh b. ʿUmar and said to him, "I found some lost property. What should I do with it?" ʿAbd Allāh said, "Publicize it!" The man said, "I have already done so." ʿAbd Allāh said, "Publicize it some more!" He said, "I already have." ʿAbd Allāh finally said, "I will not give you permission to use it for yourself. No one forced you to take possession of it."

Chapter 39. The Judicial Ruling (*Qaḍā'*) regarding a Slave Who Consumes Lost Property (*Luqaṭa*)

2209. Yaḥyā said, "I heard Mālik say, 'The rule in our view (*al-amr ʿindanā*) regarding a slave who finds lost property and consumes it before the one-year term for the public notice of lost property has expired is that the property's fair market value is an obligation attaching to his body. His master has the choice of either paying to its true owner the fair market value of the property that his slave consumed or surrendering his slave to the owner of the consumed property. If, however, the slave retains the lost property until the one-year term expires and then consumes it, its fair market value is a debt for which the slave is personally liable; it is not attached to his body, nor is his master liable in any way for it.'"

Chapter 40. The Judicial Ruling (*Qaḍā'*) regarding Lost Animals (*Ḍawāll*)

2210. According to Mālik, Yaḥyā b. Saʿīd reported from Sulaymān b. Yasār that Thābit b. al-Ḍaḥḥāk al-Anṣārī informed him that he found a camel at Ḥarra, so he bound it in its place. He then mentioned this to ʿUmar b. al-Khaṭṭāb. ʿUmar ordered Thābit to provide public notice of the bound camel three times. Thābit said to him, "This matter has kept me from working on my own farm." ʿUmar said to him, "If it is too much trouble for you, release it from the spot where you found it."

2211. According to Mālik, Yaḥyā b. Saʿīd reported from Saʿīd b. al-Musayyab that ʿUmar b. al-Khaṭṭāb once said, while resting with his back against the Kabah, "Whoever takes possession of a stray animal (*ḍālla*) is himself astray (*ḍāll*)."

2212. According to Mālik, he heard Ibn Shihāb say, "During the term of ʿUmar b. al-Khaṭṭāb, stray camels were numerous and were left alone to wander and breed, as if they were privately owned. No one interfered with them until the term of ʿUthmān b. ʿAffān. He ordered that notice be given with respect to them in order to determine their true owners, and then that they be offered for sale. In such cases, if and when a camel's true owner showed up, he would be given the price it fetched."

Chapter 41. An Act of Charity (*Ṣadaqa*) Performed by the Living on Behalf of the Deceased

2213. According to Mālik, Saʿīd b. ʿAmr b. Shuraḥbīl reported from[886] Saʿīd b. Saʿd b. ʿUbāda, from his father, that his grandfather said, "Saʿd b. ʿUbāda set out with the Messenger of God (pbuh) on a military expedition. While he was away, his mother became grievously ill in Medina. Someone said to her, 'Make out your last will and testament.' She said, 'With respect to what shall I make out a will and testament? Everything belongs to Saʿd.' She then died before Saʿd returned. When Saʿd returned to Medina, he was told of his mother's fate, so he said to the Messenger of God, 'Messenger of God, will it help her if I perform an act of charity (*ṣadaqa*) on her behalf?' The Messenger of God (pbuh) said, 'Yes.' Saʿd therefore said, 'I hereby donate such-and-such orchard in charity, for her sake,' identifying the intended orchard."

2214. According to Mālik, Hishām b. ʿUrwa reported from his father, from ʿĀʾisha, the wife of the Prophet (pbuh), that a man said to the Messenger of God (pbuh), "My mother died suddenly and unexpectedly. I believe that had she had an opportunity to speak, she would have distributed some of her property as charity. May I do so on her behalf?" The Messenger of God said, "Yes."

886 Other transmissions of Yaḥyā's recension of the *Muwaṭṭa'* give the *isnād* as follows: Saʿīd b. ʿAmr b. Shuraḥbīl b. Saʿīd b. Saʿd b. ʿUbāda, from his father, from his grandfather. This would make Shuraḥbīl, the grandson of the protagonist, Mālik's source for the report. This appears to be a more accurate chain of authorities than that given in this text, which appears to make the father of the protagonist the report's source.

2215. According to Mālik, it reached him that a Medinese man of the Banū Ḥārith b. al-Khazraj[887] gave some charity to his parents. They then died, and their son inherited the very same property—which consisted of some date palms—that he had given them as charity. He asked the Messenger of God (pbuh) whether he could reclaim those date palms. The Prophet (pbuh) said to him, "You have already been rewarded for your act of charity, so you may take them as part of your inheritance."

Chapter 42. The Rule (*Amr*) Commending Making Out a Last Will and Testament (*Waṣiyya*)

2216. According to Mālik, Nāfiʿ reported from ʿAbd Allāh b. ʿUmar that the Messenger of God (pbuh) said, "It is not proper that a Muslim with any wealth to bequeath allow even two nights to pass without having written out his last will and testament (*waṣiyya*)."

2217. Yaḥyā said, "Mālik said, 'The agreed-upon rule among us (*al-amr al-mujtamaʿ ʿalayhi ʿindanā*) is that when a testator makes out his last will and testament, whether he be in good health or on his deathbed, and it provides for the manumission of some of his slaves or for anything else, he may nevertheless change its terms in any way he wishes and do whatever he wishes in respect of his property until he dies. If he wishes to cast aside that last will and testament in its entirety and replace it with a new one, he may do so. If, however, he has designated a chattel slave (*ʿabd mamlūk*) for manumission upon his death, he has no power to change the status of such a slave. This is because the Messenger of God (pbuh) said, "It is not proper that a Muslim with any wealth to bequeath allow even two nights to pass without having written out his last will and testament."'"[888]

2218. Yaḥyā said, "Mālik said, 'Were the testator not able to change his last will and testament or to change its terms with respect to the manumission of slaves, every testator would be compelled to sequester all property specified in his last will and testament, including slaves promised manumission as well as other items of his property. Furthermore, a man might make out his last will and testament while in good health or while on a journey. Accordingly, the rule in our view about which there is no dissent (*al-amr ʿindanā alladhī lā ikhtilāfa fīh*) is that a testator is free to change all the terms of his last will and testament however he wishes, but he may not

887 The Khazraj were one of the two most important tribal groups in Medina before Islam, the other being the Aws.

888 The master's act of designating a slave for manumission binds the master, and such a slave (*mudabbar*) is consequently no longer part of the master's estate such that he could change the slave's status through his last will and testament.

retract the status of a slave after he has designated him for manumission upon his, the master's, death.'"

Chapter 43. The Enforceability of the Testamentary Dispositions (*Waṣiyya*) of Minor (*Ṣaghīr*), Dull-Witted, Insane, and Spendthrift (*Safīh*) Testators

2219. According to Mālik, ʿAbd Allāh b. Abī Bakr b. Ḥazm reported from his father that ʿAmr b. Sulaym al-Zuraqī informed him that someone said to ʿUmar b. al-Khaṭṭāb, "There is here among us a youth of the Ghassān tribe who has neared puberty and who has property. His heirs, however, are in the Levant. The only near-relative of his present here is a female paternal first cousin." ʿUmar b. al-Khaṭṭāb said, "He should make a testamentary disposition (*waṣiyya*) in her favor." ʿAmr said, "The lad then bequeathed his cousin a piece of property that goes by the name of 'Jusham's Well' (*biʾr Jusham*). The property was later sold for 30,000 dirhams. His female paternal first cousin, the one to whom he made the bequest, was known as Umm ʿAmr b. Sulaym al-Zuraqī."[889]

2220. According to Mālik, Yaḥyā b. Saʿīd reported from Abū Bakr b. Ḥazm that a youth of the Ghassān was on his deathbed in Medina, and his heirs were in the Levant. This was brought to the attention of ʿUmar b. al-Khaṭṭāb, and someone said to him, "So-and-so, a youth, is on his deathbed. Is he permitted to make a testamentary disposition?" ʿUmar said, "Yes, he should do so."

2221. Yaḥyā b. Saʿīd said, "Abū Bakr said, 'The lad was between ten and twelve years old, and he bequeathed 'Jusham's Well' to his female paternal first cousin. Her people later sold it for 30,000 dirhams.'"

2222. Yaḥyā said, "I heard Mālik say, 'The agreed-upon rule among us (*al-amr al-mujtamaʿ ʿalayhi ʿindanā*) is that the testamentary dispositions of testators who are dull-witted, spendthrifts, or insane but occasionally lucid are binding, if they were in sufficient possession of their senses to comprehend the content of their testamentary dispositions. But the last will and testament of someone who was not in sufficient possession of his senses to understand what he bequeathed and whose judgment was overcome by some defect is null and void.'"

889 In other words, the beneficiary of the youth's last will and testament was the mother of the report's original source.

Chapter 44. The Judicial Ruling (*Qaḍāʾ*) regarding the Unenforceability of a Testamentary Disposition (*Waṣiyya*) That Exceeds One-Third of the Decedent's Estate

2223. According to Mālik, Ibn Shihāb reported from ʿĀmir b. Saʿd b. Abī Waqqāṣ that his father said, "The Messenger of God (pbuh) came to pay me a visit when I was gravely ill and in extreme pain in the year of the Farewell Pilgrimage (*ḥajjat al-wadāʿ*).[890] I said to him, 'Messenger of God, the severity of my painful condition is obvious to you. My property is abundant, but I have only one heir, and she is a daughter. Shall I gift two-thirds of my estate as charity (*ṣadaqa*)?' The Messenger of God (pbuh) said, 'No.' I then said, 'How about one-half?' He said, 'No.' The Messenger of God (pbuh) then said, 'No more than one-third, and even one-third is a lot. It is better to leave your heirs well off than it is to leave them poor, begging for the people's assistance. In any case, whenever you provide support to your dependents, sincerely seeking thereby to fulfill God's commandment, you will be rewarded for it. You will be rewarded even for the food and drink you place in your wife's mouth.' I said, 'Messenger of God! Shall I be left behind to my fate here in Mecca, even as my companions return with you to Medina?'[891] The Messenger of God (pbuh) then said, 'If it is your fate to be left behind in Mecca, it may very well be that you will yet perform good deeds that further raise your honor and status. It may be that it is your fate to stay behind so that some people may profit through you, while others are harmed. O God! Perfect and complete my companions' migration and do not cause them to turn back on their heels![892] But alas, Saʿd b. Khawla was indeed wretched!' The Messenger of God (pbuh) expressed great sorrow on his account because he died in Mecca."

2224. Yaḥyā said, "I heard Mālik say, about a scenario in which a man bequeaths one-third of his property to someone, and also says to another person, 'My slave shall serve so-and-so for as long as so-and-so lives, whereupon the slave is free,' but then, upon investigation, it is discovered that the fair market value of the slave amounts to one-third of the decedent's estate: 'The fair market value of the slave's service is appraised, and the two beneficiaries divide the one-third share of the estate available for testamentary dispositions, with the one to whom the one-third of the estate was bequeathed taking his proportionate share of the one-third, and the one

890 The Farewell Pilgrimage took place in year 10 of the Hijra (632 CE), the year in which the Prophet (pbuh) died.

891 A reference to the serious nature of his illness and his fear of dying in Mecca instead of Medina.

892 In other words, the Prophet (pbuh) is asking God to allow all of his companions who had migrated with him to Medina to die there instead of turning their backs on Medina and threatening their status as immigrants.

to whom the service of the slave was bequeathed taking his proportionate share of the appraised fair market value of the slave's service.[893] In addition, each one of them takes his proportionate share of the slave's labor, or of his wage, if he earns wages. When the recipient of the slave's labor dies, the slave is manumitted.'"

2225. Yaḥyā said, "I heard Mālik say, regarding a testator who bequeaths one-third of his estate, saying, 'To so-and-so this, and to so-and-so that,' naming specific items of his property for each of them, but his heirs object, saying, 'He has gone beyond the one-third allotted to him,' 'The heirs are given a choice. They may give the beneficiaries of the testamentary dispositions their gifts and take for themselves the remainder of the estate. Alternatively, they may partition the decedent's estate for the benefit of the beneficiaries of the testamentary dispositions, giving them one-third of the decedent's estate, out of which they are entitled to satisfy their claims. They will be allowed to fulfill their claims only out of this property, whatever the extent of their claims.'"

Chapter 45. The Rule (*Amr*) That Applies to the Property of Pregnant Women, Ill People, and Those Engaged in Combat

2226. Yaḥyā said, "I heard Mālik say, 'The best view I have heard regarding the last will and testament (*waṣiyya*) of a pregnant woman, as well as all other issues related to the disposition of her property during her pregnancy and the effectiveness of such actions, is that a pregnant woman is treated in the same manner as someone who is ill. When the illness is not serious and there is no fear that it will lead to the person's death, the ill person is free to dispose of his or her property as he or she wishes. If, however, the illness is of the kind that may lead to the person's death, he or she may freely dispose of only one-third of his or her property.[894] The same rule applies to the pregnant woman. The first part of her pregnancy is all hope and joy, with no sense of illness or fear. God, Blessed and Sublime is He, says in His

893 For example, if the aggregate value of the one-third of the decedent's estate available for testamentary disposition was one hundred dinars, and the appraised fair market value of the slave's labor was fifty dinars, the beneficiaries would split the one-third in a ratio of 2:1, with the beneficiary of the testamentary disposition taking sixty-seven dinars and the recipient of the slave taking thirty-three.

894 That is, a person suffering from a life-threatening illness may not give away more than one-third of his property. He could, however, still sell his property without restriction on an arm's-length basis, the difference being that in the case of an arm's-length sale of his property he is not encroaching on the value of the estate, whereas in the case of a gratuitous transaction he is diminishing the size of the estate and thereby threatening the interests of his heirs.

Book, "We then gave her the glad tidings of Isaac, and after him, of Jacob."[895] God, Blessed and Sublime is He, also says, "She bears a light burden and it passes, until later, when she grows heavy, both of them call to God, their Lord, saying, 'If You give us a healthy child, we shall certainly be among the grateful.'"[896] Accordingly, when a woman becomes heavy with child, she is permitted to dispose of no more than one-third of her property. This restriction begins at six months. God, Blessed and Sublime is He, says in His Book, "Mothers breastfeed their children for two complete years,"[897] and God, Blessed and Exalted is He, also says, "Pregnancy and weaning last no more than thirty months."[898] So when six months have passed from the date of her pregnancy, she is permitted to dispose of no more than one-third of her property.'"

2227. Yaḥyā said, "I heard Mālik say, regarding a soldier on campaign, 'If he has been sent to the front lines and is marching to battle, he is permitted to dispose of no more than one-third of his property. As long as he is in that situation, his case is the same as that of a pregnant woman and that of the gravely ill.'"

Chapter 46. A Testamentary Disposition (*Waṣiyya*) in Favor of an Heir, and Rights of Possession (*Ḥiyāza*)

2228. Yaḥyā said, "I heard Mālik say regarding the statement of God, Blessed and Sublime is He, 'If someone is to leave any property, he should make a testamentary disposition (*waṣiyya*) in favor of his parents and next of kin,'[899] 'It has been abrogated. What was revealed in God's Book regarding the division of the decedent's estate according to fixed shares (*farāʾiḍ*) abrogated it.'"

2229. Yaḥyā said, "I heard Mālik say, 'The long-established ordinance among us about which there is no dissent (*al-sunna al-thābita ʿindanā allatī lā ikhtilāfa fīhā*) is that no testamentary disposition in favor of an heir is valid unless all the decedent's heirs ratify it. If some of them consent to it and others do not, the beneficiary may take his proportionate share of the testamentary disposition from those who consent to it, whereas those who do not take the entirety of their specified share of the estate.'"

2230. Yaḥyā said, "I heard Mālik say, regarding a scenario in which a person on his deathbed wishes to make a testamentary disposition in favor of an

895 *Hūd*, 11:71.
896 *Al-Aʿrāf*, 7:189.
897 *Al-Baqara*, 2:233.
898 *Al-Aḥqāf*, 46:15.
899 *Al-Baqara*, 2:180.

heir, so he requests his heirs' permission to do so while he is ill and has authority to dispose of only one-third of his property, and they consent to his testamentary disposition in favor of one or more of his heirs in an amount in excess of one-third of his estate: 'They do not have the right to repudiate their prior consent upon the testator's death. If they were permitted to do that, every heir would do the same, and when the testator died, they would take the property mentioned in the testamentary disposition for themselves and prevent the testamentary disposition of the one-third of his estate that he was permitted to dispose of freely from taking effect. If, however, the testator requests his heirs' permission to make a testamentary disposition in favor of an heir while still in good health, and they agree, their consent to that disposition does not bind them, and his heirs can repudiate their prior consent if they so wish. That is because when a person is in good health, he is entitled to the entirety of his property and may do with it whatever he wishes. If he so wishes, he can give away the entirety of it in charity, or give it to whomever he wishes, including one or more of his heirs.[900] The only circumstance in which his request for the heirs' permission binds them, if the heirs do in fact consent to his request, is if they consent to his request at a time when his authority over his property is limited and he is not allowed to act gratuitously except with respect to his allotted one-third of the estate. At such a time they have a greater claim to the remaining two-thirds of the estate than the testator himself does. It is in that circumstance that their agreement and their granting permission to him is binding. Accordingly, if the testator asks one of his heirs to gift the testator a portion of the heir's right in the estate when the testator is on his deathbed, and the heir agrees, but the testator does not in the end dispose of it in any fashion, it returns to the heir who gave it,[901] unless the decedent said to that heir, "So-and so is weak, and so it is my earnest wish that you give him your share of the inheritance," and he does so. That binds the heir if the decedent specified the beneficiary for the heir. If an heir gives a decedent his share of the inheritance, and the decedent disposes of only some of it in a testamentary disposition, the remainder reverts to the heir who gave it to the decedent, and whatever remains with the recipient of the testamentary disposition also reverts to the heir who gave it to the decedent when the recipient dies.'"

2231. Yaḥyā said, "I heard Mālik say, regarding a scenario in which a person makes a testamentary disposition stating that he has made a lifetime gift to

900 In other words, the heirs' consent to the testator's proposed disposition of his property while he is in good health is legally superfluous insofar as the testator remains free to do whatever he wishes with his property at that point in time.

901 In other words, it does not constitute additional property in the decedent's estate to be shared among all the heirs in accordance with their fixed claims.

one of his heirs during his lifetime but that the recipient has failed to take possession of it during the testator's lifetime, and after the testator's death the other heirs refuse to ratify the gift, that in such a case the gift reverts to the estate and the heirs divide it in accordance with their shares as specified in God's Book. That is because the deceased did not intend for the gift to be taken out of his one-third share of the estate. Therefore, the beneficiaries of the testamentary disposition are not obliged to reduce their entitlements to the decedent's one-third of the estate by the amount of that gift.'"[902]

Chapter 47. What Has Come Down regarding Transgender Men (*Mu'annath*), and Who Has the Strongest Claim to the Custody of Minor Children

2232. According to Mālik, Hishām b. ʿUrwa reported from his father that a transgender man (*mukhannath*)[903] was with Umm Salama, the wife of the Prophet (pbuh). He said to ʿAbd Allāh b. Abī Umayya,[904] while the Messenger of God (pbuh) was listening, "ʿAbd Allāh, if God grants you victory at Ṭā'if tomorrow, I will show you the daughter of Ghaylān: when she walks toward you, she is a real beauty, but when she turns her back to you, she is even more of a sight to behold!" The Messenger of God (pbuh) then said, "Men such as these are not of the sort who should be present with you in private."[905]

2233. According to Mālik, Yaḥyā b. Saʿīd said, "I heard al-Qāsim b. Muḥammad say, "ʿUmar b. al-Khaṭṭāb had a Medinese wife who bore him a son called ʿĀṣim. Sometime after his birth, ʿUmar divorced her. ʿUmar then came to Qubā' and found his son ʿĀṣim playing there in the mosque's courtyard. ʿUmar took the boy by the arm and placed him on his mount, intending to take the boy back with him to Medina. The child's grandmother caught up with them and fought with ʿUmar over the child. They went to

902 For example, a man dies leaving an estate with property worth 3,000 dinars and a last will and testament in which he leaves one-third of the estate to certain distant relations who are not his legal heirs. He also mentions in his last will and testament that A, one of his heirs, has failed to take delivery of property worth one hundred dinars. That one hundred dinars is not deemed part of the 1,000 dinars reserved for the beneficiaries of testamentary disposition. Whether or not the decedent's heirs ratify the lifetime gift of a hundred dinars to the heir, the beneficiaries of the testamentary disposition receive their full 1,000 dinars.

903 In early Arabic texts such as the *Muwaṭṭa'*, a transgender man is referred to using the terms *mu'annath* and *mukhannath* interchangeably.

904 The brother of Umm Salama.

905 The Quran's imposition of a norm of modest dress on believing women included an exception for a group of men it described as "having no desire for women" (*ghayr ulī 'l-irbati min al-rijāl*). *Al-Nūr*, 24:31. The behavior of the transgender man in this report, however, disclosed that even if he himself lacked sexual desire for women, he understood sexual attractiveness. The Prophet (pbuh) thus clarified that he did not fall under the category of those men with respect to whom believing women did not need to observe the rules of modesty.

Abū Bakr al-Ṣiddīq to resolve their dispute. 'Umar said, "He is my son," and the woman said, "He is my son." Abū Bakr then said, "Do not come between her and the boy." 'Umar did not question Abū Bakr's ruling.'" Yaḥyā said, "I heard Mālik say, 'This is the rule to which I adhere regarding that issue (*al-amr alladhī ākhudhu bihi fī dhālika*).'"

Chapter 48. Defective Goods and Bearing the Risk of Loss (*Ḍamān*) Thereof

2234. Yaḥyā said, "I heard Mālik say, regarding a man who purchases goods, be they livestock, cloth, or other merchandise, on the basis of an invalid contract of sale, resulting in an order rescinding the sale and ordering the purchaser, who has taken possession of the goods, to return them to the seller, 'The seller, the owner of the goods, is entitled to no more than their fair market value as of the date the purchaser took possession of them. He is not entitled to their fair market value as of the day the contract is rescinded.[906] That is because the purchaser bore the risk of their loss (*ḍamān*) from the day he took possession of them and the risk of any subsequent diminution in their fair market value while they remained in his possession. Conversely, any appreciation in the value of the goods or their subsequent growth accrued to him as well. It may very well be that someone takes possession of goods at a time when they are selling well and in great demand, but then the contract is rescinded at a time when demand for the goods has collapsed and no one desires them. It might be the case, for example, that the purchaser takes possession of the goods from the seller and later sells them for ten dinars, or retains them in his possession even as their price appreciates and reaches that sum, but then when the contract is rescinded and he returns the goods to the seller, their fair market value is only one dinar. He is not permitted to make off with nine dinars' worth of the seller's property.[907] Alternatively, the purchaser may take possession of the goods and sell them for only one dinar, or retain them in his possession with their fair market value being only one dinar, but by the day the contract is rescinded, their fair market value may have appreciated to ten dinars. The purchaser who took possession of the goods is not required to pay an additional nine dinars from his own property to

906 According to Mālik, if the price of the goods transferred pursuant to an invalid contract of sale changes after the purchaser takes possession and before the goods are returned to the seller, the seller is entitled only to the fair market value of the goods, not the goods themselves. In this respect, Mālik deems changes in the fair market value of goods equivalent to a change in the physical characteristics of the goods, rendering restitution of the goods to the seller impossible. Bājī, *al-Muntaqā*, 6:191.

907 This would be the result if the purchaser could simply reimburse the seller the fair market value of the goods as of the date of rescission, rather than as of the date of possession.

the seller in order to retain the goods; he must pay only their fair market value as of the day he took possession of them. A case that clarifies this rule is that of a thief who steals goods: only their fair market value on the day of the theft is taken into consideration in determining the thief's punishment. Only if that amount is great enough to require amputation of the hand is that punishment applied to him.[908] If implementation of the punishment is delayed, either because he is imprisoned until a decision is made about his final punishment or because he has fled the scene and is caught only later, the delay in implementing the punishment of amputation is not an effective reason to waive a punishment that became mandatory on the day he stole the goods in question, even if the fair market value of the goods he stole substantially decreased in the interim, nor would such a delay impose the penalty of amputation if that punishment had not been obligatory on the day the thief stole the goods, even if their fair market value rose substantially in the interim.'"

Chapter 49. Miscellaneous Reports Related to Judging (*Qaḍā'*) and Its Blameworthiness

2235. According to Mālik, Yaḥyā b. Sa'īd reported that Abū al-Dardā' wrote to Salmān al-Fārisī, saying, "Hasten to Palestine, the Holy Land." Salmān wrote back to him, saying, "Land does not make anyone holy. The only thing that makes a person holy is his deeds. Word has reached me that you have been made a doctor charged with curing people. If indeed you are successful in bringing good health to them, then blessed indeed you are. If, however, you are merely pretending to practice your craft, take care lest you kill someone and enter Hell therefor." As a result, whenever Abū al-Dardā' ruled in a dispute between two litigants, and they turned to leave, he would look at them and say, "Come back, and tell me once more your stories! A quack, by God, indeed am I!"

2236. Yaḥyā said, "I heard Mālik say, 'Whoever uses another's slave, without the permission of the slave's master, in any weighty task the like of which ordinarily demands payment of a wage is liable for any injury that befalls the slave, if the slave is injured in any way. If the slave emerges safely from the task, his master has the right to demand payment for the slave's labor. That is the rule among us (*dhālika al-amr 'indanā*).'"

2237. Yaḥyā said, "I heard Mālik say, regarding a slave who is partially manumitted, 'He is entitled to the possession of his own property, but he is

908 The scriptural penalty for theft, amputation of the hand, is conditional on the stolen property's having a minimum value of one-quarter of a gold dinar.

not entitled to act with respect to it beyond using it to secure his reasonable needs for food and clothing. If he dies, his property belongs to the person who is his part-owner.'"

2238. Yaḥyā said, "I heard Mālik say, 'The rule in our view is that as soon as a minor child attains his own property, be it cash or goods, the father of the child may, if he so wishes, charge whatever he spends on the child to the child's account.'"

2239. According to Mālik, ʿUmar b. ʿAbd al-Raḥmān b. Dalāf al-Muzanī reported that a man from Juhayna would go out in advance of the pilgrims' caravan, buy up as many riding camels as he could, and then sell them at a high price to the pilgrims. He would then set out again, marching quickly, aiming to overtake the caravan again, and repeat what he had done previously. He went bankrupt, however, and his case was brought before ʿUmar b. al-Khaṭṭāb, who said, "To proceed, then: O people! Usayfiʿ, Usayfiʿ the Juhanī,[909] cared so little for his religion and his reputation for honesty that he was content that people should know him as the man who went out ahead of the pilgrims' caravan. In fact, he eagerly sought out your credit, and you eagerly extended it to him, but now he is insolvent. Therefore, let anyone who has a claim against him come to us tomorrow morning, and we shall divide what remains of his property among them. Beware of debt! It begins in anxiety and concludes in confiscation!"

Chapter 50. What Has Come Down regarding Losses of Life and Limb Caused by Slaves

2240. Yaḥyā said, "I heard Mālik say, 'The long-established ordinance among us (*al-sunna ʿindanā*) regarding batteries (*jināya*) committed by slaves is that any injury a slave causes to a person, any thing that he takes surreptitiously, any animal in a herd that he makes off with, any dates still on the branch that he cuts down or ruins, or any theft that he commits but that does not entail amputation of the hand as punishment, is chargeable solely against the slave's body, and the compensation for it may never exceed his fair market value, be it small or great. If the master wishes, therefore, he may pay the aggrieved party the value of what his slave took or ruined or the compensation due for the injury, and retain his slave. Alternatively, if he wishes, he may surrender the slave to the victim, in which case the master is absolved of any further liability. The slave's master is free to choose either of these two options.'"

909 "Usayfiʿ" is the diminutive form of "Asfaʿ," which ʿUmar used derisively as a nickname for the man who is the subject of this report.

Chapter 51. What Gifts Are Effective

2241. According to Mālik, Ibn Shihāb reported from Saʿīd b. al-Musayyab that ʿUthmān b. ʿAffān said, "If someone makes a gift to one of his minor children, but the child is too young to take possession of his gift, the gift is nevertheless effective if the donor publicizes the gift to the child and summons witnesses to attest to it, even if it is the father himself who takes possession of it and manages it."

2242. Yaḥyā said, "Mālik said, 'The rule in our view (*al-amr ʿindanā*) is that if a father makes a gift of gold or silver to a minor son and then dies with the gift still in his own possession and care, the gift shall not be deemed effective unless the father kept the gift separate and apart from his other gold and silver, or entrusted it to another person to keep for the benefit of his son. If he did that, however, the son is entitled to the gift.'"

The Book of Judgments (*Aqḍiya*) Has Been Completed, with Abundant Praise to God and through His Help. God Grace Muḥammad and His Family.

Book 36

The Book of the Right of First Refusal (*Shufʿa*)

In the Name of God, the Merciful, the Compassionate

May God Grace Muḥammad and His Family.

Chapter 1. What Property Is Subject to a Right of First Refusal (*Shufʿa*)

2243. According to Mālik, Ibn Shihāb reported from Saʿīd b. al-Musayyab and Abū Salama b. ʿAbd al-Raḥmān b. ʿAwf that the Messenger of God (pbuh) ruled that the co-owners of a property have a right of first refusal before the property's partition. However, once the property is partitioned and boundaries delineating the co-owners' individual rights have been set out, the right of first refusal lapses. Yaḥyā said, "Mālik said, 'This is the long-established ordinance about which there is no dissent among us (*ʿalā dhālika al-sunna allatī lā ikhtilāfa fīhā ʿindanā*).'"

2244. According to Mālik, it reached him that Saʿīd b. al-Musayyab was asked whether there is an ordinance regarding the right of first refusal, and he said, "Yes; the right of first refusal applies to real property, homes, and land, and only among co-owners."

2245. According to Mālik, it reached him that Sulaymān b. Yasār held a similar view.

2246. Yaḥyā said, "Mālik said, regarding a scenario in which a man who purchases an interest in a piece of property that is owned in common by a group of people, paying for that interest with an animal, a slave, a handmaiden, or similar goods, and later one of the co-owners appears, wishing to exercise his right of first refusal but discovering that the slave or handmaiden, as the case may be, has died in the interim, and no one knows what the fair market value of the slave or the handmaiden was, with the purchaser saying, 'The slave's or handmaiden's value was one hundred dinars,' and the co-owner who seeks to exercise his right of first refusal saying, 'No, his or her fair market value was fifty dinars': 'The purchaser swears an oath that the fair market value of the goods he used to purchase his interest in the land was one hundred dinars. Unless the co-owner can produce testimony that the fair market value of the slave or the handmaiden, as applicable, was less than what the purchaser claims, he may, if he wishes, exercise his right of first refusal only by paying one hundred dinars.'"

2247. Yaḥyā said, "Mālik said, 'If a co-owner makes a gift of his share of co-owned land or his share of a co-owned house, and the recipient makes a reciprocal gift to the donor, whether in cash or in goods, the co-owners may exercise their right of first refusal to acquire that share of the land or the house, if they so wish. To do so, they must pay the recipient the fair market value of his reciprocal gift in dinars or dirhams.'"

2248. Mālik said, "If someone makes a gift of his share of a house or land owned in common with others, and he neither receives nor seeks a reciprocal gift in exchange, his co-owner does not have the right to acquire the gifted interest by paying its fair market value. This is the case as long as the donor does not receive a reciprocal gift in exchange for his gift. If, however, the donor receives a reciprocal gift, his co-owner may pay the fair market value of the reciprocal gift and acquire the gifted interest in the house or land."

2249. Yaḥyā said, "Mālik said, regarding a scenario in which a man purchases on credit an interest in land owned in common, and a co-owner wishes to acquire that interest by exercising his right of first refusal, 'If the co-owner is solvent, he may exercise his right of first refusal in accordance with the original price and credit terms. If, however, there is reason to believe that he will be unable to pay the price when it becomes due, he is permitted to exercise his right of first refusal in accordance with the original terms of the sale only if he provides a solvent and reliable guarantor having the same reputation for creditworthiness as the purchaser of the interest in the land owned in common.'"

2250. Yaḥyā said, "Mālik said, 'An absent co-owner's right of first refusal does not lapse because of his absence, even if his absence is prolonged. We do not have a specific time limit after which the right of first refusal expires.'"

2251. Mālik said, regarding a scenario in which a man dies and leaves land in his estate to his children, one of whom has children of his own, but then the child who has children dies, and one of the grandchildren sells his interest in the land: "The brother of the grandchild who is selling his interest in the land has a stronger claim to exercise the right of first refusal than do his paternal uncles who were co-owners of the land with his deceased father. That is the rule among us (*dhālika al-amr 'indanā*)."

2252. Yaḥyā said, "Mālik said, 'Each co-owner enjoys a right of first refusal proportional to his interest in the property. Each may take in accordance with his share in the property. If his interest is small, his right of first refusal is small, and if it is great, his right of first refusal is in accordance with that. That is the rule that applies if more than one of the co-owners wish to exercise their right of first refusal and they are unable to come to a mutual agreement.'"

2253. Mālik said, "As for the case of a co-owner who purchases the interest of another co-owner, and a third co-owner says, 'I wish to exercise my proportional right of first refusal with respect to that sale,' and the purchaser says, 'If you wish to take the entirety of the interest in accordance with your right of first refusal, you may do so, but if not, refrain from purchasing any of it': because the purchaser is giving his co-owner the option of purchasing the entirety of the interest and is willing to abandon his own claim in favor of the other co-owner, the other co-owner is only free either to purchase the interest in its entirety or to relinquish it in its entirety. If he acquires the entirety of the interest, he will have the strongest claim to it, but if not, his right lapses in its entirety."[910]

2254. Mālik said, regarding a scenario in which a man purchases land and makes improvements on it by, for example, planting trees or digging a well, and then another man appears, rightfully claiming that he had a right of first refusal in the sale of the land and that he now wishes to exercise that right: "He may not exercise his right of first refusal unless he reimburses the purchaser for the fair market value of the improvements the latter has made on the land. If he gives the purchaser the fair market value of his improvements, he is entitled to exercise his right of first refusal, but if he does not, his right of first refusal lapses."

2255. Mālik said, "A co-owner who sells his interest in commonly owned land or a commonly owned house and then learns that one of his co-owners wishes to exercise his right of first refusal is not permitted to defeat the latter's right of first refusal by asking the purchaser to rescind the contract, even if the purchaser agrees to rescind it. In this case the latter, if he wishes to exercise his right of first refusal, has a greater claim than the co-owner to that interest in the property, provided that he pays the price at which the co-owner first offered to sell it."

---

910 In other words, in this case, the co-owner seeking to exercise his right of first refusal is not allowed to acquire only his pro rata share of the transferred interest. He must either acquire the transferred interest in its entirety or relinquish his claim in its entirety.

2256. Mālik said, "If someone purchases an interest in a commonly owned house or commonly owned land along with some livestock and other goods, all in one deal, and a co-owner seeks to exercise his right of first refusal in the house or the land, and the purchaser says to him, 'Take everything I purchased or nothing of it, for indeed I purchased them all together,' he is not entitled to force the co-owner either to assume the entirety of his deal or to decline to exercise his right of first refusal. Rather, the co-owner may exercise his right of first refusal on the land or the house on the basis of its proportional share of the total contract price. Each item sold in the deal must be appraised individually, in proportion to the price the purchaser paid for it. The co-owner is then entitled to exercise his right of first refusal on the basis of the ratio of the fair market value of the house or the land, as applicable, to the aggregate contract price. He has no claim with respect to the livestock or the goods, unless he wishes to come to an agreement with the first purchaser in respect of those items."

2257. Mālik said, "If a co-owner sells an interest in commonly owned land, and one of his co-owners relinquishes his right of first refusal to the seller while another refuses and insists on exercising his right of first refusal, the co-owner who insists on exercising his right of first refusal must purchase the entirety of the interest transferred. He is not permitted to purchase only his proportional right to that interest and leave the rest of the interest to the purchaser."

2258. Mālik said, regarding a scenario in which a group of people are co-owners of a house, and one of them decides to sell his interest in the property while all his co-owners but one are away, and he gives that one co-owner the option to exercise his right of first refusal with respect to the entirety of the transferred interest or to relinquish it in its entirety, and the co-owner says, "I will exercise my proportional right of first refusal, but I will not interfere with the rights of my co-owners until they return, at which time they may exercise their right of first refusal. If they do, the matter is resolved, but if they relinquish their right of first refusal, I will purchase the entirety of the transferred interest at that time": "He is not allowed to do that. He either exercises his right of first refusal over the entirety of the transferred interest, or he relinquishes it in its entirety. When his co-owners return, they will be allowed to exercise their right of first refusal against him or to relinquish it if they wish. However, if this offer is made to him at the time of the original transfer, and he does not accept it, I believe that his right of first refusal lapses in its entirety."

Chapter 2. Property Not Subject to the Right of First Refusal (*Shufʿa*)

2259. According to Mālik, Muḥammad b. ʿUmāra reported from Abū Bakr b. Ḥazm that ʿUthmān b. ʿAffān said, "Once commonly owned land has been partitioned and boundaries delineating the individual rights of the co-owners have been set out, any right of first refusal (*shufʿa*) attached to the land comes to an end. Moreover, there is no right of first refusal in connection with a well that is owned in common, nor in respect of an individual date palm."[911] Mālik said, "The rule among us is in accordance with that (*ʿalā hādhā al-amr ʿindanā*)."

2260. Mālik said, "Nor is there a right of first refusal with respect to a commonly owned road, whether or not partitioning it is feasible."

2261. Mālik said, "The rule in our view (*al-amr ʿindanā*) is that there is no right of first refusal in the courtyard of a home, whether or not partitioning it is feasible."

2262. Mālik said, regarding a scenario in which a man purchases an interest in commonly owned land on the condition that he have an option to rescind the sale, and the seller's co-owners want to exercise their right of first refusal in respect of the interest that their co-owner is selling before the purchaser exercises his option to rescind, "They are not entitled to do so. They may exercise their right of first refusal only after the purchaser declines to exercise his option to rescind and affirms the sale. Only when the sale has become final and the purchaser is entitled to the property may the co-owners exercise their right of first refusal."

2263. Mālik said, regarding a man who buys a parcel of land that remains in his possession for some period of time until a second man shows up and claims that he has a share in it by way of inheritance (*mīrāth*), "If the second man establishes his claim, he continues to enjoy his right of first refusal with respect to the parcel. If the parcel is productive, its output belongs to the first purchaser until the claimant's right is established, because the first purchaser bore the risk of loss in case anything that had been planted on the parcel was destroyed or washed away by a flood. If, however, an extremely long period of time has passed, or if the relevant witnesses have died, or if both the seller and the purchaser die, or even if they are both still alive but the facts surrounding the original purchase and sale of the parcel have been forgotten due to the passage of time, the right of first refusal lapses, although any claimant whose right has been proven is entitled to his

911 The assumption here with respect to the well is that the land that it sits on is not owned in common, and with respect to the date palm that it is the only date palm in a fruit orchard.

duly established interest in the parcel. If, however, his situation is different from this because the sale of the parcel was recent but he believes that the seller intentionally concealed the price and hid it so as to defeat his right of first refusal, the parcel is to be appraised to determine its fair market value, and that is deemed to have been the contract price. Then, whatever improvements the purchaser has made to the parcel since the date he acquired the land, whether raising buildings, planting trees, or completing other improvements, are taken into account and added to the parcel's price so as to place him in a position equivalent to that of someone who bought the land for a known price and then built or planted trees on it. The holder of the right of first refusal can then exercise his right after that."

2264. Mālik said, "A right of first refusal is part of a decedent's estate to the same extent that it was part of his property when he was alive. If the decedent's heirs fear that the value of the property will be reduced if it is sold piecemeal, they are entitled to have the property sold only after it has been partitioned, so that no one has a right of first refusal that can be used against sales of the property."

2265. Mālik said, "We do not recognize a right of first refusal in connection with the sale of commonly owned slaves, handmaidens, camels, cows, yearlings (*shāt*), or any other animals. Nor is there a right of first refusal in connection with the sale of commonly owned cloth or wells surrounded by cultivated land. A right of first refusal is recognized only in connection with items that can be partitioned and are amenable to delineation by means of borders. Any property that, by its nature, is not amenable to partition is not subject to a right of first refusal."

2266. Mālik said, "Whoever buys land knowing that it is subject to a right of first refusal and knowing that the persons holding the right of first refusal are present in the jurisdiction should initiate a case against them before the responsible public official (*sulṭān*), who will either rule in their favor or will dismiss their claim and award him the property. On the other hand, if he leaves them be and does not sue them before the proper authority, while they know that he purchased the property, yet they delay in taking any action against him for a long time, I do not believe that they will be permitted, after the passage of such a long period of time, to exercise their right of first refusal."

The Book of the Right of First Refusal (*Shuf'a*) Has Been Completed, with Abundant Praise to God in the Manner That Befits Him.

Book 37

The Book of Irrigation Partnerships (*Musāqāt*)

In the Name of God, the Merciful, the Compassionate

May God Grace Muḥammad and His Family.

Chapter 1. What Has Come Down regarding Irrigation Partnerships (*Musāqāt*)

2267. According to Mālik, Ibn Shihāb reported from Saʿīd b. al-Musayyab that the Messenger of God (pbuh) said to the Jews of Khaybar[912] on the day it surrendered to him, "I leave you be as you are in your current circumstances, as long as God leaves you be, provided that we share equally the dates you produce." Saʿīd said, "The Messenger of God (pbuh) would dispatch ʿAbd Allāh b. Rawāḥa to oversee the division of the dates between them and the Messenger of God (pbuh). ʿAbd Allāh would estimate the date palms' yield before they were harvested. He would then say to them, 'If you wish, they can stay in your possession, or if you wish, I can take possession of them.' They decided to retain the output of the date palms in their possession until harvest time."

2268. According to Mālik, Ibn Shihāb reported from Sulaymān b. Yasār that the Messenger of God (pbuh) would send ʿAbd Allāh b. Rawāḥa to Khaybar, where he would divide the date crop between the Prophet (pbuh) and the Jews of Khaybar on the basis of an estimate of the date palms' yield before their harvest. The Jews amassed the jewelry of their womenfolk and said to ʿAbd Allāh, "Take these! They are yours, but lighten the burden on us when you divide the crop, and give us more than what we are due.' ʿAbd Allāh said, "By God, you Jews are among the most despicable of God's creatures in my sight, but I will not deal with you unfairly on that account. As for the bribe

912 Khaybar, an oasis town located approximately four days' march north of Medina, was a site of intense date cultivation by a Hijazi Jewish community. The Prophet (pbuh) campaigned against them after making peace with the Meccans at al-Ḥudaybiya. Khaybar surrendered after a brief siege.

that you have offered me, it is a foul thing, and we will not accept it." They said, "Indeed, this is the kind of conduct upon which the good order of the heavens and the earth is sustained."

2269. Mālik said, "If a landowner enters into a partnership with a laborer who is responsible for watering and otherwise taking care of the date palms on the owner's land in exchange for sharing in the harvest, and interspersed among the date palms is uncultivated land, whatever the laborer cultivates on such land belongs to him. A landowner's stipulation that he will cultivate the uncultivated portion of the land himself is not valid because the laborer has agreed to water and otherwise care for the cultivated land for the benefit of its owner, and the owner's stipulation results in an additional benefit to the landowner at the expense of the laborer. There is nothing objectionable, however, in the landowner stipulating that any such crop be shared between the two of them, provided that the laborer is responsible for all inputs other than the land itself, including seeds, watering, and care. If, on the other hand, the laborer stipulates that the owner must provide the seeds, the stipulation is not valid, because it entails imposition of an additional requirement on the landowner that benefits the laborer. Irrigation partnerships entail that the laborer bears the labor costs and other out-of-pocket expenses related to cultivation, with the landowner bearing no responsibility for any of these things. This is the common understanding of the irrigation partnership."

2270. Mālik said, regarding a scenario in which the flow of water from a spring that two men share to water their crops comes to a halt, and one of the two men desires to repair the spring while the other says, "I lack the resources to help repair it": "In such a case, the one who desires to repair the spring is told, 'Repair it as you see fit, including spending additional resources to complete the task, and if you are successful, all the spring's water is yours. You will have the exclusive right to use it to water your crops until such time as your neighbor reimburses you for half of what you have spent. Once he does, he again becomes entitled to take his share of the water.' The former is initially given all the water because he incurred the expenses required to repair the spring, and because if his repairs failed to restore the water's flow, his neighbor would not have to reimburse him for any of the expenses he incurred."

2271. Mālik said, "If the landowner is responsible for all the costs of cultivation, labor as well as out-of-pocket expenses, and the laborer is required to contribute only the labor of his hands, he is merely a hired hand receiving his payment as a share of the crop, and that is invalid. This is because the laborer's wage, in this case, would be indeterminate, insofar as the landowner specifies neither the amount of the wage nor the nature of the tasks that the laborer must complete. Consequently, the laborer cannot know either how much he will earn or how much work will be required of him. He cannot know whether his wage in the end will be meager or ample."

2272. Yaḥyā said, "Mālik said, 'It is not permitted for an investor in an investment partnership (*qirāḍ*)[913] or a landowner in an irrigation partnership to reserve for himself any share of the investment capital or of the date palms. This is because if he were to do so, the laborer becomes a hired hand instead of a partner in the output. The landowner might say, 'I am prepared to hand over my land to you pursuant to the terms of an irrigation partnership, provided you act as a laborer for me with respect to these particular date palms, which you will water and pollinate,' or the investor says, 'I will give you such-and-such an amount of money to invest on the condition that you perform ten dinars' worth of work for me, the returns from which will be excluded from division according to the terms of our partnership agreement.' Such conditions are invalid and nonbinding. That is the rule among us (*dhālika al-amr ʿindanā*)."

2273. Mālik said, "The long-established ordinance (*al-sunna*) regarding the stipulations that a landowner can impose on the laborer in an irrigation partnership includes stipulations such as maintenance of the orchard's walls, cleaning the spring and irrigation canals, pollinating the date palms, pruning the branches, harvesting the fruit, and similar matters, provided that the laborer receives in exchange a specified share of the crop—half, or less, or more, as they have mutually agreed. The landowner is not permitted to require the laborer to initiate structural improvements to the land, such as digging a well, installing a device for raising water from a spring, planting new trees, or building water basins at great expense."

2274. Mālik said, "Such conditions are no different from the landowner saying to someone, 'Build a structure for me here,' or 'Dig a well for me,' or 'Make a spring flow for me,' or 'Do some work for me,' in each case 'for half of my orchard's output,' at a time before the orchard's fruit has matured and become lawful for sale. Offers such as these amount to selling fruit before it has matured, and the Messenger of God (pbuh) prohibited the sale of unharvested fruit before it has matured."

913 A *qirāḍ* partnership entails an investor giving money to an entrepreneur (*ʿāmil*), who then invests it on behalf of himself and its owner, with the entrepreneur receiving compensation only out of the venture's profits, if any, according to a predetermined proportional division of the profits between the entrepreneur and the investor, such as fifty-fifty. If the venture does not realize any profit, the entrepreneur receives nothing. In that case, any property of the venture remaining after its dissolution is returned in its entirety to the investor.

2275. Mālik said, "When the fruit has matured and ripened and is licit for sale, there is nothing objectionable in the orchard's owner saying to someone, 'If you perform such-and-such tasks for me,' and specifying the tasks, 'I will give you half the produce of my orchard.' In this case, however, the owner has only employed the other party as a hired hand in exchange for a definitive and certain wage, which the prospective worker has seen and with which he is satisfied. In an irrigation partnership, by contrast, if the orchard produces no fruit, if its output fails, or if its yield is less than expected, the laborer receives only his share of the fruit that was actually realized. The hired hand, however, contracts on the basis of a specified and determinate wage. An employment contract (*ijāra*) is binding only on that basis, because an employment contract is a type of sale in which the purchaser purchases the labor of another. Accordingly, it is not a valid contract if it entails material uncertainty in the consideration (*gharar*). That is because the Messenger of God (pbuh) prohibited sales in which a material term of the contract is indeterminate or uncertain."

2276. Yaḥyā said, "Mālik said, 'The long-established ordinance with respect to irrigation partnerships among us (*al-sunna fī al-musāqāt ʿindanā*) is that they are valid and there is nothing objectionable in them with respect to the output of date palms, grapevines, olive and fig trees, pomegranates, peaches, and any fruit trees similar to them, provided that the landowner's share of the output is specified in advance, be it a half, a third, a quarter, or more or less than that.'"

2277. Yaḥyā said, "Mālik said, 'Irrigation partnerships are also valid with respect to cereal crops once their shoots have emerged from the earth and they are visible. If their owner is unable to water them, labor over them, and care for them, he, too, is permitted to enter into an irrigation partnership with respect to them.'"

2278. Yaḥyā said, "Mālik said, 'Irrigation partnerships are invalid, even on crops for which such contracts are ordinarily licit, if the fruit has already matured and ripened and is licit for sale. In such a case, an irrigation partnership can only be arranged for the subsequent growing season. An irrigation partnership involving fruit that is already licit for sale amounts to an employment contract, because the laborer works for the benefit of the landowner, tending to his fruit that has already matured and harvesting it for its owner, in exchange for a share of the orchard's output, this share being the equivalent of a wage paid in dinars and dirhams that the employer gives his employee. That is not an irrigation partnership. An irrigation partnership is contracted between the time when the date palms are pruned and the time when their fruit ripens and becomes licit for sale. An irrigation partnership with respect to fruit trees is validly contracted only when it is entered into before the fruit has matured and is licit for sale.'"

2279. Yaḥyā said, "Mālik said, 'Uncultivated land is not a proper object of an irrigation partnership. Its owner may lease it for a determinate amount of cash, in dinars or dirhams, or similar property. As for someone giving his uncultivated land to another in exchange for a third or a fourth of what the land produces that season, that transaction entails material uncertainty in the consideration and is therefore invalid. That is because the harvest may be large, or it may be poor; indeed, it may even fail entirely. In such an event, the landowner would have foregone a determinate rent that would have resulted in a binding lease contract in exchange for a mere gamble, the outcome of which—whether it will be profitable or not—he cannot know. That is prohibited. It is the equivalent of a case involving someone who hires another man to undertake a commercial journey, offering him a determinate sum, and then says, "Shall I instead give you one-tenth of my profit from the venture as your wage?" That is not licit and is prohibited.'"[914]

2280. Yaḥyā said, "Mālik said, 'No one should agree to hire himself out or to lease his land or his ship for anything other than a determinate sum, the benefit of which does not go to anyone else.'"[915]

2281. Mālik said, "The reason it is permitted to enter into an irrigation partnership with respect to an orchard of date palms but not with respect to uncultivated land is that the orchard's owner cannot sell the fruit his orchard produces until the fruit matures, whereas the owner of uncultivated land is able to lease it as-is, with nothing on it."

2282. Yaḥyā said, "Mālik said, 'The rule in our view regarding irrigation partnerships for date palms is that the term of such partnerships is up to the parties. They may contract for three or four years, or more or less than that, if they wish. That is what I have heard. All fruit trees are the equivalent of date palms in that respect. Therefore, the partners in an irrigation partnership involving other kinds of fruit trees may also validly agree to a term of several years in such contracts, to the same extent that such a term is valid with respect to date palms.'"

914 This case must be distinguished from a legitimate investment partnership whose contract entails the investor's delegation of commercial discretion to the entrepreneur. In the case of the invalid employment contract, the employee is being paid a wage out of the profits of the venture for his service in transporting the goods to market, not for the exercise of commercial judgment.

915 What Mālik appears to mean here is that when a person agrees to enter into an employment contract for an indefinite wage or to rent his property for an indeterminate amount, he is taking the risk that the entire benefit from the transaction will accrue to the other party in the event that his bet on the future turns out to have been mistaken.

2283. Yaḥyā said, "Mālik said, regarding the landowner, 'He is not permitted to take anything in compensation from his laborer, whether gold or silver, food, or anything else, as an additional consideration for the contract. Any such requirement is invalid. Nor is it permitted for the laborer to demand any additional compensation from the landowner, whether gold or silver, food, or anything else. The inclusion in the contract of any additional compensation accruing to either party is invalid. The investor in an investment partnership is in the same position. If an additional item is included in the partnership's terms as compensation to either party, both the irrigation partnership and the investment partnership are transformed into employment contracts. Any contract that entails an employment relationship, moreover, is invalid and may not be contracted if it includes material uncertainty with respect to its consideration; that is, a party does not know whether the consideration will or will not come into existence, or he does not know whether the consideration will be great or small.'"[916]

2284. Yaḥyā said, "Mālik said, regarding a man who enters into an irrigation partnership with another man in respect of an orchard in which date palms, grapevines, or similar fruit trees have been planted but parts of which remain uncultivated, 'There is nothing objectionable in entering into an irrigation partnership with respect to an orchard such as this if the portion of the land that is uncultivated is incidental relative to the fruit trees and the fruit trees represent the great bulk of the land's use; that is, if the date palms (or other fruit trees) constitute no less than two-thirds of the orchard, and the uncultivated land constitutes at most one-third. That is because the uncultivated land, in this case, is incidental to the fruit trees, which represent the real object of the contract. If, on the other hand, the cultivated portion of the land includes only a few date palms, grapevines, or similar fruit trees, which account for one-third or less of the land, while the uncultivated portion of the land constitutes two-thirds or more, the landowner is entitled to rent out the land, but handing it over within an irrigation partnership is forbidden. That is because the rule followed by the people (*min amr al-nās*) is that they enter into irrigation partnerships with respect to orchards of fruit trees, some trivial portion of which may be uncultivated, whereas they rent out uncultivated land that has a trivial

916 Under this analysis, it is invalid to stipulate a defined wage in connection with an irrigation partnership because doing so would transform the relationship from a production partnership into an employment contract. If the agreement is analyzed as an employment contract, however, it fails because the worker's wage is not specified with sufficient certainty: since the laborer's wage is contingent on the future success of the crop, he cannot know at the time of the contract what his wage will be.

number of fruit trees, just as a manuscript copy of the Quran or a sword, each gilded with silver, may be exchanged for silver, or a gold-alloyed necklace or a gold ring with precious stones may be exchanged for gold dinars. It has always been the case that such sales are valid (*lam tazal hādhihi al-buyūʿ jāʾiza*) and that people buy and sell these items on that basis. No bright line or clear rule has come down to define the outer limits of this permissibility, such that if the proportions exceeded a specific ratio the transaction would be impermissible, and if they were less than that, it would be definitely permissible. The rule in our view in respect of this issue (*al-amr fī dhālika ʿindanā*) and the practice that the people have adopted and deemed binding among them (*wa'lladhī ʿamila bihi al-nās wa-ajāzūhu baynahum*) with respect to this question is that if the gold or silver is incidental to whatever gold or silver is incorporated in the principal object of the sale, the sale of that object for gold or silver is valid. The condition is that the fair market value of the sword's blade, the copy of the Quran, or the precious stones represents two-thirds or more of the value of the item being sold, and the value of the gold or silver in the exchanged item is one-third of the item's value or less.'"

Chapter 2. Stipulating the Inclusion of Slaves in an Irrigation Partnership (*Musāqāt*)

2285. Mālik said, "The best view that has been reported regarding a laborer in an irrigation partnership is that there is nothing objectionable in the laborer stipulating that he have the right to use the landowner's slaves in performing the contract, because they are deemed to be laborers dedicated to the property and therefore are in the same position as the property itself. The only benefit the laborer in the irrigation partnership receives from them is the easing of his burden. By contrast, if the slaves are not deemed part of the property, his burden is greater. The issue in this case is similar to that in an irrigation partnership involving land whose water flows spontaneously from a spring versus one involving land whose water source requires manual lifting. No one would willingly enter, on the same terms, an irrigation partnership involving a parcel of land that, although similar with respect to trees and fertility to another parcel of land, demands heavy labor to draw its water whereas the other parcel's water comes from a continuously flowing (*wāthina*) spring, because of the ease of working the parcel with the spring compared with the difficulty involved in drawing water for the parcel without. The rule among us is in accordance with that (*ʿalā dhālika al-amr ʿindanā*). *Wāthina* refers to a spring whose water flow is constant and regular, neither shrinking in volume nor subject to periodic interruption."

2286. Yaḥyā said, "Mālik said, 'The laborer in an irrigation partnership is permitted to use the slaves attached to the property only to perform work on the landowner's property, and he is not permitted to impose on the landowner a stipulation that would allow him to use them for other purposes.'"

2287. Mālik said, "The laborer is not permitted to impose on the landowner a stipulation that the landowner provide him with slaves that he can deploy for work in the orchard, if such slaves were not already present at the time they entered into the irrigation partnership."

2288. Mālik said, "The landowner is not permitted to stipulate, in his agreement with the laborer to whom he is giving the right to cultivate his land by virtue of the irrigation partnership, that he be allowed to exclude any of the orchard's slaves from the terms of the partnership. An irrigation partnership is undertaken in respect of a piece of property in the condition it is in at the time the contract comes into effect. Accordingly, if the landowner wishes to exclude any of the orchard's slaves from the irrigation partnership, or if he wishes to include any additional slaves in it, he should do so in each case before entering into the irrigation partnership. Only after he has made such changes should he enter into the irrigation partnership, God willing. If any of the orchard's slaves then die, go missing, or become ill, however, the landowner must replace them."

The Book of Irrigation Partnerships (*Musāqāt*) Has Been Completed, with Praise to God and through His Abundant Help. God Grace Muḥammad and His Family and Grant Them Perfect Tranquility.

In the Name of God, the Merciful, the Compassionate

May God Grace Muḥammad and His Family
and Grant Them Tranquility.

Book 38

Leasing Out (*Kirā'*) Farmland

Chapter 1. Leasing Out (*Kirā'*) Farmland

2289. According to Mālik, Rabīʿa b. Abī ʿAbd al-Raḥmān reported from Ḥanẓala b. Qays al-Zuraqī, from Rāfiʿ b. Khadīj, that the Messenger of God (pbuh) prohibited the leasing out (*kirā'*) of farmland. Ḥanẓala said, "I asked Rāfiʿ b. Khadīj whether that prohibition included leases whose rents were payable in gold or silver, and he said, 'There is nothing objectionable in leasing out farmland if the rent is payable in gold or silver.'"

2290. According to Mālik, Ibn Shihāb said, "I asked Saʿīd b. al-Musayyab whether leasing out farmland in exchange for rent payable in gold or silver is permissible, and he said, 'There is nothing objectionable in that.'"

2291. According to Mālik, Ibn Shihāb reported that he asked Sālim b. ʿAbd Allāh about leasing out farmland, and he said, "There is nothing objectionable in it if the rent is payable in gold or silver." Ibn Shihāb said, "So I asked him, 'What is your view of the report that has been attributed to Rāfiʿ b. Khadīj, which prohibits the leasing out of farmland?' Sālim replied, 'Rāfiʿ exaggerated. If I had any farmland, I wouldn't hesitate to lease it out.'"

2292. According to Mālik, it reached him that ʿAbd al-Raḥmān b. ʿAwf leased some farmland that remained continuously in his possession pursuant to a lease until he died. His son said, "I always assumed the land was ours, given how long it remained in his possession, until he mentioned the lease to us on his deathbed, directing us to pay some of the rent that he still owed under the lease in an amount of gold or silver."

2293. According to Mālik, Hishām b. ʿUrwa reported from his father that he would lease out his farmland in exchange for gold or silver.

2294. Yaḥyā said, "Mālik was asked about a man who leased out his farmland in exchange for one hundred measures (*ṣāʿ*) of dates or some other agricultural produce, wheat or its like. He declared that to be prohibited."

The Book of Leasing Out (*Kirā'*) Farmland Has Been Completed, with Praise to God.

Book 39
The Book of Investment Partnerships (*Qirāḍ*)

In the Name of God, the Merciful, the Compassionate

May God Grace Muḥammad and His Family
and Grant Them Perfect Tranquility.

Chapter 1. What Has Come Down regarding Investment Partnerships (*Qirāḍ*)

2295. According to Mālik, Zayd b. Aslam reported that his father said, "'Abd Allāh and 'Ubayd Allāh, two sons of 'Umar b. al-Khaṭṭāb, set out with a detachment of the army toward Iraq. On their way back to Medina, they met Abū Mūsā al-Ash'arī, who was then the governor of Basra. He greeted them warmly and welcomed them with open arms. He then said to them, 'If only there were something I could do for you that would benefit you both!' He then said, 'Indeed, here are some funds from the public treasury that I would like to send to the Commander of the Faithful in Medina. What if I lend them to you, and you use them to purchase goods from Iraq that you can then sell in Medina? You can return the principal to the Commander of the Faithful and retain the profit for yourselves.' They said, 'We are happy to accept your offer,' and so Abū Mūsā advanced them the funds. He then wrote to 'Umar b. al-Khaṭṭāb, telling him to take the funds from them. When they arrived in Medina, they sold the goods they had acquired in Iraq at a profit. When they returned the principal sum to 'Umar b. al-Khaṭṭāb, he said, 'Did the governor lend every soldier in the army what he lent the two of you?' They said, 'No.' 'Umar then exclaimed, 'Two sons of the Commander of the Faithful? They are the ones to whom the governor lends public property? Turn over the principal and the profit.' 'Abd Allāh kept quiet, but 'Ubayd Allāh objected, saying, 'Commander of the Faithful, you are not acting fairly. Had the property's value diminished, or had it perished, we would have been liable for it.' 'Umar nevertheless said, 'Hand it over!' 'Abd Allāh remained silent, but 'Ubayd Allāh renewed his appeal. One of

'Umar's advisors, who had been seated with 'Umar at the time, then said, 'Commander of the Faithful, why don't you deem this transaction to have been an investment partnership instead of a loan?' 'Umar said, 'Very well, I will treat it as an investment partnership.' He thus took the entirety of the capital and half of the profit, and 'Abd Allāh and 'Ubayd Allāh, the two sons of 'Umar, took the remaining half of the profit."

2296. According to Mālik, al-'Alā' b. 'Abd al-Raḥmān reported from his father, from his grandfather, that 'Uthmān b. 'Affān once gave him money on the understanding that it would be the capital of an investment partnership. He was to trade using that capital, with the two of them sharing the venture's profit, if any.

Chapter 2. What Is Permissible in Connection with a Binding Investment Partnership (*Qirāḍ*)

2297. Yaḥyā said, "Mālik said, 'The well-known form that a binding investment partnership takes (*wajh al-qirāḍ al-ma'rūf al-jā'iz*) is that the entrepreneur takes capital from his partner in order to deploy it in trade without bearing the risk of its loss. The entrepreneur's reasonable expenses while he is traveling on business, such as his food and clothing and whatever else he needs, determined in view of the aggregate amount of the venture's capital, are paid out of it if the capital is sufficient to bear those expenses. If, however, the entrepreneur remains resident in his hometown, living with his own people, he is not entitled to his expenses or clothing out of the venture's capital.'"

2298. Mālik said, "There is nothing objectionable in the partners to an investment contract doing small favors for one another, if they do so freely."

2299. Mālik said, "There is nothing objectionable in the investor purchasing some of the goods that the entrepreneur acquires, if the purchase is voluntary and not a stipulation of the investment partnership."

2300. Yaḥyā said, "Mālik said, regarding an investor who gave some money to his slave and to another man on the understanding that the money would be the capital of an investment partnership that the two would manage jointly, 'There is nothing objectionable in that, and it is valid. That is because the profit belongs to the investor's slave. It is not the master's until such time as he takes it from him, if he ever does. This property is no different from the slave's other earnings.'"

Chapter 3. What Is Not Permitted in an Investment Partnership (*Qirāḍ*)

2301. Yaḥyā said, "Mālik said, 'It is not permissible for a creditor to agree to his debtor's suggestion to recharacterize the debt owed to the creditor as the capital of an investment partnership between the creditor and debtor until the creditor has first collected his debt. After doing so, the creditor can then decide whether to invest it as capital in an investment partnership or to keep it. Agreeing to the suggestion before collecting payment is prohibited only because of the risk that the debtor is insolvent and unable to pay his debt when he makes the suggestion and his actual intent is to delay repayment in exchange for paying his creditor an additional sum later.'"[917]

2302. Mālik said, regarding a scenario in which a man gave money to another on the understanding that it would be the capital of an investment partnership, and then some of the capital was lost before the entrepreneur could begin trading, but once the entrepreneur began to trade with what was left of the capital, he earned a profit, and now he wanted to calculate each partner's share of the profits on the basis of what remained of the capital after part of it was lost: "His accounting of the profits is not acceptable, and the entirety of the investor's capital must be restored out of the entrepreneur's share of the profits. Only after the investor's capital is returned to him in full do the partners divide the remaining property of the venture in accordance with the stipulated terms of their agreement in the investment partnership."

2303. Mālik said, "The only appropriate form of capital in an investment partnership is gold or silver coin. It should not be capitalized in kind using goods or retail commodities. There are sales that, although invalid for one reason or another, may not be rescinded because the positions of the parties with respect to the goods have substantially changed since the sale, and it would be impossible to rescind the transaction. Unlawful gains (*ribā*), however, must always be rescinded. It is not permitted to retain any portion of an unlawful gain, whether trivial or substantial. Partial recognition of otherwise invalid contracts of sale is permitted, but no recognition whatsoever can be given to contracts involving unlawful gain, because God, Blessed and Sublime is He, says, 'If you repent, you are entitled to the return of your capital. You are not to deal unjustly nor to be treated unjustly.'"[918]

---

917 Mālik expresses concern that the debtor's suggestion to recharacterize the debt as investment capital is a subterfuge to allow the creditor to receive payment from his debtor in excess of the principal amount due in exchange for deferring payment of the debt. This would amount to unlawful gain (*ribā*).

918 *Al-Baqara*, 2:279. According to Bājī, Mālik here draws an analogy to invalid sales to make the case that just as some sales, despite their inclusion of invalid terms, are given partial legal recognition and not rescinded in their entirety, so, too, some investment partnerships may

Chapter 4. Binding Conditions in an Investment Partnership (*Qirāḍ*)

2304. Yaḥyā said, "Mālik said, regarding a man who gave money to another on the understanding that it would be the capital of an investment partnership and imposed a condition that the entrepreneur use the capital only to purchase specific goods or prohibited the entrepreneur from purchasing specific goods, 'There is nothing objectionable in the investor conditioning his investment on the entrepreneur's agreement not to purchase specific kinds of livestock or goods. On the other hand, it is impermissible for the investor to impose on the entrepreneur the obligation that he purchase only specific kinds of goods, unless a ready supply of such goods is available year-round. In that case, there is nothing objectionable in that condition.'"

2305. Mālik said, regarding a man who gave money to another on the understanding that it would be the capital of an investment partnership, "The investor may not include a stipulation that part of the profit belong exclusively to the investor, with the entrepreneur having no claim to it, even if only for a single dirham. He is, however, permitted to stipulate that he receive half of the profit and the entrepreneur the other half, or a third, or a quarter, or less or more than that. Any specified division of the venture's profit, be it small or great, is lawful. These are the terms that Muslims use to constitute their investment partnerships (*qirāḍ al-muslimīn*). But it is impermissible for the investor to stipulate that even one dirham of the profit, much less anything more, belong to him exclusively and that only the profit that is in excess of that sum be shared between him and the entrepreneur at a ratio of fifty-fifty, for example. The investment partnerships of Muslims are not consistent with such terms (*laysa ʿalā dhālika qirāḍ al-muslimīn*)."

Chapter 5. Impermissible Conditions in an Investment Partnership (*Qirāḍ*)

2306. Yaḥyā said, "Mālik said, 'Neither is the investor permitted to stipulate an exclusive share of the profit for himself that is prior to the entrepreneur's share, nor is the entrepreneur entitled to stipulate an exclusive share of the profit for himself that excludes the investor. In addition, an investment partnership may not be concluded alongside a sale contract (*bayʿ*), a rental contract (*kirāʾ*), an employment contract (*ʿamal*), a loan (*salaf*), or

---

receive limited legal recognition even if they include some invalid terms, while others must be rescinded. An improperly capitalized investment partnership must be rescinded because it is impossible to restore the investor's capital to him at the conclusion of the partnership, thereby resulting in unlawful gain. In such a case, if the investment partnership is performed despite having been unlawfully capitalized, the entrepreneur is deemed to be an employee, not a partner, and is given a fair wage (*ujrat al-mithl*) for his services rather than a fair share of the venture's profits (*qirāḍ al-mithl*), if any. See Bājī, *al-Muntaqā*, 5:157–58.

an easement of any kind (*mirfaq*) that one party imposes on the other as a condition of entering into the investment partnership; however, it is permissible for them to give assistance freely to one another, provided that it is not stipulated in the investment partnership, and provided further that it takes the form of a favor. Neither of the parties is permitted to stipulate against the other an additional benefit that is not shared with his partner, be it in gold, silver, food, or anything else. If the agreement includes any such stipulation, the contract is transformed into an employment contract, which requires a fixed and determinate wage. When the entrepreneur takes possession of the capital, he is not permitted to stipulate that he be permitted to deal with third parties on non-arm's-length terms, whether by accepting favors or by giving favorable offers with respect to the venture's merchandise, nor may he stipulate that he be permitted to deal in the venture's merchandise for his own benefit. If, at the conclusion of the venture, the partnership's funds are plentiful and the capital has been repaid, the partners divide between themselves whatever money remains in accordance with what they stipulated. The entrepreneur bears no liability to the investor in the event no profit is realized or a loss is incurred, resulting in a diminution of the investor's capital, whether the loss is a result of the entrepreneur's permitted personal expenses or of unfavorable commercial conditions. Such losses are chargeable to the capital account that belongs to the investor. Investment partnerships are valid and binding in accordance with whatever division of profit the investor and the entrepreneur mutually agree upon, whether one-half, one-third, one-fourth, or anything more or less than that.'"

2307. Yaḥyā said, "Mālik said, 'The entrepreneur is not permitted to stipulate that he be entitled to keep the venture's capital for a stated number of years during which the investor may not call his capital. Nor is it permissible for the investor to stipulate that the entrepreneur may not dissolve the venture before the completion of a mutually agreed term. This is because an investment partnership must not be limited by a determinate term of years; rather, it requires that the investor give his money to the entrepreneur, who deploys it to trade on the investor's behalf. If either of the two decides to dissolve the venture while the capital is still uninvested, he may do so, in which case the investor receives a refund of his capital. If the investor, however, wishes to call his capital after the entrepreneur has invested it, he must wait until the entrepreneur sells the venture's assets and reduces them to cash. If the entrepreneur decides to return the investor's capital after it has been invested, he must first sell the venture's assets and reduce them to cash so that he may repay the investor in cash, just as he originally took the capital from the investor in cash.'"

2308. Mālik said, "It is not permissible for an investor who gives his money to an entrepreneur as the capital of an investment partnership to stipulate that the entrepreneur should pay the alms-tax (*zakāt*) that is due only on the investor's share of the profit. That is because such a stipulation, insofar as it would amount to a reduction in the amount of alms-tax that the investor owes in respect of his own share, would entail the investor's stipulation of a fixed share of the profit for himself, in addition to his agreed share of the venture's profit.[919] Nor is it permitted for the investor in an investment partnership to stipulate that the entrepreneur purchase only from a specific merchant. Such a condition renders the entrepreneur a mere agent working for an indeterminate wage."

2309. Mālik said, regarding a man who gave money to another on the understanding that it would be the capital of an investment partnership, stipulating that the recipient guarantee its return, "The investor is not permitted to stipulate terms in respect of his investment other than those that form the rules of the investment partnership and are in accordance with the long-established ordinances of the Muslims (*mā maḍā min sunnat al-muslimīn*) with respect to it. If the investment capital appreciates along with the protection of the guarantee, the investor will have received a benefit in addition to the profit on account of that guarantee. The profit is to be divided between them only on the basis of what it would have been had the investor made the investment without the benefit of the entrepreneur's guarantee. Further, should the capital be lost or perish, I do not believe that the entrepreneur can be held liable for the loss because a stipulation in an investment partnership holding the entrepreneur liable for losses in the capital is void."

2310. Yaḥyā said, "Mālik said, regarding a man who gave money to another on the understanding that it would be the capital of an investment

919 Assume for purposes of this example that the investor has held the minimum amount of cash in gold for the previous year (*niṣāb*), rendering him liable to pay the alms-tax. He then gives the entrepreneur 1,000 dinars as capital to invest in an investment partnership, with the profit to be divided equally between the investor and the entrepreneur. One year into the venture, the value of the investment partnership has increased to 1,100 dinars, so the investor is required to pay the alms-tax in respect of his share of this increase, fifty dinars, resulting in an obligation to pay 1.25 dinars in alms-tax. If this obligation is paid out of the partnership's funds, the value of the investment partnership is then 1,098.75 dinars, 1,000 of which represents the capital and 98.75 of which is profit subject to a fifty-fifty division at the end of the venture in accordance with the parties' stipulated agreement. By requiring the entrepreneur to pay his alms-tax obligation out of the partnership's funds, the investor is effectively taking one-half of his alms-tax obligation out of the entrepreneur's share of the profit, thereby resulting in an excess benefit in contradiction of the basic agreement to share the profit fifty-fifty. According to Mālik, this invalidates the stipulation. If, on the other hand, the entrepreneur pays the alms-tax due on the shares of both the investor and the entrepreneur, no such excess benefit results, and the condition is permissible.

partnership, stipulating that the entrepreneur use it only to purchase date palms or beasts of burden in order to acquire the date palms' output or the animals' offspring but with the intention of never selling the date palms or animals themselves, 'That stipulation is not permitted and is not consistent with the long-established ordinances of the Muslims regarding investment partnerships. It must be the case that the entrepreneur can both purchase and sell these items, just as other goods in investment partnerships are purchased and sold.'"

2311. Mālik said, "There is nothing objectionable in the entrepreneur stipulating that the investor provide him with a slave-boy as an assistant to help manage the venture's capital. If the slave-boy is no longer able to assist with the venture's capital, however, he is not to serve the entrepreneur in anything unrelated to the venture."

Chapter 6. Investment Partnerships (*Qirāḍ*) Involving Goods

2312. Yaḥyā said, "Mālik said, 'Only gold and silver coins should be used to capitalize investment partnerships. It is not permitted to capitalize an investment partnership using goods. Improperly capitalized investment partnerships come about in one of two ways: either the owner of the goods says to the entrepreneur, "Take these goods, sell them, and use the proceeds to trade, and we'll deal with one another as though we were in an investment partnership," or he says to him, "Trade using these goods, and when you cease trading, purchase goods for me that are similar to the ones I gave you originally, and if a profit is realized, we'll share it." In the first case, the investor, the owner of the goods, receives an additional benefit through these terms in the form of the entrepreneur's uncompensated labor arising out of the sale of the investor's goods, as well as the benefit of relief from assuming the expenses arising out of the sale of his goods. In the second case, it is possible that when the investor gives the entrepreneur the goods, demand is high and their price dear, but then when the entrepreneur returns to the investor like goods at the conclusion of the venture, the goods are cheap. In this case the entrepreneur might purchase the like goods for one-third of their original price, or even less. The entrepreneur would therefore make a profit equal to half the amount by which the price of the goods decreased between the beginning and the end of the venture as his share of the profit. Alternatively, the entrepreneur takes the goods at a time when their price is cheap, but through his successful trading, the partnership's assets become substantial. However, when it is time to return the goods to the investor, the price of the goods is high, so he is required to use all the venture's capital to purchase the goods the investor requires.

In such a case, his labor and commercial efforts would have been wasted. This amounts to a kind of material indeterminacy in the consideration (*gharar*)[920] that renders the arrangement invalid. If the parties do not know that investment partnerships on such terms are invalid, and they enter into an investment partnership and begin to perform it on the basis of such terms, the entrepreneur is to be given the fair wage that would have been due to an employee who performed services such as selling the investor's goods and managing and investing the proceeds. After he successfully sells the goods and invests the proceeds, the funds are deemed the capital of an investment partnership as of the day the entrepreneur took possession of them in cash. The terms of the investment partnership in this case will be those of a standard fair investment partnership (*qirāḍ al-mithl*).'"[921]

Chapter 7. Rental Contracts (*Kirā'*) in an Investment Partnership (*Qirāḍ*)

2313. Yaḥyā said, "Mālik said, regarding a scenario in which a person was given money on the understanding that it would be the capital of an investment partnership and used the money to purchase goods that he transported for sale to another town, but prices there were not favorable, so, fearing a loss if he sold the goods there, he hired transport to take the goods to another town, where he ended up selling them at a loss anyway, with the cost of the transportation to the second town exceeding the entirety of the partnership's capital: 'If what he realizes from the sale of the goods in the second town is sufficient to cover the additional transportation expenses, the matter is settled; however, if any part of the transportation contract remains unpaid after the sale of the venture's goods, the entrepreneur is liable for the balance. The investor may not be pursued for any portion of it. That is because the investor instructed the entrepreneur only to trade using the investor's own capital. Accordingly, the entrepreneur cannot hold the investor responsible for any additional sums of money. If the investor were

920 The consideration given to the entrepreneur in an investment contract is, of course, indefinite, but the contract is nonetheless valid. In the case of an investment contract capitalized with goods, however, Mālik objects that the entrepreneur's return is contingent not only on the exercise of his commercial skill but also on the future price of the goods he is required to return to the investor. This second element of indeterminacy, in Mālik's view, renders the contract's indeterminacy too great to be sustained. This is especially so given the easy solution available to the parties: the investor could sell his goods for cash and use the proceeds to capitalize the investment partnership, or he could hire the entrepreneur to sell the goods for cash on his behalf in exchange for a determinate wage and then use the proceeds to capitalize the investment partnership.

921 A standard fair investment partnership in these circumstances would mean a division of partnership profits that is consistent with prevailing market practices for valid investment partnerships similar to the invalid one that the parties attempted to execute.

responsible for that unpaid amount, it would be tantamount to deeming him personally indebted to the third party for an amount in excess of the capital he initially provided to capitalize the investment partnership. The entrepreneur is not entitled to compel the investor to accept responsibility for that.'"

Chapter 8. Breaches (*Taʿaddī*) of the Investment Partnership (*Qirāḍ*) Agreement

2314. Yaḥyā said, "Mālik said, regarding a scenario in which a man gave another money on the understanding that it would be the capital of an investment partnership, and the entrepreneur successfully invested it and realized a profit from it and then, using some or all of the profit and capital of the venture, purchased a handmaiden with whom he had sexual intercourse, as a result of which she became pregnant, and then the venture's property diminished in value: 'If the entrepreneur has money of his own, he must use it to restore the venture's capital by paying to the venture out of his own money an amount equal to the handmaiden's fair market value. If, after he satisfies that obligation, the venture has surplus funds, they are to be divided between the two of them in accordance with the terms of their initial investment partnership. If the entrepreneur lacks sufficient personal funds to reimburse the venture, however, the handmaiden must be sold and the proceeds received from her sale given to the venture in order to restore its diminished capital.'"

2315. Mālik said, regarding a scenario in which a man gave another money on the understanding that it would be the capital of an investment partnership, and that man, the entrepreneur, violated the agreement by purchasing more goods than the venture's capital could pay for using his own funds: "The investor is given a choice. If he wishes, whether the goods have been sold at a profit or at a loss or not sold at all, he may pay the entrepreneur the price he advanced for the goods and acquire them for himself. Alternatively, he may treat the entrepreneur as his partner in the goods in proportion to the entrepreneur's share of their value with respect to any future increase or diminution in their value, in accordance with any additional amount the entrepreneur advanced from his own funds to acquire them."

2316. Mālik said, regarding a man who took money from another on the understanding that it would be the capital of an investment partnership and then paid it to another man on the understanding that it would be the capital of a second investment partnership without the prior consent of the first investor, "If the second investment partnership yields a loss, the first entrepreneur is responsible for the loss, but if it realizes a profit, the first investor is entitled to his share of that profit in accordance with their initial agreement, and the first entrepreneur is entitled to receive his share of what was stipulated out of what remains of the venture's money."

2317. Mālik said, regarding an entrepreneur who violated the investment partnership agreement by borrowing money from the venture's capital and using it to purchase goods for himself, "If he earns a profit from those goods, it must be divided between them in accordance with the terms of their original agreement, but if he incurs a loss, the entrepreneur must bear it out of his own funds."

2318. Mālik said, regarding a man who gave another money on the understanding that it would be the capital of an investment partnership, but the entrepreneur borrowed some of the venture's capital to purchase goods for himself, "The investor has a choice. If he wishes, he may become the entrepreneur's partner in the goods the entrepreneur purchased using the venture's capital in accordance with the terms of their initial investment partnership agreement. Alternatively, he may abandon the goods to the entrepreneur and call his capital. This remedy applies in all cases involving an entrepreneur who violates the investment partnership agreement."

Chapter 9. Permitted Expenses in an Investment Partnership (*Qirāḍ*)

2319. Yaḥyā said, "Mālik said, regarding a man who gave another money on the understanding that it would be the capital of an investment partnership, 'If the capital is sufficient to bear the entrepreneur's personal expenses, the entrepreneur can use some of it to defray his reasonable personal expenses, such as food and clothing, in proportion to the size of the venture's capital when he travels in furtherance of the venture's affairs. He may also hire an assistant to assist him with the venture's burdens and pay him a wage out of the venture's capital, if the venture's capital is so great that he is unable to manage its affairs entirely by himself. There are tasks that someone in the entrepreneur's position is not expected to perform and the entrepreneur need not discharge himself, such as personally collecting debts, carrying goods and loading them, and similar tasks. Accordingly, the entrepreneur can use some of the capital to hire someone who will relieve him of these tasks. However, the entrepreneur is not permitted to use the venture's capital to defray his personal expenses when he is not traveling on business but rather is at home with his family. Spending from the capital is permitted only when he is traveling in furtherance of the venture's purposes and the capital is sufficient to cover such expenses. If he is trading with the venture's capital only in the town in which he resides, he is not entitled to be reimbursed for his personal expenses, such as food and clothing, from the venture's capital.'"

2320. Mālik said, regarding a scenario in which a man gave another money on the understanding that it would be the capital of an investment partnership, and the entrepreneur used the money, along with his own capital, to trade in an out-of-town venture, "His personal expenses can be defrayed out of the venture's capital and his own capital, according to the proportion of each in the entirety of the combined capital."

Chapter 10. Impermissible Expenses in an Investment Partnership (*Qirāḍ*)

2321. Mālik said, regarding a man in possession of an investment partnership's capital, from which he defrays his personal expenses and clothes himself, "He may not make any gifts from the partnership's capital, nor give any of it to a beggar or anyone else, nor deal with others on any other than an arm's-length basis. If it happens that he encounters a group of people on his travels, and they share food together on the journey, each contributing some food to their common meal, I believe there is a great deal of latitude for that, as long as he does not intend to be ostentatious. But if he is deliberately ostentatious, giving his companions substantially more than they give him without having obtained the investor's prior permission, he must disclose to the investor whatever he gave them. If the investor ratifies his action, no harm results, but if the investor refuses to ratify his action, the entrepreneur must reimburse the investor with something similar to what he gave the third parties, if that item has a reasonable substitute."

Chapter 11. Debts Contracted in Connection with an Investment Partnership (*Qirāḍ*)

2322. Yaḥyā said, "Mālik said, 'The agreed-upon rule among us (*al-amr al-mujtamaʿ ʿalayhi ʿindanā*) regarding a scenario in which a man gave another money on the understanding that it would be the capital of an investment partnership, and the entrepreneur used it to purchase goods that he then sold on credit, realizing a profit on the capital, but then the agent died before collecting the money owed to the venture, is that if his heirs wish, they may collect those debts and receive their share of the venture's profit in accordance with the terms of their father's agreement, provided that they are sufficiently trustworthy to carry out that task. If they dislike the idea of collecting the venture's debts, they may leave it to the investor to deal with the venture's debtors. They are not obliged to collect the debts themselves. They are under no obligation to collect the debts, but they also have no right to demand collection if they leave this task to the investor. If they decide to collect the debts, they are entitled to their share of the proceeds in accordance with the terms of the original agreement, as well as to their personal expenses; whatever rights their father had, they, too, have. If they are not trustworthy for the task, they are entitled to hire a trustworthy person to collect the debts. If this person collects all the capital and all the profit, they are then entitled to their father's share of the venture's profit.'"

2323. Mālik said, regarding a man who gave another money on the understanding that it would be the capital of an investment partnership, on the condition that the latter invest it personally and that he personally guarantee the payment of anything he sells on credit, "That condition binds the entrepreneur. If he sells anything on credit, he is personally responsible for its repayment."

Chapter 12. The Transport of Goods in an Investment Partnership (*Qirāḍ*)

2324. Yaḥyā said, "Mālik said, regarding a scenario in which a man gave another money on the understanding that it would be the capital of an investment partnership (*qirāḍ*), and the entrepreneur then borrowed money from the investor, or the investor borrowed money from the entrepreneur, or the investor gave the entrepreneur some goods to sell for him, or the investor gave the entrepreneur some dinars to purchase goods for him: 'There is nothing objectionable in any of these things if both parties freely agree to perform them for each other as personal favors and they are not stipulated as terms in the investment partnership, such that the investor knows that even if he had not given his capital to the entrepreneur, had he asked the entrepreneur to take his goods with him the entrepreneur would have done so, either because of their friendly personal relationship or because the request was not burdensome, and that had the entrepreneur refused his request, he would not have immediately called back his capital. Or if the entrepreneur borrowed money from the investor or agreed to transport his goods for him, he knows that even if he did not have the investor's capital in his possession, the investor would nonetheless deal with him in the same fashion, and that even if the investor had refused to comply with his request, the entrepreneur would not have returned his capital to the investor. If, on the other hand, the entrepreneur agreed to perform these services for the investor only in order to ensure that the investor kept the capital with him, or if the investor did these things only so that the entrepreneur continued to pursue the venture and did not return the capital to him, the parties to the investment partnership may not perform these actions. This is one of the things that the people of learning forbid (*huwa mimmā yanhā ʿanhu ahl al-ʿilm*).'"

Chapter 13. Loans (*Salaf*) in Connection with an Investment Partnership (*Qirāḍ*)

2325. Yaḥyā said, "Mālik said, regarding a man who lent money to another and then was asked by the borrower to consider the money he has lent him the capital of an investment partnership, 'I do not approve of entering into such an arrangement until the loan has been repaid. The lender may then choose to give the funds to the borrower as the capital of an investment partnership if he wishes, or he may refuse to do so.'"

2326. Yaḥyā said, "Mālik said, regarding a scenario in which a man gave another money on the understanding that it would be the capital of an investment partnership, and then, sometime later, the entrepreneur told the investor that he has collected the money but asked him to deem the money he holds a loan rather than the capital of an investment partnership: 'I do not approve of entering into such an arrangement until the investor has taken possession of his money. He would then be free to lend it to the man, if he so wished, or to keep it. Otherwise, I worry that in such circumstances the venture's capital might have in fact diminished, and the entrepreneur wishes to defer repaying it to the investor so that he can make up what he has lost. That is not permitted and is neither valid nor binding.'"[922]

Chapter 14. Accounting in Investment Partnerships (*Qirāḍ*)

2327. Yaḥyā said, "Mālik said, regarding a scenario in which a man gave another money on the understanding that it would be the capital of an investment partnership, and the entrepreneur successfully invested the money for a profit, and then the entrepreneur wanted to dissolve the partnership and take his share of the profit, but the investor was away on a journey: 'He has no right to take any of the venture's funds unless the investor is present. If he takes anything for himself in the investor's absence, he is liable for it until a full accounting of the venture's gains and losses has been made and the money is divided between them.'"

---

922 Technically, the venture's property that is under the entrepreneur's control is not a personal debt of the entrepreneur, which makes Mālik's reasoning in this context appear anomalous. Nonetheless, the entrepreneur owes specific obligations to the investor, including an honest accounting of the venture's operations. A failing entrepreneur may be tempted to breach such obligations and hide his failure to achieve a high rate of profit by agreeing to guarantee the capital personally through transforming it into a loan. This concern seems to be behind Mālik's refusal to permit the ex post conversion of the capital of an investment partnership into a personal loan to the entrepreneur.

2328. Mālik said, "It is not permissible for the two partners in an investment partnership to account for the venture's profits and losses, settle their accounts, and go their separate ways if the money is not in their presence. They should perform their final accounting only when the venture's money is present with them so that the investor can take possession of his capital investment in full, and then they can divide the profit between themselves in accordance with the stipulated terms of their agreement."

2329. Yaḥyā said, "Mālik said, regarding a scenario in which a man took property from another on the understanding that it would be the capital of an investment partnership and then used the venture's capital to purchase goods for the venture at a time when he was indebted to third parties, and then his creditors sought to enforce their claims against him, suing him in a foreign town in which the investor was not physically present, but in the entrepreneur's possession were goods in which substantial profit had obviously been realized, so the creditors sought an order for the sale of those goods so that they could take the entrepreneur's share of the profit to satisfy their claims against him: 'None of the venture's profit may be distributed unless the investor is present and is first repaid his capital. Only then can they divide the profit in accordance with the stipulated terms of their agreement.'"[923]

2330. Mālik said, regarding a scenario in which a man gave another money on the understanding that it would be the capital of an investment partnership, and the entrepreneur traded with it, making a profit, and then separated the capital, apportioned the profit, took his own share, and set aside the investor's share of the profit, along with the original capital amount, doing all of this in the presence of witnesses whom he had brought to attest to the accounting of the venture's profits and losses: "Division of the venture's profit is permissible only in the presence of the investor. If the entrepreneur has taken anything from the venture's funds outside the investor's presence, he must return it until the investor's capital investment has been repaid to him in full. Only then can they divide what remains of the venture's funds in accordance with the stipulated terms of their agreement."

2331. Mālik said, regarding a scenario in which a man gave another money on the understanding that it would be the capital of an investment partnership, and the entrepeneur used it and then went to the investor and said, "This is your share of the profit, and I have taken the same for myself. Your capital investment remains fully intact and is in my possession": "I

923 In other words, the creditors of the entrepreneur do not have the right to seize the entrepreneur's share of the venture's property before the venture is finally wound up and the entrepreneur receives his share of the venture's returns in cash.

do not approve of dividing the venture's property in that way. Only when the entirety of the venture's capital is present and the investor is able to account for the entirety of his invested capital and to confirm that it is intact, complete, and deliverable to him are they then permitted to divide the profit between themselves. The investor may then return the capital to the entrepreneur if he so wishes, or keep it. It is obligatory for the capital to be present, because it might be the case that some of the capital has been lost, in which case the entrepreneur fears that the investor might call it back were he to learn the truth, but since the entrepreneur wishes to keep the remaining capital in his possession, he hides the loss from the investor."

Chapter 15. Miscellaneous Reports on What Has Come Down regarding Investment Partnerships (*Qirāḍ*)

2332. Yaḥyā said, "Mālik said, regarding a scenario in which a man gave another money on the understanding that it would be the capital of an investment partnership, and the entrepreneur used the capital to purchase goods, and the investor then said to the entrepreneur, 'Sell the goods now!' but the entrepreneur refused, saying, 'I do not think it is a good time to sell,' and they could not come to an agreement about what to do: 'Neither statement shall be given any consideration; instead, people with expertise regarding such goods are consulted about the proper course of action. If they believe it is opportune to sell the goods, the goods are to be sold, but if they believe it would be more opportune to defer their sale, their sale is to be deferred.'"

2333. Mālik said, regarding a scenario in which a man took money from another man on the understanding that it would be the capital of an investment partnership and deployed it in trade, after which the investor asked the entrepreneur about the fate of his investment, and the entrepreneur said, "It is safely with me," but when the investor later discovered that the venture's capital had in fact been impaired and demanded that the entrepreneur explain what happened, the entrepreneur said that such-and-such a portion of the venture's capital had in fact perished and that he said what he did only so that the investor would not call his capital: "His statement alleging that part of the venture's capital has perished is afforded no weight, given his previous statement affirming that it was safely with him. His prior admission is taken to bind him, unless he can provide some extrinsic evidence of the destruction of the capital that would corroborate the truth of his second statement. If he is unable to provide such evidence, his prior statement is deemed dispositive, and his claim that some of the capital has perished does not serve as a defense for him. The same principle applies to a situation in which the entrepreneur says, 'I made a profit of such-and-such from the capital,' and then, when the investor asks the entrepreneur to return his capital and his share of the profit to him, the entrepreneur says, 'In fact, I did not make any profit from the venture. I only told you that I had so that you would not call your capital and instead leave it in my possession.' Such a statement does not provide a defense for the entrepreneur, and his prior statement admitting the realization of a profit is taken as conclusive against him, unless he can produce some extrinsic evidence that corroborates the truth of his second statement. Only in that case would he not be bound by his first statement."[924]

2334. Mālik said, regarding a scenario in which a man gave another money on the understanding that it would be the capital of an investment partnership, and the entrepreneur earned a substantial profit in it and then said, "I agreed to enter into an investment partnership with you on the understanding that I would take two-thirds of the profit," but the investor said, "No; it is rather the case that I agreed to enter into the investment partnership with you on the understanding that you would take only one-third of the venture's profit": "The entrepreneur is to be taken at his word, provided he swears an oath corroborating his statement, what he says is consistent with the terms on which similar investment partnerships are contracted, and his claim is similar to the customary terms in people's investment partnership agreements. But if his claim is out of the ordinary and contrary to the customary terms in people's investment partnership agreements, he is not to be taken at his word and is awarded only the share of profit that would usually be due in a similar investment partnership."

2335. Mālik said, regarding a scenario in which a man gave another man one hundred dinars on the understanding that it would be the capital of an investment partnership, and the entrepreneur then used it to contract for the purchase of some goods, but when he went to pay the hundred dinars to the owner of the goods, he discovered that it had been stolen,[925] whereupon the investor said, "Sell the goods, and if a profit is realized, it belongs to me, but if there is a loss, you must bear it, because you lost the capital," but the entrepreneur said, "Rather, you are obliged to satisfy fully the seller's

924 The ordinary rule in an investment partnership is that the entrepreneur does not personally guarantee to the investor the return of his capital. However, in circumstances in which the entrepreneur makes a representation to the investor regarding the condition of the venture that is intended to reassure the investor that all is well in order to deter the investor from exercising his right to call the capital, Mālik holds the entrepreneur personally liable for the loss on the assumption that in the absence of credible evidence to the contrary, the entrepreneur has misappropriated the funds.

925 The entrepreneur in this case purchased the goods on credit, but when he attempted to pay for the goods later, he could not because the partnership's capital had been stolen.

claim, inasmuch as I purchased the goods with your money that you gave me": "The entrepreneur is obliged to pay the seller the purchase price of the goods, and the investor is told, 'If you wish, pay the one hundred dinars to the entrepreneur, and you will be partners in the goods in accordance with the terms of the investment partnership you contracted with him with the original hundred dinars. Alternatively, you may disclaim any interest in the goods.' If the investor pays the sum to the entrepreneur, this establishes an investment partnership on the same terms as the first one, but if he refuses, the goods become the property of the entrepreneur, who is obliged to pay for them."

2336. Mālik said, regarding a scenario in which two people were partners in an investment partnership, and when they dissolved the partnership, each taking his share of the profit, the entrepreneur still had in his possession some of the venture's property that he used in the venture, such as a worn-out waterskin, a garment, or the like: "The entrepreneur is entitled to retain any item belonging to the venture that is of trivial value and of no concern to anyone. I have not heard anyone opine (*lam asmaʿ aḥadan aftā*) that he must return such an item to the investor and divide it with him. He is obliged to return to the investor only the venture's valuable property. Accordingly, if there remains anything that can be named, like a beast of burden, a camel, coarse Yemenite cloth, or anything similar to them, and it has a ready price, I believe that the entrepreneur must return whatever such items are left with him at the conclusion of the venture, unless his partner permits him to keep them."

The Book of Investment Partnerships (*Qirāḍ*) Has Been Completed. Praise Belongs to God, the Lord of the Worlds.

Book 40

The Book of Compensation (*ʿAql*) Due for Battery

In the Name of God, the Merciful, the Compassionate

May God Grace Muḥammad and His Family
and Grant Them Perfect Tranquility.

Chapter 1. The Proclamation regarding Compensation (*ʿUqūl*) Due for Battery

2337. According to Mālik, ʿAbd Allāh b. Abī Bakr b. Muḥammad b. ʿAmr b. Ḥazm reported from his father that the edict that the Messenger of God (pbuh) sent to ʿAmr b. Ḥazm[926] regarding compensation due for battery stated the following: One hundred camels for a life; one hundred camels for a nose, if completely severed; one-third of the compensation due for a life (*diya*) for a head or facial wound that reaches the brain (*maʾmūma*), and the same for a wound that pierces the abdomen (*jāʾifa*); fifty camels for the loss of an eye, a hand, or a foot; ten camels for each finger; five camels for a tooth; and five camels for a wound that exposes the skull (*mūḍiḥa*).[927]

Chapter 2. The Practice (*ʿAmal*) with Respect to the Payment of Compensation for Loss of Life (*Diya*)

2338. According to Mālik, it reached him that ʿUmar b. al-Khaṭṭāb established a monetary value for the compensation due from urban dwellers for the loss of life of a free Muslim male. For those living in regions that used gold coins, he made it 1,000 dinars, and for those who used silver coins, 12,000 dirhams. Mālik said, "The people who use gold are the Egyptians and the Levantines, and those who use silver are the Iraqis."

---

926 The Prophet (pbuh) appointed ʿAmr b. Ḥazm as his governor in Najrān, a region in the southwest of the Arabian Peninsula that had a large pre-Islamic Christian community.

927 Wymann-Landgraf understands the *maʾmūma* as "a head or facial wound that lays bare the *dura mater* of the brain." He understands the *mūḍiḥa* as a "skull wound [that] . . . lays bare the skull bone without penetrating further"; *Mālik and Medina*, 489 n. 73.

2339. According to Mālik, he heard that compensation for the loss of life of a free Muslim male was payable in instalments over three or four years. Mālik said, "Of all the views that I have heard regarding that question, three years is the one I prefer most."

2340. Mālik said, "The agreed-upon rule among us (*al-amr al-mujtamaʿ ʿalayhi ʿindanā*) is that camels are not accepted as compensation from urban dwellers for the loss of life of a free Muslim male, nor is gold or silver accepted from desert dwellers, nor is silver accepted from those who use gold coins, nor is gold accepted from those who use silver coins."

Chapter 3. The Compensation Due for Intentional Killing (*Diyat al-ʿAmd*), If Accepted by the Next of Kin in Lieu of Retaliation, and Batteries Committed by the Insane (*Jināyat al-Majnūn*)

2341. According to Mālik, Ibn Shihāb would say, "The compensation due in a case of intentional killing of a free Muslim male, when accepted by the next of kin in lieu of retaliation, is twenty-five one-year-old female camels (*bint makhāḍ*), twenty-five two-year-old female camels (*bint labūn*), twenty-five three-year-old female camels (*ḥiqqa*), and twenty-five four-year-old female camels (*jadhaʿa*)."

2342. According to Mālik, Yaḥyā b. Saʿīd reported that Marwān b. al-Ḥakam wrote to Muʿāwiya b. Abī Sufyān, telling him that an insane man had been brought before him on the accusation that he killed someone. Muʿāwiya wrote back to him, saying, "Restrain him, but do not permit retaliation to be taken against him, for the insane are not subject to retaliation (*qawad*)."

2343. Yaḥyā said, "Mālik said, 'If an adult and a minor, acting in concert, intentionally kill someone, the adult may be put to death in retaliation for the killing, whereas the child's liability is limited to half the compensation due for unlawful killing.'"

2344. Mālik said, "The same principle applies in the case of a free man and a slave who, acting in concert, intentionally kill a slave: the slave may be put to death in retaliation for the killing, whereas the free man is liable for half of the dead slave's fair market value."

Chapter 4. The Compensation Due for Unintentional Killing (*Diyat al-Khaṭaʾ*) of a Free Muslim Male

2345. According to Mālik, Ibn Shihāb reported from ʿIrāk b. Mālik and Sulaymān b. Yasār that a man of the Banū Saʿd b. Layth tribe released a horse of his, letting it gallop freely, and it trampled the legs of a man of the

Juhayna tribe. The man bled profusely from the wounds he received, and later died. ʿUmar b. al-Khaṭṭāb said to the defendants, the men of the Banū Saʿd, "Are you prepared to swear by God fifty times that he did not die as a result of the injuries he received from your kinsman's horse?" They refused and were reluctant, fearful of swearing falsely. ʿUmar then said to the victim's next of kin, "Are you yourselves willing to swear that your deceased kinsman died as a result of the injuries he received from the perpetrator's horse?" They also refused to swear the requisite oaths. ʿUmar therefore ruled that the Banū Saʿd would pay half of the compensation due for the intentional killing of a free Muslim male. Mālik said, "Judicial practice is not in accord with this report (*laysa al-ʿamal ʿalā hādhā*)."[928]

2346. According to Mālik, Ibn Shihāb, Sulaymān b. Yasār, and Rabīʿa b. Abī ʿAbd al-Raḥmān would all say, "The compensation due for the unintentional killing of a free Muslim male is twenty one-year-old female camels (*bint makhāḍ*), twenty two-year-old female camels (*bint labūn*), twenty two-year-old male camels (*ibn labūn*), twenty three-year-old female camels (*ḥiqqa*), and twenty four-year-old female camels (*jadhaʿa*)."

2347. Yaḥyā said, "Mālik said, 'The agreed-upon rule among us (*al-amr al-mujtamaʿ ʿalayhi ʿindanā*) is that retaliation (*qawad*) may not be taken against minors and that even their intentional acts are deemed unintentional until they reach puberty and criminal laws (*ḥudūd*) are applicable to them. Therefore, every act of killing for which a minor is responsible is deemed unintentional. If a minor and an adult, acting in concert, kill a free man without intent to do so, each of them is liable for half of the compensation due.'"

2348. Mālik said, "The compensation (*ʿaql*) due for someone killed unintentionally is simply an interest in property, there being no right of retaliation arising from it. It is no different from any other kind of property belonging to the deceased: his outstanding debts may be discharged from it, and it is subject to the terms of his last will and testament (*waṣiyya*). Accordingly, if the decedent has other property, and the compensation due to him constitutes one-third of his property, and he agreed to waive his right to that compensation prior to his death, the waiver would be valid and binding; but if he has no property other than his right to compensation, the waiver would be valid only with respect to one-third of the compensation due. Likewise, if he has no other property, he may make a testamentary disposition with respect to only one-third of it."

928 Mālik is here referring to the fact that ʿUmar's demand that the defendant's paternal near-relations collectively swear an oath exonerating their relative of responsibility for the victim's death is not the procedure used by courts in such a case. His comment is not a reference to the substantive verdict in the case.

Chapter 5. The Compensation (*ʿAql*) Due for Unintentional (*Khaṭa'*) Nonlethal Injuries

2349. According to Mālik, "The agreed-upon rule among them (*al-amr al-mujtamaʿ ʿalayhi ʿindahum*)[929] with respect to unintentional injuries (*khaṭa'*) is that the victim is not entitled to compensation until he heals and is restored to good health. If a person suffers a broken bone, whether a hand, a foot, or the like, as a result of an unintentional injury, and it heals and is restored to good health and is not misshapen as a result of the injury, the victim is not entitled to compensation. But if, after the break heals, the bone either has been permanently diminished or is crooked or otherwise deformed, compensation is due in proportion to the impairment. If a rule establishing the precise compensation due has come down from the Prophet (pbuh) in respect of the deformed bone, compensation should be granted in accordance with whatever the Prophet (pbuh) ordained. But if no rule establishing the precise compensation due has come down from the Prophet (pbuh) in respect of the deformed bone, nor is there a long-established ordinance (*lam tamḍi fīhi sunna*), nor is there any other precedent specifying the compensation due, the compensation due is determined through judicial discretion (*ijtihād*)."

2350. Mālik said, "No compensation is due for unintentional, nonlethal injuries to the body if the wound heals without leaving a permanent deformity. If, however, the injury results in a permanent deformity after healing, judicial discretion must be applied to determine the appropriate compensation, except in the case of a wound that pierces the abdomen (*jā'ifa*). That requires payment of compensation in an amount equal to one-third of what is due for the life of a free man."

2351. Mālik said, "No compensation is due for a wound to the body that breaks a bone (*munaqqala*) or exposes a bone (*mūḍiḥa*) if, in both cases, the wound heals without leaving a permanent deformity."

2352. Mālik said, "The agreed-upon rule among us (*al-amr al-mujtamaʿ ʿalayhi ʿindanā*) is that if a physician severs the head of the penis in the course of performing a circumcision, he is obliged to pay compensation, but this is the kind of unintentional injury in which his kin group (*ʿāqila*) bears joint responsibility for payment of the compensation due.[930] It is also the agreed-upon rule among us that whenever a physician unintentionally

929 Here Mālik is attributing the rule to unnamed third parties, in contrast to his normal practice of using the first-person plural. It is not clear from the text or the commentaries who these third parties are.

930 In certain cases, such as some types of unintentional battery, the kin group is held jointly liable for the payment of the compensation due to the victim of the battery.

causes an injury or violates ordinary standards of practice, compensation is required, and the physician's kin group bears joint responsibility for payment of the compensation due."

Chapter 6. The Compensation (*ʿAql*) Due to Women

2353. According to Mālik, Yaḥyā b. Saʿīd b. al-Musayyab would say, "The compensation due to a woman is the same as that due to a man up to one-third of the compensation due for a free Muslim male's life (*diya*). The compensation due to her on account of an injury to her finger is the same as his; the compensation due to her on account of an injury to her tooth is the same as his; the compensation due to her on account of an injury that exposes her skull (*mūḍiḥa*) is the same as his; and the compensation due to her on account of an injury that cracks her skull without exposing it (*munaqqala*)[931] is the same as his."

2354. According to Mālik, Ibn Shihāb reported, and it also reached him from ʿUrwa b. al-Zubayr, that both of them held the same view as Saʿīd b. al-Musayyab regarding the amount of compensation due to a woman, namely, that the compensation due to her is the same as that due to a man up to one-third of the compensation due for a free man's life. If the compensation that would be her due exceeds one-third of a free Muslim male's life, however, she receives half of what a similarly situated male would receive. Mālik said, "In other words, she receives the same compensation as that due to a man for an injury that exposes her bone, one that breaks it, any injury that is less serious than an injury that pierces the skull and reaches the brain (*maʾmūma*), any injury that pierces the abdomen (*jāʾifa*), and similar injuries that entail compensation equal to one-third or less of the compensation due for a free man's life. If the compensation due to her would be more than that, however, her compensation is reduced to half of what would be due to a free man for the same injury."[932]

931 Wymann-Landgraf understands the *munaqqala* to be a "cranial wound [that] . . . shatters the small bones next to the cranium but does not penetrate the brain matter"; *Mālik and Medina*, 489 n. 73.

932 One of the odd results of this rule, and one for which the Mālikīs have been roundly criticized (if not mocked), is that in certain cases, the more severe the injury, the less compensation the woman receives. For example, if a woman is injured and loses three fingers, she is entitled to thirty camels in compensation. If, however, she loses four fingers, forty camels would exceed one-third the compensation due for the life of a free man. Consequently, under the Mālikī rule, she would receive in the second case only twenty camels as compensation, even though she lost an additional finger. Zurqānī explains this anomalous result by saying that the normal rule is that the compensation due to a free woman is half of that due to a free man. However, the long-established ordinance (*sunna*) made an exception with respect to compensation obligations that were equal to or less than one-third of that due for the life of a free man, treating free men and free women similarly in those cases. Zurqānī, *Sharḥ al-Zurqānī*, 4:285.

2355. According to Mālik, he heard Ibn Shihāb say, "It has long been the established ordinance (*maḍat al-sunna*) regarding a man who injures his wife that he is required to compensate her for that injury, but he is not subject to retaliation." Mālik said, "That rule applies only in the case of unintentional injuries (*khaṭaʾ*), such as if a man strikes his wife and inflicts an injury on her that he had not intended. For example, if he gives her a lash with a whip but accidentally gouges her eye, or something similar to that."

2356. Mālik said, regarding a woman whose husband and children neither count among her male paternal near-relations (*ʿaṣaba*) nor are from her own people, "If she injures another person, neither her husband, insofar as he is of another tribe, nor her children, insofar as they are not of her people, nor her maternal half-brothers, who are not counted among her paternal near-relations, are under an obligation to contribute to the compensation due for batteries (*jināya*) that she commits. These are the people most entitled to her estate when she dies, and it has been the case since the time of the Messenger of God (pbuh) that it is only the paternal near-relations who are jointly liable to pay the compensation due for batteries. The same principle applies to a woman's freed slaves: their estates go to her children, even if they are not of her tribe, but her tribe remains obligated to pay the compensation due for any batteries that her freed slaves commit."

Chapter 7. The Compensation (*ʿAql*) Due for Killing a Fetus

2357. According to Mālik, Ibn Shihāb reported from Abū Salama b. ʿAbd al-Raḥmān b. ʿAwf, from Abū Hurayra, that a woman of the tribe of Hudhayl struck another woman of her tribe, causing her to miscarry. The Messenger of God (pbuh) ruled that the victim was entitled to receive a fine infant slave (*ghurra*), male or female, as compensation.

2358. According to Mālik, Ibn Shihāb reported from Saʿīd b. al-Musayyab that the Messenger of God (pbuh) ruled in the case of a man who killed a fetus in its mother's womb that the perpetrator was obliged to compensate her with a fine infant slave, male or female. After hearing the judgment, the defendant said, "How can I be liable to compensate for the loss of something that never drank, ate, uttered a word, or even let out a sound at birth? A thing such as that is subject to neither retaliation (*qawad*) nor compensation (*ʿaql*)." The Messenger of God (pbuh) said in response, "A man such as this is surely a companion of soothsayers."[933]

---

933 The defendant's response was expressed in rhyming prose characteristic of the speech of pre-Islamic soothsayers (pl. *kuhhān*, sing. *kāhin*). Al-Qāḍī Abū Bakr Muḥammad b. ʿAbd Allāh b. al-ʿArabī, *al-Qabas fī sharḥ Muwaṭṭaʾ Mālik b. Anas*, 3 vols. (Beirut: Dār al-Gharb al-Islāmī, 1992), 1:1000.

2359. According to Mālik, Rabīʿ b. Abī ʿAbd al-Raḥmān would say, "The fair market value of a fine infant slave (due in respect of a fetus) is fifty dinars, or 600 dirhams. The compensation (*diya*) due for the life of a free Muslim woman is 500 dinars or 6,000 dirhams."

2360. Mālik said, "Accordingly, the compensation due for the fetus of a free woman is one-tenth of that due for its mother's life, one-tenth being fifty dinars or 600 dirhams."

2361. Mālik said, "I have not heard anyone (*lam asmaʿ aḥadan*) deny that the obligation to provide compensation for killing a fetus in its mother's womb arises only after it is delivered stillborn."

2362. Mālik said, "I heard that if the fetus is born alive and then dies, compensation for loss of life is due in full. A fetus is considered to have been born alive only if it cries out at birth. If it does so and then dies, full compensation for loss of life is due."

2363. Mālik said, "We believe that the compensation due for a handmaiden's fetus is one-tenth of the fair market value of its mother."

2364. Mālik said, "If a pregnant woman intentionally kills a man or a woman, retaliation may be taken against her only after she has given birth. If, however, a pregnant woman is killed, whether intentionally or unintentionally, her killer is not required to pay any compensation for her fetus. If she was killed intentionally, her killer may be put to death, but no compensation is due for her fetus. If she was killed unintentionally, the killer's paternal kin group (*ʿāqila*) is jointly responsible for payment of the compensation due for the loss of her life, but no compensation is due for the loss of her fetus."

2365. Mālik was asked about the stillborn fetuses of Jewish and Christian women. He said, "I believe that compensation is due in an amount equal to one-tenth of that due for its mother."

Chapter 8. Circumstances in Which the Compensation Due for the Loss of Life of a Free Muslim Male (*Diya*) Is Required in Its Entirety

2366. According to Mālik, Ibn Shihāb reported that Saʿīd b. al-Musayyab would say, "The full amount of the compensation due for the loss of life of a free Muslim male is due for severing both lips of a person. If only the lower lip is severed, two-thirds of this amount is due."

2367. According to Mālik, he asked Ibn Shihāb about a partially blind man who gouges out the eye of someone who sees, and Ibn Shihāb said,

"The victim, if he wishes, may insist on retaliation (*qawad*) against the perpetrator. If he wishes, however, he may instead take the full amount of the compensation due for the loss of life, 1,000 dinars or 12,000 dirhams, as compensation for his injury."

2368. Mālik said that it reached him that the compensation for the loss of life of a free Muslim male is due for the loss of any paired body part, and that this amount is also due for the loss of a tongue. Likewise, the compensation for the loss of life of a free Muslim male is due if hearing is lost in both ears, whether or not they were severed. The same is also due if a man's penis is severed, or the two testicles.

2369. According to Mālik, it reached him that the compensation for the loss of life of a free Muslim woman is due for the loss of both of her breasts. Mālik said, "The most trivial of the injuries requiring compensation, in my opinion, are those to eyebrows and a man's breasts."[934]

2370. Mālik said, "The rule in our view (*al-amr ʿindanā*) is that if a man is injured in several parts of his body, and the resulting compensation due to him would exceed that due for the loss of life of a free Muslim male, he is nevertheless entitled to receive compensation for each of the specific injuries he has suffered. Accordingly, if he loses both of his hands, his feet, and his eyes, he receives full compensation for the loss of life of a free Muslim male three times over."

2371. Mālik said that if the sound eye of a partially blind man is unintentionally gouged out, full compensation for the loss of life of a free Muslim male is due.

Chapter 9. The Compensation (*ʿAql*) Due for an Injury to the Eye That Results in Loss of Vision

2372. According to Mālik, Yaḥyā b. Saʿīd reported from Sulaymān b. Yasār that Zayd b. Thābit would say, "If an eye is injured but is physically intact, yet there has been a loss of vision in that eye, the compensation due is one hundred dinars."

2373. Mālik was asked regarding the compensation due for the loss of the lower eyelid or the eye socket. He said, "The only resort in this circumstance is judicial discretion (*ijtihād*). If the victim's vision has suffered, however, he is entitled to compensation to the extent that his vision has been impaired."

---

934 Mālik's first statement—that the loss of every paired body part results in an entitlement to the compensation due for the loss of life of a free Muslim male—is only a general rule with some notable exceptions, such as the loss of the eyebrows and a man's breasts, as mentioned in this report.

2374. Yaḥyā said that Mālik said, "The rule in our view (*al-amr ʿindanā*) regarding an intact but blind eye that is gouged out and a paralyzed hand that is severed is that no specific amount of compensation is due; rather, it is a matter of judicial discretion."

Chapter 10. The Compensation (*ʿAql*) Due for Wounds to the Head and Face

2375. According to Mālik, Yaḥyā b. Saʿīd reported that he heard Sulaymān b. Yasār say, "A wound to the face that exposes the bone (*mūḍiḥa*) is the equivalent of one to the head, unless it permanently disfigures the face. In that case, the compensation due is increased by the difference between the compensation due for the facial wound itself and one-half of the compensation that would be due for a wound that exposes the skull. That amounts to seventy-five dinars."[935]

2376. Mālik said, "The rule in our view (*al-amr ʿindanā*) is that the compensation due for a wound that cracks the skull but does not expose it (*munaqqala*) is fifteen camels. A *munaqqala* is a wound that removes the outer lining of the bone but does not penetrate the brain. It can affect both the head and the face."

2377. Mālik said, "The agreed-upon rule among us (*al-amr al-mujtamaʿ ʿalayhi ʿindanā*) is that retaliation (*qawad*) is not permitted in the case of head wounds that pierce the skull and reach the brain (*maʾmūma*) or of wounds to the abdomen (*jāʾifa*). Ibn Shihāb said that retaliation is not permitted in the case of a head wound that pierces the skull and reaches the brain. A *maʾmūma* is any blow that pierces the skull and reaches the brain. Such a wound occurs only in the head, and it must penetrate the skull and reach the brain to receive this designation."

2378. Mālik said, "The rule in our view is that no compensation is due for any wound to the head or the face that does not expose the bone. Only if the wound is one that exposes the bone or is more severe than that does the duty to compensate arise. That is because the Messenger of God (pbuh), in the edict he sent to ʿAmr b. Ḥazm, made no mention of compensation due for wounds that do not at least expose the bone; for wounds that do, he designated five camels as compensation. Nor have any of our rulers,[936] in the past or recently, ruled that compensation is due in respect of any head wound that does not at least expose the bone."

---

935 Mālik did not adopt the view of Sulaymān b. Yasār with respect to a wound to the face that results in disfigurement. He instead left it to the judge's discretion to determine what additional compensation was due. Bājī, *al-Muntaqā*, 7:86.

936 The term used is *aʾimma*, the plural of *imām*.

2379. According to Mālik, Yaḥyā b. Saʿīd reported that Saʿīd b. al-Musayyab said, "One-third of the compensation that would be due for the loss of a limb is due if that limb suffers a piercing wound."

2380. Yaḥyā said, "I heard Mālik say, 'Ibn Shihāb disagreed with that view.'"

2381. Yaḥyā said, "I heard Mālik say, 'I do not believe there is an agreed-upon rule among us regarding the compensation due for a wound that pierces a limb (*nāfidha*). Rather, it is a matter for judicial discretion (*ijtihād*) exercised by the ruler (*imām*) or his appointed representative,[937] and there is not an agreed-upon rule among us regarding that.'"

2382. Mālik said, "The rule in our view regarding wounds to the face and the head is that only wounds that satisfy the definition of *ma'mūma* (a wound that pierces the skull and reaches the brain), *munaqqala* (a wound that cracks the skull but does not expose it), or *mūḍiḥa* (a wound that exposes the skull) are subject to fixed obligations of compensation. The compensation due for any other wound to the head or the face is a matter for judicial discretion. I do not deem wounds to either the lower jaw or the nose to qualify as wounds to the head. That is because the lower jaw and the nose are two separate bones, whereas the head is a single bone distinct from them."

2383. According to Mālik, Rabīʿa b. Abī ʿAbd al-Raḥmān reported that ʿAbd Allāh b. al-Zubayr permitted retaliation in cases involving wounds that crack and expose the skull.

Chapter 11. The Compensation (*ʿAql*) Due for the Loss of Fingers

2384. According to Mālik, Rabīʿa b. Abī ʿAbd al-Raḥmān said, "I asked Saʿīd b. al-Musayyab how much compensation is due for the loss of a woman's finger. He said, 'Ten camels.' I then said, 'How much for two fingers?' He said, 'Twenty.' I then said, 'How much for three?' He said, 'Thirty.' I then said, 'How much for four?' He said, 'Twenty.' I then said, 'The more egregious her wound and the more severe her tragedy, the lower her compensation?' He said, 'Are you an Iraqi?'[938] I said to him, 'No, but consider me either a meticulous scholar or an ignorant man seeking to learn.' He said, 'This is the established ordinance (*al-sunna*), my nephew.'"

---

937 The term *imām* may also be used in this context to designate lesser public officials who exercised power delegated to them by the head of the Islamic state.

938 This is a reference to Iraqi scholars' reputation for the use of analogy, rather than reliance on historical authority, as a principal method of legal reasoning. The questioner in this report, Rabīʿa b. Abī ʿAbd al-Raḥmān, was nicknamed "Rabīʿat al-ra'y," or "Rabīʿa the legal reasoner," because of his reputation for preferring legal reasoning to authoritative texts.

2385. Mālik said, "The rule in our view (*al-amr ʿindanā*) regarding the loss of all the fingers of a hand is that full compensation for the hand is required. That is because if the five fingers of a hand have been severed, the compensation for them is the equivalent of the compensation due for the loss of the hand itself, which is fifty camels. Ten camels are due for each finger. Accordingly, the loss of five fingers results in an obligation to pay fifty camels. In money, that amounts to thirty-three and one-third dinars for each of a finger's three joints, and in camels, it is three and one-third camels for each of a finger's three joints."[939]

Chapter 12. Miscellaneous Reports regarding the Compensation (*ʿAql*) Due for the Loss of Teeth

2386. According to Mālik, Zayd b. Aslam reported from Muslim b. Jundub, from Aslam, the freedman (*mawlā*) of ʿUmar b. al-Khaṭṭāb, that he ruled that the compensation due for the loss of a molar tooth (*ḍirs*), a broken collarbone, or a broken rib is a male camel.

2387. According to Mālik, Yaḥyā b. Saʿīd reported that he heard Saʿīd b. al-Musayyab say, "ʿUmar b. al-Khaṭṭāb ruled that the compensation due for each molar tooth is one camel, whereas Muʿāwiya b. Abī Sufyān ruled that the compensation due for each molar is five camels. ʿUmar's judgment results in undercompensation, while Muʿāwiya's judgment leads to overcompensation. Had it been me, I would have given two camels for each molar, which results in the compensation due for the loss of life of a free Muslim male (*diya*)."[940]

939 The compensation due for the loss of life of a free man is one hundred camels or one thousand dinars. The loss of a hand is half of that, fifty camels or five hundred dinars. Each finger in its entirety is one-fifth of that amount, so ten camels or one hundred dinars. Each finger, in turn, according to Mālik's analysis, consists of three parts, one for each joint of the finger. The compensation due for severing a part of the finger is determined by how many joints of the finger have been severed.

940 A normal adult mouth has thirty-two teeth, twenty of which are molars. There is agreement that the compensation due for the loss of a non-molar is five camels. Saʿīd b. al-Musayyab's opinion is based on the assumption that the loss of all thirty-two teeth should result in an obligation to pay the compensation due for the loss of a life of a free Muslim male, that is, one hundred camels. From that perspective, ʿUmar's judgment results in undercompensation, because he offered only one camel in compensation for each molar. Accordingly, under ʿUmar's rule, the loss of all teeth would result in a reimbursement of only eighty camels. Muʿāwiya's rule, on the other hand, results in overcompensation, insofar as the loss of all teeth would result in a reimbursement of 160 camels. Saʿīd's proposed rule solves this problem by modifying ʿUmar's rule so that the compensation due for each molar is two camels instead of one. As a result, the loss of all teeth produces an obligation to pay exactly one hundred camels to the victim.

2388. According to Mālik, Yaḥyā b. Saʿīd reported that Saʿīd b. al-Musayyab would say, "When a non-molar is struck and blackens from infection, full compensation for it becomes obligatory. If it is subsequently extracted, full compensation for it is due yet again."

Chapter 13. The Practice (*ʿAmal*) with Respect to Compensation (*ʿAql*) Related to Injuries to the Teeth

2389. According to Mālik, Dāwūd b. al-Ḥuṣayn reported that Abū Ghaṭafān b. Ṭarīf al-Murrī informed him that Marwān b. al-Ḥakam had once dispatched him (Abū Ghaṭafān) to ʿAbd Allāh b. ʿAbbās to ask him about the compensation due for the loss of a molar. ʿAbd Allāh said, "It is five camels." Abū Ghaṭafān said, "Marwān sent me back to ʿAbd Allāh to ask him, "Do you consider the front teeth the equivalent of the molars?" Ibn ʿAbbās replied, "Think of teeth the way you think of fingers. The compensation due for each of the fingers is the same, despite their different functions."[941]

2390. According to Mālik, Hishām b. ʿUrwa reported from his father that he deemed the compensation due for all teeth to be one and the same, making no distinction among them.

2391. Mālik said, "The rule in our view (*al-amr ʿindanā*) is that the compensation due for a tooth is the same, whether for the front teeth, the molars, or the canines. That is because the Messenger of God (pbuh) said, 'Five camels for a tooth (*sinn*).' Molars are also teeth. No tooth is more valuable than another."[942]

Chapter 14. The Compensation (*Diya*) Due for Injuries Inflicted on Slaves

2392. According to Mālik, it reached him that Saʿīd b. al-Musayyab and Sulaymān b. Yasār would say, "The compensation due for a wound to a slave that exposes his skull bone (*mūḍiḥa*) is one-twentieth of his fair market value."

---

941 Despite the report attributed to the Prophet (pbuh) mentioned at the beginning of the Book of Compensation, some scholars belonging to the Followers (the generation immediately following the Prophetic generation), such as Saʿīd b. al-Musayyab, distinguished between the compensation due for molars and that due for non-molars on the basis of their different functions. Ibn ʿAbd al-Barr, *al-Istidhkār*, 8:110. Marwān, in this report, appears to have been of that view as well, which explains why he asked his messenger, Abū Ghaṭafān, to return to Ibn ʿAbbās to clarify his position.

942 Mālik's argument is that the Arabic term *sinn* is used generically for teeth, as well as specifically for non-molars. Therefore, molars, known in Arabic as *ḍirs*, fall under the apparent sense of the Prophet's edict.

2393. According to Mālik, it reached him that Marwān b. al-Ḥakam would rule in cases involving wounds inflicted on slaves that the perpetrator was required to reimburse any resulting diminution in the slave's fair market value.

2394. Mālik said, "The rule in our view (*al-amr ʿindanā*) is that the compensation due for a wound that exposes the skull of a slave is one-twentieth of his fair market value. The compensation due for a wound that cracks a slave's skull but does not expose it (*munaqqala*) is one-fifteenth of his fair market value. The compensation due for a wound that pierces the skull and reaches the slave's brain (*maʾmūma*) or for a wound that pierces the slave's abdomen (*jāʾifa*) is one-third of the slave's fair market value. As for any injury other than these four, the compensation due is the amount by which the fair market value of the slave has been diminished. This amount is determined after the slave recovers and is restored to good health on the basis of the difference in his fair market value before and after the injury. The party who injured him is liable for the diminution in the slave's value."

2395. Mālik said, regarding a slave whose hand or foot has been broken but then heals, "The perpetrator is not liable for anything. However, if, as a result of the injury, the slave is disfigured or his fair market value has otherwise been diminished, the perpetrator is liable for the diminution in the slave's fair market value."

2396. Mālik said, "The rule in our view regarding retaliation (*qiṣāṣ*) among slaves is that the same principles that apply to free men also apply to them. The life of a handmaiden for the life of a male slave, and her injury for his injury. If a slave kills another slave intentionally, the master of the murdered slave is given the choice between having the murderer put to death and accepting the compensation (*ʿaql*) due for his murdered slave. If he elects to receive compensation for the murdered slave, he is entitled to receive the murdered slave's fair market value. In this case, if the master of the murderer wishes to pay the fair market value of the murdered slave, he may do so. Otherwise, he may surrender his culpable slave to the victim's master. If he does so, nothing else may be demanded of him. In this case, if the victim's master accepts the culpable slave and is satisfied with him, he may not then have him killed. That principle applies in all cases involving retaliation among slaves, whether involving severing of the hands, severing of the feet, or other similar acts that are the equivalent of killing with respect to a right of retaliation."

2397. Mālik said, regarding a slave who injures a Jew or a Christian, "The slave's master, if he so wishes, may pay the compensation due to the victim on behalf of the slave. Otherwise, he may surrender the slave, have him sold in a public auction, and give the proceeds of that sale in full (if the proceeds equal the compensation due) or in part (if they exceed the compensation due) to the injured Jew or Christian. In no case, however, is he permitted to hand over a Muslim slave to a Jew or a Christian."

Chapter 15. The Compensation Due to Protected People (*Diyat Ahl al-Dhimma*)

2398. According to Mālik, it reached him that ʿUmar b. ʿAbd al-ʿAzīz ruled that the compensation due when a Jewish or Christian male is killed is half of that due for the loss of life of a free Muslim male.

2399. Mālik said, "The rule in our view (*al-amr ʿindanā*) is that a Muslim is not to be killed in retaliation for the death of a non-Muslim, unless the Muslim killed him with premeditation and in cold blood (*ghīla*), in which case he is to be put to death."[943]

2400. According to Mālik, Yaḥyā b. Saʿīd reported that Sulayman b. Yasār would say, "The compensation due for killing a Zoroastrian male is 800 dirhams." Mālik said, "This is the rule among us (*wa-huwa al-amr ʿindanā*)."

2401. Mālik said, "The compensation for nonlethal injuries suffered by Jews, Christians, and Zoroastrians is calculated in proportion to the compensation due for loss of life using the same proportions as those applying to Muslims for the equivalent nonlethal injuries. The compensation for a wound that exposes the skull (*mūḍiḥa*) is therefore one-twentieth of the compensation that the members of these groups would receive for loss of life. The compensation for a head wound that pierces the skull and reaches the brain (*maʾmūma*) is one-third of their compensation for loss of life. The compensation for a wound that pierces the abdomen (*jāʾifa*) is one-third of their compensation for loss of life. The compensation for any injuries they suffer is calculated in accordance with this principle."

Chapter 16. What Renders an Individual Personally Liable to Pay Compensation (*ʿAql*)

2402. According to Mālik, Hishām b. ʿUrwa reported that his father would say, "The paternal near-relations (*ʿāqila*) are not under a joint obligation

943 Mālik here makes a distinction between intentional killing, in general, and premeditated, cold-blooded killing, which he refers to as *qatl al-ghīla*, in particular. In Mālik's view, if a Muslim kills a non-Muslim intentionally but without premeditation (e.g., he gets into a fight with a non-Muslim, and in the course of the fight he draws a weapon and kills him), he is not put to death but must pay the prescribed compensation. By contrast, were he to lie in wait for the non-Muslim and kill him unawares, he is put to death, despite the fact that his victim was a non-Muslim.

to pay compensation for an intentional killing (*qatl al-ʿamd*) committed by one of their tribe. They are jointly liable only in cases of unintentional killing (*qatl al-khaṭaʾ*)."

2403. According to Mālik, Ibn Shihāb said, "It has long been the established ordinance (*maḍat al-sunna*) that the paternal near-relations are not responsible for any portion of the compensation due for an intentional killing. They may, however, voluntarily agree to contribute."

2404. According to Mālik, Yaḥyā b. Saʿīd expressed an opinion similar to that.

2405. According to Mālik, Ibn Shihāb said, "In a case of intentional killing, if the next-of-kin of the victim waive their right to retaliation, it has long been the established ordinance that the killer must pay the compensation due for the loss of life of a free Muslim male (*diya*) out of his own property, unless his paternal near-relations agree to assist him voluntarily, of their own free will."

2406. Mālik said, "The rule in our view (*al-amr ʿindanā*) is that compensation does not become a joint obligation of the paternal near-relations unless the amount due is one-third or more of that required for the loss of life of a free Muslim male. Any compensation obligation that equals or exceeds one-third is a joint obligation of the paternal near-relations, but anything less is the personal obligation of the perpetrator."

2407. Mālik said, "The rule about which there is no dissent among us (*al-amr alladhī lā ikhtilāfa fīhi ʿindanā*) with respect to someone who commits an intentional killing or intentionally batters another person in a manner that gives rise to a right of retaliation (*qiṣāṣ*), but from whom the victim's next-of-kin or the victim (as applicable) has accepted compensation in lieu of retaliation, is that the paternal near-relations are not jointly liable for the compensation due, unless they voluntarily agree to contribute. Rather, the compensation due is the exclusive obligation of the person responsible for the killing or the injury, if he has property. If he does not have property, however, it is a debt that he owes. The paternal near-relations bear no responsibility for its payment, unless they voluntarily agree."

2408. Mālik said, "The paternal near-relations are not liable to contribute to the compensation for any self-inflicted wound, whether intentional or unintentional. That is the opinion of those with discernment among us (*raʾy ahl al-fiqh ʿindanā*). I have also never heard anyone (*lam asmaʿ anna aḥadan*) hold the paternal near-relations responsible for any part of the compensation due in respect of any intentional battery. This position is corroborated by the statement of God, Blessed and Sublime is He, in His Book, 'But for one who receives pardon from his brother, let the victim pursue payment fairly, and let the perpetrator make restitution to him as best he can.'[944] This means, as we see it, and God knows best, that whoever has agreed to accept compensation from his fellow should only pursue it fairly, and the perpetrator should pay it to him as best he can."

2409. Mālik said, "If a minor child or a woman, in each case without property of his or her own, commits a battery (*jināya*) for which the compensation due is one-third or less than that due for the loss of life of a free Muslim male, he or she is nevertheless personally liable to pay what is due to the victim out of his or her own personal property, if he or she has any. If he or she has no property, the obligation becomes a personal debt for which the paternal near-relations bear no responsibility. In addition, a child's father is not held responsible for payment of the child's obligation."

2410. Mālik said, "The rule about which there is no dissent among us is that the liability for killing a slave is determined by the slave's fair market value as of the day he is killed. Furthermore, the paternal near-relations of the perpetrator bear no responsibility to contribute anything to the payment of the slave's fair market value, be it trivial or substantial. Rather, the payment of compensation for the slave, whatever the amount may be, is the personal obligation of the perpetrator. Even if the fair market value of the deceased slave is greater than or equal to the compensation due for the loss of life of a free Muslim male, the perpetrator is nevertheless personally obliged to pay that amount out of his own property. That is because a slave, in this context, is a commodity."

Chapter 17. The Inheritance of Compensation (*'Aql*) for Battery and Accelerated Payment Thereof (*Taghlīẓ*)

2411. According to Mālik, Ibn Shihāb reported that 'Umar b. al-Khaṭṭāb exhorted the people at Minā,[945] "Whoever knows something regarding the rules of compensation (*diya*) for loss of life should come forward and tell me what he or she knows." Al-Ḍaḥḥāk b. Sufyān al-Kilābī came forward and said, "The Messenger of God (pbuh) sent me instructions to give Ashyam al-Ḍibābī's widow her share of the compensation due for the loss of her husband's life as part of her inheritance rights." 'Umar said to him, "Enter the tent and wait for me there." When 'Umar entered the tent and met him, al-Ḍaḥḥāk informed him about what had happened. Thereafter, 'Umar applied that precedent to similar cases. Ibn Shihāb said, "The killing of Ashyam was unintentional (*qatl al-khaṭa'*)."

944 *Al-Baqara*, 2:178.

945 Minā was the gathering point of the pilgrims and thus a convenient place to benefit from the collective knowledge of the community.

2412. According to Mālik, Yaḥyā b. Saʿīd reported from ʿAmr b. Shuʿayb that Qatāda, a man of the Banū Mudlij, once threw a sword at his son, striking him in the thigh. The child bled to death as a result. Surāqa b. Juʿshum went to ʿUmar b. al-Khaṭṭāb and told him what had happened. ʿUmar said to him, "Bring 120 camels to Qudayd[946] and meet me there." When ʿUmar arrived, he selected out of the 120 camels that Surāqa brought a group of thirty three-year-old female camels (*ḥiqqa*), thirty four-year-old camels (*jadhaʿa*), and forty pregnant camels (*khalifa*). He then said, "Where is the brother of the deceased?" The brother said, "Here I am." ʿUmar said to him, "Take these camels. The Messenger of God (pbuh) said, 'A killer receives nothing.'"[947]

2413. According to Mālik, it reached him that Saʿīd b. al-Musayyab and Sulaymān b. Yasār were both asked, "Is the compensation due for a killing committed during one of the sacred months accelerated?" They both said, "No, but the compensation should be increased on account of the violation of the month's sanctity." Then Saʿīd was asked, "Should the compensation due for wounds be increased, just as that for loss of life is?" He said, "Yes." Mālik said, "I think they both intended to do as ʿUmar b. al-Khaṭṭāb had done regarding the compensation demanded of the man of Banū Mudlij who struck his son."

2414. According to Mālik, Yaḥyā b. Saʿīd reported from ʿUrwa b. al-Zubayr that a Medinese man by the name of Uḥayḥa had a paternal uncle who was a minor. In fact, that paternal uncle was younger than Uḥayḥa. At the time, the paternal uncle was living with his maternal uncles. Uḥayḥa grabbed hold of him and killed him. His maternal uncles said, "We raised him from the time he was a baby until he could stand on his own two feet, through thick and thin, and then one of his paternal relations comes along and wrests him from us against our will." ʿUrwa then said, "That is why a killer may not inherit from the one he killed."

2415. Mālik said, "The rule about which there is no dissent among us (*al-amr alladhī lā ikhtilāfa fīhi ʿindanā*) is that whoever kills another intentionally (*qatl al-ʿamd*) may not inherit any of the compensation due for the loss of life, or any of the victim's estate. Nor does he preclude from the inheritance a more distant heir who would otherwise not inherit. Furthermore, anyone

946 Qudayd is a well between Mecca and Medina. ʿUmar made this request of Surāqa because he was apparently the chief of the Banū Mudlij, which was jointly responsible for payment of the compensation due for the unintentional killing of the child.

947 In other words, the father of the deceased boy is not entitled to share in the compensation due for the child's life, because he was responsible for killing him. What would have been the father's share goes to the other legal heirs of the deceased. In this case, it appears that the deceased's only other heir was his brother. Therefore, ʿUmar gave him the entirety of the compensation due for the loss of his brother's life.

who kills another unintentionally is also prohibited from inheriting any of the compensation due for the victim's loss of life. There is disagreement, however, as to whether he may inherit his share of the decedent's estate. That is because there is no reason to believe that he killed him so that he might inherit his estate or take his property. The view that I prefer is that he be allowed to inherit from the decedent's estate but not from the compensation due for the loss of his life."

Chapter 18. Miscellaneous Reports regarding Compensation (*ʿAql*) for Battery

2416. According to Mālik, Ibn Shihāb reported from Saʿīd b. al-Musayyab and Abū Salama b. ʿAbd al-Raḥmān, from Abū Hurayra, that the Messenger of God (pbuh) said, "No liability (*jubār*) arises out of damage caused by an animal; nor is there any liability in cases in which someone falls into a well or suffers an accident in a mine, and dies as a consequence. Anyone who finds treasure that was hidden away prior to the advent of Islam (*rikāz*) must pay one-fifth thereof to the public treasury." Mālik said, "*Jubār* means that no liability is attached to any of these cases."

2417. Mālik said, "Anyone leading a beast of burden by its tether, driving it along, or riding it is liable for whatever injuries the animal causes, unless the animal kicks spontaneously. ʿUmar b. al-Khaṭṭāb ruled that a person who released his horse, which subsequently injured another person, was liable to pay compensation. *A fortiori*, an even stronger case exists for holding liable a person leading, driving, or riding a beast of burden compared to a person who releases his horse."

2418. Mālik said, "The rule in our view (*al-amr ʿindanā*) regarding someone who digs a well, tethers his animal, or does anything similar to that on a public highway (*ṭarīq al-muslimīn*) is that he is liable for any resulting loss, whether injury or death, insofar as he was not permitted to use the public highway in that fashion. The compensation due for any resulting injury, as long as it is one-third or less of that due for the loss of life of a free Muslim male, is paid personally by the responsible party out of his own property. Liability for anything in excess of that is borne by his paternal near-relations (*ʿāqila*). If, however, he was permitted to do any of these things on the public highway, he is not liable for any injuries or deaths, nor must he pay any compensation. Examples of permitted usage include a man digging a well to collect rainwater and a man alighting from his beast of burden for some need and leaving it standing on the public highway momentarily. No one is required to pay compensation for any damages that might result from actions such as these."

2419. Mālik said, regarding a scenario in which a man falls into a well, and another man attempts to save him, following him down into the well, but the first man pulls the second man down, and they both fall to the bottom of the well and perish, "The first man's paternal near-relations are required to pay the compensation due for the loss of life of the second man (*diya*)."

2420. Mālik said, regarding a man who sends a child down a well or up a date palm, and the child falls to his death or is otherwise injured, "The one who sent the child is liable for what befell him, whether death or anything else."

2421. Mālik said, "The rule about which there is no dissent among us (*al-amr alladhī lā ikhtilāfa fīhi ʿindanā*) is that neither women nor children are obliged to contribute to the payment of any obligatory compensation that falls on the paternal near-relations in respect of a battery committed by one of their paternal near-relations. The obligation to pay compensation falls solely on the adult male members of the paternal near-kin."

2422. Mālik said, "Paying compensation in respect of batteries committed by freedmen (*mawālī*) is the responsibility of their paternal near-relations, if they freely agree to pay them. If they refuse, and they have a right to a pension through the public registry (*dīwān*), their obligations will be deducted from their stipends. Even if they do not have a right to a pension through the public registry, the paternal near-relations are still bound to pay the compensation due. Before the public registry existed, as was the case during the time of the Messenger of God (pbuh) and that of Abū Bakr, the paternal near-relations would nevertheless pay the obligations arising out of batteries committed by their freedmen. The public registry was established only during the time of ʿUmar b. al-Khaṭṭāb. No one is required to pay compensation for batteries committed by another person except for those committed by his own people and his own freedmen, because the right of patronage (*walāʾ*) is non-transferable, and because the Prophet (pbuh) said, 'The right of patronage belongs to the one who manumits the slave.' The right of patronage is thus a permanent form of affiliation (*nasab*)."

2423. Mālik said, "The rule in our view regarding someone who injures a domesticated animal is that the perpetrator is liable for any resulting diminution in the fair market value of the animal."

2424. Mālik said, regarding a man who is condemned to death but who, before the sentence is carried out, commits a crime subject to a mandatory penalty (*ḥadd*), "He is not subject to punishment for the second crime. His execution preempts any subsequent criminal punishment that may become due, unless he has committed slander. In this case, it is the right of the victim of slander to have the punishment enforced. People would otherwise say to the victim, 'Why didn't you have this person flogged, if indeed he slandered you?' Accordingly, I believe the slanderer must be flogged for his slander before he is executed. I do not believe, however, that he ought to be subject to any retaliation arising out of wounds that he may have inflicted on others, because the death sentence preempts everything else."

2425. Mālik said, "The rule in our view is that when a slain body is found in the territory of a people, whether in a village or anywhere else, the people living in closest proximity to where the body was found are not to be held responsible for the killing. That is because it is possible that a person may be killed and his corpse left at the door of the people, so that suspicion is cast on them. No one can be held responsible for a killing on the basis of such evidence."

2426. Mālik said, regarding a group of men consisting of contending sides who get involved in a brawl and, when it is over, discover that some of them are dead or wounded but no one knows who was responsible for what, "The best view that has been reported about this case is that payment of compensation is required, and it is the collective obligation of the side that fought those who were slain or wounded, as applicable, to pay it. However, if the slain or injured person is a bystander, all of them are collectively responsible for payment of the compensation due for the loss of his life."

Chapter 19. What Has Come Down regarding Premeditated, Cold-Blooded Killing (*Ghīla*) and Sorcery (*Siḥr*)

2427. According to Mālik, Yaḥyā b. Saʿīd reported from Saʿīd b. al-Musayyab that ʿUmar b. al-Khaṭṭāb executed five or seven people who, acting in concert, killed a man with premeditation and in cold blood. ʿUmar said, "Had all the people of Sanaa conspired in his murder, I would have put all of them to death."

2428. According to Mālik, Muḥammad b. ʿAbd al-Raḥmān b. Saʿd b. Zurāra reported that it reached him that Ḥafṣa, the wife of the Prophet (pbuh), had a handmaiden of hers who had used sorcery against her killed. Ḥafṣa had previously designated her for freedom after her death (*mudabbara*), but she nevertheless ordered that the handmaiden be killed.[948]

948 The plain sense of the Arabic report suggests that Ḥafṣa herself killed the handmaiden. The commentators themselves are uncertain as to whether she complained of the woman's sorcery to the ruler and the ruler had her put to death, or whether she acted on her

2429. Mālik said, "The sorcerer who uses sorcery, but not his client, is like the one about whom God, Blessed and Sublime is He, says in His Book, 'And they knew that whoever chooses magic will have no share in the next life.'[949] Therefore, I believe that a sorcerer—that is, the one who practices sorcery himself—must be put to death."[950]

Chapter 20. What Acts Are Sufficient to Prove Intent (*ʿAmd*)

2430. According to Mālik, ʿUmar b. Ḥusayn, the freedman (*mawlā*) of ʿĀʾisha bt. Qudāma, reported that ʿAbd al-Malik b. Marwān ruled that the next-of-kin of a man beaten to death with a stick were entitled to retaliate against the killer. The next-of-kin beat him to death with a stick.

2431. Mālik said, "The agreed-upon rule about which there is no dissent among us (*al-amr al-mujtamaʿ ʿalayhi alladhī lā ikhtilāfa fīhi ʿindanā*) is that whenever a man beats another with a stick or a rock, or strikes him intentionally, and the victim dies as a result of that blow, the killer has acted with intent, and as a result, retaliation (*qiṣāṣ*) applies."

2432. Mālik said, "Intentional killing, in our view, occurs whenever a man strikes another until he dies. Intentional killing also takes place when a man strikes another in the midst of a quarrel and departs while the other person is still alive, but he then bleeds to death. In a case like that, collective oaths (*qasāma*)[951] are required."

2433. Mālik said, "The rule in our view (*al-amr ʿindanā*) is that a group of free men may be put to death for the intentional killing of a single free male. Likewise, a group of free women may be put to death for the intentional killing of a single free woman. The same rule applies for slaves."

Chapter 21. Retaliation (*Qiṣāṣ*) for Intentional Killing

2434. According to Mālik, it reached him that Marwān b. al-Ḥakam wrote to Muʿāwiya b. Abī Sufyān, informing him that someone who had killed another while inebriated had been arrested and brought to him. Muʿāwiya replied, instructing Marwān, "He is to be put to death in retaliation."

---

own initiative, either directly or by asking a close relative to carry out the punishment. Bājī, *al-Muntaqā*, 7:116.

949 *Al-Baqara*, 2:102.

950 Mālik's rationale for putting a sorcerer to death is based on the notion that practicing sorcery, in and of itself, is a kind of unbelief.

951 Collective oaths (*qasāma*) refer to a procedure that Mālik applies to cases of intentional killing in which there is only circumstantial evidence of culpability. In this case, the next-of-kin would have to swear fifty oaths that the cause of death of the deceased was the injury suffered at the hands of the defendant before they would have the right to retaliate.

2435. Mālik said, "The best view I have heard regarding the meaning of the statement of God, Blessed and Sublime is He, 'The free for the free, and the slave for the slave,'[952] is that it refers to males. The meaning of 'The woman for the woman'[953] is that the rule of retaliation also applies to females, just as it applies to males. Accordingly, a free woman is put to death for killing another free woman, just as a free man is put to death for killing another free man. Likewise, a handmaiden is put to death for killing another handmaiden, just as a slave is put to death for killing another slave. The rule of retaliation applies to killing among women just as it applies to killing between men and women. This is because God, Blessed and Sublime is He, says in His Book, 'We ordained therein for them a life for a life, an eye for an eye, a nose for a nose, an ear for an ear, a tooth for a tooth, and wounds like for like.'[954] God, Blessed and Sublime is He, stated the rule as 'a life for a life.' Therefore, the life of a free woman is due for the life of a free man, and her injury for his injury."

2436. Mālik said, regarding a man who restrains another so that a third man can beat him, and then the third man kills him on the spot, "If the first man restrained the second believing that the third man intended to kill him, both of them are put to death. If, on the other hand, he restrained him thinking that the third man only intended to give the second man a good beating and not realizing that the third man intended to kill him, only the third man is put to death. The first man, who restrained the victim, must nevertheless be punished severely and imprisoned for a year, because he restrained him. He may not, however, be put to death."

2437. Mālik said, regarding a man who intentionally kills another or gouges out his eye but then is himself killed or has his own eye gouged out before retaliation can take place, "In this case, both the right to retaliation and the right to compensation for the loss of life (*diya*) lapse. That is because the right of the original victim was attached to the very thing that has now disappeared (that is, the perpetrator's life or eye). This is no different from a case in which a man intentionally kills another and then dies. In this case, the next-of-kin have no rights, neither to compensation nor to anything else. This is because of the statement of God, Blessed and Sublime is He, 'Equality is prescribed for you in cases involving killing: the free for the free, and the slave for the slave.'[955] The victim is entitled to retaliate only against the perpetrator. Consequently, should the perpetrator die, the victim has no claim to retaliation or compensation."

---

952 *Al-Baqara*, 2:178.
953 *Al-Baqara*, 2:178.
954 *Al-Mā'ida*, 5:45.
955 *Al-Baqara*, 2:178.

2438. Yaḥyā said, "Mālik said, 'Retaliation (*qawad*) does not apply for injuries occurring between a slave and a free man. A slave may be put to death if he intentionally kills a free man, but a free man is not to be put to death if he kills a slave, even if he does so intentionally. This is the best view that I have heard.'"

Chapter 22. Pardons (*ʿAfw*) in Cases of Intentional Killing (*Qatl al-ʿAmd*)

2439. According to Mālik, he found that the people of knowledge whose views he found satisfactory (*annahu adraka man yarḍā min ahl al-ʿilm*) would say that if a man who has sustained grievous wounds from an intentional assault declares on his deathbed that should he die of his wounds, he pardons his killer, "His declaration is valid, and he has a greater claim to his right of retaliation than do his next-of-kin after his death."

2440. Mālik said, regarding a man who pardons the perpetrator of an intentional killing (*qatl al-ʿamd*) after acquiring the right to put the perpetrator to death, "In this case, the perpetrator is not responsible to pay compensation (*ʿaql*) for the lost life, unless the party who pardons him imposes that as a condition of the pardon."

2441. Mālik said, regarding the perpetrator of an intentional killing, "If he is pardoned, he must be given one hundred lashes and imprisoned for a year."

2442. Mālik said, "If a man is the victim of an intentional killing, and the crime is proven before a judge with eyewitness testimony, and the victim has sons and daughters, and the sons agree to pardon the perpetrator but the daughters refuse, the sons' pardon binds the daughters. The daughters have no standing to object to the sons' decisions regarding whether to seek retaliation or to pardon the perpetrator."

Chapter 23. Retaliation (*Qiṣāṣ*) for Battery (*Jirāḥ*)

2443. Yaḥyā said, "Mālik said, 'The agreed-upon rule among us (*al-amr al-mujtamaʿ ʿalayhi ʿindanā*) is that whoever breaks another person's hand or leg intentionally is subject to retaliation, but there is no monetary compensation.'"

2444. Mālik said, "However, retaliation is not to be taken against a perpetrator until the victim's injuries heal. Only then may retaliation be exacted. If it turns out that the injury inflicted on the perpetrator after he recovers from it is similar to the injury that he inflicted on the victim, retaliation has been satisfied. On the other hand, if the injury of the perpetrator turns out to be worse than that which he inflicted on the victim, or even if he should die, the original victim, the one exercising the right of retaliation, bears no liability. If, after the victim exercises his right of retaliation, the perpetrator's wound heals completely whereas the original victim has been left paralyzed as a result of the perpetrator's original action, or the victim's wound has healed but left him disfigured, scarred, or maimed, the perpetrator is not subjected to a second round of retaliation. Rather, he is held liable for compensation to the extent that he has diminished the usefulness of the victim's hand. All other wounds to the body are treated in accordance with that principle."

2445. Mālik said, "If a man seeks out his wife and gouges out her eye, breaks her hand, severs her finger, or does anything like that to her, intending that outcome, she has the right to seek retaliation against him. If, on the other hand, a man strikes his wife with a rope or a whip and as a result harms her in a way that he did not desire or intend, he is liable to pay compensation for the injury that he has caused her but is not subject to retaliation."

2446. According to Mālik, it reached him that Abū Bakr b. Muḥammad b. ʿAmr b. Ḥazm authorized retaliation for someone whose thigh was broken.[956]

Chapter 24. The Compensation (*Diya*) Due for the Life of an Abandoned Freedman (*Sā'iba*) and the Liability for Batteries That He Commits

2447. According to Mālik, Abū al-Zinād reported from Sulaymān b. Yasār that a slave whom a pilgrim had manumitted and then abandoned killed the son of a man of the Banū ʿĀ'idh. The father of the deceased went to ʿUmar b. al-Khaṭṭāb, seeking compensation (*diya*) for the loss of life of his son. ʿUmar said, "He is not entitled to compensation." The father retorted, "What if it were my son who killed the man?" ʿUmar replied, "In that case, you would be obliged to pay compensation for his life." The father then said, "In that case, he is like a poisonous snake—if you leave it be, it devours you; and if it is killed, it seeks vengeance."[957]

The Book of Compensation (*ʿUqūl*) for Battery Has Been Completed, with Praise Due to God.

956 Bājī reports that this is a controversial position among Mālikīs because it is difficult to ensure proportionality in exercising such a right, and the retaliatory action is likely to destroy the perpetrator's thigh or perhaps even kill him. Bājī, *al-Muntaqā*, 7:131.

957 This is a case involving unintentional killing. A freedman abandoned by his former master lacks a relationship of patronage (*walā'*). Ordinarily, liability for batteries committed by a freedman is borne by the paternal near-relations of his patron, but in this case, the abandoned freedman had no such relationship. Therefore, ʿUmar did not authorize compensation for the loss of the child's life. Ibn ʿAbd al-Barr reports that ʿUmar's decision in this case is a matter of controversy among Muslim jurists. Ibn ʿAbd al-Barr, *al-Istidhkār*, 8:188–90.

Book 41

The Book of Collective Oaths (*Qasāma*)

In the Name of God, the Merciful, the Compassionate

May God Grace Muḥammad and His Family
and Grant Them Perfect Tranquility.

Chapter 1. The Parties Claiming the Right to Retaliation Begin the Collective Oaths (*Qasāma*)

2448. According to Mālik, Abū Laylā b. ʿAbd Allāh b. ʿAbd al-Raḥmān b. Sahl reported from Sahl b. Abī Ḥathma that some eminent men of his people informed him that ʿAbd Allāh b. Sahl and Muḥayṣa had once set out for Khaybar on account of their extreme poverty. While they were there, someone came to Muḥayṣa and reported to him that ʿAbd Allāh b. Sahl had been killed and thrown into a shallow well (*faqīr bi'r*).[958] Muḥayṣa went to the Jews of Khaybar and said, "By God, you killed him!" They said, "By God, we certainly did not!" He then departed and journeyed until he reached his people in Medina and told them what had happened. He, his brother Huwayṣa (who was the elder of the two), and his other brother ʿAbd al-Raḥmān then set out together to see the Messenger of God (pbuh). Muḥayṣa prepared to speak, because he was the one who had been to Khaybar, but the Messenger of God (pbuh) interrupted him and said, "The eldest, the eldest," meaning the eldest should speak first. So Ḥuwayṣa spoke, and then Muḥayṣa did. The Messenger of God (pbuh) then said, "Either they pay the compensation due for the loss of your companion's life, or they should prepare for war." The Messenger of God (pbuh) wrote to the Jews of Khaybar, demanding they accept responsibility for what happened. They sent him a reply, saying, "By God, we did not kill him." The Messenger of God (pbuh) said to Ḥuwayṣa, Muḥayṣa, and ʿAbd al-Raḥmān, "Are you prepared to swear oaths to vindicate your claims regarding the loss of your companion's life?" They

958 The text states that the narrator is uncertain whether the word was "a well" or "a spring" (*ʿayn*).

said, "No." He said, "Are the Jews prepared to swear for you oaths affirming their innocence?" They said, "But they are not Muslims." As a result, the Messenger of God (pbuh) decided to pay the compensation due for the loss of their companion's life himself, out of the public treasury. He dispatched one hundred she-camels to them as compensation, instructing that they be delivered to them in their own territory. Sahl remarked, "One of the red ones kicked me." Mālik said, "The term *faqīr* means well."

2449. According to Mālik, Yaḥyā b. Saʿīd reported that Bushayr b. Yasār informed him that ʿAbd Allāh b. Sahl al-Anṣarī and Muḥayṣa b. Masʿūd set out together for Khaybar. When they arrived there, each went his separate way to see to his own affairs. Then ʿAbd Allāh b. Sahl was killed. Muḥayṣa departed from Khaybar and went with his brother Ḥuwayṣa and ʿAbd al-Raḥmān b. Sahl to the Messenger of God (pbuh). ʿAbd al-Raḥmān was about to speak on account of his relationship with his deceased brother, but the Messenger of God (pbuh) said, "The eldest, the eldest," so Muḥayṣa and Ḥuwayṣa spoke instead, and they recounted what had happened to ʿAbd Allāh b. Sahl. The Messenger of God (pbuh) said to them, "Are you prepared to swear fifty oaths to vindicate your claims regarding the loss of your companion's life (or 'to vindicate your right to retaliate against the perpetrator')?" They said, "Messenger of God, we neither witnessed the killing nor were present, so we cannot swear." The Messenger of God (pbuh) said, "If the Jews swear fifty oaths denying responsibility, will it convince you of their innocence?" They said, "Messenger of God, how can we accept the oaths of nonbelievers?" Yaḥyā b. Saʿīd said, "Bushayr said that the Messenger of God (pbuh) then paid the compensation due for the loss of ʿAbd Allāh's life out of the public treasury."

2450. Mālik said, "The agreed-upon rule among us and that which I have heard from those whom I find agreeable (*al-amr al-mujtamaʿ ʿalayhi ʿindanā wa'lladhī samiʿtu mimman arḍā*) regarding collective oaths, and the rule on which the rulers of the past and the present have agreed (*wa'lladhī ijtamaʿat ʿalayhi al-aʾimma fī al-qadīm wa'l-ḥadīth*), is that the accusers who seek to impose liability are given the first chance to swear their oaths. Collective oaths apply in only two circumstances. The first is when a dying man declares, 'So-and-so killed me.' The second is when the next-of-kin are able to produce some inconclusive circumstantial evidence of the defendant's guilt. These are the only two circumstances in which accusers are entitled to swear collective oaths to prove the accused's guilt. Collective oaths are not applied, in our view, in any but these two circumstances."

2451. Mālik said, "The established ordinance about which there is no dissent among us and in respect of which the people's practice has been continuous (*al-sunna allatī lā ikhtilāfa fīhā ʿindanā wa'lladhī lam yazal ʿalayhi ʿamal al-nās*) is that when the accusers accuse someone of responsibility for a killing, whether intentional or unintentional, they are the first to take the collective oaths. The Messenger of God (pbuh) allowed the tribesmen of Banū Ḥārith to take the oath first in the case of their kinsman who was killed in Khaybar. If the accusers take the oath, they are entitled to seek retaliation against the defendant. Only one person, however, may be put to death pursuant to collective oaths, not two or more. Fifty of the deceased's male next-of-kin swear fifty oaths. If they are fewer than fifty, or some of them refuse to swear the oath, others can take substitute oaths on their behalf to complete the required number, unless one of those refusing to swear the oath is a relative who is entitled to grant a pardon to the perpetrator. If one of them refuses to swear the oath, the right to retaliation will not arise. Substitute oaths are permitted only if the next-of-kin who refuses to take the oath is not one of those male relatives of the deceased entitled to grant the perpetrator a pardon. Therefore, if even one such next-of-kin refuses to swear the oath, none of the remaining next-of-kin is entitled to swear in his place. In this situation, the obligation to swear the oaths is transferred to the defendants. Fifty of their men should swear fifty oaths. If they are not fifty, those who have already sworn are permitted to swear additional oaths to complete the required number. If there is no one to take the oath other than the accused himself, he may swear fifty times himself and be acquitted. The reason there is a difference between the procedure governing oath-taking in connection with accusations of killing, on the one hand, and that governing oath-taking in connection with claims of property, on the other, is that when a man extends credit to another, he takes steps to secure his claim by, for example, bringing witnesses to attest to the transaction, whereas when a man desires to kill another, he does not kill him in the presence of a group of people but rather tries to do it surreptitiously. If the procedure for collective oaths were applied only in cases in which there was eyewitness testimony, and were the same rules to apply to these cases as apply to cases involving property, it would be impossible to establish liability for killing, and people would be emboldened to kill one another once they knew the applicable rules of evidence. Instead, it is the case that the right to take collective oaths has been given first to the deceased's next-of-kin, so that people may be deterred from killing one another and that someone contemplating killing another may be deterred from doing so, knowing that he may be held responsible for that act by virtue of the dying man's declaration."

2452. Mālik said, regarding a scenario in which one person in a group of people is suspected of responsibility for a killing, and the deceased's next-of-kin refuse to swear their oaths and instead transfer the obligation to swear the oaths to the defendants, who constitute a numerous group, "Each member of the group must swear individually fifty oaths that he is innocent. The oaths are not to be allocated among them on the basis of their number; rather, the members of the group are exonerated only if each one of them swears fifty times. This is the best view that I have heard regarding that issue."

2453. Mālik said, "The right to swear the collective oaths belongs to the male paternal near-relations (*ʿaṣaba*) of the slain person. They are the next-of-kin who take the oaths that establish the perpetrator's guilt, and the ones by whose oaths the perpetrator is put to death."

Chapter 2. Those Among the Deceased's Next-of-Kin Who Participate in Collective Oaths (*Qasāma*) in Connection with Proving an Intentional Killing (*Qatl al-ʿAmd*)

2454. Yaḥyā said, "Mālik said, 'The rule about which there is no dissent among us (*al-amr alladhī lā ikhtilāfa fīhi ʿindanā*) is that the oaths of women are not admissible in a collective oath proceeding to prove an intentional killing, even if the slain person's only next-of-kin are females. Women have no right either to participate in the collective oath proceeding regarding an intentional killing or to grant a pardon.'"

2455. Mālik said, regarding the victim of an intentional killing, "If his male paternal near-relations (*ʿaṣaba*) or his freedmen (*mawālī*) declare, 'We are prepared to swear oaths in order to vindicate his life by exercising our right of retaliation,' that is their right."

2456. Mālik said, "Even if some of the female relations wish to pardon the killer, they are not entitled to do so. The slain man's paternal near-relations and his freedmen have a stronger claim to that right than the female relations do, because the former are the ones who vindicated his life by securing the right to retaliate for his death and who swore oaths in order to do so."

2457. Mālik said, "If, after the perpetrator's guilt has been proven, the paternal near-relations and the freedmen agree to pardon him, but the slain man's female relations refuse, saying, 'We shall not abandon our right to retaliation against the one who killed our kinsman,' the latter's objection is more worthy and of greater effect than the former's pardon. That is because someone who wishes to exercise the right of retaliation (*qawad*) has a stronger claim than those who wish to waive it once guilt has been conclusively established and the right to retaliation has been granted, whether or not those willing to pardon are male or female."

2458. Mālik said, "The minimum number of accusers required for a collective oath proceeding in a case of intentional killing is two. The oaths may be divided between the two as they wish, provided that they swear fifty oaths altogether. Once they have done so, they have proven their claim and are entitled to exercise the right of retaliation against the perpetrator. That is the rule among us (*dhālika al-amr ʿindanā*)."

2459. Mālik said, "If a group of people beat a man to death with their own bare hands, all of them may be put to death. But if the victim dies after having been beaten, collective oaths are required to prove guilt. If collective oaths take place, only one member of the group can be charged, and only he may be put to death for the killing. We have never heard of a case involving collective oaths that involved more than one accused."

Chapter 3. Collective Oaths (*Qasāma*) in Cases of Unintentional Killing (*Qatl al-Khaṭaʾ*)

2460. Mālik said, "In a collective oath proceeding to establish liability for a unintentional killing, the next-of-kin—the accusers, the ones who vindicate their claim by taking the collective oaths—must swear fifty oaths, each of them swearing a number of individual oaths determined in accordance with his proportionate share of the compensation due for the loss of the victim's life, this share being determined by the laws of inheritance. If, after the oaths are allocated among them, there are fractions of oaths that must be taken, the claimant to whom the greatest portion of the unsworn fractional oaths has been allocated is required to take them."[959]

2461. Mālik said, "If the slain person has only female heirs, they may swear the required collective oaths and become entitled to receive the compensation due for the loss of his life (*diya*). If the decedent has only one male heir, the heir may swear fifty times and become entitled to receive the compensation due. This rule applies only in cases involving unintentional killing, not in cases of intentional killing (*qatl al-ʿamd*)."

959 For example, if a man is killed leaving behind a son and a daughter as his only heirs, the son is entitled to receive two-thirds of the compensation due for the loss of his father's life, and the daughter is entitled to one-third. Accordingly, the son would be required to swear two thirds of the fifty oaths, that is, thirty-three and one-third oaths, and the daughter would be required to swear one-third of the fifty oaths, that is, sixteen and two-thirds oaths. In this case, since the daughter has been allocated two-thirds of the final oath, she, not her brother, is obligated to swear it.

Chapter 4. Inheritance in a Collective Oath Proceeding (*Qasāma*)

2462. Yaḥyā said, "Mālik said, 'If the victim's next-of-kin accept compensation for the loss of his life in lieu of retaliation, it is divided as inheritance in accordance with the Book of God, Mighty and Exalted is He. The decedent's daughters, sisters, and other female heirs inherit their shares of it. If the claims of the female heirs do not exhaust the entirety of the compensation paid for the loss of his life, what remains goes to the decedent's nearest male relations."

2463. Yaḥyā said, "Mālik said, 'If an heir of someone who died as a result of an unintentional killing wishes to collect his share of the compensation due for the loss of the decedent's life, but the other heirs are absent, he is not entitled to do so. He is not entitled to any of the compensation due, be it small or great, until the collective oath proceeding has been completed and fifty oaths have been taken. If he takes the fifty oaths himself, he is entitled to his share of the compensation due. That is because responsibility for the killing is established only once the fifty oaths have been taken, and no compensation is due until responsibility for the killing has been established. If another of the deceased's heirs shows up later, he swears a number of oaths in accordance with his share in the decedent's estate, and once he does so, he takes his share of the compensation. This procedure is followed until all the heirs have taken their respective shares. Accordingly, if a maternal half-brother shows up, he is entitled to one-sixth of the compensation and must swear one-sixth of the requisite fifty oaths. Whoever swears is entitled to his share of the compensation, and whoever refuses to swear loses his right to his share of the compensation. If some of the heirs are absent, or minors who have not yet reached puberty, the present heirs swear fifty oaths to establish the perpetrator's responsibility; then, if an absent heir later shows up or a minor heir reaches puberty, the heir swears a number of oaths in accordance with his proportional right to the compensation due as determined by his share in the decedent's estate. This is the best view I have heard.'"

Chapter 5. Collective Oaths (*Qasāma*) in Cases That Involve Slaves

2464. Yaḥyā said, "Mālik said, 'The rule in our view (*al-amr ʿindanā*) regarding slaves is that if a slave is killed, whether intentionally or unintentionally, and his master is able to produce an eyewitness to the act, he swears one oath corroborating the testimony of his witness and is then entitled to the fair market value of his slave. A collective oath proceeding is not carried out in a case involving the killing of a slave, be it intentional or unintentional. I have not heard any of the people of knowledge (*lam* *asmaʿ aḥadan min ahl al-ʿilm*) claim that a collective oath proceeding should be carried out on behalf of a slain slave. If a slave kills another slave, intentionally or unintentionally, the master of the slain slave is not obliged to institute a collective oath proceeding, nor is he obligated to take an oath at all. He is entitled to receive compensation for his deceased slave only if he has two eyewitnesses to establish responsibility for the slave's death or if he has one witness but is prepared to swear an oath corroborating that witness's testimony. This is the best view I have heard.'"

The Book of Collective Oaths (*Qasāma*)
Has Been Completed, with Praise Due to God,
and with His Assistance.

Book 42

The Book of Lapidation (*Rajm*) and Mandatory Criminal Punishments (*Ḥudūd*)

In the Name of God, the Merciful, the Compassionate

May God Grace Muḥammad and His Family and Grant Them Perfect Tranquility.

Chapter 1. What Has Come Down regarding Lapidation (*Rajm*)

2465. According to Mālik, Nāfiʿ reported that ʿAbd Allāh b. ʿUmar said, "The Jews of Medina came to the Messenger of God (pbuh) and told him that a man and a woman had engaged in illicit intercourse (*zinā*). The Messenger of God (pbuh) said to them, 'What does the Torah say about lapidation (*rajm*)?' They said, 'We publicly shame them, and then they are flogged.' ʿAbd Allāh b. Salām[960] said, 'You are lying. It speaks of lapidation.' They brought the Torah scroll and they unwound it, and one of them placed his hand over the verses of lapidation[961] and then recited what came before and after it. ʿAbd Allāh b. Salām said to him, 'Remove your hand!' The man removed his hand, and the lapidation verses appeared. They said, 'He told the truth, Muḥammad. The Torah contains the verses on lapidation.' The Messenger of God (pbuh) ordered that they be lapidated, and they were." ʿAbd Allāh b. ʿUmar said, "I saw the man lean over the woman to protect her from the stones." Yaḥyā said, "I heard Mālik say, 'In other words, he placed his body over hers so that the stones would fall on him.'"

2466. According to Mālik, Yaḥyā b. Saʿīd reported from Saʿīd b. al-Musayyab that a man of the Aslam tribe[962] came to Abū Bakr al-Ṣiddīq and said to him, "This miserable soul has committed illicit intercourse." Abū Bakr said to him, "Have you mentioned this to anyone else?" He replied, "No, I have

---

960 A Jewish convert to Islam, ʿAbd Allāh b. Salām is reported to have been knowledgeable of the Torah.

961 Cf. Deuteronomy 22:22–24.

962 Other sources identify this person as Māʿiz b. Mālik.

not." Abū Bakr said to him, "In that case, conceal it with the veil of God's protection, for God accepts the repentance of His servants." But his soul remained unsettled, so he went to ʿUmar b. al-Khaṭṭāb and repeated what he had previously told Abū Bakr. ʿUmar told him the same thing as Abū Bakr had done, but the man's soul remained unsettled, so he decided to go to the Messenger of God (pbuh). He said to him, "This miserable soul has committed illicit intercourse." Saʿīd said, "The Messenger of God (pbuh) turned his back on him three times, but the man would not stop. Finally, the Messenger of God (pbuh) summoned his family and asked them, "Is he suffering from illness? Is he mad?" They said, "Messenger of God, he is certainly of sound health and mind." The Messenger of God (pbuh) asked, "Has he ever been married?" They said, "Yes indeed, he has married, Messenger of God." Accordingly, the Messenger of God (pbuh) ordered that he be lapidated, and he was."

2467. According to Mālik, Yaḥyā b. Saʿīd reported that Saʿīd b. al-Musayyab said, "It reached me that the Messenger of God (pbuh) once said to a man of the tribe of Aslam who went by the name Hazzāl, 'Hazzāl, if only you had covered up your sin with your cloak, that would have been better for you.'" Yaḥyā b. Saʿīd said, "I reported this statement in a gathering that included Yazīd b. Nuʿaym b. Hazzāl al-Aslamī, and Yazīd said, 'Hazzāl is my grandfather, and this statement is true.'"

2468. According to Mālik, Ibn Shihāb informed him that a man confessed to having engaged in illicit intercourse during the time of the Messenger of God (pbuh). He repeated his confession four times, and then the Messenger of God (pbuh) ordered that he be lapidated, and he was. Ibn Shihāb said, "On the basis of that precedent, a man's confessions are admissible evidence against him."

2469. According to Mālik, Yaʿqūb b. Zayd b. Ṭalḥa reported from his father, Zayd b. Ṭalḥa, that ʿAbd Allāh b. Abī Mulayka informed him that a woman once went to the Messenger of God (pbuh) and told him that she had engaged in illicit intercourse and that she was pregnant. The Messenger of God (pbuh) told her, "Go away until you give birth." After she gave birth to the child, she returned. The Messenger of God (pbuh) told her, "Go away until you have suckled and weaned the child." After she finished suckling the child and weaned him, she returned. The Messenger of God (pbuh) said, "Go away until you find someone to take care of the child, and entrust the child to him." Zayd said, "She found someone to take care of the child and entrusted the child to him, whereupon she returned to the Messenger of God (pbuh), who ordered that she be lapidated, and so she was."

2470. According to Mālik, Ibn Shihāb reported from ʿUbayd Allāh b. ʿAbd Allāh b. ʿUtba that Abū Hurayra and Zayd b. Khālid al-Juhanī informed him that two men were quarreling and brought their dispute to the Messenger of God (pbuh). One of them said, "Messenger of God, resolve our dispute in accordance with God's Book!" The other man, who was the more learned of the two, said, "Indeed, Messenger of God, resolve our dispute in accordance with God's Book, and allow me to speak first." The Messenger of God (pbuh) said, "Speak," so the man said, "My son was an employee (*ʿasīf*) of this man, and he engaged in illicit intercourse with his employer's wife. He told me that my son is subject to lapidation, so I ransomed him with a hundred yearlings (*shāt*) and a handmaiden of mine. I then asked the people of knowledge about this case, and they told me that my son is in fact only subject to one hundred lashes and exile for a year. They also informed me that it is only the man's wife who is subject to lapidation." The Messenger of God (pbuh) then said, "By Him whose hand holds my soul, I will certainly resolve your dispute in accordance with God's Book. Your sheep (*ghanam*) and your handmaiden must be returned to you." He also ordered that the man's son be given one hundred lashes and that he be exiled for a year. He ordered Unays al-Aslamī to go to the employer's wife and, if she confessed to having engaged in illicit intercourse, to lapidate her. She confessed, and therefore he lapidated her. Mālik said, "*ʿAsīf* means 'employee.'"

2471. According to Mālik, Suhayl b. Abī Ṣāliḥ reported from his father, from Abū Hurayra, that Saʿd b. ʿUbāda said to the Messenger of God (pbuh), "What do you propose I do if I find a stranger alone with my wife? Shall I leave him be until I can find four witnesses and bring them to the scene?" The Messenger of God (pbuh) said, "Yes."

2472. According to Mālik, Ibn Shihāb reported from ʿUbayd Allāh b. ʿAbd Allāh b. ʿUtba b. Masʿūd that ʿAbd Allāh b. ʿAbbās said, "I heard ʿUmar b. al-Khaṭṭāb say, 'Lapidation is in God's Book; it is the obligatory punishment for males and females who engage in illicit intercourse, provided they have previously been married and proof has been provided. Either pregnancy or a confession can establish guilt.'"

2473. According to Mālik, Yaḥyā b. Saʿīd reported from Sulaymān b. Yasār, from Abū Wāqid al-Laythī, that a man came to ʿUmar b. al-Khaṭṭāb while he was in the Levant and complained to him that he had found a stranger alone with his wife. ʿUmar dispatched Abū Wāqid al-Laythī to the man's wife to investigate what had happened. When he arrived to question her, she was surrounded by a group of women. He told her what her husband had reported to ʿUmar. He then informed her that she could not be punished on the basis of her husband's accusation. She began to confess, however, and he attempted to interrupt her, reminding her of what he had told her previously, so as to get her to abandon her confession. She refused, however, and held fast to it. Therefore, ʿUmar ordered that she be lapidated, and so she was.

2474. According to Mālik, Yaḥyā b. Saʿīd reported that he heard Saʿīd b. al-Musayyab say, "When ʿUmar b. al-Khaṭṭāb departed from Minā, he alighted with his camel at al-Abṭaḥ. He then gathered a pile of pebbles, made a pillow by casting his cloak over them, and lay down on his back. He then raised his hands toward the heavens and said, "O God! I have become old and decrepit. My flock has scattered. Return me to You, without having missed or neglected anything." He then returned to Medina and gave a sermon to the people, saying, "People! Rules have been laid down for you; specific entitlements have been granted to you. You have been given a clear path, lest you wander astray, going to the right or the left." He then wrung his hands and said, "Take care that you not forget the lapidation verse, lest someone say, 'We do not see two punishments in God's Book,' for it is certainly the case that God's Messenger (pbuh) ordered lapidation, as did we. By Him whose hand holds my soul, if it were not the case that people would say, "Umar b. al-Khaṭṭāb has inserted something into the Book of God,' I would have written in God's Book, 'The old man and the old woman, lapidate them until they die.' It is certainly the case that we recited that."

2475. Mālik said, "Yaḥyā b. Saʿīd said that Saʿīd b. al-Musayyab said, 'Hardly had Dhū al-Ḥijja passed when ʿUmar b. al-Khaṭṭāb was murdered, may God have mercy on him.'" Yaḥyā said, "I heard Mālik say, "Umar's statement "the old man and the old woman" refers to a man and a woman who have been married prior to commiting illicit intercourse: lapidate them until they die.'"

2476. Mālik said that it reached him that ʿUthmān b. ʿAffān was brought a woman who had given birth to a child six months after her marriage, so he ordered that she be lapidated. ʿAlī b. Abī Ṭālib said to him, "Lapidation does not apply to her. God says in His Book, 'Pregnancy and weaning last thirty months,'[963] and He says, 'Mothers may nurse their children for up to two whole years, for whoever desires to complete the period of nursing.'[964] Accordingly, pregnancy can last six months, so she is not subject to lapidation." ʿUthmān b. ʿAffān sent a messenger to track her down and to halt enforcement of the punishment, but by the time the messenger caught up with her, the sentence had already been carried out.

963 *Al-Aḥqāf*, 46:15.
964 *Al-Baqara*, 2:233.

2477. Mālik asked Ibn Shihāb about a person who performs the act of the people of Lot.[965] Ibn Shihāb said, "He is to be lapidated, whether or not he is 'chaste' from a legal perspective (*muḥṣan*)."[966]

Chapter 2. Someone Who Confesses to Having Committed Illicit Intercourse (*Zinā*)

2478. According to Mālik, Zayd b. Aslam reported that a man confessed to having committed illicit intercourse (*zinā*) in the time of the Messenger of God (pbuh). The Messenger of God called for a whip, and a broken one was brought to him. He said, "Stronger than this." He was brought a newly fashioned whip whose knots were still taut and crisp. He said, "Weaker than this." Then he was brought a whip whose knots had frayed and softened. The Messenger of God (pbuh) then ordered that the man be flogged, and he was. He then said, "People! The time has come for you to observe God's limits. Whoever commits a foul act such as this should seek cover in God's protection and not disclose what he has done. But if he reveals his actions to us, we shall impose on him the punishment specified in God's Book."

2479. According to Mālik, Nāfiʿ reported that Ṣafiyya bt. Abī ʿUbayd told him that a man who had never been married (*bikr*) was brought to Abū Bakr al-Ṣiddīq. He was accused of having had intercourse with a handmaiden, making her pregnant. He confessed to having committed illicit intercourse. Because the man had not been previously married, Abū Bakr ordered that he be flogged as required by the mandatory punishment (*ḥadd*) specified in God's Book, and so he was. He was then exiled to Fadak.[967]

2480. Mālik said, regarding someone who confesses to illicit intercourse but then retracts his confession and says, "I didn't do it. I only said it because of this and that," and mentions some reason, "His retraction is acceptable, and the mandatory penalty is not imposed on him. That is because the mandatory punishment that is due to God becomes applicable only through two means. The first is the testimony of upright witnesses establishing the perpetrator's guilt. And the second is the perpetrator's unretracted confession. If he refuses to retract his confession, the mandatory punishment is imposed on him."

---

965 The "act of the people of Lot" is a euphemism for homosexual anal sex.

966 The penalty of lapidation applies exclusively to people who satisfy the legal condition of chastity. A person attains this status only through having previously engaged in certain forms of licit intercourse. Accordingly, even if a person is not married at the time of committing illicit heterosexual intercourse, he or she may still be subject to lapidation if he or she has previously engaged in licit intercourse. Homosexual anal intercourse, according to this report, is always punished by lapidation, regardless of the defendant's current or former marital status.

967 An oasis approximately 140 kilometers from Medina.

2481. Mālik said, "What I found the people of knowledge (*alladhī adraktu ʿalayhi ahl al-ʿilm*) saying regarding slaves who commit illicit intercourse is that exile does not apply to them."

Chapter 3. Miscellaneous Reports regarding the Mandatory Punishment (*Ḥadd*) for Illicit Intercourse (*Zinā*)

2482. According to Mālik, Ibn Shihāb reported from ʿUbayd Allāh b. ʿAbd Allāh b. ʿUtba b. Masʿūd, from Abū Hurayra and Zayd b. Khālid al-Juhanī, that the Messenger of God (pbuh) was asked about a handmaiden who had never been married and who engaged in illicit intercourse (*zinā*). He said, "If she engaged in illicit intercourse, flog her; if she then engages in illicit intercourse again, flog her; and if she engages in illicit intercourse yet again, sell her, even if only for a rope (*ḍafīr*)." Ibn Shihāb said, "I do not know whether it was the third or fourth time." Yaḥyā said, "I heard Mālik say, '*Ḍafīr* means a rope.'"

2483. According to Mālik, Nāfiʿ reported from Ṣafiyya that a slave who was supervising the slaves belonging to the public treasury forced one of the handmaidens under his supervision to have intercourse with him. ʿUmar b. al-Khaṭṭāb had him flogged and exiled him, but he did not flog the handmaiden, because the slave had raped her.

2484. According to Mālik, Yaḥyā b. Saʿīd reported that Sulaymān b. Yasār informed him that ʿAbd Allāh b. ʿAyyāsh b. Abī Rabīʿa al-Makhzūmī said, "ʿUmar b. al-Khaṭṭāb ordered me and some other youths of the Quraysh to flog handmaidens who were the property of the public treasury fifty lashes each for illicit intercourse."

Chapter 4. What Has Come Down regarding a Woman Who Has Been Raped (*Mughtaṣaba*)

2485. Mālik said, "The rule in our view (*al-amr ʿindanā*) regarding an unmarried woman who is found to be pregnant and who says, 'I was raped,' or 'I was married,' is that her statement is not credited and she is subject to the mandatory punishment (*ḥadd*) for illicit intercourse, unless she has evidence proving her claimed marriage or proving that she was raped, such as evidence that she came to the authorities bleeding, if she was a virgin, or that she was crying out for help against her rapist when she was discovered, or something similarly public that would entail deliberately exposing herself to embarrassment. If she is unable to show any of these things, she is subject to the mandatory punishment for illicit intercourse, and none of her proffered excuses is credited."

2486. Mālik said, "A raped woman may not marry until three menstrual periods have passed following the rape to exclude the possibility of pregnancy. If she has doubts regarding the regularity of her period, she may not marry until she resolves her doubts with certainty."

Chapter 5. What Has Come Down regarding the Mandatory Punishment (*Ḥadd*) for Slander (*Qadhf*), Denial of Paternity, and Indirect Slander (*Taʿrīḍ*)

2487. According to Mālik, Abū al-Zinād said, "ʿUmar b. ʿAbd al-ʿAzīz flogged a slave eighty lashes for slander." Abū al-Zinād said, "I asked ʿAbd Allāh b. ʿĀmir b. Rabīʿa about that case, and he said, 'I was alive during the terms of ʿUmar b. al-Khaṭṭāb, ʿUthmān b. ʿAffān, and the rest of the caliphs, and I never saw any of them punish a slave for slander with more than forty lashes."

2488. According to Mālik, Ruzayq b. Ḥakīm reported that a man named Miṣbāḥ asked his son for help, but the son was slow to respond. When he finally showed up, his father yelled at him, saying, "You fornicator!" Ruzayq said, "The son brought him to me to complain about what he had said, but when I was about to flog the father for slander, the son said, 'If you do actually intend to flog him, I will confess to having committed illicit intercourse (*zinā*) in order to prevent the punishment from being carried out.' When he said that, I was confused about what to do, so I wrote to ʿUmar b. ʿAbd al-ʿAzīz, who was the governor at the time, asking for his opinion. ʿUmar wrote back, telling me to give effect to the son's pardon of the father. I also wrote to ʿUmar b. ʿAbd al-ʿAzīz, asking him, "What is your view regarding a man who is slandered, or a man whose parents are slandered and one or both of them are dead?" ʿUmar wrote to me in response, "If the son grants a pardon, his pardon is effective with respect to himself. But if his parents were slandered, and one or both of them are already dead, apply the punishment that is specified in God's Book, unless the son wishes to keep the matter hidden."

2489. Yaḥyā said, "I heard Mālik say, 'That is because the slandered man might fear that if the matter were made public, witnesses might come forward. If the circumstances are as I describe them, the son's pardon is effective.'"

2490. According to Mālik, Hishām b. ʿUrwa reported that his father said, regarding a man who has slandered a group of people, "He is to be punished for slander only once." Mālik said, "Even if they disperse, he is still to be punished only once."

2491. According to Mālik, Abū al-Rijāl Muḥammad b. ʿAbd al-Raḥmān b. Ḥāritha b. al-Nuʿmān al-Anṣārī of the Banū al-Najjār reported from his mother, ʿAmra bt. ʿAbd al-Raḥmān, that two men cursed each other during the time of ʿUmar b. al-Khaṭṭāb. One of them said to the other, "By God, at least my father is not a fornicator, nor is my mother."[968] ʿUmar b. al-Khaṭṭāb consulted others to get their view on whether such a statement was slanderous. One person said, "All he has done is praise his father and his mother," whereas others said, "Certainly his father and his mother had other characteristics for which they could have been praised. We believe that you should punish him for slander." ʿUmar then ordered the man to be flogged the mandatory punishment for slander, eighty lashes.

2492. Mālik said, "In our opinion, the mandatory punishment (*ḥadd*) for slander is applicable only when the defendant has denied the plaintiff's paternity (*nafy*), engaged in explicit slander (*qadhf*), or engaged in indirect slander (*taʿrīḍ*) by making a statement by which he intends to call into doubt the plaintiff's paternity or to slander the plaintiff. Whoever makes such a statement is subject to the mandatory punishment for slander."

2493. Mālik said, "The rule in our view (*al-amr ʿindanā*) is that when a man denies another man's paternity, he is subjected to the mandatory punishment for slander. Even if the mother of the slandered plaintiff is a handmaiden, the mandatory punishment nonetheless applies to the defendant."

Chapter 6. Actions That Do Not Result in the Application of a Mandatory Punishment (*Ḥadd*)

2494. Mālik said, "The best view that has been reported regarding a man who has intercourse with a handmaiden whom he owns in part is that the mandatory punishment for illicit intercourse does not apply to his actions, and any child that results is affiliated to him. The handmaiden, however, is subject to a mandatory appraisal to determine her fair market value, and he is required to give his co-owners the fair market value of their pro rata shares in the handmaiden, upon which he becomes her sole owner. The rule among us is in accordance with this (*ʿalā hādhā al-amr ʿindanā*)."

2495. Mālik said, regarding a man who hands over his handmaiden to another man and gives him permission to have intercourse with her, "If the one to whom she was given has intercourse with her, he becomes responsible for paying her fair market value as of the day he had intercourse with her, as determined by expert appraisal, whether or not she becomes pregnant as a result. The man is not subject to the mandatory punishment for illicit intercourse because her owner gave him permission to have intercourse

968 By implication, he is suggesting that his opponent's parents were fornicators.

with her. If she becomes pregnant as a result, however, the child is affiliated to him, not to her owner at the time."

2496. Mālik said, regarding a man who has intercourse with a handmaiden belonging to his son or daughter, "The mandatory punishment for illicit intercourse does not apply to him, but he becomes responsible for paying the fair market value of the handmaiden, as determined by expert appraisal, whether or not she becomes pregnant as a result."

2497. According to Mālik, Rabīʿa b. Abī ʿAbd al-Raḥmān reported that a man set out on a journey with a handmaiden belonging to his wife and had intercourse with her, angering his wife, who complained to ʿUmar b. al-Khaṭṭāb, who then asked the man about what had happened. He said, "My wife gave her to me as a gift." ʿUmar said, "Either give me evidence supporting your claim, or I will have stones rain down on you." Rabīʿa said, "The wife admitted that she had given him the handmaiden."

Book 43
The Book of Theft (*Sariqa*)

In the Name of God, the Merciful, the Compassionate

Chapter 1. Conduct That Necessitates Amputation of the Hand

2498. According to Mālik, Nāfiʿ reported from ʿAbd Allāh b. ʿUmar that the Messenger of God (pbuh) once amputated the hand of a thief who stole a shield whose price was three dirhams.

2499. According to Mālik, ʿAbd Allāh b. ʿAbd al-Raḥmān b. Abī Ḥusayn al-Makkī reported that the Messenger of God (pbuh) said, "Amputation is not appropriate for the theft of fruit still hanging on the tree or for that of an animal grazing in the mountains; however, if an animal is taken from its enclosure or fruit is taken from a secure compartment, and the fair market value of what is taken reaches the fair market value of a shield, amputation is applicable."

2500. According to Mālik, ʿAbd Allāh b. Abī Bakr reported from his father, from ʿAmra bt. ʿAbd al-Raḥmān, that during the term of ʿUthmān b. ʿAffān, a thief stole a lemon. ʿUthmān ordered that its fair market value be appraised. Its appraised value was three dirhams on the basis of the current exchange rate of twelve dirhams for a dinar. Accordingly, ʿUthmān ordered that the thief's hand be amputated.

2501. According to Mālik, Yaḥyā b. Saʿīd reported from ʿAmra bt. ʿAbd al-Raḥmān that ʿĀʾisha, the wife of the Prophet (pbuh), said, "I'm not quite so old as to have forgotten that amputation is applicable for the theft of any item whose fair market value is greater than or equal to a quarter of a dinar."

2502. According to Mālik, ʿAbd Allāh b. Abī Bakr b. Ḥazm reported that ʿAmra bt. ʿAbd al-Raḥmān said, "ʿĀʾisha, the wife of the Prophet (pbuh), set out for Mecca accompanied by two of her freedwomen (*mawlātān*) and a slave belonging to the sons of her nephew ʿAbd Allāh b. Abī Bakr al-Ṣiddīq.

She sent a cloak from Mecca with the freedwomen. The cloak was wrapped in a piece of green cloth that had been stitched closed. The slave took the bundle, unstitched it, and took out the cloak. He put some matted wool, or a fur, in its place and sewed the bundle up again. When the freedwomen arrived in Medina, they gave the bundle to its owners. When they opened it, they found only the hide, not the cloak. They asked the two women what had happened, and they in turn asked ʿĀʾisha, the wife of the Prophet (pbuh), or they wrote to her, accusing the slave of having taken the cloak. The slave was interrogated about what had happened, and he confessed. ʿĀʾisha, the wife of the Prophet (pbuh), therefore ordered that his hand be amputated, and so it was. ʿĀʾisha said, 'Amputation is applicable for the theft of any item whose fair market value is greater than or equal to a quarter of a dinar.'"

2503. Mālik said, "The view I prefer most is that amputation is obligatory only if the fair market value of the stolen item is three dirhams or more, regardless of whether silver's rate of exchange with gold is high or low. That is because the Messenger of God (pbuh) amputated the hand of a thief who stole a shield whose fair market value was three dirhams, and because ʿUthmān amputated the hand of a thief who stole a lemon whose price was three dirhams. Of all the views I have heard regarding this question, this is the one I prefer most."

Chapter 2. What Has Come Down regarding Amputation of the Hand of a Runaway Slave Who Steals

2504. According to Mālik, Nāfiʿ reported that a runaway slave belonging to ʿAbd Allāh b. ʿUmar stole something. After the slave returned, ʿAbd Allāh sent him to Saʿīd b. al-ʿĀṣī, who was the governor of Medina at the time, to have his hand amputated for the theft. But Saʿīd refused to amputate the slave's hand. He said, "The hand of a runaway slave who steals is not to be amputated." ʿAbd Allāh b. ʿUmar said to him, "Where in God's Book did you find this condition?" ʿAbd Allāh then ordered the slave's hand to be amputated, and so it was.

2505. According to Mālik, Ruzayq b. Ḥakīm informed him that he once arrested a runaway slave who had stolen. He said, "I was unsure as to the rule that applied to him, so I sent a letter to ʿUmar b. ʿAbd al-ʿAzīz, who was the governor of Medina at the time, asking him about the case and telling him that I had heard that the hand of a runaway slave is not to be amputated if he steals while he is a fugitive. ʿUmar wrote back contradicting what I had stated in my letter, saying, "You wrote to me saying that you have heard that when a runaway slave steals, his hand is not to be amputated. But God, Blessed and Sublime is He, says in His Book, 'As to the thief, male or female:

amputate their hands, an exemplary punishment from God for what they have done, and God is Powerful, Wise.'[969] If the fair market value of what he has stolen is greater than or equal to a quarter of a dinar, his hand is to be amputated."

2506. According to Mālik, it reached him that al-Qāsim b. Muḥammad, Sālim b. ʿAbd Allāh, and ʿUrwa b. al-Zubayr would say, "If a runaway slave steals something, and the item's fair market value necessitates amputation of the hand, amputation is applicable." Mālik said, "That rule, namely, that the hand of a runaway slave is amputated if the fair market value of the stolen item necessitates amputation, is a rule about which there is no dissent among us (*al-amr alladhī lā ikhtilāfa fīhi ʿindanā*)."

Chapter 3. The Impermissibility of Interceding on Behalf of a Thief If the Case Has Reached the Ruler (*Sulṭān*)

2507. According to Mālik, Ibn Shihāb reported from Ṣafwān b. ʿAbd Allāh b. Ṣafwān that someone told Ṣafwān b. Umayya, "Whoever fails to emigrate to Medina is lost." Therefore, Ṣafwān set out for Medina. When he arrived there, he went to sleep in the mosque, using his cloak as a pillow. While he was asleep, a thief came and tried to steal his cloak from under him, but Ṣafwān grabbed the thief and took him to the Messenger of God (pbuh). The Messenger of God (pbuh) then ordered that the thief's hand be amputated, but Ṣafwān said, "This is not what I wanted, Messenger of God. I hereby give it to him freely in charity (*ṣadaqa*)." The Messenger of God (pbuh) said, "Why didn't you do that before you brought him to me?"

2508. According to Mālik, Rabīʿa b. Abī ʿAbd al-Raḥmān reported that al-Zubayr b. al-ʿAwwām once encountered a man who had caught a thief and intended to take him to the ruler. Al-Zubayr pleaded with the man to let him go, but the man said, "No, not until I take him to the ruler." Al-Zubayr said, "Once you take him to the ruler, it will be too late to plead for him. In that circumstance God curses the intercessor and the one who accepts the plea for intercession."

Chapter 4. Miscellaneous Matters Related to Amputation of the Hand

2509. According to Mālik, ʿAbd al-Raḥmān b. al-Qāsim reported from his father that a man from Yemen who had lost a hand and a foot to amputation came to Medina and presented himself to Abū Bakr al-Ṣiddīq. He complained to him that the governor of Yemen had unjustly punished him for theft. The man would observe the Night Prayer (*ṣalāt al-layl*), which led Abū Bakr

969 *Al-Māʾida*, 5:38.

to say, "By your father's life, you do not pass your nights in the manner of a thief." Then a necklace of Asmāʾ bt. ʿUmays, the wife of Abū Bakr, went missing. The man accompanied the group of people looking for the missing necklace, saying, "O God! May Your punishment fall on whoever violated the sanctity of the home of these good people." They found the missing necklace with a goldsmith, who claimed that a one-handed, one-legged man had brought it to him. The man confessed to the theft, or there were witnesses who testified against him. Consequently, Abū Bakr ordered that his left hand be amputated. Abū Bakr then said, "By God, his invocation of God against himself is more damning in my my eyes than his theft."

2510. Yaḥyā said that Mālik said, "The rule in our view (*al-amr ʿindanā*) regarding a thief who steals on multiple occasions before being arrested and brought to court is that the punishment of amputation of the hand is applied to him only once for all the prior instances of theft, provided that the mandatory punishment (*ḥadd*) for theft has not been previously applied to him. If it has been previously applied to him, however, and he then steals property that necessitates amputation, he is subject to amputation a second time."

2511. According to Mālik, Abū al-Zinād informed him that a governor of ʿUmar b. ʿAbd al-ʿAzīz arrested some people for the crime of brigandage (*ḥirāba*). However, the defendants had not killed anyone. The governor was undecided between amputating their hands or putting them to death for their crime, so he sent ʿUmar b. ʿAbd al-ʿAzīz a letter about the case. ʿUmar replied, "It is better to apply the lesser punishment."

2512. Mālik said, "The rule in our view regarding a person who steals the property of others, if the stolen property was securely stored in the marketplace, its owner had secured it in an appropriate, secure compartment, and its fair market value equals the minimum amount that necessitates amputation of the hand, is that whoever steals any property like this from a secure compartment (*ḥirz*) is subject to amputation for the crime, whether or not the owner of the goods was present with his property when it was stolen, and whether it was stolen by night or by day."

2513. Mālik said, regarding a scenario in which a person steals something in an amount that necessitates amputation, and then the stolen item is found in his possession and returned to its true owner, "His hand is still subject to amputation. If someone were to ask, 'How can his hand be amputated given that the stolen property has been taken from him and returned to its true owner?' it is because he is no different from someone who has drunk wine and on whose breath one can still smell the wine, even if he is no longer drunk. Such a person is subject to the mandatory punishment of flogging (*ḥadd*). The mandatory punishment for consuming alcoholic beverages is applied simply for drinking them, even if one does not become inebriated as a result. The drinker is punished because he drank such a drink for its intoxicating qualities. The same reasoning applies to support amputating the hand of a thief who has had the stolen item taken from him and restored to its true owner and who has not had the opportunity to benefit from it. Indeed, it was certainly the case that when he stole it, he stole it with the purpose of permanently taking it away from its owner."

2514. Mālik said, regarding a gang that breaks into a home and robs it, leaving with a bundle, a chest, a piece of wood, a basket, or something similar and carrying off the stolen loot together, "If they together remove the stolen items from where they were stored and carry them off, and the fair market value of what they make off with is equal to the minimum amount that necessitates amputation, namely, three dirhams or more, each one of them is subject to having his hand amputated. On the other hand, if each one of them individually makes off with some stolen property, only those who leave with stolen property whose fair market value is three dirhams or more are subject to amputation of the hand. However, any one of them who makes off with stolen property worth less than three dirhams is not subject to amputation."

2515. Mālik said, "The rule in our view is that if a man's house is locked up and he lives alone in it, a thief who steals from him is not subject to amputation until he exits the house completely with the stolen item. That is because in this case, the house itself is the item's secure compartment. Accordingly, the act of theft is not complete until the thief exits the house with the stolen item. If, on the other hand, someone else also lives in the house, and each one of them locks the door to his own room, each room constitutes a separate secure compartment for the property of each resident. Therefore, whoever steals anything necessitating amputation from a room in such a house and takes it into the common areas of the house has removed the stolen item completely from its secure compartment, thereby rendering the act of theft complete. He is thus liable for amputation of the hand."

2516. Mālik said, "The rule in our view regarding a slave who steals property belonging to his master is that even if the slave neither is a personal servant of the master nor has been entrusted with entry to the master's house but rather enters it surreptitiously and steals property from his master in an amount necessitating amputation, he is not subject to amputation."

2517. Mālik said, regarding a slave who neither is a personal servant of his master nor has been entrusted with entry to the master's house but rather enters it surreptitiously and steals property belonging to the master's wife in an amount necessitating amputation, "His hand is subject to amputation. The same rule applies to the wife's handmaiden: If she is neither her personal servant nor her husband's, nor has she been entrusted with entry to the house but rather enters her mistress's home surreptitiously and steals property belonging to her mistress in an amount necessitating amputation, her hand is not subject to amputation. But if the wife's handmaiden neither is her personal servant nor has been entrusted with entry to the house but then enters the home surreptitiously and steals property belonging to her mistress's husband in an amount necessitating amputation, her hand is subject to amputation. The same rule applies to a husband who steals property belonging to his wife, or a wife who steals property from her husband, in each case in an amount necessitating amputation: if the item stolen from the spouse's property was stored in a room other than their common residence or was secured in some place other than their common residence, and its amount necessitates amputation, the spouse who steals it is subject to amputation."

2518. Mālik said, regarding a minor slave-boy or a foreigner incapable of speaking Arabic, "If a stranger kidnaps such a person from his home, the kidnapper is subject to amputation. If, however, the person is kidnapped while outside his home, the kidnapper is not subject to amputation. In this case, the person is equivalent to animals grazing in the mountains and fruit hanging in the trees."[970]

2519. Mālik said, "The rule in our view regarding a graverobber is that if the fair market value of what he removes from the grave necessitates amputation, he is subject to amputation. That is because the grave is a storage facility for what is contained inside it, just as homes are secure compartments for what is contained in them. He is not subject to amputation, however, until he removes the stolen item from the grave."

970 The penalty of amputation for theft does not apply if the property's owner has not secured his possession through appropriate steps, such as placing the property under lock and key. In the case of minor slaves who cannot fend for themselves, this condition is satisfied only if their owner keeps them inside his home. If he allows them to wander about unprotected in public, and someone kidnaps them, the penalty for theft does not apply because the master has failed to secure his possession of his property. Kidnapping in such a case is still a crime, but it is not punished through amputation of the thief's hand.

Chapter 5. What Does Not Merit Amputation

2520. According to Mālik, Yaḥyā b. Saʿīd reported from Muḥammad b. Yaḥyā b. Ḥabbān that a slave stole a date palm sapling from a man's orchard and planted it in his master's. The sapling's owner went out looking for it and found it in the other man's orchard. He had the slave brought before Marwān b. al-Ḥakam and accused him of theft. Marwān put the slave in jail and had resolved to amputate the slave's hand, when the slave's master rushed off to consult Rāfiʿ b. Khadīj and obtain his opinion. Rāfiʿ informed him that he heard the Messenger of God (pbuh) say, "There is no amputation for taking either fruit or palm pith." The man said, "Marwān b. al-Ḥakam has arrested a slave of mine and wants to amputate his hand. I beseech you to come with me and inform him of what you heard from the Messenger of God (pbuh)." Rāfiʿ agreed and went with him to Marwān. When he arrived, he said, "Did you arrest a slave of this man?" Marwān replied, "Yes." Rāfiʿ then said, "What do you plan to do with him?" Marwān said, "I intend to amputate his hand as punishment for his theft." Rāfiʿ then said, "I heard the Messenger of God (pbuh) say, "There is no amputation for taking either fruit or palm pith." Upon hearing this, Marwān ordered the slave to be released, and so he was.

2521. According to Mālik, Ibn Shihāb reported from al-Sāʾib b. Yazīd that ʿAbd Allāh b. ʿAmr b. al-Ḥadramī took a slave of his to ʿUmar b. al-Khaṭṭāb and said to him, "Amputate the hand of this slave of mine, for he is a thief." ʿUmar said to him, "What did he steal?" He said, "He stole a mirror belonging to my wife, the value of which is sixty dirhams." ʿUmar said, "Release him. He is not subject to amputation. He is nothing other than a servant of yours who took some of your property."

2522. According to Mālik, Ibn Shihāb reported that a man who had embezzled some goods was brought before Marwān b. al-Ḥakam, who resolved to amputate his hand. But first he summoned Zayd b. Thābit to ask him for his opinion about the proper punishment. Zayd said to him, "Amputation does not apply for embezzlement."

2523. According to Mālik, Yaḥyā b. Saʿīd said, "Abū Bakr b. Muḥammad b. ʿAmr b. Ḥazm informed me that he once had a Nabatean man arrested for stealing some iron rings. He had the man imprisoned until such time as the Nabatean's hand could be amputated. ʿAmra bt. ʿAbd al-Raḥmān got wind of this, so she dispatched her freedwoman (*mawlāt*), Umayya, with a message for him. Abū Bakr said, 'She arrived while I was sitting with a group of people and said, "Your maternal aunt, ʿAmra, says to you, 'My dear nephew, it has been brought to my attention that you have had a Nabatean man arrested for stealing a trifle, and now you seek to have his hand amputated.'" I said,

"Yes, indeed!" Umayya said, "'Amra says to you, 'Amputation is applicable only for the theft of something whose fair market value is greater than or equal to a quarter of a dinar.'" Upon hearing this, I released the Nabatean.'"

2524. Mālik said, "The agreed-upon rule among us (*al-amr al-mujtama' 'alayhi 'indanā*) regarding slaves who confess to theft is that if a slave confesses to an act that necessitates the mandatory punishment for theft (*ḥadd*) or some other corporal punishment, his confession is effective. There is no suspicion that he would falsely subject himself to criminal punishment."

2525. Mālik said, "As for a slave who confesses to an act that results in his master's bearing monetary liability, such a confession is not effective against the master."

2526. Mālik said, "Neither a laborer nor a servant who is in the service of others and steals from his employers is subject to amputation. That is because such a person's situation is different from that of a thief. He is in the position of someone who has betrayed a trust, but a person is not subject to amputation for breach of trust."

2527. Mālik said, regarding someone who borrows a thing but then denies it, "He is not subject to amputation. Rather, he is is similar to a man to whom another man has extended credit, and then the debtor denies owing him that debt. The debtor, in such a situation, is not subject to amputation."

2528. Mālik said, "The agreed-upon rule among us regarding a thief who is discovered in a home, having gathered up property belonging to the homeowner but not having yet made off with it, is that his hand is not subject to amputation. Rather, his case is like that of a man who is found grasping a bottle of wine, intending to drink it, but who has yet to do so, and who is consequently not subject to the mandatory punishment for wine-drinking. It is also similar to the case of a man who approaches a woman, desiring to have illicit intercourse with her but not doing so, or not going so far as that with her. He, too, is not subject to the mandatory punishment for illicit intercourse."

2529. Mālik said, "The agreed-upon rule among us is that amputation does not apply for embezzlement, whether or not the fair market value of what has been taken reaches the amount necessitating amputation in the case of a theft."

The Book of Lapidation (*Rajm*) and Mandatory Punishments (*Ḥudūd*) Has Been Completed, with Praise to God As He Is Entitled to Be Praised.

In the Name of God, the Merciful, the Compassionate

May God Grace Muḥammad and His Family
and Grant Them Perfect Tranquility.

Book 44

The Book of Beverages

Chapter 1. The Mandatory Punishment (*Ḥadd*) for Wine-Drinking (*Khamr*)

2530. According to Mālik, Ibn Shihāb reported that al-Sā'ib b. Yazīd informed him that one day, ʿUmar b. al-Khaṭṭāb came out and declared, "I caught so-and-so with the smell of wine on his breath, but he claims that what he drank was mulled grape juice. I am investigating what he drank. If it was something that intoxicates, I will have him flogged." Once he confirmed that it was intoxicating, Umar had the man flogged the mandatory punishment for wine-drinking.

2531. According to Mālik, Thawr b. Zayd al-Dīlī reported that ʿUmar b. al-Khaṭṭāb sought the community's advice regarding the punishment for wine-drinking. ʿAlī b. Abī Ṭālib told him, "In our opinion, we should flog a person who drinks wine eighty times. When a man drinks, he becomes intoxicated, and when he becomes intoxicated, he rants, and when he rants, he slanders,"[971] or something similar to that. ʿUmar then imposed eighty lashes as the mandatory punishment for wine-drinking.

2532. According to Mālik, Ibn Shihāb reported that he was asked about the mandatory punishment applicable to a slave who drinks wine. He said, "It has reached me that he receives half of the punishment of a free man (and that ʿUmar b. al-Khaṭṭāb, ʿUthmān b. ʿAffān, and ʿAbd Allāh b. ʿUmar

---

971 ʿAlī's reasoning analogizes wine-drinking to slander on the theory that intoxication leads to the occurrence of slander. Because the mandatory punishment for slander is eighty lashes, he advised that the same penalty be applied for wine-drinking. In this report, ʿUmar accepts his advice.

applied to their slaves half of the punishment due to a free man if they drank wine).[972]

2533. According to Mālik, Yaḥyā b. Saʿīd reported that he heard Saʿīd b. al-Musayyab say, "God loves for everything to be pardoned, as long as it is not a mandatory punishment."

2534. Mālik said, "The long-established ordinance among us (*al-sunna ʿindanā*) is that whoever drinks an intoxicating beverage, even if he does not become intoxicated, is subject to the mandatory punishment for wine-drinking."

Chapter 2. Containers That Should Not Be Used for Steeping Dried Fruit

2535. According to Mālik, Nāfiʿ reported from ʿAbd Allāh b. ʿUmar that the Messenger of God (pbuh) once addressed the people during one of his forays. ʿAbd Allāh b. ʿUmar said, "I approached him, but he turned away before I reached him. I inquired about what he had said, and I was told, 'He prohibited steeping dried fruit in a gourd or a jug smeared with pitch.'"

2536. According to Mālik, al-ʿAlāʾ b. ʿAbd al-Raḥmān b. Yaʿqūb reported from his father, from Abū Hurayra, that the Messenger of God (pbuh) prohibited steeping dried fruit in a gourd or a jug smeared with pitch.

Chapter 3. Combinations of Fruit That Are Not to Be Steeped Together

2537. According to Mālik, Zayd b. Aslam reported from ʿAṭāʾ b. Yasār that the Messenger of God (pbuh) prohibited steeping unripened dates together with fresh ones, and dried dates together with raisins.

2538. According to Mālik, a source that he deemed reliable reported from Bukayr b. ʿAbd Allāh b. al-Ashajj, from ʿAbd al-Raḥmān b. al-Ḥubāb al-Anṣārī, from Abū Qatāda al-Anṣārī, that the Messenger of God (pbuh) prohibited drinking water in which dried dates and raisins had been steeped together, and water in which brightly colored dates and fresh dates had been steeped together. Mālik said, "That prohibition is the rule that the people of knowledge in our town have always followed (*al-amr alladhī lam yazal ʿalayhi ahl al-ʿilm bi-baladinā*). That is because the Messenger of God (pbuh) prohibited it."

---

972 The editors of the RME inserted the parenthetical language on the basis of a marginal note in the manuscript.

Chapter 4. What Has Come Down regarding the Prohibition of Wine (*Khamr*)

2539. According to Mālik, Ibn Shihāb reported from Abū Salama b. ʿAbd al-Raḥmān that ʿĀʾisha, the wife of the Prophet (pbuh), said, "The Messenger of God (pbuh) was asked about mead (*bitʿ*), and he said, 'Every beverage that intoxicates is prohibited.'"

2540. According to Mālik, Zayd b. Aslam reported from ʿAṭāʾ b. Yasār that the Messenger of God (pbuh) was asked about a beverage called *ghubayrāʾ*. He said, "There is no good in it," and prohibited it. Mālik said, "I asked Zayd b. Aslam, 'What is *ghubayrāʾ*?' He said, 'It is *usukruka*.'"[973]

2541. According to Mālik, Nāfiʿ reported from ʿAbd Allāh b. ʿUmar that the Messenger of God (pbuh) said, "Whoever drinks wine in this life and does not turn away from it in repentance before his death will be deprived of it in the Hereafter."

Chapter 5. Miscellaneous Reports regarding the Prohibition of Wine-Drinking

2542. According to Mālik, Zayd b. Aslam reported from Ibn Waʿla al-Miṣrī that he asked ʿAbd Allāh b. ʿAbbās about juice pressed from grapes. ʿAbd Allāh b. ʿAbbās said, "A man once gave the Messenger of God (pbuh) a small skin of wine. The Messenger of God (pbuh) turned to him and said, 'Don't you know that God has prohibited it?' The man said, 'No,' but the man sitting next to him whispered something to him. The Messenger of God (pbuh) asked him, 'What did you whisper to him?' The man replied, 'I advised him to sell it.' The Messenger of God (pbuh) said, 'The One who prohibited drinking it also prohibited selling it.' The man then opened the two skins and emptied their contents out."

2543. According to Mālik, Isḥāq b. ʿAbd Allāh b. Abī Ṭalḥa reported that Anas b. Mālik said, "I used to serve to Abū ʿUbayda b. al-Jarrāḥ, Abū Ṭalḥa al-Anṣārī, and Ubayy b. Kaʿb an intoxicating beverage that was produced from a combination of crushed mature dates and dried dates. One day, a man came to them and said, 'Wine-drinking has been prohibited.' Abū Ṭalḥa said, 'Anas, go break these jars.' I stood up and grabbed a mortar of ours and struck them with its base until they broke into pieces."

2544. According to Mālik, Dāwūd b. al-Ḥuṣayn reported that Wāqid b. ʿAmr b. Saʿd b. Muʿādh informed him from Maḥmūd b. Labīd al-Anṣārī that when ʿUmar b. al-Khaṭṭāb went to the Levant, the people there complained to him

973 An intoxicating beverage made by steeping either rice or corn in water.

about the epidemics endemic to that country and its unbearable conditions. They said, "The only thing that preserves our health is this intoxicating beverage." ʿUmar said, "Drink honey instead." They said, "Honey does us no good." A man of that region said, "Would you object if we made a non-intoxicating version of this beverage?" He said, "No." So they boiled the beverage until two-thirds of its liquid had evaporated, leaving only one-third. They then brought that to ʿUmar, who dipped his finger in it, then lifted up his hand and fully extended his fingers. ʿUmar said, "This mulled juice—it is like the tar that is applied to a camel's scabies!" ʿUmar allowed them to drink it. ʿUbāda b. al-Ṣāmit said, "By God, you have rendered this intoxicant lawful!" ʿUmar replied, "No, indeed, by God! O God! I will never permit them anything that You have prohibited them; nor will I prohibit them anything that You have made licit for them."[974]

2545. According to Mālik, Nāfiʿ reported from ʿAbd Allāh b. ʿUmar that some men from Iraq said to him, "Abū ʿAbd al-Raḥmān, we purchase freshly harvested dates and freshly picked grapes, and then we press them to produce wine to sell." ʿAbd Allāh said, "I call on God and His Angels and whoever hears me, be they jinn or human, to witness that I prohibit you from selling it, purchasing it, pressing it, drinking it, or serving it to others. It is an abomination, Satan's handiwork."

The Book of Beverages Has Been Completed, with Praise to God, the Lord of the Worlds.

974 By boiling the liquid until it became concentrated, they caused all the alcohol to evaporate, so the beverage was no longer an intoxicant.

In the Name of God, the Merciful, the Compassionate

Book 45

The Book of Miscellaneous Matters

Chapter 1. Supplication (*Duʿāʾ*) for Medina and Its People

2546. According to Mālik, Isḥāq b. ʿAbd Allāh b. Abī Ṭalḥa al-Anṣārī reported from Anas b. Mālik that the Messenger of God (pbuh) said, "O God! Bless them in their dealings, and grant them prosperity in everything they weigh and measure." He meant the people of Medina.

2547. According to Mālik, Suhayl b. Abī Ṣāliḥ reported from his father that Abū Hurayra said, "When the first fruit of the season had been harvested, the people would bring it to the Messenger of God (pbuh). He would then say, 'O God! Bless us in our fruit, in our city, in our dealings, and in everything we weigh and measure. O God! Abraham is Your servant, Your intimate companion (*khalīl*), and Your Prophet. I, too, am Your servant and Your Prophet. He supplicated You for the sake of Mecca, and I hereby supplicate You for the sake of Medina, with the very same supplication that he made for the sake of Mecca, twice over.' He would then call the youngest child he saw nearby and give him that fruit to eat."

Chapter 2. What Has Come Down regarding Residing in Medina and Departing from It

2548. According to Mālik, Qaṭan b. Wahb b. ʿUmayr b. al-Ajdaʿ reported that Yuḥannas, the freedman (*mawlā*) of al-Zubayr b. al-ʿAwwām, informed him that he had been sitting with ʿAbd Allāh b. ʿUmar during the time of the strife that broke out between Yazīd b. Muʿāwiya and ʿAbd Allāh b. al-Zubayr.[975] A freedwoman (*mawlāt*) of ʿAbd Allāh's came and greeted him and said, "Abū ʿAbd al-Raḥmān, I wish to leave Medina. Times are tough for us." ʿAbd Allāh said to her, "Stay put, you fool! I heard the Messenger of God (pbuh) say,

975 Zurqānī, *Sharḥ al-Zurqānī*, 4:346.

'Anyone who endures Medina's trials and tribulations shall have me as his witness or intercessor on the Day of Judgment.'"

2549. According to Mālik, Muḥammad b. al-Munkadir reported from Jābir b. ʿAbd Allāh that a bedouin man pledged his loyalty to the Messenger of God (pbuh), promising to lead his life in accordance with the rules of Islam. The man was then overcome by a fever in Medina, so he went to the Messenger of God (pbuh) and said to him, "Messenger of God, release me from my pledge." The Messenger of God (pbuh) refused. The man then went to him again, and said, "Messenger of God, release me from my pledge." The Messenger of God (pbuh) again refused. The man came yet again and said, "Release me from my pledge," but the Prophet (pbuh) again refused. The bedouin then left Medina without the permission of the Prophet (pbuh). The Messenger of God (pbuh) said, "Medina is like a blacksmith's bellows; it drives out the dross and lusters the good."

2550. According to Mālik, Yaḥyā b. Saʿīd said that he heard Abū al-Ḥubāb Saʿīd b. Yasār say that he heard Abū Hurayra say, "The Messenger of God (pbuh) said, 'I was ordered to migrate to a town that will devour all other towns. They call it Yathrib,[976] and it is Medina: it banishes the wicked, just as the blacksmith's bellows drives out the iron's dross.'"

2551. According to Mālik, Hishām b. ʿUrwa reported from his father that the Messenger of God (pbuh) said, "If anyone leaves Medina out of spite for it, God replaces him with someone better."

2552. According to Mālik, Hishām b. ʿUrwa reported from his father, from ʿAbd Allāh b. al-Zubayr, that Sufyān b. Abī Zuhayr said, "I heard the Messenger of God (pbuh) say, 'Soon Yemen will be conquered, and people will rush to take up residence there, moving with their families and with whoever chooses to follow them there, even though Medina would have been better for them, if only they understood. Soon the Levant will be conquered, and people will rush to take up residence there, moving with their families and with whoever chooses to follow them there, even though Medina would have been better for them, if only they understood. Soon Iraq will be conquered, and people will rush to take up residence there, moving with their families and with whoever chooses to follow them there, even though Medina would have been better for them, if only they understood.'"

2553. According to Mālik, Ibn Ḥimās reported from his uncle, from Abū Hurayra, that the Messenger of God (pbuh) said, "Medina shall persist in its present beautiful condition until a day comes when it is so decrepit that

976 Yathrib was the pre-Islamic name of Medina before the immigration of the Prophet (pbuh).

a dog or a wolf is left to urinate on a pillar of the mosque or on its pulpit." They said, "Messenger of God, to whom will its fruit belong at that time?" He replied, "To foraging animals—birds and predators."

2554. According to Mālik, it reached him that when ʿUmar b. ʿAbd al-ʿAzīz left Medina for Damascus when he became caliph, he turned back to look at Medina and wept. Then he said, "Muzāḥim![977] Do you share my fear that we might be among those whom Medina has expelled?"

Chapter 3. What Has Come Down regarding Declaring Medina to Be a Sanctuary

2555. According to Mālik, ʿAmr, the freedman (*mawlā*) of al-Muṭṭalib, reported from Anas b. Mālik that when Mount Uḥud came into the view of the Messenger of God (pbuh), he said, "This is a mountain that loves us, and one we love in return. O God! Abraham declared Mecca to be a sanctuary. I hereby declare all that lies between Medina's two lava fields a sanctuary."

2556. According to Mālik, Ibn Shihāb reported from Saʿīd b. al-Musayyab that Abū Hurayra would say, "If I were to see gazelles in Medina grazing, I would not even dare to frighten them. The Messenger of God (pbuh) said, 'Whatever is between Medina's two lava fields is sacrosanct.'"

2557. According to Mālik, Yūnus b. Yūsuf reported from ʿAṭāʾ b. Yasār, from Abū Ayyūb al-Anṣārī, that he once ran into some boys who had driven a fox into a corner, so he drove them away from the fox. Mālik said, "All that I know about this incident is that he said, 'Is such a thing done in the sanctuary of the Messenger of God (pbuh)?'"

2558. According to Mālik, a man said, "Zayd b. Thābit ran into me while I was at al-Aswāf,[978] where I had captured a shrike. He removed it from my hands and set it free."

Chapter 4. What Has Come Down regarding the Medinese Fever

2559. According to Mālik, Hishām b. ʿUrwa reported from his father that ʿĀʾisha, the Mother of the Believers, said, "When the Messenger of God (pbuh) came to Medina, Abū Bakr and Bilāl fell ill with fever. I visited each of them and said, 'Dearest father, how are you feeling?' and, 'Bilāl, how are you feeling?' When Abū Bakr came down with a fever, he would recite the following couplet:

---

977 Muzāḥim was a freedman of ʿUmar b. ʿAbd al-ʿAzīz. Zurqānī, *Sharḥ al-Zurqānī*, 4:356.

978 A place near al-Baqīʿ, Medina's cemetery, which lies on the outskirts of the town.

Every man awakes content in the morning, in the pleasant company
of his people,
But death is nearer to him than his sandal's strap.

Whenever Bilāl recovered from a fever, he would raise his voice and say in a plaintive tone:

Would that I knew whether I will spend another night in Mecca's
valley,
With its sweet-smelling grasses around me!
Will I one day again quench my thirst from the waters of Majanna?
Will the mountains of Shāma and Ṭafīl ever again appear before me?[979]

I then went to the Messenger of God (pbuh) and informed him of their condition and their longing for Mecca. He said, 'O God! Make Medina beloved to us, just as Mecca is, or even more so. Make it a place of good health for us, bless us in our dealings and in everything we weigh and measure, and banish its fever to al-Juḥfa.'"[980]

2560. Mālik said, "Yaḥyā b. Saʿīd told me that ʿĀ'isha, the wife of the Prophet (pbuh), said that ʿĀmir b. Fuhayra would recite:

I saw death up close before tasting it;
The coward's death comes and he is cowering with fear."

2561. According to Mālik, Nuʿaym b. ʿAbd Allāh al-Mujmir reported that Abū Hurayra said, "The Messenger of God (pbuh) said, 'Angels guard the gates of Medina; neither the plague nor the Antichrist will enter it.'"

Chapter 5. What Has Come Down regarding the Jews

2562. According to Mālik, Ismāʿīl b. Abī Ḥakīm reported that he heard ʿUmar b. ʿAbd al-ʿAzīz say, "One of the last things that the Messenger of God (pbuh) said was, 'God strike the Jews and the Christians! They prayed to the graves of their prophets. Two religions shall not remain in Arab lands.'"

2563. According to Mālik, Ibn Shihāb reported that the Messenger of God (pbuh) said, "Two religions will not live side by side in the Arabian Peninsula." Mālik said, "Ibn Shihāb said, "Umar b. al-Khaṭṭāb investigated this report diligently until he was absolutely certain that the Messenger of God (pbuh) had said it. After becoming satisified that the Prophet (pbuh) had indeed made this statement, ʿUmar ordered the Jews of Khaybar to

979 Majinna is a marketplace a few *mīls* outside of Mecca; Shāma and Ṭafīl are two mountains about thirty *mīls* outside of Mecca. Zurqānī, *Sharḥ al-Zurqānī*, 4:362.

980 A village on the caravan route between Mecca and Medina.

leave. He also ordered the Jews of Najrān and Fadak to leave. When the Jews of Khaybar left, they were not entitled to any of the fruit or the land. As for the Jews of Fadak, they were entitled to half of the fruit and half of the land, because the Messenger of God (pbuh) made peace with them on those terms. Accordingly, ʿUmar appraised the fair market value of half the fruit and half the land in terms of gold, silver, camels, ropes, and saddlebags. He gave them the fair market value of all of that, and then he ordered them to leave.'"

Chapter 6. Miscellaneous Reports regarding What Has Come Down about Medina

2564. According to Mālik, Hishām b. ʿUrwa reported from his father that when Mount Uḥud came into the view of the Messenger of God (pbuh), he said, "This is a mountain that loves us, and one we love in return."

2565. According to Mālik, Yaḥyā b. Saʿīd reported from ʿAbd al-Raḥmān b. al-Qāsim that Aslam, the freedman (*mawlā*) of ʿUmar b. al-Khaṭṭāb, informed him that he once visited ʿAbd Allāh b. ʿAyyāsh al-Makhzūmī, who was en route to Mecca. He noticed that ʿAbd Allāh had with him some water in which dried fruit had been steeped (*nabīdh*). Aslam said to him, "ʿUmar b. al-Khaṭṭāb loves this beverage." ʿAbd Allāh then poured a draught of it into a large goblet and gave it to ʿUmar. ʿUmar raised it to his mouth and took a sip. He then lifted his head up and said, "What a great drink!" He drank some more and then passed it to a man on his right. When ʿAbd Allāh turned away to leave, ʿUmar called him over and said, "Are you the one who claims that Mecca is better than Medina?" ʿAbd Allāh said, "I merely said, 'It is God's sacred precinct (*ḥaram*), His sanctuary, and the place of His House.'" ʿUmar said, "I have no objections to what you have said about the House of God, or His sacred precinct." ʿUmar then asked him again, "But are you the one who said that Mecca is better than Medina?" ʿAbd Allāh again said, "I merely said, 'It is God's sacred precinct, His sanctuary, and the place of His House.'" ʿUmar then said again, "I have no objections to what you have said about the House of God, or His sacred precinct," and he left.

Chapter 7. What Has Come Down regarding the Plague (*Ṭāʿūn*)

2566. According to Mālik, Ibn Shihāb reported from ʿAbd al-Ḥamīd b. ʿAbd al-Raḥmān b. Zayd b. al-Khaṭṭāb, from ʿAbd Allāh b. ʿAbd Allāh b. al-Ḥārith b. Nawfal, from ʿAbd Allāh b. ʿAbbās, that ʿUmar b. al-Khaṭṭāb once set out for the Levant. When he reached Sargh,[981] he met the commanding officers of his armies, Abū ʿUbayda b. al-Jarrāḥ and his fellow officers. They informed him of an epidemic that had struck the Levant. Ibn ʿAbbās said, "ʿUmar b. al-Khaṭṭāb said, 'Summon the earliest Emigrants (*muhājirūn*) to meet with me.' He summoned them so he could hear their advice, after informing them that an epidemic had struck the Levant. They disagreed among themselves about what to do. Some of them said, 'You set out to achieve a goal, and we do not believe that you should abandon it.' Others said, 'The rest of the army and the Companions of the Messenger of God (pbuh) are in your care. We do not think it right that you should plunge them into the midst of an epidemic.' ʿUmar said, 'Leave me!' He then said, 'Summon the Medinese (*anṣār*) to meet with me.' He summoned them so he could hear their advice, but they reacted in the same way as the Emigrants had. They disagreed among themselves, just as the Emigrants had done. ʿUmar said, 'Leave me.' He then said, 'Summon whoever is present here of the senior Qurayshī statesmen of the Emigrants, those who were present at Mecca's surrender.' He summoned them, and they were unanimous. They said, 'We think you should retreat and not plunge the army into the midst of an epidemic.' ʿUmar then summoned all the men and said, 'I shall certainly be departing in the morning, and so should you.' Abū ʿUbayda retorted, 'Are you fleeing from God's decree?' ʿUmar replied, 'It is not fitting that someone like you should say something like this, Abū ʿUbayda! Yes, indeed, we are fleeing from God's decree, but to nothing other than God's decree. Is it not the case that if you had a herd of camels and brought them to a valley with two slopes, one fertile and the other barren, and grazed them in the fertile one, you would be doing so in accordance with God's decree? Or if you pastured them on the barren slope instead, wouldn't you also have done that in accordance with God's decree?' ʿAbd al-Raḥmān b. ʿAwf, who had absented himself during this debate to attend to a personal matter, said, 'I know a teaching of the Prophet (pbuh) that is relevant to this matter. I heard him say, "If you hear that the plague has struck a land, do not go there. But if it strikes a land where you are already present, stay and do not flee."' So ʿUmar praised God and left."

2567. According to Mālik, Muḥammad b. al-Munkadir and Sālim b. Abī al-Naḍr, the freedman (*mawlā*) of ʿUmar b. ʿUbayd Allāh, reported from ʿĀmir b. Saʿd b. Abī Waqqāṣ that ʿĀmir heard his father, Saʿd, ask Usāma b. Zayd, "Did you ever hear the Messenger of God (pbuh) speak about the plague?" Usāma said, "The Messenger of God (pbuh) said, 'The plague is an

---

981 Sargh is a village in the Tabūk valley on the way to the Levant from Medina. Bājī, *al-Muntaqā*, 7:198.

affliction that was sent down on a group of Israelites, or some other group before them. If you hear of it striking a land, do not go there. If it strikes a land where you are already present, however, stay and do not flee.'"

2568. According to Mālik, Ibn Shihāb reported from ʿAbd Allāh b. ʿĀmir b. Rabīʿa that ʿUmar b. al-Khaṭṭāb set out for the Levant, and when he reached Sargh, he heard that an epidemic had struck the Levant. ʿAbd al-Raḥmān b. ʿAwf informed him that the Messenger of God (pbuh) said, "If you hear of an outbreak in a land in which you are already present, stay and do not flee." ʿUmar b. al-Khaṭṭāb retreated from Sargh.

2569. According to Mālik, Ibn Shihāb reported from Sālim b. ʿAbd Allāh that ʿUmar b. al-Khaṭṭāb decided to retreat on the basis of the report of ʿAbd al-Raḥmān b. ʿAwf.

2570. Mālik said, "It reached me that ʿUmar b. al-Khaṭṭāb said, 'I would rather have a single house in Rukba[982] than ten houses in the Levant.'" Mālik said, "He is referring to the assuredness of long life in the Hijaz relative to the precariousness of life in the Levant on account of the severity of the latter's epidemics."

Chapter 8. The Prohibition of the Doctrine of Free Will (*Qadar*)

2571. According to Mālik, Abū al-Zinād reported from al-Aʿraj, from Abū Hurayra, that the Messenger of God (pbuh) said, "Adam and Moses debated one another, and Adam got the better of Moses. Moses said to Adam, "Aren't you the Adam who led humanity astray and cast them out of Paradise?" Adam replied, "And aren't you the Moses to whom God gave knowledge of all things and whom God selected over all the rest of humanity to be the recipient of His message?" Moses said, "Yes, indeed!" Adam said, "So do you blame me for doing something that was decreed for me before I was even created?"

2572. According to Mālik, Zayd b. Abī Unaysa reported that ʿAbd al-Ḥamīd b. ʿAbd al-Raḥmān b. Zayd b. al-Khaṭṭāb informed him from Muslim b. Yasār al-Juhanī that ʿUmar b. al-Khaṭṭāb was asked about this verse of the Quran: "And when your Lord took from the children of Adam, from their loins, their future descendants and made them bear witness against themselves, saying to them, 'Am I not your Lord?' to which they replied, 'Yes, indeed, we do so testify!'—so that you should not say on the Day of Resurrection, 'Truly, we were heedless of this.'"[983] ʿUmar said, "I heard someone ask the

982 A place near Ṭā'if, on the way to Iraq. Bājī, *al-Muntaqā*, 7:200.

983 *Al-Aʿrāf*, 7:172. The primordial covenant between God and humanity cited in this verse is popularly referred to among Muslims as "The Day of 'Am I Not' (*alastu*)," a reference to God's rhetorical question in the verse, "Am I not your Lord?"

Messenger of God (pbuh) about the meaning of this verse, and he said, 'God, Blessed and Sublime is He, created Adam; then he rubbed His right hand on Adam's back, bringing forth from thence some of Adam's descendants. God then said, "These I created for Paradise, and they shall certainly perform the deeds of those destined for Paradise." God then rubbed Adam's back again, bringing forth from thence more of Adam's descendants. God then said, "These I created for Hell, and they shall certainly perform the deeds of those destined for Hell." A man said, "Messenger of God, what point is there, then, in man's actions?" The Messenger of God (pbuh) said, "When God creates a soul intended for Paradise, He fashions it in such a way that it acts in conformity with the deeds of those destined for Paradise. When such a soul dies, therefore, it does so while acting in conformity with the actions of those destined for Paradise. As a result, God admits it to Paradise by virtue of its actions. When God creates a soul intended for Hell, He fashions it in such a way that it acts in conformity with the deeds of those destined for Hell. When such a soul dies, therefore, it does so while acting in conformity with the actions of those destined for Hell. As a result, God consigns it to Hell by virtue of its actions."

2573. According to Mālik, it reached him that the Messenger of God (pbuh) said, "I have left you two things; if you hold fast to both, you will never go astray: the Book of God and the ordinances (*sunna*) of His Prophet."

2574. According to Mālik, Ziyād b. Saʿd b. ʿAmr b. Muslim reported that Ṭāwūs al-Yamānī said, "In my encounters with the Companions of the Messenger of God (pbuh), some of them would say, 'Everything is by virtue of God's decree.' I heard ʿAbd Allāh b. ʿUmar say, 'The Messenger of God (pbuh) said, "Everything is by virtue of God's decree, including disability and capacity (or 'capacity and disability')."'"

2575. According to Mālik, Ziyād b. Saʿd reported that ʿAmr b. Dīnār said, "I heard ʿAbd Allāh b. al-Zubayr once say in a sermon of his, 'God is both the Guide and the Tempter.'"

2576. According to Mālik, his paternal uncle Abū Suhayl b. Mālik said, "Once I was walking with ʿUmar b. ʿAbd al-ʿAzīz, and he said, 'What is your opinion of the proponents of free will (*qadariyya*)?' So I said, 'I think that you should ask them to recant their false doctrine, and if they do not, they should be put to the sword.' ʿUmar said, 'That is my opinion, too.'" Mālik said, "That is my opinion, too."

Chapter 9. Miscellaneous Reports That Have Come Down regarding People Who Uphold the Doctrine of Free Will

2577. According to Mālik, Abū al-Zinād reported from al-Aʿraj, from Abū Hurayra, that the Messenger of God (pbuh) said, "A woman must not demand, as a condition of her marriage, that her prospective husband first divorce his current wife so that she may take everything for herself. She should marry him without making such demands, and she will get whatever has been decreed for her."

2578. According to Mālik, Yazīd b. Ziyād reported that Muḥammad b. Kaʿb al-Quraẓī said, "Muʿāwiya b. Abī Sufyān once said from the pulpit, 'People, nothing can hold back what God gives, and no one can give what God holds back. The good fortune of the fortunate avails him not against God. When God wishes good for a man, He grants him deep insight into the affairs of this religion.' Muʿāwiya then said, 'I heard those very words from the Messenger of God (pbuh) while he stood on these very planks of wood.'"

2579. According to Mālik, it reached him that people would use the following expressions in describing God: "Praise be to God, the One who created everything in the fashion appropriate to it, the One whose deliberation and design is preceded by no existing thing"; "God suffices me and fulfills my needs"; "God hears those who supplicate"; and finally, "Beyond God there is nothing."

2580. According to Mālik, it reached him that people used to say, "No one dies without having exhausted whatever worldly provisions have been granted to him, so seek out your worldly provisions in a dignified manner."

Chapter 10. What Has Come Down regarding Good Character

2581. According to Mālik, Muʿādh b. Jabal said, "The last piece of advice that the Messenger of God (pbuh) offered me just as I was putting my foot in the stirrup was, 'Be upright in your interactions with people, Muʿādh b. Jabal.'"[984]

2582. According to Mālik, Ibn Shihāb reported from ʿUrwa b. al-Zubayr that ʿĀʾisha, the wife of the Prophet (pbuh), said, "Whenever the Messenger of God (pbuh) was given a choice between two things, he always chose the easier of the two, as long as it did not entail sin. If it entailed sin, no one shunned it more than he. Nor did the Messenger of God (pbuh) ever act to avenge a wrong done to himself. He acted only to avenge transgressions against God. In such cases, he would punish only for the sake of God."

984 Muʿādh was about to set off for Yemen, where he was to serve as the governor on behalf of the Prophet (pbuh).

2583. According to Mālik, Ibn Shihāb reported from ʿAlī b. Ḥusayn b. ʿAlī b. Abī Ṭālib that the Messenger of God (pbuh) said, "Part of the excellence of a man's Islam is that he minds his own business."

2584. According to Mālik, it reached him that ʿĀʾisha, the wife of the Prophet (pbuh), said, "A man once sought an audience with the Messenger of God (pbuh) while I was in the house with him. The Messenger of God (pbuh) said, 'What an ill-mannered fellow he is!' but then he let him in. It was not long before I heard the Messenger of God (pbuh) laughing with him. When the man departed, I said, 'Messenger of God, you made that uncomplimentary remark about him, but then you had a hearty laugh with him?' The Messenger of God (pbuh) said, 'The most wicked of people are certainly those with whom people interact cautiously because of their wickedness.'"

2585. According to Mālik, his paternal uncle Abū Suhayl b. Mālik reported from his father that Kaʿb al-Aḥbār said, "If you wish to know how God regards a man, look to whether he has a good reputation among his fellows."

2586. According to Mālik, Yaḥyā b. Saʿīd said, "It has reached me that through the excellence of his character a man attains the same station before God as does someone who stands for the night prayer and is thirsty from fasting during the heat of the day."

2587. According to Mālik, Yaḥyā b. Saʿīd said, "I heard Saʿīd b. al-Musayyab say, 'Do you know what is better than performing many prayers and giving much in charity?' They said, 'Do tell us.' He said, 'Mending strained relations and being wary of hatred, for its cut is deep indeed.'"

2588. According to Mālik, it reached him that the Messenger of God (pbuh) said, "I was sent to perfect good character."

Chapter 11. What Has Come Down regarding Modesty

2589. According to Mālik, Salama b. Ṣafwān b. Salama al-Zuraqī reported that Zayd b. Ṭalḥa b. Rukāna said, attributing it to the Prophet (pbuh), "The Messenger of God (pbuh) said, 'Every religion has a distinctive virtue, and the distinctive virtue of Islam is modesty.'"

2590. According to Mālik, Ibn Shihāb reported from Sālim b. ʿAbd Allāh, from ʿAbd Allāh b. ʿUmar, that the Messenger of God (pbuh) once passed by a man who was admonishing his brother about his excessive modesty. The Messenger of God (pbuh) said, "Leave him be, for modesty is a part of faith."

Chapter 12. What Has Come Down regarding Anger

2591. According to Mālik, Ibn Shihāb reported from Ḥumayd b. ʿAbd al-Raḥmān b. ʿAwf that a man went to see the Messenger of God (pbuh) and said, "Messenger of God, teach me some words to live by, but be brief, for I am forgetful." The Messenger of God (pbuh) said, "Do not get angry."

2592. According to Mālik, Ibn Shihāb reported from Saʿīd b. al-Musayyab, from Abū Hurayra, that the Messenger of God (pbuh) said, "A man's strength does not lie in his ability to throw his adversary to the ground; rather, it lies in his ability to control himself when angered."

Chapter 13. What Has Come Down regarding Shunning Others

2593. According to Mālik, Ibn Shihāb reported from ʿAṭāʾ b. Zayd al-Laythī, from Abū Ayyūb al-Anṣārī, that the Messenger of God (pbuh) said, "It is not lawful for a Muslim to shun his brother for more than three nights, with each of the two turning away when he sees the other. The better of the two is the first one to greet the other."

2594. According to Mālik, Ibn Shihāb reported from Anas b. Mālik that the Messenger of God (pbuh) said, "Do not get angry at one another; do not envy one another; do not turn your backs on one another (*lā tadābarū*); rather, be brothers, all of you, servants of God. It is not lawful for a Muslim to shun his brother for more than three nights." Mālik said, "I think that *tadābur* is nothing other than turning your back on your Muslim brother when you see him."

2595. According to Mālik, Abū al-Zinād reported from al-Aʿraj, from Abū Hurayra, that the Messenger of God (pbuh) said, "Beware of suspicion, for suspicion is the falsest speech. Do not spy or eavesdrop on one another; do not compete with one another; do not envy one another; do not hate one another; and do not shun one another. Rather, be brothers, all of you, servants of God."

2596. According to Mālik, ʿAṭāʾ b. ʿAbd Allāh al-Khurasānī said, "The Messenger of God (pbuh) said, 'Shake hands, and rancor will disappear. Exchange gifts, and you will love one another, and enmity will disappear.'"

2597. According to Mālik, Suhayl b. Abī Ṣāliḥ reported from his father, from Abū Hurayra, that the Messenger of God (pbuh) said, "The gates of the Garden are thrown open every Monday and Thursday and forgiveness is given to every Muslim who does not associate any partners with God, except for those between whom there is enmity. It is said, 'Leave these two be until they make peace. Leave these two be until they make peace.'"

2598. According to Mālik, Muslim b. Abī Maryam reported from Abū Ṣāliḥ al-Sammān that Abū Hurayra said, "People's deeds are reviewed twice a week, once on Monday and once on Thursday. Every believer is forgiven for his sins, except for those between whom there is enmity. For them it is said, 'Leave these two be until they make peace with one another.'"

Chapter 14. What Has Come Down regarding Wearing Beautiful Clothes

2599. According to Mālik, Zayd b. Aslam reported that Jābir b. ʿAbd Allāh al-Anṣārī said, "We set out with the Messenger of God (pbuh) for the raid on the Banū Anmār. While I was resting under a tree, the Messenger of God (pbuh) showed up, so I said to him, 'Messenger of God, please come into the shade.' The Messenger of God (pbuh) came and stopped in the shade. I stood up and reached for a sack of ours to find something for him. I found a small cucumber and broke it in half. I offered it to the Messenger of God (pbuh). The Messenger of God (pbuh) said, 'Where did you get this?' I said, 'We brought it with us from Medina.' There was with us another fellow who was responsible for the care of our camels. We would equip him with everything his task required, so I pulled out his equipment and gave it to him. He then turned away and set out for the camels, wearing two ragged cloaks. The Messenger of God (pbuh) took one look at him and said, 'He doesn't have any other clothes?' I said, 'Yes, indeed, Messenger of God! He has in the bag another pair of garments, which I gave him.' The Messenger of God (pbuh) said, 'Summon him, and tell him to put them on.' I told him to come back, and he put them on. He then turned around and left. The Messenger of God (pbuh) said, 'May God smite his neck![985] What is wrong with him? Isn't this much better?' The man overheard him and said, 'Messenger of God, for God's sake!'[986] The Messenger of God (pbuh) said, 'For God's sake!' The man was killed fighting for the sake of God."

2600. According to Mālik, it reached him that ʿUmar b. al-Khaṭṭāb said, "It gives me much pleasure to see the Quran reciter resplendent, wearing white garments."

2601. According to Mālik, Ayyūb b. Abī Tamīma reported that Ibn Sīrīn said, "ʿUmar b. al-Khaṭṭāb said, 'When God is generous to you, be generous to

985 A pre-Islamic Arabian expression used to express astonishment.

986 When the man heard the Prophet (pbuh) say "May God smite his neck!" he responded to the phrase's literal meaning and added "for God's sake" so that the Prophet (pbuh) could confirm that he would die a martyr. Bājī, *al-Muntaqā*, 7:219.

yourselves.' A man then donned several of his garments and prayed wearing them all."[987]

Chapter 15. What Has Come Down regarding Wearing Dyed Garments and Gold

2602. According to Mālik, Nāfiʿ reported that ʿAbd Allāh b. ʿUmar would wear garments dyed with red ocher and those dyed with saffron.

2603. Yaḥyā said, "I heard Mālik say, 'I disapprove of young male slaves wearing gold of any sort. That is because it reached me that the Messenger of God (pbuh) prohibited the wearing of gold rings. Accordingly, I disapprove of that for men, be they young or old.'"

2604. Yaḥyā said, "I heard Mālik say, regarding wraps dyed with saffron that men would wear in their houses and courtyards, 'I know nothing about them that would lead me to believe that it is prohibited to wear them, but I would rather that other garments be worn.'"

Chapter 16. What Has Come Down regarding Wearing Silk

2605. According to Mālik, Hishām b. ʿUrwa reported from his father, from ʿĀʾisha, the wife of the Prophet (pbuh), that she once dressed ʿAbd Allāh b. al-Zubayr in a silk shawl that she used to wear."

Chapter 17. Clothes That Women Are Prohibited from Wearing

2606. According to Mālik, ʿAlqama b. Abī ʿAlqama reported that his mother said, "Ḥafṣa bt. ʿAbd al-Raḥmān paid a call to ʿĀʾisha, the wife of the Prophet (pbuh). Ḥafṣa was wearing a delicate, translucent head covering. ʿĀʾisha tore it and gave her a thick one."

2607. According to Mālik, Muslim b. Abī Mūsā reported from Abū Ṣāliḥ that Abū Hurayra said, "Women who are dressed yet naked and who sashay about, drawing men's attention to themselves, shall not enter Paradise nor enjoy its scent, even though its scent may be enjoyed from a distance that requires five hundred years of travel to complete."

2608. According to Mālik, Yaḥyā b. Saʿīd reported from Ibn Shihāb that the Messenger of God (pbuh) woke up in the middle of the night, looked to the

987 According to the commentators, this report was prompted by someone asking the Prophet (pbuh) whether it was permissible to perform a required prayer while wearing only one garment, to which the Prophet (pbuh) replied, rhetorically, "And does everyone possess two garments?" A man later asked ʿUmar the same question, and ʿUmar gave the reply stated in this report, implying that if one has more than garment, one should wear them when performing a required prayer.

horizon, and said, "What blessings have been granted this evening, and what tribulations? How many a well-dressed woman in this world shall be naked on the Day of Resurrection? Arouse the womenfolk from their bedrooms."[988]

Chapter 18. What Has Come Down regarding a Man Trailing His Garment

2609. According to Mālik, ʿAbd Allāh b. Dīnār reported from ʿAbd Allāh b. ʿUmar that the Messenger of God (pbuh) said, "On the Day of Resurrection, God shall not look on anyone who drags the train of his garment out of pride."

2610. According to Mālik, Abū al-Zinād reported from al-Aʿraj, from Abū Hurayra, that the Messenger of God (pbuh) said, "On the Day of Resurrection, God does not look on someone who drags the train of his garment with pride and arrogance."

2611. According to Mālik, Nāfiʿ reported that ʿAbd Allāh b. Dīnār and Zayd b. Aslam informed him from ʿAbd Allāh b. ʿUmar that the Messenger of God (pbuh) said, "On the Day of Resurrection, God shall not look on anyone who drags the train of his garment out of pride."

2612. According to Mālik, al-ʿAlāʾ b. ʿAbd al-Raḥmān reported that his father said, "I asked Abū Saʿīd al-Khudrī about the length of a believer's garment (*izār*). He said, 'I will tell you what I know about that. I heard the Messenger of God (pbuh) say, "A Muslim's garment should reach the middle of his calves. There is no sin if it reaches down to his ankles, but anything in excess of that is sinful! Anything in excess of that is sinful! On the Day of Resurrection, God will not look on someone who drags the train of his garment with pride and arrogance."'"

Chapter 19. What Has Come Down regarding a Woman Trailing Her Garment

2613. According to Mālik, Abū Bakr b. Nāfiʿ reported from his father Nāfiʿ, the freedman (*mawlā*) of Ibn ʿUmar, that Ṣafiyya bt. Abī ʿUbayd informed him that Umm Salama, the wife of the Prophet (pbuh), said, on an occasion when the issue of the undergarment (*izār*) was brought up, "And what about a woman, Messenger of God?" He said, "She should unroll it the length of an additional handspan." Umm Salama said, "But that would leave her partially exposed." He said, "The length of a forearm, then, but no more."

988 Ibn ʿAbd al-Barr suggests that this report took place on the Night of Power (*laylat al-qadr*) and that the Prophet (pbuh) desired that his wives witness the night's blessings. Ibn ʿAbd al-Barr, *al-Istidhkār*, 8:308–9.

Chapter 20. What Has Come Down regarding Wearing Sandals

2614. According to Mālik, Abū al-Zinād reported from al-Aʿraj, from Abū Hurayra, that the Messenger of God (pbuh) said, "No one should walk around in one sandal. Either wear both of them or go barefoot."

2615. According to Mālik, Abū al-Zinād reported from al-Aʿraj, from Abū Hurayra, that the Messenger of God (pbuh) said, "When you put on sandals, begin with the right foot. When you take them off, begin with the left foot. The right foot should be the first in and the last out."

2616. According to Mālik, his paternal uncle Abū Suhayl b. Mālik reported from his father, from Kaʿb al-Aḥbār, that a man once removed his sandals. Kaʿb said to him, "Why did you take off your sandals? Perhaps you did so in reliance on your understanding of the verse 'Remove your sandals, for you are in the sacred valley of Ṭuwā.'[989] But do you have any idea what Moses' sandals were made of?" Mālik, Abū Suhayl's father, said, "I don't know what the man said in reply. Kaʿb said, 'They were made from the skin of a dead donkey.'"

Chapter 21. What Has Come Down regarding Clothing

2617. According to Mālik, Abū al-Zinād reported from al-Aʿraj that Abū Hurayra said, "The Messenger of God (pbuh) prohibited two ways of dressing and two kinds of trades. The prohibited trades are those based on touch (*mulāmasa*) and those done by tossing (*munābadha*).[990] As for manners of dress, he prohibited a man from sitting down with his legs drawn up to his chest, covered by only one piece of cloth, without another piece of cloth covering his genitals. He also prohibited a man from draping a single cloth over one of his shoulders down to the rest of his body."[991]

2618. According to Mālik, Nāfiʿ reported from ʿAbd Allāh b. ʿUmar that ʿUmar b. al-Khaṭṭāb once saw a striped silk robe offered for sale at the entrance to the mosque. He said, "Messenger of God, you should buy this robe to wear on public occasions, such as the day of the Friday Congregational Prayer (*ṣalāt al-jumuʿa*),

---

989 *Ṭāhā*, 20:12. This verse describes God speaking to Moses on Mount Sinai. Cf. Exodus 3:5.

990 A trade based on touch is when a man purchases a piece of cloth after merely touching it, without first unfolding it or examining it, or when he purchases it in the darkness of the night, without knowing what is in it. A trade done by tossing takes place when a man tosses a piece of cloth of his to another man and the latter throws his own piece of cloth to the first man, with neither of them examining the cloth each has taken. See hadith no. 2064.

991 Bājī and Zurqānī state that this manner of dressing was prohibited because it required a man to use one of his hands to hold up his garment, which meant that it was impossible for him to do anything useful with his hands without exposing his genitals. Bājī, *al-Muntaqā*, 7:228; Zurqānī, *Sharḥ al-Zurqānī*, 4:437.

and when ambassadors come to meet with you." The Messenger of God (pbuh) said, "Only someone who has no share in the next life wears such a garment." Then some robes of the very same material were given to the Messenger of God (pbuh), and he gave one of them to ʿUmar. ʿUmar then said, "Messenger of God! Are you giving me this robe after saying what you said about the robe of ʿUṭārid?"[992] The Messenger of God (pbuh) said, "I did not give it to you to wear." ʿUmar consequently gave it to a brother of his in Mecca who was still a polytheist.

2619. According to Mālik, Isḥāq b. ʿAbd Allāh b. Abī Ṭalḥa said, "Anas b. Mālik said, 'I saw ʿUmar b. al-Khaṭṭāb when he was the Commander of the Faithful. The shoulders of his garment had had been patched up three times, one patch on top of the other.'"

Chapter 22. The Physical Appearance of the Prophet (pbuh)

2620. According to Mālik, Rabīʿa b. Abī ʿAbd al-Raḥmān reported that he heard Anas b. Mālik say, "The Messenger of God (pbuh) was of moderate height, neither short nor tall. He was neither pale nor dark. His hair was neither curly nor straight. God commissioned him as His Messenger at the beginning of his fortieth year. He remained in Mecca thereafter for ten years, then was in Medina for another ten. God claimed his soul when he was sixty, and there were not twenty white hairs in his hair and beard. May God grace him and grant him His mercy and His blessings."

Chapter 23. The Physical Appearance of Jesus, the Son of Mary, and the Antichrist (*al-Dajjāl*)

2621. According to Mālik, Nāfiʿ reported from ʿAbd Allāh b. ʿUmar that the Messenger of God (pbuh) said, "I dreamed this evening that I was at the Kabah. I saw a tawny-colored man, and behold, you have never seen a tawny-colored man more handsome than he! His hair had locks that flowed down past his ears and onto his shoulders, and behold, you have never seen locks of hair as exquisite as his! He had just washed and combed his hair, and it was dripping water. He was leaning on two men (or 'on the shoulders of two men') as he circumambulated the Kabah. I asked, 'Who is this?' and I was told, 'The Messiah, the son of Mary.' Then I found myself with a man whose hair was tight and curly and who had lost his right eye, which gave it the appearance of a floating grape. I then asked, 'Who is this?' and I was told, 'This is the Antichrist.'"

---

992 His full name is ʿUṭāriḍ b. Ḥājib b. Zurāra b. ʿAdī. He was a member of the delegation sent by the tribe of Tamīm to the Prophet (pbuh). He embraced Islam and is considered one of the Companions of the Prophet (pbuh). Zurqānī, *Sharḥ al-Zurqānī*, 4:438.

Chapter 24. What Has Come Down regarding the Natural Norms of Grooming (*Fiṭra*)

2622. According to Mālik, Saʿīd b. Abī Saʿīd al-Maqburī reported from his father that Abū Hurayra said, "Five practices are characteristic of natural grooming (*fiṭra*): clipping the nails, trimming the moustache, shaving the armpits, shaving pubic hair, and circumcision."

2623. According to Mālik, Yaḥyā b. Saʿīd reported that Saʿīd b. al-Musayyab said, "Abraham was the first to establish the law of hospitality, the first to be circumcised, the first to trim his moustache, and the first to experience gray hair. He said, 'My Lord! What is this?' God, Blessed and Sublime is He, said, 'It is gravitas, Abraham.' Abraham said, 'My Lord! Increase my gravitas!'"

2624. Yaḥyā said, "I heard Mālik say, 'Trim the moustache until the edge of the lip appears—that is, the fleshy part. One should not trim more than that lest one disfigure oneself.'"

Chapter 25. The Prohibition against Eating with the Left Hand

2625. According to Mālik, Abū al-Zubayr al-Makkī reported from Jābir b. ʿAbd Allāh al-Salamī that the Messenger of God (pbuh) prohibited men from eating with the left hand, walking around in one sandal, draping a single cloth over one of their shoulders down to the rest of the body, or sitting down with their legs drawn up to their chests, revealing their genitals.

2626. According to Mālik, Ibn Shihāb reported from Abū Bakr b. ʿUbayd Allāh b. ʿAbd Allāh b. ʿUmar, from Ibn ʿUmar, that the Messenger of God (pbuh) said, "When you eat, eat and drink with your right hand, for it is Satan who eats and drinks with his left."

Chapter 26. What Has Come Down regarding the Meaning of "the Bereft" (*Masākīn*)

2627. According to Mālik, Abū al-Zinād reported from al-Aʿraj, from Abū Hurayra, that the Messenger of God (pbuh) said, "The 'bereft' (*masākīn*) are not those who wander about among the people and who are satisfied if they get a bite or two to eat, or a couple of dates." They said, "In that case, who are the 'bereft,' Messenger of God?" He said, "Someone is 'bereft' if he lacks the means to take care of himself, but the peple are unaware that he is needy. Therefore, they do not give him charity (*ṣadaqa*), and neither does he himself ask for their help."

2628. According to Mālik, Zayd b. Aslam reported from Bujayd al-Anṣārī al-Ḥārithī, from his grandmother, that the Messenger of God (pbuh) said, "Give something to the bereft, even if only a roasted hoof."

Chapter 27. What Has Come Down regarding the Gluttony of the Nonbeliever

2629. According to Mālik, Abū al-Zinād reported from al-Aʿraj that Abū Hurayra said, "The Messenger of God (pbuh) said, 'The Muslim eats enough for only one stomach, whereas the nonbeliever eats enough for seven.'"

2630. According to Mālik, Suhayl b. Abī Ṣāliḥ reported from his father, from Abū Hurayra, that the Messenger of God (pbuh) once extended hospitality to a nonbeliever. The Messenger of God (pbuh) ordered that a yearling (*shāt*) be milked for the guest, and he drank its milk. Then a second one was milked, and he drank its milk, too; then a third one was milked, and he drank that milk, too. He did not stop until he had drunk the milk of seven yearlings. The next morning, the man embraced Islam. The Messenger of God (pbuh) again ordered that a yearling be milked for the man, and it was, and he drank its milk. Then the Messenger of God (pbuh) ordered a second one to be milked for him, but the man was unable to finish its milk, whereupon the Messenger of God (pbuh) said, "The believer drinks with one stomach, and the nonbeliever drinks with seven."

Chapter 28. The Prohibition against Drinking from Silver Goblets and Blowing into a Beverage

2631. According to Mālik, Nāfiʿ reported from Zayd b. ʿAbd Allāh b. ʿUmar b. al-Khaṭṭāb, from ʿAbd Allāh b. ʿAbd al-Raḥmān b. Abī Bakr al-Ṣiddīq, from Umm Salama, the wife of the Prophet (pbuh), that the Messenger of God (pbuh) said, "Whoever drinks from a silver goblet pours the fire of Hell into his belly."

2632. According to Mālik, Ayyūb b. Ḥabīb, the freedman (*mawlā*) of Saʿd b. Abī Waqqāṣ, reported that Abū al-Muthannā al-Juhanī said, "I was with Marwān b. al-Ḥakam when Abū Saʿīd al-Khudrī showed up. Marwān asked him, 'Did you ever hear from the Messenger of God (pbuh) that he prohibited someone from blowing into a beverage?' Abū Saʿīd replied, 'Yes. A man once said to him, "Messenger of God, my thirst is not quenched in a single gulp." The Messenger of God (pbuh) said to him, "In that case, remove the cup from your mouth and take a breath." The man said, "What if I see something floating in the cup?" He said, "In that case, pour that part out."'"

Chapter 29. What Has Come Down regarding Drinking While Standing Up

2633. According to Mālik, it reached him that ʿUmar b. al-Khaṭṭāb, ʿAlī b. Abī Ṭālib, and ʿUthmān b. ʿAffān would all drink while standing.

2634. According to Mālik, Ibn Shihāb reported that neither ʿĀʾisha, the Mother of the Believers, nor Saʿd b. Abī Waqqāṣ saw anything objectionable in drinking while standing.

2635. According to Mālik, Abū Jaʿfar al-Qārī said, "I saw ʿAbd Allāh b. ʿUmar drink while he was standing."

2636. According to Mālik, ʿĀmir b. ʿAbd Allāh b. al-Zubayr reported from his father that he would drink while standing.

Chapter 30. The Long-Established Ordinance (*Sunna*) of Drinking and Passing the Vessel to the Right

2637. According to Mālik, Ibn Shihāb reported from Anas b. Mālik that the Messenger of God (pbuh) was brought some milk that had been diluted with water. Seated to his right was a bedouin, while Abū Bakr al-Ṣiddīq was on his left. He drank and then passed the vessel to the bedouin and said, "Always pass it to the one on your right."

2638. According to Mālik, Abū Ḥāzim b. Dīnār reported from Sahl b. Saʿd al-Anṣārī that the Messenger of God (pbuh) was brought a beverage, so he drank from it. A boy was seated on his right, and some old men were seated on his left. He said to the young boy, "Do I have your permission to give it to these men on my left?" The boy said, "No, Messenger of God. By God, I will not let anyone take my share of what is due to me from you." Sahl said, "The Messenger of God (pbuh) therefore passed the beverage to the boy."

Chapter 31. Miscellaneous Reports on What Has Come Down regarding Food and Beverages

2639. According to Mālik, Isḥāq b. ʿAbd Allāh b. Abī Ṭalḥa reported that he heard Anas b. Mālik say, "Abū Ṭalḥa said to Umm Sulaym, 'The voice of the Messenger of God (pbuh) is weary; I'm certain he's hungry. Do you have anything to give him?' She said, 'Yes!' She pulled out some loaves of barley bread, then wrapped them using part of a scarf of hers, and then placed the bundle in my hands. She then sent me to the Messenger of God (pbuh). I set off with the bundle and found the Messenger of God (pbuh) sitting in the mosque along with the people. I approached them, whereupon the Messenger of God (pbuh) said, 'Has Abū Ṭalḥa sent you?' I said, 'Yes!' He said, 'To invite us for food?' I said, 'Yes!' The Messenger of God (pbuh) said to those around him, 'Get up!' He left, and I went on ahead of them. I came to Abū Ṭalḥa and informed him of what had happened. Abū Ṭalḥa said, 'Umm Sulaym! The Messenger of God (pbuh) and the people are coming, and we have nothing to feed them.' She said, 'God and His Messenger know best.' Abū

Ṭalḥa left in haste and kept going until he intercepted the Messenger of God (pbuh). The Messenger of God (pbuh) continued on his way, and Abū Ṭalḥa joined him, until they finally arrived at his house. The Messenger of God (pbuh) then said, 'Umm Sulaym, what is it that you intend to give us?' She brought out the bread. He commanded that the bread be divided into small pieces, and so it was. Umm Sulaym then squeezed some fat out of a leather vessel onto the bread and added some seasoning to it. The Messenger of God (pbuh) supplicated God, using whatever phrases God wished him to use, and then said, 'Let ten people come in and eat.' Abū Ṭalḥa therefore invited ten men in, and they came in, ate their fill, and left. He then said, 'Let in another ten!' Abū Ṭalḥa invited another ten in, and they came in, ate their fill, and left. He then said, 'Let in another ten men!' Abū Ṭalḥa invited another ten in, and they came in, ate their fill, and left. He then said, 'Let in another ten!' Abū Ṭalḥa invited another ten in, and they came in, ate their fill, and left. He then said, 'Let in another ten!' Abū Ṭalḥa invited another ten in, and they came in, ate their fill, and left. The Prophet (pbuh) continued in this fashion until everyone had eaten his fill. They were around seventy or eighty men in total."

2640. According to Mālik, Abū al-Zinād reported from al-Aʿraj, from Abū Hurayra, that the Messenger of God (pbuh) said, "Food that is enough for two is enough for three, and food that is enough for three is enough for four."

2641. According to Mālik, Abū al-Zubayr al-Makkī reported from Jābir b. ʿAbd Allāh that the Messenger of God (pbuh) said, "Lock the doors, tie the waterskins, turn empty vessels upside down, cover them if they are not empty, and put out the lamps. Satan does not open a locked door, untie a sealed waterskin, or remove a vessel's cover. A mouse can cause a house to burn down with its inhabitants inside."

2642. According to Mālik, Saʿīd b. Abī Saʿīd al-Maqburī reported from Abū Shurayḥ al-Kaʿbī that the Messenger of God (pbuh) said, "Whoever believes in God and the Last Day should speak well or remain silent. Whoever believes in God and the Last Day should honor his neighbor. Whoever believes in God and the Last Day should honor his guest. For the first day and night, the host should provide his guest with the best that he possesses, but the duty of hospitality extends to no more than three days. Anything beyond that is charity (*ṣadaqa*). It is not permissible for a guest to burden his host by staying with him beyond that."

2643. According to Mālik, Sumayy, the freedman (*mawlā*) of Abū Bakr, reported from Abū Ṣāliḥ al-Sammān, from Abū Hurayra, that the Messenger of God (pbuh) said, "A man was walking along a road when suddenly he became extremely thirsty. He came across a well, so he descended to its depths, drank, and emerged. When he came out, he found a dog panting and eating the moist dust at the edge of the well because of its extreme thirst. The man said, 'This dog is as thirsty as I was.' He went back down the well, took off his leather sock, filled it with water, and then, holding the sock in his teeth, climbed back up and gave the water to the dog. God appreciated his deed and forgave his sins." The Companions asked, "Messenger of God, are we rewarded for our compassion toward animals?" He said, "There is a reward in aiding anything that has flesh and blood."[993]

2644. According to Mālik, Wahb b. Kaysān reported that Jābir b. ʿAbd Allāh said, "The Messenger of God (pbuh) dispatched a company to the coast, appointing Abū ʿUbayda b. al-Jarrāḥ as its commanding officer. They were around three hundred in number, and I was one of them. We set out, but before we had reached our destination, our provisions ran extremely low. Abū ʿUbayda ordered that all of the company's remaining provisions be collected. They amounted to no more than two bags of dates. Each day, he would give us a very small amount. Finally, the provisions were nearly exhausted, and we were rationed one date each day. Frustrated, I said, 'What good is there in one date?' He said, 'You will miss it when none are left!' We finally reached the coast, where we found a whale[994] the size of a small hillock (*ẓirb*). The company ate from it for eighteen nights. Abū ʿUbayda then ordered that two of its ribs be planted upright into the earth. He ordered a camel to be released underneath them, and it was able to pass through without touching either of them." Mālik said, "A *ẓarib*[995] is a small hillock."

2645. According to Mālik, Zayd b. Aslam reported from ʿAmr b. Saʿīd b. Muʿādh, from his grandmother, that the Messenger of God (pbuh) said, "Believing women, there is nothing that is too trivial to give your neighbor, even if it is only a roasted hoof."

2646. According to Mālik, ʿAbd Allāh b. Abī Bakr said, "The Messenger of God (pbuh) said, 'May God strike the Jews. Although they were prohibited from eating the fat, they sold it and consumed the price.'"[996]

2647. According to Mālik, it reached him that Jesus, the son of Mary, would say, "Children of Israel! Stick to pure water, wild greens, and barley bread. Stay clear of wheat bread, for you will fail to be sufficiently grateful."

---

993 The literal expression is "There is a reward for anything that has a moist liver," presumably referring to vertebrates as a class.

994 The Arabic word used here is the same as that for fish, *ḥūt*.

995 The word for "small hillock" is first vocalized as *ẓirb* and then as *ẓarib*. Both are recognized vocalizations of this word. See Zurqānī, *Sharḥ al-Zurqānī*, 4:489, and the RME, 311 n. 6.

996 Compare to Leviticus 7:23–24.

2648. According to Mālik, it reached him that the Messenger of God (pbuh) once entered the mosque and found Abū Bakr al-Ṣiddīq and ʿUmar b. al-Khaṭṭāb there. He asked them why they were there, and they both said, "We were hungry." The Messenger of God (pbuh) then said, "And I'm hungry, too." Therefore, they all set off together to Abū al-Haytham al-Tayyihān al-Anṣārī. He had some barley, so he ordered that it be prepared for them, and he got up to slaughter a yearling (*shāt*) for them. The Messenger of God (pbuh) said, "Do not slaughter a lactating female!" He slaughtered a yearling for them and poured out fresh, cold water for them out of a jug that had been hanging on a palm tree. He then brought them that food and water, and they ate and drank from it. The Messenger of God (pbuh) said, "You shall be asked about the blessings of this day."

2649. According to Mālik, Yaḥyā b. Saʿīd reported that ʿUmar b. al-Khaṭṭāb would eat bread with clarified butter. He once invited a man from the countryside to eat with him, and the man took the bread and used it to soak up every drop of clarified butter on the plate. ʿUmar said, "It is as though you were starving." The man said, "By God, I have not eaten clarified butter, nor have I seen any food cooked in it, since such-and-such a date." ʿUmar said, "I shall not eat clarified butter again until this drought is lifted and the people are able to eat as they did in former days."

2650. According to Mālik, Isḥāq b. ʿAbd Allāh b. Abī Ṭalḥa reported that Anas b. Mālik said, "I saw ʿUmar b. al-Khaṭṭāb, when he was the Commander of the Faithful, be given a measure (*ṣāʿ*) of dates. He would eat all of them, even the ones of inferior quality."

2651. According to Mālik, ʿAbd Allāh b. Dīnār reported that ʿAbd Allāh b. ʿUmar said, "ʿUmar b. al-Khaṭṭāb was asked about eating locusts. He said, 'I wish that we had a basket of them that we could eat.'"

2652. According to Mālik, Muḥammad b. ʿAmr b. Ḥalḥala reported that Ḥumayd b. Mālik b. Khutham said, "I was sitting with Abū Hurayra at his land in al-ʿAqīq. Some Medinese arrived, riding on their mounts. They dismounted, and Abū Hurayra said to me, 'Go to my mother and tell her, "Your son greets you and asks you to give us some food."' She set down three loaves on a plate, with some oil and salt. I then put the plate on my head and brought it out to them. When I served them the plate, Abū Hurayra magnified God (said 'God is great,' *Allāhu akbar*) and said, 'Praise belongs to God who satiated us with bread after we previously had only water and dates for food.' The strong, however, did not eat of the food. When they left, Abū Hurayra said, 'My nephew, be good to your flock, wipe the snot from their noses, and clean out their pen. Perform your prayers in their presence, for they are among the animals that reside in Paradise. By Him whose hand holds my soul, a time is about to come when a small group of sheep will be more beloved to their owner than Marwān's palace is to him.'"[997]

2653. According to Mālik, Abū Nuʿaym Wahb b. Kaysān said, "The Messenger of God (pbuh) was with his stepson, ʿUmar b. Abī Salama, when a plate of food was brought to him. The Messenger of God (pbuh) said to the boy, 'Say "In God's name" (*Bismi 'llāh*), and then eat the food that is closest to you.'"

2654. According to Mālik, Yaḥyā b. Saʿīd said, "I heard al-Qāsim b. Muḥammad say, 'A man came to ʿAbd Allāh b. ʿAbbās and said to him, "I take care of an orphan who has camels. Can I drink of their milk?" Ibn ʿAbbās said, "If you track down his camels when they go missing, wipe tar on those infected with scabies, repair the water basin from which they drink, and see to it that they are given enough to drink, then you may drink of their milk, so long as you cause no harm to their calves nor harm the mothers by excessive milking."'"

2655. According to Mālik, Hishām b. ʿUrwa reported from his father that he would never consume food or drink or even a medicine without first saying, "Praise be to God who guided us, fed us, satiated our thirst, and gave us the good things of the world. God is great. O God, for every evil, a blessing of Yours has found us. We therefore awake in the morning and sleep in the evening in prosperity. We ask that You perfect it and that You make us grateful for it. There is no prosperity except the prosperity You provide. There is no god except You, God of the righteous and the Lord of the worlds. Praise be to God. There is no god except God. Whatever God wills, is, and there is no power except through God. O God, bless us in what You have provided us and protect us from the punishment of Hellfire."[998]

2656. Mālik was asked, "Can a woman eat with a man other than a close relation to whom marriage is prohibited (*maḥram*) or a slave of hers?" He said, "There is nothing objectionable in that, if it is consistent with the manner in which a woman eats with men. A woman may sometimes eat with her husband and his companions who eat with him, or with her brother and his companions, in a similar fashion. It is not permissible, however, for a woman to be alone with a man whom she could potentially marry."

---

997 A reference to Marwān b. al-Ḥakam, who was the governor of Medina at that time.

998 *Al-ḥamdu lillāhi 'lladhī hadānā wa-aṭʿamanā wa-saqānā wa-naʿʿamanā. Allāhu akbar. Allāhumma alfatnā niʿmatuka bi-kulli sharr. Fa-aṣbaḥnā minhā wa-amsaynā bi-kulli khayr. Nas'aluka tamāmahā wa-shukraha. Lū khayra illā khayruk. Wa-lā ilāha ghayruk, ilāha 'l-ṣāliḥīna wa-rabbi 'l-ʿālamīn. Al-ḥamdu lillāh. Wa-lā ilāha illā 'llāh. Ma shā'u 'llāh wa-lā quwwata illā billāh. Allāhumma bārik lanā fīmā razaqtanā wa-qinā ʿadhāba 'l-nār.*

Chapter 32. What Has Come Down regarding Eating Meat

2657. According to Mālik, Yaḥyā b. Saʿīd reported that ʿUmar b. al-Khaṭṭāb said, "Avoid eating meat habitually, for it is addictive like wine."

2658. According to Mālik, Yaḥyā b. Saʿīd reported that ʿUmar b. al-Khaṭṭāb came upon Jābir b. ʿAbd Allāh, who was in the company of a porter carrying meat. ʿUmar said, "What is this?" He said, "Commander of the Faithful, we longed to have some meat, so I bought some for a dirham." ʿUmar said, "Shouldn't you rather deprive yourselves for the sake of your neighbor and your cousin? Have you thought of the meaning of this verse, 'You have squandered all of the good things given to you in this immediate life of yours, seeking enjoyment therein'?"[999]

Chapter 33. What Has Come Down regarding Wearing Rings

2659. According to Mālik, ʿAbd Allāh b. Dīnār reported from ʿAbd Allāh b. ʿUmar that the Messenger of God (pbuh) at one time used to wear a gold ring. Then the Messenger of God (pbuh) decided to discard it and said, "I shall never wear it again." ʿAbd Allāh b. ʿUmar said, "Subsequently, everyone discarded their gold rings."[1000]

2660. According to Mālik, Ṣadaqa b. Yasār said, "I asked Saʿīd b. al-Musayyab about wearing a ring. He said, 'Wear one, and tell people that I expressly gave you permission to do so.'"

Chapter 34. What Has Come Down regarding Removing Necklaces and Bells out of Fear of the Evil Eye (*al-ʿAyn*)

2661. According to Mālik, ʿAbd Allāh b. Abī Bakr reported from ʿAbbād b. Tamīm that Abū Bashīr al-Anṣārī informed him that he was with the Messenger of God (pbuh) on one of his trips. Abū Bashīr said, "The Messenger of God (pbuh) sent a representative" (ʿAbd Allāh b. Abī Bakr interrupted the report and said, "I think that Abū Bashīr said, 'and the people were already napping'"), and the representative said, "Any necklace draped around the neck of a camel, whether made of bowstring or otherwise, should be removed and broken."[1001]

---

999 *Al-Aḥqāf*, 46:19. Bājī suggests that this incident took place during a time of great want during ʿUmar b. al-Khaṭṭāb's term as caliph. Bājī, *al-Muntaqā*, 7:253.

1000 Although the text uses the word *al-nās*, which literally means "the people," the prohibition against wearing gold rings applies only to men.

1001 The commentators disagree as to the reason for this prohibition, with many, including Mālik, relating it to the pre-Islamic practice of hanging charms with the intent of warding off the evil eye. Under this interpretation, if a necklace is draped around the neck of an animal purely for the purpose of ornamentation, the prohibition does not apply. Bājī, *al-Muntaqā*, 7:255.

2662. Yaḥyā said, "I heard Mālik say, 'I think that was to ward off the evil eye.'"

Chapter 35. Performing Ablutions (*Wuḍū'*) as Protection against the Evil Eye (*al-'Ayn*)

2663. According to Mālik, Muḥammad b. Abī Umāma b. Sahl b. Ḥunayf reported that he heard his father say, "My father, Sahl b. Ḥunayf, once bathed at al-Kharrār.[1002] He removed the cloak that he was wearing as 'Āmir b. Rabī'a was looking on. Sahl had beautiful white skin. Upon seeing it, 'Āmir said to him, 'I have never seen skin as beautiful as yours, not even that of a young girl.' Sahl became severely ill on the spot, falling to the ground. Someone went to the Messenger of God (pbuh) and informed him that Sahl had fallen ill and that he would consequently not be able to set out with him. The Messenger of God (pbuh) went to see him, and Sahl informed him of what had happened with 'Āmir. The Messenger of God (pbuh) then said, 'Why do some of you kill your brethren? You should instead bless them (by saying *Tabāraka 'llāh*). The evil eye is real. 'Āmir, wash yourself to ward off its effects from Sahl.' 'Āmir washed himself in order to dissipate its effects. Sahl recovered completely and was then able to set out with the Messenger of God (pbuh)."

2664. According to Mālik, Ibn Shihāb reported that Abū Umāma b. Sahl b. Ḥunayf said, "'Āmir b. Rabī'a once saw Sahl b. Ḥunayf bathing, whereupon he said, 'I have never seen skin so beautiful, not even on a maiden cloistered away in her tent.' Sahl immediately collapsed. Someone went to the Messenger of God (pbuh) and asked him, 'Messenger of God, can you do anything for Sahl b. Ḥunayf? By God, he cannot even raise his head.' He said, 'Do you suspect that someone is responsible for this?' They said, 'Indeed, we suspect 'Āmir b. Rabī'a.' The Messenger of God (pbuh) therefore summoned 'Āmir and scolded him, saying, 'Why do some of you kill your brethren? You should instead bless them (by saying *Tabāraka 'llāh*). 'Āmir! Wash yourself to ward off its effects from Sahl.' 'Āmir therefore washed his face, hands, elbows, knees, the entirety of his feet, and his groin out of a goblet. Then he poured the remaining water over himself. Sahl recovered completely and was able to set out with the people."

However, other commentators, as the editors of the RME note, believe the prohibition to be intended to minimize the risk that the animal might choke, particularly if the necklace was made of the string of a bow, as was commonly the case before Islam.

1002 A place in Medina or its environs.

Chapter 36. Using Pious Supplications (*Ruqya*) to Ward Off the Evil Eye (*al-ʿAyn*)

2665. According to Mālik, Ḥumayd b. Qays al-Makkī said, "The two sons of Jaʿfar b. Abī Ṭālib were brought to the Messenger of God (pbuh). He said to their nursemaid, 'Why do they appear so weak and emaciated?' Their nursemaid said, 'Messenger of God, the evil eye easily finds its way to them. The only reason we have not sought to protect them with supplications is that we do not know what supplications would be agreeable to you.' The Messenger of God (pbuh) said, 'Protect them with appropriate supplications to God. If anything were to defy fate, it would be the evil eye.'"[1003]

2666. According to Mālik, Yaḥyā b. Saʿīd reported from Sulaymān b. Yasār that ʿUrwa b. al-Zubayr told him, "The Messenger of God (pbuh) once entered the house of Umm Salama, the wife of the Prophet (pbuh). There was a child weeping there, and they said that he was crying because of the evil eye." ʿUrwa said, "The Messenger of God (pbuh) said, 'Why haven't you attempted to remove its effects with appropriate supplications?'"

Chapter 37. What Has Come Down regarding the Reward of the Ill

2667. According to Mālik, Zayd b. Aslam reported from ʿAṭā' b. Yasār that the Messenger of God (pbuh) said, "When a servant of His falls ill, God, Blessed and Sublime is He, dispatches two angels to him. They pay careful attention to what the man says to his well-wishers. If, when they come to see him, he praises God and exalts Him, the angels report that to God—and He knows best. God says, 'If I claim his soul, I am obliged to deliver him to Paradise. If I choose to heal him, however, I am obliged to renew his flesh and blood and to efface his foul deeds.'"

2668. According to Mālik, Yazīd b. Khuṣayfa reported that ʿUrwa b. al-Zubayr said, "I heard ʿĀ'isha, the wife of the Prophet (pbuh), say, 'The Messenger of God (pbuh) said, "Whenever an injury befalls a believer, even if only a thorn, it offsets (or 'erases') a sin of his."'" Yazīd was uncertain as to which of the two expressions ʿUrwa used.

2669. According to Mālik, Muḥammad b. ʿAbd Allāh b. Abī Ṣaʿṣaʿa said that he heard Abū al-Ḥubāb Saʿīd b. Yasār say that he heard Abū Hurayra say, "The Messenger of God (pbuh) said, 'Whenever God wishes to bless someone, He first inflicts suffering on him.'"

1003 The specific Arabic term for supplications intended to ward off the effects of the evil eye or to cure someone of an illness is *ruqya*. Bājī reports that reciting verses of the Quran or the beautiful names of God in such a context is uncontroversial. Use of non-Islamic references or anything that smacks of polytheism (*shirk*), however, is prohibited. Bājī, *al-Muntaqā*, 7:257–58.

2670. According to Mālik, Yaḥyā b. Saʿīd reported that during the time of the Messenger of God (pbuh), a man died, and someone said, "Good for him. He died peacefully, without suffering the pain of an illness." The Messenger of God (pbuh) said, "Woe unto you! It may have been the case that had God tried him with an illness, it would have effaced his evil deeds."

Chapter 38. Seeking Protection and Treating Illness with Pious Supplications (*Ruqya*)

2671. According to Mālik, Yazīd b. Khuṣayfa reported that ʿAmr b. ʿAbd Allāh b. Kaʿb al-Sulamī informed him that Nāfiʿ b. Jubayr informed him from ʿUthmān b. Abī al-ʿĀṣī that he went to the Messenger of God (pbuh) and said, "I am in extreme pain." The Messenger of God (pbuh) said, "Rub the area with your right hand seven times and say, 'I seek refuge in God's glory and might from the evil of what I suffer.'" ʿUthmān said, "When I said it, God removed my pain. Ever since, I have told my family and others to use it when they are in pain."

2672. According to Mālik, Ibn Shihāb reported from ʿUrwa, from ʿĀʾisha, the wife of the Prophet (pbuh), that when the Messenger of God (pbuh) was ill, he would recite the last three chapters of the Quran[1004] and then breathe from his mouth onto his hands, with a little spittle, and rub his body. She said, "When his pain was too intense for him to do so, I would recite them over him, and I would rub his body with his right hand, seeking its blessing."

2673. According to Mālik, Yaḥyā b. Saʿīd reported from ʿAmra bt. ʿAbd al-Raḥmān that Abū Bakr al-Ṣiddīq once went to visit ʿĀʾisha at a time when she was ill, and he found a Jewish woman there, treating her with a supplication. Abū Bakr said, "Treat her with a supplication from the Book of God."

Chapter 39. Treating the Sick

2674. According to Mālik, Zayd b. Aslam reported that a man suffered a wound in the time of the Messenger of God (pbuh). The blood flowed profusely from the wound, and the man called for two men from the Banū Anmār tribe. The two looked at the wound, and then said that the Messenger of God (pbuh) asked them, "Which of you is the more skilled in healing?" They said, "Of what use is healing, Messenger of God?" Zayd said that the Messenger of God (pbuh) said in reply, "The One who created diseases also created their cure."

1004 Each of the last two chapters of the Quran begins with a verse in which the worshipper expressly seeks God's protection against various sources of evil. The third to last chapter of the Quran, *al-Ikhlāṣ*, is included here with the last two because it is regularly recited with the last two chapters of the Quran and because of its teachings regarding God's oneness. Zurqānī, *Sharḥ al-Zurqānī*, 4:517.

2675. According to Mālik, Yaḥyā b. Saʿīd said, "It reached me that during the time of the Messenger of God (pbuh), Saʿd b. Zurāra suffered from pain in his throat that made it difficult for him to breathe, so he cauterized the wound. He then died."

2676. According to Mālik, Nāfiʿ reported that ʿAbd Allāh b. ʿUmar was cauterized for palsy, but he was treated for the sting of a scorpion with appropriate supplications.

Chapter 40. Washing the Ill with Water to Treat Fever

2677. According to Mālik, Hishām b. ʿUrwa reported from Fāṭima bt. al-Mundhir that whenever a woman who was suffering from fever was brought to Asmā' bt. Abī Bakr in order for her to supplicate on the ill woman's behalf, Asmā' would pour water over the woman's head and down to her collar. She said, "The Messenger of God (pbuh) would tell us to bring down a fever with water."

2678. According to Mālik, Hishām b. ʿUrwa reported from his father that the Messenger of God (pbuh) said, "Fever is from the heat of Hell, so cool it with water."

Chapter 41. Visiting the Ill, and Augury (*Ṭiyara*)

2679. According to Mālik, it reached him from Jābir b. ʿAbd Allāh that the Messenger of God (pbuh) said, "When a person sets off to visit someone ill, he plunges into the depths of divine mercy. When he arrives at his destination and sits with the ill person, divine mercy settles there (or something like that)."

2680. According to Mālik, it reached him from Bukayr b. ʿAbd Allāh b. al-Ashajj, from Ibn ʿAṭiyya, that the Messenger of God (pbuh) said, "There are no such things as contagion (*ʿadwā*), ill fortune because of birds (*hām*), and serpents in a hungry belly (*ṣafar*). A sick herd should not alight with a healthy one, but a healthy herd may alight wherever it wishes." The people asked him, "Messenger of God, why is that so?" The Messenger of God (pbuh) said, "It is harmful."

Chapter 42. The Long-Established Ordinance (*al-Sunna*) regarding Hair

2681. According to Mālik, Abū Bakr b. Nāfiʿ reported from his father Nāfiʿ, from ʿAbd Allāh b. ʿUmar, that the Messenger of God ordered that the moustache be trimmed and the beard be grown.

2682. According to Mālik, Ibn Shihāb reported from Ḥumayd b. ʿAbd al-Raḥmān b. ʿAwf that he heard Muʿāwiya b. Abī Sufyān say from the pulpit, in the year in which he performed the Pilgrimage (*ḥajj*), while holding a hair extension that he took from one of his guards, "People of Medina! Where are your learned men? I heard the Messenger of God (pbuh) prohibit such things, saying, 'The Israelites perished when their womenfolk took up such habits.'"

2683. According to Mālik, Ziyād b. Saʿd reported that he heard Ibn Shihāb say, "The Messenger of God (pbuh) would at one time let his hair drape over his forehead, at whatever length God willed, but later he started to part it instead."

2684. Mālik said, "There is nothing objectionable in a man seeing the hair of his daughter-in-law or his mother-in-law."

2685. According to Mālik, Nāfiʿ reported from ʿAbd Allāh b. ʿUmar that he prohibited castration and said, "It mutilates the perfected form of God's handiwork."

2686. According to Mālik, Ṣafwān b. Sulaym reported that it reached him that the Prophet (pbuh) said, "Someone who cares for an orphan, provided he is mindful of God, and whether the orphan is his relative or a stranger to him, shall join me in Paradise, the way these two are joined." He was gesturing with his middle and index fingers.

Chapter 43. Grooming the Hair

2687. According to Mālik, Yaḥyā b. Saʿīd reported that Abū Qatāda al-Anṣārī said to the Messenger of God (pbuh), "I have a lot of hair that comes down to my shoulders. Should I comb it?" The Messenger of God (pbuh) said, "Yes, and honor it." Abū Qatāda thereafter applied oil to it twice a day, because the Messenger of God (pbuh) had told him, "Honor it."

2688. According to Mālik, Zayd b. Aslam reported that ʿAṭāʾ b. Yasār informed him, "The Messenger of God (pbuh) was in the mosque when a man with disheveled hair and a disheveled beard came in. The Messenger of God (pbuh) motioned for the man to leave the mosque, as if to tell him not to come back until he had groomed his hair and beard. The man did so and returned. The Messenger of God (pbuh) said, "Isn't it better to come to the mosque looking well-groomed, rather than disheveled as if one were Satan?"

Chapter 44. What Has Come Down regarding Dyeing the Hair

2689. According to Mālik, Yaḥyā b. Saʿīd said, "Muḥammad b. Ibrāhīm al-Taymī informed me, from Abū Salama b. ʿAbd al-Raḥmān, that ʿAbd al-Raḥmān b. al-Aswad b. ʿAbd Yaghūth, who, Abū Salama said, used to sit with them in their gatherings and whose beard and hair were grey, one day showed up, having dyed them both red. Abū Salama said, 'Everyone said to him, "This is much better." He said, "My mother, the Mother of the Believers, ʿĀ'isha, the wife of the Prophet (pbuh), sent her handmaiden, Nukhayla, to me yesterday. She told me that ʿĀ'isha insisted that I dye my hair, and that she had taken a solemn oath that I would indeed dye my hair. She also let me know that Abū Bakr al-Ṣiddīq would dye his hair."'"

2690. Yaḥyā said, "I heard Mālik say, regarding dyeing the hair black, 'I have not heard anything definitive about that, but I prefer the use of other colors. There is great latitude in whether or not to dye one's hair, God willing, and the people are not subject to any constraint with respect to it.'" Yaḥyā said, "I heard Mālik say, 'This report is proof that the Messenger of God (pbuh) did not dye his own hair. Had the Messenger of God (pbuh) dyed his own hair, ʿĀ'isha would certainly have informed ʿAbd al-Raḥmān b. al-Aswad of that fact.'"

Chapter 45. Occasions That Necessitate Seeking God's Protection

2691. According to Mālik, Yaḥyā b. Saʿīd said, "It reached me that Khālid b. al-Walīd said to the Messenger of God (pbuh), 'I suffer from nightmares.' The Messenger of God (pbuh) said to him, 'Say, "I seek protection in the perfect words of God from His wrath, from His punishment, from the evil of His servants, and from the whispering of demons, lest they afflict me."'"

2692. According to Mālik, Yaḥyā b. Saʿīd said, "When the Messenger of God (pbuh) was taken on the Night Journey, he saw an afreet chasing him with a fiery torch. Whenever the Messenger of God (pbuh) turned, he saw him. The Archangel Gabriel said to him, "Shall I teach you some words through which, were you to say them, the torch would be extinguished and the afreet would fall on his face?" The Messenger of God (pbuh) said, "Yes, indeed!" Gabriel said, "Say: 'I seek refuge in God's noble countenance and in God's perfect words, which neither the pious nor the wicked can transgress, from the evil that descends from the heavens, from the evil that ascends into them, from the evil that moves about on the earth, from the evil that emerges from underneath it, from the tribulations of both the night and the day, and from the evil of unexpected nighttime visitors, save for one that comes with good news, O Merciful One!'"[1005]

1005 *Aʿūdhu bi-wajhi 'llāhi 'l-karīm wa-bi-kalimāti 'llāhi 'l-tāmmāti 'llatī lā yujāwizuhunna barrun wa-lā fājir, min sharri mā yanzilu min al-samā'i wa-sharri mā yaʿruju fīhā, wa-sharri*

2693. According to Mālik, Suhayl b. Abī Ṣāliḥ reported from his father, from Abū Hurayra, that a man of the tribe of Aslam said, "I could not sleep last night." The Messenger of God (pbuh) said to him, "Why not?" He said, "A scorpion stung me." The Messenger of God (pbuh) said, "If only you had said when you laid down to sleep in the evening, 'I seek protection in God's perfect words from the evil of His handiwork,' it would have caused you no harm."

2694. According to Mālik, Sumayy, the freedman (*mawlā*) of Abū Bakr, reported from al-Qaʿqāʿ b. Ḥakīm that Kaʿb al-Aḥbār said, "Were it not for the fact that I recite certain words, the Jews would have transformed me into a donkey." Someone asked him, "And what are they?" He said, "I seek protection in God's glorious countenance, beyond which there is nothing greater, and in God's perfect words, which neither the pious nor the wicked can transgress, and in God's beautiful names, all of them, those that I know and those I do not, from the evil that He has created, originated, and multiplied."[1006]

Chapter 46. What Has Come Down regarding Those Who Love One Another for God's Sake

2695. According to Mālik, ʿAbd Allāh b. ʿAbd al-Raḥmān b. Maʿmar reported from Abū al-Ḥubāb Saʿīd b. Yasār that Abū Hurayra said, "The Messenger of God (pbuh) said, 'God, Blessed and Sublime is He, will say on the Day of Resurrection, "Where are those who love one another for the sake of My majesty? I shall protect them in My shade today, a day on which there is no shade except Mine."'"

2696. According to Mālik, Khubayb b. ʿAbd al-Raḥmān al-Anṣārī reported from Ḥafṣ b. ʿĀṣim that either Abū Saʿīd al-Khudrī or Abū Hurayra said, "The Messenger of God (pbuh) said, 'There are seven kinds of people whom God will protect in His shade on the day on which there is no shade except His: a just ruler (*imām*); a youth who grows up sincerely worshipping God; someone whose heart is attached to the mosque, where it abides even after he departs from it; two souls who love one another for the sake of God, having met for that purpose and parting with it; a person whose eyes overflow with tears when he remembers God in his private moments; a man who refuses the advances of a noble, beautiful woman, saying, "I fear God"; and a person who, when giving charity (*ṣadaqa*), conceals it, such that his left hand does not know what his right hand gives.'"

---

mā dharaʾa fī ʾl-arḍi wa-sharri mā yakhruju minhā, wa-min fitani ʾl-layli waʾl-nahāri wa-min ṭawāriqi ʾl-layli illā ṭāriqin yaṭruqu bi-khayr, yā raḥmān.

1006 *Aʿūdhu bi-wajhi ʾllāhi ʾl-ʿaẓīmi ʾlladhī laysa shayʾun aʿẓama minhu wa-bi-kalimāti ʾllāhi ʾl-tāmmāti ʾllatī lā yujāwizuhunna barrun wa-lā fājirun wa-bi-asmāʾi ʾllāhi ʾl-ḥusnā kullihā mā ʿalimtu minhā wa-mā lam aʿlam, min sharri mā khalaqa wa-baraʾa wa-dharaʾa.*

2697. According to Mālik, Suhayl b. Abī Ṣāliḥ reported from his father, from Abū Hurayra, that the Messenger of God (pbuh) said, "When God loves a servant of His, He says to Gabriel, 'I love so-and-so, so you should, too.' Gabriel therefore comes to love him. Gabriel then calls out to the denizens of the Heavens, 'God loves so-and-so, so you should, too.' The denizens of Heaven thus come to love him. Then they work to assure his place on earth. When God despises a servant of His . . ." Mālik said, "I am confident that what the narrator said regarding God's hatred is essentially the same."

2698. According to Mālik, Abū Ḥāzim b. Dīnār reported that Abū Idrīs al-Khawlānī said, "I entered the mosque in Damascus and saw there a young man whose teeth sparkled and around whom the worshippers had gathered. Whenever they disagreed about something, they referred it to him and would rely on his view. I therefore asked who he was, and someone told me, 'This is Muʿādh b. Jabal.' The next day, I set out early after the sun had risen for the mosque, but I found that Muʿādh had already arrived and was busy in the performance of prayer. I thus waited for him to complete his prayers. When he did, I walked straight up to him and greeted him. I said, 'By God, I certainly do love you for the sake of God.' He said, 'Do you indeed swear that it is for the sake of God?' I said, 'Certainly, I do swear that it is for the sake of God!' He said, 'Do you indeed swear that it is for the sake of God?' So I said, 'Certainly, I do swear that it is!' He then took me by the middle of my cloak, pulled me toward him, and said, 'Rejoice! For I heard the Messenger of God (pbuh) say, "God, Blessed and Sublime is He, said, 'Those who love one another for My sake, those who sit with one another in remembrance of Me, those who visit one another for My sake, and those who sacrifice what they have willingly for one another for My sake are entitled to My love.'"'"

2699. According to Mālik, it reached him that ʿAbd Allāh b. ʿAbbās would say, "Moderation, gentleness, and a goodly appearance are some of the twenty-five parts of prophethood."

Chapter 47. Dreams

2700. According to Mālik, Isḥāq b. ʿAbd Allāh b. Abī Ṭalḥa al-Anṣārī reported from Anas b. Mālik that the Messenger of God (pbuh) said, "A righteous man's auspicious dream is one of the forty-six parts of prophethood."

2701. According to Mālik, Abū al-Zinād reported from al-Aʿraj, from Abū Hurayra, a similar report from the Messenger of God (pbuh).

2702. According to Mālik, Isḥāq b. ʿAbd Allāh b. Abī Ṭalḥa reported from Zufar b. Ṣaʿṣaʿa b. Mālik, from his father, from Abū Hurayra, that when the

Messenger of God (pbuh) finished performance of the Morning Prayer (*ṣalāt al-ṣubḥ*), he would ask, "Did anyone have a dream last night?" He would also say, "Nothing will remain of prophethood after me other than auspicious dreams."

2703. According to Mālik, Zayd b. Aslam reported from ʿAṭāʾ b. Yasār that the Messenger of God (pbuh) said, "Nothing will remain of prophethood after me other than good tidings (*mubashshirāt*)." They asked, "What are these good tidings, Messenger of God?" He said, "An auspicious dream that a righteous man sees (or is made to see) is one of the forty-six parts of prophethood."

2704. According to Mālik, Yaḥyā b. Saʿīd reported that Abū Salama b. ʿAbd al-Raḥmān said, "I heard Abū Qatāda b. Ribʿī say, 'I heard the Messenger of God (pbuh) say, "An auspicious dream is from God, and a nightmare is from Satan. If someone sees something evil in his sleep, he should blow from his mouth three times, with some spittle, to his left when he awakes, seeking God's protection from the evil of his nightmare. If he does so, it will never harm him, God willing."' I used to see things in my sleep that weighed on me more heavily than mountains, but after I heard this report, I stopped worrying about them."

2705. According to Mālik, Hishām b. ʿUrwa reported that his father would say, regarding the Quranic verse "To them belong the good tidings of this life and the next"[1007] that it was a reference to auspicious dreams that the righteous see (or are made to see).

Chapter 48. What Has Come Down regarding Dice

2706. According to Mālik, Mūsā b. Maysara reported from Saʿīd b. Abī Hind, from Abū Mūsā al-Ashʿarī, that the Messenger of God (pbuh) said, "Whoever plays games of dice has disobeyed God and His Messenger."

2707. According to Mālik, ʿAlqama b. Abī ʿAlqama reported from his mother, from ʿĀʾisha, the wife of the Prophet (pbuh), that word reached her that a family who was living with her in a room of her house had some dice. She sent a message to them, saying, "If you do not get rid of the dice, I will evict you from my home." She sternly rebuked them for having dice.

2708. According to Mālik, Nāfiʿ reported from ʿAbd Allāh b. ʿUmar that whenever he found anyone in his family playing with dice, he would strike him and break the dice."

1007 *Yūnus*, 10:64.

2709. Yaḥyā said, "I heard Mālik say, 'There is no good in chess,' and he disapproved of it. I heard him express disapproval of the playing of chess and other such games, condemning them as vain. When asked about them, he would recite this verse: 'And what is there after truth but error?'"[1008]

Chapter 49. The Norms Governing Greetings

2710. According to Mālik, Zayd b. Aslam reported that the Messenger of God (pbuh) said, "The rider should greet the pedestrian, and when one member of a group returns a greeting, he does so on behalf of the whole group."

2711. According to Mālik, Wahb b. Kaysān reported that Muḥammad b. ʿAmr b. ʿAṭā' said, "I was sitting with ʿAbd Allāh b. ʿAbbās when a Yemeni man came in and said, 'Peace be upon you, and God's mercy and His blessings.'[1009] He then appended some additional words to that greeting. Ibn ʿAbbās, who by this time had gone blind, asked, 'Who is this man?' They said to him, 'This is the Yemeni man who came to visit you,' and they introduced the man to him. Ibn ʿAbbās told him, 'When greeting someone, you should add nothing after the word 'blessings.'"

2712. Yaḥyā said, "Mālik was asked, 'Should one greet a woman?' He said, "As for an old woman, I do not disapprove of greeting her. If she is young, however, I do."

Chapter 50. What Has Come Down regarding Greeting Jews and Christians

2713. According to Mālik, ʿAbd Allāh b. Dīnār reported that ʿAbd Allāh b. ʿUmar said, "The Messenger of God (pbuh) said, 'When a Jew greets you saying, "May death visit you" (*al-sāmm ʿalaykum*),[1010] reply by saying, "And the same to you!"'"

2714. Mālik was asked about whether someone who greets a Jew or a Christian should retract it. He said, "No."

Chapter 51. Miscellaneous Matters regarding Greetings

2715. According to Mālik, Isḥāq b. ʿAbd Allāh b. Abī Ṭalḥa reported from Abū Murra, the freedman (*mawlā*) of ʿAqīl b. Abī Ṭālib, from Abū Wāqid al-Laythī, that while the Messenger of God (pbuh) was sitting with the people in the

---

1008 *Yūnus*, 10:32.

1009 The Arabic transliteration of the customary greeting is *Al-salāmu ʿalaykum wa-raḥmatullāhi wa-barakātuh*.

1010 The printed edition of the RME erroneously has *al-salām ʿalaykum* rather than *al-sāmm ʿalaykum*, which is the only version of the text reported in the sources.

mosque, three people came in, two of whom approached the Messenger of God (pbuh) and one of whom went away. When the two men stopped near the Messenger of God (pbuh), they greeted him. One of them saw room in the circle of the congregants and joined it. The second man sat down behind the circle. As for the third, he turned around and walked away. When the Messenger of God (pbuh) finished what he was doing, he said, "Shall I inform you of the fate of these three? The first of them sought refuge with God, so God sheltered him. The second was bashful, so God was indulgent toward him. The third turned away, so God turned away from him."

2716. According to Mālik, Isḥāq b. ʿAbd Allāh b. Abī Ṭalḥa reported from Anas b. Mālik that he heard ʿUmar b. al-Khaṭṭāb, after replying to a man who had greeted him, ask the man, "How are you?" The man said, "I declare God's praise to you." ʿUmar said, "That is exactly what I wished to hear from you."

2717. According to Mālik, Isḥāq b. ʿAbd Allāh b. Abī Ṭalḥa reported that al-Ṭufayl b. Ubayy b. Kaʿb informed him that he would go to ʿAbd Allāh b. ʿUmar and accompany him to the market in the morning. Al-Ṭufayl said, "While we were out, ʿAbd Allāh would not cross paths with anyone, whether a purveyor of undesirable merchandise, a person selling goods, a pitiable soul, or anyone else, without greeting him. One day I came to ʿAbd Allāh, and he asked me to go with him to the market. I said to him, 'What are you planning to do there, inasmuch as you never stop to buy or sell merchandise, haggle, or sit with the market's merchants?' He said, 'Let's sit down here and talk.' Then ʿAbd Allāh said to me, 'Abū Baṭn!'[1011]—because al-Ṭufayl had a plump belly—'We set out in the morning only to greet others. We greet everyone we meet.'"

2718. According to Mālik, Yaḥyā b. Saʿīd reported that a man greeted ʿAbd Allāh b. ʿUmar, saying, "Peace be upon you, and God's mercy and His blessings, and all that goes and comes."[1012] ʿAbd Allāh b. ʿUmar said to the man, "And to you, a thousand times the like," as if that annoyed him.

2719. According to Mālik, it reached him that when one enters an abandoned home, one should say, "Peace be upon us, and on God's righteous servants."[1013]

1011 *Baṭn* is an Arabic word for the belly.

1012 The commentators disagree as to what the speaker intended by the statement "all that goes and comes" (*ul-ghādiyāt wa'l-rā'iḥāt*), with one saying that he intended the birds and others suggesting that he meant the angels who record human deeds. Bājī, *al-Muntaqā*, 7:283.

1013 *Al-salāmu ʿalaynā wa-ʿalā ʿibādi 'llāhi 'l-ṣāliḥīn.*

Chapter 52. Asking Permission to Enter

2720. According to Mālik, Ṣafwān b. Sulaym reported from ʿAṭāʾ b. Yasār that a man asked the Messenger of God (pbuh), "Messenger of God, must I ask my mother's permission before I enter the house?" He said, "Yes." The man said, "But I live with her there." The Messenger of God (pbuh) said, "Nevertheless, ask her permission." The man said, "But I serve her." The Messenger of God (pbuh) said to him, "Nevertheless, ask her permission. Do you wish to see her naked?" The man said, "No." The Messenger of God (pbuh) then said, "In that case, always ask her permission to enter."

2721. According to Mālik, a source he deemed reliable reported from Bukayr b. ʿAbd Allāh al-Ashajj, from Busr b. Saʿīd, from Abū Saʿīd al-Khudrī, that Abū Mūsā al-Ashʿarī said, "The Messenger of God (pbuh) said, 'Ask permission to enter three times. If permission is granted, you may enter, but if it is not, go away.'"

2722. According to Mālik, Rabīʿa b. Abī ʿAbd al-Raḥmān reported from several of their scholars that Abū Mūsā al-Ashʿarī sought permission to see ʿUmar b. al-Khaṭṭāb. He asked to enter three times, heard no response, and left. ʿUmar sent someone after him, and when ʿUmar saw Abū Mūsā, ʿUmar said to him, "Why didn't you enter?" Abū Mūsā said, "I heard the Messenger of God (pbuh) say, 'Ask permission to enter three times. If permission is granted, you may enter, but if it is not, go away.'" ʿUmar said, "Who else is aware of this? If you cannot bring forth anyone else to corroborate this, I will see to it that you are punished." Abū Mūsā left and kept going until he found assembled in the mosque some people who were meeting. This group was known as "the Medinese assembly" (*majlis al-anṣār*). Abū Mūsā said, "I informed ʿUmar b. al-Khaṭṭāb that I had heard the Messenger of God (pbuh) say, 'Ask permission to enter three times. If permission is granted, you may enter, but if it is not, go away.' ʿUmar said, 'If you cannot bring forth anyone else to corroborate this, I will see to it that you are punished.' If any of you has also heard this, he should come with me." They said to Abū Saʿīd al-Khudrī, "Get up and go with him." Abū Saʿīd was the youngest of them. He got up and went with Abū Mūsā and informed ʿUmar about that report. ʿUmar said to Abū Mūsā, "In fact, I never doubted you, but I fear that people may attribute statements to the Messenger of God (pbuh) that he never made."

Chapter 53. Invoking Blessings When a Person Sneezes

2723. According to Mālik, ʿAbd Allāh b. Abī Bakr reported from his father that the Messenger of God (pbuh) said, "If someone sneezes, bless him. If he sneezes again, bless him again. If he sneezes a third time, bless him a third time. If he sneezes a fourth time, however, say to him, 'You have a cold.'" ʿAbd Allāh b. Abī Bakr said, "I do not know whether it was after the third or the fourth sneeze."

2724. According to Mālik, Nāfiʿ reported that when ʿAbd Allāh b. ʿUmar sneezed, people would say, "God show mercy on you."[1014] He would reply, "God show mercy on us and on you, and may He forgive us and you."[1015]

Chapter 54. What Has Come Down regarding Statues

2725. According to Mālik, Isḥāq b. Abī Ṭalḥa reported that Rāfiʿ b. Isḥāq, the freedman (*mawlā*) of al-Shifāʾ, informed him, "ʿAbd Allāh b. Abī Ṭalḥa and I went to visit Abū Saʿīd al-Khudrī when he was ill. Abū Saʿīd said to us, 'The Messenger of God (pbuh) said to us that the angels do not enter a house in which there are statues (or "figures").'" Isḥāq was uncertain which word Abū Saʿīd used, "statues" or "figures."

2726. According to Mālik, Abū al-Naḍr reported from ʿUbayd Allāh b. ʿAbd Allāh b. ʿUtba b. Masʿūd that he went to visit Abū Ṭalḥa al-Anṣārī when he was ill. He said, "I found Sahl b. Ḥunayf there with him. Abū Ṭalḥa called for a man and asked him to remove a rug on which Sahl had been sitting. Sahl said to him, "Why are you having it removed?" Abū Ṭalḥa replied, "Because there are figures on it, and you know what the Messenger of God (pbuh) said about them." Sahl said, "But didn't the Messenger of God (pbuh) exclude drawings on a garment?" Abū Ṭalḥa said, "Yes, indeed, but removing the carpet puts me at ease."[1016]

2727. According to Mālik, Nāfiʿ reported from al-Qāsim b. Muḥammad, from ʿĀʾisha, the wife of the Prophet (pbuh), that she purchased a small cushion that had pictures on it. When the Messenger of God (pbuh) saw it, he stopped at the door and did not enter. She realized from his facial expression that there was something bothering him. She said, "Messenger of God! I turn in repentance to God and to His Messenger, but what did I do wrong?" The Messenger of God (pbuh) said, "What is this cushion doing here?" She said, "I purchased it for you, so that you may sit on it or recline on it." The Messenger of God (pbuh) said, "Those who made these pictures will be punished on the Day of Resurrection. It will be said to them, 'Bring to life what you have created.'" Then he said, "Angels do not enter a room in which there are images."

1014 *Yarḥamuka 'llāh.*

1015 *Yarḥamunā 'llāh wa-iyyākum, wa-yaghfir lanā wa-iyyākum.*

1016 Sahl was analogizing the Prophet's permission to have images on cloth to the case of images on a carpet. Abū Ṭalḥa granted the validity of the analogy but preferred to remove the carpet out of precaution.

Chapter 55. What Has Come Down regarding Eating Lizards

2728. According to Mālik, ʿAbd al-Raḥmān b. ʿAbd Allāh b. ʿAbd al-Raḥmān b. Abī Ṣaʿṣaʿa reported that Sulaymān b. Yasār said, "The Messenger of God (pbuh) once entered the house of Maymūna bt. al-Ḥārith, who had with her some lizard meat and eggs. ʿAbd Allāh b. ʿAbbās and Khālid b. al-Walīd were with him at the time. The Messenger of God (pbuh) asked her, "Where did you get this from?" She replied, "My sister Huzayla bt. al-Ḥārith gave them to me." He then told ʿAbd Allāh and Khālid, "Go ahead and eat, if you wish." The two of them said, "Won't you eat with us, Messenger of God?" He said, "Heavenly visitors from God frequent me." Maymūna then said, "Messenger of God, in that case, shall we give you some of our milk to drink?" He said, "Yes." When he finished drinking it, he said, "Where did you get this from?" She said, "My sister Huzayla gave it to me." The Messenger of God (pbuh) then said, "Do you remember your handmaiden, the one about whose manumission you sought my advice? Give her to your sister and make her available to your maternal relatives, so that she may take care of them. That would be better for you than manumitting her."

2729. According to Mālik, Ibn Shihāb reported from Abū Umāma b. Sahl b. Ḥunayf, from ʿAbd Allāh b. ʿAbbās, from Khālid b. al-Walīd b. al-Mughīra, that he once entered the house of Maymūna, the wife of the Prophet (pbuh), in the company of the Messenger of God (pbuh). A roasted lizard was served. The Messenger of God (pbuh) stretched out his hand toward it, but some of the women of the house said, "Let the Messenger of God (pbuh) know what he is about to eat." Someone said, "It is lizard, Messenger of God," whereupon he withdrew his hand. Khālid said, "Is eating it prohibited, Messenger of God?" He said, "No, but I am unaccustomed to it, insofar as it was unknown to my people, and so I find it disagreeable." Khālid said, "I then grabbed it and ate it while the Messenger of God (pbuh) looked on."

2730. According to Mālik, ʿAbd Allāh b. Dīnār reported from ʿAbd Allāh b. ʿUmar that a man called out to the Messenger of God (pbuh) and asked him, "Messenger of God, what is your view regarding lizard meat?" The Messenger of God (pbuh) said, "I neither eat it nor forbid eating it."

Chapter 56. What Has Come Down regarding the Rules That Apply to Dogs

2731. According to Mālik, Yazīd b. Khuṣayfa reported that al-Sā'ib b. Yazīd informed him that he heard Sufyān b. Abī Zuhayr, who was of the Shanū'a tribe, and a Companion of the Messenger of God (pbuh) relate the following to some people who were standing with him at the entrance to the mosque.

Sufyān said, "I heard the Messenger of God (pbuh) say, 'Whoever acquires a dog that he does not use to guard either his crops or his flock loses a portion of the reward he would have received that day for his good deeds.'" Someone interjected, "Did you hear this from the Messenger of God (pbuh)?" Sufyān said, "Yes, indeed, by the Lord of this mosque."

2732. According to Mālik, Nāfiʿ reported from ʿAbd Allāh b. ʿUmar that the Messenger of God (pbuh) said, "Whoever acquires a dog that is not fit for hunting or guarding flocks loses two portions of the reward he would have received that day for his good deeds."

2733. According to Mālik, Nāfiʿ reported from ʿAbd Allāh b. ʿUmar that the Messenger of God (pbuh) commanded that dogs be killed.

Chapter 57. What Has Come Down regarding Sheep (*Ghanam*)

2734. According to Mālik, Abū al-Zinād reported from al-Aʿraj, from Abū Hurayra, that the Messenger of God (pbuh) said, "The heart of disbelief lies in the east; arrogance and pride are the chief traits of those who breed horses and camels, the uncouth tent-dwellers; and tranquility is the chief trait of those who herd sheep."

2735. According to Mālik, ʿAbd al-Raḥmān b. ʿAbd Allāh b. ʿAbd al-Raḥmān b. Abī Ṣaʿṣaʿa reported from his father that Abū Saʿīd al-Khudrī said, "The Messenger of God (pbuh) said, 'It will soon be the case that a Muslim's best property is sheep, which he follows up and down mountain passes in search of pasture and rain, fleeing with his religion from the trials and tribulations of his day.'"

2736. According to Mālik, Nāfiʿ reported from ʿAbd Allāh b. ʿUmar that the Messenger of God (pbuh) said, "No one should milk another's livestock without the owner's permission. Would anyone be happy if someone were to come to his room, break into his pantry, and remove his food? The udders of livestock warehouse food for their owners. Therefore, no one should milk another's livestock without the owner's permission."

2737. According to Mālik, it reached him that the Messenger of God (pbuh) said, "Every prophet has also been a shepherd." Someone said, "Including you, Messenger of God?" He said, "Yes."

Chapter 58. What Has Come Down regarding Mice Falling into Clarified Butter and regarding Eating before Performing Prayer

2738. According to Mālik, Nāfiʿ reported that ʿAbd Allāh b. ʿUmar would have his supper served to him, even as he could hear, while still sitting at home, the imam recite from the Quran. He would continue his meal until he was finished.

2739. According to Mālik, Ibn Shihāb reported from ʿUbayd Allāh b. ʿAbd Allāh b. ʿUtba b. Masʿūd, from ʿAbd Allāh b. ʿAbbās, from Maymūna, the wife of the Prophet (pbuh), that someone asked the Messenger of God (pbuh) what to do if a mouse falls into a container of clarified butter. He said, "Extract its body from the butter, along with the butter surrounding it."

Chapter 59. What May Be Signs of Ill Omen (*Shu'm*)

2740. According to Mālik, Abū Ḥāzim b. Dīnār reported from Sahl b. Saʿd al-Sāʿidī that the Messenger of God (pbuh) said, "Were such things to exist, it would be in a horse, a woman, or a place of residence," meaning ill omens.

2741. According to Mālik, Ibn Shihāb reported from Ḥamza b. ʿAbd Allāh b. ʿUmar and Sālim b. ʿAbd Allāh b. ʿUmar, from ʿAbd Allāh b. ʿUmar, that the Messenger of God (pbuh) said, "Ill omens may be found in a house, a woman, or a horse."

2742. According to Mālik, Yaḥyā b. Saʿīd said, "A woman came to the Messenger of God (pbuh) and said, 'Messenger of God, we moved into a house at a time when our numbers were great and our wealth vast. Now our number has diminished and our wealth has been dissipated.' The Messenger of God (pbuh) said, 'Abandon it, for it certainly deserves blame.'"[1017]

Chapter 60. Names That Are Disfavored

2743. According to Mālik, Yaḥyā b. Saʿīd reported that the Messenger of God (pbuh) once asked about a milch camel, "Who is ready to milk her?" A man stood up, so the Messenger of God (pbuh) asked him, "What is your name?" The man said, "Murra."[1018] The Messenger of God (pbuh) said to him, "Sit down." He then asked again, "Who is ready to milk her?" and a different man stood up. The Messenger of God (pbuh) asked him, "And what is your name?" The man said, "Ḥarb."[1019] The Messenger of God (pbuh) said to him, "Sit down." He then said a third time, "Who is ready to milk her?" A third man stood up. The Messenger of God (pbuh) said, "And what is your

1017 Ibn ʿAbd al-Barr interprets this statement of the Prophet (pbuh) as a recognition on his part that the people in question believed in bad omens and that it would be practically impossible to dissuade them from this belief. Sensing this, the Prophet (pbuh) encouraged them to leave the place if, in fact, they had become convinced the place was a cause of their misfortune. Ibn ʿAbd al-Barr, *al-Istidhkār*, 8:512.

1018 *Murra* means "bitterness."

1019 *Ḥarb* means "war."

name?" The man said, "Yaʿīsh."[1020] The Messenger of God (pbuh) said to him, "Go ahead and milk her!"[1021]

2744. According to Mālik, Yaḥyā b. Saʿīd reported that ʿUmar b. al-Khaṭṭāb once asked a man, "What is your name?" The man said, "Jamra."[1022] ʿUmar said, "Who is your father?" He said, "My father is Shihāb."[1023] ʿUmar then asked him, "Of what tribe?" The man replied, "al-Ḥurqa."[1024] ʿUmar then asked him, "And where is your people's territory?" The man said, "At Ḥarrat al-Nār."[1025] ʿUmar then asked him, "Where within that territory?" The man replied, "Dhāt al-Laẓā."[1026] ʿUmar said to the man, "Quickly save your family, lest they be consumed by flames." Yaḥyā b. Saʿīd said, "It turned out to be as ʿUmar b. al-Khaṭṭāb said."

Chapter 61. What Has Come Down regarding Cupping (*Ḥijāma*) and Hiring a Cupper

2745. According to Mālik, Ḥumayd al-Ṭawīl reported that Anas b. Mālik said, "A man named Abū Ṭayba once cupped the Messenger of God (pbuh). The Messenger of God (pbuh) ordered that he should be given two kilograms (one *ṣāʿ*) of dates as compensation. He also ordered Abū Ṭayba's people to reduce what they took from him out of his earnings."[1027]

2746. According to Mālik, it reached him that the Messenger of God (pbuh) said, "If there is a remedy that is up to the challenge of an ailment, cupping (*ḥijāma*) is certainly the one."

2747. According to Mālik, Ibn Shihāb reported from Ibn Muḥayṣa al-Anṣārī of the Banū Ḥāritha that he asked permission from the Messenger of God (pbuh) to profit from the wage received by a slave of his who was a cupper. However, the Messenger of God (pbuh) prohibited him from doing so. The man continued to ask him and to seek his permission, until the Messenger

---

1020 *Yaʿīsh* means "he lives."

1021 It was common for pre-Islamic Arabs, like other groups in Late Antiquity, to use ferocious names as a means of intimidating potential enemies.

1022 *Jamra* means "ember."

1023 *Shihāb* means "comet."

1024 *Ḥurqa* means "agony" or "burning."

1025 *Ḥarrat al-nār* means "the lava field of the fire."

1026 *Dhāt al-laẓā* means "the place consumed by an inferno."

1027 Zurqānī explains the term *kharāj* in the report as referring to that portion of a slave's earnings that the slave is periodically required to give to his master. He clearly assumes that Abū Ṭayba was a slave, although the text does not expressly describe him as such. According to Zurqānī, Abū Ṭayba's people required him to give them three measures (*ṣāʿ*) of dates (approximately six kilograms), but he did not specify how often this transfer was due. If Zurqānī's interpretation of the report is accurate, it seems that the Prophet (pbuh) believed that their demands from Abū Ṭayba were unreasonable.

of God (pbuh) finally said, "Feed it to those who water your camels and date palms," meaning his slaves.[1028]

Chapter 62. What Has Come Down regarding the East

2748. According to Mālik, ʿAbd Allāh b. Dīnār reported that ʿAbd Allāh b. ʿUmar said, "I saw the Messenger of God (pbuh) pointing at the East and saying, 'There, that is the origin of strife and tribulation. There is the home of strife and tribulation from whence Satan's partisans will emerge.'"[1029]

2749. According to Mālik, it reached him that ʿUmar b. al-Khaṭṭāb wanted to set out for Iraq, but Kaʿb al-Aḥbār said to him, "Do not go there, Commander of the Faithful, for nine-tenths of all the world's sorcery resides there, and it is home to the most wicked of the jinn as well as chronic, untreatable disease."

Chapter 63. What Has Come Down regarding Killing Snakes, and What Is Said about That

2750. According to Mālik, Nāfiʿ reported from Abū Lubāba that the Messenger of God (pbuh) prohibited killing snakes found in people's houses.

2751. According to Mālik, Nāfiʿ reported from Sāʾiba, the freedwoman (*mawlāt*) of ʿĀʾisha, the wife of the Prophet (pbuh), that he prohibited killing snakes that live in houses, except for those with two stripes on their backs and those with stub tails. They cause blindness and miscarriages.

2752. According to Mālik, Ṣayfī, the freedman (*mawlā*) of Ibn Aflaḥ, reported that Abū al-Sāʾib, the freedman of Hishām b. Zuhra, said, "I went to see Abū Saʿīd al-Khudrī and found him performing prayer. I sat down to wait for him until he finished. Then I heard the sound of movement under a chair in his room. It turned out to be a snake, so I got up to kill it, but he motioned for me to sit down. When he finished the prayer, he pointed to a room in the house and said, 'Do you see that room?' I said, 'Yes!' He said, 'A newlywed youth once lived there. He set out with the Messenger of God (pbuh) on the day of the Battle of the Trench (*khandaq*). While the Messenger of God (pbuh) was there, the youth went to him and said, "Messenger of God, please let me return to visit my wife." The Messenger of God (pbuh) granted him leave but said, "Take your weapons with you, for I am concerned that

---

1028 Jurists find this report problematic since they do not believe that the profession of cupping is illegal. They consequently interpret the Prophet's (pbuh) reluctance to permit Ibn Muḥayṣa to profit from his slave's cupping wages as reflecting either an initial prohibition that was subsequently rescinded or the social disrepute of cupping. Bājī, *al-Muntaqā*, 7:298.

1029 Ibn ʿAbd al-Barr interprets this report as a prediction of the civil wars that broke out among the early Muslim community in Iraq and the territories east of it. Ibn ʿAbd al-Barr, *al-Istidkhār*, 8:519–20.

the Banū Qurayẓa[1030] might harm you." The youth then departed to visit his wife. When he arrived home, he found her outside, standing at the entrance. Jealousy took control of him, so lifted his spear to stab her. She said, "Don't be so hasty! Come inside and see what is in your room." When he entered, he discovered a snake coiled up on his bed. He plunged his spear into it, left the room, and planted the spear upright in the house. The snake twisted and turned at the end of the spear, and then the youth collapsed, dead. No one knew which one had died first, the youth or the snake. We mentioned the incident to the Messenger of God (pbuh) and he said, "There are jinn in Medina who have become Muslim. When you see any of them, leave him alone for three days; but if he continues to appear to you beyond that period of time, you may kill him, for he is a devil."'"[1031]

Chapter 64. What Should Be Said When on a Journey

2753. According to Mālik, it reached him that when the Messenger of God (pbuh) placed his foot in the stirrup at the beginning of a journey, he would say, "In the name of God. O God, you are our companion on this journey and the protector of the family that I leave behind! O God, spread out the earth for us, and make the journey easy for us! O God, I seek your protection from the hardships of this journey, from a sorrowful return, and from a distressing sight, be it in my property or in my family!"[1032]

2754. According to Mālik, a source he deemed reliable reported from Yaʿqūb b. ʿAbd Allāh b. al-Ashajj, from Busr b. Saʿīd, from Saʿd b. Abī Waqqāṣ, from Khawla bt. Ḥakīm, that the Messenger of God (pbuh) said, "Whoever alights to rest in a place should say, 'I seek protection in God's perfect words from the evil that He created.' Whoever says this will be safe from harm until he decamps."[1033]

Chapter 65. What Has Come Down regarding Traveling Alone in the Case of Men and Women

2755. According to Mālik, ʿAbd al-Raḥmān b. Ḥarmala reported from ʿAmr b. Shuʿayb, from his father, from his grandfather, that the Messenger of God (pbuh) said, "One rider is a demon, two are two demons, but three are a riding party."

1030 A powerful Jewish tribe in Medina that was allied with the Muslims but turned on them during the pagans' siege of Medina, known as the Battle of the Trench.

1031 This statement refers to the common pre-Islamic Arab belief that jinn could take on the form of snakes.

1032 *Bismi 'llāh. Allāhumma anta 'l-ṣāḥibu fī 'l-safari wa'l-khalīfatu fī 'l-ahl. Allāhumma 'zwi lanā 'l-arḍa wa-hawwin ʿalaynā 'l-safar. Allāhumma innī aʿūdhu bika min waʿthā'i 'l-safari wa-min ka'ābati 'l-munqalibi wa-min sū'i 'l-manẓari fī 'l-māli wa'l-ahl.*

1033 *Aʿūdhu bi-kalimāti 'llāhi 'l-tāmmāti min sharri mā khalaqa.*

2756. According to Mālik, ʿAbd al-Raḥmān b. Ḥarmala reported that Saʿīd b. al-Musayyab would say, "The Messenger of God (pbuh) said, 'Satan preys on the solitary and the pair, but when there are three or more, he leaves them alone.'"

2757. According to Mālik, Saʿīd b. Abī Saʿīd al-Maqburī reported from Abū Hurayra that the Messenger of God (pbuh) said, "It is not lawful for a woman who believes in God and the Last Day to travel the distance of a day and a night unaccompanied by a close male relative who is prohibited to her in marriage (*maḥram*)."

Chapter 66. What Is Commanded with Respect to Norms Governing Travel

2758. According to Mālik, Abū ʿUbayd, the freedman (*mawlā*) of Sulaymān b. ʿAbd al-Malik, reported from Khālid b. Maʿdān, who attributed to the Prophet (pbuh) that he said, "God, Blessed and Sublime is He, is gentle and loves gentleness, and He takes pleasure in it. What He gives in succor to those who pursue their ends gently is not what He gives to those who pursue their ends with violence. When you ride these dumb beasts, do not push them too far but rather allow them to rest as needed. If the land is barren, however, pass through it quickly to preserve their strength. Endeavor to travel by night, because at night distances appear shorter than they are during the day. Take care not to encamp at night along the side of the road, for it is the path of beasts and the resting spot of snakes."

2759. According to Mālik, Sumayy, the freedman of Abū Bakr, reported from Abū Ṣāliḥ, from Abū Hurayra, that the Messenger of God (pbuh) said, "Travel is a form of punishment. It deprives a man of his sleep, food, and drink. Once he has accomplished his purpose, therefore, he should hurry back to his family."

Chapter 67. The Command to Be Kind to Chattel Slaves (*Mamlūk*)

2760. According to Mālik, it reached him that Abū Hurayra said, "The Messenger of God (pbuh) said, 'A chattel slave is entitled to a reasonable amount of food and appropriate clothing, and he must not be obliged to perform tasks beyond his reasonable capacity.'"

2761. According to Mālik, it reached him that ʿUmar b. al-Khaṭṭāb would make circuits around the outskirts of Medina every Saturday, and if he found a chattel slave tasked with an overly burdensome chore, he would intervene to lighten his burden.

2762. According to Mālik, his uncle Abū Suhayl b. Mālik reported from his father that he heard ʿUthmān b. ʿAffān once say in the sermon of the Friday Congregational Prayer (*ṣalāt al-jumuʿa*), "Do not impose on a handmaiden an obligation to earn money, unless she has a skill. If you do so, she will resort to prostitution. Likewise, do not force a minor to earn money, for if he fails in that task, he will steal. Be content with what you have, for God has already provided you with sufficient means. Therefore, take care not to consume anything except that which has been obtained lawfully."

Chapter 68. What Has Come Down regarding the Chattel Slave (*Mamlūk*) and His Appearance

2763. According to Mālik, Nāfiʿ reported from ʿAbd Allāh b. ʿUmar that the Messenger of God (pbuh) said, "A slave who gives sincere counsel to his master and is devoted to the worship of God is rewarded twice over."

2764. According to Mālik, it reached him that ʿUbayd Allāh b. ʿUmar b. al-Khaṭṭāb had a handmaiden whom ʿUmar b. al-Khaṭṭāb saw dressed in the fashion of a free woman. He went to his daughter Ḥafṣa and complained, saying, "I saw your brother's handmaiden walking about among the people, dressed like a free woman!" ʿUmar disapproved of that.

Chapter 69. What Has Come Down regarding the Oath of Allegiance (*Bayʿa*) to the Ruler

2765. According to Mālik, ʿAbd Allāh b. Dīnār reported that ʿAbd Allāh b. ʿUmar said, "When we gave our oaths of allegiance to the Messenger of God (pbuh), vowing to listen and to obey, he qualified it by saying, 'To the extent of your capacity.'"

2766. According to Mālik, Muḥammad b. al-Munkadir reported that Umayma bt. Ruqayqa said, "I went to the Messenger of God (pbuh) with a group of women who gave their oath of allegiance to him under Islam. We said, 'Messenger of God, we pledge our loyalty to you, promising not to associate any deity with God, not to steal, not to fornicate or commit adultery, not to kill our children, not to engage in false and malicious calumny, and not to disobey you in any matter that is good.' The Messenger of God (pbuh) then qualified it by saying, 'To the extent of your capacity and ability.' They said, 'God and His Messenger are more merciful to us than we are to ourselves. Let us, therefore, pledge allegiance to you now, Messenger of God, by taking your hand!' The Messenger of God (pbuh) said, 'I do not shake the hands of women. It is indeed the case that my statement to a hundred women is like (*ka*) my statement to one woman (or "similar to [*mithl*] my statement to one woman").'"

2767. According to Mālik, ʿAbd Allāh b. Dīnār reported that ʿAbd Allāh b. ʿUmar sent a letter to ʿAbd al-Malik b. Marwān in which he gave his oath of allegiance. The letter said, "In the Name of God, the Merciful, the Compassionate. To proceed: To the Servant of God, ʿAbd al-Malik, Commander of the Faithful, peace be upon you. I declare to you the praise of God, the one and only god. I acknowledge my duty to hear and obey your commands in accordance with the ordinances of God and the ordinances of His Messenger, to the extent of my capacity."

Chapter 70. Disfavored Speech

2768. According to Mālik, ʿAbd Allāh b. Dīnār reported from ʿAbd Allāh b. ʿUmar that the Messenger of God (pbuh) said, "If someone says to his brother, 'You unbeliever!' one of them will certainly bear the charge."

2769. According to Mālik, Suhayl b. Abī Ṣāliḥ reported from his father, from Abū Hurayra, that the Messenger of God (pbuh) said, "If you hear someone say, 'The people have perished,' know that he is in the worst shape of them all."

2770. According to Mālik, Abū al-Zinād reported from al-Aʿraj, from Abū Hurayra, that the Messenger of God (pbuh) said, "Let no one say, 'What a baneful time!' for God Himself is time."

2771. According to Mālik, Yaḥyā b. Saʿīd reported that Jesus, the son of Mary, once crossed paths with a pig on the road. He said to it, "Go in peace!" Someone asked him, "Why are you being so polite to a pig?" Jesus replied, "I do not want my tongue to become accustomed to foul speech."

Chapter 71. The Requirement to Exercise Caution When Speaking

2772. According to Mālik, Muḥammad b. ʿAmr b. ʿAlqama reported from his father, from Bilāl b. al-Ḥārith al-Muzanī, that the Messenger of God (pbuh) said, "A man might say something that pleases God without suspecting that it will have a lasting effect, but in fact God records, as a result of what the man said, that He will remain pleased with the man until the day God meets him. Likewise, a man might say something that angers God without suspecting that it will have a lasting effect, but in fact God records, as a result of what the man said, that He will remain angry with the man until the day God meets him."

2773. According to Mālik, ʿAbd Allāh b. Dīnār reported that Abū Ṣāliḥ al-Sammān informed him that Abū Hurayra said, "A man says things heedlessly, not realizing that they will cause him to fall into the fire of Hell.

Likewise, a man says things without attaching any importance to them, but God uses his words to elevate him to Paradise."

Chapter 72. Speech That Is Disfavored on Account of Its Omission of the Remembrance of God

2774. According to Mālik, Zayd b. Aslam said, "Two men came from the east. Each of them addressed the people, who were amazed at their eloquence. The Messenger of God (pbuh) then said, 'Some speech certainly has the power of sorcery,' or 'Some speech certainly is sorcery.'"

2775. According to Mālik, it reached him that Jesus, the son of Mary, would say, "Do not accustom yourselves to speaking at length, unless you also mention God, lest your hearts become cruel. A cruel heart is distant from God, but you do not know it. Do not look at people's sins as though you were lords; rather, look to your own sins as though you were slaves. People are either enduring a trial or subject to grace. Accordingly, show mercy to those suffering a trial, and praise God for His grace."

2776. According to Mālik, it reached him that ʿĀʾisha, the wife of the Prophet (pbuh), would dispatch messengers to some members of her family after the Evening Prayer (*ṣalāt al-ʿishāʾ*), telling them, "Will you not give a rest to the angelic scribes recording your sins?"

Chapter 73. What Has Come Down regarding Backbiting

2777. According to Mālik, al-Walīd b. ʿAbd Allāh b. Ṣayyād reported that al-Muṭṭalib b. ʿAbd Allāh b. Ḥuwayṭib al-Makhzūmī informed him that a man asked the Messenger of God (pbuh), "What is backbiting?" The Messenger of God (pbuh) replied, "It is saying about a man what he would hate to hear about himself." The man said, "Messenger of God, what if it's true?" The Messenger of God (pbuh) said, "If what you are saying about him is false, that is calumny!"

Chapter 74. What Has Come Down regarding the Vices of the Tongue

2778. According to Mālik, Zayd b. Aslam reported from ʿAṭāʾ b. Yasār that the Messenger of God (pbuh) said, "Whomsoever God protects from the evil of two things will enter Paradise." A man then said, "Will you not tell us, Messenger of God?"[1034] The Messenger of God (pbuh) remained silent. The Messenger of God (pbuh) then repeated what he had said the

1034 The version of this text in the RME literally states, "Do not inform us!" However, the context, as well as other manuscript variations noted by the editors of the RME, affirm the translation that we have provided here.

first time. The man said to him again, "Will you not tell us, Messenger of God?" The Messenger of God (pbuh) remained silent. The Messenger of God (pbuh) then said it again. The man again said to him, "Will you not tell us, Messenger of God?" The Messenger of God (pbuh) then said something like it again. The man again repeated what he had said. A man standing next to him finally told him to be quiet, at which point the Messenger of God (pbuh) said, "Whomsoever God protects from the evil of two things will enter Paradise. These things are what is between his jaws and what is between his legs, what is between his jaws and what is between his legs, what is between his jaws and what is between his legs."

2779. According to Mālik, Zayd b. Aslam reported from his father that ʿUmar b. al-Khaṭṭāb went to see Abū Bakr al-Ṣiddīq and found him pulling on his tongue. ʿUmar said to him, "Stop; may God forgive you!" Abū Bakr said to him, "This has certainly led me down paths that brought me regret."

Chapter 75. What Has Come Down regarding the Private Conversation of Two People That Excludes a Third

2780. According to Mālik, ʿAbd Allāh b. Dīnār said, "I was with ʿAbd Allāh b. ʿUmar at the house of Khālid b. ʿUqba, the one in the market. A man then showed up who wanted to converse with ʿAbd Allāh b. ʿUmar in private, and we were the only three people present. ʿAbd Allāh b. ʿUmar called for another man to come, so that we would be four. He then said to me and to the man he had just called over, 'Could you two please give us some privacy? I heard the Messenger of God (pbuh) say, "When three people are together, two of them should not converse privately and exclude the third."'"

2781. According to Mālik, Nāfiʿ reported from ʿAbd Allāh b. ʿUmar that the Messenger of God (pbuh) said, "If there is a group of three people, two of them should not converse privately and exclude the third."

Chapter 76. What Has Come Down regarding Honesty and Lying

2782. According to Mālik, Ṣafwān b. Sulaym reported that a man said to the Messenger of God (pbuh), "Can I lie to my wife?" The Messenger of God (pbuh) said, "No good comes of lying." The man then said, "Messenger of God, can I promise her things and make sweet talk to her?" The Messenger of God (pbuh) then said, "There is nothing blameworthy in that."[1035]

1035 Muslim jurists distinguish lying from the breaking of promises. A lie is a false statement about something that definitively occurred in the past, whereas a promise refers to a future event that may or may not occur. A promise, therefore, may be broken (*khalaf*), but a broken promise is not a lie. The statement of the Prophet (pbuh) that there is no blame in making promises and sweet talk to one's wife assumes that the man intends to fulfill his promises. Bājī, *al-Muntaqā*, 7:314.

2783. According to Mālik, it reached him that ʿAbd Allāh b. Masʿūd would say, "Hold fast to honesty, for honesty guides one down the path of righteousness, and righteousness leads to Paradise. Shun lying, because lying leads to wickedness, and wickedness leads to Hell. Is it not the case that we commonly say in our ordinary speech, 'He spoke the truth, and he acted rightly,' and 'He lied, and he behaved wickedly'?"[1036]

2784. According to Mālik, it reached him that Luqmān was asked, "What accounts for the station that you have attained?" They meant thereby how he became a virtuous man. Luqmān said, "Truthful speech, faithfully preserving what has been entrusted to me, and minding my own business."[1037]

2785. According to Mālik, it reached him that ʿAbd Allāh b. Masʿūd would say, "When a servant of God lies continuously, his heart darkens until it becomes entirely enveloped in darkness, and then God includes his name among the liars in the divine registry."

2786. According to Mālik, Ṣafwān b. Sulaym reported that someone asked the Messenger of God (pbuh), "Can a believer be a coward?" He said, "Certainly!" Then he was asked, "Can a believer be a miser?" He said, "Certainly!" And then he was asked, "Can a believer be a liar?" He said, "Certainly not!"

Chapter 77. What Has Come Down regarding Squandering Property and Being Two-Faced

2787. According to Mālik, Suhayl b. Abī Ṣāliḥ reported from his father that the Messenger of God (pbuh) said, "God is satisfied with you when you do three things, and angry with you when you do three things. First, He is pleased with you when you worship Him without associating any other deities with Him; second, He is pleased with you when you all hold fast to God's rope; and third, He is pleased with you when you give sincere advice to those whom God has appointed to exercise authority in your affairs. But gossip, squandering wealth, and asking too many irrelevant questions—these three things make God angry with you."

2788. According to Mālik, Abū al-Zinād reported from al-Aʿraj, from Abū Hurayra, that the Messenger of God (pbuh) said, "The two-faced are among the vilest of humanity. They go to one group of people and say one thing, and then go to another group, saying the opposite."

1036 The Arabic word for honesty is *ṣidq*, and that for lying is *kadhib*. The word for righteousness is *birr*, and that for wickedness is *fujūr*. Ibn Masʿūd is pointing out that in common Arabic parlance, speaking truthfully is associated with acting righteously, and speaking falsely is associated with acting wickedly.

1037 Luqmān is a wise man who appears in the Quran and after whom one of its chapters (chap. 31) is named.

Chapter 78. What Has Come Down regarding Punishing the Many for the Actions of a Few

2789. According to Mālik, it reached him that Umm Salama, the wife of the Prophet (pbuh), asked, "Messenger of God, is it possible that we might perish, even though there are righteous people among us?" The Messenger of God (pbuh) said, "Yes, if foulness abounds."

2790. According to Mālik, Ismā'īl b. Abī al-Ḥakīm reported that he heard 'Umar b. 'Abd al-'Azīz say, "It was said that God, Blessed and Sublime is He, does not punish the many for the wrongs of a few. That is only the case, however, if the sin is not committed openly. If it is, then they all deserve punishment."

Chapter 79. What Has Come Down regarding Being Mindful of God

2791. According to Mālik, Isḥāq b. 'Abd Allāh b. Abī Ṭalḥa reported that Anas b. Mālik said, "I once set out on a walk with 'Umar b. al-Khaṭṭāb until he arrived at an orchard. He stood in the middle of the orchard, and there was only a wall separating us. I overheard him say to himself, "Umar b. al-Khaṭṭāb, Commander of the Faithful? Well done! Well done! By God, son of Khaṭṭāb! Be mindful of God, or He will certainly punish you!'"

2792. Mālik said, "It reached me that al-Qāsim b. Muḥammad would say, 'I lived with the Companions of the Prophet (pbuh), and they were not ones to be impressed by mere words.' By that he meant that only deeds are taken into account when measuring a man's worth, not his words."

Chapter 80. What to Say When One Hears Thunder

2793. According to Mālik, 'Āmir b. 'Abd Allāh b. al-Zubayr reported that when he heard thunder, he would stop talking and say, "Glory be to the One whom thunder glorifies with His praise and whom the angels glorify out of fear of Him."[1038] He would then say, "This is indeed a grave threat to all those living on earth."

Chapter 81. What Has Come Down regarding the Estate of the Prophet (pbuh)

2794. According to Mālik, Ibn Shihāb reported from 'Urwa b. al-Zubayr, from 'Ā'isha, the Mother of the Believers, that when the Messenger of God (pbuh) died, his wives had resolved to dispatch 'Uthmān b. 'Affān to Abū Bakr al-Ṣiddīq to demand their shares in the estate of the Messenger of God

1038 *Subḥāna 'lladhī yusabbiḥu 'l-ra'du bi-ḥamdihi wa'l-malā'ikatu min khīfatih.* See *al-Ra'd*, 13:13.

(pbuh), but ʿĀʾisha said to them, "Didn't the Messenger of God (pbuh) say, 'We are not to be inherited. What we leave is charity (*ṣadaqa*)'?"

2795. According to Mālik, Abū al-Zinād reported from al-Aʿraj, from Abū Hurayra, that the Messenger of God (pbuh) said, "My heirs shall not divide among themselves any gold coins that I leave behind. Anything that I leave beyond the maintenance of my wives and the provisions for my servant is charity."

Chapter 82. What Has Come Down regarding the Appearance of Hell

2796. According to Mālik, Abū al-Zinād reported from al-Aʿraj, from Abū Hurayra, that the Messenger of God (pbuh) said, "The fire that the children of Adam kindle is but a seventieth of Hell's intensity." They said, "Messenger of God, our fire would certainly be enough to punish us!" He said, "Nevertheless, Hell exceeds it by sixty-nine times."

2797. According to Mālik, his paternal uncle Abū Suhayl b. Mālik reported from his father that Abū Hurayra said, "Do you all imagine that it is red, like this fire of yours? Rather, it is blacker than tar (*qār*)," meaning pitch (*zift*).

Chapter 83. Encouraging People to Give Charity (*Ṣadaqa*)

2798. According to Mālik, Yaḥyā b. Saʿīd reported from Abū al-Ḥubāb Saʿīd b. Yasār that the Messenger of God (pbuh) said, "If a person gives charity out of wholesome earnings—and God only accepts that which is wholesome—it is as though he placed it in the very palm of the Merciful (*al-raḥmān*)[1039] for Him to nurture, in the very same way one of you might raise his foal or calf until it matures and becomes like a mountain."

2799. According to Mālik, Isḥāq b. ʿAbd Allāh b. Abī Ṭalḥa reported that he heard Anas b. Mālik say, "Abū Ṭalḥa owned the largest number of palm trees in Medina. His favorite orchard was Bīraḥāʾ. It was in front of the mosque, and the Messenger of God (pbuh) would enter it frequently and drink from its sweet water. When the verse 'You shall never attain righteousness until you give away that which you love'[1040] was revealed, Abū Ṭalḥa went to the Messenger of God (pbuh) and said, 'Messenger of God! God, Blessed and Sublime is He, says, "You shall never attain righteousness until you give away that which you love." The property I love most is Bīraḥāʾ. I hereby give it in charity, for God's sake, hoping to receive my reward from God. Use it in whatever way you wish, Messenger of God!' The Messenger of God (pbuh)

1039 *Al-raḥmān* is one of the beautiful names of God in the Islamic tradition.
1040 *Āl ʿImrān*, 3:92.

said, 'Well done, indeed! That is a profitable investment! That is a profitable investment! I have heard what you said, and I think you should give it to your near-relations.' Abū Ṭalḥa said, 'And so I will, Messenger of God.' Abū Ṭalḥa then partitioned the orchard among his near-relations and his male paternal first cousins."

2800. According to Mālik, Zayd b. Aslam reported that the Messenger of God (pbuh) said, "Give something to the beggar, even if he comes riding on a horse."

2801. According to Mālik, Zayd b. Aslam reported from ʿAmr b. Muʿādh al-Ashhalī al-Anṣārī that his grandmother said, "The Messenger of God (pbuh) said, 'Believing women, there is nothing that is too trivial to give your neighbor, even if it is only a roasted hoof.'"

2802. According to Mālik, it reached him from ʿĀʾisha, the wife of the Prophet (pbuh), that a beggar once approached her and asked her for something. She was fasting at the time. She had nothing in the house save a loaf of bread. She said to a freedwoman (*mawlāt*) of hers, "Give it to him." The freedwoman said, "But then you will have nothing to break your fast with." ʿĀʾisha again said, "Give it to him." The freedwoman said, "So I did. When evening fell, and it was time to break the fast, a family (or 'a man') who did not usually give us anything sent us a roast sheep, along with some bread. ʿĀʾisha called me over and said, 'Eat this. This is certainly better than your loaf of bread.'"

2803. Mālik said, "It reached me that a beggar once asked ʿĀʾisha, the Mother of the Believers, for some food. She was holding a bunch of grapes in her hands at the time. She said to a man there, 'Give him a bit.' The man looked at her, astonished. ʿĀʾisha said to him, "Are you surprised? I wonder how many atoms' weights[1041] there are in this one grape?"

Chapter 84. What Has Come Down regarding Refraining from Asking Others for Help

2804. According to Mālik, Ibn Shihāb reported from ʿAṭāʾ b. Yazīd al-Laythī, from Abū Saʿīd al-Khudrī, that some of the Medinese asked the Messenger of God (pbuh) for assistance. He gave them everything he had to give. He then said, "Whatever I have I will not withhold from you. Whosoever exercises restraint, God will preserve his dignity. Whosoever tries to be self-reliant, God will enrich him. Whosoever attempts to exercise fortitude,

1041 This is an allusion to the verse in the Quran that says that on the Day of Judgment, "whoever has done an atom's weight worth of good shall see it." *Al-Zalzala*, 99:7.

God will bless him with it. No one has been given a better or vaster gift than fortitude."

2805. According to Mālik, Nāfiʿ reported from ʿAbd Allāh b. ʿUmar that the Messenger of God (pbuh) said, while he was on the pulpit, preaching about charity and about refraining from asking others for help, "The upper hand is better than the lower hand. The upper hand is the one that gives, and the lower hand is the one that asks."

2806. According to Mālik, Zayd b. Aslam reported from ʿAṭāʾ b. Yasār that the Messenger of God (pbuh) once sent something to ʿUmar b. al-Khaṭṭāb, but ʿUmar refused to accept it. The Messenger of God (pbuh) asked, "Why did you refuse it?" He said, "Messenger of God, didn't you tell us that it is better that we not accept anything from anyone?" The Messenger of God (pbuh) said, "What I meant was asking others for things. As for what comes to you from others without your having first requested it, that is merely the provision that God has provided." ʿUmar then said, "By Him whose hand holds my soul, I will never ask anything of anyone, nor shall I refuse to accept anything that comes to me, if I have not asked for it."

2807. According to Mālik, Abū al-Zinād reported from al-Aʿraj, from Abū Hurayra, that the Messenger of God (pbuh) said, "By Him whose hand holds my soul! It is indeed better for a man to take his rope and collect firewood on his back than to go to a man on whom God has bestowed His favor and beg at his feet, whether he gives him something or refuses to do so."

2808. According to Mālik, Zayd b. Aslam reported from ʿAṭāʾ b. Yasār that a man from the Banū Asad said, "My family and I alighted at al-Baqīʿ, the cemetery of Medina. My family said to me, 'Go ask the Messenger of God (pbuh) for something to eat.' They then launched into a description of their pitiable state. I went to the Messenger of God (pbuh) and found there a man begging him for something. The Messenger of God (pbuh) said to him, 'I have nothing to give you.' The man turned away from him in anger and said, 'By my life! You give to whomever you wish!' The Messenger of God (pbuh) said, 'He is angry at me because I find nothing to give him. Whoever begs but has in his possession forty dirhams of pure silver (*ūqiyya*) or its equivalent in weight or value is being impertinent.' I told myself, 'A camel of ours is indeed several times more valuable than forty dirhams.' I therefore returned to my family and did not ask him for anything. Later, some barley and raisins were brought to the Messenger of God (pbuh), and he gave us some. Therefore, God delivered us from our need."

2809. According to Mālik, he heard al-ʿAlāʾ b. ʿAbd al-Raḥmān say, "An act of charity never diminishes a person's property; no servant of God forgives a wrong done to him without God increasing his standing and dignity; and no servant of God humbles himself without God honoring him." Mālik said, "I do not know whether the source of this report is the Prophet (pbuh)."

Chapter 85. Matters Prohibited in Connection with Charity (*Ṣadaqa*)

2810. According to Mālik, it reached him that the Messenger of God (pbuh) said, "It is not lawful for the family of Muḥammad to accept charity. It is usually the undesirable refuse of people."

2811. According to Mālik, ʿAbd Allāh b. Abī Bakr reported from his father that the Messenger of God (pbuh) appointed a man of the Banū ʿAbd al-Ashhal to supervise the administration of property that had been gifted as charity to the Messenger of God (pbuh). When the man came, he asked that the Prophet (pbuh) give him some of the camels that had been collected as charity. The Messenger of God became angry at the man's request, and it was obvious in his face. (One way in which his anger was known was that his eyes would become red.) The Prophet (pbuh) then said, "This man has asked me for something that puts me in an impossible position. He knows that I dislike refusing people's requests, but if I grant his, I will be granting him something to which neither he nor I have a right." The man then said, "Messenger of God, I will never ask you again to give me any property that has been dedicated to charity."

2812. According to Mālik, Zayd b. Aslam reported from his father that he said, "ʿAbd Allāh b. al-Arqam said to me, 'Show me an appropriate riding camel whose use I may request from the Commander of the Faithful.' I said, 'All right, I can give you a camel that was collected as charity.' ʿAbd Allāh b. al-Arqam said, 'Would you like a corpulent man to wash his groin and his upper thighs for you and then give the runoff to you to drink on a hot day?' I grew angry at his words and said, 'May God forgive you! How dare you say such a thing to me?' ʿAbd Allāh b. al-Arqam said, 'The camels that have been collected as charity are like the impurities of the body that are carried off in the water that people use in their baths to remove their filth.'"

Chapter 86. What Has Come Down regarding Seeking Knowledge

2813. According to Mālik, it reached him that Luqmān the Sage counseled his son, "My son, sit in the company of learned men, staying as close to them as possible. God certainly revives dead hearts through the light of wisdom, just as He revives barren land with abundant rain from the sky."

Chapter 87. What Is to Be Feared from the Supplication of Those Who Have Been Wronged

2814. According to Mālik, Zayd b. Aslam reported from his father that ʿUmar b. al-Khaṭṭāb appointed a freedman (*mawlā*) of his, who went by the name of Hunayy, as the supervisor of lands reserved for public grazing (*ḥimā*). He said, "Hunayy, do not treat people harshly, and fear the supplication of anyone who has been wronged, for God inevitably answers the supplications of those who have been wronged. Grant permission to graze for the owners of small herds of camel and sheep, and be wary of the flocks of people like Ibn ʿAffān and Ibn ʿAwf.[1042] Were their flocks to perish for want of pasture, they could return to Medina, where they have plentiful crops and date palms. By contrast, if the flock of someone who owns small herds of camel and sheep perishes, he will come to me with his children and say, 'Commander of the Faithful! Commander of the Faithful! Am I to abandon them?' God help you! Water and pasture are less dear to me than gold and silver. By God! They will conclude that I have wronged them. It is indeed their territory and their water. They won it with their blood during the Days of Ignorance prior to Islam (*jāhiliyya*), and they entered Islam with it still in their possession. By Him whose hand holds my soul, were it not for the need to provide pasture for the army's animals, I would not have reserved an inch of their territory for public grazing."

Chapter 88. The Names of the Prophet, May God Grace Him and Grant Him Tranquility

2815. According to Mālik, Ibn Shihāb reported from Muḥammad b. Jubayr b. Muṭʿim that the Prophet (pbuh) said, "I have five names: I am Muḥammad; I am Aḥmad; I am al-Māḥī, the one through whom God effaces disbelievers; I am al-Ḥāshir, the one at whose feet the people shall be gathered on the Day of Resurrection; and I am al-ʿĀqib, the final messenger of God."

1042 ʿUmar is referring to the prominent and wealthy Companions ʿUthmān b. ʿAffān and ʿAbd al-Raḥmān b. ʿAwf. He is advising his official to give preferential access to public grazing grounds to individuals with small herds over those whose flocks are numerous.

Glossary of Proper Names

Abān b. ʿUthmān (d. 105/723)
Son of the third caliph, ʿUthmān, who was the third of the Rightly Guided Caliphs. Abān b. ʿUthmān served as governor of Medina 75–82/695–702 during the reign of the Umayyad caliph ʿAbd al-Malik b. Marwān (r. 65–86/685–705).

ʿAbd Allāh b. ʿAbbās (d. 68/687)
First cousin of the Prophet Muḥammad, a prominent Companion, and an early Quranic exegete. Nicknamed Ḥabr al-Umma ("grand scholar of the community of believers") and Tarjumān al-Qurʾān ("interpreter of the Quran").

ʿAbd Allạh b. Dīnār (d. 127/745 or 136/754)
A prominent Follower and hadith transmitter.

ʿAbd Allāh b. Salām (d. 43/663)
A prominent Medinan Jewish convert to Islam during the Prophet Muḥammad's lifetime. He was reported to have been knowledgeable of the Torah; many Quranic verses praising People of the Book are said to refer to those like him.

ʿAbd Allāh b. ʿUmar b. al-Khaṭṭāb (d. 73/693)
A Companion of the Prophet Muḥammad and the son of the second caliph, ʿUmar b. al-Khaṭṭāb (r. 13–23/634–644). He is a very important source for Mālik in the *Muwaṭṭaʾ*, usually as reported to Mālik by Nāfiʿ, ʿAbd Allāh's freedman. The chain Mālik → Nāfiʿ → ʿAbd Allāh b. ʿUmar is sometimes called "the golden chain" by virtue of the high regard Muslim scholars had for the reliability of reports transmitted through this chain.

'Abd al-Malik b. Marwān (d. 86/705)
An Umayyad caliph (r. 65–86/685–705). 'Abd al-Malik was credited with numerous administrative reforms, including Arabizing the language of administration and minting the first coins of the caliphate.

'Abd al-Raḥmān b. al-Qāsim b. Muḥammad b. Abī Bakr (d. 126/744)
A Medinan Follower and hadith transmitter. The son of one of the "seven jurists of Medina."

'Abd al-Raḥmān b. 'Awf (d. 32/652)
One of the earliest converts to Islam and a member of the early group of emigrants to Abyssinia. He had a reputation as a successful trader and played a prominent role in the early caliphate after the Prophet's death.

Abū Bakr al-Ṣiddīq (d. 13/634)
One of the earliest converts to Islam and one of the Prophet's closest confidants and companions. He was also the father of 'Ā'isha, a wife of the Prophet. He served as the first caliph (r. 11–13/632–634) after the death of the Prophet.

Abū Bakr b. 'Abd al-Raḥmān b. al-Ḥārith b. Hishām (d. 93 or 94/711 or 712)
A Follower and one of the "seven jurists of Medina." He was well known for his piety and expertise in Prophetic traditions. His freedman Sumayy was an important source for Mālik in the *Muwaṭṭa'*.

Abū Bakr b. Ḥazm (d. 120/738)
An important transmitter of hadith. He was the only Anṣārī ever to serve as governor of Medina. His sons 'Abd Allāh and Muḥammad transmitted hadith from him and are also important narrators in the *Muwaṭṭa'*.

Abū Jahl b. Hishām (d. 2/624)
One of the fiercest opponents of the Prophet Muḥammad in Mecca and one of the chief persecutors of early Muslims. His actual name was 'Amr b. Hishām b. al-Mughīra, and he was known as Abū al-Ḥakam. The name "Abū al-Ḥakam" connoted wisdom and sagacity, so the early Muslims renamed him "Abū Jahl," meaning ignorant and impetuous, on account of his ferocious opposition to Islam. He died in the Battle of Badr.

Abū Salama b. 'Abd al-Raḥmān b. 'Awf (d. 94/712)
A Follower and one of the "seven jurists of Medina." A Medinan judge, he was a son of the prominent early Companion 'Abd al-Raḥmān b. 'Awf. He served as an important source for Mālik in the *Muwaṭṭa'*.

Abū Sufyān b. Ḥarb (d. 31/652)
The father of Muʿāwiya b. Abī Sufyān. He led the Meccan opposition to the Prophet Muḥammad but became a Muslim when the Prophet returned to Mecca triumphant.

Abū ʿUbayda b. al-Jarrāḥ (d. 18/639)
The general who completed the conquest of the Levant during the caliphate of ʿUmar b. al-Khaṭṭāb and later served as ʿUmar's governor there until he died from the plague in Jordan.

ʿĀʾisha bt. Abī Bakr al-Ṣiddīq (d. 58/678)
The youngest wife of the Prophet and daughter of the first caliph, Abū Bakr al-Ṣiddīq. One of the most prominent early jurists and an extremely important source of hadith.

ʿAlī b. Abī Ṭālib (d. 40/661)
The fourth caliph and the Prophet Muḥammad's cousin and son-in-law, married to the Prophet's daughter Fāṭima. He was the first *imām* of the Shīʿa.

ʿAlī b. al-Ḥusayn b. ʿAlī b. Abī Ṭālib (d. 94/712)
Also known as Zayn al-ʿĀbidīn, the great-grandson of the Prophet and the fourth *imām* of the Shīʿa.

Asmāʾ bt. Abī Bakr al-Ṣiddīq (d. 73/692)
A prominent early convert to Islam and daughter of the first caliph, Abū Bakr. She brought food and supplies to her father and the Prophet Muḥammad at the outset of their migration to Medina and later fought in the Battle of Yarmouk. She was the mother of ʿUrwa b. al-Zubayr, one of the "seven jurists of Medina," and ʿAbd Allāh b. al-Zubayr, a challenger to the Umayyad caliphate.

Bilāl b. Rabāḥ (d. 20/641)
A prominent early black slave convert to Islam. Upon his conversion to Islam, he bravely endured intense persecution at the hands of his master, Umayya b. Khalaf. Abū Bakr purchased Bilāl from his master and manumitted him. He later became the Prophet's muezzin.

Fāṭima (d. 11/632)
Daughter of the Prophet Muḥammad and wife of ʿAlī b. Abī Ṭālib.

al-Ḥajjāj b. Yūsuf (d. 95/714)
The governor of Iraq during the caliphate of ʿAbd al-Malik b. Marwān. He laid siege to ʿAbd Allāh b. al-Zubayr's forces in the Hijaz in 72/691.

al-Ḥasan b. ʿAlī b. Abī Ṭālib (d. 50/670)
Grandson of the Prophet Muḥammad, son of Fāṭima and ʿAlī b. Abī Ṭālib, and second *imām* of the Shīʿa.

Hishām b. Ismāʿīl al-Makhzūmī (d. after 87/706)
Governor of Medina in 82–86/702–5 during the reign of ʿAbd al-Malik b. Marwān, succeeding Abān b. ʿUthmān.

Hishām b. ʿUrwa b. al-Zubayr b. al-ʿAwwām (d. 146/763)
A prominent member of the second generation of Muslims, known as "the followers of the Followers" (*tābiʿū al-tābiʿīn*), and an important source for Mālik in the *Muwaṭṭa'*. He died in Baghdad after residing in Medina.

al-Ḥusayn b. ʿAlī b. Abī Ṭālib (d. 61/680)
Grandson of the Prophet Muḥammad, son of Fāṭima and ʿAlī b. Abī Ṭālib, and third *imām* of the Shīʿa. He was killed in the Battle of Karbala by forces loyal to the Umayyad caliph of the time, Yazīd b. Muʿāwiya.

Ibn Shihāb al-Zuhrī, Muḥammad b. Muslim b. ʿUbayd Allāḥ b. ʿAbd Allāh (d. 124/742)
A prominent early Muslim historian and collector of hadith. He is one of Mālik's most important sources in the *Muwaṭṭa'*.

ʿIkrima (d. 105/723)
A Follower, a freedman of Ibn ʿAbbās, and one of the primary transmitters of the latter's Quranic interpretations. He is considered one of the most important of the early Quranic exegetes.

Jaʿfar b. Muḥammad b. ʿAlī (d. 148/765)
Known as Jaʿfar al-Ṣādiq, son of Muḥammad al-Bāqir, grandson of Zayn al-ʿĀbidīn, and great-grandson of Ḥusayn b. ʿAlī. Founder of the Jaʿfarī school of law, he is revered as a scholar by Sunnīs and considered the sixth *imām* by the Shīʿa.

Kaʿb al-Aḥbār (d. 32/652)
A Jewish scholar from Yemen whose full name was Kaʿb b. Mātiʿ al-Ḥimyarī. He converted to Islam after the death of the Prophet Muḥammad and so is considered a Follower rather than a Companion. After his conversion

to Islam, he left Yemen and migrated to the Levant. According to Muslim tradition, he was responsible for introducing many elements of Jewish lore into Muslim understandings of the Quran.

Marwān b. al-Ḥakam (d. 65/685)
Governor of Medina during the caliphate of Muʿāwiya b. Abī Sufyān and later caliph in 64–65/684–685. He was a companion and secretary of the third caliph, ʿUthmān. His son, ʿAbd al-Malik, would become the fifth Umayyad caliph.

Maymūna bt. al-Ḥārith (d. 51/671)
A wife of the Prophet and maternal aunt of ʿAbd Allāh b. ʿAbbās.

Muʿādh b. Jabal (d. 18/639)
An early Companion of the Prophet who converted to Islam in his late teens. After the conquest of Mecca, the Prophet dispatched him to Yemen to serve as his governor and to instruct the people there in Islam. He is considered an early jurist, a Quranic reciter/exegete, and an important source of hadith.

Muʿāwiya b. Abī Sufyān (d. 60/680)
A member of the clan of the Banū Umayya, traditional rivals of the Prophet's clan, the Banū Hāshim. His father, Abū Sufyān, led the Meccan opposition to the Prophet Muhammad. Muʿāwiya, however, became a Muslim prior to the conquest of Mecca. He served as the governor of the Levant during the caliphates of ʿUmar b. al-Khaṭṭāb and ʿUthmān b. ʿAffān. Muʿāwiya refused to recognize ʿAlī b. Abī Ṭālib as the rightful caliph after ʿUthmān, leading to the first civil war in Islamic history. After ʿAlī's murder, Muʿāwiya was recognized as the caliph in 41/660, and he moved the capital to Damascus. He reigned until 60/680. The reign of Muʿāwiya, conventionally considered the founder of the Umayyad dynasty, marks the end of the Rightly Guided Caliphate (*al-khilāfa al-rāshida*) and the beginning of dynastic rule.

Nāfiʿ (d. 117/735)
A freedman of ʿAbd Allāh b. ʿUmar and one of Mālik's most important sources in the *Muwaṭṭaʾ*.

al-Najāshī (d. 9/630)
The Christian ruler of Abyssinia who granted asylum to some Muslims of Mecca who were suffering from persecution before the Emigration to Medina.

al-Qāsim b. Muḥammad b. Abī Bakr al-Ṣiddīq (d. 107/725)
A follower of the Followers and one of the "seven jurists of Medina." He served as an important source for Mālik in the *Muwaṭṭaʾ*.

Rabīʿa b. Abī ʿAbd al-Raḥmān (d. 136/753?)
Nicknamed "Rabīʿa the legal reasoner" (*Rabīʿat al-raʾy*), he was an important Medinese jurist and teacher of Mālik, and an important source in the *Muwaṭṭaʾ*. Sources place his death in either the fourth or the fifth decade of the second Islamic century (133/750, 136/753, or 142/759).

Saʿd b. Abī Waqqāṣ (d. 55/675)
An early convert to Islam, he converted in his late teens. He achieved renown for his military prowess and served as governor of Kufa during the caliphates of ʿUmar and ʿUthmān.

Saʿd b. ʿUbāda (d. 14/635)
A prominent Companion and the chief of the Khazraj, one of the two leading tribes of Medina before the Prophet Muḥammad's arrival. He was one of the leaders of the Anṣār, the Medinese who converted to Islam.

Ṣafiyya bt. Ḥuyayy (d. 50/670)
A Jewish convert to Islam and wife of the Prophet. He married her after the Muslims conquered the Jewish oasis town of Khaybar.

Saʿīd b. al-Musayyab (d. 94/712)
A prominent member of the Followers and one of the "seven jurists of Medina." He is an important source for Mālik in the *Muwaṭṭaʾ*.

Sālim b. ʿAbd Allāh b. ʿUmar (d. 106/724)
A prominent Follower, one of the "seven jurists of Medina," and an important source for Mālik in the *Muwaṭṭaʾ*.

Salmān al-Fārisī (d. 36/656)
A Companion of the Prophet and the first Persian to convert to Islam. He gained renown for suggesting the strategy of digging a trench around Medina in the Battle of the Trench.

Sawda bt. Zamʿa (d. 54/674)
A wife of the Prophet Muḥammad.

Sulaymān b. ʿAbd al-Malik b. Marwān (d. 99/717)
An Umayyad caliph (r. 96–99/715–717).

Sulaymān b. Yasār (d. 107/725)
A Follower and one of the "seven jurists of Medina." He served as an important source for Mālik in the *Muwaṭṭa'*.

Ṭalḥa b. 'Ubayd Allāh (d. 36/656)
One of the earliest converts to Islam. He was one of the ten individuals whom the Prophet promised Paradise.

Ṭāriq b. 'Amr (d. 73/692)
A freedman of 'Uthmān b. 'Affān who served as governor of Medina during the caliphate of 'Abd al-Malik b. Marwān.

'Ubayd Allāh b. 'Abd Allāh b. 'Utba b. Mas'ūd (d. 98/716)
A prominent Follower and one of the "seven jurists of Medina." He was the grandson of the Companion 'Utba b. Mas'ūd, who was the brother of 'Abd Allāh b. Mas'ūd. 'Ubayd Allāh served as an important source for Mālik in the *Muwaṭṭa'*.

'Umar b. 'Abd al-'Azīz b. Marwān (d. 101/720)
An Umayyad caliph who is highly esteemed in the Sunnī tradition for his learning and piety and is often referred to as the fifth Rightly Guided Caliph. Mālik includes many decisions and opinions of 'Umar b. 'Abd al-'Azīz as precedents in the *Muwaṭṭa'*.

'Umar b. al-Khaṭṭāb (d. 23/644)
The second caliph and a prominent Companion of the Prophet. He was the father of 'Abd Allāh b. 'Umar and Ḥafṣa, a wife of the Prophet. Mālik records a large number of his decisions as precedents in the *Muwaṭṭa'*.

Umm Ḥabība (d. 44/664)
Mu'āwiya's sister and a wife of the Prophet.

'Urwa b. al-Zubayr (d. 94/713)
A son of a prominent early convert to Islam, al-Zubayr b. al-'Awwām, and a prominent member of the Followers. 'Urwa was one of the "seven jurists of Medina" and an important source of legal rules for Mālik in the *Muwaṭṭa'*.

'Uthmān b. 'Affān (d. 35/656)
An early convert to Islam and one of the first Muslims to emigrate to Abyssinia to flee persecution. He was the third caliph and a son-in-law to the Prophet. His time in office was marked by political strife and

opposition, and he was eventually assassinated in 35/656. 'Uthmān is known for his integral role in commissioning the compilation of a standardized Quranic codex.

al-Walīd b. 'Abd al-Malik b. Marwān (d. 96/715)
An Umayyad caliph (r. 86–96/705–715).

Yaḥyā b. Sa'īd al-Anṣārī (d. 143/760)
A Follower and a Medinan judge. He transmitted reports from many Companions and Followers and was a student of the "seven jurists of Medina." All of the major hadith collectors transmit his narrations. He was an important source for Mālik in the *Muwaṭṭa'*.

Yaḥyā b. Yaḥyā al-Laythī (d. 234/849)
A student of Mālik and one of the most important transmitters of the *Muwaṭṭa'* to Andalusia and the Maghrib.

Zayd b. Aslam (d. 136/753)
A freedman of 'Umar b. al-Khaṭṭāb. He was a Medinan Follower and a prominent hadith transmitter and jurist. He was an important source for Mālik as well as for other early hadith narrators.

al-Zubayr b. al-'Awwām (d. 36/656)
A prominent early convert to Islam and cousin of the Prophet Muḥammad.

Glossary of Terms

ʿabd mamlūk	Chattel slave
adhān	General call to prayer
ʿadwā	Contagion
ʿafw	Pardon
ahl al-dhimma	People of the Book; protected people
ahl al-kitāb	People of the Book
akūla	Fattened animal intended for slaughter
ʿām al-fatḥ	The year of the conquest of Mecca
amān	Grant of safe passage
ʿamd	Intentional (killing or battery)
amwāl	Property
anṣār	Medinese/Helpers
ʿaqib	Descendants
ʿāqila	Paternal kin group
ʿaqīqa	Newborn sacrifice
ʿaql (sing.)/***ʿuqūl*** (pl.)	Compensation for a battery
ʿaṣaba	Male paternal near-relations
ʿatāqa	Manumission
awqiya (sing.)/***awāq*** (pl.)	Unit of measure used for silver, approximately 1,071–1,125 grams
ʿayb	Defect in a good
ʿayn	Gold or silver bullion; a specific obligation in contrast to a generic obligation; a spring
al-ʿayn	Evil eye
ayyām al-tashrīq	The three festival days following the Feast of the Sacrificial Animals; the eleventh, twelfth, and thirteenth days of Dhū al-Ḥijja

ayyim	Matron; a woman who has been married and is either divorced or widowed
ʿazl	Withdrawal prior to ejaculation; *coitus interruptus*
baghy	Rebellion
bān	Moringa tree
baraṣ	Leprosy
batta	Absolute declaration of divorce
bayʿ al-ʿariyya	Trading fresh, unharvested dates for dried ones
***bayʿ al-ʿurbān* (or *arbūn*)**	A sale involving a nonrefundable deposit
bayḍāʾ	Hulled barley
al-bayt al-ʿatīq	Literally, "the ancient house," a designation for the Kabah in Mecca
bikr	Someone who has never been married
dābba (sing.)/***dawābb*** (pl.)	Beast of burden
ḍaḥiyya or ***uḍḥiyya*** (sing.)/ ***ḍaḥāyā*** or ***aḍāḥī*** (pl.)	Animal slaughtered on the occasion of the Feast of the Sacrificial Animals on the tenth day of Dhū al-Ḥijja
al-dajjāl	Antichrist
ḍālla (sing.)/***ḍawāll*** (pl.)	Lost animal
ḍamān	Risk of loss; liability
ḍaʾn	Sheep
daʿwā	A legal claim that initiates a lawsuit
ḍawārī	Tended livestock
dayn	Debt
dhakāt	Method of slaughtering livestock to render its meat fit for consumption
dharīʿa	Pretext; ruse
dīwān	Public registry
diya	Compensation due for the unlawful killing of a free Muslim male
diyat al-ʿamd	Compensation due for intentional killing or battery
diyat al-khaṭaʾ	Compensation due for nonintentional killing or battery

du'ā'	Supplication
faḍl	Surplus property of a decedent's estate following the distribution of determinate shares (*farā'iḍ*)
fākiha	Fresh fruit
farīḍa (sing.)/***farā'iḍ*** (pl.)	Determinate share of a Quranic heir of a decedent's estate
fariyya	Slander
faskh	Annulment
ghanam	Sheep or goats
gharar	Material uncertainty in the consideration
ghīla	A man having sexual relations with his wife while she is breastfeeding; cold-blooded, pre-meditated murder
ghusl	Ritual bath to remove impurities preventing the performance of ordinary rituals
ḥabs	Something designated as an endowment
ḥadd (sing.)/***ḥudūd*** (pl.)	Mandatory criminal punishment
hady	Sacrosanct animal, usually a camel, designated for sacrifice by a pilgrim at the Kabah
ḥajb	Preemption of a more distant heir's right to inherit by an heir more closely related to the decedent
ḥajj	Pilgrimage
ḥalāl	Unrestricted state after a pilgrim completes the rites of Pilgrimage and can resume ordinary activities in terms of personal grooming, sexual intercourse, and other matters restricted during performance of the Pilgrimage
ḥamāla	Guaranty of debts
al-ḥaram	Sanctuary; usually reserved for the Meccan sanctuary, but also applied to Medina when described as the Prophetic sanctuary
ḥibā'	Gifts to the guardian of a woman, intended to persuade him to accept the suitor's offer of marriage
ḥijāma	Cupping

ḥimā	Lands reserved for public grazing
ḥirāba	Brigandage
ḥirz	Secure compartment; only if a thief steals property stored in a secure compartment is the thief subject to the penalty of amputation of the hand
ḥiwāla	Settling obligations by transfer
ḥiyāza	Rights of possession
ʿīd al-aḍḥā	Feast of the Sacrificial Animals
ʿīd al-fiṭr	Feast of Breaking the Ramaḍān Fast
ʿidda	Waiting period observed by a divorcée or a widow before she can remarry
iflās	Insolvency
ifrād	Performing only the Pilgrimage
iḥdād	Mourning a dead husband
iḥrām	Consecrated state, in which pilgrims observe special rules, such as refraining from ordinary grooming practices, sexual relations, and killing wild animals
iḥṣān	Chastity: a status attained by having sexual intercourse as a free person within a licit relationship
ijāra	Employment contract
ijtihād	Judicial discretion
ikhwa	Siblings
īlāʾ	A husband's oath to abstain from sexual relations with his wife
ʿīna	Credit sales involving food
iqāla	Rescission of a contract for the benefit of the purchaser; cancellation of a sale
iqāma	Immediate call to prayer
irkhāʾ al-sutūr	Marital privacy
istibrāʾ	Refraining from sexual relations with a woman until her menstrual period to confirm that she is not pregnant
istilām	Saluting the corners of the Kabah during circumambulation (*ṭawāf*)

iʿtikāf	Pious seclusion in a mosque during the last ten days and nights of Ramaḍān
jāhiliyya	Days of Ignorance prior to Islam
jāʾifa	Wound that pierces the abdomen
jāʾiḥa	An act of God or other calamity that destroys a crop
janāba	Ritual preclusion on account of a bodily impurity caused by menstruation or childbirth in the case of women, ejaculation in the case of men, or sexual intercourse for both men and women
janāʾiz	Funerals; corpses
janāza	Funeral bier; funeral procession
jināya	Battery
jināza	Corpse
jizāf	Estimated quantity
jizya	Annual poll-tax levied on adult non-Muslim males permanently resident in the territory of the Islamic state
judhām	Elephantiasis
jurḥ (sing.)/***jirāḥ*** (pl.)	Battery
kaffāra	Penance
kalāla	Heirs who inherit from the decedent when there are no living ascendant or descendant heirs
al-kāliʾ bil-kāliʾ	Settling one debt by means of a second debt
khalīṭ (sing.)/***khulaṭāʾ*** (pl.)	Individual owner of a herd of livestock who commingles it with others to share costs but maintains separate ownership of the animals
khaliyya; bariyya	Euphemisms for divorce
khamr	Wine
al-khandaq	Battle of the Trench
khiṭba	Proposal of marriage
khiyār	Option, including to divorce, to rescind a contract, or to choose from a menu of remedies available for a breach of contract
khulʿ	A mode of marital dissolution that entails the wife's payment of property to the husband

kirāʾ	Rental contract, whether of farmland, residential property, animals, or tools
kitāba	Manumission contract
liʿān or ***mulāʿana***	Mutual imprecation: a procedure by which a husband may formally accuse his wife of adultery
luqaṭa	Lost property found by a third party
maʿādin	Mineral wealth; mines
maḍāmīn	Fetuses in their mothers' wombs
madhī	Pre-ejaculate
maḥram	A close male relation to whom marriage is prohibited
maḥrūsa	Untended livestock
majnūn	Insane
malāqīḥ	Offspring sired by a stud
maʾmūma	Head wound that pierces the skull and reaches the brain
manbūdh	Abandoned child
manfaʿa (sing.)/***manāfiʿ*** (pl.)	Usufruct of a piece of property
mann	Free manumission of a slave or a prisoner of war
marīḍ	Ill person
maʿrūf	Acts of goodwill
mawāqīt	Designated stations along the Pilgrimage route where pilgrims must enter the consecrated state (*iḥrām*) before proceeding to Mecca
mawāt	Unused land
mawlā	Freedman
mawlāt	Freedwoman
mayta	Carrion
mīl	Unit of distance equivalent to 3,500 arm's lengths or a man's paces
minbar	Pulpit
mīrāth	Decedent's estate; a designated right to inherit from a decedent's estate
mirfaq	Easements
miskīn (sing.)/***masākīn*** (pl.)	The bereft

mithqāl	Unit of measure used for gold or silver, approximately 3.35 grams
muʿallamāt	Hounds
muʾannath/mukhannath	Transgender man
mudabbar	Slave designated for manumission upon his master's death
mudabbara	Handmaiden designated for manumission upon her master's death
mudd	Unit of measure, approximately 500 grams
mūḍiḥa	Wound that exposes the skull
mughtaṣaba	Raped woman
mughtaṣib	Rapist
muhājirūn	Emigrants
muḥallil	Man who marries a woman solely for the purpose of allowing her to remarry her previous husband
muḥāqala	Sharecropping
muḥrim	Person in the consecrated state
muḥṣan	Someone who has been previously married as a free person
muḥṣar	Someone impeded from completing the Visitation or the Pilgrimage
mukātab	Slave who is a party to a manumission contract
mukhāṭara	Betting; mutual assumption of price risk
mukhtaliʿa	Woman who has given property to her husband in exchange for a divorce
mulāmasa	Sale by touch
munābadha	Sale by tossing
munaqqala	Wound that breaks a bone or cracks the skull but does not expose it
murābaḥa	Contract of sale for goods at an agreed-upon rate of profit
murāṭala	Exchange of gold for gold and silver for silver by weight
murtahin	Secured creditor
musāqāt	Irrigation partnership
mustakraha	Raped woman

mustakrī	Lessee
mustalḥaq	A child of previously unknown paternity who is subsequently affiliated to a man who is deemed the child's father
mutʿa	Parting gift upon divorce
muzābana	Trade involving an indeterminate amount of goods
nabīdh	Water in which dried fruit has been steeped
nadhr (sing.)/***nudhūr*** (pl.)	Vow
nafal (sing.)/***anfāl*** (pl.)	Extra share of booty out of the state's one-fifth share
nafaqa	Maintenance
nāfila	Voluntary pious act
nafy	Denial of paternity
najsh	Fictitious bids
nasab	Affiliation
nasīʾa	Deferring payment
nikāḥ	Marriage
nikāḥ al-mutʿa	Temporary marriage
niyya	Intention
qaḍāʾ (sing.)/***aqḍiya*** (pl.)	Judicial ruling
qadar	Doctrine of free will
qadariyya	Proponents of free will
qadhf	Slander
qāʾif	Physiognomist
qasāma	Collective oaths used in the absence of eyewitness testimony to determine guilt in cases of intentional murder or to establish monetary liability in cases of unintentional killing
qasm	Partition of properties
qaṭāʿa	Prepayment of a manumission contract
qatl al-ʿamd	Intentional killing
qatl al-khaṭaʾ	Unintentional killing
qawad	Retaliation for intentional killing or intentional battery

qimār	Gambling
qirāḍ	Investment partnership
qirān	Performance of the Pilgrimage and the Visitation on the same trip
qiṣāṣ	Retaliation for intentional murder or intentional battery
qur' (sing.)/***aqrā'*** or ***qurū'*** (pl.)	Menstrual period
raḍāʿa	Breastfeeding
rāhin	Pledgor
rahn (sing.)/***ruhūn*** (pl.)	Pledge
rajm	Lapidation
raqaba	The *res* of the property in contrast to its usufruct (*manāfiʿ*); in the case of a slave, the slave's body, such that an obligation attached to it is the responsibility of the master
ribā	Unlawful gain
ribā al-nasī'a or ***ribā al-nasā'***	Deferred trade of food, gold, or silver
ridda	Apostasy
rikāz	Buried treasure predating the rise of Islam
riṭl	Measure of weight, approximately 280 grams in the Hijaz in Mālik's time
ruqya	Pious supplication to treat or ease suffering caused by illness
ṣāʿ	Unit of measure, approximately two kilograms
ṣadāq	Dower
ṣadaqa	Alms-tax; a gift of support; an act of charity
safīh	Spendthrift; a person who cannot prudently manage his or her property
ṣaghīr	Minor
ṣāḥib al-ʿīna	Intermediary who extends credit to finance a sale
sā'iba	Abandoned freedman
salaf	Loan; prepayment for future delivery of a commodity in a forward contract
ṣalāt al-ʿasr	Afternoon Prayer
ṣalāt al-ḍuḥā	Midmorning Prayer

ṣalāt al-fajr	Dawn Prayer preceding the obligatory Morning Prayer (*ṣalāt al-ṣubḥ*)
ṣalāt al-ʿīd	Feast Prayer
ṣalāt al-ʿishā'	Evening Prayer
ṣalāt al-istisqā'	Prayer for Rain
ṣalāt al-jamāʿa	Congregational prayer
ṣalāt al-jumuʿa	Friday Congregational Prayer
ṣalāt al-khawf	Prayer of Danger
ṣalāt al-layl	Night Prayer
ṣalāt al-maghrib	Sunset Prayer
ṣalāt al-ṣubḥ	Morning Prayer
ṣalāt al-witr	*Witr* prayer
ṣalāt al-ẓuhr	Noon Prayer
ṣalāt kusūf al-shams	Solar eclipse prayer
ṣarf	Currency exchange
sariqa	Theft
saʿy	Marching between the hillocks of Ṣafā and Marwa in Mecca in connection with the rites of the Pilgrimage or the Visitation
ṣayd	Wild animals
shafaq	Dusk
shahāda	Testimony
shahādat al-ṣibyān	Testimony of minors
shāhid	Witness
shāt	Yearling; a goat or a sheep up to the completion of its second year
shirk; sharika	Partnership
shubhāt al-nikāḥ	De facto marriage that gives rise to certain rights, obligations, and immunities but is nevertheless invalid
shufʿa	Right of first refusal
siḥr	Sorcery
siwāk	Toothbrush
ṣiyām	Fasting
sulṭān	Public official; ruler

taʿaddī	Breach of contract
tadbīr	Designation by a healthy slave owner of slaves for manumission upon his death
taghlīẓ	Accelerated payment of compensation
ṭalāq	A form of marital dissolution in which the husband unilaterally releases the wife from the obligations of the marriage contract
tamattuʿ	Performing the Pilgrimage (*ḥajj*) after performing the Visitation (*ʿumra*) during the same pilgrimage season
tamlīk	Delegation by the husband of his authority to terminate the marriage, usually to his wife but possibly to another party
tamr	Dried dates
taʿrīḍ	Indirect slander
ṭarīq al-muslimīn	Public highway
tashahhud	Recitation of the attestation of faith during prayer (*ṣalāt*)
ṭāʿūn	Plague
ṭawāf	Circumambulation of the Kabah
ṭawāf al-ifāḍa	Circumambulation of the March, a constituent element of the Pilgrimage (*ḥajj*) that must be performed by all pilgrims
ṭawāf al-wadāʿ	Farewell Circumambulation
tawliya	Repurchase of the goods of a contract by the seller at cost
tayammum	Dry ablution
thamar (sing.)/***thimār*** (pl.)	Unharvested or fresh dates
tibr	Raw gold or silver
ʿuhda	Seller's liability for defects in goods
umm walad (sing.)/ ***ummahāt al-awlād*** (pl.)	A handmaiden who has borne her master a child
ʿumra	Visitation; a lesser pilgrimage, rites performed when visiting Mecca
ʿumrā	Gift of a life estate
ʿushūr	Taxes payable by protected people

walāʿ	Patronage: a reciprocal relationship of solidarity between members of a tribe or between a manumitted slave and the manumitter
walad al-mulāʿana	Repudiated child
walad al-zinā	Illegitimate child
walīma	Wedding feast
wasaq (sing.)/***awsuq*** (pl.)	Unit of measure for cereal crops, approximately 122 kilograms
waṣiyya	Last will and testament; a testamentary disposition
wuḍūʾ	Ablutions
yamīn	Oaths; in a lawsuit, the claimant's oath
yawm al-naḥr	Day of the Slaughter of the Sacrosanct Animals; takes place on the tenth day of Dhū al-Ḥijja when pilgrims slaughter animals they have brought with them for sacrifice
yawm al-tarwiya	Day of Watering; takes place on the ninth day of Dhū al-Ḥijja when pilgrims supply themselves with water before heading out to ʿArafāt and the plains of Minā
zakāt	Alms-tax; alms
zarʿ	Grains
ẓihār	Declaring one's wife to be like the back of one's mother
zinā	Fornication; adultery

Bibliography

Primary Sources

Bājī, Sulaymān b. Khalaf al-. *al-Muntaqā sharḥ al-Muwaṭṭa'*. 7 vols. Cairo: Dār al-Kitāb al-Islāmī, n.d. Reprint of Cairo: Maṭbaʿat al-Saʿāda, 1913.

Ibn ʿAbd al-Barr, Yūsuf b. ʿAbd Allāh. *al-Istidhkār al-jāmiʿ li-madhāhib fuqahā' al-amṣār wa-ʿulamā' al-aqṭār fīmā taḍammanahu al-Muwaṭṭa' min maʿānī al-ra'y wa-'l-āthār*. Cairo: Mu'assasat al-Risāla, 1993.

Ibn al-ʿArabī, Muḥammad b. ʿAbd Allāh. *al-Qabas fī sharḥ Muwaṭṭa' Mālik b. Anas*. 3 vols. Beirut: Dār al-Gharb al-Islāmī, 1992.

Ibn Farḥūn, Ibrāhīm b. ʿAlī. *Tabṣirat al-ḥukkām fī uṣūl al-aqḍiya wa-minhāj al-aḥkām*. 2 vols. Cairo: Maktabat al-Kulliyyāt al-Azhariyya, 1986.

Ibn Ḥabīb, ʿAbd al-Malik. *al-Wāḍiḥa: Kutub al-ṣalāt wa-kutub al-ḥajj*. Edited by Miklos Muranyi. Beirut: Dār al-Bashā'ir al-Islāmiyya, 2010.

Ibn Manẓūr. *Lisān al-ʿArab*. Edited by ʿAbd Allāh ʿAlī al-Kabīr et al. 6 vols. plus 3 vols. of indexes. Cairo: Dār al-Maʿārif, [1981?]–86.

Ibn Rushd, Abū al-Walīd Muḥammad. *al-Bayān wa'l-taḥṣīl wa'l-sharḥ wa'l-tawjīh wa'l-taʿlīl fī masā'il al-Mustakhraja*. Edited by Muḥammad Ḥijjī et al. 20 vols. 2nd ed. Beirut: Dār al-Gharb al-Islāmī, 1988.

Kāndihlawī, Muḥammad Zakariyyā al-. *Awjaz al-masālik ilā Muwaṭṭa' Mālik*. 17 vols. Damascus: Dār al-Qalam, 2003.

Lane, Edward. *An Arabic-English Lexicon*. 8 vols. London: Williams, 1863.

al-Mawsūʿa al-fiqhiyya. 1st ed. 45 vols. Kuwait: Kuwaiti Ministry of Endowments, 1983.

Saḥnūn b. Saʿīd. *al-Mudawwana*. 4 vols. Beirut: Dār al-Fikr, 1986.

Shaybānī, Muḥammad b. al-Ḥasan al-. *al-Ḥujja ʿalā ahl al-Madīna*. Beirut: ʿĀlam al-Kutub, 1983.

Yafuranī, Muḥammad b.ʿAbd al-Ḥaqq al-. *al-Iqtiḍāb fī gharīb al-Muwaṭṭa' wa-iʿrābihi ʿalā al-abwāb*. Riyadh: Maktabat al-ʿUbaykān, 2001.

Yāqūt al-Ḥamawī, Shihāb al-Dīn. *Muʿjam al-buldān*. Beirut: Dār Ṣādir, 1995.

Zurqānī, Muḥammad b. ʿAbd al-Bāqī al-. *Sharḥ al-Zurqānī ʿalā Muwaṭṭa' al-Imām Mālik*. Cairo: Maktabat al-Thaqāfa al-Dīniyya, 2003.

Secondary Sources

ʿAbbās, Iḥsān. "ʿAbd al-Malik b. Marwān wa-dawruhu fī thaqāfat ʿaṣrih." *Dirāsāt* 13, no. 1 (1986): 105–13.

Abbott, Nadia. *Studies in Arabic Literary Papyri*. 3 vols. Chicago: University of Chicago Oriental Institute Publications, 1957.

Azami, Muhammad M. al-. *On Schacht's Origins of Muhammadan Jurisprudence*. Oxford: Oxford Centre for Islamic Studies and Islamic Texts Society, 1996.

Bewley, Aisha, trans. *Al-Muwatta of Imam Malik ibn Anas: The First Formulation of Islamic Law*. London: Kegan Paul, 1989. Reprint, London: Routledge, 2010.

Bravmann, M. M. *The Spiritual Background of Early Islam*. Leiden: Brill, 2009.

Brockopp, Jonathan, "Rereading the History of Early Mālikī Jurisprudence." *Journal of the American Oriental Society* 118, no. 2 (1998): 233–38.

Calder, Norman. *Studies in Early Muslim Jurisprudence*. Oxford: Clarendon Press, 1993.

Dutton, Yasin. *The Origins of Islamic Law: The Qurʾan, the "Muwaṭṭaʾ" and Madinan ʿAmal*. 2nd ed. New York: RoutledgeCurzon, 2002.

El Shamsy, Ahmed. "Rethinking *Taqlīd* in the Early Shāfiʿī School." *Journal of the American Oriental Society* 128, no. 1 (2008): 1–23.

El Shamsy, Ahmed. *The Canonization of Islamic Law: A Social and Intellectual History*. New York: Cambridge University Press, 2013.

Fadel, Mohammad. "Authority in Ibn Abī Zayd al-Qayrawānī's *Kitāb al-nawādir wa-l-ziyādāt ʿalā mā fī l-Mudawwana min ghayrihā min al-ummahāt*: 'The Chapter of Judgments' (*Kitāb al-aqḍiya*)." In *The Heritage of Arabo-Islamic Learning: Studies Presented to Wadad Kadi*, edited by Maurice A. Pomerantz and Aram A. Shahin, 207–26. Boston: Brill, 2016.

Fadel, Mohammad. "The Social Logic of *Taqlīd* and the Rise of the *Mukhtaṣar*." *Islamic Law and Society* 3, no. 2 (1996): 193–233.

Ghaly, Mohammed. *Islam and Disability: Perspectives in Theology and Jurisprudence*. London: Routledge, 2010.

Goldziher, Ignaz. *Muslim Studies*. Edited by S. M. Stern. Translated by C. R. Barber and S. M. Stern. London: Allen and Unwin, 1971.

Ḥallāq, Muḥammad Ṣubḥī b. Ḥasan. *al-Īḍāḥāt al-ʿaṣriyya lil-maqāyīs wa'l-makāyīl wa'l-awzān wa'l-nuqūd al-sharʿiyya*. Sanaa: Maktabat al-Jīl al-Jadīd, 2007.

Hallaq, Wael B. *The Origins and Evolution of Islamic Law*. New York: Cambridge University Press, 2005.

Hallaq, Wael. "Was al-Shāfiʿī the Master Architect of Islamic Jurisprudence?" *International Journal of Middle East Studies* 25, no. 4 (1993): 587–605.

Jumuʿa, Muḥammad ʿAlī. *al-Makāyīl wa'l-mawāzīn al-sharʿiyya*. Cairo: al-Quds lil-Iʿlān wa'l-Nashr wa'l-Taswīq, 2001.

Khadduri, Majid, trans. *Islamic Jurisprudence: Shāfiʿī's "Risāla."* Baltimore: Johns Hopkins Press, 1961.

Lowry, Joseph E. Review of *Die Rechtsbücher des Qairawāners Saḥnūn b. Saʿīd: Entstehungsgeschichte und Werküberlieferung*, by Miklos Muranyi. *Journal of the American Oriental Society* 123, no. 2 (2003): 438–40.

Lowry, Joseph E., trans. *The Epistle on Legal Theory: A Translation of al-Shāfiʿī's "Risālah."* New York: New York University Press, 2013.

Motzki, Harald. *Analysing Muslim Traditions: Studies in Legal, Exegetical and* Maghāzī Ḥadīth. Boston: Brill, 2010.

Opwis, Felicitas. "*Maṣlaḥa* in Contemporary Islamic Legal Theory." *Islamic Law and Society* 12, no. 2 (2005): 182–223.

Ossendorf-Conrad, Beatrix. *Das "K. al-Wadiha" des 'Abd al-Malik b. Ḥabīb: Edition und Kommentar zu Ms. Qarawiyyin 809/40 (Abwab al-Tahara)*. Stuttgart: Franz Steiner, 1994.

Rahimuddin, Muhammad. *Muwatta' Imam Malik*. Lahore: Sh. Muhammad Ashraf, 1985.

Rahman, Fazlur. *Islamic Methodology in History*. Karachi: Karachi Central Institute of Islamic Research, 1965.

Raysūnī, Aḥmad al-. *Naẓariyyat al-maqāṣid 'inda al-Shāṭibī*. 4th ed. Herndon, VA: International Institute of Islamic Thought, 1995.

Savant, Sarah. "A Tale of 3 'Versions'" (blog post). KITAB website, September 10, 2017. http://kitab-project.org/2017/09/10/a-tale-of-3-versions/.

Schacht, Joseph. *The Origins of Muhammadan Jurisprudence*. Oxford: Clarendon Press, 1959.

Swartz, Merlin. Review of *Al-Muwatta of Imam Malik ibn Anas: The First Formulation of Islamic Law*, translated by Aisha Bewley. *Middle East Studies Association Bulletin* 25, no. 1 (1991): 102–3.

Wymann-Landgraf, Umar F. Abd-Allah. *Mālik and Medina: Islamic Legal Reasoning in the Formative Period*. Boston: Brill, 2013.

Index

Index of Proper Names

Abān b. ʿUthmān, 87, 288, 300, 423, 431, 494, 539, 574
ʿAbbād b. ʿAbd Allāh b. al-Zubayr, 218
ʿAbbād b. Nusayy, 115
ʿAbbād b. Tamīm, 173, 187, 193, 378, 754
ʿAbbād b. Ziyād, 91
ʿAbd Allāh al-Ṣunābiḥī, 89, 206
ʿAbd Allāh b. ʿAbd Allāh b. al-Ḥārith b. Nawfal, 735
ʿAbd Allāh b. ʿAbd Allāh b. Jābir b. ʿAtīk, 205, 215
ʿAbd Allāh b. ʿAbd Allāh b. ʿUmar, 120–21
ʿAbd Allāh b. ʿAbd al-Raḥmān b. Abī Bakr al-Ṣiddīq, 257, 719, 748
ʿAbd Allāh b. ʿAbd al-Raḥmān b. Abī Ḥusayn al-Makkī, 719
ʿAbd Allāh b. ʿAbd al-Raḥmān b. Maʿmar al-Anṣārī, 255, 358, 761
ʿAbd Allāh b. ʿAbd al-Raḥmān b. Zayd b. al-Khaṭṭāb, 521
ʿAbd Allāh b. Abī Bakr b. Muḥammad b. ʿAmr b. Ḥazm, 44n1; ablution, 95; battery compensation, 677; bequests, 633; breastfeeding, 531, 535; charity, 784; evil eye, 754; Jews, 751; marriage, 478; legal testimony, 599; miscellaneous matters, 193, 209, 216, 245, 286, 304, 431, 620; mourning, 527; Pilgrimage, 288, 294, 343, 346–47; prayer, 126–27, 137, 140, 143, 169, 187; punishment, 719; Quran, 195; sacrificial animals, 321, 328, 378; sales, 539, 547, 563; sneezing, 766–67; vows, 393
ʿAbd Allāh b. Abī Ḥabība, 393–94
ʿAbd Allāh b. Abī Mulayka, 710
ʿAbd Allāh b. Abī Qatāda, 369
ʿAbd Allāh b. Abī Ṭalḥa, 767
ʿAbd Allāh b. Abī Umayya, 617, 638
ʿAbd Allāh b. Aḥmad b. Muḥammad b. al-Labbād, 71
ʿAbd Allāh b. Aḥmad b. Ḥanbal, 56–57
ʿAbd Allāh b. al-Arqam, 166, 784
ʿAbd Allāh b. al-Faḍl, 474, 510
ʿAbd Allāh b. al-Mughīra b. Abī Burda al-Kinānī, 368
ʿAbd Allāh b. ʿĀmir b. Rabīʿa, 87, 117, 146, 304, 544, 715, 737
ʿAbd Allāh b. ʿAmr, 374–75
ʿAbd Allāh b. ʿAmr b. al-ʿĀṣī, 125, 153, 171, 210, 321, 352, 389, 509
ʿAbd Allāh b. ʿAmr b. al-Ḥadramī, 725
ʿAbd Allāh b. ʿAmr b. ʿUthmān, 516
ʿAbd Allāh b. ʿAyyāsh b. Abī Rabīʿa al-Makhzūmī, 322, 353, 383, 714, 735
ʿAbd Allāh b. Buḥayna, 125
ʿAbd Allāh b. Bulayṭ al-Qaysī, 64
ʿAbd Allāh b. Ḥudhāfa, 321
ʿAbd Allāh b. Ḥunayn, 282
ʿAbd Allāh b. Jaʿfar, 330
ʿAbd Allāh b. Kaʿb (freedman of ʿUthmān b. ʿAffān), 97

ʿAbd Allāh b. Kaʿb b. Mālik al-Anṣārī, 606
ʿAbd Allāh b. Masʿūd: ablution, 96, 146; breastfeeding, 534; divorce, 493, 480, 519–20; loans, 585; lying, 779; Quran, 173; prayer, 146, 169; sales, 544, 586
ʿAbd Allāh b. Muḥammad b. Abī Bakr al-Ṣiddīq, 312
ʿAbd Allāh b. Nisṭās, 606
ʿAbd Allāh b. Qays b. Makhrama, 143
ʿAbd Allāh b. Rāfiʿ, 76
ʿAbd Allāh b. Rawāḥa, 649–50
ʿAbd Allāh b. Sahl, 701–2, 703
ʿAbd Allāh b. Salām, 136, 709
ʿAbd Allāh b. Thābit, 215
ʿAbd Allāh b. Umm Maktūm, 197, 516
ʿAbd Allāh b. Unays al-Juhanī, 272
ʿAbd Allāh b. Wāqid, 378
ʿAbd Allāh b. Yazīd (freedman of al-Aswad b. Sufyān), 81, 154, 199, 516, 549
ʿAbd Allāh b. Yazīd al-Khaṭmī, 339
ʿAbd Allāh b. Zayd al-Anṣārī, 109
ʿAbd Allāh b. Zayd al-Māzinī, 187, 193
ʿAbd Allāh b. Zayd b. ʿĀṣim, 83, 173n169
ʿAbd al-Bāqī, Muḥammad Fuʾād, 49, 50
ʿAbd al-Ḥamīd b. ʿAbd al-Raḥmān b. Zayd b. al-Khaṭṭāb, 601, 735, 737
ʿAbd al-Ḥamīd b. Suhayl b. ʿAbd al-Raḥmān b. ʿAwf, 548
ʿAbd al-Karīm b. Abī al-Mukhāriq al-Baṣrī, 146, 165
ʿAbd al-Karīm b. Mālik al-Jazarī, 349
ʿAbd al-Malik b. Abī Bakr b. al-Ḥārith b. Hishām, 288, 431, 478
ʿAbd al-Malik b. Jurayj, 43
ʿAbd al-Malik b. Marwān, 87n43, 288, 309n413, 337, 436, 485, 613, 697, 776
ʿAbd al-Malik b. Qurayr, 347
ʿAbd al-Raḥmān b. ʿAbd Allāh b. ʿAbd al-Raḥmān b. Abī Ṣaʿṣaʿa al-Anṣārī al-Māzinī, 110, 200, 374, 768, 769
ʿAbd al-Raḥmān b. ʿAbd al-Qārī, 121, 139–40, 196, 315, 626
ʿAbd al-Raḥmān b. Abī ʿAmra al-Anṣārī, 150–51, 427
ʿAbd al-Raḥmān b. Abī Bakr al-Ṣiddīq, 83–84, 345, 427, 496
ʿAbd al-Raḥmān b. Abī Hurayra, 389
ʿAbd al-Raḥmān b. Abī Laylā, 349
ʿAbd al-Raḥmān b. Abī Saʿīd al-Khudrī, 163
ʿAbd al-Raḥmān b. al-Aswad b. ʿAbd Yaghūth, 565, 760
ʿAbd al-Raḥmān b. al-Ḥubāb al-Anṣārī, 728
ʿAbd al-Raḥmān b. al-Mujabbar, 82, 94, 485
ʿAbd al-Raḥmān b. al-Qāsim b. Muḥammad b. Abī Bakr, 44n1; ablution, 101; alms-tax, 226; breastfeeding, 532; consecrated state, 281, 285, 292–93, 344–45; divorce, 496, 497; fasting, 268; fortitude, 217; gifts, 629; Kabah and Pilgrimage, 290, 335, 342, 346; marriage, 473–74, 482; Medina, 735; prayer, 120, 122, 146, 147, 179; theft, 721
ʿAbd al-Raḥmān b. al-Zabīr, 479
ʿAbd al-Raḥmān b. ʿAwf, 91, 105, 246, 348, 490, 511, 622, 657, 737, 785
ʿAbd al-Raḥmān b. Ḥanẓala al-Zuraqī, 413
ʿAbd al-Raḥmān b. Ḥarmala al-Aslamī, 93, 150, 255, 296, 773–74
ʿAbd al-Raḥmān b. Hurmuz, 125
ʿAbd al-Raḥmān b. Kaʿb b. Mālik al-Anṣārī, 218, 359
ʿAbd al-Raḥmān b. Muḥammad b. ʿAbd Allāh b. ʿAbd al-Qārī, 615
ʿAbd al-Raḥmān b. Sahl, 701–2
ʿAbd al-Raḥmān b. Zayd al-Anṣārī, 88
ʿAbd al-Raḥmān b. Zayd b. al-Khaṭṭāb, 521
ʿAbd al-Wārith b. Sufyān, 59, 61
ʿAbd b. Zamʿa, 617
ʿAbd Rabbih b. Saʿīd, 255, 367, 410, 512, 522

ʿAbīda b. Sufyān al-Ḥaḍramī, 390
Abraham, 169, 261n320, 747; Kabah, 312; Mecca, 731, 733
Abū ʿAbd Allāh al-Agharr, 193, 203
Abū ʿAbd Allāh al-Balansanī, 65
Abū ʿAbd Allāh al-Khawlānī, 53
Abū ʿAbd Allāh al-Khushanī, 58
Abū ʿAbd Allāh al-Ṣunābiḥī, 115
Abū ʿAbd Allāh b. ʿAbd al-Malik al-Murrākushī, 70
Abū ʿAbd Allāh b. ʿAbd Allāh b. Abī Dulaym, 58, 59, 60
Abū ʿAbd Allāh b. Abī al-Aṣbagh b. Abī al-Baḥr al-Zahrī, 63
Abū ʿAbd Allāh b. al-Ṭallāʿ, 62, 63, 66, 69
Abū ʿAbd Allāh b. Ḥamdīn, 62, 63
Abū ʿAbd Allāh b. Mufarrij, 52
Abū ʿAbd Allāh b. Rashīd al-Sabtī, 70
Abū ʿAbd Allāh Muḥammad b. ʿAbd Allāh b. Abī ʿĪsā, 64, 69
Abū ʿAbd Allāh Muḥammad b. ʿAbd Allāh b. Yaḥyā, 51
Abū ʿAbd Allāh Muḥammad b. Faraj, 73
Abū ʿAbd Allāh Muḥammad b. ʿĪsā al-Tamīmī al-Sabtī, 54, 55
Abū ʿAbd Allāh Muḥammad b. Salama al-Anṣārī, 62–63, 69
Abū ʿAbd Allāh Muḥammad b. ʿUmar b. al-Fakhkhār, 61
Abū ʿAbd al-Raḥmān. *See* Ibn ʿUmar, ʿAbd Allāh
Abū al-ʿAbbās al-Dānī, 55, 60, 61
Abū al-ʿAbbās b. al-Ghammāz, 53
Abū al-ʿĀṣ Ḥakam b. Muḥammad b. Afrānk al-Judhāmī, 57
Abū al-ʿĀṣ b. Rabīʿa b. ʿAbd Shams, 171
Abū al-Aswad Muḥammad b. ʿAbd al-Raḥmān, 289–90, 317
Abū al-Baddāḥ ʿĀṣim b. ʿAdī, 343
Abū al-Dardāʾ, 202, 206, 556, 640
Abū al-Faḍl Aḥmad Qāsim al-Tāhartī, 59, 60
Abū al-Ghayth Sālim, 368
Abū al-Ḥakam b. Najāḥ al-Lakhmī, 63
Abū al-Ḥasan b. Mughīth, 63, 64
Abū al-Ḥasan Shurayḥ, 57, 63, 64
Abū al-Ḥasan Yūnus, 59
Abū al-Ḥātim b. Ḥabbān, 45
Abū al-Haytham al-Tayyihān al-Anṣārī, 752
Abū al-Ḥubāb Saʿīd b. Yasār, 216, 555, 732, 756, 761, 781
Abū al-Maymūn al-Bajlī, 58
Abū al-Muthannā al-Juhanī, 748
Abū al-Naḍr (freedman of ʿUmar b. ʿUbayd Allāh), 44n1; ablution, 94, 97; bereavement, 216; consecrated state, 301–2; fasting, 257, 269, 320–21; funerals, 213, 219; images, 767; martyrs, 369; Night of Power, 272 prayer, 132, 141, 150, 154, 162, 163, 167; sex, 526
Abū al-Qāsim Aḥmad b. al-Qāsim b. Jābir b. ʿUbayda, 64
Abū al-Qāsim al-Mawāʿīnī, 65
Abū al-Qāsim b. Baqī, 63
Abū al-Qāsim b. Ḥabīsh, 65
Abū al-Quʿays, 532
Abū al-Rabīʿ al-Kallāʿī, 53
Abū al-Rijāl Muḥammad b. ʿAbd al-Raḥmān, 218, 346, 545, 546, 548, 621, 715–16
Abū al-Sāʾib, 118, 772
Abū al-Ṭufayl ʿĀmir b. Wāthila, 157
Abū al-Walīd al-Waqshī, 58
Abū al-Walīd b. al-Faraḍī, 52, 58
Abū al-Walīd b. Mughīth, 53, 63, 73
Abū al-Walīd Yūnus b. ʿAbd Allāh al-Ṣaffār, 69
Abū al-Zinād ʿAbd Allāh b. Dhakwān, 44n1; ablution, 83, 84, 90, 175; the bereft, 747; clothes and sandals, 744–45; currency exchange, 557; divorce, 511; dreams, 762; fasting, 262, 269; free will, 737, 739; gluttony, 748; Hell, 781; *jihād*, 357, 366; judicial matters, 601, 621, 700; marriage, 480; martyrs, 369; miscellaneous matters, 107, 218–19, 741, 750;

Muḥammad's estate, 781; prayer, 82, 119, 132, 135, 149, 152, 166, 170, 172, 390; punishment, 715, 722; sacrificial animals, 321; sales, 545, 563, 574, 582, 587–88, 595; self-reliance, 783; sheep, 769; speaking cautiously, 776; supplication, 203
Abū al-Zubayr al-Makkī Muḥammad b. Tadrus, 44n1; animals, 347, 378–79; circumambulation, 317, 327; left hand, 747; marriage, 482, 491; prayer, 157–58, 316; Satan, 750; supplication, 204
Abū ʿAmr Dhakwān, 140
Abū ʿAmra al-Anṣārī, 599
Abū ʿAmr b. Ḥafṣ, 516
Abū Asmāʾ (freedman of ʿAbd Allāh b. Jaʿfar), 330
Abū Ayyūb al-Anṣārī, 151, 191, 282, 311, 326, 339, 379–80, 733, 741
Abū Baḥr b. al-ʿĀṣ, 55, 64
Abū Bakr ʿAbbās b. Aṣbagh al-Hamadānī al-Ḥijārī, 57
Abū Bakr al-Ṣiddīq, 81, 169, 302; ablution, 88, 101; alms-tax, 222, 239; consecrated state, 281; drinking practices, 749; dyed hair, 760; funeral matters, 209–10, 214; food, 752; gifts, 626; illness, 757; inheritance, 410; *jihād*, 359, 365, 373–74; lapidation, 709–10; martyrs, 370; Medina, 733–34; parental rights, 639;prayer, 115, 116, 117, 144, 153, 168, 172, 177, 339; property, 375; punishment, 713, 721–22; speaking cautiously, 778
Abū Bakr b. ʿAbd al-Raḥmān b. al-Ḥārith b. Hishām, 161, 166, 255–56, 258, 278, 299, 498, 514, 574, 591, 592
Abū Bakr b. al-Murābiṭ, 65
Abū Bakr b. ʿAmr, 144, 245
Abū Bakr b. Ḥazm, 493–94, 633, 647
Abū Bakr b. Khayr, 54, 55–56, 57, 59, 60, 63, 64, 69, 70
Abū Bakr b. Muḥammad b. ʿAmr b. Ḥazm, 563, 592, 700, 725–26
Abū Bakr b. Nāfiʿ, 344, 744
Abū Bakr b. Rizq, 64
Abū Bakr b. Sulaymān b. Abī Ḥathma, 124, 150
Abū Bakr b. Ṭāhir al-Qaysī, 54
Abū Bakr b. ʿUbayd Allāh b. ʿAbd Allāh b. ʿUmar, 747
Abū Bakr b. ʿUthmān b. Sahl b. Ḥunayf, 215
Abū Bakr Yaḥyā b. Wāfid, 62
Abū Bashīr al-Anṣārī, 754
Abū Burda, 377
Abū Dāwūd al-Sijistānī, 57
Abū Dharr, 164–65, 355
Abū Ghaṭafān b. Ṭarīf al-Murrī, 300, 606, 627, 688
Abū Ḥanīfa, 10, 73n2, 211n242, 560n802
Abū Ḥāzim al-Tammār, 116
Abū Ḥāzim b. Dīnār, 110, 165, 168, 254, 475, 580, 749, 762, 770
Abū Ḥudhayfa b. ʿUtba b. Rabīʿa, 533
Abū Ḥumayd al-Sāʿidī, 169
Abū Hurayra: ablution, 83, 84, 85, 88, 89, 90, 175; alms-tax, 230, 245; anger, 741; the bereft, 747; compensation, 682, 694; compassion, 750; clothes and sandals, 742–45; consecrated state, 302–3, 324; divorce, 497, 509, 520; dreams, 762; fasting, 255–56, 257, 259, 261–62, 265, 269; food, 750, 752; free will, 737, 739; Fridays, 131, 136; funeral matters, 212–13, 220; gluttony, 748; grooming, 747; Hell, 781; illness, 756; *jihād*, 357, 368, 371; lapidation, 711; loving for God's sake, 761–62; Mālik b. Anas, 43; marriage, 473, 480, 490, 522–23; manumission, 425; martyrs, 369; Medina, 732–34; miscellaneous

matters, 193, 216, 219, 390, 615, 621, 728, 741, 761; Muḥammad's estate, 781; oaths, 398; prayer, 75, 76, 78, 82, 109, 114, 118, 119, 123, 129, 137, 149, 150, 152, 166–67, 170, 172, 193; precious metals, 555; punishment, 714; Quran, 199, 201–2; rain, 189; sacrificial animals, 321; sales, 546, 548, 582, 588, 592, 595; self-reliance, 783; sheep, 769; slaughtered animals, 385; slaves, 774; speaking cautiously, 776; supplication, 203, 731; toothbrushes, 107; travel, 774; Visitation, 299
Abū Idrīs al-Khawlānī, 83, 390, 762
Abū ʿĪsā b. Sahl, 61
Abū ʿĪsā Yaḥyā b. ʿAbd Allāh, 51–52, 53, 55, 61–62, 63, 66, 69, 73
Abū Isḥāq al-Lawātī, 61, 63
Abū Jaʿfar Aḥmad b. ʿAwn Allāh b. Ḥudayr al-Bazzāz, 58
Abū Jaʿfar al-Manṣūr, 7, 41
Abū Jaʿfar al-Qārī, 168, 322, 749
Abū Jaʿfar b. ʿAbd Allāh, 52–53
Abū Jahl b. Hishām, 321n437
Abū Jahm b. Hishām, 516
Abū Jahm b. Ḥudhayfa, 116, 126
Abū Juhaym, 163
Abū Laylā b. ʿAbd Allāh b. ʿAbd al-Raḥmān b. Sahl, 701
Abū Lubāba b. ʿAbd al-Mundhir, 400, 772
Abū Māʿiz al-Aslamī ʿAbd Allāh b. Sufyān, 317
Abū Marwān ʿAbd al-Malik b. al-Bājī, 63, 251n356
Abū Marwān al-Ṭabnī, 57
Abū Marwān ʿUbayd Allāh, 51, 69
Abū Masʿūd al-Anṣārī, 74, 169, 574
Abū Muḥammad (freedman of Abū Qatāda), 364
Abū Muḥammad (man from Levant), 144
Abū Muḥammad ʿAbd Allāh b. ʿAlī b. Sharīʿa al-Lakhmī (*al-rāwiya*), 57
Abū Muḥammad ʿAbd Allāh b. Ibrāhīm al-Aṣīlī al-Maghribī, 59, 60, 66
Abū Muḥammad al-Bājī, 66
Abū Muḥammad b. al-Mashshāṭ al-Aṣīlī, 55
Abū Muḥammad b. ʿAttāb, 59
Abū Muḥammad b. Billīṭ, 70
Abū Muḥammad b. Ḥazm, 64, 70
Abū Muḥammad b. Khazraj, 55–56, 59
Abū Muḥammad b. Mūjwāl al-Balansanī, 65
Abū Muḥammad Shurayḥ b. Muḥammad b. Shurayḥ al-Ruʿaynī, 70
Abū Murra, 161–62, 321, 385, 764
Abū Mūsā al-Ashʿarī, 76, 97, 534, 615–16, 659, 763, 766
Abū Muṣʿab al-Zuhrī, 9n5
Abū Nahshal b. al-Aswad, 485
Abū Nuʿaym Wahb b. Kaysān, 88, 114, 753
Abū Qatāda b. Ribʿī al-Anṣārī, 85, 167, 171, 219, 301–2, 364–5, 728, 759, 763
Abū Rāfiʿ, 300, 593–94
Abū Saʿīd (freedman of ʿĀmir b. Kurayz), 117
Abū Saʿīd al-Khudrī: alms-tax, 221, 250; bathing, 132; clothing, 744; fasting, 268; images, 767; loving for God's sake, 761; miscellaneous matters, 193, 271, 766; prayer, 109–10; precious metals, 555; Quran, 198, 200–201; sacrificial animals, 379; sales, 548, 549; self-reliance, 782; sex, 526; sheep, 769; snakes, 772
Abū Salama b. ʿAbd al-Asad al-Makhzūmī, 217
Abū Salama b. ʿAbd al-Raḥmān b. ʿAwf: ablution, 97; alms-tax, 225; compensation, 682, 694; divorce, 510, 516; dreams, 763; drinking practices, 748; fasting, 269; Fridays, 136; hair, 760; judicial matters, 601; marriage, 522–23;

miscellaneous matters, 390, 628; Night of Power, 271; nighttime supplication, 203; Pilgrimage, 347; prayer, 78, 81, 114, 119, 129, 139, 141, 142, 147, 154, 167; property, 643; Quran, 198, 199; vows, 394; wine-drinking, 729
Abū Ṣāliḥ al-Sammān, 43, 109, 119, 131, 150, 201–2, 230, 299, 357, 371, 742–43, 750, 774, 776
Abū Shākir al-Qabrī, 59
Abū Shurayḥ al-Ka'bī, 750
Abū Sufyān (freedman of Ibn Abī Aḥmad), 123, 546, 549
Abū Sufyān b. Ḥarb, 222n259, 527
Abū Suhayl b. Mālik, 44n1, 76, 112, 116, 165, 174, 269, 738, 740, 745, 775, 781
Abū Ṭalḥa al-Anṣārī, 88, 100, 126, 729, 749–50, 767, 781–82
Abū Ṭayba, 771
Abū Tha'laba al-Khushanī, 390
Abū 'Ubayd (freedman of Ibn Azhar), 178, 203
Abū 'Ubayd (freedman of Sulaymān b. 'Abd al-Malik), 115, 202, 774
Abū 'Ubayda b. al-Jarrāḥ 245, 358, 729, 736, 751
Abū 'Ubayda b. Farwa, 85
Abū Umāma b. Sahl b. Ḥunayf, 168, 211–12, 215, 606, 755, 768
Abū 'Umar Aḥmad b. Nābit al-Taghlibī, 55, 56
Abū 'Umar b. al-Ḥadhdhā' al-Tamīmī, 59, 61
Abū 'Umar b. al-Jasūr al-Umawī al-Qurṭubī, 55, 60
Abū 'Uthmān Sa'īd b. Aḥmad al-Qallās, 59
Abū 'Uthmān Sa'īd b. Naṣr, 58, 59, 60, 66
Abū 'Uthmān Sa'īd b. Salama, 62
Abū Wāqid al-Laythī, 178, 711, 764
Abū Ya'qūb Isḥāq al-Dabrī, 56
Abū Yūnus (freedman of 'Ā'isha), 154, 255
Abū Zakariyā' b. 'Ā'idh, 53
Abū Zakariyā' Yaḥyā b. Muḥammad b. Ḥusayn al-Qulay'ī, 55, 62
Adam, 136, 737–38
'Adī b. Thābit al-Anṣārī, 116, 339
'Afīf b. 'Amr al-Sahmī, 125, 151
Aflaḥ, 532
Aḥmad b. al-Muṭarrif, 62
Aḥmad b. Khālid b. al-Jabbāb Abū 'Umar al-Qurṭubī, 56, 57, 65
Aḥmad b. Salama, 62, 69
Aḥwaṣ, al-, 514
'Ā'isha bt. Abī Bakr al-Ṣiddīq: ablution, 83–84, 96–97, 98, 100, 101; alms-tax, 226–27, 237–38; amputation, 719–20; attestation of faith, 122; breastfeeding, 531–32, 534–35; charity, 782; choosing the easier option, 739; clothes, 743; consecrated state, 285, 294, 304, 307, 310, 344–45; dice, 763; divorce, 514, 515; drinking practices, 749; dyed hair, 760; fasting, 254–56, 257, 260–61, 266, 268–69, 320–21; funeral matters, 210, 213, 216, 218, 220; gifts, 626; good deeds, 174; hides, 391; illness, 756, 757; images, 767; intoxicating beverages, 729; judicial matters, 617; Kabah, 312; manumission, 427–28; marriage, 479, 496, 497, 503; Medina, 733–34; menstruation, 103–4, 105, 345–47; miscellaneous matters, 106, 192, 528; Muḥammad's estate, 780–81; oaths, 397, 400; Pilgrimage and Visitation, 289–90, 292, 318–19, 344–47, 356; pious seclusion, 275, 276, 278; prayer, 74, 75, 126, 139, 141, 142–43, 145, 147, 152–54, 156, 158, 162, 172, 182–83; Prophet's death, 210, 214; Quran, 197; sacrificial animals, 334, 378; sinning, 777; supplication, 203–4, 213; torment

of the grave, 184; wicked people, 740; women in mosques, 193
ʿĀʾisha bt. Qudāma, 222, 697
ʿĀʾisha bt. Ṭalḥa, 257
ʿAlāʾ b. ʿAbd al-Raḥmān b. Yaʿqūb, al-, 44n1, 88, 109, 117–18, 167, 206, 606, 660, 728, 744, 783
ʿAlī b. ʿAbd al-Raḥmān al-Muʿāwī, 120
ʿAlī b. Abī Ṭālib, 211n242, 222n259; ablution, 87, 94; adultery allegations, 616; consecrated state, 324; divorce, 494, 497, 500, 510; drinking habits, 748; funerals, 215; lapidation, 712; marriage, 485, 487, 519; newborn sacrifice, 382; prayer, 155, 164, 178; Pilgrimage, 290, 292, 330; sacrificial animals, 328, 380; sales, 571
ʿAlī b. al-Ḥusayn b. ʿAlī b. Abī Ṭālib, 113, 416
ʿAlī b. Ḥusayn, 158
ʿAlī b. Yaḥyā al-Zuraqī, 202
ʿAlqama b. Abī ʿAlqama, 104, 126, 220, 292, 307, 743, 763
ʿĀmir b. ʿAbd Allāh b. al-Zubayr, 171, 749, 780
ʿĀmir b. Fuhayra, 734
ʿĀmir b. Rabīʿa, 755
ʿĀmir b. Saʿd b. Abī Waqqāṣ, 174, 526, 634, 736
ʿAmr (freedman of al-Muṭṭalib), 733
ʿAmr b. ʿAbd Allāh b. Kaʿb al-Sulamī, 757
ʿAmr b. al-ʿĀṣī, 85, 99, 321
ʿAmr b. al-Ḥārith, 377
ʿAmr b. al-Jamūḥ, 374–75
ʿAmr b. al-Sharīd, 532
ʿAmr b. ʿAwf, 77
ʿAmr b. Dīnār, 738
ʿAmr b. Ḥazm, 195, 677
ʿAmr b. Kathīr b. Aflaḥ, 364
ʿAmr b. Muʿādh al-Ashhalī al-Anṣārī, 782
ʿAmr b. Rāfiʿ, 154
ʿAmr b. Saʿīd b. Muʿādh, 751
ʿAmr b. Shuʿayb, 187, 367, 524, 537, 693, 773
ʿAmr b. Sulaym al-Zuraqī, 169, 171, 633
ʿAmr b. ʿUthmān b. ʿAffān, 416
ʿAmr b. Yaḥyā al-Māzinī, 77, 83, 161, 221, 621–22
ʿAmra bt. ʿAbd al-Raḥmān: breastfeeding, 531, 535; disinterment, 218; divorce, 504, 514; illness, 757; manumission, 428; Pilgrimage, 328–29, 346; prayer, 75; pious seclusion, 275, 278; sacrificial animals, 294, 334, 378; selling dates, 545, 547, 548; slander, 716; torment of the grave, 184, 216; theft, 719, 725–26; water rights, 621; women in mosques, 193
Anas b. Mālik: ablution, 88, 90, 92; charity, 781; clothes, 746; cupping, 771; drinking practices, 749; fasting, 258, 267; food, 749–50, 752; friendliness, 741; greetings, 765; *jihād*, 371, 373; marriage, 478, 490; Medina, 733; mindfulness of God, 780; Muḥammad's appearance, 746; Pilgrimage, 291–92; prayer, 77, 116, 152, 161, 162, 188, 206; prophethood, 762; sales, 545; supplication, 731; wine, 729; year of conquest, 353
Antichrist (*al-dajjāl*), 184, 204, 734; physical appearance of, 746
ʿAqīl b. Abī Ṭālib, 77, 416
Aʿraj, al-, 44n1; ablution, 83, 84, 107, 175; the bereft, 747; clothes and sandals, 744–45; divorce, 510; dreams, 762; fasting, 261, 262, 269, 321; free will, 737, 739; gluttony, 748; Hell, 781; *jihād*, 357; marriage, 473, 480, 490; martyrs, 369; miscellaneous matters, 218–19, 588, 621, 741; Muḥammad's estate, 781; prayer, 75, 82, 119, 125, 148, 152, 157, 166,

170, 172, 207; Quran, 196, 199; Ramaḍān, 140; sacrificial animals, 321; sales, 582; self-reliance, 783; sheep, 769; speaking cautiously, 776; supplication, 203
Ashʿarī, Abū al-Ḥasan al-, 46
Ashhab b ʿAbd al-ʿAzīz, 629n885
Ashyam al-Ḍibābī, 692
ʿĀṣī b. Hishām, al-, 431
ʿĀṣim b. ʿAbd Allāh b. Saʿd, 532
ʿĀṣim b. ʿAdī al-Anṣārī, 506
ʿĀṣim b. ʿUmar b. al-Khaṭṭāb, 509, 638–39
Aslam (freedman of ʿUmar b. al-Khaṭṭāb), 284, 285, 687, 735
Asmā' bt. Abī Bakr al-Ṣiddīq, 104, 184–85, 211, 284, 285, 333, 626, 758
Asmā' bt. ʿUmays, 209, 281, 330, 722
Aswad b. Sufyān, al-, 81
ʿAṭā' b. ʿAbd Allāh al-Khurasānī, 160, 259–60, 349–50, 741
ʿAṭā' b. Abī Rabāḥ, 282, 285, 327, 333, 343, 394
ʿAṭā' b. Yasār: ablution, 86, 89, 98; alms, 238; animals, 384; consecrated state, 302–3; currency exchange, 556; divorce, 509; fasting, 256, 257; grooming, 759; illness, 756; intoxicating beverages, 729; *jihād*, 358; loans, 593; manumission, 425; Medina, 733; mosques, 174; prayer, 74–75, 81, 124, 125, 132, 163, 172, 183, 206; sacrificial animals, 379; sales, 548; self-reliance, 783; speaking honestly, 777; steeping dried fruit, 728
ʿAṭā' b. Yazīd al-Laythī, 109, 172, 202, 741, 782
ʿAtīk b. al-Ḥārith b. ʿAtīk, 215
ʿĀtika bt. Zayd b. ʿAmr b. Nufayl, 193, 257
Ayyūb b. Abī Tamīma al-Sakhtiyānī, 123, 195, 209, 228, 310, 350, 742
Ayyūb b. Ḥabīb, 748
Ayyūb b. Mūsā, 307, 400, 630
Azami, Muhammad al-, 13
Aʿẓamī, Muṣṭafā al-, 50

Bahzī, al-, 302
Bājī, Sulaymān b. Khalaf al-, 117n89, 143n131, 149n136, 184n184, 187n186, 303n400, 415n607, 509n739, 539n772, 549n792, 661n918, 700n956, 745n991
Baqī b. Mukhallad, 58, 63
Barā' b. ʿĀzib, al-, 377, 623
Barīra (freedwoman of ʿĀ'isha), 220, 428, 503
Bashīr b. Masʿūd al-Anṣārī, 74
Bashīr b. Saʿd, 169, 626
Baṣra b. Abī Baṣra al-Ghifārī, 136
Bayāḍī, Farwā b. ʿAmr al-, 116
Bewley, Aisha, 2
Bilāl b. al-Ḥārith al-Muzanī, 225, 776
Bilāl b. Rabāḥ, 80–81, 337, 733–34
Bint Khārija, Ḥabība or Malīka, 626
Bravmann, M. M., 29n48
Bujayd al-Anṣārī al-Ḥārithī, 747
Bukayr b. ʿAbd Allāh b. al-Ashajj, 156, 509, 728, 758, 766
Bushayr b. Yasār, 87, 377, 702
Busr b. Miḥjan, 151
Busr b. Saʿīd, 75, 150, 156, 163, 193, 240, 587, 766, 773
Busra bt. Ṣafwān, 95

Calder, Norman, 12, 14, 25, 31

Ḍaḥḥāk b. Khalīfa, al-, 621–22
Ḍaḥḥāk b. Qays, al-, 137, 297
Ḍaḥḥāk b. Sufyān al-Kilābī, al-, 692
Ḍamra b. Saʿīd al-Māzinī, 87, 137, 178, 526
Dāraquṭnī, Abū al-Ḥasan al-, 52, 53
Dāwūd b. al-Ḥuṣayn, 44n1; alcohol, 729; compensation, 729; consecrated state, 300; gambling, 729; gifts, 627; oaths, 606; prayer, 78–79, 123, 140, 155, 157; Quran, 196; sales, 546, 549

Devil. *See* Satan
Dhafīf, 527
Dhū al-Shamālayn (ʿUmayr b. ʿAbd ʿAmr), 124
Dhū al-Yadayn (al-Khirbāq b. ʿAmr), 123–24
Dutton, Yasin, 21n25, 31

El Shamsy, Ahmed, 21n26, 23–24, 33n61

Faḍāla b. ʿUbayd al-Anṣārī, 426
Faḍl b. ʿAbbās, al-, 308
Fāṭima bt. Abī Ḥubaysh, 105
Fāṭima bt. al-Mundhir b. al-Zubayr, 104, 184–85, 285, 333, 758
Fāṭima bt. al-Walīd b. ʿUtba b. Rabīʿa, 533
Fāṭima bt. Muḥammad, 162, 217n252; children of, 381
Fāṭima bt. Qays, 515, 516–17
Fāṭima bt. ʿUmar b. al-Khaṭṭāb, 532
Fuḍayl b. ʿUbayd Allāh, al-, 515
Furāfiṣa b. ʿUmayr al-Ḥanafī, al-, 117, 284, 449–50
Furayʿa bt. Mālik b. Sinān, al-, 523–24

Gabriel, 74, 197, 288–89, 353, 369, 760, 762
Goldziher, Ignaz, 11

Habbār b. al-Aswad, 311
Ḥabība bt. Sahl al-Anṣārī, 504
Ḥafṣa bt. ʿUmar b. al-Khaṭṭāb, 146, 153, 154, 172, 247, 254, 266, 278, 334, 503, 516, 528, 531, 532, 629, 696, 775
Ḥafṣa bt. ʿAbd al-Raḥmān, 497, 514, 743
Ḥafṣ b. ʿĀṣim, 193, 761
Ḥajjāj b. ʿAmr b. Ghaziyya, al-, 526–27
Ḥajjāj b. Yūsuf, al-, 309n413, 337
Ḥakam b. ʿAbd al-Raḥmān, al-, 52
Ḥakīm b. Ḥizām, 561–62
Hallaq, Wael, 16n20, 27n43
Ḥamza b. ʿAbd Allāh b. ʿUmar, 770
Ḥamza b. ʿAmr al-Aslamī, 258
Ḥanẓala b. Qays al-Zuraqī, 657
Ḥarām b. Saʿd b. Muḥayyiṣa, 623
Ḥārith b. Hishām, al-, 197, 261
Ḥasan b. Abī al-Ḥasan, al-, 423
Ḥasan b. ʿAlī b. Abī Ṭālib, 381–82
Ḥasan b. Muḥammad b. ʿAlī b. Abī Ṭālib, 487, 571
Hāshim b. Hāshim b. ʿUtba b. Abī Waqqāṣ, 606
Ḥāṭib b. Abī Baltaʿa, 571
Ḥawlāʾ bt. Tuwayt, al-, 141
Hazzāl, 710
Hilāl b. Usāma, 425
Hishām b. Ḥakīm b. Ḥizām, 196
Hishām b. Ismāʿīl al-Makhzūmī, 251, 574
Hishām b. ʿUrwa b. al-Zubayr b. al-ʿAwwām, 44n1, 104, 105, 106, 174; ablution, 88, 90, 92, 93, 95–96, 98–100; breastfeeding, 531; charity, 631; clothes, 743; compensation, 688, 690; consecrated state, 284, 285, 293, 302, 304; divorce, 521; dreams, 763; fasting, 257, 258–60; funeral matters, 210–11, 214–15, 218; illness, 758; judicial matters, 599, 606, 623, 638; Kabah, 312–14, 317; leasing farmland, 658; manumission, 427–28; marriage, 500, 502, 523, 524; Medina, 732, 733, 735; newborn sacrifice, 382; Night of Power, 272; oaths, 397; Pilgrimage, 318–19, 330, 332, 333, 342, 346; prayer, 76, 112, 117–18, 126, 140–41, 143, 146, 152–56, 164, 166, 170–72, 178, 179, 182, 184, 192, 206, 287, 339, 753; Quran, 197, 199; punishment, 715; sacrificial animals, 322–23, 335, 348; sales, 539; slaughtering animals, 383; supplication, 205; Visitation, 296

Ḥumayd al-Ṭawīl, 116, 258, 272, 373, 478, 490, 545, 771
Ḥumayd b. ʿAbd al-Raḥmān b. ʿAwf, 107, 201, 210, 259, 261, 315, 373, 520, 626, 741, 759
Ḥumayd b. Mālik b. Khutham, 752
Ḥumayd b. Nāfiʿ, 527–28
Ḥumayd b. Qays al-Makkī, 232, 265, 282, 285, 349, 396, 435, 524, 527, 556, 594, 756
Ḥumayda bt. Abū ʿUbayda b. Farwa, 85
Ḥumrān (freedman of ʿUthmān b. ʿAffān), 88
Hunayy (freedman of ʿUmar b. al-Khaṭṭāb), 785
Ḥusayn b. ʿAlī b. Abī Ṭālib, 330, 381–82
Ḥuwayṣa, 701–2, 703
Huzayla bt. al-Ḥārith, 768

Ibn ʿAbbās, ʿAbd Allāh: ablution, 86, 87; animals, 384, 391, 753, 768; battery compensation, 688; booty, 365, 368–69; breastfeeding, 532; consecrated state, 282, 294n385, 304, 310; divorce, 493, 509; fasting, 257–58, 265; food mishaps, 770; greetings, 764; *jihād*, 360; manumission, 431; marriage, 474, 483, 522, 523; menstruation, 104; Pilgrimage, 308, 316, 327, 350, 354, 355; plague, 735–36; prayer, 78–79, 115, 143, 146, 155, 164, 183; prophethood, 762; Ramaḍān, 253; sacrificial animals, 324; sales, 576; supplication, 204; vows, 393, 396; wine-drinking, 729; withdrawal method, 527
Ibn ʿAbd al-Aʿlā, 58
Ibn ʿAbd al-Barr, Abū ʿUmar, 50, 54–55, 58–61, 64, 66–67, 196n201, 303n400, 354n487, 368n522, 700n957, 770n1017, 772n1029
Ibn Abī al-Ḥuqayq, 359
Ibn Abī Ḥarmala, 213
Ibn Abī Khaythama, 57, 58
Ibn Abī Laylā, 349
Ibn Abī Qatāda, 85
Ibn Abī Salīṭ, 77
Ibn Abī Talīd, 55
Ibn Abī Zamanīn, Abū ʿAbd Allāh, 55, 62, 66
Ibn Abī Zayd al-Qayrawānī, Abū Muḥammad, 52–53, 57
Ibn Aflaḥ, 526, 772
Ibn al-Abbār, 70
Ibn al-Aʿrābī, 58
Ibn al-ʿArabī, Abū Bakr, 64
Ibn al-Aṣbagh al-Shaʿbānī, 65
Ibn al-Ghannām, 56
Ibn al-Mashshāṭ al-Qurṭubī, 53–55, 60–62, 66
Ibn al-Qāsim, ʿAbd al-Raḥmān, 10, 30n52, 34n64, 629n885
Ibn al-Sabbāq, 107
Ibn al-Sakan, 58, 64
Ibn al-Zubayr, ʿAbd Allāh: ʿĀʾisha's shawl, 743; civil war, 309n413, 731–32; free will, 738; judicial matters, 509, 521, 606, 686; Pilgrimage, 293, 294–95, 310, 313, 330
Ibn ʿAṭiyya, Abū Muḥammad, 61, 62, 63, 758
Ibn ʿAttāb, Abū ʿAbd Allāh, 54, 55, 61, 62
Ibn Bashkawāl, 69
Ibn Bāz, Abū Isḥāq Ibrāhīm b. Muḥammad al-Qurṭubī, 51, 55–57, 65
Ibn Dīnār, ʿAbd Allāh: alms-tax, 245, 246; breastfeeding, 534, 535; divorce, 521; eastern threat, 772; greeting Jews, 764; hoarding, 230; miscellaneous matters, 306, 429, 752; lizard meat, 768; Night of Power, 272; oath of allegiance, 775–76; Pilgrimage, 287, 344; prayer, 91, 98, 107, 120, 144–45, 161, 163, 169, 192, 199, 207; private conversations,

778; Ramaḍān, 253; rings, 754; sacrificial animals, 322, 323; sales, 556, 561, 596; speaking cautiously, 776; supplication, 205; trailing garments, 744
Ibn Farḥūn, 34n64
Ibn Fuṭays, Abū al-Muṭarrif, 52–53, 61
Ibn Ḥamdīn al-Taghlibī, 55
Ibn Ḥimās, 732
Ibn Ḥūbīl, Abū Bakr ʿAbd al-Raḥmān b. Aḥmad b. Muḥammad al-Tujībī, 54, 61
Ibn Isḥāq, 354n487
Ibn Khaṭal, 354
Ibn Lubāba, 53
Ibn Masdī, 50
Ibn Mirsā, 413
Ibn Muʿayqīb al-Dawsī, 565
Ibn Muḥammad b. ʿAmr b. Ḥazm, 95
Ibn Muḥayrīz, 144
Ibn Muḥayṣa al-Anṣārī, 771
Ibn Muḥayrīz, 526
Ibn Mukmil, 510
Ibn Muṭīʿ, 606
Ibn Qahd, 526–27
Ibn Qarqūl, 69
Ibn Shihāb al-Zuhrī: ablution, 83, 91–92, 95, 97, 99, 131; alms-tax, 222, 225, 227, 240–41, 245; anger, 741; breastfeeding, 532, 533; clothes, 743; compensation, 678–79, 681–83, 686, 691–92, 694; consecrated state, 303–4, 354; currency exchange, 558; divorce, 494–95, 498, 503–6, 509–12, 514–15, 517–20; drinking practices, 749; evil eye, 755; fasting, 254, 258–60, 265–66, 321; friendliness, 741; funeral matters, 210–12; gifts, 626, 642; hair, 759; illness, 757; inheritance, 407, 410, 416; irrigation partnerships, 649; Jews, 734; *jihād*, 359, 365, 373; judicial matters, 600, 607, 613, 616–17, 619–20, 623; Kabah, 312; lapidation, 710–11, 713; leases, 597, 657; lizard meat, 768; manumission, 423, 425; marriage, 477, 482–91, 502, 520; Medina, 733; menstruation, 104; miscellaneous matters, 107, 134, 172–73, 216, 218, 307, 353–54, 390, 391, 400, 432, 621, 628, 739–40, 747, 770, 771; modesty, 740; Muḥammad's estate, 780; Muḥammad's five names, 785; omens, 770; Pilgrimage, 297, 308, 310, 315, 337–38, 352, 355–56; pious seclusion, 275, 276, 278–79; plague, 735, 737; poll-tax, 246, 248; prayer, 74, 77, 78, 80, 82, 109, 113–15, 119, 121–22, 124–25, 129, 132–33, 139, 142, 145, 149–50, 152–53, 158–64, 168, 170, 177–78, 207, 339; property, 643; punishment, 714, 721, 725; Quran, 196, 199, 201; sacrificial animals, 324, 380; sales, 544, 549, 571, 573–74, 587, 591; self-reliance, 782; strays, 631; supplication, 203; Visitation, 296; vows, 393; wills, 634; wine-drinking, 727, 729
Ibn Sīrīn, 742
Ibn Ukayma al-Laythī, 119
Ibn ʿUmar, ʿAbd Allāh, 75n10, 133, 177; ablution, 85, 86, 90–93, 95–98, 100, 102; alms-tax, 222, 226, 230, 249–51; breastfeeding, 532, 534; castration, 759; circumambulation, 313, 316, 317; clothes, 743, 744, 745; consecrated state, 281, 282–88, 295, 301, 303, 306–7, 354; currency exchange, 556; debts, 587; dice, 763; divorce, 494, 495, 497–98, 505, 506–7, 511–13, 514, 516, 519, 521; dogs, 769; drinking habits, 749; eating habits, 387–89, 752, 769–70; fasting, 254, 258–60, 262, 264–65, 268, 277; free will, 738; funeral

matters, 210, 213–14, 216, 218; greetings, 764–65; hair, 335–37, 378; horse-racing, 372–73; illness, 758; inheritance, 629; investment parternships, 659–60; *jihād*, 360–61, 363; Kabah, 288, 312; lapidation, 709; legal testimony, 599; livestock, 769; loans, 594–95; lost property, 630; manumission, 421, 424, 426–29, 435, 436, 467; marriage, 473, 476, 482, 483, 490, 503, 523–25; martyrs, 370; Medina, 731–32; modesty, 740; Muḥammad's dream of Jesus, 746; newborn sacrifice, 381–82; oaths, 397, 399, 775–76; Pilgrimage and Visitation, 287–88, 291–92, 297, 299, 309–10, 318, 327, 332, 337–38, 341–44, 356; pious seclusion, 277; prayer, 78, 112–17, 119–21, 125, 132, 137, 142, 144–47, 149, 151–52, 158–61, 163–65, 167–71, 179, 182, 192–93, 207, 337, 353; private conversations, 778; punishment, 719, 720; Quran, 197, 199, 212, 358; Ramaḍān, 253; rings, 754; sacrificial animals, 322–24, 328–29, 334–35, 377–78, 380; sales, 539, 540, 545–46, 549, 561–64, 571–72, 579, 586, 596; self-reliance, 783; slaughtered animals, 385, 387; slaves, 544, 775; sneezing, 767; speaking cautiously, 776; supplication, 205, 206; urination, 107, 191; vows, 394; wills, 632; wine-drinking, 727–28, 729, 730; withdrawal method, 526
Ibn Umm Maktūm, 113
Ibn Waḍḍāḥ, Muḥammad al-Qurṭubī, 51, 55, 56, 57, 58, 59, 60–61, 65
Ibn Waʿla al-Miṣrī, 391, 729
Ibn Yarbūʿ al-Makhzūmī, 155
Ibrāhīm b. ʿAbd Allāh b. Abī ʿAbla, 353
Ibrāhīm b. ʿAbd Allāh b. Ḥunayn, 282
Ibrāhīm b. ʿAbd al-Raḥmān b. ʿAwf, 50
Ibrāhīm b. Abī ʿAbla, 485
Ibrāhīm b. Kulayb, 431
Ibrāhīm b. ʿUqba, 353, 533
ʿIkrima b. Abī Jahl, 327, 489–90
ʿIrāk b. Mālik, 245, 678
ʿĪsā b. Ṭalḥa b. ʿUbayd Allāh, 302, 352
Isḥāq Abū ʿAbd Allāh, 109
Isḥāq b. ʿAbd Allāh b. Abī Ṭalḥa, 44n1; ablution, 85, 90; alcohol, 729; charity, 781; clothes, 746; dreams, 762; food, 490, 749, 752; greetings, 764–65; *jihād*, 371; Medina, 731; mindfulness of God, 780; prayer, 77, 162, 191
Ismāʿīl b. Abī Ḥakīm, 98, 141, 390, 416, 734, 780
Ismāʿīl b. Muḥammad b. Saʿd b. Abī Waqqāṣ, 95, 153
ʿItbān b. Mālik, 173
ʿIyāḍ al-Sabtī, 54, 55, 61, 62, 63
ʿIyāḍ b. ʿAbd Allāh b. Saʿd b. Abī Sarḥ al-ʿĀmirī, 250

Jābir b. ʿAbd Allāh al-Anṣārī: ablution, 88, 90; clothes, 742; food, 751, 754; illness, 758; left hand, 747; Medina, 732; miscellaneous matters, 375, 606, 628; Pilgrimage, 313, 318, 320; prayer, 114, 118, 155; sacrificial animals, 378–79; Satan, 750
Jābir b. al-Aswad al-Zuhrī, 521
Jābir b. ʿAtīk, 215
Jaʿfar b. Abī Ṭālib, 756
Jaʿfar b. Muḥammad b. ʿAlī (Jaʿfar al-Ṣādiq), 44n1; divorce, 497; funeral matters, 209; legal matters, 601; newborn sacrifice, 381; Pilgrimage, 290, 292, 313, 318, 320; prayer, 138; sacrificial animals, 328, 334; Zoroastrians, 246
Jamīl b. ʿAbd al-Raḥmān al-Muʾadhdhin, 562, 605
Jayānī, Abū ʿAlī al-, 54, 57, 58, 59, 60, 61
Jesus, 746, 751, 776, 777
Judāma bt. Wahb al-Asadiyya, 535

Kaʿb al-Aḥbār, 125, 136, 163, 303, 349, 740, 745, 761
Kaʿb b. Mālik, 85, 218, 359
Kaʿb b. ʿUjra, 349–50
Kabsha bt. Kaʿb b. Mālik, 85
Kathīr b. al-Ṣalt, 286, 623
Kathīr b. Farqad, 563
Khālid b. al-Walīd, 278, 760, 768
Khālid b. Asīd, 158, 322
Khālid b. Maʿdān, 774
Khālid b. ʿUqba, 778
Khallād b. al-Sāʾib al-Anṣārī, 288
Khansāʾ bt. Khidhām al-Anṣāriyya, 482
Khārija b. Zayd b. Thābit, 286, 496, 545
Khawla bt. Ḥakīm, 487, 773
Khawwāt b. Jubayr, 181n178
Khubayb b. ʿAbd al-Raḥmān, 193, 761
Kurayb, 143, 338, 353, 523

Luqmān, 779, 784

Maʿbad b. Ḥuzāba al-Makhzūmī, 310
Maʿbad b. Kaʿb al-Salamī, 606
Maʿbad b. Kaʿb b. Mālik, 219
Maḥmūd b. Labīd al-Anṣārī, 97, 173, 729
Maḥmūd b. Rabīʿ, 173n168
Māʿiz b. Mālik, 709–10
Makhrama b. Sulaymān, 143
Malīḥ b. ʿAbd Allāh al-Saʿdī, 122
Mālik b. Abī ʿĀmir, 132, 556
Mālik b. Anas: biography, 7–8, 10;, 40, 43–44, 47; legal reasoning, 15–19, 20–22, 24, 27–33, 44–47
Mālik b. Aws b. al-Ḥadathān al-Naṣrī, 558
Manāt, 319
Manṣūr al-Ḥajabī, 400
Maʿrūf, Bashshār ʿAwwād, 49–50
Marwān b. al-Ḥakam, 95, 255–56, 310, 390, 450, 494, 496, 498, 515, 562, 606–7, 678, 688–89, 697, 725, 748, 753
Masʿūd b. al-Ḥakam, 215
Maymūna bt. al-Ḥārith, 143, 156, 300, 768, 770
Midʿam, 368
Miḥjan, 151
Miqdād b. al-Aswad, al-, 94, 290
Miṣbāḥ, 715
Miswar b. Makhrama, al-, 93, 282, 523
Miswar b. Rifāʿa al-Quraẓī, al-, 479
Moses, 737, 745
Muʿādh b. Jabal, 157, 202, 232, 372, 739, 762
Muʿādh b. Saʿd (or Saʿd b. Muʿādh), 384
Muʿāwiya b. ʿAbd Allāh b. Badr al-Juhanī, 630
Muʿāwiya b. Abī ʿAyyāsh al-Anṣārī, 509
Muʿāwiya b. Abī Sufyān, 222, 261, 285–86, 297, 371, 407, 514, 516–17, 556, 616, 678, 687, 697, 739, 759
Mughīra b. Abī Burda, al-, 85
Mughīra b. Ḥakīm, al-, 120
Mughīra b. Shuʿba, al-, 74, 91, 410
Muḥammad: ablution, 83–91, 95–96, 98, 99–101, 106–7, 143, 167, 338; adultery, 506, 616; affiliated children, 617; alms-tax, 221–22, 224–25, 235, 240, 245, 250, 358; amputation, 719–21, 725; angels, 119–20, 131, 166, 172, 203, 734, 756, 767; anger, 741, 776; apostasy, 614–15; asking permission to enter, 766; bad omens, 770; battery compensation, 657, 682, 688, 692–93, 701–2, 703; the bereft, 747; breastfeeding, 531–32, 534–35; burial of, 209–10, 214; buying back gifts, 249; camels, 630; charity, 503, 631–32, 634, 761, 781–84; children, 219; choosing the easier option, 739; Christians, 734; circumambulation, 313–14, 317; clothes, 103, 137, 155–56, 286, 742, 742n987, 743–46; compassion, 750; consecrated state, 281–83, 285–89, 294–95, 300, 301–2, 304, 306–7, 309, 344–45, 349–50; cupping, 771; currency exchange, 555–56, 558; deaths

ordered by, 354, 710–11; dice, 763; disbelievers, 615, 769; divine punishment, 780; divorce, 504, 506–7, 513–14, 516–17, 520; dogs, 769; dreams, 762–63; drinking practices, 748–50; the East, 769, 772, 777; estate of, 780–81; evil eye, 755–56; facial hair, 758; facing tragedy, 215–17; false oaths, 606; fasting, 253–58, 261–62, 266, 269, 321; feeding others, 749–50, 752, 753; floggings ordered by, 713, 714; food mishaps, 770; free will, 737–38; Fridays, 131–32, 136; friendliness and fraternity, 741–42; funeral matters, 209–10, 212–13, 215, 218–20; future followers, 88; gifts, 626, 629, 751; gluttony, 748; gold rings, 743, 754; good character, 739–40, 750; good deeds, 174; graves, 172–73, 218, 734; greetings, 764–65; hair, 759; Hell, 781; hides, 391; horses, 357–58, 372–73; hospitality, 750; hypocrites, 172; illness, 756–58; images (statues, drawings), 767; inheritance, 410, 411–12, 416; intoxicating beverages, 729; invoking God's grace on, 169–70; Jesus and the Antichrist, 746; Jews, 734–35, 751, 759, 764; *jihād*, 357–60, 361, 364–68, 371–73; journey supplication, 773; judicial matters, 599, 601; Kabah, 312–14; land rights, 620–23, 657; lapidation, 709–10; left hand, 747; legal authority, 11, 12–13, 16–17, 23, 738; liability, 694; livestock exchange, 573; lizard meat, 768; loans, 593–94; lost property and animals, 629–30; loving for God's sake, 761–62; Mālik b. Anas foretold by, 43; manumission, 421, 423, 425, 427–29, 438, 503; marriage, 300, 473–75, 479, 480, 482, 487, 490–91, 523–24; martyrs, 150, 215–16, 369–70; Medina, 731–35; menstruation, 103, 104–5; mines, 225; modesty, 740; mourning, 527–28, 529; names, 770–71, 785; newborn sacrifice, 381; Night Journey, 760; Night of Power, 271–72; nonverbal conduct, 18n22; oaths of allegiance, 775; orphans, 759; permission asked of, 526; physical appearance, 746; Pilgrimage, 285–92, 297, 308, 318–20, 330, 333, 337–38, 341, 344–46, 347n476, 352–53; pious seclusion, 271, 275, 278–79; plague, 736–37; pledges, 607; poll-tax, 246; prayer, 74–75, 80–82, 90, 91, 109–10, 112–20, 123–26, 129, 132, 133, 135, 139, 141–47, 149–55, 157–58, 161–64, 166–68, 170–75, 177, 181–85, 187–88, 191–93, 200; private conversations, 778; prohibitive payments, 574–75; property rights, 643; protection grants, 162; pumpkin, 490–91; Quran, 195–98, 201, 358, 757; revenge, 621; ritual preclusion, 255–56; sacrificial animals, 321–23, 333–34, 377–79, 380; safe passage grants, 488–89; sales, 537, 545–50, 555, 561, 569, 572, 575, 579–80, 582, 586, 591–92, 595–96, 651, 745; sandals, 744–45; Satan, 750, 772, 774; seeking God's protection, 184, 760–61; self-reliance, 782–83; shepherding, 769; slaughtered animals, 383–84, 390; slaves, 771–72, 774; snakes, 772–73, 774; sneezing, 766–67; souls of believers, 218; speaking cautiously, 776–79; steeping dried fruit, 728; supplication, 203–6, 353; tomb of, 169, 193n196; toothbrushes, 107; truth and lies, 777, 778; transgender individuals, 638; travel, 773–74; two-facedness, 779; urination, 106; Visitation, 287,

296, 299; vows and oaths, 393, 396, 398–400; water access, 620; wills, 632, 634; women, 183, 193, 743, 770, 774, 775. *See also* law: Prophetic
Muḥammad al-Bāqir, 138n122
Muḥammad b. ʿAbd Allāh b. ʿAbd al-Rahmān b. Abī Ṣaʿṣaʿa al-Anṣārī al-Māzinī, 221
Muḥammad b. ʿAbd Allāh b. Abī Maryam, 308, 568
Muḥammad b. ʿAbd Allāh b. Abī Ṣaʿṣaʿa, 756
Muḥammad b. ʿAbd Allāh b. al-Ḥārith b. Nawfal b. ʿAbd al-Muṭṭalib, 297
Muḥammad b. ʿAbd Allāh b. Yaḥyā, 53
Muḥammad b. ʿAbd Allāh b. Zayd al-Anṣārī, 169
Muḥammad b. ʿAbd al-Malik b. Ayman Abū ʿAbd Allāh al-Qurṭubī, 56–57, 58, 65
Muḥammad b. ʿAbd al-Raḥmān b. Nawfal, 535
Muḥammad b. ʿAbd al-Raḥmān b. Saʿd b. Zurāra, 696
Muḥammad b. ʿAbd al-Raḥmān b. Thawbān, 81, 291, 391, 509
Muḥammad b. Abī ʿAtīq, 496
Muḥammad b. Abī Bakr al-Ṣiddīq, 281
Muḥammad b. Abī Bakr al-Thaqafī, 291–92
Muḥammad b. Abī Bakr b. Ḥazm, 216, 413
Muḥammad b. Abī Ḥarmala, 213
Muḥammad b. al-Ashʿath, 416
Muḥammad b. ʿAlī b. Abī Ṭālib, 487
Muḥammad b. ʿAlī b. Ḥusayn, 381
Muḥammad b. al-Munkadir, 87, 88, 141, 211, 596, 732, 736, 775
Muḥammad b. al-Nuʿmān b. Bashīr, 626
Muḥammad b. ʿAmr b. ʿAlqama, 122, 776
Muḥammad b. ʿAmr b. ʿAṭāʾ, 764
Muḥammad b. ʿAmr b. Ḥalḥala al-Dīlī, 219, 354, 752
Muḥammad b. ʿAmr b. Ḥazm, 155, 547–48
Muḥammad b. Ḥabbān, 473
Muḥammad b. Ibrāhīm b. al-Ḥārith al-Taymī: ablution, 85–87; animals, 294, 302; consecrated state, 307; divorce, 512; Fridays, 136; hair, 760; judicial matters, 617; newborn sacrifice, 382; Night of Power, 271; prayer, 150, 198, 203; Quran, 116
Muḥammad b. ʿImrān al-Anṣārī, 354
Muḥammad b. Iyās b. al-Bukayr, 509
Muḥammad b. Jubayr b. Muṭʿim, 115
Muḥammad b. Kaʿb al-Quraẓī, 217, 739
Muḥammad b. Maslama al-Anṣārī, 238, 410, 622
Muḥammad b. Muslim b. Abī al-Zubayr al-Makkī, 43
Muḥammad b. Muslim b. Shihāb al-Zuhrī, 44n1
Muḥammad b. Qāsim b. Hilāl, 55, 61
Muḥammad b. Shurayḥ, 53, 64, 70
Muḥammad b. Sīrīn, 123, 195, 209, 347, 423, 568
Muḥammad b. ʿUmāra, 86, 647
Muḥammad b. ʿUqba, 222
Muḥammad b. Yaḥyā b. Ḥabbān: alms-tax, 237–38; fasting, 261, 321; marriage, 510, 526; Pilgrimage, 355; prayer, 144, 171, 191, 207, 367; Quran, 355; sales, 582; theft, 725
Muḥammad b. Yūsuf, 140
Muḥammad b. Zayd b. Qunfudh, 156
Muḥammad VI, 2, 37, 40–41, 48, 67, 71–72
Muḥayṣa b. Masʿūd, 701–2, 703
Mujāhid b. al-Ḥajjāj, 349
Mujāhid b. Jabr, 265, 556, 594
Mukhdajī, al-, 144
Mulayka, 162
Mundhir b. al-Zubayr, al-, 497
Munkadir b. Muḥammad b. al-Munkadir, al-, 207

Muntajālī, Abū 'Umar al-, 53, 54, 60, 61, 64, 69
Muranyi, Miklos, 13n13
Mūsā b. Abī Tamīm, 555
Mūsā b. Maysara, 161, 589, 763
Mūsā b. 'Uqba, 88, 288, 338
Muṣ'ab b. Sa'd b. Abī al-Waqqāṣ, 95
Musaylima b. Ḥabīb al-Ḥanafī, 196
Muslim b. Abī Maryam, 120, 742
Muslim b. Abī Mūsā, 743
Muslim b. Jundub, 687
Muslim b. Yasār al-Juhanī, 737
Muṭṭalib b. 'Abd Allāh b. Ḥuwayṭib al-Makhzūmī, al-, 777
Muṭṭalib b. Abī Wadā'a al-Sahmī, al-, 153
Muzāḥim, 733

Nāfi' (freedman of Ibn 'Umar): ablution, 85, 86, 90–93, 95, 96, 97, 98, 100, 102; alms-tax, 222, 226, 249–51; bathing, 132, 177; circumambulation, 313, 316; clothes, 743–45; consecrated state, 281–87, 295, 300–301, 306–7, 354; dice, 763; divorce, 494–95, 497, 505–6, 511, 512–14, 516; dogs, 769; eating animals, 387–89; fasting, 258–60, 262, 264–65; funeral matters, 212–14, 218, 220; hair, 335–37, 759; illness, 758; images, 767; intoxicants, 728–30; *jihād*, 359–61; judicial matters, 620; lapidation, 709; loans, 595; manumission, 421, 424, 427–28, 435, 467; marriage, 473, 476, 482, 490, 503, 523–25; martyrs, 370; miscellaneous matters, 105, 133, 197, 199, 246, 249, 277, 358, 381, 629–30, 746, 748, 767, 769, 778; mourning, 528; oaths, 397–98; Pilgrimage and Visitation, 299, 309, 318, 332, 337–38, 341–44, 353; prayer, 75, 78–80, 112, 114–17, 119, 121–22, 125, 137, 144–46, 149, 151–52, 158–61, 165, 167–68, 170–71, 179, 182, 191–92, 207; precious metals, 555; punishment, 713–14, 719–20; Ramaḍān, 255; sacrificial animals, 321–24, 326, 334, 377–78, 380; sales, 539, 545–46, 549, 556, 561, 565, 571, 586; self-reliance, 783; sheep, 769; slaughtered animals, 384–85; slaves, 775; snakes, 772; wills, 632
Nāfi' b. Jubayr b. Muṭ'im, 116, 118, 215, 474, 757
Najāshī, al-, 211
Nu'aym b. 'Abd Allāh al-Mujmir, 90, 166, 169, 202, 734
Nubayh b. Wahb, 300
Nufay' (slave of Umm Salama), 511–12
Nukhayla (handmaiden of 'Ā'isha), 760
Nu'mān Abū 'Ayyāsh al-Anṣārī, al-, 509
Nu'mān b. Bashīr, al-, 137–38, 626
Nu'mān b. Murra, al-, 170

Qabīṣa b. Dhu'ayb, 407, 410, 484–85
Qa'qā' b. Ḥakīm, al-, 105, 154, 761
Qarība bt. Abī Umayya, 496
Qāsim b. Aṣbagh al-Bayānī, 56, 58, 59, 60–61
Qāsim b. Muḥammad b. Abī Bakr al-Ṣiddīq, al-: alms-tax, 222, 237; bereavement, 217; booty, 365; camels, 753; consecrated state, 284; currency exchange, 447; divorce, 494–95, 503, 511, 514–15, 519; eating animals, 387; fasting, 320–21; images, 767; inheritance, 410; manumission, 427; marriage, 474, 479, 485–86, 491, 500, 525; mindfulness of God, 780; parental rights, 638; pious seclusion, 277; prayer, 77, 117, 118, 121, 129, 146, 147, 161, 181–82; punishment, 721; sacrificial animals, 334; sales, 547, 565, 576, 579; vows, 396
Qatāda b. al-Nu'mān, 200n215
Qatāda of Banū Mudlij, 693

Qaṭan b. Wahb b. ʿUmayr b. al-Ajdaʿ, 731
Qayjāṭī, Abū ʿAmr ʿUthmān b. Aḥmad al-, 53
Qays b. al-Ḥārith, 115

Rabīʿa b. ʿAbd Allāh b. al-Hudayr, 87, 211, 294–95, 307
Rabīʿa b. Abī ʿAbd al-Raḥmān, 44n1; ablution, 86, 103; alms-tax, 225; compensation, 686; divorce, 503, 510; fortitude, 217; inheritance, 417; legal testimony, 600; manumission, 423, 429, 449; marriage, 300, 487, 491, 501, 526; miscellaneous matters, 717, 766; Muḥammad's appearance, 746; newborn sacrifice, 381–82; Pilgrimage, 286, 327, 336; prayer, 77, 117, 118, 155, 170; property, 375, 629, 657; sacrificial animals, 379; sales, 547; theft, 721; unintentional killing, 679, 683
Rabīʿa b. Umayya, 487
Rāfiʿ b. Isḥāq, 191, 767
Rāfiʿ b. Khadīj, 491–92, 657, 725
Rahimuddin, Muhammad, 2
Rifāʿa b. Rāfiʿ al-Zuraqī, 202–3
Rifāʿa b. Simwāl, 479
Rifāʿa b. Zayd, 368
Rubayyiʿ bt. Muʿawwidh b. ʿAfrāʾ, 505
Ruqayya, 328–29
Rushayd al-Thaqafī, 482
Ruzayq b. Ḥakīm, 715, 720

Ṣaʿb b. Jaththāma al-Laythī, al-, 304
Ṣabīgh, 365
Saʿd al-Jārī, 389
Ṣadaqa b. Yasār, 120, 297, 329, 754
Saʿd b. Abī Waqqāṣ: ablution, 91, 95; death of, 83, 213, 215; eating animals, 388; fasting, 257, 260; judicial rulings, 617; Pilgrimage, 297, 318; plague, 736; prayer, 145, 164, 174; sales, 549, 555, 565; travel, 773
Saʿd b. al-Rabīʿ al-Anṣārī, 372
Saʿd b. Khawla, 634
Saʿd b. ʿUbāda, 169, 393, 427, 555, 615, 631, 711
Saʿd b. Zurāra, 758
Ṣafiyya bt. Abī ʿUbayd, 90, 344, 505, 521, 528–29, 532, 620, 713–14, 744
Ṣafiyya bt. Ḥuyayy, 346
Ṣafwān b. ʿAbd Allāh b. Ṣafwān, 721
Ṣafwān b. Sulaym, 85, 87, 132, 138, 766, 778–79
Ṣafwān b. Umayya, 488–89, 721
Sahla bt. Suhayl, 534
Sahl b. Abī Ḥathma al-Anṣārī, 181, 701–2
Sahl b. Ḥunayf, 755, 767
Sahl b. Saʿd al-Anṣārī, 749
Sahl b. Saʿd al-Sāʿidī, 110, 165, 168, 254, 475, 506, 770
Saḥnūn b. Saʿīd, 9–10, 33–34
Sāʾiba, 772
Sāʾib b. Khabbāb, al-, 524
Sāʾib b. Yazīd, al-, 140, 153, 207, 227, 248, 725, 727, 768
Saʿīd b. ʿAbd al-Raḥmān b. Ruqaysh al-Ashʿarī, 92
Saʿīd b. Abī Hind, 763
Saʿīd b. Abī Saʿīd al-Maqburī, 131, 142, 211–12, 288, 369, 425, 747, 750, 774
Saʿīd b. al-ʿĀṣī, 720
Saʿīd b. al-Musayyab: ablution, 90, 93–94, 97, 102; adultery allegations, 616; alms-tax, 225, 367; anger, 741; breastfeeding, 533; compensation, 682, 686–88, 693, 694; consecrated state, 281, 284, 301, 302, 308, 324–25; currency, 557, 559; divorce, 497, 498, 504, 505, 512, 515–16, 518, 520, 522; fasting, 255, 259–60, 263, 265; funeral matters, 211, 212; gifts, 642; good character, 740;

grooming, 747; inheritance, 416; irrigation partnerships, 647; *jihād*, 360–61, 366; judicial matters, 599, 607; killing animals, 387; lapidation, 709–10, 712; livestock exchange, 573–74; manumission, 429, 431, 450–51, 467; marriage, 474, 475, 477, 478, 480, 482, 483, 484, 486, 491, 520, 524–25; Medina, 733; miscellaneous matters, 173, 178, 202, 216, 373, 631, 657, 696; Night of Power, 272; Pilgrimage, 298; prayer, 80, 82, 113, 119, 124, 133, 142, 144, 149, 150, 151, 154, 155, 160, 171, 339; property, 643; punishment, 728; rings, 754; sacrificial animals, 324, 348; sales, 549–50, 562–63, 568, 571, 573, 580, 589, 596; slaughtered animals, 384, 385; supplication, 205; travel, 774; Visitation, 296; vows, 394
Sa'īd b. 'Amr b. Shuraḥbīl, 631
Sa'īd b. 'Amr b. Sulaym al-Zuraqī, 500
Sa'īd b. Isḥāq b. Ka'b b. 'Ujra, 523
Sa'īd b. Jubayr, 141, 146, 158, 268, 350
Sa'īd b. Sa'd b. 'Ubāda, 631
Sa'īd b. Salama, 85
Sa'īd b. Sulaymān b. Zayd b. Thābit, 496
Sa'īd b. Yasār, 144, 161
Sa'īd b. Zayd b. 'Amr b. Nufayl, 215
Salama b. 'Abd al-Raḥmān, 124
Salama b. Ṣafwān b. Salama al-Zuraqī, 740
Ṣāliḥ b. Kaysān, 158, 188, 571
Ṣāliḥ b. Khawwāt al-Anṣārī, 181
Sālim (freedman of Abū Ḥudhayfa), 533–34
Sālim b. 'Abd Allāh b. 'Umar b. al-Khaṭṭāb: ablution, 82, 93, 95, 103; breastfeeding, 532; consecrated state, 303, 336; divorce, 514–15, 519; judicial matters, 619, 620; Kabah, 312; leasing farmland, 657; marriage, 301, 474, 485; modesty, 740; mourning, 528; omens, 770; Pilgrimage, 286, 288, 310, 332, 337–38, 356; prayer, 82, 113, 114, 125, 131, 158–60, 164; plague, 737; punishment, 721; sales, 540, 587; taxes, 248
Sālim b. Abī al-Naḍr, 736
Sālim b. 'Ubayd Allāh, 158
Salmān al-Fārisī, 640
Ṣalt b. Zuyayd, al-, 94, 286
Ṣan'ānī, 'Abd al-Razzāq al-, 56
Satan, 81, 175, 201, 491, 759; bleeding, 317; Day of 'Arafa, 353; horns, 206–7; lefthandedness, 747; nightmares, 763; prayer, 110, 125, 129; protection against, 750; travelers, 774; wine, 730. *See also* Pilgrimage: casting pebbles at Devil
Savant, Sarah, 9n5
Sawda bt. 'Abd Allāh b. 'Umar, 319
Sawda bt. Zam'a, 617
Ṣayfī (freedman of Ibn Aflaḥ), 772
Schacht, Joseph, 11, 13, 20–21, 23, 32
Shabṭūn. *See* Ziyād b. 'Abd al-Raḥmān
Shaffā', al-, 150
Shāfi'ī, Muḥammad b. Idrīs al-, 10, 15–24, 32, 33n61, 34, 45; on *istiḥsān*, 19, 30
Sharīk b. 'Abd Allāh b. Abī Namir, 147, 188
Shaybānī, Muḥammad b. al-Ḥasan al-, 9n5, 10, 73n2
Subay'a al-Aslamiyya, 522–23
Sufyān b. 'Abd Allāh, 236
Sufyān b. Abī Zuhayr, 732, 768–69
Sufyān b. 'Uyayna, 43, 44–45
Suhayl b. Abī Ṣāliḥ, 44n1, 89, 398, 615, 711, 731, 741, 748, 761–62, 776, 779
Suhayl b. Bayḍā', 213
Sulaymān b. 'Abd al-Malik b. Marwān, 229
Sulaymān b. Yasār: ablution, 94, 98–99, 103, 105; alms-tax, 228, 240, 245; breastfeeding, 535; compensation, 684–85, 688, 690, 693, 700;

consecrated state, 301, 310; divorce, 505, 508, 511, 514, 519, 520, 522; evil eye, 756; fasting, 263, 321; inheritance, 408, 416, 419; irrigation partnerships, 649; judicial matters, 600, 601, 617, 630; lapidation, 711; lizard meat, 768; manumission, 435, 448–49; marriage, 300, 301, 474, 482, 484, 500, 523, 525; mourning, 528; Pilgrimage, 291, 308; prayer, 113; sacrificial animals, 326; oaths, 399; property, 643; sales, 563, 565; punishment, 714; unintentional killing, 678–79
Sumayy (freedman of Abū Bakr b. ʿAbd al-Raḥmān), 44n1; ablution, 105; compassion, 750; fasting, 255–56, 258; miscellaneous matters, 278, 761; prayer, 109, 119–20, 131, 150, 166, 201–2; travel, 774; Visitation, 299
Sunayn Abū Jamīla, 616
Surāqa b. Juʿshum, 693
Suwayd b. al-Nuʿmān, 87
Swartz, Merlin, 2n1

Ṭalamankī, Abū ʿUmar al-, 58, 61, 66
Ṭalḥa b. ʿAbd Allāh b. ʿAwf, 510
Ṭalḥa b. ʿUbayd Allāh, 174, 204, 284, 333, 353, 558
Ṭalḥa b. ʿUmar, 300
Tamīma bt. Wahb, 479
Tamīm al-Dayrī, 140
Ṭarābulsī, Abū al-Qāsim Ḥātim al-, 54, 58, 61, 66
Ṭāriq b. ʿAmr, 213
Ṭāwūs al-Yamānī, 204, 232, 738
Thābit al-Aḥnaf, 521
Thābit b. al-Ḍaḥḥāk al-Anṣārī, 630–31
Thābit b. Qays b. Shammās, 504
Thaʿlaba b. Abī Mālik al-Quraẓī, 132
Thawr b. Zayd al-Dīlī, 236, 253, 324, 327, 368, 384, 396, 522, 532, 622, 727
Thawrī, Sufyān al-, 211n242
Ṭufayl b. Ubayy b. Kaʿb, al-, 765
Ṭulayḥa al-Asadiyya, 482
Ṭulayṭilī, Abū al-Qāsim Khalaf b. Yaḥyā b. Ghayth al-, 55, 61

ʿUbāda b. al-Ṣāmit, 144, 146, 371, 730
ʿUbāda b. al-Walīd b. ʿUbāda b. al-Ṣāmit, 358
ʿUbayd Abū Ṣāliḥ (freedman of al-Saffāḥ), 587
ʿUbayd Allāh al-Khawlānī, 156
ʿUbayd Allāh b. ʿAbd Allāh b. ʿUmar b. al-Khaṭṭāb, 161, 332
ʿUbayd Allāh b. ʿAbd Allāh b. ʿUtba b. Masʿūd: consecrated state, 304; divorce, 520; fasting, 258; food mishaps, 770; hides, 391; images, 767; lapidation, 711; manumission, 425; marriage, 484; prayer, 106, 115, 137, 163, 178, 188; poll-tax, 248; punishment, 714; sales, 544; vows, 393
ʿUbayd Allāh b. ʿAbd al-Raḥmān, 201
ʿUbayd Allāh b. Abī ʿAbd Allāh, 193
ʿUbayd Allāh b. ʿAdī b. al-Khiyār, 172
ʿUbayd Allāh b. ʿUmar al-Khaṭṭāb, 476, 659–60, 775, 775
ʿUbayd Allāh b. Yaḥyā b. Yaḥyā al-Laythī, 50–53, 55, 59, 60, 65, 67, 69, 73
ʿUbayd b. Fayrūz, 377
ʿUbayd b. Ḥunayn, 201
ʿUbayd b. Jurayj, 288
Ubayy b. Kaʿb, 88, 117, 140, 265, 729
Uḥayḥa, 693
Umāma bt. Zaynab, 171
ʿUmāra b. Ṣayyād, 202, 379
ʿUmar b. ʿAbd al-ʿAzīz b. Marwān, 39, 74, 152; alms-tax, 222, 228, 229, 239; compensation, 690; divine punishment, 780; divorce, 493–94; free will, 738; inheritance, 416; Jews, 734; *jihād*, 359, 366; judicial matters, 601, 605; marriage, 476; Medina,

733; Pilgrimage, 292; poll-tax, 247; punishment, 715, 720, 722; sacrificial animals, 322; sales, 547, 592
ʿUmar b. ʿAbd al-Raḥmān b. Dalāf al-Muzanī, 641
ʿUmar b. Abī Salama, 155, 296, 753
ʿUmar b. al-Ḥakam, 425
ʿUmar b. al-Khaṭṭāb: ablution, 84–85, 87, 91, 93, 97, 98–99, 131, 195–96; affiliated children, 617–19; alms-tax, 226, 231–32, 235, 236, 238, 239, 243–45; animals, 347–48; annoying the Prophet, 197–98; apostasy, 615; breastfeeding, 534; buying back gifts, 249; clothes, 742, 745–46; compensation, 677, 692–94, 700; consecrated state, 282, 284, 285–86, 293, 300, 302–3, 307, 324, 326, 349; currency exchange, 556–57, 558–59; debt, 641; divorce, 494, 512–13, 518, 519, 520–21; drinking habits, 748; fasting, 255, 257, 259, 261, 264; food, 752, 754; free will, 737–38; funeral matters, 210–11, 213; gifts, 626–27; greetings, 765; inheritance, 407–8, 410, 411, 413, 416; intoxicating beverages, 727, 729–30; Iraq, 772; Jews, 734–35; *jihād*, 360, 364; judicial rulings, 599–600, 616, 617–18, 620, 622, 623, 630, 633, 641, 679, 687, 696; Kabah, 735; loans, 594; manumission, 424; marriage, 474, 475, 477, 482, 484–85, 487, 491, 500, 523–24; martyrs, 369, 370–71; Medina, 735; mindfulness of God, 780; miscellaneous matters, 307, 365, 659–60, 766; mosques, 174, 193; names, 771; oaths, 399; parental rights, 638–39; Pilgrimage and Visitation, 297, 299 311, 315, 316–17, 333, 340, 341–42, 344, 354; plague, 735–37; poll-tax, 246–47, 248; prayer, 75, 76, 77, 79, 112, 116, 117, 121, 132, 134, 139–40, 142, 144, 150, 160, 163, 165–66, 177–78, 178, 192, 207, 339; punishment, 710, 711–12, 714–16, 717, 725; Quran, 196, 199; sales, 539, 544, 561–62, 571; self-reliance, 783; slaves, 774–75; speaking cautiously, 778; strays, 630–31; supplication, 785
ʿUmar b. Ḥusayn, 222, 697
ʿUmar b. Muḥammad b. Zayd, 125
ʿUmar b. ʿUbayd Allāh, 167, 300
ʿUmayr (freedman of Ibn ʿAbbās), 320
ʿUmayr b. Salama al-Ḍamrī, 302
Umayya bt. Ruqayqa, 725–26, 775
Umm al-Faḍl bt. al-Ḥārith, 115, 320
Umm ʿAmr b. Sulaym al-Zuraqī, 633
Umm ʿAṭiyya al-Anṣāriyya, 209
Umm Ḥabība bt. Jaḥsh, 105n66, 286, 527
Umm Ḥakīm bt. al-Ḥārith b. Hishām, 489
Umm Hānī, 161–62
Umm Ḥarām bt. Milḥān, 371
Umm Kulthūm, 209n237, 532, 534, 626n881
Umm Qays bt. Miḥṣan, 106
Umm Salama: ablution, 86, 93, 100, 105; circumambulation, 317; clothes, 744; drinking practices, 748; evil eye, 756; fasting, 255–57; litigation, 599; manumission, 441, 511–12; marriage, 522–23; mourning, 527–29; prayer, 76, 155, 156, 217; Prophet's death, 214; transgender company, 638; wedding night of, 478
Umm Sharīk, 516
Umm Sulaym, 99–100, 347, 749–50
Unays al-Aslamī, 711
ʿUrwa b. al-Zubayr: ablution, 90, 95, 99; breastfeeding, 532, 533, 535; burial, 215; choosing the easier option, 739; compensation, 681, 690–91, 693; divorce, 503, 508, 514, 521–22; evil eye, 756; fasting, 257, 258–60; gifts, 626; illness,

756, 757, 758; inheritance, 418; judicial matters, 617; Kabah, 313–14, 317; manumission, 435, 448–49; marriage, 487, 491, 500, 502; Muḥammad's estate, 780; newborn sacrifice, 382; Pilgrimage and Visitation, 290, 293, 296, 317, 318–19, 332, 356; pious seclusion, 275; prayer, 74, 117, 121, 139, 142, 154, 156, 158, 161–62, 164, 753; punishment, 715, 721; sacrificial animals, 322–23, 335, 348; sales, 544; slaughtering animals, 383; vows, 394
Usāma b. Zayd, 333, 337, 338, 416, 517, 736
Usayd b. al-Khuḍayr, 101
ʿUṭāriḍ b. Ḥājib b. Zurāra b. ʿAdī, 746n992
ʿUtba b. Abī Waqqāṣ, 617
ʿUthmān b. Abī al-ʿĀṣī, 757
ʿUthmān b. ʿAbd al-Raḥmān, 84
ʿUthmān b. ʿAffān, 127, 132–33, 173, 330, 785; ablution, 87, 88–89, 97; alms-tax, 222, 227–28; camels, 631; consecrated state, 284, 300, 304; currency exchange, 556; divorce, 505, 510–12; drinking habits, 748; fasting, 254, 255; funeral matters, 213; gifts, 642; inheritance, 408, 416; investment partnerships, 660; judicial matters, 618; lapidation, 712; manumission, 429; marriage, 484–85, 524; Muḥammad's estate, 780; Pilgrimage and Visitation, 289, 290, 299; prayer, 77, 116, 117, 150–51, 165, 178, 339; property, 647; punishment, 715, 719; Quran, 196; sales, 540, 571; slaves, 775; wine-drinking, 727
ʿUthmān b. Ḥafṣ b. ʿUmar b. Khalda, 400, 587
ʿUthmān b. Isḥāq b. Kharasha, 410
ʿUthmān b. Maẓʿūn, 219
ʿUthman b. Ṭalḥa al-Ḥajabī, 337
ʿUwaymir al-ʿAjlānī, 506
ʿUwaymir b. Ashqar, 378

Wādī Āshī, Abū ʿAbd Allāh al-, 53, 70
Wahb b. Kaysān, 118, 751, 764
Wahb b. Masarra al-Ḥajārī, 58–61
Wahb b. ʿUmayr, 488–89
Walīd b. ʿAbd Allāh b. Ṣayyād, al-, 777
Walīd b. ʿAbd al-Malik b. Marwān, al-, 7, 229, 286, 491
Wāqid b. ʿAbd Allāh, 284–85
Wāqid b. ʿAmr b. Saʿd b. Muʿādh, 729
Wāqid b. Saʿd b. Muʿādh, 215
Wāsiʿ b. Ḥabbān, 191
Wymann-Landgraf, Umar Abd-Allah, 8, 18n22, 21–22, 27–28, 32, 677n927

Yaḥyā b. ʿAbd al-Raḥmān b. Ḥāṭib, 85, 99, 623
Yaḥyā b. Muḥammad b. Ṭaḥlāʾ, 84
Yaḥyā b. Saʿīd al-Anṣārī, 44n1, 173, 227; ablution 85, 87, 87, 93, 94, 97, 99; adultery allegations, 616; alms-tax, 229, 237, 238; breastfeeding, 533, 534; charity, 781; clothes, 743; collective oaths, 702; compensation, 684–85, 687–88, 690–91, 693; consecrated state, 281, 284, 286, 292, 294, 301–2, 307, 310, 324–25, 348–49; currency, 557; divorce, 493–94, 497, 504, 509–10, 512, 515–16, 518; dreams, 763; evil eye, 756; fasting, 257, 265, 268; food, 752–54; funeral matters, 210, 212, 214–15, 217; good character, 740; greetings, 765; grooming, 747, 759–60; horses, 373; illness, 757, 758; inheritance, 407, 410, 416, 629; *jihād*, 359–61, 364, 367–68; judicial matters, 599, 630–31, 640; lapidation, 709–12; loyalty, 358; manumission, 423, 427, 428; marriage, 475, 477,

479, 480, 483, 485, 490, 491, 523–25; martyrs, 369–71; Medina, 732, 734, 735; murder, 678, 696; names, 770–71; omens, 770; parental rights, 638; Pilgrimage, 298, 310, 320, 330, 333, 339–40, 343, 355; prayer, 75, 79, 109, 113, 116, 117–18, 121, 122, 125, 133, 137, 144, 150, 151, 152, 158–59, 161, 164, 170–71, 173, 181–82, 187, 191, 193; punishment, 714, 719, 725, 728; Quran, 196, 198; sacrificial animals, 326, 334, 348, 377–78; sales, 540, 562, 576, 592, 596; seeking protection, 760; slaughtered animals, 383–85; speaking cautiously, 776; supplication, 203, 205; vows and oaths, 394, 396, 399; wills, 633
Yaḥyā b. Saʿīd b. al-ʿĀṣī, 515
Yaḥyā b. Saʿīd b. al-Musayyab, 681
Yaḥyā b. Yaḥyā al-Laythī, 8–9, 16n21, 37, 41, 47–48, 50, 53, 56, 60, 65–68, 69, 73, 278n351
Yaʿlā b. Munya, 282
Yaʿqūb b. ʿAbd Allāh b. al-Ashajj, 773
Yaʿqūb b. Khālid al-Makhzūmī, 330
Yaʿqūb b. Zayd b. Ṭalḥa, 710
Yarfaʾ or Yarfā, 163, 413
Yazīd (freedman of al-Munbaʿith), 629
Yazīd b. ʿAbd Allāh b. al-Hādī, 136, 271, 321, 617
Yazīd b. ʿAbd Allāh b. Qusayṭ al-Laythī, 93, 385, 391, 518, 559
Yazīd b. ʿAbd al-Malik, 525
Yazīd b. Abī Sufyān, 359
Yazīd b. Jāriya al-Anṣārī, 482
Yazīd b. Khuṣayfa, 228, 756, 757, 768
Yazīd b. Muʿāwiya, 731
Yazīd b. Nuʿaym b. Hazzāl al-Aslamī, 710
Yazīd b. Rūmān, 116, 118, 140, 181
Yazīd b. Ziyād, 76, 739
Yuḥannas (freedman of al-Zubayr b. al-ʿAwwām), 731
Yūnus b. Mughīth Abū al-Walīd b. al-Ṣaffār, 52
Yūnus b. Yūsuf, 571, 733

Zabrāʾ (freedwoman of Banū ʿAdī), 503
Zayd (Abū ʿAyyāsh), 549
Zayd b. al-Khaṭṭāb, 629, 748
Zayd b. Abī Unaysa, 737
Zayd b. Aslam, 44n1, 197, 249, 302; ablution, 84, 89, 94, 103, 105; alms-tax, 238, 239, 250; animals, 384, 391; apostasy, 614; the bereft, 747; charity, 782, 784; clothes, 742, 744; compensation, 687; consecrated state, 282, 303, 349; currency exchange, 556; divorce, 514; dreams, 763; fasting, 256, 257, 264; generosity, 751; greetings, 764; grooming, 759; illness, 756, 757; inheritance, 411; intoxicating beverages, 729; investment parternships, 659; *jihād*, 357–58; livestock exchange, 573; loans, 593; marriage, 491; martyrs, 369, 370; newborn sacrifice, 381; poll-tax, 246; prayer, 74, 75, 81, 124, 142, 151, 154, 160, 161, 163, 166, 172, 183, 206, 339; punishment, 713; sales, 548, 587–88; seafood, 389; self-reliance, 783; speaking cautiously, 777–78; steeping dried fruit, 728; supplication, 205, 785
Zayd b. Ḥāritha, 533
Zayd b. Khālid al-Juhanī, 163, 188, 367–68, 599, 629, 711, 714
Zayd b. Rabāḥ, 193
Zayd b. Ṭalḥa, 710, 740
Zayd b. Thābit, 286n365; compensation, 684; divorce, 496, 511–12, 514; eating matters, 385, 390; inheritance, 407–8; marriage, 97, 476, 477, 480, 483, 526–27; Medina, 733; oaths on the

Prophet's pulpit, 606–7; prayer, 78, 150, 155, 168; punishment, 725; Quran, 196; sales, 545–46, 562, 587
Zaynab al-Thaqafiyya, 544
Zaynab bt. Abī Salama, 100, 105, 213, 317, 527–28, 599
Zaynab bt. Jaḥsh, 105, 211, 278, 527
Zaynab bt. Kaʿb b. ʿUjra, 523
Zaynab bt. Muḥammad, 209n237
Zayn al-ʿĀbidīn. *See* ʿAlī b. al-Ḥusayn b. ʿAlī b. Abī Ṭālib
Ziyād b. ʿAbd al-Raḥmān (Shabṭūn), 50, 278–79
Ziyād b. Abī Sufyān, 294
Ziyād b. Abī Ziyād, 202, 204, 353
Ziyād b. Saʿd, 240, 738, 759
Zubayr b. ʿAbd al-Rahmān b. al-Zabīr, al-, 479
Zubayr b. al-ʿAwwām, al-, 74n5, 302, 429, 485, 721, 731
Zufar b. Ṣaʿṣaʿa b. Mālik, 762
Zurayq b. Ḥayyān, 229
Zurqānī, Muḥammad al-, 50, 76n12, 143n131, 149n136, 173n167, 181n178, 745n991, 771n1027
Zuyayd b. al-Ṣalt, 98

Index of Subjects

ablution (*wuḍūʾ*), 30n54, 83–107, 195–96, 338; dry (*tayammum*), 101–4; with seawater, 85
adultery (*zinā*), 183, 418n614, 486, 711; mutual imprecation for (*liʿān*), 506–8; requirement of eyewitnesses for allegations of, 506n734, 600, 616, 711. *See also* fornication
affiliation (*nasab*), 695
afreets, 760
afterlife. *See* Hereafter
alcohol and inebriation, 379, 727–30; punishment for, 723; wine-drinking (*shurb al-khamr*), 726, 727–28
alms-tax (*zakāt*), 18, 25n35, 175, 221–51, 263n327, 358; beneficiaries of, 238–39, 245; collection and enforcement of, 239; exemptions from, 226, 245; on food, 563; prohibition of sharp dealing on, 237–38
ʿamal (practice), 21–23, 29, 31, 44, 46, 47
amr rules, 22, 27–28, 31, 32, 45–46, 104n65, 123n95
angels, 119–20, 131, 166, 172, 203, 734, 756, 767, 777, 780
animals: compassion for, 751; compensation for killing, 347–49, 623–24; eating, 387–92, 487; hides of dead, 391; liability for damages by, 694; necklaces on, 754n1001; sales of, 571–73, 595–96; slaughtering nonsacrificial, 236, 383–85; stray or lost, 629–31; wild (*ṣayd*), 301–6, 351n483, 387–92. *See also specific kinds*
animals, sacrificial (*hady*; *ḍaḥāyā*; *aḍāḥī*), 290n381, 290–91, 294–95, 297–99, 308–9, 321–30, 333–36, 347–52, 377–80, 394–95; breaking bones of, 382n544; prohibitions against, 377–78; "sacrificial" vs. "sacrosanct" distinction, 323n438, 377n535
annulment (*faskh*), 519n750
apostasy (*ridda*), 614–15
artisans, legal claims of, 624
asking permission before entering, 766
assault. *See* battery
augury (*ṭiyara*), 758
authority, discursive (*amr*) vs. historical (*sunna*), 14, 22, 25, 27–29, 33, 45–46, 123n95

backbiting, 777
barley, 242–43, 250, 549, 563
bathing (*ghusl*), 95–100, 103, 105, 107; consecrated state and, 281–82; on Feast of Breaking the Ramaḍān Fast, 177; on Friday, 131–32
battery (*jināya*; *jurḥ* [sing.]/*jirāḥ* [pl.]), 432n629; committed by slaves, 444–45, 469–72, 620, 641; compensation for, 432n629, 469–72, 677–700, 705; liability for, 690–96, 700; retaliation for (*qawad*; *qiṣāṣ*), 679, 682, 686, 689, 691, 699–700; resulting in loss of life, 677–79, 683–84, 687, 692
Battle of al-Ḥarra, 417n612
Battle of Badr, 192, 321n437, 353
Battle of Dhāt al-Riqāʿ, 181
Battle of Ḥunayn, 287n372, 296n389, 364, 366–68, 489
Battle of Qudayd, 417n612
Battle of Ṣiffīn, 417n612
Battle of the Camel, 417n612
Battle of the Trench, 182, 353, 772, 773n1030
Battle of Uḥud, 369–70, 372, 374
beasts of burden (*dawābb*), 597; liability for, 694; rental of, 612–13; wife compared to, 494n718

bereft, the (*masākīn*), 747
betting and financial risk-taking (*mukhāṭara*), 550, 580–81
beverages. *See* alcohol and inebriation
breastfeeding (*raḍāʿa*) taboos, 531–35
brigandage (*ḥirāba*), 722
burglary, 723
buried treasure (*rikāz*), 225–26, 694

camels: alms-tax on, 221, 231–35, 237, 593; Arabian vs. Bactrian, 232; as booty, 361; care of, 753; as charity, 784; as compensation for battery, 677–79, 686–88, 693, 702; marking of, 219n254; Muḥammad on, 630; purchased for meat (*jazūr*), 572; "red" (*ḥumr al-naʿam*), 165, 702; sacrificial, 321–23, 330, 377; sales and exchanges of, 571–72, 641; stray, 630–31
canonization of religious authority, 23–24
carrion (*mayta*), 384n547, 391–92
cattle (*baqar*), alms-tax on, 232–33, 237
cats, 85
cereal crops, 221–22, 242–43
charity (*ṣadaqa*), 183, 202, 221n256, 259, 378–79, 503, 761, 781–83; for the deceased, 631–32; exceptions to, 784
chastity (*iḥṣān*), 486–87; legal condition of, 713n966
chess and similar games, 764
children and minors: abandoned (*manbūdh*), 616; affiliated (*mustalḥaq*), 617–19; of divorce, 638–39; financial responsibilities of, 641; gifts for, 642; illegitimate (*walad al-zinā*), 214, 418, 424, 508, 619–20; of non-Arab mothers (*muwallad*), 487n704; orphans, 226–27, 759; pristine nature (*fiṭra*) of, 219; prohibition of retaliation against, 678, 679; repudiated (*walad al-mulāʿana*), 418; testimony of (*shahādat al-ṣibyān*), 606, 633
Christians, 432–33, 477, 486–87, 508, 615, 677n926, 683, 689–90; greeting norms for, 764; meat slaughtered by, 384, 389n556; as slaves, 416, 426, 432, 469. *See also* Jesus; People of the Book; "protected people"
circumcision, 97n56, 680, 747
clothes, 742–46; dyed, 210, 283–84, 529, 625, 743; for prayer, 137, 155–56, 742n987; women and, 529, 743–44, 775
commercial goods, alms-tax on, 228–30, 236
Companions, 12, 16, 17, 45, 46, 74n5, 77n17, 97, 768; on compassion, 751; on free will, 738; on marriage, 485; on Night of Power, 272; nonstandard readings of Quran by, 134n108; on Pilgrimage, 291, 293, 309; on plague, 736; on Treaty of al-Ḥudaybiya, 198n205. *See also individual Companions*
compensation for battery. *See under* battery
Confederates, 353n485
consecrated state (*iḥrām*), 137, 267, 280, 281–91, 293–95; contracting marriage in, 300; cupping in, 301; eating wild animals in, 301–5; killing in, 282nn357–58, 301n396, 306–7, 347–51; miscellaneous regulations on, 307–11; terms for entering and leaving, 281n354; timing of, 293, 297. *See also* animals, sacrificial
consensus (*ijmāʿ*), doctrine of, 18
contagion (*ʿadwā*), 758
corpses. *See* funeral matters
creditors, secured (*murtahin*), 607–12
crops: alms-tax on, 240–42; damaged by calamities (*jāʾiḥa*), 546, 547; damaged by livestock, 623

cupping (*ḥijāma*), 260, 301, 771–72
currency exchange (*ṣarf*). *See under* precious metals
custody, 616, 638–39

dates, 127, 259–60, 372, 649; alms-tax on, 221, 230, 240–41, 250; exceptions to alms-tax on, 243–44; sales of, 545–54, 560; ʿUmar b. al-Khaṭṭāb's fondness for, 752
Day of "Am I Not" (*alastu*), 737n983
Day of ʿArafa, 204n224, 292, 320–21, 326n441, 337; effect on Satan of, 353
Day of Judgment, 88, 110, 205, 526, 732, 782n1041
Day of Khaybar, 487
Day of Resurrection, 218, 230, 367, 369, 372, 737, 743–44, 761, 767
Day of the Slaughter of the Sacrosanct Animals (*yawm al-naḥr*), 289, 290, 311, 322, 329, 333–35, 340, 343
Day of Watering (*yawm al-tarwiya*), 288, 328n448
Days of Ignorance (*jāhiliyya*), 1, 248, 261, 319, 528, 572, 587–88, 617–18, 622, 785
Days of Minā, 321, 344, 356
debt (*dayn*), 554n797, 587–90, 607, 726; alms-tax on, 227–29; debtors' insolvency (*iflās*), 591–93, 641, 661; guaranty of, 624–26; investment parternships and, 669–70; martyrdom and, 369; owed to a decedent, 604–5
decedents' estates (*mīrāth*), 227, 605, 619, 622
defective goods, 625, 639–40
demons, 122, 269
dice. *See* gambling
divorce (*ṭalāq*), 491–92, 493–529; absolute declaration of (*batta*), 493–94, 515; conditional or suspended, 500n726; delegation of authority to wife for (*tamlīk*), 495–97; euphemisms for (*khaliyya*; *bariyya*; *bāʾina*), 494–95; maintenance (*nafaqa*) due to ex-wife, 516–17; mutual imprecation (*liʿān*) and, 506–8; parting gift upon (*mutʿa*), 511; payment from wife for (*khulʿ*), 504–5, 520; waiting period after (ʿidda), 301n395; *ẓihār* ("like back of his mother") declaration, 250n305, 262, 396, 500–502
dogs, 90, 768–69; compassion for, 751; payment for, 574–75; prohibition against eating, 390; vicious, 306–7. *See also* hounds
doubt, 12, 45–46, 89n48, 268, 304
dower. *See under* marriage
dreams, 762–63
drinking practices, 748–49
duʿāʾ. *See* supplication
"*dulūk* of the sun," 78–79
dusk (*shafaq*), 80

easements (*mirfaq*), 621–22, 663
eating restrictions, 387–92, 753
eclipses, 182–84
elephantiasis (*judhām*), 540
embezzlement, 725, 726
Emigrants (*muhājirūn*), 44, 46, 127n102, 153n140, 171, 209, 247, 736
employment contracts (*ijāra*), 597, 652–53, 654, 662, 663
endowments (*ḥabs*), 629n885
erotic dreams, 98–100, 103, 283
eschatology, 26, 167n156, 184n185
evil eye (*al-ʿayn*), 754–56

farmland leases (*kirāʾ*), 657–58
fasting (*ṣiyām*), 174, 253–70; continuous, 262; cupping while, 260; on Day of *ʿArafa*, 320–21; on day of ʿĀshūrāʾ, 260–61; on Days of Minā, 321, 356; expiation for breaking, 259–60; illness while,

262–63; kissing while, 256–58; making up missed days of, 264–68; pious seclusion and, 277; traveling while, 258–59, 263; on feast days, 261, 321; voluntary, 266–67
Feast of Breaking the Ramaḍān Fast (*ʿīd al-fiṭr*), 177–80, 261, 269, 321; alms-tax in celebration of, 249–51; pious seclusion and, 278; timing of, 253–54
Feast of the Sacrificial Animals (*ʿīd al-aḍḥā*), 177–80, 204n224, 261, 321, 377–78, 380
Festival Days (*ayyām al-tashrīq*), 321, 338, 340–41, 343
fetuses, human, compensation for killing of, 682–83
fetuses, of livestock (*maḍāmīn*), 380, 385, 573; ownership of, 464, 538; sales of, 581
five pillars of Islam, 25n35, 221n255
Followers (*tābiʿūn*), 16, 17, 39–40, 45, 74n5, 177n172, 394n568
food: destruction of another's, 614; sales and distribution of, 561–70; stories of, 749–54
fornication (*zinā*), 368, 481, 483, 486, 491, 574, 778; exemptions from punishment for, 716–17; punishment for, 709–14; slander of, 715–16. *See also* adultery
freedman (*mawlā*)/freedwoman (*mawlāt*), definition of, 75n9
free will, doctrine of (*qadar*), 737–39
Friday, importance of, 135–36
fruit: pledges of unharvested (*thamar*), 607–9; sale of, 555, 651–52; steeping dried, 728, 735
funeral matters (*janāʾiz*; *janāza*; *jināza*), 86, 209–20, 279, 374–75

gambling (*qimār*), 550, 573, 763–64
"*ghasaq* of the night," 79
ghusl. *See* bathing
gifts, 626–29, 642; buying back of, 249
gluttony (of nonbelievers), 748
goats (*ghanam*; *maʿz*). *See* sheep and goats
God's House. *See* Kabah
gold. *See* precious metals
goodwill acts (*maʿrūf*), 569
grains (*zarʿ*), alms-tax on, 240–42, 250
grapes: alms-tax on, 240–41; sales of, 549
graverobbing, 724
graves of prophets, 169, 172–73, 734
greetings, norms of, 764–65
grooming, 747, 758–59

hadith: defined, 7–8; gathering of, 39; Mālik's contribution to, 10–11, 31, 44–45, 46–47
hair: cutting during Pilgrimage and Visitation, 329, 334, 335, 336–37, 344, 758–60; dyeing, 760; shaving during Pilgrimage and Visitation, 283, 286, 308, 309, 322, 326, 330, 335–36, 344, 349–50, 378
Ḥanafī school of law, 9n5, 10, 19, 23, 73n2, 604n849, 686n938
handmaidens. *See* slaves
Hereafter, 142, 167n156, 174, 184, 203, 205
Hell, 81–82, 183, 204, 216, 218, 738; appearance of, 781; fever as heat of, 758; Ramaḍān and, 269
"helpers" (*anṣār*), 127n102, 171n164
Hijazi school of law, 23, 32
hoarding, 230
homosexuals, 638n905, 713
honesty and lying, 778–79
horses, 357–58, 366, 372–73, 694, 770
hospitality, 747, 748, 750
hounds, 305, 387–88, 575
Hour of Divine Judgment, 136
ḥudūd, 517n748, 709–17
hypocrites, 172n166, 185, 206–7

ʿīd. *See* Feast of Breaking the Ramaḍān Fast; Feast of the Sacrificial Animals

iḥrām. *See* consecrated state
ijtihād. *See* judicial discretion
illicit intercourse. *See* adultery; fornication
illness. *See* sick people
images and drawings. *See* statues and images
inheritance rights (*mīrāth*), 263n326, 401–19, 636–37; of affiliated children (*mustalḥaq*), 618–19; compensation for battery and, 692–94, 705–6; gifts and, 629, 637–38
intention (*niyya*), 268n338
insanity (*junūn*), 540, 678
insolvency (*iflās*), 591–93, 641, 661
investment partnerships (*qirāḍ*), 613, 651n913, 651n913, 659–75
Iraqi legal reasoning. *See* Ḥanafī school of law
irrigation partnerships (*musāqāt*), 649–56
Islamic calendar, 253n308
istiḥsān (juristic preference), 19, 29–30
i'tikāf, 271, 275–80

janāba. *See* ritual preclusion
Jerusalem: mosque of, 136; praying toward, 191–92
jewelry, alms-tax exemption on, 226
Jews and Judaism, 389n556, 477, 486–87, 508, 615, 649n912, 683, 689–90, 734–35, 751, 759; Banū Qurayẓa tribe, 773n1030; greeting norms for, 764; on judges, 599; magical powers of, 757, 761; Muḥammad on, 734–35, 751, 759, 764; as slaves, 426, 432; Torah, 136, 709. *See also* People of the Book; "protected people"
jihād campaigns, 26, 357–75; booty from, 361–68; prohibitions during, 358–60
jinn, 110, 136, 730, 772, 773
jizya, 246–48, 374
judicial discretion (*ijtihād*), 19, 22, 27, 33n61, 123n95, 366, 680, 684, 686
judicial rulings (*aqḍiya*), 599–642; blameworthiness of, 640; pledges and, 607–12; on rape, 613–14; witnesses and, 599–604, 606
jurisprudence: analogical reasoning in, 18, 19; "old" vs. "new," 15, 17–18, 20–21, 24

Kabah: Ancient House (*al-bayt al-'atīq*) designation, 316; construction of, 312; facing direction of, 19, 192; prayer inside, 337; saluting corners of (*istilām*), 313–14; vows to walk to, 393–96. *See also under* Pilgrimage
kidnapping, 724
kissing, 95–96, 256–58, 280, 325; the Black Stone, 314
knowledge, search for, 784

lambs (*sakhl*), alms-tax on, 236
land rights. *See* property
lapidation (*rajm*), 482, 487, 602, 709–13
last will and testament (*waṣiyya*), 617, 631, 632–38, 679
law: positive (*fiqh*), 10, 14; Prophetic (*sunna*), 15–21, 44, 277, 299, 681n932, 738; theory of (*uṣūl al-fiqh*), 10n9, 14, 33n61
left hand prohibition, 747
legal reform, 33
leprosy (*baraṣ*), 540
lessees (*mustakrī*), 612
li'ān, 506–8
litigation. *See* judicial rulings
livestock (*māshiya*; *ḥayawān*), 247, 391; alms-tax on, 222, 231–39; damage caused by, 623; exchanging of, 571–75; injury of another's, 614, 623–24; milking, 769; pledges of, 608–9
lizard meat, 768

loans (*salaf*), 554, 593–95; investment parternships and, 662, 671
lost property (*luqaṭa*), rights to, 629–30
loving for God's sake, 761–62

Mālikī school of law, 1, 2, 9, 46, 67, 72
Manicheans, 615
manumission, 249–50, 421–33, 435–61, 463–73. *See also under* slaves
marriage (*nikāḥ*), 473–92, 739; consecrated state and, 300–301; consummation time limit in, 520; de facto but invalid (*shubhāt al-nikāḥ*), 481; "of delegation" (*nikāḥ al-tafwīḍ*), 476n684; dower (*ṣadāq*) and gifts to guardian (*ḥibā'*) for, 475–77, 482, 490, 511, 613; impermissible types of, 479–86; interfaith, 477, 486, 487, 488–90, 508, 519; privacy (*irkhā' al-sutūr*) in, 477–78; nonbinding contractual stipulations in, 478–79; number of wives, limit on, 520; pious seclusion and, 279–80; proposals of (*khiṭba*), 473–74; secret, 482; stages of, 476n683; temporary (*nikāḥ al-mut'a*), 487; two arbitrators for rifts in, 519; wedding feast (*walīma*), 490–91, 521; wedding night, 478. *See also* sexual relations
martyrdom, 150, 215–16, 369–71, 742n986
measurements: of distance, 159n148, 258n316; of silver, 221n257; of length, 75n11; of weight, 96n55, 221nn257–58, 251n306, 548n791, 560n803, 578n829, 626n880
meat, eating of, 754, 768
Mecca, conquest of, 162, 258, 353–54
Medina: fever in, 733–34; importance of, 7, 731–33; as sanctuary, 733
menstruation (and lochia), 96n54, 100, 103–6; divorce and, 513–15; fasting and, 266, 279; Pilgrimage and, 295, 331, 344–47; pious seclusion and, 279; sex during, 103, 106; prostration during, 200
metaphysical realism in law, 33n61
mice, 750, 770
mines and mineral wealth (*ma'ādin*), 225
minors (*ṣaghīr*). *See* children and minors
mīrāth. *See* decedents' estates; inheritance rights
modesty, 740; ostentatious clothes, 743, 745
monetary units, 223nn160–61
moringa tree (*bān*), seeds and oil from, 308, 581–82
mourning, of dead husband (*iḥdād*), 527–29
Mudawwana, al-, 1, 9–10, 12, 33–34
murder: collective oaths on, 701–6; intentional (*qatl al-'amd*; *qatl al-ghīla*), 678, 690–91, 696–97; pardons (*'afw*) for, 699; retaliation for (*qawad*; *qiṣāṣ*), 678, 679, 690–91, 697–99; unintentional (*qatl al-khaṭa'*), 262, 678–79, 690n943, 691, 693–94, 700
Muwaṭṭa': authenticity of reports in, 11–15; authority and reason in, 14–15; definitive form of, 60, 66; importance of, 1–2, 8, 11, 40, 45–47; later reputation of, 33; on Medinese "practice" (*'amal*), 21–23, 25, 27, 29; narrative aspect of, 1, 4; "old" style jurisprudence of, 15, 16, 17; overview of, 24–34; previous Arabic editions of, 48–50, 68; previous English translations of, 1, 2, 3; recensions of, 8–9, 47; Royal Moroccan Edition of, 1, 2, 3–4, 25, 41–42, 47–49, 67–72; sourcebooks derived from, 9–10; taxonomy of texts in, 27–31; terminology of, 21–22, 27, 33; transmission of, 50–67

Nabateans, 243, 248, 725–26
natural phenomena, belief in, 188nn189–90
newborn sacrifice (*ʿaqīqa*), 381–82
Night of Power (*laylat al-qadr*), 271–72, 743n988
non-Muslims, 26, 205; inheritance and, 416–17; marriage with, 486; slaves forbidden to, 432n630, 469. *See also* People of the Book; "protected people"
nosebleeds, 93, 134

oaths (*yamīn*), 277n348, 397–400; of abstinence from sexual relations (*īlāʾ*), 497–500; of allegiance (*bayʿa*), 775–76; claimant's, 601–4; collective (*qasāma*), 26n41, 697n951, 701–7; of divorce before marriage, 519–20; penalties for broken, 250; on Prophet's pulpit (*minbar*), 606–7; for sacrificial animals, 335n464; for sales, 540; vows, difference from, 397n574
olives, alms-tax on, 241–42
omens, signs of bad, 770
orphans. *See under* children and minors

Paradise, 88, 183, 193, 201, 218, 738; Ramaḍān and, 269; two evils blocking, 777–78
pardon (*ʿafw*), 699
partnerships in business (*shirk*; *sharika*), 569, 590–91
paternity. *See* children and minors
penance (*kaffāra*), 396–99, 426–27nn626–27
penis: ablution and, 94–96, 98, 103, 106, 107; circumcision accidents and, 680
People of the Book (*ahl al-kitāb*), 247n301; compensation for injuries to, 689–90; poll-tax on, 246–48
perjury, 600
physicians, compensation from, 680–81
physiognomists (*qāʾif*), 618
Pilgrimage (*ḥajj*), 204n224, 267, 281–300, 308–56; casting pebbles at Devil, 160n149, 261n321, 283, 285n361, 286, 332–33, 342–44; chanting (*talbiya*), 287–88, 291–92, 296; circumambulation of Kabah (*ṭawāf*), 285n361, 291, 292, 293, 300, 310, 312–16; Circumambulation of the March (*ṭawāf al-ifāḍa*), 327n444, 346–47; consecrated state, 281–89, 293–300; designated stations for consecration (*mawāqīt*), 286–87, 296–97, 298, 299–300; Farewell Circumambulation (*ṭawāf al-wadāʿ*), 316–17; interference with, 308–12; march between hillocks of Ṣafā and Marwa (*saʿy*), 291n382, 292, 293, 300, 310, 315, 318–20; march from Minā to Kabah (*ifāḍa*), 286, 344; omissions and offenses, 350–52; performance for someone else, 308; performance of Pilgrimage after Visitation in one season (*tamattuʿ*), 297–99, 329n450, 356; performance of Pilgrimage and Visitation together (*qirān*), 290–91, 326; performance of Pilgrimage only (*ifrād*), 289–90; shortening prayers during, 159; stopping at ʿArafāt and Muzdalifa, 311, 322, 325, 330–32, 338–39; unrestricted state (*ḥalāl*) after, 267
pious acts, voluntary (*nāfila*), 267
pious seclusion (*iʿtikāf*), 271, 275–80
plague (*ṭāʿūn*), 735–37
pledges (*ruhūn*), 607–12, 732
pledgors (*rāhin*), 608–11
poll-tax (*jizya*) on non-Muslims, 246–48, 374
poor people. *See* bereft, the
prayer: Afternoon (*ṣalāt al-ʿasr*), 74–79, 87, 89–90, 123, 154, 157–58, 172,

182, 200, 206–7, 213, 315–16, 338, 339, 341; congregational (*ṣalāt al-jamāʿa*), 78, 112, 114, 149–56; Dawn (*ṣalāt al-fajr*), 146–47, 172; of Danger (*ṣalāt al-khawf*), 158, 181–84; Evening (*ṣalāt al-ʿishāʾ*), 76–77, 80, 109, 115–16, 142, 145, 149–51, 157–58, 170, 171, 193, 272, 338–39, 341; Feast (*ṣalāt al-ʿīd*), 177–80, 187; Friday Congregational (*ṣalāt al-jumuʿa*), 77–78, 131–38, 170, 178, 276, 338, 436, 745, 775; funeral (*ṣalāt al-jināza*), 275; Midmorning (*ṣalāt al-ḍuḥā*), 161–63; middle (*ṣalāt al-wusṭā*), 154–55; Morning (*ṣalāt al-ṣubḥ*), 74–77, 80–81, 95, 99, 109, 111–13, 117, 144, 146–47, 150–52, 155, 158n392, 165–66, 188, 192, 200, 206–7, 213, 282, 315–16, 333, 338, 340, 763; Night (*ṣalāt al-layl*), 140, 141–47, 154, 721, 740; Noon (*ṣalāt al-ẓuhr*), 75, 76, 77, 124, 126, 134–35, 155, 157–58, 170, 182, 196, 206, 338–41, 413; for Rain (*ṣalāt al-istisqāʾ*), 187–89; for solar eclipse (*ṣalāt kusūf al-shams*), 182–84; Sunset (*ṣalāt al-maghrib*), 76, 80, 87, 115, 145, 151–52, 157–59, 170, 255, 338–39, 341; *Witr* (*ṣalāt al-witr*), 142–46, 335
prayer, call to: general (*adhān*), 80n29, 81, 98, 109–13, 131, 132, 146, 151, 177; immediate (*iqāma*), 80, 90, 98, 110–13, 133, 146–47, 164, 177, 338
prayer, origin of, 74
prayer, performance of: amen (*āmīn*), 119–20; attestation of faith (*tashahhud*), 25n35; 120n90, 121–22, 125n101; clothes and grooming, 137, 155–56, 162, 759; direction (*qibla*), 137, 141, 191–93; distractions, 126–27; formal entrance, 182n180; incomplete cycles, 123–26, 129, 133–34, 171, 267; individual vs. congregational, 149–50; listening to imam, 132–33; magnification of God (*takbīr*), 101n63, 110n71, 113–15, 125, 133, 164–65, 178–79, 182, 211–12, 318, 340, 342; miscellaneous actions, 164–75; missing of, 80–81, 188; neglect of, 79–80, 93, 149; prohibitions, 82, 116, 133, 191, 206; prostration, 199–200; Quran readings, 115–19, 138, 140, 178–79, 187, 196–97, 199–200, 338; Ramaḍān and, 139–40, 142, 177–78; severe heat and, 81–82, 163; shortening and/or combining, 157–75, 337–39; sitting and standing positions, 120–26, 129, 133–34, 137, 152–53, 263; while traveling, 157–61; walking in front of others, 162–64; women's attendance, 193
prayer, supererogatory, 102, 111, 147n135
prayer, supplementary, 132, 153–54, 163, 207, 338; before and after the Feast Prayers, 179; while traveling, 161
prayer, voluntary, 142, 266
precious metals, 202, 246, 447n648; alms-tax on, 221–22, 223–26, 244; clipped coins, 557, 560; exchanging gold for silver, 555–61; leasing land for, 550
preclusion ("blocking the means"), concept of (*sadd al-dharīʿa*), 18, 30n51, 264n329
predestination, 737–39
price risks. *See* betting and financial risk-taking
profit: lawful (*fāʾida*), 223, 230, 641; unlawful (*ribā*), 556–57, 558, 562, 573, 576, 579, 587–88, 594, 661, 662n918, 671n922
prophethood, qualities of, 762–63

Prophet's Mosque, 77, 89, 106, 112, 131, 136, 139, 150, 193, 214, 261, 275
property: partition of (*qasm*), 622–23, 782; reserved for public grazing (*ḥimā*), 785; right of first refusal (*shufʿa*), 643–48; rights of converts, 374; squandering of, 779
prostitution, 574, 775
"protected people," 247n301, 248, 690
protection from evil, 760–61
public highways, 694
pulses (legumes), 242–44, 563
punishment: mandatory (*ḥudūd*), 517n748, 709–17; of the many for actions of a few, 780

Quran, 195–202, 358, 428; on amputation for theft, 720–21; on breastfeeding, 535; on "corruption in the land" (*al-fasād fī al-arḍ*), 557n800; on divorce, 493n716, 519n751; as dower, 475; on fasting, 265; on free will, 737; handling of, 195; on inheritance rights, 403–6, 412, 414–15, 418; on lapidation, 711, 712; on manumission, 426–27, 436–37; on Muḥammad's wives, 531n765; on mutul imprecation, 506n734; Night of Power in, 271n340; on pregnancy, 635–36; recitation of, 115–19, 138, 140, 178–79, 187, 196–97, 199–200, 211n244, 212, 742; on retaliation, 698; revelations of, 192, 197–98; on waiting period (*qur'*), 513n741, 514

Ramaḍān: fasting during, 174, 253–70; prayer during, 139–40, 142; timing of, 253. *See also* Feast of Breaking the Ramaḍān Fast; pious seclusion
rape, 613–14, 714–15; proof of, 714
rebellion (*baghy*), 517n748
rental contracts (*kirā'*), 657–58, 662, 666–67
retaliation. *See under* battery; murder
ribā. *See* profit: unlawful
rings, 743, 754
ritual law, 25–26; on impurities of bodily functions, 96n54
ritual preclusion (*janāba*), 96–100, 102–3, 104, 131; fasting and, 255–56

Sacred Mosque (*al-masjid al-ḥarām*), 136, 193, 289
ṣadaqa. *See* charity
safe passage, grant of (*amān*), 488–89
sales (*buyūʿ*), 537–97; advance payment for goods in, 576–78; bargaining and trading prohibitions in, 595–96; breaches of contract (*taʿaddī*) in, 612–13; on credit, 561–63, 579–80, 589–90; exchanges of goods in, 575–76; of goods at an agreed-upon rate of profit (*murābaḥa*), 583–85; of goods from inventory list, 585–86; of indeterminate amounts (*muzābana*), 549–51, 569, 581; of items by weight, 578–79; material uncertainty prohibition (*gharar*) in, 538, 545, 546n786, 550, 554, 570, 580–82, 583, 589, 597; nonrefundable deposits on (*bayʿ al-ʿurbān*), 537; right of rescission (*khiyār*) of, 586–87; seller's liability (*ʿuhda*) for defects in, 539–43, 554; by touch (*mulāmasa*) or by tossing (*munābadha*), 582–83, 745n990; two sales in one, 579–80
salutations. *See* greetings
sandals, 744–45
saʿy, meaning of, 134–35
seafood, 389–90
self-reliance, 782–84
semen, 98–99, 526–27; pre-ejaculate (*madhī*), 94
sexual relations, 97–98, 100, 103, 259, 477–78, 484–86, 503, 534, 544;

abstinence from (*īlāʾ*), 497–502; during breastfeeding (*ghīla*), 535; in consecrated state, 324–25; during divorce proceedings, 514; while fasting, 256–58, 259–60; during Pilgrimage or Visitation, 299–300, 327, 331, 344; during pious seclusion, 277, 279–80; withdrawal before ejaculation (*ʿazl*), 526–27, 620. *See also* adultery; fornication; marriage
Shāfiʿī school of law, 10
sharecropping (*muḥāqala*), 549–50
shaving the head. *See under* hair
sheep and goats (*ḍaʾn*; *ghanam*; *maʿz*), 385, 769; alms-tax on, 231–38, 240; sacrificial, 377; sales of, 551; warfare and, 362
shunning others (impoliteness, suspicion), 741–42
sick people (*marīḍ*), 263, 275, 280, 343, 510, 635, 756–58; treatment of, 757–58; visiting, 756, 758
Siege of Ṭāʾif, 489
silver. *See* precious metals
slander (*fariyya*; *qadhf*), 715–16; indirect (*taʿrīḍ*), 716; intoxication and, 727
slaves: adultery and, 507–8; alms-tax on, 245, 249–50, 251; battery committed by, 444–45, 469–72, 620, 641; chattel (*ʿabd mamlūk*) designation, 250, 435n631, 444, 484, 539, 774–75; children of, 423–24, 619–20; collective oaths and, 706–7; compensation for battery of, 688–90, 692; as compensation for causing miscarriage, 682–83; designated for manumission upon owner's death (*mudabbar*, *mudabbara*; *tadbīr*), 249–50, 426, 463–72, 632–33; divorce and, 511–12, 517; female, with children by master (*ummahāt al-awlād*), 424, 426, 437, 449, 456, 463–64; in irrigation partnerships, 655–56; legal testimony of, 601–3; in manumission contract (*mukātab*), 222, 224, 249, 423, 426, 435–61; marriage and, 486–88, 500, 502–4; masters' responsibility for, 363n509; murder and, 678, 692, 706–7; patronage (*walāʾ*) of, 423, 428–33, 453–55, 468, 503; Pilgrimage and, 332; as pledge for debt, 610; profiting from, 771–72; property rights of, 640–41; sales of, 537–44; theft by, 720–21, 723–24, 726; unpermitted use of, 640; waiting period (*ʿidda*) of, 525–26; warfare and, 363–64, 368; wine-drinking and, 727–28
sneezes, blessing for, 766–67
sorcery (*siḥr*), 696–97, 772
soothsayers, 574, 682
speaking cautiously and honestly, 776–79
spendthrifts (*safīh*), 633
spitting, 192
statues and images, 767
stoning to death. *See* lapidation
sunna ordinances, 22, 28–29, 31, 32, 46, 123n95
supplication (*duʿāʾ*), 203–6, 353; for evil eye, 756n1003; for illness (*ruqya*), 757, 758; for Medina, 731; of the wronged, 785

testamentary dispositions (*waṣiyya*), 227, 263–64; enforceability of special cases, 633–36; of slaves in manumission arrangements, 456–61, 465–67. *See also* last will and testament
testimony. *See under* children and minors; judicial rulings; slaves
theft (*sariqa*), amputation for, 623, 640, 719–26; exceptions to, 725–26
thunder, 780

toothbrushes (*siwāk*), 107
torment of the grave (*ʿadhāb al-qabr*), 184–85, 204, 212, 216
transgender people (*mu'annath/mukhannath*), 638–39
transmission of tradition, 11–13; Shāfiʿī on, 16–18
traveling, 773–74
Treaty of al-Ḥudaybiya, 198n205, 313n420, 379n540

unlawful gain (*ribā*). *See* profit: unlawful
ʿumra. *See* Visitation
urinating and defecating, 83, 88, 90, 91–92, 106–7, 166, 191, 215

Visitation (*ʿumra*), 99, 267nn334–35, 289, 296–300, 319, 329n449, 329–30; prayer during, 137, 159; slaughter of animals during, 334
vows (*nadhr*), 263–64, 265n331, 393–96

water, access to, 620–21
wheat, 550, 560–61, 563, 565–67
wills. *See* last will and testament
wine. *See* alcohol and inebriation
wiping head and ears, 90–91
wiping leather socks (*khuff*), 91–92
witnesses (*shāhid*). *See under* judicial rulings
women: bad omens and, 770; clothing prohibitions for, 529, 743, 744; collective oath ineligibility of, 704; compensation due to, 681–83; in consecrated state, 285, 289, 329; eating companions allowed for, 753; killing in warfare, prohibition of, 359; legal testimony of, 602–4, 618n866; marriage expectations of, 739; mosque behavior of, 193, 200; Muḥammad's refusal to shake hands with, 775; Pilgrimage and, 295, 331, 355, 524; property rights of, 474; seclusion of, 523–24, 51–32; travel restrictions on, 774; vows by, 399; waiting period before remarriage (*ʿidda*), 301n395, 474, 481, 482, 491, 505, 510, 512–18, 521–26, widows, 479, 482–84, 522–24; wills of, 635–36. *See also* breastfeeding; menstruation; rape; sexual relations
wounds: to head and face (*ma'mūma*; *mūḍiḥa*), 470, 677, 681, 685–86, 688–90; to stomach (*jā'ifa*), 677
wuḍū'. *See* ablution

zakāt. *See* alms-tax
ẓihār, 250n305, 262, 396, 500–502
zinā. *See* adultery; fornication
Zoroastrians, 1, 246, 247–48, 389, 390, 426, 486, 690

Harvard Series in Islamic Law, VIII
Program in Islamic Law, Harvard Law School

Previous Publications (*Islamic Legal Studies Program*)

VII. Intisar A. Rabb and Abigail Krasner Balbale (eds.), *Justice and Leadership in Early Islamic Courts* (2017)

VI. Asifa Quraishi and Frank E. Vogel (eds.), *The Islamic Marriage Contract: Case Studies in Islamic Family Law* (2008)

V. R. Michael Feener and Mark E. Cammack (eds.), *Islamic Law in Contemporary Indonesia: Ideas and Institutions* (2007)

IV. Maya Shatzmiller, *Her Day in Court: Women's Property Rights in Fifteenth-Century Granada* (2007)

III. Nurit Tsafrir, *The History of an Islamic School of Law: The Early Spread of Hanafism* (2004)

II. Peri Bearman, Rudolph Peters, and Frank E. Vogel (eds.), *The Islamic School of Law: Evolution, Devolution and Progress* (2005)

I. Gideon Libson, *Jewish and Islamic Law: A Comparative Study of Custom During the Geonic Period* (2003)